LIFT TAKE YOUR STUDYING TO THE NEXT LEVEL.

This book comes with 1-year digital access to the
Examples & Explanations for this course.

Step 1: Go to **www.CasebookConnect.com/LIFT** and redeem your access code to get started.

Access Code: EEFA232882545194

Step 2: Go to your BOOKSHELF and select your online *Examples & Explanations* to start reading, highlighting, and taking notes in the margins of your e-book.

Step 3: Select the STUDY tab in your toolbar to access the questions from your book in interactive format, designed to give you extra practice and help you master the course material.

Is this a used casebook? Access code already scratched off?

You can purchase the online *Examples & Explanations* and still access all of the powerful tools listed above. Please visit CasebookConnect.com/Catalog to learn more about Connected Study Aids.

PLEASE NOTE: Each access code provides 12 month access and can only be used once. This code will also expire one year after the discontinuation of the corresponding print title and must be redeemed before then. CCH reserves the right to discontinue this program at any time for any business reason. For further details, please see the Casebook Connect End User Agreement.

PIN: 9111149621

11792

Work of the Family Lawyer

About Wolters Kluwer Legal & Regulatory Solutions U.S.

Wolters Kluwer Legal & Regulatory Solutions U.S. delivers expert content and solutions in the areas of law, corporate compliance, health compliance, reimbursement, and legal education. Its practical solutions help customers successfully navigate the demands of a changing environment to drive their daily activities, enhance decision quality and inspire confident outcomes.

Serving customers worldwide, its legal and regulatory solutions portfolio includes products under the Aspen Publishers, CCH Incorporated, Kluwer Law International, ftwilliam.com and MediRegs names. They are regarded as exceptional and trusted resources for general legal and practice-specific knowledge, compliance and risk management, dynamic workflow solutions, and expert commentary.

ASPEN CASEBOOK SERIES

Work of the Family Lawyer

Fourth Edition

Robert E. Oliphant

Professor of Law Emeritus
Mitchell Hamline College of Law

Nancy Ver Steegh

Professor of Law
Mitchell Hamline College of Law

Wolters Kluwer

Published by Wolters Kluwer in New York.

Wolters Kluwer Legal & Regulatory Solutions U.S. serves customers worldwide with CCH, Aspen Publishers, and Kluwer Law International products. (www.WKLegaledu.com)

To contact Customer Service, e-mail customer.service@wolterskluwer.com, call 1-800-234-1660, fax 1-800-901-9075, or mail correspondence to:

>   Wolters Kluwer
>   Attn: Order Department
>   PO Box 990
>   Frederick, MD 21705

Printed in the United States of America.

 2 3 4 5 6 7 8 9 0

ISBN 978-1-4548-7004-3

Library of Congress Cataloging-in-Publication Data

Names: Oliphant, Robert E., 1938- author. | Ver Steegh, Nancy, 1953- author.
Title: Work of the family lawyer / Robert E. Oliphant, Nancy Ver Steegh.
Description: Fourth edition. ed. | New York : Wolters Kluwer, [2015] | Series: Aspen casebook series
Identifiers: LCCN 2015046823 | ISBN 9781454870043
Subjects: LCSH: Domestic relations — United States — Cases.
Classification: LCC KF505 .O43 2015 | DDC 346.7301/5 — dc23
LC record available at http://lccn.loc.gov/2015046823

Summary of Contents

PART I. STATE, FEDERAL, AND CONSTITUTIONAL REGULATION OF MARITAL RELATIONSHIPS

PART II. RESTRUCTURING PARENT-CHILD RELATIONSHIPS AT DIVORCE

PART III. FINANCIAL SUPPORT

Contents

PART I   STATE, FEDERAL, AND CONSTITUTIONAL REGULATION OF MARITAL RELATIONSHIPS   1

Chapter 2. Constitutionalizing Family Law   25

Chapter 3. Marriage Requirements   73

Chapter 4. The Divorce Process   115

PART II   RESTRUCTURING PARENT-CHILD RELATIONSHIPS AT DIVORCE   153

Chapter 5. Child Custody and Parenting Plans   155

Chapter 6. Parenting Time and Visitation 219

Chapter 7. Modifying Child Custody 257

PART 1. TRADITIONAL MODIFICATION ACTIONS 257

PART III   **FINANCIAL SUPPORT   305**

Chapter 8. Establishing Child Support   307

Chapter 9. Modification and Enforcement of Child Support   355

Chapter 13. Premarital and Postmarital Contracts   523

Chapter 14. Cohabitation Outside of Marriage   569

 **PART V**

PROTECTION OF FAMILY MEMBERS   615

Chapter 15. Intimate Partner Violence   617

PART VI	LEGAL RECOGNITION OF FAMILY RELATIONSHIPS 741

Chapter 18. Establishing Parentage   743

Chapter 19. Adoption   783

PART VII   THE CHANGING ROLE OF THE FAMILY LAWYER   863

Chapter 21. Mediation, Collaborative Law, Parenting Coordination, and Arbitration   865

Chapter 22. Professional Responsibility   905

Preface

Our primary goal in writing this 4th edition is to share the diverse body of family law with students and provide a basis for them to critically examine and discuss existing and emerging family law policy from a variety of perspectives. The casebook actively integrates history, culture, economics and other material to stimulate learning. It emphasizes 21st century issues and has been designed as a sophisticated learning and teaching tool.

This 4th edition provides clarity and focus for students and a range of pedagogic options for faculty. It was organized so that chapters may be taught individually or in a sequence that fits the particular instructor's objectives for the course. The casebook can easily fit into the pedagogical scheme of a two, three, or four credit course. It works well in a classroom setting where the instructor adopts a traditional or modified Socratic method of teaching family law and also when the professor organizes the course around problem-based material or simulation. It is at home in family law clinics where the practical exercises included at the end of every chapter can help prepare students for handling real life family law cases. The unique, focused design makes the book easily adaptable for use in an online or blended course.

In this edition, the narration is more thoroughly and narrowly focused. Some areas have been edited for greater clarity. We reduced the casebook to 22 chapters and have integrated the material from the deleted chapters into the remaining ones.

Each chapter opens with an introduction containing learning objectives and general questions intended to stimulate the interest of the student in the area to be covered. The numbered sections unfold in a logical progression that helps students view each chapter as a whole. To enhance students' understanding, the authors provide foundational context and commentary in a common sense fashion. Like focusing the lens of a camera before taking a photo, each chapter sets the scene for students and narratively fills in what otherwise might be perceived as gaps between the cases.

New in this edition are the "boxed learning/thinking modules" that we call "reflective questions." They follow almost every narrated section in the casebook. This innovative concept is intended to stimulate thought, analysis and discussion.

We also include a short list of General Principles at the end of each chapter and these summarize some of the important content covered. They are a skeleton platform from which students may develop more comprehensive understanding of the material in the chapter.

We retained and improved the chapter review problems where students have the opportunity to apply principles discussed in the main body of a chapter to more complex hypothetical situations. These problems have proven to be particularly popular with students and professors.

We continued the "Preparation for Practice" section in response to faculty who encourage students to blend substantive family law theory with real-world learning. These exercises and activities can be integrated into class sessions or conducted between class meetings.

Overall, this edition is a teaching and learning tool that provides a realistic perspective on family law. This casebook is distinct from others because the clear presentation of fundamental family law principles is integrated into the policy challenges and practical problems that are the daily "Work of the Family Lawyer."

Robert E. Oliphant
Nancy Ver Steegh

Acknowledgments

This casebook incorporates helpful suggestions from many sources, including faculty members at other law schools and adjunct faculty members with whom we have had the privilege of working with at William Mitchell College of Law. We are also grateful to our many dedicated students for their insight, feedback, and support.

Special thanks go to our spouses, Susan and Jack, for their continued patience as this book was written and revised. We are grateful for the generous support we received from Levit & James, Inc. and the use of its outstanding software in the creation of the Table of Cases. We are also grateful to our editors at Wolters Kluwer for their expertise and encouragement.

Part I

State, Federal, and Constitutional Regulation of Marital Relationships

Chapter 1

Family Law: Past and Present

1.1 INTRODUCTION

The purpose of this casebook is to share knowledge about family law and encourage critical thought and discussion about family law principles from a variety of perspectives. To achieve this purpose, we unfold the body of family law in a series of focused, individual chapters with extensive narrative, excerpts from cases, and questions designed to focus and stimulate discussion. There is a short section near the end of each chapter that provides a limited number of legal principles associated with the material. Each chapter concludes with a series of review problems and practice-focused exercises that permit a professor to provide the option of blending substantive family law and theory with practical lifelike issues.

This chapter begins with a brief discussion of the impact religion may have had on family law. It continues with a historical summary of early family law developments. Of particular interest are the Ecclesiastical courts, which were a creation of the Roman Catholic Church. It was during the twelfth and thirteenth centuries that these courts gained almost exclusive control over domestic matters in England and the European Continent. Many of the principles and practices found in family law today are remnants of the influence of these early courts.

The chapter examines many issues, including the common law and its view of the legal rights, disabilities, and responsibilities of married women. It recounts the struggles women faced to gain equality in treatment before the law.

The chapter raises several questions, including the following: Has ancient religious doctrine influenced the development of family law in the United States? What social factors other than religion may have impacted family law over the centuries? How has the law changed its view of married women in the last century? What is the purpose of marriage? What is an annulment? What is a divorce from bed and board? What is a legislative divorce? What may have led Congress and the Supreme Court to intervene in family law matters, an area of law once almost exclusively the province of state courts? What is the theoretical basis that provides governmental control of marriage and divorce? What are heartbalm statutes and why have they disappeared from use? What role does the Full Faith and Credit Clause of the Constitution play in family law interstate disputes?

> **REFLECTIVE QUESTIONS**   What are your goals for this chapter?

1.2 CULTURE: INFLUENCE OF RELIGION ON WESTERN FAMILY LAW PRINCIPLES

Most agree that early American family law reflects a "near-universal belief in a theistically ordained natural order shaped by Biblical tradition." Vivian E. Hamilton, *Expressing Community Values Through Family Law Adjudication*, 77 UMKC L. Rev. 325, 326 (Winter 2008). The Biblical traditional view, it is thought, may at times conflict and be incompatible with liberal individualism, another near-universal value incorporated into the Western culture around the seventeenth century. Vivian Hamilton, *Principles of U.S. Family Law*, 75 Fordham L. Rev. 31, 36 (2006). *See generally* Naomi Cahn & June Carbone, *Deep Purple: Shades of Family Law*, 110 W. Va. L. Rev. 459 (Fall 2007). As a result of these conflicting values and their acceptance or rejection, regional views on family law issues may at times be in sharp contrast with one another. The depth of the disagreement depends on how strongly a particular value is held. For example, the views of the religiously devout traditionalists and political conservatives with strong attachment to the Biblical tradition may differ significantly on the question of abortion or same-sex marriage from those of the less devout modernists and political liberals who have a strong association with individual liberalism.

The Biblical tradition of American family law can be traced to England and Europe of the twelfth and thirteenth centuries, if not earlier. As noted at the outset of this chapter, it was during the twelfth and thirteenth centuries that the Catholic Church gained almost exclusive control in Europe and England over family matters, including marriage, annulment, and probate. It obtained this power because of its creation of Ecclesiastical courts and the development of the canon law. (The term *canon* comes from the Greek *kanon*, which means rule or norm; it came to mean a law promulgated by Church leaders.)

The canon law was influenced by many sources, including the Bible and Roman law. Systemization of the canon law is attributable to a treatise, *Decretum*, written in 1140. *See* R. H. Helmholz, *The Development of Law in Classical and Early Medieval Europe*, 70 Chi.-Kent L. Rev. 1557, 1559 (1959). The *Decretum* became a main source of canon law until the completion of the first Code of Canon Law, which appeared in 1918.

Early Church view of marriage. The Church viewed marriage as an association created by God as part of nature to enable man and woman to "be fruitful and multiply" and to raise children in the service and love of God. Marriage was viewed as rising to the dignity of a sacrament when properly contracted between Christians. The lifelong union of body, soul, and mind within the marital estate came to symbolize the eternal union between Christ and his church. Couples who participated in this sacrament were thought to receive special graces.

Medieval annulment. Once married, the canon law provided no basis for an absolute divorce. Remarriage was not allowed. However, it recognized two types of actions associated with the concept of a divorce: divorce *a mensa et thoro* and divorce *a vinculo*. A divorce *a vinculo* had the effect of totally dissolving the marital bond. It was essentially an annulment, not a divorce as we understand that term today, and the grounds for it were extremely limited. A divorce *a vinculo* might be granted if the marriage was entered into by force, fear, fraud, or through inducement of parents, masters, or feudal or manorial lords. *See* Charles J. Reid, Jr., *The Augustinian Goods of Marriage: The Disappearing Cornerstone of the American Law of Marriage*, 8 BYU J. Pub. L. 449, 457 (2004).

Medieval divorce from bed and board. The second basis for dissolving a marriage under Church law was a divorce *a mensa et thoro*. It removed the marriage obligation but did not free the parties to remarry. A divorce *a mensa et thoro* could be granted because of a partner's adultery or cruel treatment. In ecclesiastical terms, remarriage was the equivalent of the crime of bigamy. A divorce *a mensa et thoro* approximates the modern divorce from bed and board.

Protestant Reformation. The sixteenth-century Protestant Reformation, with its assertion that human traditions had perverted the true meaning of the Bible, challenged the traditional Catholic view that an absolute divorce was unattainable. Martin Luther is sometimes credited with suggesting the possibility of a divorce when he declared that marriage was not a sacrament but a natural and social institution that fell under the natural and civil law, not under Church law. *See* Shaakirrah R. Sanders, *The Cyclical Nature of Divorce in the Western Legal Tradition*, 50 Loy. L. Rev. 407 (Summer 2004) (exploring the Protestant Revolution's rejection of indissolubility and acceptance of divorce in limited circumstances).

Parliamentary divorce. Another possible avenue of divorce crept into English law in the seventeenth century: the Parliamentary divorce. By 1670 the idea that Parliament could divorce a couple had become a part of English law. A handful of legislative divorces were granted by the English Parliament, but only to aristocrats. *See* Danaya C. Wright, *"Well-Behaved Women Don't Make History": Rethinking English Family, Law, and History*, 19 Wis. Women's L.J. 211, 212-213 (Fall

2004). It was not until 1857 that England passed a law that permitted the public to obtain an absolute divorce.

REFLECTIVE QUESTIONS	**In what ways does it appear that various ancient religious views of marriage may have influenced the development of marriage laws in the United States? Do they appear to continue to influence marriage laws today?**

1.3 CULTURE: THE COMMON LAW VIEW OF MARRIED WOMEN

The early American settlers, greatly influenced by their English roots, implemented the biblically derived concept of the unity of husband and wife. The unit was headed by the husband and it was generally accepted that a marriage could not be dissolved. However, with statehood, some jurisdictions began to enact divorce laws. However, there were few divorces and they often were difficult to attain. *See* Vivian Hamilton, *Principles of U.S. Family Law, supra.*

Wife's legal existence suspended. The common law scheme that made for unity in the marriage relations of husband and wife was extensive. *Palmer v. Turner*, 43 S.W.2d 1017, 1018 (Ky. App. 1931). To secure unity when a couple married, the wife's legal existence was suspended or extinguished. The "very legal being and existence of the woman was suspended during coverture, or entirely merged or incorporated in that of the husband." *Ibid.* A wife surrendered her property to her husband, and she was placed within her husband's keeping, so far as her civil rights were concerned. A wife could not earn for herself or contract, sue, be contracted with, or be sued, in her own right. While the wife's husband lost nothing by the marriage, the wife surrendered her property and lost her independence and identity in law.

Use of force by husband on wife. The law also gave the husband power to use such a degree of force as is necessary to make the wife behave herself and know her place. *Joyner v. Joyner*, 59 N.C. (6 Jones Eq.) 322, 325 (1862).

Owner of property. Upon marriage a husband became the owner absolutely of the wife's personal property, and any personal property she acquired during the marriage vested immediately in him. He was entitled to any rents arising from her land. *Dotson v. Dotson*, 189 S.W. 894 (Ky. 1916). He could sell, convey, or mortgage his land without her joining in the instrument with him. He had the right to select and fix her domicile, and it was her duty to accept it. When she died, he had the right to select her burial place, or to change it. *Neighbors v. Neighbors*, 65 S.W. 607 (Ky. 1901).

Services. The common law also gave a husband a proprietary interest in the services of his wife and minor children. W. Prosser, *The Law of Torts* §124, at 916 (W. Keeton 5th ed. 1984). When a wife or minor child was injured by the tort of a third party, the husband or father was entitled to recover from the tortfeasor for lost services. The action was viewed as involving a master who had lost the services of an injured servant. W. Prosser, *supra*, §125, at 931-935. Because at common law a husband and wife, in legal fiction, are one person, neither could maintain a civil action against the other based on a tort. *Carmichael v. Carmichael*, 187 S.E. 116 (Ga. App. 1936).

Purpose of marriage. Procreation was considered the primary purpose of the marriage relation. *Chavias v. Chavias*, 184 N.Y.S. 761, 762 (N.Y. 1920). A wife's principal responsibility was to the home and children, and women were seldom allowed to enter a "man's profession."

In 1872, the Supreme Court upheld the constitutionality of a state law that denied women the right to practice law solely on grounds of sex. *Bradwell v. Illinois*, 83 U.S. 130 (1872). The Court in that decision observed the following:

> [T]he civil law, as well as nature herself, has always recognized a wide difference in the respective spheres and destinies of man and woman. Man is, or should be, woman's protector and defender. The natural and proper timidity and delicacy which belongs to the female sex evidently unfits it for many of the occupations of civil life. The constitution of the family organization, which is founded in the divine ordinance, as well as in the nature of things, indicates the domestic sphere as that which properly belongs to the domain and functions of womanhood. . . .
>
> The paramount destiny and mission of woman are to fulfill the noble and benign offices of wife and mother. This is the law of the Creator. And the rules of civil society must be adapted to the general constitution of things, and cannot be based upon exceptional cases.

Id. at 141-142. The *Bradwell* decision was used to support other actions denying women civil rights. *See, e.g., United States v. Anthony*, 24 F. Cas. 829 (N.D.N.Y. 1873) (the Fourteenth Amendment did not give a woman the right to vote, and the voting by Susan Anthony was unlawful); *Robinson's Case*, 131 Mass. 376 (1881) ("[t]he conclusion that women cannot be admitted to the bar under the existing statutes of the Commonwealth is in accordance with judgments of the highest courts of the States of Illinois and Wisconsin").

Husband's duty of support. A husband had a common law duty to support his wife, which may have in part acted as a counterbalance to the legal disabilities imposed on her because of marriage and as compensation for his right to her earnings and services. If a husband refused to supply his wife with necessaries, she was authorized to purchase them on his credit, making him liable to the supplier for their costs. She had a right to have her debts before marriage paid by the husband, and she secured a life interest in one-third part of his estates of inheritance if she survived him.

REFLECTIVE QUESTIONS	What role did the "unity doctrine" play in the development of the common law of marriage in the United States? What may account for the demise of this doctrine? What may explain the *Bradwell* decision? Has the view of the purpose of marriage changed since the sixteenth century?

1.4 CULTURE: THE WOMEN'S MOVEMENT, 1900 TO DATE

Married Women's Acts. Passage of Married Women's Acts in many states around the close of the nineteenth century gave married women new rights, including the right to sue for torts committed against them, engage in business, and make contracts. In most versions of a Married Women's Act, a wife became competent to sue in her own name for injuries to herself and could retain the proceeds of those actions. Her injuries, for which she could recover judgment, included loss of her capacity to render services in the home as well as to earn money on the outside; the husband no longer had a claim for household help required because of his wife's disablement.

These statutes were often construed in a strained and grudging fashion. For example, in *Fernandez v. Fernandez*, 135 A.2d 886 (Md. 1957), the court observed that "the cases in Maryland have interpreted the [Married Women's] Act with such strictness and have given it such limited effect that we find ourselves unable to follow the authorities elsewhere without overruling our prior decision."

Congress and the Supreme Court step in. The 1960s signaled significant changes in how women were to be legally viewed in the United States as Congress and the Supreme Court began eliminating laws that discriminated against them on the basis of gender. For example, Congress enacted the 1963 Equal Pay Act and Title VII of the 1963 Civil Rights Act, which installed a policy of equal opportunity for women. In *Reed v. Reed*, 404 U.S. 71 (1971), the Court struck down an Idaho statute as unconstitutional because it gave priority to men in the administration of estates. In *Cleveland Bd. of Educ. v. LaFleur*, 414 U.S. 632 (1974), the Court invalidated a school board mandate that a teacher who became pregnant must take maternity leave. In *United States v. Virginia*, 518 U.S. 515 (1996), the Court struck down a policy that restricted admission to a public military academy to males only, stating that parties who seek to defend a gender-based classification must show an exceedingly persuasive justification. In *J.E.B. v. Alabama ex rel. T.B.*, 511 U.S. 127 (1994), the Court held that intentional discrimination on the basis of gender by state actors in use of peremptory strikes in jury selection violates the Equal Protection Clause. An Oklahoma law that permitted the sale of 3.2 beer to women over age 18 but to men only over age 21 was ruled unconstitutional in *Craig v. Boren*, 429 U.S. 190 (1976).

REFLECTIVE QUESTIONS How significant has the role of Congress and the Supreme Court been in reducing the historic discrimination against women?

1.5 STATE SOVEREIGNTY: FULL FAITH AND CREDIT CLAUSE

Among other issues, the Full Faith and Credit Clause is important in family law because it attempts to regularize recognition of marriage and divorce decisions among the states. Article IV, §1, of the Constitution commands that "Full Faith and Credit shall be given in each State to the public Acts, Records, and Judicial Proceedings of every other State," and provides that "Congress may by general Laws prescribe the Manner in which such Acts, Records and Proceedings shall be proved, and the Effect thereof." Congress has declared that judgments "shall have such faith and credit given to them in every court within the United States as they have by law or usage in the courts of the State from which they are taken." Act of May 26, 1790.

With the passage of the Full Faith and Credit Clause, the status of the several states as independent foreign sovereignties was dramatically altered. No longer was each state free to ignore rights and obligations created under the laws or established by the judicial proceedings of the others. The Full Faith and Credit Clause did this by making each state an integral part of a single nation in which rights judicially established in any part are given nationwide application.

The Full Faith and Credit Clause also established throughout the federal system the salutary principle that litigation once pursued to judgment shall be as conclusive of the rights of the parties in every other court as in that where the judgment was rendered, so that a cause of action merged in a judgment in one state is likewise merged in every other state. 28 U.S.C.A. §1738. Under the Full Faith and Credit Clause, a defendant may not a second time challenge the validity of the plaintiff's right that has ripened into a judgment, and a plaintiff may not for his single cause of action secure a second or a greater recovery. *See Hampton v. McConnel*, 16 U.S. 234 (1818).

REFLECTIVE QUESTIONS What role does the Full Faith and Credit Clause play in requiring that one state recognize a marriage legally made in another state? What problems in terms of marriage and divorce do you believe would arise without this constitutional provision?

1.6 STATE SOVEREIGNTY: REFUSAL TO RECOGNIZE SISTER STATE JUDGMENTS

Background to *Jackson v. Jackson*

The case that follows for discussion was decided more than two centuries ago. It provides a window into New York's early states' rights perspective on marriage and divorce. The case also provides a glimpse at the potential influence that religious views in New York may have had on that state's secular divorce statutes. Finally, the decision raises some interesting Full Faith and Credit Clause issues, none of which were considered in the proceeding.

Nancy Jackson married Archibald Jackson in 1800 in the state of New York. In 1803 Nancy traveled to Vermont where she sought a divorce. In her Vermont petition, Nancy alleged that Archibald abused her, beat her, and threatened her life. She also alleged that because of his severe temper she could not live with him. The Vermont court granted her a divorce and ordered Archibald to pay a total of fifteen hundred dollars for alimony.

Upon her return to New York, she asked a New York court to recognize the Vermont divorce decree and enforce the alimony provision. Archibald objected to New York assisting his ex-wife in any way. He did not, however, claim that the Vermont court that issued the divorce decree lacked jurisdiction or that there were any irregularities in the Vermont proceeding. Rather, he argued that as a matter of public policy, the New York court should not provide Nancy with a legal basis to collect alimony.

JACKSON
v.
JACKSON

Supreme Court of New York
1 Johns. 424 (1804)

SPENCER, J. . . . [T]he question at once arises, how far this court will lend its assistance to carry into effect, between its own citizens, a judgment of a foreign court, where the plaintiff has resorted to that court, with the avowed object of gaining relief in a case not provided for by our laws, and against the policy of them. I say, against the policy of our laws, because our own legislature having authorized divorces but in one case, intolerable severity of treatment does not warrant a divorce. In delivering the judgment I have formed in the present case, it is not to be understood that I mean to impugn the principle, that proper deference is due to the decisions of the courts of justice in a neighboring state, in a case properly before them, and when they do not encroach on the rights of other states.

We are not called on, in the present case, to pronounce on the legal effect of the divorce granted by the Supreme Court of Vermont. Here is a plain attempt by one of our own citizens to evade the force of our laws. The plaintiff, to obtain a divorce, which our laws do not allow, instituted her proceedings in Vermont, whilst she was an inhabitant, and an actual resident, of this state, and while her domicile continued within this state; for she was incapable, during her coverture, of acquiring a domicile distinct from that of her husband. It may be laid down as a general principle, that whenever an act is done in *fraudem legis*, it cannot be the basis of a suit in the courts of the country whose laws are attempted to be infringed. . . . The court is, therefore, of the opinion, that judgment must be given for the defendant.

DISCUSSION QUESTIONS   FOR *JACKSON v. JACKSON*

A. If the lawyer for Ms. Jackson had argued to the New York Court that the Full Faith and Credit Clause applied to this dispute, what should have been the outcome? (Note that it is not clear that the Vermont court had personal jurisdiction over the ex-husband; however, he did not raise the issue.)

B. After the decision in *Jackson*, does Ms. Jackson have any remedy available to her to collect the alimony award? Can she, for example, return to the Vermont court and ask it for assistance? Can she ignore the Vermont decree and seek a "new" divorce in New York?

C. Assume that in 2014 a Vermont court had personal jurisdiction over a couple and issued a divorce decree and awarded alimony. If the parties moved to Iowa in 2016 and became domiciled there, could an Iowa court ignore the terms of the Vermont decree?

D. Before the United States Supreme Court legalized same-sex marriage, some states recognized same-sex marriages from other states while others did not. For example, assume that a Massachusetts court married a same-sex couple who returned to Pennsylvania following the ceremony. Pennsylvania law defined marriage as a contract between one man and one woman. Did Pennsylvania have to recognize the Massachusetts marriage under the Full Faith and Credit Clause of the Constitution? Could the couple have subsequently obtained a divorce in Pennsylvania? *See Kern v. Taney*, 2010 WL 2510988 (Pa. Com. Pl. 2010) (Pennsylvania could not grant a divorce but could entertain an action to declare the relationship void); *B.S. v. F.B.*, 883 N.Y.S.2d 458 (N.Y. Sup. 2009) (civil union was not "marriage," as required to grant divorce); *Chambers v. Ormiston*, 935 A.2d 956 (R.I. 2007) (without jurisdiction to entertain divorce petition involving same-sex couple who were married in Massachusetts).

E. Until 1966, adultery remained the only recognized ground for divorce in New York. Most agree that the Roman Catholic Church most likely played a role in limiting divorce in the face of many efforts to liberalize the law prior to that time. What social or political views regarding the family, religion, and state sovereignty are implied or expressed by the decision in *Jackson*? Was there an "appropriate" separation between religion and the state when *Jackson* was decided?

1.7 PROTECTING MARRIAGE: BREACH OF PROMISE TO MARRY

The common law in the United States used both civil and criminal actions to enhance and protect marriage. One of the civil actions it adopted from the English ecclesiastical courts was the breach of promise cause of action. *Wildey v. Springs*, 47 F.3d 1475, 1479 (7th Cir. 1995). Although the cause of action is viewed as arising from the breach of a contract (the contract being the mutual promises to marry), the damages allowable resemble a tort action. For example, a plaintiff may recover for loss to reputation, mental anguish, and injury to health. A plaintiff may also recover expenditures made in preparation for the marriage and loss of the pecuniary and social advantages that the promised marriage offered. Some states allowed aggravated damages for seduction under promise to marry, and a few allowed punitive damages when the defendant's acts were malicious or fraudulent. *See* Timothy J. Sullivan, *Punitive Damages in the Law of Contract: The Reality and the Illusion of Legal Change*, 61 Minn. L. Rev. 207, 222-223 (1977).

The common law reasoned that the failure of a man to conclude a promised marriage was damaging to the reputation of the innocent woman, who was willing to go through with it. The woman was considered humiliated before the community, stigmatized because of a possible loss of virginity, and placed in a position where it might well be difficult to find another suitor.

A breach of promise to marry claim tended to serve dual ideals. First, it appealed to vestiges of the older notion that marriage was a property transaction completed after complex family negotiations. Second, it began to pay tribute to the emerging ideal that marriage was a sacred contract premised upon affection and emotional commitment.

Heartbalm claims. The breach of promise to marry action fell into a category of cases known as "heartbalm" claims. The money damages awarded to successful plaintiffs were considered balms for broken hearts. The actions were tried to a jury, which in the appropriate case, could award damages to a father for seduction and to his daughter for breach of promise to marry.

The action began to drop into disrepute by the early twentieth century. Three principal reasons are given for the decline. First, there was a concern with possible unfounded claims, given the lax standards of proof, to extort out-of-court settlements. Second, there was a concern with the excessive amount of damages that were often awarded, which prompted disdain for the actions. Finally, most concluded that the ideals that the action intended to serve were anachronistic. After all, modern women were receiving greater social and economic freedom and the loss of an initial suitor posed a lesser threat to future prospects than it might have done in the nineteenth century.

Today, an action for breach of promise to marry continues to exist in a small number of jurisdictions. *See, e.g., Finch v. Dasgupta,* 555 S.E.2d 22 (Ga. App. 2001). However, in a majority of jurisdictions, a breach of a marriage agreement is not of itself a recognized wrong, and no action may be maintained for such a breach.

REFLECTIVE QUESTIONS	What was the purpose of the breach of contract to marry cause of action under the common law? Should it remain a cause of action today or should it be abolished?

1.8 PROTECTING MARRIAGE: REMARRIAGE LIMITATIONS

There is no firmly rooted tradition in the United States that requires the government to allow either an easy divorce or a quick remarriage following a divorce. Many states initially adopted statutes that required a waiting period following a divorce before a person could remarry. It was thought that the wait might foster reconciliation by allowing the parties time to cure their marital difficulties.

Typically, a nineteenth-century state statute prohibited remarriage within six months of a divorce. A marriage entered into within a six-month period following a divorce was considered void. During that six-month interval, the parties remained husband and wife. Moreover, it was thought that the prevailing party was to conduct him- or herself as a faithful spouse until the entry of the final decree at the end of the six-month waiting period.

Some statutes were harsh. For example, in Pennsylvania an 1815 statute barred a divorced person from ever marrying a lover with whom the person had sexual relations during the former marriage. The statute declared that the "wife or husband who shall have been guilty of the crime of adultery, shall not marry the person with whom the said crime was committed during the life of the former wife or husband." When a Pennsylvania husband traveled to Maryland and married his "paramour," the Pennsylvania Supreme Court refused to recognize the marriage when the couple returned to that state because it was against public morals and contrary to the expressed public policy of the state. *In re Stull's Estate,* 39 A. 16 (Penn. 1898).

REFLECTIVE QUESTIONS	What is the purpose of statutory remarriage limitations? What role, if any, should they play today?

1.9 PROTECTING MARRIAGE: ALIENATION OF AFFECTION, CRIMINAL CONVERSATION

In addition to the breach of contract to marry cause of action already discussed, the common law strove to protect marriage by recognizing other causes of action, such as alienation of affection and criminal conversation (heartbalm actions).

An alienation of affection claim is an off-shoot of the common law tort of depriving a master of his quasi-proprietary interest in his servant. W. Page Keeton et al., *Prosser and Keeton on the Law of Torts* §124, at 916 (5th ed. 1984). Because the common law viewed women and children as property of the husband or father, this tort was extended to include their services. *Ibid.* The action eventually changed from compensation for services to compensation for loss of affection and companionship. The tort was based on the theory that a wife's body belonged to the husband and anyone who trespassed upon the husband's property by seducing his wife was liable for damages. *Tinker v. Colwell*, 193 U.S. 473, 483 (1904). A wife did not have a similar claim until much later in the development of the tort.

To prove an alienation claim, a husband had to show a valid marriage, the defendant's wrongful conduct with the spouse, a loss of consortium, and a causal connection between defendant's conduct and plaintiff's loss. Damages were awarded based on the quality and duration of the spouse's relationship. Punitive damages could be sought if a defendant's conduct was malicious and the defendant had the ability to pay.

By the 1930s, states were well on their way to eliminating many heartbalm actions. These actions were criticized as providing an uncertain basis in damages, and damages were largely punitive in nature. It was argued that the original basis for the alienation of affection claim had been removed and the action was susceptible to abuse. Moreover, such claims tended to attract a disproportionate amount of publicity. It was also thought that they presented opportunities for blackmail and were often brought merely for mercenary or vindictive reasons. *O'Neil v. Schuckardt*, 733 P.2d 693 (Idaho 1986).

By 1999, Hawaii, Illinois, Mississippi, Missouri, New Hampshire, New Mexico, North Carolina, South Dakota, and Utah maintained a cause of action for alienation of affections. Jurisdictions that retain these actions argue that the purpose of a cause of action for alienation of affection is to protect the love, society, companionship, and comfort that form the foundation of a marriage — that of consortium. *Saunders v. Alford*, 607 So. 2d 1214, 1215 (Miss. 1992).

Defenses to an alienation of affection claim. Several defenses to an alienation of affection claim are available depending upon the status of the defendant. For example, parents are privileged to alienate the affections of their child's spouse in a good faith effort to protect their child's welfare. The privilege terminates when a parent acts with ill will. It also terminates when a parent acts unreasonably under the circumstances.

The clergy could invoke religious motives as a defense to an action for alienation of affections. However, if a member of the clergy deliberately invaded the marriage, that person could be held liable, despite a religious purpose. *Bear v. Reformed Mennonite Church*, 341 A.2d 105, 107 (Pa. 1975).

REFLECTIVE QUESTIONS	**What constitutes a cause of action for an alienation of affections claim? What are the defenses? Should this cause of action be available in today's "modern world"?**

Criminal conversation. Criminal conversation is another common law heartbalm claim intended to protect marriage. Criminal conversation is usually defined as meaning that adulterous relations exist between the defendant and the spouse of the plaintiff. *Fennell v. Littlejohn*, 125 S.E.2d 408, 411 (S.C. 1962). To sustain the action, the plaintiff must establish (1) the marriage between the spouses, and (2) sexual intercourse between the defendant and the spouse during coverture. *Ibid.* At one time, criminal conversation was based on the premise that one who interfered with the husband's right to exclusive possession of his wife's body was liable in trespass to the husband for the injury done by seducing the wife. However, the basis for a common law criminal conversation claim evolved, so that the law eventually regarded its purpose to be the protection of the marriage relationship against those who might wrongfully intrude, even when the possibility of reconciliation is remote. *Id.* at 412. Under this theory, a wife also possessed the legal right to bring a corresponding action when her husband engaged in adultery. *See Rivers v. Rivers*, 354 S.E.2d 784 (S.C. 1987) (wife successfully brought an action against her husband's paramour for criminal conversation — superseded by statute).

A majority of states have acknowledged that criminal conversation, as well as alienation of affection claims, are rooted in antiquated perceptions that a wife is a chattel of her husband and have eliminated them. The actions have survived in some jurisdictions with the theory that they afford some protection to marital relationships.

REFLECTIVE QUESTIONS	**What is the distinction between an alienation of affections claim and a criminal conversion claim? Do these actions have any utility today in regulating marriage?**

1.10 REGULATING MARRIAGE AND DIVORCE

Background to *Maynard v. Hill*

Maynard v. Hill is a landmark decision that explores the legal theory that forms the basis of governmental power to regulate marriage and divorce. It also considers the question of whether a marriage contract is a private agreement between two persons or is a "status" that can be regulated by the government. *See* Steven H. Hobbs, *Love on the Oregon Trail: What the Story of* Maynard v. Hill *Teaches Us About Marriage and Democratic Self-Governance*, 32 Hofstra L. Rev. 111 (Fall 2003).

The dispute in *Maynard v. Hill* involves the validity of a legislative divorce and its impact on qualifying for a federal land grant program. In 1852-1853 marriage was a prerequisite for obtaining a large tract of public land in the Oregon Territory. *Id.* at 112. If married, an applicant received 640 acres, of which 320 acres were granted to him and 320 acres were granted to his wife in her name. Maynard was divorced during the period the statute set for qualifying for a full grant, and he received only 320 acres (the west tract). The government subsequently transferred the remaining 320 acres (the east tract) to other purchasers, one of whom was Mr. Hill. If the Court ruled that the legislative divorce was invalid, then Maynard was still married to his first wife at the time of the land grant, and Maynard's heirs argue that the east tract should also have been awarded to her rather than Hill.

Among the questions the Court is asked to consider are the following: Did the territorial legislature have the power to grant Maynard a legislative divorce? If it had the power to grant a legislative divorce, does the legislation violate the Constitution?

MAYNARD
v.
HILL

Supreme Court of the United States
125 U.S. 190 (1888)

Appeal from the Supreme Court of the Territory of Washington.

[STATEMENT OF THE CASE] This is a suit in equity to charge the defendants, as trustees of certain lands in King County, Washington Territory, and compel a conveyance thereof to the plaintiffs. The case comes here on appeal from a judgment of the Supreme Court of the Territory, sustaining the defendants' demurrer, and dismissing the complaint.

The material facts, as disclosed by the complaint, are briefly these: In 1828 David S. Maynard and Lydia A. Maynard intermarried in the State of Vermont, and lived there together as husband and wife until 1850, when they removed to Ohio. The plaintiffs, Henry C. Maynard and Frances J. Patterson, are their children, and the only issue of the marriage. David S. Maynard died intestate in the year 1873 and Lydia A. Maynard in the year 1879.

In 1850 the husband left his family in Ohio and started overland for California, under a promise to his wife that he would either return or send for her and the children within two years, and that in the meantime he would send her the means of support. He left her without such means, and never afterwards contributed anything for her support or that of the children.

On the 16th of September following he took up his residence in the Territory of Oregon, in that part which is now Washington Territory, and continued ever afterwards to reside there. On the 3d of April, 1852, he settled upon and claimed, as a married man, a tract of land of 640 acres, described in the bill, under the act of Congress of September 27, 1850, "creating the office of surveyor general of public lands in Oregon, and to provide for the survey, and to make donations to settlers of the said public lands," and resided thereon until his death.

On the 22d day of December, 1852, an act was passed by the Legislative Assembly of the Territory, purporting to dissolve the bonds of matrimony between him and his wife. The act is in these words:

An act to provide for the dissolution of the bonds of matrimony heretofore existing between D. S. Maynard and Lydia A. Maynard, his wife.

SEC. 1. Be it enacted by the Legislative Assembly of the Territory of Oregon, That the bonds of matrimony heretofore existing between D. S. Maynard and Lydia A. Maynard be, and the same are, hereby dissolved.

Passed the House of Representatives, Dec. 22d, 1852.

The complaint alleges that no cause existed at any time for this divorce; that no notice was given to the wife of any application by the husband for a divorce, or of the introduction or pendency of the bill for that act in the Legislative Assembly; that she had no knowledge of the passage of the act until July, 1853; that at the time she was not within the limits or an inhabitant of Oregon; that she never became a resident of either the Territory or State of Oregon; and that she never in any manner acquiesced in or consented to the act; and the plaintiffs insist that the Legislative Assembly had no authority to pass the act; that the same is absolutely void; and that the parties were never lawfully divorced.

On or about the 15th of January, 1853, the husband thus divorced intermarried with one Catherine T. Brashears, and thereafter they lived together as husband and wife until his death. On the 7th of November, 1853, he filed with the Surveyor General of Oregon the certificate required under the donation act of September 27, 1850, as amended by the act of the 14th of February, 1853, accompanied with an affidavit of his residence in Oregon from the 16th of September, 1850, and on the land claimed from April 3, 1852, and that he was married to Lydia A. Maynard until the 24th of December, 1852, having been married to her in Vermont in August, 1828. The notification was also accompanied with corroborative affidavits of two other parties that he had within their knowledge resided upon and cultivated the land from the 3d of April, 1852.

FIELD, J. As seen by the statement of the case, two questions are presented for our consideration: first, was the act of the Legislative Assembly of the Territory of Oregon of the 22d of December, 1852, declaring the bonds of matrimony between David S. Maynard and his wife dissolved, valid and effectual to divorce the parties; and, second, if valid and effectual for that purpose, did such divorce defeat any rights of the wife to a portion of the donation claim. . . .

When this country was settled, the power to grant a divorce from the bonds of matrimony was exercised by the Parliament of England. The ecclesiastical courts of that country were limited to the granting of divorces from bed and board. Naturally, the legislative assemblies of the colonies followed the example of Parliament and treated the subject as one within their province. And, until a recent period, legislative divorces have been granted, with few exceptions, in all the States. . . .

The facts alleged in the bill of complaint, that no cause existed for the divorce, and that it was obtained without the knowledge of the wife, cannot affect the validity of the act. Knowledge or ignorance of parties of intended legislation does not affect its validity, if within the competency of the legislature. The facts mentioned as to the neglect of the husband to send to his wife, whom he left in Ohio, any means for her support or that of her children, in disregard of his promise, shows conduct meriting the strongest reprobation, and if the facts stated had been brought to the attention of Congress, that body might and probably would have annulled the act. Be that as it may, the loose morals and shameless conduct of the husband can have no bearing upon the question of the existence or absence of power in the Assembly to pass the act.

[The] legislative power of the Territory [extends] to all rightful subjects of legislation "not inconsistent with the Constitution and laws of the United States." The only inconsistency suggested is that it impairs the obligation of the contract of marriage. Assuming that the prohibition of the federal Constitution against the impairment of contracts by state legislation applies equally, as would seem to be the opinion of the Supreme Court of the Territory, to legislation by territorial legislatures, we are clear that marriage is not a contract within the meaning of the prohibition. As was said by Chief Justice Marshall in the Dartmouth College Case, not by way of judgment, but in answer to objections urged to positions taken:

> The provision of the Constitution never has been understood to embrace other contracts than those which respect property or some object of value, and confer rights which may be asserted in a court of justice. It never has been understood to restrict the general right of the legislature to legislate on the subject of divorces.

It is also to be observed that, whilst marriage is often termed by text writers and in decisions of courts a civil contract — generally to indicate that it must be founded upon the agreement of the parties, and does not require any religious ceremony for its solemnization — it is something more than a mere contract. The consent of the parties is of course essential to its existence, but when the contract to marry is executed by the marriage, a relation between the parties is created which they cannot change. Other contracts may be modified, restricted, or enlarged, or entirely released upon the consent of the parties. Not so with marriage. The relation once formed, the law steps in and holds the parties to various obligations and liabilities. It is an institution, in the maintenance of which in its purity the public is deeply interested, for it is the foundation of the family and of society, without which there would be neither civilization nor progress. This view is well expressed by the Supreme Court of Maine in *Adams v. Palmer.* Said that court, speaking by Chief Justice Appleton:

When the contracting parties have entered into the married state, they have not so much entered into a contract as into a new relation, the rights, duties, and obligations of which rest not upon their agreement, but upon the general law of the State, statutory or common, which defines and prescribes those rights, duties, and obligations. They are of law, not contract. It was of contract that the relation should be established, but, being established, the power of the parties as to its extent or duration is at an end. Their rights under it are determined by the will of the sovereign, as evidenced by law. They can neither be modified nor changed by any agreement of parties. It is a relation for life, and the parties cannot terminate it at any shorter period by virtue of any contract they may make. The reciprocal rights arising from this relation, so long as it continues, are such as the law determines from time to time, and none other.

And again:

It is not, then, a contract within the meaning of the clause of the Constitution which prohibits the impairing the obligation of contracts. It is, rather, a social relation, like that of parent and child, the obligations of which arise not from the consent of concurring minds, but are the creation of the law itself; a relation the most important, as affecting the happiness of individuals, the first step from barbarism to incipient civilization, the purest tie of social life and the true basis of human progress.

In *Noel v. Ewing*, the question was before the Supreme Court of Indiana as to the competency of the legislature of the State to change the relative rights of husband and wife after marriage, which led to a consideration of the nature of marriage; and the court said:

Some confusion has arisen from confounding the contract to marry with the marriage relation itself. And still more is engendered by regarding husband and wife as strictly parties to a subsisting contract. At common law, marriage as a status had few elements of contract about it. For instance, no other contract merged the legal existence of the parties into one. Other distinctive elements will readily suggest themselves, which rob it of most of its characteristics as a contract, and leave it simply as a status or institution. As such, it is not so much the result of private agreement, as of public ordination. In every enlightened government, it is preeminently the basis of civil institutions, and thus an object of the deepest public concern. In this light, marriage is more than contract. It is not a mere matter of pecuniary consideration. It is a great public institution, giving character to our whole civil polity.

In accordance with these views was the judgment of Mr. Justice Story, in a note to the Chapter on marriage, in his work on the Conflict of Laws, after stating that he had treated marriage as a contract in the common sense of the word, because this was the light in which it was ordinarily viewed by jurists, domestic as well as foreign he adds:

But it appears to me to be something more than a mere contract. It is rather to be deemed an institution of society, founded upon consent and contract of the parties, and in this view it has some peculiarities in its nature, character, operation and extent of obligation, different from what belong to ordinary contracts. . . .

When, therefore, the act was passed divorcing the husband and wife, he had no vested interest in the land, and she could have no interest greater than his. Nothing had then been acquired by his residence and cultivation which gave him anything more than a mere possessory right; a right to remain on the land so as to enable him to comply with the conditions upon which the title was to pass to him. After the divorce she had no such relation to him as to confer upon her any interest in the title subsequently acquired by him. A divorce ends all rights not previously vested. Interests which might vest in time, upon a continuance of the marriage relation, were gone. A wife divorced has no right of dower in his property; a husband divorced has no right by the courtesy in her lands, unless the statute authorizing the divorce specially confers such right.

It follows that the wife was not entitled to the east half of the donation claim. To entitle her to that half she must have continued his wife during his residence and cultivation of the land. The judgment of the Supreme Court of the Territory must therefore be affirmed; and it is so ordered.

DISCUSSION QUESTIONS FOR *MAYNARD v. HILL*

A. The Court distinguishes a marriage contract from a commercial contract. What are the most significant differences between the two contracts?

B. Assume in the following hypothetical that a wife brought an action for dissolution of a marriage and the husband moved to dismiss on ground that marriage is a contract and the state dissolution statute that required the wife to petition the court for divorce interferes with the constitutional right to contract. Essentially, he claims that marriage is a contract between him and his wife and that the state is barred from interfering with the relationship. He relies on *Dartmouth College v. Woodward*, 17 U.S. 518 (1819). In that case the parties litigated whether a charter granted to certain college trustees was a contract and, if so, whether it could be altered by laws passed by the state legislature. One of several arguments against a broad construction of "contract" was that even marriage is a contract, and its obligations are affected by the laws respecting divorces. *Id.* at 625-627. The Court held that the charter was a contract. The plaintiff's wife relies on *Maynard v. Hill*. Who will most likely prevail? *See Richter v. Richter*, 625 N.W.2d 490 (Minn. App. 2001).

C. Professor C. Quince Hopkins in *The Supreme Court's Family Law Doctrine Revisited: Insights from Social Science on Family Structures and Kinship Change in the United States*, 13 Cornell J.L. & Pub. Pol'y 431, 449 (Spring 2004), makes the following observation:

> In *Maynard v. Hill*, the . . . court decided that a state legislature had the power to regulate divorce. Bracketing its analysis of the legislature's power, based in part on the

historical practice in England and the colonies allowing such control, the Court stated: "Marriage, as creating the most important relation in life, as having more to do with the morals and civilization of a people than any other institution . . . is an institution, in the maintenance of which in its purity the public is deeply interested, for it is the foundation of the family and of society, without which there would be neither civilization nor progress." Later in the opinion, the Court continued in this vein, describing marriage as "a relation the most important, as affecting the happiness of individuals, the first step from barbarism to incipient civilization, the purest tie of social life, and the true basis of human progress." . . . [T]he *Maynard* court cited to no evidence supporting what is essentially an empirical claim.

Do you agree that the Court's views in *Maynard* are essentially empirical without evidentiary support? If so, what is the significance of this observation?

1.11 STATE EXCLUSIVITY TODAY: TENSION WITH FEDERAL GOVERNMENT

It is generally accurate to say that family law today remains primarily the province of state law. In fact, the Supreme Court has stated that "the whole subject of domestic relations and husband and wife, parent and child, belongs to the laws of the States and not the laws of the United States." *Rose v. Rose*, 481 U.S. 619, 625 (1987), quoting *In re Burrus*, 136 U.S. 586, 693-694 (1890).

The Tenth Amendment's proviso that "the powers not delegated to the United States by the Constitution, nor prohibited by it to the States, are reserved to the States respectively, or to the people" was historically used to justify state exclusivity. *See Labine v. Cincent*, 401 U.S. 531 (1971). Despite this constitutional proviso, through application of the Due Process or Equal Protection Clauses of the Fourteenth Amendment, and the First Amendment, the Supreme Court has expanded constitutional protection to abortion, adoption, termination of parental rights, and other areas of family law. *See generally* Linda D. Elrod, *The Federalization of Family Law*, 6-Sum Hum. Rts. 6 (Summer 2009).

Congress has also injected itself into several areas of family law. For example, when states could not agree on which jurisdiction should decide a fiercely contested interstate custody dispute, Congress stepped in to resolve the matter by enacting the Parental Kidnapping Prevention Act of 1980 (28 U.S.C. §1738A). In other areas, such as child support, Congress enacted national legislation with a direct impact on how state courts arrive at support decisions. The Adoption and Safe Families Act (ASFA) promotes adoption of children with special needs and the Adoption Assistance and Child Welfare Act (AACWA) provides incentives to move children from long-term foster care facilities to permanent homes. The Child Abuse Prevention and Treatment Act (CAPTA) creates programs and procedures for states to address the prevention and treatment of child abuse and neglect. The Child Support Enforcement Amendments require that states participate in the federal child support program.

These are a few examples of the many provisions passed into law by Congress that impact family law. Where states appear unwilling or incapable of solving a particular family law issue, one can anticipate continued involvement by Congress. In the process, states will continue to lose their claim that the whole subject of domestic relations belongs to the laws of the States and not the laws of the United States.

REFLECTIVE QUESTIONS	What may explain the movement into family law of Congress and the Supreme Court?

General Principles

1. The Court has repeatedly described marriage as "the foundation of the family and of society, without which there would be neither civilization nor progress." In *Meyer v. Nebraska*, 262 U.S. 390, 399 (1923), the Supreme Court recognized the right "to marry, establish a home and bring up children" as central to the Due Process Clause. In *Loving v. Virginia*, 388 U.S. 1, 12 (1967), the Court stated, "The freedom to marry has long been recognized as one of the vital personal rights essential to the orderly pursuit of happiness by free men."
2. Marriage is a social relation subject to the State's police power.
3. When the contract to marry is executed by the marriage, a relation between the parties is created that they cannot change without approval from the state.
4. At common law marriage conferred upon the husband the dominion of the wife's real estate. The rents and profits belonged to him *jure mariti.* They were not only under his personal control, but they could be seized by his creditors.
5. The federal government is one of limited powers. The Constitution does not grant the federal government power over marriage; the states have the exclusive power to define marriage within their territories. However, the federal government has the power to protect individual rights such as the right to marry consistent with notions of due process and equal protection. The federal government may legislate to protect individual rights and to establish a federal floor for such rights.
6. The Full Faith and Credit Clause encourages recognition of a state's marriages in other states.
7. The tort of criminal conversation is an action brought against a person who has sexual relations with the plaintiff's spouse. The only defense is the plaintiff-spouse's consent.
8. The tort of alienation of affections is an action brought against a person who has taken actions to deprive the plaintiff of the plaintiff's spouse's affections.

The plaintiff must show that the defendant knew of the marital relationship and acted for the purpose of adversely affecting it. A majority of states have judicially or statutorily abolished the tort of alienation of affections. *See Veeder v. Kennedy*, 589 N.W.2d 610, 614 nn.3-4 (S.D. 1999).

9. A breach of promise to marry and the other heartbalm torts have been abolished in a majority of jurisdictions.

Chapter Problems

1. Sherif Girgis, Robert P. George & Ryan T. Anderson, in their article, *What Is Marriage?*, 34 Harv. J.L. & Pub. Pol'y 245, 270-271 (Winter 2011), state that "[s]ociologists David Popenoe and Alan Wolfe have conducted research on Scandinavian countries that supports the conclusion that as marriage culture declines, state spending rises. This is why the state has an interest in marriages that is deeper than any interest it could have in ordinary friendships: Marriages bear a principled and practical connection to children. Strengthening the marriage culture improves children's shot at becoming upright and productive members of society." Do you agree with the authors' conclusion that "strengthening the marriage culture improves children's shot at becoming upright and productive members of society"? If you agree, what policy measures do you suggest the state and local governments take to strengthen marriage? What unforeseen circumstances might result from your policy suggestions, if any?

2. Assume that Alma and Albert were married for ten years when Alma met Pierre. Eventually, Alma moved out of the home she occupied with Albert to live with Pierre. Albert filed for divorce and asserted a claim for alienation of affections against Pierre. Pierre has moved to dismiss Albert's claim on the ground that it fails to state a claim for relief. In 1880, how would a court treat Pierre's motion? How will a court today view his motion?

3. Assume that Orville and Shirley seek a divorce from a court in 1900. The question of which party is guilty of causing the divorce is decided by a jury in Orville's favor. A divorce decree is entered, and Shirley is prohibited from marrying as long as the decree is in force. Despite the divorce decree, Shirley marries Sam in another state a week after the divorce from Orville is final. They return to the forum state, where Shirley is immediately arrested on the felony of violating the divorce decree. Does Shirley have a defense to the crime? If the divorce action occurred in 2012, would such provisions be upheld?

4. Assume that Lady Jane and Lord Paultry were married in a sixteenth-century ceremony by the clergy in London, England. Unfortunately, the relationship broke down and each fell in love with another person and desperately wanted to marry the other person. With Lord Paultry's agreement, Lady Jane sought the services of an ecclesiastical court to obtain a divorce. Would the court grant the couple a divorce?

5. Assume that George and Ann married in Iowa in the nineteenth century. Before marriage, Ann worked as a teacher and was paid a few hundred dollars a year. After they married, she continued teaching. George insisted he was entitled to the money that Ann earned from teaching and beat Ann with a switch if she didn't turn it over to him. He then used it for gambling at the local saloon. Ann sought assistance from a common law court to prevent George from beating her and using up her salary on gambling. How successful will she be?

Preparation for Practice

1. Observe the proceedings in a Family Court in your jurisdiction. Prepare a paper containing a list of five short questions to submit to your instructor about matters you did not understand about the proceeding. Include the date and time of your observation; name of court, names of the attorneys involved, and the name of the judge you observed.

2. Contact a local family law attorney and ask for a half hour interview. During your interview, focus on asking the attorney about the problems a lawyer practicing family law typically encounters in a divorce action. Prepare a paper containing the five most challenging problems when handling a divorce that the family lawyer shared with you during the interview. In your paper, please include the date and time of your interview, name of the attorney (attorney may request anonymity), and the length of the interview. Be prepared to share the views expressed by the lawyer in your paper during class discussion.

Chapter 2

Constitutionalizing Family Law

2.1 INTRODUCTION

Many of the more remarkable changes in family law in the last 40 years or so have come as a result of constitutional decisions at both the state and federal levels. The changes are remarkable because traditionally family law was once the exclusive province of state government and controlled by local statutes and the local judiciary. As vividly illustrated in this chapter, that "local control" perspective has been seriously eroded by numerous federal constitutional rulings. *See generally* Lynn D. Wardle, *State Marriage Amendments: Developments, Precedents, and Significance*, 7 Fla. Coastal L. Rev. 403 (Fall 2005) (discussing *inter alia* constitutional protections for the family in state and federal constitutions).

In this chapter, we have collected and heavily edited six of the more important United States Supreme Court decisions affecting family law. We anticipate that these decisions will provide the primary focus for discussion in this chapter.

Some of the many questions raised by this chapter include the following: What are the different constitutional "tests" used by the Court when considering specific family law issues? When did the Court first mention that the "family" possessed constitutional rights and why was that important? What was the basis for making the practice of polygamy a criminal offense? What was the basis for the criminal laws that punished persons of different ethnic and racial backgrounds if they married? Is poverty a barrier to marriage? After the Court decisions in the last several years, what types of sexual crimes remain constitutional? What is DOMA and what is its current status? What are the reasons the majority gives in *Obergefell v. Hodges* to support its conclusion that same-sex persons may marry? Why are state constitutions sometimes used in family law disputes rather than the federal Constitution?

| REFLECTIVE QUESTIONS | What are your goals for this chapter? |

2.2 FAMILY RIGHTS AND THE COURT

The Supreme Court first mentioned the family as possessing a constitutional right in *Meyer v. Nebraska*, 262 U.S. 390 (1923). In *Meyer* the Court reviewed the conviction of a private parochial school teacher who had violated a Nebraska law that prohibited teaching any foreign language to children under age 16. The Court found the provision unconstitutional, declaring that such a law interfered with the right of parents to rear and educate their children as they saw fit. In its ruling, the Court stated that the parental right was a fundamental "liberty" specially protected by the Fourteenth Amendment to the United States Constitution.

Professor Lynn D. Wardle in *The Proposed Federal Marriage Amendment and the Risks to Federalism*, 2 U. St. Thomas L.J. 137, 176 (Fall 2004), observes that after *Meyer v. Nebraska*, "the Supreme Court rarely decided more than two constitutional cases dealing with family law issues in any given term or year." For example, from 1945 through 1964 the Court averaged fewer than two family law decisions per term. However, from 1965 through 1984 the Court was often very active, with as many as 12 family law decisions handed down in a given year. Since 1984, the Court has averaged three to four family law decisions per year. *Ibid.*

| REFLECTIVE QUESTIONS | What is the significance of *Meyer v. Nebraska* to family law? |

2.3 BARRIERS: POLYGAMY

The practice of polygamy in Utah by Mormons in the nineteenth century generated one of the earliest decisions by the United States Supreme Court dealing with the question of who can marry in America. Polygamy, practiced by some Mormons as a part of their religion, clashed with federal criminal laws that prohibited and punished such relationships.

Mormonism, which is sometimes referred to as the Latter Day Saint movement, arose in western New York, the area where its founder Joseph Smith, Jr., was raised, during a period of religious revival in the early nineteenth century. Joseph Smith claimed to have many visions involving God, Jesus, and angelic Native American prophets. These claims were often not received well by those in the community, and anti-Mormon sentiment drove the Mormons to Utah in the late 1840s. Martha M. Ertman, *Race Treason: The Untold Story of America's Ban on Polygamy,* 19 Colum. J. Gender & L. 287 (2010). At the time a vast majority of Americans were traditional Christians and believed in monogamy. Mormons, however, believed that a man could have more than one wife.

Professor Ertman suggests that the nineteenth-century ban on polygamy arose because some antipolygamists viewed Mormons as committing political treason by establishing a separatist theocracy in Utah. Other opponents saw a social treason against the nation of white citizens "when Mormons adopted a supposedly barbaric marital form, one that was natural for Asiatic and African people, but so unnatural for Whites as to produce a new, degenerate species that threatened the project of white supremacy." *Ibid.*

REFLECTIVE QUESTIONS	Based on the above brief narration, list the "worst" and "best" reasons for banning polygamy.

Background to *Reynolds v. United States*

The federal government addressed the issue of polygamy in 1862 when President Abraham Lincoln signed the Morrill Anti-Bigamy Act. The Morrill Act outlawed polygamy throughout the United States. However, the government did little to enforce the law because of its preoccupation with the Civil War.

Congress strengthened its effort to ban polygamy with the passage of the Poland Law in 1874, which increased the powers of the federal judiciary within the territory of Utah. Mormon leader Brigham Young and George Q. Cannon, the territorial delegate to Congress and advisor to Young, decided to challenge the federal government's ban on polygamy. It is believed that Young and Cannon chose Young's personal secretary, a devout Mormon and practicing polygamist, George Reynolds, as the subject for their test case. The government indicted Reynolds for bigamy, and he was subsequently convicted. His challenge to the Morrill Act as violative of his First Amendment right to freedom of religion came before the Supreme Court in 1878. In one sense, the question the Court is being asked to answer is whether a social harm apart from discrimination is the legitimate concern of the federal government. In another sense, the Court is being asked to answer the question of whether a local community could define marriage more expansively than the rest of the country.

REYNOLDS
v.
UNITED STATES

Supreme Court of the United States
98 U.S. 145 (1878)

WAITE, C.J. On the trial, . . . the accused, proved that at the time of his alleged second marriage he was, and for many years before had been, a member of the Church of Jesus Christ of Latter-Day Saints, commonly called the Mormon Church, and a believer in its doctrines; that it was an accepted doctrine of that church "that it was the duty of male members of said church, circumstances permitting, to practice polygamy; . . . that this duty was enjoined by different books which the members of said church believed to be of divine origin, and among others the Holy Bible, and also that the members of the church believed that the practice of polygamy was directly enjoined upon the male members thereof by the Almighty God, in a revelation to Joseph Smith, the founder and prophet of said church; that the failing or refusing to practice polygamy by such male members of said church, when circumstances would admit, would be punished, and that the penalty for such failure and refusal would be damnation in the life to come." He also proved that he had received permission from the recognized authorities in said church to enter into polygamous marriage. . . .

Upon this proof he asked the court to instruct the jury that if they found from the evidence that he "was married as charged — if he was married — in pursuance of and in conformity with what he believed at the time to be a religious duty, that the verdict must be not guilty." This request was refused, and the court did charge that there must have been a criminal intent, but that if the defendant, under the influence of a religious belief that it was right — under an inspiration, if you please, that it was right — deliberately married a second time, having a first wife living, the want of consciousness of evil intent — the want of understanding on his part that he was committing a crime — did not excuse him; but the law inexorably in such case implies the criminal intent. . . .

Polygamy has always been odious among the northern and western nations of Europe, and, until the establishment of the Mormon Church, was almost exclusively a feature of the life of Asiatic and of African people. At common law, the second marriage was always void (2 Kent, Com. 79), and from the earliest history of England polygamy has been treated as an offence against society. After the establishment of the ecclesiastical courts, and until the time of James I, it was punished through the instrumentality of those tribunals, not merely because ecclesiastical rights had been violated, but because upon the separation of the ecclesiastical courts from the civil the ecclesiastical were supposed to be the most appropriate for the trial of matrimonial causes and offences against the rights of marriage, just as they were for testamentary causes and the settlement of the estates of deceased persons.

By the statute of 1 James I, the offence, if committed in England or Wales, was made punishable in the civil courts, and the penalty was death. As this statute was limited in its operation to England and Wales, it was at a very early period re-enacted, generally with some modifications, in all the colonies. In connection with the case we are now considering, it is a significant fact that . . . after the passage of the act establishing religious freedom, and after the convention of Virginia had recommended as an amendment to the Constitution of the United States the declaration in a bill of rights that "all men have an equal, natural, and unalienable right to the free exercise of religion, according to the dictates of conscience," the legislature of that State substantially enacted the statute of James I, death penalty included, because, as recited in the preamble, "it hath been doubted whether bigamy or polygamy be punishable by the laws of this Commonwealth."

From that day to this we think it may safely be said there never has been a time in any State of the Union when polygamy has not been an offence against society, cognizable by the civil courts and punishable with more or less severity. In the face of all this evidence, it is impossible to believe that the constitutional guaranty of religious freedom was intended to prohibit legislation in respect to this most important feature of social life. Marriage, while from its very nature a sacred obligation, is nevertheless, in most civilized nations, a civil contract, and usually regulated by law. Upon it society may be said to be built, and out of its fruits spring social relations and social obligations and duties, with which government is necessarily required to deal. In fact, according as monogamous or polygamous marriages are allowed, do we find the principles on which the government of the people, to a greater or less extent, rests. Professor Lieber says, polygamy leads to the patriarchal principle, and which, when applied to large communities, fetters the people in stationary despotism, while that principle cannot long exist in connection with monogamy. Chancellor Kent observes that this remark is equally striking and profound. An exceptional colony of polygamists under an exceptional leadership may sometimes exist for a time without appearing to disturb the social condition of the people who surround it; but there cannot be a doubt that, unless restricted by some form of constitution, it is within the legitimate scope of the power of every civil government to determine whether polygamy or monogamy shall be the law of social life under its dominion.

In our opinion, the statute immediately under consideration is within the legislative power of Congress. It is constitutional and valid as prescribing a rule of action for all those residing in the Territories, and in places over which the United States have exclusive control. This being so, the only question which remains is, whether those who make polygamy a part of their religion are excepted from the operation of the statute. If they are, then those who do not make polygamy a part of their religious belief may be found guilty and punished, while those who do, must be acquitted and go free. This would be introducing a new element into criminal law. Laws are made for the government of actions, and while they cannot interfere with mere religious belief and opinions, they may with practices. Suppose one believed that human sacrifices were a necessary part of religious worship, would it be seriously contended that the civil government under which he lived could not interfere to prevent a sacrifice? Or if a wife religiously believed it was her duty to burn herself upon the funeral pile of her dead husband, would it be beyond the power of the civil government to prevent her carrying her belief into practice?

So here, as a law of the organization of society under the exclusive dominion of the United States, it is provided that plural marriages shall not be allowed. Can a man excuse his practices to the contrary because of his religious belief? To permit this would be to make the professed doctrines of religious belief superior to the law of the land, and in effect to permit every citizen to become a law unto himself. Government could exist only in name under such circumstances.

A criminal intent is generally an element of crime, but every man is presumed to intend the necessary and legitimate consequences of what he knowingly does. Here the accused knew he had been once married, and that his first wife was living. He also knew that his second marriage was forbidden by law. When, therefore, he married the second time, he is presumed to have intended to break the law. And the breaking of the law is the crime. Every act necessary to constitute the crime was knowingly done, and the crime was therefore knowingly committed. Ignorance of a fact may sometimes be taken as evidence of a want of criminal intent, but not ignorance of the law. The only defense of the accused in this case is his belief that the law ought not to have been enacted. It matters not that his belief was a part of his professed religion: it was still belief, and belief only.

In *Regina v. Wagstaff*, the parents of a sick child, who omitted to call in medical attendance because of their religious belief that what they did for its cure would be effective, were held not to be guilty of manslaughter, while it was said the contrary would have been the result if the child had actually been starved to death by the parents, under the notion that it was their religious duty to abstain from giving it food. But when the offence consists of a positive act which is knowingly done, it would be dangerous to hold that the offender might escape punishment because he religiously believed the law which he had broken ought never to have been made. No case, we believe, can be found that has gone so far. . . . Judgment affirmed.

DISCUSSION QUESTIONS **FOR *REYNOLDS v. UNITED STATES***

A. Professor Martha M. Ertman writes that "[t]he Court justified criminalizing Mormon polygamy in two passages that link polygamy first to 'Asiatic and African people,' then to 'stationary despotism.'" She asks why the Court was concerned about "who else, other than the Mormons, practiced polygamy, or why all three branches of government (and indeed virtually the entire nation) cared so much about a religious community in a remote part of the country[.]" Martha M. Ertman, *Race Treason: The Untold Story of America's Ban on Polygamy*, 19 Colum. J. Gender & L. 287, 293 (2010). What is your response to her query? Is the Court concerned about polygamy as a social harm? If so, is the social harm at a level that it should be a legitimate concern of the government?

B. In *Reynolds v. United States*, the Court upheld the first of four statutes that Congress passed to force Mormons to abandon the practice of polygamy. First Amendment scholars have debated the *Reynolds* division between permissible limits on conduct and impermissible limits on belief. *See* Donald L. Drakeman, *Reynolds v. United States: The Historical Construction of Constitutional Reality*, 21 Const. Comment. 697 (2004); Christopher L. Eisgruber & Lawrence W. Sager, *The Vulnerability of Conscience: The Constitutional Basis for Protecting Religious Conduct*, 61 U. Chi. L. Rev. 1245 (1994); Marci A. Hamilton, *The Belief/Conduct Paradigm in the Supreme Court's Free Exercise Jurisprudence: A Theological Account of the Failure to Protect Religious Conduct*, 54 Ohio St. L.J. 713 (1993). What is the difference between religious conduct and religious belief? Why shouldn't both belief and conduct be protected by the Constitution?

C. Opponents of polygamist relationships argue that polygamy violates the dignity of women and discriminates against them. They claim it encourages and reinforces a patriarchal conception of family life. They contend that a polygamous marriage contravenes a woman's right to equality with men and can have serious emotional and financial consequences for her and her dependents. Proponents argue that polygamous marriages often help poor women and to a lesser extent children of these women. Within impoverished societies, for example, polygamy is thought to serve a protective function for poor women — a form of social security. Polygamy has also historically served a restorative function when a significant percentage of the male population has been killed during warfare. Many reformist interpretations of Islam, for example, view the Qur'an's allowance of polygamy as inextricably linked to the protection of orphans and widows within a postwar context. Assess these arguments.

D. The *Reynolds* Court asserts that it is impossible to believe that the constitutional guaranty of religious freedom was ever intended to bar legislation prohibiting polygamy. What reasons are given by the Court to support this view? Are they persuasive? Can you add additional reasons not found in *Reynolds* in support of continuing a ban on polygamy?

E. In *Late Corp. of the Church of Jesus Christ of Latter-Day Saints v. United States*, 136 U.S. 1, 5 (1890), the Supreme Court stated, in *dictum*, that the LDS Church was a sect "contrary to the spirit of Christianity and of the civilization which Christianity has produced in the Western world." The Court also branded religious polygamy a "barbarous practice" and a "nefarious doctrine" that was "abhorrent to the sentiments and feelings of the civilized world." The Court stated that polygamy was not a religious practice but rather was "against the enlightened sentiment of mankind." In *Cleveland v. United States*, 329 U.S. 14 (1946), *reh'g denied*, 329 U.S. 831 (1946), the Court upheld the convictions of six men for transporting their plural wives across state lines in violation of the Mann Act, 18 U.S.C. §398. Justice Douglas described polygamy as "in a measure, a return to barbarism." . . . What role is the majority religion in the United States playing in these cases? What does it suggest is the relationship between a majority religion in a culture and the culture's secular law?

F. Professor Shayna M. Sigman suggests that "[o]ne reason given for the Christian prohibition against polygamy is that monogamy served as a method of decreasing the number of legitimate heirs available and increasing the amount of property that would escheat to the Roman Church." Shayna M. Sigman *Everything Lawyers Know About Polygamy Is Wrong*, 16 Cornell J.L. & Pub. Pol'y 101, 159 (Fall 2006). Is this a sufficient reason to ban polygamy?

G. Polygamy is defined as having several spouses at the same time. Bigamy is defined as contracting a second marriage while another valid marriage still exists. Because of the ease with which a divorce may be obtained, some argue that society now permits a type of legalized serial polygamy. Is there merit to this argument?

2.4 BARRIERS: MISCEGENATION

Forty of the 50 states at one time or another enacted miscegenation laws that prohibited black people from marrying white people. In the main, repeal of these laws occurred in the northern states immediately before and after the Civil War. Yet, as of 1967, with only one exception, statutes criminalizing mixed-race marriages were upheld in an unbroken line of decisions in every state where it was alleged they violated the Fourteenth Amendment to the federal Constitution. For example, in *Jackson v. Denver*, 124 P.2d 240 (Colo. 1942), the court held that "cohabitation as husband and wife under an alleged common-law marriage of a negro and a white woman, whose marriage was by statute made void, constituted 'vagrancy' within the meaning of city ordinance which defines a vagrant as any person who shall lead an immoral course of life." The Georgia Supreme Court in *Scott v. Georgia*, 39 Ga. 321 (1869), stated that "the Code of Georgia, adopted by the new Constitution, forever prohibits the marriage relation between white persons and persons of African descent." Montana held in *In re Shun T. Takahashi's Estate*, 129 P.2d 217 (Mont. 1942), that a marriage between a Japanese man and a white woman was void. Oregon's court in *In re Paquet's Estate*, 200 P. 911 (Or. 1921), held that a law prohibiting marriages "between white persons and Indians, Negroes, or Chinese, etc." is constitutional and does not discriminate between the races.

In *Lonas v. State*, 50 Tenn. 287 (1871), the State Attorney General made the following argument to justify upholding Tennessee's miscegenation laws:

> The Mosaic Law forbade the Jews to gender animals of a diverse kind together. Was there discrimination there between the horse and the ass? Would a law now against breeding mules be discrimination? If so, against which animal? Is a law against breeding mulattoes any more so? This is the substance of our law, to prevent the production of this hybrid race. To prevent violence and bloodshed which would arise from such

cohabitation, distasteful to our people, and unfit to produce the human race in any of the types in which it was created.

The Tennessee court upheld the law. The court commented that "[t]he laws of civilization demand that the races be kept apart in this country. The progress of either does not depend upon an admixture of blood. A sound philanthropy, looking to the public peace and the happiness of both races, would regard any effort to intermerge the individuality of the races as a calamity full of the saddest and gloomiest portent to the generations that are to come after us." *Id.* at 310-311.

The United States Supreme Court adopted a racist view of different races marrying during the nineteenth century. For example, it upheld the constitutionality of anti-miscegenation laws in *Pace v. Alabama*, 106 U.S. 583 (1883). In *Pace* a black man and a white woman were indicted under Alabama's criminal code for living together in a state of adultery or fornication. They were tried, convicted, and sentenced, each to two years' imprisonment in the state penitentiary. The Alabama statute was challenged as violating the Equal Protection Clause of the Constitution. The Supreme Court rejected the challenge, holding that Alabama's anti-miscegenation statute did not violate the Fourteenth Amendment because the statute treated the races equally insofar as both whites and blacks were punished in equal measure for breaking the law against interracial marriage and interracial sex.

REFLECTIVE QUESTIONS	How would you characterize the nineteenth-century courts on the issue of intermarriage of the races? Were they racist and protecting white supremacy? Uninformed or poorly educated? Following Biblical teachings? Or simply reflecting the custom and tradition in the United States at the time they decided these cases?

Background to *Loving v. Virginia*

When *Loving v. Virginia* came before the Court in 1967, there remained 17 states that punished interracial marriage, with the prohibition spelled out in various state constitutions. There was also widespread popular support for the criminal ban on marriages between the races among citizens. For example, a 1965 Gallup Poll found that 42 percent of northern whites supported bans on interracial marriage, as did 72 percent of southern whites.

Richard Loving, a white male, and Mildred Jeter, a black female, were married in Washington, D.C., in 1958 because their home state of Virginia enforced anti-miscegenation laws. Once married, they returned to Virginia. In 1959 they were arrested, prosecuted, and convicted of violating that state's anti-miscegenation law, which made it a crime to leave Virginia to evade its anti-miscegenation law and return to cohabit as husband and wife. They were each sentenced to one year in jail, with the sentence being suspended if they agreed to leave Virginia and not return for 25 years. The couple moved to Washington, D.C. In 1963 they initiated legal action challenging the constitutionality of Virginia's anti-miscegenation law. In March 1966, the Virginia Supreme Court of Appeals upheld the law. *Loving v. Commonwealth*, 147 S.E.2d 78 (Va. 1966). *See generally* Walter Wadlington, *The Loving Case: Virginia's Anti-Miscegenation Statute in Historical Perspective*, 52 Va. L. Rev. 1189 (1966). The Supreme Court agreed to review the state court ruling.

LOVING
v.
VIRGINIA
Supreme Court of the United States
388 U.S. 1 (1967)

WARREN, C.J. This case presents a constitutional question never addressed by this Court: whether a statutory scheme adopted by the State of Virginia to prevent marriages between persons solely on the basis of racial classifications violates the Equal Protection and Due Process Clauses of the Fourteenth Amendment. For reasons which seem to us to reflect the central meaning of those constitutional commands, we conclude that these statutes cannot stand consistently with the Fourteenth Amendment.

In June 1958, two residents of Virginia, Mildred Jeter, a Negro woman, and Richard Loving, a white man, were married in the District of Columbia pursuant to its laws. Shortly after their marriage, the Lovings returned to Virginia and established their marital abode in Caroline County. At the October Term, 1958, of the Circuit Court of Caroline County, a grand jury issued an indictment charging the Lovings with violating Virginia's ban on interracial marriages. On January 6, 1959, the Lovings pleaded guilty to the charge and were sentenced to one year in jail; however, the trial judge suspended the sentence for a period of 25 years on the condition that the Lovings leave the State and not return to Virginia together for 25 years. He stated in an opinion that:

> Almighty God created the races white, black, yellow, Malay and red, and he placed them on separate continents. And but for the interference with his arrangement there would be no cause for such marriages. The fact that he separated the races shows that he did not intend for the races to mix.

In upholding the constitutionality of these provisions in the decision below, the Supreme Court of Appeals of Virginia referred to its 1955 decision in *Naim v. Naim*, as stating the reasons supporting the validity of these laws. In *Naim*, the state court concluded that the State's legitimate purposes were "to preserve the racial integrity of its citizens," and to prevent "the corruption of blood," "a mongrel breed of citizens," and "the obliteration of racial pride," obviously an endorsement of the doctrine of White Supremacy. The court also reasoned that marriage has traditionally been subject to state regulation without federal intervention, and, consequently, the regulation of marriage should be left to exclusive state control by the Tenth Amendment. . . .

There can be no question but that Virginia's miscegenation statutes rest solely upon distinctions drawn according to race. The statutes proscribe generally accepted conduct if engaged in by members of different races. Over the years, this Court has consistently repudiated "(d)istinctions between citizens solely because of their ancestry" as being "odious to a free people whose institutions are founded upon the doctrine of equality." At the very least, the Equal Protection Clause demands that racial classifications, especially suspect in criminal statutes, be subjected to the "most rigid scrutiny," and, if they are ever to be upheld, they must be shown to be necessary to the accomplishment of some permissible state objective, independent of the racial discrimination which it was the object of the Fourteenth Amendment to eliminate. Indeed, two members of this Court have already stated that they "cannot conceive of a valid legislative purpose which makes the color of a person's skin the test of whether his conduct is a criminal offense."

There is patently no legitimate overriding purpose independent of invidious racial discrimination which justifies this classification. The fact that Virginia prohibits only interracial marriages involving white persons demonstrates that the racial classifications must stand on their own justification, as measures designed to maintain White Supremacy. We have consistently denied the constitutionality of measures which restrict the rights of citizens on account of race. There can be no doubt that restricting the freedom to marry solely because of racial classifications violates the central meaning of the Equal Protection Clause.

II

These statutes also deprive the Lovings of liberty without due process of law in violation of the Due Process Clause of the Fourteenth Amendment. The freedom to marry has long been recognized as one of the vital personal rights essential to the orderly pursuit of happiness by free men.

Marriage is one of the "basic civil rights of man," fundamental to our very existence and survival. To deny this fundamental freedom on so unsupportable a basis as the racial classifications embodied in these statutes, classifications so directly subversive of the principle of equality at the heart of the Fourteenth Amendment, is surely to deprive all the State's citizens of liberty without due process of law. The Fourteenth Amendment requires that the freedom of choice to marry not be restricted by invidious racial discriminations. Under our Constitution, the freedom to marry or not marry, a person of another race resides with the individual and cannot be infringed by the State. Reversed.

> **DISCUSSION QUESTIONS** FOR *LOVING v. VIRGINIA*

A. In addition to striking down the criminal statute on equal protection grounds, the Supreme Court also said it deprived the Lovings of their liberty interest under the Fourteenth Amendment. How did the Court support its liberty interest analysis?

B. In *Naim v. Naim*, 87 S.E.2d 749 (Va. 1955), the Virginia Supreme Court cited the following passage from an Indiana case, *State v. Gibson*, 36 Ind. 389, 1871 WL 5021 (Ind. 1871), where a statute made it a felony for a black and white person to marry:

> In this State marriage is treated as a civil contract, but it is more than a mere civil contract. It is a public institution established by God himself, is recognized in all Christian and civilized nations, and is essential to the peace, happiness, and well-being of society. . . . The right, in the states, to regulate and control, to guard, protect, and preserve this God-given, civilizing, and Christianizing institution is of inestimable importance, and cannot be surrendered, nor can the states suffer or permit any interference therewith. If the federal government can determine who may marry in a state, there is no limit to its power.

Do the views expressed by the court about God in the above excerpt provide support to those who argue that the miscegenation laws in the nation were based almost entirely on religious views? Note that the court in *Naim* also expressed concern about the federal government intervening in state concerns. From the perspective of the court in *Naim*, has the federal government in *Loving* inappropriately intervened in state affairs and improperly exercised its power over the state of Virginia?

C. It is suggested that miscegenation statutes "reflected a legal reaction to fears of race-mixing" and "exemplified the deep-seeded societal aversion to the notion of sexual relations between black men and white women." Marques P. Richeson, *Beyond the Final Frontier: A "Post-Racial" America? The Obligations of Lawyers, the Legislature, and the Court*, 25 Harv. BlackLetter L.J. 95, 105-106 (Spring 2009). It is also suggested that the Court held the statute in *Loving* unconstitutional because the purpose of the statute was to "sustain White Supremacy and to subordinate African-Americans and other non-Caucasians as a class." Is there support for these views in *Loving*?

D. *Loving* extended constitutional protections to interracial intimacy and set a new federal floor for individual rights throughout the nation. However, most agree that the Court recognized that the rule of law it created in *Loving* did not coincide with society's beliefs at the time. Assuming the views of a majority of the citizens of Virginia were in sharp disagreement with the Supreme Court, should the Court have surrendered to the political views of the citizens of Virginia rather than declaring miscegenation statutes unconstitutional?

2.5 BARRIERS: POVERTY, SOCIAL SECURITY, FARM SUBSIDIES, TAXES, AND MARRIAGE

Background to *Zablocki v. Redhail*

The statute considered by the Supreme Court in *Zablocki v. Redhail* was part of the revision of the Wisconsin Family Code enacted into law in 1959. The provision was designed to cover a situation where a person who was about to assume new marital responsibilities had failed to fulfill the obligation of a prior relationship where a child was born. In such a case, judicial approval was required for the marriage on the theory that this gave a judge and a family court commissioner an opportunity to emphasize the responsibility to support the present family before new obligations were incurred. The statute was expanded in 1963 to require a showing to a court by a marriage applicant that his minor children not in his custody and to whom he owed an obligation of support are not public charges or likely to become public charges.

At the time of his admission of paternity, Redhail was a minor and a high school student. From May 1972 until August 1974, he was unemployed, indigent, and unable to pay any support. He made no payments, and as of December 24, 1974, there was an arrearage in excess of $3,732. Redhail's child had been a public charge since birth and received welfare benefits in excess of $109 per month. When Redhail filed an application for a marriage license with Zablocki, the County Clerk of Milwaukee County denied the request on the basis that he did not have a court order granting him permission to marry as required by the statute. Furthermore, he was unable to provide proof that he had complied with the existing support order or proof that his child was not likely to become a public charge. Redhail challenged the denial in federal court. A three-judge panel in the Eastern District of Wisconsin heard Redhail's complaint and granted him declaratory and injunctive relief. *Redhail v. Zablocki*, 418 F. Supp. 1061 (1976). The state appealed and the issue eventually came before the Supreme Court.

Wisconsin argued that by demanding that an applicant meet the premarriage license requirements it was seeking to protect a legitimate and substantial protectable interest both as to the protection of the welfare of its minors and the marriage relationship of its residents. It also argued that the law did not create a classification based on wealth because the requirements applied generally to rich and poor alike. The fact that the requirement may affect persons differently, said the State's lawyers, did not constitute invidious discrimination; rather, such a result flows directly from the economic system, not the law.

Finally, Wisconsin claimed that the law merely withheld issuance of a license to remarry until a showing that obligations incurred from the first marriage were met. It asserted that the state's substantial interest in protecting the children of noncustodial parents provided more than a reasonable basis for the statutory classification.

Redhail's counsel argued that Wisconsin's legislative classification must be subjected to strict judicial scrutiny because it substantially abridged the right to marry, a right which is included within the constitutional right of privacy. Counsel relied heavily on *Roe v. Wade*, 410 U.S. 113 (1974), and *Loving v. Virginia*, 388 U.S. 1 (1967). Counsel also argued that Wisconsin's statute resulted in barring the plaintiffs from ever being able to obtain a marriage license because of their poverty. This wealth discrimination, argued Redhail, provided an additional justification for applying the strict scrutiny standard under the test articulated in *San Antonio Ind. School District v. Rodriguez*, 411 U.S. 1 (1973).

ZABLOCKI
v.
REDHAIL

Supreme Court of the United States
434 U.S. 374 (1978)

MARSHALL, J. At issue in this case is the constitutionality of a Wisconsin statute, Wis. Stat. §245.10(1), (4), (5) (1973), which provides that members of a certain class of Wisconsin residents may not marry, within the State or elsewhere, without first obtaining a court order granting permission to marry. The class is defined by the statute to include any "Wisconsin resident having minor issue not in his custody and which he is under obligation to support by any court order or judgment." The statute specifies that court permission cannot be granted unless the marriage applicant submits proof of compliance with the support obligation and, in addition, demonstrates that the children covered by the support order "are not then and are not likely thereafter to become public charges." No marriage license may lawfully be issued in Wisconsin to a person covered by the statute, except upon court order; any marriage entered into without compliance with §245.10 is declared void; and persons acquiring marriage licenses in violation of the section are subject to criminal penalties. . . .

II

The leading decision of this Court on the right to marry is *Loving v. Virginia*. . . .

Although *Loving* arose in the context of racial discrimination, prior and subsequent decisions of this Court confirm that the right to marry is of fundamental importance for all individuals. Long ago, in *Maynard v. Hill*, the Court characterized marriage as "the most important relation in life," and as "the foundation of the family and of society, without which there would be neither civilization nor progress." In *Meyer v. Nebraska*, the Court recognized that the right "to marry, establish a home and bring up children" is a central part of the liberty protected by the Due Process Clause, and in *Skinner v. Oklahoma ex rel. Williamson*, marriage was described as "fundamental to the very existence and survival of the race." . . .

It is not surprising that the decision to marry has been placed on the same level of importance as decisions relating to procreation, childbirth, child rearing, and family relationships. As the facts of this case illustrate, it would make little sense to recognize a right of privacy with respect to other matters of family life and not with respect to the decision to enter the relationship that is the foundation of the family in our society. The woman whom appellee desired to marry had a fundamental right to seek an abortion of their expected child, or to bring the child into life to suffer the myriad social, if not economic, disabilities that the status of illegitimacy brings. Surely, a decision to marry and raise the child in a traditional family setting must receive equivalent protection. And, if appellee's right to procreate means anything at all, it must imply some right to enter the only relationship in which the State of Wisconsin allows sexual relations legally to take place.

By reaffirming the fundamental character of the right to marry, we do not mean to suggest that every state regulation which relates in any way to the incidents of or prerequisites for marriage must be subjected to rigorous scrutiny. To the contrary, reasonable regulations that do not significantly interfere with decisions to enter into the marital relationship may legitimately be imposed. The statutory classification at issue here, however, clearly does interfere directly and substantially with the right to marry.

Under the challenged statute, no Wisconsin resident in the affected class may marry in Wisconsin or elsewhere without a court order, and marriages contracted in violation of the statute are both void and punishable as criminal offenses. Some of those in the affected class, like appellee, will never be able to obtain the necessary court order, because they either lack the financial means to meet their support obligations or cannot prove that their children will not become public charges. These persons are absolutely prevented from getting married. Many others, able in theory to satisfy the statute's requirements, will be sufficiently burdened by having to do so that they will in effect be coerced into forgoing their right to marry. And even those who can be persuaded to meet the statute's requirements suffer a serious intrusion into their freedom of choice in an area in which we have held such freedom to be fundamental.

III

When a statutory classification significantly interferes with the exercise of a fundamental right, it cannot be upheld unless it is supported by sufficiently important state interests and is closely tailored to effectuate only those interests.

Appellant asserts that two interests are served by the challenged statute: the permission-to-marry proceeding furnishes an opportunity to counsel the applicant as to the necessity of fulfilling his prior support obligations; and the welfare of the out-of-custody children is protected. We may accept for present purposes that these are legitimate and substantial interests, but, since the means selected by the State for achieving these interests unnecessarily impinge on the right to marry, the statute cannot be sustained.

There is evidence that the challenged statute, as originally introduced in the Wisconsin Legislature, was intended merely to establish a mechanism whereby persons with support obligations to children from prior marriages could be counseled before they entered into new marital relationships and incurred further support obligations. Court permission to marry was to be required, but apparently permission was automatically to be granted after counseling was completed. The statute actually enacted, however, does not expressly require or provide for any counseling whatsoever, nor for any automatic granting of permission to marry by the court, and thus it can hardly be justified as a means for ensuring counseling of the persons within its coverage. Even assuming that counseling does take place — a fact as to which there is no evidence in the record — this interest obviously cannot support the withholding of court permission to marry once counseling is completed.

With regard to safeguarding the welfare of the out-of-custody children, appellant's brief does not make clear the connection between the State's interest and the statute's requirements. At argument, appellant's counsel suggested that, since permission to marry cannot be granted unless the applicant shows that he has satisfied his court-determined support obligations to the prior children and that those children will not become public charges, the statute provides incentive for the applicant to make support payments to his children. This "collection device" rationale cannot justify the statute's broad infringement on the right to marry.

First, with respect to individuals who are unable to meet the statutory requirements, the statute merely prevents the applicant from getting married, without delivering any money at all into the hands of the applicant's prior children. More importantly, regardless of the applicant's ability or willingness to meet the statutory requirements, the State already has numerous other means for exacting compliance with support obligations, means that are at least as effective as the instant statute's and yet do not impinge upon the right to marry. Under Wisconsin law, whether the children are from a prior marriage or were born out of wedlock, court-determined support obligations may be enforced directly via wage assignments, civil contempt proceedings, and criminal penalties. And, if the State believes that parents of children out of their custody should be responsible for ensuring that those children do not become public charges, this interest can be achieved by adjusting the criteria used for determining the amounts to be paid under their support orders.

There is also some suggestion that §245.10 protects the ability of marriage applicants to meet support obligations to prior children by preventing the applicants from incurring new support obligations. But the challenged provisions of §245.10 are grossly underinclusive with respect to this purpose, since they do not limit in any way new financial commitments by the applicant other than those arising out of the contemplated marriage. The statutory classification is substantially overinclusive as well. Given the possibility that the new spouse will actually better the applicant's financial situation, by contributing income from a job or otherwise, the statute in many cases may prevent affected individuals from improving their ability to satisfy their prior support obligations. And, although it is true that the applicant will incur support obligations to any children born during the contemplated marriage, preventing the marriage may only result in the children being born out of wedlock, as in fact occurred in appellee's case. Since the support obligation is the same whether the child is born in or out of wedlock, the net result of preventing the marriage is simply more illegitimate children.

The statutory classification created by §245.10(1), (4), (5) thus cannot be justified by the interests advanced in support of it. The judgment of the District Court is, accordingly, Affirmed.

DISCUSSION QUESTIONS FOR *ZABLOCKI v. REDHAIL*

A. The Court in *Zablocki* held that a state law providing that individuals who were under an obligation to pay child support could not marry without court approval was an impermissible restriction on one's right to marry. Is the Court saying that the right to marry is part of the fundamental "right of privacy" implicit in the Fourteenth Amendment's Due Process Clause? If so, can you provide examples of when that privacy can be invaded by the state? In *Moore v. City of E. Cleveland*, 431 U.S. 494, 495-496, 506 (1977), the Court held that a city housing ordinance was an unconstitutional violation of due process where it criminalized a grandmother for living with her extended family. In his concurring opinion, Justice Brennan observed that "the ordinance unconstitutionally abridges the 'freedom of personal choice in matters of . . . family life [that] is one of the liberties protected by the Due Process Clause of the Fourteenth Amendment.'" How far does this liberty interest mentioned by Justice Brennan extend? To same-sex couples so they may marry, for example? Or, is that going too far? (*See Obergefell v. Hodges*, discussed later in this chapter.)

B. The Court conducts a two-part inquiry in *Zablocki* to determine whether the strict scrutiny or rational basis test should be applied to the state statute. It stated that "if the challenged policy imposes a direct and substantial burden on an intimate relationship, it is subject to strict scrutiny; if the policy does not impose a direct and substantial burden, it is subject only to rational basis review." It also explained that "we do not mean to suggest that every state regulation which relates in any way to the incidents of or prerequisites for marriage must be subjected to rigorous scrutiny. To the contrary, reasonable regulations that do not significantly interfere with decisions to enter into the marital relationship may legitimately be imposed." Can you create a hypothetical state regulation that does not significantly interfere with the decision to marry and would not be subject to "rigorous scrutiny"?

C. Following the Tax Reform Act of 1969, many two-wage-earner married couples were subjected to the marriage penalty, where their combined tax burden, whether they chose to file jointly or separately, was greater than it would have been if they had remained single and filed as single taxpayers. Assume that taxpayers challenge the Tax Reform Act claiming that it constitutes a "marriage penalty" and is unconstitutional because it has an adverse effect on marriage.

What constitutional test do you believe a court should apply when arriving at a ruling on this hypothetical? *See Druker v. Commissioner of Internal Revenue*, 697 F.2d 46 (2d Cir. 1982), *cert. denied*, 461 U.S. 957 (1983); *Mapes v. United States*, 576 F.2d 896 (Ct. Cl. 1978).

D. Assume that a husband and wife challenged a regulation promulgated by the secretary of agriculture that defined a husband and wife as a single person for purposes of complying with a statute limiting farm subsidy payments to $20,000 per person. Furthermore, assume that Congress had directed the secretary to define the term *person* in order to limit farm subsidy payments to farmers who kept their land idle. The married couple argued that the secretary's refusal to pay farm subsidy payments to both of them solely because of their marriage denied them equal protection of the laws under the Fifth Amendment. Is the regulation a direct and substantial burden on the freedom to marry? *See Martin v. Bergland*, 639 F.2d 647 (10th Cir. 1981). What constitutional test should a court apply to the regulation?

2.6 BARRIERS: SAME-SEX RELATIONSHIPS

Background to *Lawrence v. Texas*

Seven years before the Supreme Court granted review of *Lawrence v. Texas*, a majority ruled that a Georgia statute criminalizing sodomy was constitutional and did not infringe upon the right to privacy. *Bowers v. Hardwick*, 479 U.S. 186 (1986). Therefore, it was a surprise to many when the Court decided to review a dispute that appeared to be a matter firmly decided only a few years earlier.

The Georgia Attorney General in *Bowers v. Hardwick* had successfully argued to the Court that in order to decide whether a right is fundamental and implicit in the concept of ordered liberty, the history and traditions of our society and its institutions must be examined. In his defense, Bowers's lawyers had rejected the Attorney General's lengthy recitation of instances where homosexuality has been disapproved in western history, saying that it was beside the point. They framed the issue to the Court as "whether the State of Georgia may send its police into private bedrooms to arrest adults for engaging in consensual, noncommercial sexual acts, with no justification beyond the assertion that those acts are immoral." They argued that the Georgia statute implicates fundamental constitutional rights by regulating citizens' conduct in their own bedrooms, and involves none of the "public ramifications" that attend "sexual activity with children or with persons who are coerced either through physical force or commercial inducement." They asserted that Hardwick's conduct was quintessentially private and lies at the heart of an intimate association beyond the proper reach of state regulation.

In rejecting Bowers's challenge to the Georgia statute, Associate Justice White, writing for the Court, stated:

Sodomy was a criminal offense at common law and was forbidden by the laws of the original thirteen States when they ratified the Bill of Rights. In 1868, when the Fourteenth Amendment was ratified, all but 5 of the 37 States in the Union had criminal sodomy laws. In fact, until 1961, all 50 States outlawed sodomy, and today, States and the District of Columbia continue to provide criminal penalties for sodomy performed in private and between consenting adults. . . . Against this background, to claim that a right to engage in such conduct is "deeply rooted in this Nation's history and tradition" or "implicit in the concept of ordered liberty" is, at best, facetious.

Chief Justice Berger, who concurred in *Bowers v. Hardwick*, added:

The proscriptions against sodomy have very ancient roots. Decisions of individuals relating to homosexual conduct have been subject to state intervention throughout the history of Western civilization. Condemnation of those practices is firmly rooted in Judeo-Christian moral and ethical standards. Homosexual sodomy was a capital crime under Roman law. . . . During the English Reformation when powers of the ecclesiastical courts were transferred to the King's Courts, the first English statute criminalizing sodomy was passed. Blackstone described "the infamous crime against nature" as an offense of "deeper malignity" than rape, a heinous act "the very mention of which is a disgrace to human nature," and "a crime not fit to be named." The common law of England, including its prohibition of sodomy, became the received law of Georgia and the other Colonies. In 1816 the Georgia Legislature passed the statute at issue here, and that statute has been continuously in force in one form or another since that time. To hold that the act of homosexual sodomy is somehow protected as a fundamental right would be to cast aside millennia of moral teaching.

In his dissent in *Bowers v. Hardwick*, Justice Blackmun argued that the case was one about "being left alone."

In subsequent consideration of the sodomy statute at issue in *Bowers*, the Georgia Supreme Court held that it violated the right of privacy as guaranteed by Georgia's Constitution. *Powell v. State*, 510 S.E.2d 18 (Ga. 1998).

In *Lawrence v. Texas*, a citizen informed the Harris County, Texas, sheriff's deputies that an armed man was "going crazy" in Lawrence's apartment. The investigating officers entered the apartment and observed Lawrence and another man engaged in anal sexual intercourse. They were charged with the commission of the Class C misdemeanor offense of engaging in homosexual conduct, an offense defined by Tex. Penal Code §21.06(a) (Vernon 1994), as follows: "A person commits an offense if he engages in deviate sexual intercourse with another individual of the same sex." A Class C misdemeanor is punishable by a fine not to exceed $500.

After the petitioners were convicted and fined, they appealed to the Texas Court of Appeals. That court, relying on *Bowers v. Hardwick*, 479 U.S. 186 (1986), affirmed the conviction. The petitioners then sought review by the United States Supreme Court, which was granted.

The petitioners framed the issue to the Supreme Court as follows:

The fundamental rights question in this case turns on who has the power to make basic decisions about the specifics of sexual intimacy between two consenting adults behind closed doors. Is the decision about expressions of intimacy and choice of partner for two adults to make through mutual consent, or for the State to control through a criminal law enacted by the legislature?

The petitioners argued that the virtually unlimited power to regulate sexual intimacy claimed by Texas directly interfered with constitutionally protected intimate associations. They also argued that the relationship of an adult couple — whether heterosexual or homosexual — united by sexual intimacy is the very paradigm of an intimate association in which one finds emotional enrichment and independently defines one's identity and is protected from unwarranted state interference. They claimed that the state law impaired the protected relationship of two adults whose shared life includes sexual intimacy by regulating — or even outright forbidding — the sexual dimension of their relationship.

The State of Texas responded that the Court should permit government regulation of all sexual intimacy outside marriage, whether with another adult of the same or different sex. It argued that the states have historically prohibited a wide variety of extra-marital sexual conduct, a legal tradition inconsistent with any recognition of a constitutionally protected liberty interest in engaging in any form of sexual conduct with whomever one chooses. The state also argued that it found nothing in the Court's "substantive due process" jurisprudence that supported recognition of a constitutional right to engage in sexual misconduct outside the venerable institution of marriage. It urged the Court to not reverse its decision in *Bowers v. Hardwick*.

There were numerous *amici curiae* briefs filed with the Court. In its *amici curiae* brief, the American Psychological Association (APA) et al. argued, *inter alia*, that homosexuality is a "normal form of human sexuality," that homosexuality has no inherent association with psychopathological conditions, and that same-sex unions are largely similar to heterosexual marriages. The Center for Arizona Policy, a nonprofit organization whose president drafted Arizona's law banning same-sex marriage and actively lobbied against extending special workplace job protections based on sexual behavior, disagreed. It argued that "at best, these claims are controversial and in some cases the APA Amici's arguments are misleading or simply false."

LAWRENCE
v.
TEXAS

Supreme Court of the United States
539 U.S. 558 (2003)

KENNEDY, J. The question before the Court is the validity of a Texas statute making it a crime for two persons of the same sex to engage in certain intimate sexual conduct. . . .

We conclude the case should be resolved by determining whether the petitioners were free as adults to engage in the private conduct in the exercise of their liberty under the Due Process Clause of the Fourteenth Amendment to the Constitution. For this inquiry we deem it necessary to reconsider the Court's holding in *Bowers*. . . .

At the outset it should be noted that there is no longstanding history in this country of laws directed at homosexual conduct as a distinct matter. Beginning in colonial times there were prohibitions of sodomy derived from the English criminal laws passed in the first instance by the Reformation Parliament of 1533. The English prohibition was understood to include relations between men and women as well as relations between men and men. *See, e.g., King v. Wiseman*, 92 Eng. Rep. 774, 775 (K.B.1718) (interpreting "mankind" in Act of 1533 as including women and girls). Nineteenth-century commentators similarly read American sodomy, buggery, and crime-against-nature statutes as criminalizing certain relations between men and women and between men and men. The absence of legal prohibitions focusing on homosexual conduct may be explained in part by noting that according to some scholars the concept of the homosexual as a distinct category of person did not emerge until the late 19th century. Thus early American sodomy laws were not directed at homosexuals as such but instead sought to prohibit nonprocreative sexual activity more generally. This does not suggest approval of homosexual conduct. It does tend to show that this particular form of conduct was not thought of as a separate category from like conduct between heterosexual persons.

Laws prohibiting sodomy do not seem to have been enforced against consenting adults acting in private. A substantial number of sodomy prosecutions and convictions for which there are surviving records were for predatory acts against those who could not or did not consent, as in the case of a minor or the victim of an assault. As to these, one purpose for the prohibitions was to ensure there would be no lack of coverage if a predator committed a sexual assault that did not constitute rape as defined by the criminal law. Thus the model sodomy indictments presented in a 19th-century treatise, addressed the predatory acts of an adult man against a minor girl or minor boy. Instead of targeting relations between consenting adults in private, 19th-century sodomy prosecutions typically involved relations between men and minor girls or minor boys, relations between adults involving force, relations between adults implicating disparity in status, or relations between men and animals.

. . . The policy of punishing consenting adults for private acts was not much discussed in the early legal literature. We can infer that one reason for this was the very private nature of the conduct. Despite the absence of prosecutions, there may have been periods in which there was public criticism of homosexuals as such and an insistence that the criminal laws be enforced to discourage their practices. But far from possessing "ancient roots," American laws targeting same-sex couples did not develop until the last third of the 20th century. The reported decisions concerning the prosecution of consensual, homosexual sodomy between adults for the years 1880-1995 are not always clear in the details, but a significant number involved conduct in a public place. It was not until the 1970's that any State singled out same-sex relations for criminal prosecution, and only nine States have done so. Post-*Bowers* even some of these States did not adhere to the policy of suppressing homosexual conduct. Over the course of the last decades, States with same-sex prohibitions have moved toward abolishing them.

In summary, the historical grounds relied upon in *Bowers* are more complex than the majority opinion and the concurring opinion by Chief Justice Burger indicate. Their historical premises are not without doubt and, at the very least, are overstated. . . .

. . . In the United States criticism of *Bowers* has been substantial and continuing, disapproving of its reasoning in all respects, not just as to its historical assumptions. The courts of five different States have declined to follow it in interpreting provisions in their own state constitutions parallel to the Due Process Clause of the Fourteenth Amendment. To the extent *Bowers* relied on values we share with a wider civilization, it should be noted that the reasoning and holding in *Bowers* have been rejected elsewhere. The European Court of Human Rights has followed not *Bowers* but its own decision in *Dudgeon v. United Kingdom.* Other nations, too, have taken action consistent with an affirmation of the protected right of homosexual adults to engage in intimate, consensual conduct. The right the petitioners seek in this case has been accepted as an integral part of human freedom in many other countries. There has been no showing that in this country the governmental interest in circumscribing personal choice is somehow more legitimate or urgent. . . .

Had those who drew and ratified the Due Process Clauses of the Fifth Amendment or the Fourteenth Amendment known the components of liberty in its manifold possibilities, they might have been more specific. They did not presume to have this insight. They knew times can blind us to certain truths and later generations can see that laws once thought necessary and proper in fact serve only to oppress. As the Constitution endures, persons in every generation can invoke its principles in their own search for greater freedom.

The judgment of the Court of Appeals for the Texas Fourteenth District is reversed, and the case is remanded for further proceedings not inconsistent with this opinion. It is so ordered.

DISCUSSION QUESTIONS FOR *LAWRENCE v. TEXAS*

A. Is the Court suggesting that the historical sketches about sodomy written by the Justices in *Bowers* are inaccurate? Or, merely out of date? What public policy was reflected or furthered by criminalizing certain same-sex conduct? What public policy is reflected or furthered by the *Lawrence* decision?

B. At whom were nineteenth-century criminal sodomy indictments apparently directed and on what cultural values do you suspect these criminal statutes were based? Religious teachings? Experience? Other values? At what point in American history did laws targeting same-sex couples emerge, and is this history important to the outcome of the case?

C. The decision in *Lawrence* was six to three, with Justice O'Connor writing a concurring opinion to distinguish her views from those of the majority. She saw the issue not as one of privacy but of equality, and she would have struck down the Texas statute on equal protection grounds. She viewed the statute as unconstitutional because it made sodomy illegal only for homosexuals — heterosexuals could still engage in such activity — and she indicated that she would not have overruled *Bowers v. Hardwick.* She affirmed, however, that the behavior used to justify the Texas arrest cannot be made criminal simply because of moral concerns. Is it significant that the majority rested the decision on a substantive liberty theory involving privacy rather than placing the outcome of the decision on an equal protection basis?

D. Dissenting Justice Scalia wrote: "This [opinion] effectively decrees the end of all morals legislation. State laws against bigamy, same-sex marriage, adult incest, prostitution, masturbation, adultery, fornication, bestiality, and obscenity are likewise sustainable only in light of *Bowers*' validation of laws based on moral choices. Every single one of these laws is called into question by today's decision." Based on what has transpired since the decision, were Justice Scalia's concerns warranted? *See, e.g., 1568 Montgomery Highway, Inc. v. City of Hoover,* 45 So. 3d 319 (Ala. 2010); *United States v. Handley,* 564 F. Supp. 2d 996 (S.D. Iowa 2008); *State v. Romano,* 155 P.3d 1102 (Haw. 2007); *State v. Oakley,* 605 S.E.2d 215 (N.C. App. 2004).

E. The Court resolved the constitutionality of Texas's sodomy law in *Lawrence* by applying the rational basis test, rather than heightened scrutiny. If a fundamental right were at stake, only heightened scrutiny would have been appropriate. What is the significance of the Court selecting the lower standard of review in the context of this dispute? *See Oklahoma Educ. Assn. v. Alcoholic Bev. Laws Enforcement Commn.,* 889 F.2d 929, 932 (10th Cir. 1989).

F. Under military law, adultery is a crime under Article 134 of the Uniform Code of Military Justice (UCMJ). A servicemember is guilty of adultery if the servicemember has sexual intercourse with an individual when either of the two is married to someone else. In addition, the adulterous conduct must be prejudicial of good order and discipline in the armed forces, or be "of a nature to bring discredit upon the armed forces." It is argued by the military that prosecuting adultery (a) preserves the honor of the Armed Services, (b) maintains good order and discipline, and (c) maintains the trust and support of the American people. Katherine Annuschat, Comment, *An Affair to Remember: The State of the Crime of Adultery in the Military,* 47 San Diego L. Rev. 1161 1192-1195 (November-December 2010). After *Lawrence v. Texas,* are military regulations regarding criminal prosecution for adultery constitutional?

G. Assume in the following hypothetical that the defendant is indicted on numerous charges stemming from her alleged management and operation of a massage parlor that served as a front for illegal prostitution activity. She is charged with inducing or enticing women to travel in interstate commerce to engage in prostitution. The defendant moves to dismiss the charges, arguing that the U.S. Supreme Court's holding in *Lawrence v. Texas* necessarily renders laws prohibiting prostitution unconstitutional. What are the arguments in favor of the defendant's position? In favor of the prosecution? Most likely, how will a court rule? *See State v. Romano*, 155 P.3d 1102 (Haw. 2007); *United States v. Thompson*, 458 F. Supp. 2d 730 (N.D. Ind. 2006); *McDonald v. Commonwealth*, 630 S.E.2d 754 (Va. App. 2006).

Hollingsworth v. Perry, **133 S. Ct. 2652 (2013).** In 2000, California supporters of the "defense of marriage" movement drafted and circulated an initiative petition that ultimately appeared on the March 7, 2000, primary election ballot as Proposition 22. It did not take the form of a state constitutional amendment. Proposition 22 proposed the adoption of a new statutory provision declaring that "[o]nly marriage between a man and a woman is valid or recognized in California." At the March 7, 2000, election, the voters approved Proposition 22, and it became part of the Family Code. In 2008, the California Supreme Court struck down Proposition 22 holding that the California Constitution required the term *marriage* to include the union of same-sex couples. *In re Marriage Cases*, 183 P.3d 384 (Cal. 2008).

A new effort at preventing same-sex marriages was launched with Proposition 8 in 2008. Proposition 8 would amend the California Constitution to provide that "only marriage between a man and a woman is valid or recognized by California." On November 4, 2008, voters approved the measure and made same-sex marriage illegal in California.

The respondents, a gay couple and a lesbian couple, sued the state officials responsible for the enforcement of California's marriage laws and claimed that Proposition 8 violated their Fourteenth Amendment right to equal protection of the law. When the state officials originally named in the suit informed the district court that they could not defend Proposition 8, the petitioners, official proponents of the measure, intervened to defend it. At a bench trial, the United States District Court for the Northern District of California, 704 F. Supp. 2d 921 (N.D. Cal. 2010), held that California's Proposition 8 banning same-sex marriages violated the Due Process and Equal Protection Clauses of the United States Constitution. The Ninth Circuit affirmed and the matter was accepted for review by the Supreme Court.

The questions before the Court were: Do the petitioners have standing under Article III of the Constitution to argue this case? Does the Equal Protection Clause of the Fourteenth Amendment prohibit the State of California from defining marriage as the union of one man and one woman? All of California's officials acquiesced in the District Court ruling and refused to defend Proposition 8. The Supreme Court only addressed the standing issue. Chief Justice Roberts wrote the Court's majority opinion with Justices Kennedy, Thomas, Alito, and Sotomayor dissenting. The Court held that proponents of California's Proposition 8 banning same-sex marriage lacked standing to pursue appeals of the District Court decision, which had struck down Proposition 8.

REFLECTIVE QUESTIONS	What was the practical impact on same-sex marriage from the *Hollingsworth* decision?

Background to *United States v. Windsor*

The dispute in *United States v. Windsor* involved a same-sex couple, Edith Windsor and Thea Spyer. They met in New York City in 1963 and began a long-term relationship. They registered as domestic partners when New York City gave that right to same-sex couples in 1993. Concerned about Spyer's health, in 2007 the couple made a trip to Canada where they were legally married. They then returned to the United States and continued to reside in New York City.

When Spyer died in 2009, she left her entire estate to Windsor. The Defense of Marriage Act (DOMA) denied federal recognition to same-sex spouses. Because of DOMA, Windsor did not qualify for the marital exemption from the federal estate tax. The exemption excludes from taxation "any interest in property which passes or has passed from the decedent to his surviving spouse." 26 U.S.C. §2056(a). Windsor paid $363,053 in estate taxes and sought a refund as a surviving spouse. Her request was denied by the Internal Revenue Service. Windsor then brought a refund suit in federal court, contending that DOMA violates the principles of equal protection incorporated into the Fifth Amendment.

There were three issues before the Court: (1) Does the executive branch's agreement with the lower court that the act is unconstitutional deprive the Supreme Court of jurisdiction to decide the case? (2) Does the Bipartisan Legal Advisory Group of the House of Representatives have standing in the case? (3) Does the Defense of Marriage Act, which defines the term *marriage* under federal law as a "legal union between one man and one woman" deprive same-sex couples who are legally married under state laws of their Fifth Amendment rights to equal protection under federal law?

The excerpt from the opinion that follows concerns only DOMA, which was the third issue before the Court.

UNITED STATES v. WINDSOR

Supreme Court of the United States
133 S. Ct. 2675 (2013)

KENNEDY, J. . . . . The State's power in defining the marital relation is of central relevance in this case quite apart from principles of federalism. Here the State's decision to give this class of persons the right to marry conferred upon them a dignity and status of immense import. When the State used its historic and essential authority to define the marital relation in this way, its role and its power in making the decision enhanced the recognition, dignity, and protection of the class in their own community. DOMA, because of its reach and extent, departs from this history and tradition of reliance on state law to define marriage. " '[D]iscriminations of an unusual character especially suggest careful consideration to determine whether they are obnoxious to the constitutional provision.' " . . .

The Federal Government uses this state-defined class for the opposite purpose — to impose restrictions and disabilities. That result requires this Court now to address whether the resulting injury and indignity is a deprivation of an essential part of the liberty protected by the Fifth Amendment. What the State of New York treats as alike the federal law deems unlike by a law designed to injure the same class the State seeks to protect.

In acting first to recognize and then to allow same-sex marriages, New York was responding "to the initiative of those who [sought] a voice in shaping the destiny of their own times." . . . These actions were without doubt a proper exercise of its sovereign authority within our federal system, all in the way that the Framers of the Constitution intended. The dynamics of state government in the federal system are to allow the formation of consensus respecting the way the members of a discrete community treat each other in their daily contact and constant interaction with each other.

The States' interest in defining and regulating the marital relation, subject to constitutional guarantees, stems from the understanding that marriage is more than a routine classification for purposes of certain statutory benefits. Private, consensual sexual intimacy between two adult persons of the same sex may not be punished by the State, and it can form "but one element in a personal bond that is more enduring." *Lawrence v. Texas*, 539 U.S. 558, 567 (2003). By its recognition of the validity of same-sex marriages performed in other jurisdictions and then by authorizing same-sex unions and same-sex marriages, New York sought to give further protection and dignity to that bond. For same-sex couples who wished to be married, the State acted to give their lawful conduct a lawful status. This status is a far-reaching legal acknowledgment of the intimate relationship between two people, a relationship deemed by the State worthy of dignity in the community equal with all other marriages. It reflects both the community's considered perspective on the historical roots of the institution of marriage and its evolving understanding of the meaning of equality.

IV.

DOMA seeks to injure the very class New York seeks to protect. By doing so it violates basic due process and equal protection principles applicable to the Federal Government. . . . The Constitution's guarantee of equality "must at the very least mean that a bare congressional desire to harm a politically unpopular group cannot" justify disparate treatment of that group. In determining whether a law is motived by an improper animus or purpose, " '[d]iscriminations of an unusual character' " especially require careful consideration. . . . DOMA cannot survive under these principles. The responsibility of the States for the regulation of domestic relations is an important indicator of the substantial societal impact the State's classifications have in the daily lives and customs of its people. DOMA's unusual deviation from the usual tradition of recognizing and accepting state definitions of marriage here operates to deprive same-sex couples of the benefits and responsibilities that come with the federal recognition of their marriages. This is strong evidence of a law having the purpose and effect of disapproval of that class. The avowed purpose and practical effect of the law here in question are to impose a disadvantage, a separate status, and so a stigma upon all who enter into same-sex marriages made lawful by the unquestioned authority of the States.

The history of DOMA's enactment and its own text demonstrate that interference with the equal dignity of same-sex marriages, a dignity conferred by the States in the exercise of their sovereign power, was more than an incidental effect of the federal statute. It was its essence. The House Report announced its conclusion that "it is both appropriate and necessary for Congress to do what it can to defend the institution of traditional heterosexual marriage. . . . H.R. 3396 is appropriately entitled the 'Defense of Marriage Act.' The effort to redefine 'marriage' to extend to homosexual couples is a truly radical proposal that would fundamentally alter the institution of marriage." H.R. Rep. No. 104-664, pp. 12-13 (1996). The House concluded that DOMA expresses "both moral disapproval of homosexuality, and a moral conviction that heterosexuality better comports with traditional (especially Judeo-Christian) morality." . . . The stated purpose of the law was to promote an "interest in protecting the traditional moral teachings reflected in heterosexual-only marriage laws." Were there any doubt of this far-reaching purpose, the title of the Act confirms it: The Defense of Marriage.

The arguments put forward by BLAG are just as candid about the congressional purpose to influence or interfere with state sovereign choices about who may be married. As the title and dynamics of the bill indicate, its purpose is to discourage enactment of state same-sex marriage laws and to restrict the freedom and choice of couples married under those laws if they are enacted. The congressional goal was "to put a thumb on the scales and influence a state's decision as to how to shape its own marriage laws." . . . The Act's demonstrated purpose is to ensure that if any State decides to recognize same-sex marriages, those unions will be treated as second-class marriages for purposes of federal law. This raises a most serious question under the Constitution's Fifth Amendment.

DOMA's operation in practice confirms this purpose. When New York adopted a law to permit same-sex marriage, it sought to eliminate inequality; but DOMA frustrates that objective through a system-wide enactment with no identified connection to any particular area of federal law. DOMA writes inequality into the entire United States Code. The particular case at hand concerns the estate tax, but DOMA is more than a simple determination of what should or should not be allowed as an estate tax refund. Among the over 1,000 statutes and numerous federal regulations that DOMA controls are laws pertaining to Social Security, housing, taxes, criminal sanctions, copyright, and veterans' benefits.

DOMA's principal effect is to identify a subset of state-sanctioned marriages and make them unequal. The principal purpose is to impose inequality, not for other reasons like governmental efficiency. Responsibilities, as well as rights, enhance the dignity and integrity of the person. And DOMA contrives to deprive some couples married under the laws of their State, but not other couples, of both rights and responsibilities. By creating two contradictory marriage regimes within the same State, DOMA forces same-sex couples to live as married for the purpose of state law but unmarried for the purpose of federal law, thus diminishing the stability and predictability of basic personal relations the State has found it proper to acknowledge and protect. By this dynamic DOMA undermines both the public and private significance of state-sanctioned same-sex marriages; for it tells those couples, and all the world, that their otherwise valid marriages are unworthy of federal recognition. This places same-sex couples in an unstable position of being in a second-tier marriage. The differentiation demeans the couple, whose moral and sexual choices the Constitution protects, see *Lawrence*, 539 U.S. 558, and whose relationship the State has sought to dignify. And it humiliates tens of thousands of children now being raised by same-sex couples. The law in question makes it even more difficult for the children to understand the integrity and closeness of their own family and its concord with other families in their community and in their daily lives.

Under DOMA, same-sex married couples have their lives burdened, by reason of government decree, in visible and public ways. By its great reach, DOMA touches many aspects of married and family life, from the mundane to the profound. It prevents same-sex married couples from obtaining government health-care benefits they would otherwise receive. . . . It deprives them of the Bankruptcy Code's special protections for domestic-support obligations. . . . It forces them to follow a complicated procedure to file their state and federal taxes jointly. . . . It prohibits them from being buried together in veterans' cemeteries. . . .

For certain married couples, DOMA's unequal effects are even more serious. The federal penal code makes it a crime to "assaul[t], kidna[p], or murde[r] . . . a member of the immediate family" of "a United States official, a United States judge, [or] a Federal law enforcement officer," . . . with the intent to influence or retaliate against that official, §115(a)(1). Although a "spouse" qualifies as a member of the officer's "immediate family," §115(c)(2), DOMA makes this protection inapplicable to same-sex spouses.

DOMA also brings financial harm to children of same-sex couples. It raises the cost of health-care for families by taxing health benefits provided by employers to their workers' same-sex spouses. And it denies or reduces benefits allowed to families upon the loss of a spouse and parent, benefits that are an integral part of family security.

DOMA divests married same-sex couples of the duties and responsibilities that are an essential part of married life and that they in most cases would be honored to accept were DOMA not in force. For instance, because it is expected that spouses will support each other as they pursue educational opportunities, federal law takes into consideration a spouse's income in calculating a student's federal financial aid eligibility. . . . Same-sex married couples are exempt from this requirement. The same is true with respect to federal ethics rules. Federal executive and agency officials are prohibited from "participat[ing] personally and substantially" in matters as to which they or their spouses have a financial interest. . . . A similar statute prohibits Senators, Senate employees, and their spouses from accepting high-value gifts from certain sources, . . . and another mandates detailed financial disclosures by numerous high-ranking officials and their spouses. . . . Under DOMA, however, these Government-integrity rules do not apply to same-sex spouses.

. . .

The power the Constitution grants it also restrains. And though Congress has great authority to design laws to fit its own conception of sound national policy, it cannot deny the liberty protected by the Due Process Clause of the Fifth Amendment.

What has been explained to this point should more than suffice to establish that the principal purpose and the necessary effect of this law are to demean those persons who are in a lawful same-sex marriage. This requires the Court to hold, as it now does, that DOMA is unconstitutional as a deprivation of the liberty of the person protected by the Fifth Amendment of the Constitution.

The liberty protected by the Fifth Amendment's Due Process Clause contains within it the prohibition against denying to any person the equal protection of the laws. . . . While the Fifth Amendment itself withdraws from Government the power to degrade or demean in the way this law does, the equal protection guarantee of the Fourteenth Amendment makes that Fifth Amendment right all the more specific and all the better understood and preserved.

The class to which DOMA directs its restrictions and restraints are those persons who are joined in same-sex marriages made lawful by the State. DOMA singles out a class of persons deemed by a State entitled to recognition and protection to enhance their own liberty. It imposes a disability on the class by refusing to acknowledge a status the State finds to be dignified and proper. DOMA instructs all federal officials, and indeed all persons with whom same-sex couples interact, including their own children, that their marriage is less worthy than the marriages of others. The federal statute is invalid, for no legitimate purpose overcomes the purpose and effect to disparage and to injure those whom the State, by its marriage laws, sought to protect in personhood and dignity. By seeking to displace this protection and treating those persons as living in marriages less respected than others, the federal statute is in violation of the Fifth Amendment. This opinion and its holding are confined to those lawful marriages.

The judgment of the Court of Appeals for the Second Circuit is affirmed.

SCALIA, J. with whom **JUSTICE THOMAS** joins, and with whom **THE CHIEF JUSTICE** joins as to Part I, dissenting. . . . The majority concludes that the only motive for this Act was the "bare . . . desire to harm a politically unpopular group." Bear in mind that the object of this condemnation is not the legislature of some once-Confederate Southern state (familiar objects of the Court's scorn), but our respected coordinate branches, the Congress and Presidency of the United States. Laying such a charge against them should require the most extraordinary evidence, and I would have thought that every attempt would be made to indulge a more anodyne explanation for the statute. The majority does the opposite —

affirmatively concealing from the reader the arguments that exist in justification. It makes only a passing mention of the "arguments put forward" by the Act's defenders, and does not even trouble to paraphrase or describe them. I imagine that this is because it is harder to maintain the illusion of the Act's supporters as unhinged members of a wild-eyed lynch mob when one first describes their views as they see them.

To choose just one of these defenders' arguments, DOMA avoids difficult choice-of-law issues that will now arise absent a uniform federal definition of marriage. Imagine a pair of women who marry in Albany and then move to Alabama, which does not "recognize as valid any marriage of parties of the same sex." When the couple files their next federal tax return, may it be a joint one? Which State's law controls, for federal-law purposes: their State of celebration (which recognizes the marriage) or their State of domicile (which does not)? (Does the answer depend on whether they were just visiting in Albany?) Are these questions to be answered as a matter of federal common law, or perhaps by borrowing a State's choice-of-law rules? If so, which State's? And what about States where the status of an out-of-state same-sex marriage is an unsettled question under local law? DOMA avoided all of this uncertainty by specifying which marriages would be recognized for federal purposes. That is a classic purpose for a definitional provision.

Further, DOMA preserves the intended effects of prior legislation against then-unforeseen changes in circumstance. When Congress provided (for example) that a special estate-tax exemption would exist for spouses, this exemption reached only opposite-sex spouses — those being the only sort that were recognized in any State at the time of DOMA's passage. When it became clear that changes in state law might one day alter that balance, DOMA's definitional section was enacted to ensure that state-level experimentation did not automatically alter the basic operation of federal law, unless and until Congress made the further judgment to do so on its own. That is not animus — just stabilizing prudence. Congress has hardly demonstrated itself unwilling to make such further, revising judgments upon due deliberation.

The Court mentions none of this. Instead, it accuses the Congress that enacted this law and the President who signed it of something much worse than, for example, having acted in excess of enumerated federal powers — or even having drawn distinctions that prove to be irrational. Those legal errors may be made in good faith, errors though they are. But the majority says that the supporters of this Act acted with malice — with the "purpose" "to disparage and to injure" same-sex couples. It says that the motivation for DOMA was to "demean," to "impose inequality," to "impose . . . a stigma," ante, to deny people "equal dignity," to brand gay people as "unworthy," ante, and to "humiliat[e]" their children. . . .

I am sure these accusations are quite untrue. To be sure (as the majority points out), the legislation is called the Defense of Marriage Act. But to defend traditional marriage is not to condemn, demean, or humiliate those who would prefer other arrangements, any more than to defend the Constitution of the United States is to condemn, demean, or humiliate other constitutions. To hurl such accusations so casually demeans this institution. In the majority's judgment, any resistance to its holding is beyond the pale of reasoned disagreement. To question its high-handed invalidation of a presumptively valid statute is to act (the majority is sure) with the purpose to "disparage," "injure," "degrade," "demean," and "humiliate" our fellow human beings, our fellow citizens, who are homosexual. All that, simply for supporting an Act that did no more than codify an aspect of marriage that had been unquestioned in our society for most of its existence — indeed, had been unquestioned in virtually all societies for virtually all of human history. It is one thing for a society to elect change; it is another for a court of law to impose change by adjudging those who oppose it hostes humani generis, enemies of the human race. . . .

In my opinion, however, the view that this Court will take of state prohibition of same-sex marriage is indicated beyond mistaking by today's opinion. As I have said, the real rationale of today's opinion, whatever disappearing trail of its legalistic argle-bargle one chooses to follow, is that DOMA is motivated by " 'bare . . . desire to harm' " couples in same-sex marriages. Supra, at 2691. How easy it is, indeed how inevitable, to reach the same conclusion with regard to state laws denying same-sex couples marital status. Consider how easy (inevitable) it is to make the following substitutions in a passage from today's opinion ante, at 2694:

> "DOMA's This state law's principal effect is to identify a subset of state-sanctioned marriages constitutionally protected sexual relationships, see *Lawrence*, and make them unequal. The principal purpose is to impose inequality, not for other reasons like governmental efficiency. Responsibilities, as well as rights, enhance the dignity and integrity of the person. And DOMA this state law contrives to deprive some couples married under the laws of their State enjoying constitutionally protected sexual relationships, but not other couples, of both rights and responsibilities."

Or try this passage, from ante, at 2694:

> "[DOMA] This state law tells those couples, and all the world, that their otherwise valid marriage relationships are unworthy of federal state recognition. This places same-sex couples in an unstable position of being in a second-tier marriage relationship. The differentiation demeans the couple, whose moral and sexual choices the Constitution protects, see *Lawrence*."

 **FOR *UNITED STATES v. WINDSOR***

A. The Supreme Court held that the federal Defense of Marriage Act (DOMA) was unconstitutional. Did it also find a federal right for same-sex marriage?

B. Justice Kennedy describes why he believes the Defense of Marriage Act harms same-sex marriage. What did this analysis suggest for states that defined marriage as between one man and one woman?

C. Justice Scalia wrote that a second state-law shoe seemed likely to drop into the Court next year. He also said that Justice Kennedy's reasoning could just as easily have applied to state laws as to the federal one. Was Justice Scalia correct in his observations?

D. Around the time of this decision, approximately 37 states still had marriage restrictions. Some were in a state constitution while others were in the form of a legislative prohibition. When California became the thirteenth state to allow same-sex marriage, about 30 percent of Americans lived in jurisdictions where such marriages were legal. Until 2012, when four states voted in favor of same-sex marriage at the ballot box, same-sex marriage had either failed to gain approval or a ban on it was successful. What factors may have driven this change in perspective at the ballot box in so short a time?

E. Do you see any similarities between the *Windsor* decision and the decision in *Loving v. Virginia*?

Background to *Obergefell v. Hodges*

Massachusetts became the first state to legalize same-sex marriage following a ruling by the state's highest court in 2003. By May 2015, courts, legislatures, and voters in 36 states and the District of Columbia had legalized same-sex marriage. Meanwhile, 14 states had constitutional amendments banning gay marriage.

Same-sex marriage became legal in Florida and Alabama after federal courts struck down those states' same-sex marriage bans. However, Alabama officials refused to issue marriage licenses to same-sex couples after a ruling by the state's supreme court. This left the status of same-sex marriage in that state in limbo.

The states of Michigan, Kentucky, Ohio, and Tennessee defined marriage as a union between one man and one woman. The challengers to that definition were 14 same-sex couples and 2 men whose same-sex partners are deceased. They filed legal actions in the Federal District Courts in their home states, claiming that the state officials violate the Fourteenth Amendment by denying them the right to marry, or refusing to give full recognition to marriages lawfully performed in another state. The Federal District Courts all ruled in the challenger's favor. However, the Sixth Circuit Court of Appeals consolidated the cases and reversed the district court rulings. The Supreme Court then granted review of the Sixth Circuit ruling.

OBERGEFELL v. HODGES
Supreme Court of the United States
133 S.C. 2675 (2015)

KENNEDY, J. The Constitution promises liberty to all within its reach, a liberty that includes certain specific rights that allow persons, within a lawful realm, to define and express their identity. The petitioners in these cases seek to find that liberty by marrying someone of the same sex and having their marriages deemed lawful on the same terms and conditions as marriages between persons of the opposite sex. . . .

II

Before addressing the principles and precedents that govern these cases, it is appropriate to note the history of the subject now before the Court.

A

From their beginning to their most recent page, the annals of human history reveal the transcendent importance of marriage. The lifelong union of a man and a woman always has promised nobility and dignity to all persons, without regard to their station in life. Marriage is sacred to those who live by their religions and offers unique fulfillment to those who find meaning in the secular realm. Its dynamic allows two people to find a life that could not be found alone, for a marriage becomes greater than just the two persons. Rising from the most basic human needs, marriage is essential to our most profound hopes and aspirations.

The centrality of marriage to the human condition makes it unsurprising that the institution has existed for millennia and across civilizations. Since the dawn of history, marriage has transformed strangers into relatives, binding families and societies together. Confucius taught that marriage lies at the foundation of government. . . . This wisdom was echoed centuries later and half a world away by Cicero, who wrote, "The first bond of society is marriage; next, children; and then the family." . . . There are untold references to the beauty of marriage in religious and philosophical texts spanning time, cultures, and faiths, as well as in art and literature in all their forms. It is fair and necessary to say these references were based on the understanding that marriage is a union between two persons of the opposite sex.

That history is the beginning of these cases. The respondents say it should be the end as well. To them, it would demean a timeless institution if the concept and lawful status of marriage were extended to two persons of the same sex. Marriage, in their view, is by its nature a gender-differentiated union of man and woman. This view long has been held—and continues to be held—in good faith by reasonable and sincere people here and throughout the world.

The petitioners acknowledge this history but contend that these cases cannot end there. Were their intent to demean the revered idea and reality of marriage, the petitioners' claims would be of a different order. But that is neither their purpose nor their submission. To the contrary, it is the enduring importance of marriage that underlies the petitioners' contentions. This, they say, is their whole point. Far from seeking to devalue marriage, the petitioners seek it for themselves because of their respect—and need—for its privileges and responsibilities. And their immutable nature dictates that same-sex marriage is their only real path to this profound commitment. . . .

B

The ancient origins of marriage confirm its centrality, but it has not stood in isolation from developments in law and society. The history of marriage is one of both continuity and change. That institution — even as confined to opposite-sex relations — has evolved over time.

For example, marriage was once viewed as an arrangement by the couple's parents based on political, religious, and financial concerns; but by the time of the Nation's founding it was understood to be a voluntary contract between a man and a woman. . . . As the role and status of women changed, the institution further evolved. Under the centuries-old doctrine of coverture, a married man and woman were treated by the State as a single, male-dominated legal entity. . . . As women gained legal, political, and property rights, and as society began to understand that women have their own equal dignity, the law of coverture was abandoned. . . . These and other developments in the institution of marriage over the past centuries were not mere superficial changes. Rather, they worked deep transformations in its structure, affecting aspects of marriage long viewed by many as essential. . . .

These new insights have strengthened, not weakened, the institution of marriage. Indeed, changed understandings of marriage are characteristic of a Nation where new dimensions of freedom become apparent to new generations, often through perspectives that begin in pleas or protests and then are considered in the political sphere and the judicial process.

This dynamic can be seen in the Nation's experiences with the rights of gays and lesbians. Until the mid-20th century, same-sex intimacy long had been condemned as immoral by the state itself in most Western nations, a belief often embodied in the criminal law. For this reason, among others, many persons did not deem homosexuals to have dignity in their own distinct identity. A truthful declaration by same-sex couples of what was in their hearts had to remain unspoken. Even when a greater awareness of the humanity and integrity of homosexual persons came in the period after World War II, the argument that gays and lesbians had a just claim to dignity was in conflict with both law and widespread social conventions. Same-sex intimacy remained a crime in many States. Gays and lesbians were prohibited from most government employment, barred from military service, excluded under immigration laws, targeted by police, and burdened in their rights to associate. . . .

For much of the 20th century, moreover, homosexuality was treated as an illness. When the American Psychiatric Association published the first Diagnostic and Statistical Manual of Mental Disorders in 1952, homosexuality was classified as a mental disorder, a position adhered to until 1973. . . . Only in more recent years have psychiatrists and others recognized that sexual orientation is both a normal expression of human sexuality and immutable. . . .

In the late 20th century, following substantial cultural and political developments, same-sex couples began to lead more open and public lives and to establish families. This development was followed by a quite extensive discussion of the issue in both governmental and private sectors and by a shift in public attitudes toward greater tolerance. As a result, questions about the rights of gays and lesbians soon reached the courts, where the issue could be discussed in the formal discourse of the law.

This Court first gave detailed consideration to the legal status of homosexuals in *Bowers v. Hardwick*, 478 U.S. 186 (1986). There it upheld the constitutionality of a Georgia law deemed to criminalize certain homosexual acts. Ten years later, in *Romer v. Evans*, 517 U.S. 620 (1996), the Court invalidated an amendment to Colorado's Constitution that sought to foreclose any branch or political subdivision of the State from protecting persons against discrimination based on sexual orientation. Then, in 2003, the Court overruled *Bowers*, holding that laws making same-sex intimacy a crime "demea[n] the lives of homosexual persons." *Lawrence v. Texas*, 539 U.S. 558, 575.

Against this background, the legal question of same-sex marriage arose. In 1993, the Hawaii Supreme Court held Hawaii's law restricting marriage to opposite-sex couples constituted a classification on the basis of sex and was therefore subject to strict scrutiny under the Hawaii Constitution. . . . Although this decision did not mandate that same-sex marriage be allowed, some States were concerned by its implications and reaffirmed in their laws that marriage is defined as a union between opposite-sex partners. So too in 1996, Congress passed the Defense of Marriage Act (DOMA), 110 Stat. 2419, defining marriage for all federal-law purposes as "only a legal union between one man and one woman as husband and wife." . . .

The new and widespread discussion of the subject led other States to a different conclusion. In 2003, the Supreme Judicial Court of Massachusetts held the State's Constitution guaranteed same-sex couples the right to marry. See *Goodridge v. Department of Public Health*, 440 Mass. 309, 798 N.E.2d 941 (2003). After that ruling, some additional States granted marriage rights to same-sex couples, either through judicial or legislative processes. . . . Two Terms ago, in *United States v. Windsor*, 570 U.S. _____ (2013), this Court invalidated DOMA to the extent it barred the Federal Government from treating same-sex marriages as valid even when they were lawful in the State where they were licensed. DOMA, the Court held, impermissibly disparaged those same-sex couples "who wanted to affirm their commitment to one another before their children, their family, their friends, and their community." . . .

Numerous cases about same-sex marriage have reached the United States Courts of Appeals in recent years. In accordance with the judicial duty to base their decisions on principled reasons and neutral discussions, without scornful or disparaging commentary, courts have written a substantial body of law considering all sides of these issues. That case law helps to explain and formulate the underlying principles this Court now must consider. With the exception of the opinion here under review and one other, . . . the Courts of Appeals have held that excluding same-sex couples from marriage violates the Constitution. There also have been many thoughtful District Court decisions addressing same-sex marriage—and most of them, too, have concluded same-sex couples must be allowed to marry. In addition the highest courts of many States have contributed to this ongoing dialogue in decisions interpreting their own State Constitutions. . . .

III

Under the Due Process Clause of the Fourteenth Amendment, no State shall "deprive any person of life, liberty, or property, without due process of law." The fundamental liberties protected by this Clause include most of the rights enumerated in the Bill of Rights. . . . In addition these liberties extend to certain personal choices central to individual dignity and autonomy, including intimate choices that define personal identity and beliefs. . . .

The identification and protection of fundamental rights is an enduring part of the judicial duty to interpret the Constitution. That responsibility, however, "has not been reduced to any formula." . . . Rather, it requires courts to exercise reasoned judgment in identifying interests of the person so fundamental that the State must accord them its respect. . . . That process is guided by many of the same considerations relevant to analysis of other constitutional provisions that set forth broad principles rather than specific requirements. History and tradition guide and discipline this inquiry but do not set its outer boundaries. . . . That method respects our history and learns from it without allowing the past alone to rule the present.

The nature of injustice is that we may not always see it in our own times. The generations that wrote and ratified the Bill of Rights and the Fourteenth Amendment did not presume to know the extent of freedom in all of its dimensions, and so they entrusted to future generations a charter protecting the right of all persons to enjoy liberty as we learn its meaning. When new insight reveals discord between the Constitution's central protections and a received legal stricture, a claim to liberty must be addressed.

Applying these established tenets, the Court has long held the right to marry is protected by the Constitution. In *Loving v. Virginia*, 388 U.S. 1, 12 (1967), which invalidated bans on interracial unions, a unanimous Court held marriage is "one of the vital personal rights essential to the orderly pursuit of happiness by free men." The Court reaffirmed that holding in *Zablocki v. Redhail*, 434 U.S. 374, 384 (1978), which held the right to marry was burdened by a law prohibiting fathers who were behind on child support from marrying. The Court again applied this principle in *Turner v. Safley*, 482 U.S. 78, 95 (1987), which held the right to marry was abridged by regulations limiting the privilege of prison inmates to marry. Over time and in other contexts, the Court has reiterated that the right to marry is fundamental under the Due Process Clause. See, e.g., *M.L.B. v. S.L.J.*, 519 U.S. 102, 116 (1996); *Cleveland Bd. of Ed. v. LaFleur*, 414 U.S. 632, 639-640 (1974); *Griswold*, supra, at 486; *Skinner v. Oklahoma ex rel. Williamson*, 316 U.S. 535, 541 (1942); *Meyer v. Nebraska*, 262 U.S. 390, 399 (1923).

It cannot be denied that this Court's cases describing the right to marry presumed a relationship involving opposite-sex partners. The Court, like many institutions, has made assumptions defined by the world and time of which it is a part. This was evident in *Baker v. Nelson*, 409 U.S. 810, a one-line summary decision issued in 1972, holding the exclusion of same-sex couples from marriage did not present a substantial federal question.

Still, there are other, more instructive precedents. This Court's cases have expressed constitutional principles of broader reach. In defining the right to marry these cases have identified essential attributes of that right based in history, tradition, and other constitutional liberties inherent in this intimate bond. . . . And in assessing whether the force and rationale of its cases apply to same-sex couples, the Court must respect the basic reasons why the right to marry has been long protected. . . .

This analysis compels the conclusion that same-sex couples may exercise the right to marry. The four principles and traditions to be discussed demonstrate that the reasons marriage is fundamental under the Constitution apply with equal force to same-sex couples.

A first premise of the Court's relevant precedents is that the right to personal choice regarding marriage is inherent in the concept of individual autonomy. This abiding connection between marriage and liberty is why *Loving* invalidated interracial marriage bans under the Due Process Clause. . . . Like choices concerning contraception, family relationships, procreation, and childrearing, all of which are protected by the Constitution, decisions concerning marriage are among the most intimate that an individual can make. . . . Indeed, the Court has noted it would be contradictory "to recognize a right of privacy with respect to other matters of family life and not with respect to the decision to enter the relationship that is the foundation of the family in our society." . . .

Choices about marriage shape an individual's destiny. As the Supreme Judicial Court of Massachusetts has explained, because "it fulfils yearnings for security, safe haven, and connection that express our common humanity, civil marriage is an esteemed institution, and the decision whether and whom to marry is among life's momentous acts of self-definition." . . .

The nature of marriage is that, through its enduring bond, two persons together can find other freedoms, such as expression, intimacy, and spirituality. This is true for all persons, whatever their sexual orientation. . . . There is dignity in the bond between two men or two women who seek to marry and in their autonomy to make such profound choices. . . .

A second principle in this Court's jurisprudence is that the right to marry is fundamental because it supports a two-person union unlike any other in its importance to the committed individuals. This point was central to *Griswold v. Connecticut*, which held the Constitution protects the right of married couples to use contraception. . . .

And in *Turner*, the Court again acknowledged the intimate association protected by this right, holding prisoners could not be denied the right to marry because their committed relationships satisfied the basic reasons why marriage is a fundamental right. . . . The right to marry thus dignifies couples who "wish to define themselves by their commitment to each other." . . . Marriage responds to the universal fear that a lonely person might call out only to find no one there. It offers the hope of companionship and understanding and assurance that while both still live there will be someone to care for the other.

As this Court held in *Lawrence*, same-sex couples have the same right as opposite-sex couples to enjoy intimate association. *Lawrence* invalidated laws that made same-sex intimacy a criminal act. And it acknowledged that "[w]hen sexuality finds overt expression in intimate conduct with another person, the conduct can be but one element in a personal bond that is more enduring." . . . But while

Lawrence confirmed a dimension of freedom that allows individuals to engage in intimate association without criminal liability, it does not follow that freedom stops there. Outlaw to outcast may be a step forward, but it does not achieve the full promise of liberty.

A third basis for protecting the right to marry is that it safeguards children and families and thus draws meaning from related rights of childrearing, procreation, and education. . . . The Court has recognized these connections by describing the varied rights as a unified whole: "[T]he right to 'marry, establish a home and bring up children' is a central part of the liberty protected by the Due Process Clause." . . . Under the laws of the several States, some of marriage's protections for children and families are material. But marriage also confers more profound benefits. By giving recognition and legal structure to their parents' relationship, marriage allows children "to understand the integrity and closeness of their own family and its concord with other families in their community and in their daily lives." . . . Marriage also affords the permanency and stability important to children's best interests. . . .

As all parties agree, many same-sex couples provide loving and nurturing homes to their children, whether biological or adopted. And hundreds of thousands of children are presently being raised by such couples. . . . Most States have allowed gays and lesbians to adopt, either as individuals or as couples, and many adopted and foster children have same-sex parents. . . . This provides powerful confirmation from the law itself that gays and lesbians can create loving, supportive families.

Excluding same-sex couples from marriage thus conflicts with a central premise of the right to marry. Without the recognition, stability, and predictability marriage offers, their children suffer the stigma of knowing their families are somehow lesser. They also suffer the significant material costs of being raised by unmarried parents, relegated through no fault of their own to a more difficult and uncertain family life. The marriage laws at issue here thus harm and humiliate the children of same-sex couples. . . .

That is not to say the right to marry is less meaningful for those who do not or cannot have children. An ability, desire, or promise to procreate is not and has not been a prerequisite for a valid marriage in any State. In light of precedent protecting the right of a married couple not to procreate, it cannot be said the Court or the States have conditioned the right to marry on the capacity or commitment to procreate. The constitutional marriage right has many aspects, of which childbearing is only one.

Fourth and finally, this Court's cases and the Nation's traditions make clear that marriage is a keystone of our social order. Alexis de Tocqueville recognized this truth on his travels through the United States almost two centuries ago:

> "There is certainly no country in the world where the tie of marriage is so much respected as in America. . . . [W]hen the American retires from the turmoil of public life to the bosom of his family, he finds in it the image of order and of peace. . . . [H]e afterwards carries [that image] with him into public affairs." . . .

In *Maynard v. Hill*, 125 U.S. 190, 211 (1888), the Court echoed de Tocqueville, explaining that marriage is "the foundation of the family and of society, without which there would be neither civilization nor progress." Marriage, the Maynard Court said, has long been "'a great public institution, giving character to our whole civil polity.'" This idea has been reiterated even as the institution has evolved in substantial ways over time, superseding rules related to parental consent, gender, and race once thought by many to be essential. . . . Marriage remains a building block of our national community.

For that reason, just as a couple vows to support each other, so does society pledge to support the couple, offering symbolic recognition and material benefits to protect and nourish the union. Indeed, while the States are in general free to vary the benefits they confer on all married couples, they have throughout our history made marriage the basis for an expanding list of governmental rights, benefits, and responsibilities. These aspects of marital status include: taxation; inheritance and property rights; rules of intestate succession; spousal privilege in the law of evidence; hospital access; medical decision making authority; adoption rights; the rights and benefits of survivors; birth and death certificates; professional ethics rules; campaign finance restrictions; workers' compensation benefits; health insurance; and child custody, support, and visitation rules. . . . Valid marriage under state law is also a significant status for over a thousand provisions of federal law. . . . The States have contributed to the fundamental character of the marriage right by placing that institution at the center of so many facets of the legal and social order.

There is no difference between same- and opposite-sex couples with respect to this principle. Yet by virtue of their exclusion from that institution, same-sex couples are denied the constellation of benefits that the States have linked to marriage. This harm results in more than just material burdens. Same-sex couples are consigned to an instability many opposite-sex couples would deem intolerable in their own lives. As the State itself makes marriage all the more precious by the significance it attaches to it, exclusion from that status has the effect of teaching that gays and lesbians are unequal in important respects. It demeans gays and lesbians for the State to lock them out of a central institution of the Nation's society. Same-sex couples, too, may aspire to the transcendent purposes of marriage and seek fulfillment in its highest meaning.

The limitation of marriage to opposite-sex couples may long have seemed natural and just, but its inconsistency with the central meaning of the fundamental right to marry is now manifest. With that knowledge must come the recognition that laws excluding same-sex couples from the marriage right impose stigma and injury of the kind prohibited by our basic charter. . . .

The right to marry is fundamental as a matter of history and tradition, but rights come not from ancient sources alone. They rise, too, from a better informed understanding of how constitutional imperatives define a liberty that remains urgent in our own era. Many who deem same-sex marriage to be wrong reach that conclusion based on decent and honorable religious or philosophical premises, and neither they nor their beliefs are disparaged here. But when that sincere, personal opposition becomes enacted law and public policy, the necessary consequence is to put the imprimatur of the State itself on an exclusion that soon demeans or stigmatizes those whose own liberty is then denied. Under the Constitution, same-sex couples seek in marriage the same legal treatment as opposite-sex couples, and it would disparage their choices and diminish their personhood to deny them this right.

The right of same-sex couples to marry that is part of the liberty promised by the Fourteenth Amendment is derived, too, from that Amendment's guarantee of the equal protection of the laws. The Due Process Clause and the Equal Protection Clause are connected in a profound way, though they set forth independent principles. Rights implicit in liberty and rights secured by equal protection may rest on different precepts and are not always co-extensive, yet in some instances each may be instructive as to the meaning and reach of the other. In any particular case one Clause may be thought to capture the essence of the right in a more accurate and comprehensive way, even as the two Clauses may converge in the identification and definition of the right. . . . This interrelation of the two principles furthers our understanding of what freedom is and must become.

The Court's cases touching upon the right to marry reflect this dynamic. In *Loving* the Court invalidated a prohibition on interracial marriage under both the Equal Protection Clause and the Due Process Clause. The Court first declared the prohibition invalid because of its unequal treatment of interracial couples. It stated: "There can be no doubt that restricting the freedom to marry solely because of racial classifications violates the central meaning of the Equal Protection Clause." . . . With this link to equal protection the Court proceeded to hold the prohibition offended central precepts of liberty: "To deny this fundamental freedom on so unsupportable a basis as the racial classifications embodied in these statutes, classifications so directly subversive of the principle of equality at the heart of the Fourteenth Amendment, is surely to deprive all the State's citizens of liberty without due process of law." . . . The reasons why marriage is a fundamental right became more clear and compelling from a full awareness and understanding of the hurt that resulted from laws barring interracial unions.

The synergy between the two protections is illustrated further in *Zablocki*. There the Court invoked the Equal Protection Clause as its basis for invalidating the challenged law, which, as already noted, barred fathers who were behind on child-support payments from marrying without judicial approval. The equal protection analysis depended in central part on the Court's holding that the law burdened a right "of fundamental importance." . . . It was the essential nature of the marriage right, discussed at length in *Zablocki*, that made apparent the law's incompatibility with requirements of equality. Each concept—liberty and equal protection—leads to a stronger understanding of the other.

Indeed, in interpreting the Equal Protection Clause, the Court has recognized that new insights and societal understandings can reveal unjustified inequality within our most fundamental institutions that once passed unnoticed and unchallenged. To take but one period, this occurred with respect to marriage in the 1970's and 1980's. Notwithstanding the gradual erosion of the doctrine of coverture, . . . invidious sex-based classifications in marriage remained common through the mid-20th century. . . . These classifications denied the equal dignity of men and women. One State's law, for example, provided in 1971 that "the husband is the head of the family and the wife is subject to him; her legal civil existence is merged in the husband, except so far as the law recognizes her separately, either for her own protection, or for her benefit." . . . Responding to a new awareness, the Court invoked equal protection principles to invalidate laws imposing sex-based inequality on marriage. . . . Like *Loving* and *Zablocki*, these precedents show the Equal Protection Clause can help to identify and correct inequalities in the institution of marriage, vindicating precepts of liberty and equality under the Constitution. . . .

In *Lawrence* the Court acknowledged the interlocking nature of these constitutional safeguards in the context of the legal treatment of gays and lesbians. . . . Although *Lawrence* elaborated its holding under the Due Process Clause, it acknowledged, and sought to remedy, the continuing inequality that resulted from laws making intimacy in the lives of gays and lesbians a crime against the State. *Lawrence* therefore drew upon principles of liberty and equality to define and protect the rights of gays and lesbians, holding the State "cannot demean their existence or control their destiny by making their private sexual conduct a crime." . . .

This dynamic also applies to same-sex marriage. It is now clear that the challenged laws burden the liberty of same-sex couples, and it must be further acknowledged that they abridge central precepts of equality. Here the marriage laws enforced by the respondents are in essence unequal: same-sex couples are denied all the benefits afforded to opposite-sex couples and are barred from exercising a fundamental right. Especially against a long history of disapproval of their relationships, this denial to same-sex couples of the right to marry works a grave and continuing harm. The imposition of this disability on gays and lesbians serves to disrespect and subordinate them. And the Equal Protection Clause, like the Due Process Clause, prohibits this unjustified infringement of the fundamental right to marry. See, e.g., *Zablocki*, supra, at 383-388; *Skinner*, 316 U.S., at 541.

These considerations lead to the conclusion that the right to marry is a fundamental right inherent in the liberty of the person, and under the Due Process and Equal Protection Clauses of the Fourteenth Amendment couples of the same sex may not be deprived of that right and that liberty. The Court now holds that same-sex couples may exercise the fundamental right to marry. No longer may this liberty be denied to them. *Baker v. Nelson* must be and now is overruled, and the State laws challenged by Petitioners in these cases are now held invalid to the extent they exclude same-sex couples from civil marriage on the same terms and conditions as opposite-sex couples. . . .

V

These cases also present the question whether the Constitution requires States to recognize same-sex marriages validly performed out of State. As made clear by the case of Obergefell and Arthur, and by that of DeKoe and Kostura, the recognition bans inflict substantial and continuing harm on same-sex couples.

Being married in one State but having that valid marriage denied in another is one of "the most perplexing and distressing complication[s]" in the law of domestic relations. *Williams v. North Carolina*, 317 U.S. 287, 299 (1942). . . . Leaving the current state of affairs in place would maintain and promote instability and uncertainty. For some couples, even an ordinary drive into a neighboring State to visit family or friends risks causing severe hardship in the event of a spouse's hospitalization while across state lines. In light of the fact that many States already allow same-sex marriage — and hundreds of thousands of these marriages already have occurred — the disruption caused by the recognition bans is significant and ever-growing.

As counsel for the respondents acknowledged at argument, if States are required by the Constitution to issue marriage licenses to same-sex couples, the justifications for refusing to recognize those marriages performed elsewhere are undermined. . . . The Court, in this decision, holds same-sex couples may exercise the fundamental right to marry in all States. It follows that the Court also must hold — and it now does hold — that there is no lawful basis for a State to refuse to recognize a lawful same-sex marriage performed in another State on the ground of its same-sex character.

CHIEF JUSTICE ROBERTS, with whom **JUSTICE SCALIA** and **JUSTICE THOMAS** join, dissenting. . . . [T]his Court is not a legislature. Whether same-sex marriage is a good idea should be of no concern to us. Under the Constitution, judges have power to say what the law is, not what it should be. The people who ratified the Constitution authorized courts to exercise "neither force nor will but merely judgment."

Although the policy arguments for extending marriage to same-sex couples may be compelling, the legal arguments for requiring such an extension are not. The fundamental right to marry does not include a right to make a State change its definition of marriage. And a State's decision to maintain the meaning of marriage that has persisted in every culture throughout human history can hardly be called irrational. In short, our Constitution does not enact any one theory of marriage. The people of a State are free to expand marriage to include same-sex couples, or to retain the historic definition.

Many people will rejoice at this decision, and I begrudge none their celebration. But for those who believe in a government of laws, not of men, the majority's approach is deeply disheartening. Supporters of same-sex marriage have achieved considerable success persuading their fellow citizens — through the democratic process — to adopt their view. That ends today. Five lawyers have closed the debate and enacted their own vision of marriage as a matter of constitutional law. Stealing this issue from the people will for many cast a cloud over same-sex marriage, making a dramatic social change that much more difficult to accept.

The majority's decision is an act of will, not legal judgment. The right it announces has no basis in the Constitution or this Court's precedent. The majority expressly disclaims judicial "caution" and omits even a pretense of humility, openly relying on its desire to remake society according to its own "new insight" into the "nature of injustice." . . .

. . .

One immediate question invited by the majority's position is whether States may retain the definition of marriage as a union of two people.

Although the majority randomly inserts the adjective "two" in various places, it offers no reason at all why the two-person element of the core definition of marriage may be preserved while the man-woman element may not. Indeed, from the standpoint of history and tradition, a leap from opposite-sex marriage to same-sex marriage is much greater than one from a two-person union to plural unions, which have deep roots in some cultures around the world. If the majority is willing to take the big leap, it is hard to see how it can say no to the shorter one.

It is striking how much of the majority's reasoning would apply with equal force to the claim of a fundamental right to plural marriage. If "[t]here is dignity in the bond between two men or two women who seek to marry and in their autonomy to make such profound choices," why would there be any less dignity in the bond between three people who, in exercising their autonomy, seek to make the profound choice to marry? If a same-sex couple has the constitutional right to marry because their children would otherwise "suffer the stigma of knowing their families are somehow lesser," why wouldn't the same reasoning apply to a family of three or more persons raising children? If not having the opportunity to marry "serves to disrespect and subordinate" gay and lesbian couples, why wouldn't the same "imposition of this disability," serve to disrespect and subordinate people who find fulfillment in polyamorous relationships?

. . .

The Court's accumulation of power does not occur in a vacuum. It comes at the expense of the people. And they know it. Here and abroad, people are in the midst of a serious and thoughtful public debate on the issue of same-sex marriage. . . . This deliberative process is making people take seriously questions that they may not have even regarded as questions before.

When decisions are reached through democratic means, some people will inevitably be disappointed with the results. But those whose views do not prevail at least know that they have had their say, and accordingly are—in the tradition of our political culture—reconciled to the result of a fair and honest debate.

But today the Court puts a stop to all that.

 **FOR** *OBERGEFELL v. HODGES*

A. What are the four principles and traditions discussed by Justice Kennedy that support his conclusion that marriage is a fundamental right under the Constitution and apply with equal force to same-sex couples?

B. What was the Court's ruling on the question of whether a state must recognize a valid same-sex marriage made in another state?

C. One difference between the majority and Chief Justice Roberts's dissent is the appropriate role of the Supreme Court in a democratic society. What is the appropriate role of the Supreme Court in a democratic society?

D. In all cases where people claim to be denied equal protection or assert a violation of a right, one of the questions is whether the government had an adequate justification for its actions. Was the majority correct in striking down the state laws prohibiting same-sex marriage because no legitimate government interest is served?

E. The primary argument made by opponents of same-sex marriage, in their briefs and at oral argument, is that marriage primarily exists for procreation. Is this argument accurate? Relevant?

F. Opponents of same-sex marriage suggest that this decision is more about the romantic desires of consenting adults than about the needs or the rights of children involved to a relationship with their mother and father. Do you agree?

G. In his dissent, Chief Justice Roberts suggests that this opinion may lead to recognition of plural marital relationships. Do you agree?

H. Does this opinion mean that a religion that recognizes only a marriage between a different-sex couple can no longer refuse to conduct a marriage ceremony for a same-sex couple? If it doesn't conduct the ceremony, might it lose its federal tax exempt status? May a privately owned bakery refuse to supply a wedding cake to a same-sex couple who are about to marry?

General Principles

1. The right to marry is a fundamental right. Therefore, state restrictions on the right to marry are subject to strict scrutiny (providing the highest level of constitutional protection).
2. The strict scrutiny test requires that a restriction be "necessary to a compelling state interest" in order to survive a constitutional challenge. Classifications that directly and substantially interfere with the right to marry will be reviewed under the strict scrutiny test. (Compare *Zablocki* (total ban) with *Jobst* (loss of public benefits of $20 a month).)
3. Racial restrictions on marriage are unconstitutional.
4. In addition to the strict scrutiny test, which is applied to fundamental rights, the Supreme Court has developed two additional tests to apply where state statutes, regulations, practices, or policies are implicated. The rational basis test is the lowest level of judicial scrutiny. It requires that a restriction be reasonably related to a legitimate state objective. There is also an intermediate test that requires a restriction to be "substantially related to an important governmental objective."
5. Not all state restrictions on marriage receive heightened scrutiny. A state may promulgate reasonable restrictions that do not significantly interfere with decisions to enter into marital relationship.

6. States traditionally supported their reasons for not recognizing same-sex marriages on the basis that (a) marriage is for propagation of the species; (b) canon law and the Bible define marriages as heterosexual; (c) marriage protects the health and welfare of children; and (d) dictionaries have defined marriage as the union of a man and a woman.

7. The provisions of some state constitutions provide more expansive protection for individual rights. Because of this, gay and lesbian plaintiffs have successfully challenged state statutes barring marriage between same-sex couples using state constitutional provisions.

Chapter Problems

1. Assume that a father was convicted in a state court of intentionally failing to support his biological child. As a condition of probation for the crime, the father is to "make all reasonable efforts to avoid having another child unless he proved that he could support that child and current children." *See State v. Oakley*, 629 N.W.2d 200 (Wis. 2001), *cert. denied*, 537 U.S. 813 (2002). Is such a condition reasonably related to the defendant's rehabilitation because it will assist him in conforming his conduct to the law? Or, is the order essentially a prohibition on the right to have children and barred by *Zablocki? See* Rachel Roth, *No New Babies? Gender Inequality and Reproductive Control in the Criminal Justice and Prison Systems*, 12 Am. U. J. Gender Soc. Pol'y & L. 391 (2004).

2. It has been suggested that constitutionalization of family law seriously eroded the power of local governments to make laws for the stability of the social order, the good morals of the community, or the needs of children from broken homes. *See* Donald P. Kommers, *Propter Honoris Respectum, The Constitutionalism of Mary Ann Glendon*, 73 Notre Dame L. Rev. 1333, 1337 (May-July 1998). What arguments can you create that support and oppose this view? Which arguments are stronger?

3. Sean E. Brotherson and Jeffrey B. Teichert, in their article titled *Value of the Law in Shaping Social Perspectives on Marriage*, 3 J.L. & Fam. Stud. 23, 35 (2001), observed the following: "The law of marriage and family life in many countries has recently undergone a seismic shift, particularly in the United States. This has resulted in two countervailing legal trends. The first trend has been exemplified by a repeal of many norm-setting laws surrounding marriage and family life. Harvard scholar Mary Ann Glendon has referred to this as the 'dejuridification of marriage' or the 'withdrawal of much official regulation of marriage.' In her view, this trend has delivered a strong social message that the state has a declining interest in marriage. At the same time, the rise of autonomy theory in the law has encouraged state intervention within the family to protect individual rights. This has been referred to as the 'constitutionalization of family law.' " After reading the material in this chapter, what suggests that the states have developed a declining view of marriage? If so, what are the implications for U.S. society?

4. In *Zablocki v. Redhail*, the Supreme Court held that the right to marry is a fundamental right and that any regulation regarding marriage will receive "strict scrutiny" when it is reviewed. The Court also stated that not all state restrictions on the right to marry are to receive heightened scrutiny. For example, "reasonable regulations that do not significantly interfere with decisions to enter into the marital relationship may legitimately be imposed." *Zablocki, supra*, at 386. The Court stated that only those classifications that directly and substantially interfere with the right to marry will be reviewed under the strict scrutiny test. This decision and others have emphasized the importance of marriage to individuals and recognize that an individual's decision to marry has significant constitutional dimensions. Assume that a state decided to assess higher filing fees on persons who seek a divorce than those set in other civil cases. In your view, does the classification contravene a fundamental interest, so as to trigger heightened scrutiny, or constitute an act devoid of rationality, so as to fall short of the minimal requirements for orderly government? Does such a fee prevent a married person from divorcing and marrying another? Does it single out and discriminate against a person because he or she is married?

5. Assume the local clerk of court refuses to issue a marriage license to any same-sex couples after the *Obergefell v. Hodges* decision was handed down. The clerk asserts that she cannot issue a license because she is an Apostolic Christian and she has a sincere religious objection to same-sex marriage. Her lawyers state that the clerk believes that same-sex marriage "is not, in fact, marriage." They also state that issuing a same-sex marriage license would amount to a "searing act of validation" that would "forever echo in her conscience." The Supreme Court has refused a request by the clerk's lawyers to issue an emergency application for review. The clerk insists she has a First Amendment right to refuse to issue a marriage license. What possible legal remedies are available to same-sex couples who are refused a marriage license by this clerk?

Preparation for Practice

1. Examine your state's constitution.
    a. Does it differ from the federal Constitution? If so, in what respect?
    b. Does it have specific provisions relating to marriage? Divorce? The family?

c. Did it contain a provision preventing same-sex couples from marrying?

d. Does it contain a "common benefits" clause?

2. Review the recent decisions (last ten years or so) by your state's highest court.

a. List the cases in which the court has used a provision in your state constitution in a family law matter.

b. How was it used?

c. Why do you believe that it was used?

Chapter 3

Marriage Requirements

3.1 INTRODUCTION

This chapter contains a plethora of information, issues, and questions about state marriage requirements. The purpose of the chapter is to provide a platform from which a reader can critically analyze and discuss the need for the state marriage requirements.

Some of the questions raised by this chapter include: Is there a history of marriage discrimination based on gender? What are the benefits of marriage? What are common state marriage barriers, and do they make sense? What may account for the intervention of the Supreme Court and Congress in marriage, an area once viewed as exclusively the domain of the states? What are the reasons for minimum age requirements? Should there be mandated pre-marriage education classes? Should states mandate premarital psychological and certain physical medical exams before a couple marry? What is the purpose of solemnizing a wedding, and who should officiate as an official to solemnize a wedding? What is the putative marriage doctrine? What is a proxy marriage? What is an Enoch Arden statute?

Note as you read this chapter that state marriage regulations are divided into two broad general categories: those that are procedural and those that are substantive. For example, a state may require a couple to comply with particular licensing requirements before allowing a marriage. The licensing process is viewed as procedural and acts as formal confirmation by the state of the couple's contract to marry. State substantive regulations include descriptions of who may and may not marry. For example, state substantive regulations typically prohibit marriages where the parties are too closely related by blood.

| REFLECTIVE QUESTIONS | What are your goals for this chapter? |

3.2 HISTORIC GENDER DISCRIMINATION

Historically, state statutes discriminated against both men and women. For example, state statutes once commonly discriminated on a gender basis when setting the minimum age to marry by allowing women to marry at a younger age than men. The discrimination was justified on the ground a man's primary responsibility when he married was to provide a home and its essentials for the family and it was important for him to get a "good education and/or training" before he assumed marital responsibilities. *Stanton v. Stanton*, 517 P.2d 1010, 1012 (Utah 1974), *rev'd* 421 U.S. 7 (1975). The discrimination was also justified on the basis that "girls tend generally to mature physically, emotionally and mentally before boys." *Ibid.*

Gender distinctions regarding age were constitutionally abolished in 1975. *Stanton v. Stanton*, 421 U.S. 7 (1975). In a notation of probable jurisdiction, the Court held that the difference in Utah's statutes under which girls attained their majority at 18 but boys did not attain majority until they were 21 years of age could not survive under the Equal Protection Clause of the Fourteenth Amendment. *See also Orr v. Orr*, 440 U.S. 268, 283 (1979) (gender-based alimony statutes violated the Equal Protection Clause).

The Court has struck down several other gender-based state statutes in a variety of contexts. For example, in *Craig v. Boren*, 429 U.S. 190 (1976), the Court held that Oklahoma's gender-based differential prohibiting the sale of 3.2 beer to males under the age of 21 and females under the age of 18 violated the Equal Protection Clause. In *Reed v. Reed*, 404 U.S. 71 (1971), it held that an Idaho statute was unconstitutional because it provided that, when two individuals are otherwise equally entitled to appointment as administrator of an estate, the male applicant must be preferred to the female. In *Caban v. Mohammed*, 441 U.S. 380 (1979), the Court held that the Equal Protection Clause was violated when a mother was granted a veto over the adoption of a four-year-old girl and a six-year-old boy, but the father, who had admitted paternity and had participated in the rearing of the children, was not granted such a veto.

| REFLECTIVE QUESTIONS | What factors may account for historic gender discrimination? |

3.3 STATE INTEREST IN MARRIAGE

There is a consensus that states have a vital interest in the institution of marriage with plenary power to fix the conditions under which marital status may be created or terminated. State power to regulate marriage has been viewed, absent federal constitutional considerations, as a matter solely within the province of a state legislature. *See Estate of DePasse*, 118 Cal. Rptr. 2d 143 (Cal. App. 2002).

A century ago courts were confident in their view of the vital nature of the state interest in marriage. "Society rests upon marriage," said the Indiana court in 1901. *Franklin v. Lee*, 62 N.E. 78, 82 (Ind. App. 1901). "Society and the State [have] a vital interest in marriage," wrote the Arkansas Supreme Court in 1916. *Rowe v. Young*, 185 S.W. 438, 440 (Ark. 1916). However, courts in the twenty-first century appear less confident of the vitality of the state interest in marriage.

It has been critically suggested that this less confident view of marriage, and the state's interest in it, has to do with the transformation of marriage from an indispensable social institution to a "tool in pursuit of individual happiness." In this transformation, the state's vital interest in marriage may have been diminished. For example, Professor Maggie Gallagher writes that "the relationship between marriage and progress (much less civilization or survival), once crystal clear to courts and other educated Americans, is no longer self-evident." She asserts that by the 1980s, the Supreme Court had, at least rhetorically, transformed marriage from an indispensable social institution into a useful tool in pursuit of individual happiness. The family as a whole was increasingly described as serving primarily individual interior, symbolic, and emotional functions, and the state's interest was becoming correspondingly to promote individual liberty to define the mystery of existence for oneself in the realm of family law. Maggie Gallagher, *Rites, Rights, and Social Institutions: Why and How Should the Law Support Marriage?*, 18 Notre Dame J.L. Ethics & Pub. Pol'y 225, 226 (2004).

One area where the state's vital interest in marriage remains is found in its criminal laws. Family law relies, at least in part, on criminal law to assist in defining what marriage is and in policing marriage's normative boundaries. Melissa Murray, *Strange Bedfellows: Criminal Law, Family Law, and the Legal Construction of Intimate Life*, 94 Iowa L. Rev. 1253, 1267 (May 2009). For example, until the "late twentieth century, the criminal law in most jurisdictions prohibited fornication — sex outside of marriage — thereby highlighting marriage's role as the licensed locus for sexual activity." *Id.* at 1268-1269.

REFLECTIVE QUESTIONS	How has the state's interest in marriage changed, if it has, in the last 50 years? Explain why it has changed, if it has.

3.4 BENEFITS OF MARRIAGE

There are tangible and intangible benefits that flow from legal recognition of marriage. For example, married couples experience a certain amount of dignity and respect in the eyes of the state because they are married. They have the right to visit each other in the hospital and to make medical decisions for the other spouse when incapacitated. Married couples possess certain rights of inheritance and exemption from taxation. A surviving spouse may receive benefits under workers' compensation statutes or an employer pension plan that provides for surviving spouses. A surviving spouse may sue for compensation for the wrongful death of the other spouse. If a will leaves an estate "to my wife" or "to my husband," proof of a legally recognized marriage is essential. At the federal level, married couples receive tax, Social Security, pension, immigration, and other benefits.

REFLECTIVE QUESTIONS	Are there additional benefits to marriage that are not listed above?

3.5 MARRIAGE BARRIER: CONSANGUINITY

State legislatures have erected a number of barriers to becoming married. One of those barriers is "consanguinity." Consanguinity is defined as a "relationship by blood." *See* 3 Oxford English Dictionary 753 (2d ed. 1989) ("condition of being of the same blood; relationship by descent from a common ancestor; blood-relationship"); Black's Law Dictionary 299 (7th ed. 1999) ("relationship of persons of the same blood or origin"). The meaning of "consanguinity" is distinguished from "affinity." Consanguinity is a blood relationship, while affinity is a nonblood relationship acquired through marriage.

Courts have given several reasons to support state laws that prohibit marriages of close blood relationships. For example, in *In Commonwealth v. Otto*, 1981 WL 657 (Pa. Com. Pl. 1981), the court stated that such relationships are prohibited "for the reason that the science of genetics clearly forecasts that a child conceived out of such a relationship will more than likely be defective and for the further reason that such consanguineous relationships are virtually certain to lead to family discord and disintegration." In *Matter of Loughmiller's Estate*, 629 P.2d 156, 158 (Kan. 1981), the court wrote that "they are forbidden by ecclesiastical law (see Old Testament, Leviticus 18: 6-18); inbreeding is thought to cause a weakening of the racial and physical quality of the population according to the science of eugenics; and they prevent the sociological consequences of competition for sexual companionship among family members."

Most state criminal statutes contain provisions punishing persons within certain degrees of consanguinity who intermarry or commit adultery or fornication with each other. It is thought that many of the prohibitions have their roots in the Bible. For example, in *Ghassemi v. Ghassemi*, 998 So. 2d 731, 748 (La. App. 2008), the court stated that "Chapter 18 of the Bible's Book of Leviticus [is] the font of Western incest laws."

Universally, marriages between a parent and child or between a brother and sister are barred and such relationships are void and may result in criminal prosecution for incest. State statutes generally do not distinguish between relationships of the full and half blood, or relationships created by adoption or illegitimacy. For example, in *State v. Sharon*, 429 A.2d 1321 (Del. 1981), the parties were half-brother and half-sister by blood with the half-sister adopted and raised by a separate family. The court upheld an indictment for entering into a prohibited marriage, concluding that half-sibling relationships were included within the scope of Delaware's consanguinity law even though the prohibition was not specifically enumerated in the state statute.

First cousins. The question of whether first cousins may marry is unresolved, with about half the states barring such a marriage. Most jurisdictions prohibit marriages between an uncle and a niece. However, New York recognized a marriage between an uncle and a niece in *In re May's Estate*, 117 N.Y.S.2d 345 (N.Y. 1952). The couple, who were residents of New York where their marriage would be considered incestuous, went to Rhode Island and were legally married there. The New York court recognized the Rhode Island marriage as valid and therefore not against public policy in New York by applying the *lex loci* doctrine (i.e., the validity of a marriage is determined by the law of the place where it occurred). In *State v. Tucker*, 93 N.E. 3 (Ind. 1910), the court ruled that Indiana's statute governing marriage did not prohibit a marriage between uncle and niece by affinity.

In *Ghassemi v. Ghassemi, supra*, the Louisiana Court of Appeals held that a foreign marriage between first cousins in Iran, if valid in Iran, was valid in Louisiana and not a violation of strong public policy. The court observed:

> The marriage of first cousins has historically been regarded as in a different category from that of persons more closely related. A marriage between first cousins neither violates natural law nor is it included in the wider list of prohibited relationships set forth in Chapter 18 of the Bible's Book of Leviticus. . . .

Id. at 748.

Uncle and niece. In *Catalano v. Catalano*, 170 A.2d 726 (Conn. 1961), the court refused to recognize a marriage between an uncle and niece that was valid in Italy, the place of the marriage. It stated that the marriage was contrary to the public policy of Connecticut and therefore invalid. In *State ex rel. Miesner v. Geile*, 747 S.W.2d 757 (Mo. App. 1988), the court held that Missouri's statutory prohibition against marriage between an uncle and a niece did not prohibit marriage between uncle and niece related by adoption.

> **REFLECTIVE QUESTIONS**
>
> What reasons are given for consanguinity restrictions on marriage? Do some jurisdictions differ on the scope of the prohibition?

3.6 MARRIAGE BARRIER: AFFINITY

The doctrine of affinity is thought to have grown out of the canonical maxim that a husband and wife are one. *See* Christine McNiece Metteer, *Some "Incest" Is Harmless Incest: Determining the Fundamental Right to Marry of Adults Related by Affinity Without Resorting to State Incest Statutes*, 10 Kan. J.L. & Pub. Pol'y 262, 273 (2000). Affinity is the relationship contracted by marriage between a husband and his wife's kindred, and between a wife and her husband's kindred, in contradistinction from consanguinity, or relation by blood. *See People v. Armstrong*, 536 N.W.2d 789 (Mich. App. 1995). Texas courts have defined *affinity* as "the tie which exists between one of the spouses with the kindred of the other; thus the relations of my wife, her brother, her sisters, her uncles are allied to me by affinity and my brothers, sisters, etc. are allied in the same way to my wife. But, my brother and the sister of my wife are not allied by ties of affinity." *Pomerantz v. Rosenberg*, 593 S.W.2d 815, 817 (Tex. App. 1980).

> **REFLECTIVE QUESTIONS**
>
> What is the historic basis of the affinity prohibition on marriage? Should the prohibition be abolished?

3.7 MARRIAGE BARRIER: ADOPTED CHILDREN

Most jurisdictions bar a marriage between persons whose relationship is by adoption. The reason for the barrier rests upon concern with family harmony. Some believe that allowing such marriages will undermine the fabric of family life and detrimentally affect the social aims and purposes of the adoption process. *Marriage of Mew and M.L.B.*, 4 Pa. D. & C.3d 51 (Penn. 1977). However, it has been successfully argued that an individual's constitutionally protected right to marry trumps the state's interest in prohibiting incestuous marriages when the parties are related only by affinity as adopted brother and sister. For example, in *Israel v. Allen*, 577 P.2d 762 (Colo. 1979), the court struck down a Colorado statute on equal protection grounds that prevented two children adopted within the same family from marrying each other as adults. The court said the Colorado statute did not have a rational relationship to a legitimate state interest as applied to brothers and sisters related only by adoption. *See* Christine McNiece Metteer, *supra* at 272.

REFLECTIVE QUESTIONS	When, if ever, should children with different biological mothers and fathers adopted into the same family be allowed to marry each other?

3.8 MARRIAGE BARRIER: BIGAMY/POLYGAMY

All states have some form of bigamy statute. Bigamy is defined as having two wives or two husbands at one and the same time. *See Commonwealth v. Seiders*, 11 A.3d 495 (Pa. Super. 2010). While bigamy is defined as the act of marrying one person while legally married to another, polygamy is the state of being simultaneously married to more than one spouse. Gendered definitions are polyandry, which is the condition or practice of having more than one husband at the same time and polygyny, which is having more than one wife at a time. Criminal intent is normally required in order to convict a person of bigamy. *People v. Vogel*, 46 Cal. 2d 798, 801 (1956).

Enoch Arden statutes. Many states have enacted Enoch Arden statutes, which may act as a defense to bigamy. These statutes apply in the rare instance where a spouse remarries without having obtained a divorce from his or her partner but believes in good faith that the partner is dead. The statutes generally do not validate the subsequent marriage. Rather, they permit a spouse to remarry without criminal liability after a specified time period (five years in most American jurisdictions). The statutes take their name from the protagonist in a Tennyson poem who is shipwrecked and returns home after a long absence to find that his wife, who believed him dead, has remarried. An example of an Enoch Arden provision is Louisiana's statute declaring that a defendant will not be convicted of bigamy if he can show that his previous spouse was absent at the time of the second marriage for five successive years "without being known to such person, within that time, to be living." La. Rev. Stat. §14:76(1) (2015).

Insanity, intoxication, duress, or a belief one is divorced. Insanity, intoxication, duress, or a belief one is divorced when remarried are also possible defenses to a bigamy claim. For example, in *State v. Cain*, 31 So. 300 (1902), the court held that where a defendant, prosecuted for bigamy, undertook to show that he contracted a second marriage in the honest belief that the first had been dissolved by a decree of divorce, the burden was on him to show reasonable grounds for the belief and that he in fact held that belief.

Polygamy. Polygamy has ancient religious roots. Several of the central Biblical figures in the Old Testament were polygamists. The Jewish Talmud contains references to polygamy. It discusses, for example, how a man's estate may be distributed when he has several wives. The Prophet Muhammed had at least four wives and Sharia law recognizes that a man may have from one to four wives at a time.

In the United States, polygamy is a crime. In *Reynolds v. United States*, 98 U.S. 145 (1878), the Court held that criminal statutes punishing polygamy are not in conflict with the First Amendment to the Constitution, which prevents the government from making laws respecting a religion. The Court stated that a party's religious belief cannot be accepted as a justification for committing an overt act made criminal by the government. It reasoned that to allow a person to use religion as a barrier to prosecution would make religious beliefs superior to the law and permit every citizen to become a law unto himself. In such an instance, government would exist in name only.

Reynolds has been criticized for its strict distinction between religious beliefs and religiously motivated actions. Commentators argue that historical evidence does not support the Court's position that the Free Exercise Clause was only intended to protect beliefs. Michael W. McConnell, *The Origins and Historical Understanding of Free Exercise of Religion*, 103 Harv. L. Rev. 1410, 1488 (1990). Furthermore, subsequent Court decisions have made it clear that conduct can be protected by the First Amendment as well. In addition, the Court failed to fully articulate the state interests involved in prohibiting polygamy.

The opinion has also been criticized for failing to present any concrete proof of the dangers of polygamy, for example, that a child in a polygamous marriage is harmed or that women are exploited under the system. It is argued that religiously inspired polygamy is not any more damaging to society than de facto polygamy — multiple romantic or sexual relationships engaged in simultaneously or seriatim.

REFLECTIVE QUESTIONS   Should bigamy and polygamy be decriminalized where they remain a crime? You may want to review *Reynolds v. United States,* which is discussed in Chapter 2.

3.9 MARRIAGE BARRIER: DOMA

The Defense of Marriage Act (DOMA) was a congressional restriction on marriage that permitted states to refuse to recognize a marriage between persons of the same sex. It became federal law in 1996. 28 U.S.C. §1738. The House report on DOMA identified three governmental interests advanced by the statute: (1) in defending and nurturing the institution of traditional, heterosexual marriage; (2) defending traditional notions of morality; and (3) preserving scarce government resources.

DOMA defined marriage for purposes of federal law as a "legal union between one man and one woman as husband and wife." A "spouse" is defined as referring "only to a person of the opposite sex who is a husband or wife." DOMA required that these definitions apply "in determining the meaning of any act of Congress, or of any ruling, regulation, or interpretation of the various administrative bureaus and agencies of the United States."

In *United States v. Windsor*, 133 S. Ct. 2675 (2013), the dispute concerned the denial of the federal estate tax marital deduction for the property passing to the surviving spouse in a same-sex marriage. The Court held that §3 of DOMA, which defined "marriage" for purpose of federal law as a legal union between one man and one woman and a "spouse" as a person of opposite sex that is a husband or a wife, was unconstitutional.

REFLECTIVE QUESTIONS	*Windsor* is discussed in detail in Chapter 2. You may want to review it.

3.10 MARRIAGE BARRIER: LOSS OF SOCIAL SECURITY BENEFITS

Marriage may affect one's eligibility for Social Security Benefits. For example, in *Califano v. Jobst*, 434 U.S. 47 (1977), the Supreme Court reviewed a Social Security Act provision that provides for continuation of insurance benefits for a disabled dependent child who marries a person who is eligible for Social Security benefits. The provision discontinues benefits for a child who marries a person who is not eligible to receive Social Security benefits. The Court held that the provisions do not violate the principle of equality embodied in the Fifth Amendment's Due Process Clause.

The Court noted in *Califano v. Jobst* that "there can be no question about the validity of the assumption that a married person is less likely to be dependent on his parents for support than one who is unmarried." *Id.* at 53. Therefore, "it was rational for Congress to assume that marital status is a relevant test of probable dependency," and that termination of a child's benefits upon marriage satisfied the constitutional test. The Court stated that the general rule terminating benefits upon marriage "is not rendered invalid simply because some persons who might otherwise have married were deterred by the rule or because some who did marry were burdened thereby." *Id.* at 54. The Court concluded that the eligibility decisions were legitimate exercises of Congress's power to decide who will share in the benefits of the Social Security trust fund, and that the favored treatment of marriages between secondary Social Security beneficiaries did not violate the principle of equality embodied in the Due Process Clause of the Fifth Amendment.

REFLECTIVE QUESTIONS	Do you agree that marital status is a relevant test of probable dependency?

3.11 MARRIAGE BARRIER: POVERTY

Subtle questions of poverty, responsibility for child support, and the ability of a state to bar marriage were before the Supreme Court in *Zablocki v. Redhail*, 434 U.S. 374 (1978). In that case the Court reviewed a Wisconsin statute that prohibited any state resident under an obligation to support a minor child not in his custody from marrying without a judicial finding that the resident had met the support obligation in the past and was likely to meet it in the future. The Court found that the requirement "significantly interfere[d]" with the exercise of the right to marry because persons "who lacked the financial means to meet their support obligations" are absolutely prevented from getting married. The Court stated that "many others . . . will be sufficiently burdened by having to do so that they will in effect be coerced into forgoing their right to marry. And even those who can be persuaded to meet the statute's requirements suffer a serious intrusion into their freedom [to marry]." *Id.* at 387.

The majority, relying on a line of cases dating back to *Loving v. Virginia*, 388 U.S. 1 (1967), held that "the right to marry is of fundamental importance," and a "statutory classification [that] significantly interferes with the exercise of [this] right . . . cannot be upheld unless it is supported by sufficiently important state interests and is closely tailored to effectuate only those interests." 434 U.S. at 383. The Court reasoned that there were other avenues open to the state to obtain support for the children from the father short of barring his marriage. It stated that the statute had failed to consider the possibility that through a new marriage, the father might be better able to meet prior support obligations. The Court also stated that state classifications that directly and substantially interfere with the right to marry will be reviewed under the strict scrutiny test. It noted, however, that "reasonable [state] regulations that do not significantly interfere with decisions to enter into the marital relationship may legitimately be imposed." *Id.* at 386.

REFLECTIVE QUESTIONS	You may want to review *Zablocki* and *Loving*, which are discussed in Chapter 2.

3.12 MARRIAGE BARRIER: HOUSING DISCRIMINATION

Marriage, or the failure or inability to marry, may impact whether a person can rent a home or apartment. For example, in *State ex rel. Cooper v. French*, 460 N.W.2d 2 (Minn. 1990), the Minnesota Supreme Court was asked to apply the state's housing antidiscrimination statute to protect unmarried couples from rejection when attempting to rent apartments or homes. The statute read in relevant part:

It is an unfair discriminatory practice . . . [f]or an owner, lessee . . . to refuse to sell, rent, or lease . . . any real property because of race, color, creed, religion, national origin, sex, marital status, status with regard to public assistance, disability, or familial status.

The plaintiff sought to rent an apartment. When she applied to the landlord, she admitted that she would occasionally be visited by her fiancé. When the landlord learned of this, he refused to rent the apartment to her. The landlord justified his refusal to rent on the basis that the plaintiff and her fiancé might engage in sexual relations. He stated that he believed this would be sinful because they would be doing so without the benefit of marriage.

The Minnesota Supreme Court upheld the landlord's refusal. It construed the state statute as not intending to include discrimination on the basis of non-marital cohabitation as opposed to marital status, at least in part, because Minnesota criminalized fornication. It also interpreted Minnesota's constitutional protection of the landlord on the basis of religion as stronger than that provided by the United States Constitution. Mark Strasser, *Public Policy, Same-Sex Marriage, and Exemptions for Matters of Conscience*, 12 Fla. Coastal L. Rev. 135, 157 (Fall 2010).

A similar issue with a different outcome is *Swanner v. Anchorage Equal Rights Commn.*, 874 P.2d 274 (Alaska 1994). In that case, the landlord refused to lease properties to different individuals, who intended to occupy the apartment with a nonmarital partner. His refusal was based on his Christian religious beliefs. The plaintiffs filed a complaint with the Anchorage Equal Rights Commission. The Commission ruled that refusing to rent to unmarried couples constituted unlawful discrimination based on marital status and violated both an Anchorage ordinance and a state rental statute prohibiting such conduct. The Alaska Supreme Court affirmed the Commission's decision. It rejected the landlord's defense based on religion. It reasoned that "the governmental interest in abolishing improper discrimination in housing outweighs [the landlord's] interest in acting based on his religious beliefs." It stated that he impermissibly discriminated on the basis of marital status. The court also stated that "[a]llowing housing discrimination that degrades individuals, affronts human dignity, and limits one's opportunities results in harming the government's transactional interest in preventing such discrimination." *Id.* at 283. *See Smith v. Fair Employment & Hous. Commn.*, 913 P.2d 909, 925 (Cal. 1996).

| REFLECTIVE QUESTIONS | The States of Minnesota and California appear to disagree over the issue discussed above (housing discrimination based on religion). Which state has the (correct) (right) (best) policy? |

3.13 MARRIAGE BARRIER: TOO YOUNG TO MARRY

In a jurisdiction where a party cannot marry below a certain age under any circumstances, a marriage in violation of that prohibition will be viewed as void. For example, assume that a jurisdiction allows one to marry at age 16 with parental consent. Otherwise, one must be 18. Assume that X and Y lie about their ages and marry when X is 11 and Y is 30. Because there is no basis in law to marry at age 11, the relationship is void. This is so even if the couple continue living together as "married" for ten years. Subsequent cohabitation cannot alter the law's view that the relationship was void at the outset, and it will be treated as though it never existed.

In a jurisdiction where a party of a certain age can marry with parental consent or a court order, a marriage that proceeds without it will be viewed as voidable. In the above hypothetical if X is 17 and Y is 30, and the couple marry without parental consent or a court order, the relationship is voidable at X's option. If they continue to live together until X reaches age 18, when X could marry without parental or judicial approval, the disability is removed. In most jurisdictions and absent a statute allowing a longer period in which to obtain an annulment, X can no longer seek to void the relationship. To end the relationship after reaching age 18, X must use the jurisdiction's divorce statutes.

At what age should a state allow a person to marry? At common law, infants could validly marry — males at the age of 14 and females at 12 — and the consent of their parents was not necessary. *Bennett v. Smith*, 1856 WL 6412 (N.Y. Sup. 1856). However, by the end of the nineteenth century, state legislatures were beginning to question the advisability of allowing persons so young to marry, and statutes raising the minimum age began to appear. From the outset, the statutes appeared to conflict with the common law, and questions regarding their effect were raised. An early decision by the Supreme Court in *Meister v. Moore*, 96 U.S. 76, 80 (1877), provided state courts with guidance. Said the Court:

> In *Parton v. Henry* (1 Gray (Mass.), 119), where the question was, whether a marriage of a girl only thirteen years old, married without parental consent, was a valid marriage (the statute prohibiting clergymen and magistrates from solemnizing marriages of females under eighteen, without the consent of parents or guardians), the court held it good and binding, notwithstanding the statute. In speaking of the effect of statutes regulating marriage, . . . the court said: "The effect of these and similar statutes is not to render such marriages, when duly solemnized, void, although the statute provisions have not been complied with. They are intended as directory only upon ministers and magistrates, and to prevent as far as possible, by penalties on them, the solemnization of marriages when the prescribed conditions and formalities have not been fulfilled. But, in the absence of any provision declaring marriages not celebrated in a prescribed manner, or between parties of certain ages, absolutely void, it is held that all marriages regularly made according to the common law are valid and binding, though had in violation of the specific regulations imposed by statute."

REFLECTIVE QUESTIONS	At what age should persons be allowed to marry without parental or judicial consent? What is the minimum age persons should be allowed to marry with parental or judicial consent?

3.14 MARRIAGE BARRIER: CONSTITUTIONAL CHALLENGES TO AGE LIMITS

Age barriers to marriage contained in state statutes have not been successfully attacked on constitutional grounds. When the constitutional challenge to these statutes is raised, courts apply a rational basis test, which is the lowest level of scrutiny applied to a statute. For example, in *Moe v. Dinkins*, 533 F. Supp. 623 (S.D.N.Y. 1981), *aff'd*, 669 F.2d 67 (2d Cir. 1982), *cert. denied*, 459 U.S. 827 (1982), a New York law required parental consent before minors between ages 14 and 18 could marry. The law was challenged as violating an individual's fundamental right to marry. The court rejected the constitutional claim reasoning that the age restriction was rational because of the state's concern with unstable marriages and the inability of minors to make mature decisions. It also reasoned that the statute did not bar a marriage between the two applicants forever; rather, it delayed their marriage until they no longer required parental or judicial approval.

REFLECTIVE QUESTIONS	How have courts supported the view that age restrictions are constitutional?

3.15 MARRIAGE BARRIER: PARENTAL OR JUDICIAL CONSENT

Most states today require that both partners be 18 in order to marry without parental or judicial approval. Most states also allow persons age 16 or 17 to marry with parental consent or with a court order. However, in some jurisdictions, if the bride is pregnant, parental consent is not required if a statement is submitted to the court from a licensed physician certifying the pregnancy.

The decision in *New Jersey Div. of Youth & Fam. Servs. v. R.W.*, 641 A.2d 1124 (N.J. Super. 1994), added an interesting legal twist on parental consent to a teenage relationship. The parents, who had asked a court to allow the marriage of their 13-year-old daughter to her 19-year-old boyfriend, were charged and convicted of child abuse. The court found that they abused and neglected the child through their willful acquiescence to allow sexual intercourse between the girl and her boyfriend in their home. It observed that "consent by the minor is irrelevant; parental encouragement by allowing the child and her paramour to live together in the parental home only increases the opportunity, indeed, the likelihood, for continued abuse and exacerbates the degree of neglect." *Id.* at 1129. In *Porter v. Arkansas Dept. of Health & Human Services*, 286 S.W.3d 686 (Ark. 2008), the court determined that the parents were guilty of abuse in a neglect-dependency proceeding where they allowed their 15-year-old to date a 34-year-old man without appropriate supervision. The girl and the man had inappropriate sexual contact before their marriage, including the posting of sexually exploitative pictures on the Internet. The parents had consented to the minor female's marriage without inquiring into the male's age or background and allowed her to drop out of school and move to Mississippi.

Must both parents consent to underage marriage? There is disagreement among the states over the question of whether both parents must agree to an underage marriage. State statutes in Georgia, Iowa, Louisiana, and New Jersey require both parents to consent to a minor child's marriage, if both parents are available, unless one of them is "of unsound mind." North Carolina requires that the court appoint an attorney guardian *ad litem* for the minor and consider the opinion of both parents when determining whether marriage is in the child's best interests. Indiana requires that both parents receive notice of the hearing regarding marriage authorization, unless one parent is dead, has abandoned the petitioner, or is incompetent, the parent's whereabouts are unknown, or, if a noncustodial parent, the parent is delinquent in child support payments. Ind. Code §31-11-1-6(b)(2) (2015).

Nevada requires the consent of only a single parent to allow an underage person to marry if a court concludes there are extraordinary circumstances and the marriage is in the best interests of the minor. For example, in *Kirkpatrick v. Eighth Judicial Dist. Court ex rel. County of Clark*, 64 P.3d 1056 (Nev. 2003), the father of a 15-year-old girl sought to vacate her marriage to a 48-year-old man. Her mother had consented to the marriage, and her father did not receive notice of it. The court held that the father lacked standing to seek an annulment of the marriage.

Criteria for allowing underage marriage. As a general rule, a court may approve the marriage of an underage person only if it finds that the underage party is capable of assuming the responsibilities of marriage and the marriage will serve his or her best interests. Pregnancy alone does not establish that the party's best interests will be served by marriage. Occasionally, a court will deny an underage person the right to marry even with parental consent. *See, e.g., In re Barbara Haven*, 86 Pa. D. & C. 141 Orphans' Ct. (Penn. 1954) (court denied marriage of 14-year-old girl despite father's consent because it found only an "urgent desire" on the part of the parties to marry).

Parents waiving right to challenge marriage. Where an underage person marries without parental or judicial approval (and could be married with such approval), the parents may be deemed to have waived a right to bring an annulment action if, after learning of the marriage, they directly or indirectly acquiesce in it. For example, in *Blunt v. Blunt*, 176 P.2d 471 (Okla. 1947), the court held that the parents had waived their right to bring an annulment action because they allowed their underage son to bring his wife to their home and live in it with them following a marriage made without their consent.

UMDA. Under the Uniform Marriage and Divorce Act (UMDA) §205, a party age 16 or 17 (the Act provides alternatives) may marry with consent of both of the party's legal parents or with judicial approval.

REFLECTIVE QUESTIONS	Why shouldn't both parents be required to agree to an underage marriage before it is allowed? What is the judicial criteria for allowing an underage marriage?

3.16 STATE MARRIAGE REQUIREMENTS: PREMARITAL EDUCATION

Policymakers believe that many hasty marriages can be prevented by encouraging premarital education courses. As an incentive, some jurisdictions have proposed reducing marriage license fees for couples who received premarital education. *See, e.g.,* Ga. Code Ann. §19-3-30.1(a) (2015) ("[i]n applying for a marriage license, a man and woman who certify on the application for a marriage license that they have successfully completed a qualifying premarital education program shall not be charged a fee for a marriage license"); 43 Okla. St. Ann. §5.1(a) (2015) (clerk of court shall reduce the fee for a marriage license to persons who have successfully completed a premarital counseling program meeting the conditions specified by the state); Md. Code, Family Law, §2-404.1 (a)(1) (2015) (county may discount a marriage license fee if the couple to be married has completed, within one year before the date of the application for the license, a premarital preparation course that meets the requirements specified by the state). Where legislation has been enacted, it normally specifies that the education topics include teaching about the seriousness of marriage, conflict management skills, and the desirability of obtaining counseling if the marriage falls into difficulty. Persons recognized as qualified to act as marriage educators include members of the clergy, persons authorized to perform marriages, and marriage and family therapists. *See generally* Mark Eastburg, *Marriage Strengthening Strategies for Communities: The Greater Grand Rapids Community Marriage Policy Experience*, 9 Va. J. Soc. Pol'y & L. 224 (Fall 2001).

REFLECTIVE QUESTIONS	Should premarital education be required before parties are allowed to marry?

3.17 STATE MARRIAGE REQUIREMENTS: PREMARITAL MENTAL, PHYSICAL, AND GENETIC TESTING

The question of a person's mental and physical condition to marry has been, and continues to be, a subject of state concern. Nineteenth-century legislatures commonly erected marriage barriers for persons with certain mental conditions. For example, in 1895 the Connecticut legislature prohibited "feebleminded, imbecilic, and epileptic men and women under 45 years of age" from marrying. Matthew J. Lindsay, *Reproducing a Fit Citizenry: Dependency, Eugenics, and the Law of Marriage in the United States, 1860-1920*, 23 Law & Soc. Inquiry 541, 541 (Summer 1998). The justification for denying these persons the right to marry was usually based on the inability of the mentally deficient to enter into contracts, although it occasionally appeared the prohibition was overtly eugenic. *See* Jonathan Matloff, Comment, *Idiocy, Lunacy, and Matrimony: Exploring Constitutional Challenges to State Restrictions on Marriages of Persons with Mental Disabilities*, 17 Am. U. J. Gender Soc. Pol'y & L. 497, 498 (2009).

Persons who may be under the supervision or control of a conservator may marry in most jurisdictions with permission. *See, e.g., Howard v. MacDonald*, 851 A.2d 1142 (Conn. 2004) (no marriage license may be issued to any applicant under the supervision or control of a conservator unless the written consent of the conservator is filed with the registrar and "[a]ny person married without the consent provided for in subsection (a) of this section shall acquire no rights by such marriage in the property of any person who was under such control or supervision at the time of the marriage").

Blood tests. The physical condition of a marriage applicant has also been a subject of legislative concern. For example, venereal disease was an early concern and by the turn of the nineteenth century many state legislatures had made a person with venereal disease unfit for marriage. Nineteen states made venereal disease a bar to marriage by 1929, and ten of those required a health certificate from a physician to obtain a marriage license. Matthew J. Lindsay, *supra*; *Peterson v. Widule*, 147 N.W. 966 (Wis. 1914) (upon application for a marriage license the male party to such marriage must, within 15 days prior to the application, be examined by a physician of designated qualifications with reference to the existence or nonexistence of any venereal disease).

State marriage license regulations today often require persons desiring to marry to complete health questionnaires and submit to blood tests. The United States Supreme Court has commented on the use of blood tests, stating that

> [t]he blood test procedure has become routine in our everyday life. It is a ritual for those going into the military service as well as those applying for marriage licenses. Many colleges require such tests before permitting entrance and literally millions of us have voluntarily gone through the same . . . routine in becoming blood donors.

Breithaupt v. Abram, 352 U.S. 432, 436 (1957).

The nature and extent of information related to obtaining health certificates varies among the states, with some asking that applicants certify that they do not have a sexually transmitted disease, or, if infected, that they are not in a communicable state. In Massachusetts a medical certificate requires a showing that an individual has been examined and is free of communicable syphilis. The certificate must also indicate that a physician has offered the woman a voluntary test for susceptibility of rubella and has discussed AIDS with her.

Compulsory AIDS testing. The question of whether a couple may be compelled by a state to undergo AIDS testing before allowing them to marry remains open to debate. At one time, Louisiana and Illinois enacted statutes requiring testing for AIDS. However, both states conditioned issuance of a marriage license on passing the test, and the statutes were quickly repealed. When the Illinois bill was repealed, legislators observed that rather than submit to forced testing, hundreds of couples had traveled to neighboring states to obtain their marriage licenses.

> | REFLECTIVE QUESTIONS | What premarital medical/psychological tests, if any, should a state mandate? |

In Utah, a statute that prohibited marriage by a person afflicted with AIDS was ruled invalid because it was in conflict with the Americans with Disabilities Act (ADA). *T.E.P. v. Leavitt*, 840 F. Supp. 110 (D. Utah 1993). Presently, there appears a consensus among public health professionals that HIV testing must be voluntary and confidential. The reason given by these professionals is that this approach to AIDS testing is the only practical means of getting those at risk to test and still secure the greatest possibility of their cooperation afterwards.

3.18 STATE MARRIAGE REQUIREMENTS: MARRIAGE SOLEMNIZED BUT NO LICENSE OBTAINED

Professor Lawrence Friedman writes that state licensing of marriages did not actually develop until the need to determine eligibility for government benefits became apparent. He suggests that it was the combined goals of regulating veterans' benefits and limiting marriage and reproduction that led to the transition from common law marriage to civil marriage. Lawrence Friedman, *Private Lives: Families, Individuals, and the Law* 46 (2004); *see generally* Cynthia Grant Bowman, *A Feminist Proposal to Bring Back Common Law Marriage*, 75 Or. L. Rev. 709, 746-748 (1996).

Today, because a marriage confers legal rights and obligations on those who are recognized as "married" by the state, all jurisdictions impose specific statutory requirements on the formalities of marriage. States have typically enacted statutes declaring who may conduct a marriage ceremony, the number of witnesses required on a marriage certificate, and who will issue a marriage license. It is argued that strict compliance with state marriage statutory requirements is mandatory because the state must guard against recognition of informal relationships. However, a majority of states require only substantial compliance with marriage statutes. The majority view is that the parties' reasonable expectations should be recognized, even though there may be an imperfection in the marriage license or official application.

REFLECTIVE QUESTIONS	How important is the difference between states that strictly apply statutory requirements to marriage statutes that void a marriage where it has been solemnized but the parties failed to obtain a license, and those that apply substantial compliance to those situations?

Background to *Carabetta v. Carabetta*

In the following dispute, when the wife brought a divorce action, the husband claimed they were never legally married. The trial court granted the husband's motion to dismiss on the basis of a lack of subject matter jurisdiction. Because Connecticut did not recognize common law marriages (discussed in section 3.20), the question before the Connecticut Supreme Court was whether the alleged marriage, which lasted for more than two decades, was void because the couple had failed to obtain a marriage license.

CARABETTA
v.
CARABETTA

Supreme Court of Connecticut
438 A.2d 109 (1980)

PETERS, J. . . . The plaintiff and the defendant exchanged marital vows before a priest in the rectory of Our Lady of Mt. Carmel Church of Meriden, on August 25, 1955, according to the rite of the Roman Catholic Church, although they had failed to obtain a marriage license. Thereafter they lived together as husband and wife, raising a family of four children, all of whose birth certificates listed the defendant as their father. Until the present action [for divorce], the defendant had no memory or recollection of ever having denied that the plaintiff and the defendant were married.

The issue before us is whether, under Connecticut law, despite solemnization according to an appropriate religious ceremony, a marriage is void where there has been noncompliance with the statutory requirement of a marriage license. . . .

In determining the status of a contested marriage, we are bound therefore to examine with care the relevant legislative enactments that determine its validity. Such an examination must be guided by the understanding that some legislative commandments, particularly those affecting the validity of a marriage, are directory rather than mandatory. The policy of the law is strongly opposed to regarding an attempted marriage . . . entered into in good faith, believed by one or both of the parties to be legal, and followed by cohabitation, to be void.

The governing statutes at the time of the purported marriage between these parties contained two kinds of regulations concerning the requirements for a legally valid marriage. One kind of regulation concerned substantive requirements determining those eligible to be married. Thus General Statutes (Rev. 1949) §7301 declared the statutorily defined degrees of consanguinity within which a "marriage shall be void." . . .

The other kind of regulation concerns the formalities prescribed by the state for the effectuation of a legally valid marriage. These required formalities, in turn, are of two sorts: a marriage license and solemnization. In *Hames v. Hames*, we interpreted our statutes not to make void a marriage consummated after the issuance of a license but deficient for want of due solemnization. Today we examine the statutes in the reverse case, a marriage duly solemnized but deficient for want of a marriage license.

As to licensing, the governing statute in 1955 was a section entitled "Marriage licenses." It provided, in subsection (a): "No persons shall be joined in marriage until both have joined in an application . . . for a license for such marriage." Its only provision for the consequence of noncompliance with the license requirement was contained in subsection (e): ". . . any person who shall join any persons in marriage without having received such (license) shall be fined not more than one hundred dollars." Neither this section, nor any other, described as void a marriage celebrated without license.

As to solemnization, the governing section . . . provided in 1955:

> All judges and justices of the peace may join persons in marriage . . . and all ordained or licensed clergymen belonging to this state or any other state so long as they continue in the work of the ministry may join persons in marriage and all marriages attempted to be celebrated by any other persons shall be void; but all marriages which shall be solemnized according to the forms and usages of any religious denomination in this state shall be valid.

In the absence of express language in the governing statute declaring a marriage void for failure to observe a statutory requirement, this court has held in an unbroken line of cases . . . that such a marriage, though imperfect, is dissoluble rather than void. . . . We see no reason to import into the language "(n)o persons shall be joined in marriage until (they have applied for) a license," a meaning more drastic than that assigned in *Gould v. Gould*, [where the statute] provided that "(n)o man and woman, either of whom is epileptic . . . shall intermarry." Although the state may well have a legitimate interest in the health of those who are about to marry, *Gould v. Gould* held that the legislature would not be deemed to have entirely invalidated a marriage contract in violation of such health requirements unless the statute itself expressly declared the marriage to be void. Then as now, the legislature had chosen to use the language of voidness selectively, applying it to some but not to all of the statutory requirements for the creation of a legal marriage. Now as then, the legislature has the competence to choose to sanction those who solemnize a marriage without a marriage license rather than those who marry without a marriage license. In sum, we conclude that the legislature's failure expressly to characterize as void a marriage properly celebrated without a license means that such a marriage is not invalid. . . .

The conclusion that a ceremonial marriage contracted without a marriage license is not null and void finds support, furthermore, in the decisions in other jurisdictions. . . . In the majority of states, unless the licensing statute plainly makes an unlicensed marriage invalid, "the cases find the policy favoring valid marriages sufficiently strong to justify upholding the unlicensed ceremony. This seems the correct result. Most such cases arise long after the parties have acted upon the assumption that they are married, and no useful purpose is served by avoiding the longstanding relationship. Compliance with the licensing laws can better be attained by safeguards operating before the license is issued, as by a more careful investigation by the issuing authority or the person marrying the parties." Clark, Domestic Relations, p. 41 (1968).

There is error, the judgment is set aside and the case is remanded for further proceedings in accordance with this opinion. . . .

DISCUSSION QUESTIONS **FOR *CARABETTA v. CARABETTA***

A. The court distinguished between two types of marriage regulations. What is the significance of the distinction to the outcome of *Carabetta*?

B. If the court in *Carabetta* had ruled in favor of the husband, could the court have awarded either party alimony? Divided "marital" property?

C. In most jurisdictions, there is a presumption favoring the validity of marriage. The presumption justifies recognition of an unlicensed ceremony unless the licensing statute plainly makes an unlicensed marriage invalid. *Accounts Management, Inc. v. Litchfield*, 576 N.W.2d 233 (S.D. 1998); *Feehley v. Feehley*, 99 A. 663 (Md. 1916). However, some jurisdictions, because of specific language in the marriage statutes, refuse recognition of a marriage where there was an unlicensed ceremony.

The difference in outcomes is apparent when one compares the statutory require-ments for a valid marriage in Connecticut as outlined in *Carabetta* with those of New Jersey. Under the laws of New Jersey, a marriage is void without a state-issued marriage license. N.J. Stat. §37:1-10 (2008). Several other jurisdictions follow the New Jersey approach. *See, e.g., Nelson v. Marshall*, 869 S.W.2d 132 (Mo. App. 1993); *Moran v. Moran*, 933 P.2d 1207 (Ariz. 1996); *Harlow v. Reliance Nat'l*, 91 S.W.3d 243 (Tenn. 2002); *Parks v. Martinson*, 694 So. 2d 1386 (Ala. App. 1997). What public policy is fostered by the New Jersey statute? What public policy is fostered by the Connecticut statute discussed in the above case? Which public policy makes the most sense?

D. In *Hall v. Mall*, 32 So. 3d 682 (Fla. App. 2010), a week before the wedding the couple intended to go to the office of the county court clerk to get a marriage license. However, on that day, the prospective groom called the prospective bride at work and told her that they were not going to be able to get a marriage license because they had not agreed on the provisions of a premarital contract. The pro-spective bride was very upset by this — all of the arrangements had been made and many of the guests were already in town for the ceremony. The groom persuaded her to go ahead with the ceremony, reassuring her that "everything will be alright." The couple then participated in a full wedding ceremony performed by a minister at a church with numerous family members and friends present, complete with attendants, music, and flowers, and followed by a reception. A year after the "mar-riage" ceremony, the parties appeared before the clerk of the court and applied for and received a marriage license. However, the license was neither later solemnized nor returned to the clerk of the court to be made part of the official records of the county.

The parties referred to each other as husband and wife and two children were born of the relationship. The bride was referred to as "Mrs." in her workplace, although she had not legally changed her name. The parties continued to file separate tax returns. After six years of marriage, the wife filed for divorce. The husband responded by filing an answer and counterpetition to establish paternity. He also denied the existence of a valid marital relationship. The dispute made its way to the court of appeals.

A majority on the appellate court *en banc* held there was no valid marriage because the parties had failed to proceed under state law in good faith and were not in substantial compliance with the law. The dissent compared the lack of a mar-riage license to an unrecorded deed and pointed out that failure to record a deed does not make invalid the transfer of land. Therefore, the failure to record the marriage license does not make the marriage invalid. The majority responded that the facts were more analogous to a situation in which the parties are in nego-tiation for the purchase of land and reach agreement on a wide range of the terms of the sale yet cannot reach agreement on one final and material term. Therefore, no deed is executed and no sale is made. The dissent also argued that although Florida has abolished common law marriage, it has not abolished unlicensed mar-riages. He argued that should the state have intended to abolish unlicensed mar-riages, it must do so clearly and specifically. The dissent pointed out that if the majority ruling is followed, the couple's two children would be considered to be born out of wedlock. This result, said the dissent, is also contrary to the strong presumption of legitimacy attached to children born in wedlock. Who has the better argument, the dissent or the majority?

3.19 STATE MARRIAGE REQUIREMENTS: WHO MAY SOLEMNIZE A MARRIAGE

State statutes prescribe who and how a marriage is to be solemnized. For example, in New York a marriage is solemnized when "the parties solemnly declare in the presence of a clergyman or magistrate and the attending witness or witnesses that they take each other as husband and wife." N.Y. Dom. Rel. Law §12 (2015). Solemnization normally provides a public ritual indicating the couple has taken on a new status. The act of marriage with witnesses and a celebrant assures that there is evidence of the marriage in the form of witnesses.

Who may officiate? Who may officiate at a marriage ceremony varies from state to state. Judges and sometimes local mayors are authorized to officiate at a wedding. Minnesota permits residential school administrators of the Minnesota State Academy for the Deaf and the Minnesota State Academy for the Blind to officiate. Minn. Stat. Ann. §517.04 (2015). Religious clergy of all major denominations are usually included in state statutes listing who may officiate at a wedding. Some are specifically identified in a statute. For example, Massachusetts provides that "an authorized representative of the Spiritual Assembly of the Baha'is" and "a leader of an Ethical Culture Society which is duly established in the commonwealth and recognized by the American Ethical Union" may solemnize a wedding. Mass. Gen. Law. Ann. ch. 207, §38 (2015). Alaska includes a "commissioned officer of the Salvation Army" in a list of those who may officiate at a wedding. Alaska Stat. §25.05.261 (2015). Maine allows any member of the state bar who resides within the state to solemnize marriages. Me. Rev. Stat. 19-A §655(1)(A)(2) (2015). Montana allows lawyers to draw up a declaration of marriage for persons desiring to consummate a marriage by written declaration without solemnization. Mont. Stat. §§40-1-311, 40-1-312 (2015).

Some have questioned why states limit those who may officiate at a wedding. In *Universal Life Church v. Utah*, 189 F. Supp. 2d 1302, 1306-1307 (D. Utah 2002), the court answered that question by stating that Utah's concern over who could perform a marriage ceremony was that

> one who so cavalierly becomes a minister might not appreciate the gravity of solemnizing a marriage and might not bring to the ceremony the desired level of dignity and integrity. In addition, it is conceivable that the Legislature could rationally be concerned that an individual's decision to use such a minister might be reflective of a cavalier attitude toward the marriage relationship.

In *Universal Life Church v. Utah, supra,* a religious organization and one of its ordained Utah ministers challenged a Utah law on First and Fourteenth Amendment grounds. The Utah statute made it a criminal offense for "ministers, rabbis, or priests of any religious denomination" to join persons in matrimony if the minister was ordained over the Internet or by mail. The federal court, relying on the Equal Protection Clause of the Fourteenth Amendment, held that the statute violated the Fourteenth Amendment's Equal Protection Clause "because it prohibited ordinations over the Internet or through the mails, but permitted ordinations via facsimile, telephone, or in person by another ULC minister." Jeffrey C. Morgan, 1 *Internet Law and Practice* §25:5 (2015).

Professor Robert Rains in an analysis of *Universal Life Church v. Utah* states that the purpose of limiting who may solemnize marriage is not clear. He suggests that other professionals could bring dignity and integrity to a wedding ceremony. Robert E. Rains, *Marriage in the Time of Internet Ministers: I Now Pronounce You Married, But Who Am I to Do So?*, 14 No. 4 J. Internet L. 1, 22, 23 (2010). He asks, "Why cannot doctors, lawyers, school teachers, or, for that matter, marriage counselors, solemnize marriages?" *See also Cramer v. Commonwealth*, 202 S.E.2d 911 (Va. 1974).

Internet marriages. Note that family law attorneys were cautioned in 2007 that couples should "steer clear of Internet-ordained ministers when seeking an officiate to perform their nuptials" because of a Pennsylvania decision. Tresa Baldas, *Court Ruling Spikes Internet Ministers, Highlights Legal Issue*, 9 No. 4 N.Y. Fam. L. Monthly 1 (December 2007). In the Pennsylvania decision, the judge declared a marriage invalid because the couple had been married by an Internet-ordained minister who was unauthorized under state law to perform a wedding. *Heyer v. Hollerbush*, No. 2007 SU 2132 Y08 (York Co., Pa., Ct. C.P). *See generally* Robert E. Rains, *supra.*

REFLECTIVE QUESTIONS	Of what importance is solemnization of a marriage? When, if ever, should the failure to properly solemnize a marriage void an otherwise legal relationship? Who should be allowed to solemnize a marriage—your teacher, for example?

3.20 COMMON LAW MARRIAGE

Common law marriages are currently recognized under certain circumstances in 15 states and the District of Columbia. States that recognize common law marriage include Alabama, Colorado, Georgia (if created before January 1, 1997), Idaho (if created before January 1, 1996), Iowa, Kansas, Montana, New Hampshire (for inheritance purposes only), Ohio (if created before October 10, 1991), Oklahoma, Pennsylvania (if created before January 1, 2005), Rhode Island, South Carolina, Texas, and Utah. *See* Jennifer Thomas, Comment, *Pitfalls and Promises:*

Cohabitation, Marriage and Domestic Partnerships, 22 J. Am. Acad. Matrimonial Law. 151 (2009).

Defined. A common law marriage is typically defined as "[a] marriage that takes legal effect, without license or ceremony, when a couple live together as husband and wife, intend to be married, and hold themselves out to others as a married couple." *Lowe v. Broward County*, 766 So. 2d 1199, 1210-1211 (Fla. App. 2000) (citing Black's Law Dictionary 986 (7th ed. 1999)). When this nation was formed, the common law marriage concept was embraced by some states and rejected by others. In jurisdictions where it was adopted, a common law marriage was justified on a belief that such marriages derived from a natural right that was possessed by every human. They were promoted because public policy favored marriage over illicit relationships. They were viewed as particularly important to resolve uncertainty when cohabitants' marital status became involved in a legal struggle. Common law marriage helped protect children because children born to an unmarried couple were considered illegitimate. They also addressed the concern regarding women becoming economically dependent upon the state. A common law marriage allowed states to privatize the financial dependency of women. It is thought that the common law marriage concept expanded to western America in the nineteenth century due to the lack of religious officials to perform marriage ceremonies and the difficulty of travel.

Evidence a common law marriage exists. Although the requirements varied from jurisdiction to jurisdiction, historically a common law marriage was recognized when a person consented to marry someone who was not married to someone else, did not have a close familial relationship, and was of a minimum age. Courts looked for evidence of the following to determine whether a relationship existed: (1) an agreement of marriage *in praesenti*, (2) made by parties competent to contract, (3) accompanied and followed by cohabitation as husband and wife, (4) subsequently holding themselves out as being married, and (5) gaining a reputation as being married.

A common law marriage, where recognized, was as binding as a ceremonial marriage. If the relationship broke down, the parties had a right to file for a divorce under the jurisdiction's divorce statutes. When a partner died, the other might inherit under a will where assets are provided to the survivor, take a forced share if the survivor was unhappy with the will, or take a share of the estate under intestate succession laws if no will existed.

Concerns. As noted earlier, most states have abolished common law marriage, which reflects their concerns about them. There was a concern that common law marriages undermined the tradition and sanctity of marriage. For example, in *Sorenson v. Sorenson*, 100 N.W. 930, 932 (Neb. 1904), the court stated that "[t]his ancient doctrine is alien to the ideas and customs of our people. It tends to weaken the public estimate of the sanctity of the marriage relation. It puts in doubt the certainty of the rights of inheritance. It opens the door to false pretenses of marriage and the imposition upon estates of supposititious heirs. It places honest,

God-ordained matrimony and mere meretricious cohabitation too nearly on a level with each other." There were also concerns that common law marriages were vulnerable to fraud and perjury. *See, e.g., Wagner's Estate*, 159 A.2d 495 (Pa. 1960).

Restatement. The Restatement (Third) of Property §2.2 comment *f*, provides that a common law spouse is a spouse for purposes of intestate succession in states recognizing common law marriage.

Burden of proof. Whether the standard of proof placed on a person claiming the existence of a common law marriage is clear and convincing, or merely a preponderance, varies among jurisdictions. *Compare Nestor v. Nestor*, 472 N.E.2d 1091 (Ohio 1984) (clear and convincing) *with Callen v. Callen*, 620 S.E.2d 59 (S.C. 2005) (preponderance).

Reviving. There are those who contend that common law marriages should be revived. They believe that common law marriage protects the interests of women, particularly poor women and women of color, more effectively than any of the theories suggested to address the problems created by its absence. They also believe that most of the original reasons given to support abolition of common law marriage—fear of fraud, protection of morality and the family, racism, eugenics, and health-related issues—no longer withstand careful scrutiny. Finally, they believe that recognition of common law marriage would protect children more effectively than current paternity actions. *See* David S. Caudill, *Legal Recognition of Unmarried Cohabitation: A Proposal to Update and Reconsider Common-Law Marriage*, 49 Tenn. L. Rev. 537, 566 (1982).

REFLECTIVE QUESTIONS	Should common law marriages be abolished in all states? Or revived in all states?

3.21 COMMON LAW MARRIAGE: SHORT-TERM RELATIONSHIPS

In the usual case, a common law marriage is created when two people have lived together for a significant amount of time in a jurisdiction that recognizes such relationships and the couple remain in that jurisdiction. However, interesting questions arise if a couple visits a state that recognizes common law marriage and then they return to a jurisdiction that does not recognize such relationships. Are they now married under the common law?

Only a few state courts have been willing to recognize a common law marriage allegedly entered into by residents during a short trip to a second state that recognizes such relationships. *See, e.g., In re Estate of Pecorino*, 407 N.Y.S.2d 550 (N.Y.A.D. 1978). A majority of states do not recognize out-of-state common law marriages when a couple returns from a short visit to their home domicile. *See, e.g., Vaughn v. Hufnagel,* 473 S.W.2d 124 (Ky. App. 1971) (24-hour motel visit insufficient), *cert. denied,* 405 U.S. 1041 (1972); *In re Estate of Stahl,* 301 N.E.2d 82 (Ill. App. 1973). In *In re Binger's Estate,* 63 N.W.2d 784 (Neb. 1954), a couple residing and cohabiting in Nebraska had taken three pleasure trips to Colorado for a period of three to four days each, during which time they continued to hold themselves out as husband and wife to friends and relatives. The Nebraska court held these trips were not sufficient to create a Colorado common law marriage.

REFLECTIVE QUESTIONS	**What reasons support the majority view of courts in this country that short-term trips where the parties claim they were married under the common law of another state should not be recognized? What policy is fostered by the minority of states that will recognize such relationships? Should the law favor the minority or majority position?**

Background to *Stein v. Stein*

In *Stein v. Stein,* the surviving partner claims an interest in the deceased's estate as his common law spouse. The survivor had lived with the deceased for a little over three years in Missouri, a state that does not allow creation of common law marriages. The legal issue is whether sufficient evidence supports recognition of a common law marriage based upon the couple's short stay outside Missouri in Pennsylvania. Pennsylvania recognizes common law marriage.

STEIN
v.
STEIN

Court of Appeals of Missouri (Western Dist.)
641 S.W.2d 856 (1982)

TURNAGE, J. Nana Stein sought to establish the fact that she was the surviving spouse of John A. Stein and filed applications for allowances. . . . The facts are not in dispute. About September, 1978, Nana started living with John in his apartment near the Blue Ridge Mall in Kansas City. They had met while Nana was a waitress in a restaurant in the Mall. In April, 1979, Nana and John took a bus tour, with other senior citizens, of the East. This tour lasted about three weeks and went through several states, including Pennsylvania. Nana's contention was that she and John exchanged rings and marriage vows in Philadelphia on one night. . . . [I]t is undisputed that Nana and John held themselves out as husband and wife, both before and after the tour, and lived together in John's apartment for about fifteen months.

It is further undisputed that John and Nana were residents of Missouri and were domiciled in this state during the entire time that they lived together. Their only absences were temporary while on the bus tour and for other trips for short visits with relatives of both. The resolution of this case is greatly simplified by the decision of the Southern District in *Hesington v. Hesington*, 640 S.W.2d 824 (1982). *Hesington* held . . . that Missouri will not recognize a marriage in a common law form between Missouri residents even though the marriage is alleged to have occurred in a state which recognizes common law marriage. The basis of that decision is §451.040.5, RSMo 1978, which declares that common law marriages hereafter contracted shall be null and void. *Hesington* held that to forbid common law marriage in this state but recognize a strictly common law marriage of residents of this state on a sojourn in a common law state would defeat the very purpose of the statute. In *Hesington*, Missouri residents went into Oklahoma, which does recognize common law marriage, and purported to exchange marriage vows. They thereafter held themselves out as husband and wife, but all the time they were domiciled in Missouri and actually resided in this state. The court held that the recognition of such a marriage would violate the public policy of this state as expressed in §451.040.5 when it involves Missouri residents, even though the circumstances of such marriage occurs in a state recognizing common law marriage.

The facts in this case are almost identical to those in *Hesington*. Here the parties were residents of Missouri and they were on a sojourn in Pennsylvania, which does recognize common law marriage. Nana contends the exchange of marriage vows in Pennsylvania constituted a valid common law marriage under the laws of that state. The judgment denying recognition of a common law marriage is affirmed.

DISCUSSION QUESTIONS FOR *STEIN v. STEIN*

A. What public policy does the court's refusal to recognize a common law relationship in this case fulfill? Is nonrecognition rational? Fair? Would the outcome have been different if the couple were residents of a state that allowed common law marriages for several years before moving to Missouri? What benefits, if any, did the survivor lose because of the refusal to recognize the relationship?

B. Assume that a husband and wife were married for 40 years when Alzheimer's began to seriously affect the husband to a point where his wife was no longer able to care for him in their home. The wife's attorney advised her that if she got a divorce, her husband, a veteran, would have immediate Title XIX medical assistance under the federal Medicaid statute without "wiping out" the couple's entire assets.

The divorce petition was granted with the court stating that there had been a breakdown of the marital relationship to the extent that the legitimate objects of matrimony have been destroyed and there remained no reasonable likelihood that the marriage could be preserved, and that all conciliation proceedings should be, and were, waived by the court. The decree ordered that the marital relationship that had existed between the parties was set aside and each of the parties was restored to "the full privileges and immunities of a single person." The divorce decree also restored the wife's former maiden name.

The wife continued to care for her now ex-husband on a daily basis following the divorce even though he was confined to a nursing home. About four months after the divorce, the veteran died and the ex-wife sought veterans' benefits as his surviving spouse. She argued that this jurisdiction recognized common law marriages, which it did. She contended that at the time of the veteran's death, they were in a common law marriage. The government challenged the relationship and the matter went to court. On these facts, how should a court rule? Should it make a difference to the outcome of the hypothetical if the couple were in good health at the time of the divorce but continued to live together as husband and wife for ten years after the divorce until the veteran died?

C. In those jurisdictions where common law marriage has been abolished, it is argued that the abolition has a particularly negative impact on Social Security benefits for women for two reasons. Women have a greater life expectancy than men and men earn higher wages than women. Jennifer Thomas, *supra* at 164. Because women generally outlive their husbands and depend on Social Security survivor benefits in retirement, women who live in states that have abolished common law marriages are unable able to collect benefits, even if they have lived with their male partners and held themselves out as being married. "The collection of wrongful death benefits also negatively affects women because women are more likely to be economically dependent on men. When a woman loses her husband, she is left to survive without the high wage earner's support." *Ibid.* Are these arguments sufficient to encourage revival of common law marriages in those states that no longer allow them? Alternatively, should the federal government establish its own common law marriage standards for awarding Social Security benefits regardless of state marriage laws? Can the lack of uniformity among the states on this issue be justified? *See generally* Cynthia Grant Bowman, *A Feminist Proposal to Bring Back Common Law Marriage,* 75 Or. L. Rev. 709 (Fall 1996).

3.22 PROXY MARRIAGE

Marriages by proxy are rare and ordinarily require at least one party to be present for the wedding ceremony. Montana is the only state that once provided for double proxy marriages — meaning that neither party needed to be present at the actual ceremony. Maurice Possley, *Marriage by Proxy Booming in Montana,* Montana Law. 32 (June/July 2007). Stand-ins represented the bride and groom. Because Montana was inundated with double-proxy marriage requests from military members and others all over the world, in 2007 it altered its proxy marriage law to require that one of the parties to such a marriage be either a Montana resident or a member of the military on active duty.

The question of whether a proxy marriage conducted in violation of a provision of local law is necessarily void has been answered in the negative, at least in one decision. *Barrons v. United States*, 191 F.2d 9 (9th Cir. 1951). In *Barrons*, a proxy marriage was upheld in Nevada where it was conducted in the absence of the serviceman groom. The proxy ceremony was celebrated before a regularly ordained minister. Nevada law declared that a marriage was invalid if the parties failed to declare, in the presence of the judge, minister, or magistrate, and the attending witnesses, that they take each other as husband and wife; and in every case there shall be at least two witnesses present.

The Nevada statute could literally be construed as requiring that the declaration of marriage be made by the parties personally, and that a proxy marriage by its very nature is invalid. However, the Ninth Circuit held that if the serviceman failed to appear personally for his proxy marriage, the failure was a defect that at most rendered the marriage voidable. As a consequence, if the marriage was not annulled by his wife and the serviceman died while in military service, the serviceman's father could not attack its validity and defeat the right of the serviceman's widow to the benefits provided under the national service life insurance policy. *See State v. Anderson*, 239 Or. 200, 204 (1964) (if a proxy ceremony were defective, the parties could annul the marriage, but the government had no grounds for stepping in and invalidating the marriage).

UMDA. The Uniform Marriage and Divorce Act (UMDA) §206(b) recognizes proxy marriages if the proxy acts with written authorization.

REFLECTIVE QUESTIONS	What requirements should a legislature mandate when drafting a proxy marriage statute?

3.23 COVENANT MARRIAGE

Despite covenant marriage legislative proposals in about two dozen states, only three have adopted covenant marriage legislation: Louisiana (1997), Arizona (1998), and Arkansas (2001). Louisiana's Covenant Marriage Act forms the model for other states considering enacting such legislation. It is reported that only 1 to 2 percent of couples marrying in Arkansas, Arizona, and Louisiana since covenant marriage was legalized have chosen that option. Edward Stein, *Looking Beyond Full Relationship Recognition for Couples Regardless of Sex: Abolition, Alternatives, and/or Functionalism*, 28 Law & Ineq. 345, 364, n.109 (Summer 2010).

If couples seeking to marry in the three states that have adopted covenant marriage decide to execute a covenant marriage contract, they undergo mandatory premarital counseling that stresses the seriousness of marriage. There is also a premarital signing of a Declaration of Intent requiring couples to make all reasonable efforts to preserve the marriage, including marriage counseling in the event of difficulties. There are specific provisions that provide for a limited number of grounds for divorce. Shahar Lifshitz, *Married Against Their Will? Toward a Pluralist Regulation of Spousal Relationships*, 66 Wash. & Lee L. Rev. 1565, 1632 (Fall 2009). For example, the Declaration of Intent for couples provided in Louisiana's Covenant Marriage Statute reads in part:

> We do solemnly declare that marriage is a covenant between a man and a woman who agree to live together as husband and wife for so long as they both may live. We have chosen each other carefully and disclosed to one another everything which could adversely affect the decision to enter into this marriage. We have received premarital counseling on the nature, purposes, and responsibilities of marriage. We have read the Covenant Marriage Act, and we understand that a Covenant Marriage is for life. If we experience martial difficulties, we commit ourselves to take all reasonable efforts to preserve our marriage, including marital counseling. With full knowledge of what this commitment means, we do hereby declare that our marriage will be bound by Louisiana law on Covenant Marriages and we promise to love, honor, and care for one another as husband and wife for the rest of our lives.

La. Rev. Stat. §9:273(A)(1) (2015).

A divorce under a covenant contract requires either an agreed-upon two-year separation or one of a limited set of circumstances — such as adultery, abuse, imprisonment for a felony, or abandonment. The typical state covenant marriage law also allows married couples to renew their vows and to recast their marriage under terms of the covenant. Proponents of covenant marriage believe it will reduce the divorce rate and make a marriage more durable because of the premarital steps taken by the couple.

Critics of covenant marriage express concern that the parties may have unequal bargaining power and undertake a marriage to which they are not committed. There is also concern that parties may select a covenant marriage to satisfy the demands of their particular religious affiliation. Furthermore, the parties might view a "regular" noncovenant marriage as an inferior marital form of marriage, which may lessen the validity of the standard marriage. Finally, there is concern that covenant marriages may increase litigation and the likelihood of spousal abuse. *See* Jeanne Louise Carriere, *"It's Déjà Vu All Over Again": The Covenant Marriage Act in Popular Cultural Perception and Legal Reality*, 72 Tul. L. Rev. 1701, 1714-1718, 1741-1742 (1998).

REFLECTIVE QUESTIONS	**What state policy is promoted by a covenant marriage statute? Should all states adopt covenant marriage statutes?**

3.24 PUTATIVE MARRIAGE

The term *putative marriage* (*matrimonium putativum*) refers to the specific instance where a void marriage is recognized with limited legal consequences despite its invalidity. In order for a court to recognize the existence of a putative marriage, one or both of the parties must be innocent of the existing impediment and must be acting in good faith at all times during the existence of the putative marriage. A putative marriage is terminated by the death of either of the parties or removal of the impediment.

Children born of a putative marriage are considered legitimate. *Curtin v. State*, 238 S.W.2d 187, 190 (Tex. Crim. App. 1951). Jurisdictions have legislatively provided for an innocent putative spouse with most of the marital rights flowing from the relationship. *See, e.g., Wagner v. County of Imperial*, 193 Cal. Rptr. 820 (Cal. App. 1983) (putative spouse entitled to sue for wrongful death of other spouse); *Thomason v. Thomason*, 776 So. 2d 553 (La. App. 2000) (wife who learned of defect when husband filed for divorce given status of putative spouse); *Johnson v. Commissioner of Revenue*, 1979 WL 1142 (Minn. Tax 1979) (a putative marriage is viewed as virtually identical to a legal marriage under Minnesota law; therefore, a putative marriage should not be thought of as inferior to a valid marriage).

UMDA. Under the Uniform Marriage and Divorce Act (UMDA) §209, any person who has cohabited with another to whom he or she is not legally married in the good faith belief that the individual was married to that person is a putative spouse until knowledge of the fact that he or she is not legally married terminates the person's status and prevents acquisition of further rights. A putative spouse acquires the rights conferred upon a legal spouse, including the right to maintenance following termination of the status, whether or not the marriage is prohibited (§207) or declared invalid (§208).

Because good faith is the test, a person may have more than one putative spouse at the same time. UMDA, *Commentary*, §209. A putative spouse and a legal spouse may be able to claim from a single estate or from other funds legally available to a spouse. A court will usually apportion property and other financial incidents of marriage between the legal and putative spouse, or among putative spouses. It is suggested that a fair and efficient apportionment standard is likely to be related to the length of time each spouse cohabited with the common partner. *Ibid.*

Restatement. The Restatement (Third) of Property §2.2 comment *e* provides that "[un]less precluded by applicable statute, a putative spouse is treated as a legal spouse for purposes of intestacy."

Community property jurisdictions. The putative spouse doctrine is recognized in community property states. For example, in California, the putative spouse doctrine was recognized as an equitable corollary of the community property system, which California inherited from Spanish civil law and formally adopted by statute in 1850. *See generally* Raj Rajan, *The Putative Spouse in California Law*, 11 J. Contemp. Legal Issues 95, 97 (2000).

The community property system rests on the concept that marriage is a partnership, and the property and earnings acquired during a valid marriage are the property of both partners in equal shares. *In re Marriage of Bonds*, 5 P.3d 815 (Cal. 2000). The putative spouse doctrine extends this partnership concept to innocent parties of an invalid marriage. For example, in *Vallera v. Vallera*, 134 P.2d 761 (Cal. 1943), the court considered it "well settled that a woman who lives with a man as his wife in the belief that a valid marriage exists, is entitled upon termination of their relationship to share in the property acquired by them during its existence." *Id.* at 783. The purpose of the doctrine is to protect the expectations of innocent parties and achieve results that are equitable, fair, and just. *Caldwell v. Odisio*, 299 P.2d 14 (Cal. 1956). California courts have applied the doctrine to a claim under an omitted spouse statute and to recognize a claim for an intestate share by an unmarried cohabitor. *See, e.g., Estate of Sax*, 263 Cal. Rptr. 190 (Cal. App. 1989); *Estate of Leslie*, 689 P.2d 133 (Cal. 1984).

REFLECTIVE QUESTIONS	Describe the kind of evidence that should be produced in court to establish a claim that a person is a putative spouse.

3.25 CONFIDENTIAL MARRIAGE

A "confidential marriage" exists in California. In that state, couples can marry either by public marriage or through a confidential marriage. Ashley E. Rathbun, Comment, *Marrying into Financial Abuse: A Solution to Protect the Elderly in California*, 47 San Diego L. Rev. 227, 238 (February/March 2010). To establish a confidential marriage under California law, a couple who are not minors must first live together as husband and wife, although the statute does not specify the required length of time a couple must live together before marrying. *See* Cal. Fam. Code §500 (2015). A relationship involving occasional intercourse will not create a confidential marriage. Neither being or having a "mistress" is sufficient to qualify as living together as husband and wife for purposes of creating a confidential marriage. Rathbun, *supra* at 239, n.65.

The primary purpose of the California confidential marriage law is to shield the parties and their children, if any, from the publicity of a marriage recorded in the ordinary manner, and to encourage unmarried persons who have been living together as man and wife to legalize their relationship. The process associated with a confidential marriage eliminates some of the procedural requirements, such as filing a health certificate or obtaining a license. The parties must be of marriageable age, not minors, and must be living together. California law also requires that a ceremony of solemnization and a record of the marriage be on file with the county clerk. *See* Cal. Fam. Code §§500-536 (2015). Although California requires that the marriage be recorded, the records are private and may be inspected only upon a showing of "good cause." Cal. Fam. Code §511 (2015). A confidential marriage is unavailable to domestic partners.

REFLECTIVE QUESTIONS	**What do you believe is the purpose of California's confidential marriage statute? Should states outside California enact such a provision into their family law codes?**

3.26 SHAM MARRIAGE

Sham marriages are created without the intent to live together as a husband and wife. Aliens have attempted to use sham marriages to gain citizenship in the United States. *See, e.g., Ogbolumani v. Napolitano,* 557 F.3d 729 (7th Cir. 2009). In *United States v. Rubenstein,* 151 F.2d 915, 919 (2d Cir. 1945), the court described a sham marriage as follows:

> If the spouses agree to a marriage only for the sake of representing it as such to the outside world and with the understanding that they will put an end to it as soon as it has served its purpose to deceive, they have never really agreed to be married at all. They must assent to enter into the relation as it is ordinarily understood, and it is not ordinarily understood as merely a pretense, or cover, to deceive others.

There is disagreement among the federal circuits over the question of intent when the government is seeking to prove the existence of a sham marriage. The Fourth, Fifth, Sixth, Seventh, and Tenth Circuits have held that the government is not required to show that a defendant lacked intent to establish a life with his spouse — and thus jury instructions suggesting otherwise are contrary to law. *See United States v. Sonmez,* 777 F.3d 684 (4th Cir. 2015). The First, Eighth, and Ninth Circuits, on the other hand, have held that a defendant cannot be convicted of marriage fraud unless the government proves that the person did not intend to establish a life with his or her spouse — and thus jury instructions to that effect must be given. *See United States v. Yang,* 603 F.3d 1024, 1026 (8th Cir. 2010); *Cho v. Gonzales,* 404 F.3d 96, 102-103 (1st Cir. 2005); *United States v. Orellana-Blanco,* 294 F.3d 1143, 1151 (9th Cir. 2002).

The Ninth Circuit has explained that

> motivations are at most evidence of intent, and do not themselves make the marriages shams. Just as marriages for money, hardly a novelty, or marriages among princes and princesses for reasons of state may be genuine and not sham marriages, so may marriages for green cards be genuine. Intent to obtain something other than or in addition to love and companionship from that life does not make a marriage a sham. Rather, the sham arises from the intent not to establish a life together.

Orellana-Blanco, 294 F.3d at 1151.

> | REFLECTIVE QUESTIONS | Explain the disagreement among the federal circuits over how a jury should be charged in a criminal case involving a sham marriage. |
> |---|---|

3.27 PRISONER MARRIAGE

The Supreme Court has said that the right to marry extends to all individuals, including prisoners. Although states may impose reasonable regulations on prisoners that do not significantly interfere with the decision to enter into the marital relationship, if a law directly or substantially interferes with the right to marry, it must be drafted to meet the Constitution's compelling state interest test.

The leading Supreme Court decision on prisoner marriage is *Turner v. Safley*, 482 U.S. 78 (1987). In *Safley*, the prisoners sought to overturn prison regulations that conditioned their right to marry on the warden's approval. The regulation barred marriages of inmates except when there was a pregnancy or a nonmarital child was to be born. Prison officials argued that the restriction was related to the state's interest in rehabilitation of the inmate and to prison security issues. The prisoners argued that a warden could not reject a marriage request unless "compelling" reasons existed to deny it.

In arriving at its decision, the Court recognized that when a person is incarcerated for a crime, the state is able to burden the prisoner's liberty with additional restrictions. However, it made clear that normally a state may not completely bar prisoners from marriage. It stated that the important attributes of marriage remain, despite prison, including emotional bonding and receipt of government benefits conditioned on marriage.

The Court found that the state regulation under review barring all inmate marriages was not reasonably related to any state interests. The Court ruled that on the facts before it allowing a prisoner to marry would cause minimal security problems. It stated that the fundamental right to marry was more compelling than the arguments made by the state for the prison regulations barring the creation of the relationship.

Incidental interference with the right to marry does not give rise to a constitutional claim if there is "some justification" for the interference. *Williams v. Wisconsin*, 336 F.3d 576, 582 (7th Cir. 2003); *Keeney v. Heath*, 57 F.3d 579, 580-581 (7th Cir. 1995). For example, in *Williams v. Wisconsin, supra,* a parolee brought a §1983 action challenging a state ban on international travel, which prevented him from journeying to the Philippines to marry a woman with whom he had been corresponding. The court upheld the travel restriction. It observed that no one had forbidden Williams from getting married or from marrying his pen pal. "At most," reasoned the court, "the state's rule has affected either the timing or the place of his marriage plans. This type of incidental interference with the right to marry does not give rise to a constitutional claim if there is 'some justification' for the interference." *Williams, supra* at 582.

REFLECTIVE QUESTIONS
When may prisoners marry, if ever?

3.28 MARRIAGE AS EMANCIPATING A MINOR

Most states have statutes declaring that marriage emancipates a minor and relieves the minor's parents of further responsibility for the minor's support. Emancipation generally means freeing a child for all the period of his or her minority from the care, custody, control, and service of the child's parents; the relinquishment of parental control; the conferring on the child of the right to his or her own earnings; and the termination of the parent's legal obligation to support the child.

Emancipation is never presumed, and the burden is upon the party asserting it to show facts proving the emancipation. *Ragan v. Ragan*, 931 S.W.2d 888, 890 (Mo. App. 1996).

Emancipation can be accomplished in one of three ways: (1) by express parental consent, (2) by implied parental consent, or (3) by a change of the child's status in the eyes of society. *Denton v. Sims*, 884 S.W.2d 86, 88 (Mo. App. 1994). The third method is most often shown by the child entering the military or marrying. The question as to when a child is emancipated depends on the particular facts and circumstances of each case.

What is the obligation of a parent when a minor marries and then divorces before reaching age 18 and is without support? Most likely the minor can successfully claim parental support until reaching majority. *See* Christina Baine DeJardin, *Pitfalls Await Emancipated Parents*, 16 J. Contemp. Legal Issues 311, 314 (Fall 2007); *Church v. Church*, 657 P.2d 151 (Okla. 1982).

REFLECTIVE QUESTIONS
What facts *might* persuade a judge that a minor who is neither married nor in the military service is emancipated?

3.29 PRESUMPTION OF MOST RECENT MARRIAGE

When two parties claim they are married to the same spouse, the law generally presumes the most recent marriage is valid. *Mayo v. Ford*, 184 A.2d 38, 41 (D.C. App. 1962). The party asserting the invalidity of the marriage has the burden of rebutting the presumption by conclusive evidence. *See Caddel v. Caddel*, 486 S.W.2d 141 (Tex. App. 1972). The presumption continues over another presumption until proof that it was ended by death or divorce. *Gordon v. Railroad*

Retirement Bd., 696 F.2d 131 (D.C. Cir. 1983); *Teamsters Local 639 Employer's Pension Trust v. Johnson*, 1992 WL 2000075 (D.C. 1992).

 **REFLECTIVE QUESTIONS** Of what value is the presumption of most recent marriage?

3.30 NAME CHANGE AFTER MARRIAGE

When a woman married at common law, she assumed her husband's surname. The assumption was based on custom rather than the law. When a couple marry today, a woman may retain her birth name or adopt her husband's surname, absent fraudulent intent. A husband may also assume his wife's maiden name if he chooses to do so.

REFLECTIVE QUESTIONS What is the value of the name change principle mentioned above? If you marry, will you and your partner take identical surnames? Hyphenated surnames? Retain your surnames, or do something else?

3.31 MARITAL RAPE

At common law, a husband could not be found guilty of raping his wife. A wife was considered to have given implied consent to intercourse. She was also considered property, and her identity merged with her husband. The family was private, and the fictitious view of marital unity was strong. *See Shunn v. State*, 742 P.2d 775 (Wyo. 1987); Jill Elaine Hasday, *Contest and Consent: A Legal History of Marital Rape*, 88 Cal. L. Rev. 1373, 1375-1376 (2000). Moreover, rape could not occur because it required a lack of consent and the marriage relationship was a contractual obligation of irrevocable consent. Finally, some argued that marital rape should not be recognized because it prevented reconciliation of the spouses. *See* Emily J. Sack, *Is Domestic Violence a Crime? Intimate Partner Rape as Allegory*, 24 St. John's J. Legal Comment. 535, 552 (Spring 2010).

Most jurisdictions today have either abolished or limited the marital rape exception by statute or court ruling. For example, in *People v. Liberta*, 474 N.E.2d 567 (N.Y. 1984), *cert. denied*, 471 U.S. 1020 (1985), the New York Court of Appeals rejected the anachronistic views about the subservient role of a woman relative to her husband as the rational basis for the marital rape exception. It held that the marital rape exemption in New York's penal law violated equal protection under the New York Constitution. Note that in much of Asia and the Middle East, the marital rape exception endures. Amanda C. Pustilnik, *Violence on the Brain: A Critique of Neuroscience in Criminal Law*, 44 Wake Forest L. Rev. 183, 227 (Spring 2009).

| REFLECTIVE QUESTIONS | **What social changes have occurred in the United States over the last half century that may have caused the law to change its traditional view of marital rape?** |

3.32 SPOUSAL TESTIMONIAL PRIVILEGE

Generally, under the law in most jurisdictions, once a couple marry, a husband cannot be examined at a trial for or against his wife without her consent, nor can a wife be examined for or against her husband without his consent. The purpose of the marital testimonial privilege is to promote family harmony by precluding one spouse from testifying against the other without consent. It is also "premised upon the belief that the marital union is sacred and that its intimacy and confidences deserve legal protection." *State v. Rollins*, 675 S.E.2d 334, 337 (N.C. 2009). The privilege only applies to conversations held during the marriage. One common exception to the rule provides that the marital privilege does not apply to a criminal action or proceeding for a crime committed by one spouse against the other. *State v. Zais*, 790 N.W.2d 853 (Minn. App. 2010).

| REFLECTIVE QUESTIONS | **Do the reasons for the spousal testimonial privilege make sense in today's world? Should it be expanded to persons who cohabit much like a husband and wife but do not formally marry?** |

3.33 RECOGNIZING MARRIAGES FROM FOREIGN NATIONS

Recognition of marriages made in other nations has created a number of legal issues for courts in this country. The Supreme Court has said that

> [m]arriages not polygamous or incestuous, or otherwise declared void by statute, will, if valid by the law of the State where entered into, be recognized as valid in every other jurisdiction.

Loughran v. Loughran, 292 U.S. 216, 223 (1934). This rule is based upon the general principle that the capacity or incapacity to marry depends on the law of the place where the marriage is celebrated, and not on that of the domicile of the parties. For example, in *Gamez v. Industrial Commission*, 559 P.2d 1094 (1976), the Arizona Court of Appeals held that if a marriage entered into in Mexico was invalid in Mexico then it was to be considered invalid in Arizona.

Restatement. The Restatement (Second) of Conflicts §§283-284 states that a marriage satisfying requirements of the state where contracted is valid everywhere unless it violated the strong public policy of another state which had the most significant relationship to the spouses and the marriage at the time of the marriage. Furthermore, a state should usually give the same incidents to a valid foreign marriage that it gives to a marriage contracted within its territory.

Polygamous foreign marriages. When courts are faced with a problem involving a polygamous marriage recognized in a foreign country but not in the United States, they may, under certain circumstances, unbundle the relationship and enforce certain parts of it. While they may not necessarily recognize the foreign marriage for the purpose of providing a divorce, they may recognize the marriage for the purpose of a declaration of the legitimacy of children or for inheritance. They might also enforce an alimony decree from a foreign state where the husband legally married two wives. The American court could justify its decision on the basis that it has no interest in becoming a haven for foreign debtors fleeing alimony decrees from courts of another country.

In *Estate of Bir*, 188 P.2d 499 (Cal. App. 1948), the deceased husband was survived by two wives who had legally married him in India, which allowed polygamous marriages. When he died in California, the question was how to divide his estate between the surviving wives. The California court held that no public policy would be affected by dividing his estate between them, particularly since neither wife contested the right of the other to share the estate and they were the only interested parties. Thus, the marriages were considered valid in California to the extent of allowing wives to share the deceased's estate equally. *Cf. Rosales v. Battle*, 7 Cal. Rptr. 3d 13 (Cal. App. 2003) (concubinage in Mexico not the same as marriage, and unmarried claimant lacked standing to claim a part of the decedent's estate).

Policy reflected in state statute. The existence of a strong public policy against recognition of a foreign relationship is usually reflected in a specific state statute. For example, in *K. v. K.*, 393 N.Y.S.2d 534 (Fam. Ct. 1977), the couple married in Poland. However, they failed to follow Polish law because the wife's prior marriage had not been dissolved. Under Polish law she was a bigamist. When the wife sought support from a New York court where the couple had been living, the court applied Polish law and held that because the marriage was invalid in Poland, it was also invalid in New York.

Isn't the ruling in *Estate of Bir* contrary to a strong public policy? Should polygamous marriages, legal in other nations, be recognized in the United States for all purposes?

General Principles

1. Marriage is a contract and a status. *Maynard v. Hill,* 125 U.S. 190 (1833).
2. Void marriages are those that society deems contrary to public morals and violative of deeply held core values and include incestuous and bigamous relationships. Voidable marriages are relationships deemed less offensive to society, and the decision to void these relationships usually rests with the partner who possesses the legal disability.
3. Under the common law doctrine of nonintervention, courts are reluctant to involve themselves in an ongoing marriage because of a desire to preserve marital harmony.
4. Under the general rule of *lex loci,* a marriage valid where performed is valid everywhere, unless it is repugnant to the public policy of the domicile of the parties or is contrary to a state's positive laws.
5. Most jurisdictions impose specific statutory requirements on the formalities of marriage, that is, who may conduct a marriage ceremony, the number of witnesses required on a marriage certificate, and who may issue a marriage license. A majority of jurisdictions require only substantial compliance with state marriage statutes, not strict, literal compliance.
6. The purpose of solemnizing a marriage is to provide public notice and a permanent public record of the marriage. It may also satisfy a religious tradition and acts to impress on the couple the seriousness of marriage.
7. Consanguinity barring marriage exists in all jurisdictions. Consanguinity is a blood relationship.
8. Affinity is the relation contracted by marriage between a husband and his wife's kindred, and between a wife and her husband's kindred, in contradistinction from consanguinity, or relation by blood.
9. Although all states prohibit the marriage of relatives within certain degrees of kinship, most also prohibit marriage if the relationship is due to adoption.
10. Most jurisdictions today have either abolished or limited the marital rape exception by statute or court ruling.

Chapter Problems

1. Assume that Paula and David wish to marry but refuse to participate in blood tests for syphilis prior to marriage, as required by state statute. They contend that mandating such a test violates their First Amendment right to free exercise of religion under the Constitution because withdrawing blood from a body is contrary to their religious beliefs. Will a court require them to undergo the tests before marriage?

2. Assume that Pam and Donald were each 17 years of age when they lied about their ages on a marriage application and were secretly married by a justice of the peace. In their jurisdiction, persons age 16 and 17 can marry with permission of the court or one of their parents. Persons over 18 can marry without court or parental permission. Is the relationship between Pam and Donald void or voidable? If voidable, who may bring the action to void the relationship?

3. Assume that a 15-year-old daughter informs her parents that she intends to marry her 26-year-old volleyball coach. Also assume that in this jurisdiction, the state marriage statute bars anyone younger than 16 from marrying under any condition. The daughter and volleyball coach travel to Nevada where they obtain valid permission from the daughter's mother to marry. (Nevada allows 15-year-olds to marry with permission.) The two marry. When the daughter's father finds out about the marriage, he brings an action to void the relationship on the ground his permission was not obtained. What factors will determine the result in this dispute?

4. Doris marries Mike, who was still married to Sally. Doris had no knowledge of Mike's marriage to Sally. The state brings a criminal action against Doris for bigamy. Doris moves to dismiss the charge on the ground she had no knowledge that Mike was married when she married him. Doris also brings a divorce action. Will Doris most likely be convicted of a crime? Can Doris obtain a divorce, and if so, what type of divorce will it be?

5. Assume that Phyllis and Doug have lived together for 15 years without benefit of marriage in a jurisdiction that does not recognize common law marriage. They held themselves out as husband and wife, signed legal documents as husband and wife, and held joint bank accounts as husband and wife. When Doug dies without a will, Phyllis seeks her intestate share of Doug's estate as a surviving spouse under the law that applies to married couples. Phyllis produces evidence that a year before Doug died, the two of them took a three-week vacation in a state where common law marriages are recognized. During the trip, Phyllis claims that the couple exchanged rings and marriage vows in this jurisdiction. Phyllis seeks to have the court in the jurisdiction that does not recognize common law marriages recognize the out-of-state common law marriage for purposes of probating the estate. Will Phyllis most likely be successful?

6. Assume that Wanda, age 17, and Roy, age 20, decide to live together as husband and wife in a jurisdiction that recognizes common law marriages. Also, assume that the jurisdiction has the following statute: "The period of minority extends in all persons to the age of eighteen (18) years." A second statute states that "persons 18 years of age or older may marry." There are no statutory exceptions to the statutes. Wanda's mother challenges the marriage, stating that because Wanda is not emancipated, she cannot marry. Has the common law marriage emancipated Wanda?

7. Assume that Jane and George participated in a marriage ceremony. They applied for and were issued a marriage license prior to the ceremony, and the minister signed their marriage license at the ceremony. However, the parties never filed the license with the county clerk's office after the ceremony. When Jane seeks a divorce, George claims they were never married because they failed to file the license with the county clerk. The relevant state statute reads as follows: "(a) Any person obtaining a license under the provisions of this act shall be required to return the license to the office of the clerk of the county court within sixty (60) days from the date of license." Most likely, how will a court decide the question of whether they were legally married?

8. Assume that State X promulgates a statute that provides that women at age 18 and men at age 19 may marry without parental consent. Would such a statute be constitutional?

Preparation for Practice

1. Visit the local family court clerk's office and obtain blank copies of a marriage application. What are the answers to the following questions?

   a. Who may officiate at a marriage ceremony?
   b. How much does a marriage license cost?
   c. What educational materials, if any, does the clerk's office provide a marriage applicant?
   d. What medical tests are required, if any? What are suggested?
   e. Is premarital counseling required? Advised?
   f. If an applicant is indigent, is the filing fee waived?
   g. What is the waiting period before a couple can be married?

2. Compare the provisions in your state that prevent a person from marrying with those of another state you select.

   a. Are they identical?
   b. If they differ, in what respects do they differ?

Chapter 4

The Divorce Process

4.1 INTRODUCTION

This chapter surveys the history of divorce law from the earliest of times to the present. It compares and contrasts traditional common law views of divorce with those of the present day and provides an overview of divorce law in the United States as it exists today. It covers issues related to a divorce proceeding including older common law defenses to a divorce. It examines the grounds for a no-fault divorce, discusses religious objections to divorce, and asks on what basis a state should recognize a foreign divorce decree. It provides insight into a divisible divorce proceeding and touches upon such issues as marital rape and the marital testimonial privilege.

Some of the many questions raised by this chapter include the following: Have ancient divorce customs and practices influenced secular divorce law in the United States? What is the distinction between an annulment and a divorce from bed and board? What was a parliamentary divorce, and is the concept used today in the United States? What is the historical derivation of fault? Why was fault important to common law divorce law, and what were some of the common defenses to a common law divorce action? What were the reasons that caused all jurisdictions in the United States to enact no-fault divorce provisions? Typically, what grounds must be shown before a no-fault divorce will be granted? Does a state's adoption of no-fault divorce mean that fault may not be used to award alimony or attorneys' fees or divide marital property? What is a covenant marriage, and does it prevent persons from filing a no-fault divorce petition? When may a religious belief prevent a secular divorce, if ever? What is a "summary divorce" proceeding? Does an indigent have a right to be represented at public expense at a contested divorce hearing? When is a jury trial allowed in a divorce action? What is the history of discrimination in public employment against persons who divorce? What is a divisible divorce? When will a state recognize a divorce that took place outside the United States? What is the distinction between a void and voidable marriage?

> **REFLECTIVE QUESTIONS**   What are your goals for this chapter?

4.2 HISTORY: DIVORCE IN ANCIENT TIMES

Historians report that the concept of one divorcing a spouse has existed in some form for centuries. For example, under Athenian law, Greek husbands and wives could go their separate ways after merely filing notice of their intent with a magistrate. Mary Frances Lyle & Jeffrey L. Levy, *From Riches to Rags: Does Rehabilitative Alimony Need to Be Rehabilitated?*, 38 Fam. L.Q. 3, 4, n.2 (Spring 2004).

It is believed that marriage in early Roman times consisted of an agreement between families. Men married in their mid-twenties; women married in their early teens. When reaching marrying age, parents consulted with friends to find suitable partners with a goal of improving the family's wealth or class. Roman divorce was as simple as marriage. Marriage was a private matter and was a declaration of intent to live together. A divorce was a declaration of a couple's intent not to live together and apparently required only that they declare their decision to divorce before witnesses. *See generally* Shaakirrah R. Sanders, *The Cyclical Nature of Divorce in the Western Legal Tradition*, 50 Loy. L. Rev. 407-410 (Summer 2004). Roman divorce was apparently quite common among persons in the upper classes. When a wife divorced, she could expect to receive the return of her dowry and the protection of her father.

Historians suggest that divorce may have assumed formality of sorts when the Roman emperor Caesar Augustus promulgated the *Lex Julia de Adulteris coërcendis* (17 B.C.). These laws are claimed to be an attempt to increase population by encouraging marriage and procreation. They established adultery as a private and public crime. A provision required that a divorcing couple execute a writing that renounced their marriage — making divorce something more than an informal dissociation.

Adultery. When it came to adultery, Roman law treated men and women differently. Under the *Lex Julia*, a wife found guilty of adultery in a special court known as the *quaestio* might sacrifice the return of her dowry. Women could not bring criminal actions for adultery against their husbands, but men were permitted to bring such actions against their wives.

Medieval Church view of divorce. The Christian era experienced removal of divorce from the European legal codes and their replacement by Church law as applied by its ecclesiastical courts. By the reign of Edward the Confessor (1042-1066 A.D.), English clergy had gained authority to decide all matters relating to marriage and divorce.

The Church's religious views of marriage and divorce were incorporated into canon law and enforced by the ecclesiastical courts. The Church taught that marriage was a sacrament and indissoluble except by death. These beliefs were founded on the Gospels. *See, e.g.,* Matthew 19:5-6, 19:3-9 ("Wherefore they are no more twain, but one flesh. What therefore God hath joined together, let not man put asunder"); Luke 16:18 ("Anyone who divorces his wife and marries another woman commits adultery, and the man who marries a divorced woman commits adultery"); Mark 10:11 ("Whoever divorces his wife and marries someone else commits adultery against her"); Ephesians 5:30-31 ("For this cause shall a man leave his father and mother, and shall be joined unto his wife, and they two shall be one flesh"); I Corinthians 7:10-11 ("To the married I give this command (not I, but the Lord): A wife must not separate from her husband. But if she does, she must remain unmarried or else be reconciled to her husband. And a husband must not divorce his wife"); and Romans 7:2-4 ("For the woman which hath an husband is bound by the law to her husband so long as he liveth; but if the husband be dead, she is loosed from the law of her husband"). As a consequence, it was impossible to obtain a divorce in countries controlled by the Church courts.

Medieval view of divorce from bed and board. When marriage vows were broken by adultery or acts of cruelty that rendered further cohabitation unsafe, the Church courts permitted spouses to live apart from each other. This was accomplished by awarding the innocent party a divorce *a mensa et thoro*, that is, a divorce from bed and board. The decree of divorce *a mensa et thoro* did not sever the marital ties.

The ecclesiastical courts required a showing that one of the parties was at fault before a divorce from bed and board was allowed, and adultery was the most common allegation. In addition to breaking a religious commandment, adultery by a wife was viewed as serious because of the possibility of interposing spurious children into the family bloodline and degrading her husband's honor. A husband who committed adultery was viewed in a different light. His wife was generally expected to submit to his infidelities, which did not threaten her or her children's legal status. It appears that only if the husband's behavior became intolerably outrageous could a wife seek a divorce *a mensa et thoro* from the ecclesiastical courts.

Medieval view of an annulment. An annulment of the relationship could be obtained from an ecclesiastical court by obtaining a divorce *a vinculo*. This action was an annulment, not a divorce as we understand that term today. It was extremely limited. Generally, a divorce *a vinculo* was permitted only if the relationship was entered into by force, fear, fraud, or through inducement of parents, masters, or feudal or manorial lords. If granted, it severed all ties between the couple.

<table>
<tr><td>REFLECTIVE
QUESTIONS</td><td>Have any of the medieval views related to divorce survived to the twenty-first century in the United States?</td></tr>
</table>

4.3 HISTORY: PROTESTANT REFORMATION

The sixteenth-century Protestant Reformation questioned the Church's teachings in a number of areas. In particular, the Reformers challenged the Church's view of marriage, arguing that it was not a sacrament in the Roman sense; rather, it was a natural and social institution. The Reformation is generally credited with also challenging the theory that absolute divorce was not possible. Don S. Browning, *Modern Law and Christian Jurisprudence on Marriage and Family*, 58 Emory L.J. 31, 46 (Fall 2008) ("Luther rejected the sacramental view of marriage, thus opening Christian jurisprudence to more realistic possibilities of divorce").

Despite the Reformation and the separation of the Anglican Church from Rome in 1534 with Parliament declaring Henry VIII the head of the church, Anglican religious doctrine regarding marriage and divorce remained little changed. *See generally* Joel A. Nichols, *Multi-Tiered Marriage: Ideas and Influences from New York and Louisiana to the International Community*, 40 Vand. J. Transnat'l L. 135, 143-144 (January 2007). The newly established Anglican Church courts continued to exercise jurisdiction over matters of marriage and divorce, much like that exercised when the courts were controlled by Rome. An effort to reform marriage and divorce did not begin in England until the passage of legislation in 1835-1836 that allowed marriages to be contracted under the supervision of a civil authority rather than only by the Church courts. Additional reforms occurred in 1857 with the passage of the Matrimonial Causes Act, which allowed for an absolute divorce, addressed child custody, and shifted jurisdiction over issues of marriage and divorce law from the Church to the civil courts.

<table>
<tr><td>REFLECTIVE
QUESTIONS</td><td>Was the Reformation period in history important to the development of the concept of divorce?</td></tr>
</table>

4.4 HISTORY: PARLIAMENT/LEGISLATIVE DIVORCE

By 1670 the idea that Parliament could divorce a couple had become a part of English law. A handful of legislative divorces were granted by the English Parliament, but only to aristocrats. *See* Danaya C. Wright, *"Well-Behaved Women Don't Make History": Rethinking English Family, Law, and History*, 19 Wis. Women's L.J. 211,

212-213 (Fall 2004). The English view that Parliament, a legislative body, could divorce persons by private act was followed by many jurisdictions early in this nation's history. *See, e.g., Maynard v. Hill,* 125 U.S. 190, 206 (1888) ("until a recent period, legislative divorces have been granted, with few exceptions, in all the states"). However, by the time of the Civil War, 33 of 37 states prohibited divorce by private legislative act. Neal R. Feigenson, *Extraterritorial Recognition of Divorce Decrees in the Nineteenth Century,* 34 Am. J. Legal Hist. 119, 122, n.19 (April 1990). Gradually, legislative divorce vanished from the lexicon of divorce actions in the states. It was replaced by statutes permitting an absolute divorce on a variety of grounds.

REFLECTIVE QUESTIONS	Is there a role for the legislative divorce concept today?

4.5 HISTORY: COLONIAL AMERICA

The American colonists brought marriage and divorce laws with them from their home countries. New England and northern colonies settled by Puritans (heirs of the Calvinist traditions), relied on civil authorities to address matters of marriage and divorce. Joel A. Nichols, *supra* at 145-146. However, colonies such as Virginia, with a well-established Anglican Church, incorporated religious requirements into its law. For example, until the Revolutionary War, Virginia required that "a religious marriage ceremony, according to the rites of the Church of England" be held for those wishing to marry. *Ibid.* In general, whether parties could divorce in colonial America depended on the region where they lived, with the southern colonies generally subscribing to the strict English view that marriage was for life and forbidding an absolute divorce. *See generally* Lawrence Friedman, *A History of American Law,* 181-183 (1973) (discussing the treatment of divorce in the various colonies and states). Some of the colonial legislatures allowed a divorce by private act; such divorces were not confined to any particular grounds.

REFLECTIVE QUESTIONS	Does it appear that the English view of marriage and divorce was influential on colonial America?

4.6 FAULT-BASED DIVORCE ACTIONS UNDER THE COMMON LAW

Fault was an integral component of the Ecclesiastical courts in England. It was also an integral component of divorce law as it developed in the United States. Fault was essential to establish a ground for divorce and for making a property division and/or alimony award. Jury trials were often held with the jury determining who was at fault.

Adultery. Adultery was one of the first common fault-based grounds for divorce recognized in state courts. Evidence supporting the claim was difficult to obtain because the act was committed in private. In response to this difficulty, courts usually allowed circumstantial evidence to buttress an adultery claim. To establish adultery, the evidence had to show (1) a disposition on the part of the defendant and the paramour to commit adultery, and (2) an opportunity to commit the offense. *Goldschmiedt v. Goldschmiedt*, 265 A.2d 264 (Md. 1970). For example, proof that a wife was seen entering a hotel room on several afternoons arm-in-arm with a man not her husband was normally considered circumstantial proof of adultery.

Over time, fault-based grounds other than adultery worked their way into various state statutes. Common grounds for an absolute divorce found in early state statutes included desertion, mental cruelty, habitual drunkenness, and cruel and inhuman treatment.

Desertion. Desertion in most state statutes was a fault-based claim that required the following: (1) a physical separation, (2) separation without the consent and against the will of the other spouse, and (3) a separation without justification. *Matter of Lorenzo's Estate*, 602 P.2d 521 (Haw. 1979). The common law took the view that, in the absence of evidence to the contrary, there is a presumption that a physical separation of husband and wife is with the consent of the husband and not against his will. *Id.* at 528. The common law might punish a wife who unlawfully deserted her husband by ordering that she lose any interest in his property should they divorce. *Id.* at 524.

Constructive desertion. Constructive desertion provided another fault-based ground for divorce. Constructive desertion involved the situation where a party justifiably separated from his or her spouse. The essential element of constructive desertion is that one spouse brought about a separation from the other spouse because of the latter's misconduct. The misconduct may have consisted of cruelty arising from physical abuse or other acts that affected and impaired the health of a petitioner and made living together intolerable. *Edwards v. Edwards*, 356 A.2d 633 (D.C. 1976). Even when the behavior did not rise to the level of cruelty or excessively vicious conduct, some courts ended violent marriages on the ground of constructive desertion. *See Painter v. Painter*, 688 A.2d 479, 488 (Md. App. 1997) ("Due to the seriousness of the problem of domestic violence in our society, . . . [we] again emphasize that a woman is not required to be a homicide victim in order to establish the elements of constructive desertion").

Mental and physical cruelty. Mental and physical cruelty are fault-based grounds for divorce found in many state statutes. Where cruelty was alleged, some early common law courts required that actual or threatened physical violence occur before a divorce was granted. This requirement has eventually ebbed with courts allowing mental cruelty to support a divorce action. Some courts have required that the claimed mental cruelty pose a psychological danger to the plaintiff's well-being.

> **REFLECTIVE QUESTIONS** **Why was fault considered important in early divorce law?**

4.7 AFFIRMATIVE DEFENSES TO FAULT-BASED DIVORCE UNDER THE COMMON LAW

Unclean hands. There were a number of affirmative defenses to a divorce action under the common law. The defenses were related in one way or another to a party's "fault." For example, the unclean hands defense required that the petitioning party enter court without serious fault. It was sometimes used as a defense in mental cruelty or desertion cases when the petitioner's own acts were questionable. *See Sisk v. Sisk*, 902 So. 2d 1237 (La. App. 2005).

Recrimination. An affirmative defense closely resembling the unclean hands defense was recrimination. A party asserting this defense claimed that the complaining party was guilty of an offense that would in fact justify the defendant in obtaining a divorce. For example, a defendant could assert that the petitioning spouse had committed adultery. If proven, a common law court would refuse to grant a divorce. *See Rankin v. Rankin*, 124 A.2d 639 (Pa. Super. Ct. 1956).

Condonation, collusion, and connivance. Condonation, collusion, and connivance were also affirmative defenses to a divorce action at common law. Condonation represented an expressed or implied forgiveness of the marital misconduct. It was usually conditional and based on a promise not to repeat the offense. *See P.K. v. R.K.*, 820 N.Y.S2d 844 (Sup. Ct. 2006). Collusion, as a defense, was an agreement by the two parties to create a false-fact situation upon which a divorce could be granted. Connivance, a defense often used in adultery actions, was defined as consent by one party to the adulterous act of the other.

Insanity. Insanity was recognized as a defense under certain circumstances. For example, in *Wolfe v. Wolfe*, 258 P.2d 1211 (Wash. 1953), the court found that the husband was not entitled to divorce on ground of cruel and inhuman treatment where wife had been adjudicated insane more than two years prior to institution of the divorce action and her competency had not been restored.

> **REFLECTIVE QUESTIONS** **What appears to be the primary purpose of the common law defenses listed above?**

4.8 NO-FAULT DIVORCE: ORIGIN

It may be of historical interest that it is claimed that the Bolshevik rulers of the Soviet Union were among the first authorities to institute a system of "no-fault" divorce. This occurred following the Russian Revolution in 1917. Frank Gibbard, *Divorce by Jury: Governor Gilpin's Matrimonial Ordeal*, 37-Jan Colo. Law. 51, 52, n.17 (January 2008). Soviet dictator Joseph Stalin later removed many of the Bolshevik "liberalized measures" involving divorce. *Ibid.*

Separate and apart. In the United States no-fault divorce of sorts existed in some jurisdictions before what many refer to as "the no-fault revolution." These jurisdictions had enacted statutes permitting spouses who had been living "separate and apart" for a period of time to divorce without proving fault.

Reasons for "no-fault" statutes. The modern no-fault revolution began in the late 1960s and continued into the 1970s. No-fault proponents argued that "no-fault divorce more accurately reflected modern conceptions of terminating marital relations than did the prior laws." Lynn D. Wardle, *No-Fault Divorce and the Divorce Conundrum*, 1991 BYU L. Rev. 79, 95. They claimed that, in many cases, by the time the parties arrived at court, they had already divided their property, lived apart for many years, and had little to dispute. Despite the obvious breakdown of the relationship, the party seeking a divorce had to prove that grounds existed, and witnesses had to be produced to prove that the other party was at fault. The requirement of sworn testimony was followed, even when the other party failed or refused to appear at the divorce hearing. The result was that many divorce proceedings were considered a sham. In other proceedings, where fault dictated the amount of property to be divided, moral judgments about which party was right or wrong ignored the complexity of the underlying causes of a marital dispute. It was argued that the process made the eventual outcome of a divorce action speculative rather than reasonably certain.

No-fault proponents also asserted that divorce was a private matter that the state had no legitimate interest to restrict when the marriage was irretrievably broken and the parties had agreed to terminate the marriage. They claimed that requiring divorcing parties to disclose "'the most intimate and often embarrassing details of marital life' [was] 'abhorrent to the community,' violated the spirit of family privacy, and worked only to 'demean the marriage relationship, humiliate the parties, and damage the residual family relationships.'" Joseph Goldstein, *On Abolition of Grounds for Divorce: A Model Statute and Commentary*, 3 Fam. L.Q. 75, 82-83 (1969). It was also claimed that no-fault divorce represented a "cultural rise of individual liberty within the family" and allowed "the parties involved to assess the viability of the marriage." Note, Jane Biondi, *Who Pays for Guilt? Recent Fault-Based Divorce Reform Proposals, Cultural Stereotypes and Economic Consequences*, 40 B.C. L. Rev. 611, 614 (1999). Reformers argued that courts should move away from assigning blame between the spouses for the failure of the marriage and focus instead on the needs of the members of the family unit in the settlement of financial issues. *Dixon v. Dixon*, 319 N.W.2d 846, 851 (Wis. 1982).

Success of no-fault. California became the first state to adopt no-fault divorce when then Governor Ronald Reagan signed a no-fault provision into law in September 1969. It was also during this early period in the development of no-fault that the National Conference of Commissioners on Uniform State Laws promulgated a model act, the Uniform Marriage and Divorce Act (UMDA), which contained no-fault features. Proponents of no-fault legislation were eventually successful in convincing legislators in all 50 states to adopt some form of no-fault basis for divorce. New York became the last state to adopt the no-fault concept as a part of its domestic relations code in 2010.

In general, the no-fault legislation required consideration of the marriage as a whole and made the possibility of reconciliation an important issue. The change from fault to no-fault was thought to induce a more conciliatory and less charged atmosphere. It was hoped that this change would facilitate resolution of the other issues involved in a divorce and perhaps effect reconciliation.

REFLECTIVE QUESTIONS	List the potential advantages of a no-fault divorce statute.

4.9 NO-FAULT DIVORCE: OPPOSITION

There has been, and continues to be, opposition to "no-fault" divorce. Critics are concerned that it has made marriage obligations "illusory because no penalties can be exacted for breach of any marital promises." Margaret F. Brinig & Steven M. Crafton, *Marriage and Opportunism*, 23 J. Legal Stud. 869, 879 (June 1994). As a consequence, "there is therefore no incentive other than a moral obligation or a feeling of affection to prevent either party from engaging in postcontractual opportunism." *Ibid.* Critics are also concerned that parties to marriage contracts are free to act opportunistically at minimal cost. *Ibid. See generally* Mark Ellman, *The Misguided Movement to Review Fault Divorce, and Why Reformers Should Look Instead to the American Law Institute*, 11 Int'l J.L., Pol'y & Fam. 216 (1997).

Critics express concern that no-fault divorce has hurt children by increasing divorce rates and by leaving custodial parents with fewer resources. *See* Robert M. Gordon, *The Limits of Limits on Divorce*, 107 Yale L.J. 1435, 1436 (March 1998). It is claimed that sharply curtailing or eliminating no-fault divorce will significantly reduce these harms.

REFLECTIVE QUESTIONS	Do you agree with the concerns expressed by no-fault opponents?

4.10 NO-FAULT DIVORCE: NEW YORK'S STRUGGLE

Background to *Molinari v. Molinari*

As already noted, New York was the last state in the United States to maintain that allegations of fault were necessary if a family court was to grant a divorce. In *Molinari v. Molinari*, Jeffrey Molinari's lawyer struggled to persuade the trial court judge that there had been a constructive abandonment by his client's wife for one or more years. The New York Supreme Court judge (in New York the Supreme Court is a trial court) shares his frustration in this short opinion with the absence of no-fault as a ground for divorce as he struggles to determine whether a divorce should be granted on the basis of constructive abandonment.

MOLINARI
v.
MOLINARI

Supreme Court of New York
2007 WL 1119894 (N.Y. Sup. 2007)

ROSS, J. . . . . In this case involving allegations of constructive abandonment, as a matter of law, all four of our Appellate Divisions have steadfastly held that the refusal or failure to engage in marital relations must be unjustified, willful and continued, despite repeated requests from the other spouse for resumption of cohabitation. Not only must the absence of relations be for more than one year, but there must be repeated requests for conjugal relations, which requests were unjustifiably, willfully and continuously refused. . . .

A cursory determination of the grounds issue here would only deflect a recurring dilemma to the public at large. In an all-too-frequent occurrence, matrimonial courts are faced with innumerable instances where efficacious resolution of economic issues and custody determinations are back-seated and delayed by fault (grounds) trials. The party without resources to afford such litigation, or, the party who chooses not to aggressively allege the faults of his/her spouse, is often at a tactical disadvantage—simply because an opposing party seeks to impose financial leverage or exacting personal animus, due to the current statutory scheme to establish grounds for divorce in New York State.

The Court of Appeals maxims of a "level playing field" and "litigation parity" are doctrines that are conceptually important, but which are significantly impeded by the current antiquated statutory scheme of fault-based divorce in New York State—the significant cost and delay, resulting from such trials, in many cases, are precluding access to our courts or making the process wholly more acrimonious by fostering and encouraging the embellishment of a spouse's wrongdoing as to grounds, often with immeasurable effects upon a divorcing household.

This case vividly illustrates the direct impact that New York's fault-based divorce statute has on the manner and speed in which matrimonial matters proceed. Here, while litigating the issue of grounds, these parties were relegated to motion practice, amendment of pleadings, contemplation of withdrawal of the action and seeking a divorce in another jurisdiction, filing jury demand, conferences, and ultimately, trial of the matter. These proceedings relating to fault have endured since January, 2005.

. . . Notwithstanding the controverted issue of the circumstances surrounding the departure of the plaintiff from the marital home, and even acknowledging that there is no written separation agreement between the parties, Mr. Molinari would be entitled to be granted a judgment of divorce, on these limited facts alone, in 49 states — with New York being the only exception. . . .

A recent survey of divorce statutes for the fifty states, Puerto Rico, the U.S. Virgin Islands and the District of Columbia indicates that 35 jurisdictions recognize some form of Irreconcilable Differences or Irretrievable Breakdown of the marriage as a basis of ending the marital relationship, 6 jurisdictions recognize Incompatibility as a basis of ending marriages and 11 jurisdictions permit living separate and apart without legal proceedings or the finding of fault as a basis for divorce. Only New York requires the finding of fault or the living apart pursuant to a legal document as the basis for a divorce. . . .

Accordingly, it is ORDERED, that determination of the grounds issue in this matter will be stayed until legislative determination of Bill A03027, or further order of this Court.

 **FOR *MOLINARI v. MOLINARI***

A. The court lists various grounds for a no-fault divorce found outside New York. Which no-fault ground would you have urged the State of New York to adopt? Or would you have urged New York to remain a fault jurisdiction? Would you also have urged the New York legislature to eliminate consideration of fault when considering property division and support?

B. Assume that a state set the grounds for a no-fault divorce as requiring an agreed upon voluntary 12-month separation or an involuntary 2-year separation. Furthermore, assume that the state does not recognize either irreconcilable differences or irretrievable breakdown as grounds for a no-fault divorce. Are there advantages to this approach to no-fault? Disadvantages? *See Payne v. Payne*, 707, 366 A.2d 405, n.1 (Md. App. 1976).

C. The court suggests that a process without a no-fault basis for a divorce adversely impacts "the manner and speed in which matrimonial matters proceed." Should "speed" in obtaining a divorce be a relevant consideration?

4.11 NO-FAULT DIVORCE: VARYING GROUNDS

As already observed, the grounds for a no-fault divorce vary among jurisdictions. Some states require a showing that there are "irreconcilable differences" between the parties. Others define no-fault as a breakdown of the marital relationship resulting in the parties living apart for a statutory period. Some states are said to be pure no-fault jurisdictions; others are termed mixed, with legislatures adding a no-fault ground such as "living separate and apart" to their fault-based grounds. Among the grounds approved by various state legislatures are the following: living separate and apart for a specified period of time, incompatibility, irreconcilable differences, and irretrievable breakdown of the marriage.

When irretrievable breakdown is recognized as a no-fault ground for divorce, a party's testimony alone may be a sufficient basis for finding an irretrievable breakdown of a marriage. *See, e.g., Hagerty v. Hagerty*, 281 N.W.2d 386, 388 (Minn. 1979). Often a no-fault statute will require proof that there is "no reasonable prospect of reconciliation." *See, e.g., Moore v. Moore*, 654 N.E.2d 904 (Ind. App. 1995). A statute that requires proof of "no reasonable prospect of reconciliation" and "serious marital discord adversely affecting the attitude of one or both of the parties" before a marriage can be dissolved does not allow "divorce on demand." *Richter v. Richter*, 625 N.W.2d 490, 493 (Minn. App. 2001).

REFLECTIVE QUESTIONS	**What ground would you select from the grounds listed above to support issuance of a no-fault divorce decree?**

4.12 SCOPE OF "NO-FAULT" DIVORCE STATUTES

As jurisdictions enacted no-fault as a ground for divorce, there remained questions about its scope. For example, did no-fault extend to an award of alimony? Did no-fault apply to awarding marital property? The answer to these questions from various jurisdictions is mixed.

In those jurisdictions that merely added no-fault to the traditional fault grounds, such as adultery and desertion, the concept of fault in terms of alimony awards or property division was retained as a part of family law jurisprudence. For example, Rhode Island's property division statute requires a court to consider the conduct of the parties during the marriage. R.I. Gen. Laws, §15-5-16.1 (2015). In Virginia, the use of fault is sanctioned where it has an economic effect upon the marital property or its value. *Marion v. Marion*, 401 S.E.2d 432 (Va. 1991); *see Chapman v. Chapman*, 498 S.W.2d 134, 137 (Ky. 1973) (fault is not to be considered in determining whether a spouse is entitled to maintenance but it may be considered insofar as the amount is concerned; fault could be considered in the distribution of assets because the legislature had failed to change the property distribution statute, when it adopted no-fault divorce, to expressly preclude fault from consideration). In Michigan, marital misconduct remains one of several relevant factors that a trial court must consider to reach an equitable property division. *Sparks v. Spark*, 485 N.W.2d 893 (Mich. 1992).

On the other hand, New Hampshire has held that in a no-fault divorce, marital misconduct may not be considered in property division. *Boucher v. Boucher*, 553 A.2d 313 (N.H. 1988). The Iowa Supreme Court stated that not only must the "guilty party" concept be eliminated as a factor, but evidence of the conduct of the parties insofar as it tends to place fault for the breakdown of the marriage on either spouse must also be rejected as a factor in awarding a property settlement or an allowance of alimony or support money. *In re Marriage of Tjaden*, 199 N.W.2d 475, 477 (Iowa 1972); *see Hartland v. Hartland*, 777 P.2d 636, 642 (Alaska 1989) (marital misconduct does not justify granting unequal percentages of the marital estate).

> **REFLECTIVE QUESTIONS**
>
> What might justify drafting a no-fault statute that permits a couple to divorce without a showing of fault but allows a court to set support and divide property based on the relative fault of a party in causing the breakdown of the marriage? Or, is there no justification for making this distinction?

4.13 NO-FAULT DIVORCE: COVENANT MARRIAGE

In the three states that have enacted covenant marriage statutes (Arizona, Arkansas, Louisiana), parties entering into these relationships cannot use no-fault provisions if they seek to end the relationship. Statutes in these jurisdictions normally allow covenant divorces only after a period of separation and/or proof the other party is at fault because of domestic violence, adultery, or abandonment.

> **REFLECTIVE QUESTIONS**
>
> Would allowing persons who contracted a covenant marriage to use no-fault as a basis for divorce defeat the purpose of the covenant marriage statutes? Is a refusal to allow the use of no-fault as a ground for divorce when a covenant marriage contract has been executed merely upholding a contract?

4.14 SUMMARY DIVORCE PROCEDURES

Several states provide for a simplified, or summary, divorce or dissolution procedure. Summary divorce is governed by statute and begins by the filing of a joint complaint or petition. The procedure is not adversarial, and the parties are required to have determined all property issues before beginning the proceeding. Summary divorce cannot determine child custody.

Nevada allows a summary divorce if the following conditions are met: (1) The couple have lived separate and apart for more than one year. (2) They have no children. (3) They have reached an agreement regarding property distribution. (4) They have waived a right to spousal maintenance. If the conditions are all met, the couple may file a joint petition, and divorce judgment will be entered ten days later. Nev. Rev. Stat. §125.181 (2015), et seq. *See* Katherine Shaw Spahta, *The Last One Hundred Years: The Incredible Retreat of Law from the Regulation Of Marriage*, 63 La. L. Rev. 243, 274 (Winter 2003).

REFLECTIVE QUESTIONS	What appear to be the limitations on using the summary divorce procedure?

4.15 DIVORCE ACTIONS AND JURY TRIAL RIGHT

The question of whether parties seeking a divorce have a right to a jury trial to decide the factual disputes is tied to the historic treatment of marital matters by English equity courts and the existence of jury trial provisions regarding marital matters in state statutes and constitutions. As a general principle, a jury trial is available only if it was available at common law. Marital disputes were not considered issues to be resolved by the common law. Rather, they were viewed as equitable in nature. *See* John K. Matsumoto, *Why No Right to Jury Trial in Marital Dissolution Actions?*, 11 J. Contemp. Legal Issues 202, 204 (2000). A state can alter this general view by enacting a statute providing for a jury trial in divorce action or including such a provision in the state constitution.

There are a few jurisdictions where a jury trial is used to determine some portion of a divorce action. They include Texas, Georgia, Louisiana, New York, and Tennessee. *See, e.g., Bernholc v. Bornstein*, 898 N.Y.S.2d 228 (N.Y.A.D. 2010); *Lenz v. Lenz*, 79 S.W.3d 10 (Tex. 2002); *Kautter v. Kautter*, 685 S.E.2d 266 (Ga. 2009); *Delaney v. Delaney*, 339 So. 2d 945 (La. App. 1976); *Montesi v. Montesi*, 529 S.W.2d 720 (Tenn. App. 1975). *See also* Jeffrey F. Ghent, Annotation, *Right to Jury Trial in State Court Divorce Proceedings*, 56 A.L.R.4th 955, 964 (1987) & Supp. 2003.

REFLECTIVE QUESTIONS	Why shouldn't those states that don't allow jury trials in divorce actions enact statutes allowing them?

4.16 JOINDER OF TORT ACTIONS WITH A DIVORCE COMPLAINT

As a general rule, a plaintiff in a tort action seeking damages has a constitutional right to a trial by jury in a state court. However, as noted above, there is no right to a jury trial in a divorce action in most jurisdictions. How should a court treat the situation when a spouse files a complaint for divorce and also joins a tort claim such as assault against the other partner in a jurisdiction that does not allow a jury trial in a divorce action? The answer is mixed. At least nine states have answered the question by prohibiting joinder of tort and divorce actions. Some states, such as New Jersey, apparently require that all claims be joined. *See generally* Pamela Laufer-Ukeles, *Reconstructing Fault: The Case for Spousal Torts*, 79 U. Cin. L. Rev. 207, 246 (Fall 2010).

> **REFLECTIVE QUESTIONS**   **What is the potential benefit to a party of joining tort claims with a divorce action?**

4.17 COLLUDING TO OBTAIN DIVORCE

Background to *Vandervort v. Vandervort*

The *Vandervort* case involves the elderly and a divorce on the ground of incompatibility. "Incompatibility" is expressly made a ground for divorce under the "no-fault" statutes in some jurisdictions. *See, e.g., Robert J.T. v. Peggy J.T.*, 492 A.2d 855 (Del. 1985). However, in other jurisdictions, incompatibility is not recognized as an independent ground for divorce. *See, e.g., Nance v. Nance*, 548 So. 2d 87 (La. App. 1989). In *Vandervort*, the Oklahoma court recognizes incompatibility as a ground for a divorce but questioned its applicability to the facts of the case.

Roger and Patricia Vandervort faced a problem that is becoming common to many middle-class Americans as they age: How do they preserve their marital assets in the face of a catastrophic illness? The couple decided to divorce and to divest Patricia of nearly all her marital property in anticipation of her eventual need for care in a nursing home because she was suffering from multiple sclerosis. Both Roger and Patricia believed that Patricia's single status and complete lack of assets would enable her to receive Social Security disability income and Medicaid to pay for her nursing home care. Roger agreed to care for Patricia until she required nursing home care. A divorce judgment was obtained on the grounds of incompatibility when Roger presented an uncontested petition to the court with an attached waiver signed by Patricia.

However, shortly after they were divorced, Patricia claimed that Roger stopped caring for her, and she went to live with her parents. Roger alleged that Patricia abandoned him to live with her parents. She moved to vacate the divorce judgment. The trial judge vacated the judgment on the ground that Roger and Patricia had obtained a fraudulent divorce for the sole purpose of increasing Patricia's public benefits. Roger challenged the ruling.

VANDERVORT
v.
VANDERVORT

Court of Appeals of Oklahoma
134 P.3d 892 (Okla. 2006), *cert. denied* (Mar. 28, 2006)

REIF, J. . . . The [original divorce] petition signed by Husband affirmatively represented that incompatibility was the ground upon which divorce should be granted, while the "consent decree" signed by both parties reflected their mutual agreement that incompatibility existed between them. However, at the time the divorce was sought and granted, Husband and Wife intended to return to their Texas County residence where they were to continue living together with Husband providing and caring for Wife. In fact, they did so for a short time after the divorce. These facts belie their claim of incompatibility.

The statutory ground of incompatibility does not permit the court to dissolve a marriage merely because its termination is desired by one or both parties. Incompatibility [cannot be] dependent in application upon an agreement or stipulation between the parties, and thus furnish a vehicle for a consensual divorce which the law did not intend.

Actionable incompatibility is determined to exist when there is such a conflict of personalities as to destroy the legitimate ends of matrimony and the possibility of reconciliation. Incompatibility must be established by proof, objective in its character, of causes to which marital disharmony is attributed [and cannot be] bottomed on a mere subterfuge or after-thought [without] a substantial foundation. . . .

In cases where parties to a divorce collude to procure a judgment and one party later seeks to vacate that judgment, the law generally "will leave them where it finds them." However, the Oklahoma Supreme Court has also observed that "where the jurisdiction of the court is invoked and obtained by a fraudulent 'concoction' and the fraud is consummated through the instrumentality of a court of justice, it would impeach the moral sense and that of justice that courts be not protected against such fraud."

We conclude the case at hand falls under the latter rule rather than the former. The parties here colluded to misrepresent incompatibility as a ground for divorce (when they actually intended to continue cohabitating) and, in turn, used the sham divorce to deceive public agencies concerning Wife's eligibility for public benefits. It not only offends public policy for parties to obtain a divorce on a concocted ground, but it also offends public policy to use such a divorce for financial gain. Rather than leave the parties where we find them, we believe equity and justice require they be returned to the state of matrimony. The trial court's judgment accomplishes that purpose.

GABBARD, dissenting. This case is a good example of how bad facts sometimes make bad law.

I do not disagree with the majority's analysis of the facts in this case. It finds that Husband and Wife acted together to fraudulently obtain a divorce in Oklahoma County knowing that they were not residents of that county and were not incompatible. The parties were dealing with a problem common to many middle-class Americans: How do couples preserve their marital assets in the face of a catastrophic illness? Their solution was to obtain a divorce in which Husband received virtually all the marital property, thereby qualifying Wife for government assistance when her progressive illness caused her health to deteriorate to the point that she needed nursing home care. Husband promised to care for her in the home until that time. Only after Husband allegedly breached his promise of care did Wife move to set aside the decree. That relief should not be granted.

As the majority and the trial court have concluded, this case involves mutual fraud. It is not a case in which one spouse practices fraud upon the other in order to obtain an advantageous divorce settlement. Where both parties have participated in fraud upon the court, 24 Am.Jur.2d Divorce 896 and Separation §438 (1998) sets forth the general rule:

> [A] spouse who participates in the fraudulent procurement of a divorce decree, and who freely enjoys the fruits of the decree, will be unable to have it set aside under a rule allowing actions for relief from judgments procured by fraud. . . .

A court of equity will ordinarily refuse to vacate a decree of divorce where its aid is made necessary by the fault or neglect of the applicant. This rule is based on sound public policy and has been followed by Oklahoma courts since 1910. . . .

Here, Wife was not incompetent at the time of the decree, nor did Husband fraudulently promise to care for her in order to obtain an advantageous divorce decree. On the contrary, the evidence clearly establishes that Wife wanted this divorce, participated in obtaining it, and did not seek relief from it until she suffered from an unanticipated event—Husband's alleged refusal to care for her. This alleged conduct occurred after the decree was entered. . . .

Because the majority's decision is contrary to established precedent and public policy, and provides an unnecessary and inappropriate remedy, I dissent.

DISCUSSION QUESTIONS FOR *VANDERVORT v. VANDERVORT*

A. Who is the defrauded party in this case? The state? The ex-wife? If they committed a federal or state fraud, why isn't that a matter for the respective social welfare agencies — not this court?

B. The dissent in *Vandervort* cited *Green v. James*, 296 P. 743 (Okla. 1931), where the Oklahoma Supreme Court refused to grant equitable relief to either fraudulent party, stating: "It would be a special novelty for a plaintiff to address the tribunal with the defendant and I have been playing a trick on this court, but I discovered he has got the better of me, so please turn the tables on him." *Id.* at 746. Isn't that exactly what happened in *Vandervort?* In other words, while the couple may have deceived the court when they obtained their divorce, why should the judgment be vacated to most likely benefit the wife who participated in the deception and is unhappy with the after-the-fact judgment?

C. The Court noted in *Vandervort* that "[t]he statutory ground of incompatibility does not permit the court to dissolve a marriage merely because its termination is desired by one or both parties." Why shouldn't it?

D. How is "incompatibility" defined within the meaning of the Oklahoma statute? Does incompatibility refer to petty quarrels and minor bickering? *See Lillis v. Lillis*, 563 P.2d 492, 495-496 (Kan. App. 1977) ("incompatibility may be broadly defined as such a deep and irreconcilable conflict in the personalities or temperaments of the parties as makes it impossible for them to continue a normal marital relationship. The conflict of personalities and dispositions must be so deep as to be irreconcilable and irremediable. Petty quarrels and minor bickerings are clearly not sufficient to meet this standard"); *Marino v. Marino*, 576 So. 2d 1196 (La. App. 1991) ("Conduct sufficient to support a separation under LSA-C.C. art. 138(3) must include substantial acts of commission or omission violative of marital duties and responsibilities; mutual incompatibility, fussing and bickering is insufficient"). Doesn't the behavior of the parties in *Vandervort* following the entry of the divorce decree support the view that they were incompatible?

E. After this decision, what advice should a lawyer give an aging married client faced with a medical crisis that will drain all of the client's assets and will eventually leave the client and the client's partner impoverished? If it is clear that one option that may protect much of your client's assets is to obtain a divorce so the ill partner becomes impoverished and eligible for government assistance, should a lawyer advise the client to take such action? Is such action fraud? Unethical? *See generally In re Marriage of Collins*, 200 N.W.2d 886. 890 (Iowa 1972) ("The criteria for dissolution now is a breakdown of the marriage relationship to the extent that the legitimate objects of matrimony have been destroyed and it would, therefore, appear collusion is no longer relevant to this criteria. In truth, if it were demonstrated the parties were in collusion to bring about a termination of the marriage relationship, it would further evidence the fact of the marriage breakdown").

4.18 RELIGION AND DIVORCE: BELIEF VERSUS PRACTICE

Freedom of religion has a dual aspect: freedom to believe and freedom to act in exercise of such belief. The federal and state constitutions place the freedom of belief (or rights of conscience) beyond government control or interference. Accordingly, under the Free Exercise Clause of the First Amendment, the freedom of belief is absolute and inviolate. *Bowen v. Roy*, 476 U.S. 693, 699 (1986). As Justice Jackson wrote in *West Virginia State Bd. of Educ. v. Barnette*, 319 U.S. 624, 642 (1943):

> If there is any fixed star in our constitutional constellation, it is that no official, high or petty, can prescribe what shall be orthodox in politics, nationalism, religion, or other matters of opinion or force citizens to confess by word or act their faith therein.

On the other hand, freedom to act in the exercise of a religious belief is not an absolute right, and it may be regulated for the protection of society. *Cantwell v. Connecticut*, 310 U.S. 296, 304 (1940) (state may by general and non-discriminatory legislation regulate the times, the places, and the manner of soliciting upon its streets, and of holding meetings thereon; and may in other respects safeguard the peace, good order and comfort of the community, without unconstitutionally invading the liberties protected by the Fourteenth Amendment). Some religious acts and practices by individuals must yield to the common good. *Bowen v. Roy*, 476 U.S. 693, 702 (1986) ("Religious beliefs can be accommodated, but there is a point at which accommodation would radically restrict the operating latitude of the legislature"). In *United States v. Lee,* 455 U.S. 252 (1982), the Court held that a religious belief in conflict with payment of taxes afforded no basis for resisting a tax imposed on employers to support social security system.

 **REFLECTIVE QUESTIONS** — What is the importance of the distinction between the freedom to believe and the freedom to act in the exercise of a religious belief?

Background to *Hogan v. Hogan*

In *Hogan v. Hogan,* religious issues arose during the divorce proceeding. The case involves an Ohio couple, Kathleen Ann Hogan and Clifford Floyd Hogan, who had been married for 15 years when Kathleen sought a divorce. They had two children, ages eight and ten. At the divorce hearing, Kathleen testified that she suffered mental and physical abuse by Clifford. Clifford opposed the divorce alleging that it would infringe on his state and federal constitutional right to freely exercise his religion. He testified that he sincerely believed that divorce was sinful under church law and that marriage was indissoluble in the eyes of his religion. He stated that he believed that the divorce would not be recognized by his church. The trial judge granted the divorce and Clifford appealed.

HOGAN
v.
HOGAN

Court of Appeals of Ohio
747 N.E.2d 299 (Ohio App. 2000)

VALEN, J. In his sole assignment of error, appellant argues that the trial court lacked jurisdiction to enter a divorce decree. . . .

Section 7, Article I of the Ohio Constitution states:

> All men have a natural and indefeasible right to worship Almighty God according to the dictates of their own conscience.

This court has previously determined that a claim of violation of religious rights under the Ohio Constitution should be considered pursuant to a three-part test adopted by the Ohio Supreme Court. . . . The test is first, whether a defendant's religious beliefs are sincerely held; second, whether the regulation at issue infringes upon a defendant's constitutional right to freely engage in the religious practices; and third, whether the state has demonstrated a compelling interest for enforcement of the regulation and that the regulation is written in the least restrictive means.

The first part of the tripartite test requires a determination of whether a person's religious beliefs are sincere. Appellant asserts that he genuinely holds the religious beliefs of the Roman Catholic Church. At the conclusion of appellant's testimony at the February 1 hearing, the trial judge told appellant that he had "great respect for [his] personal convictions" and characterized appellant's concerns as "sincere." However, even if we concede that appellant's religious beliefs are sincere, we find that appellant's argument does not meet the second and third parts of the test.

Appellant fails to satisfy the second part of the three-part test because he has not demonstrated that divorce infringes upon his constitutional right to freely engage in the Catholic faith. Appellant insists that to undergo a divorce would force him to violate his religious beliefs. On the one hand, appellant insists that to be divorced is a "mortal sin" in the eyes of the Catholic Church and that being divorced will undermine his opportunity to continue to practice his faith. On the other hand, appellant argues that according to the Catholic faith, a marriage that is sacramental and consummated is indissoluble. After the trial judge stated that it had to grant the divorce in this case, appellant asked the trial judge, "And are you . . . in agreement that our Roman Catholic Religion still allows us to be married?" The trial judge responded that he had no position as to the beliefs of the Roman Catholic Church. By suggesting that a divorce under Ohio law may not necessarily be acknowledged under the Catholic Church as a divorce but may be treated as a continued marriage, appellant fails to unequivocally show that his legal divorce will infringe upon his right to freely engage in his religious practice.

Moreover, appellant has not successfully challenged the divorce statute under the third part of the tripartite test because it is apparent that the state has a compelling interest in enforcing divorce and that the divorce statute is written in the least restrictive way possible. It has been commented:

> For as long as one need remember, the legislature has treated marriage and divorce as proper subjects of the legislative police power. Statutory regulation has governed qualifications and eligibility for marriage, . . . [and] grounds for divorce [.] . . . [S]tate actions regulating marriage and its incidents are so unassailably constitutional that only the quixotic would challenge them.

Appellant has not provided us any reason that divorce, which involves the dissolution of marriage, a legal relationship existing under Ohio law, should not be regulated by the state. Appellant cannot demonstrate that the state of Ohio lacks a compelling interest for enforcement of divorce. Moreover, appellant does not argue that the divorce statute is not written in the least restrictive means. . . .

Appellant also insists that the trial court improperly impinged upon his right to free exercise of religion under the United States Constitution by issuing this divorce decree. The First Amendment to the United States Constitution states:

> Congress shall make no law respecting an establishment of religion, or prohibiting the free exercise thereof. . . .

The divorce statute is a statute of general application. This court has previously found that "neutral or generally applicable state actions are subjected to a lower level of scrutiny under the [United States Constitution's] First Amendment's Free Exercise Clause than they are under the Ohio's Free Exercise Clause." . . . Therefore, because appellant cannot demonstrate that his right to free exercise under the Ohio Constitution had been violated, he cannot show that his right to free exercise under the First Amendment to the United States Constitution has been violated.

The trial court properly issued a divorce decree upon demonstration that the parties have lived separate and apart without interruption for one year. Appellant has failed to show that his right to free exercise as provided by the Ohio Constitution and the United States Constitution has been violated.

DISCUSSION QUESTIONS FOR *HOGAN v. HOGAN*

A. This court determined that a claim of violation of religious rights should be considered pursuant to a three-part test. Examine and explain the three-part test. The court also states that "the state has a compelling interest in enforcing divorce." What is that compelling interest?

B. The First Amendment has never been interpreted as an absolute proscription on the governmental regulation of religious practices. In addition to their free exercise rights, parents have a fundamental right to educate their children, including the right to communicate their moral and religious values. However, a parent's actions are not insulated from a domestic relations court's inquiry just because they are based upon religious beliefs, especially actions that will harm a child's mental or physical health. Thus, a parent may not shield his actions from the court's scrutiny by claiming religious motivations for those actions. Assume that a father who describes himself as a devout Christian who firmly believes in a literal reading of the Bible is given restricted visitation with his children following a divorce. He argues that the trial court based its decision to restrict his visitation solely on his strongly held religious beliefs in violation of his constitutional right of freedom of religion under the First Amendment to the United States Constitution. He claims that his comments to the children about his ex-wife's relationship with another man "are simply a reflection of his religious views, which include the Biblical teachings on adultery," and as such cannot be taken into account by the court. How will a court analyze his argument? *See Willis v. Willis,* 775 N.E.2d 878 (Ohio App. 2002).

C. Assume that a court ordered a noncustodial parent in a divorce action to pay 40 percent of his child's tuition at a private Catholic school. The noncustodial parent challenges the order asserting that requiring him to pay tuition for his son to attend a religious school violates the First and Fourteenth Amendments to the United States Constitution. He contends that the court is aiding one religion and compelling him to support a place of worship against his consent in violation of the Establishment Clause of the Constitution. Most likely, how will a court treat the objection? *See Smith v. Null,* 757 N.E.2d 1200 (Ohio App. 2001) (divorce statutes permitting support awards above and beyond standard amount allowed order that noncustodial parent pay a portion of child's private school tuition, even though public schools were available).

4.19 RELIGION AND DIVORCE: JEWISH LAW AND ACCESS TO A DIVORCE

Under traditional Jewish law, a civil divorce is not sufficient to dissolve a marriage. Only a religious divorce, which is provided by obtaining from the Beth Din a signed writ of divorce called a "Get," completely dissolves the marriage for a person who wishes to remarry within the Orthodox Jewish religion. *Lang v. Levi,* 16 A.3d 980 (Md. App. 2011). A Beth Din generally consists of a panel of three rabbis who preside over religious matters including divorce, conversion, and general commercial or business matters involving Jews. Traditionally, only the husband has the power to grant or withhold the "Get." The rabbinic authorities may not compel the husband to grant the "Get" if he does not wish to do so. Until a woman receives a "Get" she may not remarry within her religion. If she does remarry without the "Get," the new marriage is not considered valid, the woman is considered an adulterer, and any children from the new marriage are considered from a religious perspective illegitimate. *See generally Elmora Hebrew Center, Inc. v. Fishman,* 593 A.2d 725, 729-732 (N.J. 1991).

REFLECTIVE QUESTIONS	**Does the refusal of rabbinic authorities to allow a "Get" prevent a party from proceeding to obtain a divorce in a state court?**

4.20 MODERN DIVORCE FROM BED AND BOARD

A bed-and-board divorce is likely found in most, if not all, state statutes and is often referred to as a "legal separation." The rationale advanced to support the practice of granting bed-and-board divorces is the need to provide support and other incidental remedies for a spouse or for individuals who, for religious or other reasons, do not seek to sever the matrimonial bond. *Hamel v. Hamel,* 426 A.2d 259, 261 (R.I. 1981).

Concern has been directed at bed-and-board divorce actions because they allegedly create a situation in which the parties receive the burdens, but not the benefits, of the marriage relationship in that they are living apart but are still bound by marital ties. In many jurisdictions a divorce from bed and board may also include an award of custody, child support, property division, and alimony.

REFLECTIVE QUESTIONS	**Given the concern about bed-and-board divorce actions, do they serve any useful function in a modern society?**

4.21 IMPOSITION OF SPECIAL FEES IN DIVORCE ACTIONS

The practice of charging additional fees when a couple files for divorce has been challenged. For example, in *Browning v. Corbett,* 734 P.2d 1030 (Ariz. App. 1986), a special $12 fee attached to a divorce filing, which was distributed between a domestic violence shelter fund and a child abuse prevention and treatment fund, was challenged. It was argued that due process and equal protection was violated because the fee raised funds for a program that was not court-related. In rejecting the challenge, the court reasoned that the state had a legitimate interest in providing assistance to victims of domestic abuse and in attempting to reduce occurrences of child abuse. Because victims of domestic violence and child abuse frequently come from broken homes, it was considered rational to raise funds for programs to assist these victims by requiring parties to marriage dissolution actions to pay an additional fee when filing. The court said it could not find in either federal or state constitutions a provision that requires court filing fees to be applied only to court-related functions.

Minnesota, North Dakota, and Texas have adopted the Arizona rationale. However, Oklahoma, Illinois, and Louisiana have rejected the collection of fees for non-judicial programs. Oklahoma held that requiring a portion of fees paid to court clerks in civil actions to be credited or deposited to accounts of certain nonjudicial programs violated the state constitution's open courts provision. *Fent v. State ex rel. Dept. of Human Services*, 236 P.3d 61 (Okla. 2010). *See Crocker v. Finley*, 459 N.E.2d 1346 (Ill. 1984); *Safety Net for Abused Persons v. Segura*, 692 So. 2d 1038 (La. 1997). In Louisiana the court held the fee collection statute constituted a "tax," and violated that state's constitutional right of access and separation of powers provisions because the fees were not related to the administration of justice.

REFLECTIVE QUESTIONS	Why should additional fees to support social programs be added to divorce filings when they are not added to probate and other filings with a clerk's office?

4.22 INDIGENT'S ACCESS TO DIVORCE PROCESS

An indigent person is denied due process of law if a state refuses to allow that person to bring a divorce action unless court fees are first paid. *Boddie v. Connecticut*, 401 U.S. 371 (1971). The Court in *Boddie* reasoned that marriages were created by state laws and dissolutions were provided only through access to the judicial process provided by the state. Therefore, it would be a denial of due process to deny to an indigent person the use of the judicial machinery provided by the state.

Publication. In *Deason v. Deason*, 296 N.E.2d 229 (N.Y. 1973), the court held that an indigent plaintiff seeking a divorce could not be denied access to the courts solely on the basis of her inability to pay court fees and costs, which included publication costs that were an expense payable by plaintiff to a third person other than a public officer. The court said that burden in relation to publication costs of an indigent plaintiff should fall upon the local government absent any legislation on the subject. *See State ex rel. Blevins v. Mowrey*, 543 N.E.2d 99 (Ohio 1989) (indigent plaintiff in divorce action could require appropriate public officials to effect service of process by publication without prepayment of costs of publication); *Dugan v. Dugan*, 570 S.W.2d 183 (Tenn. 1979) (service by registered mail to defendant's last address and posting in three places in lieu of publication); *Johnson v. Johnson*, 329 A.2d 451 (D.C. App. 1974) (must publish in least expensive newspaper on a single occasion).

Right to counsel. There is no Sixth Amendment constitutional right to be represented by counsel in a divorce proceeding. *Haller v. Haller*, 423 N.W.2d 617 (Mich. App. 1988). In *In re Smiley*, 330 N.E.2d 53 (N.Y. 1975), the court stated that "*Boddie* does not support, or by rationale imply, an obligation of the State to assign, let alone compensate, counsel as a matter of constitutional right." However, New York's Family Court Act §262(a) (2015) provides the Family Court with a limited power to assign counsel for indigent persons in specifically enumerated cases, including those where "the parent of any child [is] seeking custody or contesting the substantial infringement of his or her right to custody of such child." Judges have discretion to appoint counsel to represent parties in a divorce action.

REFLECTIVE QUESTIONS	Should free counsel be provided to indigents involved in divorce actions, at least in some circumstances, such as when custody of a minor child is disputed? Or, when a spouse is imprisoned and cannot appear at various divorce proceedings?

4.23 MAY A CHILD DIVORCE A PARENT?

In *Ryan v. Ryan*, 677 N.W.2d 899 (Mich. App. 2004), a daughter, who was a minor at the time, attempted to "divorce" her parents. The court held that the daughter lacked standing. The court also held that the trial court did not have subject matter jurisdiction over the minor's divorce complaint against her parents, explaining that "a court only has jurisdiction over the dissolution of a marriage between a man and a woman." *Id.* at 908. It reasoned that because a marriage is defined by statute as "inherently a unique relationship between a man and a woman," it necessarily followed that there could be no divorce between a child and his or her parents. *Ibid.* The court also stated that permitting the action to proceed would improperly interfere with the parents' fundamental liberty interest to make decisions concerning care, custody, and control of the child.

REFLECTIVE QUESTIONS	Do you agree with the reasoning of the *Ryan* court?

4.24 DISCRIMINATION IN PUBLIC EMPLOYMENT BECAUSE OF DIVORCE

Public employees are protected from discrimination in the employment arena should a divorce somehow become related to an adverse employment decision. The reason for this is that decisions of the Supreme Court have firmly established that matters relating to marriage and family relationships involve privacy rights that are constitutionally protected against unwarranted governmental interference. *See, e.g., Roe v. Wade*, 410 U.S. 113, 152-153 (1973). The Court has categorized these matters as among the personal decisions protected by the right to privacy and recognized that freedom of personal choice in matters of marriage and family life is a liberty protected by the Due Process Clause of the Fourteenth Amendment. *Zablocki v. Redhail*, 434 U.S. 374, 384-385 (1978) (citing *Cleveland Board of Education v. LaFleur*, 414 U.S. 632, 639-640 (1974)). Given the associational interests that surround the establishment and dissolution of the marital relationship, adjustments such as divorce and separation are said to be naturally included within the umbrella of protection accorded to the right of privacy. *United States v. Kras*, 409 U.S. 434, 444 (1975).

An example of the protection afforded by the Constitution is illustrated by *Littlejohn v. Rose*, 768 F.2d 765 (6th Cir. 1985). In that case, the court held that if a public school teacher was denied reemployment by a school board because of her involvement in a divorce, this would violate her constitutional right to privacy. Another somewhat related example is *Adkins v. Board of Education of Magoffin County, Kentucky*, 982 F.2d 952 (6th Cir. 1993). In that case, the plaintiff was denied employment with a school board simply because of her marriage to a person whom her employer disliked. The court stated that "[w]hile the plaintiff had no contractual right to a job, she could not be deprived of her public employment for exercising a constitutional right." *Id.* at 955. Similarly, in *Montgomery v. Carr*, 101 F.3d 1117, 1127 (6th Cir. 1996), the court stated that "[i]f the only motivation for a public official in taking some adverse employment action against a public employee is the public employee's protected activity, then regardless of the level of scrutiny applied, such action is unconstitutional."

REFLECTIVE QUESTIONS	What changes in U.S. society may explain the fairly recent court decisions protecting persons who divorce who hold public employment from being fired because of the divorce?

4.25 FOREIGN DIVORCE DECREES: COMITY

Occasionally, when a relationship breaks down, one spouse may seek a jurisdiction outside the United States in which to obtain a divorce. In general, a valid judgment rendered in a foreign nation after a "fair trial" in a contested proceeding will be recognized in the United States. Restatement (Second) of Conflict of Laws §98 (1971). Whether a trial is "fair" is a fact question for the reviewing court.

Limits on Full Faith and Credit Clause. The Full Faith and Credit Clause of the Constitution does not apply to divorces outside the United States. *Hilton v. Guyot*, 159 U.S. 113, 163-164 (1895). Article IV, §1, of the United States Constitution declares that "Full Faith and Credit shall be given in each State to the public Acts, Records, and judicial Proceedings of every other State." Because of Article IV, courts look to at least two possibilities for recognition of the foreign divorce. One is for a state court to apply the doctrine of comity to the dispute. The second is for the state court to apply the theory of estoppel.

Comity. As a general rule a court may but "is not required to, recognize a divorce decree from a foreign country under the discretionary doctrine of comity." Before a court will apply comity to a request to recognize a divorce decree, it will ask three questions: First, does recognition violate the strong public policy of the forum state? *See Dreher v. Budget Rent-A-Car System, Inc.*, 634 S.E.2d 324 (Va. 2006). Second, does recognition prejudice the state's own rights or the rights of its citizens? *America Online, Inc. v. Nam Tai Electronics, Inc.*, 571 S.E.2d 128 (Va. 2002). Third, would recognition leave the court in a position where it is unable to render complete justice? *See* 16 Am. Jur. 2d *Conflict of Laws* §13 (2010).

REFLECTIVE QUESTIONS	Describe the discretionary "doctrine of comity."

4.26 FOREIGN DIVORCE DECREES: THE DOMICILE ISSUE

A majority of state courts refuse to recognize a divorce obtained in a foreign country where neither party was a domiciliary of that country. *Cvitanovich-Dubie v. Dubie*, 231 P.3d 983 (Haw. App. 2010). Because states have statutory provisions for a divorce that require either domicile or a period of physical presence within the state before a divorce is granted, the majority reason that it would be a violation of a state's public policy to recognize a divorce where neither party was domiciled in the jurisdiction where it was granted. The Tennessee Supreme Court took a minority view and upheld the validity of a Dominican divorce decree issued to Memphis residents in *Hyde v. Hyde*, 562 S.W.2d 194 (Tenn. 1978), on the basis of comity. In that case, the wife, who remained a resident of Tennessee at the time, obtained an ex parte divorce in the Dominican Republic. However, the greater weight of authority nationwide supports the notion that courts generally should not extend comity to a divorce decree issued by a court in a foreign country where neither party to the divorce was a domiciliary of that country.

REFLECTIVE QUESTIONS	Do you agree with the majority or minority view on the domicile issue? Or, might recognition turn on the particular facts of the case, that is, all parties agree that the divorce was legal in the foreign nation even though under state policy it is invalid?

4.27 FOREIGN DIVORCE DECREES: THE ESTOPPEL THEORY

Application of the doctrine of estoppel is an alternative theory upon which a court in a rare instance may recognize a foreign divorce, which is otherwise invalid. *See generally Stephen C. Glassman, The Tangled International Divorce Web, Recognition and Enforcement at Home,* 9-SPG Fam. Advoc. 4 (Spring 1987). When considering whether to apply this doctrine, courts will carefully examine the facts that suggest failure to recognize the divorce may result in an inequitable (unfair) result. *See* Restatement (Second) of Conflict of Laws §12.

For example, in *Mayer v. Mayer,* 311 S.E. 2d 659 (N.C. App. 1985), the wife sued her second husband for divorce and asked for alimony and attorney's fees. The second husband asserted that his wife's divorce from her first husband in the Dominican Republic, which as her lawyer he had actively helped procure, was invalid. Therefore, he reasoned he did not have to pay alimony. The wife argued that her husband should be estopped from questioning the validity of the Dominican Republic divorce since (a) he participated in her procurement of the invalid divorce; (b) all parties relied upon the divorce's validity until he abandoned her; and (c) a contrary result would create a marriage at will by her husband, who could end the marital relationship at any time he desired without any obligation on his part toward his wife. The court held that the husband was estopped from denying the validity of that divorce. It said that under the quasi-estoppel doctrine, one is not permitted to injure another by taking a position inconsistent with prior conduct, regardless of whether the person had actually relied upon that conduct. *See generally* Homer Clark, *Estoppel Against Jurisdictional Attack on Decrees of Divorce,* 70 Yale L.J. 45 (1960).

In another estoppel case, *Scherer v. Scherer,* 405 N.E.2d 40 (Ind. App. 1980), the husband filed a petition for divorce in Indiana and prayed for an equitable distribution of property. The wife answered and asserted several defenses, including an allegation that a prior Dominican Republic divorce decree barred the Indiana proceeding.

The husband argued that because neither spouse was a good faith domiciliary in the Dominican Republic at the time their divorce decree was rendered, the divorce decree is invalid in Indiana. The court held that the husband's inconsistent conduct before and after the foreign divorce estopped him from attacking the Dominican Republic decree in Indiana.

The court in *In re Shank's Estate,* 316 P.2d 710 (Cal. App. 1957), stated that "no particular set of facts is necessary to invoke an equitable estoppel," in response to the husband's argument that estoppel has only been applied against a party who has induced the securing of an invalid divorce, participated in the proceeding itself, or remarried with knowledge of the facts. *Id.* at 711. In *Shank's,* the husband had actual notice of the foreign divorce action but did not appear in person or by counsel. Subsequent to the divorce, he "acquiesced in and relied upon the Mexican decree of divorce and conducted himself as if said decree were valid and effective," through acts including the purchasing of real property in his own name as a "single man," establishing a meretricious relationship with another woman, and living separately from his wife. *Id.* at 711-712. The court held he was estopped after his wife's death from challenging the validity of the Mexican divorce.

REFLECTIVE QUESTIONS	Describe a situation where a court might look favorably on the use of equitable estoppel in a divorce action.

4.28 DURATIONAL RESIDENCY REQUIREMENTS

A state may impose a durational residency requirement before a couple may divorce. The purpose of such a provision is "to prevent divorce-minded couples from shopping for favorable residence requirements." *Wallace v. Wallace*, 320 P.2d 1020, 1022-1023 (1958).

What constitutes legitimate state interests in imposing durational requirements was discussed by the Supreme Court in *Sosna v. Iowa*, 419 U.S. 393 (1975) (applying the rational basis test to Iowa durational requirement). In upholding Iowa's one-year residency requirement for divorce actions, the Court said that divorce proceedings affect marital rights, property rights, and often custody of children. The importance of these consequences is such that the state "may insist that one seeking to initiate such a proceeding have the modicum of attachment to the State required here." *Id.* at 407. The Court observed that "[s]uch a requirement additionally furthers the State's parallel interests both in avoiding officious intermeddling in matters in which another State has a paramount interest, and in minimizing the susceptibility of its own divorce decrees to collateral attack." *Ibid.* Furthermore, because jurisdiction over divorce proceedings is founded upon domicile, Iowa could protect its judgments from collateral attack by such a requirement.

REFLECTIVE QUESTIONS	Why aren't durational residency requirements unconstitutional?

4.29 EX PARTE DIVISIBLE DIVORCE

American law recognizes the doctrine of divisible divorce. Under this doctrine, a forum may issue a valid divorce decree based on "domicile" jurisdiction over one party while lacking the authority to determine issues of financial responsibility because the court did not have personal jurisdiction over a second party. The court assumes *in rem* jurisdiction over the marital status of the parties and changes that status from "married" to "not married."

Assuming proper notice is given, a divisible divorce judgment must be afforded full faith and credit outside the state issuing the decree. Issues such as alimony and attorneys' fees remain subject to litigation in a state having personal jurisdiction over both parties to the marriage. *Estin v. Estin*, 334 U.S. 541, 543-549 (1948); *see Marriage of Moore & Ferrie*, 18 Cal. Rptr. 2d 543 (Cal. App. 1993) (community property interests not adjudicated by Ohio dissolution judgment subject to litigation in subsequent California action). For example, the Supreme Court of Oklahoma said in *Powers v. District Court of Tulsa County*, 227 P.3d 1060, 1075 (2009), that "in the absence of *in personam* jurisdiction over one spouse an *ex parte* divisible divorce decree may change the marital status of appearing and non-appearing spouses, but a divisible divorce is ineffectual to alter economic interests and certain other legal interests of the spouses."

| **REFLECTIVE QUESTIONS** | Define an ex parte divisible divorce. |

Background to *Scott-Lubin v. Lubin*

The husband was a Florida resident. A divorce action was begun in Florida in 2005 by his wife. When she was unable to locate her husband, the trial court granted her permission to notice the suit by publication. The husband did not answer the petition, and a default final judgment of dissolution of marriage was entered in 2006. The trial court also awarded the wife the marital residence, two of the couple's three cars, permanent alimony, and attorneys' fees and costs.

In 2008, the wife filed a motion to enforce the final judgment. In response, the husband's counsel filed a notice of appearance in the case. The husband then appeared pro se at the hearing before a general magistrate on June 5. At the hearing, the husband participated and told the magistrate that he had not paid because he "was not aware of the entry of the Final Judgment." The trial court adopted all of the recommendations of the general magistrate that the husband pay all alimony arrearages and court costs on July 14, 2008.

On June 8, the husband's lawyer filed a motion to vacate the final judgment pursuant to Florida's Rules of Civil Procedure. The trial court found that the husband was never personally served with a petition for dissolution of marriage. Since the husband was never served, the trial court ruled that it lacked jurisdiction to resolve the claims regarding alimony, the marital residence, and other matters pertaining to the parties' assets and liabilities. The trial court concluded that the final judgment entered in 2006 was void, "except as to the granting of the Dissolution of Marriage itself." The wife appealed.

The appellate court framed the issue as whether the trial court erred in setting aside a final judgment, where the trial court found that it lacked personal jurisdiction over the husband, despite the fact that the husband actively participated in the proceedings.

SCOTT-LUBIN
v.
LUBIN

Court of Appeals of Florida (4th District)
49 So. 3d 838 (2010)

LEVINE, J. . . . Generally, service of process by publication, like in the present case, would not be sufficient to determine issues related to alimony and property. Constructive service of process confers only in rem or quasi in rem jurisdiction upon the court.

With respect to issues surrounding the dissolution of a marriage, the Florida Supreme Court stated, in pertinent part, the following:

> The concept of "divisible divorce" . . . recognizes that a dissolution proceeding has two separable aspects, that which relates to the marital res and that which relates to the property rights and obligations of the parties. While constructive service is sufficient for an adjudication of the former, personal jurisdiction is generally required for a determination of the latter.

However, in this case, because the husband voluntarily appeared and participated at the hearing before the general magistrate, he has waived his right to challenge the court's jurisdiction. It is well established that if a party takes some step in the proceedings which amounts to a submission to the court's jurisdiction, then it is deemed that the party waived his right to challenge the court's jurisdiction regardless of the party's intent not to concede jurisdiction. . . . Thus, the trial court erred in setting aside the final judgment on the grounds of lack of personal jurisdiction, inasmuch as the husband participated in this case without raising a contemporaneous objection to the court's exercise of jurisdiction.

The fact that the husband did not appear and participate in the case until after rendition of the final judgment is irrelevant. The husband's post-judgment participation at a hearing, along with his counsel's notice of appearance, without a simultaneous objection to service of process, would still result in a waiver of the husband's right to contest the trial court's exercise of personal jurisdiction.

We conclude that the husband's actions constituted submission to the jurisdiction of the circuit court, and the trial court's vacatur of the final judgment was in error. We reverse and remand for reinstatement of the final judgment. Reversed and remanded.

> **DISCUSSION QUESTIONS** FOR *SCOTT-LUBIN v. LUBIN*
>
> **A.** What was the problem with how the trial judge handled the original divorce action?
>
> **B.** Once the trial judge subsequently vacated the divorce judgment, what was the situation with regard to an award of alimony and distribution of property? Without the reversal on appeal, would the ex-wife have been required to return the property to her ex-husband?
>
> **C.** Did the court of appeals adequately consider the fact that the ex-husband appeared *pro se* at the hearing in June in its opinion?
>
> **D.** Can you argue that this was a decision in which the court reached a practical result but not necessarily a correct legal result?
>
> **E.** How would you have decided the jurisdictional issue if you were a judge hearing the matter on appeal?

4.30 ANNULMENT VERSUS DIVORCE

This chapter has focused to this point on divorce actions. On rare occasions, a party may seek to annul a marriage rather than obtain a divorce. The annulment may be sought for religious or other reasons.

Today, annulment actions are most commonly found in immigration and Social Security disputes, where a marriage either qualifies or disqualifies an individual from eligibility for certain benefits. *See, e.g., S.K. v. F.K.*, 26 Misc. 3d 1238(A), Slip Copy, 2010 WL 979701 (Table) (N.Y. Sup. 2010) (immigration fraud); *Brown v. Cowell*, 19 So. 3d 1171 (Fla. App. 2009) (immigration fraud); *Everetts v. Apfel*, 214 F.3d 990 (8th Cir. 2000) (Social Security). Annulments are also associated with efforts to void a marriage following the death of an individual where a fight has erupted over the distribution of the decedent's estate. *See Campbell v. Thomas*, 897 N.Y.S.2d 460 (N.Y.A.D. 2010).

When a party seeks to annul a marriage rather than obtain a divorce under a state dissolution provision, the issue is often whether the relationship is void or voidable. Voidable marriages are relationships deemed less offensive to society, and the decision to end these relationships usually rests with the partner who possesses the legal disability. Examples of voidable relationships include marriages of persons with serious mental disabilities, persons with physical disabilities making it impossible to perform sexual intercourse, or persons who are too young to marry without parental or judicial approval and who fail to obtain such approval. A voidable marriage is valid for all purposes until the party entitled to assert its voidability timely raises the issue and it is annulled by a competent court. *Brewer v. Miller*, 673 S.W.2d 53 (Tenn. App. 1984). It is possible for a voidable marriage to be ratified and to ripen into a valid marriage.

Void defined. Void marriages are those that society deems contrary to public morals and violating deeply held core values. These include incestuous and bigamous relationships. A void marriage is viewed in most jurisdictions as one that is invalid for all purposes from the moment of its inception, whether or not it has been so declared in a court of law. *In re Karau's Estate*, 80 P.2d 108 (Cal. App. 1938). It is treated as if it never existed, and its invalidity may be shown collaterally in any proceeding where it becomes an issue. *Ibid. See Hunt v. Hunt*, 100 P. 541, 542 (Okla. 1909) ("A marriage is void when it has no legal effect, confers no marital or property rights, imposes no duties or liabilities, and is incapable of subsequent ratification. Marriages are void when declared so by statute, and when there is a valid prior marriage undissolved.").

Importance of void/voidable distinction. The importance of the void/voidable distinction is illustrated by the ruling in *McConkey v. McConkey*, 215 S.E.2d 640 (Va. 1975). There the couple divorced, and the ex-wife was awarded alimony. She then married one Sykes, which resulted in alimony from her first marriage being terminated by statute. She subsequently filed an annulment action, claiming that the marriage between her and Sykes was void because of his fraud, and she prevailed. The trial court order stated that her marriage to Sykes was "null, void and of no effect," and she sought reinstatement of the alimony from her first husband. The Virginia Supreme Court denied her request for reinstating alimony. It reasoned that her marriage to Sykes was not *void ab initio* because there was no evidence that the marriage ceremony was invalid. It concluded that the "annulment was based upon fraud on the part of Sykes, so that the marriage was voidable if [the wife] desired to have it annulled." *Id.* at 641.

Toler v. Oakwood Smokeless Coal Corp., 4 S.E.2d 364, 368 (Va. 1939), provides another example of the importance of the void/voidable distinction. Martha Toler honestly, but mistakenly, believed that her husband had been killed in West Virginia. She then married Raymond Toler. When he was killed in an industrial accident, Martha sought workers' compensation benefits as Toler's wife/dependent. The court denied her request when it discovered that she had not divorced her first husband and he was alive. It reasoned that her second marriage was bigamous and, therefore, *void ab initio*. It observed that "[a] void marriage confers no legal rights, and, when it is determined that the marriage is void, it is as if no marriage had ever been performed. . . . A voidable marriage differs from a void marriage in that [the voidable marriage] may be afterwards ratified by the parties . . . and usually is treated as a valid marriage until it is decreed void."

The Utah Court of Appeals considered the void/voidable distinction in *In re Marriage of Kunz*, 136 P.3d 1278 (Utah App. 2006). There, the court concluded that an alleged sham immigration marriage between a husband and his legal wife would be voidable, not automatically void. It reasoned that the Utah legislature had failed to include immigration-motivated marriages among those deemed void in its statutory scheme; therefore, they were merely voidable, that is, valid until nullified.

| REFLECTIVE QUESTIONS | Illustrate the importance of determining whether an annulled relationship is void or voidable. |

General Principles

1. The concept of divorce has existed for centuries.

2. English ecclesiastical courts distinguished between an absolute divorce, which was never granted, a divorce from bed and board (divorce *a mensa et thoro*), and an annulment (divorce *a vinculo*).

3. Comity is a discretionary legal doctrine that governs whether a court of the United States will recognize a divorce decree rendered by a court of a foreign country.

4. A majority of jurisdictions take the view that they may charge special fees for couples filing for a divorce. These fees are in addition to the normal fees charged for a civil action. When challenged on constitutional grounds, a court will most likely apply the rational basis test instead of the strict scrutiny test to determine whether they may be levied.

5. Under the Free Exercise Clause of the First Amendment, the freedom of religious belief is absolute and inviolate. While a state cannot interfere with religious beliefs and opinions, it may interfere with religious practice and conduct. The state may, for example, grant a divorce over the deeply held religious objection of one of the parties.

6. A court in an ex parte divorce has "in rem" jurisdiction over the status of the parties (the status being that they are married).

7. Personal jurisdiction over a defendant is not required to terminate a marriage if the party seeking the divorce is domiciled in the forum state. A party must, of course, satisfy due process by providing appropriate notice of the proceeding.

8. Appropriate notice to a defendant in a divorce action is "notice reasonably calculated under all the circumstances, to apprise interested parties of the pendency of the action and afford them an opportunity [to be heard]." *Mullane v. Central Hanover Bank & Trust Co.*, 339 U.S. 306, 314 (1950).

9. If a court issues a divorce decree when it does not have personal jurisdiction over the defendant, it may not determine any economic issues such as alimony, property division, child support, or attorneys' fees.

Chapter Problems

1. Assume two Pakistani citizens who were married in Pakistan and, after residing in Maryland for more than 20 years, divorced in Maryland in accordance with Pakistani law. The couple resolved property issues between themselves, and neither seeks a Maryland divorce in order to save money. Each former spouse then remarries in Maryland and resides with the new spouse in Maryland. Each former spouse is charged with bigamy in violation of Maryland Code (2002), §10-502 of the Criminal Law Article. Each raises the Pakistani divorce as a defense. Will Maryland recognize their defense? *See Aleem v. Aleem,* 931 A.2d 1123 (Md. App. 2007).

2. Assume that Alice brings an action to divorce David alleging extreme mental cruelty. The two have been married for 20 years and have two children of the marriage. David opposes the divorce, claiming Alice is seeking a divorce based on his religious beliefs, not any of his actions. At the divorce trial, Alice testifies that she feels depressed, frustrated, lost, abandoned, and hurt because David's religion has become like a "mistress." According to Alice, David told her on several occasions that she would not live in paradise on earth if she was a nonbeliever and that she would "just lay in the dirt." She claims she cannot have a normal conversation with David, as he continually states he is there to teach her and the children about how to live a religious life. David is no longer involved in their former family practices because his religious views do not allow him to celebrate holidays and birthdays or be concerned with other worldly things. She also is concerned over the adverse impact David's religious views are having on their children. She specifically worries about some of his beliefs; for example, he would never permit the children to have a blood transfusion should it be necessary, or to have a measles vaccination.

David claims the United States Constitution and the state constitution prevent his religious beliefs from forming the basis of grounds for divorce. The trial judge grants the divorce on the grounds of extreme mental cruelty, and David appeals asserting his constitutional claim. How will an appellate court most likely rule on the appeal?

3. Assume that the parties were married for ten years when the husband petitioned to dissolve the marriage. Under the local divorce statute in the husband's state, a marriage may be dissolved if there has been an "irretrievable breakdown of the marriage relationship." An "irretrievable breakdown" occurs when "there is no reasonable prospect of reconciliation." If the parties dispute that the marriage has broken down, a court's finding of irretrievable breakdown must be supported by evidence that (1) the parties have lived separate and apart for a period of not less than 180 days immediately preceding the commencement of the proceeding, or (2) there is serious marital discord adversely affecting the attitude of one or both of the parties.

The wife testifies at the trial that she had tried for several years to urge her husband to seek treatment for alcoholism. Finally, when he continued to refuse to seek treatment, she asked him to leave their home. The husband moved out and a few weeks later filed for a divorce. The husband testified that he had made several unsuccessful attempts at reconciliation between the time he filed for divorce and the date set for trial. He testified that there was no hope of reconciliation. The wife testified that the marriage could be saved if the husband was treated for alcoholism, but she was not otherwise willing to take him back. Given the language of the state statute, is there a basis for the trial court awarding the husband a divorce on the grounds of irretrievable breakdown of the marriage relationship? Or, should the trial judge order the husband to undergo treatment for alcoholism and stay any further divorce proceeding until he has completed the treatment?

4. Assume the year is 1920 and Cecil seeks a divorce from Mary on the grounds that she deserted him by leaving their home with their children and moving in with her mother. Mary denied Cecil's claim and asserts a counterclaim asking for a divorce and claiming as grounds constructive desertion. The questions of fact will be tried to a jury and the state statute requires that there be a finding of fault before a divorce decree can be entered.

The parties were married for 20 years and had 2 children. Cecil testified at the trial that there were marital problems between the parties prior to the time Mary left the home, including continuous arguments and verbal abuse. He also testified that he refused Mary's numerous attempts to get him to leave the home in the months before she left. She once threw his clothes out a window, and on another occasion offered him $500 her mother had given her if he would sign a letter saying he was leaving for good. He refused. She told Cecil that she was dissatisfied with him because he spent too much time with the children, was lazy, and didn't make much money. One day, while Cecil was at work, she moved out without notice with the children.

Mary also testified that for three years before she moved out, Cecil subjected her and the children to constant verbal abuse, threats, and physical pushing and shoving. She testified that her reasons for leaving the marital home were as follows: "I had begun to lose weight. I could not sleep. I had diarrhea most of the time. I stayed anxious and just really felt that I was going to be ill if I continued to stay in that situation. I feared for my children." Mary's physician testified that he saw her once shortly after she left the family abode complaining of nausea, chills, and diarrhea. He concluded that the cause was nonviral gastroenteritis and anxiety. A few weeks before trial, the physician again saw Mary and testified that she appeared to have lost weight and complained of inability to sleep. The physician concluded that the cause was "anxiety and depression about divorce" and prescribed an anxiety-reducing drug.

Cecil agreed that there were continuous arguments and verbal abuse between the parties, but he denied any physical abuse and attributed the marital problems to the wife's conduct. The parties' children corroborated Cecil's accounts as to many of the confrontations between Cecil and Mary. Will an all male jury most likely find grounds for divorce exist for Cecil or Mary? How would a judge decide the issue today?

5. Assume for the purposes of this hypothetical only that it is 2009, the state is New York, and Ronald and Wanda had been married for five years when they began to experience marital difficulties. Also assume for the purposes of this hypothetical that the only basis for a divorce is proof of adultery. The parties separated, and Wanda sued Ronald for a divorce, alleging as her ground that Ronald had committed adultery. (Assume for the purposes of this problem only, that the only basis for divorce is adultery.)

Wanda testified that she suspected Ronald was having an affair with Roxanne. She testified that Ronald and Roxanne would speak to each other regularly on the telephone. Both Ronald and Roxanne were in the same military unit and often sent on special-duty assignments in various parts of the country. On one occasion, Wanda claims that Ronald told her he was going on a special military weekend assignment but that Roxanne was to remain on base. However, after leaving Ronald at the airport to catch his plane for the weekend assignment, Wanda came back to the airport and discovered the two of them talking to each other. She did not see whether they both boarded the same airplane.

Wanda recalled that on one occasion after she and Ronald had separated, that she arrived around 8:00 in the morning and watched Roxanne's apartment for approximately five hours. She said that she saw Ronald go in and out of the apartment and load and unload boxes from Roxanne's vehicle. She later telephoned Ronald on his cellular telephone and asked him what he was doing that day; he claimed he was with his father fixing up an old car.

There was also evidence presented during the trial that both Wanda and Ronald had been friends with Roxanne for a significant period prior to the divorce action. Wanda had spent time with Roxanne, and Ronald and Wanda had often eaten dinner with Roxanne when Ronald and Roxanne were required to travel on temporary duty assignments for the military. Will a court grant Wanda a divorce on the ground of adultery?

6. Assume that David and Pauline are married for five years when their relationship breaks down. David admits to having an affair with Alice during the marriage, and Pauline admits to having an affair with Russell during the marriage. Pauline files her divorce action in a jurisdiction that allows a divorce when there has been an irretrievable breakdown of the marriage relationship. David brings a motion to dismiss Pauline's divorce action on the grounds that (1) no divorce should be granted where both parties are at fault, (2) Pauline condoned David's behavior, which he asserts is a defense, and (3) he believes that with counseling the parties' marriage will survive. Pauline has refused to participate in counseling. Most likely, how will a court rule on David's motion? How would a court have ruled a hundred years ago?

Preparation for Practice

1. Prepare a script for two classmates who will role-play husband and wife. In your script outline the following: They have been married ten years when they agree to dissolve their marriage. H is moving to another state 1,000 miles away. The two issues they stringently disagree on involve a canoe and the dog. The couple received a red canoe from some friends as a wedding present, and it has been regularly used by them on outings. Sam, their five-year-old black standard poodle, has been raised by them since he was six weeks old. Both are extremely attached to Sam and the red canoe and intend to litigate the issue if they can't settle it. Give both role players some leeway to add some realistic facts to their relationship.

   Conduct a ten-minute mediation session focusing on the two issues. Have the mediation session videotaped and later critiqued by your instructor or a practicing mediator. What is the desirable result of the mediation? As a mediator, what is your role? What did you achieve, if anything, in ten minutes?

   Then, conduct a ten-minute arbitration session. Have the arbitration session videotaped and later critiqued by your instructor or a lawyer experienced in arbitration. How do mediation and arbitration differ?

2. Take the same facts from the above hypothetical problem. This time select a single classmate to represent the lawyer of the party you decide not to represent. Assume the two of you as lawyers are meeting with your client's permission to resolve the canoe/poodle dispute. Your client has directed you to "get the canoe and the poodle." The other side has directed the attorney to "get the canoe and the poodle at any cost." What is the worst outcome of this meeting? The best? What is a desirable result? Is there a difference in outcomes depending on whether you select mediation, arbitration, or let the lawyers "do it"? Overall, is the only solution to litigate the two issues?

3. Prepare a short paper explaining when courts in your jurisdiction will recognize a divorce between American citizens that took place in a foreign country. Explain what facts may cause them to refuse recognition.

4. Prepare a PowerPoint presentation explaining the grounds in your jurisdiction that are available for divorce.

Restructuring Parent-Child Relationships at Divorce

Chapter 5

Child Custody and Parenting Plans

5.1 INTRODUCTION

This chapter surveys decision making about the care and living arrangements of children following separation or divorce of the parents. The welfare of children is usually the primary concern of parents as they separate, and there is much that a family law attorney can do to promote healthy adjustment. Parents may want information about how children at various developmental stages experience separation and divorce and ways that they can ease the overall stress on children. The family law attorney plays a key role in early identification and appropriate handling of parenting issues linked to intimate partner violence, substance abuse, and mental health concerns.

As you read this chapter, please consider the following questions: How might divorce impact children? What are the legal technical terms for various child custody arrangements? How is the best interest of the child standard applied? What role do experts play in child custody cases? What are the pros and cons of statutory presumptions with respect to child custody and access? What special needs might families have when there has been intimate partner violence or child abuse?

REFLECTIVE QUESTIONS	Imagine that you are a divorcing parent. What would you want to know from your attorney?

5.2 CONTEXT: DIVORCE AND CHILDREN

Because nearly 50 percent of marriages end in divorce, researchers estimate that 40 percent of children have experienced or will experience the divorce of their parents. *See* Stephen J. Bahr, *Social Science Research on Family Dissolution: What It Shows and How It Might Be of Interest to Family Law Reformers*, 4 J.L. & Fam. Stud. 5 (2002). A frequently cited study suggests that children's adjustment to divorce may be linked to factors such as the absence of the noncustodial parent, the adjustment of the custodial parent, the conflict between the parents, economic hardship, and stressful life changes. *See* Paul R. Amato, *Children's Adjustment to Divorce: Theories, Hypotheses, and Empirical Support*, 55 J. Marriage & Fam. 23 (1993).

At separation or divorce, parents work to restructure their parenting relationship while simultaneously facing individual financial and emotional challenges. Some research shows that 25 percent of parents ease into a co-parenting relationship; half disengage for a while and then become more cooperative; but 25 percent remain at odds with each other. *See* Carla B. Garrity & Mitchell A. Baris, *Caught in the Middle* 27 (1994). Parents in the latter group are more likely to be struggling with issues such as intimate partner violence, substance abuse, serious mental illness, or child abuse.

The majority of parents reach agreement on parenting issues, and only a fraction of child custody disputes are resolved through trial. The published cases in this chapter arise from that small percentage of cases, and it is important to remember that they are atypical in that regard.

> **REFLECTIVE QUESTIONS** | What factors may affect a child when parents separate or divorce?

5.3 CONTEXT: ALTERNATIVE DISPUTE RESOLUTION PROCESSES

In recent years, court systems have adopted decision-making processes and approaches aimed at reducing conflict and helping parents establish workable post-divorce parenting relationships. *See* Joan B. Kelly & Robert Emery, *Children's Adjustment Following Divorce: Risk and Resilience Perspectives*, 52(4) Fam. Rel. 352 (2003). Processes such as parenting education, mediation, collaborative law, and cooperative negotiation equip some parents to fashion parenting arrangements tailored to meet the unique needs of their children. Because parents are most familiar with the needs of their children, they are most likely to know which arrangements will be workable for all concerned.

Some courts offer a continuum of processes and services for families. As a result, lawyers often work with other professionals and sometimes assume roles such as the following: parenting educator (offering programs designed to educate parents about the impact of divorce on children, parenting after divorce, and conflict resolution); mediator (a neutral third party who facilitates discussion so that parents can problem-solve and resolve conflicts); parenting coordinator (helps parents make day-to-day decisions about matters such as scheduling and transportation and in some cases exercises limited decision-making authority); best interests attorney/guardian *ad litem* (investigates, reports to the court, and advocates for the interests of the child); and attorney for the child (advocates based on the child's expressed wishes). These roles are discussed in more detail in Chapters 21 and 22.

While facilitative processes work well for many families, participation can be unsafe and ill advised for others. Consequently, parents must make informed decisions about whether and when to participate. For example, families whose members experience child abuse, intimate partner violence, substance abuse, or mental illness may require court intervention to provide safety and accountability. At any given time they may or may not be in a position to negotiate freely and make autonomous decisions in the long-term interests of children.

Attorneys play an important role in explaining dispute resolution processes to clients and helping them to decide which, if any, process might be beneficial. They also prepare clients to participate and they often represent clients during dispute resolution sessions.

REFLECTIVE QUESTIONS	How does representing a family law client in an alternative dispute resolution process differ from representing a client in a family court matter where the judge is the decision maker?

5.4 CONTEXT: INTIMATE PARTNER VIOLENCE PROTOCOLS

Domestic abuse may have a profound impact on children and must be taken into account when fashioning parenting and access arrangements. Consequently, all family lawyers should implement a protocol for screening for a history of intimate partner violence. Screening protocols offer multiple opportunities for disclosure and may involve a combination of confidential face-to-face interviews, use of questionnaires and screening tools, observation and check-in, and documentary review. Failing to implement a screening protocol in family practice may constitute attorney malpractice. *See* Margaret Drew, *Lawyer Malpractice and Domestic Violence: Are We Revictimizing Our Clients?*, 39 Fam. L.Q. 7 (2005).

If there is some indication that intimate partner violence may be an issue, an attorney should take steps to understand its nature and context, determine the implications for children and parenting, and account for it in child custody and access arrangements. Gabrielle Davis, *A Systematic Approach to Domestic Abuse-Informed Decision-Making in Family Law Cases*, 53 Fam. Ct. Rev. 562 (2015).

See also Peter Jaffe et al., *Custody Disputes Involving Allegations of Domestic Violence: Toward a Differentiated Approach to Parenting Plans*, 46 Fam. Ct. Rev. 500 (2008).

> **REFLECTIVE QUESTIONS** | Why is it important for family law attorneys to screen all clients for domestic violence?

5.5 PARENTING ARRANGEMENTS: LABELS AND TERMINOLOGY

Court orders regarding child custody and access have traditionally incorporated the following terms: *sole legal custody* (one parent has authority to make major decisions such as those regarding medical treatment, religion, and education); *joint legal custody* (parents share major decisions); *sole physical custody* (the child resides primarily with one parent who is responsible for routine daily care); and *joint physical custody* (the child maintains a residence in both homes). Some states have adopted parenting plan legislation under which parents may choose to forgo the use of traditional labels, create their own labels, or choose terms such as *on-duty* and *off-duty* parent or *residential* and *nonresidential* parent.

Parenting plans are written agreements, approved by the court, that contain parenting time schedules, decision-making protocols, parenting ground rules, mechanisms for dispute resolution, and financial arrangements for the child. Parenting plans vary substantially and may involve a high degree of co-parenting, or they may be drafted to ensure little, if any, contact between the parents.

The following list defines a continuum of typical parenting arrangements that may be captured under various labels and terminology: *co-parenting* (both parents parent cooperatively, sometimes in a joint legal and physical custody arrangement); *parallel parenting* (contact between the parents is minimized in order to protect the children from conflict); *supervised exchange* (physical exchange of the children takes place in the presence of a third party to avoid conflict or violence between the parents); *supervised access* (parenting time takes place in a supervised setting); and *no contact* (when children are at risk and no meaningful relationship is possible, parenting time may not be allowed). Peter Jaffe et al., *supra*. As discussed later in this chapter, families with a history of serious conflict, intimate partner violence, or child abuse and neglect require carefully structured parenting arrangements with an emphasis on safety.

> **REFLECTIVE QUESTIONS** | Do you favor the use of parenting plans? How detailed should they be? When might a parenting plan be too detailed?

Background to *Rivero v. Rivero*

As various parenting arrangements have proliferated, courts have struggled to capture them under traditional labels. As noted above, some states allow parents to create their own parenting labels and some commentators have endorsed doing away with labels altogether. In the case below, the Supreme Court of Nevada takes a different approach, one characterized by the dissent as overly formulaic.

RIVERO
v.
RIVERO

Supreme Court of Nevada
216 P.3d 213 (2009)

GIBBONS, J. We are asked to resolve several custody and support issues on appeal. Preliminarily, the parties dispute the definition of joint physical custody.

Although the divorce decree provided Ms. Rivero with custody five days each week and Mr. Rivero with custody two days each week, the district court concluded that the parties actually intended an equal timeshare. The district court noted that it was "just trying to find a middle ground" between what the divorce decree provided and what the parties actually wanted regarding a custody timeshare. Further, the court found that the decree's order for joint physical custody was inconsistent with the decree's timeshare arrangement because the decree's five-day, two-day timeshare did not constitute joint physical custody. In its order, the district court concluded that the parties intended joint physical custody and ordered an equal timeshare.

The Family Law Section requests that this court define all types of legal and physical custody to create a continuum in which it is clear where one type of custody ends and another begins. It argues that such definitions will provide much needed clarity and certainty in child custody law. Our discussion of child custody involves two distinct components of custody: legal custody and physical custody. The term "custody" is often used as a single legal concept, creating ambiguity. To emphasize the distinctions between these two types of custody and to provide clarity, we separately define legal custody, including joint and sole legal custody, and then we define physical custody, including joint physical and primary physical custody.

I. LEGAL CUSTODY

Legal custody involves having basic legal responsibility for a child and making major decisions regarding the child, including the child's health, education, and religious upbringing. Sole legal custody vests this right with one parent, while joint legal custody vests this right with both parents. Joint legal custody requires that the parents be able to cooperate, communicate, and compromise to act in the best interest of the child. In a joint legal custody situation, the parents must consult with each other to make major decisions regarding the child's upbringing, while the parent with whom the child is residing at that time usually makes minor day-to-day decisions.

Joint legal custody can exist regardless of the physical custody arrangements of the parties. Also, the parents need not have equal decision-making power in a joint legal custody situation. For example, one parent may have decision-making authority regarding certain areas or activities of the child's life, such as education or healthcare. If the parents in a joint legal custody situation reach an impasse and are unable to agree on a decision, then the parties may appear before the court "on an equal footing" to have the court decide what is in the best interest of the child.

II. PHYSICAL CUSTODY

Physical custody involves the time that a child physically spends in the care of a parent. During this time, the child resides with the parent and that parent provides supervision for the child and makes the day-to-day decisions regarding the child. Parents can share joint physical custody, or one parent may have primary physical custody while the other parent may have visitation rights.

The type of physical custody arrangement is particularly important in three situations. First, it determines the standard for modifying physical custody. Second, it requires a specific procedure if a parent wants to move out of state with the child. Third, the type of physical custody arrangement affects the child support award. Because the physical custody arrangement is crucial in making these determinations, the district courts need clear custody definitions in order to evaluate the true nature of parties' agreements. Absent direction from the Legislature, we define joint physical custody and primary physical custody in light of existing Nevada law.

A. Joint Physical Custody

Ms. Rivero and the Family Law Section assert that this court should clarify the definition of joint physical custody to determine whether it requires a specific timeshare agreement. The Family Law Section suggests that we define joint physical custody by requiring that each parent have physical custody of the child at least 40 percent of the time. In accordance with this suggestion, and for the reasons set forth below, we clarify Nevada's definition of joint physical custody pursuant to Nevada statutes and caselaw and create parameters to clarify which timeshare arrangements qualify as joint physical custody.

Although Nevada law suggests that joint physical custody approximates an equal timeshare, to date, neither the Nevada Legislature nor this court have explicitly defined joint physical custody or specified whether a specific timeshare is required for a joint physical custody arrangement. In fact, even the terminology is inconsistent. This court has used the following phrases to describe situations where both parents have physical custody: shared custodial arrangements, joint physical custody, equal physical custody, shared physical custody, and joint and shared custody. Given the various terms used to describe joint physical custody and the lack of a precise definition and timeshare requirement, we now define joint physical custody and the timeshare required for such arrangements.

1. Defining Joint Physical Custody

"In determining custody of a minor child . . . the sole consideration of the court is the best interest of the child." NRS 125.480(1). The Legislature created a presumption that joint legal and joint physical custody are in the best interest of the child if the parents so agree. The policy of Nevada is to advance the child's best interest by ensuring that after divorce "minor children have frequent associations and a continuing relationship with both parents . . . and [t]o encourage such parents to share the rights and responsibilities of child rearing." To further this policy, the Legislature adopted the statutes that now comprise NRS Chapter 125 to educate and encourage parents regarding joint custody arrangements, encourage parents to cooperate and work out a custody arrangement before going to court to finalize the divorce, ensure the healthiest psychological arrangement for children, and minimize the adversarial, winner-take-all approach to custody disputes.

Although NRS Chapter 125 does not contain a definition of joint physical custody, the legislative history regarding NRS 125.490 reveals the Legislature's understanding of its meaning. Joint physical custody is "[a]warding custody of the minor child or children to BOTH PARENTS and providing that physical custody shall be shared by the parents in such a way to ensure the child or children of frequent associations and a continuing relationship with both parents." This does not include divided or alternating custody, where each parent acts as a sole custodial parent at different times, or split custody, where one parent is awarded sole custody of one or more of the children and the other parent is awarded sole custody of one or more of the children.

2. The Timeshare Required for Joint Physical Custody

The question then remains, what constitutes joint physical custody to ensure the child frequent associations and a continuing relationship with both parents? Our law presumes that joint physical custody approximates a 50/50 timeshare. This court has noted that the public policy, as stated in NRS 125.490, is that joint custody is presumably in the best interest of the child if the parents agree to it and that this policy encourages *equally* shared parental responsibilities.

Although joint physical custody must approximate an equal timeshare, given the variations inherent in child rearing, such as school schedules, sports, vacations, and parents' work schedules, to name a few, an exactly equal timeshare is not always possible. Therefore, there must be some flexibility in the timeshare requirement. The question then becomes, when does a timeshare become so unequal that it is no longer joint physical custody? Courts have grappled with this question and come to different conclusions. For example, this court has described a situation where the children live with one parent and the other parent has every-other-weekend visitation as primary physical custody with visitation, even when primary custody was changed for one month out of the year and the other parent would revert back to weekend visitations. In *Wright*, 114 Nev. at 1368, 970 P.2d at 1071, this court described an arrangement where the parents had the children on a rotating weekly basis as joint physical custody.

Similarly, the California Court of Appeal has held that "[physical] custody one day per week and alternate weekends constitutes liberal visitation, not joint [physical] custody." *People v. Mehaisin*, 101 Cal. App. 4th 958, 124 Cal. Rptr. 2d 683, 687 (2002). Likewise, when the mother has temporary custody and the father has visitation for a one-month period, the parties do not have joint physical custody. Rather, the father has a period of visitation, and the mother has sole physical custody thereafter. Just as Nevada has defined joint physical custody as requiring an equal timeshare, the California Court of Appeal noted that joint physical custody includes situations in which the children split their time living with each parent and spend nearly equal time with each parent. Some jurisdictions have adopted bright-line rules regarding the timeshare requirements for joint physical custody so that anything too far removed from a 50/50 timeshare cannot be considered joint physical custody.

We conclude that, consistent with legislative intent and our caselaw, in joint physical custody arrangements, the timeshare must be approximately 50/50. However, absent legislative direction regarding how far removed from 50/50 a timeshare may be and still constitute joint physical custody, the law remains unclear. Therefore, to approximate an equal timeshare but allow for necessary flexibility, we hold that each parent must have physical custody of the child at least 40 percent of the time to constitute joint physical custody. We acknowledge that the Legislature is free to alter the timeshare required for joint physical custody, but we adopt this guideline to provide needed clarity for the district courts. This guideline ensures frequent associations and a continuing relationship with both parents. If a parent does not have physical custody of the child at least 40 percent of the time, then the arrangement is one of primary physical custody with visitation. We now address how the courts should calculate the 40-percent timeshare.

3. Calculating the Timeshare

The district court should calculate the time during which a party has physical custody of a child over one calendar year. Each parent must have physical custody of the child at least 40 percent of the time, which is 146 days per year. Calculating the timeshare over a one-year period allows the court to consider weekly arrangements as well as any deviations from those arrangements such as emergencies, holidays, and summer vacation. In calculating the time during which a party has physical custody of the child, the district court should look at the number of days during which a party provided supervision of the child, the child resided with the party, and during which the party made the day-to-day decisions regarding the child. The district court should not focus on, for example, the exact number of hours the child was in the care of the parent, whether the child was sleeping, or whether the child was in the care of a third-party caregiver or spent time with a friend or relative during the period of time in question.

Therefore, absent evidence that joint physical custody is not in the best interest of the child, if each parent has physical custody of the child at least 40 percent of the time, then the arrangement is one of joint physical custody.

B. Defining Primary Physical Custody

We now discuss primary physical custody to contrast it with joint physical custody and to clarify its definition. A parent has primary physical custody when he or she has physical custody of the child subject to the district court's power to award the other parent visitation rights. The focus of primary physical custody is the child's residence. The party with primary physical custody is the party that has the primary responsibility for maintaining a home for the child and providing for the child's basic needs. This focus on residency is consistent with NRS 125C.010, which requires that a court, when ordering visitation, specify the "habitual residence" of the child. Thus, the determination of who has primary physical custody revolves around where the child resides.

Primary physical custody arrangements may encompass a wide array of circumstances. As discussed above, if a parent has physical custody less than 40 percent of the time, then that parent has visitation rights and the other parent has primary physical custody. Likewise, a primary physical custody arrangement could also encompass a situation where one party has primary physical custody and the other party has limited or no visitation. . . .

PICKERING, J., concurring in part and dissenting in part.

I respectfully dissent. While I agree that this case presents an opportunity to establish helpful precedent, I disagree with the majority's assessment of the record facts and the law that should apply to them.

This appeal grows out of a stipulated divorce decree. Two family court judges upheld the decree's stipulation for joint physical custody. The only modification either judge made was to adjust the child's residential timeshare arrangement slightly. After taking testimony from the parents, both of whom work, the second judge determined that the parents' days off differed perfectly. Thus, each parent could have the child while the other was at work, minimizing the time the child had to spend in day care, if a one-day adjustment to the residential timeshare was made.

I do not find in the original stipulated decree the inflexible 5/2 timeshare the majority does. After providing for "joint legal custody and joint physical care, custody and control" of the parties' daughter, the original decree provided for the father to have the child "each Sunday at 7 P.M. until Tuesday at 9:00 P.M. *in addition to any time agreed on by the Parties."* (Emphasis added.) The residential timeshare, as adjusted, provided for the father to have the child from "Sunday at 1 P.M. until Wednesday at 2 P.M."—thus adding a day to the father's allotted two days and two hours per week but deleting the provision giving him such additional "time agreed on by the Parties" (who were having trouble agreeing to anything). The second family court judge made an express, on-the-record finding that, as adjusted, the residential timeshare arrangement was consistent with the stipulated decree's provision for joint physical custody—and in the child's best interest. The timeshare adjustment also obviated the mother's argument that the court should not have approved the stipulated decree's provision for a *Wright*-based offset, by which the parties had voluntarily agreed neither would pay child support to the other.

This strikes me as a sensible, maybe even Solomon-like solution. Instead of upholding the family court's exercise of sound discretion, however, the majority reverses and remands these parents to the family court for more litigation. On remand, the family court is directed to establish the exact percentage of time the child has spent with each parent over the course of the past year; to then apply a newly announced 40-percent formula on which joint physical custody and future child support will depend; and thereafter to enter formal findings, beyond those stated in the decree and in open court, respecting these and other matters.

I submit that this result and the underlying formula the majority adopts are contrary to statute and case precedent. The family court interpreted its decree in a way that was fair, supported by the record, and consistent with applicable law. A sounder result would be to recognize the distinction other courts have drawn between true custody modification and residential timeshare adjustments and support the family court's sound exercise of discretion as to the latter in this case.

DISCUSSION QUESTIONS FOR *RIVERO v. RIVERO*

A. According to the Supreme Court of Nevada, what is sole legal custody? What is sole physical custody? What is joint legal custody? What is joint physical custody? How can the arrangements be combined?

B. Why did the Family Law Section seek specific definition of "where one type of custody ends and another begins"?

C. What arguments are made by the dissent? Do you find them persuasive? Why?

D. Are bright-line approaches and definitions consistent with the notion of individualized determinations of custody and access?

E. How do you think the decision in this case will affect negotiation of custody and access issues? Does it encourage parents to apportion time mathematically rather than focus on the needs of children? In the alternative, does it clarify choices for parents?

F. Do custody and access labels matter? How?

G. The ALI refers to "custodial responsibility" rather than using the terms "custody" and "visitation." ALI, *Principles of the Law of Family Dissolution: Analysis and Recommendations* §2.03(3), comment 3 (2002). Do you agree with this approach? Why or why not?

5.6 HISTORICAL PRESUMPTIONS: PATERNAL, MATERNAL, PRIMARY CARETAKER

The effort to make individualized determinations concerning children's living arrangements following separation of the parents is a relatively recent development in the law. Historically, custodial arrangements were based on a one-size-fits-all approach involving presumptions. Historic presumptions restricted the exercise of judicial discretion by imposing custodial arrangements based on certain parental characteristics such as sex or caretaker status.

Background to *Ex parte Devine*

Under English common law, which was adopted by early American courts, fathers were presumed to be better able to care for minor children and they were consequently awarded legal and physical custody of them. However, by the 1930s, courts began adopting the "tender years" or maternal presumption. In the following case, *Ex parte Devine*, the Alabama Supreme Court considers whether the tender years doctrine violates the Equal Protection Clause of the Constitution. In its analysis, the court reviews common law presumptions, discusses the history of the tender years doctrine, and remands the case for an individualized consideration of the needs of the child. In its decision to abandon the tender years doctrine, the court creates a list of 12 factors for trial judges to consider when determining custody in divorce cases.

EX PARTE DEVINE
Supreme Court of Alabama
398 So. 2d 686 (1981)

Pursuant to Rule 10(e) of the Alabama Rules of Appellate Procedure, the petitioner/ father (appellant below) and respondent/mother (appellee below) filed the following stipulations of fact to serve in lieu of the record on appeal:

> [The parties] were married on December 17, 1966, and separated on March 29, 1979.
>
> The two children born of the parties during their marriage, viz: Matthew Patrick Devine, a son, born June 29, 1972, and Timothy Clark Devine, a son, born June 25, 1975 (the custody as to both of whom the Court has awarded to Alice Beth Clark Devine) are children of "tender years" as contemplated by the "tender years" doctrine or presumption.
>
> Alice Beth Clark Devine graduated from the Woman's College of Georgia in Milledgeville, Georgia, in 1962, receiving a B.S. degree with a major in Business Administration and a minor in Business Education. Since her graduation, Mrs. Devine has taught high school for 2 years at Margaret McAvoy High in Macon, Georgia; worked at the Georgia Rehabilitation Center for at least 2 years; was an instructor at the Augusta Area

Technical School in Georgia for 2 years; was an instructor trainer with the Army at Fort Gordon, Georgia for approximately 2 years; taught in high school at Notasulga, Alabama, for one year; directed a media library and taught classes for the Department of Rehabilitation at Auburn University for approximately 2 years; in 1975 commenced employment with the U.S. Army at Fort McClellan, Alabama, where she was employed continuously through the time of the trial of this cause as an Educational Specialist with a GS-11 rating earning in excess of $20,000 annually as salary (plus additional fringe benefits), and at the time of the trial Mrs. Devine indicated that she intended to remain employed at Fort McClellan or at some similar employment after the trial.

Mrs. Devine was 38 years of age at the time of the trial of this cause. Christopher P. Devine was born on January 15, 1937, and at the time of the trial he was a member of the faculty and head of the Guidance and Counseling Department at Jacksonville State University, Jacksonville, Alabama. At the time of the trial, the older son had just completed the first grade at the said University's Elementary Laboratory School and the younger son was enrolled in the said University's Nursery Laboratory School. . . .

[T]here exists in Alabama law a presumption that when dealing with children of tender years, the natural mother is presumed, in absence of evidence to the contrary, to be the proper person to be vested with custody of such children. This presumption, while perhaps weaker now than in the past, remains quite viable today. . . . Based upon the evidence presented at trial, the presumption of fitness discussed above and the court's opinion that it was in the children's best interest that they be in the custody of their mother, custody was placed subject to plaintiff's liberal visitation rights. . . .

The sole issue presented for review is whether the trial court's reliance on the tender years presumption deprived the father of his constitutional entitlement to the equal protection of the law. In resolving this issue, we feel it is necessary to consider the historical development of the tender years presumption and re-examine its modern efficacy in light of recent pronouncements by the United States Supreme Court.

At common law, it was the father rather than the mother who held a virtual absolute right to the custody of their minor children. This rule of law was fostered, in part, by feudalistic notions concerning the "natural" responsibilities of the husband at common law. The husband was considered the head or master of his family, and, as such, responsible for the care, maintenance, education and religious training of his children. By virtue of these responsibilities, the husband was given a corresponding entitlement to the benefits of his children, i.e., their services and association. It is interesting to note that in many instances these rights and privileges were considered dependent upon the recognized laws of nature and in accordance with the presumption that the father could best provide for the necessities of his children:

Undoubtedly, the father has primarily, by law as by nature, the right to the custody of his children. This right is not given him solely for his own gratification, but because nature and the law ratifying nature assume that the author of their being feels for them a tenderness which will secure their happiness more certainly than any other tie on earth. Because he is the father, the presumption naturally and legally is that he will love them most, and care for them most wisely. And, as a consequence of this, it is presumed to be for the real interest of the child that it should be in the custody of its father, as against collateral relatives, and he, therefore, who seeks to withhold the custody against the natural and legal presumption, has the burden of showing clearly that the father is an unsuitable person to have the custody of his child.

Hibbette v. Baines, 29 So. 80 (1900). As Chief Justice Sharkey more eloquently stated in his dissenting opinion in *Foster v. Alston*, 7 Miss. (6 How.) 406, 463 (1842):

> We are informed by the first elementary books we read, that the authority of the father is superior to that of the mother. It is the doctrine of all civilized nations. It is according to the revealed law and the law of nature, and it prevails even with the wandering savage, who has received none of the lights of civilization.

By contrast, the wife was without any rights to the care and custody of her minor children. By marriage, husband and wife became one person with the legal identity of the woman being totally merged with that of her husband. As a result, her rights were often subordinated to those of her husband and she was laden with numerous marital disabilities. As far as any custodial rights were concerned, Blackstone stated the law to be that the mother was "entitled to no power (over her children), but only to reverence and respect." 1 W. Blackstone, *Commentaries on the Law of England* 453 (Tucker ed. 1803).

By the middle of the 19th century, the courts of England began to question and qualify the paternal preference rule. This was due, in part, to the "hardships, not to say cruelty, inflicted upon unoffending mothers by a state of law which took little account of their claims or feelings." W. Forsyth, *A Treatise on the Law Relating to the Custody of Infants in Cases of Difference Between Parents or Guardians* 66 (1850). Courts reacted by taking a more moderate stance concerning child custody, a stance which conditioned a father's absolute custodial rights upon his fitness as a parent. Ultimately, by a series of statutes culminating with Justice Talfourd's Act, 2 and 3 Vict. c. 54 (1839), Parliament affirmatively extended the rights of mothers, especially as concerned the custody of young children. Justice Talfourd's Act expressly provided that the chancery courts, in cases of divorce and separation, could award the custody of minor children to the mother if the children were less than seven years old. This statute marks the origin of the tender years presumption in England.

In the United States the origin of the tender years presumption is attributed to the 1830 Maryland decision of *Helms v. Franciscus*, 2 Bland Ch. (Md.) 544 (1830). In *Helms*, the court, while recognizing the general rights of the father, stated that it would violate the laws of nature to "snatch" an infant from the care of its mother:

> The father is the rightful and legal guardian of all his infant children; and in general, no court can take from him the custody and control of them, thrown upon him by the law, not for his gratification, but on account of his duties, and place them against his will in the hands even of his wife. . . . Yet even a court of common law will not go so far as to hold nature in contempt, and snatch helpless, puling [whimpering] infancy from the bosom of

an affectionate mother, and place it in the coarse hands of the father. The mother is the softest and safest nurse of infancy, and with her it will be left in opposition to this general right of the father.

Thus began a "process of evolution, perhaps reflecting a change in social attitudes, (whereby) the mother came to be the preferred custodian of young children and daughters. . . ." Foster, *Life with Father: 1978*, 11 Fam. L.Q. 327 (1978). . . .

At the present time, the tender years presumption is recognized in Alabama as a rebuttable factual presumption based upon the inherent suitability of the mother to care for and nurture young children. All things being equal, the mother is presumed to be best fitted to guide and care for children of tender years. . . . To rebut this presumption the father must present clear and convincing evidence of the mother's positive unfitness. . . . Thus, the tender years presumption affects the resolution of child custody disputes on both a substantive and procedural level. Substantively, it requires the court to award custody of young children to the mother when the parties, as in the present case, are equally fit parents. Procedurally, it imposes an evidentiary burden on the father to prove the positive unfitness of the mother.

In recent years, the tender years doctrine has been severely criticized by legal commentators as an outmoded means of resolving child custody disputes. Several state courts have chosen to abandon or abolish the doctrine, noting that the presumption "facilitates error in an arena in which there is little room for error." *Bazemore v. Davis*, 394 A.2d 1377 (D.C. 1978). . . . Only one court has expressly declared the presumption unconstitutional. *State ex rel. Watts v. Watts*, 350 N.Y.S.2d 285 (1973). Nevertheless, some form of the presumption remains in effect in at least twenty-two states. In twenty states the doctrine has been expressly abolished by statute or court decision, and in four other states its existence is extremely questionable. In four states the presumption remains in effect despite a state's equal rights amendment or statutory language to the contrary. As far as Alabama is concerned, the trial court correctly noted that the presumption, "while perhaps weaker now than in the past, remains quite viable today."

It is safe to say that the courts of this state, like the courts of sister states, have come full circle in resolving the difficult questions surrounding child custody. At common law, courts spoke of the natural rights of the father. Now they speak of the instinctive role of the mother.

The question we are confronted with is not dissimilar to the question confronting the English courts over 150 years ago: Is it proper to deny a parent the custody of his or her children on the basis of a presumption concerning the relative parental suitability of the parties? More specifically, can the tender years presumption withstand judicial scrutiny under the Fourteenth Amendment to the United States Constitution as construed in recent decisions by the Supreme Court of the United States?

The appellate courts of this state have held that the tender years presumption is "not a classification based upon gender, but merely a factual presumption based upon the historic role of the mother," *Hammac v. Hammac*, 19 So. 2d 392 (1944). These statements indicate that the courts in the forties had not developed the sensitivity to gender-based classifications which the courts by the seventies had developed. In *Orr v. Orr*, 440 U.S. 268, (1979), the United States Supreme Court held that any statutory scheme which imposes obligations on husbands, but not on wives, establishes a classification based upon sex which is subject to scrutiny under the Fourteenth Amendment. The same must also be true for a legal presumption which imposes evidentiary burdens on fathers, but not on mothers. The fact that the presumption discriminates against men rather than women does not protect it from judicial scrutiny.

. . . [W]e conclude that the tender years presumption represents an unconstitutional gender-based classification which discriminates between fathers and mothers in child custody proceedings solely on the basis of sex. . . . [T]he tender years doctrine creates a presumption of fitness and suitability of one parent without any consideration of the actual capabilities of the parties. The tender years presumption, . . . imposes legal burdens upon individuals according to the "immutable characteristic" of sex. By requiring fathers to carry the difficult burden of affirmatively proving the unfitness of the mother, the presumption may have the effect of depriving some loving fathers of the custody of their children, while enabling some alienated mothers to arbitrarily obtain temporary custody. Even so, a gender-based classification, although suspect, may be justified if it is substantially related to a significant state interest.

Admittedly, the State has a significant interest in overseeing the care and custody of infants. In fulfilling this responsibility in child custody proceedings, the courts of this state, in custody determinations, have applied the "best interests of the child" rule. . . . We are convinced that the tender years presumption rejects the fundamental proposition . . . that "maternal and paternal roles are not invariably different in importance." . . . Even if mothers as a class were closer than fathers to young children, this presumption concerning parent-child relations becomes less acceptable as a basis for judicial distinctions as the age of the child increases. Courts have come to rely upon the presumption as a substitute for a searching factual analysis of the relative parental capabilities of the parties, and the psychological and physical necessities of the children. The presumption has thus become what one writer refers to as an "anodyne" for the difficult decisions confronting the court. Roth, *The Tender Years Presumption in Child Custody Disputes*, 15 J. Fam. L. 423, 438 (1976). However, as Justice White correctly observed in *Stanley v. Illinois*, 405 U.S. 645, (1972), "(p)rocedure by presumption is always cheaper and easier than individualized determination." In view of the fact that the welfare of children and competing claims of parents are at stake, such a means of determination cannot be justified.

The trial court's custody decree conclusively shows that the tender years presumption was a significant factor underlying the court's decision. Confronted with two individuals who were equally fit (i.e., all things being equal), the trial court awarded custody to the mother.

Accordingly, the judgment of the Court of Civil Appeals affirming the lower court decree and affirming the constitutionality of the tender years presumption is hereby reversed. The case is due to be remanded to the trial court with directions that the court consider the individual facts of the case. The sex and age of the children are indeed very important considerations; however, the court must go beyond these to consider the characteristics and needs of each child, including their emotional, social, moral, material and educational needs; the respective home environments offered by the parties; the characteristics of those seeking custody, including age, character, stability, mental and physical health; the capacity and interest of each parent to provide for the emotional, social, moral, material and educational needs of the children; the interpersonal relationship between each child and each parent; the interpersonal relationship between the children; the effect on the child of disrupting or continuing an existing custodial status; the preference of each child, if the child is of sufficient age and maturity; the report and recommendation of any expert witnesses or other independent investigator; available alternatives; and any other relevant matter the evidence may disclose. . . . Only in this way will the court truly consider the best interests of the Devine children.

TORBERT, CHIEF JUSTICE (dissenting).

The majority of the Justices on this Court have voted to abolish the tender years doctrine for all purposes in this state. I believe that decision goes too far, and I would retain the doctrine as a factor to be considered in deciding to which parent custody should be awarded.

The well-being of the child is the paramount consideration in determining its custody. The focus in a child custody hearing is on the child's welfare and best interest, not on the parents or their personal rights. Custody of one's child is not a prize to be fought for; rather it is a responsibility imposed by the court under appropriate conditions or restrictions the court sees fit to impose. . . . Gender may be an inappropriate factor to consider in bestowing a benefit, but it should be a factor in determining which parent will have primary custody of a very small child.

We are not faced here with the type of problem dealt with in *Orr*, *Frontiero*, and *Reed*, i.e., a rule by which one gender was given absolute preference over the other. The tender years doctrine, as the majority correctly stated, has evolved over the years into a factor to be considered in child custody determinations, rather than a compelling presumption. I believe it is valid as such, and should be retained in its present form.

 **FOR *EX PARTE DEVINE***

A. At common law, which parent had a virtual absolute right to custody of a minor child? How was this view of custody rationalized? What was Blackstone's view of the role of a mother relative to her children?

B. Trace the tender years doctrine to its origin.

C. Prior to this case, what burden of proof was required of a father to overcome the tender years doctrine? Did courts consider the tender years presumption to be a gender presumption?

D. The court stated that trial judges had improperly relied on the application of the tender years presumption. What was the basis for this criticism?

E. Does *Ex parte Devine* prohibit the trial court from considering the age of the children? Or, does it merely prohibit the consideration of a presumption in favor of the mother's custody based on the age of the children?

F. The dissenting judge argued that the majority decision went "too far" and that the tender years doctrine should be retained as one of many factors to be considered in awarding custody. Do you agree? *See* Alexandra Selfridge, *Equal Protection and Gender Preference in Divorce Contexts over Custody*, 16 J. Contemp. Legal Issues 165 (2007).

G. In the final paragraph of the decision, the court lists various factors for the lower court to consider in awarding custody. Assume that you are the judge when the case is remanded, and use the factors set forth by the Supreme Court to make a decision in the *Devine* case. What would you decide? Are there additional facts you would want to know?

H. List some of the benefits and costs of using presumptions to determine child custody. From a policy perspective, do you favor use of presumptions in custody cases? *See* Nancy Ver Steegh & Diana Gould-Saltman, *Joint Legal Custody Presumptions: A Troubling Legal Shortcut*, 52 Fam. Ct. Rev. 263 (2014).

Background to *Pikula v. Pikula*

As legislatures adopted the best interests test and courts repudiated the maternal preference, critics became concerned that long-term mother-child relationships would be uprooted and that children would be harmed as a result. Commentators predicted that fathers might threaten custody litigation in order to induce mothers to accept less than adequate financial settlements. As a result of these concerns and others, some states adopted a statutory preference in favor of the parent defined as the primary caretaker. In Minnesota, a presumption favoring the primary parent was adopted by the Minnesota Supreme Court in the 1985 case of *Pikula v. Pikula*, despite the fact that the term *primary caretaker* did not appear in the child custody statutes in force at the time. Although some states retain primary caretaker status as a best interests factor, it is no longer used as a preference. Nevertheless, the extent to which one parent has acted as the primary caretaker of young children may still be given significant weight by courts.

PIKULA
v.
PIKULA

Supreme Court of Minnesota
374 N.W.2d 705 (1985)

WAHL, J. This matter concerns the propriety of the custody award of two minor children in the judgment and decree dissolving the marriage of Kelly Jo Pikula and Dana David Pikula. Both parents sought custody of their daughters, aged 4 and 2. After a two day trial, the trial court awarded custody to Dana, the father.

Kelly and Dana Pikula were married on March 29, 1980, when Kelly was 17 and Dana 20. At the time of their marriage, their older daughter, Tiffany, was 8 months old. Prior to Tiffany's birth, Kelly and Dana had lived with Kelly's sister, Denise, in St. Paul. After the baby was born, the family moved to Brainerd, Dana's hometown, where they had frequent contact with Dana's parents and sisters. The Pikula family is closely knit, with Dana's parents at the center of the family. The family members visit each other frequently and spend holidays together. Two of the three adult Pikula children work for their father, and the parents continue to assist the adult children financially. Dana took a job with his father's trucking company, working a split shift as a driver. Kelly had a second daughter, Tanisha, in 1981, and finished high school while taking care of the children and managing the home.

[B]oth Kelly and Dana were imperfect parents. Dana and members of his family testified Kelly occasionally had trouble controlling her temper with the two girls, was somewhat ambivalent about her role as mother, and was a poor housekeeper. Kelly did not dispute she was sometimes dissatisfied and frustrated, but by her own account and by the testimony of Dana and his family, she was a good mother. She testified her dissatisfactions were rooted in her relationship with Dana and in Dana's problems with alcohol which at times resulted in physical displays of temper and verbal abuse. These problems persisted throughout the marriage and became particularly severe after Tanisha, their second child, was born. Dana was hospitalized during this period after injuring his hand by putting his fist through a door. He initially agreed to undergo counseling at that time, but soon stopped attending because he "didn't feel he had a problem with other people." He did attend AA meetings for a period, but began drinking again after five or six months. According to the report prepared by the custody evaluator, Dana continues to have problems with chemical dependency.

Kelly and her sisters also testified Dana's drinking in part precipitated the couple's separation. At the time Dana began drinking again, Dana forced Kelly and the children to leave her sister Renee's home in St. Paul where Kelly had been visiting with the children. Dana appeared at the house at around 9 P.M. and insisted Kelly and the girls leave immediately with him. When Kelly resisted, he took the children, put them in the car, and then dragged Kelly out of the house. In the meantime, Renee's boyfriend came out of the house and hit Dana on the arm with a baseball bat. Kelly said the children were watching this scene from the car, and once they were underway, Dana drove recklessly, shouted at her, and prevented her from comforting the children. Dana denies he used physical force, had trouble operating the car, or kept Kelly from the children. Kelly's sisters stated, though, they were sufficiently concerned to report the incident to the police.

Kelly did not remain in the home long after their return from St. Paul. She said Dana told her he was going to keep her there and he intended to take the children away so she would know what it was like to be alone. He was angry at her for not taking his side against her sister's boyfriend. Kelly then left the home and moved into the Women's Center of Mid-Minnesota, a shelter for battered women, where she continued to live until the time of the trial.

During this time, the couple agreed to a joint custody arrangement until custody was judicially determined. The arrangement was an uneasy one. For a time, the children remained in the family home while Kelly and Dana alternated living there on a four-day rotation schedule. Kelly began bringing the children to the shelter for her custody period, however, when tensions between Kelly and Dana escalated.

The recommendations of three professional social workers were also before the trial court. All three recommended that custody be awarded to Kelly. Social worker Jean Remke met with Kelly and Dana together or separately four times. In her view, both Kelly and Dana are somewhat emotionally immature. In Remke's opinion Kelly is "decidedly the most functional parent," because she seemed more capable of "putting herself aside to attend to the physical and emotional needs of others," while Dana repeatedly used the children in efforts to control their mother, and showed "no signs of really understanding this and no signs of altering his behavior."

Social worker Louise Seliskl had extensive contact with Kelly at the shelter, both through individual counseling and observation. Seliski also found Kelly had been a fit mother to the two girls and believed she would continue to provide a loving and supportive environment for them. She said she observed affection between Kelly and the children, that Kelly never used excessive discipline, and that the children were always clean. Seliski terminated therapy with Kelly because Kelly was "handling her life as well as anyone could expect her to handle it" and had no significant psychological problems or chemical dependency. It was Seliski's recommendation that custody be given to Kelly.

The reports prepared by Remke and Seliski were included in the custody evaluation prepared by social worker Nancy Archibald. The evaluation also included reports of interviews with the parties, their families, neighbors and friends, a church premarital evaluation, and letters of recommendation. In Archibald's opinion, the views expressed by Remke and Seliski were supported by her interviews with Kelly and Dana. She also recommended, based on all the data, that custody be awarded to Kelly with reasonable visitation provided to Dana.

Evidence was also introduced at trial concerning the custodial environment each parent would provide the children. Kelly testified she intended to move with the children to her sister's home in Maplewood until she could find employment and move into her own apartment. Dana objected to this plan, and testified that Kelly's sister had used marijuana and characterized some of her sister's friends as "bikers." Dana testified that he intended to remain in Brainerd if he were awarded custody of the girls. He continued to work a split shift at the time of trial, and his schedule required him to leave Brainerd at 3:00 A.M. for Wadena, lay over in Wadena from 7:00 A.M. until 3:00 P.M., and return to Brainerd at 7:00 P.M. Occasionally, he would return to Brainerd during his layover, permitting him to spend several hours at home. The child care responsibilities were principally borne by Dana's mother, however, and the children frequently spent the night with her and were cared for by her during the day.

Based on this record, the trial court initially made two key findings of fact in awarding custody to Dana. These [amended] findings stated as follows:

> . . . Amended Finding 11. That there is a strong, stable, religious family group relationship within the Pikula family, including respondent and the children, that has been developed, nurtured and cultivated over the years. It has stood like a bedrock through the depression years and post-war years of plenty and permissiveness. This environment has inbred in the family, including respondent, a unity, respect, loyalty and love that for the most part has been destroyed and lost in most modern American families. It is in the best interests and welfare of the children that their custody be awarded to respondent, who shares these attributes and who will assure that these children will be raised in the present cultural, family, religious and community environment of which they have been and are integral parts, which environment affords them stability, appropriate socializing and family orientation. The children are properly adjusted to their current home situation, broadly defined, and to the greater community within which they have lived virtually their entire lives, the children behave well and have extensive and qualitative contacts with significant persons within this environment, respondent's personal environment continues to stabilize and improve and is presently satisfactory, as well as gives indications of continuing stability, and it is desirable that the children's continuity with respondent and significant other persons and institutions here be maintained, respondent offering a permanent, well-established, concerned and involved, as well as supporting home for the children, the overall health of those who likely will here affect the mental, physical, emotional, educational, cultural and religious growth of the children is good, and respondent is inclined to, has and likely will continue to care for the children and raise them in their religion, creed and culture.
>
> Amended Finding 12. That the environment in which petitioner finds herself is almost the exact opposite of that in which respondent lives and will raise the children, it would subject the children to considerable uncertainty and instability in home, community, culture, persons and religion, should custody be awarded to petitioner, and further, such an award would disrupt, curtail and likely end the children's nurturing and constant contacts with the environment, persons and institutions now significantly and positively affecting their lives, petitioner's behavior and practices of child rearing as well as her interest in her children are at least subject to serious question and doubt, and it would not be in the children's best interest to award their custody to petitioner.

The Court of Appeals, in reversing, held that the trial court had abused its discretion in awarding custody of the children to Dana on the facts of this case. . . .

The trial court's findings regarding Kelly's fitness as a custodial parent are troubling in light of the whole record. The court found Kelly's environment would "subject the children to considerable uncertainty and instability in home, community, culture, persons and religion," that granting Kelly custody would sever the children's relationship with the Pikula family, and that Kelly's "behavior and practices of child rearing as well as her interest in her children are at least subject to serious question." Each of these findings was contradicted by evidence submitted by Kelly, and inconsistent with testimony from Dana and his family that Kelly was a good mother. In fashioning these findings, the trial court also discredited the custody evaluator's report and the recommendations of two other professional counselors. The trial court is not, however, bound to adhere to such expert testimony if it believes it is outweighed by other evidence. While the grounds for the trial court's failure to consider this evidence are not apparent, given our limited scope of review we cannot conclude there was not sufficient evidence on the record to outweigh it. We therefore hold that the evidence was adequate to support the findings which the trial court did make.

We conclude, however, that the trial court erred in determining that custody of the children should be awarded to Dana on the basis of the facts that were found. . . .

The guiding principle in all custody cases is the best interest of the child. The importance of emotional and psychological stability to the child's sense of security, happiness, and adaptation that we deemed dispositive in *Berndt* is a postulate embedded in the statutory factors and about which there is little disagreement within the profession of child psychology. For younger children in particular, that stability is most often provided by and through the child's relationship to his or her primary caretaker, the person who provides the child with daily nurturance, care and support. As we further noted in *Berndt* a court order separating a child from the primary parent could thus rarely be deemed in the child's best interests. Courts in three other states have reached similar conclusions in construing their custody statutes and rules. *Garska v. McCoy*, 278 S.E.2d 357 (W. Va. 1981); *In re Maxwell*, 456 N.E.2d 1218 (1982); *VanDyke v. VanDyke*, 618 P.2d 465 (1980); see also *Commonwealth ex rel. Jordan*, 448 A.2d 1113 (1982). . . . While at one time the tender years doctrine was universally adopted in the state courts, most jurisdictions have repudiated the doctrine as sex discriminatory. A recent survey of state laws lists 38 states which have rejected the presumption, four which retain "tiebreaker" versions, and eight states with doubtful or unique laws.

The primary parent preference, while in accord with the tender years doctrine insofar as the two rules recognize the importance of the bond formed between a primary parent and a child, differs from the tender years doctrine in significant respects. Most importantly, the primary parent rule is gender neutral. Either parent may be the primary parent; the rule does not incorporate notions of biological gender determinism or sex stereotyping. In addition, the rule we fashion today, we believe will encourage co-parenting in a marriage unlike the tender years doctrine which, for fathers, meant that whatever function they assumed in the rearing of their children would be deemed irrelevant in a custody contest.

We follow the reasoning of those states in adopting the rule that when both parents seek custody of a child too young to express a preference, and one parent has been the primary caretaker of the child, custody should be awarded to the primary caretaker absent a showing that parent is unfit to be the custodian.

Continuity of care with the primary caretaker is not only central and crucial to the best interest of the child, but is perhaps the single predicator of a child's well-being about which there is agreement, and which can be competently evaluated by judges. The other indicia of a child's best interests set forth in section 518.17, while plainly relevant to a child's well-being and security, are, by contrast, both inherently resistant of evaluation and difficult to apply in any particular case. Subdivision 1 (g) and (h) require judges to assess the proposed custodians' "mental and physical health," and "capacity and disposition" to give the child "love, affection, and guidance." A trial court is further required to consider all other "relevant factors" in reaching its decision. We are mindful that trial courts, seeking to apply these factors to reach an intelligent determination of relative degrees of fitness, must aspire to a "precision of measurement which is not possible given the tools available to the judges." Moreover, as one author has observed, "[e]mpirical findings directly or indirectly relevant to questions for which judges deciding difficult [custody] cases need answers are virtually nonexistent." The legislature, in enacting Minn. Stat. §518.167 (1984), which permits trial courts to order professional custody evaluations, has recognized the special needs of judges in that regard. That custody evaluations may not adequately provide a judge with such needed insight in particular cases, however, is embedded in the rule that such evaluations may be disregarded when outweighed by other evidence.

This inherent lack of objective standards aside from primary parent status in custody determinations has several related effects which are not in the best interests of children. Imprecision in the application of the law may result in "wrong" results, and in unpredictability of outcome. Parents already estranged may be tempted to use a threatened custody contest strategically when neither parent can predict with any certainty which parent will ultimately be awarded custody. The availability of such strategies cannot in any sense be viewed as in the best interests of the children involved.

This situation is exacerbated by the fact that the two parents may be unequally situated with respect to other matters at issue in the negotiation process. A parent who has remained at home throughout a marriage to raise the children will often have sacrificed economic and educational opportunities in order to perform that role, and he or she will likely be in greater need of economic support upon dissolution of a marriage. A spouse in that position has only one issue available to "concede" in the division of marital assets: custody of the children. At the same time, as the *Garska* court observed, "uncertainty of outcome is very destructive of the position of the primary caretaker parent because he or she will be willing to sacrifice everything in order to avoid the terrible prospect of losing the child in the unpredictable process of litigation." Moreover, in practical fact, many primary caretakers may simply be unable to afford the expense of litigation at all, further weakening their bargaining position when the uncertainty in the outcome of a trial is necessarily high. The rule we fashion today should largely remove the issue of custody from the arena of dispute over such matters, and prevent the custody determination from being used in an abusive way to affect the level of support payments and the outcome of other issues in the proceeding.

The inherent imprecision heretofore present in our custody law has, in turn, diminished meaningful appellate review. We have repeatedly stressed the need for effective appellate review of family court decisions in our cases, and have required specificity in written findings based on the statutory factors. We are no less concerned that the legal conclusion reached on the basis of those findings be subject to effective review. We recognize the inherent difficulty of principled decision making in this area of the law. Legal rules governing custody awards have generally incorporated evaluations of parental fitness replete with ad hoc judgments on the beliefs, lifestyles, and perceived credibility of the proposed custodian. It is in these circumstances that the need for effective appellate review is most necessary to ensure fairness to the parties and to maintain the legitimacy of judicial decision making.

For these reasons, the recognized need for stability in children's lives, the uncertainty of other indicia of a child's best interests in custody decisions, and the pressing need for coherent decision making on the trial court level and for effective appellate review—we hold the factors set forth in section 518.17, subd.1, require that when both parents seek custody of a child too young to express a preference for a particular parent and one parent has been the primary caretaker, custody be awarded to the primary parent absent a showing that parent is unfit to be the custodian. We adopt the indicia of primary parenthood set forth in *Garska* to aid trial courts in determining which, if either, parent is the primary caretaker:

> While it is difficult to enumerate all of the factors which will contribute to a conclusion that one or the other parent was the primary caretaker parent, nonetheless, there are certain obvious criteria to which a court must initially look. In establishing which natural or adoptive parent is the primary caretaker, the trial court shall determine which parent has taken primary responsibility for, inter alia, the performance of the following caring and nurturing duties of a parent:
>
> 1. preparing and planning of meals;
> 2. bathing, grooming and dressing;
> 3. purchasing, cleaning, and care of clothes;
> 4. medical care, including nursing and trips to physicians;
> 5. arranging for social interaction among peers after school, i.e., transporting to friends' houses or, for example, to girl or boy scout meetings;
> 6. arranging alternative care, i.e., baby sitting, day-care, etc.;
> 7. putting child to bed at night, attending to child in the middle of the night, waking child in the morning;
> 8. disciplining, i.e., teaching general manners and toilet training;
> 9. educating, i.e., religious, cultural, social, etc.; and,
> 10. teaching elementary skills, i.e., reading, writing and arithmetic. . . .

When the facts demonstrate that responsibility for and performance of child care was shared by both parents in an entirely equal way, then no preference arises and the court must limit its inquiry to other indicia of parental fitness. Once the preference does arise, however, the primary parent should be given custody unless it is shown that the child's physical or emotional health is likely to be endangered or impaired by being placed in the primary parent's custody.

The indicia of primary parenthood set forth above make plain that a parent who has performed the traditional role of homemaker will ordinarily be able to establish primary parent status in a custody proceeding involving young children. That this is so reflects no judgment by this court on the competence or fitness of parents who choose or are compelled to fashion less traditional divisions of labor within a family. Our decision today merely encompasses our understanding of the traumatic impact on children of separation from the primary caretaker parent. Nor do we mean to suggest that a parent who works outside the home may not be deemed the primary parent. We would expect that, as between any two parents, one will be the primary parent even if neither conforms to the more traditional pattern of one parent working outside the home and one within it.

Turning to the facts of this case, we conclude that the matter must be remanded for a determination of which, if either, parent was the primary caretaker of the children at the time the dissolution proceeding was commenced.

The Court of Appeals is affirmed in part in reversing the trial court's award of custody to the father, reversed in part in awarding custody to the mother, and the matter is remanded for proceedings consistent with the rule set out in this opinion.

DISCUSSION QUESTIONS FOR *PIKULA v. PIKULA*

A. What was the court's holding? Based on the facts presented, which parent would you characterize as the primary parent?

B. What objective criteria did the court develop to identify the parent who has functioned as the primary caretaker?

C. What does the court see as the single crucial predictor of a child's well-being?

D. How does the court see the application of the primary caretaker doctrine affecting a custody decision where the two parents are financially or otherwise unequally situated?

E. Could a parent who works outside the home be considered to be the primary caretaker of young children? Why or why not?

F. Five years after the decision was announced, the Minnesota legislature eliminated the primary caretaker presumption. What arguments must have persuaded the legislature to take this course of action?

G. How does the primary caretaker presumption differ from the tender years doctrine?

H. The court suggests that the absence of objective standards in custody disputes has several unrelated effects. What are those effects?

I. The American Law Institute (ALI) urges parents to create a parenting plan voluntarily at the time of divorce. However, if the parties do not agree, the ALI proposes allocating parental responsibility to "approximate" the proportion of caretaking done by each parent prior to the divorce. How does this approach compare to the primary caretaker presumption? *See* ALI, *Principles of the Law of Family Dissolution: Analysis and Recommendations* §2.08 (2002). West Virginia, which previously used the primary caretaker presumption, has adopted a modified version of the approximation standard. W. Va. Code §48-9-206 (2011).

J. The trial court decided not to accept the recommendation of three experts. What was the basis for the recommendations of these experts? The court states: "Moreover, as one author has observed, '[e]mpirical findings directly or indirectly relevant to questions for which judges deciding difficult [custody] cases need answers are virtually nonexistent.'" If that was the case in 1985, has the situation changed? What is the role of empirical research in the family court? The court bases its decision on the need for children to have stability and continuity of care. Should the court provide an empirical basis for concluding that stability and continuity of care are more important for children than factors such as frequent contact with both parents?

5.7 BEST INTERESTS STANDARD: THE ROLE OF THE EXPERT

Background to *McIntosh v. McIntosh*

As the tender years maternal preference fell into disuse, the best interests of the child test was widely adopted and remains the dominant legal standard today. Typical statutes based on the Uniform Marriage and Divorce Act (UMDA) §402 list various factors for the court and the parties to consider in making a case-by-case determination concerning the needs of the child or children.

The factors are intended to guide exercise of judicial discretion, but in practice their application can be challenging. Judges sometimes feel ill-equipped to make determinations and they sometimes seek expert evaluation by a neutral mental health professional. The following case provides an example of judicial analysis of statutory best interest factors and illustrates the role of expert testimony in the process.

McINTOSH
v.
McINTOSH

Court of Appeals of Michigan
768 N.W.2d 325 (2009)

KELLY, J.

I. BASIC FACTS AND PROCEDURAL HISTORY

The parties met in the early 1990s when defendant was plaintiff's boss at a Hot 'n Now business. At the time, defendant had a son, Keegan, from a previous relationship. The parties lived together before getting married on October 2, 2004. Their son, Jordan, was born on May 5, 2006.

On July 5, 2007, plaintiff filed his verified complaint for divorce and moved for an *ex parte* order awarding him sole legal and physical custody of Jordan. He alleged that the parties separated on May 31, 2007, and that because of Keegan's presence in the home, he feared for his and Jordan's safety. On July 5, 2007, the trial court entered an *ex parte* order awarding the parties joint custody of Jordan, with Jordan's residence to be with plaintiff and for defendant to have reasonable parenting time. Defendant was precluded from overnight parenting time when Keegan was present. . . . The trial court ultimately entered a consent order modifying the *ex parte* order to provide for an equal division of physical custody.

Numerous difficulties arose with respect to the parenting time schedule, resulting in several show cause hearings and in parenting time exchanges occurring at the local police station. The trial court referred the case to the Kalamazoo County FOC for a child custody and parenting time evaluation and recommendation. Laura Kracker, a limited license psychologist at Kalamazoo Psychology, L.L.C., performed psychological evaluations of the parties. In the final report, Kracker recommended that the parties continue to share joint legal and physical custody of Jordan. . . . On April 8, 2008, in a written opinion, the trial court awarded defendant sole legal and physical custody of Jordan.

III. PSYCHOLOGICAL EVALUATION

Plaintiff argues that the trial court erred by "ignoring" and refusing to implement the recommendation from the psychological evaluation, which recommended continuing the shared 50/50 custodial arrangement. We disagree. Plaintiff mistakes the proper use and role of a psychological evaluation. While trial courts may consider psychological evaluations, and, at their discretion, afford them the weight they deem appropriate in accord with the Michigan Rules of Evidence, psychological evaluations are not conclusive on any one issue or child custody factor. The ultimate resolution of any child custody dispute rests with the trial court. (See "[T]he Child Custody Act [MCL 722.21 et seq.] requires the circuit court to determine independently what custodial placement is in the best interests of the children.")

In declining to adopt the recommendation of the FOC report and psychological report, the trial court stated:

> This case had a lot of contact with the Court since the summer of 2007. And as cases go, documents were filed by both sides and there were conferences by both sides. What was very evident throughout this entire case from the very beginning of the filing of the complaint of—for divorce, up until the closing argument of counsel was that the father, Plaintiff in this case, was on a very focused mission to remain in control of the case and at all costs the child of the parties to the extent that he denied the child seeing the mother in the beginning of the case and for periods of time until an order was entered saying that the mother was to be allowed to see the child.
>
> I will confess that none of that quite hit home to this judge until the actual trial, until I heard the parties testify. I was greatly impacted by the testimony in this case in my decision and the evidence. As far as I understand, the law in Michigan, there is nothing that says that a judge making a custody decision has to rubberstamp what the Friend of the Court evaluation does and, in fact, sadly what I am learning by my number of years on the bench is that many times these evaluators that we trust to give us an open-minded opinion, what they end up doing is rubberstamping temporary orders that are issued by Courts on very limited information or temporary orders that are entered because the parties agree on something in the beginning of the case.
>
> I was not expecting the testimony or the evidence that I got at trial. At the most, I think at the most, [plaintiff's counsel] would have to be—acknowledge this, at the most, I said probably will follow the recommendation of joint. Probably, because that's very often what I do, and if they had a 50/50 situation, that's probably the way the evidence would be. That's probably the most that I said because that's how I saw it at the time before trial, and I fully expected that the end result, that we would have wasted our time at trial, I fully expected that the end result would be that I would say, okay, I've heard all this testimony. Now the father's gonna have 50-percent of the time and mother's gonna have 50-percent of the time, which was recommended.
>
> Instead, when I reflected on the testimony and the evidence, and went back to the pleadings in this case, I was shocked. Totally shocked to see that it was not meritorious at all to agree with the Friend of the Court evaluation, and there's nothing under the law that says I have to agree. . . .

We commend the learned trial court's reasoning in this matter. Although the parties' agreement to admit Kracker's report allowed the trial court to *consider* the psychological evaluation, the trial court, as it recognized, was not in any way compelled to adopt its recommendation. Rather, a trial court may consider all the competent evidence presented at the hearing in arriving at its own custody decision and give each the weight as it deems appropriate. . . . Here, the trial court properly considered the psychological evaluation in light of all the other evidence presented and determined that the FOC's recommendation was not appropriate. The trial court did not err by refusing to implement the FOC's recommendation.

IV. AWARD OF SOLE LEGAL AND PHYSICAL CUSTODY

In order to resolve a child custody dispute, a trial court must evaluate the best interests of the child in light of the factors in MCL 722.23:

"[B]est interests of the child" means the sum total of the following factors to be considered, evaluated, and determined by the court:

(a) The love, affection, and other emotional ties existing between the parties involved and the child.

(b) The capacity and disposition of the parties involved to give the child love, affection, and guidance and to continue the education and raising of the child in his or her religion or creed, if any.

(c) The capacity and disposition of the parties involved to provide the child with food, clothing, medical care or other remedial care recognized and permitted under the laws of this state in place of medical care, and other material needs.

(d) The length of time the child has lived in a stable, satisfactory environment, and the desirability of maintaining continuity.

(e) The permanence, as a family unit, of the existing or proposed custodial home or homes.

(f) The moral fitness of the parties involved.

(g) The mental and physical health of the parties involved.

(h) The home, school, and community record of the child.

(i) The reasonable preference of the child, if the court considers the child to be of sufficient age to express preference.

(j) The willingness and ability of each of the parties to facilitate and encourage a close and continuing parent-child relationship between the child and the other parent or the child and the parents.

(k) Domestic violence, regardless of whether the violence was directed against or witnessed by the child.

(l) Any other factor considered by the court to be relevant to a particular child custody dispute.

Plaintiff has not challenged the trial court's finding that the parties were equal with respect to a number of best interests factors in MCL 722.23. Specifically, plaintiff only challenges the trial court's findings with respect to best interests factors f, j, k, and l, primarily on the basis of the trial court's finding that plaintiff is an alcoholic. Plaintiff asserts that there is not a scintilla of competent evidence to establish his alcoholism. We disagree.

Plaintiff has a long history of alcohol use. Defendant testified that plaintiff's alcohol use was a problem even before the marriage. She testified that he became violent and angry when he drank. She found out when they were seeing a marriage counselor that plaintiff was hiding liquor at the marital residence. In the beginning of 2007, plaintiff admitted that he was an alcoholic and he had a relapse in May 2007. On one occasion, defendant found plaintiff passed out in bed with a bottle of vodka next to him. On the date of the "first exchange" for defendant to have overnight parenting time with Jordan, she could tell that plaintiff had been drinking from the way that he tossed Jordan in the air and because she could "smell it" and saw that his eyes were glassy. Plaintiff also testified that he abused alcohol for a while, but only classified a four- to six-month period as a "problem." He conceded hiding alcohol and attending Alcoholics Anonymous (AA) meetings for seven or eight months beginning in January 2007. He also planned to attend additional AA meetings.

The trial court properly considered this evidence in evaluating factor f, "[t]he moral fitness of the parties involved." MCL 722.23(f). Our Supreme Court has indicated that having a drinking problem is a type of conduct that bears on how one functions as a parent, which can be considered under the moral fitness factor. Giving deference to the trial court's assessment of the credibility of witnesses, its finding that this factor should favor defendant on the basis of plaintiff's unresolved alcohol problem is not against the great weight of the evidence.

Plaintiff's challenge to the trial court's finding on factor j, "willingness and ability of each of the parties to facilitate and encourage a close and continuing parent-child relationship between the child and the other parent . . . ," MCL 722.23(j), is without merit. The trial court mentioned plaintiff's "controlling behavior and alcoholic behavior, at this point" in finding that plaintiff "would do everything in his power to interfere with and upset the parent/child relationship of the mother." Moreover, the trial court considered the entire case history in concluding that this factor favored defendant. Plaintiff was found to have withheld Jordan from defendant without cause, to have reported defendant to the police and protective services, and, "overall, [to have] behaved in a manner designed to cause upset, and influence the mother/child relationship in this case." The trial court made other findings with respect to the proceedings, which included its entry of an *ex parte* order in November 2007 for plaintiff to return Jordan to defendant. Considering the evidence as a whole, the trial court's decision to weigh factor j in favor of defendant is not against the great weight of the evidence. There was record evidence to support the trial court's finding that plaintiff was unwilling or unable to facilitate and encourage a close relationship between defendant and Jordan.

With respect to factor k, "[d]omestic violence, regardless of whether the violence was directed against or witnessed by the child," MCL 722.23(k), the trial court found:

> There was evidence that there was at least one incident of domestic violence in the home perpetrated by the father against the mother. This is not surprising given his testimony regarding his relationship with alcohol. There was at least one conviction for domestic violence in the history of their relationship. Although the father tried to show that the mother had violent behavior, the only testimony was that she threw a glass at the father on one occasion. There was no other testimony of domestic violence perpetrated by the mother against the father.
>
> The mother testified that the father had been abusive throughout the marriage, which would explain in part the apparent traumatized behavior of the older boy in the home.

Considering defendant's testimony that she was physically assaulted by plaintiff, as well as plaintiff's own testimony admitting that he was "probably" physically assaultive toward defendant on two occasions, we find no basis for disturbing the trial court's finding that the domestic violence factor favored defendant.

Factor l is "[a]ny other factor considered by the court to be relevant to a particular child custody dispute." MCL 722.23(l). Factor l is a "catch-all" provision. Contrary to plaintiff's argument on appeal, the trial court did not expressly weigh this factor in favor of defendant. Rather, the court used factor l to comment on various matters, including the parties' love for their son and plaintiff's conduct during this case, which were already considered under other factors or affected its decision to change the joint custody arrangement. The trial court also used factor I to comment on arguments raised at trial regarding defendant's parenting skills with respect to her teenaged son, finding that plaintiff also had substantial involvement in the teenaged son's life before and after plaintiff became his stepfather, but did not weigh any "parenting skills" factor in favor of either party. It also addressed relevant circumstances when assessing the "[a]ny other factor" in MCL 722.23(l). It found that plaintiff, "failed, to this date, to understand or admit how inappropriate his behavior was at the time of the initial filing of this case, and how it resulted in an act of cruelty perpetrated on the minor child." Overall, the trial court's findings with respect to factor I are consistent with its decision to weigh the parties the same with respect to the love and affection factor in MCL 722.23(a) and the "guidance" factor in MCL 722.23(b), but to weigh factor j in favor of defendant. We are not persuaded that the trial court's findings with respect to factor I are against the great weight of the evidence.

Considering the circumstances and evidence presented, the court did not abuse its discretion by finding clear and convincing evidence to award defendant sole legal and physical custody.

DISCUSSION QUESTIONS FOR *McINTOSH v. McINTOSH*

A. What best interests factors were in dispute? Do you agree with the judge's application of the factors to the facts in this case?

B. Given the facts of this case, what arguments might each parent make with respect to the best interests factors not specifically analyzed on appeal?

C. In your view is the statutory list of factors adequate? What factors would you add or delete?

D. What is the standard of review on appeal? Why does the appellate court give so much deference to the findings of the trial court?

E. Despite the popularity and sex-neutral approach of the best interests standard, critics allege that it promotes litigation because outcomes are difficult to predict with accuracy. Do you favor continued use of the best interests test? If so, why? If not, what standard would you use instead?

F. What is the appropriate role of expert testimony in child custody decision making? What arguments can you make in support of the idea that judges should defer to expert opinion? What arguments can you make in support of limiting the role experts play in custody and access cases? Are there due process considerations?

G. Sometimes parents retain a mental health professional to help craft parenting arrangements and advise them concerning the needs of their children at the time of separation or divorce. How does this professional role differ from that of performing a court ordered custody evaluation?

H. One of the factors to be considered in this case was "moral fitness of the parties." Do you agree with the trial court that an alcohol problem is evidence of moral unfitness? How much time would need to go by without incident before moral fitness might be viewed as restored?

5.8 BEST INTERESTS STANDARD: THE NEXUS TEST AND POST-SEPARATION SEXUAL RELATIONSHIPS

Background to *Piatt v. Piatt*

Under the Uniform Marriage and Divorce Act (UMDA), courts deciding custody cases are discouraged from considering parental conduct that does not have a nexus to the parent's relationship with the child. Section 402 states: "The court shall not consider conduct of a proposed custodian that does not affect his relationship to the child." This "nexus test" is sometimes applied in cases involving subsequent sexual relationships of either or both parents. In *Piatt v. Piatt*, the court considers the relevance of the post-separation relationships of the parents.

PIATT
v.
PIATT

Court of Appeals of Virginia
499 S.E.2d 567 (1998)

FITZPATRICK, J. . . . The parties' settlement agreement . . . provided that a custody evaluation would be performed by Dr. Christopher D. Lane. In his report, Dr. Lane recommended that the parties share joint legal custody and that wife have primary physical custody with liberal visitation for husband. Dr. Lane based his recommendation in part on "the assessment of [wife's] parenting abilities as being demonstrably broader in scope at this time than those of Mr. Piatt and in the perceived greater responsiveness of [the child] to her." Dr. Lane also testified that his assessment of both parties' parenting skills and commitment to parenting "would be consistent with a high level of devotion to the care of [the] child."

At trial, both parents presented evidence concerning their post-separation relationships with third parties. The evidence established that husband had been involved in one heterosexual relationship and wife had participated in two homosexual relationships following the parties' separation. Husband and his female friend testified that their involvement was serious, and they planned marriage with the full support of husband's family. Wife acknowledged that she was "experimenting" and still dealing with the issue of her sexual orientation, and that as a result, her relationship with her father had been damaged.

Dr. Lane filed a supplemental report in which he reviewed several studies on the effects of homosexuality on children. He testified that "[t]here seems to be no credible documentation of damage to children" from being raised by a homosexual parent. Dr. Lane also indicated that wife "is still struggling with her own sexual identity," and her "family is reverberating" from her "very angry estrangement from her father."

The trial court ruled from the bench, finding that wife "is still in a turmoil, which is continuing and has continued over the last two years. This turmoil is as to her sexual orientation and how her life should go forward." The court agreed with Dr. Lane that "both parents have good parenting skills. They both love their daughter, and their daughter loves both of them." However, the trial court expressed doubt about the credibility of wife's testimony and concluded:

> I have to balance these things out. And there is no easy answer, but I believe that the father is better qualified at this point to be the primary caretaker of the child. I believe there is more stability in his surroundings and in his home. There is support on both sides of the family, but there is probably a little bit more support on the side of the father. . . .
>
> I am going to make it joint custody, because I do not want anybody to think that they do not have a say in raising the child. The primary custodian will be the father.

The trial court awarded joint legal custody of the child, with husband having primary physical custody and wife having ten days per month visitation plus vacations and alternate holidays.

Wife contends the trial court erred in treating her two post-separation relationships as having an adverse effect upon the child, but not so treating husband's relationship. However, the record discloses no finding that either party's post-separation sexual behavior had an adverse effect upon the child. Rather, the trial court treated the parties' post-separation sexual behavior as evidence supporting its conclusion that husband provided a more stable home environment for the child. Consequently, wife's contention is without merit. . . .

In general, a court examines the sexual conduct of a parent to determine whether it has had any adverse impact on the child. *See Brown v. Brown*, 199, 237 S.E.2d 89, 91 (1977) ("in determining the best interest of the child, the court must decide by considering all the facts, including what effect a nonmarital relationship by a parent has on the child"). Here both parents' relationships were facts for the trial court to consider, but the record does not reflect that those relationships provided the basis for the custody award.

The trial court referred to wife's post-separation sexual relationships and her "experimentation" not as having a direct negative impact on the child, but as manifestations of wife's inner "turmoil" and "lack of control." These characteristics have a direct bearing on wife's ability to provide a stable home environment and to "meet the emotional, intellectual and physical needs of the child." . . .

The evidence supports the trial court's conclusion that wife's home environment was less stable than husband's. The record demonstrates that wife often left the child in the care of others while she pursued recreational trips and activities. She occasionally took the child with her without regard to the child's bedtime or evening routine. Wife was unsure whether she would remain in her condo after the one-year lease ended. She dated several individuals and admitted to two sexual relationships. Furthermore, wife's family relationships were strained.

The court contrasted the stability of wife's home environment with that provided by husband. The evidence shows that husband developed a routine for the child. He maintained his residence in the marital home, where the child had lived her entire life. He was involved in a long-term relationship with another woman and was planning for marriage. He had the full support of his parents and his brother and sister-in-law. His relatives provided day care for the child and her young cousin.

All of these facts led the trial court to conclude that, while it was clear that neither parent was unfit, husband could provide a more stable environment for the child. The trial court recognized the commitment of both parents to the child by ordering joint custody, and the physical custody arrangement provided wife with liberal visitation. The parties acknowledged that their previous shared custody arrangement failed. Credible evidence supports the trial court's award of joint custody with primary placement of the child with husband. . . .

For the foregoing reasons, we affirm.

ANNUNZIATA, J., dissenting.

. . . The evidence shows, as wife contends, that the trial court treated wife's sexual conduct differently from that of husband. First, the trial court's finding that wife had engaged in "promiscuity while still married," but that husband had not, is not supported by the evidence. . . . Neither party's relationships could reasonably be described from the record as "indiscriminate," "frequent and diverse," or "transient." In fact, the relationship in which wife was involved at the time of the hearing had lasted five months longer than husband's relationship. Wife's first relationship ended before her second relationship began. The record contains no evidence of other sexual relationships by either party. The court's assignment of the label of "promiscuity" to wife's two serial, monogamous relationships, to distinguish her conduct from that of husband, is not supported by the evidence.

. . . The record contains no evidence that wife's conduct, comprised [*sic*] of two same-sex relationships in eighteen months, had any effect on the parties' child. At the time of the hearing, the child was less than four years old, and neither party introduced evidence that the child was aware of wife's relationships. Husband testified that, to his knowledge, wife had never exposed the child to any intimate relationship with another woman. Indeed, the evidence affirmatively proved that no displays of affection of a sexual nature took place between wife and her partner in front of the child, that wife's partner did not live at the wife's home, and that wife had no plans to have her partner live in the home at any time. While the evidence showed that wife was "struggling" with her sexual identity, no evidence proved that the wife's "struggle" affected her ability to parent the child. Indeed, the evidence is to the contrary. Not only did expert testimony establish that wife's parenting skills were "demonstrably broader in scope . . . than those of [husband]," the court found the wife's parenting skills were equal to those of the husband. The absence of evidence showing any effect of wife's sexual conduct on the child supports wife's contention that the trial judge applied different standards when evaluating the parties' post-separation sexual conduct.

DISCUSSION QUESTIONS FOR *PIATT v. PIATT*

A. Did the trial court make a finding that the wife's sexual behavior adversely affected the child? How did the trial court link the wife's post-separation sexual relationships to the child?

B. What facts seemed to persuade the appellate court that primary placement of the child with the father was in the child's best interests?

C. In her dissent, Judge Annuziata states that there is no evidence indicating that the wife's same-sex relationships had an effect on the child. What facts does the dissent use to support this assertion?

D. Commentator J. Amy Dillard writes that Judge Annuziata was extensively questioned concerning her opinion in the *Piatt* case at her judicial reappointment hearing: "The treatment of Annunziata prompted some Democrats to express concerns that reappointing judges based on their ideologies undermined judicial independence. Some Republicans agreed. Because the reappointment hearing for Annunziata was unusually long and exceptionally political, the potential for chilling other judges from acting in accordance with the Canons, but in conflict with majority political opinion, looms large." J. Amy Dillard, *Separate and Obedient: The Judicial Qualification Missing from the Job Description*, 38 Cumb. L. Rev. 1, 24-27 (2007-2008). Should judges be questioned about specific decisions at reappointment? What is the role of judicial independence?

E. A custody evaluation was performed by Dr. Lane, who testified as an expert in the case and recommended that the parties "share joint legal custody and that wife have primary physical custody with liberal visitation for husband." Why do courts seek expert testimony in child custody cases? Why did the court decide not to adopt the recommendation of this expert?

F. In the decision the court states, "The court agreed with Dr. Lane that 'both parents have good parenting skills. They both love their daughter, and their daughter loves both of them.'" If that is the case, could this matter have been resolved without going to trial? How should courts decide cases where both parents are skilled and caring?

G. Under what factual circumstances would you conclude that a parent's post-marital sexual relationship has a nexus to the parent's relationship with the child and would adversely impact the child?

5.9 BEST INTERESTS STANDARD: THE COOPERATIVE PARENT FACTOR AND INTIMATE PARTNER VIOLENCE

Background to *Ford v. Ford*

In awarding legal and physical custody, many states consider the extent to which a proposed custodial parent will encourage contact with the other parent. Legislatively, these are known as "cooperative" or "friendly-parent" statutes, and they are designed to increase the likelihood that a child will maintain strong relationships with both parents after divorce. Thus in determining the best interests of the child, a court may favor the parent most likely to support continued contact with the other parent. Unfortunately, in some cases children may be endangered by ongoing contact with one of the parents, and in such situations friendly-parent provisions should not be invoked. For example, in the next case, *Ford v. Ford*, a father who committed acts of domestic violence was awarded primary residential custody of a child because the mother discouraged "frequent and continuing contact" with him as required under a Florida friendly-parent statute.

FORD

v.

FORD

Court of Appeals of Florida
700 So. 2d 191 (1997)

POLEN, J. Tara Ford appeals a final judgment of dissolution that awarded primary residential custody of the parties' then twenty month old daughter, Kylee, to the former husband. . . .

The majority of testimony adduced during the six-day final dissolution hearing concerned the issue of custody of Kylee and focused on domestic violence, with the primary focus on two distinct domestic disputes occurring on May 7, 1994, and

October 26, 1994, the latter of which immediately preceded the parties' final separation. Several witnesses provided testimony regarding this violence, including Kay Jones, a Custody Evaluator who completed a court-ordered custody/visitation evaluation. Ms. Jones' eleven-page report contained a summary of her observations, numerous discussions with the parties and witnesses, and her ultimate recommendations.

The report details the May domestic dispute, after which the husband entered the Family Violence Intervention Program at the Parent-Child Center. The May dispute occurred on Mother's Day. The couple invited the husband's family to their house for a barbecue, but it was cancelled when the husband called his grandmother's house at 10:00 A.M. The husband's family traveled to the couple's house, and when they arrived the husband ran out of the house screaming, and told his family they better get in the house before he tore off his wife's head. The husband took a walk with his sister-in-law and told her he hit his wife again.

Rita Clark, director of the Family Violence Intervention Program, testified the husband participated in the program for a time. During his intake, the husband listed violence and abuse as his major problem areas and indicated his spouse was the "victim" of his domestic violence. Ms. Clark explained the husband's childhood was typical of someone with a family violence background. He reported his mother was abusive toward him, and he was jailed at one point for violence against his parents. The husband stated he was married once before, and reported violence against his first wife. Clark testified regarding occasions when the husband engaged in "victim blaming," where the perpetrator of physical violence states they are the victim of violence. She stated the husband told her he was working on trying to change.

The husband's conversations with Ms. Jones demonstrate his inconsistent and incomplete explanation of past events and the parties' history together. The husband reported to Ms. Jones that he was married twice before, his first marriage lasting eleven days and his second marriage lasting one year, yet he could not remember the last names of either wife or where or when he was divorced. When asked to supply a copy of each divorce decree, he stated he could only find his first divorce decree. He told Ms. Jones his first wife was abusive. When entering the Family Violence Intervention Program, the husband reported he was married only once before, and perpetrated violence against his previous wife.

The October 26, 1994, incidence of violence involved the husband throwing the wife on the floor. The wife testified he began kicking her in the chest, ribs, and legs. The wife ran out of the house and called the police, eventually leaving the house because she feared for her safety, as well as that of her daughter. The husband stated he slapped the wife, but only after she kicked him. He explained how he "lowered [the wife] to the floor," not "like she was a ninety year old woman," but he "didn't slam her to the floor either." Following the October 26th incident, the husband phoned Michelle Lampert and told her the wife left because he hit her.

A prior incidence of violence occurred when the wife was four to five months pregnant. The former wife explained the husband was upset because she chose to attend her last day of work as an Emergency Medical Technician. The husband threw her on the floor of her closet, shoving her in the stomach, and kicking her in the side. The husband recounted the incident as involving an argument, after which the wife threatened to abort the baby, and then began hitting herself in the stomach with a fist. The husband testified he restrained the former wife from this self-abuse by holding her wrists, and lowered her to the ground, holding her there for a period of time.

The former husband's testimony regarding domestic violence is revealing. The former husband told Ms. Jones the former wife was abusive. He explained he entered counseling because he "wanted more behavior management for her" and volunteered to attend the Family Violence Intervention Program "because I sought it out as an abused husband." He told Ms. Jones he was the victim in their relationship.

When questioned during the final hearing regarding the discrepancy between his deposition testimony, in which he testified he did not strike the wife, and his hearing testimony in which he admitted slapping his wife only twice and pulling her hair "certainly more than twice," the husband explained he was "being very specific" during his deposition. He justified the discrepancy by stating he defined "strike" to mean "to blow or to strike with an object, like a champagne bottle hitting a ship." He explained that because he had not hit his wife with an object, he responded to deposition questions by stating he did not "strike" his wife.

When asked why a woman weighing just over 100 pounds would regularly hit and kick a man weighing 165 pounds as the former husband alleged, he testified he could only speculate the reason was because his wife could not control her anger.

The husband admitted to Ms. Jones that he took the couple's Ford Mustang from the former wife's grandmother's home late one night after they separated, and knew the Ford Explorer he left in its place was "probably" going to be repossessed. Indeed, the car was repossessed the day before a scheduled May 27, 1995, visit, leaving the wife unable to transport Kylee to the husband for visitation, as she was required to do. The wife telephoned the husband, who agreed to drive to the wife's home in Miami. He appeared at the wife's home with several people and a video camera, explaining he wanted "to prove the [wife] was withholding visits."

In completing her evaluation, Ms. Jones recommended the former wife should have primary residential custody of Kylee because the former wife was more emo-tionally stable and would provide a better home setting for Kylee because the former wife lived with her father and grandmother in Miami.

In the Final Judgment of Dissolution, the trial court ordered the parents to share parental responsibility of Kylee, and awarded primary physical residence to the former husband. It found the mother manipulated visitation during the litigation to the detriment of the father, using Kylee as leverage, concluding the father would be most likely to allow frequent and continuing contact between Kylee and the non-residential parent. The court found the child more closely bonded to the Mother, explaining this bonding was partly a function of the length of time Kylee spent with the Mother. It found both parties equally capable of providing for Kylee. The court did not address the continuity of residence factor, and found the permanence of the existing or proposed custodial home was insignificant in that neither party had a significantly permanent family unit.

Importantly, the court found the parties' physical health equal, but as to the issue of the parties' mental health, found:

Neither parent is mentally ill. Both parents were in need, are in need and will be in need of therapy and both have shown a willingness to obtain therapy. Parenting for both parents will continue to be difficult until their therapy helps them deal with the hard feelings that they have for each other. This factor favors the Father more than the Mother.

Finally, the court found the factor regarding willingness and ability to facilitate and encourage a close continuing relationship between the child and the other parent favored the father over the mother. . . .

We are troubled not only by the absence of any meaningful analysis of the extensive evidence of domestic violence, but also by the apparent misapplication of record evidence to the statutory factors contained in section 61.13(3), Florida Statutes (1995). That statute provides:

> 61.13 Custody and support of children; visitation rights; power of court in making order. . . .
> (3) For purposes of shared parental responsibility and primary residence, the best interests of the child shall include an evaluation of all factors affecting the welfare and interests of the child, including, but not limited to:
> (a) The parent who is more likely to allow the child frequent and continuing contact with the nonresidential parent. . . .
> (g) The mental and physical health of the parents. . . .
> (j) The willingness and ability of each parent to facilitate and encourage a close and continuing parent-child relationship between the child and the other parent. . . .

Section 61.13(3), Fla. Stat. (1995).

As to factors (3)(a) and (j), the trial court's expressed concern regarding difficulties encountered in visitation reflects a problem commonly occurring in cases where evidence demonstrates a pattern of domestic violence. The trouble occurs when a court attempts to harmonize the non-abusive parent's conduct with "friendly parent" provisions. Here, the trial court failed to offset what it perceived to be the mother's violation of Florida's friendly-parent provisions, with what was recognized in the temporary order as the mother's "justifiable reason to fear the Husband." This failure resulted in an unbalanced final judgment that found "the Mother has manipulated the visitation during this litigation to the detriment of the Father," and failed to recognize the probability that the mother's actions were justified.

While the former husband himself eventually admitted perpetrating violence against the former wife, the former husband's allegations of the former wife's violence stood unsubstantiated. The husband's unsupported accusations do not rise to the level of competent, substantial evidence required to support a fact finder's determination. Evidence relied on to support an ultimate finding should be sufficiently relevant and material that a reasonable mind would accept it as adequate to support the conclusion reached. The husband's mere accusations fall short of this standard.

As to factor (g), the record is devoid of competent substantial evidence supporting the trial court's finding this factor favored the father over the mother. To the contrary, this record is replete with testimony demonstrating the long history of abuse perpetrated by the former husband against the former wife, violence he sought help in controlling. The trial court's finding to the contrary is unsupportable. Reversed.

DISCUSSION QUESTIONS **FOR *FORD v. FORD***

A. How is the existence of domestic violence relevant to decision making about child custody under the statute used in this case? What does being a perpetrator of domestic violence indicate about the father's ability to parent? Was the child present during any of the incidents described? Why does that matter? In about half of families experiencing domestic violence, children are also physically abused. Does the court inquire about that possibility here? *See* Jeffrey L. Edleson, *Should Childhood Exposure to Adult Domestic Violence Be Defined as Child Maltreatment Under the Law?*, in Protecting Children from Domestic Violence 8 (Peter G. Jaffe et al. eds., 2004).

B. Are there other situations where the "friendly-parent" provision should not apply? Are there situations where one parent should discourage contact with the other parent? How could you redraft the statute used in this case to prevent its application in such situations? Should the factor be deleted altogether?

C. The abuse of discretion standard is one of the most difficult for an appellant to satisfy; however, the court of appeals found that the trial court's custody determination was arbitrary and unreasonable with respect to the weight accorded the testimony offered, and the court's findings. What facts did the court of appeals rely upon in reaching this decision? Does use of the abuse of discretion standard vest too much discretion in a trial judge who may or may not be versed in family dynamics and issues such as domestic violence?

5.10 BEST INTERESTS STANDARD: ASCERTAINING THE WISHES OF THE CHILD

Background to *Ynclan v. Woodward*

The Uniform Marriage and Divorce Act (UMDA) expressly provides for consideration of the child's wishes in determining custody. However, a judge must first determine that a child has sufficient maturity to express a meaningful preference. Research indicates that most judges seriously consider the preferences of older teenagers but do not attach importance to the views of infants and toddlers. Not surprisingly, judges vary in how they weigh the views of children in between those ages, although there is a relationship between the age of the child and the significance judges attach to the child's preference. Barbara A. Atwood, *The Child's Voice in Custody Litigation: An Empirical Survey and Suggestions for Reform*, 45 Ariz. L. Rev. 629 (2003).

Sometimes the child's views are communicated through a professional conducting a child custody evaluation, but in other cases a judge may interview a child in chambers. In the case below, the Supreme Court of Oklahoma discusses the circumstances under which an *in camera* interview may be held and the extent to which parents should have access to a transcript of the interview.

YNCLAN
v.
WOODWARD

Supreme Court of Oklahoma
237 P.3d 145 (2010)

KAUGER, J. It appears that Nancy Ynclan (the mother) and Nolan Shawn Ynclan (the petitioner/father) were married on Valentine's Day 1996. The couple had four children born in 1996, 1997, 1999, and 2004, and on February 27, 2008, the mother filed for divorce from the father in Garfield County District Court.

The matter proceeded to trial on January 14 and January 30, 2009. On the second day of trial, the trial judge interviewed the three oldest children, in chambers, without counsel or the parents being present. However, a court reporter was present to take notes. The three interviews lasted less than fifteen minutes. The mother insists that counsel for both sides agreed not to be present in the interview, but that written questions were submitted. According to the father, after the interview, he promptly made an informal request for the transcript of the children's interviews and tendered his cost deposit. This request was denied and at the conclusion of the trial, the court granted the divorce and awarded the mother custody of the children.

The father argues that 20 O.S. Supp. 2007 §106.4(A) and 43 O.S. Supp. 2002 §113(C), taken collectively, require that *in camera* interviews of children in custody proceedings be transcribed and that the statutes also require the trial court to allow the parents to review such transcripts. In other words, he alleges that the transcripts may not be sealed from either the parties or their attorneys. . . .

The procedure of a trial judge conducting a private, *in camera* interview with a child, depending upon age and maturity, has been widely used as a means of discovering the child's custodial preference. The purposes of conducting an interview in private, rather than in open court in the presence of the parents include:

1) elimination of the harm a child might suffer from exposure to examination and cross-examination and the adversarial nature of the proceedings generally;
2) reduction of added pressure to a child to an already stressful situation;
3) enhancement of the child's ability to be forthcoming;
4) reduction of the child's feeling of disloyalty toward a parent or to openly choose sides;

5) minimization of the emotional trauma affecting the child, by lessening the ordeal for the child;
6) protection of the child from the tug and pull of competing custodial interests; and
7) awarding custody without placing the child in an adverse position between the parents.

Obviously, the purpose of such a hearing is not to lessen the ordeal for the parents, but, rather, to lessen the ordeal for the child. Nor is it intended to make a secret of the basis for the court's findings. The preference of the child is only one of many factors to be considered when determining the child's best interest concerning custody. It should never be the only basis for determining custody. Nor should a child be directly asked where the child would rather live because specifically asking preference provides an opportunity for parental manipulation or intimidation of the child as well as an opportunity for the child to manipulate the parents. It also gives the child the impression that their preference is "the" deciding factor for custody. Rather, the trial court should conduct such an interview so as to discern the child's preference, while at the same time, being sensitive to how the child is coping with the divorce, the pressures put on the child by the divorce and stating a preference, as well as to ascertain the motive of the child in stating a preference. When the trial court determines the child's best interest will be served by considering the child's preference, whether to hold such an interview is generally within the trial court's discretion. . . .

In spite of the due process implications, *in camera* interviews are widely used as a means of discovering a child's custodial preference. In most cases, if the parents consent or agree to the interview, a trial court may hold an *in camera* custody preference interview without the parents. If a parent does not object to the procedure at the time of the interview, then any objection is generally waived on appeal. Even when consent is given, the courts usually protect the parents' due process rights by either allowing or requiring the parents' lawyers to be present during the interview or at least allowing the lawyers to either submit or ask questions, or both. However, if the parent is acting *pro se,* the *pro se* parent is excluded from the interview altogether.

Other various procedures have been developed, in attempts to resolve the conflict between the parental due process rights with the child's right to be heard. For instance, a number of states require, either by statute or judicial holding, that *in camera* conversations with children must be recorded. In other states, the presence of a court reporter can be waived, or the record must be made only if requested by the parties.

Taken together, 20 O.S. Supp. 2007 §106.4(A) and 43 O.S. Supp. 2002 §113 do not fully resolve the conflicts between the parental due process rights of having an *in camera* interview transcribed with the child's right to be heard. For instance, 43 O.S. Supp. 2002 §113, does not expressly address parental consent to holding an *in camera* interview. What it does do is:

1) require the court to determine that the best interest of the child will be served by expressing preference;
2) generally give the trial court discretion to consider a child's preference unless if the child is of sufficient age, [presumably 12 or older], in which case the court is required to consider the expression of preference or other testimony;

3) expressly allow counsel to be present, but provides that if the lawyers are not allowed in the interview, the reasons for their exclusion must be expressly stated by the trial court;

4) in no case is the child's preference binding on the court or the only factor the court should consider;

5) if the child is of sufficient age to form an intelligent preference, and the court does not follow the child's preference, the court shall make specific findings of fact supporting such action if requested by either party and

6) either party may also request that a transcript of the in chamber proceedings be made, but the statutes do not address whether or if the party is entitled to access of the transcript.

In order to provide a proper balance of parental due process rights with the child's right to be heard, we hereby adopt the following guidelines for trial courts to utilize when planning to conduct an *in camera* custodial or visitation child preference interview:

1) If the trial court or the parties consider the possibility of an *in camera* interview of the children, then the trial court, pursuant to 43 O.S. 2001 §113, must make and state on the record its preliminary determinations concerning whether the child's best interest is served by conducting such an *in camera* interview and whether the child is of a sufficient age to form an intelligent preference.

2) If the parents consent to the interview being in chambers, or otherwise waive their own presence, the judge may proceed with an *in camera* interview.

3) If one or both parents object to being excluded, the trial court must consider whether the parents want counsel present. This consideration should include whether to allow counsel to be present, allow counsel to question the child, or allow counsel to submit questions to be asked. Whether the trial court allows the counsel to participate in the questioning or submit questions is within the trial court's discretion. If no objection is made regarding this issue, the parties waive objection to the issue on appeal. If the judge proceeds with an *in camera* interview without counsel present, pursuant to 43 O.S. 2001 §113, the reason for counsel's exclusion must be stated on the record.

4) The next issue to be considered on the record is whether either or both parents request that a court reporter be present. If a request for a court reporter is made, the court reporter must be present and the interview shall be recorded — otherwise the parties waive objection to the issue on appeal.

Once a record is made, the question becomes whether it must be made available to the parties, and if so when? Again, the procedures vary from state to state. In some states, the record must be made available to the parties. In other words, the record may be sealed from the parties, but must be made available for appellate review in an effort to protect the children's confidentiality, while still providing a basis of appellate review to protect the parents' due process rights. Transcribing the matter and making it available to the court, but not to the parties, could satisfy the due process requirement stated in 20 O.S. Supp. 2007 §106.4(A). Rarely are the parties completely precluded from ever knowing what transpired in the interview.

Our research reveals one New Jersey case directly on point, and we agree with its result. In *Uherek v. Sathe*, 391 N.J. Super. 164, 917 A.2d 306, 308 (2007), *cert. denied by Uherek v. Uherek*, 192 N.J. 72, 926 A.2d 856 (2007), the court addressed whether a father, nearly four years after dissolution of marriage, was entitled to transcripts of the trial judge's *in camera* interview with the parties' child. The New Jersey rule, like Oklahoma's statute 43 O.S. Supp. 2002 §113, allowed for transcripts to be provided to counsel and the parties upon the payment of costs. . . .

Like the father in *Uherek, supra,* the petitioner here does not seek the transcript to rely on for an appeal of the custody dispute. In fact, no appeal has been lodged regarding custody. Rather, he seeks the transcript merely to satisfy his curiosity. We agree with the rationale utilized by the New Jersey court, and decline to create a right to transcripts pursuant to 43 O.S. Supp. 2002 §113 absent a pending custody dispute. Accordingly, we hold that unless a parent or the parents appeal the custody or visitation determination, due process does not require that either parent have access to the transcript of the *in camera* interview of the children merely to satisfy their curiosity.

WATT, J., dissenting:

I dissent both from today's opinion and from the proposed rule change. Although the majority gives lip service to a plethora of reasons why an *in camera* interview serves the child's best interests, today, its opinion and proposed rule change may well sound the death knell to the utilization of this invaluable tool in future contested child custody matters. I also cannot agree with the immediate implementation of rule changes to causes in the appellate pipeline, altering the rules midstream in situations which involve the raw emotions of youth who have already been through the difficult rigors associated with placement proceedings.

The opinion and rule change most certainly destroy the foundational principle for courts to conduct "*in camera* hearings" with the children which principle is also the basis for any custody decision, that being "the best interests of the child/children." Today's order not only robs the trial court of its discretion but also destroys the court's most vital tool in making decisions with regard to custody and that is obtaining the trust of the child or children. No longer can a judge promise that degree of protection of CONFIDENTIALITY so that a child will be more likely to be forthright and honest in expressing his or her views during these *in camera* proceedings.

I would adopt the rationale expressed in *Myers v. Myers,* 170 Ohio App. 3d 436, 867 N.E.2d 848, where the court stated, as follows:

> The requirement that the *in camera* interviews be recorded is designed to protect the due-process rights of the parents. The due-process protection is achieved in this context by sealing the transcript of the in camera interview and making it available only to the court for review. This process allows appellate courts to review the *in camera* interview proceedings and ascertain their reasonableness, while still allowing the child to "feel safe and comfortable in expressing his opinions openly and honestly, without subjecting the child to any additional psychological trauma or loyalty conflicts."

Accordingly, the sealing of the transcript and its inclusion in the record on appeal for review by the appellate courts in Oklahoma and using an abuse of discretion standard of review would protect the rights and best interests of the children while also affording the parents their right of due process.

By today's opinion and rule change, absent a complete waiver by all of the parties, "*in camera* hearings" as we have known them for decades will disappear.

With today's pronouncement and rule change, either parent need only file their petition in error, pay the filing fee, and obtain and pay for a copy of the transcript and then be free to "beat the child/children over the head with it" for comments made to the judge in chambers. When there is no appeal, the proposed rule allows parents to request that the trial court release the transcript when no appeal is filed. No responsible parent would want access to hearing results unless they intended to, at some future date, use it against the child or a former spouse.

Under today's order, thousands of children, at best, will leave the courthouses across this state with a bitter taste in their mouth for the judicial system or, at worst, result in mental or physical scarring that will remain for the rest of their lifetime.

Furthermore, instead of protecting the children and acting in their best interest, warring parents, consumed with bitterness for one another will now use their children as weapons in their domestic battle with the opposing spouse.

Finally, without any way to determine how many children will be affected by having their innermost thoughts revealed to warring parents, the majority imposes changes upon parents, children, and trial courts to which they had no notice when it makes the guidelines applicable "in all future cases including those already in the appellate pipeline." In the past, when rule changes have been imposed on the unsuspecting litigant, the rules have been made applicable in the cause and prospectively to all petitions for certiorari filed thirty (30) days after final publication in the Oklahoma Bar Journal.

DISCUSSION QUESTIONS FOR *YNCLAN v. WOODWARD*

A. What should a judge consider in deciding whether a child has sufficient maturity to express a custodial preference? At what age did the court in this case presume that a child is sufficiently mature?

B. Why do judges conduct interviews in chambers rather than asking a child's preference in open court?

C. Under the ruling in this case, who might be present during an interview? Must a record be made of an interview?

D. Under what conditions would a parent have access to the transcript of an *in camera* interview?

E. On what basis does the dissenting judge disagree with the majority decision? Do you agree with the majority or with the dissent? Why?

F. Do you think children should ever be asked about their custodial preference? Why or why not? When might a less direct approach (discussing the child's concerns about his or life subsequent to divorce, etc.) make more sense?

G. What are the pros and cons for obtaining the child's views through a neutral expert as opposed to an *in camera* interview? Which do you think a child might prefer?

H. When parents attend mediation or use another collaborative process, there are a variety of ways that children can have involvement or input. For example, after parents have crafted a parenting time arrangement, a teenager may be invited to a mediation session to discuss its workability from his or her perspective. Under what circumstances would this seem preferable to an *in camera* interview? When might a more formal judicial interview be more appropriate? *See* Joan B. Kelly, *Psychological and Legal Interventions for Parents and Children in Custody and Access Disputes: Current Research and Practice*, 10 Va. J. Soc. Pol'y & L. 129 (2002); Jennifer McIntosh et al., *Child-Focused and Child-Inclusive Divorce Mediation: Comparative Outcomes from a Prospective Study of Postseparation Adjustment*, 46 Fam. Ct. Rev. 105 (2008) (child-inclusive mediation promoted developmental recovery of children).

5.11 BEST INTERESTS STANDARD: CONSIDERATION OF RACE, RELIGION, AND DISABILITY

Courts have examined the extent to which race, religion, and disability can be considered in determining the best interests of the child. Courts may not use race as a sole or decisive factor in making child custody decisions. *See Palmore v. Sidoti*, 466 U.S. 429 (1984). Although courts may not favor one religious tradition over another, judges can nevertheless consider parental religious behavior that affects the health and well-being of children. *See Hicks v. Cook*, 288 S.W.3d 244 (Ark. App. 2008). *See also Gribeluk v. Gribeluk*, 991 N.Y.S.2d 117 (App. Div. 2014) (court can consider child's religious ties). Similarly, courts may not discriminate against parents with disabilities but they may consider the effect of parental disability on a child. *See Arneson v. Arenson*, 670 N.W.2d 904 (S.D. 2003).

| REFLECTIVE QUESTIONS | Create a hypothetical involving custody of a minor child involved in a divorce where a court might consider religion as a factor in deciding which parent should receive physical custody. Create a hypothetical where religion would not be a consideration when a court is determining physical custody. |

5.12 PRESUMPTIONS AND PREFERENCES: THE "NATURAL" PARENT

Barring unfitness, "natural" parents are entitled to custody over "third parties" such as stepparents and grandparents. This presumption has historical roots, but unlike the paternal, maternal, and primary caretaker presumptions discussed previously, the natural parent presumption remains in widespread use today. It is based on constitutional recognition of a parent's abiding interest in the care and control of his or her children. The purpose of the presumption is to assure that the parents of a child have superior decision making, custody, and access rights over nonparents. The presumption may be overcome only by showing that the legal parents are unfit to care for the child.

Many people are comfortable with the general premise of the natural parent presumption, even though in practice it means that children remain with parents who are fit, but perhaps not as capable of parenting as an interested grandparent or other relative. Difficult situations may arise when an absent parent returns and seeks physical custody of a child who has lived with a third party for an extended period of time. *See* Elizabeth Barker Brandt, *De Facto Custodians — A Response to the Needs of Informal Kin Caregivers?*, 38 Fam. L.Q. 291 (2004). In response the ALI recommends softening the natural parent presumption by broadening the definition of "parent" to include parents by estoppel and de facto parents. *See* ALI, *Principles of the Law of Family Dissolution: Analysis and Recommendations* §2.03(b), (c) (2002).

REFLECTIVE QUESTIONS	What are some policy arguments in favor of and against maintaining the natural parent presumption?

5.13 PRESUMPTIONS AND PREFERENCES: JOINT LEGAL AND PHYSICAL CUSTODY

Background to *In re Marriage of Hansen*

States take different approaches to the issue of joint legal and physical custody. Some states have adopted presumptions that joint legal custody, and/or to a lesser extent, joint physical custody is in the best interests of children. Other states presume that such arrangements are in the best interests of children when specifically requested by parents. Some states have a statutory "preference" for joint legal and/or physical custody. Still other states have no expressed preference but consider each case on its merits. In *In re Marriage of Hansen*, the Iowa Supreme Court explores the issue of joint legal and physical custody at some length, including a detailed analysis of relevant social science literature.

IN RE MARRIAGE OF HANSEN
Supreme Court of Iowa
733 N.W.2d 683 (2007)

APPEL, J. Lyle and Delores were married on September 4, 1987. The marriage lasted approximately eighteen years. At the time of trial, Lyle was forty-five years of age and Delores was forty-six. Two children were born of the marriage, Miranda, who was twelve years old at the time of the district court proceedings, and Ethan, who was eight.

At all times prior to the filing of the divorce petition, Delores was the primary caregiver. Lyle, alternatively, was the main breadwinner. For example, during the course of the marriage Delores attended parent-teacher conferences on a regular basis, while Lyle did not. The vast majority of the time, it was Delores who helped the children with their homework. Lyle admits that she was better at it, particularly math. During the marriage, Lyle missed important childhood events because of social activities or work-related assignments. When the children were in infancy, Delores opened a day care center in their home. Later, when family finances became an issue, she held full-time employment outside the home. After the parties' separation, however, Lyle has become more involved in the lives of the children.

The record developed at trial reveals serious marital stress. The record demonstrates a history of recurrent arguments, excessive consumption of alcohol, allegations of infidelity and sexual misconduct, and allegations of domestic abuse. Unfortunately, at least some of these contretemps were in front of the children. It was not a pleasant proceeding. . . .

The record further reveals that Delores tended to acquiesce to Lyle when there were disagreements. For example, when Delores was pregnant with Miranda, she wanted to attend child-birthing classes, but Lyle stated that *he* had already undergone training and that, as a result, the classes were not needed. When Delores began operating a child care center out of their home, Lyle insisted on reviewing applicant backgrounds and controlled which children could utilize the service. He further demanded that parents or custodians pick up their children by 5:00 p.m. sharp. Delores did not agree with these practices, but felt she had no choice but to acquiesce. In addition, Delores asked Lyle if he would participate in marital counseling, but he refused, stating that he did not believe in counseling. Delores testified that she agreed to temporary joint physical care prior to trial only because she did not feel she could stand up to her husband. Delores expressed concern that if she disagrees with Lyle, he becomes angry and intimidating.

The parties appear to have different approaches to child rearing. Delores wants the children to be active in the Methodist church and other extracurricular activities. While not being overtly resistant, during the course of the marriage, Lyle did not encourage these kinds of activities. The parties also have different approaches to discipline. Lyle claims to have been the disciplinarian in the marital home. The record reveals that there are occasions when Lyle believed that discipline needed to be more severe than Delores was willing to impose. Lyle acknowledged that, at times, he is overprotective. As Lyle admitted, there are some things that he might let the children do that Delores might not, and vice versa.

At trial, Lyle expressed concern that Delores will expose their children to her family, which he finds highly dysfunctional. Delores testified that her father abused her as a child, but they have reconciled sufficiently to maintain an ongoing relationship. Lyle's concern, however, extends beyond the father, as other members of Delores' family have been convicted of child endangerment and drug offenses. Delores counters that when the children visit her family, it is always under her supervision.

Prior to trial, the parties were apparently able to work out the scheduling issues inherent in a joint physical care arrangement. There was not always agreement, however, on matters related to the children. For instance, when one child experienced unexpected academic difficulties, Delores believed professional counseling would be of help. Lyle disagreed, once again stating that he did not believe in professional counseling. Delores acquiesced, and counseling was not obtained. On another occasion, the kids called their mother and asked to be picked up because Lyle was angry that they had not cleaned their rooms, and had slammed the kitchen door, breaking its glass pane. Moreover, Delores testified that Miranda told her she desired a more stable living arrangement with a home base.

While much of the record in this case is unattractive, it is clear that both Lyle and Delores love their children. They are both capable of making substantial contributions to their lives. The record further reveals that the children are bright and generally well-adjusted.

A. CUSTODY AND CARE ISSUES

1. Legal Framework

On appeal, no party contests the district court's award of joint legal custody. With respect to the children, Delores seeks to overturn the district court's ruling awarding joint physical care to both parties. She seeks physical care. Lyle, however, seeks physical care, but in the event this does not occur, is willing to accept joint physical care in the alternative.

At the outset, it is important to discuss the differences between joint legal custody and joint physical care. "Legal custody" carries with it certain rights and responsibilities, including but not limited to "decisionmaking affecting the child's legal status, medical care, education, extracurricular activities, and religious instruction." Iowa Code §598.1(3), (5) (2005). When joint legal custody is awarded, "neither parent has legal custodial rights superior to those of the other parent." *Id.* §598.1(3). A parent who is awarded legal custody has the ability to participate in fundamental decisions about the child's life.

On the other hand, "physical care" involves "the right and responsibility to maintain a home for the minor child and provide for routine care of the child." *Id.* §598.1(7). If joint physical care is awarded, "both parents have rights to and responsibilities toward the child including, but not limited to, shared parenting time with the child, maintaining homes for the child, [and] providing routine care for the child. . . ." *Id.* §598.1(4). The parent awarded physical care maintains the primary residence and has the right to determine the myriad of details associated with routine living, including such things as what clothes the children wear, when they go to bed, with whom they associate or date, etc.

If joint physical care is not warranted, the court must choose a primary caretaker who is solely responsible for decisions concerning the child's routine care. Visitation rights are ordinarily afforded a parent who is not the primary caretaker. . . .

4. Review of the Traditional Approach to Joint Physical Care

While we find that the Iowa legislature has not overridden prior case law regarding joint physical care, we nonetheless believe that the notion that joint physical care is strongly disfavored except in exceptional circumstances is subject to reexamination in light of changing social conditions and ongoing legal and research developments. Increasingly in Iowa and across the nation, our family structures have become more diverse. While some families function along traditional lines with a primary breadwinner and primary caregiver, other families employ a more undifferentiated role for spouses or even reverse "traditional" roles. A one-size-fits-all approach in which joint physical care is universally disfavored is thus subject to serious question given current social realities.

In addition, the social science research related to child custody issues is now richer and more varied than it was in the past. In the past, many scholars and courts rejected joint physical care based on the influential writings of Joseph Goldstein, Anna Freud, and Albert J. Solnit. These scholars utilized attachment theory to emphasize the need to place children with a single "psychological parent" with whom the children had bonded. Joseph Goldstein, Anna Freud, & Albert J. Solnit, *Beyond the Best Interests of the Child* 98 (1979). Although the research upon which the "psychological parent" attachment theory was based rested upon studies of infants, it was also thought to apply throughout the life cycle of a child. Shelley A. Riggs, *Is the Approximation Rule in the Child's Best Interests?*, 43 Fam. Ct. Rev. 481, 484 (2005).

The psychological parent approach stressed the important role of a strong, caring parent-child dyad and embraced what is sometimes termed a monotropic view of infant-child bonding. Robert F. Kelley and Shawn L. Ward, *Social Science Research and the American Law Institute's Approximation Rule*, 40 Fam. Ct. Rev. 350, 355-359 (2002); Peggy Cooper Davis, *The Good Mother: A New Look at Psychological Parent Theory*, 22 N.Y.U. Rev. L. & Soc. Change 347, 360 (1996). The "psychological parent" approach based on attachment theory seems to have influenced a number of courts. *Pikula v. Pikula*, 374 N.W.2d 705, 711 (Minn. 1985), *superseded by statute*, Minn. Stat. §248.2 (1989). . . .

Attachment theory that emphasizes primary relationships continues to have strong advocates. Riggs, 43 Fam. Ct. Rev. at 482-490; James G. Dwyer, *A Taxonomy of Children's Existing Rights in State Decision Making About Their Relationship*, 11 Wm. & Mary Bill Rts. J. 845, 913 (2003); Mary Ann Mason, *The Custody Wars: Why Children Are Losing the Legal Battle, and What We Can Do About It*, 116 (1999). The validity of the parent-child dyad or monotropic view of attachments, however, has been subject to substantial question. Many scholars now view infants as capable of attaching to multiple caregivers and not simply one "psychological parent." Michael E. Lamb, *Placing Children's Interest First: Developmentally Appro-priate Parenting Plans*, 10 Va. J. Soc. Pol'y and L. 98, 109-113 (2002). Further, a growing body of scholarship suggests that the continued presence and involvement of both parents is often beneficial to the lives of children and not necessarily detrimental as believed by many adherents of the "psychological parent" theory. *Id.* at 100 (citing disadvantages of children growing up in fatherless families, including psychological adjustment, behavior and achievement at school, educational attain-ment, employment trajectories, and income generation); Michael T. Flannery, *Is "Bird Nesting" in the Best Interest of Children?*, 57 SMU L. Rev. 295, 302 (2004) (most commentators agree that, generally, children benefit from continued contact with both parents after a divorce).

As a result, a substantial body of scholarly commentary now challenges the blanket application of the monotropic psychological parent attachment theory to avoid joint physical care. For example, reputable scholars have stated that,

> despite literature that suggests moderate correlations between conditions of early rearing and classes of later outcomes—for example, with respect to attachment and parental bonding—experts' ability to make specific predictions, given specific conditions (let alone ambiguous ones!) is weak to negligible.

Thomas M. Horner & Melvin J. Guyer, *Prediction, Prevention, and Clinical Exper-tise in Child Custody Cases in Which Allegations of Child Sexual Abuse Have Been Made*, 25 Fam. L.Q. 217, 248 (1991). Some academic observers suggest that joint physical care may be a way to encourage continued involvement of both spouses in the lives of the children. Matthew A. Kipp, *Maximizing Custody Options: Abolishing the Presumption Against Joint Physical Custody*, 79 N.D. L. Rev. 59 (2003); Stepha-nie N. Barnes, *Strengthening the Father-Child Relationship Through a Joint Custody Presumption*, 35 Willamette L. Rev. 601 (1999). They cite a wide range of studies to suggest that children may be better off with joint physical care than other arrangements.

The current social science research cited by advocates of joint custody or joint physical care, however, is not definitive on many key questions. To begin with, there are substantial questions of definition and methodology. Such criticisms include: samples that only examine parents who voluntarily choose joint custody, the use of small and homogenous groups, the skewing of samples toward middle-class parents with higher incomes and education, the lack of control groups, and the lack of distinction between "joint custody" arrangements and traditional sole cus-tody with visitation, and the failure to differentiate the effects of preexisting parental characteristics from the effects of custody type. Jana B. Singer & William L. Reyn-olds, *A Dissent on Joint Custody*, 47 Md. L. Rev. 497, 507 (1988); *see also* Diane N. Lye, *What the Experts Say: Scholarly Research on Post-Divorce Parenting and Child Wellbeing*, Report to the Washington State Gender and Justice Commission and Domestic Relations Commission 4-2 (1999) (research fraught with methodological difficulties and severe limitations) [hereinafter Lye, Report]; Daniel A. Krauss & Bruce D. Sales, *Legal Standards, Expertise, and Experts in the Resolution of Contested*

Child Custody Cases, 6 Psychol. Pub. Pol'y & L. 843, 850 (2000) (noting myriad of conceptual and methodological problems).

Further, the data is conflicting or ambiguous. As noted by one recent academic observer, the research to date on the benefits of joint physical care is inconclusive and has produced mixed results. Stephen Gilmore, *Contact/Shared Residence and Child Well-Being: Research Evidence and Its Implications for Legal Decision Making*, 20 Int'l J.L. & Pol'y & Fam. 344, 352-353 (2006); *see also* Krauss & Sales, 6 Psychol. Pub. Pol'y & L. at 857-858 (recent empirical studies of joint custody have not been able to demonstrate a substantial positive effect on postdivorce child adjustment when joint physical care is compared with other custodial arrangements).

An exhaustive review commissioned by the Washington State Supreme Court Gender and Justice Commission and the Domestic Relations Commission examined the many studies related to child custody issues. The review concluded that the available research did not reveal any particular post-divorce residential schedule to be most beneficial to children. While the review concluded that the research did not demonstrate significant advantages to children of joint physical care, the research also did not show significant disadvantages. Lye, Report at Summary.

While it seems clear that children often benefit from a continuing relationship with both parents after divorce, the research has not established the amount of contact necessary to maintain a "close relationship." Preeminent scholars have noted that "surprisingly, even a fairly small amount of close contact seemed sufficient to maintain close relationships, at least as these relationships were seen from the adolescents' perspective." Eleanor E. Maccoby, et al., *Postdivorce Roles of Mothers and Fathers in the Lives of Their Children*, 7 J. Fam. Psychol. 24, 24 (1993); *see also* Michael E. Lamb, *Noncustodial Fathers and Their Impact on the Children of Divorce in the Postdivorce Family: Children, Parenting, and Society* 105, 111 (Ross A. Thompson & Paul R. Amato eds., 1999) (causal link between frequency of father-child contact and child's adjustment to parental divorce "much weaker than one might expect"); Valarie King, *Variation in the Consequences of Nonresident Father Involvement for Children's Well-Being*, 56 J. of Marriage & Fam. 963, 970-971 (1994) (benefit to child not related to quantity of visits), *as cited in* American Law Institute, *Principles of the Law of Family Dissolution* §2.02 cmt. f. (2000) [hereinafter *Principles*]; Gilmore, 20 Int'l J.L. & Pol'y & Fam. at 358 (not contact per se but the nature and quality of contact are important to children's adjustment).

There is thus growing support for the notion that the quality, and not the quantity, of contacts with the noncustodial parent are the key to the well-being of children. Quality interaction with children can, of course, occur within the framework of traditional visitation and does not occur solely in situations involving joint physical care.

At present, the available empirical studies simply do not provide a firm basis for a dramatic shift that would endorse joint physical care as the norm in child custody cases. Nonetheless, in light of the changing nature of the structure of families and challenges to the sweeping application of psychological parent attachment theory, we believe the joint physical care issue must be examined in each case on the unique facts and not subject to cursory rejection based on a nearly irrebuttable presumption found in our prior cases. Gilmore, 20 Int'l J.L. & Pol'y & Fam. at 360-361 (the law should eschew the use of presumptions in the process of deciding post-separation parenting regimes); Krauss & Sales, 6 Psychol. Pub. Pol'y & L. at 857 (empirical research does not support presumptions to resolve custody disputes); Lye, Report at 4-1 (circumstances of each family are unique, recognition of unique circumstances central to good post-divorce parenting choices). . . .

In considering whether to award joint physical care where there are two suitable parents, stability and continuity of caregiving have traditionally been primary factors. . . . We continue to believe that stability and continuity of caregiving are important factors that must be considered in custody and care decisions. As noted by a leading scholar, "past caretaking patterns likely are a fairly reliable proxy of the intangible qualities such as parental abilities and emotional bonds that are so difficult for courts to ascertain." Bartlett, 35 Willamette L. Rev. at 480. While no post-divorce physical care arrangement will be identical to predissolution experience, preservation of the greatest amount of stability possible is a desirable goal. In contrast, imposing a new physical care arrangement on children that significantly contrasts from their past experience can be unsettling, cause serious emotional harm, and thus not be in the child's best interest.

As a result, the successful caregiving by one spouse in the past is a strong predictor that future care of the children will be of the same quality. . . . Conversely, however, long-term, successful, joint care is a significant factor in considering the viability of joint physical care after divorce. . . .

Stability and continuity concepts have been refined in the recent literature and expressed in terms of an approximation rule, namely, that the caregiving of parents in the post-divorce world should be in rough proportion to that which predated the dissolution. Elizabeth S. Scott, *Pluralism, Parental Preference, and Child Custody*, 80 Cal. L. Rev. 615, 617 (1992). Recently, the American Law Institute's *Principles of Family Law*, published in 2000, adopted the general rule that custodial responsibility should be allocated "so that the proportion of custodial time the child spends with each parent approximates the proportion of time each parent spent performing caretaking functions for the child prior to the parents' separation. . . ." *Principles* §2:08, at 178. A reporter of the ALI Project on Family Dissolution that produced *Principles* suggests that the ALI approximation rule is gender neutral, focuses on historical facts rather than subjective judgments, and is, in most cases, likely to provide an environment that is in the best interest of the child. Bartlett, 35 Willamette L. Rev. at 480-482.

We do not, however, adopt the ALI approximation rule in its entirety. Iowa Code section 598.41(3) and our case law requires a multi-factored test where no one criterion is determinative. Any wholesale adoption of the approximation rule would require legislative action. *See* W. Va. Code Ann. §48-9-206(a) (2007).

Nonetheless, we believe that the approximation principle is a factor to be considered by courts in determining whether to grant joint physical care. By focusing on historic patterns of caregiving, the approximation rule provides a relatively objective factor for the court to consider. The principle of approximation also rejects a "one-size-fits-all" approach and recognizes the diversity of family life. Finally, it tends to ensure that any decision to grant joint physical care is firmly rooted in the past practices of the individual family. . . .

A second important factor to consider in determining whether joint physical care is in the child's best interest is the ability of spouses to communicate and show mutual respect. A lack of trust poses a significant impediment to effective co-parenting. Eleanor E. Maccoby & Robert H. Mnookin, *Dividing the Child: Social Costs and Legal Dilemmas of Custody* 276 (1992) [hereinafter Maccoby & Mnookin]. Evidence of controlling behavior by a spouse may be an indicator of potential problems. *McGee v. McGee*, 224 A.D.2d 832, 835, 637 N.Y.S.2d 816 (N.Y. App. Div. 1996) (citing domineering attitude); *Kline v. Kline*, 686 S.W.2d 13, 15-16 (Mo. Ct. App. 1984) (citing power struggles and hostility). Evidence of untreated domestic battering should be given considerable weight in determining custody and gives rise to a presumption against joint physical care. Iowa Code §598.41(2)(c); *Hynick*, 727 N.W.2d at 579; *In re Marriage of Daniels*, 568 N.W.2d 51, 55 (Iowa Ct. App. 1997).

Third, the degree of conflict between parents is an important factor in determining whether joint physical care is appropriate. Joint physical care requires substantial and regular interaction between divorced parents on a myriad of issues. Where the parties' marriage is stormy and has a history of charge and countercharge, the likelihood that joint physical care will provide a workable arrangement diminishes. It is, of course, possible that spouses may be able to put aside their past, strong differences in the interest of the children. Reality suggests, however, that this may not be the case. Maccoby & Mnookin at 284 (expressing deep concern in cases where there is substantial parental conflict); *The Wingspread Report and Action Plan, High-Conflict Custody Cases*, 39 Fam. Ct. Rev. 146, 146 (2001) ("[h]igh-conflict custody cases seriously harm the children involved").

In short, a stormy marriage and divorce presents a significant risk factor that must be considered in determining whether joint physical care is in the best interest of the children. The prospect for successful joint physical care is reduced when there is a bitter parental relationship and one party objects to the shared arrangement. *Burkhart v. Burkhart*, 876 S.W.2d 675, 680 (Mo. Ct. App. 1994) (allegations of infidelity and breach of trust); *Braiman v. Braiman*, 44 N.Y.2d 584, 407 N.Y.S.2d 449, 378 N.E.2d 1019, 1021 (N.Y. 1978) (court ordered joint custody involving embattled and embittered parents, accusing one another of vices and wrongs, can only enhance familial chaos). As noted in the Washington state review, there is evidence that high levels of child contact with a nonresidential father are beneficial to children in low conflict families, but harmful to children in high conflict families. Lye, Report at 4-17; *see also* Kelly & Ward, 40 Fam. Ct. Rev. at 364 ("much of the research on shared parenting that finds positive effects finds them in the context of postdivorce parental relationships in which high levels of conflict are absent").

Conflict, of course, is a continuum, but expressions of anger between parents can negatively affect children's emotions and behaviors. Hildy Mauzerall, Patricia Young, & Debra Alsaker-Burke, *Protecting of the Children of High Conflict Divorce: An Analysis of the Idaho Bench/Bar Committee to Protect Children of High Conflict Divorce's Report to the Idaho Supreme Court*, 33 Idaho L. Rev. 291, 305 (1997). Even a low level of conflict can have significant repercussions for children. Robert E. Shepherd, Jr., *Legal Dispute Resolution in Child Custody: Comments on Robert H. Mnookin's "Resolving Child Custody Disputes" Conference Presentation*, 10 Va. J.

Soc. Pol'y 89, 91 (2002). Courts must balance the marginal benefits obtained from the institution of a joint physical care regime as compared to other alternatives against the possibility that interparental conflict will be exacerbated by the arrangement, to the detriment of the children. Elizabeth Scott & Andre Derdeyn, *Rethinking Joint Custody*, 45 Ohio St. L.J. 455, 457 (1984). . . .

A fourth important factor in determining whether joint physical care is in the best interest of the children, particularly when there is a turbulent past relationship, is the degree to which the parents are in general agreement about their approach to daily matters. *Burham*, 283 N.W.2d at 275 (*citing Dodd v. Dodd*, 93 Misc. 2d 641, 647, 403 N.Y.S.2d 401 (N.Y. Sup. Ct. 1978) for the proposition that even joint legal custody assumes "agreement about child rearing practices"); *Burkhart*, 876 S.W.2d at 680 (where record does not show commonality of ideas about child rearing, joint physical care inappropriate); *Horton v. Horton*, 891 A.2d 885, 892 (R.I. 2006) (lack of agreement on discipline a factor). It would be unrealistic, of course, to suggest that parents must agree on all issues all of the time, but in order for joint physical care to work, the parents must generally be operating from the same page on a wide variety of routine matters. The greater the amount of agreement between the parents on child rearing issues, the lower the likelihood that ongoing bitterness will create a situation in which children are at risk of becoming pawns in continued post-dissolution marital strife.

While the above factors are often significant in determining the appropriateness of joint physical care, we do not mean to suggest that they are the exclusive factors or that these factors will always be determinative. This court has stated, despite application of a multi-factored test, that district courts must consider the total setting presented by each unique case. *In re Weidner*, 338 N.W.2d 351, 356 (Iowa 1983) (each case to be considered upon its peculiar circumstances). The above factors present important considerations, but no iron clad formula or inflexible system of legal presumptions. . . .

In summary, we believe that statements in the case law indicating that joint physical care is strongly disfavored are overbroad. . . . While we believe that in many contested cases, the best interests of the child will not be advanced by joint physical care, the courts must examine each case based on the unique facts and circumstances presented to arrive at the best decision.

5. Best Interests of Children in this Case

Having examined the entire record, we hold that this is not a case where joint physical care is in the best interest of the children in light of the primary caregiving responsibilities of Delores, the communication and respect issues, the contentiousness of the marriage, and the lack of agreement on daily matters. We conclude that the best interest of the children will be advanced by awarding physical care to Delores rather than to award joint physical care.

At the same time, Lyle has an important role to play in his children's lives. No one questions his devotion to them and their need for his guidance and support. A responsible, committed, nonresident parent, with good parenting skills, has the potential to engage in a high-quality relationship with his or her child and to positively impact the child's adjustment. Gilmore, 20 Int'l J.L. & Pol'y & Fam. at 352. . . .

We expect Delores to support Lyle's relationship with the children as required by Iowa Code section 598.41(5)(*b*). Through liberal visitation and the exercise of joint legal custody, the children can realize the benefits of Lyle's continued involvement in their lives.

DISCUSSION QUESTIONS **FOR *IN RE MARRIAGE OF HANSEN***

A. How does the court define the terms *legal custody* and *physical care*?

B. On what basis did many scholars in the past reject joint physical care?

C. The validity of the parent-child dyad or monotropic view of attachments has been subject to substantial question. What is the shift among some social scientists regarding the attachment theory? *See* Marsha Kline Pruett et al., *Parental Separation and Overnight Care of Young Children, Part I: Consensus Through Theoretical and Empirical Integration*, 52 Fam. Ct. Rev. 240 (2014).

D. What are potential benefits of joint physical care cited by some social scientists?

E. The court describes current social science research regarding joint physical custody as "not definitive on many key questions" and states that the data is "conflicting or ambiguous." What problems with the literature does the court identify? What did the court conclude from its survey of the social science literature?

F. Should social science literature inform public policy making at the legislative or judicial level? What studies are worthy of consideration? Who should decide? *See* Robert F. Kelly & Sarah H. Ramsey, *Assessing and Communicating Social Science Information in Family and Child Judicial Settings: Standards for Judges and Allied Professionals*, 45 Fam. Ct. Rev. 22 (2007).

G. Should lawyers who handle child custody cases be conversant with relevant empirical research? Why or why not? Should parents be informed about the impact of divorce on children? Should lawyers be prepared to counsel clients on such issues? Why or why not?

H. The court cites "growing support" for the assertion that quality of parent-child contact is more strongly associated with the well-being of children than quantity of contact. The court then states: "Quality interaction with children can, of course, occur within the framework of traditional visitation and does not occur solely in situations involving joint physical care." Is there an argument that quality of contact is related to quantity of contact? Do you agree with the court's statement?

I. Empirical research from Australia suggests that some parents are more likely to successfully share care than others:

> It [shared care] was a parenting arrangement that proved viable for a small and distinct group of families, who shared the following profile: electing a shared arrangement, as opposed to having legally enforceable orders to adopt such an arrangement; geographical proximity (within a moderate car trip); the ability of parents to get along sufficiently well; a business-like working relationship between parents; child-focused arrangements; a commitment by everyone to make shared care work; family-friendly work practices for both mothers and fathers; financial comfort (particularly for women); and shared confidence that the father is a competent parent.

Jennifer E. McIntosh, *Legislating for Shared Parenting: Exploring Some Underlying Assumptions*, 47 Fam. Ct. Rev. 389 (2009). Parents who successfully share physical care tend to have older children and are more likely to live near each other and take a respectful, flexible approach to arrangements. *See* Jennifer McIntosh et al., *Post-Separation Parenting Arrangements: Patterns and Developmental Outcomes for Infants and Children*, Report to the Australian Government Attorney-General's Department (2010). What are the implications of this research for policy making about joint physical custody presumptions?

J. The court delineates four factors to be considered in deciding whether to award joint physical custody. What are those factors?

K. What is the approximation rule? Does the court adopt it in this case?

L. How are custodial presumptions inconsistent with making individualized determinations under the best interests standard? What assumptions underlie custodial presumptions? Are the assumptions true for all families? *See* Nancy Ver Steegh & Diana Gould-Saltman, *Joint Legal Custody Presumptions: A Troubling Legal Shortcut*, 52 Fam. Ct. Rev. 263 (2014).

5.14 PRESUMPTIONS AND PREFERENCES: INTIMATE PARTNER VIOLENCE

As discussed in more detail in Chapter 15, some states have adopted rebuttable presumptions against awarding legal and/or physical custody to perpetrators of intimate partner violence. For example, §401 of the Model Code on Domestic and Family Violence provides: "In every proceeding where there is at issue a dispute as to the custody of a child, a determination by the court that domestic or family violence has occurred raises a rebuttable presumption that it is detrimental to the child and not in the best interest of the child to be placed in sole custody, joint legal custody, or joint physical custody with the perpetrator of family violence." State statutes vary considerably concerning the showing required to trigger application of the presumption and the proof needed to rebut it. *See* Margaret F. Brinig et al., *Perspectives on Joint Custody Presumptions as Applied to Domestic Violence Cases*, 52 Fam. Ct. Rev. 271 (2014).

REFLECTIVE QUESTIONS	**Do you favor adoption of presumptions against awarding legal or physical custody to perpetrators of intimate partner violence? Why or why not?**

5.15 PARENTING PLANS: JUDICIAL REVIEW

Background to *Vollet v. Vollet*

The vast majority of child custody cases are resolved by agreement. Although parents are often in the best position to develop workable parenting plans, courts retain the authority to review child custody arrangements to assure that they are in the best interests of the child. In the following case the appellate court reviews a trial judge's refusal to approve a "noncohabitation/overnight guest restriction" clause contained in the parties' agreed parenting plan.

VOLLET
v.
VOLLET

Court of Appeals of Missouri
202 S.W.3d 72 (2006)

LOWENSTEIN, J. The record here reveals the following. Cindy Vollet ("Wife") filed a petition for dissolution of her marriage to Kevin Vollet ("Husband"). The parties agreed on the division of their marital and non-marital property and debts, and agreed to joint custody of their three minor children (ages two and five), alternating on a week-on-week-off basis. . . . Joint Exhibit 2, marked as Exhibit B and submitted to the court, was a non-cohabitation/overnight guest restriction, signed by both parties that provided:

Neither party shall cohabitate with or permit anyone, not a relative, to stay overnight at any time in which the Minor Children are in his or her physical custody, or for any periods of temporary custody/visitation. Furthermore, both parties agree that when either is in a relationship with another individual, both parties shall make that individual aware of the terms of this parenting plan so as to allow that individual to be able to participate for the betterment of the minor children and to insure that individual does not interfere with the terms of this agreement.

In the event that either party to this Agreement brings an action for failure to perform any of the obligations imposed by this Agreement on him or her, or for enforcement or clarification of the Agreement, the prevailing party in such action shall have the right to recover his or her attorney's fees and litigation costs reasonably expended in prosecuting or defending the action.

The parties asked the court to incorporate the terms of Exhibit B into their Separation Agreement, and include its terms in the judgment. . . . However, the court rejected Joint Exhibit 2, the non-cohabitation/overnight guest restriction, as part of the judgment, stating:

The reason I'm not approving or incorporating Joint Exhibit B — or Joint Exhibit 2 is that you both walk away from this as single individuals. And neither one of you — the best interest of the children should control. And I expect everyone to use the same good judgment as anybody uses. But neither of you should have that sort of control or have custody depending on that sort of control. . . .

I'm not incorporating that into this judgment *or any other judgment that I issue.* If there's ever a situation that under the law qualifies for modification, so be it. That'll be governed by general law in the best interest of the child — children. I'm not going to incorporate that as a special provision. (emphasis added).

Husband contends in Point I that the trial court abused its discretion in refusing to include the parties' Joint Exhibit B in the judgment because the ruling is contrary to the best interest of the minor children. Although the parties to a dissolution proceeding are authorized pursuant to Section 452.325, R.S. Mo. 2000 to enter into a written separation agreement containing provisions for the maintenance of either of them, the disposition of any property owned by either of them, and the custody, support, and visitation of their children, "[p]rovisions regarding the custody, support and visitation of minor children are not binding on the trial court, and cannot act to preclude or limit the court's authority regarding those provisions in the dissolution decree." . . . "As a result, orders pertaining to the custody of minor children become the special obligation of the judge who must act upon evidence adduced in the case. Such evidence must be recorded in order that a meaningful review of child custody orders can be had. . . ."

In Exhibit B, Husband and Wife agreed to a non-cohabitation/overnight guest restriction as part of the parenting plan. At the dissolution hearing, Wife testified briefly regarding the terms of Exhibit B and requested that the court incorporate it into the Separation Agreement and approve it. However, "[a]greements between parents regarding minor children are only advisory." . . . "[S]uch agreements do not bind the court, because the court is ordered to make a determination of the child's best interest by looking at all relevant factors, including the eight enumerated factors in §452.375." "Agreement between, or stipulation by the parties does not relieve the court of this responsibility." . . .

Pursuant to Section 452.375.2, R.S. Mo. 2000, "[t]he court shall determine custody in accordance with the best interests of the child." At the dissolution hearing, there was no evidence as to what would be in the best interests of the children. Specifically as to Exhibit B, Wife's testimony merely acknowledged the content of the exhibit. There was no testimony offered as to why Exhibit B was in the best interests of the children, such as to ensure a proper custodial environment or promote a stable environment for the children. Whether the court includes the exhibit in the Separation Agreement and in the judgment and decree of dissolution should be based on the pole-star consideration in every child custody matter — the best interests of the children. . . . The court in the case at bar stated: "I'm not incorporating that [Exhibit 2] into this judgment or any other judgment that I issue." It is clear from the record that the trial court did not consider the best interests of the children in rejecting the language of the agreement. The court merely said it would reject the contents of the proposal "as part of any judgment."

In *Buschardt*, the father appealed a judgment modifying custody, visitation, and support of the minor child. It was the court, not the parties, that ordered that both parties were prohibited from having an adult of the opposite sex, to whom they were not lawfully wed or related, spend the night with them during periods of custody or visitation. As one issue on appeal, the father argued that the trial court's rulings as to custody and visitation resulted from the trial court's bias against him because he was living with a woman to whom he was not lawfully married or related. The trial judge stated on the record that he was restricting visitation if cohabitation occurred "because he had a policy to include such a provision in every decree when cohabitation was an issue." As this court then noted: The effect of cohabitation, like any other factor, must be determined on a case-by-case basis, always with the purpose in mind of determining the best interests of the children. . . . A judge's decision on visitation is to be an exercise of the judge's discretion after properly weighing all the relevant facts, not a decision based on a predetermined policy. By having a policy that a certain provision is to be entered in every case, the judge abused his discretion by failing to exercise it. The primary consideration for the court in a custody or visitation determination is, without question, the best interest of the children.

Conversely, if a judge has a predetermined policy that a certain provision will never be incorporated into a custody decree, he has "abused his discretion by failing to exercise it." Although the situation in *Buschardt* is different, i.e., there the court insisted on a no cohabitation clause and here the court refused to insert such a provision in the decree, the reasoning in *Buschardt* applies here. Because the trial judge abused his discretion by arbitrarily rejecting Exhibit B without determining whether inclusion of the exhibit in the parenting plan was in the best interests of the children, the case must be reversed and remanded for the trial court to consider additional evidence upon which to make this determination. Point I is sustained.

DISCUSSION QUESTIONS FOR *VOLLET v. VOLLET*

A. Why do courts review parenting arrangements that the parties have agreed upon? Is this sound public policy or unnecessary interference with parenting decisions?

B. Did the clause at issue in this case serve the best interests of the children? What reason did the trial judge give for refusing to incorporate the cohabitation agreement?

C. On what basis does the court distinguish the facts of this case from those in *Buschardt*, where a similar provision was incorporated into a divorce decree?

D. What do you think will happen when the case is remanded?

E. Should parents be allowed to agree to parenting plan terms that a court could not or would not be likely to order? For example, could parents agree that neither will move out of the jurisdiction? Could they agree not to remarry? Could they agree not to have additional children in their new relationships? Should courts allow or enforce such agreements?

General Principles

1. Legal custody involves responsibility for decision making regarding major issues such as the child's religion, health, and education. Physical custody involves the residence and day-to-day physical care of the child. Legal and/or physical custody may be exercised by one parent or shared by the parents.
2. The historic paternal presumption presumed fathers were better suited to receive custody of children. The tender years presumption presumed mothers were better suited to care for younger children. These gendered presumptions were later determined to violate the Equal Protection Clause of the Constitution.
3. Most jurisdictions use the "best interest" test for making child custody determinations. The test requires individualized consideration of the needs of every child, but it has, for this reason, been criticized for being too discretionary and unpredictable in application.
4. The historic primary caretaker presumption and the proposed approximation standard illustrate the importance placed on providing stability and continuity for children while also taking into account the relative commitment of each parent to the performance of daily child-rearing tasks.

5. In most jurisdictions conduct of a parent, such as cohabitation, will only be relevant to determining the best interests of the child if it has an adverse effect on the child.

6. One factor in determining the best interests of the child may be the willingness of parents to promote an ongoing relationship with the other parent. Application of cooperative parent provisions is problematic in families with a history of intimate partner violence.

7. A majority of jurisdictions consider intimate partner violence as a factor in the application of the best interests standard or they have adopted a preference or presumption regulating custody and parenting time when intimate partner violence has occurred.

8. Among other factors in determining best interests, courts will consider the custodial preferences of children with sufficient maturity to express a meaningful preference.

9. While race, religion, and physical disability cannot be individually determinative factors in awarding custody, they may be considered if they detrimentally affect the child.

10. States vary considerably concerning the extent to which they allow or encourage use of joint legal and physical custody of children.

11. Although most parents reach agreement about parenting arrangements, before they are finalized courts review agreements and proposed parenting plans to assure that they are in the best interests of children.

Chapter Problems

1. Assume that a legislator asks you to draft a statute regarding joint child custody (legal and physical). As a policy matter, what approach do you favor? Will you create presumptions? Will you use custody labels? Will you require creation of parenting plans? Why? What specific language would you recommend?

2. Assume that Ann and Scott have two children who are age 10 and age 15 at the time of the divorce. Both parents are fit and suitable parents, and each seeks sole physical custody of the children. Should the children be consulted as to their wishes? Why or why not? If the children are consulted, who should meet with them, where should the discussion take place, and who should be present?

3. Assume that Joe and Marie are both 19 years old when they seek a divorce. They married when they were both 18, and they have one child. While they are both adequate parents in that they provide for the child's basic needs, Marie's mother thinks that the child would be better off in her custody. Assume that Marie's mother seeks custody of the child and assume that Marie's mother is, in fact, a better parent than either Marie or Joe. Will a court award custody to Marie's mother?

4. Assume that Joanna and Paulo have two children who are eight and ten years old at the time of the divorce. They are both devoted parents, and they are committed to assuring that the children have strong relationships with both of them. They agree to share joint legal and physical custody, but before the divorce is final, Paulo is transferred and ends up living approximately 100 miles away from Joanna. They reach a new agreement incorporating a plan for the children to alternate residences each year. Assume that you are the judge asked to approve this arrangement. What would you decide and why? *See Headrick v. Headrick*, 916 So. 2d 610 (Ala. Civ. App. 2005) (disapproving annually alternating residence); *Mundy v. Devon*, 2006 WL 902233 (Del. Supr. 2006) (approving alternating primary residence).

5. Using the list of potential child custody and access arrangements in section 5.5, create fictional families for whom each arrangement would be suitable.

Preparation for Practice

1. Find the child custody and parenting time statutes used in your state. Is the best interests of the child standard used? Are specific factors enumerated? Are there any custody-related presumptions? How are various custody and access arrangements defined?

2. Locate a sample parenting plan form by going online or using a law library. How comprehensive are the provisions? What would you add or delete? Would it be usable by an unrepresented party?

3. Find out if your jurisdiction has a self-help center for unrepresented parents. How do parents find out about it? What assistance is available? How is it funded?

4. Assume that a judicial commission retains you to draft a list of recommended qualifications for judges who will sit on the family court bench. What will you recommend in terms of education, training, and experience? Why? *See* Natalie Anne Knowlton, *The Modern Family Court Judge: Knowledge, Qualities, and Skills for Success*, 53 Fam. Ct. Rev. 203 (2015).

5. As discussed in this chapter, a court may appoint a mental health professional to complete a custody evaluation. In this capacity, the mental health professional makes specific recommendations based on his or her evaluation of the case. Because judges typically give these evaluations substantial weight, concerns have arisen with respect to accountability, qualifications, and quality assurance. Professional groups such as the Association for Family and

Conciliation Courts have developed and published model professional standards for custody evaluators. *See* Task Force for Model Standards of Practice for Child Custody Evaluation, *Model Standards of Practice for Child Custody Evaluation*, 45 Fam. Ct. Rev. 70 (2007). Review and critique the Model Standards. How might a lawyer use the Model Standards when reviewing a custody evaluation?

6. Assume that you are interviewing a new client who is very angry with her spouse. She directs you to do everything you can to make her husband suffer during and after the divorce process. Specifically, she wants you to delay the divorce, make sure that her husband has limited access to the children, and obtain a financial award wholly unfavorable to him. The couple has two young children. Assume that both are fit parents. How will you advise this client? What information will you provide to her? What will you do or not do on her behalf? For the response of one professional group, see the American Academy of Matrimonial Lawyers, *The Bounds of Advocacy* at http://www.aaml.org/library/publications/19/bounds-advocacy (last visited October 19, 2015).

7. Assume that a state legislative committee retains you to prepare a report on the pros and cons of legislation creating a joint legal custody presumption and/or a joint physical custody presumption. Explain your analysis.

Chapter 6

Parenting Time and Visitation

6.1 INTRODUCTION

This chapter explores how children's relationships with various adults are structured following the separation or divorce of the parents. The first part of the chapter concerns parental access to children, specifically the allocation, enforcement, restriction, and modification of parenting time. The second part of the chapter surveys the legal recognition of children's relationships with adults such as grandparents, stepparents, and some same-sex partner caregivers. These relationships may continue informally, but courts will only enforce ongoing contact under certain circumstances.

As you read, consider questions such as the following: How should parents structure parenting time for a nonresidential parent? When and how should courts enforce, restrict, or modify a nonresidential parent's access to children? When and under what conditions should courts become involved in enforcing contact with adults other than parents?

REFLECTIVE QUESTIONS	What are your goals for this chapter?

6.2 PARENTING TIME: TERMINOLOGY

Historically, one parent usually exercised sole physical custody of the children and the nonresidential parent was granted *visitation*. In recent years states have replaced the term *visitation* with *parenting time* and other similar designations. The change in terminology is intended to affirm the importance of children's ongoing relationships with both parents when those relationships are safe and appropriate. The ALI has taken the additional step of recommending that the terms *custody* and *visitation* be replaced with the single term *custodial responsibility*. ALI, *Principles of the Law of Family Dissolution: Analysis and Recommendations* §2.03 (2002).

Parenting time encompasses a wide variety of parenting arrangements. For example, parenting time can refer to the time that a joint physical custodian spends with children as well as time that a nonresidential parent spends with children.

REFLECTIVE QUESTIONS	The use of the term *visitation* when referring to time spent with a parent has been criticized. What is the basis of the concern?

6.3 PARENTING TIME: RIGHTS AND ENFORCEMENT

Right to parenting time. Parents have a constitutionally protected liberty interest in ongoing contact with their children. *See Meyer v. Nebraska*, 262 U.S. 390 (1923), and *Pierce v. Society of Sisters*, 268 U.S. 510 (1925). This liberty interest is reflected in §407(a) of the UMDA, which provides that a "parent not granted custody of the child is entitled to reasonable visitation rights unless the court finds, after a hearing, that visitation would endanger seriously the child's physical, mental, moral, or emotional health." Under the UMDA, courts and parents often had difficulty agreeing on the meaning of "reasonable visitation" and many states now require that specific and detailed parenting time arrangements be included in court orders. Some states have adopted presumptions related to allocation of parenting time. *See* Minn. Stat. §518.175 subd. 1(g) (2014) (rebuttable presumption of 25 percent parenting time).

Enforcement of parenting time. When parents experience problems with parenting time after separation or divorce, it may be because the arrangement was not appropriately structured or the parenting plan was not sufficiently detailed to meet the needs of the children and parents. (Development of parenting plans is discussed more fully in Chapter 5.) If problems arise, parents may revisit the parenting plan to incorporate more specific and less problematic terms.

Payment of child support and the exercise of parenting time are legally unrelated obligations. Consequently, parents do not have the option of unilaterally withholding child support if parenting time is wrongfully denied. In that event, a parent may seek compensatory parenting time or file a contempt of court action.

REFLECTIVE QUESTIONS	Do you think that a parent should be allowed to withhold parenting time if the other parent doesn't pay child support?

Background to *Miller v. Smith*

Although a sole legal and physical custodian has the right to make major and day-to-day decisions on behalf of the child, those rights do not extend to all aspects of the noncustodial parent's time with the child. Although most parents defer to each other's wishes for the good of the children, for some children parenting time disagreements become a source of persistent stress. In *Miller v. Smith* the mother was granted sole legal and physical custody of the child at the time of divorce. The parties returned to court for the third time concerning the details of the parenting time schedule, specifically whether the father was required to transport their six-year-old daughter to gymnastics during his parenting time with her.

MILLER
v.
SMITH

Supreme Court of Vermont
989 A.2d 537 (2009)

Mother . . . filed a motion, asking the court to clarify that father must bring the child to her scheduled activities on his visitation days. . . . The court . . . explained that the family court could not referee the details of how the child spent her time with father. Father was an adult and during his time with B.S. he would have to make decisions about the child's activities. The court expected that father would respect the child's wishes, but in the end, it was a private matter that the court would not supervise. The court noted that any other approach was unthinkable. The court had no ability or any role in deciding if gymnastics on Tuesdays were better for the child than an afternoon spent at father's house. If the court issued an order requiring father to take the child to after-school activities, the parties would then be back with an endless stream of disputes over the value and reasonableness of various activities. The court could provide blocks of time to each parent. Within reason, how each parent spent that time was left to the individual parent who was caring for the child at the time. Mother appealed from this decision.

The family court acted well within its discretion in refusing to police the child's recreational activities during her visitation with father. Our decision in *Gazo v. Gazo*, 166 Vt. 434, 697 A.2d 342 (1997), is instructive. In that case, we recognized that the parent who does not have physical responsibility for a child "has a right to some measure of parent-child contact unless the best interests of the child[] require otherwise." *Id.* at 444, 697 A.2d at 348. The court may impose conditions on visitation if clearly required by the child's best interests, which is not to suggest that the custodial parent can impose restrictions unilaterally. *Id.* at 444-445, 697 A.2d at 348. "If the custodial parent desires that restrictions be imposed, she must ask the court to impose them." *Id.* at 445, 697 A.2d at 348. As we observed in *Gazo*, "[w]ithout mutual tolerance and understanding, these rights of visitation can become a nightmare for both parents and a disaster for the child or children involved." In this case, the court specifically rejected mother's proposed restrictions, and we find no abuse of the family court's discretion in ruling on this motion to clarify. Mother essentially argues that she has the right to control the child's activities during father's visitation. This is the "nightmare" situation we foretold in *Gazo*. If the custodial parent were allowed to establish routines and restrictions within a noncustodial parent's time at her whim, the contact with father would be little more than a babysitting function with mother having filled the time with instructions and conditions. There are certainly times when the parent awarded parental rights and responsibilities will want to establish conditions, such as where the child has a strict vegetarian diet but the noncustodial parent gives the child hamburger each night of a visit, the mother could ask the court to consider making adherence to a vegetarian diet mandatory. However, to allow the custodial parent to schedule the child for time that is supposed to be spent with the noncustodial parent ignores the legislative mandate that children should continue "to have the opportunity for maximum continuing physical and emotional contact with both parents." 15 V.S.A. §650. It would also, as the trial court aptly noted, bring the parties back before the court "with an endless string of disputes over the reasonableness and value of sports, music lessons, gymnastics classes and friends' birthday parties." As the family court explained, it "can provide blocks of time to each parent. Within reason, how each spends it has to be left to the individual decision of the parent who is caring for [the child] at the time." *Affirmed.*

DISCUSSION QUESTIONS FOR *MILLER v. SMITH*

A. Why did the court refuse to intervene concerning the father's exercise of parenting time?

B. Because the mother was the sole legal and physical custodian of the child, could she not decide to enroll the child in gymnastics? On what basis could the father interfere with that decision?

C. The case is silent concerning the wishes of the child. Should the outcome have been different if the child was heartbroken about missing gymnastics? Why or why not?

D. In some states neutral third-party professionals such as parenting coordinators or parenting time expediters are appointed to work with parents who have continuing disputes of this nature. Would that have been helpful here?

6.4 PARENTING TIME: WISHES OF THE CHILD

After separation or divorce, parents are expected to actively encourage and support a child's relationship with the other parent. While most children want regular contact with a nonresidential parent, it is not always beneficial for them. As discussed in the following sections, contact restrictions may be warranted, particularly in some situations involving child abuse, intimate partner violence, substance abuse, and child abduction.

Absent restrictions on parenting time, children are not free to decline to spend time with a nonresidential parent. When children oppose spending time with a parent, further inquiry is needed to determine the cause of the concern and what intervention or restrictions might be appropriate.

REFLECTIVE QUESTIONS	If a child resists spending time with a noncustodial parent, should the child be forced to do so? Should the age of the child be a significant factor?

6.5 PARENTING TIME RESTRICTIONS: RELIGIOUS PRACTICE

When one parent is designated as the legal custodian, that parent has the right to make major decisions for the child such as those involving medical care, education, and choice of religion. The other parent is expected to support the decisions made by the legal custodian. If the parent without legal custody undermines or ignores the choices made by the parent with legal custody, the legal custodian may place restrictions on the exercise of parenting time. For example, in the case of *Wood v. DeHahn*, the parties came from different religious backgrounds, and the court was asked to place restrictions on the noncustodial parent's use of parenting time. Specifically, the custodial parent, a practicing Mormon, challenged the right of the noncustodial parent to take the children to Catholic services on Christmas, Easter, and Mother's Day.

WOOD
v.
DEHAHN

Court of Appeals of Wisconsin
571 N.W.2d 186 (1997)

PHILLIP, J. DeHahn, a practicing Mormon, appeals the trial court's order denying his request to restrict his former wife, Michelle Wood, a Catholic, from taking their children to Catholic services on Christmas, Easter and Mother's Day. DeHahn notes that our statutes give him, as legal custodian of the children, the right to make all major decisions concerning the children's upbringing, including religion. He further notes that the statutes require the noncustodial parent to act in a manner "consistent" with the legal custodian's choice of religion. DeHahn reads the statutes to therefore give him, not the trial court, the right to decide whether an action by his former spouse is inconsistent with the way he is raising the children regarding religion, and the trial court's job is to enforce his decision unless it is found harmful to the children. . . .

After DeHahn and Wood were divorced in 1991, DeHahn was awarded sole legal custody of their two minor children. DeHahn is a member of the Church of Latter Day Saints, commonly referred to as the Mormon church, and is raising the two children as Mormons. . . .

DeHahn is correct when he observes that as the parent having sole legal custody, he has the exclusive right to choose the religion for the children. Furthermore, Wood, as the noncustodial parent, has no right to participate in the choice of religion for the children and her actions must be consistent with the decision made by DeHahn. . . .

In DeHahn's view, he not only has the power to decide what religion the children shall be brought up with, but he also has the unfettered right to manage that choice absent a showing of harm. DeHahn effectively contends that training young minds is a form of indoctrination and any action by his former wife which he believes to be inconsistent with that training must be enjoined by court order if he so insists.

Deciding whether the statute gives the legal custodian the right to determine what is inconsistent and what is not is a question of statutory interpretation and, therefore, a question of law. . . .

DeHahn recognizes that the issue is one of statutory interpretation. And he concedes that he is unable to find any language in the statute which gives him, and not the court, the right to determine what action is inconsistent with his major life choice. As Wood points out, however, there is such legal authority. She correctly cites §767.01(1), Stats., which gives circuit courts "authority to do all acts necessary and proper" in actions affecting the family.

We agree that not only does this statutory authority give the court the power to place restrictions on visitation, but the converse is also true; the court has the discretion to decline to place restrictions on visitation. Case law supports this statement. Matters relating to visitation are committed to the discretion of the trial court. Thus, it is the court's responsibility to determine if the noncustodian's actions are inconsistent such that it is necessary and reasonable to fashion a restrictive order to protect the legal custodian's major life choice. . . .

Here, the children continue to be practicing Mormons. The mother takes the children to church three times a year. There is no evidence that the mother is attempting to teach her children so as to dissuade them from being practicing Mormons. There is no evidence that the children are being subverted. It is not enough that DeHahn disapproves of the children going to a church that is not of his faith. He must convince the court that the action of going to another church cannot stand together with his authority to choose one religion over another religion. He must show how a restrictive order is reasonably necessary in order to protect his choice of religion for the children. As the moving party, he has that burden. He has failed to meet his burden.

Lange v. Lange, 502 N.W.2d 143 (Ct. App. 1993), is a study in contrast. The mother in *Lange* was the sole legal guardian and her choice of religion was the Lutheran church. The father, who was Catholic, opposed the mother's choice and convinced the children that because their mother was Lutheran, she was going to hell and had effectively caused the children to reject the mother's choice. Moreover, the father had ignored earlier orders to refrain from imposing his religious views on the children, stating that he followed God's orders, not the court's.

The trial court restricted the father's visitation rights in order to protect the mother's choice of religion. We upheld the trial court's restriction on the father's visitation rights as a reasonable use of its discretion because the record contained ample evidence supporting a finding that the father was acting inconsistently with the mother's choice.

The court wrote that because it was the father's intent to impose his choice of religion on the children, he was thereby subverting the mother's choice.

We do not have those facts here. The court made a "reasonableness" determination that going to a church service three times a year was not contrary to the children's religious upbringing in the Mormon faith. We are comfortable with the court's judgment and hold that there was no misuse of discretion.

 **FOR *WOOD v. DEHAHN***

A. The parties agreed that the visitation statute required that the noncustodial parent act in a manner "consistent" with the legal custodian's choice of religion. What reasons are given by the court to support its view that allowing the children to attend church with the noncustodial parent three times a year over the custodial parent's objection does not violate this general principle? What if the noncustodial parent took the children to church on five occasions? Ten occasions? Every other weekend?

B. Assume that you are negotiating and drafting a parenting plan in a case where the divorcing parents come from different religious traditions. How would you approach the negotiation, and what sort of terms would you consider including in the final parenting plan? Could the situation in *DeHahn* have been avoided? How?

C. When one parent seeks to control the other parent's religious interaction with the child, are there First Amendment implications? *See* Kent Greenawalt, *Child Custody, Religious Practices, and Conscience*, 76 U. Colo. L. Rev. 965 (2005); Jeffrey Shulman, *Spiritual Custody: Relational Rights and Constitutional Commitments*, 7

J.L. & Fam. Stud. 317 (2005); Eugene Volokh, *Parent-Child Speech and Child Custody Speech Restrictions*, 81 N.Y.U. L. Rev. 631 (2006).

D. Is this case distinguishable from the preceding case, *Miller v. Smith*? Why or why not?

6.6 PARENTING TIME RESTRICTIONS: COHABITATION, SEXUAL PREFERENCE, AND HIV STATUS

Analogous to the application of the nexus test in child custody proceedings, courts are not generally receptive to attempts to restrict parenting time based on attributes or conduct of a parent that does not directly and adversely affect the child. Consequently without a showing of endangerment to a child's physical or emotional health, parenting time will not usually be restricted based on the sexual preference or HIV status of a parent or because a parent cohabits with someone of the opposite sex.

> **REFLECTIVE QUESTIONS** Under what factual circumstances might parenting time be restricted because of a parent's cohabitation with a new partner?

6.7 PARENTING TIME RESTRICTIONS: SUBSTANCE ABUSE, CHILD ABUSE, INTIMATE PARTNER VIOLENCE, CHILD ABDUCTION

Under UMDA §407(a) the noncustodial parent is entitled to reasonable parenting time unless it would "endanger seriously the child's physical, mental, moral, or emotional health." Consequently, courts will limit or restrict parenting time if a parent with concerns about the exercise of parenting time can demonstrate that the child will be harmed or endangered. This may occur if the parent has a history of child abuse, intimate partner violence, alcohol and substance abuse, or child abduction.

Typical restrictions of parenting time include imposition of supervised parenting time, denial of overnight contact, supervised exchange, and limitation on the amount of time spent with the child. In determining what contact might be appropriate, psychologists advise consideration of the risks and benefits to the child. For example, contact with an abusive parent may re-traumatize a child, but in other cases safe access may help a child develop a more realistic view of his or her relationship with a parent. *See* Janet Johnston et al., *In the Name of the Child:*

A Developmental Approach to Understanding and Helping Children of Conflicted and Violent Divorce 323 (2009).

When parenting time is supervised, a friend or family member may be ordered to remain present during parenting time or contact with the child may take place at a formal supervised visitation center. Supervised visitation centers have been described as follows:

> Supervised visitation is contact between a noncustodial parent and his or her "child overseen by a trained third party in a controlled environment. . . ." . . . The service allows children to safely maintain family attachments and reduces children's sense of abandonment when they are removed from their parents' care.
>
> During the 1990s, courts began to expand the use of supervised visitation programs to help address a variety of other family dysfunctions found in many cases involving divorce or disputed custody. These frequently recurring problems include substance abuse, mental illness, threats of abduction, and domestic violence. Instead of prohibiting contact between parents accused of wrongdoing and their children, courts began to order families to use visitation programs to enhance family safety during contact, while other services were offered to reduce family problems.

Nat Stern & Karen Oehme, *A Comprehensive Blueprint for a Crucial Service: Florida's New Supervised Visitation Strategy*, 12 J.L. & Fam. Stud. 199, 201 (2010). Unfortunately the availability of such services has been curtailed due to funding cutbacks.

When fashioning parenting time arrangements for families who have experienced intimate partner violence, it is vital to consider the nature and context of the abuse and the specific implications for contact with the child. *See* Gabrielle Davis, *A Systematic Approach to Domestic Abuse-Informed Decision-Making in Family Law Cases*, 53 Fam. Ct. Rev. 562 (2015); Peter G. Jaffe et al., *Custody Disputes Involving Allegations of Domestic Violence: Toward a Differentiated Approach to Parenting Plans*, 46 Fam. Ct. Rev. 500 (2008).

 **REFLECTIVE QUESTIONS**   **Why might a parent object to supervised parenting time? When and under what conditions should the requirement of supervision be terminated?**

Background to *Pratt v. Pratt*

A parent who seeks to restrict the exercise of parenting time has the burden of showing that the child's physical, mental, or emotional health would be seriously endangered by unrestricted contact with the other parent. This is a heavy burden and courts scrutinize restrictions with great care. In the case of *Pratt v. Pratt*, the court agrees that supervision is needed as a result of the mother's substance abuse issues, but the appellate court determines that the arrangement ordered by the trial court did not sufficiently protect her right to contact with the child.

PRATT
v.
PRATT

Court of Civil Appeals of Alabama
56 So. 3d 638 (2010)

MOORE, J., Susanne M. Pratt ("the mother") appeals from a judgment of the Montgomery Circuit Court ("the trial court") divorcing her from John W. Pratt ("the father") and awarding her supervised visitation with the parties' three children. We affirm in part and reverse in part.

The pertinent evidence at trial, when viewed in a light most favorable to the findings of the trial court, indicates that the mother had developed health problems following the birth of the parties' three children that caused her lethargy and other disabling symptoms, which sometimes prevented her from properly caring for the children. The mother used narcotic and other medications to treat those health problems, resulting in what one expert considered a substance-abuse problem, which another expert described as an "iatrogenic addiction." The mother appeared to overcome those problems after the parties separated, which allowed her to start working as a nurse and permitted her to exercise custody of the children uneventfully for a period. However, in early December 2008, the mother experienced a seizure-like episode and lost consciousness late at night while at her home in Montgomery with the children and her father. Following that episode, the father obtained custody of the children while the mother remained hospitalized. Upon her discharge several days later, the mother's treating physicians, who did not definitively diagnose the cause of the episode but suspected it may have arisen from the mother's medically unsupervised attempt to withdraw from all of her medications, recommended that the mother cease using narcotic medications; however, at the time of trial, the mother continued to use narcotic medications prescribed by her pain-management physician. Some evidence suggested that the mother had also obtained prescription medications from other physicians without coordinating with her primary doctor. All the expert testimony on the subject recommended that, due to her unresolved health and prescription-drug-use problems, the mother should have supervised visitation with the children.

The trial court entered its judgment of divorce on June 24, 2009. In that judgment, the trial court, among other things, divorced the parties, awarded the parties joint legal custody of the children, awarded the father primary physical custody of the children, and awarded the mother supervised visitation. In reference to the mother's supervised visitation, the judgment stated:

> 3. . . . The [mother] shall have supervised visitation with the children and said visitation shall be supervised by Roger and Gloria Burk. The counselor, Laurie Mattson Shoemaker, shall prepare guidelines to be given to the supervisors for the supervised visitation.
>
> 4. The schedule of supervised visitation may be upon agreement of the parties, however, said visitation shall occur no less than once every two weeks, beginning June 26, 2009. The location and length of visits are at the discretion of the [father] and the

supervising party, however, each visit should last at least two hours and should be held in as "home-like" a setting as possible, so that the children feel comfortable.

We initially address the mother's argument that the trial court exceeded its discretion in ordering supervised visitation based on its concern that the mother had developed an addiction to prescription pain medication. From our reading of her brief, the mother does not complain that the trial court did not have sufficient evidence before it to support its concern that the children could be at risk while visiting the mother due to her prescription-drug-use problem. Rather, the mother contends that the trial court should have protected the children by using means other than supervised visitation that would be less intrusive on the parent-child relationship.

"The trial court has broad discretion in determining the visitation rights of a noncustodial parent, and its decision in this regard will not be reversed absent an abuse of discretion." In exercising its discretion over visitation matters, "'[t]he trial court is entrusted to balance the rights of the parents with the child's best interests to fashion a visitation award that is tailored to the specific facts and circumstances of the individual case.'" A noncustodial parent generally enjoys "reasonable rights of visitation" with his or her children. However, those rights may be restricted in order to protect children from conduct, conditions, or circumstances surrounding their noncustodial parent that endanger the children's health, safety, or well-being. In fashioning the appropriate restrictions, out of respect for the public policy encouraging interaction between noncustodial parents and their children, *see* Ala. Code 1975, §30-3-150 (addressing joint custody), and §30-3-160 (addressing Alabama Parent–Child Relationship Protection Act), the trial court may not use an overbroad restriction that does more than necessary to protect the children.

In *Ex parte Thompson*, our supreme court recently endorsed supervised visitation as a reasonable means of protecting the child of a noncustodial parent who was suffering from, among other problems, an unresolved substance-abuse condition when the evidence showed that unsupervised visitation would have subjected the child to an unreasonable risk of harm. The mother argues that, in this case, the trial court could have adequately addressed its safety concern for the children by simply ordering that she refrain from using prescription drugs. In *Jackson v. Jackson*, 999 So. 2d 488 (Ala. Civ. App. 2007), a plurality of this court concluded that a mother, who was accused of having in the past occasionally used marijuana for recreational use outside the presence of her children, should have been allowed unsupervised visitation subject to a prohibition against exposing the children to any illegal drug use. However, the facts of this case differ significantly from those in *Jackson*. The mother in this case uses narcotic and other prescription medications daily, which use has adversely affected her ability to parent the children in the past and the cessation of which may have caused or contributed to her prior "black-out" episode while in her home with the children. In *Ratliff*, we found it unreasonable to restrict a mother from using prescription drugs designed to control her mental-health problems while visiting with her children because such a restriction could actually endanger the children. For that same reason, we conclude that the trial court in this case could not have merely ordered the mother to refrain from using her prescription medications while visiting with the children.

Because the trial court reasonably could have concluded that supervised visitation was necessary to protect the children from an unreasonable risk of physical or emotional harm emanating from the condition of the mother, and because the trial court reasonably could have rejected as inadequate the less intrusive means of protection advocated by the mother, we find that the trial court did not exceed its discretion in awarding the mother supervised visitation with the children.

The mother next contends that the manner in which the trial court structured its award of supervised visitation granted the father so much discretion over her right to visitation that the father, in essence, may effectively veto that right. Although the trial court specified that the mother was to receive, at a minimum, two hours of visitation every two weeks, the trial court did not specify the location or the length of the mother's visits. Rather, the trial court granted the father and the visitation supervisors the exclusive discretion to determine the location of the visitation and whether the mother's visits should be extended beyond the minimum two-hour period. Additionally, although the trial court's judgment did not expressly grant the father the right to dictate the time at which the mother's visits are to be held, the judgment places considerable discretion in the father by requiring his agreement as to the timing of the visitation. Thus, whether the discretion granted to the father and/or the visitation supervisors violates Alabama law is squarely before this court.

Although Alabama law originally found no problem with vesting a custodial parent with complete discretion over the visitation of the noncustodial parent, over time our appellate courts began to recognize that divorced parties often disagree regarding visitation matters, and that a custodial parent should not be allowed to unilaterally limit or restrict the noncustodial parent's visitation. This court eventually held that a visitation order awarding " 'reasonable visitation with the minor children at the discretion of the [custodial parent]' " generally should not be allowed because it authorizes the custodial parent to deny visitation altogether, which would not be in the best interests of the children.

. . . [T]his court has repeatedly held that a judgment awarding visitation to be supervised by the custodian of the child, without establishing a minimal visitation schedule for the noncustodial parent, impermissibly allows the custodian to control all visitation. . . . [A]n order of visitation granting a custodian so much discretion over a visitation schedule that visitation could be completely avoided if the custodian so desired should be deemed to be an award of no visitation and to be in violation of the rights of the noncustodial parent.

This court, however, has affirmed awards of unspecified visitation based on the agreement of the parties when the trial court also provides that, in the event of disagreement, "standard visitation" or some other specified visitation would be imposed.

Thus, a judgment awarding visitation that guarantees the noncustodial parent a specified visitation schedule, while granting the custodian discretion to allow for additional visitation, does not necessarily violate the rights of the noncustodial parent. The propriety of the judgment depends on whether the noncustodial parent has a sufficient, specified visitation schedule to rely upon, independent of the custodial parent's discretion.

Applying the rationale of the above-cited cases to the visitation schedule established for the mother in this case, we agree with the mother that the visitation schedule is unduly vague and that it, in fact, fails to provide her with any schedule at all. As noted above, the mother is guaranteed to receive only two hours of visitation every two weeks; she has no guarantee when or where those visits will occur. Because the time and location of her visits are expressly within the discretion of the father (as well as within the discretion of the visitation supervisors), the mother has no recourse should the father elect to schedule those visits at a time and location prohibitive for the mother. Because the trial court has cloaked the father's decisions with such broad discretion, the father's lack of cooperation in providing the mother with a reasonable visitation schedule would not be readily addressable by a contempt action.

We also reiterate that " '[t]he *trial court* is entrusted to balance the rights of the parents with the child's best interests to fashion a visitation award that is tailored to the specific facts and circumstances of the individual case.' " That judicial function may not be delegated to a third party. A trial court is not empowered to delegate its judicial functions even to another governmental agency.

The trial court's visitation award, as written, vests the father and the visitation supervisors with nearly complete discretion in determining when, where, and how the mother exercises her current visitation rights; it also grants a third party the right to decide when and if the mother's visitation rights should be expanded. Because those are nondelegable determinations for the trial court, we reverse those portions of the trial court's judgment and remand the cause for the trial court to establish a sufficiently specific visitation order for the mother.

We affirm the trial court's judgment to the extent it required the mother's visitation with the children to be supervised. We reverse the trial court's judgment to the extent it granted the father and the visitation supervisors the authority to determine the location and timing of the mother's visits and to determine whether to increase the length of the mother's visits.

 **FOR *PRATT v. PRATT***

A. What danger to the children did the court deem sufficient to restrict the access rights of the mother? Do you agree with the assessment of the court? Why or why not?

B. Could the safety of the children have been protected through means less intrusive than supervised parenting time? What other arrangements might the mother have preferred?

C. For what length of time should parenting time be supervised? Should the restriction go forward indefinitely? What if the mother successfully seeks treatment?

D. What was the problem with having the parenting time take place at the discretion of the father? What argument can you make that this was a suitable solution from a practical perspective?

E. What is the trial court required to do on remand? What would a "sufficiently specific" parenting time look like in this case?

6.8 PARENTING TIME RESTRICTIONS: INCARCERATED PARENT

Background to *Etter v. Rose*

In extreme cases a parent may request no contact between the other parent and the child or children. Not surprisingly courts hesitate to so totally restrict a parent's constitutional right to contact with the child.

Particularly difficult questions arise when children are young and a parent is incarcerated for a long period of time. For example, in the case of *Culver v. Culver*, 82 A.D.3d 1296 (N.Y. App. Div. 2011), the court approved a lower court decision granting limited parenting time with a preschool girl by a father convicted of committing sex offences against other children. The court summarized the testimony of the mother's expert as follows:

> Steven Wood, a licensed mental health counselor and clinical specialist with significant experience in child and adolescent therapy testified for the mother and disagreed. Specifically, Wood asserted that because the child is beginning to reach the age at which she will begin forming substantive memories, visiting her father in prison may damage her future relationship with him. In Wood's opinion, the child does not have sufficient life experience to be able to go through the process of visiting a maximum security prison. Wood also concluded that, while the individual processes the child would have to go through to visit the father would not — in themselves — be traumatic, the cumulative effect of such an experience would be. Yet, Wood also concluded that the child was stable, did not demonstrate an increased vulnerability to social trauma and did not express a fear of her father and that, although the child did not feel abandoned by her father, any child who had a parent disappear could develop a feeling of abandonment.

In contrast, the expert retained by the father reached a different set of conclusions:

> Family Court found "persuasive and reasoned" the report and testimony of Jerold Grodin, a licensed psychologist with significant experience in the field of child psychology, who testified for the father. Grodin opined that visitation with the father, even at

his correctional facility, would be "healthful and safe" and in the child's best interests because the child seems to be comfortable in new situations and is quite inquisitive, and also because of the inherent need for any child to maintain contact with both parents. His interaction with the child also revealed a bond between the child and father and a desire on the part of the child to contact the father. Grodin discussed how children who are separated from their parents, without a clear understanding, tend to develop feelings of abandonment. Grodin further concluded that visitation would not be traumatic for the child and that it could be facilitated by therapeutic counseling.

See also Matter of Flood v. Flood, 63 A.D.3d 1197 (Sup. Ct. App. Div. N.Y. 2009) ("Visitation with a noncustodial parent is presumed to be in the children's best interests, although the presumption can be overcome with evidence that visitation would be detrimental to the children's welfare. A parent's incarceration, by itself, does not vitiate this presumption.").

In the following case, *Etter v. Rose*, an incarcerated father seeks to exercise parenting time while in prison, over the objection of the mother.

ETTER
v.
ROSE

Superior Court of Pennsylvania
684 A.2d 1092 (1996)

TAMILIA, J. Michael L. Etter appeals from the March 25, 1996, Order denying his request for visitation with his minor son at the prison where appellant is presently incarcerated. The court reasoned it would not be in the child's best interests to allow such visitation, and it is the court's policy to deny a request for a minor's visitation with an inmate when the custodial parent objects.

Appellant argues the court abused its discretion by denying his request for visitation in that the court erred by applying the "best interest" standard and improperly based its decision on personal and biased opinions. Appellant also contends the court's policy of denying visitation when the custodial parent objects contravenes the legislature's intent to guarantee a child's continued contact with both parents and unconstitutionally denies visitation without allowing him the opportunity to respond to the objections of the child's mother.

When considering a request for visitation, the primary concern of the court is what is in the best interest and permanent welfare of the child. This determination will be made on a case-by-case basis and premised on a weighing of all factors which legitimately affect the child's physical, intellectual, moral and spiritual well-being. The trial court had before it for consideration appellant's petition and mother's response. In denying appellant's request, the trial judge reasoned a "prison is not conducive to establishment of a positive parent/child relationship. . . ."

While encouraging an on-going, healthy parent/child relationship is certainly an aim of the judicial system, of paramount concern must be, after considering all factors, what is best for the child. We cannot agree that the trial court carefully weighed all factors in determining the best interests of the child. Rather, the court established a policy which consisted of one factor, the wishes of the mother, the custodial parent. By doing so, the court did not consider the best interests of the child but created two categories of visitation, that approved by the mother and that not approved by the mother. Although in general we believe "[v]iolation of the laws with its resulting confinement subsumes very serious restrictions on the freedom to do many things and to exercise many rights, the least of which is to have a normal relationship with one's family[,]" . . . in this case, the result is illogical and inconsistent in that the child is permitted to visit his step-father, who is also in prison, but not his natural father because he would suffer trauma by prison visitation with him.

While there is no case law which permits denial of visitation with a parent because of incarceration alone, we believe there is a basis for creation of a presumption, to be rebutted by the prisoner parent, that such visitation is not in the best interest of the child. Appellant must, however, be afforded a hearing in which both parties are permitted to establish the relative benefits or harm to the child occasioned by visitation with father while in prison. All relevant factors must be considered, including age of the child, distance and hardship to the child in traveling to the visitation site, the kind of supervision at the visit, identification of the person(s) transporting him and by what means, the effect on the child physically and emotionally, whether the father has and does exhibit a genuine interest in the child, whether he maintained reasonable contacts in the past and any other relevant matters impinging on the child's best interest. We emphasize that . . . the trial court is not obliged to require the attendance of appellant at any further hearing.

Appellant has indicated to this Court that he will be eligible for parole from his current term of incarceration in January, 1997. Since the likelihood is present that partial custody will be granted to father, it would be appropriate to explore seriously visitation before his release.

We find the trial court abused its discretion and committed error in refusing visitation without fully exploring the merits of the petition. Accordingly, we reverse the Order denying appellant's request for visitation with his minor son while incarcerated and remand for a hearing consistent with this Opinion.

DISCUSSION QUESTIONS FOR *ETTER v. ROSE*

A. How might a child be harmed by visiting a parent in prison? How might a child benefit from visiting a parent in prison?

B. The court states, "While there is no case law which permits denial of visitation with a parent because of incarceration alone, we believe there is a basis for creation of a presumption, to be rebutted by the prisoner parent, that such visitation is not in the best interest of the child." Is the court creating a rebuttable presumption that such visitation is not in the best interest of the child? What is the purpose of the seven factors set forth by the court? Who has the burden of proof?

C. The court reasons that the father must be afforded a hearing, but the court also states that the trial court is "not obliged to require the attendance of appellant at any further hearing." Does this mean that the father will be granted a hearing but will not be allowed to personally attend it?

6.9 PARENTING TIME: MODIFICATION

Parenting time arrangements are subject to modification by the court because a child's situation may change dramatically from the time of the parent's separation or divorce until the child reaches majority. Parents often agree to changes and submit agreed modifications for approval by the court.

The Uniform Marriage and Divorce Act allows for modification in the best interests of the child but provides that "the court shall not restrict a parents' visitation rights unless it finds that the visitation would endanger seriously the child's physical, mental, moral, or emotional health." UMDA §407.

REFLECTIVE QUESTIONS

The UMDA suggests that parenting time should be restricted if it would seriously endanger the child. Is this standard different than the best interests of the child standard?

Background to *Baber v. Baber*

Sometimes a parent seeks to modify a parenting time order because of behavior exhibited by the other parent while parenting time is being exercised. This typically occurs in cases involving intimate partner violence, child abuse, child abduction, and as in the case below, substance abuse.

BABER
v.
BABER

Supreme Court of Arkansas
2011 WL 478622

On April 27, 2009, appellee filed a motion to modify visitation, contending that material changes in circumstances had occurred since the parties last appeared before the circuit court and that these changes warranted the court's placing restrictions on appellant's visitation. In her motion, appellee made the following allegations: (1) appellant tested positive for THC on August 19, 2008; (2) appellee had reason to believe that appellant submitted himself to drug and alcohol tests in conjunction with the medical review board's suspension of his medical license and, although appellee requested copies of the tests from appellant, appellant refused to furnish the results to her; (3) appellee was contacted by a female friend of appellant's who informed her that appellant was not sober; (4) appellant admitted to drinking alcohol during his visitation with the parties' son, despite a provision in the parties' settlement agreement that prohibited appellant from drinking alcohol at any time during his visitation periods; (5) appellant has stated that his consumption of alcohol is not a problem and has expressed his intent to continue drinking alcohol; (6) appellant has exercised his visitation rights sporadically; and (7) appellant sent the parties' minor son home with third parties, who were strangers to their son and to appellee, rather than meet appellee at a public location to exchange him for visitation, and appellee was concerned that appellant avoided the visitation exchange to prevent her from observing that he was under the influence of drugs or alcohol. Appellee added that, based upon appellant's history of drug and alcohol abuse and the foregoing events, she suspected that appellant was under the influence of drugs or alcohol and therefore suspended his visitation pursuant to the parties' settlement agreement.

Appellant responded and denied that material changes in circumstances existed to warrant a modification of visitation. Specifically, he denied that his medical license was suspended or that it was suspended due to drug and alcohol use, denied that he consumed alcohol while the minor children were present, and denied that he was attempting to avoid a visitation exchange with appellee when he allowed his son to ride with friends. Pleading affirmatively, appellant asserted that appellee had unreasonably suspended visitation in violation of the divorce decree for the sole purpose to harass, embarrass, and punish him and asserted that she should be held in contempt of court. He further asserted that he should be given unqualified visitation to the children

We now consider appellant's contention that the circuit court erred in modifying visitation. Appellant admits that he consumes alcohol, that he has received inpatient treatment for alcohol abuse, and that he drank alcohol at a time when his son was visiting. He states that he drank two beers at his birthday party after his son had gone to bed, and he concedes that this action was a mistake that he should not have made and will not make again. Appellant also admits that he violated the divorce decree when he consumed alcohol when his son was visiting. Still, appellant contends that the circuit court's order modifying visitation must be reversed because the circuit court altered visitation as a sanction for his violation of the decree with no consideration whatsoever of changed circumstances and the best interests of the children.

A circuit court maintains continuing jurisdiction over visitation and may modify or vacate those orders at any time when it becomes aware of a change in circumstances or facts not known to it at the time of the initial order. Although visitation is always modifiable, to promote stability and continuity for the children and to discourage repeated litigation of the same issues, courts require more rigid standards for modification than for initial determinations. Thus, the party seeking a change in visitation has the burden to demonstrate a material change in circumstances that warrants such a change.

The primary consideration regarding visitation is the best interest of the child. Important factors the court considers in determining reasonable visitation are the wishes of the child, the capacity of the party desiring visitation to supervise and care for the child, problems of transportation and prior conduct in abusing visitation, the work schedule or stability of the parties, and the relationship with siblings and other relatives. Fixing visitation rights is a matter that lies within the sound discretion of the circuit court.

Upon review of the circuit court's findings, we are not persuaded by appellant's assertion that the circuit court modified visitation for the sole purpose of "punishing" him. When the divorce decree was entered, appellant, who had a history of drug and alcohol abuse, agreed to abstain from using drugs and alcohol while his children were visiting. He completed treatment at Talbott Recovery and, based on the record of his stay there, demonstrated a desire to be drug and alcohol free. But evidence at the hearing showed that appellant was no longer committed to abstaining from drugs and alcohol. Marable testified that she and appellant drank alcohol together the day he arrived home from treatment and continued to drink alcohol together every day for the next three weeks. She also stated that appellant used marijuana when they were together. Finally, in violation of the divorce decree, appellant admitted that he consumed alcoholic beverages when his son was visiting. This evidence demonstrated a material change in circumstances.

 **FOR** *BABER v. BABER*

A. What legal standard does the court use to decide whether parenting time should be modified?

B. Who has the burden of proof with respect to the modification? What evidence was produced?

C. If the father had a substance abuse problem at the time of the divorce, what is the change in circumstances?

D. What modifications do you think might be appropriate in this case?

6.10 VISITATION: GRANDPARENTS

When couples separate or divorce, they redefine and restructure their parenting relationship, either through agreement or court intervention. However, the separation of the parents also impacts the child's relationships with grandparents, stepparents, and other adults who may have cared for the child. Historically, these adults remained involved with the child only if the legal parents facilitated contact. More recently the law has recognized and enforced some of these relationships under some conditions.

REFLECTIVE QUESTIONS	How much deference should be given to the decision-making authority of parents in the context of grandparent visitation? Should the best interests of the child be the primary focus?

Background to *Troxel v. Granville*

Grandparents historically had access to grandchildren only if facilitated by the children's parents. However, as divorce became more common and grandparents lived longer, organized grandparent groups lobbied for enforceable grandparent visitation statutes, and by 1994 every state had adopted one.

In 2000 the Supreme Court dramatically changed the legal landscape for grandparent visitation with the issuance of the decision in *Troxel v. Granville*. Subsequent to *Troxel*, many states reexamined their grandparent and third-party visitation statutes to determine whether they unconstitutionally infringed on the right of fit parents to make decisions about the care and custody of minor children.

> Changes in state laws following *Troxel* have come from legislatures and court decisions. Some states modified their third-party visitation statutes to provide more explicit protections for the rights of parents. . . . After *Troxel*, at least six state supreme courts struck down grandparent visitation statutes as overly broad (*see, e.g.*, Florida, Hawaii, Illinois, Iowa, Michigan, Washington). But in other states, the courts added requirements of what grandparents must show before being granted court-ordered visitation, and, thus, the constitutionality of the statutes was upheld. *See, e.g.*, Arkansas, Colorado, Connecticut, Kansas, Maryland, Massachusetts, Minnesota.

Jeff Atkinson, *Shifts in the Law Regarding the Rights of Third Parties to Seek Visitation and Custody of Children*, 47 Fam. L.Q. 1, 5 (2013).

In *Troxel*, the paternal grandparents of two children born outside of marriage sought visitation rights after their son, the father of the children, committed suicide. The children's mother challenged their effort, arguing that the Washington statute permitting grandparent visitation created an unconstitutional interference with her fundamental right to rear the children.

TROXEL
v.
GRANVILLE
Supreme Court of the United States
530 U.S. 57 (2000)

O'CONNOR, J. Section 26.10.160(3) of the Revised Code of Washington permits "[a]ny person" to petition a superior court for visitation rights "at any time," and authorizes that court to grant such visitation rights whenever "visitation may serve the best interest of the child." Petitioners Jennifer and Gary Troxel petitioned a Washington Superior Court for the right to visit their grandchildren, Isabelle and Natalie Troxel. Respondent Tommie Granville, the mother of Isabelle and Natalie, opposed the petition. The case ultimately reached the Washington Supreme Court, which held that §26.10.160(3) unconstitutionally interferes with the fundamental right of parents to rear their children.

I

Tommie Granville and Brad Troxel shared a relationship that ended in June 1991. The two never married, but they had two daughters, Isabelle and Natalie. Jennifer and Gary Troxel are Brad's parents, and thus the paternal grandparents of Isabelle and Natalie. After Tommie and Brad separated in 1991, Brad lived with his parents and regularly brought his daughters to his parents' home for weekend visitation. Brad committed suicide in May 1993. Although the Troxels at first continued to see Isabelle and Natalie on a regular basis after their son's death, Tommie Granville informed the Troxels in October 1993 that she wished to limit their visitation with her daughters to one short visit per month.

In December 1993, the Troxels commenced the present action by filing a petition to obtain visitation rights with Isabelle and Natalie. The Troxels filed their petition under two Washington statutes, Wash. Rev. Code §§26.09.240 and 26.10.160(3) (1994). Only the latter statute is at issue in this case. At trial, the Troxels requested two weekends of overnight visitation per month and two weeks of visitation each summer. Granville did not oppose visitation altogether, but instead asked the court to order one day of visitation per month with no overnight stay. In 1995, the Superior Court issued an oral ruling and entered a visitation decree ordering visitation one weekend per month, one week during the summer, and four hours on both of the petitioning grandparents' birthdays.

Granville appealed, during which time she married Kelly Wynn. Before addressing the merits of Granville's appeal, the Washington Court of Appeals remanded the case to the Superior Court for entry of written findings of fact and conclusions of law. On remand, the Superior Court found that visitation was in Isabelle and Natalie's best interests:

> The Petitioners [the Troxels] are part of a large, central, loving family, all located in this area, and the Petitioners can provide opportunities for the children in the areas of cousins

and music. The court took into consideration all factors regarding the best interest of the children and considered all the testimony before it. The children would be benefitted from spending quality time with the Petitioners, provided that time is balanced with time with the childrens' [*sic*] nuclear family. The court finds that the childrens' [*sic*] best interests are served by spending time with their mother and stepfather's other six children.

Approximately nine months after the Superior Court entered its order on remand, Granville's husband formally adopted Isabelle and Natalie.

The Washington Court of Appeals reversed the lower court's visitation order and dismissed the Troxels' petition for visitation, holding that nonparents lack standing to seek visitation under §26.10.160(3) unless a custody action is pending. The Washington Supreme Court granted the Troxels' petition for review and agreed with the Court of Appeals' ultimate conclusion that the Troxels could not obtain visitation of Isabelle and Natalie pursuant to §26.10.160(3). The court rested its decision on the Federal Constitution, holding that §26.10.160(3) unconstitutionally infringes on the fundamental right of parents to rear their children. We granted certiorari.

II

The demographic changes of the past century make it difficult to speak of an average American family. The composition of families varies greatly from household to household. While many children may have two married parents and grandparents who visit regularly, many other children are raised in single-parent households. In 1996, children living with only one parent accounted for 28 percent of all children under age 18 in the United States. Understandably, in these single-parent households, persons outside the nuclear family are called upon with increasing frequency to assist in the everyday tasks of child rearing. In many cases, grandparents play an important role. For example, in 1998, approximately 4 million children — or 5.6 percent of all children under age 18 — lived in the household of their grandparents.

The nationwide enactment of nonparental visitation statutes is assuredly due, in some part, to the States' recognition of these changing realities of the American family. Because grandparents and other relatives undertake duties of a parental nature in many households, States have sought to ensure the welfare of the children therein by protecting the relationships those children form with such third parties. The States' nonparental visitation statutes are further supported by a recognition, which varies from State to State, that children should have the opportunity to benefit from relationships with statutorily specified persons — for example, their grandparents. The extension of statutory rights in this area to persons other than a child's parents, however, comes with an obvious cost. For example, the State's recognition of an independent third-party interest in a child can place a substantial burden on the traditional parent-child relationship. Contrary to Justice Stevens' accusation, our description of state nonparental visitation statutes in these terms, of course, is not meant to suggest that "children are so much chattel." Rather, our terminology is intended to highlight the fact that these statutes can present questions of constitutional import. In this case, we are presented with just such a question.

Specifically, we are asked to decide whether §26.10.160(3), as applied to Tommie Granville and her family, violates the Federal Constitution.

The Fourteenth Amendment provides that no State shall "deprive any person of life, liberty, or property, without due process of law." We have long recognized that the Amendment's Due Process Clause, like its Fifth Amendment counterpart, "guarantees more than fair process." *Washington v. Glucksberg*, 521 U.S. 702, 719 (1997). The Clause also includes a substantive component that "provides heightened protection against government interference with certain fundamental rights and liberty interests."

The liberty interest at issue in this case — the interest of parents in the care, custody, and control of their children — is perhaps the oldest of the fundamental liberty interests recognized by this Court. More than 75 years ago, in *Meyer v. Nebraska*, 262 U.S. 390, 399, 401 (1923), we held that the "liberty" protected by the Due Process Clause includes the right of parents to "establish a home and bring up children" and "to control the education of their own." Two years later, in *Pierce v. Society of Sisters*, 268 U.S. 510, 534-535 (1925), we again held that the "liberty of parents and guardians" includes the right "to direct the upbringing and education of children under their control." We explained in Pierce that "[t]he child is not the mere creature of the State; those who nurture him and direct his destiny have the right, coupled with the high duty, to recognize and prepare him for additional obligations." We returned to the subject in *Prince v. Massachusetts*, 321 U.S. 158 (1944), and again confirmed that there is a constitutional dimension to the right of parents to direct the upbringing of their children. "It is cardinal with us that the custody, care and nurture of the child reside first in the parents, whose primary function and freedom include preparation for obligations the state can neither supply nor hinder."

In subsequent cases also, we have recognized the fundamental right of parents to make decisions concerning the care, custody, and control of their children. *See, e.g., Stanley v. Illinois*, 405 U.S. 645, 651 (1972) ("It is plain that the interest of a parent in the companionship, care, custody, and management of his or her children come[s] to this Court with a momentum for respect lacking when appeal is made to liberties which derive merely from shifting economic arrangements"); *Wisconsin v. Yoder*, 406 U.S. 205, 232 (1972) ("The history and culture of Western civilization reflect a strong tradition of parental concern for the nurture and upbringing of their children. This primary role of the parents in the upbringing of their children is now established beyond debate as an enduring American tradition"); *Quilloin v. Walcott*, 434 U.S. 246, 255 (1978) ("We have recognized on numerous occasions that the relationship between parent and child is constitutionally protected"); *Parham v. J.R.*, 442 U.S. 584, 602 (1979) ("Our jurisprudence historically has reflected Western civilization concepts of the family as a unit with broad parental authority over minor children. Our cases have consistently followed that course"); *Santosky v. Kramer*, 455 U.S. 745, 753 (1982) (discussing "[t]he fundamental liberty interest of natural parents in the care, custody, and management of their child"); *Glucksberg, supra*, at 720 ("In a long line of cases, we have held that, in addition to the specific freedoms protected by the Bill of Rights, the liberty specially protected by the Due Process Clause includes the righ[t] to direct the education and upbringing of one's children" (citing *Meyer* and *Pierce*)). In light of this extensive precedent, it cannot now be doubted that the Due Process Clause of the Fourteenth Amendment protects the fundamental right of parents to make decisions concerning the care, custody, and control of their children.

Section 26.10.160(3), as applied to Granville and her family in this case, unconstitutionally infringes on that fundamental parental right. The Washington nonparental visitation statute is breathtakingly broad. According to the statute's text, "[a]ny person may petition the court for visitation rights at any time," and the court may grant such visitation rights whenever "visitation may serve the best interest of the child." §26.10.160(3). That language effectively permits any third party seeking visitation to subject any decision by a parent concerning visitation of the parent's children to state-court review. Once the visitation petition has been filed in court and the matter is placed before a judge, a parent's decision that visitation would not be in the child's best interest is accorded no deference. Section 26.10.160(3) contains no requirement that a court accord the parent's decision any presumption of validity or any weight whatsoever. Instead, the Washington statute places the best-interest determination solely in the hands of the judge. Should the judge disagree with the parent's estimation of the child's best interests, the judge's view necessarily prevails. Thus, in practical effect, in the State of Washington a court can disregard and overturn any decision by a fit custodial parent concerning visitation whenever a third party affected by the decision files a visitation petition, based solely on the judge's determination of the child's best interests.

Turning to the facts of this case, the record reveals that the Superior Court's order was based on precisely the type of mere disagreement we have just described and nothing more. The Superior Court's order was not founded on any special factors that might justify the State's interference with Granville's fundamental right to make decisions concerning the rearing of her two daughters. To be sure, this case involves a visitation petition filed by grandparents soon after the death of their son — the father of Isabelle and Natalie — but the combination of several factors here compels our conclusion that §26.10.160(3), as applied, exceeded the bounds of the Due Process Clause.

First, the Troxels did not allege, and no court has found, that Granville was an unfit parent. That aspect of the case is important, for there is a presumption that fit parents act in the best interests of their children. As this Court explained in Parham:

> [O]ur constitutional system long ago rejected any notion that a child is the mere creature of the State and, on the contrary, asserted that parents generally have the right, coupled with the high duty, to recognize and prepare [their children] for additional obligations. The law's concept of the family rests on a presumption that parents possess what a child lacks in maturity, experience, and capacity for judgment required for making life's difficult decisions. More important, historically it has recognized that natural bonds of affection lead parents to act in the best interests of their children.

Accordingly, so long as a parent adequately cares for his or her children (i.e., is fit), there will normally be no reason for the State to inject itself into the private realm of the family to further question the ability of that parent to make the best decisions concerning the rearing of that parent's children.

The problem here is not that the Washington Superior Court intervened, but that when it did so, it gave no special weight at all to Granville's determination of her daughters' best interests. More importantly, it appears that the Superior Court applied exactly the opposite presumption. . . .

The decisional framework employed by the Superior Court directly contravened the traditional presumption that a fit parent will act in the best interest of his or her child. In that respect, the court's presumption failed to provide any protection for Granville's fundamental constitutional right to make decisions concerning the rearing of her own daughters. *Cf., e.g.*, Cal. Fam. Code Ann. §3104(e) (West 1994) (rebuttable presumption that grandparent visitation is not in child's best interest if parents agree that visitation rights should not be granted); Me. Rev. Stat. Ann., Tit. 19A, §1803(3) (1998) (court may award grandparent visitation if in best interest of child and "would not significantly interfere with any parent-child relationship or with the parent's rightful authority over the child"); Minn. Stat. §257.022(2)(a)(2) (1998) (court may award grandparent visitation if in best interest of child and "such visitation would not interfere with the parent-child relationship"); Neb. Rev. Stat. §43-1802(2) (1998) (court must find "by clear and convincing evidence" that grandparent visitation "will not adversely interfere with the parent-child relationship"); R.I. Gen. Laws §15-5-24.3(a)(2)(v) (Supp. 1999) (grandparent must rebut, by clear and convincing evidence, presumption that parent's decision to refuse grandparent visitation was reasonable); Utah Code Ann. §30-5-2(2)(e) (1998) (same); *Hoff v. Berg*, 595 N.W.2d 285, 291-292 (N.D. 1999) (holding North Dakota grandparent visitation statute unconstitutional because State has no "compelling interest in presuming visitation rights of grandparents to an unmarried minor are in the child's best interests and forcing parents to accede to court-ordered grandparental visitation unless the parents are first able to prove such visitation is not in the best interests of their minor child"). In an ideal world, parents might always seek to cultivate the bonds between grandparents and their grandchildren. Needless to say, however, our world is far from perfect, and in it the decision whether such an intergenerational relationship would be beneficial in any specific case is for the parent to make in the first instance. And, if a fit parent's decision of the kind at issue here becomes subject to judicial review, the court must accord at least some special weight to the parent's own determination.

Finally, we note that there is no allegation that Granville ever sought to cut off visitation entirely. Rather, the present dispute originated when Granville informed the Troxels that she would prefer to restrict their visitation with Isabelle and Natalie to one short visit per month and special holidays. Significantly, many other States expressly provide by statute that courts may not award visitation unless a parent has denied (or unreasonably denied) visitation to the concerned third party. *See, e.g.*, Miss. Code Ann. §93-16-3(2)(a) (1994) (court must find that "the parent or custodian of the child unreasonably denied the grandparent visitation rights with the child"); Ore. Rev. Stat. §109.121(1)(a)(B) (1997) (court may award visitation if the "custodian of the child has denied the grandparent reasonable opportunity to visit the child"); R.I. Gen. Laws §15-5-24.3(a)(2)(iii)-(iv) (Supp. 1999) (court must find that parents prevented grandparent from visiting grandchild and that "there is no other way the petitioner is able to visit his or her grandchild without court intervention").

Considered together with the Superior Court's reasons for awarding visitation to the Troxels, the combination of these factors demonstrates that the visitation order in this case was an unconstitutional infringement on Granville's fundamental right to make decisions concerning the care, custody, and control of her two daughters. . . .

There is thus no reason to remand the case for further proceedings in the Washington Supreme Court. As Justice Kennedy recognizes, the burden of litigating a domestic relations proceeding can itself be "so disruptive of the parent-child relationship that the constitutional right of a custodial parent to make certain basic determinations for the child's welfare becomes implicated." In this case, the litigation costs incurred by Granville on her trip through the Washington court system and to this Court are without a doubt already substantial. As we have explained, it is apparent that the entry of the visitation order in this case violated the Constitution. We should say so now, without forcing the parties into additional litigation that would further burden Granville's parental right. We therefore hold that the application of 26.10.160(3) to Granville and her family violated her due process right to make decisions concerning the care, custody, and control of her daughters. Accordingly, the judgment of the Washington Supreme Court is affirmed.

DISCUSSION QUESTIONS FOR *TROXEL v. GRANVILLE*

A. How much visitation did the grandparents request? What did the trial court order?

B. Was this a dispute about how much time the grandparents could spend with the child or whether the grandparents could see the child at all? Could this matter have been resolved in mediation or through negotiation? Why do you think it resulted in extensive litigation?

C. The Supreme Court states that it is "difficult to speak of an average American family." What is the basis of the Court's conclusion?

D. Describe the liberty interest at issue in this case.

E. On what basis does the Supreme Court conclude that the Washington non-parental visitation statute is "breathtakingly broad"? What does the statute provide?

F. What weight did the trial court give to the mother's determination of her daughters' best interests?

G. Should the "best interests" of a child be given priority over the "wishes" or "control" of a parent as to whom the child should see? Is the visitation for the benefit of the child? Should the child have any rights in this situation?

H. Assume that a legislator asks you to draft a grandparent visitation statute that will pass constitutional scrutiny after *Troxel*. What provisions will you include or not include?

I. According to Prof. Garza, *Troxel* has apparently done little to encourage state uniformity with respect to grandparent and third-party visitation statutes:

> The variety among the individual third-party visitation statutes is even more apparent after *Troxel*. While most states limit third-party visitation to grandparents, many include great-grandparents, stepparents, siblings, and third parties who have a significant relationship with the child. For those states that permit third-party visitation, only some states define what is necessary to establish the significant or existing relationship required. Further, some states do not rely on third-party visitation statutes to award visitation; instead, they use the common law doctrines of de facto parenthood, *in loco parentis*, or psychological parenthood. In addition, even though part of the ultimate holding in *Troxel* articulated a longstanding constitutional presumption that a parent is fit and acts in a child's best interests, twenty-one states do not have such a presumption via statute or common law. Most statutes use a "best interests of the child" standard in third-party visitation cases, but only some states provide factors to be considered by the court, leaving the best interests standard open to interpretation by individual courts. In addition, only a few states require a showing of harm as discussed in *Troxel*.

Sonya C. Garza, *The Troxel Aftermath: A Proposed Solution for State Courts and Legislatures*, 69 La. L. Rev. 927, 940-941 (2009). Do you think the judges deciding *Troxel* meant to spawn diverse statutory approaches or was that an unintended consequence of the decision?

J. Some courts have ruled that grandparent visitation statutes do not apply to great-grandparents. Do you think it is appropriate to make this distinction? Why or why not? *See Lott v. Alexander*, 134 So. 3d 369 (2014) (great-grandparents could not seek visitation under grandparent visitation statute); *In re M.D.E.*, 297 P.3d 1058 (2013) (great-grandparent lacked standing). *But see In re Dayton*, 2015 WL 1828039 (2015) (great-grandparents had standing).

6.11 VISITATION: STEPPARENTS

At common law stepparents had no right to ongoing contact with stepchildren after divorcing the legal parent of the children. Even today, stepparents lack enforceable relationships with stepchildren unless they are able to invoke a state third-party visitation statute or de facto or *in loco parentis* status. A small minority of states have adopted statutes addressing stepparent visitation. Jeff Atkinson, *Shifts in the Law Regarding the Rights of Third Parties to Seek Visitation and Custody of Children*, 47 Fam. L.Q. 1, 7 (2013) (California, Illinois, Kansas, New Hampshire, Oregon, Tennessee, Virginia, and Wisconsin).

> **REFLECTIVE QUESTIONS** Should children have a right to visitation with a stepparent after divorce or separation? Should children have a right to visitation with stepsiblings? Why or why not?

6.12 VISITATION: UNMARRIED SAME-SEX PARTNER

Background to *SooHoo v. Johnson*

In addition to grandparents, caring adults such as stepparents and individuals who have cared for a child may seek visitation. These relationships were typically not recognized at common law, and such requests are not necessarily granted today. However, state third-party visitation statutes may provide an avenue for maintaining contact under such circumstances. In the next case, *SooHoo v. Johnson*, the Minnesota Supreme Court considers the constitutionality and applicability of a third-party visitation statute to a case involving an unmarried same-sex couple. After the couple separated, the partner who was not related to the children biologically or through adoption sought visitation with them.

SOOHOO
v.
JOHNSON

Supreme Court of Minnesota
731 N.W.2d 815 (2007)

PAGE, J. Appellant Marilyn Johnson appeals from the judgment of the district court granting respondent Nancy SooHoo's petition seeking visitation with Johnson's two minor children pursuant to Minn. Stat. §257C.08, subd. 4 (2006), which allows the court to grant reasonable visitation to a person with whom the child has resided for at least two years. . . .

Johnson and SooHoo, who lived together and jointly owned a house in Minneapolis, ended a 22-year relationship in the fall of 2003. During the course of that relationship, Johnson adopted two children from China. When Johnson adopted the first child, both she and SooHoo traveled to China. When Johnson adopted the second child, SooHoo remained in Minneapolis and cared for the first child while Johnson went to China. SooHoo did not adopt either of the children, but the record indicates that Johnson and SooHoo co-parented the children, recognized themselves as a family unit with two mothers, and represented themselves to others as such. For example, SooHoo took maternity leave to care for both children upon their arrival in the United States. SooHoo also participated in the selection of child-care providers and schools for the children and shared in the daily parenting responsibilities, including dropping off and picking up the children from day care, helping with school projects and homework, preparing meals for the family, taking the children to doctors['] appointments (including authorizing the children's immunizations), coordinating extracurricular activities and play dates, providing the sole care while Johnson was away on business, and taking the children to California to visit Soo-Hoo's extended family, all without apparent objection by Johnson. The record further reflects that the children referred to SooHoo as "mommy," and referred to SooHoo's parents as their grandparents. In the information provided to the children's schools, Johnson listed SooHoo as mother number two and listed the last name of one of the children as Johnson-SooHoo. SooHoo attended the children's parent-teacher conferences with Johnson, during which both women signed off on the teacher's goal setting report as "Parent/Guardian."

The relationship between Johnson and SooHoo dissolved after a domestic incident that resulted in reciprocal orders for protection. The district court order against SooHoo barred SooHoo from residing at or visiting the home she owned with Johnson. During the five or six months after the court issued the reciprocal orders for protection, SooHoo was allowed to see the children for a total of only 48 hours.

In late 2003, SooHoo filed a petition seeking sole physical and legal custody of the children. In the alternative, she sought visitation. . . . Ultimately, the court awarded SooHoo visitation, which, in addition to weekly visitation, included a holiday visitation schedule that divided the major holidays between SooHoo and Johnson and an extended period of visitation during the summer months. The court also ordered that SooHoo employ a therapist to address her differential attention to the children and that Johnson "employ a counselor (or continue with existing counseling) to address her tension and anxiety relative to the [children]." In awarding visitation, the court concluded that Minn. Stat. §257C.08, subd. 4, withstood constitutional muster. The court of appeals affirmed. . . .

I

Johnson first challenges the constitutionality of Minn. Stat. §257C.08, subd. 4, arguing that it violates her right to due process. Section 257C.08, subdivision 4, provides that a third party (excluding foster parents), who resided in a household with a child for two or more years but no longer resides with the child, may petition the court for an order granting reasonable visitation with the child. Before a court may grant visitation, the statute requires it to determine: (1) that visitation with the third party would be in the child's best interest; (2) that the third party and the child have established "emotional ties creating a parent and child relationship"; and (3) that granting the third-party visitation would not interfere with the relationship between the custodial parent and the child. Minn. Stat. §257C.08, subd. 4(1)-(3).

The U.S. Supreme Court has explained that the substantive due process rights provided by the Fourteenth Amendment afford "heightened protection against government interference with certain fundamental rights and liberty interests." *Washington v. Glucksberg*, 521 U.S. 702, 720 (1997). A parent's right to make decisions concerning the care, custody, and control of his or her children is a protected fundamental right. *Troxel v. Granville*, 530 U.S. 57, 65, (2000). Johnson contends that section 257C.08, subdivision 4, is unconstitutional on its face and as applied in this case because it violates her rights as a fit parent to decide the care, custody, and control of her children.

In *Troxel*, the Supreme Court struck down as unconstitutional a Washington statute that granted "[a]ny person" standing to petition for visitation at "any time" so long as visitation was in the best interests of the child. *Troxel*, 530 U.S. at 61, 73. . . . The Supreme Court declared the Washington statute unconstitutional as applied but declined to address whether third-party visitation statutes are per se unconstitutional. *Id.* at 73. . . . In addition, the Court set out three guiding principles necessary for a third-party visitation statute to survive a constitutional challenge: (1) the statute must give some special weight to the fit custodial parent's decision regarding visitation; (2) there can be no presumption in favor of awarding visitation; and (3) the court must assert more than a mere best-interest analysis in support of its decision to override the fit parent's wishes. *Id.* at 69-70. These guiding principles ensure that third-party visitation statutes are narrowly tailored to the governmental interest in protecting the general welfare of children. . . .

Johnson first contends that third-party visitation statutes like section 257C.08, subdivision 4, are unconstitutional per se because they fail to give proper deference to a fit parent's decision regarding visitation. A facial challenge to the constitutionality of a statute requires a showing that " 'no set of circumstances exists under which the Act would be valid.' " *Ohio v. Akron Ctr. for Reprod. Health*, 497 U.S. 502, 514 (1990). . . . But the Supreme Court in *Troxel* declined to hold that third-party visitation statutes are per se unconstitutional. *Troxel*, 530 U.S. at 73. And we believe that in expressly declining to hold that third-party visitation statutes are per se unconstitutional, the Court recognized that there may be instances when the state may constitutionally intrude upon a fit parent's right to the care, custody, and control of the parent's child and order visitation against the parent's wishes. *Id.* We believe such is the case with section 257C.08, subdivision 4, and we reject Johnson's argument on this point.

We therefore turn to an analysis of the language of the statute. . . . In order to survive strict scrutiny, a law must advance a compelling state interest and must be narrowly tailored to further that interest. . . . As to the first prong of the strict scrutiny analysis, Johnson asserts that the state "does not have a compelling interest in second guessing the determinations of a fit-parent as to what is in the best interest of her children." Johnson centers this argument on her fundamental right to the care, custody, and control of her children. That right, however, is not absolute. The Supreme Court has long recognized that states may intrude on parental rights in order to protect the "general interest in the youth's well being." *Prince v. Massachusetts*, 321 U.S. 158 (1944). The Court explained in *Prince* that "the state as *parens patriae* may restrict the parent's control by requiring school attendance, regulating or prohibiting the child's labor, and in many other ways. [T]he state has a wide range of power for limiting parental freedom and authority in things affecting the child's welfare." *Id.* at 166-167. The Court has also explained that "the relationship of love and duty in a recognized family unit is an interest in liberty entitled to constitutional protection." . . . It follows then, that a state, in its role as *parens patriae*, has a compelling interest in promoting relationships among those in recognized family units (for example, the relationship between a child and someone *in loco parentis* to that child) in order to protect the general welfare of children. . . .

We turn next to whether the requirements of section 257C.08, subdivision 4, are narrowly drawn to further the state's compelling interest. Initially, we note that section 257C.08, subdivision 4, is, on its face, more narrowly drawn than the Washington statute at issue in *Troxel.* The Washington statute allowed courts to award visitation to any person at any time so long as it was in the child's best interests. In contrast, section 257C.08, subdivision 4, limits the class of individuals who may petition for visitation to those persons who have resided with the child for two years or more (excluding foster parents). In addition to that threshold requirement, the statute further narrows the class of those who may be awarded visitation to petitioners who have "established emotional ties creating a parent and child relationship." Minn. Stat. §257C.08, subd. 4(2). We read this requirement as mandating that the petitioner stand *in loco parentis* with the child. As we have previously explained:

> The term "*in loco parentis*," according to its generally accepted common-law meaning, refers to a person who has put himself in the situation of a lawful parent by assuming the obligations incident to the parental relation without going through the formalities necessary to legal adoption and embodies the two ideas of assuming the parental status and discharging the parental duties.

. . . Therefore, unlike the statute at issue in *Troxel,* the requirements that the petitioner have resided with the child for two or more years and have a parent-child relationship with the child substantially limits the class of individuals who may successfully petition for visitation. Section 257C.08, subdivision 4, is further narrowly tailored by providing that before a court may order visitation, the court must find that visitation is in the best interests of the child and that visitation will not interfere with the custodial parent's relationship with the child.

But section 257C.08, subdivision 4, does not specify the level of proof required or who bears the burden of proving the requirements of section 257C.08, subdivision 4. We believe that in order to afford due deference to the fit custodial parent, the burden of proof must be on the party seeking visitation, and the standard of proof must be clear and convincing evidence. We base this conclusion on the following analysis. The Supreme Court has explained that "the minimum standard of proof tolerated by the due process requirement reflects not only the weight of the private and public interests affected, but also a societal judgment about how the risk of error should be distributed between the litigants." *Santosky v. Kramer,* 455 U.S. 745, 755, (1982). The balancing test set forth by the Court in *Mathews v. Eldridge* guides our determination regarding the minimum standard of proof required in these cases. 424

U.S. 319, 335 (1976). That balancing test requires us to weigh: (1) "the private interests affected by the proceeding"; (2) "the risk of error created by the State's chosen procedure"; and (3) "the countervailing governmental interest supporting use of the challenged procedure." *Santosky*, 455 U.S. at 754.

Looking at the first *Mathews* factor, the Supreme Court has explained that the clear and convincing evidentiary standard is mandated when the individual interests in the proceeding are "'particularly important'" and "'more substantial than mere loss of money.'" . . . The Court has specifically explained that a parent's right to the care, custody, and control of his or her child is "an interest far more precious than any property right." . . . We have also observed that parents have a fundamental right to the care, custody, and control of their children that should not be interfered with except for "'grave and weighty reasons.'" . . .

As for the second factor, the Supreme Court has explained that proceedings that "employ imprecise substantive standards that leave determinations unusually open to subjective values of the judge" magnify the risk for erroneous deprivation of private interests. *Santosky*, 455 U.S. at 762. Section 257C.08, subdivision 4, requires the district court to make subjective determinations regarding what is in the best interests of the child, whether the petitioner and child established a parent-child relationship, and whether visitation would interfere with the parental relationship. As explained in *Troxel*, one of the dangers of utilizing a best-interest analysis is the potential for a court to make the decision based entirely on the court's subjective estimation without regard to the fit parent's wishes. *Troxel*, 530 U.S. at 67.

Finally, the government interest in this case under the third *Mathews* factor is the state's interest as *parens patriae* in the welfare of the child. As we have already explained, the state's interest as *parens patriae* in the welfare of the child and in promoting relationships among recognized family units is compelling.

Balancing the interests involved in a petition for third-party visitation, we conclude that requiring the party seeking visitation to prove the requirements of subdivision 4 by clear and convincing evidence is necessary to protect against the risk of erroneously depriving a parent of his or her interest in the care, custody, and control of his or her children. Therefore, we must strike Minn. Stat. 257C.08, subd. 7 (2006), as unconstitutional. Subdivision 7 requires the district court to grant third-party visitation unless the court finds by a preponderance of the evidence after a hearing that visitation would interfere with the custodial parent's relationship with the child. We read the plain language of subdivision 7 as impermissibly placing the burden on the custodial parent to prove that visitation would interfere with the parent-child relationship. The parent's fundamental right to the care, custody, and control of his or her child carries with it the presumption that the parent is acting in the best interest of the child and requires deference to the parent's wishes. *Troxel*, 530 U.S. at 70. Accordingly, placing the burden on the parent to prove no interference violates that fundamental right. Further, subdivision 7's preponderance of the evidence standard is not sufficient to protect parents against the risk of an erroneous deprivation of their parental rights.

Because Minn. Stat. §257C.08, subd. 4, limits the class of individuals who may be granted third-party visitation to those who have a longstanding parent-child relationship with the child and prohibits the district court from granting visitation if the visitation is not in the child's best interest or interferes with the custodial parent's relationship, and because we conclude that the petitioner has the burden of proof by clear and convincing evidence, we also conclude that it is narrowly drawn to the state's compelling interest in protecting the general welfare of children by preserving the relationships of recognized family units. We therefore hold that Minn. Stat. §257C.08, subd. 4, is not unconstitutional on its face.

Turning then to the district court's application of section 257C.08, subdivision 4, to the facts in this case, we reject Johnson's as-applied challenge to the constitutionality of section 257C.08, subdivision 4. In order to make this determination, we look first at whether the court applied the legal framework set forth in section 257C.08, subdivision 4. If so, we then must determine whether the circumstances of this case are such that the Constitution requires a more rigorous legal framework. *See Troxel*, 530 U.S. at 68 (noting that the trial court's order "was not founded on any special factors that might justify the State's interference" with the parent's fundamental rights).

Here, the district court applied the legal framework set forth in section 257C.08, subdivision 4, which we have just held to be constitutional on its face. The court awarded visitation after finding that SooHoo resided with the children for more than two years, that SooHoo was *in loco parentis* with the children, and that SooHoo and the children had developed emotional ties creating a parent-child relationship. The court then determined that visitation with SooHoo was in the children's best interest after giving special weight to Johnson's wishes regarding visitation. Finally, the court determined that granting visitation with SooHoo would not interfere with Johnson's relationship with the children. Although the court stated, presumably based on the language of subdivision 7, that the burden of proof on this element rested with Johnson, the court went on to explain that regardless of who bore the burden of proof, the evidence in the record strongly demonstrated that visitation with SooHoo would not interfere with Johnson's relationship with her children. Having concluded that SooHoo carried her burden of proving all the elements required under section 257C.08, subdivision 4, the court awarded a visitation schedule that it deemed reasonable in light of the circumstances of the case and the relationship between SooHoo and the children.

Because we conclude that the district court applied the correct legal framework, we next look at whether the facts of this case are such that section 257C.08, subdivision 4, cannot be constitutionally applied to Johnson. Johnson has not identified, and we have not found, any facts in this case that support a holding that section 257C.08, subdivision 4, was unconstitutionally applied to Johnson. Accordingly, we conclude that the court's application of section 257C.08, subdivision 4, was constitutional and, therefore, we reject Johnson's argument that section 257C.08, subdivision 4, is unconstitutional as applied to her.

II

We next address Johnson's argument that the district court abused its discretion in the amount of visitation it awarded SooHoo. Johnson's primary argument is that the amount of visitation is unreasonable because it is commensurate with that which a court would award a noncustodial parent. She also argues that the amount of visitation is not reasonable because it interferes with her parental relationship with her children. . . .

Although Johnson forcefully argues that the amount of visitation awarded is unreasonable because it is commensurate with that which would be awarded to a noncustodial parent, Johnson cites no authority, nor have we found any authority, for the proposition that an award of visitation to a third party that is commensurate with what would be awarded to noncustodial parents is inherently unreasonable.

Minnesota Statutes §257C.08, subd. 4, allows the district court to grant reasonable visitation. Generally, the reasonableness of an award of visitation turns on the specific facts and circumstances of each case. The district court, having heard the witnesses, is in the best position to determine what is reasonable under the circumstances. Given the evidence presented in the record before us, and the court's broad discretion, we are not in a position to say, based on our standard of review, that the court's findings are clearly erroneous or that the court abused its discretion. Here, the court carefully reviewed the applicable law and then applied that law to the facts contained in the record. As for Johnson's argument that the visitation award is unreasonable because it interferes with her parental relationship with the children, it is enough to say, as discussed above, that the visitation awarded does not interfere with Johnson's parental relationship. Therefore, we affirm the court's visitation award.

 **FOR** *SOOHOO v. JOHNSON*

A. What facts support SooHoo's argument that she co-parented the children involved in this dispute?

B. On what basis did Johnson challenge the constitutionality of Minnesota's visitation statute?

C. The court states that the Supreme Court has set out three guiding principles necessary for a third-party visitation statute to survive constitutional challenge. What are those three guiding principles?

D. What level of constitutional scrutiny did the court apply to the visitation statute?

E. Johnson asserted that the state "does not have a compelling interest in second guessing the determinations of a fit-parent as to what is in the best interests of her children." What was the court's response to this argument?

F. Johnson argued that the visitation statute was not sufficiently narrowly drawn to further the state's compelling interests. What was the court's response to this argument?

G. On whom does this court place the burden of proof when visitation is an issue? What is the level of proof required?

H. The balancing test set forth by the Supreme Court in *Mathews v. Eldridge* was used by the court to guide its determination regarding the minimum standard of proof required in these cases. What does the balancing test require the courts to weigh?

I. The court concluded that requiring the party seeking visitation to prove the requirements of subdivision 4 of the visitation statute by clear and convincing evidence is necessary to protect against the risk of erroneously depriving a parent of his or her interest in the care, custody, and control of his or her children. Summarize how the three *Mathews* factors were utilized to reach this decision.

J. On what basis did the court hold subdivision 7 of the visitation statute unconstitutional?

K. When the court considered whether the visitation statute, as applied in this case, was unconstitutionally applied, it concluded it was not. On what basis did the court reach this conclusion?

L. How was the Minnesota statute at issue in this case different from the Washington statute in *Troxel*? Did these differences lead to different outcomes in the two cases?

M. In future similar cases, what does the petitioning party need to prove? By what standard of proof? Give examples of the type of evidence that a petitioner might present.

N. Would the outcome of this case have been different if (a) the state had not adopted a third-party visitation statute? (b) SooHoo had legally adopted the children? (c) Johnson had not objected to the visitation? (d) the parties had participated in mediation? *See* Deborah L. Forman, *Same-Sex Partners: Strangers, Third Parties, or Parents? The Changing Legal Landscape and the Struggle for Parental Equality*, 40 Fam. L.Q. 23 (2006); Jennifer L. Rosato, *Children of Same-Sex Parents Deserve the Security Blanket of the Parentage Presumption*, 44 Fam. Ct. Rev. 74 (2006).

O. The *SooHoo* case took place before same-sex marriage was legal in Minnesota. Would the legal posture and the outcome of the case have been different if SooHoo and Johnson had been legally married? Why or why not?

General Principles

1. Historically, one parent exercised sole physical custody of the children and the nonresidential parent was granted visitation.
2. Parents have a constitutionally protected liberty interest in ongoing contact with their children.
3. A parent without legal custody is expected to support the decisions made by the legal custodian.
4. A parent must demonstrate that the child will be harmed or endangered by contact with the other parent for a court to limit or restrict parenting time.
5. To modify a final parenting time order the parent seeking a change has the burden of demonstrating a material change in circumstances warranting such a change.
6. Historically, grandparents had access to grandchildren only if facilitated by the children's parents.
7. The relationships of caring adults such as grandparents, stepparents, and individuals who have cared for a child were not recognized at common law, and today states vary considerably concerning whether, and under what conditions, they will grant such requests.

Chapter Problems

1. Assume that two parents divorce when their son is 15 years old. Under the parenting plan, the boy lives primarily with his father, but the parents have agreed that he will stay with his mother on weekends. The boy resents the mother's new relationship and is busy with school activities and friends. He initially resists staying at the mother's home and eventually refuses to stay there on weekends. If the mother seeks your advice, how will you advise her? As a matter of policy, should the wishes of the child be considered? When? *See* Barbara Jo Fidler & Nicholas Bala, *Children Resisting Postseparation Contact with a Parent: Concepts, Controversies, and Conundrums*, 48 Fam. Ct. Rev. 10 (2010).

2. Should parenting time be viewed as a parental entitlement or as a benefit for the child? Imagine a situation where a noncustodial parent fails to exercise parenting time. Should the child be able to require the parent to do so? *See In re Marriage of Osborn*, 135 P.3d 199 (Kan. App. 2006) (child lacked standing to modify parenting time).

3. Assume that A and B have one child during their marriage. When they divorce, the child, C, lives primarily with A. B remarries and has two more children. C spends substantial time with B and with C's half-siblings. B is sent to prison, and his wife refuses to allow C to visit with C's half-siblings. Does C have a constitutional or common law right to visit with the half-siblings? *See Barger ex rel. E.B. v. Brown*, 134 P.3d 905 (Okla. App. 2006).

4. Assume that you are asked to give an advisory opinion on the constitutionality of the following state statute: "The court shall, upon petition filed by a grandparent of a minor child, award reasonable rights of visitation to the grandparent with respect to the child when it is in the best interest of the minor child if: (a) One or both parents of the child are deceased; (b) The marriage of the parents of the child has been dissolved; (c) A parent of the child has deserted the child; (d) The minor child was born out of wedlock and not later determined to be a child born within wedlock as provided in §742.091; or (e) The minor is living with both natural parents who are still married to each other whether or not there is a broken relationship between either or both parents of the minor child and the grandparents, and either or both parents have used their parental authority to prohibit a relationship between the minor child and the grandparents." What is your opinion? *See Beagle v. Beagle*, 678 So. 2d 1271 (Fla. 1996).

Preparation for Practice

1. Assume that you represent a parent who will be exercising parenting time. What specific topics should be covered in the parenting plan with respect to parenting time? What provisions might you suggest including?

2. Locate two parenting plan forms by going online or looking in the law library. How do the provisions about parenting time compare? Are there important similarities and differences?

3. Does your state have a third-party visitation statute? Locate it and determine whether a stepparent, grandparent, or other individual could seek visitation with a child.

4. A parents' group retains you to draft proposed legislation to authorize post-divorce visitation for stepparents. Draft a statute and annotate it with your explanation of what is included and why.

Chapter 7

Modifying Child Custody

PART 1: TRADITIONAL MODIFICATION ACTIONS

7.1 INTRODUCTION: OBJECTIVES

This chapter has three parts: The first part focuses on the legal issues associated with a traditional in-state custody/parenting plan modification request. The second part focuses on issues created when a custodial parent seeks to modify an existing custodial order or parenting plan by relocating to another jurisdiction. The third part examines the Uniform Child Custody Jurisdiction Enforcement Act (UCC-JEA). The UCCJEA is a complex model act intended to assist states when drafting legislation dealing with the question of which of two or more states has jurisdiction to decide an interstate child custody issue.

The chapter should help with the legal analysis of a variety of child custody modification problems. It should also provide sufficient information so one can recognize and discuss the challenges associated with child custody modification requests involving in-state, out-state, and interstate disputes.

This chapter raises many questions, including the following: What role does *res judicata* play in preventing child custody modification requests? What are the reasons for statutory moratoriums on bringing custody modification actions? Who bears the burden of proof in a modification action and does it differ when a third party is seeking to modify a child custody order? What must be shown by the moving party before a court will even grant an evidentiary hearing in a custody dispute? What are some of the changed circumstances a court will recognize as requiring a hearing and possibly a change in child custody? Will a court grant a change of custody because a child support obligor fails to pay child support payments? Will a court grant a change of custody because a custodial parent with-holds court-ordered parenting time from the noncustodial parent? How does the constitutional right to travel affect a custodial parent who wants to move to another state with the child or children? How does the model UCCJEA attempt to resolve interstate child custody issues as to which of two or more states may have juris-diction to hear a modification dispute?

> **REFLECTIVE QUESTIONS**   What are your goals for this chapter?

7.2 INTRODUCTION: A WIDE VARIETY OF MODIFICATION REQUESTS

A wide variety of child custody modification requests are brought into the nation's family courts on a regular basis. The most common modification request asks for a change in an order that originally awarded sole physical custody of a minor child to one parent and now seeks to place physical custody in the other parent. Less common is a request to change a sole physical custody award to a joint physical custody arrangement. Occasionally, a request is made to modify legal custody, although when this motion is brought, it is usually accompanied with a request that physical custody also be modified.

Modification may also be sought where the parents originally received joint legal and physical custody and one of them seeks to modify the original order giving that parent sole physical custody of the child or children.

> **REFLECTIVE QUESTIONS**   List some of the various types of child custody modification requests that courts are asked to resolve.

7.3 BARRIERS TO MODIFICATION HEARING: *RES JUDICATA*

Res judicata plays an important role when a family court is asked to modify an existing child custody order. Black's Law Dictionary (9th ed. 2009) defines *res judicata* in part as follows:

> An issue that has been definitively settled by judicial decision. . . . An affirmative defense barring the same parties from litigating a second lawsuit on the same claim, or any other claim arising from the same transaction or series of transactions

and that could have been — but was not — raised in the first suit. The essential elements are (1) an earlier decision on the issue, (2) a final judgment on the merits, and (3) the involvement of the same parties, or parties in privity with the original parties. Restatement (Second) of Judgments §§17, 24 (1982). — Also termed *res adjudicata*; claim preclusion; doctrine of *res judicata*.

Once a family court child custody order has been entered by a court with jurisdiction over the parties, that order is considered *res judicata* of the facts and circumstances existing at the time it became final. After a final custody order is entered, a family court may consider modifying it only if it finds that a material or substantial change in circumstances affecting the interest and welfare of the child or children has occurred since the custody order was entered. *Sanchez v. Hernandez*, 45 So. 3d 57, 60-61 (Fla. App. 2010). It is important to recognize that under *res judicata* principles, a purportedly changed circumstance cannot be one that the court contemplated at the time of the earlier determination. *Ebach v. Ebach*, 757 N.W.2d 34, 36 (N.D. 2008).

REFLECTIVE QUESTIONS	What role does *res judicata* play when a family court is asked to change a custody order?

7.4 BARRIERS TO MODIFICATION HEARING: MORATORIUMS

Courts believe that children involved in a divorce should be provided with as much stability as possible. To provide stability, state statutes often contain time limitations during which a child custody modification motion cannot be brought after an initial custody order has been entered. The time limitation is usually referred to as a "moratorium" and typically it is for a period of either one or two years.

UMDA. Section 409(a) of the Uniform Marriage and Divorce Act (UMDA) contains a suggested two-year moratorium before a motion to modify a custody decree can be brought. *See In re F.A.G.*, 148 P.3d 375 (Colo. 2006). The commissioner's notes following §409 of the UMDA state that most experts believe that ensuring the decree's finality is more important than determining which parent should be custodian. Section 409(a) of the UMDA is designed to maximize finality and ensure continuity for the child without jeopardizing the child's interest. It is also designed to prevent a noncustodial parent from attempting to punish a former spouse by bringing frequent and unfounded attempts to change an existing prior custody order shortly after it was entered.

Endangerment exception. A custody modification motion alleging endangerment of a child is an exception to a two-year moratorium and can be brought at any time. UMDA §409(a) is consistent with this exception by requiring the movant for change, if he brings the motion within two years of a prior custody order, to show much greater urgency for a change than the usual best interests standard.

REFLECTIVE QUESTIONS	What are some of the reasons for a custody modification moratorium?

7.5 STANDARDS FOR MODIFYING CUSTODY: UMDA

The UMDA has been influential in suggesting to state legislatures the standards to apply in custody modification disputes. For example, §409(b) states that sole physical custody may be modified on one of three grounds: (1) upon a showing that the present custodial parent agrees to the modification request; or (2) that the child has been integrated in the petitioner's family with the consent of the custodial parent; or (3) that the child's present environment seriously endangers his physical, mental, moral, or emotional health and that the harm likely to be caused by a change of environment is outweighed by its advantages.

Agreement. The first ground for modification under the UMDA presents few problems. This is especially true where the parties have voluntarily executed a written agreement to modify custody. A written agreement might be set aside if it can be shown that a party was coerced into signing it; however, such claims are rare.

Voluntary integration. The second ground for modification under the UMDA is voluntary integration. Voluntary integration is not an issue when the parties agree that they have voluntarily integrated a child into the noncustodial parent's family. However, when parties dispute whether voluntary integration actually occurred, a court must conduct a fact-specific inquiry in an effort to determine who is providing the most accurate information about the alleged integration. The result is sometimes unexpected. For example, in *Gibson v. Gibson*, 471 N.W.2d 384, 386 (Minn. 1991), the court held that there had not been integration into the father's family despite the fact that the child had resided with his father for 17 months. The court found that the child was allowed to live with his father all these months only because his mother was financially unable to care for him and understood, when she allowed the child to remain with his father, that the arrangement was to be temporary.

Most courts agree that integration requires something more than merely expanding visitation. *In re Marriage of Chatten*, 967 P.2d 206 (Colo. App. 1998). It includes the performance of normal parental duties such as washing clothes, providing meals, attending to medical needs, assisting with homework, and guiding the child or children physically, mentally, morally, socially, and emotionally. In addition, the amount of time spent by a child with the proposed custodial parent should be of sufficient duration so that the child has become settled into the home of that parent as though it were his or her primary home. *See In re Marriage of Pontius*, 761 P.2d 247 (Colo. App. 1988).

Endangerment. The third basis for modification under the UMDA is endangerment. The party asserting endangerment must establish four elements to make out a prima facie case of endangerment: (1) Circumstances have changed involving the child or custodial parent; (2) the modification would be in the best interests of the child; (3) the child's physical or emotional health or emotional development is endangered by his or her present environment; and (4) the harm associated with the proposed change in custody would be outweighed by the benefits of the change.

REFLECTIVE QUESTIONS	An endangerment claim can be brought at any time despite the existence of a statutory moratorium. Why?

7.6 STANDARDS FOR MODIFYING CUSTODY: ALI MODEL ACT

The American Law Institute (ALI) recommends that an existing custody order be modified upon a showing of (1) a substantial change in the circumstances (relating to the child or one or both parents) on which the parenting plan was based that makes modification necessary to the child's welfare, or (2) harm to the child. ALI *Principles* §2.15(1) & (2) (2002). The ALI *Principles* allow a modification when it is "necessary to the child's welfare" rather than when it is in the "best interests" of the child.

REFLECTIVE QUESTIONS	The ALI Model Act uses the phrase "necessary to the child's welfare" rather than "best interests" when a modification of an existing child custody order is sought. Is there a significant difference in the meaning of these two phrases?

7.7 STANDARDS FOR MODIFYING CUSTODY: BURDEN OF PROOF

Courts generally apply a more rigid standard to a custody modification request than they do when making an initial custody determination. The more rigid standard is justified on the basis that it is needed to promote stability and continuity for the child or children and to discourage repeated litigation of issues already decided.

The burden of proof in a modification action may vary from a preponderance of evidence in some jurisdictions to clear and convincing evidence in others. *See, e.g., Mercier v. Mercier*, 11 So. 3d 1283, 1286 (Miss. 2009) (proof by a preponderance of the evidence); *In re Marriage of Smithson*, 943 N.E.2d 1169, 1172 (Ill. App. 2011) (clear and convincing evidence).

Modifying a joint custody award. The standards for modifying an existing *joint custody* award differ from those that are applied when a change is requested in an existing sole custody award. They also may differ from state to state. For example, the New York standard for modifying an existing joint custody award is when "the relationship between joint custodial parents has deteriorated to the point where they simply cannot work together in a cooperative fashion for the good of their children." *Ehrenreich v. Lynk*, 903 N.Y.S.2d 549 (N.Y. 2010). In contrast to New York, Missouri has declared that a court shall not modify a joint custody decree "unless . . . it finds, upon the basis of facts that have arisen since the prior decree or that were unknown to the court at the time of the prior decree, that a change has occurred in the circumstances of the child or his custodian and that the modification is necessary to serve the best interest of the child." *Hightower v. Myers*, 304 S.W.3d 727, 733 (Mo. 2010).

No presumption. Most states agree that there is no presumption regarding the fitness of either parent in a change of custody request when the parents have been provided in a judgment or decree joint physical custody of a child or children. *See, e.g., Buck v. Buck*, 279 S.W.3d 547 (Mo. App. 2009). In these cases, courts will usually apply a best interests test to decide whether the joint custody arrangement should be modified. *See, e.g., M.A.J. v. S.B.*, 73 So. 3d 1287 (Ala. 2011); *Jordan v. Rea*, 212 P.3d 919 (Ariz. 2009).

Request alone may be sufficient. Courts generally agree that a request by one of the parties to terminate a joint physical custody order by itself provides a sufficient basis to conclude that circumstances have changed so as to warrant a possible modification. *See In re Marriage of Lasky*, 678 N.E.2d 1035 (Ill. 1997). Some courts reason that application of a heightened burden of proof in joint physical custody cases is unnecessary because it should be self-evident when one party has brought a motion to change custody that joint custody is no longer in the best interest of the child.

Third parties. In most states, where third parties such as grandparents seek to modify an existing custody order, statutes typically require that they produce clear and convincing proof to support their request. *Polasek v. Omura*, 136 P.3d 519 (Mont. 2006). The higher standard is justified on the basis that courts must apply close scrutiny to any infringement on a person's right to parent a child.

In situations where a custodial parent seeks to modify an existing custody order that has granted a third party custodial rights to children, courts may sometimes shift the burden of proof to the third party to show by clear and convincing evidence that the parent's allegations cannot be sustained. For example, in *In re A.M.*, 251 P.3d 1119 (Colo. App. 2010), the child's parents moved to end or modify visitation with the child's grandparents. The court placed the burden of disproving the parental modification request by clear and convincing evidence on the grandparents.

REFLECTIVE QUESTIONS	**Should courts apply different burdens of proof when a change in custody is requested where the parties were originally awarded joint physical custody versus when one party was originally awarded sole custody?**

7.8 STANDARDS FOR MODIFYING CUSTODY: SCOPE OF REVIEW

The scope of the review to determine whether a change is warranted in an existing child custody order varies from state to state. For example, when deciding the question of the best interests of a child in a custody modification hearing in New York, the examination by the court is broad and determined by a review of the "totality of the circumstances." *Eschbach v. Eschbach*, 436 N.E.2d 1260 (N.Y. 1982). Factors a New York court may consider include, *inter alia*, (1) the original placement of the child, (2) the length of that placement, (3) the child's desires, (4) the relative fitness of the parents, (5) the quality of the home environment, (6) the parental guidance given to the child, (7) the parents' financial status, and (8) the parents' ability to provide for the child's emotional and intellectual development.

Court and legislatures outside New York take a somewhat different approach when it comes to stating what must be shown before a modification request is granted. For example, the court in *Wood v. Wood*, 29 So. 3d 908, 911 (Ala. App. 2009), stated that a party seeking a change in custody must show that the change "will materially promote [the] child's welfare." In *Horton v. Parrish*, 461 S.W.3d 718 (Ark. 2015), the court said that "once the trial court determines that the threshold requirement of a material change in circumstances since the last order of custody has been met, the trial court must then determine who should have custody with the sole consideration being the best interest of the children." Minnesota's legislature says that "the court shall not modify a prior custody order or a parenting plan provision which specifies the child's primary residence unless it finds, upon the basis of facts, including unwarranted denial of, or interference with, a duly established parenting time schedule, that have arisen since the prior order or that were unknown to the court at the time of the prior order, that a change has occurred in the circumstances of the child or the parties and that the modification is necessary to serve the best interests of the child." Minn. Stat.

§518.18 (2015). The statute goes on to state that custody will not be changed absent agreement, integration into the noncustodian's home, or the child's present environment endangers the child's physical or emotional health or impairs the child's emotional development, and the harm likely to be caused by a change of environment is outweighed by the advantage of a change to the child.

In Alabama there is a three-part test requiring the noncustodial parent seeking a change of custody to demonstrate (1) that he or she is a fit custodian; (2) that material changes that affect the child's welfare have occurred; and (3) that the positive good brought about by the change in custody will more than offset the disruptive effect of uprooting the child. *K.U. v. J.C.,* — So. 3d —, 2015 2015 WL 5918742 (Ala. App. 2015). In Tennessee, when a residential parenting schedule is sought to be modified, the petitioner must prove by a preponderance of the evidence a material change of circumstance affecting the child's best interest. In this jurisdiction, a material change of circumstance does not require a showing of a substantial risk of harm to the child. A material change of circumstance for purposes of modification of a residential parenting schedule may include, but is not limited to, significant changes in the needs of the child over time, which may include changes relating to age; significant changes in the parent's living or working condition that significantly affect parenting; failure to adhere to the parenting plan; or other circumstances making a change in the residential parenting time in the best interests of the child. *Hoover v. Hoover,* Slip Copy, 2015 WL 4737413 (Tenn. App. 2015).

REFLECTIVE QUESTIONS	Create a hypothetical illustrating a situation where there has been a material change in circumstances of the custodial parent but it has not affected the child in the custodial parent's care.

7.9 PROCEDURE: PERSUADING A COURT TO GRANT AN EVIDENTIARY HEARING

The conditions under which a family court will grant a full evidentiary hearing when a modification request is received vary. In general courts will initially rely on affidavits attached to moving papers asking for a full evidentiary hearing when deciding whether to grant the request. *See, e.g., O'Loughlin v. Sweetland,* 900 N.Y.S.2d 127 (N.Y.A.D. 2010). The affidavit procedure is used to discourage calendaring an insubstantial evidentiary hearing when a modification request is made. The affidavit cannot simply assert the statutory requirements for modification of the existing custody decree. It must contain facts that support the modification request. *See, e.g., Yvonne S. v. Wesley H.,* 245 P.3d 430 (Alaska 2011); *West v. West,* 664 S.W.2d 948, 949 (Ky. App. 1984). In general, a moving party is entitled to an evidentiary hearing if the party establishes a prima facie case by alleging in supporting affidavits sufficient facts that if uncontradicted would support a modification. *Volz v. Peterson,* 667 N.W.2d 637 (N.D. 2003).

Does the procedure described above that must be followed in order to obtain an evidentiary hearing put a premium on drafting skills when preparing affidavits?

7.10 EVIDENCE OF CHANGED CIRCUMSTANCES: THREAT TO CHILD'S HEALTH

Background to *Lizzio v. Jackson*

In New York, courts follow a fairly common set of principles in modification disputes. First, they don't need to reach the question of the best interests of the child unless a change of circumstances is proven. Second, once a court determines that a change in circumstances has been shown, the matter proceeds and the court decides whether the evidence indicates "a real need for a change in order to insure the child's best interest." *Matter of Kamholtz v. Kovary*, 620 N.Y.S.2d 576 (N.Y.A.D. 1994). The latter determination necessitates an inquiry into a number of factors relevant to the child's best interest, including the following: (1) a parent's fitness and ability to provide for the child's intellectual, emotional, and psychological development; (2) the length and quality of the preexisting custody arrangement; and (3) the quality of the parent's home environment and the child's prospects for the future. A court may also consider a child's social activities, economic provision, and personal desires.

In *Lizzio v. Jackson*, the ex-wife received primary (physical) custody of the two children of the marriage at the time the couple separated. Six years after the original separation and five years after the divorce judgment was entered, the ex-husband asked the trial court to grant primary custody of both children to him based on the allegation that the custodial parent was exposing their son, an asthmatic, to second-hand cigarette smoke.

LIZZIO
v.
JACKSON

Supreme Court of New York
226 A.D.2d 760 (1996)

CARDONA, J. . . . The issue in this proceeding is whether there were sufficient facts before Family Court to warrant granting petitioner's request for a change of custody. Following their separation in 1988, the parties entered into a separation agreement which contained a joint custodial provision with physical custody of the two children with respondent and visitation to petitioner. This custody arrangement was incorporated in the parties' 1991 divorce judgment. In January 1994, petitioner commenced this proceeding contending that custody of both children should be transferred to him, on various grounds, but primarily based on the allegation that respondent was exposing their son, an asthmatic, to second-hand cigarette smoke. Family Court granted the petition to the extent of awarding primary physical custody to petitioner, prompting respondent's appeal.

Initially, we must disagree with Family Court's conclusion that, in seeking to modify the parties' prior custody arrangement, petitioner was not required to show a change in circumstances. As this Court has noted, "[a] change in an established custody arrangement should be allowed only upon a showing of sufficient change in circumstances demonstrating a real need for a change in order to insure the child's best interest." The determination necessitates an inquiry into a number of factors relevant to the child's best interest, including the quality of the parents' home environments, the length of time the present custody arrangement was in place, relative fitness and ability to provide the requisite intellectual and emotional development for the child.

[I]t appears from Family Court's decision that it focused exclusively on respondent's smoking. Family Court concluded that "[b]ut for that issue and the health risk that smoking poses, the [c]ourt would continue the custody arrangement as the parties agreed some years ago." Although we understand, appreciate and agree with the court's concern in that regard, a review of the record compels us to conclude that this factor alone did not warrant a change in physical custody.

The parties' son was diagnosed with asthma in 1986, prior to their separation, and in 1990 was also diagnosed with various allergies which included cigarette smoke. Respondent has always smoked and was doing so when the parties divorced in 1991. In addition, although petitioner claimed that the son's health was deteriorating and that his asthma attacks were more frequent, there is no evidence in the record supporting these assertions. It is not disputed that respondent smoked in her son's presence until petitioner commenced this proceeding. At that time, Family Court issued a temporary restraining order prohibiting either parent from exposing the son to tobacco smoke. It is also not disputed that since then, respondent and her current husband smoke outside or on the back porch.

In our view, while we find that there was insufficient evidence to change physical custody, given the fact that the son is asthmatic and has been diagnosed as being allergic to cigarette smoke, both parents shall continue to observe Family Court's order directing adherence to the instructions of their son's allergist. We stress that our determination is based on the fact that respondent's smoking did not warrant a change in custody and should in no way be construed as reflecting negatively on petitioner's ability to parent the children.

Ordered that the order is modified, on the law and the facts, without costs, by reversing so much thereof as awarded physical custody of the parties' children to petitioner; physical custody of the parties' children awarded to respondent, both parties shall continue to observe Family Court's order directing adherence to the instructions of their son's allergist, and matter remitted to the Family Court of Fulton County for further proceedings not inconsistent with this Court's decision; and, as so modified, affirmed.

DISCUSSION QUESTIONS   FOR *LIZZIO v. JACKSON*

A. A court, when determining whether to modify child custody, need not reach the question of the best interests of the child unless a change of circumstances is shown. Events representing a change of circumstance must have been unanticipated and must have arisen since the last order was entered. Applying these principles to this case, were there events that arose since the last custody order that were not anticipated by the moving party?

B. What additional evidence might the attorney for the father have sought to support his claim that there had been a substantial change of circumstances? If the father's attorney was successful at persuading the court that a substantial change in circumstances had occurred, what would the attorney next have to prove?

C. Assume in the following hypothetical that after the mother and father divorce, mother is awarded physical and legal custody of their nine-year-old son. The son has some behavior problems that require substantial amounts of care and attention. A year after the divorce, father remarries. His wife is a traditional homemaker and remains at home. Mother obtains a job at a food market near her home as a maintenance worker and works there about 45 hours a week. She hires a babysitter to care for her son before and after school. Father brings a modification action seeking legal and physical custody. He asserts in his moving papers that while he works 50 hours a week, his new wife will provide complete care for the boy. Mother argues that father has demonstrated that he has "abdicated his parental duties" to a third party and the child will be spending most of his time with a stranger, his stepmother. Will a court grant the father an evidentiary hearing on his allegations? If a hearing is held, will a court most likely modify custody? *See Matter of Bogert v. Rickard*, 604 N.Y.S.2d 331 (N.Y. 1993) (held that modification not warranted where custodial father, who remarried, worked and noncustodial mother did not, father continued to provide loving, stable home environment, limited his work hours, adjusted work schedule, and declined promotion to accommodate personal care of children).

7.11 EVIDENCE OF CHANGE IN CIRCUMSTANCES: MILITARY DEPLOYMENT

Given the current state of our armed forces and the military commitments requiring the deployment and redeployment of our nation's soldiers, the dilemma confronting divorced military parents of young children as to how best to advance the care of those children in the absence of one parent is a recurring problem. Some states, such as Florida, provide that if a custody modification is filed as a result of a parent being deployed because of military service, the court may not modify a previous order that changes time-sharing as it existed on the date the parent was deployed. An exception exists that allows a court to enter a temporary order to amend the custody arrangement if there is clear and convincing evidence that the temporary modification is in the best interests of the child.

California provides that "[a] party's absence . . . shall not, by itself, be sufficient to justify a modification of a custody . . . order if the reason for the absence . . . is the party's activation to military service and deployment out of state." Cal. Fam. Code §3047 (West 2005). Arizona does not consider "military deployment of a custodial parent a change of circumstances that materially affects the welfare of the child if the custodial parent has filed a military family care plan and if the military deployment is less than six months." Ariz. Rev. Stat. Ann. §25-411B (2009). Kansas similarly permits the parties to enter into a parenting plan in contemplation of military deployment and provides a presumption "that the agreement is in the best interests of the child." Kan. Stat. Ann. §60-1630(e) (2008).

Limited inquiry. In *In re Marriage of E.U. and J.E.*, 152 Cal. Rptr. 3d 58 (Cal. App. 2012), the court stated that when it is asked to enforce reinstatement of the established parenting plan upon a deployed parent's return from military service, it should conduct a limited best interests inquiry. It went on to say that the court's analysis of the child's best interests should be restricted to serious concerns such as the child's young age at the time of the servicemember's deployment. It also suggested that a transitional period may be needed to ease the child back into the original parenting arrangement.

| REFLECTIVE QUESTIONS | Do you see any problem with the test established in *In re Marriage of E.U. and J.E.*? What if the returning servicemember suffers from mental or physical health problems that impair his or her ability to parent? |

Background to *Faucett v. Vasquez*

In the case that follows, *Faucett v. Vasquez*, the father had custody of the child and was being deployed. The child's mother brought a custody modification action and framed her claim as against the father's new wife — a third party to the action. The new wife would be caring for the minor child while the father was deployed. The mother's strategy in framing the issue in this way was to gain a presumption favoring her as the natural parent and to avoid having to bear the threshold burden of establishing changed circumstances. The father argued that the dispute was between him and his ex-wife, not between his ex-wife and his new wife.

FAUCETT
v.
VASQUEZ

Superior Court of New Jersey, Appellate Division
984 A.2d 460 (N.J. Super. 2009)

MESSANO, J. This case presents a question of first impression in this State. In particular, must a parent seeking modification of a court order regarding custody of her child bear the threshold burden of establishing changed circumstances that affect the welfare of the child, when the court-ordered parent of primary residence (PPR) is a member of the United States military about to be deployed for a year away from home? . . .

Plaintiff and defendant were married on January 11, 1997, and divorced on December 11, 2001. Their union produced a son, Billy, who was born in 1997. . . . In 2002 . . . the court entered [an] order that provided: 1) joint legal custody . . . ; 2) plaintiff would be the PPR except [defendant would] be the [PPR] during school summer vacations; 3) During school summer vacations [defendant would] have custody approximately 70% of the summer vacation and [plaintiff] approximately 30% of the time; and 4) defendant would have the child for [three] weekends each month as determined by the parties. . . .

In January 2009, defendant sought, by order to show cause, the immediate transfer of custody because of plaintiff's impending deployment as a military reservist, initially out of state, but thereafter, overseas. . . . Defendant . . . noted that plaintiff's wife, who was also in the military, sometimes had to leave home during the work week, resulting in all three children being left in the care of plaintiff's parents. Defendant argued that she provided the preferred living arrangement for [Billy] in his father's absence and suggested that upon plaintiff's return from service, the parties could re-evaluate the child's needs.

Defendant further claimed that if Billy did not live with her during plaintiff's absence, it would negatively impact him emotionally, though she provided no details or support for that conclusion. She stated that she was open to reasonable visitation arrangements so her son could continue to see his step-family and his paternal family. In sum, defendant sought "full residential custody of [Billy]" while plaintiff was deployed overseas, along with reasonable child support.

Plaintiff opposed the motion. He noted that he would be deployed in February 2009 for one year or less. He claimed that Billy was extremely close to his step-siblings, and all three children lived and played together well. Before being deployed to Iraq, plaintiff was to spend the first three months of his active duty in the United States. He noted that he would be accorded one extended leave which would permit him to return home and see his son. He also explained that while stationed in Iraq, it would be difficult to contact home, and it would be even more difficult if he had to contact defendant to speak to his son. Plaintiff took the opportunity to add that defendant's house was a mess, that several people lived with her, and that Billy often did not have a place to sleep when he stayed with her. Plaintiff agreed to allow extra [parenting] time for . . . defendant while he was deployed.

In a reply certification, defendant alleged that plaintiff's wife strongly believe[d] that [Billy] should move in with defendant while plaintiff was deployed. Defendant also alleged that plaintiff's wife told her that the couple was experiencing severe marital problems, and that plaintiff's parents were behind the opposition to any change in custody. She denied the allegations plaintiff made about the condition of her home and her care of Billy. . . .

The judge concluded that there was no need for a change of custody to immediately occur. He noted that Billy was in the same school he ha[d] always attended, was near his friends, and was having his medical needs met. The child did not report any problems with the care provided by plaintiff's wife.

. . . [T]he judge decided to increase defendant's parenting time to every weekend and all school holidays. He increased defendant's summer parenting time, ordering Billy to reside with her all summer, except for two weekends each month. The judge also ordered a custody evaluation after which he anticipated either party could apply again for modification of his order. This appeal ensued. . . .

Defendant's argument may be distilled to an essential point. In seeking modification of the 2002 order, she need not demonstrate a change of circumstances that affect Billy's welfare, because, as between herself and plaintiff's current wife, defendant is presumed to be entitled to custody of her son. Since plaintiff did not rebut this presumption by demonstrating defendant was unfit, or that exceptional circumstances existed, the judge erred in not awarding her immediate residential custody of Billy while plaintiff was deployed on active military duty.

Plaintiff's retort is that the dispute is not between defendant and a third-party, but, rather between two natural parents. Since he is the PPR, defendant bore the burden of demonstrating changed circumstances that affected Billy's welfare such that modification was warranted. Plaintiff contends defendant failed to do this, and the judge correctly determined not to alter the status quo. . . .

In *Watkins v. Nelson*, 748 A.2d 558 (N.J. 2000), the Court was called upon to decide the appropriate standard to apply in a custody dispute between a child's father, the plaintiff, and her maternal grandparents, the defendants. The child's mother had died shortly after giving birth, and the child had thereafter been raised by the defendants. The defendants refused the father's request for custody and filed an action . . . seeking an order granting them custody of their granddaughter. The Court noted that even upon the death of the custodial parent, the statute precludes the surviving non-custodial parent's automatic accession to custody of his or her child. Instead, the Family Part is empowered to consider the custody issue during the time period between the death of the custodial parent and the ultimate transfer of custody.

In such disputes, the Court enunciated the analytic framework as follows:

> [I]t is the relationship of the child to the person seeking custody that determines the standard to be used in deciding the custody dispute. When the dispute is between two fit parents, the best interest of the child standard controls because both parents are presumed to be equally entitled to custody.
>
> The child's best interest rebuts the presumption in favor of one of the fit parents. But, when the dispute is between a fit parent and a third party, only the fit parent is presumed

to be entitled to custody. In that context, the child's welfare is protected because the presumption in favor of the fit parent is rebuttable. Once the presumption in favor of a fit parent is rebutted . . . , the child's best interest is advanced by not awarding custody to the parent. Viewed in that context, in custody determinations between a fit parent and a third party, . . . the child's best interests become a factor only after the parental termination standard has been met, rather than the determinative standard itself. . . .

In this case, plaintiff's current wife, who defendant argues is the analogous third-party in the *Watkins* framework, is not seeking custody of Billy. In our view, this distinction is critical. Unlike the father in *Watkins* who faced the denial of custody and a significant curtailment of his parental rights, defendant in this case faces no such consequences. Indeed, she continues to share legal custody of Billy with plaintiff, and the judge significantly increased her parenting time.

There are other reasons why the parental presumption ought not to apply when the PPR is facing *temporary* military deployment. In *Watkins*, the custodial parent's death created an unalterable set of circumstances. The child in that case could never be reunited with the parent who previously had exercised primary, albeit short-lived, custody. That is clearly not the case here. Instead, plaintiff will hopefully return from his deployment in good health and in a relatively short, finite period of time, after which he can resume his relationship with Billy as before.

Lastly, in *Watkins*, neither the deceased mother nor the plaintiff/father had ever sought a court order defining their custodial relationship with their child. As a result, the Court was affirming the basic tenet that as between a third-party and a natural parent, the parent need not bear the initial burden of proving that it was in the child's best interests to award him custody because he provided a better home than that provided by the interested third-party. . . .

We might assume that the difficult questions posed by this appeal are being raised in courtrooms throughout the United States, and that decisional law from our sister jurisdictions could provide us with guidance. However, no reported decision was brought to our attention by either party, and our own independent research has disclosed few that discuss the issues in this context. . . .

In one case, . . . *In re Marriage of DePalma*, 176 P.3d 829, 831 (Colo. App. 2007), *cert. denied*, 2008 WL 434613 (Colo. Feb. 19, 2008), . . . the appellate court first noted that in determining a custodial dispute between a parent and a nonparent, Colorado courts recognize a presumption that a biological parent has a first and prior right to the custody of his or her child. However, the court noted that because the dispute was between mother and father, and not between mother and stepmother, the presumption that a parent has a first and prior right to the custody of his or her child was not implicated. . . . Thus, when two fit parents disagree, the court must weigh the wishes of both to determine what is in the child's best interests. The appellate court then rejected the mother's contention that the trial court effectively granted parenting time to the stepmother or that it had extended special rights to the stepmother. . . .

[T]he Supreme Court of Kansas rejected application of the parental presumption to a custody dispute between a father, who was the custodial parent and about to be deployed to Korea for one year, and the children's mother, also in the military but soon to retire. *In re Marriage of Rayman*, 273 Kan. 996, 47 P.3d 413, 414 (2002). Noting the custody dispute was between two parents, the court determined "the parental preference doctrine [is] not applicable to the facts of [the] case." Likening the facts presented to "temporary changes which relate to nonmilitary custodial relationships[,]" the court affirmed the trial court's decision denying the mother's modification request, and maintaining primary custody with the father during his absence.

We are firmly convinced that the distinctions we have raised between the facts presented in *Watkins* and those presented here, and the limited jurisprudence from our sister states, require us to reject defendant's argument that the parental presumption applies to this dispute such that she was entitled to immediate residential custody of Billy solely because of plaintiff's military deployment. In this regard, we conclude the motion judge appropriately denied defendant's motion.

. . .

We are hard-pressed to see how defendant did not, in the first instance, establish that a significant change of circumstances in Billy's life was about to occur because of that plaintiff will be physically separated from Billy for twelve months, with very little contact in the interim. He acknowledged in his certification that it would be difficult to contact his son. Thus, it is undisputed that plaintiff will not exercise traditional custody over Billy for a significant period of time. In this sense, the circumstances of Billy's day-to-day residential custody have clearly changed, albeit temporarily, since the entry of the 2002 order. . . .

Plaintiff's pending deployment for an entire year, in itself, was a circumstance of such magnitude, and likely to affect Billy's welfare, that defendant need not have awaited the passage of time and the consequences of plaintiff's absence vis-à-vis their son, to seek modification. In other words, if legal or residential custody is contested, a parent's military deployment and absence from the home for a significant period of time is sufficient for the Family Court to "order an investigation of the [situation]," in search of a "meaningful solution to serve the best interests of the child." This is not to say that the non-deploying parent is necessarily entitled to modification; we only hold that defendant in this case established a *prima facie* case for modification and the matter should have been set down for a plenary hearing.

As a result, we must reverse the order of dismissal and remand the matter for further proceedings.

 **FOR** *FAUCETT v. VASQUEZ*

A. The noncustodial parent argued that she need not demonstrate a change of circumstances that affects the child's welfare, because, as between herself and the custodial parent's current wife, she is presumed to be entitled to custody of her son. She also argued that because the custodial parent did not rebut this presumption by demonstrating she was unfit, or that exceptional circumstances existed, the trial judge erred in not awarding her immediate residential custody of the child while the custodial parent was deployed on active military duty. What is the court's response to these arguments?

B. According to this court, when the modification dispute is between a fit parent and a third party, who is presumed to be entitled to custody? What reasons support such a presumption? When the modification dispute is between two fit parents, is the custodial parent entitled to a presumption that he or she should retain custody?

C. The court states that the existing arrangements in which a child has thrived should be disturbed only if the court finds "compelling circumstances." Given the facts in the opinion, does it appear that there are compelling circumstances to alter the existing custody arrangement?

D. Kentucky promulgated a statute declaring that unless the child is endangered, "any court-ordered modification of a child custody decree, based in whole or in part on the active duty of a parent or a de facto custodian as a regular member of the United States Armed Forces deployed outside the United States; or any federal active duty of a parent or a de facto custodian as a member of a state National Guard or a Reserve component; shall be temporary and shall revert back to the previous child custody decree at the end of the deployment outside the United States or the federal active duty, as appropriate." Ky. Rev. Stat. §403.340 (2011). How would this statute affect the outcome of this case if it were applied to it? Should other jurisdictions follow Kentucky in regard to creating similar provisions to protect divorced military personnel?

E. When weighing all of the factors that go into a modification decision, which of the following is the most important and should receive the greatest weight from the trial judge? Bonding? Continuity? Remarriage of the custodial parent? Religious compatibility? The new family consisting of the child and custodial parent? Mental stability of parent? Financial stability of parent?

7.12 EVIDENCE OF CHANGED CIRCUMSTANCES: DENIAL OF OR INTERFERENCE WITH VISITATION

When should denial or interference with court-ordered visitation warrant a change in custody? The answer is that unwarranted denial of or interference with duly established visitation may constitute contempt of court and may result in a modification of custody. However, the unwarranted denial of or interference with visitation is usually viewed as only one of many factors to consider when a custody modification action is brought. It is well established that alteration of an established custody arrangement will be ordered only upon a showing of a change in circumstances that reflects a real need for change to ensure the best interest of the child. In extreme cases, courts may modify custody where the custodial parent has repeatedly interfered with the noncustodial parent's visitation rights if modification is in the best interest of the child. *See Egle v. Egle*, 715 F.2d 999 (5th Cir. 1983), *cert. denied*, 469 U.S. 1032 (1984).

REFLECTIVE QUESTIONS	**Why shouldn't the unwarranted interference with a visitation provision in a divorce decree automatically result in a change of custody at the request of the noncustodial parent?**

7.13 EVIDENCE OF CHANGED CIRCUMSTANCES: OLDER TEENAGER'S PREFERENCE

An older teenage child's custody preference for living with the noncustodial parent is given considerable weight in determining whether an existing custody order should be modified. *Ross v. Ross*, 477 N.W.2d 753, 756 (Minn. App. 1991). However, courts generally agree that a teenager's preference to live with the noncustodial parent is not absolute. *See, e.g., Maxwell v. Maxwell*, 37 P.3d 424, 426 (Alaska 2001).

Courts also appear to be in general agreement that a request by a mature child for a change in custody in and of itself may constitute a significant change in circumstances justifying a full hearing on the matter. *See, e.g., Volz v. Peterson*, 667 N.W.2d 637 (N.D. 2003).

REFLECTIVE QUESTIONS	**Should custody be modified because a mature teenager demands that a change occur?**

7.14 EVIDENCE OF CHANGED CIRCUMSTANCES: FAILURE TO PAY CHILD SUPPORT

Most jurisdictions will not allow a modification of custody merely because the noncustodial parent has failed to pay child support. *See, e.g., Green v. Krebs*, 245 Ga. App. 756 (2000). Courts focus on the best interests of a child or children, and it may not be in their best interests to alter an existing custody order because the noncustodial parent failed to make support payments. *See Ex parte McLendon*, 455 So. 2d 863 (Ala. 1984). The remedy is for the custodial parent to bring a contempt action to enforce the existing child support court order.

Note that a party who is in contempt for failure to pay child support is usually not entitled to a hearing on a motion to modify a divorce decree unless the party purges him- or herself of the contempt. *Rodriquez v. Rodriquez*, 249 P.3d 413 (Idaho 2011).

| REFLECTIVE QUESTIONS | **Why shouldn't a noncustodial parent who fails to pay reasonable child support be punished by automatically allowing visitation arrangements with the child or children to be modified on request of the custodial parent?** |

PART 2: RELOCATION

7.15 RELOCATION ISSUES MAY ARISE WHEN A COURT IS INITIALLY DECIDING CUSTODY OR WHEN A MODIFICATION OF AN EXISTING ORDER IS SOUGHT

The issue of the custodial parent seeking to relocate to a city or state distant from that of the noncustodial parent comes before a family court in at least two contexts. The first is when a request is brought to relocate as a part of an initial custody decision. The second is when a request to relocate is brought after the initial custody order was issued.

The number of relocation requests by a custodial parent has continued to increase as our society has become increasingly mobile and migratory. In fact, "the number of relocation cases has continued to expand at an astounding rate." David V. Chipman & Mindy M. Rush, *The Necessity of "Right to Travel" Analysis in Custodial Parent Relocation Cases*, 10 Wyo. L. Rev. 267 (2010).

Deciding a relocation request is challenging and usually controls the family structure for years to come. For example, if the court allows a mother to relocate to another jurisdiction with the minor child in her care, this normally ends a noncustodial father's regular weekly visits with the child. However, if the court denies the mother's relocation request, the relationship between the mother and the child will be dramatically altered, should the mother decide to relocate to another jurisdiction without the child. If the mother decides to remain in the forum jurisdiction rather than change the relationship with the child by relocating, the consequences to her may be a loss of a major job opportunity, separation from a new spouse, or inability to move to an area where her extended family lives. The situation becomes more difficult when the mother and father enjoy a close, warm, loving relationship with the child and both are capable parents.

Adding to the difficulty of understanding and applying the law in relocation disputes is the failure of the 50 states to adopt uniform legislation concerning this issue. For example, some state relocation statutes provide rebuttable presumptions favoring relocation; others provide rebuttable presumptions against relocation. Some jurisdictions place the burden of showing relocation is in the best interests of the child on the relocating parent; others place the burden on the nonrelocating parent to show relocation is not in the child's best interests. *See generally* Sally Adams, *Avoiding Round Two: The Inadequacy of Current Relocation Laws and a Proposed Solution*, 43 Fam. L.Q. 181 (Spring 2009).

> **REFLECTIVE QUESTIONS**
>
> What may explain the inability of states to agree on whom to place the burden of proof in a relocation dispute and whether a presumption should favor the custodial parent, the noncustodial parent, or no one?

7.16 CONSTITUTIONAL RIGHT TO TRAVEL

One question a family court must resolve in relocation disputes is how the constitutional right to travel affects a custodial parent's request to relocate to another state or nation outside the United States. Does the Constitution protect a custodial parent's right to travel? A second related question is whether the constitutional right to travel provides authority for the custodian to travel with the custodial child.

The answer to the first question is clear: The custodial parent has a constitutional right to individually relocate. In *Shapiro v. Thompson*, 394 U.S. 618, 630 (1969) *overruled on other grounds* by *Edelman v. Jordan*, 415 U.S. 651, 671 (1974), the Supreme Court recognized an individual's constitutional right to travel. The Court, citing *United States v. Guest*, 383 U.S. 745, 757 (1969), stated that "[t]he constitutional right to travel from one State to another occupies a position fundamental to the concept of our Federal Union. It is a right that has been firmly established and repeatedly recognized." In *Saenz v. Roe*, 526 U.S. 489 (1999), the Supreme Court declared that an individual's right to interstate travel is guaranteed by the Privileges and Immunities Clause of the Fourteenth Amendment of the United States Constitution.

The answer to the second question is that there is no constitutional right of a custodial parent to automatically travel to another state with the child or children in the parent's custody. The issue in relocation cases in general is the extent to which parental needs and desires are intertwined with the child's best interests. A court must determine the best interest of the child while weighing a majority time parent's right to travel with the custodial child and a minority time parent's right to parent.

> **REFLECTIVE QUESTIONS**
>
> If a custodial parent's constitutional right to travel cannot be interfered with, on what constitutional basis may a state nevertheless refuse to allow that parent to relocate to a distant place with the child or children in that parent's physical custody?

7.17 SOCIAL SCIENCE CONFLICT OVER RELOCATION

When deciding a relocation request, courts have looked to social science research for help in assessing the impact that relocation may have on the child or children. Researchers generally agree that children's lives are altered by even the most amicable of divorces and that a high level of parental conflict has a destructive impact on children. Linda D. Elrod & Milfred D. Dale, *Paradigm Shifts and Pendulum Swings in Child Custody: The Interests of Children in the Balance*, 42 Fam. L.Q. 381, 384-385 (Fall 2008).

Researchers disagree over the depth of the impact on the child and the parents when relocation is the issue. For example, the late Dr. Judith S. Wallerstein argued for a presumption favoring the custodial parent's relocation request, subject only to a court's power to restrain a move that would prejudice the welfare of the child. She said that courts should recognize that the child and the custodial parent have formed a "new family unit" following divorce. Furthermore, courts should reasonably anticipate that once the new family unit is formed the future may include a new marriage, an important job opportunity, or a return to the help provided by an extended family in the rearing of the child by a single parent. She implied that what is good for the new family unit as a whole is good for the custodial child. She stated that imposing a choice of relocating without a child can be severely detrimental to the psychological and economic well-being of the custodial parent over many years. She also stated that it is unrealistic to expect that a family in contemporary American society, whether intact or divorced, will remain in one geographic location for an extended period of time. Judith S. Wallerstein & Tony J. Tanke, *To Move or Not to Move: Psychological and Legal Considerations in the Relocation of Children Following Divorce*, 30 Fam. L.Q. 305, 314-315 (Summer 1996). *See also* Janet M. Bowermaster, *Sympathizing with Solomon: Choosing Between Parents in a Mobile Society*, 31 U. Louisville J. Fam. L. 791, 884 (1992) (custodial parents should be allowed to relocate with their child in good faith to pursue "their best opportunities").

Dr. Wallenstein's research and views have been criticized. For example, Dr. Richard A. Warshak argues that the assumption made by Dr. Wallerstein that allowing relocation will be rewarding for the relocating parent is not necessarily true. He writes that:

> The new relationship may fail. Graduate school may not be what the parent expected. The new job could be short-lived. Relationships with extended family can become strained. And the children's difficulties adjusting to the move and separation from their other parent might cast a pall on the parent's satisfaction with the new circumstances. In the event that the relocation disappoints the custodial parent, the children could experience the diminished parenting Wallerstein refers to, without the protective buffering effect of frequent contact with the non-custodial parent.

Richard A. Warshak, *Social Science and Children's Best Interests in Relocation Cases: Burgess Revisited*, 34 Fam. L.Q. 83, 99 (2000). Others have criticized

Dr. Wallerstein's research as anecdotal, and without scientific sampling or rigorous double-blind methodologies to ensure correction for any researcher bias. Moreover, critics contend that her subjects are not necessarily typical because they came from predominantly white, upper-middle-class backgrounds and were well educated, which raises questions about application of her findings to other groups. *See* Robert Pasahow, *A Critical Analysis of the First Empirical Research Study on Child Relocation*, 19 J. Am. Acad. Matrimonial Law. 321, 335 (2005).

REFLECTIVE QUESTIONS	Do the social scientists have the key to the impact an out-of-state move will have on a child or children? Is there too much focus on the parents rather than the children?

7.18 RELOCATION PRESUMPTIONS AND STANDARDS

Relocation is an area where state policy making varies tremendously. Not only do states take different approaches to the issue, they also seem to periodically alter their views on whether to encourage or discourage parental geographical moves.

Favoring custodial parent. The use of presumptions favoring the custodial parent or the noncustodial parent vary among jurisdictions. The presumptions may also change from time to time, in apparent response to the state legislature and/or state court changing philosophy about relocation. For example, California appears to favor the custodial parent's removal request. In that state, a parent who has been awarded physical custody of a child is not required to show that a proposed relocation move is necessary. Instead, he or she has the right to change the residence of the child, subject to the power of the court to restrain a removal that would prejudice the rights or welfare of the child. *See In re Marriage of LaMusga*, 12 Cal. Rptr. 3d 356 (Cal. 2004).

State ambivalence. Some states can't make up their mind about which of the two parties to favor when it comes to a relocation request. For example, Minnesota favored the custodial parent from 1983 to 2006. During that period, it held that a custodial parent was presumptively entitled to relocate with the minor child. It placed a high burden of proof on the party opposing relocation to establish that removal would endanger the child's physical or emotional health and was not in the best interests of the child. Or, in the alternative, the noncustodial parent had to produce evidence that the purpose of the move was to interfere with the visitation rights of that parent. *Auge v. Auge*, 334 N.W.2d 393 (Minn. 1983). However, the Minnesota legislature changed its relocation standard in 2006. In doing so, it reversed the presumption favoring relocation and placed the burden on the custodial parent to demonstrate that the benefits of the move outweighed its detriments. *Goldman v. Greenwood*, 748 N.W.2d 279 (Minn. 2008).

Favoring noncustodial parent. Alabama favors the noncustodial parent with a rebuttable presumption that a change of principal residence of a child is not in the best interest of the child. In that state, the relocating parent bears the initial burden of proof of overcoming the presumption by showing that relocation is in a child's best interests. If that burden is met, the burden then shifts to nonrelocating parent to show the relocation is not in the child's best interests. Ala. Code §30-3-169.4 (2015). In New York, a parent seeking permission to relocate with a child has the burden of establishing by a preponderance of the evidence that the proposed relocation is in the child's best interests. *Murphy v. Peace*, 899 N.Y.S.2d 493 (N.Y.A.D. 2010). Similarly, in North Dakota the burden of proof is placed on the relocating party to show that relocation of the child with the parent is legitimate and in the best interests of the child. *Maynard v. McNett*, 710 N.W.2d 369 (N.D. 2006).

No precise formula. Vermont adopted the relocation standard set forth in ALI *Principles* §2.17(1). *Hawkes v. Spence*, 878 A.2d 273 (Vt. 2005). Under Vermont's standard, "relocation is a substantial change of circumstances justifying a reexamination of parental rights and responsibilities only when the relocation significantly impairs either parent's ability to exercise responsibilities the parent has been exercising or attempting to exercise under the parenting plan." *Ibid.* This determination involves "no precise formula," but requires the court to consider factors including "the amount of custodial responsibility each parent has been exercising and for how long, the distance of the move and its duration, and the availability of alternative visitation arrangements." *Ibid.*

Neutral. Colorado has no presumption for or against relocation. Both parents bear the burden to demonstrate the move is or is not in the child's best interests. *In re Marriage of Ciesluk*, 113 P.3d 135 (Colo. 2005).

REFLECTIVE QUESTIONS	When a custodial parent makes a relocation request, should the law presume it is in the best interests of the new family consisting of the custodial parent and child or children to allow the request? Or, should the law presume it is not in the best interests of the child or children to allow the request? Or, should the law be neutral?

7.19 RELOCATING FROM STATE TO STATE

Background to *Curtis v. Curtis*

The facts in *Curtis v. Curtis* are not disputed. The parties were divorced in 2006, in Falls City, Nebraska. Falls City is a small Nebraska town with a population of about

4,000 people located only a few miles from the Missouri border. At the time of the divorce, Ryonee Curtis was granted primary physical custody of her minor child, with the parties sharing joint legal custody. She also was awarded the right to live in the couple's small, mortgaged home with her ex-husband receiving ownership and the mortgage. The home was later foreclosed upon and she and her daughter went to live with Scott McCann and his three children in a house owned by him.

Scott McCann also owned lakefront property at Big Lake, Missouri. He decided to sell his Falls City property and build a new home in Big Lake. The property on which the new home was to be built is located about 17.6 miles from Falls City. Arrangements were made for Ryonee, her daughter, and Scott and his children to rent a house in Big Lake while the new home was under construction. When Ryonee asked the court for permission to move to Big Lake, her ex-husband objected and a hearing was set.

At the hearing, Ryonee testified that given her financial situation, she believed it would be difficult for her to obtain housing in Falls City similar to the house Scott was building. She estimated that she could only afford $200 for rent even though she worked full-time at a grocery store. She said she received $1,500 a year from her ex-husband, presumably as part of the division of the marital estate. She also testified that her ex-husband provided $460 per month in child support and paid 60 percent of day care expenses.

She agreed that if the court allowed the move, the child would continue to attend school in Falls City and she would continue her current employment in Falls City. She also agreed that the visitation schedule that the child had with her father would not significantly change. Finally, if the court refused to allow her to move with her daughter to Big Lake, she would remain in Nebraska with the child.

The ex-husband, Ryan Curtis, argued that Ryonee's desire to continue to cohabit with Scott was not a legitimate reason to allow her to relocate. Ryan testified that the child's family and friends were all in Falls City, she attended school and day care in Falls City, and had lived in Falls City her entire life. He also argued that instability or uncertainty was created because Scott could determine whether Ryonee and the child could come or go at the Big Lake house.

CURTIS
v.
CURTIS

Court of Appeals of Nebraska
759 N.W.2d 269 (2008)

CARLSON, J. . . .

Under the circumstances revealed by the evidence in this case, we conclude that Ryonee's desire to continue living with her current boyfriend is not a legitimate reason to remove Jordyn from Nebraska. Career advancement and remarriage are commonly found legitimate reasons for a move in removal cases, but they do not compose the exclusive list of legitimate reasons. Clearly, Ryonee's desire to move from Nebraska is not based on an employment opportunity for her or Scott and is not based on remarriage. Ryonee's sole reason for wanting to move is her desire to continue living with Scott as she has been doing since moving out of the marital home. Because Scott is selling his house in Falls City where Ryonee and Jordyn have been living, Ryonee and Jordyn have to find someplace else to live. However, Ryonee has not demonstrated a legitimate reason as to why their new home has to be with Scott in Missouri.

Ryonee testified that given her financial situation, it would be difficult for her to obtain housing in Falls City similar to the house Scott is going to build in Missouri. While it could be true that Scott's new house might provide newer or more spacious housing for Ryonee and Jordyn than Ryonee would be able to afford on her own, there is no evidence that Ryonee cannot find or cannot afford suitable housing in Falls City. Ryonee testified that she could only afford $200 a month in rent. There is no evidence in the record regarding her income or her expenses. We do know, however, that she receives $1,500 a year from Ryan, as well as $460 per month in child support. We also know that Ryan is renting a house in Falls City for $200 per month. She does not allege that she is unable to find suitable housing for $200 per month in Falls City or that she even looked into whether housing for $200 per month was available, and if so, whether such housing was suitable for her and Jordyn. Thus, she has not shown that she cannot afford housing on her own or that living with Scott in Missouri is her only available housing option.

Because Ryonee has failed to satisfy the initial threshold of showing a legitimate reason to move, it is not necessary for this court to determine if it is in Jordyn's best interests to move to Missouri with Ryonee, nor is it necessary to address Ryan's remaining assignments of error. . . . We find that the district court abused its discretion in granting Ryonee's request to remove Jordyn from Nebraska because Ryonee failed to meet her burden of proof to demonstrate that her reason for leaving Nebraska constituted a legitimate reason for removal. Accordingly, we reverse the district court's order granting Ryonee's application for removal.

DISCUSSION QUESTIONS FOR *CURTIS v. CURTIS*

A. This court overturned the trial judge's order, which had allowed the custodial mother to relocate 17.6 miles from the noncustodial parent and Falls City. The basis of the ruling was a finding that the mother's desire to relocate to live with her boyfriend was not a "legitimate reason" to allow relocation outside Nebraska. Do you agree with this reasoning?

B. It is suggested that a custodial parent's constitutional right to interstate and intra-state travel is rarely analyzed by courts in relocation cases. David V. Chipman & Mindy M. Rush, *The Necessity of "Right to Travel" Analysis in Custodial Parent*

Relocation Cases, 10 Wyo. L. Rev. 267, 270 (2010). It is also suggested that a failure by courts to recognize and analyze a parent's constitutional right to travel will, at times, yield absurd results. *Ibid.* The court in this case did not discuss the constitutional right of the mother to relocate in the opinion. Should the court have considered this issue before making a ruling? Moreover, since the child was not harmed and the father's visitation schedule was not altered, is it logical to conclude that the state of Nebraska has a policy of keeping its children within its borders? *See, e.g., Vanderzee v. Vanderzee*, 380 N.W.2d 310, 311 (Neb. 1986) ("Generally, the best policy in divorce cases is to keep minor children within the jurisdiction. . . ."). Would a constitutional analysis of the custodial parent's right to travel have altered the outcome?

C. How would courts in California, Pennsylvania, and Vermont most likely have approached this case?

D. It has been suggested that placing restrictions on relocation chills the custodial parent's constitutional right to travel. In response to this argument, one court commented on a mother's relocation petition stating that as a mother she "does not accept the notion that she placed a chill on her right to travel when she bore and started to raise two children. She does not want this court to restrict her legal right to travel. She does not realize that her right to travel, though not legally, was from a practical point of view restricted when she chose to play the role of mother years ago." Anne L. Spitzer, *Moving and Storage of Postdivorce Children: Relocation, the Constitution and the Courts*, Ariz. St. L.J. 1, 25 n.195 (1985) (quoting *Bezou v. Bezou*, No. 81-11606 (C.D.C. Orleans June 3, 1983)). Do you agree with the trial judge's perspective on motherhood and a mother's right to travel?

7.20 MODEL RELOCATION STANDARD: AMERICAN LAW INSTITUTE (ALI)

The American Law Institute's *Principles of the Law of Family Dissolution* ("ALI *Principles*") recognizes a number of "legitimate" purposes for relocation. *See generally* Janet Leach Richards, *Resolving Relocation Issues Pursuant to the ALI Family Dissolution Principles: Are Children Better Protected?*, 2001 BYU L. Rev. 1105, 1112-1117. The *Principles* reflects a concern for balancing a child's relationship with both custodial and noncustodial parents and generally favor relocation.

The ALI *Principles* §2.17 states, in relevant part:

1. The relocation of a parent constitutes a substantial change in circumstances under 2.15(1) only when the relocation significantly impairs either parent's ability to exercise responsibilities the parent has been exercising or attempting to exercise under the parenting plan. When changed circumstances are shown, the court should try to revise the parenting plan to accommodate the relocation without changing the proportion of custodial responsibilities each parent is exercising. If that is impractical, the court

should modify the parenting plan in accordance with the child's best interests and in accordance with the following principles:

a. The court should allow a parent who has been exercising the clear majority of custodial responsibility to relocate with the child if the parent shows that the relocation is for a valid purpose, in good faith, and to a location that is reasonable in light of the purpose.

i. The court should recognize any of the following purposes for a relocation as valid: (1) to be close to significant family or other sources of support; (2) to address significant health problems; (3) to protect the safety of the child or another member of the child's household from a significant risk of harm; (4) to pursue a significant employment or educational opportunity; (5) to be with one's spouse or domestic partner who lives or has a significant opportunity in the new location; (6) to significantly improve the family's quality of life. The relocating parent has the burden of proving the validity of any other purpose.

ii. The court should find that a move for a valid purpose is reasonable unless its purpose is shown to be substantially achievable without moving, or by moving to a location that is substantially less disruptive of the other parent's relationship to the child.

b. If the parent does not establish that the purpose for the relocation is valid, in good faith, and to a location that is reasonable in light of the purpose, the court should order modifications most consistent with the child's best interests. The court should reallocate primary custodial responsibility, effective if the relocation occurs unless the relocating parent demonstrates that the child's best interests would be served by relocating with the parent.

c. If neither parent has been exercising a clear majority of custodial responsibility, the court should modify the plan in accordance with the child's best interests, taking into account all relevant factors including the effects of the relocation on the child.

d. The court should deny the request of custodial responsibility to enable the parent to relocate with the child if the parent has been exercising substantially less custodial responsibility for the child than the other parent, unless the reallocation is necessary to prevent harm to the child.

e. The court should minimize the impairment to a parent-child relationship caused by a parent's relocation through alternative arrangements for the exercise of custodial responsibility appropriate to the parent's resources.

Would application of the ALI custody modification standard have changed the outcome of the Nebraska Court of Appeals decision in the *Curtis v. Curtis* case discussed above?

7.21 MODEL RELOCATION STANDARD: UNIFORM MARRIAGE AND DIVORCE ACT

The Uniform Marriage and Divorce Act addressed original custody determinations, §402, visitation, §407, and custody modification, §409. However, the drafters did not specifically address relocation. A relocation study group was in the process of developing standards in 2008, and was expected to recommend the formulation of uniform legislation. *See Unif. Relocation of Children Act*

(Natl. Conference of Commrs. on Unif. State Laws, Draft 2008). However, in 2009, the commission decided to discontinue drafting a Uniform Relocation Act. Sally Adams, *Avoiding Round Two: The Inadequacy of Current Relocation Laws and a Proposed Solution,* 43 Fam. L.Q. 181, n.6 (Spring 2009).

REFLECTIVE QUESTIONS	What possible reason might have caused the commissioners to discontinue drafting a Uniform Relocation Act?

7.22 MODEL RELOCATION STANDARD: AMERICAN ACADEMY OF MATRIMONIAL LAWYERS

The American Academy of Matrimonial Lawyers proposed a Model Relocation Act (AAML) in 1998. It was to serve as a template for states to use when enacting their own relocation statutes. *See Harrison v. Morgan,* 191 P.3d 617 (Okla. App. 2008); Am. Acad. of Matrimonial Lawyers, *Proposed Model Relocation Act,* 15 J. Am. Acad. Matrimonial Law. 1 (1998). The act lists several factors that the trial court should consider before allowing the relocation of a child.

Under the AAML, when a move is contemplated, a relocating parent must notify the nonrelocating parent within 60 days of a proposed change of address, and the notice must include the reasons for the move and a proposed revised visitation. Proposed Model Relocation Act §203(b)(5)-(6). If there is no objection to the relocation or a new visitation plan within 30 days, the relocation goes forward. *Id.* §301.

Should the nonrelocating parent object, a hearing is conducted where the court will consider the following eight factors: (1) the nature, quality, extent of involvement, and duration of the child's relationship with the parents, other adults, and siblings; (2) the age, developmental stage, and needs of the child and the likely impact the relocation would have on the child's physical, educational, and emotional development; (3) the feasibility of preserving the relationship between the nonrelocating parent and the child through suitable visitation arrangements; (4) the child's preference, taking into consideration the age and maturity of the child; (5) whether there is an established pattern of conduct by the relocating parent either to promote or thwart the relationship of the child and the nonrelocating parent; (6) whether the relocation of the child will enhance the general quality of life for both the relocating parent and the child; (7) the reasons of each person for seeking or opposing the relocation; and (8) any other factor affecting the best interests of the child. §405.

The proposal also contains three options a legislature should consider when deciding where to assign the burden of proof. The first option places the burden on the relocating parent to show that the proposed relocation is made in good faith and in the best interests of the child. *Id.* §407. The second option places the burden on the nonrelocating parent to show that the proposed relocation is not made in good faith or is not in the best interests of the child. The final option contains a burden-shifting approach where the relocating parent must initially show that the proposed relocation is made in good faith. Once that is done, the burden shifts to the nonrelocating parent to show that the proposed relocation is not in the best interests of the child.

REFLECTIVE QUESTIONS	Which of the three burden of proof options contained in the AAML Model Act do you favor?

7.23 RELOCATION STANDARD: JOINT LEGAL AND PHYSICAL CUSTODY

Background to *Mason v. Coleman*

Mason v. Coleman involves parties who divorced in Massachusetts and shared joint legal and physical custody of their two minor children. In June of 2002, the ex-husband and his current wife moved from Massachusetts to New Hampshire, which placed him approximately 17 miles from where his children were attending school in Massachusetts. A month later, the ex-husband filed a motion in Massachusetts asking for modification of the custody arrangement. He requested, among other things, that his ex-wife be restrained from moving to New Hampshire from Massachusetts, that the children continue to be enrolled in school in Massachusetts, and that he receive sole physical custody of the two children.

In her answer to her ex-husband's motion, the ex-wife asked for permission to move with the children to New Hampshire. She also asked that the original custody order be modified so that she received sole physical custody of the children. The matter was tried and the trial judge rejected the ex-wife's relocation request to move with the children to New Hampshire and continued the shared custody arrangement. She appealed.

MASON
v.
COLEMAN

Supreme Judicial Court of Massachusetts
850 N.E.2d 513 (Mass. 2006)

COWIN, J. . . . Under the [original divorce] agreement, the parents divided physical custody of the children approximately equally. The parties agreed to move within twenty-five miles of Chelmsford, and agreed that, in light of uncertainty as to where each would locate in Massachusetts, the children would attend school in the district of the mother's residence.

Some years passed, and each parent remarried. The mother and father obtained modification of the divorce decree by the Probate and Family Court as required by their changing needs. The father eventually relocated to Nashua, New Hampshire, approximately seventeen miles from Chelmsford [Massachusetts]. The mother objected privately but had little advance notice of the move and did not file suit to prevent it.

Weeks after the father gave notice of his plan to move to Nashua, the mother gave notice of her intent to relocate with the stepfather to Bristol, New Hampshire. The mother's parents live in Bristol; she planned to move into her parents' home with her family and eventually into her own home nearby. The stepfather's children from a previous marriage (of whom the stepfather had joint custody) and his former wife were also to move to Bristol, and the stepfather promised them that he would follow.

In 2002, testing revealed that the older child, then ten years old, had attention deficit disorder/attention hyperactivity disorder and related learning problems. Although kind and athletic, he lacked appropriate social skills and had trouble making friends. As a result of medication, the hard work of both parents, and a dedicated school staff, the child was able to succeed in fifth grade.

The Chelmsford [Massachusetts] school district has initiated a student accommodation plan for the child, and his middle school has established an "active and effective support system for him." The judge found that the child is making "great strides" both socially and educationally in his middle school. The judge further found that, based on the State's standardized achievement tests, the Chelmsford school system is one of the better school systems in the Commonwealth, and that the Bristol, New Hampshire, middle school ranks below the State average on New Hampshire's standardized achievement test. The judge concluded that, in light of the disruptions to his developmental process that would be occasioned by the challenges of a new home, school, and sibling, and reduction in the time spent with the father, the move to New Hampshire would be "detrimental" to the older child's socialization and education.

In addition to the developmental issues, the judge found that the mother's children claimed one of them was inappropriately touched by the son of the mother's new husband. The allegation caused considerable acrimony between the mother and father. This tension left the child, who subsequently recanted and then reasserted his claim of abuse, feeling "scared about his role in the family" and "emotionally harmed" by his parents' ongoing conflict.

When the mother informed the father of her intention to move to New Hampshire, the father refused to consent to removal of the children from the Commonwealth and filed a complaint for modification of the divorce decree in the Probate and Family Court seeking, among other things, sole physical custody and a temporary order enjoining the mother from removing the children from the Commonwealth. The mother counterclaimed for modification granting her sole physical custody and for a temporary order permitting the planned relocation to Bristol, New Hampshire.

A probate judge allowed the father's temporary order enjoining removal and other judges issued orders not material here. After some time, and a four-day trial, a different judge weighed the best interests of the children and determined that removal to New Hampshire in the manner requested by the mother was not in the best interests of the children and thus would not be authorized by the court. The judge found that Chelmsford schools were preferable to those of Bristol, particularly for the child with special needs; that uprooting the children would be detrimental to their interests; that the move would cause a reduction of the father's parenting time that would not be in the children's interests; that misconduct allegations against a stepsibling weighed against increased time in the mother's household; and that there was insufficient evidence of financial imperative to justify the mother's move to Bristol. The judge determined that the father's move to Nashua did not provide ground for the relief requested by the mother, and the judge did not award sole physical custody to either party, deciding instead to order continued shared legal and physical custody. The mother appealed. . . .

. . . True joint custody is divisible into two components: shared legal custody and shared physical custody. . . . Shared legal custody carries "mutual responsibility and involvement by both parents in major decisions regarding the child's welfare including matters of education, medical care and emotional, moral and religious development." This contrasts to sole legal custody, which gives to only one parent these rights and responsibilities. Shared physical custody contemplates that "a child shall have periods of residing with and being under the supervision of each parent . . . assur[ing] . . . frequent and continued contact with both parents." This contrasts to sole physical custody which generally reflects that the children reside with only one parent "subject to reasonable visitation by the other parent." *Id.*

Although the General Laws state that there is no presumption "either in favor or against shared . . . custody at the time of trial on the merits," such an arrangement is generally appropriate only if the parties demonstrate an ability and desire to cooperate amicably and communicate with one another to raise the children.

> Joint custody is synonymous with joint decision making and a common desire to promote the children's best interests. It is understandable, therefore, that joint custody is encouraged primarily as a voluntary alternative for relatively stable, amicable parents behaving in mature civilized fashion. . . . [I]n order to be effective joint custody requires . . . a willingness and ability to work together to reach results on major decisions in a manner similar to the way married couples make decisions.

Shared physical custody in particular carries with it substantial obligation for cooperation between the parents. Such an arrangement, by its nature, involves shared commitment to coordinate extensively a variety of the details of everyday life. Shared physical custody necessitates ongoing joint scheduling and provision for supervision and transportation of children between homes, schools, and youth activities. It is thus incumbent on a parent who has been awarded joint physical custody to recognize that the viability of the endeavor is dependent on his or her ability and willingness to subordinate personal preferences to make the relationship work. While a joint physical custody agreement remains in effect, each parent necessarily surrenders a degree of prerogative in certain life decisions, e.g., choice of habitation, that may affect the feasibility of shared physical custody. . . .

Where physical custody is shared, the "best interest" calculus pertaining to removal is appreciably different from those situations that involve sole physical custody. Where physical custody is shared, a judge's willingness to elevate one parent's interest in relocating freely with the children is often diminished. No longer is the fortune of simply one custodial parent so tightly interwoven with that of the child; both parents have equal rights and responsibilities with respect to the children. The importance to the children of one parent's advantage in relocating outside the Commonwealth is greatly reduced. ALI *Principles of the Law of Family Dissolution, supra* at §2.17(1), (4)(c) . . . recently adopted by the ALI, supports the view that where "neither parent has been exercising a clear majority of custodial responsibility," the effect of the relocation on the child is a "relevant factor" in determining the child's best interests.

Where physical custody is shared and neither parent has a clear majority of custodial responsibility, the child's interests will typically "favor protection of the child's relationships with both parents because both are, in a real sense, primary to the child's development." Distant relocation often impedes "frequent and continued contact" with the remaining joint custodian.

Joint physical custody need not necessarily be impeded by relocation outside the Commonwealth. In some cases, distance between the parents may not greatly increase as a result of removal. In addition, there are significant differences in the individual tolerances of the custodians and the children. It is a question for a judge, taking into account all of the facts, whether an increase in travel time between households and schools brought about by removal, and other burdens of distance, will significantly impair either parent's ability to exercise existing responsibilities, and ultimately whether removal is in a child's best interests.

. . . The order [here] is based on the judge's findings that the children's best interests would be negatively affected by this move. She made detailed written findings that their current schools were superior, that uprooting the children would be difficult for them, that the move would impair the father's parenting to the detriment of their interests, that potential misconduct by other siblings in the mother's household weighed against increased physical custody by the mother, and that any financial or other advantage of the move to the mother was unclear. From this the judge determined that it was not in the children's best interests to be removed to Bristol, New Hampshire.

The mother disagrees with the judge's weighing of the evidence. . . . The mother advances several arguments with regard to the judge's findings of fact, none of which is persuasive. The judge was not required to adopt the opinions of a guardian *ad litem*, therapist, psychologist, school official, and other evaluator, each of which were different from those of the judge in certain particulars. . . . Her findings regarding the situation are warranted by the evidence and, based on them, her conclusion that removal is not in the children's best interests is not an abuse of discretion.

The mother contends in passing, without citation to directly relevant judicial authority, that the judge's refusal to authorize removal of the children from the Commonwealth offended her right to freedom of movement pursuant to the Fifth and Fourteenth Amendments to the United States Constitution. To the contrary, G.L. c. 208, §30, does not restrict the mother's right of travel, only her right to remove children within the law's scope. The judge here determined that removal would clearly not serve the best interests of the children. Thus, we are satisfied that the mother's travel was not unconstitutionally impeded by the application of G.L. c. 208, §30. . . . For the foregoing reasons, the judgment of the Probate and Family Court is affirmed.

DISCUSSION QUESTIONS FOR *MASON v. COLEMAN*

A. Shared physical custody carries with it substantial obligation for cooperation between the parents. After the trial and appeal in this matter, is it reasonable to assume there will no longer be substantial cooperation between the parents? If not, isn't a better solution to the dispute to award sole physical custody to one of the parents?

B. What factor seems to be the most persuasive to the trial judge? Was it, for example, the comparative quality of the present and proposed school district? Or, were there other "more persuasive" considerations?

C. The guardian *ad litem* apparently recommended that the mother be permitted to relocate to Bristol, New Hampshire, that the father's custody be concentrated on nonschool days, and that the mother should occasionally provide round-trip transportation to a midway point between the residences. Others who testified at the trial, including a therapist, psychologist, and school official, appeared to support the mother's relocation request. On what basis might the court have rejected those opinions?

D. The mother contends that the court's refusal to authorize removal of the children from the Commonwealth offended her right to freedom of movement pursuant to the Fifth and Fourteenth Amendments to the United States Constitution. The court responded that the ruling did not restrict her right of travel, only her right to remove children within the law's scope. Do you agree with the mother or the court? Doesn't the court's ruling "chill" the mother's constitutional right to travel?

E. In Massachusetts, when parents have joint legal custody, but the mother, for example, has physical custody, the "real advantage" test applies. This test allows a parent who has been exercising the clear majority of custodial responsibility to relocate with the child if that parent shows that the relocation is for a valid purpose, in good faith, and to a location that is reasonable in light of the purpose. Under the "real advantage" test, once it is found that there is a genuine, recognizable advantage to the custodial parent from the move, the inquiry then turns to whether the move is consistent with the children's best interests. The advantages to the custodial parent do not disappear, but instead remain a significant factor in the equation. *Abbott v. Virusso*, 862 N.E.2d 52 (Mass. App. 2007). Assume a court awarded joint legal and physical custody of a child to a couple, but as a practical matter the facts demonstrate that the mother was providing for the child 60 percent of the time. Under these circumstances, if the mother seeks to relocate to another jurisdiction, does the "real advantage" test apply? What if the child lived 70 percent of the time with the mother?

F. Professor Theresa Glennon suggests that relocation was favored in the 1990s and 2000s, but the current trend is moving away from a presumptive right to relocate toward requiring the custodial parent to prove the move is in the child's best interests. Theresa Glennon, *Divided Parents, Shared Children — Conflicting Approaches to Relocation Disputes in the USA*, 4 Utrecht L. Rev. 55, 57 (2008). What factors may account for the trend?

G. Professor Glennon also suggests that when relocation is sought for economic reasons and is denied because of the other parent's objections, that the noncustodial parent should be obligated to provide compensation. Theresa Glennon, *Still Partners? Examining the Consequences of Post-Dissolution Parenting*, 41 Fam. L.Q. 105, 139 (2007) ("I propose that courts have explicit authority to consider an economic remedy when they deny relocation. This remedy should be based on an income-sharing model that would recognize that at least some of the financial burden should be shared"). Would such a result protect the interests of the custodial parent and limit the economic harm the custodial parent suffers and the gender discrimination implicit in it? Should this suggestion be implemented as legislation? *See also* Cynthia Starnes, *Mothers as Suckers: Pity, Partnership, and Divorce Discourse*, 90 Iowa L. Rev. 1513, 1518, n.4 (2005) (proposing a "parenting-partnership" model that requires income sharing during "the unfinished parental work of raising minor children").

PART 3: THE UNIFORM CHILD CUSTODY JURISDICTION ENFORCEMENT ACT (UCCJEA) AND PARENTAL KIDNAPPING PREVENTION ACT (PKPA)

7.24 HISTORY

In part 3 of this chapter, the focus is on how courts, Congress, and state legislatures have struggled to arrive at a solution to determine which of two or more states has jurisdiction to modify an existing child custody decision.

Common law. Under the common law, jurisdiction to determine an interstate child custody dispute was based on a child's domicile. This meant, in almost all cases, the appropriate jurisdiction to decide the matter was the child's father's domicile. The reason for this rested on the common law principle that a child took the father's domicile. *See Wilcox v. Wilcox*, 862 S.W.2d 533, 538 (Tenn. App. 1993).

The inflexibility of the domicile rule made it unworkable. The rule, if strictly applied, could leave a court without authority to act in the best interest of a child who was before it in a jurisdiction other than where the father was domiciled. In some situations, it was apparent that the child was in need of the court's immediate protection. However, the domicile rule tied the hands of the court to do anything.

In response to the perceived need to protect children, jurisdictions began rejecting the domicile rule and applying a more flexible approach, which was based on physical presence of a child or children within the jurisdiction of a court. The premise of this theory was that an inquiry into a child's welfare could best be carried on in the location where the child was physically present.

The presence theory was criticized as placing a premium on removing a child from the domiciliary state and encouraging forum shopping.

REFLECTIVE QUESTIONS	What is the basis for criticizing the "domicile" and "presence" theories when applied to interstate custody disputes?

7.25 THE SUPREME COURT MUDDIES THE WATERS

As interstate competition in conflicting child custody awards increased throughout the nation, some hoped that the United States Supreme Court would remedy the situation by holding that the "first state to act" (i.e., the state that first entered a custody order) was entitled to enforcement of that custody order under the Full Faith and Credit Clause. The Supreme Court eventually had the opportunity to make such a ruling in *May v. Anderson*, 345 U.S. 528 (1953). However, the Court rejected the "first state to act" theory. Rather, a plurality of the Court held that a custody order is not entitled to full faith and credit if the rendering state lacked personal jurisdiction over one of the parties.

In a concurring opinion in *May v. Anderson*, Justice Frankfurter suggested that even if full faith and credit is not constitutionally required in an interstate custody dispute, comity should be extended to foreign child custody decrees to avoid child snatching, forum shopping, and the like. While several state courts acted on Justice Frankfurter's suggestion, "comity in child custody cases turned out to be more honored in the breach than in the application, as local courts found ways to avoid enforcement of existing out-of-state orders on one legal pretext or another." *Wilcox v. Wilcox*, 862 S.W.2d 533, 538 (Tenn. App. 1993).

Note that the personal jurisdiction perspective of the Court in *May* was ignored by the National Conference of Commissioners on Uniform State Laws

(NCCUSL) when the UCCJEA and its predecessor, the UCCJA, were drafted. Congress also ignored *May* when enacting the PKPA. *See* Homer Clark, *Domestic Relations* 792, n.1 (2d ed. 1985).

REFLECTIVE QUESTIONS	Describe the conflict in custody theories found in *May v. Anderson.*

7.26 THE FIRST MODEL ACT: UCCJA

The first significant effort to encourage the development of uniform interstate custody standards among states came in 1968 when NCCUSL promulgated a model provision that it called the Uniform Child Custody Jurisdiction Act. The avowed purpose of the model act was to eliminate interstate competition over custody matters, child snatching, and unauthorized holdovers following authorized visitation periods. The model act applied to initial custody decisions and subsequent modification efforts.

REFLECTIVE QUESTIONS	What was the purpose of the UCCJA?

7.27 CONGRESS STEPS IN, FOLLOWED BY THE UCCJEA

After a decade, it became clear that the efforts of the Commissioners on Uniform State Laws to persuade states to uniformly adopt the UCCJA had failed. Congress then stepped in to try to resolve the conflict among the states. In 1980 Congress drafted the Parental Kidnapping Prevention Act (PKPA). 28 U.S.C. §1738A. PKPA preempts state law and requires that full faith and credit be given to foreign custody decrees, to the extent that the other state's "child custody determination [was] made consistently with the provision of [the PKPA]." 28 U.S.C. §1738A(a). PKPA controls in any case where there is a conflict between federal and state law. *Guardianship of Gabriel W.*, 666 A.2d 505 (Me. 1995).

The PKPA gives exclusive jurisdiction to the child's home state, and "[h]ome state" is defined as the state in which the child lived with his parent or parents for "at least six consecutive months." 28 U.S.C. §1738A(b)(4); *see Atkins v. Atkins*, 823 S.W.2d 816 (1992).

In addition to prioritizing home state jurisdiction, the PKPA mandates exclusive continuing jurisdiction in the state initially issuing the decree if that state remains the residence of the children or any contestant and provided that state has not declined to exercise jurisdiction. 28 U.S.C. §1738A(f).

UCCJEA. In 1997 the Commissioners on Uniform State Laws promulgated the Uniform Child Custody Jurisdiction and Enforcement Act (UCCJEA). 9 Unif. L. Ann. (Part 1B) 649 (1999). The goal of the UCCJEA was to reconcile the differences between the UCCJA and the PKPA.

The UCCJEA followed the contours of the PKPA and gave priority to home state jurisdiction. It also restricted the use of emergency jurisdiction to temporary orders and restricted the exercise of custody modification to a forum that possessed continuing jurisdiction over the last custody judgment or order. The UCCJEA clarified the meaning of child custody determination to encompass all custody and visitation decrees (temporary, permanent, initial, and modification) and expanded the definition of child custody proceedings to include those related to divorce, separation, abuse and neglect, dependency, guardianship, paternity, termination of parental rights, and protection from domestic violence. Some version of the UCCJEA has been adopted in all states.

REFLECTIVE QUESTIONS	What is the significance of the following statement in the context of interstate custody disputes? "PKPA is preemptive, and controls in any case where there is a conflict between federal and state law."

7.28 THE PREEMPTION DOCTRINE IN THE CONTEXT OF PKPA

The federal preemption doctrine is an important consideration when a state version of the UCCJEA clashes with a provision of the PKPA. As a general rule, because federal law is the supreme law of the land under the Supremacy Clause of the United States Constitution, Article VI, Clause 2, state laws that interfere with or are contrary to federal law are invalidated under the preemption doctrine. When such a conflict occurs, the reviewing court is limited by the Supremacy Clause to a determination of whether Congress has positively required by direct enactment that state law be preempted. *Hisquierdo v. Hisquierdo*, 439 U.S. 572, 581 (1979). Before a state law governing domestic relations will be overridden, the Court has said that it must do major damage to clear and substantial federal interests. *United States v. Yazell*, 382 U.S. 341 (1966). "The relative importance to the State of its own law is not material when there is a conflict with a valid federal law, for the Framers of our Constitution provided that the federal law must prevail." *Free v. Bland*, 369 U.S. 663, 666 (1962).

REFLECTIVE QUESTIONS	Illustrate how the preemption doctrine can be applied with a hypothetical.

Background to *Scott v. Somers*

In *Scott v. Somers*, the question is whether the PKPA prevents Connecticut courts from reviewing and modifying a custody decision issued by the State of Florida.

SCOTT
v.
SOMERS

Court of Appeals of Connecticut
903 A.2d 663 (2006)

BISHOP, J. Congress enacted the Parental Kidnapping Prevention Act (PKPA), 28 U.S.C. §1738A, to avoid jurisdictional competition and conflict in matters of child custody and visitation and to promote cooperation between state courts. See Pub. L. No. 96-611, 94 Stat. 3569, §7(c). This case involves the authority of a Connecticut court to modify a child custody determination rendered by a court of another state. The defendant, Jacklyn A. Somers, appeals from the judgment of the trial court modifying a Florida order and awarding custody of the minor child to the plaintiff, Matthew A. Scott. . . .

The child of the unmarried parties was born in New Haven on July 19, 1999. They all resided in Connecticut until February or March, 2001, when they moved to Melbourne, Florida. On November 19, 2002, in response to a motion for temporary relief filed by Somers, a Florida court found Florida to be the child's home state and granted Somers temporary primary custody of the child subject to the visitation rights of Scott.

On August 31, 2004, Scott filed an action for custody of the child in New Haven Superior Court. In his application for custody, Scott represented that the child had resided with him in Connecticut since May, 2003, that both he and the child have a significant connection to Connecticut and that there is substantial evidence in Connecticut concerning the child's present or future care, protection, training and personal relationships. Scott also indicated that Somers previously had been awarded temporary custody of the child by a Florida court.

On October 14, 2004, citing the Uniform Child Custody Jurisdiction and Enforcement Act (UCCJEA), the Connecticut court issued an order awarding temporary custody of the child to Scott "until further order of the court regarding jurisdiction." On October 24, 2004, the court held a telephone conference with the Florida court to discuss jurisdiction of the proceedings. Counsel for all of the parties participated in this conference. The courts recognized that there was a factual dispute as to the circumstances of the child's presence in Connecticut and did not agree which state had jurisdiction.

The Florida court had before it a very different set of facts. Somers represented to the Florida court the following: In November, 2003, she took the child to Tennessee to visit the child's grandmother; Scott took the child from the grandmother, and took her to Connecticut and refused to return her to Florida; Somers went to Connecticut in 2004 to retrieve the child and stayed there until June when Scott promised that he would return the child to Florida by July 19, 2004, the child's fifth birthday; Scott did not return the child to Florida by July 19; and, despite her efforts, she was denied contact with the child from June, 2004, until approximately three weeks prior to the October 24, 2004, telephone conference.

In the midst of this jurisdictional stalemate, on November 12, 2004, the Connecticut court issued an order retaining jurisdiction over this case and the minor child and, on November 29 and 30, 2004, held a final hearing on Scott's application for custody. The court found that the child resided in Connecticut with Scott, that returning her to Somers' care would place her at risk of neglect or abuse and that it was in the child's best interest to modify Florida's custody determination. Accordingly, the court exercised jurisdiction in accordance with . . . the UCCJEA, and awarded permanent sole legal and physical custody of the child to Scott, subject to visitation by Somers. The court also retained jurisdiction, pursuant to the UCCJEA, over the child and all orders affecting custody and parental access. This appeal followed.

. . . The jurisdictional provisions of the PKPA, codified at 28 U.S.C. §1738A, essentially impose on states a federal duty, under enumerated standards derived from the UCCJA, to give full faith and credit to the custody decrees of other states and amounts to a federal adoption of key provisions of the UCCJA for all states. . . . To the extent that the PKPA and the UCCJA conflict, the Supremacy Clause of the United States constitution mandates that the PKPA preempts the state's enactment of the UCCJA. . . . Arguably, Connecticut's version of the UCCJEA would provide Connecticut with jurisdiction to modify Florida's custody order. As will be explained in more detail, however, Connecticut does not have jurisdiction because the PKPA requires the Connecticut court to examine Florida law in making its jurisdictional assessment. Florida, however, has no statutory provision parallel to §46b-115m(b) of the Connecticut UCCJEA. Rather, Florida law provides that Florida, as the originating state and the continuing residence of Somers, has exclusive, continuing jurisdiction over this matter. In this circumstance, the PKPA requires that the Connecticut court defer to the Florida court's continuing jurisdiction.

The governing principle of the PKPA requires that "authorities of every State shall enforce according to its terms, and shall not modify except as provided in subsection (f), (g), and (h) of this section, any custody determination or visitation determination made consistently with the provisions of this section by a court of another State." 28 U.S.C. §1738A(a). Section 1738A(d) then provides the crucial presumption of continuing jurisdiction and expresses its clear intent to reserve the modification of child custody determinations to the state of initial rendition.

Section 1738A(f), the exception to the prohibition on modification contained in subsection (a), "restates the same presumption [of continuing jurisdiction], but in terms of an interdiction of assertions of jurisdiction by a second state when the first state's jurisdiction continues." It provides:

> A court of a State may modify a determination of the custody of the same child made by a court of another State, if (1) it has jurisdiction to make such a child custody determination;

and (2) the court of the other State no longer has jurisdiction, or it has declined to exercise such jurisdiction to modify such determination. 28 U.S.C. §1738A(f).

The PKPA thus preserves to the state that initially enters a child custody determination that is valid under its own law and is consistent with the PKPA the sole prerogative to modify that determination, as long as any modification would also be valid under its own law and either the child or a contestant continues to live in the state. Thus, "the PKPA anchor[s] exclusive modification jurisdiction in the original home state as long as the child or one of the contestants remains in that state." . . .

"The effect of §§1738A(d) and 1738A(f) is to limit custody jurisdiction to the first state to properly enter a custody order, so long as two sets of requirements are met. First, the PKPA defines a federal standard for continuing exclusive custody jurisdiction: the first state must have had proper initial custody jurisdiction when it entered its first order (according to criteria in the [PKPA]) and it must remain 'the residence of the child or any contestant' when it later modifies the order. [T]he [PKPA] incorporates a state law inquiry: in order to retain exclusive responsibility for modifying its prior order the first state must still have custody jurisdiction as a matter of its own custody law." . . . Even if the federal and state criteria for continuing jurisdiction are met, the court in the state that first had jurisdiction can, if it chooses, voluntarily relinquish jurisdiction in favor of a court better situated to assess the child's needs. Accordingly, the PKPA explicitly limits the circumstances under which a state that might otherwise have jurisdiction over a child custody dispute is required to defer to the state that originally issued the custody order. With these principles in mind, we turn to the case at hand.

Here, it is undisputed that Florida initially exercised jurisdiction in this case in conformity with the PKPA. It is also undisputed that Somers continues to reside in Florida. Thus, the only remaining question is whether Florida continues to have jurisdiction under its law. Florida has enacted a version of the UCCJEA that provides that Florida has exclusive, continuing jurisdiction over its child custody determinations until "(a) [a] court of this state determines that the child, the child's parents, and any person acting as a parent do not have a significant connection with this state and that substantial evidence is no longer available in this state concerning the child's care, protection, training, and personal relationships; or (b) [a] court of this state or a court of another state determines that the child, the child's parent, and any person acting as a parent do not presently reside in this state." Fla. Stat. Ann. §61.515(1) (West 2005). Because Somers continues to reside in Florida, the Florida court has exclusive, continuing jurisdiction over its custody determination, under Florida law, until a Florida court determines that significant connections do not exist in Florida. Thus, a party seeking to modify Florida's custody determination must obtain an order from Florida stating that it no longer has jurisdiction. This was not done in the present case and, therefore, Connecticut did not have jurisdiction to modify Florida's order.

There is also nothing in the record to indicate that Florida relinquished its jurisdiction. To the contrary, following the October 24, 2004, telephone conference, the Florida court determined that it had jurisdiction and awarded primary residential custody of the child to Somers. Thus, notwithstanding the strictures of the PKPA, we are faced with two conflicting custody orders resulting from a jurisdictional quagmire. Relying on the action taken by the court of his or her respective state of residence, neither party participated in the proceedings of the other state. Somers did not participate in the Connecticut proceedings, and Scott did not participate in the Florida proceedings. Therefore, regrettably, because each order is based only on the version of events presented by the party present in each state, neither order is fully informed as contemplated by the PKPA.

The judgment is reversed and the case is remanded with direction to dismiss this matter for lack of jurisdiction.

DISCUSSION QUESTIONS   **FOR *SCOTT v. SOMERS***

A. The Connecticut father argued that Connecticut should exercise jurisdiction because of the state's longstanding public policy to protect children who reside there and are at risk for abuse and neglect. He asserted that if the child was returned to Florida, she was at risk of neglect and/or abuse. He claimed that Connecticut's policy to protect children created an exception to the application of interstate comity as it relates to a child custody modification action. He also argued that the child in this dispute had resided in Connecticut for more than 13 months at the time of the contested proceeding. He concluded that the best interests of the child were to allow the Connecticut court to proceed and award him sole legal and physical custody. Weigh the father's arguments. How valid are they? Is strict application of the preemption doctrine in this particular case warranted where abuse and dependency claims are made? Were the best interests of the child really protected by the Connecticut ruling?

B. Multiple cases from other jurisdictions have uniformly held that the PKPA preempts state judgments allegedly modifying foreign custody decrees. *See Richardson v. Richardson*, 644 A.2d 472, 475 (Me. 1994) (subsection (f) of 28 U.S.C. §1738A is sole basis for modification of decree of another state); *Walsh v. Walsh*, 458 N.Y.S.2d 835, 840 (N.Y. Sup. 1983) (Texas modification of New York decree violated the PKPA). Given the PKPA, was it necessary for the Uniform Commissioners on State Laws to draft the UCCJEA and urge its adoption by the states?

7.29 CONTINUING JURISDICTION: INITIAL CUSTODY AWARD

Once an initial child custody determination is made, exclusive, continuing jurisdiction generally remains with the court that issued the order or decree. *Atchison v.*

Atchison, 664 N.W.2d 249 (Mich. App. 2003). Should a foreign court be asked to modify an order issued by the decreeing court, the foreign court usually conducts a three-step process. First, it determines whether the decreeing court (the court making the initial custody determination) has lost its jurisdiction. Second, if the decreeing court has lost exclusive continuing jurisdiction, the foreign court must decide whether it has jurisdiction to make a custody determination under the circumstances of the case. *See Staats v. McKinnon*, 206 S.W.3d 532, 548 (Tenn. App. 2006). Finally, if the foreign court determines that it has subject matter jurisdiction under the first two steps of the jurisdictional analysis, it then determines whether it may or must decline to exercise its jurisdiction on one of the three grounds specified in the UCCJEA. *Ibid.*

> **REFLECTIVE QUESTIONS**   What is the three-step process briefly outlined above?

7.30 HOME STATE UNDER THE UCCJEA

The UCCJEA gives home state jurisdiction priority in initial child custody proceedings. A court has home state jurisdiction if it was the home state on the day the custody action was filed or at any time during the six months preceding the filing. *See Rosen v. Celebrezze*, 883 N.E.2d 420, 427-428 (Ohio 2008) (explaining that despite some confusing language in the definitional section, this consecutive six-month period can be either immediately preceding the filing or at any time during the preceding six months). Where a child with home state status in one state is moved for any reason to a second state, the child will not lose home state status in the first state or gain it in the second for another six months. *Stephens v. Fourth Judicial Dist. Court*, 128 P.3d 1026, 1029 (Mont. 2006); UCCJEA §201(a)(1), Comment, §201.

Significant connection. A state has "significant connection" jurisdiction where no other state has home state or extended home state jurisdiction, or "a court of the home state of the child has declined to exercise jurisdiction on the ground that this State is the more appropriate forum," and "the child and the child's parents, or the child and at least one parent or person acting as a parent, have a significant connection with this State concerning the child's care, protection, training, and personal relationships." UCCJEA §201(a)(2).

When a child has no home state or when a home state declines jurisdiction, another state court may exercise jurisdiction if the child has sufficient ties to the state and substantial evidence concerning the child is available in the state. UCCJEA §206(a). A child need not be physically present in a state for the state to exercise significant connection jurisdiction. More than one state may have jurisdiction on this basis, but only one state may exercise jurisdiction.

UCCJEA §206(b). The UCCJEA resolves the conflict in favor of the first-filed proceeding.

REFLECTIVE QUESTIONS	Under what circumstances may a state exercise "significant connection" jurisdiction?

7.31 STATUS JURISDICTION

A state court can compel a person to appear and defend a civil suit only if the defendant has minimum contacts with the state such that the assertion of jurisdiction would be fair and reasonable. However, in divorce and child custody actions, state courts often assert jurisdiction over a defending spouse who lacks such contacts by applying the status exception. Advocates of the status exception for child custody rely on *Shaffer v. Heitner*'s footnote 30 as justification for their view. *Shaffer v. Heitner*, 433 U.S. 186, 208 n.30 (1977) ("We do not suggest that jurisdictional doctrines other that those discussed in text, such as the particularized rules governing adjudications of status, are inconsistent with the standard of fairness."); Rhonda Wasserman, *Parents, Partners, and Personal Jurisdiction*, 1995 U. Ill. L. Rev. 813. The footnote suggests that the "particularized rules governing adjudications of status" might satisfy due process even in the absence of minimum contacts.

Although the UCCJEA is a subject matter statute, many jurisdictions adopting the model act have concluded that a court has jurisdiction to render a custody decision even when it lacks personal jurisdiction over one of the parties. *See generally Hollowell v. Tamburo*, 991 So. 2d 1022 (Fla. App. 2008). This is accomplished by applying the status theory to a custody proceeding. *In Interest of S.A.V.*, 837 S.W.2d 80 (Tex. 1992). Advocates consider the status theory in custody proceedings as similar to a "divisible divorce." Recall that a jurisdiction may divorce a couple (change status) without personal jurisdiction over both parties. *Estin v. Estin*, 334 U.S. 541, 546-547 (1948) (distinguishing marital status as falling within jurisdictional status exception to minimum contacts test). In a custody dispute, the connection between the state and the child is viewed as a sufficient nexus to give it jurisdiction to decide the issue. *See In re R.W.*, 39 A.3d 682, 693 (Vt. 2011) (justifying parent's relationship with child as legal relationship capable of status-based adjudication). The custody proceeding is an action *in rem*. The *res* is the status of the infant.

When a court with subject matter jurisdiction lacks personal jurisdiction over a party decides to exercise status theory jurisdiction and proceeds to adjudicate custody it is limited in the relief it may grant. The well-accepted principle is that without personal jurisdiction, a court may not award marital property, set child support, or establish alimony. *Latta v. Latta*, 654 So. 2d 1043 (Fla. App. 1995).

<table>
<tr>
<td>

REFLECTIVE QUESTIONS

</td>
<td>

What is the importance of the development of the status theory in terms of normally requiring personal jurisdiction over all parties to a child custody dispute before a binding order can be issued?

</td>
</tr>
</table>

General Principles

1. A court that issues an initial custody order with jurisdiction over the parties has continuing power to hear and modify that order, even if one party moves to another jurisdiction.

2. In most jurisdictions, the party seeking modification must meet a higher standard than that used at the initial custody hearing. Courts reason that a higher standard is needed because of the potential effect of unwarranted and repeated custody hearings on the stability of the children and the custodial family.

3. States that have adopted the Uniform Marriage and Divorce Act (UMDA) require a showing of consent, integration, or serous endangerment of a child's physical, moral, or emotional health before a modification request will be granted. UMDA §409.

4. The UMDA provides a moratorium of two years on bringing custody modification motions absent a showing of endangerment. UMDA §409(a).

5. In most jurisdictions, when a motion is made to modify a joint physical custody order, courts apply the best interests of the child or children standard. In these situations, a judge's willingness to elevate one parent's interest in relocating freely with the children is often diminished. Jurisdictions use differing standards in relocation disputes, with some jurisdictions requiring a showing of "exceptional circumstances before allowing" a custodial parent to relocate to another jurisdiction with the minor child or children. A minority of jurisdictions presume a relocation is in the best interests of a custodial child.

6. The American Law Institute (ALI) provides that a custodial parent should be permitted to relocate as long as he or she can show that the relocation is in good faith and for a legitimate purpose and is to a location that is reasonable in light of that purpose. ALI *Principles* §2.20(4)(a).

7. When it comes to a constitutional right to travel, some courts will distinguish between the right to travel of the custodial parent as an individual and the best interests of a minor child.

8. The purpose of the UCCJEA is to resolve and prevent jurisdictional conflicts between states in custody matters. The purpose of the PKPA is to determine which custody decrees are entitled to full faith and credit.

9. If there are differences between a state UCCJEA and the PKPA, under the Supremacy Clause, the PKPA (a federal statute) trumps the UCCJEA.

Chapter Problems

1. Assume the following: Joan and John divorce in a no-fault jurisdiction. They have one child, age nine, and Joan is awarded physical (residential) custody of the child. John receives reasonable visitation. A year after the divorce, John seeks to modify custody on the ground that Joan is having an affair with Tim, who has moved in and is living with her. John argues that the relationship is detrimental to their son. In an affidavit submitted with his request for a full hearing, John states that Joan's conduct is immoral and renders Joan an unfit custodian. This jurisdiction has adopted §409(a) of the Uniform Marriage and Divorce Act (UMDA), which bars modification proceedings for two years absent certain conditions. The trial judge asks the following questions of the lawyers: (a) Does §409(a) bar John from bringing an action? (b) Has John submitted sufficient support for his action that requires the court to order a full hearing? (c) If there has been a change in circumstances, what standard should the court apply when deciding whether to modify the current custody arrangement?

2. Assume that Pete and Patty divorce and that Patty is awarded sole physical custody of their daughter, Melissa, age four. Three months after the divorce, Patty is seriously injured in an automobile accident. For the next four months, Melissa lives full time with Pete and Pete's mother, who has moved into Pete's home to provide care for Melissa when Pete is working. When Patty has sufficiently recovered from her injuries, she is confined to a wheelchair. She asks Pete to return Melissa. Pete refuses and brings a motion asking the court to award him primary care of the child. He contends that he is now providing Melissa with her own room, she has been enrolled in an excellent day care facility, she has expressed a desire to live with him permanently, and Patty's confinement to a wheelchair will make it difficult for her to care for Melissa. The trial judge, in a jurisdiction that has adopted the UMDA, asks the following questions: (a) Is the action time barred? (b) Has there been a change of circumstances? (c) If there has been a change in circumstances, on what basis can Pete seek to have the original order modified?

3. Assume that Mom and Dad were divorced when their only child was seven years old. Mom received sole physical (primary) custody of the child. At the time of the original custody proceeding, Dad admitted that he was an alcoholic and was unable to provide appropriate care for the child. Three years later, Dad brings a motion seeking a court order that he be awarded primary custody of the child.

At the modification hearing, Dad acknowledged that he is an alcoholic but testified that he has been abstinent from alcohol since the divorce, although he is not presently in treatment. His AA counselor supported Dad's testimony. Dad is employed as a delivery person for an office supply company and owns a home subject to a mortgage. Dad also has a supportive extended family with whom the child is close, including Dad's mother who lives with him most of the year and Dad's sisters who live in his neighborhood.

Evidence indicated that while Mom has primary physical custody of the child, the child witnessed numerous incidents of severe domestic violence and alcohol abuse by Mom and her live-in boyfriend. Two such incidents resulted in the arrest and incarceration of the boyfriend. Another incident prompted Mom to bring the child to Dad's home, where the child remained for four months. Notably, Mom visited the child only once during this entire period. At the time of the hearing, Mom's boyfriend was undergoing court-ordered inpatient treatment for alcohol abuse and intended to resume his residence with Mom and the child upon release. He had also successfully completed an anger management course. The child, although age seven, was interviewed by the court. He indicated to the judge that he was aware of the violence in the household and expressed fear of the boyfriend. However, he refused to express a desire to live with either parent. How should a court rule on the modification request? *See Holden v. Tillotson*, 716 N.Y.S.2d (N.Y. 2000).

4. Assume that Mom and Dad divorce after ten years. The trial judge awards sole physical (primary) custody to Mom of their three-year-old girl. In making the decision, the court pointed out that Dad was a drug addict, unemployed, and not undergoing treatment for his drug problem.

Four years later, Dad brings a motion asking the court to modify the custody award to give him sole (primary) custody of the minor child. Evidence indicates that Dad has been in a drug-counseling program for two years and has been abstinent from using drugs for the past year. A counselor supported his position. Dad has been employed for five months at a hamburger franchise. Dad's mother now lives with him and has a close relationship with the child.

Evidence indicated that Mom left the child home alone on one occasion when she was only six years old and often sent her to school inappropriately dressed and unkempt. Mom apparently ignored attempts by the child's teacher to address these issues. At the time of the hearing, Mom had been evicted from one apartment for failing to pay rent and was unemployed. She was behind in rent payments for her current apartment. Although the child was diagnosed with breathing problems subsequent to the parties' separation, both Mom and her boyfriend continue to smoke cigarettes, although not in the child's presence. Mom testified that Dad had never paid child support of any kind and continued to refuse to pay support. She explained that she was doing the best she could with the assistance of the welfare department. Should a court modify custody?

5. Assume that Mom and Dad live in Arizona for several years and that Mom files for a divorce in that state and seeks custody of their minor child. While the divorce action is pending in the Arizona court, Dad takes the minor child and moves to Pennsylvania. After a few weeks in Pennsylvania, Dad also files a divorce action and requests custody of the minor child. Mom challenges the jurisdiction of a

Pennsylvania court to render a custody decision citing a provision in the UCCJEA and 28 U.S.C. §1739(A)(g) of PKPA. Assuming that Arizona and Pennsylvania have both adopted identical provisions of the UCCJEA, how should a Pennsylvania court rule and why?

Preparation for Practice

1. Retrieve a recent reported custody modification decision made by your jurisdiction's highest court. Using the facts in that decision and ones you may add, and guided by your local family court and civil procedure rules, draft a typical set of documents a lawyer would submit to a trial court asking for a change in custody. These documents might include a notice of motion, motion, and supporting affidavits, depending on your jurisdiction's requirements. The documents may be reviewed for feedback by your instructor or an attorney practicing family law.

2. Prepare a PowerPoint presentation that explains the reasoning used by your jurisdiction in allowing or refusing relocation in its three most recent reported decisions. Be prepared to post your presentation online for your class and instructor to review.

Financial Support

Chapter 8

Establishing Child Support

8.1 INTRODUCTION

This chapter explores the legal obligation of parents to financially support their children. Adequate financial support for a minor child involved in a divorce or a parentage determination is crucial to the well-being of the child. In addition to monthly payments, provision must be made for medical expenses and the cost of child care.

As you read this chapter, consider the following questions: Who has an obligation to pay child support? How is the amount of child support determined? What parental income is considered available for child support? Does the amount of child support vary depending on parenting arrangements?

REFLECTIVE QUESTIONS	**What are your goals for this chapter?**

8.2 HISTORY: ELIZABETHAN POOR LAWS

The common law accorded a child no legally enforceable support right. Blackstone wrote that the "insuperable degree of affection" between parent and child was a sufficient guarantor of parental support to obviate the need for legal sanctions. The common law approach was also based, in part, on a general reluctance to pierce the legal unity of the family.

The Elizabethan Poor Laws, passed at the beginning of the seventeenth century, contain some of the earliest statements regarding the legal obligation of a parent to support a child. The laws were the result of economic conditions that created a large class of landless, often destitute laborers, and they transformed a moral duty of family support into legal obligations. They were one of the first efforts to create a public welfare program that was funded through taxation. The laws provided direct financial assistance only to those incapable of self-help, with a consequence that children were often indentured as apprentices.

The industrial age altered the perspective of the family, with courts imposing a paternal support obligation that was enforceable on behalf of a child and that applied whether or not the child was in danger of becoming a public charge. Statutory divorce laws, the Married Women's Property Acts, and the basis to claim alimony developed during this period and heralded a shift away from the view of the family as a unified legal entity.

REFLECTIVE QUESTIONS	Why do you think that the obligation was placed on the state to ensure that minor children received financial support when their parents were unable or unwilling to provide support? What was the philosophy about supporting children before the state intervened?

8.3 TRADITIONAL FOCUS OF STATE LAW

In the United States, parents are primarily responsible for bearing the cost of raising minor children. Over the last century, states struggled to develop methods of calculating child support awards that are fair to both parents and provide sufficiently for the child:

> Fifty years ago, the right to child support was based on the recognized principle that every child has the right to be supported by his or her parents. Child support orders, however, were based on the amorphous twin precepts of an obligor's ability to pay as weighed against the needs of the child (reminiscent of the maxim, "From each according to his abilities, to each according to his need").

Laura W. Morgan, *Child Support Fifty Years Later*, 42 Fam. L.Q. 365, 365-366 (2008).

The Uniform Marriage and Divorce Act (UMDA) provides that either or both parents may be ordered to pay a reasonable amount of child support based on the financial resources of each parent and the child; the standard of living the child would have enjoyed; and the physical, emotional, and educational needs of the child. UMDA §309. Under the UMDA, judges exercised extensive discretion and, not surprisingly, child support orders varied widely and were difficult to predict even within a single jurisdiction.

Over the past 50 years, the legal landscape with respect to child support has changed dramatically. Primarily as a result of federal intervention, states adopted mandatory child support guidelines. Consequently, judges no longer exercise so much discretion and, in contrast to other areas of family law, uniformity and predictability are valued over in-depth consideration of individual needs.

If parents do not meet the basic needs of children, the state provides support in the form of public assistance. As a result, development of the law regarding child support has been driven largely by the requirements of public assistance programs. For example, one of the first federal interventions into the child support arena was to require public assistance recipients to cooperate in obtaining and enforcing child support orders. *See* Child Support and Establishment of Paternity Act of 1974, 42 U.S.C. §§651-655. Similarly, states initially adopted child support guidelines in order to preserve federal funding for Aid to Families with Dependent Children (AFDC). *See* 42 U.S.C. §§651, 667(a)-(b) (1984). Thus, although the child support system is administered pursuant to state law, those laws and their enforcement have been substantially shaped by federal public welfare policy.

REFLECTIVE QUESTIONS	Mandatory child support guidelines were created because of federal intervention. Why did the federal government intervene in an area traditionally left to the states?

8.4 ROLE OF THE FEDERAL GOVERNMENT

In the 1970s, the federal government began collecting national data regarding child support awards and payments. The impetus for this effort was concern over rising rates of single parenting and welfare dependence. From this data, a number of federally mandated programs were created. For example, the 1975 Child Support Enforcement Act aimed to assist states with child support collections to meet three objectives: (1) reducing public expenditures on welfare by obtaining child support from noncustodial parents on an ongoing basis; (2) helping families obtain support so they could get off and stay off public assistance; and (3) stimulating state action to establish paternity for children born outside marriage so that child support could be obtained for them.

In 1984 Congress mandated that every state seeking federal funding for its welfare program establish advisory child support guidelines. *See* 42 U.S.C. §§651, 667(a)-(b) (1984). The Family Support Act of 1988 strengthened the guidelines by requiring that they operate as rebuttable presumptions of the correct support amount. The legislation also mandated that any deviation from the presumptive amount be supported by a decision maker's specific findings, in writing or on the record, as to why the guideline amount would be unjust or inappropriate in a particular case.

The Omnibus Budget Reconciliation Act of 1993 required states to create a rebuttable or conclusive presumption of paternity where genetic testing indicated a man was the father of a child born outside of marriage. It also modified the Employee Retirement Income Security Act (ERISA) to require that employers make group health care coverage available to the noncustodial children of their employees. In an effort to address interstate child support issues, Congress enacted the Full Faith and Credit for Child Support Orders Act (FFCCSOA) in 1994 for the purpose of establishing national standards to facilitate the payment of child support, discourage interstate conflict over inconsistent orders, and to avoid jurisdictional competition. FFCCSOA requires "that state courts afford full faith and credit to child support orders issued in other states and refrain from modifying or issuing contrary orders except in limited circumstances."

The Welfare Reform Act of 1996 contained a number of child support provisions, one of which established a national system for tracking employment and required reporting of new hires within 20 days with information forwarded to the Federal Case Registry and the Federal Parent Locator Service (FPLS). The act mandated that states adopt a version of the Uniform Interstate Family Support Act by January 1, 1998, and required that states adopt expedited procedures. It also encouraged states to use liens, seizures of funds, license suspension, and administrative subpoenas to collect outstanding child support. In 1996 the federal government, through the Personal Responsibility and Work Opportunity Reconciliation Act, expanded the FPLS's services to include a National Directory of New Hires and a Federal Case Registry of Support Orders.

REFLECTIVE QUESTIONS	This section outlines various child support–related programs created by the federal government. Do some appear to be more important than others? Would you do away with any of them?

8.5 GUIDELINES: REBUTTABLE PRESUMPTION

Prior to the widespread adoption of child support guidelines, judges exercised considerable discretion in making awards. Statutes such as the UMDA provided little concrete guidance to judges, and child support awards were extremely unpredictable. As a result, cases were difficult to settle, and similarly situated obligors were sometimes subject to drastically different support orders.

As noted above, the federal government initially sought uniformity in child support awards in cases where the child was a recipient of public assistance. Advisory guidelines were developed by the states and implemented as part of an ongoing effort to reduce public assistance expenditures. These guidelines eventually became mandatory, and they were applied to all children, not only those receiving public assistance. *See* Child Support Enforcements Amendments of 1984, Pub. L. No. 98-378, 98 Stat. 1305; Family Support Act, 42 U.S.C. §667(b)(2).

State guidelines constitute a rebuttable presumption that the amount of support calculated under the guidelines is correct. Although one or both parents can seek a deviation from the guidelines amount, courts rigorously apply them. For example, the Alaska Supreme Court summarized the high standard required for court approval of deviations from the guidelines, even when the parties have agreed to them:

> Rule 90.3(c) states that a superior court "may vary the child support award as calculated under the other provisions of this rule for good cause upon proof by clear and convincing evidence that manifest injustice would result if the support award were not varied." The superior court "must specify in writing the reason for the variation, the amount of support which would have been required but for the variation, and the estimated value of any property conveyed instead of support." Rule 90.3(c) explains that the good cause requirement "may include a finding that unusual circumstances exist which require variation of the award in order to award an amount of support which is just and proper for the parties to contribute toward the nurture and education of their children."

Laughlin v. Laughlin, 229 P.3d 2002 (Alaska 2010). When deviations are approved, they are likely to involve upward deviations for items such as extraordinary medical expenses or special educational needs.

REFLECTIVE QUESTIONS	What is the legal and practical significance of the rebuttable presumption regarding the guidelines support amount?

8.6 GUIDELINES: STATE MODELS

States have adopted child support guidelines based on different underlying models. A majority of states use some form of the *income shares* approach. The goal of this model is to provide the child with the same proportion of support that he or she would have had if the family had remained living together. Under the income shares approach, state guidelines dictate a support amount based on the combined incomes of the parents, and that amount is prorated between the parents based on the percentage of combined income attributable to each of them.

In contrast some states use the *percentage-of-income* child support model. Under this method, the nonresidential parent pays a state-mandated percentage of his or her income for child support. The actual percentage of income paid varies depending on the number of children and the income of the obligor.

A few jurisdictions use variations on these models, such as the more complicated Melson formula. *See, e.g., Dalton v. Clanton*, 559 A.2d 1197 (Del. 1989) (explaining origin, principles and application of Melson formula in Delaware).

The American Law Institute (ALI) proposes an enhanced model of child support, which contains a formula derived from that used in Massachusetts. The formula provides for a preliminary assessment and then applies a reduction mechanism. *See* American Law Institute, *Principles of the Law of Family Dissolution: Analysis and Recommendations* §3.04, comment b (2000). Some believe that if the

ALI *Principles* was adopted, the amount of child support awards in most states would increase, "particularly those involving small families of modest means in which the residential parent, usually the mother, has a lower income than the nonresidential parent." Leslie Joan Harris, *The Proposed ALI Child Support Principles*, 35 Willamette L. Rev. 717, 718 (1999).

Although state guidelines constitute a rebuttable presumption that the amount of support awarded is correct, considerable legal judgment is exercised in the application of the guidelines. For example, parents may seek deviations from the guidelines, obligors may contest the definition of income, and under certain conditions courts may impute income to obligors. As will be seen in this chapter, despite the complexity of the guidelines, some questions remain unanswered or are answered quite differently in each state.

REFLECTIVE QUESTIONS	What are the policy reasons for allowing state variation in the operation of child support guidelines?

8.7 PERCENTAGE-OF-INCOME MODEL

Under the percentage-of-income child support model, the obligor pays a mandated percentage of his or her net income in child support. Net income is typically calculated by deducting items such as taxes, health insurance premiums, reasonable pension payments, child support paid to prior children, and maintenance payments stemming from prior relationships. Living expenses are not deducted when arriving at net income for the purpose of child support calculation. The income of the primary physical custodian is not explicitly considered, although the income shares model assumes that parent will provide substantial in-kind support.

Background to *Zabloski v. Hall*

The percentage of income paid by the obligor changes based on the number of children and the obligor's income level. Some state statutes place a ceiling on the amount of income that is considered available for child support purposes. Consequently, a middle-class obligor with one child may pay the same amount of child support as a multimillionaire with one child. In contrast, other states allow child support orders to rise with the obligor's income, based on the theory that children should be able to enjoy the standard of living they experienced during the marriage. *Ladwig v. Ladwig*, 785 N.W.2d 664, 518 (Wis. App. 2010) (high-income obligor with "equal placement" ordered to pay $8,455 per month in child support).

In *Zabloski v. Hall*, the court considers a situation where the mother seeks an upward deviation from the guidelines payment amount because while she lives in relative poverty, the father of the child is a rock star with a substantial income. At the time of the case, Daryl Hall was a member of Hall & Oates, a duo with eight number-one singles. The court calculates child support using the percentage-of-income model.

ZABLOSKI
v.
HALL

Court of Appeals of Minnesota
418 N.W.2d 187 (1988)

CRIPPEN, J. Andrea Zabloski and public authorities commenced this parentage action against respondent Daryl Hall in April 1984. Prior to trial, Hall acknowledged paternity. The only remaining issues involved setting the amount of child support and awarding attorney fees to Zabloski and the child's appointed guardian *ad litem.*

Zabloski and Hall have never been married to each other, nor have they ever resided together. Their relationship consisted of a single sexual encounter early in 1983. Their son was born on January 8, 1984.

Zabloski is currently 24 years old and lives in Duluth. She also has a minor daughter who was born in June 1985. She and her two children live in a small one-bedroom apartment. Zabloski was on public assistance from October 1983 until October 1986, when she began receiving temporary child support from Hall. Her monthly income during that time consisted of approximately $437 in A.F.D.C. benefits and an average of $120 in food stamps. Since the birth of her daughter, she has also received $95 per month in child support, an amount which she expects will soon increase to $250 per month.

At trial, Zabloski presented evidence of the needs of her household. She submitted a proposed monthly budget of $3,143 based on the purchase of an $80,000 three-bedroom home, a new car, monthly food expenditures of $400, and monthly spending of $800 for her son (including $175 for clothing, $200 for toys/books, $125 for school needs, $53 for musical training/supplies, and $300 monthly toward the purchase of a $9,000 piano). Experts retained by both parties testified that the amount of money a parent spends on a child is largely a matter of personal choice. Zabloski's expert testified that on a net monthly income of $43,000, approximately 13 percent or $5,590 per month would be spent on a 3-year-old child, with an increase to 25 percent at age 6. An economist testifying on Hall's behalf concluded that at an annual income of $29,338, approximately 25 percent or $611 per month would be needed to support one child in a family of three or four. Utilizing other statistics, that amount decreased to $427 per month. Hall is 40 years old and resides in Millbrook, New York, in a three-bedroom home located on 160 acres of land. He is unmarried and has no other children. He is an entertainer who has achieved commercial success, and his current net income approximates $1.4 million per year, or $116,000 per month. He testified by deposition that most of his personal monthly expenses of $8,250 are for travel and business related needs. Hall further described his personal lifestyle as "frugal" and "simple." He indicated that he would want his son Darren to live in a similar manner and to grow up as he did, without expensive music lessons or tutoring.

The trial court granted custody of the child to his mother. Hall was ordered to pay child support of $1,000 per month, to provide health and dental coverage for Darren, and to pay for any uninsured medical or dental expenses. Absent an upward deviation, no higher award is provided under statutory child support guidelines. Minn. Stat. §518.551, subd. 5(a) (1986). Hall was also directed to reimburse St. Louis County $20,763.93 for A.F.D.C. payments and medical expenditures. The court awarded Zabloski and the guardian all attorney fees and costs incurred through the time of trial, an amount totaling $62,241.63. Post trial, $11,563 in back support was awarded directly to Zabloski and additional attorney fees of $500 were awarded to both Zabloski and the guardian. On appeal, Zabloski and the guardian contend the ongoing child support award is unsatisfactory.

The statutory child support guidelines are a starting point for the determination of a support award. Where an obligor's net monthly income is $4,000 or above, the guidelines set child support for one child at $1,000. Minn. Stat. §518.551, subd. 5(a) (1986). The statute further provides:

> Absent an agreement of the parties on the award, the court shall order child support in accordance with the guidelines and the other factors set forth in paragraph (b) and any departure therefrom. . . .

Thus, while the statute provides for departure above or below the guidelines amount, it states that a court deciding to deviate must make express findings on the reasons for deviation, based on the factors set out in Minn. Stat. §518.551, subd. 5(b). In this case, Zabloski and the guardian argue that the trial court abused its discretion by failing to fully consider Hall's standard of living, the factor listed in subdivision 5(b)(1).

In this case, the trial court's findings address not only the father's income, assets, and expenses, but also the mother's earning ability, living circumstances, and the child's personal needs. It found that if Zabloski were to complete her high school education, she would still be able to "generate only minimum or slightly above minimum wage income." It found that the child "appears to be a child of above-average intelligence who suffers from no mental, physical or emotional disabilities, and does not require any special attention or special care or training." In its memorandum, the court elaborated: "[T]here is nothing in the record herein showing this minor child to have any particular, special, unusual or distinctive needs, either physical, mental, emotional or educational. Indeed, he is a normal, ordinary, healthy three-year-old. He has no significant medical problem requiring treatment, no learning disability requiring special education, nor any other special need requiring an unusual level of support."

In support of its decision not to deviate, the trial court identified several reasons which are persuasive. First, after reciting Zabloski's claimed needs, the court found that she "has not prepared or presented to this Court an estimate of how much of this proposed budget would represent the actual monthly expenses of the minor child." Based on the evidence submitted by the experts at trial regarding the amount of income which would normally be spent on a normal child, the court determined that the personal needs of the child are much less than the total sum claimed necessary by the mother for the child and family. Thus, the court determined that the child's personal needs did not exceed $1,000 per month.

The court next made a distinction between the support which is legally required to be provided under the guidelines and the freedom of a parent to choose whether additional contributions are to be given. In this sense, the legislature has effectively declared that a child's needs are normally not higher than $1,000 per month.

The court finally implied that while the mother's needs may be considered, it would be inappropriate to use a child support obligation to upgrade her standard of living. In this sense, a distinction was made between the mother's needs and the standard of living to be enjoyed by a family. The maximum appropriate award under the guidelines effectively suggests a normal "cap" on the use of support to upgrade a child's standard of living. Examination of the trial court's findings and memorandum in this case satisfy us that Hall's standard of living was properly considered. Judgment affirmed.

 **FOR *ZABLOSKI v. HALL***

A. Describe the emotional and legal relationship of the mother and father in this case.

B. Until the mother began receiving temporary child support from the father, what was her average monthly income? What was the father's approximate annual income?

C. List the items in the mother's proposed monthly budget.

D. What reasons did the court give with respect to the decision not to deviate from the child support guidelines?

E. If the parents in this case had married and stayed together, the child would undoubtedly have experienced a much higher standard of living. Should the financial circumstances and opportunities of the child be so drastically affected by the marital status of the parents? Should it make a difference that the child was conceived during a one-night stand rather than during an intact marriage?

F. Under the percentage-of-income method of child support calculation, the mother's income was not considered under the guidelines. Instead, it is assumed that the mother would pay for items such as shelter and food, which are not covered by the father's payment. Did that assumption work to the disadvantage of the child in this case? Under the income shares model (discussed in the following section), the incomes of both parents would be relevant. Assuming that the cap remained in place, might use of the income shares method have made a difference?

G. Rock star Mick Jagger allegedly had a nonmarital child with a Brazilian model. In June 2000, it was reported that she sought $35,000 a month in child support. He argued that child support should be no more than $5,600 per month. If you were a legislator, what sort of legislation would you propose to govern such situations? Would you include a cap on income available for child support? If so, where would you place the cap? Would you allow deviation from the guidelines based on the standard of living of the obligor? Would you except high-income families from using the guidelines? How would your analysis differ if the obligor had an unusually low standard of living?

8.8 THE INCOME SHARES MODEL

Background to *Voishan v. Palmer*

Unlike the percentage-of-income method used in the previous case, the income shares model takes the income of both parents expressly into account. Each parent pays his or her proportionate share of a guideline amount derived from the state-estimated cost of raising a child at the parent's combined income level. The theory behind the income shares model is that the proportion of parental income allocated for child-related expenses should approximate what the child would have received if the parents lived together.

Similar to the issue in *Zabloski*, the court in *Voishan v. Palmer* considers a situation where the combined income of the parties is higher than the upper limit set under the guideline schedule. But, in *Voishan* the court calculates support under the income shares model rather than the percentage of income model used in *Zabloski*.

VOISHAN
v.
PALMER

Court of Appeals of Maryland
609 A.2d 319 (1992)

CHASANOW, J. John and Margaret Voishan were divorced on June 26, 1981, by decree of the Circuit Court for Anne Arundel County. Margaret was awarded custody of their two daughters and John was ordered to pay $250 per week toward the girls' support.

Over four years later, an order dated October 7, 1985, increased the amount of John's obligation for the support of both children to $1,400 per month. On March 8, 1991, the circuit court's intercession was again sought to address John's request to find Margaret in contempt for violating the visitation order as well as Margaret's motion to modify child support. The Honorable Raymond G. Thieme, Jr., presided at that hearing and shortly thereafter entered an order finding that Margaret was not in contempt of court. That order also increased John's child support obligation for the one daughter who was still a minor from $700 per month to $1,550 per month. John then appealed the modification of child support to the Court of Special Appeals. Because of the important issues raised on appeal, this Court granted certiorari before consideration by the intermediate appellate court.

This dispute requires the Court, for the first time, to address Maryland Code, (1984, 1991 Repl. Vol.) Family Law Article §§12-201 et seq. (the "guidelines"). The General Assembly enacted these guidelines in 1989 to comply with federal law and regulations. See 42 U.S.C. §§651-667 (1982 & 1984 Supp. II) and 45 C.F.R. §302.56 (1989). The federal mandate required that the guidelines be established and "based on specific descriptive and numeric criteria and result in a computation of the support obligation." After considering several different models recommended by the Advisory Panel on Child Support Guidelines, the General Assembly chose to base Maryland's guidelines on the Income Shares Model. The conceptual underpinning of this model is that a child should receive the same proportion of parental income, and thereby enjoy the standard of living, he or she would have experienced had the child's parents remained together. Accordingly, the model establishes child support obligations based on estimates of the percentage of income that parents in an intact household typically spend on their children. Consistent with this model, the legislature constructed the schedule in §12-204(e), which sets forth the basic child support obligation for any given number of children based on combined parental income. Following the Income Shares Model, Maryland's guidelines first require that the trial judge determine each parent's monthly "adjusted actual income." Section 12-201(d) states: Adjusted actual income means actual income minus:

(1) preexisting reasonable child support obligations actually paid;
(2) except as provided in §12-204(a)(2) of this subtitle, alimony or maintenance obligations actually paid; and
(3) the actual cost of providing health insurance coverage for a child for whom the parents are jointly and severally responsible.

After determining each parent's monthly "adjusted actual income," the judge then adds these two amounts together to arrive at the monthly "combined adjusted actual income" of the parents. Having calculated the combined adjusted actual income of the parents, the judge can then determine whether that figure falls within the range of incomes found in the schedule of §12-204(e). If the figure is within the schedule, the judge then locates the corresponding "basic child support obligation" for the given number of children. Where the monthly income falls between two amounts set forth in the schedule, §12-204(c) dictates that the basic child support obligation is the same as the obligation specified for the next highest income level. The judge then divides this basic child support obligation between the parents in proportion to each of their adjusted actual incomes. The judge must then add together any work-related child care expenses, extraordinary medical expenses, and school and transportation expenses and allocate this total between the parents in proportion to their adjusted actual incomes. The amount of child support computed in this manner is presumed to be correct, although this presumption may be rebutted by evidence that such amount would be unjust and inappropriate in a particular case.

In the instant case, evidence was presented at the March 8, 1991, hearing that John now earns $145,000 per year, while Margaret's annual income is $30,000. John does not contend that his actual income should be reduced by any expenses identified in §12-201(d). Therefore, he computes a "combined adjusted actual income" of $175,000 a year or $14,583 per month in his argument to this Court. This combined income exceeds $10,000 per month, which is the highest income provided for in §12-204(e). The legislature addressed this situation in §12-204(d), which says: "If the combined adjusted actual income exceeds the highest level specified in the schedule in subsection (e) of this section, the court may use its discretion in setting the amount of child support."

. . . John contends that the $1,550 monthly child support award is inconsistent with the spirit and intent behind the Income Shares Model, and concludes that Judge Thieme abused his discretion in awarding that amount. John maintains that Judge Thieme accurately found that the parties' earnings created a ratio of 83 to 17 for John's and Margaret's respective percentages of their $175,000 combined annual income. John contends, however, that Judge Thieme erred in the manner in which he applied these percentages to arrive at the amount of $1,550 per month for John's share of the obligation. Judge Thieme examined expense sheets for each of the parties and concluded that the "reasonable expenses of the child" were $1,873 each month. The judge then calculated 83% of that figure and rounded John's share of the obligation down to $1,550.

John argues here, as he did below, that a "reasonable approach" would have been for the trial judge to assume that the maximum basic child support obligation listed in the schedule is not only applicable to combined monthly incomes of $10,000, but also applies to those in excess of $10,000 per month. Under the schedule in §12-204(e), the maximum basic child support obligation of $1,040 per month is presumptively correct for parties who have a combined monthly income of $10,000. John argues that $1,040 per month should also provide the presumptively correct basic child support obligation for all combined monthly incomes over $10,000. While we believe that $1,040 could provide the presumptive minimum basic award for those with combined monthly incomes above $10,000, we do not believe that the legislature intended to cap the basic child support obligation at the upper limit of the schedule. Had the legislature intended to make the highest award in the schedule the presumptive basic support obligation in all cases with combined monthly income over $10,000, it would have so stated and would not have granted the trial judge discretion in fixing those awards. Further, John's proposed approach creates an artificial ceiling and itself defeats the guidelines' policy that the child enjoy a standard of living consonant with that he or she would have experienced had the parents remained married. We are unpersuaded by John's argument that the legislature meant for all children whose parents earn more than $10,000 per month to have the same standard of living as those whose parents earn $10,000 per month. Alternatively, John argues that Judge Thieme should have extrapolated from the guidelines to determine what the support obligation would have been had the schedule extended up to the parties' $14,583 monthly income. John notes that at the upper levels in the guidelines, the basic child support obligation for one child increases by $5 for every $100 rise in combined adjusted actual income. Extrapolating on that basis, John argues that the basic child support obligation would be $1,270 per month ($4,583/100 × $5 plus $1,040).

John also acknowledges that under the guidelines, in addition to the basic child support obligation — whatever that is computed to be — he has an obligation to pay 83% of the additional work-related child care expenses which, in the instant case, are $400 per month. Taking 83% of the $1,270 basic child support obligation plus 83% of the $400 work-related child care expenses, John argues, renders his portion of his daughter's support to be $1,386 per month. Although slightly more generous than his earlier argument, which would leave the judge with no discretion, John's second contention is essentially that this Court should significantly restrict the judicial discretion granted by §12-204(d) and allow judges very little latitude in deviating from the extrapolation method. John asks this Court to hold that Judge Thieme abused his discretion when he set the award $164 higher than the amount computed by John's strict extrapolation theory. While we believe that the trial judge should consider the underlying policies of the guidelines and strive toward congruous results, we think that Judge Thieme did not abuse his discretion in fixing the amount of this award. . . .

While we reject John's argument that Judge Thieme abused his discretion because he placed too little reliance on John's suggested mechanical extrapolation from the schedule, we also decline to adopt the position taken by the Maryland Chapter of the American Academy of Matrimonial Lawyers (the AAML) in their amicus curiae brief. The AAML basically argues that Judge Thieme abused his discretion because he placed too much reliance on a mechanical application of the guidelines. The AAML contends that the economic data from which the figures in the schedule were derived did not include empirical evidence of the actual household expenditures for children of high-income parents. Because the research and data used in constructing the Income Shares Model did not contemplate these high-range combined parental incomes, the AAML argues, the model provides no assistance in calculating the proper amount of child support. Thus, the AAML concludes, "the trial court erred when it applied a rigid formula (relative percentage of parents' income)."

We do not believe that the legislature intended that the schedule in §12-204(e) "govern" a judge's discretion by dictating a cap or mechanical extrapolation. However, we also do not believe that the legislature intended that the principles from which the schedule was derived should be ignored when a judge exercises discretion under §12-204(d).

While awards made under §12-204(d) will be disturbed only if there is a clear abuse of discretion, a reviewing court must also be mindful that the federal call for child support guidelines was motivated in part by the need to improve the consistency of awards. Thus, the trial judge has somewhat more latitude than that argued by John, but not the unguided discretion of pre-guidelines cases as advocated by the AAML. Rather, we agree with the Attorney General's position that the guidelines do establish a rebuttable presumption that the maximum support award under the schedule is the minimum which should be awarded in cases above the schedule. Beyond this the trial judge should examine the needs of the child in light of the parents' resources and determine the amount of support necessary to ensure that the child's standard of living does not suffer because of the parents' separation. Further, the judge should give some consideration to the Income Shares method of apportioning the child support obligation. Consequently, we conclude that Judge Thieme properly exercised his discretion in receiving evidence of the parents' financial circumstances, considering the needs of the child, and then apportioning the "reasonable expenses of the child."

DISCUSSION QUESTIONS FOR *VOISHAN v. PALMER*

A. In this case, did application of the income shares model provide the child with the same standard of living that the child would have enjoyed if the parents had remained married?

B. The case includes a brief discussion of how work-related child care expenses might be paid. What is proposed? Why do you suppose that child care expenses are not included in the guidelines amount but rather involve a separate calculation?

C. The court states that in its amicus brief, the American Academy of Matrimonial Lawyers asserts that "the economic data from which the figures in the schedule were derived did not include empirical evidence of the actual household expenditures for children of high-income parents. Because the research and data used in constructing the Income Shares Model did not contemplate these high-range combined parental incomes . . . the model provides no assistance in calculating the proper amount of child support." Is it possible to construct a single set of guidelines that will treat children of all income levels fairly? If guidelines are based on evidence of actual household expenditures on children, what factors should come into play? Would you favor consideration of factors such as the age of the children, the number of children in the family, and the standard of living of the parents?

D. Which model of calculating child support do you prefer? Why?

8.9 MEDICAL SUPPORT AND CHILD CARE EXPENSES

At the time of separation or divorce, consideration must be given to provision of medical care for the child or children. In some states medical expenses are included in the basic child support calculation, but in others support for medical expenses entails a separate calculation. *See Bare v. Bare*, 994 A.2d 487 (Md. Ct. Spec. App. 2010); *In re H.J.W.*, 302 S.W.3d 511 (Tex. Ct. App. 2009). Practically speaking, decisions about insurance coverage may be influenced by which parent has best access to dependent coverage. Sometimes parents divide insurance costs in proportion to their incomes. Any medical expenses not covered by insurance or extraordinary expenses will also be apportioned.

The states have not given uniform treatment to the issue of payment for child care expenses. Some states have created a formula that results in each parent paying a proportional share of the child care expenses. Other states deduct the expense from the obligor's gross income before child support is calculated. Still others consider child care expenses as a basis for deviating from the guidelines and awarding the obligee additional support.

REFLECTIVE QUESTIONS	Why do states differ with respect to how they deal with medical and child care expenses? How do you think those expenses should be handled?

8.10 INCOME AVAILABLE FOR CHILD SUPPORT: OVERTIME

Background to *Welter v. Welter*

No matter which guidelines model is used, questions arise concerning what constitutes "income" for the purpose of child support calculation. Definitions of gross income usually include items such as wages, tips, bonuses, profit sharing, investment income, deferred compensation, and severance pay. *See* Paula Woodland Faerber, *Empirical Study: A Guide to the Guidelines: A Longitudinal Study of Child Support Guidelines in the United States*, 1 J.L. & Fam. Stud. 151 (1999).

Despite the fact that most statutes contain carefully drafted definitions of income, courts are left to grapple with situations that may not have been contemplated by legislators. For example, in *Welter v. Welter*, a child support award is to be based on "all salary and wages" and the court must decide whether this definition includes payment for overtime work.

WELTER

v.

WELTER

Court of Appeals of Wisconsin
711 N.W.2d 705 (2006)

CANE, C.J. Larry and Carolyn Rae Welter were married on October 3, 1998, and divorced on May 3, 1999. While married, they had one child together. . . . The court commissioner's order indicates that he excluded the overtime income as a general policy when calculating Larry's gross income and subsequent child support obligation. Counsel noted, and it is not disputed that, this "Court Commissioner . . . has a policy of not including overtime. I think that's fairly widely known within the family law community."

The circuit court followed the court commissioner's decision, finding "The Court Commissioner's . . . policy of not including overtime is correct." The court reasoned,

> I do feel and I felt this way in divorce cases and so forth, it seems to, particularly if overtime is voluntary, that's the only opportunity a person has to get ahead on their own bills and so forth. And so if Mr. Welter is working diligently and earning a lot of overtime pay to pay his current obligations and . . . if he has other children . . . I think he ought to be entitled to do that. I think his basis of paying on his . . . regular pay and his longevity pay is fair, but I really disagree with going after overtime.

Child support determinations are within the trial court's discretion and will not be reversed absent an erroneous exercise of discretion. . . . Wisconsin law requires that child support obligations be expressed as a fixed sum unless the parties stipulate otherwise, Wis. Stat. §767.25(1)(a), based upon a percentage of gross income and assets calculation (the percentage standard). Wis. Stat. §767.25(1j). Gross income includes, among other things, all salary and wages. Wis. Admin. Code §DWD 40.02(13)(a)1 (Dec. 2003).

The court has the discretion to deviate from the percentage standard based on the facts of each case if its application would be unfair to the child or any of the parties. Wis. Stat. §767.25(1m). To determine fairness, sixteen different factors are considered, which relate to the circumstances surrounding the parents, the child or any of the parties. *Id.* The sixteen factors include a catch-all factor, which states the court may modify the child support obligation based on "[a]ny other factors which the court in each case determines are relevant." Wis. Stat. §767.25(1m)(i). If the court deviates from the percentage standard, the court shall state in writing or on the record the amount of support that would be required by using the percentage standard, the amount by which the court's order deviates from that amount, its reasons for finding that use of the percentage standard is unfair to the child or party, its reasons for the amount of modification and the basis for the modification. Wis. Stat. §767.25(1n). Thus, although the circuit court is not required to precisely follow the percentage standard, "it must articulate its reasoning process for the decision to remain within the support guidelines or to deviate from them." *Rumpff v. Rumpff*, 688 N.W.2d 699.

We agree with the Agency that the circuit court erred when it upheld the court commissioner's decision to exclude overtime pay as a general policy without exception when applying the percentage standard. Overtime income clearly constitutes a portion of salary and wages, and Wisconsin law does not exclude overtime income in the application of the percentage standard. *See* Wis. Admin. Code §DWD 40.03(1) (Dec. 2003). Further, the court and the court commissioner could have deviated from the percentage standard if they considered the above factors and articulated their reasoning regarding why its normal application would be unfair to the child or the parties. *See Rumpff*, 688 N.W.2d 699.

We recognize there may be circumstances when overtime income may be excluded from the gross pay of a spouse if it would be unfair to the parties or other factors supported exclusion. However, here the circuit court and the court commissioner simply applied a general policy against including overtime income in the application of the percentage standard. It is erroneous for a court commissioner or a court to set forth a general policy regarding the calculation of a child support obligation when the law calls for an exercise of discretion. *See In re Steven J.S.*, 515 N.W.2d 719 (Ct. App. 1994) ("The trial court properly exercises its discretion if it articulates its reasons, bases its decision on facts of record and the correct legal standards, and the [child support] award is neither excessive nor inadequate"). Thus, we reverse and remand with directions to the circuit court to analyze the facts and apply the proper legal standards when exercising its discretion on whether to exclude overtime income.

DISCUSSION QUESTIONS FOR *WELTER v. WELTER*

A. What method of calculating child support was used in this case?

B. The court makes a distinction between excluding overtime pay as a matter of policy and excluding overtime pay as a deviation from the child support guidelines. Is this a significant distinction?

C. What arguments could be made to support the obligor's position that overtime income should not be available for child support purposes? What arguments could be made that overtime income should be considered when awarding child support? Should all overtime income be treated the same way?

8.11 IMPUTATION OF INCOME AVAILABLE FOR CHILD SUPPORT

As a part of their employment compensation, some parents receive in-kind benefits in lieu of salary or wages. For example, a child support obligor who works at a resort may receive "free" lodging while so employed. This is a form of income to the obligor, but it is unlikely to appear on the obligor's paycheck. Such income usually falls within the state definition of income available for child support and consequently courts will ascribe or impute an amount of income to the obligor and base the child support award on it. Nevertheless, some benefits associated with employment are less clear. For example, the Supreme Court of Vermont affirmed that a tuition benefit flowing from a parent's employment at a private school was not gross income because it did not reduce the parent's living expenses. *Kelly-Whitney v. Kelly-Whitney*, 15 A.3d 138 (Vt. 2011).

Courts may impute income to obligors in circumstances where the court finds that the obligor is voluntarily unemployed or underemployed. This is a very fact-specific determination but courts typically examine factors such as the following:

> Oklahoma follows the rule that "equity will normally not favor reduction of a child support obligation where the parent's financial condition is due to his/her fault, or voluntary wastage or dissipation of his/her talents and assets." . . . Title 43 O.S. Supp. 2009 §118B (D)(2) specifically allows trial courts to impute income to a spouse in determining child support, if it is equitable. In doing so, courts may consider a number of factors: (a) "whether a parent has been determined by the court to be willfully or voluntarily underemployed or unemployed," taking into consideration the impact of additional training or education; (b) "when there is no reliable evidence of income"; (c) a parent's "past and present employment"; (d) a parent's "education, training, and ability to work"; (e) a parent's lifestyle; (f) a parent's role as caretaker of a handicapped or seriously ill child or relative of the parent; or (g) any additional factors deemed relevant to the particular circumstances of the case.

Parnell v. Parnell, 239 P.3d 216 (Okla. Civ. App. 2010).

REFLECTIVE QUESTIONS   In *Parnell*, the court lists a number of considerations for deciding whether to reduce a child support obligation. Are these fair considerations?

Background to *Carolan v. Bell*

In the following case, *Carolan v. Bell*, the Maine Supreme Court considers whether to impute income to a parent for rent, health benefits, and voluntary underemployment. The court explains factors typically considered in such situations.

CAROLAN
v.
BELL

Supreme Judicial Court of Maine
916 A.2d 945 (2007)

ALEXANDER, J. Carolan and Bell are the parents of a son, now seven years old. Carolan has no other children. Bell has a thirteen-year-old daughter from a previous relationship. . . . The court ordered shared parental rights and responsibilities. . . .

Carolan has a high school diploma and a technical school degree for work in a dental laboratory. In the past she has worked for various dental laboratories and has worked in the service industry. At the time of hearing, Carolan was working as a dental assistant and earning $13.50 per hour. Carolan's employer's office is closed on Fridays; therefore she works approximately thirty-three to thirty-five hours per week, Monday through Thursday. She then takes her son to school on Friday, a twenty-eight-mile trip, and typically volunteers at the school that day.

Carolan testified that her employer covers her health insurance costs, but because the health insurance premiums have risen, she has not received a pay raise in two years. She was unaware of how much her employer actually pays to maintain her health insurance. Carolan rents a small single-family home that is owned by her parents. She pays $1,000 per month in rent and pays for all of the utilities. Her oil bill for the 2005-2006 season was over $1,000. Carolan hopes to eventually purchase this home from her parents. Her parents previously rented the home for $1,300 per month.

Testimony indicated that Bell lives rent-free in a home owned by his employer, Bell Farms, which is his family's corporation. A real estate broker testified that the fair rental value of the property was $900 to $1,000 per month, although Bell claimed that it is much less. The corporation owns several vehicles that Bell uses for personal purposes. The corporation also pays most of his expenses, including his utility bills and insurance. Bell's employer also pays for his children's health insurance. Bell presented exhibits indicating that Bell's employer would pay $214.85 per month for a single person insurance plan and $386.73 per month for a parent and child(ren)'s plan. . . .

Carolan argued that her gross income should be her income that is reported on her W-2 and that the court should not impute any additional income to her. Bell argued that the court should impute additional income to Carolan for: (1) the difference between her rent and the rent charged the prior tenant; (2) the value of the health insurance that Carolan's employer pays for her; and (3) voluntary under-employment. The court adopted Bell's suggestions for imputing income in its findings and order addressing child support. This case requires us to consider the limits of a court's discretion to impute income to establish annual gross income for child support calculation purposes pursuant to 19-A M.R.S. §2001(5) (2006). When calculating gross income for child support purposes, the court may consider income from any "ongoing source." 19-A M.R.S. §2001(5)(A). The law authorizes the court to impute additional income in certain circumstances, such as when a parent is voluntarily unemployed or underemployed, 19-A M.R.S. §2001(5)(D), or when the parent, as an employee, receives in-kind payments or services, in lieu of wages, in the course of his or her employment, 19-A M.R.S. §2001(5)(B). . . .

A. INCOME IMPUTED FOR VALUE OF RENT REDUCTION

We have held that income from an "ongoing source" includes money received from educational grants for living expenses. . . . However, gross income does not include money received as a gift, where the donor has no legal obligation to continue "ongoing" payment. . . .

Here, the difference between the rent Carolan paid and the rent paid by the previous tenant cannot be considered income from an ongoing source pursuant to 19-A M.R.S. §2001(5)(A). Although her monthly rent may be $300 less than the previous tenant's, the $1,000 rent is hardly an insubstantial sum. There is no evidence in the record that Carolan's rent payments are significantly less than prevailing rental rates for similar properties in the area. Even if the record included evidence of a significant variance between actual rent paid and prevailing rates in the area, the court would be engaging in considerable speculation if it were to impute income, or loss of income, based on a finding that a particular rent payment was significantly more, or less, than the prevailing, or "economic," rental rate that should be assessed for a particular unit. Further, there is no evidence in the record that Carolan's parents have a legal obligation to continue the $1,000 per month rental rate. The court erred by imputing the value of the difference between Carolan's rent and the rent of the previous tenant in Carolan's gross income calculation.

B. INCOME IMPUTED FOR VALUE OF HEALTH INSURANCE

Gross income includes "income from an ongoing source, including, but not limited to . . . expense reimbursements or in-kind payments received by a party in the course of employment or self-employment or operation of a business if the expense reimbursements or in-kind payments reduce personal living expenses." 19-A M.R.S. §2001(5)(A)-(B). . . . In the present case, subsection (5)(B) provided the authority for the court to include the value of Bell's rent-free housing, use of vehicles, and other payments for his living expenses in calculating his gross income, because the value of these items was received by Bell in lieu of wages in the course of his employment and reduced his personal living expenses. Here, we need not address, as a general matter, whether a court may include the amount an employer contributes to an employee's health insurance plan when calculating gross income.

Carolan's testimony that she receives employer-paid health insurance in lieu of a wage increase supports the court's conclusion that the health insurance payments are "in-kind benefits" subject to imputation to gross income pursuant to section 2001(5)(B). This result provides similar treatment for Carolan's and Bell's employer-paid health benefits. Thus, the court did not err in its treatment of employer-paid health benefits to impute income to each party pursuant to subsection (5)(B).

While there was no evidence of the actual amount of Carolan's employer's health insurance payments, the court did not err in finding that the value of Carolan's health insurance benefits was $2,578. The court arrived at this amount by multiplying Bell's employer's monthly rate for single employees, $214.85, by twelve. Using this amount to infer the value of Carolan's employer's payments was reasonable and not an abuse of discretion.

C. INCOME IMPUTED FOR EIGHT ADDITIONAL HOURS OF WORK

Pursuant to the Child Support Guidelines, income may be imputed when a person is found to be underemployed, subject to conditions specified in section 2001(5)(D). Paragraph D states in pertinent part: "Gross income may include the difference between the amount a party is earning and that party's earning capacity when the party voluntarily becomes or remains unemployed or underemployed, if sufficient evidence is introduced concerning a party's current earning capacity."

The determination of whether a party is voluntarily underemployed is a question of fact that we review for clear error. . . . If a parent is voluntarily underemployed, the court's decision to impute income or apply the parent's earning capacity, rather than his or her current income, is discretionary. . . .

In this record, there is no dispute that Carolan's job is what would be considered full-time employment with benefits. Her employment as a dental assistant properly utilizes her education and experience. She works thirty-three to thirty-five hours per week, and works virtually all of the hours that are available from her employer. Her employer's office is closed on Fridays. Like many other employees in today's economy, she does not work a full forty-hour week. However, a person who works such a schedule is not thereby "underemployed" as a matter of fact or law for purposes of section 2001(5)(D). A parent who has a full-time job consistent with the parent's education and experience, but who works less than a forty-hour week, is not, thereby subject to having his or her income recalculated to a forty-hour per week equivalent for child support calculation purposes. Carolan's employment, although a few hours less than a forty-hour week, is consistent with her training and experience, and utilizes all available hours provided by her employer. The finding of voluntary underemployment was a clear error. Therefore, the court abused its discretion by imputing an additional eight hours of income to Carolan when calculating her gross income.

 **DISCUSSION QUESTIONS** **FOR** *CAROLAN v. BELL*

A. Although the dissent is not reproduced here, the dissenting judge argued that Carolan performed yard work and painting in return for receiving a reduction in rent. If this was the case, should the rent reduction be considered income?

B. With respect to the imputation of the value of the employer-paid health benefits, the dissenting judge stated: "I write separately on this point to note that there is no requirement that a party prove that, in the absence of the health insurance, the employer would have paid the employee compensation in an amount equal to the value of the benefit provided." Should such proof be required? Why or why not?

C. What argument can be made that Carolan's decision to work only four days per week is voluntary underemployment? Would the result have been different if her employer remained open on Friday? What if her employer decides to close on Thursdays as well?

D. The court states, "While there was no evidence of the actual amount of Carolan's employer's health insurance payments, the court did not err in finding that the value of Carolan's health insurance benefits was $2,578." Should there have been evidence about the value of the health insurance payments? Who had the burden of proof on this issue?

E. Should parents who stay at home with children or who cut back on work hours to care for children have income imputed to them? Why or why not?

8.12 LOW-INCOME OBLIGORS

Most low-income obligors are involuntarily unemployed or underemployed and state guidelines include adjustments or self-support reserves that apply to them. In such cases the guideline support amount may be reduced to allow a low-income obligor to meet his or her subsistence needs.

Some commentators express concern that low-income adjustments and self-support reserves can have a detrimental impact on children in need of support. *See* Stacy Brustin, *Child Support: Shifting the Financial Burden in Low-Income Families*, 20 Geo. J. on Poverty L. & Pol'y 1 (2013). Other commentators suggest that entry of a child support order that an obligee is unable to pay results in substantial arrearages and "insurmountable debt" that harms family relationships. Jacquelyn Boggess et al., *What We Want to Give Our Kids*, Center for Family Policy & Practice and Center for Community Economic Development 2-3 (2014), available at http://www.cffpp.org/publications/whatwewanttogiveour-kids.pdf (last visited July 2, 2015).

REFLECTIVE QUESTIONS	**How should policy makers balance children's need for support and the subsistence needs of a low-income obligor?**

8.13 JOINT PHYSICAL CUSTODY AND PARENTING TIME OFFSETS

As more parents share physical custody, courts and legislatures have considered how child support guidelines should be administered in situations where children spend substantial time with each parent. States have taken different approaches to adjusting child support amounts — some states provide parenting time "offsets" to guideline support and others allow downward deviations to the guideline amount.

The idea of reducing an obligor's payment based on time spent with children has been criticized because some expenses (other than food and utilities) are not linked to residential time. For example, items such as clothing, school supplies, sports equipment, and music lessons may be paid for by either parent, regardless of the amount of time spent with the child. Unfortunately, child support guidelines incorporating shared parenting offsets sometimes do not require any allocation of specific expenses between the parents. Stephen K. Erickson, *If They Can Do Parenting Plans, They Can Do Child Support Plans*, 33 Wm. Mitchell L. Rev. 827 (2007). In reaction to this concern, New Jersey views basic support as consisting of three parts:

> "[B]asic child support" consists of three consumption categories: (1) fixed expenses (representing 38% of the child support amount); (2) variable expenses (representing

37% of the child support amount), and (3) controlled expenses (representing 25% of the child support amount). "Fixed expenses" are those incurred even when the child is not residing with the parent. Housing-related expenses, like dwelling, utilities, household furnishings and household care items, are considered fixed costs. . . . "Variable costs" are incurred only when the child is with the parent. This category includes transportation and food. . . . The fixed and variable expenses must be met by both parents and each parent's responsibility is determined based upon their relative incomes and the time each spends with the child. . . .

"Controlled expenses," however, are different. These expenses include items like clothing, personal care, entertainment and other miscellaneous expenses. The Guidelines assume that controlled expenses are only incurred by the parent of primary residence. Accordingly, controlled expenses are apportioned between the parties based on their income shares, "not in relation to time spent with the children."

Wunsch-Deffler v. Deffler, 968 A.2d 713 (N.J. 2009).

Background to *Sanjari v. Sanjari*

The court in *Sanjari v. Sanjari* confronts a situation where the parents share joint physical custody of their two minor children and the court must determine child support. The father asserts that the trial court treated him as a visiting parent rather than a joint physical custodian when it came to calculating support.

SANJARI
v.
SANJARI

Court of Appeals of Indiana
755 N.E.2d 1186 (2001)

BAILEY, J. Amir and Alison were married on February 11, 1982. Two children were born of the marriage. On August 9, 1999, Alison petitioned for dissolution of the marriage. . . . On August 22, 2000, the trial court conducted a final hearing.

Alison and Amir agreed to a permanent award of joint legal custody and joint physical custody of their children, with each parent having the children in his or her care 50 percent of each two-week period of time. They also amicably agreed to a division of their personal property out-of-court. The remaining marital assets consisted of the marital residence, one vehicle, a pension, business equipment and cash. However, the marital debt substantially exceeded the value of the assets.

At the hearing, the parties disputed the value of the residence and the appropriate amount of credit, if any, to be allocated to Amir for anticipatory tuition payments to a private school that the children ultimately did not attend. At the conclusion of the hearing, the trial court ordered that the children remain in public school and allocated no credit to Amir for tuition payments. Amir was ordered to pay child support in graduated amounts of $175.00 and $215.00 weekly. The marital residence, valued at $90,000.00, was awarded to Alison and she was ordered to pay the first and second mortgages totaling $94,764.00. Purportedly, the property distribution resulted in a negative asset award to each party with Alison having the larger negative balance. No equalization order was entered. . . .

Amir contends that his child support order is erroneous because it incorporates a deviation from the Indiana Child Support Guidelines ("Guidelines") for visitation rather than contemplating his status as a custodial parent. Regarding child custody and child support, the Decree of Dissolution provides in pertinent part:

> The parties are awarded the joint legal and physical custody of the minor children, to-wit: [A.S.], date of birth October 8, 1988, and [M.S.], date of birth September 11, 1992. The court is of the opinion that the parties are able to agree on periods of custody for each parent which are approximately equal in time and that no order for visitation will be entered. . . .

Absent the shared custody of the children and based on the child support guidelines, the support obligation of the husband would be $221.00 per week, after granting the normal 10 percent credit for visitation (child support worksheet attached as Exhibit 1).

The court, because of the additional time spent with the children over and above the regular guidelines of the court, finds that a deviation from the guidelines is in order and now sets support to be paid by the husband at $175.00 per week beginning on June 16, 2000, and ending September 1, 2000. Beginning September 1, 2000, the husband's income increases to $83,000.00 per year ($1,596.00 per week), increasing the support, by chart, to $268.00 per week. Again, allowing credit for extra visitation, the court sets support to be paid by the husband at $215.00 per week beginning September 8, 2000. The thrust of the order is that Alison is treated as the custodial parent and Amir is treated as the noncustodial parent who exercises visitation. Such is contrary to the parties' agreement for joint physical custody, adopted and incorporated by the trial court into the Decree of Dissolution.

The Guidelines do not directly address the calculation of child support in circumstances where the parents have been awarded joint physical custody of their children. Nevertheless, in this situation we find instructive the following Commentary to Guideline 6 concerning split custody:

> In those situations where each parent has physical custody of one or more children (split custody), it is suggested that support be computed in the following manner:
>
> 1. Compute the support a father would pay to a mother for the children in her custody as if they were the only children of the marriage.
> 2. Compute the support a mother would pay to a father for the children in his custody as if they were the only children of the marriage.
> 3. Subtract the lesser from the greater support amount.
> 4. The parent who owes the greater amount of support pays the difference computed in step 3, above.

The practical effect on child rearing expenses where each parent has two children half-time would presumably be analogous to the effect on expenses where each parent has one child full-time, the situation described in the foregoing Commentary. However, we do not suggest that all other support calculation methods are foreclosed in joint physical custody situations. As the Commentary to Guideline 6 states "infinite possibilities exist in terms of time spent with each parent, travel between parents and other considerations."

Here, however, the record reflects that the parents spend equal time with their children and live in the same geographical area. Moreover, there is no testimony that either parent incurs extraordinary medical expenses or extraordinary expenditures on behalf of the children. Finally, the child support worksheets in the record reflect that neither parent has a legal duty of support for a dependent other than the children of this marriage. Under these circumstances, we remand for a calculation of child support obligations of both parents consistent with the methodology described in the Commentary to Guideline 6. . . . Finally, Amir claims that the trial court erroneously failed to recognize his payment of school tuition as the payment of marital debt. We disagree.

Generally, the marital pot closes on the date the dissolution petition is filed. Therefore, debts incurred by one party after the dissolution petition has been filed are not to be included in the marital pot. Here, the record reflects that Amir desired that the children be withdrawn from public school and enrolled in a private school. Amir, in his individual capacity, executed a contract for tuition payments after the date of separation. The children did not attend the private school at any time and the trial court ordered that the children were to attend Elkhart Community Schools in the future. We find no abuse of discretion in the trial court's refusal to include an individual contractual obligation, incurred after the date of marital separation, within the marital pot. We remand for recalculation of child support in light of the parties' joint physical custody award.

DISCUSSION QUESTIONS FOR *SANJARI v. SANJARI*

A. How much significance should be given to the label "sole physical custody"? For example, where the divorce decree provides that one party has sole physical custody of a child, should a court consider applying the formula developed in this case if the child spends 40 percent of his or her time with the noncustodial parent? What if the child spends 45 percent of his or her time with the noncustodial parent? Or 30 percent?

B. Should child support always be apportioned between parents according to the estimated percentage of time the child or children spend with each of their parents? Does such a system provide incentive for parents to seek additional time with children in order to make lower child support payments? Is this problematic?

What if the obligor who received a parenting time offset doesn't exercise all of his or her parenting time?

C. Mediators sometimes work with families to develop an agreed detailed budget for the children. The parents are asked to agree on a fair way to share the costs outlined in the budget, often based on their relative incomes. Then responsibility for specific expenses is assigned to each parent. Depending on the allocation of costs and the relative incomes of the parents, money may or may not exchange hands between them. How might such an arrangement be squared with existing child support guidelines? Should judges approve such agreements? What special findings might be required?

8.14 CHILDREN FROM OTHER RELATIONSHIPS (NONJOINT CHILDREN)

Situations where a parent has an existing support obligation for a child or children from another relationship present difficult decisions concerning the allocation of available support among them. States may give priority to the children of the original family by not reducing existing support awards when subsequent children are born, or states may equalize payments among children from both families:

> In practice, in calculating support orders for subsequent children under the "first family first" policy, judicial deference is ordinarily given to existing support orders for children born from prior relationships. As of 2004, at least forty state guidelines "provide that a parent's preexisting order is to be subtracted from the parent's income prior to the determination of support." . . .
>
> "Equalization," the second way to allocate child support among families, calls for "equal treatment of all the children of a particular parent" on the basis that "[h]ad the parents stayed together and produced additional children, there would have been adjustments and a likely reduction in the resources available for the first child."

Adrienne Jennings Lockie, *Multiple Families, Multiple Goals, Multiples Failures: The Need for "Limited Equalization" as a Theory of Child Support*, 32 Harv. J.L. & Gender 109, 140-141 (2009). Guidelines adjustments may be limited to prior-born children for whom a parent is paying support or encompass nonjoint children residing with the parent. Jane C. Benohr, *Child Support Guidelines and Guidelines Reviews: State Differences and Common Issues*, 47 Fam. L.Q. 327, 343 (2013).

| REFLECTIVE QUESTIONS | Is the "first family first" policy realistic? Are there fairness concerns for children born in the second family? |

Background to *Beck v. Beck*

In *Beck v. Beck*, a father seeks a downward departure from the guidelines because he is supporting two children from other relationships. The Maryland statute allows the court to consider obligations to other children as a potential reason to deviate from the presumptive child support amount.

BECK
v.
BECK

Court of Special Appeals of Maryland
885 A.2d 887 (2005)

MEREDITH, J. The father and the mother were married on May 29, 1992. During the course of their marriage, two children were born. The father and the mother were granted a judgment of absolute divorce on April 18, 2001. At the time of the divorce, the mother was awarded legal custody and primary physical custody of the two children, and the circuit court ordered the father to pay child support of $608.45 per month.

In addition to the two marital children, the mother has a 13-year-old minor from a previous relationship living in her household, and the father has a 16-year-old minor from a previous relationship living in his household. The father has a fourth child, born after the divorce, for whom he is paying $300 per month in child support. . . . During a hearing on November 1, 2004, the circuit court found that the father's child support obligation for his post-marriage child was not relevant because the child support guidelines allow a deduction only for pre-existing child support obligations. The circuit court entered an order dated November 4, 2004, in which the court, after finding that the guideline amount was $816.17 per month, departed downward from the guideline amount and ordered the father to pay child support in the amount of $700 per month. The circuit court justified its downward departure from the guideline amount with a conclusory finding that it was "because of the presence in the [father's] house of an older half-sibling whom he supports [that it is] in the best interests of [the Becks' marital children] that the [father] be able to adequately support the older half-sibling."

F.L. §12-202(a)(1) requires a court to use the child support guidelines "in any proceeding to establish or modify child support, whether *pendente lite* or permanent." As the Court of Appeals explained in *Petrini v. Petrini*, 336 Md. 453, 460, 648 A.2d 1016 (1994):

> The purpose of the guidelines was to limit the role of the trial courts in deciding the specific amount of child support to be awarded in different cases by limiting the necessity of factual findings that had been required under pre-guidelines case law. The legislature also intended the guidelines to remedy the unconscionably low levels of many child

support awards when compared with the actual cost of raising children, to improve the consistency and equity of child support awards, and to increase the efficiency in the adjudication of child support awards.

"There is a rebuttable presumption that the amount of child support which would result from the application of the guidelines . . . is the correct amount of child support to be awarded," F.L. §12-202(a)(2)(i), but that "presumption [of correctness] may be rebutted by evidence that the application of the guidelines would be unjust or inappropriate in a particular case." F.L. §12-202(a)(2)(ii); *Knott v. Knott*, 146 Md. App. 232, 251, 806 A.2d 768 (2002).

F.L. §12-202(a)(2)(iii) sets forth a non-exhaustive list of factors that may be brought to the circuit court's attention by the parent seeking to rebut the presumption of correctness of the guidelines, and provides: . . .

> (iii) In determining whether the application of the guidelines would be unjust or inappropriate in a particular case, the court may consider:
> 1. the terms of any existing separation or property settlement agreement or court order; . . . and
> 2. the presence in the household of either parent of other children to whom that parent owes a duty of support and the expenses for whom that parent is directly contributing.

Although the statute specifies that the circuit court may consider "the presence in the household of either parent of other children to whom that parent owes a duty of support," F.L. §12-202(a)(2)(iii)(2), the child support statute was amended in 2000 to further specify that this factor may not provide the *sole* basis for rebutting the presumption that the child support guideline is correct. F.L. §12-202(a)(2)(iv); *Gladis v. Gladisova*, 856 A.2d 703 (2004); *Lacy v. Arvin*, 780 A.2d 1180 (2001).

The statute also provides that if "the court determines that the application of the guidelines would be unjust or inappropriate in a particular case, the court shall make a . . . finding on the record stating the reasons for departing from the guidelines," F.L. §12-202(a)(2)(v), including, among other points, a statement that explains "how the finding serves the best interests of the child." F.L. §12-202(a)(2)(v)(C). . . . More specifically, F.L. §12-202(a)(2)(v) provides: . . .

> (v) 1. If the court determines that the application of the guidelines would be unjust or inappropriate in a particular case, the court shall make a written finding or specific finding on the record stating the reasons for departing from the guidelines.
> 2. The court's finding shall state:
> A. the amount of child support that would have been required under the guidelines;
> B. how the order varies from the guidelines;
> C. how the finding serves the best interests of the child; and
> D. in cases in which items of value are conveyed instead of a portion of the support presumed under the guidelines, the estimated value of the items conveyed.

As was stated in *Horsley, supra*, 132 Md. App. at 29, 750 A.2d 692, "[t]o justify a departure from the Guidelines, . . . more than the loose use of labels is needed."

In short, a downward departure is justified only when the circuit court finds that the guideline amount is unjust or inappropriate in a particular case. F.L. §12-202(a)(2)(ii). And even when the guideline amount is found by the circuit court to be unjust or inappropriate, the circuit court must also find, in writing or on the record, that the downward departure is in the best interests of the child receiving the child support. F.L. §12-202(a)(2)(v)(C).

As noted at the outset, the circuit court's findings in the Becks' case relative to the downward departure from the guideline amount were sparse, consisting of a comment on the record that "[the father] has the half-sibling of [the Becks'] children he is raising and I think it's in [the Beck children's] best interest that that child [*i.e.*, their half-sibling] should be supported in a reasonable manner." This finding satisfies neither the requirement of F.L. §12-202(a)(2)(iv) that there be a reason *other than* the presence of another child in the household, nor the requirement of F.L. §12-202(a)(2)(v) that the departure serve the best interests of the child who is receiving the support. The similar finding that was incorporated into the written order of November 4, 2004, suffers from the same deficiencies. . . .

In sum, the father had the burden to rebut the presumption that the guidelines amount of support was correct. Merely having two other children is not enough to rebut the presumption.

DISCUSSION QUESTIONS FOR *BECK v. BECK*

A. The court states, "And even when the guideline amount is found by the circuit court to be unjust or inappropriate, the circuit court must also find, in writing or on the record, that the downward departure is in the best interests of the child receiving the child support." How did the trial court justify the downward deviation? Did the court address the best interests of the child for whom the support was being ordered? Can you make an argument that the deviation was in the best interest of that child?

B. How should support be allocated among children? Should subsequent children be entitled to less support than prior-born children? In a part of the decision not included here, the court focuses on an argument made in a concurring/dissenting opinion in *Dunlap v. Fiorenza*, 738 A.2d 312 (1999), that subsequent children might require less support "when a family has one child, the family needs a place to live, including a bedroom for the child. If the number of children in the family increases, the family may still make do in the same living space by having the children share the bedroom and bathroom. Other costs, such as utilities, are also largely fixed, regardless of whether there is one child or more than one in the home." Do you agree? If a downward deviation is appropriate in cases involving a subsequently born child, should that policy be incorporated into the guidelines rather than being handled as a deviation?

C. As a matter of public policy, when do you think downward deviations from the presumptive child support amount should be allowed? For example, courts are generally disinclined to grant deviations because the obligor has debts. Should it matter if the debts are for medical bills incurred during the marriage or for an expensive new car? For what other reasons might an obligor seek a deviation?

8.15 DURATION OF SUPPORT: AGE, HIGHER EDUCATION, EMANCIPATION

Child's age. In most jurisdictions child support orders remain in force until a child turns 18 or completes secondary school, whichever occurs later. As discussed below, exceptions exist if the child becomes emancipated or goes on active military duty.

Higher education. Parents are not generally obligated to pay support for children over 18 who are enrolled in college, community college, or technical school. Some states prohibit courts from ordering support under these circumstances, but other states have statutes authorizing courts to order financial support for students participating in post-secondary educational programs. In states where courts cannot order educational support, settlement agreements incorporating provisions for support during post-secondary education may nevertheless be enforced as a contractual obligation. *See Ex parte Christopher*, 145 So. 3d 60 (Ala. 2013) (statute did not authorize court to order educational support for child over the age of 19); ALI, *Principles of the Law of Family Dissolution: Analysis and Recommendations* §3.12 (2002) ("Providing for a Child's Life Opportunities"); Ryan C. Leonard, *New Hampshire Got It Right: Statutes, Case Law and Related Issues Involving Post-Secondary Education Payments and Divorced Parents*, 4 Pierce L. Rev. 505 (2006).

Emancipation. The duration of child support may be limited or an existing order may be terminated if the child dies or becomes emancipated. A child may be considered emancipated in situations where the child marries, enters the military, gives birth, or cohabits outside of the parental home. *See* Chadwick N. Gardner, *Don't Come Cryin' to Daddy! Emancipation of Minors: When Is a Parent "Free at Last" from the Obligation of Child Support?*, 33 U. Louisville J. Fam. L. 927 (1995).

REFLECTIVE QUESTIONS	Do you think that states should mandate four years of continued child support if a child over the age of 18 is enrolled as a full-time student at an accredited college?

Background to *Oeler v. Oeler*

Decisions about the duration of support, especially with respect to emancipation, are quite fact-specific. In the case below, the Supreme Court of Pennsylvania considers whether a parent has a continuing obligation to support a high school student who chooses to live on her own against the wishes of her father, the child support obligor.

OELER
v.
OELER

Supreme Court of Pennsylvania
594 A.2d 649 (1991)

ZAPPALA, J. This appeal presents a question of first impression of whether a parent can be compelled to support a minor child who unilaterally chooses to reside in her own apartment.

As do most domestic cases, this one has a long court-related history beginning in 1974 when the parties separated and continuing since then with various support-related proceedings. At the time of separation, the parties had three minor children, two sons and one daughter. When this most recent controversy arose, both sons were in college and no longer the subject of the existing support order entered on April 1, 1975. Only Paula, age 17, remained a subject of the original support order which had been modified due to various changes in circumstances.

Although the record is void of any custody orders, it appears undisputed that at least prior to 1985, the father had primary physical custody of his daughter, Paula. Based upon this order, Paula lived with her father from January, 1985 through May, 1986. Because the father resided outside of the Allen High School jurisdiction, the father paid Paula's tuition to enable her to continue to attend that high school. Notwithstanding the existing order and without modifying that order, Paula moved back with her mother in June of 1986, where she remained until late December of 1987.

On or about December 29, 1987, the parties entered into a support stipulation, which was incorporated into an order of court of the same date. According to the stipulation, the father's support obligation for Paula was set at $900.00 per month retroactive to June 15, 1987. Furthermore, in accordance with the parties' stipulations, the court included the following provisions in its order of December 29, 1987:

1. Should actual physical custody of Paula Oeler change from the Plaintiff to Defendant or any third party in the future, this Order shall be automatically subject to review.
2. In the event that Paula Oeler shall no longer be in actual physical custody of the Plaintiff, the Defendant, Richard Oeler, shall begin immediately to pay $300.00 per month.

Apparently, on the same day the court was entering this modified support order, the mother was relocating to New Haven, Connecticut. Based upon this move and the fact that Paula no longer resided with the mother, on December 31, 1987, the father filed for a modification of his support payments in accordance with paragraph 2 of the December 29, 1987, Order of Court.

At some point prior to the mother's move, the father was advised by his daughter that her mother intended to relocate to Connecticut to pursue an internship at Yale University Art Gallery. The father then advised his daughter that she was welcome to reside with him in order to complete her high school education at Allen High School. During their conversation, Paula indicated to her father that she and her mother intended to make arrangements for Paula to live with a local family until graduation. Based upon this representation, the father indicated he would provide monetary assistance to the family that Paula resided with, so long as he deemed that family appropriate. When Paula and her mother were unable to secure a temporary living arrangement with a family in Allentown near the school, they unilaterally and without any notice or discussion with the father, entered into a lease for an apartment for Paula. Paula's apartment was a one-bedroom apartment in a three-apartment building in Allentown with a monthly rental of $335.00 per month. Thereafter, Paula's mother sought reimbursement of expenses incurred by Paula, from the father.

During the hearing, testimony was given by the parties and their daughter. All parties agreed that the father was willing to have Paula reside with him at his expense to enable her to complete her final year of high school at Allen High School. The mother testified that in good conscience she could not or would not force her daughter Paula to live with her father. To do so, the mother felt it would effectively be taking advantage of her daughter because by making this forced living arrangement, the mother would then be free to pursue her own goals or opportunities and that being her desire to receive an internship at Yale University Art Gallery. Paula testified that she did not want to live with her father because she and her stepmother did not get along. Specifically, her stepmother was "too neat" for her, which meant everything had to be "picked up and put away" which was contrary to her style of living. Although she also indicated that she wanted to live closer to her friends, she admitted that her father's house was only ten to fifteen minutes from her school by car.

Based upon this record, the trial court concluded that the father had made his home available to his daughter and that she had no justifiable reason for refusing to live with him. Furthermore, the court noted that the mother and daughter unilaterally made alternative living arrangements without any consultation with the father. [T]he trial court concluded that Paula's action in refusing her father's offer prevented her from reaping any financial gains.

At common law, the duty of a parent to support his child was conditioned upon a parent receiving love, affection and assistance from that child. Contrary to the common law, today, the duty to support a minor child is absolute.

It is quite clear from reviewing this record that the father is not refusing to support his daughter. Rather, he is refusing to allow his daughter to dictate the proper allocation of support monies. In other words, the father is willing to provide housing, food, clothing and an education for his daughter. The disagreement arises because

Paula wants to reside under her own roof at her father's expense. In granting the father's termination of support request, the trial court believed that Paula offered no justifiable reason for not living with her father. We agree. In essence, the best interest of Paula would not be served by permitting her to reside alone.

The decision of the trial court is reasonable and in complete accord with traditional values of child rearing. What the Supreme Court of Massachusetts cogently stated over a century and a half ago is still applicable today.

> Where a child leaves his parents' house, voluntarily to avoid the discipline and restraint so necessary for the due regulations of families, he carries with him no credit; and the parent is under no obligation to pay for his support.

Angel v. McLellan, 16 Mass. 28, 31 (1819). That Supreme Court further commented that to permit the minor, at his election, to depart from his parents' house, with power to charge that parent with his support, would tend to the destruction of all parental authority, and invert the order of family government.

[W]e can find no fault in the trial court's disposition of this matter. The trial court neither misapplied existing law or values nor exercised its judgment in an unreasonable manner. Accordingly, we must reverse the order of the Superior Court and affirm the order of the Court of Common Pleas of Lehigh County.

DISCUSSION QUESTIONS FOR *OELER v. OELER*

A. During the hearing, all parties agreed that the father was willing to have Paula reside with him at his expense in order to enable her to complete her final year of high school. What was the response of the mother to this offer? What was Paula's response?

B. The court states, "At common law, the duty of a parent to support his child was conditioned upon a parent receiving love, affection and assistance from that child. Contrary to the common law, today, the duty to support a minor child is absolute." What appears to be the difference, if any, between the common law duty to support a child and the court's view of the duty to support as it exists today? Was the duty to support in this case viewed as a conditional one?

C. The court ruled that the father was not obligated to pay child support because the daughter offered "no justifiable reason" for living by herself and because it was not in Paula's best interests to live alone. Do you agree with the court's analysis on this point? Are there justifiable reasons for not living with a parent, such that a court would impose a support obligation on the parent?

8.16 DURATION OF SUPPORT: ADULT CHILDREN WITH SPECIAL NEEDS

Background to *Haxton v. Haxton*

In some cases, child support is extended beyond minority if the "child" has special needs. For example in the case of *Gersten v. Gersten*, 219 P.3d 209 (Ariz. Ct. App. 2009), the court awarded continuing support for a disabled adult child under an Arizona statute authorizing support for a child whose disability began before the age of majority and who is unable to live independently and support him-or herself.

Nevertheless, continuing support is not always granted. For example, the Court of Appeals of Kansas did not extend beyond minority a parent's support obligation in a case involving a severely disabled 19-year-old with cerebral palsy, reasoning that the trial court lacked statutory or common law authority to make such an order. *Doney v. Risley*, 201 P.3d 770 (Kan. Ct. App. (2009).

The court in *Haxton v. Haxton* explores whether a father could be ordered to provide $225 in monthly support for a mentally handicapped son who was over the age of majority and was not attending school. In reaching a decision the judge reviewed the history and purpose of child support.

HAXTON
v.
HAXTON

Supreme Court of Oregon
705 P.2d 721 (1985)

ROBERTS, J. . . . The rights and responsibilities of family members toward each other are regulated by many of our statutes. Parental support obligations toward minor children after dissolution are addressed in ORS 107.095, 107.105, 107.108 and 107.135. The criminal code prohibits child abandonment and neglect by those adults, most often the parents, with a responsibility to maintain the child. Our laws punish a parent's failure to support a child financially. ORS 163.555. . . .

Of particular relevance to the present case is the development of two civil statutes, ORS 416.061 and ORS 109.010, both of which address the duty of close family members, defined differently in the two statutory schemes, to support indigent relatives. Both statutes set forth a similar duty of support. However, their historical antecedents, purposes and development indicate that these statutes were enacted to address separate social concerns. ORS chapter 416, the relative responsibility law, has its origins in the Elizabethan poor laws of 1601. These laws constituted one of the first systems of public welfare for the poor. ORS 109.010 represents private familial obligations that developed in America independently of England.

STATUTORY DUTY OF SUPPORT

The Elizabethan poor laws, including the provision requiring family members to support their needy relatives, provided a model for the systems of public support found in most American jurisdictions, including our own and those of New York. The Elizabethan poor laws came into being in response to the demise of the power and wealth of religious institutions, which ha[d] assumed the burden to support the poor, and the subsequent unrest manifested in widespread vagrancy and begging that unassuaged poverty engendered. Professor tenBroek writes that the poor laws culminated the process of shifting the burden to alleviate poverty "from the ecclesiastical, private and voluntary to the civil, public and compulsory."

In the Elizabethan system, support of the poor was achieved by taxation and was regulated at the county level. As a corollary, these statutes included features intended to reduce the burden on the public treasury. For example, the poor laws mandated forced labor at fixed wages for all paupers capable of working. They relocated the poor to the parishes of their birth and limited their mobility. They provided criminal sanctions for vagrancy, begging and refusing to work if able. Finally, they compelled financially able relatives to contribute to the support of family members who were public charges.

COMMON LAW DUTY OF SUPPORT

While it is doubtful that English common law recognized enforceable familial obligations of support apart from the Elizabethan poor laws, such was not the case in the United States. Early American cases recognized the parents', specifically the father's, duty to support his children. The duty of support, which was examined in a variety of contexts, was often said to exist as a matter of common law and independently of statute. . . .

Johnson v. Barnes, supra, made explicit reference to the difference between the English common law, which did not recognize a parental duty of support, and the American common law, which recognized such a duty. The court noted the uncertainty or nonexistence of the English common law duty but was "not prepared to say that this rule has been adopted in this country. . . ." 29 N.W. 759. *Gilley v. Gilley, supra*, acknowledged the minority American position, similar to England's, that no duty of support existed outside of statute but applied the "settled" state law that such a duty existed and was enforceable.

Plaster v. Plaster, supra, elaborated in dictum that the duty of support should also extend into the child's adulthood "if from physical debility and impaired health, the boy is unable to earn a livelihood, and must depend upon others for support. . . ." *Porter v. Powell, supra*, reasoned that the parental obligation of support is not grounded in the duty of the child to serve the parent but on the inability of the child to care for itself. Therefore, the parent has a "legal as well as moral duty" to support his child "when [she is] unable, from infancy, disease or accident, to earn her own necessary support. . . ." We have found no case squarely addressing the parental duty to support adult incapacitated children before 1854, the date of enactment of the predecessor to ORS 109.010. Whether the common law recognized a duty to support such children before this time is inconclusive. However, the language of the statute proposed in New York and adopted in this state indicates that "children" is not a term limited to those of minority age but rather connotes an ongoing relationship among family members. . . .

[T]wo separate duties of familial support appeared in the first code of Oregon. When the code commission presented its report on the draft code to the Oregon Territorial Legislature in 1853, the duty now found in ORS 109.010 was placed among the civil laws, and the relative responsibility law, now ORS 416.061, was set forth under the heading "Support of the Poor,". . . . The placement of two duties of familial support in different sections of the code, one public in nature, the other civil and private, mirrors the independent development of the duties of support in the United States. The relative responsibility statute, and the overall scheme of public support for the poor of which it is a part have been amended throughout the years but the basic premise that certain relatives are liable to relieve the public burden of support of the poor has remained unchanged. The obligation, originally enforced by counties, Statutes of Oregon 1854, p. 463, is now enforced by a state agency. ORS 416.100. The current relatives' responsibility statute is found under the Adult and Family Services title in the Recovery of Assistance Payments Chapter. ORS 416.061. The statutes reflect changes resulting from administrative expansion. However, despite the change in form and structure from the early Elizabethan poor laws, the purpose of relieving the burden for support of the poor through enforcement actions against relatives brought by the government on behalf of the public remains the same. . . .

From this background it can be seen that the parents' duty of support in ORS 109.010 stated a legal obligation recognized by many American states. To the extent that the duty derives from common law, it was capable of enforcement even before some states codified it. Oregon took over that codification in what is now ORS 109.010. Father argues that the legal obligation, standing alone, is not enforceable in the absence of explicit enforcement procedures and that enforcement procedures that exist now by statute limit the duty of support. This argument would only be correct if the legislature, when it enacted the obligation, prescribed a particular method of enforcement at the same time, or if the legislature later enacted enforcement procedures intended to be exclusive. . . .

Other states have recognized that the parental duty of support extends to adult incapacitated children. *Crain v. Mallone*, 113 S.W. 67 (1908), held that an incompetent adult son's share of his mother's estate should not be reduced by the amount of support his mother provided him during his majority. The court stated:

> The duty and obligation of a parent to care for his offspring does not terminate when the child arrives at age or becomes an adult; nor is it limited to infants and children of tender years. An adult child may from accident or disease be as helpless and incapable of making his support as an infant, and we see no difference in principle between the duty imposed upon the parent to support the infant and the obligation to care for the adult, who is equally, if not more, dependent upon the parent. In either case the natural as well

as the legal obligation is the same, if the parent is financially able to furnish the necessary assistance.

In *Schultz v. Western Farm Tractor Co.*, 190 P. 1007 (1920), the court upheld the amount awarded to an adult incompetent son for the wrongful death of his father, under the theory that the father owed a duty of support to his son so long as the son was disabled:

> Doubtless the legal duty of a parent to support his normal children ceases at the age of majority, but the rule is not the same with respect to his defective children, whether the defect be mental or physical. To these he owes a continuing obligation of support, which ceases only when the necessity for support ceases.

Similarly, in *Borchert v. Borchert*, 45 A.2d 463 (1946), the court indicated that the parents' duty of support extended to an adult handicapped child, but modification of a decree of child support was not the appropriate procedure by which to enforce the duty. In dictum, the court acknowledged:

> The doctrine of liability in a father to support an incapacitated adult child seems to have permeated the courts of this country, in many cases without any statutory enactment to support it. The obligation is set out in a great many cases, often in those judicial expressions known as obiter dicta. . . . However vague and unsatisfactory such statements are, it must be concluded, in view of the many decisions so holding, that there is now a tendency in this country, whether based upon local statutes or upon a modern judicial expansion of the common law, to recognize a duty imposed upon a parent to support his incapacitated child.

Prosser v. Prosser, 157 P.2d 544 (1945), is almost identical to the instant case. Mother sued on behalf of her 22-year-old incapacitated daughter for support from the child's father. The court granted relief, describing the action as one to enforce a common law duty of a parent to support and maintain his children. The court stated: "It is a generally accepted rule that where a child on becoming of age is in such a feeble and dependent condition physically or mentally as to be unable to support himself the parental obligations and duties toward such a child remain unchanged."

CONCLUSION

A duty of support appears among our earliest laws. No limitations were placed on the enforcement of that duty when it was first enacted, nor have any been imposed with subsequent amendments. We hold that a statutory duty of parental support exists and may be enforced in a direct action by this mentally handicapped adult child against his parent. The trial court below properly allowed the child to maintain an action against his father and awarded support.

DISCUSSION QUESTIONS FOR *HAXTON v. HAXTON*

A. The Elizabethan Poor Laws came into being in response to the declining role of what institution? How were the Poor Laws intended to reduce the burden on the public treasury?

B. On whom did the early common law place a duty of support? The court states that there is an explicit difference between the English and American common law majority rule when it came to a duty of child support. What is that difference?

C. On what basis did the common law consider extending a support obligation into a child's adulthood?

D. The father argued that the legal obligation to support his adult child, standing alone, was not enforceable in the absence of explicit enforcement procedures and that the existing enforcement procedures limited the duty of support. What was the court's response to this argument?

E. Assume that you represent the father in this case. What arguments would you make on his behalf? In this jurisdiction, must a parent support an incapacitated child for life? Should any aspect of this burden be shifted to the community?

F. What reasons justify the requirement that parents support minor children until they are adults? Does the same reasoning apply with respect to whether adult children should be required to support elderly parents who are "feeble and dependent"? Should filial responsibility laws be enforced as aggressively as child support laws? Why or why not?

G. Aside from a possible legal duty to support family members, what are the informal moral expectations of financial support in your family? How far do they extend? Are your obligations coterminous with the law or is more expected?

8.17 DEATH OF THE OBLIGOR

The duty to support minor children is not terminated by the death of the obligor. This policy recognizes that the child's need for support is in no way lessened by the death of a parent.

Section 316(c) of the UMDA provides that a parent's child support obligation is terminated "by the emancipation of the child but not by the death of a parent obligated to support the child. When a parent obligated to pay support dies, the amount of support may be modified, revoked, or commuted to a lump sum payment to the extent just and appropriate in the circumstances."

Under UMDA §316(c) the parties or the court may provide for the contingency of the premature death of the parent in the original decree. If this does not occur, the UMDA permits courts to modify support provisions after the death of the parent. In this way, the UMDA encourages divorcing parents to assure support for their children during their entire minority. UMDA Commissioners' Note to §316(c).

In practice, child support provisions often include the purchase of life insurance, the proceeds of which would be used to support the child in the event that the obligor dies prematurely.

REFLECTIVE QUESTIONS	Do you think that the duty of child support should continue beyond the death of the obligor? Why or why not?

8.18 TAX TREATMENT

The Internal Revenue Service does not consider child support payments as income to the recipient, nor are they viewed as allowable deductions from the payor's gross income.

8.19 BANKRUPTCY

Filing for bankruptcy protection does not allow a discharge of past-due child support obligations. Any past, present, or future payments owed for child support cannot be included as a debt and cannot be discharged in a bankruptcy proceeding.

REFLECTIVE QUESTIONS	Do you think that child support arrearages should ever be dischargeable in bankruptcy? Why or why not?

8.20 EQUITABLE ESTOPPEL: STEPPARENT OBLIGATION TO SUPPORT

At common law a stepparent had no duty to support stepchildren, and today a stepparent is not obligated to support a stepchild absent a specific statutory provision or very unusual circumstance. A few jurisdictions have imposed special support duties on a stepparent, although those duties end when the stepparent divorces the custodial parent. *See, e.g.*, Wash. Rev. Code §26.16.205, N.D. Stat. §14-09-09 (West 2015). Furthermore, the income of a stepparent is generally not considered when calculating child support under state guidelines.

REFLECTIVE QUESTIONS	**Why do you think that stepparents were not required to support stepchildren under the common law?**

Background to *Thacker v. Thacker*

Only a handful of jurisdictions have imposed duties on former stepparents on the theory of equitable estoppel. *See L.S.K. v. H.A.N.*, 813 A.2d 872 (Pa. Super. Ct. 2002). In *Thacker v. Thacker*, the former wife posits two theories, including an estoppel argument, with the hope of obtaining child support for her daughters.

THACKER
v.
THACKER

Court of Appeals of Missouri (2010)
311 S.W.3d 402

MITCHELL, P.J. Wife, a Russian school teacher, met Husband, a retired physician, over the Internet on November 30, 2005. The two communicated by Internet and then by telephone two to three times per week. In June of 2006, Husband traveled to Russia to meet Wife in person and to meet her daughters. Husband and Wife had discussed the possibility of marriage prior to Husband's arrival in Russia, and while he was there, he asked Wife to marry him. She accepted Husband's proposal because she loved him and thought that he would make a good husband for her and a good father for her daughters. Husband had also recently purchased a house, and he excitedly showed Wife pictures that he had taken of the house and of his car.

After Husband returned to the United States, he kept in contact with Wife over the telephone and the Internet. The e-mail messages that Husband sent to Wife professed his love for her and his excitement over the prospect of their becoming a family. One e-mail message sent in August of 2007 suggested that Wife would pick out a new Toyota Sequoia when she arrived in the United States and included photos of the vehicle in various available colors.

In January of 2008, Husband submitted Affidavits of Support to the Department of Homeland Security stating that Husband intended to contribute to the support of Wife and her daughters, that he would marry Wife and adopt her daughters, and that they would be a family. Husband also sent a letter to the American Embassy in Russia to facilitate Wife's visa. The letter stated his intention to marry Wife and provided financial information regarding Husband's assets and income. Husband suggested to Wife that she have her ex-husband sign away his parental rights to Wife's daughters to facilitate her visa.

Anticipating her move to the United States and her marriage to Husband, Wife sold her apartment in Russia, perhaps for a discounted price, and sold many of her possessions and several of her daughters' possessions. She wanted to be ready to leave Russia as soon as her visa was approved. After making travel preparations, Wife sent all of the remaining proceeds from the sale of her assets to Husband in the United States.

Wife and her daughters arrived in the United States at the end of January 2008. Wife and her daughters immediately moved in with Husband. Wife's daughters, ages thirteen and sixteen, were frightened to live in Husband's house because there was no solid fence around the house, as there apparently is around most Russian homes, and because they believed that they heard noises in the attic or outside of their windows.

Wife's youngest daughter, R.K., was particularly frightened and had trouble sleeping. Wife testified that in mid-February, R.K. asked whether she might come in and sleep in Husband's and Wife's bedroom. Husband agreed to allow R.K. to sleep with them, but only if she slept in the middle. At about four o'clock in the morning, R.K. awoke Wife and was visibly upset. R.K. reported to Wife that Husband had touched her inappropriately. Wife confronted Husband about the incident the next morning and he denied R.K.'s story, suggesting she had just had a bad dream. Husband assured Wife that, in any event, it would not happen again, and Wife decided to forgive Husband and give him another chance because she loved him and did not want to return to Russia.

Wife married Husband March 29, 2008, but the marriage was troubled. Wife testified that she did not like the way Husband spoke to her, Husband's frequent pornography viewing, Husband's constant demands for sex, the presence of Husband's loaded firearms in the house, and Husband's taking photos of her daughters. Husband testified that Wife was never happy, that she complained about the house, and that he was disappointed that Wife's interest in sex seemed to decrease after the marriage. He stated that he did not like the attitudes of Wife's teenage daughters and did not believe that they helped enough around the house.

On May 29, 2008, a Missouri Department of Social Services worker visited the Thackers' home because someone had reported the February alleged incident between Husband and R.K. An investigation was conducted and all family members were interviewed. Wife and the Social Services worker testified that the Social Services worker advised Wife that she should remove her daughters from the house immediately or that Husband should leave the house, but that the girls would not be allowed to stay in the home with Husband. Wife took the girls and moved into a shelter. A few days later Wife attempted to reconcile with Husband, but he refused and petitioned the court for dissolution of the marriage. Wife filed a counter-petition seeking spousal maintenance and child support on the theory that Husband's representations to the Department of Homeland Security in January of 2008 evidenced an express contract between Husband and Wife that Husband would provide financial support for Wife and her daughters and, arguably, that Wife and her daughters relied, to their detriment, on Husband's representations promising support, so that Husband should be estopped from denying any obligation to support them after the dissolution.

The trial court entered a judgment dissolving the marriage. At the time the judgment was issued, Wife had obtained a social security number and was employed as a teaching assistant, earning a gross monthly income of $1,058.21. The trial court found that when Wife accepted Husband's proposal of marriage in June of 2006, Husband had not made representations to Wife that he would adopt her children and treat them as his own. The trial court further found that neither Husband's affidavits of support submitted to the Department of Homeland Security in January of 2008 nor his letter to the American Embassy in Russia established the existence of an express or implied contract to provide support to Wife and her daughters in the event of the couple's divorce. As to Wife's estoppel theories, the trial court found that life for Wife and her daughters in Russia was difficult; that Wife had not received support from her ex-husband for her daughters; and that Wife and her daughters wanted to come to the United States and chose to remain. Thus, any reliance by Wife and her daughters on Husband's promises of support was not to their detriment.

Generally, a step-parent must provide support for his or her step-children so long as the step-children reside in the same house as the step-parent. §453.400.1. The obligation for the step-parent to provide support ends, however, when the step-children no longer live with the step-parent. Of course, a couple may contract to have child support continue even after the step-child no longer lives with the step-parent.

For Wife to establish that she and Husband expressly contracted for Husband to continue supporting Wife's daughters after he was no longer statutorily required to do so, Wife would have to have established that, in exchange for her promise to marry Husband, or for some other consideration, Husband promised to Wife that he would support her daughters, even if they no longer lived with him. Wife testified at the trial that she married Husband because she loved him and because she thought that he would make a good father and a good husband, and not specifically because Husband had promised to support her daughters. In fact, all of the evidence of Husband's promises or intentions that Wife provided to the trial court originated well after Wife had accepted Husband's marriage proposal. Therefore, we agree with the trial court's conclusion that Wife's agreement to marry Husband was not, in this case, consideration for an express contract for Husband's support of Wife's daughters. Point denied.

Wife's second point on appeal is that the trial court erred in failing to order child support for Wife's daughters based upon her theory of estoppel. . . . Our courts have held that support obligations may be imposed based upon an estoppel theory. Estoppel cases center upon promises of support made either directly to the children, or to the children's parent. To establish a claim for child support on an estoppel theory, Wife would have to have proven: (1) that Husband promised to support Wife's daughters; (2) that Wife (or her daughters) had relied on Husband's promise *to their detriment*; (3) that Husband expected or should have expected such reliance; and (4) that injustice resulted from the reliance that only enforcement of the promise could cure.

In *Stein*, 831 S.W.2d at 689, a couple had agreed to adopt a baby from Korea. The wife in the dissolution proceeding sought an award of support for the child from her husband based upon an estoppel theory. The Eastern District of this court held that, because the child was not worse off having been adopted by the wife and brought to the United States than she had been as an orphan in Korea, there had been no showing of detrimental reliance upon the husband's promises to support the child.

In this case, even assuming that Wife and her daughters had relied upon promises of support made by Husband in deciding to come to the United States, substantial evidence exists to support a finding by the trial court that such reliance was not to the detriment of either Wife or her daughters. Wife testified that her life in Russia was not easy. Although she owned an apartment in Russia, she had to work two jobs to support herself and her daughters. The girls' father did not contribute to their support, and at one time Wife had to sell some of her jewelry to provide for her daughters. Wife testified that her life in the United States was difficult also, yet she had made no attempts to return to Russia with her daughters despite having return plane tickets. On the contrary, Wife had hired an immigration lawyer to facilitate her staying in the United States, and one of her daughters testified at trial that she also wanted to stay in the United States. The trial court's conclusion that Wife failed to meet her burden with respect to her estoppel claim was supported by substantial evidence and was not against the weight of the evidence.

DISCUSSION QUESTIONS	FOR *THACKER v. THACKER*

A. Explain the Wife's express contract claim. Why did the lower court reject the claim?

B. Explain the Wife's estoppel argument. What elements did she need to prove?

C. On what basis does the court reject the Wife's estoppel claim?

D. Do you think this case was correctly decided? Why or why not?

E. As a matter of public policy, should states obligate stepparents to pay child support? Why or why not?

8.21 EQUITABLE ESTOPPEL: UNMARRIED SAME-SEX PARENTS

Background for *H.M. v. E.T.*

In the following case biological mother seeks child support from a former same-sex partner for a child conceived by artificial insemination. The court is asked to determine whether the doctrine of equitable estoppel could apply.

H.M.
v.
E.T.

Supreme Court of New York, Appellate Division
76 A.D.3d 528 (2010)

The petitioner, H.M., a Canadian citizen, and the biological mother of the subject child, filed a petition pursuant to the Uniform Interstate Family Support Act (Family Ct. Act art. 5-B), seeking to obtain child support from E.T., her former same-sex partner with whom she allegedly agreed to conceive a child through artificial insemination by donor (hereinafter AID), and upon whose promise of support she allegedly relied in so conceiving the child.

The doctrine of equitable estoppel has long been invoked to prevent a putative father, who has established a relationship with a child, from denying paternity in order to avoid paying support. . . . The " 'paramount' concern in such cases 'has been and continues to be the best interests of the child' " . . . Consistent with this principle, this Court has acknowledged that application of the doctrine of equitable estoppel would be appropriate, if determined to be in the best interests of the child, even under circumstances in which the child's "true paternity [was] not in issue."

Indeed, this Court and other courts have employed the doctrine of equitable estoppel, sometimes in conjunction with that of implied contract, to hold parties responsible for paying child support, not only in the absence of a biological or adoptive connection to the subject child, but in the absence of an established parent-child relationship, where those parties agreed either to adopt the child or to cause the child's conception through AID. This Court's decision in *Wener*, holding that a husband could be required, under the "dual foundation" of equitable estoppel and implied contract, to support a child whom he had neither fathered nor adopted (*Wener*, 35 A.D.2d at 53, 312 N.Y.S.2d 815), was later sanctioned by the Court of Appeals in (*Matter of Baby Boy C.*, 84 N.Y.2d 91, 101-103, 615 N.Y.S.2d 318, 638 N.E.2d 963). In permitting a husband to revoke his consent to joint adoptions of children already taken into his wife's care, the Court of Appeals, relying upon *Wener*, reasoned that "denial of the adoptions by [the husband][would] not leave the children or [the wife] as their guardian without recourse to an appropriate economic remedy."

Therefore, this Court has previously employed the "implied promise-equitable estoppel approach" . . . to preclude a man with no biological or adoptive connection to a child from disavowing a relied-upon, implied promise to support the child, thus preventing the man from leaving the child without the support of two parents, as originally contemplated. By parity of reasoning, we hold that where the same-sex partner of a child's biological mother consciously chooses, together with the biological mother, to bring that child into the world through AID, and where the child is conceived in reliance upon the partner's implied promise to support the child, a cause of action for child support under Family Court Act article 4 has been sufficiently alleged.

In accordance with the foregoing, we conclude that sufficient allegations have been raised in H.M.'s petition, warranting a hearing in the Family Court on the issue of whether E.T. should be equitably estopped from denying her responsibility to support the subject child.

DISCUSSION QUESTIONS FOR *H.M. v. E.T.*

A. In what other circumstances have courts in this jurisdiction applied the doctrine of equitable estoppel?

B. What arguments against application of the doctrine of equitable estoppel were likely made by the potential obligor?

C. Should courts require express written agreements to support in such cases? Why or why not?

D. Is this case distinguishable from the preceding case, *Thacker v. Thacker?* Explain.

General Principles

1. The common law accorded a child no legally enforceable support right.
2. Over the last century, states struggled to develop methods of calculating child support awards that are fair to both parents and provide sufficiently for the child.
3. Although the child support system is administered pursuant to state law, those laws and their enforcement have been substantially shaped by federal public welfare policy.

4. Both parents bear responsibility for support of live children while they are minors. In most jurisdictions child support orders remain in force until a child turns 18 or completes secondary school, whichever occurs later.

5. State guidelines constitute a rebuttable presumption that the amount of support awarded is correct. Although one or both parents can seek a deviation from the guidelines amount, courts rigorously apply them.

6. A majority of states use some form of the income shares model of calculation. Under the income shares approach, state guidelines dictate a support amount based on the combined incomes of the parents, and that amount is prorated between the parents based on the percentage of combined income attributable to each of them.

7. Some states use the percentage-of-income child support model where the non-residential parent pays a state-mandated percentage of his or her income for child support. The actual percentage of income paid varies depending on the number of children and the income of the obligor.

8. For the purpose of child support calculation, gross income usually includes items such as wages, tips, bonuses, profit sharing, investment income, deferred compensation, and severance pay.

9. At common law a stepparent had no duty to support stepchildren, and today a stepparent who has married a custodial parent but has not adopted the custodial parent's child is typically not legally obligated to support the child.

10. Some jurisdictions have held that children of unmarried same-sex couples have a right to support from both same-sex parents.

11. The Internal Revenue Service does not consider child support payments as income to the recipient, nor are they viewed as allowable deductions from the payor's gross income.

Chapter Problems

1. Most states do not impose a legal obligation to support stepchildren. From a public policy point of view, why do you believe that is the case? Can you make an argument that stepparents should have an obligation to support stepchildren with whom they reside? Would factors such as the length of the relationship, the age of the children, and the relative wealth of the stepparent make a difference under your analysis?

2. UMDA §309 provides that either or both parents can be ordered to pay a reasonable amount in child support based on the following factors: the child's financial resources; the financial resources of the parents; the standard of living the child would have enjoyed; and the child's physical and emotional needs. Assume that you are a judge applying UMDA §309 to the following situation (assume that child support guidelines have not yet been developed in your state). The parties have two children, ages 10 and 15. The parents agree that the father will have primary physical custody of the children. Under the definition of income available for child support in your state, the mother has $6,000 per month in income and the father has $3,000 per month in income. How much will you order the mother to pay in child support? Without discussing this problem beforehand, compare your child support award with one made by another student in the class. Are they the same or different? Why?

3. Describe three situations where, if you were a judge, you would grant a downward deviation in child support. List three situations where you would grant an upward deviation in child support. Do you think that any of these situations warrant incorporation into the child support guidelines, or should they be handled as deviations? Why?

4. Assume that Roger and Gail divorced and that Gail was ordered to provide support for their only child, Russell. Under state law, when Russell reached 18, Gail's support obligation would end. However, Roger asked the court to continue the child support and produced medical evidence that Russell suffered from a serious attention deficit disorder and dyslexia. An expert testified that Russell would need much more education in order to become self-supporting. Most likely, how will a court rule on Roger's extension request?

5. Assume that Alice and Tim divorce and Alice is the primary physical custodian of their son, Joe. Tim pays child support of $750 per month. Tim wins the lottery and is paid a lump sum of $50,000 after taxes. Alice seeks an increase in child support on behalf of Joe. What arguments will she make in support of the motion? What arguments will Tim make in opposition to the motion?

6. Assume that Maria and Carl are divorced and that they have two minor children. Maria is ordered to pay child support. During the summer she works at a resort making minimum wage. However, she is provided with lodging and two meals per day. Carl asks the court to impute the value of the lodging and meals. What will he argue? How will Maria respond?

Preparation for Practice

1. Locate the child support guidelines statute used in your state and answer the following questions:

   a. What model of calculating child support does it use?
   b. How is "income" for the purpose of calculating support defined?
   c. How is the issue of high-income obligors handled?
   d. How does the statute deal with children from prior relationships?
   e. How are child care expenses and medical support dealt with?
   f. Is there a parenting time offset and/or does the statute specifically address calculation in cases involving joint physical custody?

2. Create the facts for a hypothetical family and calculate the child support payment under the statute in your state.

3. Does your state have an online child support calculator? Try using it to calculate support for a hypothetical family.

4. The Elizabethan Poor Laws were an early attempt to establish a legal duty to financially support relatives who could not support themselves. Ever since their passage, debate has ensued concerning the extent to which parents and children have an obligation to support each other. Some 30 states have laws on the books that require adult children to support indigent parents. However, these filial responsibility laws are seldom enforced. *See* Seymour Moskowitz, *Filial Responsibility Statutes: Legal and Policy Considerations*, 9 J.L. & Pol'y 709 (2001). Further illustrating the link between support of family members and public assistance policy, some commentators speculate that state filial responsibility laws might be more aggressively enforced if the Medicaid program held adult children responsible for expenditures made on behalf of indigent elderly parents. *See* Shannon Frank Edelstone, *Filial Responsibility: Can the Legal Duty to Support Our Parents Be Effectively Enforced?*, 36 Fam. L.Q. 501 (2002). In sharp contrast, the duty of parents to financially support minor children continues to be the focus of intense scrutiny and activity. What are the policy pros and cons of enforcing statutes requiring adult children to support indigent parents? What is your opinion on the issue?

Chapter 9

Modification and Enforcement of Child Support

9.1 INTRODUCTION

This chapter focuses on two situations where courts become involved with child support issues after a final support order has been entered in a divorce or parentage action. The first part of the chapter considers the circumstances under which an existing child support order can be modified. The second part of the chapter explores efforts to enforce existing child support orders.

As you read, you may want to consider questions such as these: When can an existing child support order be changed? What legal standard would a court apply when requested to modify a child support order? What happens if an obligor fails to make child support payments? What enforcement options does the other parent have? What happens when an obligor who is in arrears resides in a different state?

> **REFLECTIVE QUESTIONS** What are your goals for this chapter?

9.2 MODIFICATION STANDARD: SUBSTANTIAL CHANGE IN CIRCUMSTANCES

Once child support has been established, unforeseen future developments may necessitate an increase or decrease in an existing order. As a general principle, jurisdictions modify child support orders when there is a substantial change in circumstances that makes the original award unfair or, in some jurisdictions, unconscionable.

If parents divorce when a child is young, the financial needs of the child and the circumstances of the parents are likely to change significantly before the child reaches majority. While most orders incorporate regular cost-of-living increases, future unanticipated changes may necessitate modification of an existing child support award. A substantial change in circumstances may be the result of fluctuation in a parent's financial situation, an increase in income, job loss, or a large inheritance. Modification may also be warranted, for example, when a child incurs major medical expenses or develops special needs.

	What are some unforeseen circumstances, in addition to those listed above, that may occur after entry of a child support order and lead to a request for modification?

9.3 MODIFICATION STANDARD: PRESUMPTION

Courts are available to assist parents in making needed child support modifications; however, they do not want to be besieged by such requests. Consequently, some states have adopted standards for modification that are quite stringent. For example, the Uniform Marriage and Divorce Act (UMDA) §316(a) provides that child support may be modified "only upon a showing of changed circumstances so substantial and continuing as to make the terms unconscionable."

Other states have adopted presumptions that come into play when modification is sought based on an obligor's increase in income. Typically, legislation provides that a change in income resulting in a 20 percent change in the child support order will be presumed to constitute a substantial change in circumstances sufficient to warrant modification of the current child support award.

REFLECTIVE QUESTIONS	Why might a legislature select the figure of 20 percent as the threshold change in income required to seek modification of a child support order? Why not 10 percent or 30 percent?

Background to *MacLafferty v. MacLafferty*

MacLafferty v. MacLafferty involves parents who have filed multiple post-decree actions concerning parenting time and child support. In this instance the court is required to interpret and apply a child support modification statute, and in so doing, the court considers the legislative history of the provisions.

MacLAFFERTY
v.
MacLAFFERTY

Supreme Court of Indiana
829 N.E.2d 938 (2005)

SULLIVAN, J. The marriage of William P. MacLafferty ("Father") and Donna J. MacLafferty ("Mother") was dissolved on June 30, 1995. Physical custody of the couple's two children was awarded to Mother. Since then, Mother and Father have been back to court a number of times with disputes over child support, parenting time, and other issues. In the proceeding immediately prior to the litigation at hand, Father's prior child support obligation of $406 per week was modified by court order dated April 17, 2002, to $364 per week plus six percent of any bonus income earned.

Father filed a petition to modify the April 17, 2002, order on October 28, 2002, requesting that his support obligation be decreased because Mother had obtained full-time employment, and her income had increased. According to the trial court, obtaining full-time employment caused Mother's income for child support purposes to increase from $324 per week ($16,848 annualized) to $709 ($36,868 annualized). Father's income for child support purposes also increased during this time period, from $2,287 per week ($118,924 annualized) to $2,407 ($125,164 annualized); none of these amounts include bonuses.

Father's petition also sought changes in parenting time and the treatment of the children's summer camp expenses and requested that Mother be directed to comply with various provisions of prior court orders concerning parenting time.

After a hearing on April 14, 2003, the court granted Father's petition on July 10, 2003. The court's order reduced Father's child support obligation to $313 per week (plus 6% of any bonus income earned), a 14% reduction from the previous amount, and granted Father the other relief he sought with respect to parenting time (including the directives to Mother relating to compliance) and children's summer camp expenses. Mother appealed, but the Court of Appeals affirmed. . . .

Our review of the support modification order at issue here is controlled by Indiana Code Section 31-16-8-1. In relevant part, the statute provides:

> Provisions of an order with respect to child support . . . may be modified or revoked. . . . [M]odification may be made only:
> (1) upon a showing of changed circumstances so substantial and continuing as to make the terms unreasonable; or
> (2) upon a showing that:
> (A) a party has been ordered to pay an amount in child support that differs by more than twenty percent (20%) from the amount that would be ordered by applying the child support guidelines; and
> (B) the order requested to be modified or revoked was issued at least twelve (12) months before the petition requesting modification was set.

Ind. Code §31-16-8-1 (2004). While the statute presents alternative methods of seeking modification—compliance with Subsection (1) or, in the alternative, compliance with Subsection (2)—only Subsection (1) is available to Father here. This is because the amount that Father would be ordered to pay applying the Indiana Child Support Guidelines, Ind. Child-Support Guideline 3 (West 2003), differed by less than 20% (in fact, as noted above, only 14%).

Father had the burden here of establishing changed circumstances so substantial and continuous as to make the terms of the April 17, 2002, order unreasonable. . . . The trial court found that burden satisfied and ordered a reduction in Father's support obligation as well as granting the other relief requested. Father now characterizes Mother's appeal as a "thinly veiled attempt to convince this court to reweigh the evidence and to substitute its judgment for that of the trial court."

We begin this review with some reflections on the legislative history of Indiana Code section 31-16-8-1. From its original enactment in 1973 until 1997, the statute consisted only of the substance of current subsection (1), *i.e.*, it permitted modifications only where the requisite "changed circumstances" showing was made. It had long been held that this provision demonstrated the Legislature's determination to limit the "vexatious litigation which accompanies the dissolution of a marriage." *Lankenau v. Lankenau*, 365 N.E.2d 1241, 1244 (1977). Effective July 1, 1997, the Legislature added Subsection (2), thereby providing an entitlement to modification where the two specific, bright-line requirements—the 20% change and 12-month time period—have been met. 1997 Ind. Acts 1 §8.

Our interpretation of the Legislature's action in 1997 is that it wanted to provide a bright-line for parents and for courts as to when a parent would be entitled to modification in his or her child support obligation solely on grounds of change in income. The Legislature seems to be saying that if more than a year had passed since the last modification, and one parent's income has changed so much that his or her obligation under the Child Support Guidelines would change by 20%, a parent is entitled to modification. The Legislature left in place the opportunity for a parent to request modification at any time and for any reason so long as—but only if—the parent could show changed circumstances "so substantial and continuing as to make the terms [of the prior order] unreasonable." Ind. Code §31-16-8-1(1) (2004).

In addition to providing a bright-line test for a parent who seeks modification solely on grounds of change in income, it seems to us that, as a practical matter, the Legislature has effectively established a bifurcated standard for modification, Subsection (2) covering situations where a parent seeks modification solely on grounds of change in income and Subsection (1) covering all other situations (including situations alleging a change in income and one or more other changes). It is true that, as a matter of pure logic, a parent could seek modification solely on grounds of change in income under Subsection (1)—indeed, Father does so here. But we do not believe that the Legislature would consider a change in circumstances standing alone (*i.e.*, without any other change in circumstances) that would change one parent's child-support payment by less than 20% to be "so substantial and continuing as to make the terms [of the prior order] unreasonable." Indeed, it is hard to see the reason the Legislature would have enacted subsection (2) at all if a parent could receive a modification under Subsection (1) where the only changed circumstance alleged would change one parent's payment by less than 20%. Nevertheless, we do not hold that a modification may never be made . . . under subsection (1) where the changed circumstance alleged is a change in one parent's income that only changes one parent's payment by less than 20%. There may be situations where a variety of factors converge to make such a modification permissible under the terms of the statute. While we do not find this case to be such a situation, we do not foreclose such a possibility.

The trial court here concluded "that Mother's change to full-time employment and the increase in her income attributable thereto constitutes a substantial and continuing change of circumstances sufficient to find that the previous Court Order regarding Support and Visitation is now unreasonable." Appellate review is facilitated when trial courts state the reasons for their decisions but the trial court here did not give any explanation as to why it considered this change to have been "so substantial" (or, for that matter, "continuing") that the terms of its previous order had been rendered unreasonable. We do not find it to have been so. Mother's income did increase as a result of her becoming employed on a full-time basis, but the increase only amounted to $375 per week during a period of time when Father's weekly income increased $120 (not including any bonuses that he earned of which 6% were to be paid in child support). Even after the change here, Mother's income was quite modest compared to Father's: Father's income (excluding bonuses) was approximately 3-1/4 times that of Mother. We hold that the change alleged here was not so substantial as to render the terms of the prior order unreasonable.

Father identifies two cases that he says stand for the proposition "that changes in the relative financial resources of both parents alone may be sufficient to modify a child support order." *Harris v. Harris*, 800 N.E.2d 930, 938 (Ind. Ct. App. 2003), *transfer denied*, 812 N.E.2d 798 (2004). That proposition is true, of course, only when the changes are so substantial and continuing as to render the terms of the prior support order unreasonable. The two cases Father cites each involve changes far more substantial than the one before us. In the first, the changed circumstances included the facts that Father had lost a very lucrative job; successfully sued his former employer; and relocated to Colorado where he secured another very lucrative position. In addition, Mother, who apparently did not have regular employment at the time the prior support order was entered, had secured a regular position, working out of her home, for an annual salary of $90,000 (plus a $500 monthly car allowance). *Id.* In the second case, the changed circumstances included the facts that Mother had become employed on a full-time basis "significantly" increasing her income while Father's income had significantly declined. In addition, of the couple's three children in Mother's custody at the time the prior support order was entered, one had become emancipated and another lived with Father. *Kirchoff v. Kirchoff*, 619 N.E.2d 592, 596 (Ind. Ct. App. 1993). We find no support for Father's claim in either of these cases.

Having previously granted transfer, thereby vacating the opinion of the Court of Appeals, we now reverse the trial court; vacate the provisions of its order dated July 10, 2003, reducing Father's child support payment; and order that Father's child support payment be restored to $364 per week (the amount established by the trial court in its April 17, 2002, order), effective July 10, 2003.

<table>
<tr><td>**DISCUSSION QUESTIONS**</td><td>FOR *MacLAFFERTY v. MacLAFFERTY*</td></tr>
</table>

A. The court believes that the legislature added two "bright-line" requirements in an effort to curb "vexatious litigation." What were the two requirements? Do you think that these requirements will reduce post-decree litigation? Why or why not?

B. When would subsection (1) of the statute providing for modification "upon a showing of changed circumstances so substantial and continuing as to make the terms unreasonable" apply? List three examples of changes where this court might approve modification under subsection (1).

C. The court notes that "Mother and Father have been back to court a number of times with disputes over child support, parenting time, and other issues." Assume that the father contacts you to represent him in another post-decree matter, how would you counsel him? Will you suggest filing another action in court?

9.4 MODIFICATION APPLICATIONS: CHANGE IN EMPLOYMENT

In some situations where there is arguably a change in circumstances, a court may nevertheless refuse to modify a support obligation. For example in *Steele v. Neeman*, 206 P.3d 384 (Wyo. 2009), the Supreme Court of Wyoming held that a poor relationship between a child and his father, which included lack of visitation, was not sufficient reason to modify a support order. The court concluded as follows: "A parent is supposed to be a 'financial resource' for his/her child. It is a responsibility of parenthood. This responsibility exists regardless of visitation or negative feelings between a parent and child." *Id.* at 388. In *Lazenby v. Bunkers*, 2010 WL 2634743 (Ohio App. 2010), the Court of Appeals of Ohio determined that the wife's remarriage "to a man of substantial means" did not constitute a substantial change in circumstances because there remained a continuing disparity between the incomes of the parents.

Courts scrutinize situations where an obligor becomes voluntarily unemployed or willingly assumes a lower-paying position. Courts are concerned about the financial repercussions for the child and whether the change is motivated by an obligor's desire to avoid paying support. For example in the case of *Adams v. Adams*, 2010 WL 1997774 (Ark. App. 2010), an obligor resigned his appointment as a college English professor in order to attend law school. The trial court judge did not take evidence but nevertheless concluded that "he knew of no basis in the law that would allow the court to excuse a parent's child-support obligations because a parent quit his or her job 'to do something different.'" *Id.* However, on appeal the case was reversed and remanded so a determination could be made concerning whether the obligor's decrease in income was "due to the fault, voluntary wastage, or dissipation of one's talents or assets." *Id. But see Olson v. Mohammadu,* 81 A.3d 215 (Conn. 2013) (income reduction associated with father's voluntary relocation to be near child could constitute change in circumstances for child support modification).

REFLECTIVE QUESTIONS Is a child support obligor who quits a part-time job at a fast food restaurant to enroll in law school underemployed? Should the obligor's child support payment be reduced while the obligor attends law school?

Background to *In re Little*

In the next case, *In re Little,* the court considers whether an obligor's voluntary decision to leave his employment to become a full-time student constitutes a change in circumstances sufficient to warrant a downward modification of child support. The court analyzes problems associated with use of the "good faith" test.

IN RE LITTLE
Supreme Court of Arizona
975 P.2d 108 (1999)

McGREGOR, J. The parties divorced in November 1995. The court ordered appellant Billy L. Little, Jr., an Air Force lieutenant, to pay $1,186 per month for the support of his two young children. In August 1996, appellant resigned his commission in the Air Force, a position that paid $48,000 in yearly salary plus benefits, and chose to enroll as a full-time student at Arizona State University College of Law rather than to seek employment.

Upon leaving the Air Force, appellant petitioned the court to reduce his child support obligation to $239 per month. The trial court concluded that appellant had failed to prove a substantial and continuing change of circumstances in accordance with Arizona Revised Statutes (A.R.S.) §25-327.A and 25-503.F, and denied his request for modification. The trial court specifically found that appellant voluntarily left his employment to further his own ambition; that he failed to consider the needs of his children when he made that decision; and that to reduce his child support obligation would be to his children's immediate detriment and their previously established needs. The trial court did reduce appellant's child support obligation to $972 per month on the ground that appellee Lisa L. Little had acquired a higher paying job. The court of appeals, applying a good faith test to determine whether appellant acted reasonably in voluntarily leaving his employment, held that the trial court abused its discretion in finding that appellant's decision to terminate his employment and pursue a law degree was unreasonable. . . .

A number of other jurisdictions have considered the issue that confronts us. Courts in sister jurisdictions have applied one of three tests to determine whether to modify a child support order when a parent voluntarily terminates his or her employment. The first of these tests, the good faith test, "considers the actual earnings of a party rather than his earning capacity, so long as" he or she acted in good faith and not "primarily for the purpose of avoiding a support obligation" when he or she terminated employment. The second test, designated the strict rule test, "disregards any income reduction produced by voluntary conduct and looks at the earning capacity of a party in fashioning a support obligation." The third test, referred to as the intermediate test, balances various factors to determine "whether to use actual income or earning capacity in making a support determination." Each of the tests evidences its own strengths and weaknesses, and each reflects the public policy of its adopting jurisdiction.

Other jurisdictions have detected three fundamental flaws in the good faith test, which assigns the highest value to the obligor parent's individual freedom of choice. First, the test erroneously "assumes that a divorced or separated party to a support proceeding will continue to make decisions in the best overall interest of the family unit," when often, in fact, the party will not. Second, the test fails to attach sufficient importance to a parent's existing obligation to support his or her children. As one court explained, the good faith test allows a parent to be "free to retire, take a vow of poverty, write poetry, or hawk roses in an airport, if he or she sees fit," provided only that his or her motivation for acting is not to shirk a child support obligation. Third, once the party seeking a downward modification provides a seemingly good faith reason for leaving employment, the burden of proof often shifts to the party opposing the reduction to then show that the reason given is merely a sham. Even if the burden of proof does not shift, the trial court is still left with the difficult task of evaluating a party's subjective motivation. While all those factors influence our decision to reject the good faith test, we regard the primary shortcoming of the good faith test as being its focus upon the parent's motivation for leaving employment rather than upon the parent's responsibility to his or her children and the effect of the parent's decision on the best interests of the children.

The strict rule test also contains a fatal flaw. This test is too inflexible because it considers only one factor, the parent's earning capacity, in determining whether to modify a child support order when a parent voluntarily leaves employment. We decline to adopt the strict rule test because it allows no consideration of the parent's individual freedom or of the economic benefits that can result to both parent and children from additional training or education.

We reject both these extreme approaches and instead adopt an intermediate balancing test that considers a number of factors, consistent with A.R.S. §25-327.A, 25-503.F, 25-501.C, and the Guidelines. Arizona law prescribes that "the obligation to pay child support is primary and other financial obligations are secondary." A.R.S. §25-501.C. Thus, the paramount factor a trial court must consider in determining whether a voluntary change in employment constitutes a substantial and continuing change in circumstances sufficient to justify a child support modification is the financial impact of the parent's decision on the child or children the support order protects. If a reduction in child support due to a noncustodial parent's voluntary decision to change his or her employment status places a child in financial peril, then the court generally should not permit a downward modification.

In many instances, the impact on the children will not be so severe as to place the children in peril. In those circumstances, courts must consider the overall reasonableness of a parent's voluntary decision to terminate employment and return to school. The answers to several questions will provide relevant information. The court should ask whether the parent's current educational level and physical capacity provide him or her with the ability to find suitable work in the marketplace. If so, the decision to leave employment is less reasonable. See *Patterson v. Patterson*, 432 P.2d 143, 148 (1967) (refusing to reduce a father's child support award on the grounds that "no showing was made that he lacked the ability or capacity to work" and because a father's obligation to his children "cannot be diminished because he preferred to be idle rather than industrious or [that] . . . his own improprieties caused a diminution in his medical practice income"). In contrast, answers to other questions make the parent's decision to leave employment more reasonable. If the additional training is likely to increase the parent's earning potential, the decision is more likely to be found reasonable. See Guidelines 4.e.2; see also *Rubenstein v. Rubenstein*, 655 So. 2d 1050, 1052 (Ala. Civ. App. 1995) (holding that the trial court did not abuse its discretion in failing to impute additional income to a father who, while completing a residency program that would increase his future income potential, continued to fulfill his current support obligation). The court should also consider the length of the parent's proposed educational program, because it matters whether the children are young enough to benefit from the parent's increased future income. See *Overbey v. Overbey*, 698 So. 2d 811, 815 (Fla. 1997) (considering as a factor in its refusal to reduce a father's child support obligation the fact that "the older child will reach majority before the father finishes school" and the younger child will do so "only a few years thereafter"). The court also should inquire whether the parent is able to finance his or her child support obligation while in school through other resources such as student loans or part-time employment. See *Baker v. Grathwohl*, 646 N.E.2d 253, 255 (Ohio App. 1994) (discussing the fact that the trial court was not convinced that the obligor father would not be able to obtain part-time employment during law school). Finally, the court should consider whether the parent's decision is made in good faith, as a decision to forego [*sic*] employment and return to school usually will not be reasonable or made in good faith if the parent acts to avoid a child support obligation.

We do not intend to suggest that the factors listed above are exhaustive of the relevant areas of inquiry. The primary task for a trial court is to decide each case based upon the best interests of the child, not the convenience or personal preference of a parent. We believe the balancing test described above comports not only with Arizona's public policy, but also with a national policy trend that favors strictly enforcing child support obligations. Several states, including Alabama, Florida, Maine, Montana, New Mexico, Ohio, and Virginia, recently have held that a parent's voluntary return to school does not justify a downward modification of his or her child support obligation. Moreover, the federal government has passed laws recognizing that the duty to support one's children is paramount. For instance, federal bankruptcy law excepts debts "to a child of the debtor, for support of such child, in connection with a separation agreement, divorce or other order of a court of record" from discharge in bankruptcy proceedings. Recently enacted federal criminal legislation provides that a parent who "wilfully fails to pay a support obligation with respect to a child who resides in another State shall be punished" by fine and/or up to six months imprisonment for the first offense, and by fine and/or up to two years imprisonment for subsequent offenses. 18 U.S.C.A. §228 (West Supp. 1998). In addition, Congress authorized the Bureau of Justice Assistance to provide grants to states "to develop, implement, and enforce criminal interstate child support legislation and coordinate criminal interstate child support efforts." 42 U.S.C.A. §3796cc (West 1994). The court of appeals, rather than look to this development in public policy, instead relied upon a forty-year-old decision, *Nelson v. Nelson*, 357 P.2d 536 (Ore. 1960), to support its holding. In *Nelson*, the court held that a father "may in good faith make a change in occupation, fully aware that the change will reduce his ability to meet his financial obligations to his children."

We reject the reasoning of *Nelson* for several reasons. First, its holding elevates a parent's wishes and financial status above the best interests of his children. Second, the decision clearly contradicts our state legislature's statutory mandate that "the obligation to pay child support is primary and all other financial obligations are secondary." A.R.S. §25-501.C. Moreover, we disagree with the notion that attending school full-time and fulfilling one's child support obligation are mutually exclusive options, given that a divorced or separated parent can fill income gaps by participating in student financial aid programs and/or obtaining part-time employment. The court of appeals erred when it relied on *Nelson*.

Applying the balancing test to the facts involved here, we conclude that the trial court did not abuse its discretion when it refused appellant's request for a downward modification of his child support obligation.

 **DISCUSSION QUESTIONS**   **FOR *IN RE LITTLE***

A. The court discusses three tests that are used to determine whether to modify a child support order when a parent voluntarily terminates employment. What are the three tests?

B. What problems does the court discuss with respect to each of the tests? Which of the three possible tests do you believe is the most appropriate for use in most child support modification disputes?

C. Which test does the court adopt? Why?

D. The court discusses the case of *Nelson v. Nelson*. On what basis does the court reject the reasoning in that case?

E. The ALI provides that income should not be imputed if a parent's unemployment or underemployment is the result of a parent's "pursuit of education, training, or retraining in order to improve employment skills so long as the pursuit is not unreasonable in light of the circumstances and the parent's responsibility for dependents." American Law Institute, *Principles of the Law of Family Dissolution: Analysis and Recommendations* §3.14(5)(a) (2002). How does this standard differ from those discussed in this case?

F. Similar imputation questions arise when an obligor becomes unemployed. If you were a judge presented with a request for a downward deviation due to an obligor's unemployment, would it matter to you why the obligor became unemployed? What if the obligor was laid off? What if the obligor was injured and could no longer perform the same job? What if the obligor was very unhappy in his or her current position? What if the obligor retired? Are any of the three tests discussed in *In re Little* relevant to your analysis?

9.5 MODIFICATION: ORAL AGREEMENTS, RETROACTIVITY

Background to *Hunt v. Hunt*

In many cases, parents agree to child support modifications. Nevertheless, parental modification agreements are subject to approval by the court, and they are not enforceable until his occurs. Modifications are typically made retroactive only to the date of service of the motion for modification. In the following case, the parties made an oral agreement modifying child support but no subsequent court action was undertaken to make it enforceable.

HUNT
v.
HUNT

Court of Appeals of Oregon
242 P.3d 682 (2010)

BREWER, C.J. The parties' marriage was dissolved in April 2000. The dissolution judgment required husband to pay the unsegregated sum of $392 per month in child support for the parties' two minor children. The parties' son died in July 2002 at the age of nine. The parties thereafter reached an oral agreement to reduce husband's support obligation for the parties' surviving daughter to $200 per month. However, that agreement was never formally documented or reduced to the form of a judgment modifying the dissolution judgment. Thus, the obligation of $392 per month continued to accrue. . . . Father appears *pro se* on appeal, and some of his arguments are less clear than we would prefer. . . . Unfortunately for father, the trial court correctly denied his request for relief from the arrearage claim in the two primary respects that he urges on appeal. ORS 107.135 provides, in part:

> (6) Any modification of child or spousal support granted because of a change of circumstances may be ordered effective retroactive to the date the motion for modification was served or to any date thereafter.
> (7) The judgment is final as to any installment or payment of money that has accrued up to the time the nonmoving party, other than the state, is served with a motion to set aside, alter or modify the judgment. The court may not set aside, alter or modify any portion of the judgment that provides for any payment of money, either for minor children or for the support of a party, that has accrued before the motion is served. . . .

Father did not file and serve a motion to modify the child support obligation before the parties' daughter reached age 18. Accordingly, the court had no authority to enforce the parties' oral agreement to reduce the support obligation to $200 per month. ORS 107.135(6), (7); *see also Thomsen and Thomsen*, 167 Or. App. 218, 223, 2 P.3d 432 (2000) ("[I]t is well settled that we may modify support awards for minor children only from the date of the motion for modification forward; all amounts previously in arrears have become judgments and may not be modified, except in very narrow circumstances not at issue here.").

DISCUSSION QUESTIONS FOR *HUNT v. HUNT*

A. Why do you think that courts decline enforcement of oral agreements to modify child support? What might happen if they did otherwise? Did the mother deny the existence of the oral agreement in this case? Do you think it should have been enforced?

B. Why might states adopt statutory provisions limiting the retroactivity of modifications of child support?

C. The court states that the father was ordered to pay the "unsegregated sum of $392 per month in child support for the parties' two minor children." What is the significance of the fact that the award was unsegregated? Would the result in this case have been different if the awards for the two children were segregated? Why or why not?

D. The court notes that "Father appears *pro se* on appeal, and some of his arguments are less clear than we would prefer." The number of unrepresented parties in family court has risen dramatically—what special obligations, if any, should courts have in dealing with them? Might the result have been different in this case if the father had been represented?

E. At the time a child support award is entered, parents typically cannot waive the right to seek modification. For example, in the case of *Fernandez v. Fernandez*, 222 P.3d 10310 (Nev. 2010), the Supreme Court of Nevada refused to enforce a stipulation making child support nonmodifiable. The court reasoned that trial courts have continuing jurisdiction in child support matters and that Nevada courts were, in fact, required to review child support awards every three years. The court noted that it might have ruled differently had Nevada statutes expressly provided that parties could incorporate nonmodification stipulations. Do you think parents should be able to agree that child support awards cannot be modified? What are the policy arguments in favor of and against such an approach?

9.6 ENFORCEMENT: CONTEMPT OF COURT

Historically, custodial parents were left to their own devices to collect unpaid child support. While remedies such as contempt were available, a needy obligee often could not afford to bring an action against the obligor. However, in 1974, Congress enacted Title IV-D of the Social Security Act, which created a federal-state partnership aimed at establishing and enforcing child support orders. Although originally focused on child support cases where children were public assistance recipients, in 1984, IV-D services became available for the benefit of all children. *See* 42 U.S.C. §651 et seq.

REFLECTIVE QUESTIONS	What is the justification for extending the focus of the federal-state child support partnership beyond children receiving public assistance?

Background to *Leger v. Leger*

Obligees may bring a private civil action on behalf of a child to hold an obligor in contempt of court for failure to comply with a child support order. Typically, an action is brought seeking to have the obligor held in civil contempt so that the obligor can purge the sentence by making back child support payments. However, if criminal contempt is sought, all of the rights of an accused in a criminal case must be afforded the defendant. In *Leger v. Leger*, the court discusses the difference between civil and criminal contempt.

LEGER
v.
LEGER

Court of Appeals of Louisiana
808 So. 2d 632 (2001)

WEIMER, J. [Defendant moved] to reduce child support and terminate alimony alleging a change of circumstances. [His ex-wife asked that he be found in] contempt for failure to pay child support and alimony. . . . When the parties appeared before the court . . . they informed the court that a stipulation covering most issues had been reached. . . . The only matter left to be tried was the contempt. Following the hearing, the trial judge found Mr. Leger in contempt for failure to pay his child support and ordered that he serve 14 days in jail. . . .

Constructive contempt of court is any contempt other than a direct one. Constructive contempt includes the willful disobedience of any lawful judgment of the court. . . . The penalty which may be imposed for contempt of court for disobeying an order for the payment of child support or spousal support is a fine of not more than five hundred dollars or imprisonment for not more than three months, or both. LSA-R.S. 13:4611(1)(d). To find a person guilty of constructive contempt, it is necessary to find that he or she violated the order of court intentionally, knowingly, and purposely, without justifiable excuse. . . .

Review of the record indicates that Mr. Leger was involved in an automobile accident during November 1998. He filed a [motion] to terminate alimony and reduce child support on December 2, 1998. He provided a disability certificate dated November 5, 1998, from Dr. Paul M. Doty indicating that he was totally incapacitated for an undetermined period due to a dislocated shoulder and a fractured navicular. According to the stipulation reached by the parties, Mr. Leger owed $5,500 in past due child support and alimony as of the date of the filing. Because of the amount of the past due support owed, a substantial portion of the arrearages accrued prior to the injuries he suffered in the automobile accident. He acknowledged that he had only paid $100 since the date of the filing of the [motion].

Also, according to the stipulation Mr. Leger's income had decreased from $47,982 in 1997 to $28,770 in 1998. Additionally, because of the automobile accident, he was unable to work and his income was limited to $1,846 a month in compensation payments. Testimony adduced at the hearing on the [motion] for contempt indicated the decrease in income had resulted from employment with a different company as well as the decline in the amount of work available. Mr. Leger was employed as a crane mechanic. He testified that he did not carry medical insurance at work because he could not afford it. He acknowledged he had not attempted to discuss the need to reduce the support payments with Ms. Leger; he simply had not paid the support due.

Mr. Leger also testified that he and another woman identified as his fiancée have an infant son who has significant medical bills and will require surgery. He admitted he had not paid anything on that debt, but acknowledged that he had received some bills. Considering the evidence before the court, we cannot say the trial court erred in finding Mr. Leger in contempt for failure to pay alimony and child support. . . .

[T]he contempt proceeding in this matter was criminal in nature since the court assigned a determinate jail sentence. Nevertheless, Mr. Leger was afforded all constitutional protections. He had notice of the hearing, he was present at the hearing, and he was represented by counsel. When called to testify, he willingly took the stand and answered questions regarding his failure to pay support as ordered by the court. There was no objection to the manner in which the proceeding was conducted. His guilt was established beyond a reasonable doubt. Following the hearing, when the court imposed sentence, counsel for defendant requested that the sentence be delayed as the defendant was due to be in Miami with his infant child the following week. The court denied the request. There was no objection raised as to the sentence being imposed without a "purge clause" nor was there an objection that the contempt proceeding had been a criminal contempt proceeding since the court ordered incarceration without an ability to purge.

If the contempt proceeding is in the nature of a civil proceeding, but without the constitutional safeguards afforded to a criminal defendant, a sentence of incarceration without affording the defendant the opportunity to purge the sentence would be impermissible. See *Feiock*, 485 U.S. at 632. However, if the constitutional safeguards are afforded the defendant, including proof of the contempt beyond a reasonable doubt, no opportunity to purge the sentence is required. In this matter, we find the defendant was afforded proper constitutional protections and his guilt of being in contempt was established beyond a reasonable doubt. The judgment of the court ordering Mr. Leger to serve fourteen days in jail is affirmed. . . .

Children cannot live on light and air; they need and are entitled to not only love and affection, but also the financial support of their parents. This financial support obligation is based on the needs of the children and the ability of the parents to provide support. LSA-C.C. art. 141. . . .

For the foregoing reasons, the judgment of the trial court finding defendant in contempt and sentencing him to fourteen days in parish prison is affirmed.

DISCUSSION QUESTIONS FOR *LEGER v. LEGER*

A. What was Mr. Leger's factual defense to the contempt citation?

B. Why is this proceeding criminal rather than civil? If a contempt action is criminal, what constitutional protections are afforded a defendant?

C. If you were the attorney seeking to collect the unpaid child support in this case, would you have brought an action for civil or criminal contempt? Why? How would you counsel the mother regarding the advisability of each remedy?

D. If you had been Mr. Leger's counsel, how would you have advised him concerning his options and possible courses of action? After serving his sentence, does he still have to pay the past-due child support?

E. According to some commentators, "[f]athers struggling with joblessness and low incomes make up a significant share of parents who have been court-ordered to pay child support. One in four parents who are ordered to pay child support debt have no income, and another 31 percent have annual incomes below roughly $12,700. These parents are subject to the workings of the child support system regardless of their income or employment status." Jacquelyn Boggess et al., *What We Want to Give Our Kids*, Center for Family Policy & Practice and Center for Community Economic Development 2-3 (2014), available at http://www.cffpp.org/publications/whatwewanttogiveourkids.pdf (last visited July 2, 2015). What is likely to be the long-term effect of contempt actions on these fathers?

Background to *Turner v. Rogers*

Most child support contempt proceedings seek to have the obligor held in civil, rather than criminal, contempt of court. Although the obligor technically holds the keys to the jail cell door, he or she may nevertheless spend substantial time in confinement. In *Turner v. Rogers*, the Supreme Court of the United States considered whether an indigent obligor has a right to counsel when faced with incarceration pursuant to a civil contempt proceeding.

TURNER
v.
ROGERS

Supreme Court of the United States
131 S. Ct. 2507 (2011)

BREYER, J., delivered the opinion of the Court.

South Carolina's Family Court enforces its child support orders by threatening with incarceration for civil contempt those who are (1) subject to a child support order, (2) able to comply with that order, but (3) fail to do so. We must decide whether the Fourteenth Amendment's Due Process Clause requires the State to provide counsel (at a civil contempt hearing) to an *indigent* person potentially faced with such incarceration. We conclude that where as here the custodial parent (entitled to receive the support) is unrepresented by counsel, the State need not provide counsel to the noncustodial parent (required to provide the support). But we attach an important caveat, namely, that the State must nonetheless have in place alternative procedures that assure a fundamentally fair determination of the critical incarceration-related question, whether the supporting parent is able to comply with the support order.

South Carolina family courts enforce their child support orders in part through civil contempt proceedings. Each month the family court clerk reviews outstanding child support orders, identifies those in which the supporting parent has fallen more than five days behind, and sends that parent an order to "show cause" why he should not be held in contempt. . . . The "show cause" order and attached affidavit refer to the relevant child support order, identify the amount of the arrearage, and set a date for a court hearing. At the hearing that parent may demonstrate that he is not in contempt, say, by showing that he is not able to make the required payments. . . . If he fails to make the required showing, the court may hold him in civil contempt. And it may require that he be imprisoned unless and until he purges himself of contempt by making the required child support payments (but not for more than one year regardless).

In June 2003 a South Carolina family court entered an order, which (as amended) required petitioner, Michael Turner, to pay $51.73 per week to respondent, Rebecca Rogers, to help support their child. (Rogers' father, Larry Price, currently has custody of the child and is also a respondent before this Court.) Over the next three years, Turner repeatedly failed to pay the amount due and was held in contempt on five occasions. The first four times he was sentenced to 90 days' imprisonment, but he ultimately paid the amount due (twice without being jailed, twice after spending two or three days in custody). The fifth time he did not pay but completed a 6-month sentence.

After his release in 2006 Turner remained in arrears. On March 27, 2006, the clerk issued a new "show cause" order. And after an initial postponement due to Turner's failure to appear, Turner's civil contempt hearing took place on January 3, 2008. Turner and Rogers were present, each without representation by counsel.

The hearing was brief. The court clerk said that Turner was $5,728.76 behind in his payments. The judge asked Turner if there was "anything you want to say." Turner replied,

> Well, when I first got out, I got back on dope. I done meth, smoked pot and everything else, and I paid a little bit here and there. And, when I finally did get to working, I broke my back, back in September. I filed for disability and SSI. And, I didn't get straightened out off the dope until I broke my back and laid up for two months. And, now I'm off the dope and everything. I just hope that you give me a chance. I don't know what else to say. I mean, I know I done wrong, and I should have been paying and helping her, and I'm sorry. I mean, dope had a hold to me.

The judge then said, "[o]kay," and asked Rogers if she had anything to say. After a brief discussion of federal benefits, the judge stated,

> If there's nothing else, this will be the Order of the Court. I find the Defendant in willful contempt. I'm [going to] sentence him to twelve months in the Oconee County Detention Center. He may purge himself of the contempt and avoid the sentence by having a zero balance on or before his release. I've also placed a lien on any SSI or other benefits.

The judge added that Turner would not receive good-time or work credits, but "[i]f you've got a job, I'll make you eligible for work release." When Turner asked why he could not receive good-time or work credits, the judge said, "[b]ecause that's my ruling."

The court made no express finding concerning Turner's ability to pay his arrearage (though Turner's wife had voluntarily submitted a copy of Turner's application for disability benefits). . . . Nor did the judge ask any follow-up questions or otherwise address the ability-to-pay issue. After the hearing, the judge filled out a prewritten form titled "Order for Contempt of Court," which included the statement: "Defendant (was) (was not) gainfully employed and/or (had) (did not have) the ability to make these support payments when due." But the judge left this statement as is without indicating whether Turner was able to make support payments.

While serving his 12-month sentence, Turner, with the help of *pro bono* counsel, appealed. He claimed that the Federal Constitution entitled him to counsel at his contempt hearing. The South Carolina Supreme Court decided Turner's appeal after he had completed his sentence. And it rejected his "right to counsel" claim. The court pointed out that civil contempt differs significantly from criminal contempt. The former does not require all the "constitutional safeguards" applicable in criminal proceedings. And the right to government-paid counsel, the Supreme Court held, was one of the "safeguards" not required.

Turner sought certiorari. In light of differences among state courts (and some federal courts) on the applicability of a "right to counsel" in civil contempt proceedings enforcing child support orders, we granted the writ. . . .

We must decide whether the Due Process Clause grants an indigent defendant, such as Turner, a right to state-appointed counsel at a civil contempt proceeding, which may lead to his incarceration. This Court's precedents provide no definitive answer to that question. This Court has long held that the Sixth Amendment grants an indigent defendant the right to state-appointed counsel in a *criminal* case. . . . And we have held that this same rule applies to *criminal contempt* proceedings (other than summary proceedings).

But the Sixth Amendment does not govern civil cases. Civil contempt differs from criminal contempt in that it seeks only to "coerc[e] the defendant to do" what a court had previously ordered him to do. . . . A court may not impose punishment "in a civil contempt proceeding when it is clearly established that the alleged contemnor is unable to comply with the terms of the order." . . . And once a civil contemnor complies with the underlying order, he is purged of the contempt and is free. [H]e "carr[ies] the keys of [his] prison in [his] own pockets."

Consequently, the Court has made clear (in a case not involving the right to counsel) that, where civil contempt is at issue, the Fourteenth Amendment's Due Process Clause allows a State to provide fewer procedural protections than in a criminal case. . . .

Civil contempt proceedings in child support cases constitute one part of a highly complex system designed to assure a noncustodial parent's regular payment of funds typically necessary for the support of his children. Often the family receives welfare support from a state-administered federal program, and the State then seeks reimbursement from the noncustodial parent. . . . Other times the custodial parent (often the mother, but sometimes the father, a grandparent, or another person with custody) does not receive government benefits and is entitled to receive the support payments herself.

The Federal Government has created an elaborate procedural mechanism designed to help both the government and custodial parents to secure the payments to which they are entitled. . . . These systems often rely upon wage withholding, expedited procedures for modifying and enforcing child support orders, and automated data processing. . . . But sometimes States will use contempt orders to ensure that the custodial parent receives support payments or the government receives reimbursement. Although some experts have criticized this last-mentioned procedure, and the Federal Government believes that "the routine use of contempt for non-payment of child support is likely to be an ineffective strategy," the Government also tells us that "coercive enforcement remedies, such as contempt, have a role to play." . . . South Carolina, which relies heavily on contempt proceedings, agrees that they are an important tool.

We here consider an indigent's right to paid counsel at such a contempt proceeding. It is a civil proceeding. And we consequently determine the "specific dictates of due process" by examining the "distinct factors" that this Court has previously found useful in deciding what specific safeguards the Constitution's Due Process Clause requires in order to make a civil proceeding fundamentally fair. *Mathews v. Eldridge*, 424 U.S. 319, 335, (1976) (considering fairness of an administrative proceeding). As relevant here those factors include (1) the nature of "the private interest that will be affected," (2) the comparative "risk" of an "erroneous deprivation" of that interest with and without "additional or substitute procedural safeguards," and (3) the nature and magnitude of any countervailing interest in not providing "additional or substitute procedural requirement[s]." . . .

The "private interest that will be affected" argues strongly for the right to counsel that Turner advocates. That interest consists of an indigent defendant's loss of personal liberty through imprisonment. The interest in securing that freedom, the freedom "from bodily restraint," lies "at the core of the liberty protected by the Due Process Clause." . . . And we have made clear that its threatened loss through legal proceedings demands "due process protection." . . .

Given the importance of the interest at stake, it is obviously important to assure accurate decisionmaking in respect to the key "ability to pay" question. Moreover, the fact that ability to comply marks a dividing line between civil and criminal contempt, reinforces the need for accuracy. That is because an incorrect decision (wrongly classifying the contempt proceeding as civil) can increase the risk of wrongful incarceration by depriving the defendant of the procedural protections (including counsel) that the Constitution would demand in a criminal proceeding. . . . And since 70% of child support arrears nationwide are owed by parents with either no reported income or income of $10,000 per year or less, the issue of ability to pay may arise fairly often. . . .

On the other hand, the Due Process Clause does not always require the provision of counsel in civil proceedings where incarceration is threatened. And in determining whether the Clause requires a right to counsel here, we must take account of opposing interests, as well as consider the probable value of "additional or substitute procedural safeguards." . . .

Doing so, we find three related considerations that, when taken together, argue strongly against the Due Process Clause requiring the State to provide indigents with counsel in every proceeding of the kind before us.

First, the critical question likely at issue in these cases concerns, as we have said, the defendant's ability to pay. That question is often closely related to the question of the defendant's indigence. But when the right procedures are in place, indigence can be a question that in many—but not all—cases is sufficiently straightforward to warrant determination *prior* to providing a defendant with counsel, even in a criminal case. Federal law, for example, requires a criminal defendant to provide information showing that he is indigent, and therefore entitled to state-funded counsel, *before* he can receive that assistance. . . .

Second, sometimes, as here, the person opposing the defendant at the hearing is not the government represented by counsel but the custodial parent *un*represented by counsel. See Dept. of Health and Human Services, Office of Child Support Enforcement, Understanding Child Support Debt: A Guide to Exploring Child Support Debt in Your State 5, 6 (2004) (51% of nationwide arrears, and 58% in South Carolina, are not owed to the government). The custodial parent, perhaps a woman with custody of one or more children, may be relatively poor, unemployed, and unable to afford counsel. Yet she may have encouraged the court to enforce its order through contempt. (Rogers asks court, in light of pattern of nonpayment, to confine Turner.) She may be able to provide the court with significant information. (Rogers describes where Turner lived and worked.) And the proceeding is ultimately for her benefit.

A requirement that the State provide counsel to the noncustodial parent in these cases could create an asymmetry of representation that would "alter significantly the nature of the proceeding." . . . Doing so could mean a degree of formality or delay that would unduly slow payment to those immediately in need. And, perhaps more important for present purposes, doing so could make the proceedings *less* fair overall, increasing the risk of a decision that would erroneously deprive a family of the support it is entitled to receive. The needs of such families play an important role in our analysis. . . .

Third, as the Solicitor General points out, there is available a set of "substitute procedural safeguards," which, if employed together, can significantly reduce the risk of an erroneous deprivation of liberty. They can do so, moreover, without incurring some of the drawbacks inherent in recognizing an automatic right to counsel. Those safeguards include (1) notice to the defendant that his "ability to pay" is a critical issue in the contempt proceeding; (2) the use of a form (or the equivalent) to elicit relevant financial information; (3) an opportunity at the hearing for the defendant to respond to statements and questions about his financial status, (*e.g.,* those triggered by his responses on the form); and (4) an express finding by the court that the defendant has the ability to pay. In presenting these alternatives, the Government draws upon considerable experience in helping to manage statutorily mandated federal-state efforts to enforce child support orders. It does not claim that they are the only possible alternatives, and this Court's cases suggest, for example, that sometimes assistance other than purely legal assistance (here, say, that of a neutral social worker) can prove constitutionally sufficient. But the Government does claim that these alternatives can assure the "fundamental fairness" of the proceeding even where the State does not pay for counsel for an indigent defendant.

While recognizing the strength of Turner's arguments, we ultimately believe that the three considerations we have just discussed must carry the day. In our view, a categorical right to counsel in proceedings of the kind before us would carry with it disadvantages (in the form of unfairness and delay) that, in terms of ultimate fairness, would deprive it of significant superiority over the alternatives that we have mentioned. We consequently hold that the Due Process Clause does not *automatically* require the provision of counsel at civil contempt proceedings to an indigent individual who is subject to a child support order, even if that individual faces incarceration (for up to a year). In particular, that Clause does not require the provision of counsel where the opposing parent or other custodian (to whom support funds are owed) is not represented by counsel and the State provides alternative procedural safeguards equivalent to those we have mentioned (adequate notice of the importance of ability to pay, fair opportunity to present, and to dispute, relevant information, and court findings).

We do not address civil contempt proceedings where the underlying child support payment is owed to the State, for example, for reimbursement of welfare funds paid to the parent with custody. Those proceedings more closely resemble debt-collection proceedings. The government is likely to have counsel or some other competent representative. Cf. *Johnson v. Zerbst*, 304 U.S. 458, 462-463, (1938) ("[T]he average defendant does not have the professional legal skill to protect himself when brought before a tribunal with power to take his life or liberty, *wherein the prosecution is presented by experienced and learned counsel*" (emphasis added)). And this kind of proceeding is not before us. Neither do we address what due process requires in an unusually complex case where a defendant "can fairly be represented only by a trained advocate." . . .

The record indicates that Turner received neither counsel nor the benefit of alternative procedures like those we have described. He did not receive clear notice that his ability to pay would constitute the critical question in his civil contempt proceeding. No one provided him with a form (or the equivalent) designed to elicit information about his financial circumstances. The court did not find that Turner was able to pay his arrearage, but instead left the relevant "finding" section of the contempt order blank. The court nonetheless found Turner in contempt and ordered him incarcerated. Under these circumstances Turner's incarceration violated the Due Process Clause.

We vacate the judgment of the South Carolina Supreme Court and remand the case for further proceedings not inconsistent with this opinion.

JUSTICE THOMAS, with whom **JUSTICE SCALIA** joins, dissenting.

. . . For the reasons explained in the previous two sections, I would not engage in the majority's balancing analysis. But there is yet another reason not to undertake the *Mathews v. Eldridge* balancing test here. That test weighs an individual's interest against that of the Government. *Id.*, at 335, 96 S. Ct. 893 (identifying the opposing interest as "the Government's interest"); *Lassiter*, 452 U.S., at 27, (same). It does not account for the interests of the child and custodial parent, who is usually the child's mother. But their interests are the very reason for the child support obligation and the civil contempt proceedings that enforce it.

When fathers fail in their duty to pay child support, children suffer. See Cancian, Meyer, & Han, *Child Support: Responsible Fatherhood and the Quid Pro Quo*, 635 Annals Am. Acad. Pol. & Soc. Sci. 140, 153 (2011) (finding that child support plays an important role in reducing child poverty in single-parent homes); cf. Sorensen & Zibman, *Getting to Know Poor Fathers Who Do Not Pay Child Support*, 75 Soc. Serv. Rev. 420, 423 (2001) (finding that children whose fathers reside apart from them are 54 percent more likely to live in poverty than their fathers). Nonpayment or inadequate payment can press children and mothers into poverty. M. Garrison, *The Goals and Limits of Child Support Policy, in Child Support: The Next Frontier* 16 (J. Oldham & M. Melli eds.2000); see also Dept. of Commerce, Census Bureau, T. Grall, *Custodial Mothers and Fathers and Their Child Support: 2007*, pp. 4-5 (2009) (hereinafter *Custodial Mothers and Fathers*) (reporting that 27 percent of custodial mothers lived in poverty in 2007).

The interests of children and mothers who depend on child support are notoriously difficult to protect. *See, e.g., Hicks v. Feiock*, 485 U.S. 624, 644, (1988) ("The failure of enforcement efforts in this area has become a national scandal."). Less than half of all custodial parents receive the full amount of child support ordered; 24 percent of those owed support receive nothing at all. *Custodial Mothers and Fathers* 7; see also Dept. of Health and Human Services, Office of Child Support Enforcement, FY 2008 Annual Report to Congress, App. III, Table 71 (showing national child support arrears of $105.5 billion in 2008). In South Carolina alone, more than 139,000 noncustodial parents defaulted on their child support obligations during 2008, and at year end parents owed $1.17 billion in total arrears. *Id.*, App. III, Tables 73 and 71.

That some fathers subject to a child support agreement report little or no income "does not mean they do not have the ability to pay any child support." Dept. of Health and Human Services, H. Sorensen, L. Sousa, & S. Schaner, *Assessing Child Support Arrears in Nine Large States and the Nation* 22 (2007) (prepared by The Urban Institute) (hereinafter *Assessing Arrears*). Rather, many "deadbeat dads" "opt to work in the underground economy" to "shield their earnings from child support enforcement efforts." Mich. Sup. Ct., *Task Force Report: The Underground Economy* 10 (2010) (hereinafter *Underground Economy*). To avoid attempts to garnish their wages or otherwise enforce the support obligation, "deadbeats" quit their jobs, jump from job to job, become self-employed, work under the table, or engage in illegal activity. See Waller & Plotnick, *Effective Child Support Policy for Low-Income Families: Evidence from Street Level Research*, 20 J. Pol'y Analysis & Mgmt. 89, 104 (2001); Assessing Arrears 22-23.

Because of the difficulties in collecting payment through traditional enforcement mechanisms, many States also use civil contempt proceedings to coerce "deadbeats" into paying what they owe. The States that use civil contempt with the threat of detention find it a "highly effective" tool for collecting child support when nothing else works. Compendium of Responses Collected by the U.S. Dept. of Health and

Human Services Office of Child Support Enforcement (Dec. 28, 2010), reprinted in App. to Brief for Sen. DeMint et al. as *Amici Curiae* 7a; *see id.*, at 3a, 9a. For example, Virginia, which uses civil contempt as "a last resort," reports that in 2010 "deadbeats" paid approximately $13 million "either before a court hearing to avoid a contempt finding or after a court hearing to purge the contempt finding." *Id.*, at 13a-14a. Other States confirm that the mere threat of imprisonment is often quite effective because most contemners "will pay . . . rather than go to jail." *Id.*, at 4a; see also *Underground Economy* C-2 ("Many judges . . . report that the prospect of [detention] often causes obligors to discover previously undisclosed resources that they can use to make child support payments").

This case illustrates the point. After the family court imposed Turner's weekly support obligation in June 2003, he made no payments until the court held him in contempt three months later, whereupon he paid over $1,000 to avoid confinement. Three more times, Turner refused to pay until the family court held him in contempt — then paid in short order.

Although I think that the majority's analytical framework does not account for the interests that children and mothers have in effective and flexible methods to secure payment, I do not pass on the wisdom of the majority's preferred procedures. Nor do I address the wisdom of the State's decision to use certain methods of enforcement. . . .

I would affirm the judgment of the South Carolina Supreme Court because the Due Process Clause does not provide a right to appointed counsel in civil contempt hearings that may lead to incarceration. As that is the only issue properly before the Court, I respectfully dissent.

 **DISCUSSION QUESTIONS** **FOR *TURNER v. ROGERS***

A. What is the holding of the Court in this case? To whom and under what conditions does it apply?

B. What are the three prongs of the *Mathews* test utilized by the Court and how does the Court analyze each?

C. What is the significance of the obligor's ability to pay? How does it figure into the Court's analysis?

D. Under the reasoning of the Court, why does it matter if the obligee is represented by counsel?

E. What "substitute procedural safeguards" does the Court identify?

F. According to the dissent, how does the majority's analytical framework fail to "account for the interests that children and mothers have in effective and flexible methods to secure payment"? Do you agree?

G. Both the majority and the dissent cite research regarding child support obligors who do not pay support in a timely way. What assertions are made and what are the policy implications of the research?

H. Commentators have criticized use of civil contempt in child support enforcement proceedings because if a parent is unable to pay, support will not be collected and family relationships may be harmed. Use of criminal contempt has similarly been critiqued:

> The legal failure represented by incarceration of indigent parents for contempt is — if possible — even greater than the social and economic failure. Criminal contempt is supposed to be a punishment for willful misbehavior, not for an absence of funds. Civil contempt is supposed to be used to coerce a person to do something that he is able, but unwilling, to do. In either case, if the contemnor's failure to pay the sums ordered by the court is simply a result of inability to pay, his incarceration can only be characterized as imprisonment for being poor.

Elizabeth G. Patterson, *Civil Contempt and the Indigent Child Support Obligor: The Silent Return of Debtor's Prison*, 18 Cornell J.L. & Pub. Pol'y 95, 97-98 (2008). Do you agree that incarceration constitutes a serious legal failure? Why or why not? Do you think the Court's decision in *Turner* will ease these concerns?

I. Commentators have also expressed concerns about the detrimental effects of child support enforcement on low-income families:

> While society and the law expect *all* fathers to support their children financially, low-income fathers are not able to meet this norm of economic fatherhood. However, some low-income fathers contribute in other ways — by buying diapers, clothing, toys, and groceries for their children. Some also do a fair amount of caretaking — they take their children to school, help them with homework, take them to the doctor, or spend time with them while the mother works. These contributions facilitate paternal engagement but they do not count as child support for purposes of the law. Fathers who make in-kind and caretaking contributions are pursued for payment of child support in the same way as parents who have no contact with their children and contribute nothing to their upbringing. Many scholars have shown that the law's aggressive pursuit of child support payments may drive low-income fathers away from their children by signaling that their worth as fathers is measured by financial contributions that they are unable to make.

Solangel Maldonado, *Shared Parenting and Never-Married Families*, 52 Fam. Ct. Rev. 632, 635-636 (2014). At the same time, a child's need for support doesn't diminish because a parent is unable to pay child support. How should the law balance these interests?

9.7 ENFORCEMENT: COLLECTION METHODS, STATE PROSECUTION, BANKRUPTCY

Collection tools. States have adopted a number of collection methods including the following: wage withholding, interception of tax refunds, garnishment, credit bureau reporting, driver's license suspension, recreational license suspension (hunting and fishing), publication of "most wanted" list of "deadbeat" obligors, occupational license suspension (real estate agents, lawyers, barbers), passport denial, seizure of financial awards such as workers' compensation payments and lottery winnings, and wage assignments.

Criminal prosecution. All states have statutes authorizing criminal prosecution of obligors who willfully fail to pay child support as ordered. *See* Wis. Stat. §948.22 (2) providing that intentional failure to pay support can be charged as a Class I felony.

Lack of relief in bankruptcy. Unpaid child support is not dischargeable in bankruptcy. *See* Janet Leach Richards, *A Guide to Spousal Support and Property Division Claims Under the Bankruptcy Abuse Prevention and Consumer Protection Act of 2005*, 41 Fam. L.Q. 227 (2007).

REFLECTIVE QUESTIONS	**Why do you think that so many collection tools have been enacted? In what circumstances are they likely to be most effective or ineffective?**

9.8 ENFORCEMENT ACROSS STATE BOUNDARIES: CRIMINAL PROSECUTION

The Child Support Recovery Act of 1992 (CSRA) and the Deadbeat Parents Punishment Act of 1998 (DPPA) establish criminal penalties for willfully delinquent obligors who have children residing in other states. 18 U.S.C. §228(a) provides:

> **(a) Offense.** — Any person who —
> **(1)** willfully fails to pay a support obligation with respect to a child who resides in another State, if such obligation has remained unpaid for a period longer than 1 year, or is greater than $5,000;
> **(2)** travels in interstate or foreign commerce with the intent to evade a support obligation, if such obligation has remained unpaid for a period longer than 1 year, or is greater than $5,000; or
> **(3)** willfully fails to pay a support obligation with respect to a child who resides in another State, if such obligation has remained unpaid for a period longer than 2 years, or is greater than $10,000; (shall be punished as provided in subsection (c).)

The constitutionality of the Child Support Recovery Act was upheld in *United States v. Hampshire*, 95 F.3d 999 (10th Cir. 1997), where a father was sentenced under the act to two years' probation and was ordered to pay $38,804 in restitution. The appellate court ruled that the act did not violate the Commerce Clause:

> In enacting the CSRA, Congress made explicit findings concerning the impact of delinquent parents on interstate commerce. In 1989, approximately $5 billion of $16 billion in child support obligations were not honored. About one-third of the unpaid child support obligations involved a delinquent father who lived in a different state than his children. Delinquent parents used the multistate system to evade enforcement efforts by individual states. Accordingly, in enacting the CSRA, Congress sought "to strengthen, not to supplant, State enforcement."

Id. at 1004.

REFLECTIVE QUESTIONS	Do you think the punishments under the CSRA are too extreme? Why or why not?

9.9 MODIFICATION AND ENFORCEMENT ACROSS STATE AND NATIONAL BOUNDARIES: UIFSA

In today's mobile society, parents may divorce in one state but eventually reside in other states. Complex jurisdictional issues are presented if modification or enforcement of an existing order becomes necessary. The Uniform Interstate Family Support Act (UIFSA) addresses such situations by providing uniform jurisdictional standards for state courts. Ideally, there should be only one valid court order governing the child support obligation for a given child. *See* John J. Sampson, *Uniform Interstate Family Support Act (2001) with Prefatory Note and Comments (with Still More Unofficial Annotations)*, 36 Fam. L.Q. 329 (2002). UIFSA includes provisions requiring states to cooperate in establishing and enforcing child support orders.

The Supreme Court of Rhode Island recently reviewed the history and purpose of UIFSA:

> The UIFSA was adopted by the General Assembly in 1997. This Court has yet to address its provisions. We begin by looking to the history and purpose of the act and seek guidance from the holdings of our sister jurisdictions. In the late 1980s and early 1990s, Congress sought to address the problem of an inefficient nationwide system of family law jurisprudence that allowed for multiple and often inconsistent child-support orders. . . . In 1994, Congress enacted the Full Faith and Credit for Child Support Orders Act (FFCCSOA); and in 1996, as a condition to the award of certain

federal funding, Congress required that all states enact the most recent version, the UIFSA, promulgated by the National Conference of Commissioners on Uniform State Laws (NCCUSL). . . . Together these acts created a "single-order system" whose purpose was "(1) to facilitate the enforcement of child support orders among the [s]tates; . . . (2) discourage continuing interstate controversies over child support . . . [and] (3) avoid jurisdictional competition and conflict among [s]tate courts. . . ."

"The scheme of the UIFSA is for a court with personal jurisdiction over the obligor to establish a support order and to retain jurisdiction to enforce or modify the order until the occurrence of certain conditions which terminate jurisdiction in the issuing state and provide the basis for jurisdiction in another state." . . . These goals are implemented through the "definitional concept called 'continuing, exclusive jurisdiction[.]'" "Although the UIFSA never speaks explicitly of 'subject matter jurisdiction,' the terms that it does use — 'jurisdiction' and 'continuing exclusive jurisdiction' — are simply alternative ways of referring to subject matter jurisdiction and its territorial limitations." . . .

Sidell v. Sidell, 18 A.3d 499 (R.I. 2011). The UIFSA has substantially improved the ability of recipients to collect child support from obligors located in other states.

Sometimes parents seek to enforce child support orders across international boundaries. In 2007, the United States became a signatory to the Hague Convention on the International Recovery of Child Support and Other Forms of Family Maintenance, and as a consequence, the National Conference of Commissioners on Uniform State Laws amended the UIFSA. National Conference of Commissioners on United States Law, *Uniform Interstate Family Support Act (last amended or revised in 2008) with Prefatory Note and Comments*, 43 Fam. L.Q. 75 (2009). The purpose of the amendments is to promote "recognition and enforcement of support orders across national boundaries." Battle Rankin Robinson, *Integrating an International Convention into State Law: The UIFSA Experience*, 43 Fam. L.Q. 61, 62 (2009).

REFLECTIVE QUESTIONS	What is the purpose of UIFSA?

Background to *In re Marriage of Amezquita & Archuleta*

In *In re Marriage of Amezquita & Archuleta*, the parties were divorced in New Mexico and the mother and children moved to California. The mother registered the New Mexico order in California and brought an action to enforce the order and to modify it. The father concedes that California has jurisdiction to enforce the child support order, but he argues that the modification action should be heard in New Mexico because California lacks subject matter jurisdiction.

IN RE MARRIAGE OF AMEZQUITA & ARCHULETA
Court of Appeals of California
124 Cal. Rptr. 2d 887 (2002)

NICHOLSON, P.J. . . . The parties, who have three children (born in 1981, 1984, and 1987), were divorced in 1990. The New Mexico decree set child support payable from Mark A. Amezquita (Husband) to Roberta D. Archuleta (Wife) at $600 per month. In September 1999, Wife, who had moved to California with the children, registered the out-of-state support order in Sacramento and obtained an order to show cause for a modification of the support. She filed a declaration stating that Husband, an employee of the United States Air Force, was living in San Pedro, California. The pleadings were served on Husband personally within California.

Husband, in *propria persona*, filed a responsive declaration stating that he did not consent to the requested order but would consent to an order to "be specified after advisement by legal counsel." Soon thereafter, counsel for Husband filed a declaration and memorandum of points and authorities seeking to amend the responsive pleading so as not to admit that the court had jurisdiction over the support matter. Counsel asserted Husband was misled into filing the responsive pleading by a court employee and by the office of opposing counsel and that New Mexico is the only state with jurisdiction to modify the support order.

Husband is a sergeant in the Air Force assigned to active duty in California. He maintains a New Mexico driver's license. He votes and files income tax returns there. Husband holds, in his words, a "residual interest" in his parents' home in New Mexico and intends to return to that state when he retires from the military. . . . A California court may modify another state's child support order "[i]f all of the parties . . . reside in this state and the child does not reside in the issuing state. . . ." (Fam. Code, §4962, subd. (a).) If these conditions are not met, the California court does not have subject matter jurisdiction to make the modification. . . .

Family Code section 4962 was borne of section 613 of the Uniform Interstate Family Support Act (UIFSA); they are identical in every way relevant to this case. The Legislature adopted the UIFSA in 1997. Drafted by the National Conference of Commissioners on Uniform State Laws (NCCUSL), the UIFSA was imposed on the states by Congress as a condition to receiving federal funding of child support enforcement efforts. (42 U.S.C. §666.)

Family Code section 4962 is just one piece of the UIFSA, which was meant to insure that, in the words of the NCCUSL, "only one valid support order may be effective at any one time," even though the parties and their children may move from state to state. With that in mind, we turn to section 205 of the UIFSA, which was adopted in California as Family Code section 4909 and in New Mexico as section 40-6A-205. It provides: "A tribunal of this State issuing a support order consistent with the law of this State has continuing, exclusive jurisdiction over a child-support order: (1) as long as this State remains the residence of the obligor, the individual obligee, or the child for whose benefit the support order is issued; or (2) until all of the parties who are individuals have filed written consents with the tribunal of this State for a tribunal of another State to modify the order and assume continuing, exclusive jurisdiction." The NCCUSL referred to this section as "perhaps the most crucial provision in UIFSA."

Under this section, which we will refer to as Family Code section 4909, New Mexico retains "continuing, exclusive jurisdiction" if that state is Husband's "residence." If New Mexico's jurisdiction is exclusive, then, by definition, California does not have jurisdiction. In other words, under the UIFSA, it is assumed that a person cannot have more than one residence. This, however, does not comport with the more general definition of residence noted above, allowing for multiple residences. Instead, "residence," for the purpose of the UIFSA, must mean "domicile," of which there can be only one.

Interpreting "reside in this state" in Family Code section 4962 to mean "are domiciled in this state" does not stretch the meaning of the words used beyond an acceptable, plain-meaning limit. When section 4962 was adopted in 1997, the Legislature was aware, at least constructively, that courts have interpreted "residence" to mean "domicile" in the family law context. When legislation has been judicially construed and subsequent statutes on a similar subject use identical or substantially similar language, the usual presumption is that the Legislature intended the same construction, unless a contrary intent clearly appears. Furthermore, as noted above, the goal of the UIFSA to prevent states from issuing conflicting support orders would be thwarted by a conclusion that a person can maintain more than one residence for the purpose of applying section 4962. This is the only interpretation that promotes, and does not defeat, the purpose of the UIFSA.

On this record, Husband is domiciled in New Mexico, even though he is stationed in California on military assignment. Counsel for Wife conceded it is "probably reasonable to assume New Mexico is his domicile." As noted above, a person's domicile is "the place where he intends to remain and to which, whenever he is absent, he has the intention of returning. . . ." Although Husband has lived in California for several years on military assignment, the record is uncontradicted that he does not intend to remain here after retirement and, instead, intends to return to New Mexico. He retains his New Mexico driver's license, and he votes and pays taxes there.

During argument in the trial court, counsel for Wife contended that asserting jurisdiction over child support modification in California is not unfair to Husband. She argued: "[T]here's nothing unfair about litigating a modification of support here when [Husband] has lived here for five years, when [Wife] has lived here with the children . . . since . . . June of 1998. There's . . . just nothing inherently unfair about proceeding here when everybody is living here. Regardless of where his domicile is, he's been here for five years, living here."

While fairness to the parties may have been an ideal sought after by the NCCUSL and, later, our Legislature when the UIFSA was written and adopted, it is not the overriding princip[le] and cannot be invoked to overcome the purpose of maintaining order in the enforcement and modification of support orders. Here, Husband is domiciled in New Mexico, the "issuing state" of the original child support order, and therefore "resides" in that state for the purpose of applying the UIFSA. New Mexico retains "continuing, exclusive jurisdiction" over child support and California does not have jurisdiction to modify New Mexico's order.

While we find the trial court did not have jurisdiction to modify the New Mexico support order, it had jurisdiction to enforce that order because Wife properly registered the order in California. (Fam. Code, §4959.) Husband concedes this point.

The trial court's order is reversed as to modification of the New Mexico support order. To the extent the order directs Husband to pay on the arrearage under the New Mexico order, the current order is affirmed.

DISCUSSION QUESTIONS FOR *IN RE MARRIAGE OF AMEZQUITA & ARCHULETA*

A. In what state was the divorce decree issued? Nine years after the divorce, to what state did the ex-wife move and upon arrival, what relief did she seek in terms of child support?

B. What was the legal consequence of the husband's responding to his ex-wife's legal action in California?

C. On what basis does California have subject matter jurisdiction to modify another state's support order?

D. On what basis does the UIFSA provide that a state has exclusive jurisdiction over a child support order? May a party have more than one residence under the UIFSA?

E. Of what importance to the outcome of this case is it that the court construes *residence* in the context of the UIFSA to mean *domicile*?

F. On what basis did the court reject the ex-wife's fairness argument?

G. After this decision, where must the wife go to obtain a modification of the existing child support award? Is New Mexico the only jurisdiction where the action can be heard?

H. Assume for the purposes of this question that California requires an obligor to pay child support until the child reaches age 18. Also assume for this question that New Mexico requires that support for a child continue until age 21. If the husband registers the New Mexico order in California, will he be allowed under the UIFSA to stop payment when the youngest child reaches age 18?

General Principles

1. Child support orders can usually be modified when there is a substantial change in circumstances that makes the original award unfair or, in some jurisdictions, unconscionable.

2. Courts scrutinize situations where an obligor seeks a modification of child support after becoming voluntarily unemployed or underemployed. Courts are concerned about the financial repercussions for the child and whether the change is motivated by the obligor's desire to avoid paying support.

3. Parental agreements to modify support are subject to approval by the court and they are not enforceable until this occurs.

4. When granted, modification orders are typically made retroactive only to the date of service of the motion for modification.

5. Contempt actions for child support enforcement may involve either civil or criminal contempt.

6. States have adopted a number of collection methods providing for specific sanctions and suspensions including the following: wage withholding, interception of tax refunds, garnishment, credit bureau reporting, driver's license suspension, recreational license suspension (hunting and fishing), publication of "most wanted" list of "deadbeat" obligors, occupational license suspension (real estate agents, lawyers, barbers), passport denial, seizure of financial awards such as workers' compensation payments and lottery winnings, and wage assignments.

7. States may criminally charge and prosecute delinquent child support obligors. The Child Support Recovery Act of 1992 (CSRA) and the Deadbeat Parents Punishment Act of 1998 (DPPA) also establish criminal penalties for willfully delinquent obligors who have children residing in other states.

8. The Uniform Interstate Family Support Act (UIFSA) contains uniform jurisdictional standards for state courts with the goal of having only one valid court order governing the child support obligation for a given child.

Chapter Problems

1. Assume that Pauline and David divorce after 15 years of marriage. Pauline is awarded sole physical custody of their only child, and David is ordered to pay child support. Assume that David moved to another state immediately after the divorce and has been living there for the past five years. Since the divorce, David has not paid any child support, and Pauline has not made an effort to collect it from him. The child is now 17 years old. Pauline comes to your office, located in the state where the divorce decree was entered, and asks you whether she can collect back child support and seek an upward modification in the current amount. She says, "David has a new job that pays lots of money." What are Pauline's options? What advice will you give her?

2. Assume that a mother is ordered to make monthly child support payments. She is convicted of a crime and sentenced to prison. She moves for a downward modification of the award based on the changed circumstance of her incarceration. What arguments will she make? What arguments might be made in opposition? How might a court rule? *See A.M.S. ex rel. Farthing v. Stoppleworth*, 694 N.W.2d 8 (N.D. 2005).

3. Despite the best efforts of state and federal governments, many children are not receiving ordered support. What may be some of the reasons for obligors' continued failure to pay outstanding child support?

4. Assume that the child support obligor petitions the court to reduce his $1,000 monthly child support obligation to $250 per month. The support is for two children, ages 7 and 12. Petitioner is currently working as a pharmacist and has been accepted into medical school. At the hearing, the court determines that the petitioner is proceeding in good faith. Should the court allow the reduction in child support?

5. Assume that when Juanita and Carlos divorce, Carlos is required to pay $500 a month in child support for their one child, age 10. Following the divorce, Carlos is advised by the leaders of his church that he should commit himself to two years of missionary work in Asia. Carlos seeks an order reducing his monthly child support obligation to $100. How might a court rule?

6. A child support obligation is not treated the same as other judgments in civil disputes. For example, a defendant's license to drive an automobile cannot be suspended for failure to pay an outstanding civil judgment obtained in a tort or contract action. What is different about child support actions? Should the enforcement provisions used in child support actions be extended to other civil proceedings?

Preparation for Practice

1. Perform an Internet search for child support enforcement assistance in your state. What services are available for parents to whom child support is owed?

2. Visit the website of the Office of Child Support Enforcement, U.S. Department of Health and Human Services at http://www.acf.hhs.gov/programs/cse/. What resources and information is available?

3. If a lawyer represents a child support obligee and collects past due support on his or her behalf, can the lawyer ethically retain a percentage of the recovery in fees? Why or why not?

Chapter 10

Establishing Spousal Support

10.1 INTRODUCTION

This chapter explores spousal support awards sought at the time of divorce. *Spousal support*, *alimony*, and *maintenance* are terms used interchangeably to describe the obligation of one spouse to provide income to the other spouse during and after divorce. The chapter following this one discusses how and when existing spousal support awards may be modified or terminated.

As you read this chapter, consider questions such as the following: How has spousal support been viewed historically? How have changing gender roles affected public policy with respect to spousal support? What is the purpose of spousal support? Under what conditions is spousal support awarded? How is the amount of spousal support determined?

REFLECTIVE QUESTIONS	What are your goals for this chapter?

10.2 DUTY TO SUPPORT: DOCTRINE OF NECESSARIES

The conceptual basis of spousal support has deep historical roots, and the topic consequently provides an interesting vehicle for examining the changing roles of family members over time. Judicial decisions regarding spousal support often reflect different perspectives on marriage and divorce. For example, historically husbands and wives were considered to be one person, and the husband had a duty to support the wife throughout her life unless she committed adultery or left the marital home without provocation. Today spouses are viewed as equal partners, and it is no longer assumed that the husband will provide for the wife upon divorce. As a consequence, court decisions regarding spousal support and its duration have become more complicated and more difficult to predict.

REFLECTIVE QUESTIONS	Why do you think that courts historically barred a wife from receiving alimony if she committed adultery?

Background to *North Carolina Baptist Hospitals, Inc. v. Harris*

Historically, when couples married, the bride and her dowry became the property of her husband. Under the Unity Doctrine they became one person, and the wife had few, if any, rights. As a result of her legal disability, the husband was liable to third parties who supplied the wife with essential items or "necessaries." During the 1900s wives began to gain control over some property as Married Woman's Acts were enacted. However, statutes incorporating the doctrine of necessaries remained in effect. In *North Carolina Baptist Hospitals, Inc. v. Harris*, the court is confronted with the question of how or whether to apply the doctrine of necessaries in modern society. Should the duty of support remain the obligation of the husband, or does this violate equal protection?

NORTH CAROLINA BAPTIST HOSPITALS, INC.
v.
HARRIS

Supreme Court of North Carolina
354 S.E.2d 471 (1987)

MEYER, J. On 20 January 1982 defendant Donnie Harris was admitted to plaintiff North Carolina Baptist Hospital for medical treatment. This treatment was in fact provided. It was stipulated by the parties that the treatment was necessary for the health and well-being of Mr. Harris.

At the time of Mr. Harris' admission to the hospital, the hospital's business office submitted to his wife, defendant Vern Dell Harris, a form to sign authorizing treatment. Vern Dell signed this form in her husband's name, "by Vern Dell Harris." She declined to sign as guarantor. The trial judge found as a fact that Vern Dell neither requested her husband's admission to the hospital, anticipated that he would be admitted, nor agreed to pay for the services.

The hospital charged $3,303.61 for the services provided to defendant Donnie Harris. Neither Donnie nor Vern Dell has paid this bill to date.

We are called upon in this case to decide whether, in the absence of an express undertaking on her part, a wife may be held responsible for the necessary medical expenses incurred by her husband. . . .

At common law it was the duty of the husband to provide for the necessary expenses of his wife. This duty arose from the fact of the marriage, not from any express undertaking on his part. The doctrine of necessaries was a recognition of the traditional status of the husband in the marital relationship as the financial provider of the family's needs, and has been enforced even where the husband was incompetent, or where the wife was financially capable of providing for her own needs. It is well settled that "doctrine of necessaries" applies to necessary medical expenses.

A corresponding duty on the part of the wife has also been a feature of the common law. She was obliged to provide domestic services which pertain to the comfort, care, and well-being of her family and consortium to her husband. *Ritchie v. White*, 35 S.E.2d 414 (1945).

The traditional allocation of marital rights and duties was based at least in part on the legal disability of married women to manage their own financial affairs. At early common law, the property of a woman vested in her husband at the point of marriage. As early as 1837, however, the legislature began taking steps to reduce the control of the husband over his wife's property. Thus, a wife could dispose of her property to her husband if the court could be assured, during a privy examination, that the transaction was entered into voluntarily. With the Constitution of 1868, the legislature provided for the right of the wife to dispose of her property to third parties, although still requiring the consent of the husband. Transactions between the spouses were presumed to be the result of the husband's control over the wife as late as 1891.

Even after the enactment of the "Martin Act," 1911 Sess. Laws ch. 109 (now N.C.G.S. §52-2), giving a married woman the right to dispose of her own property without the permission of her husband, and N.C.G.S. §47-14.1, abolishing the privy examination, the judge-made doctrine of necessaries continued to provide financial protection for married women. Several commentators have noted a resulting dis-equilibrium in the law: wives share their husbands' freedom to contract and are additionally entitled to financial support, while no longer being required to provide the traditional domestic services. As Professor Lee noted:

> The husband's common law duty to support his wife and minor children was partly balanced by the wife's duty to render services in the home. But the law can enforce the former, not the latter.

2 R. Lee, N.C. Family Law §131, at 128 (4th ed. 1980).

We have consistently held that a wife is responsible for her own necessaries upon her express contract or on equitable principles when the husband was unable to pay, notwithstanding her husband's concurrent liability. It appears that this Court has not addressed the question of whether a wife may also be liable for the necessary medical expenses of her husband. A review of those cases in which other jurisdictions have reached this issue, and of our state's public policy as expressed through legislation, persuades us that the doctrine of necessaries should be expanded to include this situation.

Most jurisdictions reaching this issue have held that the doctrine of necessaries should be applied in a gender-neutral fashion. Some states have eliminated it from their common law altogether. *See, e.g., Condore v. Prince George's County* (Maryland), 425 A.2d 1011 (1981); *Schilling v. Bedford County Memorial Hospital, Inc.* (Virginia), 303 S.E.2d 905 (1983). Other jurisdictions have expanded the doctrine to apply equally to either gender. *See, e.g., Jersey Shore Medical Center-Fitkin Hospital v. Baum's Estate*, 417 A.2d 1003 (1980); *Richland Memorial Hospital v. Burton* (South Carolina), 318 S.E.2d 12 (1984). Still other jurisdictions have imposed liability on the wife where the husband is unable to pay for his own necessaries. *See, e.g., Borgess Medical Center v. Smith* (Michigan), 386 N.W.2d 684 (1986); *Marshfield Clinic v. Discher* (Wisconsin), 314 N.W.2d 326 (1982). One jurisdiction reaching this issue recently has held that the common law doctrine, as historically applied, is still the law. *See Shands Teaching Hosp. and Clinics, Inc. v. Smith*, 497 So. 2d 644 (Fla. 1986). We agree with plaintiff that the trend is toward a gender-neutral application of the doctrine. . . . Our concern here must be with the policy of North Carolina as evinced by the actions of our legislature. . . .

The defendant wife relies on *Presbyterian Hospitals v. McCartha*, 310 S.E.2d 409, disc. rev. improvidently allowed, 312 N.C. 485, 322 S.E.2d 761 (1984). There the Court of Appeals, under facts similar to the ones at bar, determined that a wife was not liable for the medical expenses of her husband. The court reasoned that since the hospital was looking to the husband for payment and not relying on the wife's credit, there was no basis in law or equity for her to be held liable.

A review of several historical developments in the law of our state indicates a trend toward "gender neutrality." Many of the statutory provisions that formerly applied only to males now apply to both genders. Thus, N.C.G.S. §14-322, which had provided for criminal sanctions against males for non-support, now applies to either gender. There is no longer a statutory presumption that the husband is the supporting spouse for alimony purposes. No longer is the duty to support children the sole primary responsibility of the father. N.C.G.S. §50-13.4(b) (1984).

We followed the legislative trend toward gender neutrality in our recent case of *Mims v. Mims*, 305 N.C. 41, 286 S.E.2d 779 (1982). There, we considered the judge-made rule that where a wife buys property and puts it in her husband's name, a resulting trust in the property arises in her favor; yet where the husband buys property and puts it in his wife's name, the law presumes it to have been a gift to her. We noted that this rule arose in our courts sitting in equity to protect the interests of the wife, whom the law presumed to be controlled by her husband in financial matters. In deciding that this gender-biased rule was no longer in keeping with the modern concept of the marriage and with recent legislative trends already alluded to, we said:

> These notions no longer accurately represent the society in which we live, and our laws have changed to reflect this fact. No longer must the husband be, nor is he in all instances the sole owner of the family wealth. No longer is the wife viewed as "little more than a chattel in the eyes of the law." *Nicholson v. Hospital*, 266 S.E.2d 818, 820 (1980). No longer in all cases is the husband the supporting and the wife the dependent spouse. No longer is the wife thought generally to be under the domination of her husband. *Mims v. Mims*, 286 S.E.2d at 785.

We find that the reasoning in *Mims* is sound and applies equally well to the judge-made gender-biased rule requiring a husband to pay for the necessaries of his wife, but relieving her of a reciprocal duty. We therefore hold that a wife is liable for the necessary medical expenses provided for her husband. To the extent that the Court of Appeals opinion in *McCartha*, 66 N.C. App. 177, 310 S.E.2d 409, conflicts with our ruling, that case is overruled. . . .

Having held that the doctrine of necessaries applies equally to both spouses, we turn to the question of whether the dismissal of plaintiff's action against Vern Dell Harris was proper. In order to make out a prima facie case against a spouse for the recovery of expenses incurred in providing necessary medical services to the other spouse, the following must be shown:

1. medical services were provided to the spouse;
2. the medical services were necessary for the health and well-being of the receiving spouse;
3. the person against whom the action is brought was married to the person to whom the medical services were provided at the time such services were provided; and
4. the payment for the necessaries has not been made.

Turning to the facts in the present case, it appears that all of the elements of a prima facie case have been proven or stipulated to by the parties and that no affirmative defenses have been shown. The trial judge found as facts, and the parties so stipulated, that services were provided to defendant Donnie Harris; that these services were necessary to his health and well-being; that Donnie Harris was married to Vern Dell Harris at the time that the services were provided; that the outstanding balance for the services was $3,303.61; and that the payment for those services has not been made. We conclude, therefore, that plaintiff is entitled to recover of Vern Dell Harris $3,303.61, the cost of the medical services provided for her husband by plaintiff.

We, therefore, reverse the decision of the Court of Appeals, vacate the judgment of the trial court, and remand the case to the Court of Appeals for further remand to the District Court, Yadkin County, for entry of judgment for $3,303.61, plus interest, in favor of plaintiff against Vern Dell Harris.

DISCUSSION QUESTIONS FOR *NORTH CAROLINA BAPTIST HOSPITALS, INC. v. HARRIS*

A. What was the common law view concerning provision of necessaries? What reasons did the court give to justify this view?

B. What were the duties of husband and wife at common law?

C. According to this decision, what are the elements of a prima facie case with respect to provision of necessaries?

D. What reasons did the court give to justify changing the common law view of necessaries? How have courts modified the doctrine?

E. The common law view of necessaries was developed during an era when marriage was viewed as permanent and divorce was rare and based strictly on fault. Today divorce is much more common and easy to accomplish. Does this mean that spouses should have fewer financial obligations to each other? Should families continue to be viewed as an economic unit?

F. Under this court's approach to necessaries, are there areas other than medical services to which the doctrine may apply? What purchases would you view as necessary today?

10.3 DUTY TO SUPPORT: CHANGING GENDER ROLES

Historically, spousal support was gender-based, and support obligations were imposed only on husbands. However, in 1979 the Supreme Court ruled that an Alabama statute awarding spousal support only to wives violated the Equal Protection Clause. *Orr v. Orr*, 440 U.S. 268 (1979). The Court determined that sex was not a "reliable proxy for need."

The *Orr* case was decided during an era of major change in the employment status of married women. Between 1960 and the late 1980s, the number of working married women increased from 28 percent to 68 percent. J. Thomas Oldham, *Changes in the Economic Consequences of Divorces, 1958-2008*, 42 Fam. L.Q. 419, 424 (2008). Nevertheless wives earned less in part due to the "wage gap" and the fact that many worked part time. *Id.* at 424-425.

During the last half of the twentieth century, the legal and societal landscape changed dramatically and so quickly that couples who married under one set of societal expectations found themselves divorcing under another. Change worked to the particular disadvantage of long-term homemakers, who faced new expectations of self-support as they were forced and expected to make an economic "clean break" from their spouses.

Appellate decisions from this era evidence the trend away from permanent spousal support awards and toward short-term "rehabilitative" awards. For example, the 1977 decision in *Cashman v. Cashman*, 256 N.W.2d 640 (Minn. 1977), involved the ex-wife of a judge who bore 12 children during a 28-year traditional marriage and suffered from various health problems. Despite her age and time away from her employment as a nurse, the trial court granted only temporary spousal support. The appellate court reversed, holding that Mrs. Cashman's outmoded skills, the length of the marriage, and Mrs. Cashman's medical problems justified a permanent award.

REFLECTIVE QUESTIONS	For the purpose of establishing spousal support, should a situation involving a spouse with outmoded skills who is suffering from medical problems and coming out of a long-term marriage be viewed differently than a healthy, working spouse who is divorcing after a short marriage?

Background to *Otis v. Otis*

Three years after the *Cashman* decision discussed above, the Minnesota Supreme Court considered the spousal support claim of another long-term homemaker. In *Otis v. Otis*, the court referred specifically to the "new" provisions of the Uniform Act, which required a threshold finding of need before a spousal support award was made.

The *Otis* court chronicles changes that occurred in the intervening years between the *Cashman* and *Otis* decisions, including a developing national trend toward rehabilitative spousal support awards. According to one study, in 1978, 74 percent of spousal support awards made to employed wives married for ten years or more were permanent awards. However, by 1984, only 31 percent of these awards were permanent awards. Martha Garrison, *Good Intentions Gone Awry: The Impact of New York's Equitable Distribution Law on Divorce Outcomes*, 57 Brook. L. Rev. 620, 703 (1991). This is a remarkable amount of change over a relatively short period of time.

Otis v. Otis involves the affirmance of a three-year temporary spousal support award. The ex-husband earned $120,000 per year, the marriage lasted for 25 years, and the ex-wife was a traditional homemaker capable of earning $12,000 to $18,000 per year. She had "abandoned a promising career as an executive secretary in order to fulfill the expected, traditional role of wife and hostess for a rising and successful business executive." Because she was in good health, could obtain a job, and was viewed as no longer dependent on her husband, the court upheld a three-year award of spousal support.

OTIS
v.
OTIS

Supreme Court of Minnesota
299 N.W.2d 114 (1980)

TODD, J. The parties were married on June 6, 1954. At the time of the marriage, Mrs. Otis was a skilled executive secretary, earning a substantial income. She left her employment to give birth to the parties' only child and has remained absent from the employment market since that time. Mr. Otis has achieved a high degree of success in the business world and is employed by Control Data Corporation as an executive vice president. At the time of the divorce, Mrs. Otis was 45 and Mr. Otis was 46 years of age. The divorce decree divided the property of the parties as follows:

[Mrs. Otis received property as follows:]

Household furniture	$ 13,000.00
Clothing, jewelry, etc.	$ 9,000.00
Interest in real estate partnership	$ 25,000.00 (cost)
Equity in leased automobile	$ 1,000.00
Cash	$ 21,400.00 (net)
Equity in homestead	$ 35,000.00
Control Data stock (2,923 shares)	$121,304.50
Total:	$225,704.50

[Mr. Otis received property as follows:]

Household furniture	$ 13,000.00
Clothing, jewelry, etc.	$ 2,500.00
Interest in real estate partnership	$ 25,000.00 (cost)
Porche automobile	$ 10,000.00
Cash	$ 7,500.00
Profit sharing plan — cash value	$ 1,300.00
Life insurance policies — cash value	$ 20,000.00
Control Data stock (6,827 shares) (net value)	$131,320.50
Total:	$210,620.50

Mr. Otis was also awarded his substantial interest in his vested pension plan. In addition, he was awarded property in Greece valued at $85,000 which he had inherited.

At the time of the divorce, Mr. Otis received an annual salary in excess of $120,000, plus bonuses. The trial court found that Mrs. Otis was in good health and had held a highly paid secretarial job in the past. Further, the court found that Mrs. Otis, with some additional training, is capable of earning $12,000 to $18,000 per year. In addition to the property settlement outlined above, Mrs. Otis was awarded as "alimony" the sum of $2,000 per month, commencing December 1, 1978, through and until the last day of 1980, and $1,000 per month, commencing on January 1, 1981, through and until the last day of 1982. Thereafter, no further "alimony" must be paid. In recent years, courts have retreated from traditional attitudes toward spousal support because society no longer perceives the married woman as an economically unproductive creature who is "something better than her husband's dog, a little dearer than his horse." Traditionally, spousal support was a permanent award because it was assumed that a wife had neither the ability nor the resources to become self-sustaining. However, with the mounting dissolution rate, the advent of no-fault dissolution, and the growth of the women's liberation movement, the focal point of spousal support determinations has shifted from the sex of the recipient to the individual's ability to become financially independent. This change in focus has given rise to the concept of rehabilitative alimony, also called maintenance, spousal support, limited alimony, or step-down spousal support. The Missouri Court of Appeals expressed the concerns concisely:

> The most that can be accurately said about the amount to be granted is that it is neither the policy of the law to give the spouse receiving maintenance a lifetime annuity nor to reduce her to menial labor to eke out an existence.

The Florida Court of Appeals, which has had various occasions to consider alimony questions, has adopted an approach similar to that of the Uniform Act. The [Florida] court has recognized the distinction between permanent alimony and rehabilitative alimony (maintenance):

> Under the circumstances, the [Florida] trial court erred in awarding permanent rather than rehabilitative alimony. As we have previously stated: "The public policy under the new law which the legislature passed and which therefore we must apply seems to be that if the spouse has the capacity to make her own way through the remainder of her life unassisted by the former husband, then the courts cannot require him to pay alimony other than for rehabilitative purposes."

The public policy of the State would be utterly frustrated by an award of permanent alimony where it affirmatively appears that the wife has not only the capacity but also the desire to be self-supporting.

More recently that court [Florida] emphasized, in setting aside a 20-year award of alimony, that rehabilitative alimony must be of reasonable duration: Rehabilitative alimony is not a substitute for either unemployment compensation or retirement benefits. The award is clearly an incentive to assist one in reclaiming employment skills outside the home which have atrophied during the marital relationship. It was not meant to remove the recipient from the job market. When a wife has completed her maternal role, and provided she is in good health, she should make every effort to rehabilitate herself within a reasonable time thereafter, and when she has done so, rehabilitative alimony is to be discontinued.

The Florida Court has also indicated that a substantial difference in the earning capacities of the spouse does not justify continuing alimony once a spouse has become self-supporting: In view of the foregoing, under the applicable law the ability of the husband to pay does not justify continuation of the alimony where, as here, the rehabilitated wife is shown to have become self-supporting.

We are now faced in Minnesota with new legislation which effects a substantial change in the role of the courts in awarding periodic or lump-sum payments to a divorced spouse. Minnesota decisions decided prior to this time provide only minimal help in passing on the validity of trial court awards under the new act. Rather, the focus of this court must now be on a determination of the two basic standards established by the new legislation; namely, we must determine if the spouse seeking maintenance—

> a. Lacks sufficient property, including marital property apportioned to him, to provide for his reasonable needs, especially during a period of training or education, and
> b. Is unable to support himself through appropriate employment or is the custodian of a child whose condition or circumstances make it appropriate that the custodian not be required to seek employment outside the home.

In construing the Uniform Act provision, the Kentucky Court of Appeals concluded that the statute required satisfaction of the conditions of both subsections.

Applying these standards to the findings of the trial court which we are bound to accept in the absence of a transcript, we conclude that the decision of the trial court is not clearly erroneous.

OTIS, J. dissenting. In my opinion it is manifestly unjust and inappropriate to deprive a wife of an expectancy on which she had a right to rely after a marriage of 25 years and accordingly I respectfully dissent.

Recognizing a wife's contribution to her husband's career, this court has held that the support to which a divorced wife is entitled is not limited to that which will provide her with the bare necessities of life. She can expect a sum which will maintain her at a standard of living commensurate with what she and her husband enjoyed at the time of the dissolution.

The parties were married in June 1954. Today, respondent is a vice-president of Control Data Corporation, earning more than $120,000 per year. Appellant has not been employed since her son was born, at which time she abandoned a promising career as an executive secretary in order to fulfill the expected, traditional role of wife and hostess for a rising and successful business executive. She performed this role so well that in 1977 she was selected to serve as hostess to the board of directors of Control Data Corporation during a week-long meeting in Greece, which was her homeland and that of her husband. When her husband was being considered for his present position, appellant was herself interviewed to determine whether she could fill the role required of her in her husband's business career. A number of years previously she had been anxious to resume a career of her own. Her husband forbade it stating that he was "not going to have any wife of mine pound a typewriter."

There is no showing that at her age, now approximately forty-seven, she can be gainfully employed at her prior occupation after a lapse of more than twenty years. As we said in *Bollenbach*, "[the wife's] role in the particular situation of these parties was to expend her youth and intelligence and talents in the home and with her children and in family-related activities of which her husband approved."

DISCUSSION QUESTIONS FOR *OTIS v. OTIS*

A. The court observes that "traditionally, spousal support was a permanent award because it was assumed that a wife had neither the ability nor the resources to become self-sustaining. However, with the mounting dissolution rate, the advent of no-fault dissolution, and the growth of the women's liberation movement, the focal point of spousal support determinations has shifted from the sex of the recipient to the individual's ability to become financially independent. This change in focus has given rise to the concept of rehabilitative alimony, also called maintenance, spousal support, limited alimony, or step-down spousal support." When, if ever, might this court award permanent spousal support?

B. The court suggests that public policy would be "utterly frustrated by an award of permanent alimony." The dissenting judge states, "Recognizing a wife's contribution to her husband's career, this court has held that the support to which a divorced wife is entitled is not limited to that which will provide her with the bare necessities of life." Is the new policy to limit spousal support to provision of the bare necessities of life? Does UMDA §308 encourage such an approach? Should the standard of living during the marriage be considered?

C. Five years after this opinion was rendered, the Minnesota court system reconsidered its view of spousal support awards in long-term, traditional marriages. This happened in response to state legislation enacted in direct response to decisions such as this one. If Ms. Otis had been divorced in 1985, she might well have received permanent monthly support. When courts and legislatures have different views on matters of public policy, how should they be resolved?

D. What would happen to Ms. Otis today? According to Professor Cynthia Lee Starnes:

> Many of the primary caregivers at work in today's home are going about their business unaware that if their marriages end they are likely to become the law's suckers, set free to alone bear the long-term costs of the role they thought was part of marital teamwork. Archaic alimony laws are to blame. Alimony is often the only available tool for ensuring that divorce does not impose all the long-term costs of marital roles on caregivers while freeing the other spouse to enjoy all the long-term benefits. Yet, in its current incarnation, alimony is not up the task before it. Beset by myths, disdain, and neglect, the law of alimony inspires orders that are unpredictable, inconsistent, short-lived, and uncommon.

Cynthia Lee Starnes, *The Marriage Buyout: The Troubled Trajectory of U.S. Alimony Law* 185 (2014). If spouses agree that one will work less in order to nurture children or care for elderly parents, are there ramifications at the time of divorce? What is fair in this circumstance?

10.4 RATIONALES FOR SPOUSAL SUPPORT

The law of spousal support remains controversial and unsettled in part because of the lack of consensus concerning its purpose. Should it satisfy need? Serve as a bridge to self-support? Reimburse for financial and other sacrifices? Punish for marital fault?

On the other hand, from a policy-making perspective, perhaps it is important that the concept of spousal support remains sufficiently flexible to further a variety of purposes based on the various situations of former spouses. For example, a statute recently passed in Massachusetts provides for general term alimony (based on economic independence), rehabilitative alimony, reimbursement alimony, and transitional alimony. *See* Charles P. Kindregan, Jr., *Reforming Alimony: Massachusetts Reconsiders Postdivorce Spousal Support*, 46 Suffolk U. L. Rev. 13, 28-37 (2013).

REFLECTIVE QUESTIONS	Do you think that spousal support has a place in modern times? Why or why not? Under what conditions would you deem it appropriate?

10.5 PURPOSE OF SPOUSAL SUPPORT: NEED AND THE UMDA PROVISIONS

The Uniform Marriage and Divorce Act (UMDA) was influential in the development of the law of spousal support, and several provisions were adopted by many states during the 1970s. UMDA §308 provides for a two-step analysis regarding spousal support awards. Under UMDA §308(a), the court considers need, specifically whether the spouse seeking support "(1) lacks sufficient property to provide for his reasonable needs; and (2) is unable to support himself through appropriate employment or is the custodian of a child whose condition or circumstances make it appropriate that the custodian not be required to seek employment outside the home." If need is not established, no support is awarded.

If need is established, under UMDA §308(b), the court decides amount and duration of support based on the following factors: "(1) the financial resources of the party seeking maintenance including marital property apportioned to him, his ability to meet his needs independently, and the extent to which a provision for support of a child living with the party includes a sum for that party as custodian; (2) the time necessary to acquire sufficient education or training to enable the party seeking maintenance to find appropriate employment; (3) the standard of living established during the marriage; (4) the duration of the marriage; (5) the age and physical and emotional condition of the spouse seeking maintenance; and (6) the ability of the spouse from whom maintenance is sought to meet his needs while meeting those of the spouse seeking maintenance."

REFLECTIVE QUESTIONS	From a policy perspective, should "need" or "standard of living" be the primary consideration when deciding spousal support? Why or why not?

10.6 PURPOSE OF SPOUSAL SUPPORT: REHABILITATION

Today courts tend to fashion spousal support awards geared toward a specific purpose. For example, rehabilitative support is designed to enable a former spouse to gain training and education in order to become financially independent. Reimbursement spousal support compensates a spouse for financial sacrifices made during the marriage. Courts that view divorce as analogous to breach of a contract or dissolution of a partnership may employ spousal support as a tool to apportion financial consequences more fairly. As discussed later in this chapter, in some states spousal support may also serve to compensate a spouse who suffered from a partner's marital misconduct.

REFLECTIVE QUESTIONS	Is there a difference between rehabilitative support and reimbursement support?

Background to *Cox v. Cox*

In *Cox v. Cox*, the court considers a spousal support request based on a long-term marriage where one spouse earns more than the other. The court examines different types of spousal support, including limited-duration, rehabilitative, and reimbursement support, and analyzes statutory factors related to amount and duration. The ex-wife, who finished law school but did not pass the bar exam, challenges the award of limited-duration spousal support.

COX

v.

COX

Superior Court of New Jersey
762 A.2d 1040 (2000)

CARCHMAN, J.A.D. . . . Plaintiff Margaret M. Cox and defendant Harry E. Cox were married in 1977. Their child, Heather, currently a college student, was born in 1979. In 1996, the parties separated, and a dissolution complaint was filed. During the marriage, defendant worked as a crane operator earning approximately $120,000 per year in gross salary including regular overtime, or approximately $7,800 per month net of taxes and other mandated deductions. After Heather completed the first grade, plaintiff returned to work and earned approximately $13,000 to $14,000 per year working at various part-time jobs as a data entry clerk, bank teller, and cosmetics salesperson. Plaintiff's resumption of employment represented the parties' mutual decision and was necessitated by their need for additional funds to support the household.

In 1989, plaintiff began attending Rutgers University, and earned her undergraduate degree in 1995. She continued to work during college, earning approximately $6,000 a year. In 1995, plaintiff enrolled in law school, and earned her law degree in 1998. She did not work during law school and incurred approximately $100,000 in debt to finance her education. After graduating, and during the pendency of the trial, plaintiff served a one-year term as a judicial law clerk at a salary of $30,000 per year. Unfortunately, her first attempt to pass the New Jersey bar examination was unsuccessful. However, following her clerkship, plaintiff secured employment at a law firm at a salary of $33,000 per year. Although plaintiff's reply brief and a letter filed pursuant to R. 2:6-11(d), state that her two subsequent attempts to pass the bar examination were unsuccessful and that she was recently terminated from her position at the law firm, we do not consider this information on appeal, as it is not part of the record below.

According to plaintiff, she and defendant "had a nice standard of living" during the marriage. They vacationed once every two years, and dined out two or three times a week. Plaintiff indicated that she no longer dines out, and that her "standard of living has substantially dropped" with respect to housing, clothing, and transportation. Although the parties then owned a house in Delran, plaintiff rented an apartment that was more accessible to public transportation and thus more convenient to her work. During the marriage, defendant worked approximately eighty to ninety hours per week. At the time of trial, he earned $25 per hour but claimed that the mental and physical stress of the job have started to take a toll on his health. At the conclusion of the trial, the judge found that as of March 22, 1998, defendant earned $1,392 in weekly net income and had reasonable weekly expenses of approximately $553. Thus, exclusive of child support, alimony, Heather's school loan payments, and life insurance payments, defendant had a weekly surplus of $839. The judge found that plaintiff earned $640 per week and had reasonable monthly expenses of $3,035 per month. However, the judge concluded that plaintiff incurred an extraordinary rental expense of $1,000 monthly for her apartment and observed that plaintiff had a deficit of approximately $66 per month without alimony.

Most significantly, the judge found that this was a long-term marriage, and there was substantial disparity between the parties' incomes. Nevertheless, the judge ordered limited duration alimony in the amount of $200 per week for a period of five years "to enable the plaintiff to establish herself as an attorney." . . .

The award of alimony to a divorcing spouse is provided for by statute:

> after judgment of divorce or maintenance . . . the court may make such order as to the alimony or maintenance of the parties . . . as the circumstances of the parties and the nature of the case shall render fit, reasonable and just.

N.J.S.A. 2A:34-23. If the judge determines that permanent alimony is not warranted, further specific findings setting forth the judge's reasons for that determination must be made. Consideration of any other form of alimony, including limited duration alimony, may follow only after those determinations and findings have been made. Clearly, limited duration alimony is neither an available option nor an appropriate remedy in all dissolution cases. In considering alimony applications under the new statutory scheme, judges should bear in mind that an award of limited duration alimony must reflect the underlying policy considerations which distinguish this form of alimony from rehabilitative and reimbursement alimony. Conceptually, limited duration alimony is more closely related to permanent alimony than to rehabilitative or reimbursement alimony. The latter two types of alimony represent forms of limited spousal support for specified purposes; once the purpose is achieved, entitlement to that form of alimony ceases. Permanent and limited duration alimony, by contrast, reflect the important policy of recognizing that marriage is an adaptive economic and social partnership, and an award of either validates that principle.

A noted scholar has described the principle and its application to alimony awards:

> According to the marital partnership principle, the married couple forms an economic unit. The contributions of both husband and wife to this unit are valuable regardless of whether the contributions are financial or nonfinancial. . . .

The prevailing principle in fixing an alimony award . . . was recently reiterated by the Supreme Court: "the goal of a proper alimony award is to assist the supported spouse in achieving a lifestyle that is reasonably comparable to the one enjoyed while living with the supporting spouse during the marriage."

Any award of alimony requires an analysis of the statutory factors to be considered in setting the amount and duration of an award, including:

1. The actual need and ability of the parties to pay;
2. The duration of the marriage;
3. The age, physical and emotional health of the parties;
4. The standard of living established in the marriage and the likelihood that each party can maintain a reasonably comparable standard of living;
5. The earning capacities, educational levels, vocational skills, and employability of the parties;
6. The length of absence from the job market of the party seeking maintenance;
7. The parental responsibilities for the children;
8. The time and expense necessary to acquire sufficient education or training to enable the party seeking maintenance to find appropriate employment . . . ;
9. The history of the financial or non-financial contributions to the marriage by each party . . . ;
10. The equitable distribution of property ordered and any payments on equitable distribution, directly or indirectly, out of current income, to the extent this consideration is reasonable, just and fair;
11. The income available to either party through investment[s] . . . ;
12. The tax treatment and consequences to both parties of any alimony award . . . and
13. Any other factors which the court may deem relevant.

The most commonly expressed rationale for permanent alimony is:

1. To compensate for benefits conferred on the other spouse by being responsible for homemaking and child rearing. The primary benefit is increased earning capacity of

the other spouse who, while enjoying family life, was free to devote all productive time to income production.

2. To compensate for the opportunity costs of homemaking. This is primarily lost earning capacity through the years of major responsibility for the home, either not being employed or holding employment subject to the needs of the family. Courts recognize this opportunity cost when they refer to the fact that the claimant for alimony had remained in the home in the traditional role of full-time homemaker. There is, also, a cost in lessened opportunity for remarriage which is greater for women than men and which increases the longer the marriage lasts.

In short, "a transfer of earning power" occurs during a traditional marriage in which the homemaker spouse's efforts increased the other's earning capacity at the expense of her own. Alimony is an award formulated to compensate for that transfer by sufficiently (fairly) meeting reasonable needs for support not otherwise met by property division and personal income.

Limited duration alimony is to be awarded in recognition of a dependent spouse's contributions to a relatively short-term marriage that nevertheless demonstrated the attributes of a "marital partnership." In determining whether to award limited duration alimony, a trial judge must consider the same statutory factors considered in any application for permanent alimony, tempered only by the limited duration of the marriage. All other statutory factors being in equipoise, the duration of the marriage marks the defining distinction between whether permanent or limited duration alimony is warranted and awarded. . . .

We also question the judge's requirement that the parties return in two years to review the status of plaintiff's award. While on its face, such an order would appear to benefit plaintiff, on reflection, it inures to her detriment. The alimony statute clearly confines the scope of permissible modifications to limited duration alimony awards based upon changed or nonoccuring circumstances to amount only, absent unusual circumstances warranting a change in duration. N.J.S.A. 2A:34-23(c). By requiring a review after two years, presumably requiring plaintiff to show why the award should be continued for the full five-year period as originally ordered, the trial judge has shifted the burden from the paying spouse to seek modification, to the receiving spouse to continue the alimony awarded.

In sum, we conclude that the award of limited duration alimony here was inappropriate. The nature of the award was, in fact, rehabilitative, and it failed to account for the various contributions of plaintiff as a homemaker, child-rearer, and "marital partner" for the duration of this twenty-two year marriage.

Because we are ordering a remand and requiring the trial judge to consider all of the relevant statutory factors, we need not determine whether the award of $200 per week was an appropriate amount. We observe, however, that while defendant is responsible for Heather's college costs, plaintiff is burdened with the cost of her own higher education debts. The trial judge's findings on this issue failed to carefully analyze the financial impact and duration of those significant obligations, as well as to make the clear and definitive findings as to the parties' marital standard of living which are essential to any permanent alimony award determination.

Reversed and remanded for further proceedings consistent with this opinion.

DISCUSSION QUESTIONS FOR *COX v. COX*

A. For how many years were Margaret and Harry married? Should the length of a marriage influence the outcome of an alimony award? Why or why not?

B. Under UMDA §308(a), does the wife meet the initial need-based threshold for an award of spousal support?

C. Which of the 13 statutory factors listed by the court should receive the greatest weight when deciding the amount and duration of an award? Or should each factor receive equal weight?

D. This court distinguishes between durational, permanent, rehabilitative, and reimbursement spousal support. What are the major characteristics of each? When should each be used?

10.7 PURPOSE OF SPOUSAL SUPPORT: COMPENSATION, CAREGIVING, AND THE ALI

The American Law Institute proposes that spousal support be awarded as compensation for losses in earning capacity and standard of living, particularly where one spouse has disproportionately cared for children or other relatives. American Law Institute, *Principles of the Law of Family Dissolution: Analysis and Recommendations* §5.01 et seq. (2002).

Rather than attempting to define or establish need when awarding spousal support, the American Law Institute (ALI) takes a conceptually different approach by focusing on compensation for loss. As stated in ALI, *Principles of the Law of Family Dissolution* §5.02 comment a (2001):

> The principal conceptual innovation of this Chapter is therefore to recharacterize the remedy it provides as *compensation for loss* rather than *relief of need*. A spouse frequently seems in need at the conclusion of a marriage because its dissolution imposes a particularly severe loss on him or her. The intuition that the former spouse has an obligation to meet that need arises from the perception that the need results from the unfair allocation of the financial losses arising from the marital failure. This perception

explains why we have alimony, and why all alimony claims cannot be adjudicated by reference to a single standard of need.

Section 5.03 delineates types of losses to be compensated, including assumption of a disproportionate share of care giving, investment in the earning capacity of the other spouse, and changes in standard of living. *See* James Herbie DiFonzo, *Toward a Unified Field Theory of the Family: The American Law Institute's Principles of the Law of Family Dissolution*, 2001 BYU L. Rev. 923.

Research supports the assertion that acting as a primary caretaker takes a toll on the ultimate earning capacity of the caregiving parent:

> The parent who decides to be the primary caregiver in many instances either quits work for a period or takes part-time work in order to be able to fulfill child-care responsibilities. Because of such career choices, the primary caretaker's career is impacted. That parent loses seniority, and skills erode. Only 34% of married women with children younger than age six work full time.
>
> The impact on the primary caretaker's career prospects can be significant. One investigator found that female nonmothers earned 90% of what men earned at age 30; in contrast, mothers earned an average 70% of the male wage. Twenty years ago, another investigator found that a primary caretaker's lifetime earnings were reduced, on average, by $22,000, $43,000, and $64,000 for raising one, two, or three children, respectively. Another study found an average wage penalty of approximately 7% per child for American women.

J. Thomas Oldham, *Changes in the Economic Consequences of Divorces, 1958-2008*, 42 Fam. L.Q. 419, 425-426 (2008) (citations omitted). One commentator has suggested creating a new form of support, "chalimony," for caregivers of children with disabilities or chronic health conditions. *See* Karen Syma Czapanskiy, *Chalimony: Seeking Equity Between Parents of Children with Disabilities and Chronic Illnesses*, 34 N.Y.U. Rev. L. & Soc. Change 253 (2010).

REFLECTIVE QUESTIONS	Do you agree with the ALI approach? How is it different from the UMDA approach?

10.8 PURPOSE OF SPOUSAL SUPPORT: REIMBURSEMENT AND APPORTIONMENT OF INEQUITY

Background to *Haugan v. Haugan*

Courts are sometimes faced with situations where one spouse has forgone the immediate enjoyment of earned income to enable the other to pursue advanced education on a full-time basis. Typically, the sacrifice is made with the expectation that the parties will share a higher standard of living in the future. Because the income of the working spouse is used for living expenses, there is usually little accumulated marital property to be divided if the dissolution occurs prior to the attainment of the financial rewards concomitant with the advanced degree or professional license. Furthermore, the working spouse may not be entitled to statutory spousal support because of the demonstrated ability of self-support. Because the equities weigh heavily in favor of providing a remedy to the working spouse in such a situation, the courts have struggled to find theories upon which relief can be granted. The court in *Haugan v. Haugan* discusses various creative approaches to providing spousal support in such a situation.

HAUGAN
v.
HAUGAN

Supreme Court of Wisconsin
343 N.W.2d 796 (1984)

ABRAHAMSON, J. The couple, Patricia and Gordon Haugan, were married on August 4, 1973. About a month later the husband entered medical school and the wife began gainful employment. Each already had a bachelor's degree. For the first four years of their marriage the wife taught elementary school while the husband attended medical school in South Dakota and then in Minnesota. The wife's total earnings of between $26,187 and $28,974 supported the couple during these four years. The husband received a stipend of $2,200 and borrowed money to pay education expenses.

The wife continued to teach school for the next three years of their marriage while the husband, having graduated from medical school, was in a medical residency in Chicago. The husband's aggregate earnings for that three-year period were between $49,254 and $49,548, and the wife's were between $43,339 and $45,056. In addition to working full time outside the home, the wife performed virtually all of the household duties over the seven years.

In 1980, in anticipation of the husband's completing his medical training and beginning his practice of medicine, the couple bought a house in Green Bay, Wisconsin, and the wife resigned from her teaching job. On May 13, 1980, however, about two months before the husband completed his medical residency, the couple separated. In August 1980 the husband began practicing pediatric medicine in Green Bay at an annual salary of $48,000 ($4,000 a month) plus bonuses, for a total annual compensation of $55,498. The wife was unemployed until February 1981, when she began a job with IBM in Green Bay at an annual salary of $19,680 ($1,640 a month). Between August 1980 and August 1981 the husband voluntarily paid the wife a total of $10,150 ($817 a month in temporary maintenance plus half of a joint income tax refund of $693).

The wife testified that at the time of the marriage she and her husband shared the expectation that she would support him while he obtained his medical education and that he would support her after he began his medical practice, allowing her to pursue the career of a homemaker, wife, and mother. The husband argued that the record did not establish a "mutual agreement" since it contained no evidence of a written or formalized agreement. The trial court concluded that "no mutuality of such 'contract' had been established" and that the wife's expectation was "not an express or implied contractual arrangement." Nonetheless, cognizance must be taken of the fact that the husband had a general idea of the wife's expectations.

The couple's total assets were valued at $124,133. The couple's total liabilities at the time of the divorce amounted to approximately $126,176, thus exceeding the value of the assets. . . .

All of the debts of the parties — the debts the husband incurred before marriage, the debts the parties incurred during marriage, and the debts the husband incurred for medical education — were assigned to the husband.

The trial court's explanation of its division of the marital property — assets and liabilities — was limited. The trial court stated that although it was not enumerating all the factors set forth in secs. 767.255 and 767.26, Stats. 1981-82, it had considered all the statutory factors and it intended to award the wife more than 50 percent of the marital property.

The trial court denied the wife's request for maintenance payments on the grounds that her post-divorce income would exceed her pre-divorce income and she would not be in financial need after the divorce.

On appeal from the portion of the judgment denying maintenance and awarding property division, the court of appeals affirmed the judgment of the circuit court. The problem this case poses is not uncommon. University degree–divorce decree cases are frequent. In many marriages, while one spouse pursues an undergraduate, graduate, or professional degree or license, the other works to support the couple and forgoes his or her own education or career and the immediate benefits of a second income which the student spouse might have provided. The couple typically expects that the degree will afford them a higher shared standard of living in the future. That standard of living is never realized by the supporting spouse when the marriage breaks up just as the newly educated spouse is beginning the long-awaited career. In addition, little marital property has accumulated, because the couple's income was used for education and living expenses.

In a marriage of significant duration, the marital partners share the return on their investment in the marriage. When the marriage ends in divorce the accumulated property is divided according to law and maintenance may be awarded.

But in a marital partnership where both parties work toward the education of one of the partners and the marriage ends before the economic benefit is realized and property is accumulated, it is unfair under these circumstances to deny the supporting spouse a share in the anticipated enhanced earnings while the student spouse keeps the degree and all the financial rewards it promises. As this court has recognized, "in a sense," the degree "is the most significant asset of the marriage" and "it is only fair" that the supporting spouse be compensated for costs and opportunities foregone [*sic*] while the student spouse was in school. A compensatory award to the supporting spouse can ensure that both marital partners, and not only the one who has received the education, participate in the financial rewards attributable to the enhanced earnings of the student spouse. The legislature recognized in the Divorce Reform Act of 1977 that the wife or husband who invested in a spouse's education should be compensated upon divorce. The legislature said that "a spouse who has been handicapped socially and economically by his or her contributions to a marriage shall be compensated for such contributions at the termination of the marriage insofar as this is possible."

Such compensation may be accomplished under the statutes through maintenance payments, property division, or both. Sec. 767.26, Stats. 1981-82, which governs maintenance payments, provides that the trial court may consider, among other factors, "the educational level of each party at the time of marriage and at the time the action is commenced," and "the contribution by one party to the education, training or increased earning power of the other." Sec. 767.255, Stats. 1981-82, which governs property division, directs the trial court to presume that the marital property is to be divided equally between the parties but authorizes the trial court to alter this presumed division after considering such factors as "the contribution by one party to the education, training or increased earning power of the other," and "the earning capacity of each party."

In exercising its broad discretion in rendering a fundamentally fair and equitable decision in each case, the trial court has the difficult task of quantifying the value of the supporting spouse's and student spouse's contributions to the marriage and determining the rights and responsibilities of the parties on divorce. Because circumstances vary so much from case to case, this court cannot set down a formula for the trial court to apply in assigning a dollar value to each partner's contribution. We can, however, suggest several approaches for the trial court to consider in reaching its decision as to a maintenance award, property division, or both for the supporting spouse. These approaches are illustrative only; there are other approaches.

One approach the trial court may consider is the cost value approach whereby it calculates the value of the supporting spouse's contributions, not only in terms of money for education and living expenses but also in terms of services rendered during the marriage. In this case, for example, the wife worked full time outside the home and also performed the household duties, and the fair market value of those homemaking services might be considered along with her financial input. Furthermore, the trial court should consider adjusting the value of the supporting spouse's contributions by a fair rate of return or for inflation. Such an award is restitutionary in nature; it does not account for a return on the supporting spouse's investment in terms of a share in the future enhanced earnings of the student spouse.

On review the wife in this case urges that the trial court should have calculated the contributions she made to the support of her student husband by using the cost value approach set forth in *DeLa Rosa v. DeLa Rosa*.

Although this court in *Lundberg* did not directly address the question of calculating the costs of support to determine compensation to the supporting spouse, we did refer to *DeLa Rosa v. DeLa Rosa*. In *DeLa Rosa*, the Minnesota court developed the following formula for awarding such compensation to the working wife:

working spouse's financial contributions to joint living expenses and educational costs of student spouse

less

1/2 (working spouse's financial contributions plus student spouse's financial contributions less cost of education)

equals

equitable award to working spouse.

DeLa Rosa, *supra*, 309 N.W.2d at 759.

Using this formula, the wife in this case asserts that she contributed $69,526 to $74,030 in earnings to the marriage; that her husband contributed earnings and stipends of $51,454 to $51,748; that the direct costs of his medical education were $18,220; and that he contributed medical school loans of $13,457 (valued as of the trial date). Applying these figures to the *DeLa Rosa* formula, the wife calculates her contribution as $13,000, without including interest, adjustments for inflation, or her non-financial contributions. The wife introduced evidence at trial that the value of the $13,000 contribution indexed for inflation is $28,560.

A second approach is looking at opportunity costs. The trial court may in determining the award to the supporting spouse consider the income the family sacrificed because the student spouse attended school rather than accepting employment. In this case the wife introduced evidence that the husband's increased earnings during the seven-year marriage had he not pursued medical education and training would have been $45,700 after taxes, or $69,800 indexed for inflation.

A third approach enables the trial court to consider compensating the supporting spouse according to the present value of the student spouse's enhanced earning capacity. This approach recognizes the spouse's lost expectation of sharing in the enhanced earning capacity; it gives the supporting spouse a return on his or her "investment" in the student spouse measured by the student spouse's enhanced earning capacity. In this case an economist, called as a witness by the wife, estimated the value of the husband's enhanced earning capacity to be $266,000. The economist's figure was the product of multiplying the husband's after-tax annual enhanced earnings of $13,000 (the difference between the husband's annual salary as a physician and the 1979 mean salary for white college-educated males in his age group) by 32.3 (estimated years remaining in the husband's expected working life) discounted to its present value. Using this calculation the wife asserts she would be entitled to one half of the present value of the husband's enhanced earning capacity, or $133,000.

Because many unforeseen events may affect future earnings, this third approach has been subject to criticism. Calculations of the expected stream of income may not take into account such variables as market opportunities, individual career choices and abilities, and premature death. Other approaches are, however, subject to criticism for giving the student spouse a windfall and for failing to recognize the supporting spouse's lost expectations.

Another approach is a variation of the labor theory of value suggested by wife's counsel at oral argument. Under this approach the trial court considers the value of the supporting spouse's contribution to the marriage at one half of the student spouse's enhanced yearly earning power for as many years as the supporting spouse worked to support the student. Under this theory the wife's contribution might be valued at $45,500 (one half of $13,000 × 7), which perhaps should be discounted to present value.

As stated before, no mathematical formula or theory of valuation settles the case. Each case must be decided on its own facts. The guiding principles for the trial court are fairness and justice. . . .

In this case we conclude that the trial court abused its discretion in three respects: it improperly based its denial of maintenance on the wife's lack of need; it failed to articulate fully its reasoning as to denial of maintenance and as to the property division; and the award was clearly inadequate to compensate the wife under the circumstances of this case.

In making its determination as to maintenance, the trial court denied maintenance to the wife stating that the wife was young, in good health, and lacked financial need. This reasoning is contrary to *Lundberg* in which we held that even though the wife was not in need she might be awarded maintenance to compensate her for her contribution to the husband's education, training, and enhanced earning capacity.

While the trial court specifically stated that it considered the husband's enhanced earning capacity, it did not explain why it nevertheless denied maintenance to the wife. In determining maintenance payments, the trial court is supposed to consider the educational level of the parties at the time of marriage and divorce, the contribution by one party to the education, training or increased earning power of the other, and the property division. Sec. 767.26(3)(4)(9), Stats. 1981-82. In this case these factors point toward awarding maintenance, yet the trial court denied maintenance.

Although the trial court stated that "this record requires other than a fifty/fifty division," it failed to explain how it would compensate the wife for her contribution to the husband's education and how it arrived at the property division as a form of compensation. The legislature has directed the trial court to divide the marital property equally between the parties but has authorized the trial court to alter this distribution after considering such factors as the contribution of each party to the marriage, giving appropriate economic value to each party's contribution in home-making, the contribution by one party to the education, training, or increased earning power of the other, the earning capacity of each party, and the maintenance payments. Sec. 767.255(3)(5)(6)(8), Stats. 1981-82.

In the trial court's division of property the wife received approximately 50 percent of the assets and was held responsible for none of the debts. Thus the wife might be viewed as having received more than the statutory 50 percent presumptive share of property through her release from debts. To calculate the amount of benefit she may have received from her release from debt, we must analyze the debts the husband assumed upon the divorce. We do not view the wife as benefiting from the husband's assumption of the education expenses, the land contract liability, or the real estate taxes. Since the husband received both the enhanced earning capacity and the home (in which he had lived during the separation), he should rightfully pay the education expenses, the land contract balance, and the real estate taxes. These debts go along with the assets.

The wife did, however, benefit when the trial court required the husband to pay the joint marital debt of approximately $28,000 incurred for acquisition of property and living expenses. The wife's share of this debt would apparently be $14,000. Indeed on review the wife acknowledges that she received an approximate $14,000 benefit from the trial court's assignment of debts, but she asserts that the release from debts is inadequate to compensate her for contributing total financial and homemaking support of the family unit for four years, contributing almost one half of the financial support of the unit for three years, and foregoing [sic] the husband's earnings during this period and his enhanced earnings in the future.

The husband argues, in effect, that the $14,000 the wife received in excess of the 50-50 marital property division is adequate compensation for her contribution since her total financial contribution during the marriage was $18,000 to $22,000 more than the husband's and that one half of this sum is attributable to his support and one half to hers. The husband therefore argues that the wife was compensated $14,000 for her financial contribution to her husband of $9,000 to $12,000.

We are not persuaded by the husband's reasoning. His calculation ignores the wife's non-financial contribution to the marriage and does not include a rate of return on the wife's contribution or adjustment for inflation or consideration of her lost expectation of sharing in his enhanced earning capacity to which she contributed. Using only a factor for inflation, the wife estimates her $13,000 contribution to the marriage as being worth $28,000 at the time of divorce. Thus the wife asserts on review that in addition to the release from liability of $14,000, she is entitled to an additional award of at least $14,000.

The husband further argues that the award puts the wife in the same position after divorce as she was in before marriage. She leaves the marriage with some property and a job. She did not want further education and was not thwarted in the enjoyment of a career. We are not persuaded by this reasoning because it fails to address the issue which this court has recognized in the university degree– divorce decree cases, namely, that concepts of fairness and equity require that the supporting spouse be compensated when the student spouse leaves the marriage with an earning capacity substantially increased through the other spouse's efforts and sacrifices and the supporting spouse leaves the marriage with little property and a lower earning capacity than the student spouse. Although the trial court may not be able to compensate the wife in this case by giving her the opportunity to pursue the career she wanted as a homemaker and parent, the court can compensate her for the contribution she made in supporting the couple while the husband pursued his professional education. According to the record the wife's contribution was valued between $13,000 (without adjustment for interest and inflation) and $133,000.

Where the marriage terminates before the parties benefited economically from the university degree or license acquired during the marriage and before substantial assets are accumulated, an award of 50 percent or even more of the marital property is unlikely to compensate the supporting spouse fully. The wife would have received 50 percent of the property even if she had not supported her husband financially while he was in school. The award in this case which denied maintenance, divided the assets equally, and relieved the wife of approximately $14,000 in debts seems insufficient compensation for her significant financial and non-financial contributions to this marriage over a seven-year period, her lost expectation of sharing in his enhanced earning capacity, and the valuations of her contribution. Decision of the court of appeals is reversed; judgment of the circuit court vacated in part; cause remanded to the circuit court for further proceedings.

DISCUSSION QUESTIONS FOR *HAUGEN v. HAUGEN*

A. Would spousal support likely be awarded in this case under UMDA §308? Why or why not?

B. The court says that if both parties to a marriage "work toward the education of one of the partners and the marriage ends before the economic benefit is realized and property is accumulated, it is unfair under these circumstances to deny the supporting spouse a share in the anticipated enhanced earnings while the student spouse keeps the degree and all the financial rewards it promises." How will the future enhanced earnings be calculated? Isn't this mere speculation?

C. Explain the cost-value approach.

D. Explain the opportunity-cost approach.

E. Explain the compensation according to the present value of the student spouse's enhanced-earning-capacity approach.

F. Explain the variation of labor theory of value.

G. On what basis did the appellate court conclude that the trial court had abused its discretion?

H. What rationale did the court use in this case to reject the claim that an award of 50 percent or more of the property would adequately compensate the wife?

I. New Jersey provides for reimbursement alimony, which permits a court to consider a financial award based on household expenses, educational costs, school travel expenses, and other contributions. It limits the recovery, however, to monetary contributions that the supporting spouse made with the mutual and shared expectation that both parties would derive increased income and material benefits from the education. *See Mahoney v. Mahoney*, 453 A.2d 527 (N.J. 1982); *Hill v. Hill*, 453 A.2d 537 (N.J. 1982). Does this approach differ from that used by the court in *Haugen*?

10.9 PURPOSE OF SPOUSAL SUPPORT: THE ROLE OF MARITAL FAULT

Most early American courts and legislatures assumed that the husband had a life-long duty of support. By the beginning of the twentieth century, courts commonly awarded a divorced wife personal and real property, usually up to the value of one-third of the personal estate of the husband, and the value of her dower in his real estate. Most jurisdictions prohibited support of any kind if the wife committed adultery, and legislation in most states mandated that the courts examine the "character and situation" of the parties who came before them asking for divorce. Under the fault-based system, spousal support was seen as a kind of damage award because the other spouse had breached his or her marital obligation, and a wife who was found to be at fault generally forfeited any right to support. In this way, spousal support or lack thereof, served as compensation to an injured spouse.

REFLECTIVE QUESTIONS	Why did common law courts examine both the "character and situation" of the parties before deciding whether to award spousal support?

Background to *Riley v. Riley*

Despite the advent of no-fault divorce, approximately half of the states today consider fault when making spousal support awards. Linda D. Elrod & Robert G. Spector, *A Review of the Year in Family Law 2013-2014: Same-Sex Couples Attain Rights to Marry and Parent*, 48 Fam. L.Q. 609, 654-55 (2015). The court in *Riley v. Riley* explains the role of fault in its decision to award higher spousal support payments.

RILEY
v.
RILEY

Court of Appeals of Utah
138 P.3d 84 (2006)

BILLINGS, J. Husband and Wife were married in February 1992 in Fairbanks, Alaska. . . . In July 1994, the family moved to Kaysville, Utah, where Wife continued her work in the child and family services field and obtained a master's degree. . . . After Husband and Wife moved to Utah, Husband pursued a career as a commercial pilot. . . . In 1999, Husband had an extramarital affair, resulting in the birth of a son in

Houston, Texas, on February 4, 2000. Due to Husband's pattern of sustained deception, Wife was unaware of the affair or the child until she opened a letter addressed to Husband from the State of Texas in April 2001. After Wife learned of the affair and the child, Husband and Wife sought counseling to deal with the resulting marital problems. Husband and Wife agreed that as a condition of the parties remaining together, Husband would not have contact with his newly born son or the son's mother.

In spring 2003, Husband asked Wife what they would do if the son lost his mother. Wife informed Husband that he would have to give up his parental rights to the child. In response, Husband decided to leave the marriage. Husband moved to Houston, Texas, agreeing to pay Wife $900 each month until they sold their house in Utah. The couple sold their house on December 1, 2004. . . .

The trial court found that Husband set forth his monthly expenses at $4,655, $750 of which was for food and entertainment. The trial court determined that, despite the fact that some of Husband's expenses were inflated, he still had more than $2,000 left over each month based on earnings of $6,800. Therefore, the trial court concluded that Husband had the ability to provide support to Wife.

Throughout the marriage, Wife's earning potential remained relatively stable. At the time the parties married, Wife was earning approximately $50,000 a year working for the State of Alaska. Her 2004 W-2 showed a gross income of $46,919.64. Wife reported her 2005 expected gross income as approximately $50,000. Although Wife occasionally performed outside contract services, the court found that her income from these services was minimal. The trial court found Wife's monthly earnings to be $4,153. At the time of trial, Wife had $23,000 in a 401(k) account. There was a loan against this account in the amount $11,500.

Wife set forth expenses totaling $4,491, including $400 per month in legal fees. The court found that Wife's monthly expenses were $4,491, $338 more than her income of $4,153 per month. Therefore, the court found Wife was in need of support.

The trial court also found that Husband and Wife contributed significantly different amounts toward family expenses over the course of the marriage. Husband earned approximately $205,688, plus $22,500 in VA benefits, while Wife earned approximately $502,645. In addition to her earnings, Wife liquidated several of her premarital assets to contribute to family expenses. The trial court found that Wife earned and contributed approximately $275,000 to $300,000 more than Husband over the course of the marriage.

Finally, the trial court determined that Wife was more credible than Husband. Specifically, the trial court found that while Wife had been frank with the court, Husband had been unwilling to admit facts that he should have admitted. For example, during trial, Husband denied having fathered an additional child around the time of his separation from Wife. Husband did acknowledge, however, that he was involved with the child's mother and that this child was covered by his medical insurance. The trial court therefore concluded that Husband had either lied about fathering a second child out of wedlock or he had defrauded the insurance company, either of which reflected poorly on his credibility.

In its decision, the trial court acknowledged it had given consideration to the issue of fault. Specifically, the court noted that: (1) during the course of the marriage, Husband committed adultery and fathered an out-of-wedlock child; (2) Husband hid this from Wife for nearly two years, during which time he paid child support; (3) Wife found out about Husband's affair and his new son when she opened a letter from the State of Texas that was addressed to Husband; (4) these circumstances constituted grounds for extreme mental anguish and distress for Wife; and (5) Husband may have fathered an additional child outside his marriage to Wife, and he was evasive and deceitful about the existence of such a child. The trial court concluded that the divorce would not have taken place but for Husband's acts of adultery.

Based on the above findings, the trial court ordered Husband to pay Wife alimony in the amount of $900 per month, not to exceed the duration of the marriage — approximately 156 months. . . .

Under Utah Code section 30-3-5, the trial court must consider, at a minimum, the following factors in determining alimony:

> (i) the financial condition and needs of the recipient spouse; (ii) the recipient's earning capacity or ability to produce income; (iii) the ability of the payor spouse to provide support; (iv) the length of the marriage; (v) whether the recipient spouse has custody of minor children requiring support; (vi) whether the recipient spouse worked in a business owned or operated by the payor spouse; and (vii) whether the recipient spouse directly contributed to any increase in the payor spouse's skill by paying for education received by the payor spouse or allowing the payor spouse to attend school during the marriage.

Utah Code Ann. §30-3-5(8)(a) (Supp. 2005).

Additionally, in determining an alimony award, "the court may consider the fault of the parties." *Id.* §30-3-5(8)(b). Further, [w]hen a marriage of long duration dissolves on the threshold of a major change in the income of one of the spouses due to the collective efforts of both, that change shall be considered in . . . determining the amount of alimony. If one spouse's earning capacity has been greatly enhanced through the efforts of both spouses during the marriage, the court may make a compensating adjustment in . . . awarding alimony. *Id.* §30-3-5(8)(e).

Here, considering all of the foregoing factors, the trial court awarded Wife $900 per month in alimony, well above the shortfall between her demonstrated monthly expenses and her monthly income. In determining the amount of alimony, the trial court explicitly stated it had considered Husband's fault. We conclude the trial court did not abuse its discretion in awarding Wife a $900 per month alimony award. . . .

Finally, Husband maintains the trial court abused its discretion in granting Wife an alimony award of $900 per month because, in doing so, the trial court was attempting to punish Husband for his misdeeds. Utah statutory law expressly provides that a trial court "may consider the fault of the parties in determining alimony." Utah Code Ann. §30-3-5(8)(b). Certainly the facts of this case — Husband's engagement in extramarital affairs and his prolonged deceitful conduct that led to the divorce—present precisely the type of situation where the legislature intended the trial court to consider fault. Indeed, Husband's fault goes a long way in explaining the propriety of a $900 per month alimony award, even though such an award would be too high if only economic factors were considered.

In the present case, the trial court carefully explained its reasons for granting the alimony award. Those reasons are consistent with the factors set out in Utah Code section 30-3-5(8). *See id.* §30-3-5(8). Specifically:

> [The trial court] f[ound] that the facts of this case justif[ied] consideration of [Husband's] fault. [It] deem[ed] it necessary to consider that factor in fairness to [Wife]. It [was] not the [trial c]ourt's intent to apply strict punitive measures so as to unfairly or inequitably burden [Husband]. Nevertheless, [Wife][was] entitled to certain relief based upon her needs, [Husband's] ability to pay, his fault, the efforts of [Wife] in furthering [Husband's] career, and the sacrifice/liquidation of [Wife's] pre-marital assets in order to further [Husband's] career opportunities.

Accordingly, we conclude the trial court did not abuse its discretion in granting Wife a $900 per month alimony award.

DISCUSSION QUESTIONS FOR *RILEY v. RILEY*

A. What factors is a court required to consider when making a spousal support award under the Utah statutes governing this case?

B. The husband in this case argues that he is being "punished" for his misconduct. Is that one of the purposes of considering fault when a spousal support award is made? What other policy reasons support consideration of fault when making awards?

C. Many states do not consider a party's fault when determining spousal support and the UMDA specifically provides that spousal support awards should be made "without regard to marital misconduct," UMDA §308(b). What is this likely rationale for such an approach?

D. Do you think that martial fault should be a consideration in spousal support? Why or why not? *See Clark v. Clark*, 57 A.3d 1 (N.J. Super. 2012) (remand to consider wife's economic fault); *Sorey v. Sorey*, 757 S.E.2d 518 (N.C. App. 2014) (abandonment of marital home); *Mick-Skaggs v. Skaggs*, 411 S.C. 94 (S.C. App. (2014) (denial of alimony due to adultery).

10.10 AMOUNT OF SPOUSAL SUPPORT: IMPUTATION OF INCOME

Background to *In re the Marriage of Scheuer v. Scheuer*

Sometimes a spouse voluntarily reduces his or her income and then seeks to pay a lower amount of spousal support than he or she might otherwise be ordered to provide. In the next case, the court is confronted with a soon-to-be-former spouse who said that "he would rather just quit his job than pay maintenance." Not surprisingly the court imputes a substantial amount of income to him.

IN RE THE MARRIAGE OF SCHEUER
v.
SCHEUER

Court of Appeals of Wisconsin
711 N.W.2d 698 (2006)

HOOVER, P.J. Bradley and Cora Lee Scheuer were married July 29, 1978. Cora petitioned for divorce on April 23, 2003. The couple had two children, but both were adults at the time of the divorce.

Bradley had been employed at Andersen Windows for twenty-three years, earning approximately $20 an hour. Cora, employed at Wood Goods, was earning around $12.70 an hour. On May 6, 2003, the court commissioner entered a temporary maintenance order, with Bradley paying Cora $300 per month.

In December 2003, the parties had their first appearance before the trial court. One issue was whether maintenance should be reduced or terminated because Bradley had lost his job in July. He had been terminated, and Cora alleged he had been fired for misconduct on the job. According to Cora's testimony, Bradley had told her he would rather just quit his job than pay maintenance. She also stated he had repeated disciplinary problems at work, particularly with his supervisors, and had been ordered to attend anger management classes. Bradley admitted he skipped work for five days in a row, although he asserted he had taken vacation days. The court eventually suspended maintenance as of January 1, 2004, and ordered Bradley to seek work. Bradley later found a new job paying $11.74 per hour.

As part of the final divorce decree, however, the trial court imputed an annual earning capacity of $41,875, or $20.13 per hour, to Bradley. The trial court explained:

> I'm finding that your earning capacity is $20 per hour and that is based on the fact that you were in a job in which you had long-time job security, and an opportunity to continue had it not been for your own misconduct, and your misconduct was the sole reason for your termination and for the now demonstrated and claimed actual lower earnings. Had you not committed misconduct you would have been continuing at a rate of at least $20 per hour.

Based on the imputed earning capacity, the court ordered Bradley to pay maintenance for fifteen years: $400 per month for the first five years, $500 per month for the second five years, and $600 per month for the third five years.

Maintenance serves two purposes: to support the recipient spouse in a manner reflecting the needs and earning capacities of the parties — the support objective — and to ensure a fair and equitable financial arrangement between the spouses — the fairness objective. . . . This rule, however, is subject to a "shirking" exception. When shirking is established, it is appropriate to consider the obligor's earning capacity instead of his or her actual earnings. To support a shirking determination, the trial court "need find only that a party's employment decision to reduce or forego [*sic*] income is voluntary and unreasonable under the circumstances." *Chen v. Warner*, 695 N.W.2d 758 (2005). Ordinarily, the legal question of reasonableness is a question of law, but because the trial court's legal conclusion is so intertwined with the factual findings necessary to support it, we should give weight to the trial court's ruling. *Van Offeren*, 496 N.W.2d 660. Therefore, we review a shirking determination as a question of law, but one to which we pay appropriate deference. . . .

Bradley asserts it was improper to impute his earning capacity without expert testimony about his actual capacity. Aside from the fact that he never attempted to offer such testimony, Bradley cites absolutely no authority for his proposition. We need not address arguments unsupported by reference to legal authority. *Kruczek v. Department of Workforce Dev.*, 692 N.W.2d 286 (Ct. App. 2004). Further, under the facts of this case, expert testimony was not necessary to assist the court in determining Bradley's earning capacity. The trial court properly considered Bradley's demonstrated earning ability — the wage he had been earning at Andersen Windows — in determining his earning capacity for calculating maintenance.

Bradley complains that the trial court never found he was shirking, nor did it determine he intentionally lost his job to avoid paying maintenance. But "shirking" does not require a finding the obligor reduced his or her earnings for the purposes of avoiding the maintenance obligation, nor must the court specifically use the word "shirking." *See Smith v. Smith*, 501 N.W.2d 850 (Ct. App. 1993). The test is whether the reduction in actual earnings was voluntary and unreasonable under the circumstances. *Id.* There is no set list of factors which are decisive in a shirking determination. However, perhaps the most common factor accompanying such a finding is a voluntary of self-inflicted change in financial circumstances. For example, in such cases . . . [the obligor] *has been fired or demoted for misconduct* . . . or by some other means has brought about his or her reduced ability to pay support. *Wallen v. Wallen*, 407 N.W.2d 293 (Ct. App. 1987).

In this case, the court found Bradley's actual earnings were reduced because of his voluntary misconduct at Andersen Windows, thus justifying use of imputed earning capacity. The court also found Bradley's misconduct at work resulted from his unwillingness to deal realistically and reasonably with his divorce and was the sole reason he was terminated. We discern no clear error in the trial court's factual findings and, accordingly, we agree with its implicit conclusion of Bradley's unreasonableness. Thus, the trial court did not erroneously exercise its discretion in setting a maintenance award based on imputed, rather than actual earning capacity.

> **DISCUSSION QUESTIONS**   FOR *IN RE THE MARRIAGE OF SCHEUER v. SCHEUER*
>
> **A.** How does the court define "shirking"?
>
> **B.** What are other factual examples of "shirking"?
>
> **C.** Does it make policy sense to impute income in such cases? What is the likelihood that the former husband will pay the amount ordered?

10.11 AMOUNT OF SPOUSAL SUPPORT: STATUTORY GUIDELINES

Because of the unpredictable nature of spousal support awards, some states and jurisdictions have begun to adopt spousal support guidelines that are analogous to guidelines used in child support cases. *See* Twila B. Larkin, *Guidelines for Alimony: The New Mexico Experiment*, 38 Fam. L.Q. 29 (2004) (discussing guidelines used in jurisdictions in California, Pennsylvania, Michigan, Virginia, Arizona, Nevada, Oregon, and Kansas).

Computer software. Some family practitioners are "cautiously" using computer software to calculate the approximate amount of alimony a client will receive or pay using a variety of formulas. Some practitioners worry that if mathematical alimony formulas are developed, lawyers and judges may rigidly apply them.

AAML formula. A report from the American Association of Matrimonial Lawyers suggests the following framework: Take 30 percent of the payor's gross income minus 20 percent of the payee's gross income. That amount, when added to the gross income of the payee, should not exceed 40 percent of the combined gross incomes of the parties. The AAML suggests calculating duration of the award by multiplying the length of the marriage by a certain numerical factor.

ALI formula. In 2002, the American Law Institute recommended that states create formulas for determining alimony, including the adoption of presumptions and guidelines. *See* American Law Institute, *Principles of the Law of Family Dissolution: Analysis and Recommendations* §§5.05-5.07 (2002). When setting the amount and duration, the ALI recommends a formula based on a percentage of the difference in the spouses' post-divorce income, with payments made for a period of time linked to the length of the marriage. The ALI views alimony as compensation for economic loss incurred by a spouse as a result of the marriage, including lost employment and educational opportunities leading to disparities in post-divorce earning capacities.

Arguments favoring the development of alimony formulas. Some commentators believe that formulas might lower the legal costs associated with a divorce by allowing the parties and their lawyers to more accurately estimate the amount of alimony a court would order. They believe that more certainty would enhance perceptions of fairness.

Example. The use of the formula was approved by Maricopa Superior Court in Arizona in 2002. The formula rests on a "duration factor," which is described as .015 times the number of years of marriage. Thus, for a 10-year marriage, the duration factor is .015 × 10 = .15. Fifteen percent is then taken times the difference in the parties' incomes. If the husband earns $7,500 and the wife earns $1,500 per month, the presumptive alimony is 15 percent × $6,000, or $900 per month. That number is then multiplied by the difference in the parties' incomes to render the final amount.

Assume the husband's income at the time of dissolution is $100,000 annually, or $8,333 per month. The wife's income is $15,000 annually, or $1,250 per month. The duration of the marriage is 20 years. The wife is 40 years old at the time of dissolution.

Result: $2,125 monthly for 6-10 years.
Post-award incomes: Husband, $6,208; Wife, $3,375.
(A) The duration factor equals 0.015 × 20, or 0.30.
(B) The guideline amount is then calculated this way: $8,333–$1,250 = $7,083 (the difference between husband's and wife's income). $7,083 × 0.3 = $2,125 monthly spousal maintenance (calculated or rounded to nearest whole dollar).
(C) Calculation of the award's duration: The guideline duration for a marriage of 20 years is 20 × 0.3–0.5 = 6.0–10.0 years.

Unanswered questions. In his analysis of various spousal support guidelines methodologies, Professor Oldham raises important questions for consideration:

> If one is inclined to consider formulas, a number of issues need to be addressed: Would the formula apply to only some types of marriages or all marriages? Should different formulas be created for those divorcing with or without minor children? When, if ever, should the formula not apply? Should claimants have to show that they incurred career damage, such as by assuming the role of primary caretaker of a child for a substantial period? Should there be income levels above which the formula should not apply? Should there be a maximum amount established so that, when the aggregate amount of the recipient's salary and any child support and spousal support received reached that amount, there should be no additional support?

J. Thomas Oldham, *Changes in the Economic Consequences of Divorces, 1958-2008,* 42 Fam. L.Q. 419, 443 (2008).

Do you favor the use of spousal support formulas?

Background to *Boemio v. Boemio*

While most spousal support guidelines are statutory, in the following case a trial court used guidelines promulgated by the American Academy of Matrimonial Lawyers. The obligor claimed that the trial court failed to apply the appropriate Maryland statute and instead substituted the AAML guidelines analysis.

BOEMIO
v.
BOEMIO

Court of Appeals of Maryland
994 A.2d 911 (2010)

ADKINS, J. Petitioner Boemio and Respondent Seixas were married on October 12, 1985, in the District of Columbia and shortly thereafter made their home in Silver Spring, Maryland. The couple had two children within the first five years of the marriage. In 1988, Boemio earned a Master's of Business Administration in finance from George Washington University. This was his second post-graduate degree, as he had already earned a master's degree in economics prior to the marriage. The same year he began his MBA studies, Boemio obtained a position at the Federal Reserve Board. He remains in the Board's employ to this day, leaving only to take a two-year assignment with a Swiss bank.

Seixas had completed high school and one year of college instruction. For much of the marriage, she worked as a retail manager for CVS. That job, however, required 45- to 55-hour work weeks and was, according to Seixas, "very stressful" and "physically strenuous[.]" Consequently, she took a less demanding administrative assistant position, along with a $10,000 pay cut. Boemio's six figure salary and Seixas' supplemental income afforded the couple what the trial court characterized as a "securely middle class" existence. It was "comfortable, but not extravagant." They incurred little consumer debt and managed to pay off the mortgage on their Silver Spring home.

Middle-class comfort, however, did not make for a successful marriage. Boemio moved out of the marital home in January 2006. Divorce proceedings began on May 26, 2006, when Boemio filed for divorce in the Circuit Court for Montgomery County, Maryland. In June 2007, Seixas filed an Amended Countercomplaint for Absolute Divorce, seeking use and possession of property, child support, alimony, and other relief.

During a two-day trial before the Honorable Michael D. Mason, Seixas claimed that she was not self-supporting and needed alimony to maintain herself. Boemio argued that Seixas was able to support herself without alimony. The court delivered its decision via oral opinion on July 19, 2007. It found that Seixas would not be able to maintain her accustomed lifestyle without alimony and that an unconscionable disparity existed and would continue to exist between the two parties. Thus, the trial court awarded Seixas $3,000 per month in indefinite alimony.

II. ANALYSIS

Title 11 of the Family Law Article governs alimony. See FL §11-101 to 11-112. In particular, FL Section 11-106 guides courts when crafting the amount and duration of an alimony award. In making this determination, a trial court must consider the twelve factors enumerated in FL Section 11-106(b). Additionally, FL Section 11-106(c) permits a court to award indefinite alimony, if it finds that:

> (1) due to age, illness, infirmity, or disability, the party seeking alimony cannot reasonably be expected to make substantial progress toward becoming self-supporting; or
> (2) even after the party seeking alimony will have made as much progress toward becoming self-supporting as can reasonably be expected, the respective standards of living of the parties will be unconscionably disparate.

Boemio contests the trial court's indefinite alimony award of $3,000 per month to Seixas. Specifically, he contends that the trial court erred by "abandon[ing]" an analysis of the twelve factors required under subsection (b) and the considerations in subsection (c), and instead relied exclusively on the AAML guidelines to fashion the award. . . .

The AAML guidelines consist of two formulas, one to calculate the amount of an alimony award, and the other to establish its duration. See Mary K. Kisthardt, *Rethinking Alimony: The AAML's Considerations for Calculating Alimony, Spousal Support or Maintenance*, 21 J. Am. Acad. Matrimonial Law. 61, app. A (2008). The guidelines also provide "deviation factors" that may signal a necessary adjustment to the recommended amount or duration. To compute the amount of alimony, the adjudicator is to take 30% of the payor's gross income and subtract from it 20% of the payee's income. This amount, however, cannot exceed 40% of the combined gross income of the parties when added to the gross income of the payee. To determine the duration of the award, the AAML guidelines suggest multiplying the length of the marriage by one of the following factors: for zero to three years, a factor of 0.3; for three to ten years, a factor of 0.5; for ten to twenty years, a factor of 0.75; and for more than twenty years, permanent alimony. In this case, the formulas produced a permanent alimony award of $3,816 per month. The trial court, however, rejected that amount as too much. Instead it awarded Seixas $3,000 per month.

A. Amount

. . . The second prong of Boemio's attack on the court's use of the AAML guidelines is more direct—he insists that because the court noted what the alimony award *would have been* under the guidelines, it must have relied exclusively on the AAML guidelines to calculate the final judgment. We are not persuaded by his logic. The Circuit Court clearly engaged in the required considerations under Section 11-106(b). Boemio conveniently ignores the court's statements that the guidelines were "not authoritative[,]" were used "for informational purposes only[,]" and "[did not] control the Court's decision." Nor does he acknowledge the court's express rejection of the $3,816 amount as "excessive." In short, Boemio has failed to prove his charge that the court completely discarded its obligatory FL Section 11-106(b) analysis.

To be sure, the Circuit Court consulted the AAML formulas, and a careful reading of the transcript compels the conclusion that the AAML guidelines played a role in its decision. "Playing a role" is different from being the exclusive or dispositive criterion. Yet, we still must decide whether a court's substantive consideration of these guidelines, along with the FL Section 11-106 factors, is a legitimate exercise of the Circuit Court's discretion.

It is well-settled that Section 11-106 does not preclude a trial court from considering other factors in addition to the twelve mentioned. . . . As the introductory language of subsection (b) provides, "[i]n making the determination, the court shall consider *all* the factors necessary for a fair and equitable award, *including* [the twelve listed]." . . . ("As the prefatory language in subsection (b) makes plain, the court is not restricted to a consideration of the factors that are expressly listed."). While the statute provides factors, it gives the court little guidance on how to translate them into dollars. We believe that *if* the guidelines reasonably direct the court to a fair and equitable award without supplanting or frustrating any one of the twelve enumerated statutory considerations, a court may refer to them as an aid in translating its statutorily mandated analysis into a dollar amount.

In deciding whether use of monetary guidelines like the AAML's will supplant or frustrate the statutory guidelines, we first consider what role monetary guidelines will play when applied in the context of a statute directing use of evaluative factors, but without direction as to how they translate into a monetary amount. Commentators have addressed the practical difficulties for judges and litigants when such statutory criteria are the only resource available:

> Of the three financial issues raised by divorce — asset division, child support, and spousal maintenance — the question of alimony is typically the least predictable and the most contentious. . . . On the issue of child support, while there remains room for bargaining by higher-income parents, most couples settle within the shadow, if not by strict application, of statutory child support guidelines. Only with regard to alimony is there no fixed frame of reference for discussions.
>
> Spousal support negotiations are particularly difficult because of the absence of any objective standard for judging fairness or predicting outcomes. **Statutes simply list factors for trial courts to consider without providing any guidance as to how the judge should weigh or apply them.** Without predictable judicial parameters, the parties cannot readily assess the risks and benefits of pushing forward to trial, thereby making private resolutions problematic. . . .
>
> At first reading, these legislative guidelines for awarding alimony appear fair and appropriate. Closer inspection, however, reveals that the statutory criteria are so broad,

idiosyncratic, or unclear in purpose or direction that they actually provide little practical guidance for — or limitation upon — judicial discretion.

The majority of the statutory factors are laudable but imprecise, such as the instruction for a judge to take into account "a history of the contributions to the marriage by each party." . . .

[T]he statutes are [also] uniformly silent as to the manner in which the factors should be utilized to calculate an award. Not a single jurisdiction among those that list multiple alimony considerations ranks the factors' relative significance or weight. Not a single statute explains how judges should apply the criteria. The result is that both the trial and appellate courts look to a hodgepodge of factors, weighing them in an unspecified and unsystematic fashion, rendering it impossible for couples or their counsel to predict with any degree of certainty what the actual alimony award might or should be.

Robert K. Collins, *The Theory of Marital Residuals: Applying an Income Adjustment Calculus to the Enigma of Alimony*, 24 Harv. Women's L.J. 23, 23, 32-33 (2001) (emphasis added).

Numerous courts across the country have resorted to non-legislative formulas as aids in crafting alimony awards. *See generally* Virginia R. Dugan & Jon A. Feder, *Alimony Guidelines: Do They Work?*, 25 Fam. Advoc. 20 (2003) (describing the alimony guidelines developed in twelve different jurisdictions, including California, Florida, Maine, Michigan and Texas). For example, Maricopa County, Arizona, frames its alimony awards around a "duration factor," which is 0.015 times the number of years of the marriage. That number is then multiplied by the difference in the parties' incomes to render the final amount. In Kansas, several counties use what is known as the "Johnson County Guidelines," which provide that alimony should be twenty percent of the difference between the parties' gross monthly incomes when there are minor children and twenty-five percent of the difference when there are no children. The Fairfax County Virginia Bar Association recommends that spousal support equal thirty percent of the payor's income minus fifty percent of the payee's income in cases where there is no child support. Where there is child support being paid, the formula is twenty-eight percent of the payor's income minus fifty-eight percent of the payee's income.

These guidelines provide predictability for both counsel and clients, increasing litigant satisfaction: "Experienced attorneys in California, where guidelines have been used [since 1977], have found clients accept the concept of guidelines much more readily than broad ranges of results when guidelines are not used." . . . We do not mention these examples to indicate that the specific numeric formulas are necessarily right for Maryland. We use them to demonstrate that many courts, with statutes setting forth evaluative criteria, have considered it beneficial to utilize monetary guidelines as an aid in reaching their decisions.

The AAML guidelines were the result of more than two years of data-gathering by the AAML Commission. After extensively reviewing guidelines being used in jurisdictions around the country, the Commission discovered that the common denominators in all were the income of the spouses and the duration of the marriage. Thus, the AAML guidelines focused on those two factors. The formula was then tested against seven other guidelines that were being used or had been proposed, and the result fell within the norm. Also, "[r]ecognizing that certain circumstance[s] would render an award based solely on the [AAML formula] unfair, the Commission also included factors that would suggest a deviation." As the AAML explained in the introduction to the guidelines, "[t]he proposed considerations are designed to be used in conjunction with state statutes that first determine eligibility for an award. They are not intended to replace existing state public policy regarding eligibility for an award." . . .

We believe that the AAML recommendations are the product of a careful study by a professional organization of knowledgeable practitioners, which are reasonable in approach, and do not supplant FL Section 11-106 or frustrate its goals. We consider these, and other legitimate and neutral guidelines, helpful to judges making alimony awards in Maryland. Therefore, we conclude that the court did not err in consulting those guidelines after conducting its statutory analysis. Rather, the court made an effort to be fair and equitable, as well as being mindful of the benefits of consistency in alimony awards for family law practitioners, litigants, and judges. We wish to be clear, however, that our decision in this case does not mandate the use of any guidelines by circuit courts in performing their Section 11-106 analyses. As we explained in *Solomon*, "each case must be evaluated on its facts and not on some fixed minimum or universal standard.". . . . Thus, in applying FL Section 11-106(b), circuit court judges may wish to consult no monetary guidelines, one particular set of guidelines, or a combination of guidelines. The knowledge, experience and judgment of the circuit court judges are the best determinants for making awards that are "fair and equitable" under FL Section 11-106(b).

DISCUSSION QUESTIONS FOR *BOEMIO v. BOEMIO*

A. How is spousal support calculated under the AAML guidelines? How is the process different from the method provided in the Maryland statute?

B. What other spousal support guidelines does the court discuss? How do they differ from one another?

C. Why does the court look to the AAML guidelines?

D. Do you think it was improper for the court to use guidelines not contained in the Maryland statutes? Why or why not?

E. Do you think that guidelines will become more widely adopted in the future? Why or why not?

F. What problems do you foresee with use of spousal support guidelines? Do you agree with Professor Starnes, who states as follows:

Some legal actors have responded to the dysfunction of current alimony law by endorsing alimony guidelines, but the lack of consensus on an underlying theory of alimony confounds efforts to identify a mathematical formula for generating the numbers that populate these guidelines. If guidelines numbers are predictable, they are not necessarily equitable or consistent across jurisdictions. The absence of an underlying theory also leaves alimony vulnerable to myth, misconception, and hype — all of which characterize a new, energized anti-alimony reform movement that has reignited sentiments popular forty years ago.

Cynthia Lee Starnes, The Marriage Buyout: The Troubled Trajectory of U.S. Alimony Law 129 (2014).

10.12 DURATION OF SPOUSAL SUPPORT: LENGTH OF MARRIAGE, STATUTORY LIMITS

Spousal support awards are more commonly made in favor of low-income wives after a long-term marriage is ended. *See* Marsha Garrison, *How Do Judges Decide Divorce Cases? An Empirical Analysis of Discretionary Decision Making*, 74 N.C. L. Rev. 401, 469 (1996). There is some but not total agreement among jurisdictions concerning how long a couple needs to be married to consider the relationship "long-term" for the purpose of awarding spousal support. In *Mobley v. Mobley*, 18 So. 3d 724 (Fla. App. 2009), a Florida trial court denied a wife's request for rehabilitative spousal support because the parties had been married for only ten years. The appellate court remanded the case for fact finding pursuant to the statutory factors for determining spousal support:

> A ten-year marriage falls within the gray area in which there is neither a presumption for or against alimony. *See Walker v. Walker*, 818 So. 2d 711, 713 (Fla. 2d DCA 2002) (stating that a twelve-year marriage is in the gray area for which there is no presumption for or against alimony); *Bailey v. Bailey*, 617 So. 2d 815, 816 (Fla. 2d DCA 1993) (treating eight-year marriage as in the gray area for purposes of alimony); *Kellerman v. Kellerman*, 659 So. 2d 1390, 1390 (Fla. 3d DCA 1995) (stating the parties' marriage of less than seven years was a short-term marriage). The trial court erred as a matter of law in denying alimony on the basis that the parties were married for ten years.

Id. at 727-728.

A few states statutorily limit the duration of spousal support awards. For example, the Maine spousal support states as follows:

> **2. Types of spousal support.** The court may, after consideration of all factors set forth in subsection 5, award or modify spousal support for one or more of the following reasons.
>   **A.** General support may be awarded to provide financial assistance to a spouse with substantially less income potential than the other spouse so that both spouses can maintain a reasonable standard of living after the divorce.

(1) *There is a rebuttable presumption that general support may not be awarded if the parties were married for less than 10 years as of the date of the filing of the action for divorce. There is also a rebuttable presumption that general support may not be awarded for a term exceeding 1/2 the length of the marriage if the parties were married for at least 10 years but not more than 20 years as of the date of the filing of the action for divorce* [emphasis added].

(2) If the court finds that a spousal support award based upon a presumption established by this paragraph would be inequitable or unjust, that finding is sufficient to rebut the applicable presumption.

B. Transitional support may be awarded to provide for a spouse's transitional needs, including, but not limited to:

(1) Short-term needs resulting from financial dislocations associated with the dissolution of the marriage; or

(2) Reentry or advancement in the work force, including, but not limited to, physical or emotional rehabilitation services, vocational training and education.

C. Reimbursement support may be awarded to achieve an equitable result in the overall dissolution of the parties' financial relationship in response to exceptional circumstances. Exceptional circumstances include, but are not limited to:

(1) Economic misconduct by a spouse; and

(2) Substantial contributions a spouse made towards the educational or occupational advancement of the other spouse during the marriage.

Reimbursement support may be awarded only if the court determines that the parties' financial circumstances do not permit the court to fully address equitable considerations through its distributive order pursuant to section 953. . . .

19-A Me. Rev. Stat. Ann. §951-A (2013). *See also* 13 Del. C. §1512(d) (for marriages less than 20 years, spousal support not to "exceed 50% of the term of the marriage"); Utah Code Ann. 1953 §30-3-5(8)(j) (2013) (without extenuating circumstances spousal support limited to number of years of marriage); Mass. Gen. Laws Ann. ch. 208, §49 (2012) (time limits based on length of marriage).

REFLECTIVE QUESTIONS	What are arguments for and against legislative adoption of durational limits on spousal support?

10.13 TAX CONSEQUENCES

Background to *Dewbrew v. Dewbrew*

Because the vast majority of divorce cases are settled, most spouses reach agreement on the issue of spousal support. To further settlement, many practitioners and mediators use financial software to prepare budgets and create hypothetical alternatives for spouses to consider. Depending on the complexity of the case, a neutral financial planner may be retained to advise the couple concerning their financial options.

The tax implications of spousal support and child support are important considerations for planning. As explained in *Dewbrew v. Dewbrew*, spousal support payments are deductible from the taxable income of the payor, and they are includable as income to the recipient. For tax purposes spousal support is defined as any cash payment made pursuant to a written divorce or separation agreement so long as there is no liability to make the payment after the death of the payee spouse and the spouses are not members of the same household at the time the payment is made.

DEWBREW
v.
DEWBREW

Court of Appeals of Indiana
849 N.E.2d 636 (2006)

RILEY, J. . . . Tina and Appellee-Petitioner, Herbert A. Dewbrew (Herbert), were married on January 13, 1990. During their marriage, two daughters were born: B.D., born on January 22, 1991, and C.D., born on August 26, 1996. . . .

In their Property Settlement and Custody Agreement, merged into the dissolution decree, the parties provided in Article III, Support of the Children and Exemptions, as follows: "1. *General Support:* As a result of the parenting time anticipated no support shall be paid by either party." At the same time, Article IV, Settlement of Property and Debts, states in paragraph five:

Husband agrees to make alimony payments to the wife as follows:

1. $3,000.00 per month starting the first day of the month in which wife moves into 1675 W. Foxcliff, and continuing for 5 years.
2. Starting in the [s]ixth year husband's payments to wife shall be reduced to $1,000.00 per month for [f]ive (5) years at which time said payments shall terminate.

At the motion's hearing, Herbert clarified that the alimony was in fact a combination of alimony and child support. He testified, in pertinent part, that:

[HERBERT]: What we had talked about was that [Tina] would get a thousand dollars a month, and [B.D.] would get a thousand dollars a month, and [C.D.] would get a thousand dollars a month for the first five years, and that would give [Tina] time to get on her feet and get her schooling done and whatever she was going to do, and then the five years after that it would go down to a thousand dollars a month for [C.[D].] . . .

[COUNSEL]: And why would, why would it go down to a thousand dollars? . . .

[HERBERT]: Cause [B.D.] would be eighteen and on her own, and I'd already agreed to pay for all her schooling. And Tina would have, well she said what she was going to do was go back to night school and graduate from that, and then go to college. . . .

Initially, we note that the trial court's Order contains contradictory conclusions. On the one hand, the trial court determined that the instant case did not require a calculation of child support because of the anticipated parenting time of both parties, while on the other hand, the trial court clearly stated that child support was nevertheless included in the settlement agreement because a portion of Tina's alimony payments were actually destined by the parties to be used for the benefit of the children. We disagree with Herbert's argument that although the trial court found credible Herbert's explanation that a portion of Tina's alimony payments "were actually intended by the parties to be used by Tina for the children," it did not conclude that these payments were effectively child support. Herbert's argument amounts to nothing more than mere semantics: payments made by one party to another after a dissolution of marriage and which are destined for the use or support of minor children are properly characterized as child support. . . .

Pursuing the best interests of B.D. and C.[D]., Tina argues that alimony and child support payments trigger different tax consequences. As a recipient of alimony payments, Tina maintains that she must include the entire amount in the calculation of her gross income where they are taxed under the prevalent tax bracket. However, child support payments, if sufficiently identifiable, are not taxable. Accordingly, Tina asserts that by not separating out her alimony payment from the child support, the minor children's support payments are diminished by the payment of taxes.

In determining whether the incorporation of child support in Tina's alimony payment is against the best interests of the children, we first need to establish whether the alimony, stipulated in the parties' property settlement agreement, connotes spousal maintenance or a property settlement as they involve different tax treatments. However, in the instant case, alimony belies an interpretation which equates the term with spousal maintenance.

Relying on our decision in *Legge v. Legge*, 618 N.E.2d 50, 50-51 (Ind. Ct. App. 1993), we defined an alimony provision in *DeBoer v. DeBoer*, 669 N.E.2d 415, 421 (Ind. Ct. App. 1996), *trans. denied*, as constituting spousal maintenance where the settlement agreement unambiguously provided definite terms as to the amount, length, and manner of payment. Likewise here, the payments are clearly delineated with regard to amount and duration and are contingent upon the passage of a certain time period to decrease in amount paid. Accordingly, the term alimony as used by the parties actually dictates a finding that the payments are made for spousal maintenance support.

As a general rule child support payments and spousal maintenance in divorces and judicial separations are treated differently in the Internal Revenue Code. An individual may deduct from his or her taxable income the payments he or she made during a taxable year if those payments are for spousal maintenance. I.R.C. §215(a), *Kean v. Commissioner of Internal Revenue*, 407 F.3d 186, 189 (3d Cir. 2005). Consequently, the recipient of the payments must include the amounts when calculating his or her gross income. I.R.C. §61(a)(8). On the other hand, where child support is specifically designated or fixed in the settlement agreement, the amount is not deductible by the payor spouse, nor taxable to the recipient. *See* I.R.C. §71(b); *Abramo v. Commissioner of Internal Revenue*, 78 T.C. 154, 160, 1982 WL 11069 (U.S. Tax Ct. 1982). In other words, since no taxes are withheld on the amount paid as child support, the entire sum can be used for the benefit of the child.

In the case before us, all parties testified that Herbert wanted to take care of his daughters and intended to support them. At the motion's hearing, Herbert himself testified that part of the payment characterized as spousal maintenance should go towards the support of the children. However, by neglecting to separately designate the child support and instead mingling it with the spousal maintenance payment, Herbert not only raises his deductible taxable amount but, at the same time, deprives his children from some financial support by making the support payments taxable. Accordingly, even though Herbert promised his children a certain support to maintain their lifestyle, at the end of the day, they receive less than they are due. Based on the difference in tax treatment between spousal maintenance payments and child support, we conclude that the inclusion of child support within the amount of spousal maintenance is against the welfare and interest of the children. *See Cox*, 833 N.E.2d at 1080. Consequently, we are left with a clear conviction that the trial court made a mistake by refusing to set aside the parties' property settlement and custody agreement with regard to the child support payments. *Id.* Therefore, we remand to the trial court with the instruction to distinguish the child support from the spousal maintenance and calculate the appropriate amount of support in accordance with the child support guidelines.

DISCUSSION QUESTIONS FOR *DEWBREW v. DEWBREW*

A. What are the implications for Tina if the appellate court upholds the trial judge's decision to allow the agreement?

B. The court concludes that including child support within maintenance is improper. What is the court's rationale?

C. Why is it important to delineate child support, spousal support, and property division clearly in a settlement agreement? How are they different from each other?

D. Spousal support payments are deductible by the payor and are considered income to the recipient. If the payor is in a significantly higher tax bracket than the recipient, can payment of spousal support result in tax savings? Could this make more income available for support?

10.14 BANKRUPTCY

Alimony, maintenance, support, and property settlement obligations incurred during divorce proceedings are generally protected against discharge in bankruptcy. *See* Mark F. Scurt, *Bankruptcy Intersects Family Law*, 40-JUN Md. B.J. 44 (2007).

General Principles

1. Historically, husbands and wives were considered to be one person and the husband had a duty to support the wife throughout her life unless she committed adultery or left the marital home without provocation.
2. Many states now apply the doctrine of necessaries in a gender-neutral fashion, but some states have eliminated it.
3. In 1979 the Supreme Court ruled that an Alabama statute awarding spousal support only to wives violated the Equal Protection Clause. *Orr v. Orr*, 440 U.S. 268 (1979).
4. The UMDA provision regarding spousal support requires courts to make a threshold determination of need before considering factors related to amount and duration.
5. Spousal support awards have various purposes, including relief of need, rehabilitation, compensation for loss, apportionment of inequity, and recognition of marital fault.
6. Courts may impute income for the purpose of paying spousal support to a spouse who is voluntarily unemployed or underemployed.
7. Some states have adopted spousal support guidelines for the purpose of calculating the amount and duration of support.
8. Spousal support payments are deductible from the taxable income of the payor and they are includable as income to the recipient.

Chapter Problems

1. The UMDA, the ALI, and jurisdictions with spousal support guidelines have taken distinctly different approaches to determining spousal support. What are the advantages and disadvantages of each approach? Which do you favor?

2. Assume that P (mother) and D (father) have two children and are seeking a divorce after ten years of marriage. By agreement of the parties, P has not worked outside the home so that she could be available to home-school the children. P is now 30 years old, and she seeks spousal support because she plans to continue to home-school the children, she has few marketable skills, and she has never worked full time. D believes that P should obtain employment, and he objects to the spousal support payment. How would this case be analyzed under the UMDA? How would you analyze this case under the ALI proposal? If you were the judge, how would you rule? If you were a mediator working with this couple, how would you approach this issue? *See Taylor v. Taylor*, 2007 WL 474053 (Ark. 2007).

3. When courts consider spousal support awards, they often place great weight on the length of the marriage. How long do you believe a couple should be married before their relationship is defined as long term? How is the length of the marriage relevant to the analysis under the UMDA? How is the length of the marriage relevant to the analysis under the ALI approach?

4. Assume the same facts as presented in the *Haugan* case. Also assume that the jurisdiction has legislatively adopted the ALI compensation-for-loss approach. How would the *Haugan* case be analyzed? What is the likely result?

5. When Harry and Hana divorce, Harry persuades Hana to accept spousal support and not ask for child support for their 15-year-old child. Hana is unemployed, and Harry's annual income is over $200,000. Harry promises to provide spousal support that would normally exceed the total a court would order in spousal support and child support. They agree that the spousal support will cease when their child graduates from high school. Do you foresee any future tax difficulty for either party to this agreement?

Preparation for Practice

1. Locate the spousal support statute(s) for your state. What types of spousal support might be awarded?

2. Does your state have a statute governing provision of necessaries? If so, what does it provide?

3. If your state legislature contacted you to brief them on spousal support legislative reforms, what would you recommend?

Chapter 11

Modification of Spousal Support

11.1 INTRODUCTION

This chapter discusses when and under what conditions spousal support orders may be modified. In cases where a spousal support order is currently in effect, or where the court has expressly reserved subject matter jurisdiction over the issue, a spousal support award may be modified as certain circumstances change. Typical circumstances warranting review of the award include changes in the obligor's income, increased need by the recipient, remarriage of the recipient, or the death of one of the parties.

Of course, not all divorces include a spousal support order — a court may deny spousal support or the parties may expressly waive it at the time of divorce. If the divorce decree is silent concerning spousal support and the court does not reserve jurisdiction over the issue, spousal support cannot be later awarded. But if jurisdiction over the issue of spousal support is reserved, future modification may be allowed. For example, a court might reserve the question of spousal support when a long-term, traditional marriage ends and both parties are unemployed. At a future date, when one of the parties is employed, the court could award support.

As you read this chapter, the following questions might come to mind: Under what conditions can a spousal support award be changed? What happens if the spouse paying spousal support loses income or dies? What happens if the recipient remarries, cohabits, or wants to extend an award? Can the parties agree at the time of divorce that the court will be prohibited from modifying a spousal support award? Why might they want to prevent modification?

> **REFLECTIVE QUESTIONS**   What are your goals for this chapter?

11.2 LEGAL STANDARDS FOR MODIFICATION, BURDEN OF PROOF, RETROACTIVITY

States differ concerning the legal standard for modification of spousal support. Many require evidence of a substantial change in circumstances sufficient to render the original award unfair. Some states require a higher showing, similar to the Uniform Marriage and Divorce Act (UMDA), which contains a very restrictive legal standard for modification. The UMDA §316 provides for modification only on "a showing of changed circumstances so substantial and continuing as to make the terms unconscionable."

Although modification standards vary from jurisdiction to jurisdiction, courts typically approach the issue of modification using a four-step analysis. First, courts examine the judgment to determine whether there is jurisdiction to hear the request. A court has jurisdiction to modify a judgment if at the time of the original award it possessed personal jurisdiction over the parties and an award of spousal support was made or if the issue was reserved.

The second stage of the proceeding involves presenting evidence showing that there has been a substantial change in circumstances on the part of either party. Courts generally take the view that an award should be modified only upon clear proof of facts showing a substantial change of circumstances from those existing at the time of the dissolution or prior modification. In most jurisdictions, the evidence must demonstrate that the change was not contemplated at the time of final judgment of dissolution. If the change was foreseeable, courts will usually dismiss the motion for a modification. Whether a change in circumstances is substantial enough to warrant court intervention often turns on the facts of the case. However, modification will not be granted based on circumstances that existed at the time of the original order. Consequently, modification is not an appropriate remedy for a party who regrets making a "bad bargain."

If the moving party successfully proves that there has been a substantial change in circumstances, then the court takes the third step, in which the moving party must prove that the substantial change in circumstances makes the original award unreasonable and unfair, although jurisdictions may differ on the exact language or standard applied to this step of the proceeding.

Once the moving party has satisfied the court that a modification is warranted, the fourth stage in the modification proceeding involves setting the exact amount of increase or decrease in maintenance. Trial courts are generally asked to consider all relevant factors, including the criteria for an award of maintenance found in the state statute.

The party seeking to modify an existing order bears the burden of meeting the applicable legal standard. If the modification is granted, it is generally not made retroactive beyond the date of the filing of the motion for modification.

REFLECTIVE QUESTIONS	**How significant is the distinction between the UMDA unconscionability standard and the unfairness standard when applied to spousal support modification requests?**

Background to *Metcalf v. Metcalf*

In *Metcalf,* the Supreme Court of Nebraska considers a situation where an obligor has twice moved for modification of an existing spousal support award. The court discusses the standard for modification in Nebraska and considers the time period during which changed circumstances must have occurred.

METCALF
v.
METCALF

Supreme Court of Nebraska
769 N.W.2d 386 (2009)

McCORMACK, J., Kenneth and Rita Jo Metcalf were divorced in 1999, and in the decree of dissolution entered on March 18, 1999, the district court ordered Kenneth to pay Rita alimony of $2,000 per month for a period of 120 months beginning April 1. In the original dissolution decree, Kenneth's monthly gross income was determined to be $8,211 per month, or $98,532 per year. Rita's income was determined to be $1,337 per month, or $16,044 per year.

On March 31, 2005, Kenneth filed a complaint seeking a reduction of his alimony obligation, alleging that since 1999, his income decreased and Rita's income increased. The court held a hearing on the matter on December 20, 2005, and on January 26, 2006, the court entered an order denying modification. The court concluded that Kenneth failed to prove a material and substantial change in circumstances had occurred to warrant modification. Kenneth did not appeal this order, but instead, on March 15, he filed a second complaint for modification of alimony.

The district court held an evidentiary hearing regarding Kenneth's second complaint to modify alimony. Rita filed a motion *in limine* asking the court to exclude any evidence presented at the first modification hearing that would show that there had been a material change in circumstances warranting a reduction in alimony. Rita asserted that any such evidence was barred by collateral estoppel. The court limited the evidence at the second hearing, allowing only evidence of changes which occurred after December 20, 2005, the date the first hearing was held.

An evidentiary hearing was held before the district court in the current modification proceedings on October 15, 2007. Kenneth has worked as a chiropractic physician for 23 years. Kenneth is currently married, and his wife is employed as a nurse. Kenneth testified with respect to his current health, indicating that he has issues with "arthritic changes" in his knees and hands which limit him to a degree in his work as a chiropractor and that he has recently experienced problems with dizziness. While Kenneth had health insurance at the time of the divorce in 1999, he did not have health insurance at the time of the second modification hearing, because he does not have funds to pay for insurance.

Before becoming a chiropractor, Kenneth was a licensed funeral director and embalmer. At the time of the second modification hearing, Kenneth had investigated other employment with three local funeral firms because of the diminishing income in his current profession. Kenneth hoped to find employment within the limitations of his current physical issues, but he has not been able to find employment with a funeral firm that would eliminate the need for lifting and carrying associated with that business.

At the second modification hearing, the court took judicial notice of the original divorce decree and certain other exhibits, which were received into evidence at the first modification hearing. These exhibits show that Kenneth's average yearly income for 1996 through 2004 was $112,703 ($114,918 in 1996, $98,533 in 1997, $95,000 in 1998, $99,787 in 1999, $140,981 in 2001, $159,091 in 2002, $44,070 in 2003, and $149,244 in 2004; no income for 2000 was shown on the exhibit). The court also took judicial notice of Kenneth's 2004 tax return, showing income of $149,244, and a financial statement Kenneth submitted to his bank dated May 24, 2005, which showed that Kenneth's income was $80,000. . . .

Kenneth also explained how his financial state had changed since the first modification proceeding. Kenneth had a retirement account of approximately $35,000, but he cashed it in incrementally starting in 2003, attempting to avoid bankruptcy. Kenneth eventually filed a chapter 7 bankruptcy petition and received a discharge. However, Kenneth still owes $21,000 to the Internal Revenue Service that was not discharged, and he is making payments of $250 per month to pay off that debt.

Additionally, Kenneth deeded his home back to the mortgage lender after foreclosure proceedings were initiated, and he gave back the 2004 Dodge Durango he was leasing. He now drives a 1996 Toyota Camry with approximately 140,000 miles on it. Because of Kenneth's alleged decrease in income, Kenneth no longer has health insurance. Kenneth also had to eliminate his full-time employee position in 2006. Further, Kenneth testified that he has continued to experience a gradual decline in new patients and services rendered, but Kenneth provided no explanation as to why he was losing patients. At the time of the second hearing, Kenneth testified that his net income was about $3,000 per month.

Kenneth was also questioned about his criminal history. In 1995, Kenneth was found guilty of debauching a minor, a Class I misdemeanor. Rita argues that if Kenneth's income has decreased, it is likely a result of his criminal history, which is a result of his own wrongdoing, and that therefore, modification is not warranted.

At the second modification hearing, Rita testified about her financial situation, and the court took judicial notice of Rita's income tax returns for 2003 and 2004. Her tax returns show income of $39,267 for 2003 and $64,708 for 2004. These amounts do not include the $24,000 in alimony Rita received in each of those years. Rita's net income in 2005 was $9,408, and in 2006, Rita suffered a net loss of $37,867. In the first 8 months of 2007, Rita's net income was $10,708. Rita cashed in her IRA in the amount of $23,800 to meet her monthly living expenses of $3,633.

At the time of the parties' divorce, Rita owned a beauty salon. Thereafter, Rita owned a dry cleaning business, and in 2005, she and her son opened a coffee shop. Since then, they opened another coffee shop. Rita and her son also acquired some investment property which cost $195,000. Rita testified that she relied upon her alimony award when she purchased the investment property and that without the alimony, she would not be able to make payments of both interest and principal. A few years before the second modification hearing, Rita refinanced her home to obtain part of the money for the land purchase, borrowing $110,000 against her house.

After considering the evidence, the court entered an order dismissing Kenneth's second complaint to modify alimony. The court concluded that because Kenneth failed to appeal the January 2006 order, which dismissed his first complaint for modification, Kenneth was required to show a material change in circumstances since January 26, 2006. The court also concluded that Kenneth failed to show a material change in circumstances in the 2 to 3 months between January and March 2006. Kenneth appealed, and the Court of Appeals affirmed, concluding that the district court was correct to require Kenneth to show a material change in circumstances since the time his prior request for modification was denied. . . .

Alimony orders may be modified or revoked for good cause shown. Good cause means a material and substantial change in circumstances and depends upon the circumstances of each case. Good cause is demonstrated by a material change in circumstances, but any changes in circumstances which were within the contemplation of the parties at the time of the decree, or that were accomplished by the mere passage of time, do not justify a change or modification of an alimony order. The moving party has the burden of demonstrating a material and substantial change in circumstances which would justify the modification of an alimony award.

To determine whether there has been a material and substantial change in circumstances warranting modification of a divorce decree, a trial court should compare the financial circumstances of the parties at the time of the divorce decree, or last modification of the decree, with their circumstances at the time the modification at issue was sought. However, there is some confusion about the time period that must be considered to determine whether there has been a change in circumstances in cases where there has been a previous attempt to modify alimony prior to the current motion. This is an issue of first impression for this court.

We determine that in cases where there has been a previous attempt to modify support, the court must first consider whether circumstances have changed since the most recent request for modification. But when considering whether there has been a *material and substantial* change in circumstances justifying modification, the court will consider the change in circumstances since the date of the last order establishing or modifying alimony. In other words, a judgment for alimony may be modified only upon a showing of facts or circumstances that have changed since the last order granting or denying modification was entered. But once some change has been established since the last request, the analysis focuses on the change in circumstances since alimony was originally awarded or last modified. We adopt this rule because it recognizes the force of res judicata; modification will be considered only when there has been a change in circumstances since the last request for modification. But if there has been no change, modification is not justified, because the request is essentially the same as the last request.

In this case, the Court of Appeals' majority concluded that the issue of whether a change in circumstances occurred between the time of the entry of the decree and the modification proceeding was fully litigated. And as such, the Court of Appeals' majority held that the district court did not err in limiting its review to whether a material change in circumstances had occurred since the last modification proceeding. We agree with the Court of Appeals' majority that the district court was correct by limiting its review to only the change in circumstances occurring since the first modification proceeding. However, any change in circumstances occurring since the first modification proceeding should have been compared to the original decree when determining whether the change in circumstances was a material and substantial change warranting modification.

Any changes in Kenneth's circumstances that occurred prior to the first modification proceeding are settled, and the doctrine of res judicata prevents the district court from considering any change based on those circumstances. But the initial alimony award was not affected by the first modification proceeding, and Kenneth is currently paying alimony based upon the circumstances as they existed in 1999. As such, the change in circumstances, if any, occurring after the first modification proceeding must be compared to the parties' financial circumstances at the time of the initial divorce decree to determine whether there has been a material and substantial change in circumstances warranting a modification of Kenneth's alimony obligation.

In this case, the district court and the Court of Appeals concluded that the parties' circumstances were about the same as they were at the first modification proceeding, and thus, the Court of Appeals concluded that Kenneth failed to establish that there was any change in circumstances from the first modification to the current modification. The establishment of changed circumstances is necessary in order to modify alimony. Our de novo review of the record reveals that the district court's determination that Kenneth failed to show that his circumstances changed from the previous modification to the current modification proceeding was not an abuse of discretion. As such, we conclude that because nothing has changed since the first modification proceeding, Kenneth's motion to modify alimony was properly denied.

We conclude that when there has been one or more previous modification proceedings, the court should first determine whether there has been any change in circumstances arising after the most recent modification proceeding. If circumstances have changed since the time of the most recent request for modification, then the court should consider the change in circumstances since the original decree or order affecting alimony to determine whether there has been a material and substantial change. If there has been no change between the most recent modification request and the current request, the current modification is barred by *res judicata*. Based on our review of the record, Kenneth has failed to prove that the circumstances have changed since the most recent modification request. Since the circumstances are the same as they were at the prior modification proceeding, Kenneth's request is barred by *res judicata*.

DISCUSSION QUESTIONS FOR *METCALF v. METCALF*

A. What legal standard for modification did the court use? How does it compare to the standard in UMDA §316?

B. What facts support Kenneth's argument that the spousal support award should be changed? What facts support Rita's claim that the spousal support award should not be modified?

C. What did the court hold concerning which time frame was relevant to the court's determination?

D. What policy considerations might support the court's holding in this case?

11.3 CHANGE IN THE CIRCUMSTANCES OF THE OBLIGOR: DEATH, RETIREMENT

Unless expressly provided otherwise in the divorce decree, the obligation to pay ongoing (as opposed to lump sum) spousal support ceases upon the death of the obligor. UMDA §316(b). However, short of death, various changes may occur in the life of the obligor that might meet the state standard for modification. Couples may agree to modification, but in some cases courts are asked to determine whether modification is warranted.

Sometimes a change in circumstances is clearly unanticipated and unforeseen, such as if an obligor becomes disabled in an accident or a long-time permanently employed obligor is suddenly laid off. However, other life events may be contemplated or predictable at the time of the divorce, and courts are reluctant to change or terminate spousal support in such cases.

An obligor may seek to decrease or terminate payment of spousal support when he or she retires from full-time employment. For example in *Pierce v. Pierce*, 916 N.E.2d 330 (2009), the Supreme Court of Massachusetts considered a husband's complaint to terminate his spousal support payment when he voluntarily retired from his law firm after previously serving as an Associate Justice of the Massachusetts Superior Court. He urged the court to create a rebuttable presumption that spousal support should terminate when an obligor voluntarily retires at the customary age of 65 years. The court declined to do so, holding that all of the statutory factors should be considered in each case and that the age of the obligor could not be viewed in isolation from other facts. *See also Daunhauer v. Daunhauer*, 295 S.W.3d 154 (Ct. App. Ky. 2009) (examining "the totality of the circumstances surrounding the retirement").

REFLECTIVE QUESTIONS	What is the policy underlying the termination of spousal support when an obligor dies? How might a lawyer protect a client against losing spousal support if this occurs?

Background to *In re Arvenitis*

In the next case, *In re Arvenitis*, the court considers whether the retirement of the obligor, 12 years after the divorce, constitutes a substantial change in circumstances warranting modification of the spousal support award.

IN RE ARVENITIS
Supreme Court of New Hampshire
886 A.2d 1025 (2005)

NADEAU, J. The following facts appear on the record before us. The parties were divorced pursuant to a stipulated decree dated March 10, 1992. At that time, the plaintiff and defendant were fifty-one and fifty years old respectively. The final stipulation provided that "[t]he defendant shall pay to the plaintiff as alimony the sum of Five Hundred dollars ($500.00) per week payable weekly, for her support."

In April 2004, the defendant petitioned to modify the parties' divorce decree to, among other things, terminate his obligation to pay alimony. The defendant alleged that he would be turning sixty-three years old that August and was planning to retire. The trial court denied the defendant's petition, finding that he failed to prove "that a substantial change in circumstances ha[d] arisen since the initial award, making the current support amount either improper or unfair." *Giles v. Giles*, 618 A.2d 286 (1992) (quotation omitted). Specifically, the court found that the defendant could not "claim that he was not aware[, at the time the stipulation was executed,] of the fact that he would retire." . . .

RSA 458:14 (2004) provides that "[e]xcept as otherwise provided in RSA 458:19, I and VII, the court, upon proper application and notice to the adverse party, may revise and modify any order made by it, may make such new orders as may be necessary, and may award costs as justice may require." This provision grants the trial court the "power to modify orders concerning alimony upon a proper showing of changed circumstances." . . . When making the determination whether an order should be modified, "the trial court must take into account all of the circumstances of the parties, including the terms of the stipulation."

In *Laflamme*, we clarified that the divorce decree and incorporated stipulations "must be interpreted in light of the facts and circumstances known to the parties and the court at the time the court issued the decree, along with future facts or circumstances known or reasonably anticipated to occur in the future." *Laflamme*, 144 N.H. at 527, 744 A.2d 1116. We further stated that "[c]hanges to a party's condition that are both anticipated and foreseeable at the time of the decree cannot rise to the level of a substantial change in circumstances sufficient to warrant modification of an alimony award." . . .

The defendant asks us, in part, to "address the question of whether voluntary retirement may ever be a factor to be considered in a request for termination of alimony." The trial court appears to have interpreted *Laflamme* to mean that voluntary retirement can never constitute a substantial change in circumstances justifying a termination of alimony because it can always be "reasonably anticipated to occur in the future." . . . *Laflamme* should not be construed so broadly. There, we reversed the modification of alimony where the trial court had found, and the obligor spouse did not dispute on the record before us, "that he knew at the time of the divorce that he would be retiring in a few years," yet nevertheless "agreed to pay the plaintiff alimony in exchange for his receipt of substantially more than half of the marital assets." . . . We noted that the post-divorce changes the obligor spouse experienced "were foreseeable and *actually anticipated.*" . . .

The trial court's order appears to be based on a premise that foreseeability alone takes voluntary retirement out of the realm of changed circumstances. The stipulation in this case, executed twelve years prior to the petition to terminate alimony, was silent on the issue of retirement. The defendant represents that his retirement "was not anticipated at the time of the divorce," and the trial court made no specific factual finding to the contrary. In fact, the defendant represents, and the plaintiff does not dispute, that the trial court refused to hear evidence regarding the parties' circumstances. Moreover, the trial court applied the concept of foreseeability more broadly than we have under similar circumstances. In *Gnirk v. Gnirk*, 589 A.2d 1008 (1991), we held that where the parties divorced four years prior to the time their oldest child would make the decision to attend college, college expenses were not reasonably foreseeable at the time of divorce. We refused to extend *Morrill v. Millard (Morrill)*, 570 A.2d 387 (1990), which held that increased expenses that were "fully foreseeable" to the parties at the time they negotiated their divorce stipulation did not constitute a substantial change in circumstances justifying a modification of child support. Specifically, we stated that the argument "that the potential for incurring college expenses for the parties' children was 'fully foreseeable' " at the time of the divorce "inappropriately extends *Morrill* to cover events which are merely possibilities at the time a stipulation is negotiated." *Gnirk*, 589 A.2d 1008.

Finally, we note that our overarching concern in *Laflamme* was that the master and the trial court had "overlooked the equities of the case." . . . We believe that the interpretation the trial court appears to have placed on *Laflamme* could potentially overlook the equities of this and other cases. We therefore reiterate that under *Laflamme*, a change in circumstances that is "*both* anticipated and foreseeable at the time of the decree" does not constitute a substantial change in circumstances warranting a change in alimony. . . . A determination that a change in circumstances was "actually anticipated," is a factual finding that must be based on evidence. If there is any genuine dispute as to the material facts, an evidentiary hearing will normally be required. Because the trial court failed to hear evidence and make a factual finding as to whether the defendant's retirement was actually anticipated at the time of the divorce, we vacate and remand for an evidentiary hearing.

Should the trial court, on remand, find that the defendant's retirement was not both actually anticipated and foreseeable, it will have to determine whether retirement, alone or in conjunction with other changes alleged by the defendant, constitutes a substantial change in circumstances justifying a termination of alimony. We agree with the Supreme Court of Florida that:

> Although it would be a better practice to incorporate consideration of retirement and what will happen in the event of retirement in an agreement or final judgment, . . . silence in that regard should not preclude consideration of a reasonable retirement as part of the total circumstances in determining if sufficient changed circumstances exist to warrant a modification of alimony.

In determining whether a voluntary retirement is reasonable, the court must consider the payor's age, health, and motivation for retirement, as well as the type of work the payor performs and the age at which others engaged in that line of work normally retire. . . . Based upon th[e] widespread acceptance of sixty-five as the normal retirement age, . . . one would have a significant burden to show that a voluntary retirement before the age of sixty-five is reasonable. Even at the age of sixty-five or later, a payor spouse should not be permitted to unilaterally choose voluntary retirement if this choice places the receiving spouse in peril of poverty. . . .

 **FOR *IN RE ARVENITIS***

A. The court discusses the standard it established in *Laflamme* for determining whether a change of circumstances has occurred. What is that standard?

B. As this court construes *Laflamme*, could voluntary retirement ever constitute a substantial change in circumstances?

C. On remand, what does the trial court need to determine? What is the legal standard to be applied and what factual findings are necessary?

D. As a matter of public policy, should spousal support payments be reduced at retirement? If the couple had stayed together, would their joint income likely have decreased at the time of retirement? Should the amount an obligor pays in spousal support be reduced if the obligor elects to retire early? What if this results in a hardship to the recipient? What if the recipient is much younger in age than the obligor?

E. Professor Kindregan summarizes state views on retirement as a grounds for modification as follows:

> Currently no consensus exists in the United States on whether the retirement of an alimony obligor may serve as a basis for modifying the obligation. A number of states consider retirement of an alimony obligor as a potential factor in modification of alimony, but reported cases suggest reluctance to do so. Some courts have determined specific formulas to resolve the retirement issue. Other courts have shown a greater willingness to reduce or eliminate alimony in relation to declining health, rather than the obligor's independent decision to retire. The Massachusetts statute is unusual because it seems to accept the obligor's reaching the full retirement age as set out by the Social Security Administration as presumptively controlling the termination of his or her obligation, except in cases where the court, in entering the order, set a different standard for good cause shown or when there has been a showing by clear and convincing evidence of good cause shown for continuance of the order.

Charles P. Kindregan, Jr., *Reforming Alimony: Massachusetts Reconsiders Postdivorce Spousal Support*, 46 Suffolk U. L. Rev. 13, 25 (2013). Which approach do you favor?

11.4 CHANGE IN CIRCUMSTANCES OF THE RECIPIENT: INHERITANCE, REMARRIAGE, COHABITATION

A substantial change in circumstances rendering a spousal support order unfair or unconscionable may result from changes in the situation of the recipient. The recipient may experience a substantial increase or decrease in income for a number of reasons. For example in *Timberlake v. Timberlake*, 947 N.E.2d 1250 (Ct. App. Ohio 2011), a modification action was triggered when a recipient of spousal support inherited assets from her parents. The obligor argued that spousal support should be terminated, but the court rejected his argument, reasoning that the parents' death was foreseeable and had been contemplated during the divorce settlement process. Consequently, the court did not terminate the spousal support payments

The obligation to pay spousal support generally ceases if the recipient remarries. As provided in UMDA §316(b), "Unless otherwise agreed in writing or expressly provided in the decree, the obligation to pay future maintenance is terminated upon the death of either party or the remarriage of the party receiving maintenance."

Challenging questions arise if a recipient does not remarry but instead cohabits subsequent to divorce. State rules vary but many states analyze whether the need of the former spouse is changed as a result of the cohabitation. Twila L. Perry, *The*

"Essentials of Marriage": Reconsidering the Duty of Support and Services, 15 Yale J.L. & Feminism 1, 26 (2003). *See Schuchard v. Schuchard*, 292 S.W.3d 498 (Mo. Ct. App. 2009) (trial court should have considered change in need due to the financial contribution of the wife's same-sex partner).

In *Remillard v. Remillard*, 999 A.2d 713 (Conn. 2010), the Supreme Court of Connecticut considered the appeal of a former wife who sought to terminate her spousal support payments to her ex-husband based on his cohabitation with another woman even though they were not engaged in a sexual or romantic relationship. The separation agreement provided that spousal support payments would terminate if the ex-husband cohabited with an "unrelated female." *Id.* at 348. The court upheld the trial court's definition of "the term 'cohabitation' as requiring a sexual or romantic relationship." *Id.* at 720.

Some states statutorily authorize termination of spousal support payments when the recipient cohabits. *See, e.g.,* S.C. Code 1976 §20-3-150 (West 2005). Nevertheless, the Court of Civil Appeals of Alabama held that a statute providing for termination of spousal support payments if the recipient "is living openly or cohabiting with a member of the opposite sex," did not apply to cohabitation with a same-sex partner. *J.L.M. v. S.A.K.*, 18 So. 3d 384, 388 (Ct. App. Ala. 2009).

REFLECTIVE QUESTIONS	Is termination of spousal support when a former spouse cohabits with another following divorce consistent with the purpose of spousal maintenance?

Background to *Cermak v. Cermak*

In the following case, the North Dakota Supreme Court considers a situation where an obligor moves to terminate spousal support based on the cohabitation of the recipient but the relevant North Dakota statute is silent on the issue.

CERMAK
v.
CERMAK

North Dakota Supreme Court
569 N.W.2d 280 (1997)

VANDE WALLE, Chief Justice. The Cermaks were married in June of 1964. Duane was granted a divorce from Loretta on January 11, 1995. In an Amended Judgment of January 23, 1995, the district court ordered Duane to pay Loretta permanent spousal support in the amount of $600 per month. The Judgment provided the permanent support was to cease upon the death or remarriage of

Loretta. Duane had asked the district court to include a clause that would terminate spousal support upon the cohabitation of Loretta, but the court did not do so.

In mid-1995, Loretta sold the real property she received under the terms of the Amended Judgment and took up residence with a man whom she had been seeing during the pendency of the divorce proceeding. Although Loretta moved in with the paramour while the prior appeal was pending, the effect of the "live-in" relationship was never reviewed by this Court.

Duane challenges the district court's ruling that (a) termination of his spousal support obligation is not warranted because cohabitation is not the same as remarriage, and (b) reduction is inappropriate because the same reasons for granting support still exist today. . . .

Loretta Cermak acknowledges she is in a "live-in" relationship with another man. But merely cohabiting is insufficient to create a marital relationship in our State. North Dakota abrogated common law marriages shortly after statehood. N.D.C.C. §14-03-01 (Supp. 1997) (providing only marriages entered into pursuant to state law are valid). See *Schumacher v. Great Northern Ry. Co. et al.*, 136 N.W. 85, 86 (1912) (noting the 1890 legislature clearly intended to abrogate nonceremonial marriages). Unless the statutory requirements are met, the fact of cohabitation alone is insufficient to create a legally recognized marriage. However, Duane argues Loretta's relationship is so much like a remarriage it is sufficient to invoke the provision in the Amended Judgment terminating his spousal support obligation.

Here, although the Amended Judgment provided for termination upon the death or remarriage of Loretta, it made no mention of cohabiting. While other state legislatures have specifically provided for cohabitation as a ground for termination of spousal support, North Dakota has not enacted a similar law. Absent such a provision we will not attach marital obligations to a nonmarital relationship. In the present case, Duane asks us to interpret remarriage in a manner that recognizes a new relationship, a de facto marriage, having all the hallmarks of a common law marriage. To do so would in effect recognize a common law marriage when it has been specifically abrogated by our state legislature.

We agree with the district court that this relationship has none of the permanent benefits of a marriage. The Supreme Court of Maine stated the rationale for a "termination-upon-remarriage" clause in *Mitchell v. Mitchell*, 418 A.2d 1140, 1143 (Me. 1980). "[I]t is against public policy in the ordinary case for one man to be supporting the wife of another who has himself assumed the legal obligation for her support." However, as the Maine Supreme Court recognized, "[t]his reasoning does not apply to the case of an unmarried cohabitant receiving alimony. Though unmarried cohabitants may voluntarily contribute to each other's support, they have no legal obligation to pay." In the case at bar, Duane asks us to interpret the divorce decree in a way that would leave Loretta with an uncertain means of support. The length of Loretta's relationship is unknown; it may last until her death, or may sour tomorrow. On this record, any support Loretta may receive from her cohabitant is provided from his benevolence and comes with no reciprocal or continuing obligation.

Duane argues other states have held cohabiting so similar to remarriage that it terminates spousal support. Specifically, Duane refers us to the case of *Hammonds v. Hammonds*, 641 So. 2d 1211 (Miss. 1994). In *Hammonds*, however, the Mississippi Supreme Court abandoned the automatic termination Duane suggests here. Prior to the *Hammonds* case, the courts in Mississippi terminated spousal support solely on the basis of cohabitation. See, e.g., *McRae v. McRae*, 381 So. 2d 1052, 1055-1056 (Miss. 1980) (holding former spouse's abode with a man who was not her husband forfeited her right to future alimony). In *Hammonds*, Mississippi joined the modern trend among jurisdictions in holding cohabitation cannot be the sole basis for termination of spousal support. *Hammonds*, 641 So. 2d at 1217 (advising "that in determining the effect of post-divorce cohabitation on a recipient spouse's alimony entitlement, financial, rather than moral aspects of the cohabitation are to be considered"). . . .

Duane's argument effectively asks us to adopt the antiquated view and terminate Loretta's spousal support solely on the basis of her unmarried cohabitation. We refuse the invitation to turn back the clock on a watch that has not even been set. We adopt the modern view that cohabitation cannot be the sole basis for termination of spousal support at least where cohabitation is not included as a condition for termination in the divorce decree. Accordingly, we hold a recipient spouse's unmarried cohabitation is not a remarriage and is insufficient, alone, to terminate a permanent spousal support obligation.

Alternatively, Duane Cermak claims the district court erred in refusing to reduce his spousal support obligation. The district court's determination as to whether there has been an unforeseen material change in circumstances justifying a reduction of support is a finding of fact that will not be set aside on appeal unless it is clearly erroneous.

Loretta R. Cermak claims her "live-in" relationship was contemplated by Duane and the court prior to the issuance of the Amended Judgment in this case. A change of circumstances must be unforeseen at the time of the original divorce decree. That is to say the change must not be contemplated by the parties at the time of the divorce. The record on appeal clearly establishes Duane asked the district court to include a "termination-upon-cohabitation" clause in the Amended Judgment. The district court did not do so, and its refusal to do so was not raised as an issue in the prior appeal. Obviously, Duane contemplated Loretta's future live-in relationship. Thus, a reduction in Duane's spousal support obligation is not warranted under a theory of change of circumstances.

Furthermore, Duane merely alleges Loretta's live-in relationship reduces her financial needs. The party claiming a material change in circumstances has occurred bears the burden of proof. *Wheeler*, 548 N.W.2d at 30. A "[m]aterial change [is] something [that] substantially affects the financial abilities or needs of a party." Duane concludes the change is material because Loretta is sharing expenses with her cohabitant. This argument assumes a decreased need automatically occurs when a recipient spouse cohabits. We are not prepared to make such an assumption without evidence establishing a material change in financial needs has actually occurred. See *Myhre v. Myhre*, 296 N.W.2d 905, 909 (S.D. 1980) (refusing to assume decreased need automatically occurs when a recipient spouse cohabits). The district court's finding that nothing has changed since the original decree is not clearly erroneous. The District Court Order is affirmed.

 **FOR *CERMAK v. CERMAK***

A. According to the original judgment, when was spousal support to cease?

B. Duane argued that Loretta's relationship is so much like a remarriage that it is sufficient to invoke the provision in the Amended Judgment terminating his spousal support obligation. What was Loretta's response to this argument?

C. What rationale does the court accept for the "upon-marriage" clause?

D. The court states that it is adopting the "modern view" regarding cohabitation. What is the "modern view" according to the court?

E. Was there an argument that Duane failed to make that might have been more successful? What evidence might he have produced?

F. As observed in the opinion, Duane had asked the district court to include a clause that would terminate spousal support upon the cohabitation of Loretta, but the trial court did not do so, and its refusal was not raised as an issue in his earlier appeal. The court states that because Duane contemplated Loretta's future live-in relationship, a reduction in Duane's spousal support obligation is not warranted under a theory of change of circumstances. Do you agree with this analysis? Is it consistent with the analysis in *In re Arvenitis*?

11.5 CHANGE IN CIRCUMSTANCES OF THE RECIPIENT: EXTENSION OF AWARD

Courts will generally not modify spousal support if (a) there was no award in the original divorce and jurisdiction over the issue was not expressly reserved by the court; or (b) there was a spousal support award in the divorce but it has expired. Simply stated, in both situations there is no existing award to modify.

REFLECTIVE QUESTIONS	**Could a former spouse seek support after being seriously injured in a car accident if the divorce judgment and decree is silent on the issue of spousal support?**

Background to *Wessels v. Wessels*

In *Wessels v. Wessels*, the recipient was awarded rehabilitative spousal support for a period of five years. However, due to continued health problems, the recipient was not able to rehabilitate herself and become gainfully employed. Just days prior to the expiration of the rehabilitative award, the recipient filed a petition to continue the support payments or convert the rehabilitative spousal support to a permanent award.

WESSELS
v.
WESSELS

Supreme Court of Iowa
542 N.W.2d 486 (1995)

HARRIS, J. Can rehabilitative alimony, set to terminate at a given time, be extended and made permanent by reason of unforeseen changed circumstances?

James and Yvonne Wessels were married in 1966 while he was a medical student and she was a nursing student. After receiving her degree in 1968 Yvonne worked to help support the couple while James completed medical school. After graduating from medical school James practiced at several army bases as part of his military service. Yvonne continued to work until the birth of a son in 1970 and a daughter a year later. The parties then decided she would fulfill the role of the traditional homemaker and take care of the children and family while her husband pursued his medical career. Both children are now grown, although a conservatorship has been established for the daughter due to her learning disability. James serves as the conservator.

The marriage eventually deteriorated, and in May 1986, after twenty-one years, the parties were granted a dissolution. The dissolution decree adopted the parties' stipulation which, among other things, provided that (1) James would pay Yvonne rehabilitative alimony in the amount of $3,100 per month for a period of sixty months; (2) James would pay Yvonne $700 per month (up to a two-year maximum) if she attended a full-time, postgraduate program; and (3) Yvonne would make every reasonable effort to become self-sufficient. The language was carefully crafted to specify that the alimony was rehabilitative.

. At the time the dissolution stipulation and decree were drafted, Yvonne had already begun to experience psychiatric problems. She sought treatment from a psychiatrist beginning in 1985 and underwent extensive evaluation at a widely respected psychiatric clinic in 1986. She was diagnosed as suffering from major depression and chronic posttraumatic stress disorder. Her psychiatric problems also caused her to have certain physical ailments, including reflux esophagitis, ulcers, hiatal hernia, chronic lower back pain, psoriasis, and Raynaud's disease.

Yvonne's life since the dissolution has gone into a drastic downward spiral. But only by hindsight, in view of what has transpired since entry of the decree, can it be said that it was unrealistic to hope she could become self-supporting. We are convinced, although James obviously feels otherwise, that her failure has not been for lack of effort. She attempted to enroll in college to pursue a master's degree in special education, and actually began classes in the fall term of 1987. She was however rejected from the masters' program due to inadequate undergraduate grades, and was subsequently forced from her studies due to a psychiatric episode that led to hospitalization.

Rather than returning to her studies, Yvonne entered the work force. Beginning in May 1988 she was employed for three months at a restaurant as a cashier and custodian, and later by a hospital where she worked as a nurse. Then, following a job-related injury, she was assigned to the hospital pharmacy. The hospital placed her on medical leave of absence in November of 1991 at the time of still another psychiatric hospitalization.

In all Yvonne has had twelve psychiatric hospitalizations since the dissolution and has been treated by several psychiatrists in the Des Moines area. Although her primary diagnosis of chronic posttraumatic stress disorder and depression has remained the same, her condition has badly deteriorated. She has been receiving social security disability benefits and long-term disability benefits from her employer. Her current treating psychiatrist states she is not currently capable of holding a job. It is the medical opinion of the physician who completed the medical portion of her disability application in 1991 that Yvonne cannot be rehabilitated and will never work again. Yvonne continues to live in the comfortable family home she was awarded in the dissolution decree. Also residing there is a man with numerous physical ailments who pays $300 monthly rent. Except for alimony Yvonne's only other income is $400 in monthly social security disability benefits and, at the time of hearing, $785 in monthly disability payments derived through Yvonne's hospital employment. In contrast James' professional career as an anesthesiologist has flourished. His income in 1993 was expected to reach $300,000. He also expected to receive an additional $100,000 in income that year from investments.

Under the dissolution decree the last payment of rehabilitative alimony was due in May 1992. On April 30, 1992, Yvonne filed her petition to modify the decree. She asserted that, because her health problems prevented her from obtaining employment as contomplated in the stipulation and agreement, rehabilitative alimony should be continued or converted into permanent alimony. She also requested assistance for her medical bills, and attorney's fees.

After trial on the merits the district court concluded "Yvonne's worsening psychiatric problems, the lack of health insurance benefits, her increased medical expenses, her unemployability, the increased financial resources of James and the reduced assets of Yvonne" constituted a significant change in circumstances warranting modification of the decree. The court ordered James to continue to pay alimony of $3,100 per month to Yvonne until the death of either party or until otherwise ordered by the court. Due to Yvonne's inability to manage funds, however, the court ordered the alimony to be paid into a court-supervised trust for Yvonne's benefit. The court also ordered James to pay one-half of Yvonne's uninsured medical expenses and $10,000 of Yvonne's attorney's fees. . . .

James contends the trial court exceeded its authority in modifying the initial decree because rehabilitative alimony payable for a limited period cannot be extended and converted into traditional alimony. . . . We have distinguished rehabilitative alimony from permanent alimony, explaining that the former was fashioned as a method of supporting an economically dependent spouse through a limited period of re-education or retraining following a dissolution, thereby creating opportunity and incentive for that spouse to become self-supporting. *In re Marriage of Francis*, 442 N.W.2d 59 (Iowa 1989). We noted:

> Because self-sufficiency is the goal of rehabilitative alimony, the duration of such an award may be limited or extended depending on the realistic needs of the economically dependent spouse, tempered by the goal of facilitating the economic independence of the ex-spouse. As in the case of "traditional" alimony, payable for life so long as a spouse is incapable of self-support, a change in status . . . may alter the support picture and warrant a modification. *Id.* at 64 (citations omitted).

We have held that alimony provided in a dissolution decree, even though terminated by a subsequent modification order, can thereafter be reinstated. It was important that the initial decree awarded some alimony because where no alimony is initially awarded the decree cannot be modified to allow any. Finally, in *In re Marriage of Marshall*, 394 N.W.2d 392 (Iowa 1986), we held that, in extraordinary circumstances, a court holds the power under Iowa Code section 598.21(8) to modify a dissolution decree to reinstate alimony payments after the payor spouse had met his obligations under the initial decree, even though the period set for alimony payments in the original decree had expired.

Under our cases there are some rare situations where, notwithstanding an agreement and decree to the contrary, later occurrences are so extreme in their nature as to render the initial understanding grossly unfair and therefore subject to change. We do not envision situations of this kind to be common; they will exist only when the subsequent changes demand that the original order cannot, in fairness and equity, continue to stand. The onset of cancer under the facts in *Marshall* is an example. We think Yvonne's deteriorating condition is another.

These holdings easily support the authority of the trial court here, on proper showing, to modify the initial decree. We say "easily support" because, unlike the facts in *Marshall*, here there was no gap between the ending of the alimony obligation under the initial decree and the application to modify. That is, Yvonne's application to modify, as previously mentioned, preceded the ending of the original obligation.

We next consider whether Yvonne has in fact demonstrated the unusual change of circumstances necessary to justify this extraordinary modification. Anyone seeking modification of the dissolution decree holds the burden to establish entitlement by a preponderance of the evidence. The changed circumstances must not have been in the contemplation of the court when the original decree was entered. The changes must be more or less permanent and continuous, not temporary. The initial decree is entered with a view to reasonable and ordinary changes that may be likely to occur. *In re Marriage of Skiles*, 419 N.W.2d 586, 589 (Iowa App. 1987) (medical problems associated with the aging process are in contemplation and knowledge of trial court).

Without doubt the rehabilitative alimony was provided in the present case in the belief that, through additional education, training, and work experience Yvonne would be able to obtain a full-time job and become self-supporting. The decree also declared it was Yvonne's responsibility to make every reasonable effort to achieve this goal. Obviously Yvonne has not met the goal of self-sufficiency but we have already found she made a good-faith attempt to do so. We reject James' contention that her deteriorated condition is due to her own life style choices.

Yvonne is currently not capable of holding a job and we are persuaded she will not become able to do so. This permanent deteriorated condition is a material and substantial change not contemplated by the court at the time of the initial decree. And, most importantly, it qualifies as the sort of rare and unique change that demands the extraordinary relief Yvonne seeks. The trial court was correct in so finding.

On our de novo review we agree with the terms of the modification order. James contends the trial court lacked the power to require him to pay for half of Yvonne's uncovered medical expenses. We disagree, noting that Iowa Code section 598.21(8)(c) provides for modifications when there are "changes in the medical expenses of a party." Both parties appeal from that part of the modification order that directed James to pay $10,000 toward Yvonne's $28,200 in accumulated attorney's fees. We find no abuse.

DISCUSSION QUESTIONS FOR *WESSELS v. WESSELS*

A. What did the stipulation adopted by the parties provide? Under the dissolution decree, when was the last payment of rehabilitative spousal support due?

B. What distinction does the court make between permanent and rehabilitative spousal support?

C. Would the result in this case have been different if Yvonne filed for modification of the spousal support award a few days after it had expired instead of a few days before? Does the court discuss this in the opinion?

D. This case involved an award of rehabilitative spousal support. What was the substantial change in circumstances making the original award unfair? Who had the burden of proof and what showing was required?

E. Under what circumstances should a rehabilitative award be extended? What if the recipient does not take reasonable steps toward rehabilitation? What if a recipient who is required to do so diligently attends school and receives a degree but is unable to find a job due to market changes?

11.6 ENFORCEMENT OF NONMODIFICATION STIPULATIONS

Because most divorces are settled by the parties, the issue of spousal support is most likely to be negotiated. Typically, parties will prepare budgets and consider sample scenarios before reaching an agreement.

Some potential obligors are hesitant to agree to even a short-term spousal support payment because of the potential for later modification and continuation of the order, as seen in *Wessels*. However, potential obligors may be more inclined to agree to some payment of spousal support if the recipient waives the right to subsequently modify or extend the order. As a matter of public policy, the option to make and rely on such agreements promotes settlement of cases.

Under the UMDA §306(b) courts are bound by the parties' agreement with respect to spousal support unless the court finds that the agreement is unconscionable. Furthermore, agreements "set forth in the decree are enforceable by all remedies available for enforcement of a judgment, including contempt, and are enforceable as contract terms." UMDA §306(e). With respect to agreements preventing modification of spousal support, UMDA §306(f) provides: "Except for terms concerning the support, custody, or visitation of children, the decree may expressly preclude or limit modification of terms set forth in the decree if the separation agreement so provides." Thus, as a matter of public policy, the UMDA provides strong support for approving and enforcing settlements reached by the parties.

In *Rose v. Rose*, 795 N.W.2d 611 (Mich. App. 2010), the court recounted the public policy supporting enforcement of nonmodification agreements:

> (1) Nonmodifiable agreements enable parties to structure package settlements, in which alimony, asset divisions, attorney fees, postsecondary tuition for children, and related matters are all coordinated in a single, mutually acceptable agreement; (2) finality of divorce provisions allows predictability for parties planning their postdivorce lives; (3) finality fosters judicial economy; (4) finality and predictability lower the cost of divorce for both parties; (5) enforcing agreed-upon provisions for alimony will encourage increased compliance with agreements by parties who know that their agreements can and will be enforced by the court [citing *Staple v. Staple*, 616 N.W.2d 219 (Mich. App. 2000)].

Id. at 614. Nevertheless, courts sometimes have concerns about enforcing nonmodification agreements.

Do you think that divorcing spouses should be able to preclude future modification of a spousal support award?

Background to *Karon v. Karon*

In the next two cases, courts examine nonmodification stipulations and rule on their enforceability. In *Karon v. Karon*, the court considers whether to enforce a stipulation incorporated in a judgment and decree that purports to divest the court of jurisdiction over the issue of modification.

KARON
v.
KARON

Supreme Court of Minnesota
435 N.W.2d 501 (1989)

YETKA, J. Howard F. and Frima M. Karon married on December 21, 1952. Howard commenced a dissolution proceeding in 1979, and the parties executed a stipulation on June 27, 1981. The court entered its judgment and decree on August 28, 1981, incorporating the terms of the stipulation.

Both documents provided that Howard would pay Frima $1,200 per month for 6 years and $600 per month for 4 years thereafter. Both documents also stated:

> Except for the aforesaid maintenance, each party waives and is forever barred from receiving any spousal maintenance whatsoever from one another, and this court is divested from having any jurisdiction whatsoever to award temporary or permanent spousal maintenance to either of the parties.

Moreover, the stipulation states that the parties

> hereby mutually release each other from all rights, claims and other obligations arising out of or during the course of their marriage relationship, except as specifically set forth elsewhere in this Stipulation.

Howard worked as the vice president of sales at Ed Phillips & Sons Co. before the dissolution. In January 1980, he became senior vice president of sales with a gross annual income of $79,337. In 1985, he earned $111,440 taxable income. In 1986, Howard estimated his 1986 gross salary at $126,000. In addition, Howard has been accruing interest in a deferred payment plan since 1981. The plan will be worth approximately $625,000 in 1995 if he stays with his company until that time.

Frima worked as a sales representative for women's sportswear. Beginning in the mid-1960's [*sic*], she worked at various companies. In 1981, she earned $16,924; in 1984, she earned $13,956; and she estimated her 1985 income as "negligible" because her job had been eliminated. Conditions in the industry precluded her from finding similar employment, and in November 1985, she worked part-time in a bakery for $5 per hour. In 1986, Frima took a real estate course and began selling real estate at Edina Realty. She earned no money during her first year of work. In September 1986, she had an IRA valued at $26,500.

In late 1985, Frima moved the court for a modification of the maintenance award, requesting permanent maintenance of $3,500 per month. Howard challenged the court's authority to modify the maintenance provision, arguing that the parties had waived any alteration of maintenance in the stipulation and that the court had divested itself of jurisdiction to alter the decree. A referee held that Minn. Stat. §518.64 (Supp. 1985) granted it such authority and ordered that it would hear the modification motion on the merits after a discovery period. The district court affirmed this order.

After the completion of discovery, a referee heard the merits of the motion and ruled that a substantial change in circumstances had occurred, warranting a maintenance modification pursuant to section 518.64. The referee determined, however, that Frima had the capacity to earn $1,000 per month and thus increased maintenance to $1,500 per month rather than the $3,500 requested. The referee also made the award permanent because Frima had an uncertain future earning capacity. Finally, the referee awarded Frima $1,000 in attorney fees. The district court affirmed the referee's order. . . .

The parties have confused and compounded numerous issues, but we believe the question before us is whether one of the adult parties to a stipulation in a dissolution matter made in 1981, which was approved by the trial court and which settled all issues, including maintenance, and which further provided that the parties expressly waived any right to maintenance except as provided in the original agreement, may now re-open the issue of maintenance to seek an increase therein. The trial court allowed reconsideration of the maintenance issue and the court of appeals affirmed.

Howard argues that the terms of the original judgment and decree denied the court any further jurisdiction over the issue of maintenance. The language of the judgment and decree purports to divest jurisdiction. Section 518.64, however, states that the court may modify a maintenance award upon petition of a party. Minn. Stat. §518.64, subd. 1 (1984). The court must decide, therefore, whether the maintenance issue was *res judicata* or whether the court correctly modified the maintenance award under section 518.64 regardless of the original order's language.

Initially, the legal doctrines at issue need clarification. Howard, in essence, argues that the form of *res judicata* known as direct estoppel precludes relitigation of the maintenance issue. Direct estoppel is issue preclusion in a second action on the same claim. The seminal issue, therefore, becomes whether the original decree constituted a final judgment in the dissolution on the maintenance issue. If so, it should have had the *res judicata* effect of preventing the court from hearing the modification motion. Phrased in other words, we must decide whether the district court properly divested itself of jurisdiction over the issue in 1981.

It is not the parties to the stipulation who have divested the court of ability to relitigate the issue of maintenance. The court had the authority to refuse to accept the terms of the stipulation in part or in toto. The trial court stands in place and on behalf of the citizens of the state as a third party to dissolution actions. It has a duty to protect the interests of both parties and all the citizens of the state to ensure that the stipulation is fair and reasonable to all. The court did so here and approved the stipulation and incorporated the terms therein in its decree. . . .

Amicus for the Family Law Section of the Minnesota State Bar Association stated at oral argument that setting aside the stipulation and decree is insulting and demeaning to women. Counsel who argued on behalf of the association is a woman. She took that position in response to counsel for respondent's implication that women involved in divorce cannot understand or act to protect their rights even when represented by counsel; therefore, the state must protect them in the manner it protects children in the role of *parens patriae.*

Amicus's argument is compelling. Moreover, what effect would affirmance have on other contracts entered into by married women? Would such a decision supporting the respondent ultimately lead to turning the clock back, outlawing not only antenuptial agreements, but also allowing parties to contest the validity of all instruments and contracts entered into on behalf of married women? Would we also question the validity of deeds of conveyances and purchases of expensive personal property? Where would the protection end? In short, intelligent adult women, especially when represented by counsel, must be expected to honor their contracts the same as anyone else. Any other holding would result in chaos in the family law field and declining respect for binding agreements as well.

[W]e reverse the modification of the original dissolution decree and remand to the trial court with instructions to enforce the terms of that initial dissolution decree.

COYNE, J., dissenting. Consider that not unlikely event that a woman entering into a stipulation identical to that presented shortly thereafter suffers a totally disabling illness that threatens to quickly exhaust all of her available resources and that, during the same period, her former husband enjoys a substantial increase in income. I am simply unable to reconcile the majority decision with either the clearly stated legislative mandate contained in Minn. Stat. §518.64 or the cumulative decisional authority of this court supporting the principle that awards of spousal maintenance are, upon motion, subject to the continuing jurisdiction and scrutiny of the trial courts.

Admittedly, the language of the original judgment and decree, as well as the parties' stipulation, purports to divest the court of any jurisdiction to modify the provision for spousal maintenance. The majority has accepted Howard's contention that the judgment and decree should be given *res judicata* effect, precluding relitigation or reconsideration of the maintenance issue. However, 60 years ago, in a somewhat different context, this court refused to give *res judicata* effect to language in a divorce decree which purported to divest the court of jurisdiction over maintenance. Although there have been many changes in family law over the intervening 60 years, we have consistently recognized that jurisdiction over marriage dissolution is statutory. Since dissolution jurisdiction is statutory, the corollary of the observation that the district court has no power except that delegated by statute, is that the district court cannot divest itself of the power validly delegated by statute.

 **DISCUSSION QUESTIONS** FOR *KARON v. KARON*

A. What was the parties' original agreement with respect to modification of the spousal support award?

B. Does this court adopt the view that parties can divest a court of jurisdiction?

C. Compare the views of the majority and the dissent. Is the dissent arguing that parties in this jurisdiction cannot, by stipulation, limit the duration of spousal support absent a specific statute permitting such limitation? What public policy would be fostered if the dissent's view regarding modification is followed? What public policy is furthered by the majority's view?

D. In response to this decision, the Minnesota Legislature promulgated a statute that permits parties to agree to expressly preclude or limit maintenance. To do so through a stipulation, the court must make specific findings that the stipulation is fair and equitable, is supported by consideration described in the findings, and that full disclosure of each party's financial circumstances has occurred and the stipulation must be made a part of the judgment and decree. What potential abuses and hardships was the legislature trying to prevent by passing this statute?

E. In a subsequent Minnesota case, parties with a valid *Karon* waiver agreed to subsequent modifications of spousal maintenance that were approved by the court. When one of the parties sought to vacate the modification orders, the Minnesota Supreme Court agreed, stating, "Given that the parties' *Karon* waiver is valid, the district court did not have jurisdiction to issue the modification orders." Do you agree with this outcome? Why or why not? *See Gossman v. Gossman*, 847 N.W.2d 718 (Minn. App. 2014).

Background to *Maddick v. Deshon*

Section 11.4 of this chapter discussed termination of spousal support when a recipient remarries. In this case the court considers whether a nonmodification stipulation can prevent statutory termination of a spousal support award based on the remarriage of the recipient.

MADDICK
v.
DESHON

Court of Appeals of Missouri
296 S.W.3d 519 (2009)

ALOK AHUJA, J., Respondent Joseph Maddick ("Husband") and Appellant Roberta DeShon ("Wife") were married in July 1983. Their marriage was dissolved in October 2003. The judgment included a provision requiring Husband to pay Wife periodic, modifiable maintenance of $500 per month.

A year later, the parties entered into a stipulation to modify the judgment. The parties agreed that the child of the marriage had become emancipated. The parties also agreed that Wife's expenses had increased. The stipulation also provided:

The parties agree that the periodic modifiable maintenance should be increased to the amount of Seven Hundred Fifty Dollars ($750.00) per month, effective September 1, 2004, for a period of seven (7) years as non-modifiable contractual maintenance. . . . *The maintenance obligation herein should terminate upon Respondent's death.* (Emphasis added.)

On October 26, 2004, the court entered a modified judgment setting forth the stipulation. The court then decreed:

That the Petitioner shall pay to Respondent the sum of Seven Hundred Fifty Dollars ($750.00) per month for non-modifiable contractual maintenance. Said payments shall commence September 1, 2004, for a period of seven (7) years as non-modifiable contractual maintenance. . . . *Said maintenance obligation shall only terminate upon the death of Respondent or September 30, 2011, whichever occurs first.* (Emphasis added.)

Wife remarried on September 29, 2007. Shortly thereafter, Husband filed a motion to again modify the dissolution decree. He alleged that Wife's remarriage constituted a substantial and continuing change of circumstances, and sought to have his maintenance obligation terminated as of the date of Wife's remarriage.

After hearing evidence in September 2008, the circuit court entered its Judgment Modifying Decree of Dissolution of Marriage. The court sustained Husband's motion to terminate maintenance after finding "that there was no written agreement or court order extending [Husband's] obligation to pay maintenance past the date of [Wife's] remarriage." Wife appeals.

The issue in this case is whether the parties' written stipulation or the October 2004 modified judgment rebuts the statutory presumption, created by §452.370.3, that maintenance terminates upon the receiving spouse's remarriage. Wife contends that the unambiguous language of both the stipulation and the modified judgment rebuts the statutory presumption and obligates Husband to continue paying maintenance despite her remarriage. Alternatively, Wife argues that the language in the stipulation was ambiguous, and that the court erred in excluding extrinsic evidence that would have resolved the ambiguity.

Section 452.370.3 provides in relevant part:

Unless otherwise agreed in writing or expressly provided in the judgment, the obligation to pay future statutory maintenance is terminated upon the death of either party or the remarriage of the party receiving maintenance.

. . . Wife emphasizes that the modified judgment expressly sets forth the "only" two events which would terminate Husband's maintenance obligation. She argues that the court expressly provided the exclusive circumstances which would terminate Husband's maintenance obligation, and thereby excluded Wife's remarriage as a termination event. Thus, according to Wife, the judgment "expressly provides" that maintenance will *not* terminate upon her remarriage.

Wife's argument is not without force. The trial court's modified judgment purports to specify the "only" events which will terminate Husband's obligation to pay maintenance. By expressly (and seemingly exhaustively) cataloguing the circumstances in which maintenance will terminate, and including in that listing only one of the three termination events listed in §452.370.3, it is at least arguable that the court "expressly provided otherwise" than the presumptive statutory scheme (under which maintenance terminates on the death of either spouse, or the recipient spouse's remarriage).

We do not write on a blank slate, however. Despite the appeal of Wife's argument, we believe it is foreclosed by controlling Missouri decisions construing §452.370.3. While none of those cases involves language of a decree purporting to identify the "only" circumstances in which maintenance will terminate, their reading of §452.370.3 requires a decree to expressly extend maintenance beyond remarriage before the statutory presumption is defeated. Giving the language of those cases its plain meaning, a decree must expressly and affirmatively provide that maintenance continues beyond the events listed in §452.370.3, or else the occurrence of those events will terminate the paying spouse's obligations.

Thus, in *Cates,* the Missouri Supreme Court interpreted §452.370.3 to provide that the statutory presumption is rebutted "by a decree of dissolution *expressly extending the obligation to pay future statutory maintenance beyond* the death of either party or *the remarriage of the receiving party.*" 819 S.W.2d at 734 (emphasis added); *id.* at 736 (finding statutory presumption unrebutted where "[w]e find no language in [the decree] *expressly* extending Larry's obligation to continue the monthly payments due on the maintenance in gross award beyond Rochelle's remarriage").

Two years later, the Supreme Court interpreted *Cates* as holding that, "[b]ecause the decree and separation agreement *did not address the effect of remarriage,* this Court . . . concluded that the statute should control and that the payments should terminate." *Glenn v. Snider*, 852 S.W.2d 841, 843 (Mo. banc 1993) (emphasis added). . . .

As we read these plain (and repeated) holdings, in order to rebut the statutory presumption that maintenance terminates upon the receiving spouse's remarriage, a dissolution decree must expressly refer to the receiving spouse's possible future remarriage, and must expressly provide that maintenance payments shall continue beyond that contingency.

Although not dispositive, this reading of §452.370.3 is confirmed by the uniform statute from which the Missouri provision is derived, and by cases from other jurisdictions which have adopted similar provisions. The relevant language of §452.370.3 is adopted from §316(b) of the Uniform Marriage and Divorce Act, 9A Part II U.L.A. 102 (1998). The comment to §316(b) makes clear that the statutory presumption will only be defeated by an affirmative statement in a dissolution decree extending maintenance beyond remarriage or death:

> Subsection (b) authorizes the parties to agree in writing or the court to provide in the de[c]ree that maintenance will continue beyond the death of the obligor or the remarriage of the obligee. In the absence of such an agreement or provision in the decree, this section sets the termination date for the obligation to pay future maintenance.

Cases from other jurisdictions which have adopted §316(b) reach the same result: a decree must expressly provide that maintenance continues despite the receiving spouse's remarriage in order to defeat the presumptive termination of maintenance at that time. Although our research concerning out-of-state caselaw has not been exhaustive, we note that at least one such decision involves decretal language bearing a striking similarity to the language at issue here. In *In re Marriage of Roth*, 865 P.2d 43 (1994), a divorce decree provided that "[o]nly in the event of the death of either the Respondent or Petitioner prior to June 15, 1993 shall this obligation to pay spousal maintenance terminate." Like here, the receiving spouse argued "that the word 'only' clearly and unambiguously excludes any event other than death from terminating spousal support." The court rejected this argument, relying on the holding of an earlier Washington Supreme Court decision: " 'In the hopes of discouraging dubious interpretation of questionable decretal language, we hold . . . that the decree must specifically mention remarriage in order to overcome the presumption. Specific decretal language means just that.' " Thus, under Washington law, "[the statute] mean[s] just what [it] say[s]: 'express provision' means use of the word 'remarriage,' " the statute "require[es] the specific mention of remarriage to continue spousal support beyond remarriage." *Roth* concluded that a decree specifying that maintenance would terminate "[o]nly in the event of the death of either [party]" did not meet this standard: "Here, neither the dissolution agreement nor any other agreement provides that maintenance is to continue past remarriage; remarriage therefore terminated the obligation." . . .

In this case, the October 2004 modified judgment did not refer to remarriage. We recognize that the court's statement that Husband's "maintenance obligation shall only terminate upon the death of [Wife] or September 30, 2011" supports *an inference* that the court intended that no other event would terminate Husband's obligation. Nonetheless, such an inference cannot satisfy the requirement that a decree of dissolution "expressly extend[] the obligation to pay future statutory maintenance beyond . . . the remarriage of the receiving party." *Cates*, 819 S.W.2d at 734.

The Supreme Court made the following cautionary observation in *Cates*, which has been repeated in later cases: "Given the unambiguous language of [§452.370.3], it is difficult to imagine that the careful drafter would fail to state the intent of the parties when failure to do so results in termination of maintenance." 819 S.W.2d at 738. That admonition is as apt today as it was eighteen years ago.

 **FOR** *MADDICK v. DESHON*

A. What were the specific terms of the nonmodification stipulation?

B. What was the former wife's interpretation of the clause? What was the former husband's interpretation of the clause?

C. If you were drafting the agreement in this case, what language would you use if you represented the former wife or the former husband?

D. Do you think the court made the correct decision in this case? Why or why not?

E. In *Blum v. Koster*, 919 N.E.2d 333 (Ill. 2009), the Supreme Court of Illinois held that a court could not, without an express agreement of the parties, make spousal support nonmodifiable. What is the likely public policy behind the decision? Do you think that a court should be able to enter a spousal support order that cannot be modified? Why or why not?

General Principles

1. States differ concerning the legal standard for modification of spousal support but many require evidence of a substantial change in circumstances sufficient to render the original award unfair.
2. The party seeking to modify an existing order bears the burden of meeting the applicable legal standard. If the modification is granted, it is generally not made retroactive beyond the date of the filing of the motion for modification.
3. Payment of periodic spousal support typically terminates on the death of either the obligor or the recipient.
4. When an obligor retires, courts will look at the totality of circumstances, including the foreseeability of the retirement, when determining whether to reduce or terminate spousal support payments.
5. The obligation to pay spousal support generally ceases if the recipient remarries, but the obligation does not necessarily end if the recipient cohabits outside of marriage.
6. Courts will generally not modify spousal support if (a) there was no award in the original divorce and jurisdiction over the issue was not expressly reserved by the court; or (b) there was a spousal support award in the divorce but it has expired.
7. An agreement not to modify spousal support may provide an obligor with assurance that a rehabilitative or limited duration spousal support order will not become permanent.

Chapter Problems

1. Assume that P and D divorce. They have been married for ten years and D plans to return to college to obtain a degree in teaching. As a part of the divorce settlement approved by the court, P agrees to pay D rehabilitative spousal support for four years. D returns to college and, while making good progress toward a degree,

begins cohabiting with X. The divorce decree is silent on the issue of cohabitation, and it is not addressed in the state statute. X has an excellent job and provides financially for D. P files for modification alleging that D no longer needs spousal support. What arguments will P and D make to the court?

2. Assume that P and D divorce. P has been a full-time homemaker for 15 years and has worked part time as a piano teacher. The court awards P permanent spousal support. A year after the divorce, P obtains full-time employment as a music teacher, and D moves to decrease or terminate the spousal support award. What arguments will each make? Which do you find more persuasive?

3. Assume that P and D divorce in State X, which has adopted a provision identical to UMDA §308 (discussed in the previous chapter). Under that section, spousal support is awarded only if the proposed recipient: "(1) lacks sufficient property to provide for his reasonable needs; and (2) is unable to support himself through appropriate employment. . . ." D is awarded permanent spousal support. Five years after the divorce, P's income doubles, and D seeks an increase in support. What arguments will P and D make? Which do you find more persuasive?

4. In *Sills v. Sills*, 2007 WL 1500812 (Utah App. 2007), the court considered whether the parties, through a nonmodification agreement incorporated into the decree, could divest the court of jurisdiction to modify spousal support. The court stated as follows:

> The language . . . does not denote that a court is divested of its statutorily granted jurisdiction where parties have waived their right to modify. Rather, . . . [it] merely reflects the rule that courts are more reluctant to overturn specific and knowing waivers of property distribution rights and thus require a movant to show more than changed circumstances—i.e., the movant must demonstrate compelling reasons—for the court to modify and override the parties' waiver.

How is this analysis different from that used by the court in *Karon v. Karon*? Which reasoning is more sound?

5. Professor Cynthia Lee Starnes argues that the alimony remarriage-termination rule is not rationally based. She asserts as follows:

> More contemporary alimony rationales—from fault-based damage awards to no-fault need-based models, from partnership models to the American Law Institute's loss-sharing scheme—provide no explanation for termination of alimony upon remarriage and, in fact, provide compelling arguments against termination. The sense of impropriety and indignation that infuse occasional judicial efforts to explain the rule only confirm the suspicion that the roots of the remarriage-termination rule lie in archaic principles of coverture, which cast a wife not as a marital partner, but rather as a man's burden, dependent on her husband for protection and survival until the next man comes

along to relieve him of the task. This vision of burdened men and incapacitated women makes a dispiriting statement about husbands and wives and about the institution of marriage itself. If the remarriage-termination rule can be explained only in such pejorative terms, it should not endure.

Do you agree with her analysis? *See* Cynthia Lee Starnes, *One More Time: Alimony, Intuition, and Remarriage-Termination Rule*, 81 Ind. L.J. 971 (2006).

Preparation for Practice

1. Does your state have a statute governing the use and enforceability of non-modification agreements? If so, what are its terms?

2. Work with a partner to draft an enforceable nonmodification stipulation.

3. Work with a partner to draft an unenforceable nonmodification agreement.

4. Imagine that you are engaged in negotiating a divorce and you represent a high-income client who is divorcing a very low-income spouse. How might you use the tax deductibility of spouse support and a nonmodification stipulation to structure a spousal support agreement?

Part IV

Distribution of Property

Chapter 12

Division of Property at Divorce

12.1 INTRODUCTION: OVERVIEW

When a marriage dissolves and the parties are unable to amicably agree over how their marital property is to be divided, the matter is of necessity resolved by a family court judge. This chapter focuses exclusively on the legal issues a court may face when deciding to whom property should go.

Several theories and concepts are used by jurisdictions in the United States when awarding property upon divorce. This chapter provides basic information about these concepts and theories, including a history of their development. It also provides challenging problems where the concepts and theories may be applied and tested within a practical analytic framework.

Some of the questions considered by this chapter include the following: How do courts treat passive and active increases or decreases in the value of property? What are the definitions of marital and nonmarital property? What role does marital "fault" play in making property awards? What is transmutation? What is goodwill? Should courts place a property value on a law degree or other professional degree earned while married when a couple divorce? How should homemaker contributions, stock, pensions, and various compensation awards be valued?

REFLECTIVE QUESTIONS	What are your goals for this chapter?

12.2 HISTORY: TITLE SYSTEM

Three property distribution systems have been used at various times in the United States to divide the marital assets of a divorcing couple: (1) the separate title system; (2) the community property system, which is used today in 9 jurisdictions; and (3) the equitable distribution system, which is used today in over 40 jurisdictions. Each of these property distribution systems is discussed below, beginning with the title system.

Title system. At common law, a majority of states used the title system to distribute marital property when a divorce occurred. This system provided that each party was entitled to retain title to an asset that he or she acquired during the marriage. A result of strict application of this theory was that a "spouse obtained an ownership interest in the other's property only upon the latter's death through the operation of dower, curtesy, or a statutory forced share. Thus, through chance or calculated title holding, one spouse could emerge from divorce owning all the property acquired during marriage." Laurie L. Malman, *Unfinished Reform: The Tax Consequences of Divorce,* 61 N.Y.U. L. Rev. 363, 373 (June 1986).

The title system was criticized as unjust, especially in a traditional family setting where most of the property was titled in the husband's name. For example, should a divorce occur, a traditional homemaker did not have a right to share in the property acquired by her income-earning husband. She (almost always the wife) was left with little but a claim for alimony, which often proved difficult initially to obtain and then later challenging to enforce. The title system did not recognize a homemaker's contributions to the marriage. In those rare instances where both spouses worked outside the home and the husband's income was placed into investments in his name while the wife's earnings were devoted to family expenses, upon divorce, the husband received all the investments.

The unfair treatment of a homemaker under the title-based system was a driving force in bringing about major reform in divorce law over the past half-century. This has resulted in title-based jurisdictions moving to some form of an equitable distribution system when a couple divorce. The title-based system is no longer used in any states.

Note that there were possible legal avenues available that could avoid the harsh treatment a wife received in a title system state. For example, a father could create a trust for his daughter, or make a premarital settlement that would protect his daughter should a divorce occur. As a practical matter, such arrangements were confined to the wealthy, landed classes.

| REFLECTIVE QUESTIONS | What is the criticism of a title-based property system when a divorce occurs? |

12.3 HISTORY: COMMUNITY PROPERTY SYSTEM

The community property theory, used in this country in its earliest form in several western states, is an outgrowth of the civil law influence of France, Spain, and Mexico. *See Roberts v. Wehmeyer*, 218 P. 22, 25 (Cal. 1923). Today, Arizona, California, Idaho, Louisiana, New Mexico, Nevada, Texas, and Washington are recognized as community property states. In 1986, Wisconsin adopted a version of the Uniform Marital Property Act and is a considered a community property state. *See* Doris J. Freed & Timothy B. Walker, *Family Law in the Fifty States: An Overview*, 19 Fam. L.Q. 331, 354-355 (1986).

The community property partnership concept applies during a marriage, upon dissolution of the marriage, or upon the death of one of the partners. In general, both spouses are vested in all the property acquired during the marriage, other than property that by statute is specifically excluded from the community, such as a gift to one partner but not the other, or an inheritance to one partner but not the other. Some jurisdictions allow earnings on nonmarital property to remain the individual's separate property; others do not. The increase in the value of a party's separate property resulting from that party's effort during marriage is usually considered community property. *See Cockrill v. Cockrill*, 601 P.2d 1334, 1336 (Ariz. 1979).

Presumption. In general, a community property state considers a marriage a partnership, and each spouse possesses an undivided one-half interest in property acquired by spousal labor during the relationship. It is presumed that property possessed by either spouse during a divorce is community property. For example, the Texas Family Code states that "[p]roperty possessed by either spouse during or on dissolution of marriage is presumed to be community property." The Code also states that "[t]he degree of proof necessary to establish that property is separate property is clear and convincing evidence." Vernon's Tex. Code Ann., Tex. Fam. Code §3.003 (2015). Community property is divided when a marriage is dissolved, and each partner is entitled to immediate control over that partner's community property interest.

REFLECTIVE QUESTIONS	When it comes to ownership of marital property, what appears to be the philosophical view of a community property state? How does it differ from a title system approach?

12.4 EQUITABLE DISTRIBUTION SYSTEM: TERMS AND CONCEPTS

As noted earlier, the title system has been replaced in more than 40 states with the equitable distribution theory. The concept of equitable distribution is a corollary of the principle that marriage is a joint enterprise whose vitality, success, and endurance is dependent on the conjunction of multiple components, only one of which is financial. The nonremunerated efforts of raising children, making a home, performing a myriad of personal services, and providing physical and emotional support are among other noneconomic ingredients of the marital relationship. The noneconomic contributions are viewed as essential to its nature and maintenance as are the economic factors, and courts and legislatures believe that their worth is entitled to substantial recognition.

The extent to which each party contributes to the marriage is measurable not only by the amount of money contributed to it, but also by a whole complex of financial and nonfinancial components. Equitable distribution recognizes that when a marriage ends, each of the spouses, based on the totality of the contributions made to the marriage, has a stake in and right to a share of the marital assets accumulated because they represent the capital product of what was essentially a partnership entity.

Tracing. In most equitable distribution jurisdictions, the nonmarital claimant bears the burden of properly tracing claimed nonmarital funds to a marital use or account. For example, in *Jackson v. Jackson*, 765 S.W.2d 561 (Ark. 1989), the court found that a one-half interest that the former wife purchased with nonmarital funds during the marriage remained her nonmarital real estate. The funds used to purchase the real estate were directly traceable through a joint checking account. This overcame the presumption of ownership of the property as tenants by entirety.

Marital property defined. In most states, marital property is broadly defined. For example, in New York, marital property is defined as ". . . all property acquired by either or both spouses during the marriage and before the execution of a separation agreement or the commencement of a matrimonial action, regardless of the form in which title is held. . . ." Dom. Rel. L. §236B(1)[c] (2015). Ohio defines marital property as "[a]ll real and personal property that currently is owned by either or both of the spouses, including, but not limited to, the retirement benefits of the spouses, and that was acquired by either or both of the spouses during the marriage; [a]ll interest that either or both of the spouses currently has in any real or personal property, including, but not limited to, the retirement benefits of the spouses, and that was acquired by either or both of the spouses during the marriage; and [unless otherwise excepted] all income and appreciation on separate property, due to the labor, monetary, or in-kind contribution of either or both of the spouses that occurred during the marriage." Ohio Rev. Code §3105.171 (2010).

Most state statutes include pensions and retirement investments acquired or earned during the marriage as martial property and equity in property built up during the marriage.

Presumptions. State statutes in most equitable distribution jurisdictions presume that all property acquired legally or equitably during a marriage by either party is marital property. For example, Minnesota law states that "all property acquired by either spouse subsequent to the marriage and before a decree of legal separation is presumed to be marital property. . . ." Minn. Stat. §518.54, subd. 5 (1984).

Overcoming the presumption. The presumption that all property acquired during the marriage is marital property is not unassailable. It can be overcome by producing sufficient evidence showing that an item is nonmarital property.

Presumption of equal division. States have also created presumptions regarding an award of marital property when a couple divorce. For example, in Wisconsin a trial court is to presume that all marital property should be divided equally, although the court may deviate from an equal division if it is necessary to render equitable and fair results. *Gibbs v. Gibbs*, 862 N.W.2d 902 (Table) (Wis. App. 2015). In West Virginia a court presumes that all marital property is to be divided equally between the parties, but may alter this distribution after considering several factors listed in the statute such as homemaker and child care services. *Mark V.H. v. Dolores J.M.*, 752 S.E.2d 409 (W. Va. 2013). In New Hampshire a presumption exists that an equitable division is an equal division. *See, e.g.*, N.H. Rev. Stat. §458:16-a (2015) (court shall presume that an equal division is an equitable distribution of property, unless the court establishes a trust fund or unless the court decides that an equal division would not be appropriate or equitable after considering several factors).

Defining nonmarital property. Nonmarital property is generally defined by statute as including real or personal property, acquired by either spouse before, during, or after the existence of their marriage, which (a) is acquired as a gift, bequest, devise, or inheritance made by a third party to one but not to the other spouse; (b) is acquired before the marriage; (c) is acquired in exchange for or is the increase in value of property; (d) is acquired by a spouse after the valuation date; or (e) is excluded by a valid antenuptial contract. For example, in *Dubord v. Dubord*, 579 A.2d 257 (Me. 1990), the court found that funds from the wife's investments used to purchase the marital residence were nonmarital property. This finding overcame the statutory presumption that all property acquired subsequent to marriage was marital property.

Active versus passive appreciation. When discussing property values in equitable distribution jurisdictions, many courts and commentators refer to the increase in value attributable to the efforts of the spouses as "active appreciation." However, if the increase in property value is attributable to inflation and general economics and market conditions, they refer to the increase as "passive appreciation." It has been suggested that while this definition appears relatively clear, that "sophisticated attempts to distinguish active appreciation from passive appreciation of an asset may call for expert testimony and byzantine formulas beyond the reach of all but the well-heeled client." Bea Ann Smith, *The Partnership Theory of Marriage: A Borrowed Solution Fails*, 68 Tex. L. Rev. 689, 736-737 (March 1990).

REFLECTIVE QUESTIONS	What type of evidence would you seek to produce at a hearing to persuade a court that certain property is nonmarital property rather than marital property?

12.5 COMMUNITY PROPERTY JURISDICTIONS: MARITAL AND NONMARITAL CONCEPTS

Marital property defined. Community property jurisdictions provide broad definitions of *marital* similar to those definitions found in most equitable distribution jurisdictions. For example, California defines marital property as "all property, real or personal, wherever situated, acquired by a married person during the marriage while domiciled in this state is community property." Cal. Fam. Code §760 (2015). It is noted that sometimes courts within the same states, whether considered an equitable distribution jurisdiction or a community property state, appear to arrive at inconsistent characterizations. Mary Moers Wenig, *Increase in Value of Separate Property During Marriage: Examination and Proposals*, 23 Fam. L.Q. 301, 318 (1989) ("examination of the cases reveals inconsistency not explainable by the statutes; inconsistency from state to state, within a state from case to case, and from asset to asset within a case").

Nonmarital property. Separate nonmarital property in community property jurisdictions usually includes the following: (1) property owned by either spouse before marriage; (2) property acquired by a spouse after the marriage by gift or inheritance; and (3) property acquired after the marriage in exchange for separate property.

Factors determining whether property is nonmarital. In community property jurisdictions, factors that may determine whether property is nonmarital or community are the time of the property's acquisition, operation of various presumptions, particularly those concerning the form of title, and whether spouses have transmuted or converted the property from separate to community or vice versa. *See In re Marriage of Haines*, 39 Cal. Rptr. 2d 673 (Cal. App. 1995).

California, a community property jurisdiction, considers jointly acquired marital assets as divisible in a divorce but does not consider nonmarital property as a part of the community. For example, in *Heilman v. Heilman*, 266 P.2d 148 (Cal. App. 1954), furniture purchased during the marriage by the wife from separate funds was not considered community property. In *Mears v. Mears*, 4 Cal. Rptr. 618 (Cal. App. 1960), part of the purchase price of stock came from the proceeds of sale of furniture, which the wife inherited from her father and part from community funds. The court allocated to the separate and community property the respective percentage of the contributions to the purchase price.

Retirement benefits. All of the community property states apportion retirement benefits. Most use time-based apportionment; one state, Louisiana, uses a contribution-based apportionment.

REFLECTIVE QUESTIONS	**List some types of property that will probably be considered nonmarital by a court in a community property jurisdiction.**

12.6 PROPERTY DIVISION: UMDA INFLUENCE

The Uniform Marriage and Divorce Act (UMDA) has influenced many states in drafting property distribution statutes to be used upon divorce. The original version of section 307 of the UMDA and the current version set out alternative approaches for identifying the property and the basis for their division. Section a is set out below.

Section 307, *Alternative A* (for jurisdictions that are not community property states) declares as follows:

> (a) In a proceeding for dissolution of a marriage . . . the court, without regard to marital misconduct, shall . . . equitably apportion between the parties the property and assets belonging to either or both however and whenever acquired, and whether the title thereto is in the name of the husband or wife or both. In making apportionment the court shall consider the duration of the marriage, any prior marriage of either party, any antenuptial agreement of the parties, the age, health, station, occupation, amounts and sources of income, vocational skills, employability, estate, liabilities, and needs of each of the parties, custodial provisions, whether the apportionment is in lieu of or in addition to maintenance, and the opportunity of each for future acquisition of capital assets and income. The court shall also consider the contribution or dissipation of each party in the acquisition, preservation, depreciation, or appreciation in value of the respective estates, and the contribution of a spouse as a homemaker or to the family unit.

Alternative B (for community property states), states as follows:

> In a proceeding for dissolution of the marriage . . . the court shall assign each spouse's separate property to that spouse. It also shall divide community property, without regard to marital misconduct, in just proportions after considering all relevant factors including:
>
> 1. Contribution of each spouse to acquisition of the marital property, including contribution of a spouse as homemaker;
> 2. Value of the property set apart to each spouse;
> 3. Duration of the marriage; and
> 4. Economic circumstances of each spouse when the division of property is to become effective, including the desirability of awarding the family home or

the right to live therein for a reasonable period to the spouse having custody of any children.

Equitable versus equal distribution. "Equitably," as used by the UMDA, does not necessarily mean "equal." *Mercatell v. Mercatell*, 854 A.2d 609 (Pa. Super. 2004); *Zelnik v. Zelnik*, 573 N.Y.S.2d 261, 272 (N.Y.A.D. 1991).

REFLECTIVE QUESTIONS	What is the distinction between the use of the words "equal" and "equitable" in a jurisdiction that adopted the UMDA?

12.7 PROPERTY DIVISION: ALI APPROACH

The American Law Institute (ALI) *Principles of the Law of Family Dissolution*, published in 2002, divides property into marital and nonmarital shares. The ALI *Principles* allows only marital property to be distributed upon divorce.

The ALI *Principles* recharacterizes separate property as marital property if the parties are involved in a long-term marriage. A court can void the recharacterization by making written findings that preservation of the separate character of the property is necessary to avoid substantial injustice. ALI *Principles* §4.18.

ALI Presumption. The ALI *Principles* establishes a presumption that favors dividing marital property equally. The presumption can be rebutted by a showing that a spouse in a divorce proceeding is entitled to compensation for reasons that would justify an award of spousal support. ALI *Principles* §4.09 (2002).

REFLECTIVE QUESTIONS	Do you agree with the ALI view that a court may recharacterize separate nonmarital property as marital property if the parties are involved in a long-term marriage?

12.8 VALUING PROPERTY: GENERALLY

When valuing and distributing property in a contested dissolution, a family court judge has three tasks: First, the judge must create and complete a list of all the assets involved in the action so that it can be determined which are subject to distribution as marital property and which are nonmarital. Second, once the list is prepared, the next step is to place a reasonable value on the assets. Finally, the court determines on an equitable basis how the assets should be distributed.

At what point should property be valued? For purposes of dividing and valuing marital property, a family court judge must consider at what point in the relationship the marriage has ended and the property of each spouse thereafter is "separate property." The possibilities include the following and are decided on a state-by-state basis:

1. The date the complaint or petition to dissolve the relationship was filed. *See, e.g., Painter v. Painter*, 320 A.2d 484, 495 (N.J. 1974); *Genovese v. Genovese*, 920 A.2d 660 (N.J. Super. 2007).
2. The date the divorce decree is entered. *Fuentes v. Fuentes*, 247 F. Supp. 2d 714 (D.V.I. 2003).
3. The date the parties separated. *Deitz v. Deitz*, 436 S.E.2d 463 (Va. App. 1993); *In re Estate of Osicka*, 461 P.2d 585 (Wash. App. 1969).
4. The date of trial. *Reynolds v. Reynolds*, 109 S.W.3d 258 (Mo. App. 2003).
5. The date a stipulation regarding value was made.

Once the divorce decree is entered, courts will not value the property. *See Bain v. Bain*, 553 So. 2d 1389 (Fla. App. 1990). The reason is that a subsequent change in the property's value following the decree could be due to one of the party's nonmarital labor or efforts.

Given the various options listed above, which date do you believe is the most appropriate to select as the date for valuing marital property?

12.9 FAULT

There is not a national consensus on the use of fault when considering distribution of property. Several jurisdictions hold that fault is not a relevant issue when awarding property. *See, e.g., Howard S. v. Lillian S.*, 876 N.Y.S.2d 351 (N.Y. 2009); *Chalmers v. Chalmers*, 320 A.2d 478, 482-483 (N.J. 1974); *Eaton v. Eaton*, 447 A.2d 829 (Me. 1982); *Jones v. Jones*, 334 N.W.2d 492 (S.D. 1983).

Some jurisdictions consider fault is relevant when awarding property. For example, in *Beede v. Beede*, 440 A.2d 283 (Conn. 1981), the court considered all the evidence presented by each party, including the causes for its breakdown. In this case the court focused on the husband's adultery as cause of dissolution when dividing the marital property. *See Peters v. Peters*, 283 S.E.2d 454 (Ga. 1981) (conduct of the parties during the marriage and with reference to the cause of the divorce is relevant and admissible on the issue of equitable property division); *Bohl v. Bohl*, 657 P.2d 1106 (Kan. 1983) (district court has the duty to divide marital property in a just and reasonable manner considering *inter alia* the question of fault, when determined).

UMDA. The UMDA §307 excludes "marital misconduct" as a factor when distributing marital property.

Should fault ever be considered by a court when dividing marital property?

12.10 ECONOMIC MISCONDUCT

Economic misconduct has been defined as "involving marital assets, such as intentional waste or a selfish financial impropriety, coupled with a purpose unrelated to the marriage." *Gershman v. Gershman*, 943 A.2d 1091, 1097 (Conn. 2007). It is a factor courts will consider when dividing marital property in most jurisdictions. For example, in *Quinn v. Quinn*, 641 A.2d 180 (Me. 1994), the court held that a husband's unilateral transfer of property purchased with marital funds to the parties' adult children for nominal consideration was economic misconduct, and should have been taken into account by the trial court when arriving at an alimony award. *In Deidun v. Deidun*, 606 S.E.2d 489 (S.C. App. 2004), economic misconduct was found where the wife ran up credit card and other debts without informing her husband. In *Walstad v. Walstad*, 837 N.W.2d 911 (N.D. 2013), the court held that the secreting of assets was a clear and blatant form of economic misconduct. An award of 70 percent of marital property to a 52-year-old wife and award of 30 percent to 62-year-old husband was said to be warranted on the ground that husband had engaged in economic misconduct in light of his tangled financial records, gambling activities, and attempted secretion of monies and his evasiveness. *Conceicao v. Conceicao*, 611 N.Y.S.2d 318 (N.Y. App. 1994).

Whether a party's misconduct is so serious that it impacts the distribution of property is determined on a case-by-case basis. For example, in *K. v. B.*, 784 N.Y.S.2d 76 (N.Y. App. 2004), when the husband liquidated marital assets, including the children's investment funds, for his own purposes, this was considered economic fault. However, when the wife liquidated some mutual funds to repay investors in her law firm, this was not considered economic fault.

Create an example that would convince a court that a party's misconduct was so serious that the other party should receive far more marital property because of the misconduct.

12.11 MINGLED ASSETS: APPRECIATION OF NONMARITAL PROPERTY GENERALLY

Appreciation in community property states. How should a court treat the increase of separate value of an asset during a marriage that is due to market forces?

How should it treat the increase of separate value of an asset that is due to the financial or in-kind contributions of both the husband and wife? As a general rule, community property and equitable distribution property jurisdictions approach the answers to these questions somewhat differently. The difference apparently rests on the purpose of the classification.

Inception of title rule. Community property states generally follow the "inception of title" rule. *See Barnett v. Barnett*, 67 S.W.3d 107, 111 (Tex. 2001). Under this rule, the character of an asset is determined when it is acquired. It is thought that the inception of title rule, although arbitrary, is more conducive to uniformity and a degree of certainty when a court is faced with dividing property in a divorce action. *McCurdy v. McCurdy*, 372 S.W.2d 381 (Tex. App. 1963).

Passive forces. In a community property jurisdiction, if the increase in value is attributable to market forces, the increase takes the same character as the original capital investment in the asset. Separate property that increases in value during the marriage because of market forces continues to be considered separate property, and the community has no claim to it. However, if the increase in value of separate property is attributable to the investment of community funds or the labor of one of the spouses, the community is entitled to reimbursement for the value of the contribution.

California applies two different approaches when considering the increased value of separate property where the increase is due to passive forces (which creates more separate property) and partly due to community funds or efforts (for which the community is entitled to reimbursement). Two cases, *Pereira v. Pereira*, 103 P. 488 (Cal. 1909), and *Van Camp v. Van Camp*, 199 P. 885 (Cal. App. 1921), set out California's dual approach. The California Supreme Court has described the difference between the *Pereira* and *Van Camp* formulas in *Beam v. Bank of America*, 98 Cal. Rptr. 137, 141 (Cal. 1971), as follows:

> Over the years our courts have evolved two quite distinct, alternative approaches to allocating earnings between separate and community income in such cases. One method of apportionment first applied in *Pereira v. Pereira* . . . and commonly referred to as the *Pereira* approach, "is to allocate a fair return on the [husband's separate property] investment [as separate income] and to allocate any excess to the community property as arising from the husband's efforts." . . . The alternative apportionment approach, which traces its derivation to *Van Camp v. Van Camp* is "to determine the reasonable value of the husband's services . . . , allocate that amount as community property, and treat the balance as separate property attributable to the normal earnings of the [separate estate]." . . .

The California Supreme Court also explained that there is no fixed formula for determining the community property interest in a spouse's separate property business, and that the trial court should choose the approach that results in substantial justice.

In *Pereira*, the trial judge allocated all the "gains" from a business after marriage to the community, but the California Supreme Court reversed. It reasoned that the "capital" of the business was "undoubtedly" the owner spouse's separate estate and, further, "some of the profits were justly due to the capital invested." *Id.* at 488. Therefore, under *Pereira*, a court allocates a fair return on the spouse's separate property investment and considers it as separate income. Any excess is allocated to the community property as arising from the spouse's efforts.

Under the *Van Camp* formula, a fair salary for a spouse's labor is calculated. If the spouse was paid less than the amount calculated, the community receives enough of the increase to make up the difference, and the rest of the increase in value is separate property. Although a court has discretion to choose whatever formula will effect substantial justice, the *Van Camp* formula is usually applied when the appreciation in value is primarily attributable to community efforts; the *Pereira* formula is usually used when the primary cause is due to market factors.

Appreciation in equitable distribution jurisdictions. Most equitable distribution states follow the principle that an increase in the value of nonmarital property attributable to the efforts of one or both spouses during their marriage, like the increase resulting from the application of marital funds, is marital property. It is a result of the active participation of the spouse in the increase in value of the property. Conversely, an increase in the value of nonmarital property attributable to inflation or to market forces or conditions retains its nonmarital character. *Antone v. Antone*, 645 N.W.2d 96 (Minn. 2002). This is usually considered passive appreciation.

Transmutation concept. The transmutation concept is sometimes used by courts in both equitable and community property jurisdictions when deciding whether property is marital or nonmarital. *See* William A. Reppy, Jr., *Debt Collection from Married Californians: Problems Caused by Transmutations, Single-Spouse Management, and Invalid Marriage*, 18 San Diego L. Rev. 143 (1981). "Transmutation" is defined as follows: "A change in the nature of something: esp., in family law, the transformation of separate property into marital property, or of marital property into separate property." Black's Law Dictionary 1638 (9th ed. 2009). Transmutation has been described as a broad term used to describe arrangements between spouses that change the character of property from separate to community and vice versa. *Ustick v. Ustick*, 657 P.2d 1083, 1091 (Idaho App. 1983).

Transmutation occurs when separate property is treated in such a way as to give evidence of an intention that it become marital property. *Batson v. Batson*, 769 S.W.2d 849, 858 (Tenn. App. 1988). Transmutation may be effected by an agreement between the parties or by the affirmative act or acts of the parties. An example of transmutation is for a spouse to purchase property with separate funds but to take title in joint tenancy. Another example is simply placing separate property in the names of both spouses.

When determining whether transmutation has taken place, a trial judge may consider the following: (1) the expressed intent of the parties insofar as it can be reliably ascertained; (2) the source of the funds, if any, used to acquire the property;

(3) the circumstances surrounding the acquisition of the property; (4) the dates of the marriage, the acquisition of the property, the claimed transmutation, and the breakup of the marriage; (5) the inducement for and/or purpose of the transaction which gave rise to the claimed transmutation; and (6) the value of the property and its significance to the parties.

ALI view. The American Law Institute's *Family Dissolution Principles* provides that the increase in value of separate property is marital if it is attributable to a spouse's labor. However, it remains separate if the increase in value is due to other causes. In mixed cases, the *Principles* recommends an approach similar to that used in *Pereira*. ALI, *Principles of the Law of Family Dissolution* §§4.04, 4.05 (2002).

The American Law Institute's *Principles of the Law of Family Dissolution* provides that separate property is gradually converted to marital property as it is held over the course of the marriage. ALI *Principles* §4.12. The rationale for this principle is that as the parties' lives grow together over the years, they will increasingly expect and intend to share their economic fortunes fully. *See* Carolyn J. Frantz & Hanoch Dagan, *Properties of Marriage*, 104 Colum. L. Rev. 75, 113-114 (2004). Frantz and Dugan explain that "over time, spouses feel less need and less desire to guard against the possibility of divorce and remarriage." *Id.* at 114.

Frantz and Dagan go beyond existing statutes and the ALI *Principles* and argue that separate property should be transmuted into marital property regardless of intent when the property is used during marriage. Their view is that marriage should be understood as an "egalitarian liberal community" and that property division rules should be based on this understanding. *See also* Shari Motro, *Luck, and Love: Reconsidering the Sanctity of Separate Property*, 102 Nw. U. L. Rev. 1623 (2008) (providing a formula for automatically converting separate property into shareable marital or community property as the marriage lengthens).

REFLECTIVE QUESTIONS	How is the "inception of title" rule used? Define the transmutation concept discussed above. When under the ALI *Principles* is separate property converted to marital property?

12.12 MINGLED ASSETS: SOURCE OF FUNDS RULE

In equitable distribution jurisdictions the characterization of property as nonmarital or marital depends upon the source of each contribution. Unfortunately, the "source of funds" rule is not uniformly applied among the equitable distribution states. *See, e.g.*, Brett R. Turner, 3 Equit. Distrib. of Property, 3d Appendix A (2010) ("Arkansas cases have essentially ignored the source of funds rule").

The "source of funds" rule provides that when an asset increases in value caused by market or other passive forces during a marriage, its value is allocated between the parties proportionately according to the contributions of separate and marital funds. Using this approach, a party retains as separate property the amount the party contributed towards acquisition of an asset plus the increase on that investment due to passive appreciation. *See Knowles v. Knowles*, 588 A.2d 315 (Me. 1991).

For example, in *Horsley v. Horsley*, 490 S.E.2d 392 (Ga. 1997), the court applied the "source of funds" rule to the equitable division of a home that was brought into a marriage. The Georgia Supreme Court stated that equity required a determination of the contribution of the spouse who brought the home to the marriage, and then a weighing of that contribution against the total nonmarital and marital investment in the property. It explained:

> [A] spouse contributing nonmarital property is entitled to an interest in the property in the ratio of the nonmarital investment to the total nonmarital and marital investment in the property. The remaining property is characterized as marital property and its value is subject to equitable distribution. Thus, the spouse who contributed nonmarital funds, and the marital unit that contributed marital funds each receive a proportionate and fair return on their investment.

Id. at 393.

Source of funds: Joint title. As a general rule, the "source of funds" rule is ordinarily not available to characterize as nonmarital property any property that was transferred to joint title during the marriage. It is felt that tracing the parties' contributions to classify the property as marital or nonmarital ignores the effect of the joint titling of property and is incompatible with the partnership concept of marriage. *Whiting v. Whiting*, 396 S.E.2d 413 (W. Va. 1990).

Entireties theory. In some jurisdictions, donative intent is presumed when a spouse uses separate funds to furnish consideration for property titled as an entireties estate. *McLean v. McLean*, 374 S.E.2d 376, 381-382 (N.C. 1988). The transfer is viewed as evidence of specific intent on the part of the donor. The presumption that the property is jointly owned in these jurisdictions can be rebutted only by clear, cogent, and convincing evidence. *Ibid.* Rebuttal of the presumption would then result in application of traditional source of funds analysis.

REFLECTIVE QUESTIONS | Define the "source of funds" rule discussed above. Is it available where property is jointly titled?

12.13 MINGLED ASSETS: COMMINGLING SEPARATE PROPERTY

Equitable distribution jurisdictions. During a marriage, nonmarital property may become commingled with marital property. For example, in *Alston v. Alston*, 555 So. 2d 1128 (Ala. App. 1989), the court held that a spouse's inheritance, when commingled with marital assets, became marital property. In making its decision, the court noted that the determination of whether separate, nonmarital assets, over which it exercises exclusive control, is a matter for the trier of fact. *See Popowich v. Korman*, 900 N.Y.S.2d 297 (N.Y. 2010) (because of the commingling in the brokerage account of plaintiff's separate property with other property acquired during the marriage, the entire account should be deemed marital property).

Tracing. In order for property to maintain its nonmarital character, it must be kept separate from marital property or, if commingled, it must be readily traceable. *Wopata v. Wopata*, 498 N.W.2d 478 (Minn. App. 1993).

Tracing in community property jurisdictions. As a general rule, commingling of nonmarital and community property does not necessarily convert the separate property to community property. *Batra v. Batra*, 17 P.3d 889 (Idaho 2001). So long as the separate property is identifiable through direct tracing or accounting, commingling of such separate property with community property does not convert the separate property into community property. In *Josephson v. Josephson*, 772 P.2d 1236, 1239 (Idaho App. 1989), *overruled on other grounds*, *Bell v. Bell*, 835 P.2d 1331 (Idaho App. 1992), the court explained the commingling doctrine:

> Where the parties have commingled their separate and community funds in a bank account, and treat them as one fund, it all becomes community property. The commingling doctrine is a special application of the general presumption that all property acquired during the marriage is community property. The party who asserts that the property is separate has the burden of persuasion, and must prove the property is separate with reasonable certainty and particularity. This may be accomplished through evidence of tracing or accounting.

The California Court of Appeals in *In re Marriage of Braud*, 53 Cal. Rptr. 2d 179, 194 (Cal. App. 1996), found that the husband was entitled to reimbursement for any contributions to improvements of the family home to the extent he could trace the contributions to a separate property source. It observed that "the tracing runs through a commingled checking account into which [the husband] undisputedly deposited $10,000 of his inheritance, but into which the parties also regularly deposited his community property paychecks throughout the period of remodeling. Of course, the mere commingling of separate property and community property funds does not alter the status of the respective property interests, provided that the components of the commingled mass can be adequately traced to their separate property and community property sources."

REFLECTIVE QUESTIONS	What is the relationship between commingling and tracing? Create an example where because of tracing a court will most likely find that there existed separate nonmarital property in a commingled bank account.

12.14 MINGLED ASSETS: APPRECIATION OF HOMESTEAD

Background to *Woosnam v. Woosnam*

Woosnam v. Woosnam, 587 S.W.2d 262 (Ky. Ct. App. 1979), is included here for discussion because it is one of the earliest decisions in the nation to consider the apportionment of marital and nonmarital property where the increase in value of a residence is due to inflationary forces. In *Woosnam*, the court sitting in an equitable distribution jurisdiction considers the amount of nonmarital property to be awarded to the spouse who purchased a home before the marriage, which was then sold during the marriage. A second home was purchased using funds from the sale of the first home.

WOOSNAM
v.
WOOSNAM

Court of Appeals of Kentucky
587 S.W.2d 262 (Ky. App. 1979)

GUDGEL, J. This is an appeal from a portion of a judgment entered in a divorce action. Appellant Patricia Woosnam claims the chancellor erred in his determination of the amount of nonmarital property to be restored to her. . . .

Patricia and Kenneth Ray Woosnam, appellee, were married April 17, 1970. At the date of their marriage Patricia owned a house and lot at 3414 Surrey Drive, Owensboro, against which there was an existing mortgage indebtedness of $9,466.23. It had been purchased for $12,500.00. Kenneth moved into the house after their marriage and the parties resided there together.

Six years later, the Surrey Drive house was sold for $19,175.00, and the entire net proceeds from the sale, after payment of the balance of Patricia's remaining mortgage indebtedness and expenses, were reinvested in another house at 2118 Carriage Drive. This property was purchased for $23,000.00. The parties resided together in this house until their separation on January 25, 1978. The chancellor found the Surrey Drive property had a fair market value of $13,300.00 on the date the parties married and the Carriage Drive property a fair market value of $37,500.00 shortly after their separation.

The chancellor determined that Patricia had a nonmarital interest in the Surrey Drive property of $3,833.77 on the date of marriage. This sum equals the net equity in the property on that date based on its value of $13,300.00 and a mortgage indebtedness of $9,466.23. He then determined that this sum equaled 28.8% of the property's value at the date of marriage and awarded her as nonmarital property that percentage of its sales price of $19,175.00 or $5,587.20. The Carriage Drive house was ordered sold with the net proceeds to be applied first in satisfaction of

Patricia's claim for nonmarital property with the balance of the remaining equity to be divided equally as marital property. There was conflicting evidence regarding sums expended for permanent improvements made to both houses, but the chancellor made no findings as to the amount of these improvements and did not consider them in making his award.

Patricia's sole contention on this appeal is that the chancellor erred in determining the amount of nonmarital property to be restored in her pursuant to KRS 403.190. She relies upon this Court's decision in *Robinson v. Robinson*, Ky. App., 569 S.W.2d 178 (1978). In that case we held that if either spouse owns property subject to indebtedness prior to the marriage, the net equity in that property shall be considered nonmarital property at the time of separation in the proportion which the net equity at the date of marriage bears to the value of the property at the date of marriage. In making his award of nonmarital property, the chancellor determined in accordance with *Robinson* that Patricia was entitled to have restored to her 28.8 percent of the value of the Surrey Drive house as of the date of its sale. However, he further ruled that all of the increased value of the Carriage Drive house at the date the parties separated was the result of "joint efforts" or "team efforts" and was thus marital property. We believe that the latter finding is clearly erroneous and reverse.

KRS 403.190(2)(b) specifically exempts as marital property any property acquired in exchange for property acquired before the marriage. Subsection (2)(e) of KRS 403.190 exempts as nonmarital property, property acquired before the marriage to the extent that the increase in value of the property did not result from the efforts of the parties during the marriage. These statutes mandate restoration to the spouse having a nonmarital interest in property owned at the date of marriage, the appreciated value of that same interest in any property acquired in exchange during the marriage, not attributable to the joint efforts of the parties. The only requirement is that the spouse prove that the nonmarital funds have been reinvested in the property acquired in exchange.

In the case before us the evidence established beyond all doubt that Patricia's nonmarital funds from the Surrey Drive property were reinvested in the Carriage Drive property.

The chancellor found, however, that the increase in the value of the Carriage Drive house between the date of its purchase and the date of the parties' separation ($14,500.00) was attributable to the "joint efforts" or "team efforts" of the parties. We can find no evidence in the record to support this finding. Kenneth argues that his expertise in the real estate market permitted the parties to purchase the Carriage Drive house at less than its market value, but introduced no evidence to establish a value at the date the parties acquired it higher than its purchase price. There was evidence the parties' expended sums for permanent improvements, ordinarily attributable to joint efforts, but the chancellor made no findings as to the amount of these improvements. Accordingly, since we find no evidence to support the chancellor's finding that the appreciated value of the Carriage Drive house was attributable to the "joint efforts" or "team efforts" of the parties, the judgment must be reversed.

Upon remand, the chancellor should first determine, using the formula in *Robinson*, the value of Patricia's nonmarital interest in the Surrey Drive property at the date it was sold. Then, a new ratio should be determined with the value of

Patricia's nonmarital interest in the Surrey Drive property being the numerator and the value or purchase price of the Carriage Drive property being its denominator. The new ratio should then be applied to the value of the Carriage Drive property at the date of separation to determine the value of Patricia's nonmarital interest to be restored to her.

The method described above permits the spouse having a nonmarital interest in property at the date of marriage to realize additional appreciation in the value of that interest after reinvestment, in proportion to its value at the date of separation. To hold, as the chancellor did in this case, that the entire increase in value at separation is attributable to joint efforts of the parties, assumes none of the increased value can be attributed to inflationary factors, when in all probability most of the increased value is directly attributable to inflation. The whole rationale for the rule in *Robinson* is to award the spouse having a nonmarital interest in property his or her proportionate share of any increase in the value of that interest during the marriage. . . .

This case is further complicated by the fact that there was evidence as to sums expended for permanent improvements made to both properties during the marriage. As noted previously, the chancellor made no findings as to the amount of these improvements, even though the sums expended for this purpose are properly attributable to the parties' joint efforts and will constitute marital property. Accordingly, upon remand, the chancellor should make specific findings as to the value of these improvements.

A question then arises as to the method by which these improvements shall be taken into account in applying the ratios set out above in determining Patricia's nonmarital interest in the Carriage Drive property. We believe the answer is obvious.

Since the portion of the sales price of the Surrey Drive property attributable to sums expended for permanent improvements constitutes marital property, their value should be deducted from the sales price prior to applying the proper ratio specified above. Likewise, the value of improvements made to the Carriage Drive house should be deducted from its value at the date of separation prior to applying the proper ratio. The judgment appealed from is reversed and remanded for further proceedings consistent with this opinion.

DISCUSSION QUESTIONS FOR *WOOSNAM v. WOOSNAM*

A. Using *Woosnam v. Woosnam*, the Minnesota Supreme Court adopted a formula for determining what share of the increased value is attributable to the investment of nonmarital property in a marital asset. *Schmitz v. Schmitz*, 309 N.W.2d 748 (Minn. 19891). The Minnesota formula reads as follows: "The present value of a nonmarital asset used in the acquisition of marital property is the proportion the net equity or contribution at the time of acquisition bore to the value of the property at the time of purchase multiplied by the value of the property at the time of separation. The remainder of equity increase is characterized as marital property and is distributed according to Minn. Stat. §518.58." *Brown v. Brown*, 316 N.W.2d 552, 553 (Minn. 1982); *see Faus v. Faus*, 319 N.W.2d 408, 412 (Minn. 1982). Apply this formula to the following: P purchased a home for $10,000 prior to marriage paying $3,000 down. P took out a $7,000 mortgage. On the day of her marriage to D, the mortgage on the house was down to $5,000. When P and D divorced, the home was valued at $20,000 and the mortgage was paid off. How will a court apportion the value of the home?

B. Assume for this hypothetical that the wife contributed $5,000 of separate property to buy a house one week before marriage. The house had a value of $20,000 at that time and the wife took out a $15,000 mortgage. At the date of divorce, the mortgage has been reduced — by marital funds — by $5,000 and the house had increased in value to $30,000. Under the formula used by Kentucky in *Woosnam*, the separate property share of the home at the date of divorce is determined by the percentage of ownership the separate property contribution represented to the value of the asset at the date of acquisition. Do the calculations showing the net nonmarital value of the home at the time of divorce.

C. Assume for this hypothetical that in an equitable distribution jurisdiction, H purchased a home for $100,000 just prior to marriage. H paid $50,000 down and obtained a $50,000 mortgage for the remainder. On the day H and W married, the home is valued at $100,000 and there is a $50,000 mortgage to be paid off. Five years after the marriage, H and W divorce and the home purchased by H has a market value of $200,000. Using the theory developed in *Woosnam*, how much of the home's value is H's nonmarital property?

D. Assume for this hypothetical that in an equitable distribution jurisdiction, W purchased a home for cash just prior to her marriage to H for $100,000 (no mortgage). H and W were married for ten years when they divorced. At the time of the divorce, the home was valued at $200,000. Using the theory developed in *Woosnam*, how much of the home's value is W's nonmarital property? How might a court in Maine treat this issue?

E. Assume for this hypothetical that in an equitable distribution jurisdiction, W purchased a home for $90,000 two years before W married H. W made a $10,000 down payment and took out an $80,000 mortgage. On the date W and H married, the home had a fair market value of $100,000 and the mortgage was now $70,000. Using the theory developed in *Woosnam*, what is W's nonmarital interest on the date of the marriage? Can you think of another theory to apply?

12.15 MINGLED ASSETS: HOMEMAKER'S CONTRIBUTIONS

How should homemaker services be valued when a marriage dissolves? Traditionally, a stay-at-home spouse was not seen as making a significant contribution to the estate by his or her homemaker services. Only where a spouse made "direct" contributions, such as actively managing the other spouse's separate property or making financial contributions toward the enhancement of such property, was the spouse entitled to share in the appreciation of that asset to the extent attributable to his or her efforts.

REFLECTIVE QUESTIONS	What may explain the reason a traditional stay-at-home spouse historically was not viewed as making a significant contribution to the marital estate?

Background to *Wood v. Wood*

In *Wood v. Wood*, the court is asked to determine whether a spouse's indirect contributions as a homemaker and parent may be considered by the court in awarding a percentage of the appreciation of the other spouse's separate property. The wife argued that the legislative intent inherent in New York's equitable distribution statute reflects the view that the institution of marriage is a joint enterprise whose success is dependent on a variety of factors, financial and otherwise. She contended that the function of equitable distribution is to ensure that when a marriage comes to an end, each of the spouses, based on his or her relative contributions, will be entitled to a share of the family assets accumulated while the marital relationship endured. To this end, the equitable distribution statute gives recognition to the essential supportive role played by the wife in the home.

The husband argued that in this four-year marriage any increase in the value of his medical practice was his separate property and not subject to equitable distribution. He claimed that his wife never worked at his medical office and did nothing to increase the value of his professional practice.

WOOD
v.
WOOD

Supreme Court of New York
465 N.Y.S.2d 475 (1983)

GEILER, J. This [case] raises the issue of whether a spouse's contributions as a parent and homemaker may be considered by the court in awarding said spouse a share in the appreciation in value of the other spouse's separate property which appreciation has occurred since the inception of the marriage to the date of the commencement of the divorce action.

Defendant in this four-year marriage is seeking an order directing that his medical practice is separate property and that any increase in the value of the claimed separate property subsequent to the date of his marriage to plaintiff herein is also separate property, and, as such, is not property subject to equitable distribution. Defendant claims that plaintiff never worked at defendant's medical office and has done nothing to increase the value of his professional practice.

1077 DRL §236(B)(5)(a) provides that:

> The court, in an action wherein all or part of the relief granted in divorce . . . shall determine the respective rights of the parties in their separate or marital property, and shall provide for the disposition thereof in the final judgment.

DRL §236(B)(1)(c) defines "marital property" as:

> All property acquired by either or both spouses during the marriage and before the execution of a separation agreement or the commencement of a matrimonial action, regardless of the form in which title is held. . . .

Among the items defined in the term "separate property" is the increase in value of separate property,

> except to the extent that such appreciation is due in part to the contributions or efforts of the other spouse (DRL §236(B)(1)(d)(3)).

DRL §236(B)(5) goes on to list ten factors that the court is mandated to consider in making an equitable distribution of the parties' marital property and one of such factors is the direct and indirect contributions made to the acquisition of marital property by the party not having title, including contributions and services as a spouse, parent, wage earner and homemaker, and to the career or career potential of the other party (DRL §236(B)(5)(d)(6)).

Accordingly, based on a liberal reading of the above sections of DRL §236(B), the court holds that appreciation in separate assets from the inception of the marriage to the date of the commencement of a divorce action constitutes marital property to the extent that such appreciation is due to the contributions or efforts of the non-titled spouse and the contributions to the accumulation of such appreciation may be direct or indirect.

The meaning of "indirect contribution," however, is yet subject to definition. There are situations where the non-titled spouse surely makes a contribution to the increase in value, as where he or she helps build up a business owned by the titled spouse, or manages the finances, trades securities or real estate or has made other significant direct contributions to enhance the value of the other's separate property. But will the fact that one of the parties was a homemaker, parent and companion qualify as an "indirect" contribution as opposed to the more normally thought of "indirect" contributions such as preparing social events for the business, appearing with the titled spouse at business related social functions, etc.?

A recent development in Canada, where this issue has seen much play is most illuminating. The Supreme Court of Canada in construing certain sections of the Ontario Family Law Reform Act held that a wife did not necessarily have to prove a "direct" contribution to the appreciation in a husband's separately owned business in order to receive a share in the value of the appreciation of said business which occurred from the time of the inception of the marriage. Regrettably, the Canadian Supreme Court then withdrew and excluded home and child care as an indirect contribution. Canadian commentators and this court feel that a more liberal approach is necessary for a truly "equitable" distribution on divorce.

The concept of equitable distribution borrows from the community property states the premise that when a couple marries, the parties enter into, *inter alia*, an economic partnership and the wife accordingly should be rewarded for her labors in the home.

The concept of equitable distribution is a corollary of the principle that marriage is a joint enterprise whose vitality, success and endurance [are] dependent upon the conjunction of multiple components, only one of which is financial. The nonremunerated efforts of raising children, making a home, performing a myriad of personal services and providing physical and emotional support are, among other noneconomic ingredients of the marital relationship, at least as essential to its nature and maintenance as are the economic factors, and their worth is consequently entitled to substantial recognition. Thus, the extent to which each of the parties contributes to the marriage is not measurable only by the amount of money contributed to it during the period of its endurance but, rather, by the whole complex of financial and nonfinancial components contributed. The function of equitable distribution is to recognize that when a marriage ends, each of the spouses, based on the totality of the contributions made to it, has a stake in and right to a share of the marital assets accumulated while it endured, not because that share is needed, but because those assets represent the capital product of what was essentially a partnership entity.

Accordingly, the court holds that summary judgment is denied. The issue of whether the defendant's medical practice is property subject to equitable distribution is referred to the trial court for determination. The issues of spousal contributions to the husband's separately titled business, their existence and their value shall be an element to be proved by plaintiff at the trial of this action.

 **FOR *WOOD v. WOOD***

A. List the direct and indirect contributions a homemaker spouse may make to a relationship. Which of these contributions should be considered when a court is dividing property when the relationship is dissolved? Can care, love, and companionship be considered an indirect contribution to a marriage and be valued when dividing property?

B. On remand, how will the court value the contributions of the homemaker in *Wood*? Should the plaintiff prepare a list of the jobs a homemaker carries out and value each of them? For example, should housecleaning be compared to maid service at a hotel or contract house cleaning? Should child care include teaching? Nursing care? Babysitting? Chauffeur? Alternatively, should the homemaker be analogized to a manager who has the responsibility of hiring persons to carry out all these tasks?

C. It has been generally agreed that a homemaker displaced through divorce often suffers an immediate and dramatic decline in economic status. Cynthia Starnes, *Divorce and the Displaced Homemaker: A Discourse on Playing with Dolls, Partnership Buyouts and Dissociation Under No-Fault*, 60 U. Chi. L. Rev. 67, 79 (Winter 1993). For example, it has been estimated that in the first year after divorce, women and children average a 73 percent decline in their standard of living, while men enjoy a 42 percent rise. *Id.* at n.48. The result has been that displacement plunges a homemaker into poverty. *Ibid.* Are Professor Starnes's observations, made in 1993, still valid? If not, why not? If so, does this suggest that an equal division of marital assets is seldom equitable?

D. *In Rubin v. Rubin*, 481 N.Y.S.2d 172 (N.Y. 1984), the court concluded that the plaintiff's wife was not entitled to share in the appreciation in value of her husband's separate property business interest in a closely held corporation because her spousal contributions during the marriage of seven years were limited to playing "bridge and tennis." *Wood v. Wood* was not mentioned. In *Borg v. Borg*, 491 N.Y.S.2d 659 (N.Y. 1985), the defendant wife's claim for a share in the appreciation that had occurred in the value of the plaintiff's separately owned printing business during the parties' six-month marriage was denied "[s]ince defendant failed to establish that the business appreciated in value due to her contribution." In *Billington v. Billington*, 489 N.Y.S.2d 89 (1985), the defendant wife's claim for the separate asset appreciation was also denied since she failed to allege that said assets appreciated in value as a result of her contributions or efforts. Do these cases suggest that in a jurisdiction like New York a finding of a causal connection between appreciation in a separate property asset and the nontitled spouse's indirect contributions as a homemaker and parent may depend on a variety of factors including the length of the marriage, the relationship between the parties, the type of services actually performed by the nontitled spouse, and the nature of the separate property? Are such considerations contrary to *Wood v. Wood*? Are they consistent with the partnership theory of marriage?

E. What if a spouse who anticipates a coming divorce begins to give away property to children, parents, or grandparents? Does the other spouse have a remedy during the marriage? At the time of divorce?

12.16 CHALLENGES: VALUING GOODWILL

This is an area in flux. Goodwill is an intangible asset of a marriage. Goodwill is associated with a spouse's business or professional practice (e.g., law, medicine, or other business). Goodwill represents the reputation of the business that signifies the probability of future earnings. Courts have defined goodwill as "nothing more than the probability that the old customers will resort to the old place." *In re Marriage of Brooks*, 742 S.W.2d 585, 586 (Mo. App. 1987).

Enterprise goodwill. The concepts of "enterprise goodwill" and "personal goodwill" are used by many courts in deciding whether to include goodwill as a marital asset when valuing and distributing marital property. In *May v. May*, 589 S.E.2d 526, 541 (W. Va. 2003), the court provided the following definition of enterprise goodwill:

> Enterprise goodwill attaches to a business entity and is associated separately from the reputation of the owners. Product names, business locations, and skilled labor forces are common examples of enterprise goodwill. The asset has a determinable value because the enterprise goodwill of an ongoing business will transfer upon sale of the business to a willing buyer. . . .

See generally Courtney E. Beebe, *The Object of My Appraisal: Idaho's Approach to Valuing Goodwill as Community Property in* Chandler v. Chandler, 39 Idaho L. Rev. 77, 83-84 (2002). In *Frazier v. Frazier*, 737 N.E.2d 1220, 1225 (Ind. App. 2000), the court said that "enterprise goodwill is based on the intangible, but generally marketable, existence in a business of established relations with employees, customers and suppliers, and may include a business location, its name recognition and its business reputation."

Personal goodwill. The court in *May v. May, supra*, defined "personal goodwill":

> [P]ersonal goodwill is associated with individuals. It is that part of increased earning capacity that results from the reputation, knowledge and skills of individual people. Accordingly, the goodwill of a service business, such as a professional practice, consists largely of personal goodwill.

See Diane Green Smith, *Till Success Do Us Part: How Illinois Promotes Inequities in Property Distribution Pursuant to Divorce by Excluding Professional Goodwill*, 26 J. Marshall L. Rev. 147, 164-165 (1992) (calculating personal goodwill).

A majority of states differentiate between "enterprise goodwill" and "personal goodwill." *Gilman v. Hohman*, 725 N.E.2d 425, 429 (Ind. App. 2000). Courts in these states take the position that personal goodwill is not marital property, but that enterprise goodwill is marital property. *See, e.g., Powell v. Powell*, 648 P.2d 218 (Kan. 1982); *Nail v. Nail*, 486 S.W.2d 761 (Tex. 1972); *Holbrook v. Holbrook*, 309 N.W.2d 343 (Wis. App. 1981).

Some courts do not attempt to distinguish between personal and enterprise goodwill. These jurisdictions have taken the position that both personal and enterprise goodwill in a professional practice constitute marital property. *See, e.g., Poore v. Poore*, 331 S.E.2d 266 (N.C. App. 1985). A minority of courts have taken the position that neither personal nor enterprise goodwill in a professional practice constitutes marital property. *See, e.g., Singley v. Singley*, 846 So. 2d 1004 (Miss. 2002) ("[w]e join the jurisdictions that adhere to the principle that goodwill should not be used in determining the fair market value of a business, subject to equitable division in divorce cases").

For those who argue that the consideration of goodwill in dividing marital assets is appropriate, a common denominator is equity. They contend that if professional goodwill exists and if it was developed during a marriage, it is considered marital property. They also contend that denying a spouse's interest in marital property would be both unfair and unjust. *See Prahinski v. Prahinski*, 540 A.2d 833 (Md. 1988); Alan S. Zipp, *Divorce Valuation of Business Interests: A Capitalization of Earnings Approach*, 23 Fam. L.Q. 89 (1989).

REFLECTIVE QUESTIONS	Create an example of "enterprise goodwill" and "personal goodwill."

12.17 CHALLENGES: CLOSELY HELD CORPORATIONS

Background to *Nardini v. Nardini*

In *Nardini v. Nardini*, the court is asked to value and divide a small family business upon the termination of a 31-year marriage. Marguerite Nardini, in addition to being a homemaker, had been a periodic bookkeeper for the family business for 29 years. Her husband, Ralph, argued that Marguerite made few direct contributions to the growth of the business and that her indirect contributions should receive little, if any, consideration when dividing the business.

The court discusses what portion of a closely held family business is marital and what is nonmarital. It explores various theories about valuing a small business and examines how they were applied in this case. It asks the following questions: (1) How should a court allocate the increase in value of nonmarital property attributable to the physical improvement of the property through application of marital funds and marital effort? (2) How should it value the increase in value of nonmarital property attributable to the increase in equity by application of marital funds to reduce mortgage indebtedness? (3) How should it treat an increase in the value of nonmarital property attributable to inflation and market forces?

NARDINI
v.
NARDINI

Supreme Court of Minnesota
414 N.W.2d 184 (1987)

COYNE, J. . . . Critical to the appropriate distribution of property owned at the time of the dissolution of the parties' marriage are the valuation of the primary business of the parties and its characterization as marital or nonmarital. The record discloses that both prior to and during the marriage, Ralph was engaged in the sale and maintenance of fire protection equipment. He claims that in 1949, prior to his marriage, he purchased a 50% interest in the whole of Chemical Sales & Service, a sole proprietorship, from Peter Dietsch for $2,500 and that he continued in the employ of the business for several years servicing equipment. Marguerite disputes the fact that Ralph's purchase was as extensive as he claimed, contending instead that he bought an interest only in that portion of the business which was engaged in servicing fire extinguishers. Despite this dispute, the record is devoid of any evidence offered by either party of the value of the business, its sales or assets at the time of either the claimed purchase or the marriage.

At the time of the marriage in 1953 Ralph was a uniformed service employee who worked for a salary. Periodically, Marguerite assisted in keeping the books of the business. In 1956, the Nardinis purchased Dietsch's remaining interest for $12,500 and incorporated the business. . . . While Ralph manages the business and continues to call on customers, the business now has 12 full-time employees and engages 3 independent contractors. At the time of dissolution of the marriage, Ralph held 60% of the shares of Nardini of Minnesota, and Marguerite held the other 40% of the shares.

. . . [The parties] were unable to agree on either the value of Nardini of Minnesota or its character as marital or nonmarital property. Moreover, while Ralph attributes the great financial success of the business to his "key man" effort alone, Marguerite asserts that she too contributed greatly by her years of periodic employment with the company, her extensive civic and social involvements, and her provision of a traditional marital home during the years of growth. We therefore scrutinize the record for evidence on these claims and disputes.

To determine the value of Nardini of Minnesota, Marguerite's expert, Steven Thorp, employed a comparison analysis, examining specific characteristics and financial information of similar companies. In comparing the Nardini business to publicly traded companies and taking into account factors unique to the Nardini operation, he valued Nardini of Minnesota at $725,213.

John Hawthorne, Ralph's expert witness, estimated value by both a comparison analysis and an examination of similarly structured small fire equipment dealers operating in the metropolitan area. He, too, noted and factored the unique Nardini characteristics, but he estimated the total value of Nardini of Minnesota at $350,000. He then assumed that one-half the value was excepted nonmarital property and reduced the remaining one-half value to reflect a lack of operational control in a one-half interest. He ultimately opined that a one-half interest had a value of $135,135. Separately, Hawthorne estimated liquidation value of the corporation at $391,456. While he acknowledged that this valuation exceeded the sale valuation, he reasoned that the risks and expenses attendant on liquidation must be considered in estimating the market value of the company as a going business.

The record clearly demonstrates Ralph's contributions to the growth of the business. Working within the company since 1949 and functioning as its president and salesperson, Ralph has developed the business contacts and personally claims responsibility for 50% to 60% of the sales based upon his personal relationships with customers and his hard work. Marguerite's contributions were less tangible, taking the form of sporadic bookkeeping services and substantial community involvement, including active volunteer work and service on the Little Canada City Council. Moreover, as indicated, she provided a stable home and family life which permitted Ralph to devote his efforts to business achievements.

The trial court found that Ralph owned a one-half interest in the common stock of Nardini of Minnesota as nonmarital property and assigned a market value of $135,135 to that one-half interest. The trial court found that the other one-half interest in the common stock of Nardini of Minnesota was marital property, which the court also valued at $135,135. . . .

A. VALUATION OF THE FAMILY BUSINESS

. . . When the parties cannot agree on a division of the marital property, just and equitable division of an asset included in the marital property of the parties can be accomplished in one of three ways: (1) If the asset is readily divisible, the court can divide the asset and order just and equitable distribution in kind; (2) the court can order the sale or liquidation of the asset and make a just and equitable division of the proceeds of sale or liquidation; or (3) the court can determine the value of the asset, order distribution of the entire asset to one of the parties, and order the recipient to pay to the other spouse a just and equitable share of the value of the asset.

Whatever the method, the goal is to place both parties in the optimum position. The choice of methods usually depends on the type of asset to be divided. While the first method may be an eminently suitable way to divide the shares of publicly owned corporations, it is an unlikely choice if the corporation is closely held. The second method has the advantage of certainty and may be necessary for equitable division when an indivisible asset constitutes the bulk of the marital property. Sale or liquidation of a family-owned business may be appropriate if, for example, the parties are at or near retirement age or the dissolution of the marriage may adversely affect the business. The third method, which is in essence a forced sale by one spouse to the other in which the court sets the selling price and the terms of payment, has the greatest potential for error and unfairness, particularly where the asset is the major marital asset. It is the third method of division which gives rise to this appeal.

. . . The book value of Nardini of Minnesota at December 31, 1984, was $565,598. The corporation held cash and cash equivalents totaling more than $100,000 and its net accounts receivable exceeded $300,000. Absent an unnoted change in accounting methods, inventory was carried at the lower of cost (first-in first-out method) or market. Current liabilities, including current installments of long term debt, were less than $80,000. The consultants' estimates of the market value of Nardini of Minnesota varied from $725,000 to $350,000. The one consultant also testified that the value of a one-half interest in the common stock of the corporation must be reduced from $175,000 to $135,135 to reflect a lack of control. While we are cognizant of the difficulty and the imprecision of valuing a closely held corporation, nevertheless it is apparent that a valuation which assumes that either Marguerite or Ralph would be willing participants in a sale of Nardini of Minnesota to a third party for a price of $270,270—a sum no greater than the corporation's cash and cash equivalent, Ralph's annual salary and benefits and one year's net corporate income—is unrealistic.

First, for purposes of valuing marital property, there is no justification for discounting an undivided interest in a corporation all of whose shares are owned by one or both spouses. Although shares may be transferred from one spouse to the other, whenever the court is called on to value a business, neither any corporate asset nor any fraction of the shares of the corporation will actually be sold to an outsider. Generally, as occurred here, the corporate shares are awarded to the spouse more actively engaged in the business of the corporation, and the management and operation of the business continue essentially unchanged. In this context the establishment of a fair market value contemplates nothing more than the assignment of a fair and reasonable value to the family business as a whole to allow equitable apportionment of the marital property.

Second, Ralph's appraiser testified that the amount which could be realized by liquidating the corporation significantly exceeded its market value as a going business. Nevertheless, the trial court adopted the lesser value, which it further discounted for lack of control. The value of a family business as marital property cannot be less than a sum equal to the net proceeds which could be realized from the forced sale of the tangible assets of the business and the collection or assignment of intangibles such as accounts receivable, and after payment of all liabilities. If the corporation is to continue in operation under the management of one of the owner-spouses even though the liquidation value of the business is greater than its value as a going business, assigning the corporation the lesser value as a going business patently disadvantages the spouse who must relinquish his or her interest in the corporation and unfairly benefits the spouse to whom the marital interest in the corporation is awarded. Moreover, inasmuch as Nardini of Minnesota is a thriving and vital corporation with cash and cash assets in excess of liabilities, the worst-case scenario suggested by "down and dirty" liquidation is not a suitable measure of market value. (Ralph's appraiser considered $407,859 a "realistic" liquidated value for Nardini of Minnesota. His "down and dirty" liquidation figure was $391,456.) While the relinquishment of his or her interest in the family business is in effect a forced sale, the court must determine the value of the business as if the transaction were a sale of the entire business by a willing seller to a willing buyer.

There is, of course, no universal formula for determining the value of a closely held business. No matter how experienced and objective the appraiser, the valuation of a business is an art, influenced by various subtle and subjective factors. While book value may be an appropriate starting point in valuing a business such as Nardini of Minnesota, with its high liquidity and modest investment in machinery and equipment, whatever the starting point, other factors, such as the following, must be taken into consideration before a reasonable valuation can be made:

1. The nature of the business and the history of the enterprise from its inception.
2. The economic outlook in general and the condition and outlook of the specific industry in particular.
3. The book value of the stock and financial condition of the business.
4. The earning capacity of the company.
5. The dividend-paying capacity.
6. Whether or not the enterprise has goodwill or other intangible value.
7. Sales of the stock and the size of the block of the stock to be valued.
8. The market price of stocks of corporations engaged in the same or similar line of business having their stocks traded in a free and open market.

In any case a sound valuation requires not only the consideration of all relevant facts but also the application of common sense, sound and informed judgment, and reasonableness to the process of "weighing those facts and determining their aggregate significance."

Viewed in the light of the foregoing principles, it is apparent that by failing to take into consideration the relevant facts and the fundamental factors appropriate for use and analysis in the value of a closely held corporation, the trial court abused its discretion. We remand for determination of the fair and reasonable value of Nardini of Minnesota in accordance with the principles enunciated in this opinion.

B. ALLOCATION OF MARITAL AND NONMARITAL INTERESTS

. . . Here the trial court determined that Ralph had acquired a one-half interest in the business now known as Nardini of Minnesota before he and Marguerite were married and declared that one-half of the present value of Nardini of Minnesota is nonmarital property. At first glance the result seems to comport with the statute, which provides in rather straightforward terms that property acquired before the marriage and the increase in value of such property is nonmarital property.

The simplicity of the statutory definition is, however, rather deceptive, for the language seems out of harmony with the modern definition of property as a bundle of divisible rights and offers little direction with respect to resolving the complex valuation questions frequently encountered in marriage dissolution cases. The statutory language does not distinguish between increases in value that occur prior to the marriage and increases that occur during the marriage. Neither does it make any distinction based on either the nature or the cause of the increase in value. That is, the statutory language does not distinguish between realized and unrealized gain and does not distinguish between increases due to the efforts of one or both of the spouses and increases from causes unrelated to the efforts of either of them.

In order to resolve the ambiguities which surface on any attempt to determine the value of property and its character as marital or nonmarital property, the terms "acquired before marriage" and "increase" in the definitions of nonmarital property have generally been interpreted in a manner consonant with the policy underlying the dissolution statutes. . . .

. . . At least one jurisdiction . . . has treated the increase in value of nonmarital shares of a closely held corporation as marital property. There the court distinguished between an increase in value attributable to the efforts of the parties and an increase in value attributable to inflation and general economic and market conditions. . . .

. . . [I]n *Schmitz v. Schmitz*, we held that a homestead comprised both marital and nonmarital interests. The husband had provided the down payment on the duplex in which the parties lived and paid the mortgage payments from the rental income from the other unit. The determination was based on the analysis in *Woosnam v. Woosnam*, recognizing the marital character of appreciation attributable to the joint or team efforts of the spouses with respect to property purchased in part with nonmarital funds. . . .

We hold that the increase in the value of nonmarital property attributable to the efforts of one or both spouses during their marriage, like the increase resulting from the application of marital funds, is marital property. Conversely, an increase in the value of nonmarital property attributable to inflation or to market forces or conditions, retains its nonmarital character. The principle may be illustrated by this hypothetical:

> Let us assume that on the date of their marriage John owned real estate then valued at $30,000 but subject to a $20,000 mortgage. Jane owned 300 shares of XYZ Co. On the date of marriage the market value of the publicly traded, unencumbered shares was $25 per share or $7,500.
>
> Expending marital funds for materials and hired labor but doing most of the work themselves, soon after their marriage John and Jane built an addition to the building on John's property, increasing its value by $10,000 — from $30,000 to $40,000. During the course of the marriage, the parties used marital funds to pay the mortgage balance down to $4,000. At the time of the dissolution the market value of the real estate was $100,000.

. . . [It] must be recognized that there are three kinds of "increase" involved in the example: (1) the increase in value attributable to the physical improvement of the property through application of marital funds and marital effort; (2) the increase in value attributable to the increase in equity by application of marital funds to reduce the mortgage indebtedness; and (3) the increase in value attributable to inflation and market forces. The hypothetical assumes an investment of cash and of property and services having a cash value in the total amount of $40,000. Whatever amount John may have invested in the property prior to the marriage, on the date of the marriage his nonmarital equity in the property was $10,000. During the marriage the parties contributed marital funds and labor in the construction of an addition which increased the value of the property by $10,000. In addition, the parties undertook payment of the $20,000 mortgage balance with marital funds, reducing the unpaid balance to $4,000. The present value of John's nonmarital interest is the proportion his net equity at the time of marriage ($10,000) bore to the aggregate of the value of the property on the date of the marriage ($30,000) plus the value of the addition on its completion ($10,000). The interests will then be apportioned as follows:

1. $10,000 divided by $40,000 = .25.
2. $100,000 × .25 =$25,000 (John's nonmarital interest).
3. $100,000 −$25,000 =$75,000 (marital interest).

The net value of the property, however, is only $96,000 ($100,000 − $4,000 mortgage balance). Because the parties undertook payment of the mortgage debt with marital funds, reduction of the marital interests by the amount of the mortgage balance ($75,000 − $4,000 = $71,000) is appropriate. Thus, $71,000 is marital property and $25,000 is John's nonmarital property, all to be justly and equitably distributed. . . .

At the time of the dissolution, Jane owned 800 shares of XYZ Co., which then had a market value of $40 per share or $32,000. The increase in the number of shares is the result of a 2 for 1 split which increased Jane's holdings from 300 to 600 shares. The additional 200 shares were acquired through the reinvestment of cash dividends paid during the marriage. Jane claims all 800 shares of XYZ Co. as her nonmarital property.

> . . . The phrase "increase in value" used in subsection (b)(5) is not intended to cover the income from property acquired prior to marriage. Such income is marital property. Similarly, income from other non-marital property acquired after the marriage is marital property. . . . Unif. Marriage and Divorce Act §307 comment at 204 (1970).

The intent of the drafters of the UMDA §307 commentary at 204 (1970) indicates that a stock dividend or split is nonmarital property:

> a stock dividend or split, the value of which is determined by market forces, does not increase the shareholder's proportionate ownership interest in the corporation and is not usually regarded as income.
>
> Cash dividends, on the other hand, would be considered a return on the investment or income and, therefore, be marital property.

Thus, Jane's 300 original shares and the 300 shares received in the stock split, having a total value of $24,000, would be Jane's nonmarital property, and the 200 shares purchased by reinvesting dividends and having a present value of $8,000 would be marital property.

Of course, investments do not always increase in value. If the value of Jane's 800 shares of XYZ Co. were worth only $10 per share at the time of the dissolution, Jane's 600 nonmarital shares would be worth only $6,000, less than the value of the 300 shares Jane owned when she married John. The 200 shares purchased with marital funds would have a present value of only $2,000.

The active/passive management distinction is certainly useful in avoiding the harsh results that would flow from viewing a business that was the economic cornerstone of a long-term marriage as separate property simply because the business, in some form, began to take shape before the marriage. . . .

This formula, designed to apportion marital and nonmarital interests in a specific parcel of residential real estate, usually the homestead of the parties, may also be used to apportion interests in certain other kinds of property, such as publicly traded stock, the value of which depends on forces outside the marital partnership.

Although the parties cast their differences in terms of the extent to which the efforts of each enhanced the value of the business, there is no dispute that the present value of the stock of Nardini of Minnesota is attributable to the efforts of the marital partners over the course of more than 30 years of marriage. Certainly, the business did not prosper of its own accord. Ralph's $2,500 purchased a one-half interest in a business which consisted of a truck, a carbon dioxide tank, various tools and manuals and, according to Ralph, "that's about it."

Given the nature of the assets of the business in 1949 and of the corporate assets today, the increase in the value of the business cannot be reasonably attributed to market conditions. There can be little doubt that more than 35 years of essentially prosperous and mildly inflationary economic conditions provided a favorable climate in which a budding business could grow and flower. But a business, like a garden, must be tended if it is to flourish. The economic life of the truck and carbon dioxide tank of 1949 has long since ended; and were it not for the personal efforts contributed by the spouses, the investment would have withered and died with the truck and the tank. What Ralph really invested in was the opportunity to turn his talents toward the development of an enterprise in which he had a personal stake.

The stated capital of the corporation formed after the 1956 acquisition of the Dietsch interest is only $2,000. The corporate financial statements make no reference to paid-in surplus. Whether business assets were transferred to the corporation at a zero basis or retained by the Nardinis and did not become corporate assets is not apparent from the record. By December 31, 1984, the book value of the corporate shares had increased to $565,598. Thus, in addition to the corporate income distributed to Ralph and Marguerite as salary, pension plan contributions and other fringe benefits, on December 31, 1984, the corporation had retained earnings of $563,598 (all of which were, of course, earned during the marriage). It seems to us that the nature of income generated through the efforts of the marital partners is not changed by its retention as shareholder equity in a wholly owned corporation. Whether the business be carried on as a family corporation or a partnership or a sole proprietorship, income earned during the marriage, whether distributed or undistributed and reinvested in the business, is marital property.

The fundamental error in the trial court's apportionment of marital and nonmarital interests in Nardini of Minnesota lies in the assumption that because Ralph purchased a one-half interest in a business prior to the marriage, his nonmarital interest should forever be one-half of the value of the business. The assumption ignores the fact that the events of the past 31 years have diluted the significance of the original nonmarital interest: Ralph's $2,500 investment in 1949 has been dwarfed by the overall success of the business. Even though we regard the formula developed in [valuing residential property upon divorce] unsuitable for apportioning the marital and nonmarital interests in a business which has been in the family over the course of a long-term traditional marriage, owns no real estate and has little in the way of physical assets, and whose success has depended on the efforts of the marital partners, the general principle underlying [decisions valuing residential property upon divorce] — that the present value of each interest is essentially proportionate to the amounts of the respective investments — suggests an appropriate basis for apportioning the marital and nonmarital interests in Nardini of Minnesota. While Ralph invested $2,500 in the business in 1949, the record here reveals that over the course of more than 31 years the marital partnership reinvested in Nardini of Minnesota $563,598 of retained earnings in addition to the $12,500 paid for Dietsch's interest in the business — money which could have been used for the acquisition of marital assets of a different kind. Nearly the entire present value of Nardini of Minnesota, then, should be apportioned as marital interest, which under the facts of this case the trial court has properly allocated to the parties in equal shares.

Reversed and remanded.

DISCUSSION QUESTIONS FOR *NARDINI v. NARDINI*

A. Ralph Nardini attributed the financial success of the business to his "key man" effort alone. He claimed that working within the company since 1949 and functioning as its president and salesperson, he developed the business contacts and personally claims responsibility for 50 to 60 percent of the sales based upon his personal relationships with customers and his hard work. What did Marguerite contend were her contributions to the business? With whom did the Minnesota Supreme Court agree and why?

B. Marguerite and Ralph each retained experts to value the company. What value did each expert place on the business and how did the experts arrive at the figures they presented to the court? What were the theories used by the experts in their valuation of the business?

C. The court in *Nardini* sets out three options that may be used by a court to divide marital property when the parties cannot agree on the value of a closely held business. It did not mandate a particular method. What are the three options and what appear to be the advantages of each method?

D. The court articulated eight factors that it felt should be considered when arriving at a reasonable value of a closely held corporation. What are the eight factors? Is any one of the factors more important than any other?

E. What is the rationale for the court's conclusion that "the entire present value of Nardini of Minnesota" should be apportioned as marital interest? Is it persuasive?

F. As the court in *Nardini* pointed out, the Commissioner's Note to the original draft of §307 of the Uniform Marriage and Divorce Act states in part: "The intent of the drafters indicates that a stock dividend or split is nonmarital property: a stock dividend or split, the value of which is determined by market forces, does not increase the shareholder's proportionate ownership interest in the corporation and is not usually regarded as income. Cash dividends, on the other hand, would be considered a return on the investment of income and, therefore, be marital property." Is the distinction persuasive?

12.18 CONTINGENT FEE CONTRACTS

Background to *In re Marriage of Estes*

In re Marriage of Estes considers the question of how to value contingent fee cases worked on or acquired by a lawyer during a marriage. A minority of jurisdictions hold that because of the nature of contingent fee cases, they are too speculative to value accurately and should not be considered marital property or part of the community for distribution. *See generally Beasley v. Beasley*, 518 A.2d 545, 554 (Pa. 1986).

The *Estes* court asks whether a value should be placed on a contingent fee case when the case had not yet been tried or settled. The attorney for the husband in *Estes* argued that contingent fee contracts should not be included in the marital estate because they depend on an uncertain event. As such, he claimed no obligation, or fee entitlement, is created until and unless the actual happening of the event. Second, he asserted that even if such a contract creates a contemporaneous right to enforce it upon the happening of the event, any such right is only one of a specific enforcement and not a retroactive vesting to the contract's creation. To this end, the attorney for the husband claimed that the client could revoke the contingent fee agreement with the attorney or the client's death would terminate the attorney-client relationship and concomitantly the attorney's entitlement to a fee. Finally, he contended that a contingent fee contract has no ascertainable value prior to successful completion of the case.

IN RE MARRIAGE OF ESTES
Court of Appeals of Washington
929 P.2d 500 (1997)

SCHULTHEIS, Acting Chief Judge. Yong Estes appeals the dissolution decree contending the court should have included her attorney husband's contingency fee cases as marital assets. Mr. Estes filed a petition for dissolution in December 1993. The parties had been married for 10 years, and separated in October 1993. They have no children.

. . . Mr. Estes's gross income from his law practice in 1992 was $61,400. At the time of separation he had accounts receivable of $77,689.90. In addition he had been working on five or more personal injury cases in which his fee was contingent on the amount of any actual recovery. He testified in one case his client had made a settlement offer of $1.2 million, which had not yet been accepted or rejected. Because of the uncertainty of the outcome in any of his contingency fee cases, he testified that they had no value.

Ms. Estes was employed in the banking industry during much of the marriage. She obtained additional training and certification as a travel agent but never obtained gainful employment in that field. At the time of trial she was employed as a part-time bank teller earning $7.25 per hour. . . .

The court found the rights to contingency fees had no value and awarded them to Mr. Estes. The court awarded Mr. Estes assets valued at $188,352, and liabilities of $10,469, for a net property distribution of $177,883. The court awarded Ms. Estes assets of $209,855, including a payment of $60,000 from Mr. Estes, secured by a judgment lien. The court found Ms. Estes was in need of maintenance and awarded her $1,000 per month, to terminate upon her receipt of $73,631 from Mr. Estes, and noted the purpose of the unequal property division was to provide for her needs in lieu of additional maintenance. The decree of dissolution was entered on July 25, 1994. Ms. Estes moved for reconsideration, and following denial of her motion filed notice of appeal.

On September 6, 1994, Mr. Estes obtained a tentative settlement agreement in one of his contingency fee cases. Under the final agreement he received a contingency fee of $178,640.72. Mr. Estes did not disclose the fact of the settlement or the amount of his contingency fee to Ms. Estes prior to the trial court's ruling on her motion for reconsideration. Ms. Estes learned of the settlement agreement in July 1995. She moved to vacate the dissolution decree, alleging the amount of the contingency was newly discovered evidence that showed misrepresentation as to the value of the case. The motion was denied, and she appealed. . . .

Ms. Estes argues the court erred in finding the right to those fees had no value. Mr. Estes testified the value of the contingent fees was zero. He also indicated that in one case he had made a $1.2 million settlement offer on behalf of his client. The latter evidence suggests that while the value of the contingent fees would be difficult if not impossible to ascertain, they had some value. The difficulty of valuation, without more, does not preclude the court from awarding contingent fees; the proceeds of a contract obtained during the marriage in the conduct of the community's business may be awarded to both parties and divided between them when received.

This is the approach followed in the majority of jurisdictions that have considered the matter.

The Supreme Court of Georgia held contingent fee agreements are not marital assets, reasoning that the difficulty in ascertaining their value at the time of the divorce action rendered them "too remote, speculative and uncertain. . . ." *Goldstein v. Goldstein*, 414 S.E.2d 474, 476 (1992). The Illinois, Pennsylvania, and Oklahoma courts have similarly concluded difficulties in ascertaining the value of contingent fee agreements precludes their classification as marital assets. *In re Tietz*, 605 N.E.2d 670 (1992); *In re Zells*, 572 N.E.2d 944 (1991); *Musser v. Musser*, 909 P.2d 37 (Okla. 1995); *Beasley v. Beasley*, 518 A.2d 545 (1986). The *Zells* court also reasoned that an award of unearned attorney fees to the nonattorney wife would pose an "impermissible ethical conflict" violating the rule prohibiting sharing legal fees with nonlawyers. 572 N.E.2d at 945.

An attorney should not be required to place a value on contingency fee cases not yet tried or settled. The difficulty of valuing contingent fees is readily solved by abiding the outcome of the underlying actions and determining the portion of any ultimate recovery attributable to the marital community based on the time devoted to the case before and after separation. Nor is it apparent that an obligation to share with a former spouse a portion of a fee to be received in the future, if limited to that portion of the fee earned by the attorney's efforts during the marriage, would implicate the evils contemplated by the rule of ethics that prohibits sharing fees with nonattorneys. Fees earned during marriage are community property, necessarily shared with a nonattorney spouse; this has never been viewed as a violation of the rules of professional conduct.

The court's finding that Mr. Estes's right to contingency fees had no value, and its award to him of the entirety of any fees subsequently collected, is contrary to law. The proceeds of any contingency fee agreements obtained during the marriage in the conduct of the community's business should be awarded to both parties and divided between them, when received, "based upon the percentage of the number of hours worked during the marriage bears to the total number of hours worked in earning the fee. . . ." The trial court should have awarded to both parties the right to receive contingency fees, to be divided upon receipt. . . .

Reversed and remanded for further proceedings consistent with this opinion.

DISCUSSION QUESTIONS FOR *IN RE MARRIAGES OF ESTES*

A. What reasons are found in this opinion to support the view that a court should not include a contingent fee as a marital asset when parties divorce? Is the reasoning persuasive?

B. What was the court's response to the claim that sharing a portion of a contingent fee with a nonlawyer violated the rules of professional conduct?

C. The court established that the proceeds of any contingent fee agreements obtained during the marriage in the conduct of the community's business should be awarded to both parties and divided between them, based upon the percentage of the number of hours worked during the marriage bears to the total number of hours worked in earning the fee. How will a court compute the time worked on a case if a lawyer fails to keep careful hourly records? *See Mitlyng v. Mitlyng*, not reported in P.3d, 122 Wash. App. 1017 (Wash. 2004).

D. The opinion contains the competing views of several jurisdictions regarding when and how to value contingent fees. *Compare Garrett v. Garrett*, 683 P.2d 11166 (Ariz. 1983), with *Roberts v. Roberts*, 689 So. 2d 378 (Fla. 1997) (pending contingent fee cases in husband's law office could not be included in distribution of parties' marital property in divorce action). Which of the views appears to achieve the most equitable outcome when parties divorce?

12.19 DEGREES AND LICENSES

During a marriage, one spouse may contribute earnings and services to the relationship while the other spouse is spending most of his or her time obtaining a professional degree or license. Usually, the supporting spouse considers the contribution as looking toward the future when the partners will benefit from a significantly improved standard of living. When the relationship breaks down before the improved standard of living is achieved, the question is how should the supporting spouse's contributions be viewed?

When addressing that question, courts will ask the following: Is a license or degree an asset that is subject to distribution when the parties divorce? Is it a mere expectancy that has little or no value as an asset? The answers to these questions turn on the jurisdiction considering the issue. The majority view appears to be that an advanced degree is not marital property. Rather, it is a cumulative product of many years of previous education, combined with diligence and hard work. It may not be acquired by the mere expenditure of money. It is an intellectual achievement that may potentially assist in the future acquisition of property. *In re Marriage of Horstmann*, 263 N.W.2d 885 (Iowa 1978), *citing Marriage of Graham*, 555 P.2d 527 (Colo. App. 1976). However, it possesses none of the attributes of property in the usual sense of that term and cannot be equitably valued and divided. *Holbrook v. Holbrook*, 309 N.W.2d 343 (Wis. App. 1981).

Note that while a majority of jurisdictions do not consider a professional degree or license acquired by one of the parties during marriage as marital property, these jurisdictions usually consider giving the supporting spouse additional compensation because of its existence. The compensation may be in form of restitution, alimony, or other recompense.

 **REFLECTIVE QUESTIONS**

When it comes to a valuing a professional degree or license obtained during a marriage, what reasons support the majority view that it is not marital property?

Background to *O'Brien v. O'Brien*

New York is a minority jurisdiction and the *O'Brien* decision is probably the leading ruling in the nation on the degree/license issue. Note that the decision is based on portions of New York's Equitable Distribution law, which provides that a court consider the efforts one spouse has made to the other spouse's career. *See* N.Y. Dom. Rel. L. §236(B)(5) (McKinney 1985). The analysis in *O'Brien* is illustrative of the equitable concerns of the working spouse who contributes to the other spouse's career; however, it has a limited application beyond New York.

O'BRIEN
v.
O'BRIEN

Court of Appeals of New York
489 N.E.2d 712 (1985)

SIMONS, J. In this divorce action, the parties' only asset of any consequence is the husband's newly acquired license to practice medicine. The principal issue presented is whether that license, acquired during their marriage, is marital property subject to equitable distribution under Domestic Relations Law §236 (B) (5). . . .

Plaintiff and defendant married on April 3, 1971. At the time both were employed as teachers at the same private school. Defendant had a bachelor's degree and a temporary teaching certificate but required 18 months of postgraduate classes at an approximate cost of $3,000, excluding living expenses, to obtain permanent certification in New York. She claimed, and the trial court found, that she had relinquished the opportunity to obtain permanent certification while plaintiff pursued his education. At the time of the marriage, plaintiff had completed only three and one-half years of college but shortly afterward he returned to school at night to earn his bachelor's degree and to complete sufficient premedical courses to enter medical school. In September 1973 the parties moved to Guadalajara, Mexico, where plaintiff became a full-time medical student. While he pursued his studies defendant held several teaching and tutorial positions and contributed her earnings to their joint expenses. The parties returned to New York in December 1976 so that plaintiff could complete the last two semesters of medical school and internship training here. After they returned, defendant resumed her former teaching position and she remained in it at the time this action was commenced. Plaintiff was licensed to practice medicine in October 1980. He commenced this action for divorce two months later. At the time of trial, he was a resident in general surgery.

During the marriage both parties contributed to paying the living and educational expenses and they received additional help from both of their families. They disagreed on the amounts of their respective contributions but it is undisputed that in addition to performing household work and managing the family finances defendant was gainfully employed throughout the marriage, that she contributed all of her earnings to their living and educational expenses and that her financial contributions exceeded those of plaintiff. The trial court found that she had contributed 76% of the parties' income exclusive of a $10,000 student loan obtained by defendant. Finding that plaintiff's medical degree and license are marital property, the court received evidence of its value and ordered a distributive award to defendant.

Defendant presented expert testimony that the present value of plaintiff's medical license was $472,000. Her expert testified that he arrived at this figure by comparing the average income of a college graduate and that of a general surgeon between 1985, when plaintiff's residency would end, and 2012, when he would reach age 65. After considering Federal income taxes, an inflation rate of 10% and a real interest rate of 3% he capitalized the difference in average earnings and reduced the amount to present value. He also gave his opinion that the present value of defendant's contribution to plaintiff's medical education was $103,390. Plaintiff offered no expert testimony on the subject.

The court, after considering the life-style that plaintiff would enjoy from the enhanced earning potential his medical license would bring and defendant's contributions and efforts toward attainment of it, made a distributive award to her of $188,800, representing 40% of the value of the license, and ordered it paid in 11 annual installments of various amounts beginning November 1, 1982 and ending November 1, 1992. The court also directed plaintiff to maintain a life insurance policy on his life for defendant's benefit for the unpaid balance of the award and it ordered plaintiff to pay defendant's counsel fees of $7,000 and her expert witness fee of $1,000. It did not award defendant maintenance.

The Equitable Distribution Law contemplates only two classes of property: marital property and separate property. . . . The former, which is subject to equitable distribution, is defined broadly as "all property acquired by either or both spouses during the marriage and before the execution of a separation agreement or the commencement of a matrimonial action, regardless of the form in which title is held" Plaintiff does not contend that his license is excluded from distribution because it is separate property; rather, he claims that it is not property at all but represents a personal attainment in acquiring knowledge. He rests his argument on decisions in similar cases from other jurisdictions and on his view that a license does not satisfy common-law concepts of property.

Neither contention is controlling because decisions in other States rely principally on their own statutes, and the legislative history underlying them, and because the New York Legislature deliberately went beyond traditional property concepts when it formulated the Equitable Distribution Law. Instead, our statute recognizes that spouses have an equitable claim to things of value arising out of the marital relationship and classifies them as subject to distribution by focusing on the marital status of the parties at the time of acquisition. Those things acquired during marriage and subject to distribution have been classified as "marital property" although, as one commentator has observed, they hardly fall within the traditional property concepts because there is no common-law property interest remotely resembling marital property.

Having classified the "property" subject to distribution, the Legislature did not attempt to go further and define it but left it to the courts to determine what interests come within the terms of section 236(B)(1)(c).

We made such a determination in *Majauskas v. Majauskas*, 474 N.Y.S.2d 699, 463 N.E.2d 15, holding there that vested but unmatured pension rights are marital property subject to equitable distribution. Because pension benefits are not specifically identified as marital property in the statute, we looked to the express reference to pension rights contained in section 236(B)(5)(d)(4), which deals with equitable distribution of marital property, to other provisions of the equitable distribution statute and to the legislative intent behind its enactment to determine whether pension rights are marital property or separate property. A similar analysis is appropriate here and leads to the conclusion that marital property encompasses a license to practice medicine to the extent that the license is acquired during marriage. . . .

The determination that a professional license is marital property is also consistent with the conceptual base upon which the statute rests. As this case demonstrates, few undertakings during a marriage better qualify as the type of joint effort that the statute's economic partnership theory is intended to address than contributions toward one spouse's acquisition of a professional license. Working spouses are often required to contribute substantial income as wage earners, sacrifice their own educational or career goals and opportunities for child rearing, perform the bulk of household duties and responsibilities and forego [*sic*] the acquisition of marital assets that could have been accumulated if the professional spouse had been employed rather than occupied with the study and training necessary to acquire a professional license.

In this case, nearly all of the parties' nine-year marriage was devoted to the acquisition of plaintiff's medical license and defendant played a major role in that project. She worked continuously during the marriage and contributed all of her earnings to their joint effort, she sacrificed her own educational and career opportunities, and she traveled with plaintiff to Mexico for three and one-half years while he attended medical school there. The Legislature has decided, by its explicit reference in the statute to the contributions of one spouse to the other's profession or career that these contributions represent investments in the economic partnership of the marriage and that the product of the parties' joint efforts, the professional license, should be considered marital property. . . .

Plaintiff's principal argument, adopted by the majority below, is that a professional license is not marital property because it does not fit within the traditional view of property as something which has an exchange value on the open market and is capable of sale, assignment or transfer. The position does not withstand analysis for at least two reasons. First, as we have observed, it ignores the fact that whether a professional license constitutes marital property is to be judged by the language of the statute which created this new species of property previously unknown at common law or under prior statutes. Thus, whether the license fits within traditional property concepts is of no consequence. Second, it is an overstatement to assert that a professional license could not be considered property even outside the context of section 236 (B).

A professional license is a valuable property right, reflected in the money, effort and lost opportunity for employment expended in its acquisition, and also in the enhanced earning capacity it affords its holder, which may not be revoked without due process of law. That a professional license has no market value is irrelevant. Obviously, a license may not be alienated as may other property and for that reason the working spouse's interest in it is limited. The Legislature has recognized that limitation, however, and has provided for an award in lieu of its actual distribution.

Plaintiff also contends that alternative remedies should be employed, such as an award of rehabilitative maintenance or reimbursement for direct financial contributions. The statute does not expressly authorize retrospective maintenance or rehabilitative awards and we have no occasion to decide in this case whether the authority to do so may ever be implied from its provisions. It is sufficient to observe that normally a working spouse should not be restricted to that relief because to do so frustrates the purposes underlying the Equitable Distribution Law. Limiting a working spouse to a maintenance award, either general or rehabilitative, not only is contrary to the economic partnership concept underlying the statute but also retains the uncertain and inequitable economic ties of dependence that the Legislature sought to extinguish by equitable distribution. Maintenance is subject to termination upon the recipient's remarriage and a working spouse may never receive adequate consideration for his or her contribution and may even be penalized for the decision to remarry if that is the only method of compensating the contribution. As one court said so well, "[the] function of equitable distribution is to recognize that when a marriage ends, each of the spouses, based on the totality of the contributions made to it, has a stake in and right to a share of the marital assets accumulated while it endured, not because that share is needed, but because those assets represent the capital product of what was essentially a partnership entity," *Wood v. Wood*, 119 Misc. 2d 1076, 1079. The Legislature stated its intention to eliminate such inequities by providing that a supporting spouse's "direct or indirect contribution" be recognized, considered and rewarded.

Turning to the question of valuation, it has been suggested that even if a professional license is considered marital property, the working spouse is entitled only to reimbursement of his or her direct financial contributions. By parity of reasoning, a spouse's down payment on real estate or contribution to the purchase of securities would be limited to the money contributed, without any remuneration for any incremental value in the asset because of price appreciation. Such a result is completely at odds with the statute's requirement that the court give full consideration to both direct and indirect contributions "made to the acquisition of such marital property by the party not having title, including joint efforts or expenditures and contributions and services as a spouse, parent, wage earner and homemaker."

If the license is marital property, then the working spouse is entitled to an equitable portion of it, not a return of funds advanced. Its value is the enhanced earning capacity it affords the holder and although fixing the present value of that enhanced earning capacity may present problems, the problems are not insurmountable. Certainly they are no more difficult than computing tort damages for wrongful death or diminished earning capacity resulting from injury and they differ only in degree from the problems presented when valuing a professional practice for purposes of a distributive award, something the courts have not hesitated to do.

The trial court retains the flexibility and discretion to structure the distributive award equitably, taking into consideration factors such as the working spouse's need for immediate payment, the licensed spouse's current ability to pay and the income tax consequences of prolonging the period of payment and, once it has received evidence of the present value of the license and the working spouse's contributions toward its acquisition and considered the remaining factors mandated by the statute, it may then make an appropriate distribution of the marital property including a distributive award for the professional license if such an award is warranted. When other marital assets are of sufficient value to provide for the supporting spouse's equitable portion of the marital property, including his or her contributions to the acquisition of the professional license, however, the court retains the discretion to distribute these other marital assets or to make a distributive award in lieu of an actual distribution of the value of the professional spouse's license.

DISCUSSION QUESTIONS FOR *O'BRIEN v. O'BRIEN*

A. According to the court, what was the principal objective of the nine-year marriage? Is identifying the "objective" important to the outcome of the case?

B. The lower appeals court limited application of the New York statute to a professional who was in an established practice. What was this court's response to that view? Which view is more persuasive?

C. What was the plaintiff's principal argument against valuing the medical degree? Is the argument persuasive?

D. The court provided two reasons why the plaintiff's principal argument should fail. What are they? Are they sound?

E. Since the *O'Brien* ruling, New York has had numerous opportunities to apply the reasoning in that case to other dissolution actions. For example, in *Elkus v. Elkus*, 572 N.Y.S.2d 901 (App. Div. 1991), the celebrity status of a skilled opera singer was found to be a marital asset subject to equitable distribution. In *Mitnick v. Rosenthal*, 260 A.D.2d 238, 239 (N.Y. 1999), the court held that the wife's fellowships were properly found to be subject to equitable distribution upon evidence that they enhanced her earning capacity. In *Hougie v. Hougie*, 261 A.D.2d 161, 162 (N.Y. 1999), the court held that defendant's enhanced earning capacity as an investment banker was subject to equitable distribution, regardless of whether or not such a career requires a license, and that the Series 7 securities license, which is necessary to trade securities in the United States, that he obtained during the marriage should be taken into account in determining his enhanced earning capacity. In *Murtha v. Murtha*, 264 A.D.2d 552, 553 (N.Y. 1999), the court held that the husband's Chartered Financial Analyst certification enhanced his earning capacity, and although not a prerequisite for employment and/or advancement, was subject to equitable distribution because he was promoted after receiving it and his compensation more than doubled. In *Judge v. Judge*, 48 A.D.3d 424 (N.Y. 2008), the court held that defendant's MBA degree was a marital assert subject to equitable distribution, explaining that an academic degree may constitute a marital asset subject to equitable distribution, even though the degree may not necessarily confer the legal right to engage in a particular profession, since the record demonstrated that the degree substantially increased the wife's future earnings.

In other cases, the court has held that the portion of the value of a spouse's enhanced earning capacity resulting from the education acquired during the marriage is a marital asset. Hence, for example, in *McAlpine v. McAlpine*, 176 A.D.2d 285 (N.Y. 1991), the court held that only that portion of the husband's fellowship represented by the last five examinations could be treated as marital property since the fellowship, which required the study of mathematics and the successful passage of ten examinations, was largely obtained premaritally, and defendant graduated from college and passed five of the examinations before he was married. Similarly, in *Hickey v. Hickey*, 256 A.D.2d 383 (N.Y. 1998), the court held that since plaintiff's nursing license was a result, in part, of an educational process which began before the marriage, it could not, in its entirety, be distributed as marital property, and remitted the matter for a hearing to determine the number of credits earned by plaintiff toward the license before the marriage, and to recalculate defendant's share of the license. *See also* Cal. Fam. Code §2641 (b)(1) (West 2004) (providing for reimbursement of the community for contributions to the education or training of a party that substantially increases the earning capacity of that party).

Are the New York/California approaches to valuing degrees and licenses fair? Shouldn't other jurisdictions adopt them?

F. In *Simmons v. Simmons*, 708 A.2d 949 (1998), the Connecticut Supreme Court concluded that a medical degree earned by one spouse during the marriage was not property. It reasoned that while an advanced degree could be considered property under traditional property principles, such a degree was not property for equitable distribution purposes because "an advanced degree entails no presently existing, enforceable right to receive any particular income in the future." *Ibid.* It said that the degree represents "nothing more than an opportunity for the degree holder, though his or her own efforts, in the absence of any contingency that might limit or frustrate those efforts, to earn income in the future." In other words, although an advanced degree has certain characteristics of property, the potential for future income related thereto was too speculative for the degree to be considered divisible marital property. Accordingly, it concluded that a medical degree properly was classified as expectancy, and therefore was not subject to equitable distribution. *Ibid.* Do you agree with the reasoning of the Connecticut Supreme Court?

ALI. The ALI *Principles* follows the majority rule in the nation and does not treat the earning capacity of a license or degree acquired during marriage as a divisible asset. Instead, the *Principles* provides for "compensatory payments" that can be used to reimburse a supporting spouse for the financial contributions made to the other spouse's education or training. ALI *Principles* §§4.07, 5.12. Note that the education must have been completed in less than a specified number of years (set out in a rule of statewide application) before the filing of the dissolution petition. *Id.* §5.12.

> ### REFLECTIVE QUESTIONS
>
> Illustrate how ALI "compensatory payments" might be determined by a trial judge.

12.20 TORT AND COMPENSATION AWARDS

How to fairly value and divide tort and compensation awards to a spouse who was injured during the marriage has been a challenge to courts and legislatures. For example, in a community property state such as California, a lump sum permanent disability award received prior to separation was considered the injured spouse's separate property to the extent it was meant to compensate for the injured spouse's diminished earning capacity (and/or medical expenses) after separation. *Raphael v. Bloomfield,* 6 Cal. Rptr. 3d 583 (Cal. App. 2003). The *Raphael* court noted that a portion of the lump sum award received during the marriage represented future benefits, and not owed during the marriage. *See Hatcher v. Hatcher,* 933 P.2d 1222 (Ariz. 1997) (lump sum disability proceeds which represented compensation for a husband's loss of earning ability during marriage is community property, while remainder of lump sum payment was the husband's separate property).

Most equitable distribution of property jurisdictions conduct an "analytic" approach to classifying a settlement or recovery for a spouse's personal injury claim that occurred during the marriage as marital or separate property of the injured spouse. Kurtis A. Kemper, 109 A.L.R.5th 1 (2003). This approach requires an examination of the components of the settlement or recovery to determine the purpose of each component of the settlement or recovery. *See Newborn v. Newborn,* 754 A.2d 476 (Md. App. 2000) (analytical approach, as opposed to mechanical or unitary approaches, was the appropriate method to determine whether husband's personal injury settlement was marital property, where his injury occurred prior to separation). In *Newborn,* the court held that all of the proceeds from the settlement were the separate and nonmarital property of husband except (1) monies that were paid to reimburse the Newborns for medical expenses; (2) monies paid to reimburse Mr. Newborn for wages he lost as a result of the accident prior to September 1981 — when he returned to work; (3) monies paid to reimburse Ms. Newborn for wages she would have earned if she had not stayed home to care for her husband; and (4) monies paid to the Newborns for their joint claim for loss of consortium. *Id.* at 491.

REFLECTIVE QUESTIONS	**List the three approaches used by courts to classify a settlement or recovery for a spouse's personal injury claim that occurred during the marriage.**

Background to *Lopiano v. Lopiano*

In *Lopiano v. Lopiano*, the issue is whether the trial court properly assigned a portion of a spouse's unliquidated personal injury award incident to dissolution of marriage. While married, Mr. Lopiano was severely injured and as a result of a negligence claim, a jury returned a verdict of $2,820,000. The award was reduced to $800,000 by the trial judge. The trial court found that Mr. Lopiano's personal injury award was property subject to equitable distribution and ordered him to pay his spouse 25 percent of the net recovery to be received.

Mr. Lopiano challenged the trial judge's decision. He argued that the order was unfair because (1) the portion of the award attributable to pain and suffering should not have been included as property subject to division; (2) the portion of the award representing lost wages should not have been included; (3) the trial court's inclusion of the pain and suffering and future earnings portions of the award violated his right to equal protection under Connecticut's constitution.

LOPIANO
v.
LOPIANO

Supreme Court of Connecticut
752 A.2d 1000 (1998)

KATZ, J. . . . The parties were married on May 6, 1967. . . . Unfortunately, in February, 1992, while at work, he sustained severe physical injuries causing him to be 100 percent physically disabled. He pursued a negligence action in New York, which, in 1996, resulted in the following jury award: $750,000 for past pain and suffering; $1,600,000 for future pain and suffering over the next twenty-nine years; $80,000 for past loss of earnings; $375,000 for future loss of earnings; and $15,000 for past medical expenses; totaling $2,820,000. This sum was reduced by $423,000 based upon a finding that the plaintiff was 15 percent negligent, leaving a net jury award of $2,397,000. The trial judge in the negligence action reduced the awards for pain and suffering, and made the following allocations: $150,000 for past pain and suffering; $400,000 for future pain and suffering; $75,000 for past loss of wages; and $175,000 for future loss of wages; leaving the plaintiff an award totaling $800,000. . . .

The trial court determined that the plaintiff's personal injury award was property subject to equitable distribution and issued the following financial orders:

(1) the plaintiff must pay to the defendant $100 weekly as periodic alimony until the defendant's remarriage, the death of either party, further court order or upon her receiving her share of the plaintiff's judgment or award from his personal injury action;
(2) the plaintiff must pay to the defendant 25 percent of the net recovery received by the plaintiff by judgment or settlement of that action; and
(3) when the plaintiff receives his net recovery, he shall pay to the defendant's attorney the sum of $10,000 as an allowance to defend this dissolution action.

The plaintiff makes three claims in connection with the trial court's distribution to the defendant of a percentage of his personal injury award. Specifically, he claims that the trial court should not have included as property subject to dissolution . . . the portion of his personal injury award received as compensation for pain and suffering on the basis that such payments are compensation for personal losses. He next claims that the trial court improperly included as property the portion of his personal injury award received as compensation for post dissolution lost wages. Finally, he claims that the inclusion by the trial court of both of these items violated his rights to equal protection under . . . the constitution of Connecticut. . . .

There are marked differences in the treatment of proceeds from personal injury recoveries among the various jurisdictions. For purposes of distribution in a dissolution proceeding, there are three approaches to classifying personal injury awards or settlements. The first approach is to classify any such award or settlement as the personal and entirely separate property of the injured spouse.

The second approach, the analytic approach, requires an evaluation of the purpose of the compensation in the determination of the character of the award or settlement as "marital" or "personal" property. Under this approach, pain and suffering is personal, compensation for lost wages and medical expenses incurred during the course of the marriage is marital, while compensation for future economic losses is deemed nonmarital. This approach of distinguishing between the economic and noneconomic components of a personal injury award is the overwhelming method of classification in community property states. It has also been applied in a number of equitable distribution states.

The third approach, and the more modern trend, is the literal or mechanistic approach, which provides that, regardless of the underlying purpose of the award or the loss it is meant to replace, if the award or settlement was acquired during the marriage, it is deemed to be marital property. . . .

None of these approaches mirrors exactly how courts in this state view their authority in dissolution proceedings. In Connecticut, the trial court's authority to reach a party's right of action arises from the fact that such a right may be characterized as property. Characterization of the right of action as personal, or characterization of what the recovery was intended to address as personal, does not affect the divisibility of the settlement or award in dissolution proceedings because the trial court retains the authority to distribute both jointly held and individually held property.

Although it is not improper for the trial court to consider the actual source or ownership of an asset, these are but two factors to be considered in reaching an equitable division in dissolution proceedings. The fact that a particular asset belongs to one spouse may cause the trial court to be predisposed to awarding it to its named owner; however, if the marital estate is otherwise insufficient to maintain the other spouse, the court must be able to exercise its discretion in arriving at an equitable distribution, taking into consideration the needs and assets of both parties. The failure to interpret property broadly . . . could result in substantial inequity where, for example, a spouse who recovers a substantial amount in a personal injury action is left with income-producing assets, bought solely with money from the award, and the uninjured spouse is left destitute. Such a result clearly would be contrary to the purposes of [Connecticut law] and would not be in keeping with the equitable nature of dissolution proceedings under that section.

Unlike provisions in effect in many other jurisdictions that limit distributions to property based upon how and when it was acquired, [Connecticut law] does not draw such distinctions. In our view, the legislative decision to recognize all forms of presently existing interests as property subject to distribution at the time of dissolution is well considered. Therefore, while the plaintiff's award for his pain and suffering was undeniably his personal property, it was nevertheless subject to the court's authority for purposes of this dissolution action. We do not decide that the award in this case must have been divided, only that it was the trial court's function to weigh the factors relevant to the needs of the parties and the circumstances of the case in order to determine what portion, if any, of the award should be distributed to the defendant.

DISCUSSION QUESTIONS FOR *LOPIANO v. LOPIANO*

A. The plaintiff makes three claims in connection with the trial court's distribution to the defendant of a percentage of his personal injury award. What are they and are they persuasive?

B. The court discussed the differences in the treatment of proceeds from personal injury recoveries among the various jurisdictions in the nation? Which of the jurisdictions appears to achieve the most equitable (fair) outcome in a divorce action?

C. The court stated that while the plaintiff's award for his pain and suffering was undeniably his personal property, it was nevertheless subject to the court's authority for purposes of this dissolution action. On remand, how should a court value and divide the personal injury award including the award for pain and suffering?

12.21 PREMARITAL COHABITATION

Property acquired during premarital cohabitation is generally not considered marital property when the cohabiting parties marry and then divorce. For example, in *Crouch v. Crouch*, 410 N.E.2d 580 (Ill. App. 1980), before she married, the wife left college and abandoned her own career to help her husband in his gallery business. When they divorced she claimed she had obtained a premarital property right in the gallery. In rejecting her claim, the court said that "[t]he heart of the petitioner's claims to the disputed property is that she was in some form a partner in the art gallery business and in equity and good conscience should be compensated for her work benefiting the business prior to their marriage. Her plight, however compelling, has no available remedy under the Illinois Marriage and Dissolution of Marriage Act." *Id.* at 583. Similarly, in *Grishman v. Grishman*, 407 A.2d 9 (Me. 1979), the trial court erred in concluding that an interest in real estate acquired by the husband while the parties were unmarried cohabitants was marital property. The court noted that the Maine dissolution statute expressly defines "marital property" in terms of "property acquired by either spouse subsequent to the marriage." *Id.* at 12.

It may be possible, on rare occasions, to persuade a court that property acquired "in anticipation of marriage" is marital property. For example, in *In re Marriage of Airman*, 530 P.2d 1012 (Colo. App. 1974), a family residence was selected and acquired within a few days of the parties' marriage in contemplation of that marriage. The court held the residence and all the equity in it should be treated as marital property. It reasoned that in order to obtain the status of separate property, it must appear that the property was acquired prior to marriage with the intent that it become the separate property of the person making the separate property claim. It found a contrary intent from the record before it.

In *Rolle v. Rolle*, 530 A.2d 847 (N.J. Super. 1987), the question was whether assets acquired by a party in contemplation of marriage prior to and during a substantial period of cohabitation followed by a marriage are subject to equitable distribution in accordance with New Jersey statutes. The court held that the state's equitable distribution statute did not allow recognition of the assets as marital property. However, it also held that equitable remedies such as resulting trust, constructive trust, *quantum meruit*, quasi contract, and transmutation are available, under proper factual circumstances, to a spouse laying claim to assets acquired by other spouse during period of cohabitation prior to marriage.

REFLECTIVE QUESTIONS	When, if ever, may a court consider premarital cohabitation as involving marital property where the cohabiting parties marry and then divorce?

12.22 DEBTS: DIVIDING DEBTS

Marital debts defined. Marital debts are generally defined as those debts incurred during the marriage for the joint benefit of the parties, or the acquisition of marital property. *Mondelli v. Howard*, 780 S.W.2d 769 (Tenn. App. 1989). In *Mondelli* the court stated that when deciding who should pay a debt, it examines the following: (1) the debt's purpose; (2) which party incurred the debt; (3) which party benefitted from incurring the debt; and (4) which party is best able to repay the debt.

Liability of separate property. As a general rule, each spouse's separate property is liable for his or her debts. In a community property state, community property is only liable for community debts. In some jurisdictions, where courts are permitted to allocate marital debts on an "equitable" basis, they may take separate debts into account when determining who is able to pay outstanding debts.

Joint benefit test. Some courts have applied a "joint benefit" test to characterize debts incurred during periods of separation as marital if they were incurred to pay family living expenses. Others have rejected this characterization. For example, in *Alford v. Alford*, 120 S.W.3d 810, 813 (Tenn. 2003), the court rejected the "joint benefit" test stating it would "create substantial confusion and difficulty in determining what debts would meet the standard. For example, if one spouse incurs debt during the marriage to purchase a new automobile, would the purchase be for the joint benefit of both parties? If the automobile was used to drive children to school, would that change the result? The 'joint benefit' test would require trial courts to go through a difficult and unnecessary inquiry, and we decline to adopt it."

Proportionality scheme. Some courts may consider using either an equal division scheme or a proportionality scheme when dividing debts. The equal division scheme is found in jurisdictions that have a statutory equal division presumption. The presumption is applied to debts as well as assets. *See Thomson v. Thomson*, 661 S.E.2d 130, 136 (S.C. App. 2008). The proportionality scheme is considered for use in some jurisdictions to allocate debts in proportion to the parties' ability to pay them. The result is that the party with the most income generally receives most of the debts. *See, e.g., Kocsis v. Kocsis*, 28 S.W.3d 505 (Mo. App. 2000); *Schmaltz v. Schmaltz*, 586 N.W.2d 852 (N.D. 1998).

Third parties. An order or agreement between spouses regarding the allocation of debts does not bind creditors. The remedy for a party failing to pay a debt that the party was ordered by the trial judge in the divorce decree to pay is for the other party to bring a contempt action. *See, e.g., Srock v. Srock*, 466 P.2d 34, 35-36 (Ariz. App. 1970).

Agreement. A nonmarital debt becomes a marital debt if the nonincurring spouse agrees to accept liability. *See In re Marriage of Welch*, 795 S.W.2d 640 (Mo. App. 1990); *Schneider v. Schneider*, 761 S.W.2d 760 (Mo. App. 1988).

> | REFLECTIVE QUESTIONS | When, if ever, may a divorce decree that clearly allocates payment of debt incurred during the marriage to one party but not the other bind the third party to whom the debt is owed? |
> |---|---|

12.23 GIFTS IN CONTEMPLATION OF MARRIAGE

An engagement is usually a happy period for a couple looking toward marriage. However, circumstances may drastically alter the relationship and the planned engagement may be cancelled. When this occurs, the parties may demand the return of gifts made during the engagement period, claiming they were gifts in contemplation of marriage.

Five views: Still married to someone else. When considering gifts in contemplation of marriage, there are five approaches that courts use. *Cooper v. Smith*, 800 N.E.2d 372, 376 (Ohio App. 2003). Under the first approach, a donor is denied recovery if the donee was legally married to someone else at the time the donor and donee became engaged. *See Morgan v. Wright*, 133 S.E.2d 341 (Ga. 1963); *Lowe v. Quinn*, 267 N.E.2d 251 (N.Y. 1971). This approach theorizes that an agreement to marry where one party is already married is void as against public policy.

***Inter vivos* gifts.** The second approach treats all gifts exchanged during the engagement period as irrevocable *inter vivos* gifts. *Albinger v. Harris*, 48 P.3d 711 (Mont. 2002). This approach adheres to general gift law, which provides that an *inter vivos* gift is irrevocable once complete. Courts adopting this approach refuse to imply a condition on the gifts simply because they were given during the engagement period. It is thought that this approach encourages a donor to think twice before giving extravagant gifts. It also does not allow a donor to recover a gift because he or she later regrets having given it. It is argued, however that this approach works an injustice on unsuspecting donors who are deceived by donees who are unjustly enriched.

Engagement ring and all other gifts. The third approach, which appears to be the majority rule, considers an engagement ring as a conditional gift while all other gifts are viewed as irrevocable *inter vivos* gifts unless they were expressly conditioned on the subsequent marriage. *See Heiman v. Parrish*, 942 P.2d 631 (Kan. 1997); *Albanese v. Indelicato*, 51 A.2d 110 (N.Y. 1947); *Gikas v. Nicholis*, 71 A.2d 785 (N.H. 1950). This approach recognizes that an engagement ring symbolizes the couple's promise to marry. Because of that symbolic significance, it implies a condition with respect to the engagement ring only. It recognizes that in the natural course of events it would be unusual for the donor to give the engagement ring upon the expressed condition that marriage was to ensue. This approach recognizes that the other gifts lack the symbolic significance of the engagement ring and refuses to allow the donor to recover a gift simply because he or she later regrets having given it.

No recovery. It is the theory of these cases that the so-called heartbalm statutes not only bar breach of marriage contracts but any other proceeding that directly or indirectly arises out of the breach. Under that view, gifts in contemplation of marriage may not be recovered even though unjust enrichment may result to the donee. The results of these cases have been almost uniformly criticized as being unnecessary and undesirable. *Gikas v. Nicholis*, 71 A.2d 785 (N.H. 1950).

No-fault. The fifth approach is closely related to the conditional gift theory. Gifts given in contemplation of marriage are returned to the donor if the marriage does not occur, regardless of who might be at fault in ending the engagement. Courts adopting this approach conclude that the policy statements that govern a no-fault jurisdiction's approach to a broken marriage are equally relevant to a broken engagement.

REFLECTIVE QUESTIONS — Which of the various views listed above regarding the return of an engagement ring and other gifts is the better approach? Why? When should fault be considered, if ever, when an engagement is broken off?

12.24 PENSIONS: ERISA

Pensions are considered property that may be distributed when a marriage dissolves. The distribution is controlled by a comprehensive federal statute, the Employee Retirement Income Security Act (ERISA) of 1974, 29 U.S.C. §1000 et seq.

ERISA has been the subject of two Supreme Court decisions in which the question was whether it preempted state succession law. In the first decision, *Boggs v. Boggs*, 520 U.S. 833 (1997), Dorothy Boggs died in 1979, one year after she made a purported testamentary gift to her sons of her community property interest in her husband's undistributed pension plans. Her husband remarried. Upon his retirement in 1985, he received various benefits from his employer's retirement plans, including a lump sum savings plan distribution, which he rolled over into an IRA; shares of stock from the company's employee stock ownership plan; and a monthly annuity payment. After the husband's death in 1989, his sons from his first marriage contested the right of the second wife, Sandy Boggs, to the corpus and interest on the IRA, arguing the earlier testamentary gift from Dorothy Boggs vested ownership of a portion of the IRA in the sons.

The Supreme Court held that the purported testamentary transfer violated 29 U.S.C. §1056(d)(1)—the so-called anti-alienation provision of ERISA. In considering the issue, the Court weighed the importance of the state community property law, which — it acknowledged — "is a commitment to the equality of husband and wife and reflects the real partnership inherent in the marital relationship," against the importance of §1055 of ERISA, which mandates a qualified joint and survivor annuity in order "to ensure a stream of income to surviving spouses." 520 U.S. at 839-843. The Court concluded:

> ERISA's solicitude for the economic security of surviving spouses would be undermined by allowing a predeceasing spouse's heirs and legatees to have a community property interest in the survivor's annuity. Even a plan participant cannot defeat a nonparticipant surviving spouse's statutory entitlement to an annuity. It would be odd, to say the least, if Congress permitted a predeceasing nonparticipant spouse to do so. Nothing in the language of ERISA supports concluding that Congress made such an inexplicable decision. Testamentary transfers could reduce a surviving spouse's guaranteed annuity below the minimum set by ERISA (defined as 50% of the annuity payable during the joint lives of the participant and spouse). . . .
>
> In the face of this direct clash between state law and the provisions and objectives of ERISA, the state law cannot stand.

In the second decision, *Egelhoff v. Egelhoff*, 532 U.S. 141 (2001), the Court held that a state of Washington statute, which provided that the designation of a spouse as the beneficiary of a nonprobate asset is revoked automatically upon divorce, was expressly preempted by ERISA to the extent that it applies to ERISA plans. "ERISA's pre-emption section, 29 USC §1144(a), states that ERISA 'shall supersede any and all State laws insofar as they may now or hereafter relate to any employee benefit plan' covered by ERISA." *Id.* at 146.

In *Egelhoff* children from an intestate's first marriage sued the intestate's second wife, whose marriage to the decedent had been dissolved shortly before his death, The children claimed entitlement to life insurance proceeds and pension plan benefits. The State of Washington had a beneficiary redesignation statute that provided:

> If a marriage is dissolved or invalidated, a provision made prior to that event that relates to the payment or transfer at death of the decedent's interest in a nonprobate asset in favor of or granting an interest or power to the decedent's former spouse is revoked. A provision affected by this section must be interpreted, and the nonprobate asset affected passes, as if the former spouse failed to survive the decedent, having died at the time of entry of the decree of dissolution or declaration of invalidity.

Wash. Rev. Code §11.07.010(2)(a) (1994). Because the Washington statute required that plan administrators "pay benefits to the beneficiaries chosen by state law, rather than to those identified in the plan documents," the statute implicated an area of core ERISA concern. *Egelhoff, supra* at 147. The Supreme Court found that the state statute ran counter to ERISA's provisions that a plan shall "specify the basis on which payments are made to and from the plan," *Id., quoting* 29 U.S.C. §1102(b)(4), and that the plan fiduciary shall administer the plan "in accordance with the documents and instruments governing the plan," *Id., quoting*

29 U.S.C. §1104(a)(1)(D), making payments to a beneficiary "designated by a participant or by the terms of the plan." *Id., quoting* 29 U.S.C. §1002(8).

REFLECTIVE QUESTIONS	What is the significance of the *Egelhoff* and *Boggs* rulings in terms of spousal protection under a pension plan and divorce? Federal supremacy?

12.25 PENSIONS: QDRO

A Qualified Domestic Relations Order (QDRO) permits a retirement plan to be divided between divorcing spouses. A QDRO is a type of order often entered in a divorce proceeding and its terms must be recorded in the judgment and/or marital settlement agreement. QDROs apply to defined contribution and defined benefit plans.

To be valid. To be valid, a QDRO must specify (a) the name and last known mailing address of the participant and alternate payee; (b) the amount or percentage of the participant's benefits to be paid by the plan to each such alternate payee, or the manner in which such amount or percentage is to be determined; (c) the number of payments or period to which such order applies; and (d) each plan to which such order applies.

A QDRO meets the above requirements only if it (a) does not require the plan to provide a type or form of benefit, or any option, not otherwise provided under the plan; (b) does not require the plan to provide increased benefits on the basis of actuarial value; and (c) does not require the plan to pay benefits to an alternate payee that are already required to be paid to another alternate payee under another order previously determined to be a QDRO.

REFLECTIVE QUESTIONS	When is a QDRO necessary?

12.26 PENSIONS: MILITARY RETIREMENT BENEFITS

The Uniformed Services Former Spouse's Protection Act (USFSPA), 10 U.S.C. §1408 (2000), was enacted in reaction to *McCarty v. McCarty*, 453 U.S. 210 (1981). In *McCarty*, the United States Supreme Court ruled that military retirement benefits are the separate property of the retiree. The USFSPA overrules *McCarty* retroactively and allows a state court to apply its own law to determine the divisibility of military retirement benefits upon divorce. It also facilitates enforcement of a divorce decree by permitting payment to be made directly to the former spouse without the need for periodic garnishment actions.

REFLECTIVE QUESTIONS	What is the importance of the USFSPA to divorced military spouses?

12.27 BANKRUPTCY

The Bankruptcy Abuse Prevention and Consumer Protection Act (BAPCPA), which became effective October 17, 2005, generated sweeping amendments to the Bankruptcy Code. In terms of the relationship between family and bankruptcy courts, BAPCPA enhanced the rights of domestic creditors through increased protection and enforcement rights in bankruptcy and expanded the jurisdiction of family courts to adjudicate the rights of these domestic creditors in concurrent bankruptcy and divorce proceedings.

Significantly, under BAPCPA §523(a)(5), all marital-related debt, including obligations arising from property settlement agreements, are automatically considered nondischargeable. Determination of nondischargeability under §523(a)(5) is a question of federal law, and a bankruptcy court must make an independent finding as to whether an obligation labeled "support" is actually in the nature of support as that term is defined under federal law. Whether a debt is actually in the nature of support is determined by examining the intent of the parties at the time of the divorce. *See In re Swartz*, 339 B.R. 497 (Bankr. W.D. Mo. 2006). The factors that bankruptcy courts typically consider in making this determination include (1) the label used for the debt at issue (although this is not dispositive); (2) the income and needs of the parties at the time the obligation was created; (3) the amount and type of property division; (4) the number and frequency of payments of the award; (5) any waiver of alimony or maintenance in the agreement or decree; (6) the availability of state court modification and enforcement procedures; and (7) the tax treatment of the obligation. *See Norton Bankr. L. and Prac.* 2D §47:35 (2005).

REFLECTIVE QUESTIONS	What is the importance of the following statement: "All marital-related debt, including obligations arising from property settlement agreements, are automatically considered nondischargeable" in a bankruptcy proceeding?

General Principles

1. At common law, all property titled in the name of the spouse who acquired it was normally awarded to that spouse. This was typically the husband. A majority of states have replaced the common law title system with an equitable distribution scheme.

2. Courts traditionally awarded property on the basis of (1) who was at fault for the breakup, (2) who was most in need, or (3) the standard of living the parties enjoyed during the marriage. In general, modern courts divide property on the theory that a marriage is an economic relationship.

3. Community property is the marital property regime found in nine states: Arizona, California, Idaho, Louisiana, Nevada, New Mexico, Texas, Washington, and Wisconsin. Community property is usually defined as all property, other than that excluded by statute that defines separate property, acquired after marriage by either husband or wife, or both. In general, in a marriage in these jurisdictions, each spouse holds an undivided half interest in the community. Community property regimes view a marriage as a partnership.

4. The American Law Institute (ALI) *Principles of the Law of Family Dissolution* §4.18, characterizes separate property as marital property for the dissolution of long-term marriages (unless the trial judge makes findings that preserving the separate character of the property is necessary to avoid substantial injustice). The theory is that the characterization carries out the reasonable expectations of the parties in long-term marriages.

5. The Uniform Marriage and Divorce Act §307 asks a court to consider four factors when arriving at a division of marital property: (1) the contribution of each spouse to that property (including homemaking services); (2) the value of the property set apart to each spouse; (3) the duration of the marriage; and (4) the economic circumstances of each spouse at the time of dissolution, including the desirability of awarding the family home to the primary custodian of the children.

6. The Uniform Marriage and Divorce Act considers marital property as property acquired by the parties subsequent to the marriage but does not include property that is (1) acquired by gift or inheritance, (2) exchanged for separate property, or (3) subject to a valid agreement of the parties. UMDA §307(b).

7. Most equitable distribution jurisdictions divide only marital property, although a minority may divide both separate and marital property.

8. Almost all jurisdictions refuse to treat degrees and professional licenses that enhance a spouse's earning capacity as marital property. However, courts may take degrees and licenses into account when awarding alimony or property.

9. Jurisdictions that treat degrees and professional licenses as marital property are criticized because (1) they lack the traditional attributes of property (cannot be bought or sold); (2) their future earning capacity is speculative; (3) they are the product of only one spouse's intelligence and skills; and (4) valuation would

result in forcing one spouse to work to pay the other, a kind of involuntary servitude.

10. *Transmutation* is a general term used to describe arrangements between spouses to convert property from separate property to community property and vice versa.

Chapter Problems

1. Assume that at the time of the dissolution, Jane owned 800 shares of XYZ Co., which then had a market value of $40 per share or $32,000. The increase in the number shares is the result of a 2-for-1 split that increased Jane's holdings from 300 to 600 shares. The additional 200 shares were acquired through the reinvestment of cash dividends paid during the marriage. Jane claims all 800 shares of XYZ Co. as her nonmarital property. How will a court rule in an equitable distribution jurisdiction value the stock? Will a court in a community property jurisdiction come up with a different result?

2. Assume that Alice and Bobby married just before Bobby began law school. Alice worked to support both of them while Bobby spent all his time at his studies. Bobby graduated at the top of his class and was hired by a prestigious law firm. He falls in love with his legal secretary and divorces Alice. There is little property to divide. Alice asks the court to consider Bobby's law degree as an asset. Most likely, how will a court in a majority of jurisdictions rule on Alice's request?

3. Assume that Pauline and Joseph were married in 1907, and after ten years they separated. Pauline brought an action to divorce Joseph. During the marriage, Pauline was a traditional homemaker while Joseph ran the family blacksmith shop. The home and the shop are in Joseph's name. Pauline asks that the court divide the property in an equitable fashion. This jurisdiction applies the title theory to distribution of marital assets. How will a court rule on Pauline's request?

4. Assume the facts that are stated in Problem 3 above, with the following changed assumption. Assume that the divorce takes place in a community property jurisdiction in 1920. Would the court recognize Pauline's claim?

5. Cooper, whose engagement broke up when he sued his former fiancée's mother because of an auto accident, is now suing his fiancée, asking that the court return a car and an engagement ring he gave her in anticipation of their marriage. His former fiancée contends that Cooper should not recover the gifts because they were *inter vivos* gifts. How will a court in a majority of jurisdictions most likely rule?

6. Assume Roy purchased a painting for $500 before his marriage to Pam. At the time of the marriage it was worth $500. During the marriage the painting increases in value to $5,000. What portion, if any, is considered marital property in an equitable distribution jurisdiction? What portion will be considered community property in a state like Texas or California?

7. Assume Roy purchased a painting for $500 before his marriage to Pam. At the time of the marriage it was worth $500. After marriage, and immediately before restoration, it is valued at $500. To restore the painting, $500 of marital funds is used. After the restoration, the painting is valued at $2,000. What are the competing marital and nonmarital interests in the painting?

8. Assume that Pat purchases a car for $10,000 just before marriage, paying $5,000 down. Assume that on the date of the marriage, $5,000 is owed, and the market value of the car is $10,000. Pat makes all the payments on the car during the marriage from Pat's paycheck, and Pat produces checks to prove this allegation. Title is also in Pat's name only. Assume upon divorce the car is valued at $5,000. In an equitable distribution jurisdiction such as New York, what portion, if any, is marital? Will a community property jurisdiction such as Texas arrive at a different result?

9. Assume that on the date of John's marriage to Joan that he owns a home valued at $30,000 that is subject to a $20,000 mortgage. What is John's approximate nonmarital equitable percentage in the home at the moment before the couple marries if John still owes $20,000 on the home? If John and Joan live in the home for 40 years and the mortgage is paid off by Joan in the tenth year of their marriage, what is John's approximate nonmarital equitable interest in the home? Can you argue that after 40 years, there was no longer an expectation of a marital/nonmarital division if the couple divorced? Would your argument be treated more favorably in an equitable distribution jurisdiction or a community property jurisdiction?

10. Assume that Pam purchased a home before her marriage to Don for $50,000. At the time of the purchase, Pam made a $10,000 cash payment and took out a $40,000 mortgage. When Pam and Don married, the home had a market value of $50,000, but Pam's mortgage on it was only $10,000. When the couple dissolved their marriage, the home had a market value of $100,000 and no mortgage. Determine Pam's nonmarital interest in the home in an equitable distribution jurisdiction. How will it be valued in a community property jurisdiction?

11. Assume that Roger and Jamie were married for 20 years when the marriage dissolved. During the marriage Jamie received a legacy from her mother of $50,000. She purchased stock with the money. At the time of the divorce, the stock was valued at $100,000. Roger claims that he has a marital interest in the stock. The court is advised that this jurisdiction has adopted the UMDA. Under the UMDA, how will a court treat Roger's claim?

12. Assume that in an equitable distribution jurisdiction H purchased a home for $30,000. At the time of his marriage to W, H owed $20,000 on the home. Soon after their marriage H and W built an addition to the home on H's property, increasing its value by $10,000 — from $30,000 to $40,000. During the course of the marriage, the parties used marital funds to pay the mortgage balance down to $4,000. At the time of the dissolution the market value of the real estate was $100,000. Can you calculate H's nonmarital equity in the property on the date of H's marriage? Will the calculations differ depending on whether you are in an equitable distribution jurisdiction or a community property jurisdiction?

Preparation for Practice

1. Prepare a PowerPoint slide presentation in which you illustrate through the use of court-accepted mathematical formulas how a family court in your jurisdiction might treat appreciation of stock, a family home, a vested pension, and the goodwill in a small business when a couple divorce after 30 years of marriage. Be prepared to post your presentation to Blackboard or other similar electronic program for the use of all of the members of your class.

2. Prepare a short written scenario for a hypothetical client who is a lawyer. Include in the script that the client opened a one-person law firm two years after the client and his wife married. During the entire time of the marriage, the wife remained a homemaker caring for their two children. After ten years of marriage, the couple are divorcing. The client is coming to you to ask advice about how to value his law firm in the divorce. He is especially concerned about "goodwill." Ask a classmate to role-play the client. Videotape a 15-minute interview in which you focus on explaining how the law firm will most likely be valued by the trial judge in a community property jurisdiction. Ask your instructor or a family law attorney to critique your interview.

Chapter 13

Premarital and Postmarital Contracts

13.1 INTRODUCTION

This chapter explores the background, development, and application of premarital contracts. A short section near the end of the chapter addresses postmarital contracts. The chapter provides an opportunity to consider the practical implications of the use of premarital contracts, which are agreements signed at a time when persons are about to marry. The chapter also provides an opportunity to examine, digest, and debate the somewhat complex legal principles and differing philosophies that family courts apply when resolving challenges to enforcement of these agreements.

The chapter considers the following questions: What is the reason that until quite recently courts and legislatures limited premarital contracts to use only upon the death of a party? Why did courts and legislatures extend their use to divorce? What kind of premarital contract requests will most courts refuse to honor? When are premarital contract provisions unconscionable? Can premarital contracts be used to limit alimony, child support, and attorneys' fees should a couple divorce? What disclosures must be made at the time a premarital contract is executed? How much time should a party be given to review a premarital contract before signing it? What is the "second look" doctrine, and does it interfere with the right of competent adults to make contracts?

Jurisdictions use a variety of labels for premarital contracts, including *premarital, antenuptial,* or *prenuptial* agreements. Black's Law Dictionary 1220 (8th ed. 2004) states that a premarital contract is also labeled as an *antenuptial* or *premarital* agreement.

There is general agreement that states vary widely on the approach to premarital agreements. Some states are extremely protective of the rights of potentially vulnerable parties to these contracts. Other states are extremely pro-enforcement.

| REFLECTIVE QUESTIONS | What are your goals for this chapter? |

13.2 HISTORY

Agreements made between parties contemplating marriage have existed in some form in almost every culture throughout the world for well over 2,000 years. Mary Lou Miller Wagstaff, *Premarital Agreements*, DMC FL-CLE 2-1, 2-2 (9th ed. 2010). For example, dowry contracts were executed by Middle Eastern tribal families. The concept "traveled to ancient Greece and later established its roots in European history as the familiar process whereby a woman's family negotiated with her intended husband's family to provide a certain amount of money, goods, animals, or land to the husband to be set aside so that the woman would not become impoverished in the event of a divorce or the husband's death." *Ibid.*

The ancient Jewish *ketubah*, which was entered into before the marriage, controlled the obligations of the parties to each other during the marriage. It also contained a provision for support in the event of a divorce. *Ibid.* Sephardic Jewish women are said to have carried their dowry with them in the form of jewelry sometimes covering almost every area of their bodies. In some parts of the Arab world the marriage contract requires that the husband give the wife *sadaq*, which is a material gift that becomes hers to keep to compensate for the fact that her husband can pronounce a divorce at any time. *See also* C.M.A. McCauliff, *The Medieval Origin of the Doctrine of Estates in Land: Substantive Property Law, Family Considerations, and the Interests of Women*, 66 Tul. L. Rev. 919 (1992).

Tudor England. Premarital contracts in somewhat the same form as we know them today appeared as early as the sixteenth-century Tudor period in England. Both the chancery and law courts passed on their validity, and they were of sufficient importance to be included in the original Statute of Frauds of 1677. *See generally Wilson v. Wilson*, 185 N.W. 97 (Iowa 1921).

Older United States view. Prior to the 1970s, a premarital contract in the United States was typically executed when the parties were contemplating a second marriage and one or both had substantial property and children from a first marriage to whom they wanted their property to go upon their deaths. A premarital contract prior to 1970 was strictly limited to the distribution of property at the time of the death of one of the parties to the relationship; one could never be used to cover the possibility of a divorce. *See* Judith T. Younger, *Perspectives on Antenuptial Contracts,* 40 Rutgers L. Rev. 1059, 1061 (1988).

Denigrate marriage. The early courts took the view that a premarital contract that contemplated and/or made provision for divorce violated public policy. They reasoned that the public's interest in the enforcement of the spousal duty of support should not be thwarted by a premarital provision that bore little or no reasonable relationship to the subsequent circumstance of the parties. Premarital contracts were also thought to denigrate marriage and encourage divorce. Furthermore, courts "questioned the quality of the bargaining process through which such agreements were reached, presuming that wives-to-be did not have the ability or presence of mind to provide contractual consent. Courts feared that women, confronted with the superior bargaining power of their husbands, would unwittingly contract away their right to support. . . ." Rachel S. Arnow-Richman, *Bargaining for Loyalty in the Information Age: A Reconsideration of the Role of Substantive Fairness in Enforcing Employee Noncompetes,* 80 Or. L. Rev. 1163, 1227-1228 (Winter 2001).

Modern view of use of premarital contracts. Premarital contract law began to change its view of the utility of such agreements upon divorce in the United States during the early 1970s, as evidenced by the Florida Supreme Court decision in *Posner v. Posner,* 233 So. 2d 381 (Fla. 1970). The *Posner* decision challenged the commonly accepted view that premarital contracts could not be used in contemplation of a possible future divorce. In concluding that they could be used upon divorce, the court reasoned that the ratio of marriages to divorces had reached a "disturbing rate," and divorce had become a commonplace fact of life. It stated that premarital contracts were no more likely to encourage divorce than premarital contracts made by parties in contemplation of death. After the *Posner* decision, jurisdictions throughout the United States began to retreat from the view that a premarital contract could only be enforced upon the death of a spouse. *See generally* Doris J. Freed & Timothy B. Walker, *Family Law in the Fifty States: An Overview,* 19 Fam. L.Q. 331, 438 (1985-1986).

REFLECTIVE QUESTIONS	What may explain the expansion of premarital contracts from use only upon death of a party to possible use at the time a couple divorce? What purpose did they serve when they were limited to application only following the death of a party?

13.3 CRITICAL CONCERNS

It has been observed that "premarital agreements are not neutral documents because they can be consciously used by either party to a marriage for the purpose of reaping financial gain" and may impact "gender dynamics, during and after marriage." Leah Guggenheimer, *A Modest Proposal: The Feminomics of Drafting Premarital Agreements*, 17 Women's Rts. L. Rep. 147, 148 (Spring 1996). A premarital contract has been described as "the world's most unromantic document." Margaret Ryznara & Anna Stepień-Sporek, *To Have and to Hold, for Richer or Richer: Premarital Agreements in the Comparative Context*, 13 Chap. L. Rev. 27 (Fall 2009). Premarital contracts envision "the end of a marriage not yet begun," and require that "prospective couples must divide property not yet acquired." *Ibid.* It is a time when the couple have strong positive thoughts about the relationship and its future, which is sometimes described as "blind optimism." Barbara A. Atwood & Brian H. Bix, *New Uniform Law for Premarital and Marital Agreements*, 46 Fam. L.Q. 313, 319 (Fall 2012). Often, the prospective couple understandably do not have a solid understanding of the law of marital property or spousal maintenance, particularly if they have not been married and previously divorced. Despite the lack of knowledge, the as yet unmarried couple "must select a legal framework governing their marriage and divorce" and lawyers "are often invited to participate in the negotiations, fuelling prospective spouses in their demands." Atwood & Bix, *supra.* For many, the process is simply too distasteful, and they forgo the opportunity to create a premarital contract. For others, the realization that a large percentage of marriages end in divorce is the catalyst driving them to insist on a premarital contract to protect their property interests should the relationship founder and a divorce occur.

Instruments of oppression? Professor Judith T. Younger has suggested that premarital agreements "attractive in theory as giving power to parties to craft their own bargains, are becoming instruments of oppression in practice." Judith T. Younger, *Lovers' Contracts in Courts: Forsaking the Minimum Decencies*, 13 Wm. & Mary J. Women & L. 349, 427 (2007). She has outlined several possible approaches to these agreements that should be considered if a just result is to be achieved.

First, she suggests that courts should consider enforcing "only those contracts for which both sides had independent representation." *Ibid.* Second, she suggests that courts and legislatures should consider enacting a rule for two kinds of contracts: agreements that leave dependent spouses on welfare and those that fail to provide for reasonable support for homemaker spouses. Using her approach, contracts leaving a spouse in either of these situations would be deemed unconscionable as a matter of law and therefore unenforceable. *Ibid.*

Third, she suggests that jurisdictions should consider requiring advance judicial approval at the time of execution of the contract. Approval would be based on a court's determination that the contract is in the best interests of the parties and that they understand the governing principles and rules. *Ibid.* Finally, she suggests that jurisdictions should cease to enforce these agreements altogether and use them only as advisory. *Ibid.*

REFLECTIVE QUESTIONS   **What problems, if any, do you see with Professor Younger's suggestions?**

13.4 EQUITABLE AND COMMUNITY PROPERTY SPOUSAL PROTECTION SCHEMES

States in the United States are divided into two marital property schemes that, absent a premarital agreement, generally protect a spouse from becoming impoverished when there is a divorce or a death. The majority of states apply an equitable distribution scheme, while nine states have adopted some form of a community property scheme.

Community property schemes to protect spouse. Community property schemes view the married partners as co-owners of the community property. Absent a premarital agreement, the community property scheme protects a partner from impoverishment at death or divorce, assuming that a community estate exists. When the marital community ends, each spouse owns an equal share of the community property. *See generally* Raymond C. O'Brien, *Integrating Marital Property into a Spouse's Elective Share*, 59 Cath. U. L. Rev. 617 (Spring 2010).

Equitable distribution protection of spouse. Equitable distribution schemes recognize a marriage as an economic partnership. Should a divorce occur, property is usually distributed on an equitable rather than an equal basis. A family court identifies with specificity the property owned by the parties, classifies it as marital or separate, and then divides the marital property either equally or according to equitable factors. *Nix v. Nix*, 341 S.E.2d 116, 118 (N.C. App. 1986).

Absent a premarital agreement, equitable distribution jurisdictions also protect a spouse from impoverishment upon the death of a partner. Most jurisdictions have adopted an elective-share statute that gives a surviving spouse an election when a partner dies. The survivor may take under either the decedent's will, if one exists, or renounce the will and take a fractional share of the decedent's estate.

REFLECTIVE QUESTIONS	Absent a premarital agreement, how have most states attempted to protect a divorced or surviving spouse from impoverishment?

13.5 REASONS FOR DRAFTING PREMARITAL CONTRACTS

There are many reasons given to explain why couples may draft a premarital contract that can be applied should they divorce or one of them dies. For example, it can be used as an estate planning tool or it can provide for children of a former marriage and effectuate a desire to pass certain property on to them. Some spouses may want to pass family heirlooms or the family business to members of the family, rather than to a nonfamily partner.

A premarital contract may play a psychological role of sorts by attempting to remove family and spousal doubts about the motive for a marriage, with the written document acting as assurance that the poorer partner is entering the marriage for love and not for money. It may minimize family tensions and ensure that adult children and other relatives are protected in the event of death or divorce. It may also be seen as requiring parties to discuss economic issues prior to marriage, which may help promote a stable marriage. In some instances, a party may have experienced an extraordinarily unhappy divorce and may believe that a premarital contract can help avoid the emotional trauma and financial costs that accompanied the former divorce should the new marriage fail.

Premarital contracts usually address the following issues:

1. Giving up any right (by inheritance or any other legal right) to take property from the deceased spouse's estate.
2. Giving up the right to dispute the will of a deceased spouse.
3. Giving up the right to claim ownership of specific property that would ordinarily be considered marital property in the event of a divorce.
4. Giving up the right to seek financial support from the other spouse in the event of a divorce.

REFLECTIVE QUESTIONS	**What are the strongest reasons supporting the use of a premarital contract? What are the weakest reasons for its use?**

13.6 ALIMONY: WAIVING

There is a split in authority among the states as to whether a premarital agreement may control the issue of alimony. Most states allow a waiver of alimony (alimony is also often referred to as "maintenance" or "support") if the waiver is explicit. A minority of jurisdictions refused to allow premarital contracts to control alimony, holding that provisions attempting to do so are void *per se*. Other jurisdictions allow a premarital contract to waive alimony but subjected the contract to a review for fairness at the time of enforcement. *See generally* Amberlynn Curry, *The Uniform Premarital Agreement Act and Its Variations Throughout the States*, 23 J. Am. Acad. Matrimonial Law. 355 (2010).

Comparing the approaches of Tennessee and South Dakota to premarital contracts may shed some light on the changing complexion of the question of whether alimony provisions in premarital contracts should be enforced. Tennessee, for example, allows a premarital contract to waive or limit alimony if entered into freely and knowledgeably, with adequate disclosure, without undue influence or overreaching. However, it will not enforce the contract at the time of a divorce if to do so makes the spouse a public charge. *Cary v. Cary*, 937 S.W.2d 777 (Tenn.

1996). On the other hand, South Dakota has held that provisions in a premarital agreement purporting to limit alimony obligations are against public policy and not enforceable. *Connolly v. Connolly*, 270 N.W.2d 44 (S.D. 1978). The South Dakota Supreme Court reasoned that conditions affecting a spouse's entitlement to alimony cannot accurately be foreseen and the public interest in a spouse's duty of support should not be thwarted by these agreements. The justices also felt that an alimony provision in a premarital agreement may bear no reasonable relationship to the subsequent situation of the parties, which made it void.

REFLECTIVE QUESTIONS	Should competent adults who voluntarily sign these contracts expect that courts will enforce them even if the provisions are significantly unfair to one of the parties?

13.7 BARRIERS TO USE: CHILDREN

Adult parties to a premarital agreement may contract regarding matters, including their personal rights and obligations, not in violation of public policy. Children, however, receive special protection.

Child support. All jurisdictions agree that the right of a child to support from a parent may not be adversely affected by a premarital agreement. Therefore, a provision in a premarital contract eliminating a party's potential future child support obligation is void as against public policy.

Child custody. Likewise, when determining child custody, the best interest of a child or children, rather than that of the parents, is a court's paramount concern. Children are seen as far more important than the subjects of alimony and property settlements, and courts believe that they have a duty to make an independent determination of custody. Consequently, a court cannot be bound by custody agreements entered into prior to marriage that govern custody of future-born children. Even if the premarital contract mandated joint custody, this provision may not affect a trial court's obligation to determine custody and parenting time in accordance with the best interests of the children. *See Edwardson v. Edwardson*, 798 S.W.2d 941, 946 (Ky. 1990).

REFLECTIVE QUESTIONS	Why shouldn't a court be bound by the terms of a premarital agreement regarding future children if the parties to the agreement are competent adults and voluntarily sign it?

13.8 BARRIERS TO USE: ESSENTIAL MARRIAGE OBLIGATIONS

Occasionally, a lawyer is asked to include provisions in a premarital contract that attempt to change the essential obligations of the marriage contract. Most courts see such provisions as contrary to public policy and unenforceable. The reason for the reticence to enforce this type of provision begins with the principle that when a marriage occurs, it creates a status in which the state is vitally interested and under which certain rights and duties incident to the relationship come into being, irrespective of the wishes of the parties.

For example, in *Graham v. Graham*, 33 F. Supp. 936 (D. Mich. 1940), the court refused to enforce an agreement declaring that the wife would pay the husband $300 a month during marriage to adjust financial matters between them so in the future there would be no arguments as to what money the husband would receive. In *Michigan Trust Co. v. Chapin*, 64 N.W. 334 (Mich. 1895), the court refused to enforce an agreement where the husband promised to pay his wife a specified sum per year for keeping house. In *Mirizio v. Mirizio*, 140 N.E. 605 (Mich. 1926), the court refused to enforce a provision in a premarital contract stating that the parties will not live together after marriage. An agreement to waive the right to defend against a future divorce action was held contrary to public policy in *McHugh v. McHugh*, 436 A.2d 8 (Conn. 1980).

Restatement. The Restatement of the Law of Contracts §587 declares that "a bargain between married persons or persons contemplating marriage to change the essential incidents of marriage such as to forgo sexual intercourse is not enforceable."

Criminal violations. Obviously, a premarital agreement cannot violate criminal laws. For example, a provision to supply a spouse with an illegal substance or to participate in a crime of some sort would be void.

Attorneys' fees. Public policy involving the use of premarital contracts may implicate attorneys' fees associated with a possible future divorce. For example, the South Dakota Supreme Court held in *Walker v. Walker*, 765 N.W.2d 747 (S.D. 2009), that a provision in a premarital agreement waiving attorneys' fees was contrary to public policy. It reached this decision by reasoning that it had earlier determined that public policy precluded a waiver of alimony in premarital agreements. *Sanford v. Sanford*, 694 N.W.2d 283, 293 (S.D. 2005). It viewed its decision precluding a waiver of attorneys' fees as a logical extension of its decision to not allow alimony to be waived.

| REFLECTIVE QUESTIONS | Why do courts refuse to uphold provisions in premarital contracts that go to the "essentials" of the marriage? What are some examples of the "essentials" of a marriage contract that courts refuse to enforce? |

13.9 BARRIERS TO USE: WAIVING RETIREMENT BENEFITS

The use of premarital agreements to waive retirement benefits implicates federal Law. For an effective waiver of retirement benefits, the waiver must comply with the Employee Retirement Income Security Act of 1974 (ERISA) and the Retirement Equity Act of 1984 (REA), 29 U.S.C. §1001 et seq. The REA amended ERISA to provide protection to spouses and dependents of employees and this act must be considered when addressing retirement benefits in premarital agreements.

Section 417(a)(2) of the Internal Revenue Code, as amended by REA, provides that a spouse may waive a right to a qualified plan benefit if the waiver meets the following requirements:

1. The waiver must be in writing;
2. The election must designate a beneficiary (or a form of benefits) that may not be changed without spousal consent, or the consent of the spouse expressly permits designations by the participant without any requirement of further consent by the spouse;
3. The spouse's consent must acknowledge the election's effect; and
4. The spouse's signature must be witnessed by a plan representative or a notary public.

29 U.S.C. §1055(c) (1988); IRC §417(a) (1988); *Hurwitz v. Sher*, 982 F.2d 778 (2d Cir. 1992).

REFLECTIVE QUESTIONS	What is the primary purpose of §417(a)(2) of the Internal Revenue Code?

13.10 COMPARING PREMARITAL AND COMMERCIAL CONTRACTS

There are clear differences between a premarital and commercial contract. First, the state has a greater interest in a premarital contract than in a commercial contract. Because of its interest, the state assumes the role of *parens patriae* with respect to protecting the children of the relationship and, in some cases, protecting the distribution of marital and nonmarital property. Judith T. Younger, *Perspectives on Antenuptial Contracts*, 40 Rutgers L. Rev. 1059, 1061 (1988). Second, at the time a premarital contract is made, courts view the relationship between the parties as confidential, not as an arms' length transaction. Third, in contrast to most business contracts, the parties to a premarital contract may be unevenly matched in bargaining power.

A premarital contract is also considered executory — that is, it is to be performed in the future — in the context of a personal relationship that the parties have yet to experience. It is possible that at some point in the future that changed circumstances may make enforcing the contract unfair. Furthermore, premarital contracts set aside otherwise applicable public policies while commercial agreements do not.

> **REFLECTIVE QUESTIONS** | What are the most significant differences between a premarital contract and a commercial contract?

13.11 CONSIDERATION

Because a premarital agreement is considered a contract, what is the consideration for executing it? The answer is that most courts today regard the marriage alone as consideration for the agreement. *See, e.g., Estate of Gillilan v. Estate of Gillilan*, 406 N.E.2d 981, 988 (Ind. App. 1980); *Friedlander v. Friedlander*, 494 P.2d 208, 300 (Wash. 1972); *Wilson v. Wilson*, 170 A.2d 679, 685 (Me. 1961). This does not mean the parties are not free to bargain for additional performance in return for their own promise to forgo certain financial advantages that would normally come with the marriage. *In re Estate of Thompson*, 812 N.W.2d 726 (Iowa 2012); *see Harllee v. Harllee*, 565 S.E.2d 678, 684 (N.C. App. 2002) (holding that additional consideration recited in the premarital agreement in the form of defendant's promise to pay plaintiff $10,000.00 subjected defendant to liability for breach); *see also Schultz v. Duitz*, 69 S.W.2d 27, 30 (Ky. App. 1934) ("A marriage contract may be supported by the mutual promise of the parties — the promise of one to marry the other. But if the contracting parties choose to pay or promise an additional consideration, they will be bound thereby just the same as in commercial transactions.").

UPAA. Under §2 of the Uniform Premarital Agreement Act (UPAA), a marriage is viewed as consideration for a premarital contract.

No consideration. In a growing number of states, a premarital contract may be created without consideration. For example, in Connecticut, consideration for a premarital agreement is not required. However, a premarital agreement must be in writing and both parties must sign. Conn. Gen. Stat. §46b-36c (2015). Likewise, after its execution, a premarital agreement can be amended or revoked, in a writing signed by both parties, with or without consideration. Conn. Gen. Stat. §46b-36f (2015). *See* Ill. 750 ILCS 10/3 (West 2010) (no consideration required).

<table>
<tr><td>REFLECTIVE QUESTIONS</td><td>Shouldn't the consideration for a premarital contract be something other than the marriage itself? Why have some states drafted statutes declaring that no consideration is required in order for a contract to be enforced?</td></tr>
</table>

13.12 COMPARED TO OTHER CONTRACTS: CONFIDENTIAL RELATIONSHIP

The question of whether a prospective spouse is in a confidential relationship when signing a premarital contract has received varying responses. Some jurisdictions presume the parties to be in a confidential relationship as a matter of law. *See, e.g., In re Estate of Kinney,* 733 N.W.2d 118 (Minn. 2007); *DeMatteo v. DeMatteo,* 762 N.E.2d 797, 810 (Mass. 2002). In other jurisdictions, a presumption does not exist. *See, e.g., In re Marriage of Bonds,* 5 P.3d 815, 831 (Cal. 2000); *Mallen v. Mallen,* 622 S.E.2d 812, 815 (Ga. 2005). Finally, a few jurisdictions determine whether a confidential relationship exists based on the specific facts of the case. *See, e.g., Butler v. Butler,* 347 A.2d 477, 480 (Pa. 1975).

Obviously, a court's view of a whether a confidential relationship exists is important. If a court finds or presumes that a confidential relationship existed at the time the contract was signed, it may make the following assumptions: First, the contract was not a typical arms' length contract transaction. Second, because it was not a typical arms' length transaction, the parties were in a fiduciary relationship. Finally, the fiduciaries were under a mandatory duty to act in good faith with a high degree of fairness and disclosure of all circumstances that materially bear on the premarital contract. *See, e.g., Gross v. Gross,* 464 N.E.2d 500, 509 (Ohio 1984).

<table>
<tr><td>REFLECTIVE QUESTIONS</td><td>What is the significance of a court finding that a confidential relationship existed at the time a premarital contract was signed?</td></tr>
</table>

Background to *Kline v. Kline*

Kline v. Kline provides a historical perspective on premarital contracts. It involves a premarital contract executed between Gabriel Kline and Ann Hendricks. The contract recited that Kline and Hendricks intended to marry and that Kline was seised of a dwelling-house and tract of land occupied by him and Hendricks and that he was "possessed of certain effects and property."

The contract stated that in case Kline died before Hendricks that she should have a life estate in the north end of the dwelling-house; the kitchen; one room and entry on the second floor; half the garret, cellar, and garden; and $40 per annum out of his estate. The contract was executed with Hendricks signing by her mark.

Following Kline's death, Ms. Hendricks challenged the contract, claiming Kline had not informed her of the true nature and extent of his property or her property rights in his property upon his death. Although the contract was read to Hendricks when it was executed, she did not speak English. At Kline's death, his personal estate amounted to $8,991.45; ten lots of real estate, that sold for $6,369; and the dwelling-house and lot, which were valued at $800.

The trial judge instructed the jury as follows:

> The question involved in this case is, whether an antenuptial agreement entered into between Gabriel Kline and the defendant, on the 21st of March 1850, is valid. It is contended by defendant, that a confidential relation existed between Gabriel Kline and her, and that it was incumbent on the plaintiffs to show that Gabriel Kline fully informed her of the amount and extent of the property owned by him before the execution of the agreement; otherwise there can be no recovery by the plaintiffs.

The judge also instructed the jury that

> [t]he woman was bound to exercise her judgment and take advantage of the opportunity that existed to obtain information; if she did not do so it was her own fault. The parties were dealing at arms' length. He was not bound to disclose to her the amount or value of his property.

This part of the jury instruction was challenged when it was given and is assigned as error on appeal.

KLINE
v.
KLINE

Supreme Court of Pennsylvania
57 Pa. 120 (1868)

SHARSWOOD, J. . . . There is perhaps no relation of life in which more unbounded confidence is reposed than in that existing between parties who are betrothed to each other. Especially does the woman place the most implicit trust in the truth and affection of him in whose keeping she is about to deposit the happiness of her future life. From him she has no secrets; she believes he has none from her.

To consider such persons as in the same category with buyers and sellers, and to say that they are dealing at arms' length, we think is a mistake. Surely when a man and woman are on the eve of marriage, and it is proposed between them, as in this instance, to enter into an antenuptial contract upon the subject of "the enjoyment and disposition of their respective estates," it is the duty of each to be frank and unreserved in the disclosure of all circumstances materially bearing on the contemplated agreement. . . .

If . . . this agreement was intended to debar the wife of all future right to any share of her husband's estate in case she survived him, it was a most unequal and unjust bargain. It holds out the idea in the recital that his only property was the house and lot he then occupied, while the jury might have inferred from the evidence that he was worth at that time ten times its value. It bestows on her a portion of the house for life, with her own household goods which she owned before marriage, and the small annuity of $40 a year or about 11 cents a day to feed and clothe her, to find medical attendance and nursing for her when sick, and to bury her decently when she died. If, as has happened, she should find herself a solitary widow, without children, at the advanced age of seventy, such a pittance leaves her to be an object of private charity or public relief.

To say that she was bound when the contract was proposed to exercise her judgment, that she ought to have taken advantage of the opportunity that existed to obtain information, and that if she did not do so it was her own fault, is to suggest what would be revolting to all the better feelings of woman's nature. To have instituted inquiries into the property and fortune of her betrothed, would have indicated that she was actuated by selfish and interested motives. She shrank back from the thought of asking a single question. She executed the paper without hesitation, and without inquiry. She believed that he would propose nothing but what was just, and she had a right to exercise that confidence. She lived with him seventeen years, for aught that appears, as an affectionate and faithful helpmeet, and no doubt largely assisted in accumulating the fortune—at least of $15,000—of which he died in possession according to the evidence.

We think there was error in the charge, and accordingly, the Judgment is reversed.

DISCUSSION QUESTIONS FOR *KLINE v. KLINE*

A. Why didn't the prospective wife in *Kline v. Kline* take advantage of the opportunity to obtain more information regarding the nature and extent of her future husband's property before she signed the premarital agreement? If she did not, is that a sufficient reason to void the contract? Does the fact that marriage was often characterized by courts during this period as involving "sacred obligations" play any role in how the court viewed the premarital relationship? *See generally* Note, *Wife's Right to Set Aside Voluntary Ante-Nuptial Conveyances*, 27 Harv. L. Rev. 474, 475 (1914).

B. In *Porreco v. Porreco*, 811 A.2d 566 (Pa. 2002), the court held that a husband's misrepresentation as to the value of the engagement ring made during the process of forming their premarital agreement did not constitute fraud. The majority stated there was no justifiable reliance by the wife on his statement about the value of the ring because she could have had the ring appraised before they married. The dissent asked: "She was 19, he was nearly 30 years older; was it unreasonable for her to believe what he told her?" Does this Pennsylvania decision overrule *Kline*? Or is it distinguishable? Do you agree with the dissent?

C. Assume for this hypothetical that the year is 1900. The decedent left a will in which he provided for the payment of $2,500 dollars to his wife pursuant to a premarital contract in which she waived all claims and rights in his estate. The premarital agreement was entered into 7 years prior to his death, when the widow was 56 and the deceased 76. The widow was illiterate and unable to speak English, and executed the agreement by making a mark. The parties appeared at a synagogue before the marriage ceremony was performed and a Hebrew teacher prepared the contract. The widow contends that she did not understand what she was doing and that no information was given or statement made to her showing the value of her husband's estate. However, she admitted that she knew her late husband owned a house in which they subsequently lived, but she denied that she was aware that he owned any personal property other than a small undertaker business. The deceased's property, all of which is to go to his son under the terms of the premarital contract, is valued at about $10,000. Should (could) a court void the contract? *See In re Gorback's Estate*, 96 Super. 527 (Pa. Super. 1929); *Serbus v. Serbus*, 324 N.W.2d 381 (Minn. 1982).

D. Assume for this hypothetical that the year is 2012 and both parties were represented by counsel prior to their marriage. They executed a premarital contract after two weeks of negotiation. Under the terms of the contract, Husband would pay Wife a lump sum amount according to the length of the marriage. If the divorce occurred after 5 years but before 10 years from the date of marriage, Husband would pay Wife $250,000; if the divorce occurred after 10 years but before 15 years of marriage, he would pay her $500,000; if the divorce occurred after 15 years of marriage, he would pay her $500,000, plus a percentage of his gross salary over a period of 4 years. After 15 years of marriage, the Wife moved out to live with a neighbor with whom she had fallen in love. Divorce proceedings were instigated. Wife challenged the premarital agreement on the ground her Husband failed to disclose a beneficial interest in his deceased father's trust, which at trial was estimated to be worth $1 million dollars. Two issues are presented to the court. First, should evidence that the divorce is W's fault be allowed at trial on the question of the validity of the contract? Or, to reduce the amount of money to be paid per the agreement? Second, should the court void the premarital agreement because of fraud, that is, the failure to disclose the trust? *See Griffin v. Griffin*, 94 P.3d 96 (Okla. App. 2004).

13.13 PROCEDURE: CAPACITY

The parties to a premarital agreement must have the capacity to execute it. This means that they must be of legal age and possess sufficient mental capacity to be considered legally competent. A premarital agreement made by a person without the requisite capacity will not be enforced. *See generally Crosby v. Crosby*, 362 P.2d 3 (Kan. 1961).

Presumption. A person is presumed to be competent at the time a premarital contract is signed, and the burden of proving incompetence rests with the party asserting incapacity. *Dornemann v. Dornemann*, 850 A.2d 273, 282 (Conn. 2004); *Estate of Obermeier*, 540 N.Y.S.2d 613 (N.Y.A.D. 1989). The test for capacity is generally a determination of whether the individual was unable to comprehend the nature of the transaction and make a rational judgment with respect to the transaction. *See In re Estate of Menahem*, 847 N.Y.S.2d 903 (N.Y. Sur. Ct. 2007).

 **REFLECTIVE QUESTIONS** | **If a person is considered competent at the time a premarital contract is executed, doesn't that imply the contract was voluntary? If so, is the section immediately following in this chapter that considers voluntariness necessary?**

13.14 PROCEDURE: VOLUNTARILY EXECUTED

When deciding whether a premarital agreement was voluntarily executed, a court will examine all of the facts and circumstances surrounding its execution. In *In re Marriage of Bonds*, 5 P.3d 815 (Cal. 2000) (superseded by statute as indicated in *In re Marriage of Cadwell-Faso and Faso*, 119 Cal. Rptr. 3d 818 (Cal. App. 2011)), the court identified the following factors that a court might consider when deciding whether a contract was signed voluntarily:

(1) Coercion that may arise from the proximity of execution of the agreement to the wedding, or from surprise in the presentation of the agreement.
(2) The presence or absence of independent counsel or of an opportunity to consult independent counsel.
(3) Inequality of bargaining power — in some cases indicated by the relative age and sophistication of the parties.
(4) Whether there was full disclosure of assets.
(5) The extent of the parties' understanding of the rights being waived under the agreement or at least their awareness of the intent of the agreement.

> | REFLECTIVE QUESTIONS | Would you eliminate any of the factors listed above? Would you add any factors to the list? |

13.15 PROCEDURE: STANDARD PREMARITAL CONTRACT REQUIREMENTS

Generally, any kind of property right that would accrue by virtue of marriage, including equitable distribution rights and testamentary rights, may be waived by a premarital contract absent a state statute to the contrary. In most jurisdictions, the following are typical legal requirements that must be met to ensure the validity of a premarital contract.

1. The contract must be in writing.
2. Both parties must enter into the contract only after full disclosure of holdings.
3. The parties must intend that the contract be a full discharge of rights of inheritance from the estate of the other and a waiver of any marital rights, should the couple divorce.
4. There must be fair consideration in exchange for the waiver of rights of inheritance or other statutory rights.
5. Additionally, case law seems to require that each spouse be advised by a separate attorney regarding his or her rights and liabilities under such a contract, or, at a minimum, have the opportunity to do so.

> | REFLECTIVE QUESTIONS | Which of the five factors listed above is the most important? Would you add anything to the list? Delete anything from the list? |

Background to *Lawrence v. Lawrence*

The following case is technical in the sense that it was chosen for discussion because of a question about how many witnesses are needed to properly execute a premarital contract under a Georgia statute. It is intended to stimulate discussion about some of the practical issues a lawyer faces when gathering the parties in his or her office to sign the premarital contract. Without a statute, it appears there is no formal requirement for a notary or witnesses to be present. C.J.S., *Husband and Wife* §61. However, even if there is no such requirement, many lawyers suggest premarital contracts should be executed with formalities similar to executing a will. Furthermore, some lawyers suggest a court reporter should be present to record the proceeding with a videotape showing execution of the agreement with the lawyers asking the parties relevant questions.

LAWRENCE
v.
LAWRENCE

Supreme Court of Georgia
687 S.E.2d 421 (2009)

NAHMIAS, J. . . . [Georgia law states that] "[e]very marriage contract in writing, made in contemplation of marriage, . . . must be attested by at least two witnesses." Ms. Lawrence correctly notes that the antenuptial agreement was attested by only one witness and claims that it is therefore void.

This Court has repeatedly recognized that an antenuptial agreement that purports to settle alimony issues is classified under Georgia law as a contract "made in contemplation of divorce," not a contract "made in contemplation of marriage." *Dove v. Dove*, 647, 680 S.E.2d 839 (2009). The distinction may seem somewhat semantic, but it is well established in the law of Georgia and the rest of the nation. As a leading treatise on the law of contracts explains:

> Historically, the validity of premarital agreements often depended upon whether they were to be effective only upon death or also upon divorce, perhaps most courts taking the view that an antenuptial agreement which contemplated and made provision for divorce thereby violated public policy, while one which only encompassed provision for property interests during marriage or upon death did not.

5 Williston on Contracts §11:8. While all states now hold that agreements in contemplation of divorce do not necessarily violate public policy, the distinction between agreements in contemplation of divorce and agreements in contemplation of marriage or death has continued.

The antenuptial agreement in this case addresses alimony. Moreover, it refers explicitly to the possibility of divorce, explaining that the parties want the agreement to govern in that event:

> While the parties hereto contemplate a lasting marriage, terminated only by the death of one of the parties hereto, they also recognize the unfortunate possibility that their marriage might be terminated by way of divorce or other dissolution during the lifetime of both parties as both parties hereto have had previous divorces from other spouses, and both parties hereto recognize and readily accept the potential frailty of their relationship. In the event of such a dissolution or termination of their marriage during the lifetime of both parties by way of divorce or other dissolution, . . .

Consequently, the antenuptial agreement at issue is clearly a contract made in contemplation of divorce, not a contract made in contemplation of marriage. As such, it is not subject to the dual attestation requirement of OCGA §19-3-63. . . . Accordingly, the trial court did not err in upholding the validity of the antenuptial agreement against the challenge under OCGA §19-3-63.

| DISCUSSION QUESTIONS | FOR *LAWRENCE v. LAWRENCE* |

A. The court distinguishes between contracts made in contemplation of marriage and those made in contemplation of divorce. Do you agree with the court's distinction? Is the answer that antenuptial agreements relating to issues settling property rights at death are made in contemplation of marriage, because such agreements are considered to be an inducement to marriage? Is the fact here that the antenuptial agreement specifically addressed alimony, and explicitly referred to the possibility of divorce, make it a contract "made in contemplation of divorce," rather than in contemplation of marriage? If so, is this a distinction worth retaining?

B. Assume for this hypothetical that a jurisdiction enacts a statute that reads as follows:

> An antenuptial contract must be in writing, executed in the presence of two witnesses and acknowledged by the parties, executing the same before any officer or person authorized to administer an oath under the laws of this state.

Assume that H and W execute such an agreement prior to their marriage. After ten years, they begin divorce proceedings. At the trial, W challenges the premarital agreement on the ground that only one person witnessed the agreement. W argues that the absence of a second witness makes the antenuptial agreement, on its face, invalid and unenforceable. H argues that two persons witnessed the agreement, that is: First, the one person both agree was there as a witness. Second, the notary who notarized the signature of the witness and that of each party. Should H or W prevail? *See Siewert v. Siewert*, 691 N.W.2d 504 (Minn. App. 2005).

C. Assume the hypothetical facts outlined in B above. Also assume that H argues that the statute does not preclude the parties from serving as each other's witness. W contends that the statute requires "independent" witnesses. Who has the better argument?

13.16 PROCEDURE: FULL AND FAIR DISCLOSURE OF ASSETS

As observed earlier, courts in a majority of jurisdictions regard the parties to a premarital contract as having a confidential relationship of mutual trust that demands the exercise of the highest degree of good faith, candor, and sincerity in all matters bearing on the proposed agreement. *See, e.g., Cannon v. Cannon*, 865 A.2d 563 (Md. 2005); *Rosenberg v. Lipnick*, 389 N.E.2d 385, 388 (Mass. 1979); *Wiley v. Iverson*, 985 P.2d 1176 (Mont. 1999). In these jurisdictions, the courts take the position that the burden is not on either party to inquire into the others assets; rather, the burden is on each party to inform the other prospective partner of existing assets.

A minority of jurisdictions treat the parties as involved in an arms' length relationship on the theory that parties who are not yet married are not presumed to share a confidential relationship. *See, e.g., DeLorean v. DeLorean*, 511 A.2d 1257 (N.J. Super. 1986), *quoting In re Marriage of Dawley*, 551 P.2d 323, 355 (Cal. 1976). These jurisdictions impose a duty on each spouse to inquire and investigate the financial condition of the other making the disclosure requirement less demanding.

General knowledge insufficient. Most jurisdictions place a duty on each party to a premarital contract to disclose the amount, character, and value of individually owned property. However, the nature and extent of that disclosure differs from jurisdiction to jurisdiction. For example, some courts take the view that general knowledge of a party's financial condition is not sufficient to satisfy the obligation of full disclosure generated by the confidential relationship between prospective spouses. *Schumacher v. Schumacher*, 388 N.W.2d 912 (Wis. 1986); *McHugh v. McHugh*, 436 A.2d 8 (Conn. 1980); *Friedlander v. Friedlander*, 494 P.2d 208 (Wash. 1972).

General knowledge sufficient. Other jurisdictions appear to accept the view that general knowledge of another's wealth and assets is sufficient to validate a premarital agreement. For example, in *Harbom v. Harbom*, 760 A.2d 272 (Md. App. 2000), the court said that the disclosure need not be a drastically sweeping one, and the wife need not know the husband's exact means so long as she has a general idea of his property and resources. In *Pajak v. Pajak*, 385 S.E.2d 384 (W. Va. 1989), the court said that it is sufficient if the party against whom the agreement is to be enforced had a general idea of the other party's financial condition and there was no fraud or concealment that had the effect of inducing the party into entering an agreement that otherwise would not have been made. *See Laird v. Laird*, 597 P.2d 463 (Wyo. 1979); *In re Estate of Lopata*, 641 P.2d 952, 955 (Colo. 1982); *In re Estate of Thies*, 903 P.2d 186 (Mont. 1995).

Contracts before an engagement. When considering the validity of premarital contracts, some courts may distinguish between contracts executed before a formal engagement and those executed after a formal engagement. For example, in *In re Sokolowski*, 597 N.E.2d 675 (Ill. App. 1992), the court upheld the contract because (1) there was no fraud, duress, or coercion; (2) the subsequent marriage was sufficient consideration; and (3) because the parties were not engaged to be married until after the agreement was signed. The Tennessee Supreme Court has held that because an engagement to marry creates a confidential relationship between the contracting parties, a premarital agreement entered into after the engagement must be attended by the utmost good faith. *Baker v. Baker*, 142 S.W.2d 737, 748 (1940).

REFLECTIVE QUESTIONS	Is the distinction discussed by the Illinois court in *Sokolowski* sound?

13.17 PROCEDURE: THE NECESSITY OF COUNSEL

Among factors considered in a court's procedural fairness determination of a premarital contract is whether independent counsel represented each party at the time it was executed. A majority of jurisdictions consider the absence of independent counsel as one factor among many when deciding whether to enforce a premarital contract. *See, e.g., In re Estate of Kinney*, 733 N.W.2d 118, 124 (Minn. 2007); *In re Estate of Lutz*, 563 N.W.2d 90, 98 (N.D. 1997).

A typical example of how a majority of courts approach their analysis of a premarital contract where only one party is represented is *Panossian v. Panossian*, 569 N.Y.S.2d 182 (N.Y.A.D. 1991). In that case, the court ruled that the absence of independent counsel did not warrant setting aside the contract being challenged by the wife. The court found that the lawyer selected by the husband, who prepared the premarital contract, provided the parties with a copy of the document, and read each of the provisions aloud prior to its execution. At the trial where the contract was challenged, the wife stated that she had willingly signed the contract in consideration of her husband's wishes, and acknowledged that she was aware that the portent of the agreement was that neither party would request anything from the other in case of divorce. The court found the record devoid of any evidence of coercion or undue influence exercised on the part of the attorney.

Another example is *In re Marriage of Bonds*, 5 P.3d 815 (Cal. 2000). In that case a foreign-born, unrepresented wife signed a premarital contract on the eve of her wedding to major league baseball player Barry Bonds. The wife waived all her rights to community property. The marriage broke down after seven years, and at their divorce trial, the wife challenged the voluntariness of the premarital contract. The California Supreme Court found the agreement voluntary and criticized the intermediate appellate court, which had ruled the contract was entered involuntarily. The California Supreme Court said the lower court had given too much weight to Mrs. Bonds's lack of representation when the contract was signed.

Following the court's decision in *Bonds*, the California legislature amended that state's law declaring that a premarital agreement will be deemed involuntary unless the court makes certain specified findings, including a finding that the challenger was represented by independent counsel at execution of the agreement or, after being advised to consult independent counsel, executed a written waiver of such representation. *See* Cal. Fam. Code §1615(c)(1) (2015.) To validate the contract, a court must also find that an unrepresented challenger was fully informed of the terms and basic effect of the agreement as well as the rights and obligations he or she was giving up by signing. The California statute also requires a writing signed by an unrepresented challenger stating that the terms and effect of the agreement were explained to her and naming the person who gave the explanation.

The Washington Supreme Court has held that when a premarital contract is executed and it is "patently unreasonable," independent counsel is required. *In re Estate of Crawford*, 730 P.2d 675 (Wash. 1986). The court also placed the responsibility on the represented party's attorney to advise the unrepresented party of the wisdom of obtaining independent counsel.

The West Virginia Supreme Court explained the value of a lawyer representing each party when a contract was executed in *Gant v. Gant*, 385 S.E.2d 384 (W. Va. 1989). It wrote:

> Advice of independent counsel at the time parties enter into a prenuptial agreement helps demonstrate that there has been no fraud, duress or misrepresentation, and that the agreement was entered into knowledgeably and voluntarily, [but] such independent advice of counsel is not a prerequisite to enforceability when the terms of the agreement are understandable to a reasonably intelligent adult and both parties have had the opportunity to consult with independent counsel.

REFLECTIVE QUESTIONS	Why shouldn't states require independent counsel for both parties before a premarital contract can be upheld? Shouldn't states also require a court to approve the agreement before it can go into effect?

13.18 PROCEDURE: SUFFICIENT TIME TO REVIEW CONTRACT

The amount of time a party has to review a premarital contract is another factor that courts will consider when deciding whether to uphold it. For example, in *Gordon v. Gordon*, 25 So. 3d 615 (Fla. App. 2009), the contract was presented to the prospective wife ten days prior to the wedding. The court ruled that she was not subjected to duress, coercion, or overreaching, finding that ten days prior to the marriage was sufficient time for the wife to exercise the opportunity to review the agreement and to seek the advice of legal counsel if she chose to do so. It also observed that the wife had a high level of education and business acumen, and, having twice married, she understood the significance of the document she was about to sign and chose not to seek the advice of a lawyer.

However, in *Pember v. Shapiro*, 794 N.W.2d 435 (N.D. 2011), the court found that over a five-hour period the parties were pressed to execute an entire premarital agreement from scratch, complete the wedding ceremony with the justice of the peace, eat lunch, and get to a bank before it closed. The court stated:

> While this hectic schedule in itself does not invalidate the agreement's enforceability, it is a strong indicator of the haphazard manner in which this agreement was put

together. The parties' hurriedly gave a lawyer, hired by the wife, information for the agreement. The wife testified she couldn't remember whether any modifications were made after it was drafted, but the husband said there were none. Further, when the wife was asked whether she had discussed her premarital property with her husband beforehand, she testified, "I didn't actually talk to Dale about it. I just signed the contract." The husband told the court he did not understand the agreement when it was signed or when asked about it at trial.

Id. at 447. The court concluded that because of the confusion surrounding the unfamiliar and inflexible terms in the agreement, and its rapid formation and execution, the parties were unable to give proper consent as required under North Dakota law.

The premarital agreement was voided in *Faiman v. Faiman*, 2008 WL 5481382 (Conn. Super. 2008). The agreement had been prepared by the wife's future husband's attorney, and the first time she saw the final draft was minutes before she was asked to sign it. This was only three days before the wedding. *See also McHugh v. McHugh*, 436 A.2d 8 (Conn. 1980).

In *Hoag v. Dick*, 799 A.2d 391 (Me. 2002), a premarital agreement was held invalid when it was presented to wife on her wedding day. The court concluded that under the circumstances, she was deprived of any opportunity to obtain advice from independent legal counsel.

Size and formality of wedding. The Ohio Supreme Court considers the size and formality of the impending wedding important. In *Fletcher v. Fletcher*, 628 N.E.2d 1343 (Ohio 1994), it said that where the impending wedding is small and informal, it is reasonable for the trial court to conclude that the wedding could have been postponed to allow for consultation with an attorney regarding the proposed premarital contract.

REFLECTIVE QUESTIONS	Why shouldn't all states enact a statute that voids any premarital contract that is not finalized and signed at least two weeks before a wedding?

13.19 ENFORCEMENT ISSUES: UNCONSCIONABLE CONTRACTS

The following is a list of factors considered relevant in most jurisdictions to determine whether a premarital contract is unconscionable at the time it was executed: (1) the disadvantaged party's opportunity to seek independent counsel; (2) the relative sophistication of the parties in legal and financial matters; (3) the temporal proximity between the introduction of the premarital agreement and the wedding date; (4) the use of highly technical or confusing language or fine print; and (5) the use of fraudulent or deceptive practices to procure the disadvantaged party's assent to the agreement. *In re Marriage of Shanks*, 758 N.W.2d 506, 517-518 (Iowa 2008); *Marsh v. Marsh*, 949 S.W.2d 734, 741 (Tex. App. 1997).

In *Peters-Riemers v. Riemers*, 644 N.W.2d 197 (N.D. 2002), the court held a premarital agreement unconscionable for the following reasons: (1) It was given to the wife only three days before the marriage. (2) The wife did not have the benefit of independent legal advice prior to signing the agreement. She was required to read the agreement in the same room, at the same table, where her husband and his attorney sat, causing a coercive environment. Her reading of the agreement was cursory, and her understanding of its consequences limited. (3) The husband failed to provide his wife with a fair and reasonable disclosure of his property and financial obligations and evidenced an "abject disability" to make honest financial disclosures. For example, he disclosed a "net worth" of $473,724 in the premarital agreement. However, just a matter of months earlier, on loan applications, he had disclosed a net worth of $1,341,500, $683,683, and $706,178.

Short period of support. According to the Kentucky Supreme Court, the fact that a premarital contract provides for a very short period of alimony should the parties divorce does not make the contract unconscionable on its face. *Gentry v. Gentry*, 798 S.W.2d 928 (Ky. 1990). The court stated that the short period of support suggested that the parties did not foresee a lengthy marriage.

REFLECTIVE QUESTIONS	What are the most important factors a court will consider when deciding whether a premarital contract is unconscionable?

13.20 ENFORCEMENT ISSUES: REASONABLENESS OF PREMARITAL CONTRACTS

Background to *Simeone v. Simeone*

Simeone v. Simeone, 581 A.2d 162, 167 (1990), expresses a minority perspective on premarital contracts. It is widely discussed and is included here to provide an opportunity to compare its view with those of a majority of jurisdictions. The court in this case decided that Pennsylvania would no longer inquire into whether the terms of the premarital agreement were fair or whether the parties had informed understandings of the rights they were surrendering. The court concluded that challenges to premarital contracts would be the same as those available for conventional contract agreements, that is, duress, unconscionability, and misrepresentation. In its opinion, the court rejects earlier Pennsylvania decisions that had suggested that premarital contracts would be approved only if they either "made an adequate provision for [a spouse]" or provided for "full and fair disclosure [of the] general financial pictures of the parties [and] the statutory rights [being relinquished]." Howard Fink & June Carbon, *Between Private Ordering and Public Fiat: A New Paradigm for Family Law Decision-Making*, 5 J.L. & Fam. Stud. 1, 20-21 (2003).

SIMEONE
v.
SIMEONE

Supreme Court of Pennsylvania
581 A.2d 162 (1990)

FLAHERTY, J. . . . At the time of their marriage, in 1975, appellant was a twenty-three year old nurse and appellee was a thirty-nine year old neurosurgeon. Appellee had an income of approximately $90,000 per year, and appellant was unemployed. Appellee also had assets worth approximately $300,000. On the eve of the parties' wedding, appellee's attorney presented appellant with a premarital agreement to be signed. Appellant, without the benefit of counsel, signed the agreement. Appellee's attorney had not advised appellant regarding any legal rights that the agreement surrendered. The parties are in disagreement as to whether appellant knew in advance of that date that such an agreement would be presented for signature. Appellant denies having had such knowledge and claims to have signed under adverse circumstances, which, she contends, provide a basis for declaring it void.

The agreement limited appellant to support payments of $200 per week in the event of separation or divorce, subject to a maximum total payment of $25,000. The parties separated in 1982, and, in 1984, divorce proceedings were commenced. Between 1982 and 1984 appellee made payments which satisfied the $25,000 limit. In 1985, appellant filed a claim for alimony *pendente lite.* A master's report upheld the validity of the premarital agreement and denied this claim. Exceptions to the master's report were dismissed by the Court of Common Pleas of Philadelphia County. The Superior Court affirmed. *Simeone v. Simeone*, 380 Pa. Super. 37, 551 A.2d 219 (1988).

. . . The present agreement did expressly state . . . that alimony *pendente lite* was being relinquished. It also recited that appellant "has been informed and understands" that, were it not for the agreement, appellant's obligation to pay alimony *pendente lite* "might, as a matter of law, exceed the amount provided." Hence, appellant's claim is not that the agreement failed to disclose the particular right affected, but rather that she was not adequately informed with respect to the nature of alimony *pendente lite.* . . .

[Former premarital contract] decisions [by this court] rested upon a belief that spouses are of unequal status and that women are not knowledgeable enough to understand the nature of contracts that they enter. Society has advanced, however, to the point where women are no longer regarded as the "weaker" party in marriage, or in society generally. Indeed, the stereotype that women serve as homemakers while men work as breadwinners is no longer viable. Quite often today both spouses are income earners. Nor is there viability in the presumption that women are uninformed, uneducated, and readily subjected to unfair advantage in marital agreements. Indeed, women nowadays quite often have substantial education, financial awareness, income, and assets.

. . . [T]he law has advanced to recognize the equal status of men and women in our society. *See, e.g.*, Pa. Const. art. 1, §28 (constitutional prohibition of sex discrimination in laws of the Commonwealth). Paternalistic presumptions and protections that arose to shelter women from the inferiorities and incapacities which they were perceived as having in earlier times have, appropriately, been discarded. . . .

Contracting parties are normally bound by their agreements, without regard to whether the terms thereof were read and fully understood and irrespective of whether the agreements embodied reasonable or good bargains. . . . Based upon these principles, the terms of the present premarital agreement must be regarded as binding, without regard to whether the terms were fully understood by appellant.

[W]e find no merit in a contention raised by appellant that the agreement should be declared void on the ground that she did not consult with independent legal counsel. To impose a per se requirement that parties entering a premarital agreement must obtain independent legal counsel would be contrary to traditional principles of contract law, and would constitute a paternalistic and unwarranted interference with the parties' freedom to enter contracts.

Further, the reasonableness of a premarital bargain is not a proper subject for judicial review. . . . [E]arlier decisions required that, at least where there had been an inadequate disclosure made by the parties, the bargain must have been reasonable at its inception. . . . Some have even suggested that prenuptial agreements should be examined with regard to whether their terms remain reasonable at the time of dissolution of the parties' marriage.

By invoking inquiries into reasonableness, however, the functioning and reliability of prenuptial agreements is severely undermined. Parties would not have entered such agreements, and, indeed, might not have entered their marriages, if they did not expect their agreements to be strictly enforced. If parties viewed an agreement as reasonable at the time of its inception, as evidenced by their having signed the agreement, they should be foreclosed from later trying to evade its terms by asserting that it was not in fact reasonable. Pertinently, the present agreement contained a clause reciting that "each of the parties considers this agreement fair, just and reasonable." . . .

Further, everyone who enters a long-term agreement knows that circumstances can change during its term, so that what initially appeared desirable might prove to be an unfavorable bargain. Such are the risks that contracting parties routinely assume. Certainly, the possibilities of illness, birth of children, reliance upon a spouse, career change, financial gain or loss, and numerous other events that can occur in the course of a marriage cannot be regarded as unforeseeable. If parties choose not to address such matters in their prenuptial agreements, they must be regarded as having contracted to bear the risk of events that alter the value of their bargains.

We are reluctant to interfere with the power of persons contemplating marriage to agree upon, and to act in reliance upon, what they regard as an acceptable distribution scheme for their property. A court should not ignore the parties' expressed intent by proceeding to determine whether a prenuptial agreement was, in the court's view, reasonable at the time of its inception or the time of divorce. These are exactly the sorts of judicial determinations that such agreements are designed to avoid. Rare indeed is the agreement that is beyond possible challenge when reasonableness is placed at issue. . . .

. . . [W]e do not depart from the longstanding principle that a full and fair disclosure of the financial positions of the parties is required. Absent this disclosure, a material misrepresentation in the inducement for entering a prenuptial agreement may be asserted. Parties to these agreements do not quite deal at arms' length, but rather at the time the contract is entered into stand in a relation of mutual confidence and trust that calls for disclosure of their financial resources. . . . It is well settled that this disclosure need not be exact, so long as it is "full and fair." In essence therefore, the duty of disclosure under these circumstances is consistent with traditional principles of contract law.

Appellant's final contention is that the agreement was executed under conditions of duress in that it was presented to her at 5 P.M. on the eve of her wedding, a time when she could not seek counsel without the trauma, expense, and embarrassment of postponing the wedding. . . .

Although appellant testified that she did not discover until the eve of her wedding that there was going to be a prenuptial agreement, testimony from a number of other witnesses was to the contrary. Appellee testified that, although the final version of the agreement was indeed presented to appellant on the eve of the wedding, he had engaged in several discussions with appellant regarding the contents of the agreement during the six-month period preceding that date. Another witness testified that appellant mentioned, approximately two or three weeks before the wedding that she was going to enter a prenuptial agreement. Yet another witness confirmed that, during the months preceding the wedding, appellant participated in several discussions of prenuptial agreements. And the legal counsel who prepared the agreement for appellee testified that, prior to the eve of the wedding, changes were made in the agreement to increase the sums payable to appellant in the event of separation or divorce. He also stated that he was present when the agreement was signed and that appellant expressed absolutely no reluctance about signing. It should be noted, too, that during the months when the agreement was being discussed appellant had more than sufficient time to consult with independent legal counsel if she had so desired. . . . Order affirmed.

The concurring opinion of Mr. Justice Papadakos is not included.

McDERMOTT, J., dissenting. . . . Let me begin by setting forth a common ground between my position in this matter and that of the majority. There can be no question that, in the law and in society, men and women must be accorded equal status. I am in full agreement with the majority's observation that "women nowadays quite often have substantial education, financial awareness, income, and assets." However, the plurality decision I authored in *Estate of Geyer*, 516 Pa. 492, 533 A.2d 423 (1987), as well as the Dissenting Opinion I offer today, have little to do with the equality of the sexes, but everything to do with the solemnity of the matrimonial union. I am not willing to believe that our society views marriage as a mere contract for hire. On the contrary, our Legislature has set forth the public policy which must guide this Court:

"The family is the basic unit of society and the protection of the family is of paramount public concern." In this Commonwealth, we have long declared our interest in the stability of marriage and in the stability of the family unit. Our courts must seek to protect, and not to undermine, those institutions and interests which are vital to our society. . . .

In my view, one seeking to avoid the operation of an executed pre-nuptial agreement must first establish, by clear and convincing evidence, that a full and fair disclosure of the worth of the intended spouse was not made at the time of the execution of the agreement. This Court has recognized that full and fair disclosure is needed because, at the time of the execution of a pre-nuptial agreement, the parties do not stand in the usual arms' length posture attendant to most other types of contractual undertakings, but "stand in a relation of mutual confidence and trust that calls for the highest degree of good faith. . . ." In addition to a full and fair disclosure of the general financial pictures of the parties, I would find a pre-nuptial agreement voidable where it is established that the parties were not aware, at the time of contracting, of existing statutory rights which they were relinquishing upon the signing of the agreement. It is here, with a finding of full and fair disclosure, that the majority would end its analysis of the validity of a pre-nuptial agreement. I would not. . . .

At the time of dissolution of the marriage, a spouse should be able to avoid the operation of a pre-nuptial agreement upon clear and convincing proof that, despite the existence of full and fair disclosure at the time of the execution of the agreement, the agreement is nevertheless so inequitable and unfair that it should not be enforced in a court of this state. Although the spouse attempting to avoid the operation of the agreement will admittedly have a difficult burden given the standard of proof, and the fact of full and fair disclosure, we must not close our courts to relief where to enforce an agreement will result in unfairness and inequity. The majority holds to the view, without waiver, that parties, having contracted with full and fair disclosure, should be made to suffer the consequences of their bargains. In so holding, the majority has given no weight to the other side of the scales: the state's paramount interest in the preservation of marriage and the family relationship, and the protection of parties to a marriage who may be rendered wards of the state, unable to provide for their own reasonable needs. Our sister states have found such treatment too short a shrift for so fundamental a unit of society.

Thus, I believe that the door should remain open for a spouse to avoid the application of a pre-nuptial agreement where clear and convincing proof establishes that the result will be inequity and unfairness under the circumstances of the particular case and the public policy of this state. I would emphasize that there are circumstances at the inception of marriage that render a pre-nuptial agreement not only fair and equitable, but a knowing and acceptable reservation of ownership. Such are usually the circumstances surrounding a second marriage. One coming to a second marriage may reserve property created in a previous union, to satisfy what they think a proper and just disposition of that property should be, for children of that prior marriage, or other relations or obligations they feel it a duty to observe. Likewise, one of wealth or property entering a marriage need stake no more on its success than what is fair and reasonable independent of the value of their wealth. That is to say that one's previous wealth is not in itself a criterion of fairness. One is not required to give all they brought for an agreement to be reasonable. So too may one properly reserve things given them as heirlooms, or things of peculiar meaning expressly stated, so long as their value is not increased or preserved as a result of efforts or sacrifice by the union. . . .

It is also apparent that, although a pre-nuptial agreement is quite valid when drafted, the passage of time accompanied by the intervening events of a marriage, may render the terms of the agreement completely unfair and inequitable. While parties to a pre-nuptial agreement may indeed foresee, generally, the events which may come to pass during their marriage, one spouse should not be made to suffer for failing to foresee all of the surrounding circumstances which may attend the dissolution of the marriage. Although it should not be the role of the courts to void pre-nuptial agreements merely because one spouse may receive a better result in an action under the Divorce Code to recover alimony or equitable distribution, it should be the role of the courts to guard against the enforcement of pre-nuptial agreements where such enforcement will bring about only inequity and hardship. It borders on cruelty to accept that after years of living together, yielding their separate opportunities in life to each other, that two individuals emerge the same as the day they began their marriage. . . .

The majority is concerned that parties will routinely challenge the validity of their pre-nuptial agreements. Given the paramount importance of marriage and family in our society, and the serious consequences that may accompany the dissolution of a marriage, we should not choose to close the doors of our courts merely to gain a measure of judicial economy. Further, although I would continue to allow parties to challenge the validity of pre-nuptial agreements, I would not alter the burden of proof which has been required to sustain such a challenge. . . .

I would remand this matter to provide the appellant with an opportunity to challenge the validity of the pre-nuptial agreement on two grounds. Although alimony *pendente lite* was mentioned in the pre-nuptial agreement, appellant should have an opportunity to establish that the mere recitation of this legal term did not advise her of the general nature of the statutory right she was relinquishing with the signing of the agreement. Appellant must establish this lack of full and fair disclosure of her statutory rights with clear and convincing evidence. Further, I would allow appellant the opportunity, with the same standard of proof, to challenge the validity of the pre-nuptial agreement's support provisions, relating to alimony *pendente lite* and alimony, for undue unfairness and inequity.

DISCUSSION QUESTIONS FOR *SIMEONE v. SIMEONE*

A. The majority justifies the decision by stating that earlier Pennsylvania premarital opinions were based on the assumption that "spouses are of unequal status." Now, according to the majority, spouses involved in premarital contracts have equal status. However, does equal status also mean parties have equal bargaining power? Has the majority gone too far in removing protection from an overreaching spouse?

B. The dissent argues that despite the existence of full and fair disclosure at the time of the execution of the agreement, if the contract is so inequitable and unfair it should not be enforced. Isn't this a wise policy in this area of the law? If so, why did the majority apparently reject this argument? What if a widow or widower is left virtually penniless by such a contract? What if a widow or widower is left a ward of the public because of such a contract?

C. The dissent also argues that while parties to a prenuptial agreement may indeed foresee, generally, the events which may come to pass during their marriage, one spouse should not be made to suffer for failing to foresee all of the surrounding circumstances which may attend the dissolution of the marriage. In other words, the dissent is suggesting that public policy should require a review of the contract when the couple divorce from an equitable perspective. Would such a policy essentially vitiate the efficacy of these contracts?

D. Are some women disadvantaged in some situations when it comes to premarital contracts? For example, do contracts, especially when a second or third marriage is concerned, disadvantage some women because the men are often older, more experienced in financial affairs, and wealthier? *See* Gail F. Brod, *Premarital Agreements and Gender Justice*, 6 Yale J.L. & Feminism 229, 234-252 (1994).

E. When considering whether alimony may be waived by a premarital contract, the Georgia Supreme Court has said: "Under the three-part test for an enforceable antenuptial agreement . . . reiterated by this Court many times . . . , the party seeking enforcement bears the burden of proof to demonstrate that: (1) the antenuptial agreement was not the result of fraud, duress, mistake, misrepresentation, or nondisclosure of material facts; (2) the agreement is not unconscionable; and (3) taking into account all relevant facts and circumstances, including changes beyond the parties' contemplation when the agreement was executed, enforcement of the antenuptial agreement would be neither unfair nor unreasonable." *Lawrence v. Lawrence*, 687 S.E.2d 421, 423 (Ga. 2009). In what way does Georgia's approach to premarital contracts differ from the approach used in Pennsylvania? Which is the better approach?

F. The South Dakota Supreme Court held in *Connolly v. Connolly*, 270 N.W.2d 44 (S.D. 1978), that provisions in a prenuptial agreement purporting to limit alimony obligations are against public policy and therefore not enforceable. How does South Dakota's approach to waiver of alimony differ from that of Georgia and Pennsylvania? Which of the three jurisdictions has the better public policy?

G. *Simeone v. Simeone* has been criticized for allowing the courts to withdraw "from the business of policing the reasonableness of premarital bargains." *Family Law — Prenuptial Agreements — Pennsylvania Supreme Court Rejects Substantive Review of Prenuptial Agreements*, 104 Harv. L. Rev. 1399 (April 1991). Should other state courts follow Pennsylvania's lead and generally withdraw from policing premarital contracts?

H. The court in *Simeone* did not accept the argument that premarital agreements should be declared void if one party failed to have independent counsel. Wouldn't such a requirement protect the public interest in the fairness of such contracts?

13.21 ENFORCEMENT ISSUES: SECOND LOOK DOCTRINE

In many jurisdictions the second look doctrine is associated with a substantive fairness review of a premarital contract at the time it is to be enforced. Courts find that reviewing a premarital contract for substantive fairness is a challenge. Professor Judith Younger, when describing substantive fairness, wrote: "As it applies to the terms of the agreement, it is not a substitution of the court's notions of what is right for the parties' bargain. It is 'amorphous,' made on a case by case basis and the standard is variously described as 'reasonable,' 'fair,' 'not unconscionable,' and 'equitable.'" Judith T. Younger, *A Minnesota Comparative Family Law Symposium, Antenuptial Agreements*, 28 Wm. Mitchell L. Rev. 697, 701 (2001).

It is argued that a substantive fairness review at the time of enforcement intrudes upon the right of mature adults to freely contract with respect to the allocation of property and other rights. Courts that have employed a substantive fairness review usually limit invalidation of contract provisions to those that could not have reasonably been foreseen and that have become so one-sided as to be oppressive or unconscionable. For example, New Jersey has held that substantive fairness of prenuptial agreements is properly determined at the time of enforcement. *Rogers v. Gordon*, 961 A.2d 11 (N.J. Super. A.D. 2008). In an earlier decision, the New Jersey court held that "[a]n agreement which would leave a spouse a public charge or close to it, or which would provide a standard of living far below that which was enjoyed both before and during the marriage would probably not be enforced by any court." *Marschall v. Marschall*, 477 A.2d 833, 841 (N.J. Super. 1984). The court in *Marschall* noted that although "the applicable measure for judicially fixed support is the standard of living during the marriage, there does not seem anything inherently 'unfair' in an antenuptial agreement which uses a different standard — perhaps the somewhat lower standard at which one spouse lived before the marriage." *Ibid.*

| REFLECTIVE QUESTIONS | Does the second look doctrine intrude upon the right of mature adults to freely contract with respect to the allocation of property and other rights? |

Background to *Austin v. Austin*

Austin v. Austin concerns the substantive fairness of a waiver of alimony in a pre-marital agreement. To answer whether the premarital contract is substantively fair and reasonable, the court asks two broad questions: First, what were the circumstances that existed at the time the parties signed the contract? Second, what are the circumstances of the parties at the time of the divorce?

AUSTIN
v.
AUSTIN

Supreme Court of Massachusetts
839 N.E.2d 837 (2005)

IRELAND, J. . . . The parties met in 1984 and lived together from 1986 until 1988. They were married in May, 1989. Two days prior to the marriage . . . the couple executed the agreement. . . .

. . . A key provision was that, if the marital residence was owned solely by the husband at the time of separation, although the wife would have to vacate the home, the husband was required to assist the wife in relocating and to give the wife "support based upon such considerations as the length of the marriage, their present employment, whether any children were born to the marriage and such other factors as are cognizable under domestic relations and property laws of the jurisdiction in which the parties last resided." Both parties waived alimony from the other.

Over the course of their twelve-year marriage, the couple had one child, born in 1991. By agreement, the wife stayed home as a full-time mother, helping out occasionally at the family's restaurant, which opened in 1999, and other businesses. In addition, in 1995, the couple bought a house . . . , which was the marital home at the time the wife filed for divorce in 2001. During the marriage, the family enjoyed "an upper class lifestyle." . . .

After a trial on the merits of the divorce, the judge divided the marital assets. Relevant to our discussion is the fact that the wife was awarded, among other things, the marital home, valued at $1,275,000, $525,000 in cash, and her Lexus automobile (subject to a loan balance of $24,575). The judge also awarded the wife $500 per week in child support and $1,000 per week in alimony. The husband's appeal from the alimony provision is the sole issue before this court.

. . . Antenuptial agreements that waive alimony are not "per se against public policy and may be specifically enforced." *Osborne v. Osborne*, 428 N.E.2d 810 (1981). However, to be enforceable, the agreement must be valid at the time of execution and must also be fair and reasonable at the time of divorce. *DeMatteo v. DeMatteo*, 762 N.E.2d 797 (2002). In order to be valid at the time of execution, the judge must determine whether "(1) [the agreement] contains a fair and reasonable provision as measured at the time of its execution for the party contesting the agreement; (2) the contesting party was fully informed of the other party's worth prior to the agreement's execution, or had, or should have had, independent knowledge of the other party's worth; and (3) a waiver by the contesting party is set forth." *Id.* . . . In determining whether an agreement was fair and reasonable at the time of execution, "reference may appropriately be made to such factors as the parties' respective worth, . . . ages, . . . intelligence, literacy, business acumen, and prior family ties or commitments." An agreement, even a one-sided agreement that leaves the contesting party with "considerably fewer assets" and imposes a "far different lifestyle after divorce" than she had during the marriage, is fair and reasonable unless "the contesting party is essentially stripped of substantially all marital interests." *DeMatteo v. DeMatteo.* . . .

Where an agreement is valid at the time of execution, a judge must take a second look at its provisions at the time of divorce. . . . At that time, the agreement will be enforced "unless, due to circumstances occurring during the course of the marriage, enforcement . . . would leave the contesting spouse 'without sufficient property, maintenance, or appropriate employment to support' herself." . . .

In concluding that the agreement was not fair and reasonable as to alimony for the wife at the time of its execution, the [trial] judge stated: "Although at the time it may have been reasonable to forgo alimony because she was employed and was young and healthy, . . . it was not fair and reasonable at the time of execution for [the wife] to forgo all possible alimony and support given the great disparity of earning potential of the parties." The wife was employed at a department store in Boston, and the husband had various business interests. The judge noted that the wife entered the marriage intending to build a life with the husband and "rightfully believed that what they built together would belong to both of them," but that the husband made "it his mission . . . to prevent the creation of joint marital assets." . . .

The judge's findings do not permit the conclusion that the wife was "essentially stripped of substantially all marital interests," which is the standard required to declare an agreement invalid at its execution. . . . Disparity of income that has the potential to leave one spouse in an essentially different lifestyle is not a valid basis for determining that the agreement was invalid at its execution. Moreover, "[w]here there is no evidence that either party engaged in fraud, failed to disclose assets fully and fairly, or in some other way took unfair advantage of the confidential and emotional relationship of the other when the agreement was executed, an agreement will be valid unless its terms essentially vitiate the very status of marriage."

Here there is no evidence of the husband's taking unfair advantage of the wife at the time the agreement was executed. The wife's attorney drafted the agreement, after he had advised her not to sign an agreement prepared by the husband's attorney. Furthermore, as discussed, the judge found that the wife was fully aware of her rights and knowledgeable about alimony, property division, and child support. The agreement provided that the wife's separate premarital property would remain hers and not be incorporated into marital assets. . . . The agreement permitted the wife a joint interest in marital assets and provided that "any appreciation on the marital home or such home as the parties reside as their last marital home at the time of separation, whether due to market forces or capital investment," be divided as a marital asset, even if the husband held sole title to the property. Most important, the agreement entitled the wife to relocation and "support" from the husband if there were no jointly owned marital home at the time of a divorce, "based upon such considerations . . . as are cognizable under domestic relations and property laws" of the relevant jurisdiction. In short, the agreement provided for either funds from a capital asset or access to support, utilizing standard factors such as those now codified in Massachusetts in G.L. c. 208, §34. When they were married, the couple resided in the husband's condominium unit. Therefore, it was reasonably foreseeable that a home owned by the husband would exist in the event of a divorce. There is nothing in this record that would allow us to conclude that the agreement vitiated the status of marriage by stripping the wife of "substantially all marital interests." . . . Accordingly, the agreement was valid at the time it was executed. Had the wife been dissatisfied with the terms of the agreement, she could have refused marriage.

Our conclusion that the agreement is valid requires us "to consider whether there is any reason not to enforce it." . . . [T]he [trial] judge also found that the agreement concerning alimony was invalid at the time of divorce. He stated that the wife had spent ten of the twelve years of marriage as a homemaker, completely dependent on the husband, and given her lack of education, was "not in a position to secure income which would maintain the lifestyle that she achieved [for her and her daughter] during the marriage."

In the *DeMatteo case*, the court held that the so-called "second look" at the agreement "is to ensure that the agreement has the same vitality at the time of the divorce that the parties intended at the time of its execution." The agreement must be enforced unless circumstances such as the mental or physical deterioration of the contesting party, or erosion of promised support by inflation, would lead the court to conclude that the agreement was not conscionable and that its "enforcement . . . would leave the contesting spouse 'without sufficient property, maintenance, or appropriate employment to support herself.' " . . .

Here, there has been no physical or mental deterioration of the wife. She was self-supporting during a period of separation prior to their marriage. The wife has the marital home worth $1,275,000 and was awarded $525,000 in cash. She was allowed to keep many of the contents of the marital home, including jewelry acquired since the marriage worth $74,000. Given the assets she has been awarded, we cannot say that the agreement leaves the wife without sufficient property and maintenance. . . . [W]e conclude that the agreement is enforceable and vacate the judge's order to award the wife alimony.

GREANEY, J. (dissenting, with whom **SPINA, J.,** joins). The court today denies a woman, in her fifties, with a high school education, low potential earning capacity, and a child to raise, her right to receive alimony. . . . Significantly, at [the time the contract was signed], the wife did not simply agree to take less than what she might have received under G.L. c. 208, §34. Instead, she relinquished her right to both alimony and any claim on the husband's assets, essentially giving up substantially all marital interests. The wife, in substance, was given nothing under the agreement. The agreement contemplated only potential marital assets that might be acquired after marriage. . . .

DISCUSSION QUESTIONS FOR *AUSTIN v. AUSTIN*

A. The "second look" test adopted in Massachusetts holds that once the agreement is found to be valid, a court may still consider whether to enforce it. What factors may exist at the time of enforcement that will persuade a Massachusetts court to reject the contract? Is this good public policy? What is Massachusetts's philosophical perspective on this issue?

B. Isn't the dissent correct that the wife received nothing under the agreement when it was signed? Doesn't that make the consideration inadequate? Therefore, isn't the agreement unfair, if not unconscionable?

C. Why do you suspect that many jurisdictions have not yet adopted the Massachusetts "second look" doctrine?

D. A Massachusetts court will not allow a premarital contract to waive or limit child support but will allow it to waive or limit alimony. How strong is the argument that because the mother is awarded custody of the child in *Austin*, allowing a waiver of alimony will affect the raising of the child? Should it follow that in cases where there are minor children in the custody of a party to a nonmarital agreement, alimony cannot be waived as to that person?

E. The court in *Austin* distinguishes the consideration for a separation agreement and the consideration for a premarital contract. What is the distinction and does it make sense?

13.22 RELIGIOUS PROVISIONS

Premarital agreements containing religious provisions have received a mixed reception by the courts. If a contract contains a section where the parties agree to raise children in a particular faith, that provision will usually not be upheld. *See, e.g., In re Marriage of Weiss*, 49 Cal. Rptr. 2d 339 (Cal. App. 1996); *In re Marriage of Nuechterlein*, 587 N.E.2d 21 (Ill. App. 1992); *In re Marriage of Wolfert*, 598 P.2d 524 (Colo. App. 1979).

In *Odatalla v. Odatalla*, 810 A.2d 93 (N.J. Super. 2002), the court was asked to enforce an Islamic premarital contract called a "*mahr* agreement." Prior to their religious marriage ceremony, the parties entered into this agreement, which obligated the husband to pay "one golden pound coin" to the wife during the religious ceremony and, thereafter, a "postponed ten thousand U.S. dollars." *Id.* at 95. The husband complied with the prompt payment of the one golden pound coin, and, upon seeking a divorce, the wife sought enforcement of the postponed ten thousand dollar payment. The court found that the agreement could be enforced "based upon neutral principles of law and not on religious policy or theories." The court explained that because no doctrinal issue was involved, there could be no constitutional infringement. The court further explained that enforcement of the secular parts of the written agreement is consistent with the constitutional mandate for a free exercise of religious beliefs.

In *Ahmed v. Ahmed*, 261 S.W.3d 190 (Tex. App. 2008), the court refused to enforce a *mahr* agreement. The husband had contracted to give his wife $50,000 either at the time of the marriage or deferred in the event of a divorce. The court found that because the parties participated in a valid civil wedding ceremony six months before signing the *mahr* agreement, they were already spouses when it was executed. The court held that they were not "prospective spouses" as required by the Texas premarital statute.

New York courts have enforced the secular portions of premarital agreements between Orthodox Jews. *Avitzur v. Avitzur*, 446 N.E.2d 136 (N.Y.) *cert. denied*, 464 U.S. 817 (1983).

| REFLECTIVE QUESTIONS | How would you state the "rule of law" that flows from the above cases? |

13.23 BURDEN OF PROOF

The states do not agree on whom the burden of proof should be placed in premarital contract disputes. Before statutes replaced the common law, some courts shifted the burden in a premarital contract dispute depending on how consideration for the contract was viewed. For example, in *In re Estate of Kinney*, 733 N.W.2d 118, 126-127 (Minn. 2007), the court observed that the common law placed the burden of proof on the proponent of a premarital contract when a court found that the parties were in a confidential relationship and the contract was not supported by adequate consideration. The consideration was not the marriage, which many courts had said was sufficient consideration for these contracts. Rather, the court considered the amount of property and allowance given the poorer spouse as the consideration for the contract.

The *Kinney* decision discussed above accurately reflects the approach taken by many common law courts. When an inadequate allowance for the poorer spouse was found in a premarital contract, the common law court shifted the burden of proof to the proponent of the contract and employed a presumption that the contract was fraudulent because of a lack of consideration. In those cases where a common law court found that the contract was supported by adequate consideration, the burden was placed on the party challenging the contract to persuade the court that it should not be enforced. *See Christians v. Christians*, 44 N.W.2d 431 (Iowa 1950).

Alimony. Some courts continue to utilize a shifting burden model for some aspects of premarital agreements. For example, in Illinois, if the provisions made for the spouse receiving alimony in a premarital contract are largely disproportionate to the value of the other spouse's estate, there arises a presumption of concealment of the assets. *In re Estate of Hopkins*, 520 N.E.2d 415 (Ill. App. 1988). In such a case, the burden of proof to uphold the contract shifts to the party who claims it is valid.

Other issues. Maryland has held that when there is neither full disclosure nor actual knowledge and the allowance to the party waiving rights is unfairly disproportionate to the worth of the property involved, the party seeking to uphold the agreement must shoulder the burden to prove that it was entered into voluntarily, freely, and with full knowledge of its meaning and effect. *Cannon v. Cannon*, 865 A.2d 563, 572 (Md. 2005). Tennessee takes the view that an antenuptial agreement is not enforceable unless the party seeking to uphold the agreement proves, by a preponderance of the evidence, either that a full and fair disclosure of the nature, extent, and value of the spouse's holdings was provided to the spouse seeking to avoid the agreement, or that disclosure was unnecessary because the spouse seeking to avoid the agreement had independent knowledge of the full nature, extent, and value of the proponent spouse's holdings. *In re Estate of Baker*, 207 S.W.3d 254 (Tenn. App. 2006).

New York courts place the burden of proof on the party seeking to set aside a premarital agreement. It has said that the party bears a very high burden of showing that the agreement is manifestly unfair and that this unfairness was the result of overreaching on the part of the other party to the agreement. *Panossian v. Panossian*, 569 N.Y.S.2d 182 (N.Y.A.D. 1991).

UPAA. The Uniform Premarital Agreement Act (UPAA) places the burden of proof on the party seeking to avoid enforcement of the premarital agreement. Uniform Premarital Agreement Act §6. The UPAA departs from the presumption and burden shifting traditionally used to determine whether "fair disclosure" has been provided. *See In re Estate of Martin*, 938 A.2d 812 (Me. 2008). In doing so, the UPAA reflects greater social acceptance of and comfort with premarital agreements than existed at common law.

REFLECTIVE QUESTIONS	When challenged, should the burden be on the proponent of the premarital contract to prove it is legal? Or, should the burden be on the challenger to prove it is illegal? Or, should there be a shifting burden of some kind?

13.24 MODEL ACT: UNIFORM PREMARITAL AGREEMENT ACT (UPAA)

A model act, the Uniform Premarital Agreement Act (UPAA), was drafted in 1983 by the National Conference of Commissioners on Uniform State Law. The

Uniform Premarital and Marital Agreements Act, which was promulgated by the Commissioners in 2012, is intended to replace the UPAA. It is discussed in section 13.25.

The Commissioners explained the reason for the 1983 UPAA in a prefatory note:

> The number of marriages between persons previously married and the number of marriages between persons, each of whom is intending to continue to pursue a career, is steadily increasing. For these and other reasons, it is becoming more and more common for persons contemplating marriage to seek to resolve by agreement certain issues presented by the forthcoming marriage. However, despite a lengthy legal history for these premarital contracts, there is a substantial uncertainty as to the enforceability of all, or a portion, of the provisions of these contracts and a significant lack of uniformity of treatment of these contracts among the states. The problems caused by this uncertainty and nonuniformity are greatly exacerbated by the mobility of our population.

9B West's U.L.A. (1987) UPAA, Prefatory Note, p. 36; *see generally*, Stephanie Barkholz Casteel, *Planning and Drafting Premarital Agreements*, SR042 ALI-ABA 531 (June 13-18, 2010). The UPAA states that agreements pertaining to property rights on divorce or death are enforceable unless the party against whom enforcement is sought proves (a) that he or she did not execute the agreement voluntarily; or (b) that the agreement was unconscionable when made and that, before execution of the agreement, he or she (1) was not provided a fair and reasonable disclosure of the property or financial obligations of the other party, (2) did not voluntarily and expressly waive, in writing, any right to disclosure of the property or financial obligations of the other party beyond the disclosures provided, and (3) did not have, or reasonably could not have had, an adequate knowledge of the property and financial obligations of the other party.

Note that the term *unconscionable* used in the UPAA was derived from the Uniform Marriage and Divorce Act (UMDA). In the note to §306 of the UMDA, the term is described as encompassing overreaching, concealment of assets, or sharp dealings inconsistent with the obligations of marital partners to deal fairly with each other.

A valid premarital contract under the UPAA must be in writing, as must any amendments and revocations to the agreement. The only consideration required for a premarital contract to be enforceable is that the couple marry. The UPAA does not recognize postmarital contracts. A contract will be rejected if it is not executed voluntarily, meaning that it will fail if it is the product of fraud, duress, coercion, or overreaching. The UPAA does not define these concepts.

The UPAA places the burden of proof upon the challenger of a contract to show involuntariness at the time it was executed. This includes proof supporting a claim that the contract is unconscionable and/or lacks appropriate disclosure and/or the signor lacked fair knowledge of the other's financial circumstances. Once the challenger provides evidence that the contract is unfair or unreasonable, given the circumstances of the parties, a presumption arises that either the defending spouse concealed his or her assets and holdings or that the challenging spouse lacked knowledge of the other's finances. The burden of proof then shifts to the defending spouse to rebut these presumptions by showing that full disclosure was made or that the challenging spouse had an approximate knowledge of the character and extent of the other's income and property.

Under UPAA §6(a)(2), a court may not consider the alleged unconscionability of the agreement unless it first finds there was no fair and reasonable financial disclosure, voluntary waiver of such disclosure, and the challenging party did not have, or reasonably could not have had an adequate knowledge of the other party's property and financial obligations. Uniform Premarital Agreement Act §6(a)(2). Under this section of the UPAA, an agreement that is "merely" unconscionable — that is, one that is unconscionable, but the other factors of subsection (1)(b) have not been proven — will not be struck down as invalid. *In re Marriage of Rudder*, 217 P.3d 183, 189 (Or. App. 2009); *In re estate of Martin*, 938 A.2d 812 (Me. 2008).

REFLECTIVE QUESTIONS	How does the burden of proof shift under the UPAA when a premarital contract is challenged?

13.25 MODEL ACT: UNIFORM PREMARITAL AND MARITAL AGREEMENTS ACT

The Uniform Premarital and Marital Agreements Act (UPMAA) was completed by the Uniform Law Commissioners in 2012. It is described as "harmonizing the standards in existing uniform acts governing premarital and marital agreements (Uniform Premarital Agreement Act, Uniform Marital Property Act, Uniform Probate Code, and Model Marriage and Divorce Act)." However, as of April 2015, only two states, Colorado and North Dakota, have adopted the UPMAA. *See* Barbara A. Atwood & Brian H. Bix, *A New Uniform Law for Premarital and Marital Agreements*, 46 Fam. L.Q. 313, 315 (Fall 2012).

The new model act is said to parallel the general structure of the prior law while strengthening the procedural fairness requirements. *Id.* at 33. It also contains some newly structured definitions of premarital and marital agreements, "a nuanced formulation of access to independent counsel, and a safe-harbor warning for unrepresented parties." These were intended to further the Commissioners' commitment to informed decision making and a fair process. The following is a short list of a few of the differences between the UPAA and the UPMAA.

1. The UPMAA establishes a more demanding standard for the validity of an agreement entered into during marriage than that applicable to premarital agreements in the UPAA. For example, an agreement executed during marriage is not enforceable if the spouse challenging the agreement proves that the agreement

was not executed voluntarily, that the agreement was unconscionable when made, or that there was a lack of adequate financial disclosure. Financial disclosure requirements in the UPMAA are somewhat expanded in the UPAA.

2. Parties are free to choose the law governing not only the interpretation and construction of an agreement, but also its validity and enforceability.

3. The act requires that if the other party is represented by legal counsel, the challenger must have the financial ability to retain a lawyer. The ability to retain a lawyer can be shown either from his or her own assets or by virtue of the other party's payment of reasonable counsel fees. The drafters believe that this new requirement levels the playing field if only one party initially has a lawyer.

4. The drafters state that the main change in the unconscionability provision of the UPMAA, relative to the UPAA, is that unconsionability at the time of signing is now sufficient by itself to invalidate an agreement. Under the UPAA if a challenger demonstrated an agreement was unconscionable, there also had to be a showing of inadequate financial disclosure.

REFLECTIVE QUESTIONS	Which of the new provisions in the UPMAA do you consider the most important?

13.26 MODEL ACT: AMERICAN LAW INSTITUTE (ALI) PRINCIPLES

The American Law Institute (ALI) *Principles of the Law of Family Dissolution: Analysis and Recommendations* views marriage as a partnership and require that premarital contracts meet standards of procedural and substantive fairness if they are to be enforced. *See generally Marriage as Contract and Marriage as Partnership: The Future of Antenuptial Agreement Law*, 116 Harv. L. Rev. 2075, 2098 (May 2003). The ALI *Principles* creates a rebuttable presumption that a premarital contract is valid if (1) it was executed at least 30 days prior to the marriage; (2) both parties had, or were advised to obtain, counsel and had the opportunity to do so; and (3) if one of the parties did not have counsel, the agreement contained understandable information about the parties' rights and the adverse nature of their interests. ALl *Principles* §7.04(e)(a)(b) and (c).

REFLECTIVE QUESTIONS	Can you explain what the ALI may have meant when it used the phrase "understandable information" in its *Principles*?

13.27 MODEL ACT: RESTATEMENT (THIRD) OF PROPERTY

Section 9.4 of the Restatement (Third) of Property applies to both premarital and marital agreements dealing with the elective share and other spousal statutory rights arising on death. The Restatement gives the parties a right to waive their "right of election" to take against the will by entering into a contract, agreement, or waiver to that effect before or after marriage. It can be a very important section where the husband and wife are planning their estates. Section 9.4 reads as follows:

§9.4 Premarital or Marital Agreement

(a) The elective share and other statutory rights accruing to a surviving spouse may be waived, wholly or partially, or otherwise altered, before or during marriage, by a written agreement that was signed by both parties. An agreement that was entered into before marriage is a premarital agreement. An agreement that was entered into during marriage is a marital agreement. Consideration is not necessary to the enforcement of a premarital or a marital agreement.

(b) For a premarital or marital agreement to be enforceable against the surviving spouse, the enforcing party must show that the surviving spouse's consent was informed and was not obtained by undue influence or duress.

(c) A rebuttable presumption arises that the requirements of subsection (b) are satisfied, shifting the burden of proof to the surviving spouse to show that his or her consent was not informed or was obtained by undue influence or duress, if the enforcing party shows that:

Before the agreement's execution, (i) the surviving spouse knew, at least approximately, the decedent's assets and asset values, income, and liabilities, or (ii) the decedent or his or her representative provided in timely fashion to the surviving spouse a written statement accurately disclosing the decedent's significant assets and asset values, income, and liabilities; and either the surviving spouse was represented by independent legal counsel; or If the surviving spouse was not represented by independent legal counsel, (i) the decedent or the decedent's representative advised the surviving spouse, in timely fashion, to obtain independent legal counsel, and if the surviving spouse was needy, offered to pay for the costs of the surviving spouse's representation; and (ii) the agreement stated, in language easily understandable by an adult of ordinary intelligence with no legal training, the nature of any rights or claims otherwise arising at death that were altered by the agreement, and the nature of that alternation.

The commentary to the Restatement states that "[a]mong the material facts that are to be considered [when deciding whether to enforce the agreement] is the amount that the agreement provides for the surviving spouse. That amount may be considered in relation to the decedent's financial condition when the agreement was executed or in relation to the portion of the decedent's estate granted to the surviving spouse by the elective-share statute and other spousal statutory rights arising on death. Also to be considered is the financial and family situation of both parties when the agreement was executed." Commentary, Restatement (Third) of Property: Wills & Other Donative Transfers (2011).

 What is the significance of the discussion in the commentary to the Restatement regarding consideration? (It may be useful to review the earlier section on consideration.)

13.28 POSTNUPTIAL CONTRACTS

A postnuptial agreement is a contract entered into after marriage by a husband and wife involving the property rights of the parties. Such agreements were impossible in England under the common law system because of the unity theory of marriage, which considered spouses a single person embodied in the husband. *See* Judith T. Younger, *Lovers' Contracts in the Courts: Forsaking the Minimum Decencies in Contract*, 13 Wm. & Mary J. Women & L. 349, 353 (Winter 2007). However, they were valid and enforceable in this country in equity, and under the Married Women's Property Acts.

A postnuptial agreement has been used in some jurisdictions to limit or eliminate an alimony award should the couple divorce. *See, e.g., Clanton v. Clanton*, 592 N.Y.S.2d 783 (N.Y.A.D. 1993). In a New York ruling, an agreement that a husband would provide financial and residential assistance to his wife's two disabled sons from a previous marriage in exchange for her waiver of her right to the parties' entire marital residence upon a future separation or divorce, was held not unfair or unreasonable. The agreement was affirmed even though there was evidence that the wife agreed to the modification only because of husband's threat of separation. *Webb v. Webb*, 851 N.Y.S.2d 828 (N.Y. 2007) (husband agreed to convey property into a trust for the benefit of defendant's two disabled sons).

In *Ansin v. Craven-Ansin*, 929 N.E.2d 955 (Mass. 2010), a postmarital agreement was upheld. In making its ruling, the court stated that such agreements are enforceable if careful scrutiny by the judge determines at a minimum the following:

1. Each party has had an opportunity to obtain separate legal counsel of their own choosing.
2. There was no fraud or coercion in obtaining the agreement.
3. All assets were fully disclosed by both parties before the agreement was executed.
4. Each spouse knowingly and explicitly agreed in writing to waive the right to a judicial equitable division of assets and all marital rights in the event of a divorce.
5. The terms of the agreement were fair and reasonable at the time of execution and are fair and reasonable at the time of divorce.

In some states, postnuptial agreements are specifically authorized by statute. *See, e.g.,* N.Y. Dom. Rel. L. §236(B)(3); Minn. Stat. §519.11, sub.(1)(a).

Consideration. Because postnuptial agreements are contracts and subject to ordinary principles of contract interpretation, absent specific statutory provisions to the contrary, there must be consideration for them. Consideration exists if there is a "benefit to the promisor or a detriment to the promisee" and "[i]t is enough that something is promised, done, forborne or suffered by the party to whom the promise is made as consideration for the promise made to him." *Hamer v. Sidway*, 545, 27 N.E. 256 (N.Y. 1891). Because the circumstances surrounding postnuptial agreements are said to be pregnant with the opportunity for one party to use the threat of dissolution to bargain him- or herself into positions of advantage, they are carefully scrutinized. *Bedrick v. Bedrick*, 17 A.3d 17, 26 (Conn. 2011). The Appellate Division of the New Jersey Superior Court has noted that a wife "face[s] a more difficult choice than [a] bride who is presented with a demand for a prenuptial agreement. The cost to [a wife is] . . . the destruction of a family and the stigma of a failed marriage." *Pacelli v. Pacelli*, 725 A.2d 56 (N.J. Super.), *cert. denied*, 735 A.2d 572 (1999).

Business deals? Courts have also observed that postnuptial agreements "should not be treated as mere 'business deals.' " *Stoner v. Stoner*, 819 A.2d 529 (Penn. 2003). They recognize that, just like prospective spouses, "parties to these agreements do not quite deal at arm's length, but rather at the time the contract is entered into stand in a relation of mutual confidence and trust. . . ." *Id.* at 533. "Ordinarily and presumptively, a confidential relation or a relationship of special confidence exists between husband and wife. It includes, but is not limited to, a fiduciary duty between the spouses, of the highest degree." 41 Am. Jur. 2d 72, *Husband and Wife* §69 (2005).

Limitations. A postnuptial agreement cannot bind a court in determining the amount of child support a party is to pay for the care of a minor child. It also cannot determine custody of a child, should the marriage dissolve.

Trend. The trend in the United States is to recognize postmarital contracts, with a majority of jurisdictions holding that they are enforceable. To be enforceable, most jurisdictions agree that they cannot be incident to a contemplated separation or divorce, and must be free from fraud, coercion, or undue influence. Each party must act with full knowledge of the property involved and his or her rights and consider the settlement fair and equitable.

REFLECTIVE QUESTIONS	What public purpose do postnuptial agreements serve? What are some of the concerns with these contracts?

General Principles

1. Premarital contracts were historically limited to use only upon death of a spouse.
2. Premarital contracts today can be used upon divorce or death of a spouse.
3. Parties to traditional commercial contracts are bound by them without regard to whether the terms are reasonable or whether they are understood.

4. Premarital contracts are governed by requirements such as disclosure and fairness because of society's heightened concern with marriage and divorce.

5. Premarital contracts are executory, that is, they are to be performed in the future when changed circumstances may make them unfair.

6. Premarital contracts with terms regarding child support are not enforceable.

7. Premarital contracts regarding child custody are not enforceable.

8. The Statute of Frauds requires that a premarital contract be in writing and signed by the party who executed the document. Some state statutes may require that they be witnessed by two independent witnesses.

9. A premarital contract will generally be upheld if (1) it is entered voluntarily (without undue pressure or duress); (2) there is full and fair disclosure of the assets of the parties; (3) the parties had an opportunity to consult with counsel; and (4) it is reasonable.

10. States are not in agreement over the issue of utilizing premarital contracts to limit or exclude spousal support. A majority of states will allow limits or exclusions of alimony under certain conditions.

Chapter Problems

1. Few, if any, jurisdictions have concluded that a premarital contract should be subject to the "second look" doctrine upon the death of one of the parties. Do you believe that the same "second look" doctrine employed by several courts to premarital contracts when used upon divorce should also be applied upon the death of a party? If so, what arguments will you make in support of your position? Alternatively, explain why the "second look" doctrine should not be used upon the death of a party to a premarital contract.

2. Assume that Pauline and David executed a premarital contract in which David, who was unemployed at the time, specifically agreed to make no claim for any community property. The premarital contract read as follows: "David waives and renounces any and all rights that, and to which, he would otherwise be entitled to because of his marriage to Pauline, whether present or future rights, to any and all property which Pauline has now, or which she may acquire in the future, whether the same be real, personal, or mixed property, or of any kind or nature and wherever situated." Ten years later, their marriage breaks down. During their marriage, Pauline experienced a huge increase in her earnings. However, David, in fact, is still unemployed and living at a near poverty level, and seeks alimony. David challenges the contract. What arguments will the parties make in this dispute, and how will a court most likely rule in a jurisdiction that applies the "second look" doctrine? How will Pennsylvania most likely rule?

3. Assume that two days before their marriage 75-year-old Albert and 40-year-old Polly enter into a premarital contract by which "in consideration of an immediate payment to Polly of a Mercedes Benz automobile valued at $35,000 she waives all rights to inherit or share in any of nonmarital or marital property owned by Albert." The contract fails to state in detail the extent of his assets but contains language to the effect that "Albert's property is valued at several million dollars." In addition to the property waiver, the contract also states that "In consideration of an immediate payment to Polly of $30,000, Polly waives any right to receive alimony, either temporary or permanent, should the parties divorce." Polly rejects in writing the opportunity to obtain independent counsel to review the contract and signs it in Albert's lawyer's office after reviewing it for an hour. Albert dies after two years of marriage. Polly seeks her intestate share of Albert's estate, valued at $20 million dollars under the state's elective share statute. Albert's heirs claim the premarital contract bars her legal action. She has no job, no savings, and no income. She challenges the premarital contract that provided her with little, if anything, upon the death of Albert. Who will normally have the burden of persuading the court the contract is valid? How will a majority of courts in this country most likely rule?

4. Sally and Sam execute a premarital contract that provides that, in the event of divorce, the court shall require that they will have joint legal and joint physical custody of any children born to the marriage. After ten years and two children, the couple divorce. Sally challenges the child custody provision in the contract. What will she argue?

5. Assume that a month before their wedding, lawyer Bob presents Barbara with a draft of a premarital contract in which she waives any and all rights to his property acquired before or after the marriage. Attached to the contract is a partial list of Bob's assets. Barbara has been Bob's legal secretary for a dozen years and has handled most of his professional and personal affairs. Barbara is offered the opportunity to consult with a lawyer, but because of her love for Bob she waives the opportunity. The marriage lasts 15 years and they have 2 children. When they divorce, Barbara challenges the contract. How will a court in Pennsylvania most likely rule on her challenge? Will a Massachusetts court most likely rule differently?

6. Assume that prior to their marriage five years ago in California, a couple, H and W, executed a premarital contract waiving alimony. A waiver of spousal support was sanctioned at the time by the California legislature. *In re Marriage of Bellio*, 129 Cal. Rptr. 2d 556, 558 n.1 (Cal. App. 2003) (UPAA effective as of 1 January 1986 in California). The agreement does not contain a standard provision found in most of these agreements making it clear what state law will apply if a court is asked to enforce the contract. Assume that at the time the premarital contract was executed, North Carolina did not allow such agreements to be used for a divorce. The parties move to North Carolina after residing in California for six months of their marriage. Five years later, the marriage breaks down. The parties are domiciled in North Carolina. H seeks to enforce the premarital contract in a North Carolina court, arguing that California law applies; W argues that the contract is not enforceable because at the time it was executed, North Carolina law clearly forbade such agreements. Both parties agree that unless the premarital agreement at issue "appears clearly to have been intended to be performed elsewhere, the construction is to be governed by the law of the place where it is intended to be performed." *Hicks v. Skinner*, 71 N.C. 539, 545 (1874). H argues California law applies and the contract is enforceable. W argues that North Carolina law applies and it is not enforceable. Most likely, how will a court rule? *See Boudreau v. Baughman*, 368 S.E.2d 849, 857-858 (1988); *Morton v. Morton*, 332 S.E.2d 736 (N.C. App. 1985).

Preparation for Practice

1. Select a classmate and ask him or her to play the role of a client who is financially poor but who in three weeks is about to marry a multimillionaire. Write a short script for the hypothetical client. Include in the script the fact that the client has already obtained a copy of the premarital contract and it waives the client's right to alimony and all death benefits. The client receives lump sum payments (nothing else) of $25,000 if the marriage last five years; $50,000 if the marriage lasts ten years; and $75,000 if the marriage lasts more than ten years. The client's current net assets are not more than $5,000.

   Assume that the client has come to you seeking legal advice on whether to sign a premarital contract. Set up a 15-minute video interview. During the interview, consider what suggestions you can make that will assist in preventing, or at least reducing, irrational decision making on the client's part when signing the premarital agreement. Explain the possibility to the client that a premarital agreement will not be enforceable in the future if your jurisdiction has accepted the "second look" doctrine — but be cautious. Have the interview between you and your client videotaped but limit the interview to no more than 15 minutes. When finished, ask your instructor or a family lawyer to critique the interview.

2. Assume that you were just hired as your first job out of law school as an associate in a small family law firm in your town. You have been asked as your first assignment by a senior partner to draft an outline of the important areas to cover in a premarital contract to be used on death or divorce. The outline will be discussed at the weekly meeting of partners and associates. The senior partner explains to you that the outline should cover at a minimum the following: (a) parties' names and addresses; (b) the number of marriages this will be for each party; and (c) the purpose of the contract (i.e., to govern the parties' rights in the event of death, divorce, or both). She says that the agreement should also state that (a) each party has made full financial disclosure to the other, (b) that each party had the advice of independent counsel of his or her choosing in the preparation and execution of the agreement, and that (c) each

party accepts the terms of the agreement as fair and reasonable. Another junior associate has suggested that you include topics such as life insurance coverage for the surviving spouse, any lump sum payment or installment payment, any creation of a trust for the life of the surviving spouse, the formula for determining spousal benefits the parties wish to utilize (including "adjusted gross estate" plus adjusted taxable gifts, disposition of joint tenancies, increasing benefits based on length of marriage and benefits for others beside spouse (children or parents)), the timing and method of any payment, and the waiver of statutory rights, including intestate share, elective share, survivor's allowance, and wrongful death recovery. Because the contract is to address a possible divorce, be sure to include provisions about support, property division, and division of liabilities.

Assume that your jurisdiction allows alimony to be waived and that the court has ruled that a waiver must be clear and comprehensive. Other issues that have been suggested to you by a form book include tax filing statutes, provisions for breach by either party and the consequences of a breach of the contract, waiver of retirement benefits, as well as other benefits that result from the marital status. Also, it is suggested that you indicate what state law will apply to the contract and its effective date.

Draft a comprehensive outline of a premarital contract to be used upon death or divorce. Be prepared to post it to Blackboard so that it can be shared with your classmates and your instructor.

3. Prepare a PowerPoint slide presentation explaining the "second look" doctrine. Be prepared to post it to the class website and/or show and discuss it during class.

Chapter 14

Cohabitation Outside of Marriage

14.1 INTRODUCTION

This chapter considers the legal issues that may arise when unmarried persons, living together much like a married couple, end their relationship. Because a growing number of persons choose this lifestyle, it is an area of the law that has drawn increased attention from courts and legislatures. Unfortunately, the law is in transition and lacks uniformity.

This chapter is relevant but potentially less important in the minority of jurisdictions that recognize common law marriages. Those jurisdictions most likely resolve many of the issues raised in this chapter because they recognize common law marriages and have a well-developed statutory framework to guide judges in resolving support and property division issues. The challenge for jurisdictions that do not recognize common law marriages is to decide whether "married-like" couples will receive legal redress of any kind when their relationship ends.

The chapter touches on the cultural changes that have led several courts and legislatures to move from a position where cohabiting parties received no legal redress for issues associated with cohabitation to one where the law provides limited recognition and redress. It extensively considers the *Marvin* doctrine and its influence on cohabitation law in jurisdictions outside California.

Some of the questions raised by this chapter include the following: Why should courts provide redress to persons who live together much like a husband and wife when they have the option to marry and receive significant statutory protection should they divorce? How do courts determine that an agreement between single persons living together and having sex is not meretricious? Technically, what type of consideration is accepted as legitimate by courts to support the creation of contracts made by cohabitants? What is the "Marvin doctrine" and do courts outside California follow it? In a cohabitation dispute, when, if ever, should a court award palimony, which is payment similar to alimony? When, if ever, may cohabitants recover on tort claims such as loss of consortium? Should Dead Man's statutes apply to testimony by cohabitants when claiming a portion of an estate of a deceased partner? When should federal courts refuse to hear cohabitation contract disputes by application of the domestic relations exception to subject matter jurisdiction?

> **REFLECTIVE QUESTIONS**   What are your goals for this chapter?

14.2 A GROWING ACCEPTANCE OF COHABITATION PUSHES COURTS TO PROVIDE REDRESS

The present-day inclination of many courts and legislatures to provide redress to cohabitants battling over property and support reflects a cultural phenomenon that many trace to the 1960s. In that period, increasing numbers of adults began openly living together, much as husband and wife, without a traditional marriage ceremony or a state-sanctioned marriage license. It was also during that period that most perceive that society's attitude toward marriage, family formation, and sexual companionship began to undergo a cultural transformation. Concomitantly, the social stigma associated with nonmarital cohabitation and childbearing began to weaken as the numbers of unmarried cohabitants escalated.

By June 2011, cohabitation was reported at an all-time high, with the number of opposite-sex couples living together rising 13 percent in a year's time, from 6.7 million in 2009 to 7.5 million in 2010. According to a U.S. Census study, the increase was directly connected with the recession and a cohabitant's employment status. Unmarried couples made up 12 percent of U.S. couples in 2010, a 25 percent increase in 10 years. Two-thirds of the cities with the largest shares of unmarried couples were in the Northeast and Midwest.

> **REFLECTIVE QUESTIONS**   What do you see as the future for cohabitation in the United States? Will it become the norm with marriage viewed as not very necessary?

14.3 DEFINING COHABITATION

The definitions of "cohabitation" are not necessarily terms of art; rather, they are descriptions to assist fact-finders to determine whether the circumstances surrounding individual relationships can be categorized for some legal purpose. The American Heritage Dictionary (3d ed. 1994) defines cohabitation as "(1) To live together as spouses; and (2) To live together in a sexual relationship when not legally married." Ballantine's Law Dictionary (3d ed. 1969) defines cohabitation as "[a] dwelling together of man and woman in the same place in the manner of husband and wife." Black's Law Dictionary 296 (9th ed. 2009) defines cohabitation as "[t]he fact or state of living together, esp. as partners in life, usu. with the suggestion of sexual relations."

Courts have provided additional definitional guidance. In Oregon, for example, the court of appeals has stated that "cohabit" does not refer to simply living in the same residence. "[I]t refers to a domestic arrangement between a man and woman who are not married to each other, but who live as husband and wife, in that, for more than a brief period of time, they share a common domicile and living expenses and are sexually intimate." *In re C.M.C.*, 259 P.3d 938, 940 (Or. App. 2011). Thus, "[p]ersons cohabiting with each other" refers to persons living in the same residence in a relationship akin to that of spouses. *Ibid.*

The term *cohabitation* is not so broad as to cover persons who are mere roommates or who live in the same apartment building. *See, e.g., State v. Benesh*, 781 N.W.2d 302 (Iowa App. 2010).

REFLECTIVE QUESTIONS | What facts may help distinguish between those unmarried couples who are living together much as though they are married and those that are "merely living together"?

14.4 REASONS FOR COHABITATION

There are many reasons given to explain why persons may choose to cohabit without the benefit of marriage. One reason is that that society is increasingly accepting cohabitation as an alternative living arrangement to marriage. As the acceptance level increases, a greater number of children are raised in cohabiting households. As a result of their family experience, those children may consider that cohabitation is the "norm" rather than marriage and reject marriage as adults.

There may also be financial and housing advantages for young, single persons who are dating. Sharon Sassler, *The Process of Entering into Cohabiting Unions*, 66 J. Marriage & Fam. 491, 491 (2004). Cohabitation may be viewed as an alternative to dating or to being single, which permits the partners to develop a mature relationship while sharing finances. Some may view cohabiting as a kind of trial marriage to determine each person's compatibility with the other. There are also couples who may not have the resources for a wedding ceremony and decide to live together without formal state recognition. *See* Cynthia Grant Bowman, *Social Science and Legal Policy: The Case of Heterosexual Cohabitation*, 9 J.L. & Fam. Stud. 1, 15 (2007). Divorced persons may also be "screening candidates for remarriage or seeking an alternative to marriage." *Ibid.* Retired persons may be cohabiting for convenience and economy or because they have no particular reason to marry. Low-income mothers may be making rational use of cohabitation to support themselves and their children. *Ibid.*

REFLECTIVE QUESTIONS	What are some of the "strongest" reasons that may explain why a couple decide to cohabit rather than marry?

14.5 COMPARING BENEFITS OF COHABITATION VERSUS MARRIAGE

When it comes to "benefits," marriage and cohabitation are distinguishable concepts. While there are many state and federal laws that provide benefits to a married spouse, a cohabitation relationship is not the same as marriage and cohabitants are not spouses. Cohabitants are not included within state marriage, divorce, or estate statutes. For example, the law in all jurisdictions regards the duty to support one's spouse as an essential incident of marriage. However, states generally refuse to impose this duty on persons who cohabit without marrying. *See, e.g., In re Marriage of Pendleton and Fireman*, 5 P.3d 839, 852 (Cal. 2000). Unmarried cohabitants cannot take advantage of benefits provided by the tax law to married couples, including the marital deduction, joining in gifts, or rollover of an IRA into a spouse's name. They are generally barred from asserting a claim for loss of consortium and are not covered under family medical and car insurance policies unless specifically named. When a cohabitant's partner dies, the survivor is not entitled to receive a statutory portion of the estate or to take a statutory portion of the estate against a will.

Note that several states have recognized a cohabitant's right to benefits under workers' compensation schemes. *See, e.g.*, California, Louisiana, Maryland, Michigan, New Jersey, and Oregon.

REFLECTIVE QUESTIONS	What benefits do cohabitants forfeit when they refuse to marry?

14.6 THE COMMON LAW VIEW OF COHABITATION

Background to *Baker v. Couch*

This case provides historical insight into how all courts in the United States once viewed unmarried couples who lived together much like a husband and wife. The common law firmly rejected applying marriage law to cohabitating partners and was quick to invalidate contracts between unmarried cohabitants. The common law held that contracts having an immoral object were unenforceable on the ground of public policy, which relied heavily upon prevailing social attitudes. *Baxter v. Wilburn*, 190 A. 773 (Md. 1937). For example, in the case for discussion that follows, *Baker v. Couch*, Paul Couch, a 23-year-old man, and Alma Baker, a woman in her early thirties, lived together for a period in an intimate adulterous relationship. Couch had been married and divorced previously, and Baker had been married three times. The legal dispute the court is asked to resolve involves promissory notes in Baker's possession that were obtained by her from Couch. Couch is asking the court for an order requiring that Baker return them, claiming they were obtained through undue influence. Baker claims that they were a gift.

The evidence produced at trial included a written contract that the couple executed concerning the notes. Couch claims the document is unlawful because it was executed without consideration. However, the primary issue before the court is whether it will provide relief to either party where the evidence indicates they were involved in an immoral relationship. The court is concerned that the immoral relationship formed the basis of consideration for the contract, which for this court, if true, makes the contract unenforceable.

BAKER
v.
COUCH

Supreme Court of Colorado
221 P. 1089 (Colo. 1924)

BURKE, J. . . . One allegation . . . is that defendant promised, if the case was dismissed, to "resume meretricious relations with said plaintiff." This plaintiff was about 23 years of age. He says in his pleadings that he was without business judgment or experience. The record before us seems to confirm that assertion. But that he was not otherwise unsophisticated is indicated by evidence that he had at least one other similar affair and had previously been married.

Defendant was some eight years his senior, and, aside from any irregular attachments, had three times embarked upon the matrimonial sea under legal sanction. The first husband had died, the second was divorced, and the third was in process of separation on the grounds of bigamy. Plaintiff did not appear at the trial, and his story of the affair must be gleaned from his pleadings. Defendant testified that the illicit relations between the parties began almost with their acquaintance, had continued for some time, when the notes were delivered to her, and that those relations, past and future, were the consideration for the delivery.

Prior to the execution of the alleged contract . . . defendant . . . was being advised by a "law student," who apparently had not yet taken up the subject of legal ethics. Said contract, upon which one of the defenses is based, recited that its consideration was "love and affection"; but if any deity presided over this affair, it is very evident that it was not Athenian Venus, but Babylonian Ishtar. That contract closes with the following:

> Party of the first part [defendant] agrees to permit the party of the second part [plaintiff] to call at her home at reasonable hours and to continue the friendship already begun, until such time as the parties hereto agree to terminate this agreement.

We have been compelled to carefully examine the entire nauseous mess disclosed by this record. . . . [W]e are of the opinion that the consideration and the sole consideration, for the original delivery of the notes to defendant . . . was past, present, and future illicit relations between the parties. Under such circumstances no recovery could be had. The law is well settled, and the authorities practically unanimous.

Where the contract or transaction in question is . . . immoral, and there is mutual misconduct of the parties with respect thereto, neither law nor equity will aid to enforce, revoke, or rescind. To such disputes the courts will not listen, and the parties thereto they will leave in the exact position in which they have placed themselves. It is immaterial whether information of such illegality comes from plaintiff or defendant, or is disclosed by pleadings or evidence. For the foregoing reasons the judgment is reversed, and the cause remanded to the district court, with directions to dismiss the action.

DISCUSSION QUESTIONS FOR *BAKER v. COUCH*

A. If one applies the reasoning of this court to a divorce action brought by a plaintiff who committed adultery before filing for the divorce, would the court hear the dispute? If the answer is "no," does this make the courts at this time in history the moral policemen of society?

B. In the following hypothetical, assume that Farmer A has a horse that he wants to sell. Farmer B has money to purchase the horse and is willing to part with the money to purchase A's horse. This is a transaction. A and B's manifestations refer to each other — the horse for the money. Party B is seeking Party A's horse in exchange for her money, and vice-versa. *See* Danielle Kie Hart, *Contract Formation* *and the Entrenchment of Power*, 41 Loy. U. Chi. L.J. 175, 204-205 (Fall 2009). Apply this hypothetical to the facts in *Baker v. Couch*. Was there a transaction between Baker and Couch? What did the parties bargain for? What distinguishes the hypothetical from the facts in *Baker v. Couch*?

C. In *Baker v. Sockwell*, 251 P. 543 (Colo. 1926), Alma Baker attempted to force the holder of some of the same promissory notes described in *Baker v. Couch* to deliver them to her. *Id.* at 544-545. The Colorado court held that it would not assist Baker in her attempt to collect the notes because of the means she used to obtain title to them. Is the court once again acting as a "moral policeman"? If so, where did the court most likely obtain the values it is applying to the dispute? (What is the relationship, if any, between secular law and social morality?)

D. The Colorado Supreme Court eventually overruled *Baker v. Couch* in *Salzman v. Bachrach*, 996 P.2d 1263 (Colo. 2000), stating the following: "Although we find the rule of law in these earlier cases persuasive to some degree, social norms and behaviors have changed to such an extent that we now join the majority of courts in other states in holding that nonmarried cohabiting couples may legally contract with each other so long as sexual relations are merely incidental to the agreement. Furthermore, such couples may ask a court for assistance, in law or in equity, to enforce such agreements." Does the change in moral perspective suggest that the early law was being guided by something other than reason and logic?

14.7 CONSIDERATION FOR A COHABITATION CONTRACT

A cohabitation contract, as with any contract, must identify the parties to the agreement, acknowledge that they are legally competent, and set out the purpose of the contract. There must also be adequate consideration for the contract.

Consideration defined. Consideration for any contract is defined as a "bargained for legal benefit or detriment." *DiPasquale v. Costas*, 926 N.E.2d 682, 696 (Ohio App. 2010). Consideration is also defined as "[t]he inducement to a contract; the cause, motive, price, or impelling influence which induces a contracting party to enter into a contract." Black's Law Dictionary 161 (5th ed. 1979). It is said that if something is bargained for, consideration is present. "To be 'bargained for' means that 'the parties' manifestations must have reference to each other, i.e., that they be reciprocal.'" Danielle Kie Hart, *supra* at 204-205.

Restatement. The Restatement (Second) of Contracts states that something is bargained for "if it is sought by the promisor in exchange for his promise and is given by a promise in exchange for that promise." Restatement (Second) of Contracts §71(2) (1981). It also states that with certain exceptions, "any performance which is bargained for is consideration." Restatement (Second) of Contracts §72 (1981).

Illegal consideration as a part of the contract. The law has generally accepted the view that where the main consideration for a contract is illegal, such as sex for an indivisible promise, the contract will not be enforced. For example, a person who provides services as a housekeeper is normally barred from recovery on the bargain if cohabitation or sexual activity was contemplated as an *integral part* of the bargain and actually took place. *Walker v. Gregory*, 1860 WL 524 (Ala. 1860); *see Pizzo v. Goor*, 857 N.Y.S.2d 526 (N.Y.A.D. 2008).

Love, affection. In the context of cohabitation contracts, love, and affection are not viewed by courts as adequate consideration for an implied or express contract. Furthermore, a moral obligation alone does not constitute consideration. *Stone v. Lynch*, 315 S.E.2d 350, 354 (N.C. App. 1985), *aff'd*, 325 S.E.2d 230 (N.C. 1985).

Severable homemaker servicers. In *Carroll v. Lee*, 712 P.2d 923, 926 (Ariz. 1986), the court held that homemaking services that are severable from the meretricious relationship constitute consideration that can support an implied agreement between two parties who are unmarried cohabitants. *See Salzman v. Bachrach*, 996 P.2d 1263 (Colo. 2000); *Wilcox v. Trautz*, 693 N.E.2d 141 (Mass. 1998); *Crooke v. Gilden*, 414 S.E.2d 645 (Ga. 1992).

REFLECTIVE QUESTIONS	Can a court realistically sever the meretricious behavior in a relationship from other matters when considering a cohabitation agreement? If so, how is this done?

14.8 THE MARVIN DOCTRINE: "MARVIN I" (THE MAIN CASE)

Background to *Marvin v. Marvin*

This section and the two that follow trace the *Marvin* case from beginning to end. In this way, one can obtain a complete picture of the dispute and its eventual conclusion. The California Supreme Court initially remanded the case to the trial court, and the decision by the trial court is discussed. The decision by the trial court on remand was appealed, and the ruling by the court of appeal is summarized. At that point, the case came to an end.

Lee Marvin died in 1987. He was a well-known Hollywood actor who won a Best Actor Oscar in 1965 for his role in the Western spoof, *Cat Ballou*. He had met Michelle Triola, a 31-year-old stand-in and extra dancer, on the set of *Ship of Fools* in 1964, and they were lovers until they parted in 1970. Marvin remained married to his first wife for a considerable time while living with Triola. When his marriage was eventually dissolved, Marvin renewed a relationship with his former teenage sweetheart, Pamela Feeley, and they married in 1970. Marvin continued to send money to Michelle Triola for a year and a half after his second marriage. When he stopped sending her funds, she sued claiming that they had agreed to share the proceeds from his earnings during the nearly six years they had lived together.

At the trial, Triola's lawyer argued that his client had the same rights as a married spouse even though Triola and Lee Marvin had never married. Although the court doesn't use the term, the lawyer is credited with coining the term *palimony* to designate the money he claimed his client was owed from alimony.

Marvin's lawyer argued that the court should not recognize the alleged oral contract between Marvin and Triola. He asserted that recognition was contrary to existing public policy because the relationship was immoral and any consideration for a contract, if it existed, rested on this immoral foundation. He also argued that enforcement was barred by the Statute of Frauds, which required that contracts for marriage settlements be in writing. Finally, he claimed that Triola's claim was similar to a breach of promise to marry action, a heartbalm cause of action that had been abolished in California and most other jurisdictions.

MARVIN
v.
MARVIN

Supreme Court of California, *en banc*
557 P.2d 106 (Cal. 1976)

TOBRINGER, J. . . . Plaintiff avers that in October of 1964 she and defendant "entered into an oral agreement" that while "the parties lived together they would combine their efforts and earnings and would share equally any and all property accumulated as a result of their efforts whether individual or combined." Furthermore, they agreed to "hold themselves out to the general public as husband and wife" and that "plaintiff would further render her services as a companion, homemaker, housekeeper and cook to defendant."

Shortly thereafter plaintiff agreed to "give up her lucrative career as an entertainer [and] singer" in order to "devote her full time to defendant as a companion, homemaker, housekeeper and cook"; in return defendant agreed to "provide for all of plaintiff's financial support and needs for the rest of her life."

Plaintiff alleges that she lived with defendant from October of 1964 through May of 1970 and fulfilled her obligations under the agreement. During this period the parties as a result of their efforts and earnings acquired in defendant's name substantial real and personal property, including motion picture rights worth over $1 million. In May of 1970, however, defendant compelled plaintiff to leave his household. He continued to support plaintiff until November of 1971, but thereafter refused to provide further support.

On the basis of these allegations plaintiff asserts two causes of action. The first, for declaratory relief, asks the court to determine her contract and property rights; the second seeks to impose a constructive trust upon one half of the property acquired during the course of the relationship. . . .

Plaintiff's complaint states a cause of action for breach of an express contract.

In *Trutalli v. Meraviglia* (1932), we established the principle that nonmarital partners may lawfully contract concerning the ownership of property acquired during the relationship. We reaffirmed this principle in *Vallera v. Vallera* (1943), stating that "If a man and woman [who are not married] live together as husband and wife under an agreement to pool their earnings and share equally in their joint accumulations, equity will protect the interests of each in such property." . . .

Defendant . . . principally relies on the contention that the alleged contract is so closely related to the supposed "immoral" character of the relationship between plaintiff and himself that the enforcement of the contract would violate public policy. He points to cases asserting that a contract between nonmarital partners is unenforceable if it is "involved in" an illicit relationship or made in "contemplation" of such a relationship. A review of the numerous California decisions concerning contracts between nonmarital partners, however, reveals that the courts have not employed such broad and uncertain standards to strike down contracts. The decisions instead disclose a narrower and more precise standard: a contract between nonmarital partners is unenforceable only to the extent that it explicitly rests upon the immoral and illicit consideration of meretricious sexual services. . . .

Although the past decisions hover over the issue in the somewhat wispy form of the figures of a Chagall painting, we can abstract from those decisions a clear and simple rule. The fact that a man and woman live together without marriage, and engage in a sexual relationship, does not in itself invalidate agreements between them relating to their earnings, property, or expenses. Neither is such an agreement invalid merely because the parties may have contemplated the creation or continuation of a nonmarital relationship when they entered into it. Agreements between nonmarital partners fail only to the extent that they rest upon a consideration of meretricious sexual services. . . .

The three cases cited by defendant which have declined to enforce contracts between nonmarital partners involved consideration that was expressly founded upon illicit sexual services. In *Hill v. Estate of Westbrook*, the woman promised to keep house for the man, to live with him as man and wife, and to bear his children; the man promised to provide for her in his will, but died without doing so. Reversing a judgment for the woman based on the reasonable value of her services, the Court of Appeal stated that "the action is predicated upon a claim which seeks, among other things, the reasonable value of living with decedent in meretricious relationship and bearing him two children. The law does not award compensation for living with a man as a concubine and bearing him children. As the judgment is at least in part, for the value of the claimed services for which recovery cannot be had, it must be reversed." Upon retrial, the trial court found that it could not sever the contract and place an independent value upon the legitimate services performed by claimant. We therefore affirmed a judgment for the estate.

In the only other cited decision refusing to enforce a contract, the contract "was based on the consideration that the parties live together as husband and wife." Viewing the contract as calling for adultery, the court held it illegal.

The decisions demonstrate that a contract between nonmarital partners, even if expressly made in contemplation of a common living arrangement, is invalid only if sexual acts form an inseparable part of the consideration for the agreement. In sum, a court will not enforce a contract for the pooling of property and earnings if it is explicitly and inseparably based upon services as a paramour. [H]owever, if sexual services are part of the contractual consideration, any severable portion of the contract supported by independent consideration will still be enforced.

The principle that a contract between nonmarital partners will be enforced unless expressly and inseparably based upon an illicit consideration of sexual services not only represents the distillation of the decisional law, but also offers a far more precise and workable standard than that advocated by defendant.

Similarly, in the present case a standard which inquires whether an agreement is "involved" in or "contemplates" a nonmarital relationship is vague and unworkable. Virtually all agreements between nonmarital partners can be said to be "involved" in some sense in the fact of their mutual sexual relationship, or to "contemplate" the existence of that relationship. Thus defendant's proposed standards, if taken literally, might invalidate all agreements between nonmarital partners, a result no one favors. Moreover, those standards offer no basis to distinguish between valid and invalid agreements. By looking not to such uncertain tests, but only to the consideration underlying the agreement, we provide the parties and the courts with a practical guide to determine when an agreement between nonmarital partners should be enforced. . . .

In summary, we base our opinion on the principle that adults who voluntarily live together and engage in sexual relations are nonetheless as competent as any other persons to contract respecting their earnings and property rights. Of course, they cannot lawfully contract to pay for the performance of sexual services, for such a contract is, in essence, an agreement for prostitution and unlawful for that reason. But they may agree to pool their earnings and to hold all property acquired during the relationship in accord with the law governing community property; conversely they may agree that each partner's earnings and the property acquired from those earnings remains the separate property of the earning partner. So long as the agreement does not rest upon illicit meretricious consideration, the parties may order their economic affairs as they choose, and no policy precludes the courts from enforcing such agreements. . . .

[W]e believe that the prevalence of nonmarital relationships in modern society and the social acceptance of them, marks this as a time when our courts should by no means apply the doctrine of the unlawfulness of the so-called meretricious relationship to the instant case. As we have explained, the nonenforceability of agreements expressly providing for meretricious conduct rested upon the fact that such conduct, as the word suggests, pertained to and encompassed prostitution. To equate the nonmarital relationship of today to such a subject matter is to do violence to an accepted and wholly different practice.

We are aware that many young couples live together without the solemnization of marriage, in order to make sure that they can successfully later undertake marriage. This trial period, preliminary to marriage, serves as some assurance that the marriage will not subsequently end in dissolution to the harm of both parties. We are aware, as we have stated, of the pervasiveness of nonmarital relationships in other situations.

The mores of the society have indeed changed so radically in regard to cohabitation that we cannot impose a standard based on alleged moral considerations that have apparently been so widely abandoned by so many. Lest we be misunderstood, however, we take this occasion to point out that the structure of society itself largely depends upon the institution of marriage, and nothing we have said in this opinion should be taken to derogate from that institution. The joining of the man and woman in marriage is at once the most socially productive and individually fulfilling relationship that one can enjoy in the course of a lifetime.

We conclude that the judicial barriers that may stand in the way of a policy based upon the fulfillment of the reasonable expectations of the parties to a nonmarital relationship should be removed. As we have explained, the courts now hold that express agreements will be enforced unless they rest on an unlawful meretricious consideration. We add that in the absence of an express agreement, the courts may look to a variety of other remedies in order to protect the parties' lawful expectations. . . .

The judgment is reversed and the cause remanded for further proceedings consistent with the views expressed herein.

DISCUSSION QUESTIONS FOR *MARVIN v. MARVIN*

A. What is the consideration for the contract between Marvin and Triola? Was there detrimental reliance by Triola on Marvin's alleged promise? Was Triola induced into entering a contract with Marvin?

B. What is the "narrow" and "precise" standard the *Marvin* court adopts when considering whether contracts between nonmarital partners should be enforced? Is the standard "workable" in the sense that all agreements between nonmarital partners involve to some extent a mutual sexual relation, or contemplate the existence of that sexual relationship?

C. According to *Marvin*, there are numerous theories upon which cohabiting litigants may pursue their claims against former partners. Among them are express oral agreements, implied agreements, and partition actions. Since the *Marvin* decision, some of these theories have been adopted by courts. *See, e.g., Donovan v. Scuderi*, 443 A.2d 121, 125-126 (Md. App. 1982); *Kinkenon v.*

Hue, 301 N.W.2d 77, 80-81 (Neb. 1981); *Carroll v. Lee*, 712 P.2d 923, 926-927 (Ariz. 1986); *Libby v. Lorrain*, 430 A.2d 37, 38-39 (Me. 1981); *Carlson v. Olson*, 256 N.W.2d 249, 255 (Minn. 1977). Other legal theories recognized in *Marvin* that might be used in cohabitant disputes include joint venture, constructive trust, and resulting trust.

Assume for this hypothetical that P and D cohabit in a state that does not recognize common law marriage. D convinced P to let her manage all of partner P's stock and investment accounts. To make the management easier, D asks P to transfer title of the accounts to D. After ten years, the relationship breaks down and P and D cannot agree on who owns the stock and investment accounts. The lawyer for P is considering which of three theories to select for her action against D: (1) a constructive trust theory, which is used when one partner holds title to specific property, but in fairness, the property should be transferred to the other partner; (2) a resulting trust theory, which is based on a theory that when one person holds property for the benefit of another, but never intended the other to have an equitable or beneficial interest in the property; and (3) a joint venture theory, which is used when there is a joint interest in the property by the parties sought to be held as partners. In a joint venture, there must exist either an expressed or implied agreement showing that the parties intended to share in the profits and losses of the venture. Furthermore, there must also be actions and conduct showing co-operation in the project. Which of the three theories appears most likely to succeed? *See* Kim Willoughby, Lewis v. Lewis *and Non-Married Partner Litigation*, 39-Jan Colo. Law. 33, 35 (January 2010).

D. The liberal *Marvin* theories of recovery have not been accepted by all jurisdictions. Some require an express contract, whether oral or written. *See, e.g., Levar v. Elkins*, 604 P.2d 602 (Alaska 1980); *Dominguez v. Cruz*, 617 P.2d 1322 (N.M. Ct. App. 1980); *Morone v. Morone*, 413 N.E.2d 1154 (N.Y. 1980). Other jurisdictions require a written contract. Some jurisdictions rejected the theory that a quasi-marital contract between unmarried cohabitants, whether of opposite sexes or the same sex, could be enforced at all. *See, e.g., Rehak v. Mathis*, 238 S.E.2d 81 (Ga. 1977). Rhode Island has stated that it has never recognized a palimony claim. *See Norton v. McOsker*, 407 F.3d 501, n.6 (1st Cir. 2005).

The ruling by New Hampshire in *Tapley v. Tapley*, 449 A.2d 1218 (N.H. 1982), raises interesting discussion issues. The parties lived together without marriage for ten years. The female partner performed housekeeping chores, including preparation of meals, laundering, care and cleaning of the home, keeping the financial books, payment of bills, banking, shopping, showing their rental property, and caring for the male's infant child on weekends. In addition, the parties opened joint checking accounts, shared medical insurance, and represented themselves as married on official documents. The female received total support from the defendant except for child support from her former husband, monetary gifts from her parents, and small sums she earned from outside-the-home work. The defendant also supported the female's daughter for two years subsequent to her eighteenth birthday when her natural father's support payments to her had stopped. The female sought reasonable compensation and permanent support for the household services she rendered to the defendant during the period of their cohabitation on theories of implied contract and *quantum meruit.* The New Hampshire court rejected her claims. What might have been the basis for rejecting the plaintiff's claims? How would a California court most likely rule on the plaintiff's claims?

E. Assume for this hypothetical that P and D cohabit for six years before their relationship falls apart. They have two children born to them during the relationship. In a written document, executed and notarized during the time they cohabited, P agrees that should the couple's relationship end, D will receive legal custody of their two children. After the breakup, P challenges the custody provision. How will a court most likely rule on this contract? *See Linda R. v. Ari Z.,* 895 N.Y.S.2d 412, 414 (N.Y.A.D. 2010). Could the contract be used to at least show intent to confer parental rights on D? *See Mullins v. Picklesimer,* 317 S.W.3d 569 (Ky. 2010); *In re Mullen,* 924 N.E.2d 448, 461 (Ohio App. 2009).

F. The *Marvin* court states that "nothing we have said in this opinion should be taken to derogate" marriage. Isn't the fact that the court gives cohabiting couples rights to enforce implied contracts itself a derogation of marriage?

G. Some argue that the *Marvin* doctrine gives unmarried partners greater freedom to arrange their economic and other aspects of their relationship than most states allow married partners. Does it? If so, isn't this unfair to married partners?

14.9 MARVIN DOCTRINE: "MARVIN II," TRIAL JUDGE'S FINDINGS ON REMAND

In summary, the California Supreme Court held in *Marvin I* the following: (a) Agreements between nonmarital partners fail only to the extent that they rest on illicit sexual services; (b) the rights of Marvin's wife were not impaired because those rights were already fixed by her divorce action; (c) the contract being reviewed was not a marital settlement; (d) agreements between cohabiting couples to pool earnings and provide support are not barred by the abolition of the breach of promise to marry statutes; (e) express agreements between cohabiting couples will be enforced except to the extent that such contracts rest on unlawful consideration; (f) implied agreements (both implied-in-fact and implied-in-law) are enforceable to protect the fulfillment of the parties' reasonable expectations; and (g) courts may examine the conduct to the parties to fashion relief through creation of a constructive trust, resulting trust, or *quantum meruit.* The court then remanded the *Marvin* decision back to the trial court for reconsideration.

Trial judge's findings. On remand, the trial judge found that the parties never agreed during their cohabitation that they would combine their efforts and earnings or would share equally in any property accumulated as a result of their efforts, whether individual or combined. It also found that they never agreed that the plaintiff would relinquish her professional career as an entertainer and singer in order to devote her efforts full time to defendant as his companion and homemaker.

The trial court concluded that (1) the defendant never had any obligation to pay plaintiff a reasonable sum as and for her maintenance; (2) the plaintiff suffered no damage resulting from her relationship with defendant, including its termination, and thus defendant did not become monetarily liable to plaintiff at all; (3) the plaintiff actually benefited economically and socially from the cohabitation of the parties, including payment by defendant for goods and services for plaintiff's sole benefit in the approximate amount of $72,900, payment by defendant of the living expenses of the two of them of approximately $221,400, and other substantial specified gifts; (4) a confidential and fiduciary relationship never existed between the parties with respect to property; (5) the defendant was never unjustly enriched as a result of the relationship of the parties or of the services performed by plaintiff for him or for them; and (6) the defendant never acquired any property or money from plaintiff by any wrongful act.

Rehabilitation/living expenses award. The most controversial finding by the trial court was its rehabilitation determination. The trial court found that the plaintiff at the time of the trial had been recently receiving unemployment insurance benefits, and that it was doubtful that she could return to the career she had enjoyed before the relationship of the parties commenced, namely, that of singer. It found that the plaintiff was in need of rehabilitation, that is, to learn new employable skills, and that she should be able to accomplish such rehabilitation in two years. It awarded her $104,000, saying it was not only necessary for rehabilitation, but also for her living expenses (including her debts) during this period of rehabilitation. It found that the defendant had the ability to pay this sum "forthwith." *Marvin v. Marvin*, 5 Fam. L. Rep. 3077 (1979). Lee Marvin again appealed.

REFLECTIVE QUESTIONS	Of all the findings listed above, which are the most important to Michelle Triola? Which are the most important to Lee Marvin?

14.10 MARVIN DOCTRINE: "MARVIN III," FINAL APPELLATE COURT REVIEW OF TRIAL JUDGE'S FINDINGS

In *Marvin v. Marvin*, 176 Cal. Rptr. 555 (Cal. App. 1981), the court of appeal relied heavily on four of the trial court's findings in reversing the judgment: (1) The plaintiff benefited economically and socially from her relationship with the defendant and had suffered no damage therefrom, even with respect to its termination; (2) the defendant never had any obligation to pay the plaintiff a reasonable sum as and for her maintenance; (3) the defendant had not been unjustly enriched by reason of the relationship or its termination; and (4) the defendant had never acquired anything of value from the plaintiff by any wrongful act.

Given the trial court's findings, the court of appeal concluded that the $104,000 for "occupational rehabilitation" was an abuse of discretion. It stated that the award merely established that the plaintiff had a need for rehabilitation and that the defendant had the ability to respond to that need. "This is not enough," said the court. "The award, being nonconsensual in nature, must be supported by some recognized underlying obligation in law or in equity. A court of equity admittedly has broad powers, but it may not create totally new substantive rights under the guise of doing equity." *Id.* at 559.

REFLECTIVE QUESTIONS	Do you agree with the appellate court ruling discussed above?

14.11 MARVIN DOCTRINE: REJECTED IN ILLINOIS

The most influential case rejecting the *Marvin* doctrine is probably *Hewitt v. Hewitt*, 394 N.E.2d 1204 (Ill. 1979). In *Hewitt*, a woman cohabitant sought a one-half share in the property accumulated during the relationship. She and the defendant were students at Grinnell College in Iowa when she became pregnant. The defendant told her that they were already husband and wife and would live as such, therefore, no formal marriage ceremony or license was necessary. He also said that he would "share his life, his future, his earnings and his property" with her. The parties immediately announced to their respective parents that they were married and for the next 15 years held themselves out as husband and wife. Three children were born to the relationship.

At the hearing in this matter, the woman testified that in reliance on the defendant's promises she devoted her efforts to his professional education and his establishment in the practice of pedodontia and obtained financial assistance from her parents for this purpose. She also assisted him in his career with her own special skills, and although she was given payroll checks for these services, she placed them in a common fund. She claimed that the defendant, who was without funds at the time of the marriage, as a result of her efforts, earned over $80,000 a year when their relationship ended and had accumulated large amounts of property, owned either jointly with her or separately. She also testified that she gave him every assistance a wife and mother could give, including social activities designed to enhance his social and professional reputation.

The trial judge rejected her claims. The judge believed that Illinois law and public policy required that the claims be based on a valid marriage. The dispute then went to an intermediate Illinois appellate court, which reversed the trial judge. The appellate court stated that because the parties had outwardly lived a conventional married life, the plaintiff's conduct had not "so affronted public policy that she should be denied any and all relief." It held that the plaintiff's complaint stated a cause of action on an express oral contract. The appellate court adopted the reasoning of the California Supreme Court in *Marvin v. Marvin*. The decision was then taken for review by the Illinois Supreme Court.

The Illinois Supreme Court rejected the woman's claims. It observed the following:

> There are major public policy questions involved in determining whether, under what circumstances, and to what extent it is desirable to accord some type of legal status to claims arising from such relationships. Of substantially greater importance than the rights of the immediate parties is the impact of such recognition upon our society and the institution of marriage. Will the fact that legal rights closely resembling those arising from conventional marriages can be acquired by those who deliberately choose to enter into what have heretofore been commonly referred to as "illicit" or "meretricious" relationships encourage formation of such relationships and weaken marriage as the foundation of our family-based society? In the event of death shall the survivor have the status of a surviving spouse for purposes of inheritance, wrongful death actions, workmen's compensation, etc.? And still more importantly: what of the children born of such relationships? What are their support and inheritance rights and by what standards are custody questions resolved? What of the sociological and psychological effects upon them of that type of environment? Does not the recognition of legally enforceable property and custody rights emanating from nonmarital cohabitation in practical effect equate with the legalization of common law marriage at least in the circumstances of this case?

The court reasoned that:

> The real thrust of plaintiff's argument here is that we should abandon the rule of illegality because of certain changes in societal norms and attitudes. It is urged that social mores have changed radically in recent years, rendering this principle of law archaic. It is said that because there are so many unmarried cohabitants today the courts must confer a legal status on such relationships. This, of course, is the rationale underlying some of the decisions and commentaries. . . . If this is to be the result, however, it would seem more candid to acknowledge the return of varying forms of common law marriage than to continue displaying the naiveté we believe involved in the assertion that there are involved in these relationships contracts separate and independent from the sexual activity, and the assumption that those contracts would have been entered into or would continue without that activity.

The court concluded that the "plaintiff's claims are unenforceable for the reason that they contravene the public policy, implicit in the statutory scheme of the Illinois Marriage and Dissolution of Marriage Act, disfavoring the grant of mutually enforceable property rights to knowingly unmarried cohabitants."

Has Illinois rejected *Hewitt*? A 2014 decision by the Appellate Court of Illinois, First District, Fifth Division, has called the viability of *Hewitt* somewhat into question. *Blumenthal v. Brewer*, 24 N.E.3d 168 (2014). In that decision, the trial judge had applied *Hewitt* when rejecting a cohabitant's claim for a portion of property obtained while she and her partner lived together. On appeal, the plaintiff identified numerous changes in Illinois law, which the plaintiff argued had caused public policy to shift dramatically in the ensuing 35 years since *Hewitt*. According to the plaintiff, *Hewitt* was no longer good law in Illinois. The court of appeals seemed to agree holding that the former partner could bring common law claims for unjust enrichment and *quantum meruit* in relation to the real property that was in dispute.

Only a handful of jurisdictions have accepted the *Hewitt* view. *See, e.g., Merrill v. Davis*, 673 P.2d 1285 (N.M. 1983); *In re Estate of Alexander*, 445 So. 2d 836 (Miss. 1984); *Grishman v. Grishman*, 407 A.2d 9, n.6 (Me. 1979).

> **REFLECTIVE QUESTIONS**   Do you agree with the analysis of the Illinois court in *Hewitt*?

14.12 MARVIN DOCTRINE: ALI PERSPECTIVE

The American Law Institute (ALI) in its *Principles of the Law of Family Dissolution: Analysis and Recommendations* (2002) appears to have abandoned *Marvin*'s contract theory approach to resolving cohabitation disputes. Shahar Lifshitz, *A Potential Lesson from the Israeli Experience for the American Same-Sex Marriage Debate*, 22 BYU J. Pub. L. 359, 378-379 (2008). The *Principles* treats unrelated parties without a common child as *presumed* domestic partners if they share a common household for a minimum of three years. The presumption may be rebutted by evidence that the parties did not "share a life together as a couple." Parties may also be treated as domestic partners if one of them can produce evidence showing that they shared a common household and a life together for a "significant period of time," even if that time is less than the minimum periods set in the other provisions. *See* ALI, *Principles of the Law of Family Dissolution* §6.01. When domestic partners dissolve their relationship, property and compensatory payment (alimony) remedies are comparable to those available upon dissolution of a marriage. *Ibid.* The ALI *Principles* would extend equally to same-sex and opposite-sex cohabiting couples.

Section 6.03 of the ALI *Principles* lists 13 factors that are intended to assist courts in deciding whether a couple shared a life together. Among these factors are intermingling finances, becoming economically dependent, having defined tasks, dividing roles between partners, raising children jointly, and making statements regarding the relationship or participation in commitment ceremonies.

REFLECTIVE QUESTIONS | How does the ALI approach to cohabitation agreements differ from the more traditional contract approach used by many courts?

14.13 MARVIN DOCTRINE: PALIMONY

Background to *Devaney v. L'Esperance*

Devaney v. L'Esperance is considered a "palimony" case, which in general terms is a claim similar to alimony. The dispute involves a woman who brought suit against a man who was married and living with his wife during the plaintiff's 20-year relationship with him. She is seeking to enforce promises of support he allegedly made to her during their relationship. He defends the lawsuit on the ground they never cohabited in a husband-wife like relationship. The trial court ruled in favor of the man and the woman appealed. The Superior Court, Appellate Division, 918 A.2d 684, affirmed. The woman then sought review in the New Jersey Supreme Court. The two most important questions presented to the court were: First, is cohabitation an indispensable element of a palimony action? Second, was the evidence submitted to the trial judge sufficient to establish that the couple had a "marital-type" relationship?

DEVANEY v. L'ESPERANCE

Supreme Court of New Jersey
949 A.2d 743 (N.J. 2008)

WALLACE, J. . . . Plaintiff and defendant were involved in an intimate relationship. During the course of their twenty-year relationship, defendant, who was married, continued to live with his wife and never cohabited with plaintiff. However, he promised to divorce his wife, marry plaintiff, and have a child with her. Defendant's promises were not fulfilled and his relationship with plaintiff eventually ended.

Plaintiff filed a palimony complaint against defendant, asserting a breach of a promise to support her for life. The trial court denied relief because the parties essentially had a dating relationship rather than a marital-type relationship that was needed to support a palimony claim. The Appellate Division affirmed solely because the parties never cohabited. We granted certification to address whether a party may prove a cause of action for palimony absent cohabitation.

. . . In 1983, plaintiff, Helen Devaney, then twenty-three years old, began working for defendant, Francis L'Esperance, Jr., as a receptionist for his ophthalmology medical practice. At that time, defendant was fifty-one years old and had been married to his current wife for approximately twenty years. Plaintiff and defendant embarked on a romantic relationship. Although plaintiff was aware that defendant was married, she believed that he would divorce his wife.

In the beginning of their relationship, plaintiff lived in a variety of places, all of which were rented in her own name and mostly self-financed. At some point, defendant began paying plaintiff's telephone bill and gave her money for various other things. Plaintiff, however, remained largely self-sufficient during this period of their relationship. She continued working for defendant in various capacities, at first full-time, and then part-time.

For about ten years, plaintiff and defendant saw each other regularly and would spend vacations together. However, when the parties were not traveling, they rarely stayed overnight together. Defendant frequently had dinner at plaintiff's house, but he invariably returned home to his wife.

Plaintiff testified that defendant repeatedly told her that he would divorce his wife and marry her. In 1993, plaintiff terminated her employment with defendant and pursued educational opportunities. Shortly thereafter, plaintiff moved to Connecticut. A year later, she moved to Seattle, Washington, where she remained for approximately three years. Plaintiff testified that her decision to move was based primarily on defendant's unfulfilled promise to divorce his wife. During her stay in Seattle, plaintiff frequently spoke by telephone with defendant and requested money from him. Defendant would send her approximately four hundred dollars a month to cover her incidental expenses. During the time that plaintiff lived in Seattle, defendant visited her six or seven times.

In 1997, defendant asked plaintiff to return to the East Coast. Plaintiff testified that defendant promised that he would "make things right" by divorcing his wife, marrying plaintiff, and having a baby with her. She testified that she agreed to move back after defendant showed her a separation agreement that was signed by both defendant and his wife. Plaintiff also testified that defendant promised to buy her a home.

Plaintiff returned to New Jersey in 1997, and moved into a North Bergen condominium that defendant leased for her. In 1999, defendant purchased the condominium unit and plaintiff continued to reside there. Defendant also purchased a car that plaintiff used; gave her money for various expenses; and paid for her undergraduate and graduate education. Plaintiff ultimately received a Master's degree.

Despite the increased support that defendant provided to plaintiff, the parties saw each other no more than two or three evenings at the condominium for dinner each week and sometimes one day on the weekend. During the seven years that plaintiff lived in the condominium, defendant spent only six or seven nights there.

In 2003, the parties considered having a child together. However, at some point, plaintiff learned that she would have difficulty conceiving a child. Defendant also changed his mind about wanting to have another child in August 2003 and conveyed that to plaintiff.

Finally, defendant told plaintiff that he wanted to discontinue the relationship. Plaintiff continued to live in the North Bergen condominium, and in December

2003, she began a relationship with another man. In February 2004, defendant attempted to visit the condominium when plaintiff's new boyfriend was present, but defendant was denied entrance by plaintiff.

Shortly thereafter, defendant sought to remove plaintiff from the condominium and filed an action for ejectment. Eventually, the trial court granted defendant possession of the condominium and the judgment was affirmed on appeal.

Plaintiff filed a complaint for palimony in October 2004, and defendant filed an answer. Following discovery, a bench trial was held. The Family Part judge issued an oral opinion in which she denied plaintiff's complaint for palimony. The judge found that defendant had made "general promises" to plaintiff that he would take care of her and that "things would work out," and that plaintiff used those promises to sustain her belief that they would eventually live together. Further, although over the years plaintiff became financially dependent on defendant, defendant never promised to provide plaintiff with lifetime financial support.

The trial judge rejected plaintiff's contention that the parties entered into an implied agreement for support, and citing *In re Estate of Roccamonte*, 808 A.2d 838 (2002), found that such an agreement requires that the parties have entered into a "marital-type" relationship. The judge cited several factors that contributed to her conclusion that the parties' relationship was not akin to a marriage. The judge considered that the parties had not cohabited, had not spent significant periods of time together, and had not demonstrated an intention to commingle property. The judge also found that although defendant did visit with plaintiff's family, the parties did not hold themselves out to the public as husband and wife and plaintiff did not attend social gatherings with defendant's friends, family, or colleagues.

In addition, the judge found that plaintiff's contributions to the relationship were not similar to those a wife would make in a marriage. Although plaintiff provided defendant with companionship and helped with some of his personal and business matters, the judge found no evidence that those actions were more than a typical dating relationship. Finally, the judge denied plaintiff's request for counsel fees because the equities weighed against such an award.

Plaintiff appealed. The Appellate Division affirmed the trial court's decision denying plaintiff palimony. . . . The panel held that under New Jersey law, cohabitation is an essential element to a cause of action for palimony and because the parties never lived together, plaintiff was not entitled to the requested relief. The panel also affirmed the denial of plaintiff's claim for counsel fees. We granted plaintiff's petition for certification.

II

Plaintiff argues that the Appellate Division erroneously held that cohabitation is an indispensable element of a palimony cause of action. She contends that consistent with *Roccamonte, supra*, in which the Court defined a marital-type relationship as "the undertaking of a way of life in which two people commit to each other," 174 N.J. at 392, 808 A.2d 838, cohabitation is a relevant, but not a necessary, factor. Plaintiff contends that the parties' relationship satisfied *Roccamonte* because they committed to each other, provided companionship, and met each other's financial, emotional, physical, and social needs. Plaintiff asserts that her entering into such a relationship and subsequently conducting herself in accordance with its unique character was consideration in full measure to make defendant's promise of lifetime support enforceable. She also argues that the parties' attempt to conceive a child was evidence of a marital-type relationship and that equity requires an award of palimony because she devoted herself to defendant for almost twenty years in reliance on defendant's promises that he would divorce his wife, marry plaintiff, and have a child with her. Further, she contends that whether she is entitled to counsel fees should await the ultimate disposition of this matter.

In contrast, defendant argues that the Appellate Division's holding is correct because the law is "settled" that cohabitation is a prerequisite to a claim for palimony, and the fact that he was married and living with his wife during the entire course of the parties' relationship weighs against the finding of a marital-type relationship. He notes that under *Roccamonte*, a critical ingredient to a marital-type relationship is that two people commit to each other, foregoing other liaisons and opportunities and that did not happen in this case. Moreover, defendant argues that an attempt to have a child should not create an entitlement to palimony because there is no public interest in promoting childbearing in the context of an adulterous relationship. In addition, he contends that plaintiff was enriched by the fact that he paid for her education, and she is now capable of supporting herself. Defendant contends that soon after the parties broke up, she met another man, and became engaged to marry him, and therefore, there is no evidence of a "profound dependency" on defendant. Finally, defendant argues that the Appellate Division correctly upheld the trial judge's determination that neither party should receive counsel fees as a reasonable exercise of discretion.

III

Preliminarily, we trace our history of a cause of action for palimony, which in general terms is a claim for support between unmarried persons. We first recognized such a cause of action in *Kozlowski v. Kozlowski*, 403 A.2d 902 (1979). Prior to that decision, our courts would not enforce support agreements between unmarried individuals or married persons who lived together with someone other than their spouses because they were considered meretricious.

In *Kozlowski*, both the defendant and the plaintiff were married to other persons when the defendant induced the plaintiff to leave her husband and come live with him. The parties lived as a normal family unit for approximately six years. During that time, three of the four children of the two families came to live with the couple in their new home. Although a serious disagreement caused them to separate for a week, the defendant wanted to resume the relationship and promised to take care of and provide for the plaintiff for the rest of her life if she would return. The plaintiff agreed and the parties resumed their relationship for about nine more years before the defendant broke it off for another woman.

The plaintiff filed suit against the defendant, seeking, among other things, future support for life. The trial court found that the defendant expressly agreed to support the plaintiff for the rest of her life and that such a promise was enforceable. While the appeal was pending in the Appellate Division, this Court certified the appeal. The Court acknowledged the changing mores that resulted in many unmarried persons living together and adopted the view expressed by the California Supreme Court, which declared:

> In summary, we believe that the prevalence of nonmarital relationships in modern society and the social acceptance of them, marks this as a time when our courts should by no means apply the doctrine of the unlawfulness of the so-called meretricious relationship to the instant case. As we have explained, the nonenforceability of agreements expressly providing for meretricious conduct rested upon the fact that such conduct, as the word suggests, pertained to and encompassed prostitution. To equate the nonmarital relationship of today to such a subject matter is to do violence to an accepted and wholly different practice.
>
> We are aware that many young couples live together without the solemnization of marriage, in order to make sure that they can successfully later undertake marriage. This trial period, preliminary to marriage, serves as some assurance that the marriage will not subsequently end in dissolution to the harm of both parties. We are aware, as we have stated, of the pervasiveness of nonmarital relationships in other situations.
>
> The mores of the society have indeed changed so radically in regard to cohabitation that we cannot impose a standard based on alleged moral considerations that have apparently been so widely abandoned by so many.
>
> We conclude that the judicial barriers that may stand in the way of a policy based upon the fulfillment of the reasonable expectations of the parties to a nonmarital relationship should be removed. As we have explained, the courts now hold that express agreements will be enforced unless they rest on an unlawful meretricious consideration.

[*Id.* at 902 (*quoting Marvin v. Marvin*, 557 P.2d 106, 122 (1976).]

The Court recognized that such an agreement may be expressed or implied because the "[p]arties entering this type of relationship usually do not record their understanding in specific legalese." The Court concluded that "an agreement between adult parties living together is enforceable to the extent it is not based on a relationship proscribed by law, or on a promise to marry."

Three years later, the Court applied the *Kozlowski* principles in *Crowe v. DeGioia*, 447 A.2d 173 (1982). There, the plaintiff met the defendant in 1960 when she was separated from her husband. The defendant was single and agreed that the plaintiff and her seven children could live with him. The plaintiff alleged that the two lived together for twenty years in a relationship that was akin to a marriage and that the defendant told her that "he would take care of her and support her for the rest of her life." When the defendant broke off the relationship, he promised to give her a good settlement, but never did. The plaintiff filed a complaint seeking support and temporary relief. The trial court granted temporary relief, but the Appellate Division reversed. After reaffirming that the plaintiff was not entitled to alimony because the parties were not married, this Court applied traditional equitable principles to authorize preliminary relief. The Court explained that

> [t]he inability to fit [the] plaintiff's claim for temporary relief into the conventional category of a matrimonial action is not a bar to relief. To achieve substantial justice in other cases,

we have adjusted the rights and duties of parties in light of the realities of their relationship. Increasing numbers of unmarried couples live together. . . . Although [the] plaintiff need not be rewarded for cohabitating with [the] defendant, she should not be penalized simply because she lived with him in consideration of a promise for support. Our endeavor is to shape a remedy that will protect the legally cognizable interests of the parties and serve the needs of justice.

[*Id.* at 173 (internal citations omitted).]

Thus, the Court affirmed the trial court's grant of preliminary relief and remanded for a plenary hearing to resolve the factual dispute.

The most recent case in which this Court addressed palimony is *Roccamonte, supra*, 808 A.2d 838. In that case, the issue was whether the promise of support for life was enforceable against the decedent's estate. Each party was married to another person when they met in the 1950's. The parties began a relationship and eventually lived together off and on until the plaintiff sought to end the relationship because the defendant refused to divorce his wife and marry her. The plaintiff moved to California in mid-1960, but returned when the defendant promised that he would financially support her for the rest of her life if she would come back to him. The plaintiff agreed. She divorced her husband and the parties lived together as if they were husband and wife until the defendant's death.

However, the defendant never divorced his wife. Although the defendant promised the plaintiff that if he were to die first he would provide for her during her lifetime, he died intestate. The plaintiff received the proceeds of a life insurance policy on the defendant's life and some other assets, but she believed that the defendant failed to keep his promise to support her for life. The plaintiff commenced a palimony action in October 1995 against the defendant's estate seeking a "lump-sum support award." The trial court ultimately granted the estate's motion for summary judgment, and dismissed the complaint. The Appellate Division reversed, and remanded for a hearing on the plaintiff's entitlement to support on a contract theory. A bench trial was held, and the trial court rejected the plaintiff's theories and dismissed the complaint. The Appellate Division affirmed.

This Court reviewed its prior palimony cases and explained that such highly personal contracts require that the Court take special care to "determine whether such a contract has been entered into and what its terms are." The Court made clear that the fundamental principle of New Jersey's palimony cases is that "the formation of a marital-type relationship between unmarried persons may, legitimately and enforceably, rest upon a promise by one to support the other." The Court expressly declared that "the entry into [a marital-type relationship] and then conducting oneself in accordance with its unique character is [sufficient] consideration" to enforce a promise for support. Importantly, the Court defined a marital-type relationship as one

in which people commit to each other, foregoing other liaisons and opportunities, doing for each other whatever each is capable of doing, providing companionship, and fulfilling each other's needs, financial, emotional, physical, and social, as best as they are able. And each couple defines its way of life and each partner's expected contribution to it in its own way. Whatever other consideration may be involved, the entry into such a relationship and then conducting oneself in accordance with its unique character is consideration in full measure.

[*Id.* at 838.]

The Court noted that because the trial court had not properly applied the palimony principles of *Kozlowski* and *Crowe*, it would exercise original jurisdiction and determine if the defendant made an express or implied contract to support the plaintiff. The Court scrutinized the record and found that the evidence supported the conclusion that the defendant promised to support the plaintiff for life. The Court explained that

[i]t is not disputed that [the defendant's] final break from his family and his marital-like relationship with [the] plaintiff resulted from his successful efforts to induce [the] plaintiff's return to him after she had moved to California to make a new life for herself because she had despaired of [the defendant's] willingness ever to divorce his wife and marry her. There is no reasonable inference that can be drawn from her abandonment of that plan at his insistence and the resulting reunion other than that she relied on his representations, express or implied, that her future would be neither prejudiced nor compromised. It is also beyond dispute that [the defendant] was concerned for [the] plaintiff's economic well-being and provided for her lavishly during their twenty-five years together as well as during the first extended period of their relationship. . . . The promise, clearly implied, if not express, that he would see to it that she was adequately provided for during her lifetime . . . seems to us to have been both the corollary for and the condition of their relationship for the last quarter century of [the defendant's] life.

[*Ibid.*]

The Court remanded the matter to the trial court for a determination of the level of support to be awarded to the plaintiff.

We turn now to the present case. The question we have not previously addressed is whether the parties may have a marital-type relationship, which is the underpinning of the consideration needed to support a claim for palimony, when they have not cohabited. The panel below and several other published Appellate Division opinions have interpreted our jurisprudence to require cohabitation as an indispensable element of a palimony action.

We do not read our jurisprudence as being so confining to make cohabitation a necessary requirement to a successful claim for palimony. Rather we opt for a more flexible approach that seeks to achieve substantial justice in light of the realities of the relationship. It is the promise to support, expressed or implied, coupled with a marital-type relationship that are the indispensable elements to support a valid claim for palimony.

Indeed, whether the parties cohabited is a relevant factor in the analysis of whether a marital-type relationship exists, and in most successful palimony cases, cohabitation will be present. We recognize, however, that palimony cases present highly personal arrangements and the facts surrounding the relationship will determine whether it is a marital-type relationship that is essential to support a cause of action for palimony. There may be circumstances where a couple may hold themselves out to others as if they were married and yet not cohabit (i.e., couples who are separated due to employment, military, or educational opportunities and who do not cohabit). The trier of fact must consider the realities of the relationship in the quest to achieve substantial justice. Therefore, in addressing a cause of action for palimony, the trial judge should consider the entirety of the relationship and, if a marital-type relationship is otherwise proven, it should not be rejected solely because cohabitation is not present.

Just as important, "[w]e have recognized that Family Part judges have developed a special expertise in dealing with family and family-type matters." That is, the Family court is well-equipped to consider highly personal facts and to determine whether a plaintiff's claim for support based on a marital-type relationship has merit.

The trial judge in the present case exemplified that expertise. In concluding that the parties did not enjoy a marital-type relationship, the judge found that the parties did not live together; they did not spend significant periods of time together; they did not commingle their property or share living expenses; and they did not hold themselves out to the public as husband and wife. The trial judge correctly considered the lack of cohabitation as a factor in reaching its determination and appropriately analyzed all of the factors of the highly personalized relationship between the parties, including the fact that defendant continued to live with his wife. Consequently, in rejecting plaintiff's argument of an implied contract to support her for life, the judge concluded that the marital-type relationship that informs the basis of a valid contract was lacking. As the trial judge so aptly phrased it, "the parties' relationship was best characterized as a dating relationship."

In summary, we hold that cohabitation is one of the many factors a trial judge should consider in determining whether a plaintiff has proven a marital-type relationship to support a cause of action for palimony. In these highly personalized cases, it is conceivable that a plaintiff, even in the absence of cohabitation, may establish a marital-type relationship and prove a cause of action for palimony. In the present case, however, there was sufficient credible evidence for the trial judge to reject plaintiff's palimony claim.

. . . As modified, the judgment of the Appellate Division affirming the trial court's rejection of plaintiff's claim for palimony is affirmed.

LONG, J. concurring. . . . My concern is that the Court's broad requirement of a marital-type relationship, which is entirely appropriate in an implied contract case such as this, will be carried over and bar enforcement of an express contract for lifetime support based on some other type of consideration. Under contract law, plaintiffs who have acted in reliance on an express promise for support and who have provided consideration other than conformance with marital roles are nevertheless entitled to recover.

The point is that, under our established case law, like every other person, a participant in a non-marital romantic relationship may recover in contract if she can show that she incurred a detriment in reliance on an express promise of support, that that promise was breached, and that she was damaged thereby. . . .

To be sure, to succeed on a claim of an express promise for lifetime support will be difficult because those kinds of representations are rarely made in the presence of witnesses and are usually denied by the putative promisor when the relationship breaks down. Nevertheless, in a case in which a plaintiff in fact proves an express promise of lifetime support, and that she provided the agreed upon consideration, she should not be barred from recovery based on the absence of a marital-type relationship.

RIVERA-SOTO, J. concurring in the result. As a threshold matter, Alabama, Idaho, Oklahoma, South Carolina and Utah recognize common law marriages, and, for that reason, do not allow palimony claims.

The vast majority of states that do not acknowledge common law marriages also have rejected a cause of action for palimony, although most have allowed parties to recoup either assets brought into the relationship or the value of the services they have provided to the relationship. Thus, even though Alaska does not explicitly recognize a *Marvin*/palimony cause of action, it does allow for the division of property acquired during cohabitation, noting that "to the extent it is ascertainable, intent of the parties should control the distribution of property accumulated during the course of cohabitation." Arkansas too does not recognize a palimony claim; although it forbids common law marriages under its laws, Arkansas does recognize common law marriages validly formed elsewhere. Connecticut expressly states that "no right to palimony exists under Connecticut law." However, Connecticut "[c]ourts will enforce a contract, express or implied, between nonmarital partners, and may employ equitable remedies to enforce those agreements where necessary." Delaware likewise rejects palimony claims, particularly when one of the parties is already married.

Georgia explicitly rejects any palimony claims. Illinois jettisons palimony claims as surrogates for outlawed common law marriages. Although it does not recognize palimony claims, Iowa allows unmarried cohabitants to enforce property claims based on "a recognized legal theory outside marriage to support the claim." Kansas disallows a palimony claim, but provides for "equitable division of the property accumulated by the parties during the period they were living together, a view also shared by Mississippi, Montana, New Hampshire, South Dakota and West Virginia. Kentucky rejects palimony claims for a straightforward and logical reason: "[w]ere it otherwise, the courts, in effect, would be reinstituting by judicial fiat common law marriage which by expressed public policy is not recognized." Louisiana too rejects palimony claims. Holding that "[i]t is not right to treat unmarried people as if they were married[,]" Maine does not recognize a palimony claim, but does allow recovery for "business [-]related services" and for "domestic services performed solely to allow the defendant to devote more time to his business. Maryland bars a palimony cause of action based on a continued sexual relationship, or a promise to marry "whether attired in the full raiment of the prohibited action or disguised as another type of action." Michigan explicitly rejects, as a matter of public policy, the palimony cause of action set forth in *Marvin, supra.*

New York does not enforce contracts implied from the relationship of unmarried cohabitants, but does enforce express contracts for the distribution of earnings and assets acquired during the cohabitation. Ohio "decline[s] to follow [*Marvin*, and like decisions] insofar as they recognize a new legal status for persons living together without benefit of marriage[,]" holding that "[t]here is no precedent in Ohio for dividing assets or property based on mere cohabitation without marriage[.]" Tennessee and Vermont do not allow palimony claims, but do enforce claims for property acquired during the relationship on a partnership theory

Several states—Arizona, Colorado, Hawaii, Indiana, Massachusetts, Missouri, Nebraska, Nevada, New Mexico, North Carolina, Oregon, Pennsylvania, Rhode Island, Washington and Wyoming—do not explicitly address whether a palimony claim for support is cognizable, focusing instead on whether assets acquired during the non-marital cohabitation relationship are divisible. . . .

Two states, by statute, have required that palimony claims must satisfy the statute of frauds in order to be enforceable. Minnesota provides that

> [i]f sexual relations between the parties are contemplated, a contract between a man and a woman who are living together in this state out of wedlock, or who are about to commence living together in this state out of wedlock, is enforceable as to terms concerning the property and financial relations of the parties only if: (1) the contract is written and signed by the parties, and (2) enforcement is sought after termination of the relationship.

[Minn. Stat. §513.075 (2007).]

Its legislature made that point clear when it enjoined that

> [u]nless the individuals have executed a contract complying with the provisions of section 513.075, the courts of this state are without jurisdiction to hear and shall dismiss as contrary to public policy any claim by an individual to the earnings or property of another individual if the claim is based on the fact that the individuals lived together in contemplation of sexual relations and out of wedlock within or without this state.

[Minn. Stat. §513.076 (2007).]

Texas likewise provides that a

> promise or agreement [made on consideration of marriage or on consideration of nonmarital conjugal cohabitation] is not enforceable unless the promise or agreement, or a memorandum of it, is (1) in writing; and (2) signed by the person to be charged with the promise or agreement or by someone lawfully authorized to sign for him.

[Tex. Bus. & Com. Code Ann. §26.01 (2007).]

. . . The lesson to be gleaned is clear: nowhere—save for those limited instances where a claim for palimony is based on a writing confirming an agreement of support—can a palimony claim be sustained absent proof of cohabitation. The rationale undergirding that obvious rule is equally self-evident: because they are easy to allege yet inherently contrary to fundamental legal concepts that have governed our jurisprudence for centuries, palimony claims must be viewed with great skepticism and must be subjected to harsh and unremitting scrutiny. It is to how this Court has guarded against sham palimony claims that I now turn. . . .

IV

It is against that backdrop—one that is neither explored nor analyzed by the majority, either in respect of its reasoning or its ultimate implications—that the majority announces the unceremonious discard of cohabitation as a prerequisite for a palimony cause of action. No doubt, there is a strong emotional basis for a palimony claim. . . .

Yet, as we have been well warned, it is the very nature of a palimony claim that commands caution and strict proof requirements, and a distinct cohabitation requirement stands as a formidable bulwark against emotion-based yet meritless claims.

Because the majority concedes that plaintiff cannot satisfy even the lesser standard the Court sets forth, the end result in this case is the dismissal of plaintiff's palimony claim. That result should have been reached for a different reason—because plaintiff has failed to prove the element of cohabitation necessary to sustain a palimony claim—and not for the reasons tendered by the majority. Therefore, I concur solely in the result.

DISCUSSION QUESTIONS FOR *DEVANEY v. L'ESPERANCE*

A. The majority opinion states that it is the promise to support, expressed or implied, coupled with a marital-type relationship, that are the indispensable elements to support a valid claim for palimony. The majority opinion also states that cohabitation is only one of many factors a trial judge should consider when determining whether a plaintiff has proven a marital-type relationship to support a cause of action for palimony. Didn't the plaintiff meet that standard? What additional evidence would have convinced the majority in *Devaney v. L'Esperance* that a marital-like relationship standard was met? For example, does the standard require the demonstrable act of setting up a household together in contrast to an extra-marital affair? Does setting up a household signify that the parties have entered into a relationship that may result in a significant and long-term commitment of family assets? How does cohabitation differ from "commitment" and cohabitation from a "marital-type relationship"?

B. The majority opinion states that "it is conceivable that a plaintiff, even in the absence of cohabitation, may establish a marital-type relationship and prove a cause of action for palimony." Can you provide an example to illustrate what the court means by this statement?

C. Outline Justice Long's concerns as expressed in his concurring opinion. Can you provide an example of the type of cohabitation dispute that Justice Long is describing in his opinion that is of concern to him?

D. Justice Rivera-Soto also writes a concurring opinion. In it he asserts that the majority has discarded cohabitation as a barrier against meritless claims. Does cohabitation provide a measure of advance notice and warning, to both parties to a relationship, and to their respective family members, that legal and financial consequences may result from that relationship? Therefore, isn't the Justice correct when he asserts cohabitation is necessary to every cohabitation claim? *See Levine v. Konvitz,* 897 A.2d 1061 (N.J. Super. 2006).

E. Does *Devaney v. L'Esperance* allow parties to make private agreements analogous to marriage contracts? If so, of what value is a traditional marriage contract? If a palimony promise survives the promisor's death, isn't the palimony promisee in a better position than that of a divorced wife, whose right to receive alimony normally ceases upon the obligor's death? Is this fair?

F. *In re Estate of Roccamonte,* discussed in *Devaney,* involved a 25-year relationship during which the man remained married to his wife with whom he had two children. Although the man lived with the plaintiff and supported her lavishly, he always filed joint income tax returns with his wife and supported their children. He did not make a will. When he died intestate, his cohabitant brought a claim against the estate alleging that he had promised to support her for the rest of her life. After a seven-year legal struggle, the New Jersey Supreme Court considered her claim. By this time, she was 77 and living in poverty on food stamps. It held that because the deceased had made an oral promise to support her for the rest of her life, the promise could be enforced against his estate. (It noted it was not alimony.) Explain the difference in outcome between *Roccamonte* and *Devaney.*

G. In *Thomas v. LaRosa,* 400 S.E.2d 809 (W. Va. 1990), when the parties stopped cohabiting, Ms. Thomas alleged that her partner had breached an oral contract that he would support her and her children from a previous marriage. During the cohabitation, the partner had provided her with a monthly stipend, covered household expenses, and supported and educated her children. At all times the male was married to another woman. The court held that agreements, express or implied, made between adult, nonmarital partners for future support, even when such contracts are not explicitly and inseparably founded on sexual services, are not enforceable. While observing that it would enforce legitimate business contracts, the court viewed the contract in this dispute as a contract for a common law marriage. Because common law marriages are not recognized in West Virginia, it would not recognize this agreement. Do you agree with the reasoning of the West Virginia court? *See Featherston v. Steinhoff,* 575 N.W.2d 6, 9 (Mich. App. 1997).

H. It has been suggested that courts should recognize the growing number of cohabitants and accommodate their relationships in various areas of the law, including expanding recognition into the criminal law context of the marital communication privilege. It is argued that doing so is consistent with the purpose behind the privilege (which is to protect the harmony of a relationship throughout its duration), the tendency among states to extend rights and obligations between cohabiting couples, and does not create a significant administrative burden on courts. Julia L. Cardozo, *Let My Love Open the Door: The Case for Extending Marital Privileges to Unmarried Cohabitants*, 10 U. Md. L.J. Race, Religion, Gender & Class 375, 398 (Fall 2010). Do you agree with this suggestion?

14.14 EXPRESS CONTRACTS

Background to *Soderholm v. Kosty*

As already observed, not all jurisdictions have accepted the sweeping approach used to resolve cohabitation disputes pioneered by the *Marvin* court. New York is one of those states. The case for discussion that follows, *Soderholm v. Kosty*, involves college students who cohabited for a time together, and it contains the reasons for New York's cautious approach to recognition of these contracts.

SODERHOLM
v.
KOSTY

Justice Court of Village of Horseheads, New York
676 N.Y.S.2d 850 (N.Y. 1998)

BROCKWAY, VILLAGE JUSTICE. Plaintiff Soderholm brings this Small Claims action seeking restitution in the amount of $2,500.00, arising out of moneys spent by plaintiff during cohabitation with Kosty.

There is no dispute that the parties, both students at Corning Community College at the time, decided to reside together and did so commencing in September of 1994. The relationship eventually soured and resulted in the break-up of the parties in December of 1995. During this time, the parties engaged in a sexual relationship as well. An attempt at reconciliation in February of 1996 failed. Soderholm attempts collection of $2,239.59 together with $260.41 as compensation for telephone calls, a certified letter and "time wasted" in collection thereof.

Plaintiff kept fairly detailed notes regarding some of the various expenses of living during the time in question. This included some apparently contemporaneous entries of such items as magazines, school books, movie rentals, gasoline, utilities, rent, and some of defendant's car payments. With the exception of a 10/20/94 $25.00 payment to Soderholm in Kosty's handwriting, none of these entries are initialed or otherwise agreed to by Kosty in writing. They are, in essence, self-serving. The more sizable claims, generally documented by way of plaintiff's check entries, include $770.25 for Kosty's share of the rent (representing four of the sixteen months during which they resided together); $647.43 for car payments (representing payments to Binghamton Savings Bank towards four of sixteen months of defendant's car payments); and $311.00 (representing a payment to Prudential, a car repair bill, and a plane ticket). Those sums total $1,728.68. Soderholm bases his claim for reimbursement on both implied and express contract theory and on an "unjust enrichment" theory. It is not disputed that during this period of time plaintiff often used defendant's vehicle, including its use on a trip to North Carolina for a job interview. It should be noted that Kosty was employed during the periods in question.

The complex and varied relationships between men and women, when they come to an end, oft leave a bitter residue and a smoldering irritation for which the salve, often the only soothing balm, is cash. It is a poor substitute for love, affection or attention, but for many its satisfactions are longer lasting. The termination of this informal "cohabitation" relationship sounds in what has been dubbed "palimony" or "companiomony."

With respect to plaintiff's claim under the theory of an implied contract, the court dismisses same. Such a claim in the surrounding of a cohabiting relationship is not only against New York's public policy (as evidenced by the 1933 abolition of common law marriages) but runs into too great a risk of error for a court, in hindsight, ". . . to sort out the intentions of the parties and to fix jural significance to conduct carried out within an essentially private and generally noncontractual relationship. . . ."

This court similarly dismisses any claim sounded in "unjust enrichment." Although justice courts do have equitable powers to, in effect, create an implied contract based in equity, it must be shown that a defendant was (i) enriched; (ii) that the enrichment was at plaintiff's expense and (iii) that equity and good conscience require defendant to return the money or the property to the plaintiff. In the instant case, it cannot be said, given the overall situation and the relationship between the parties, that defendant was unequivocally enriched, or, even if she were, that equity and good conscience would require restitution to the plaintiff. Defendant testified that there were numerous dinners, groceries, movies, clothes for plaintiff, and the like that she paid for on many occasions. Additionally, we know that as a matter of human experience, goods, services and financial advances are frequently rendered between two people not for remuneration but because they value each other's company or because they find it a caring, convenient or rewarding thing to do. The same can be said for most expenses in a "cohabitation" relationship. Given the usual "give and take" normally associated with cohabitation, and the giving and receiving by both here of love, affection, gifts and the like, it cannot be said that equity and good conscience cry out for fiscal adjustment.

Finally, plaintiff asserts that there was an express contract, obviously verbal in nature, which warrants reimbursement to him. . . . [W]hile cohabitation without marriage does not give rise to the property and financial rights which normally attend the marital relation, neither does cohabitation disable the parties from making an agreement within the normal rules of contract law. Nevertheless, even an express contract alleged to be verbal in nature presents problems of proof. Particularly in the context of cohabitation, it is subject to a greater risk of emotion-laden afterthought, fraud, ambiguity, and bitterness.

In the instant matter, the court finds that the plaintiff has sustained the necessary burden of proof only with respect to defendant's share of the rent. Uncontroverted testimony established that Kosty was a co-lessee with regard to the apartments they rented. Apparently, she paid her share of the rent the other twelve months. The evidence is sufficient to spell out Kosty's intent to be bound not only to the landlord but to plaintiff as well. This arrangement is little different from mere college roommates agreeing to share rental costs—clearly an enforceable obligation. No evidence was presented negating this intent.

But with respect to the other claims, while defendant's own testimony indicated that she would on occasion state that she would pay plaintiff "the money" "if she had it" at some vague future point in time ("when she got it"), any alleged understanding regarding these other items are absolutely too ambiguous to be called contractual. Basic contract law requires that a contract spell out a meaningful exchange of promises, clear in their intent and manner of execution. It is not for courts to fashion a contract where the parties have neglected to do so themselves. In this case, the plaintiff, years after the events, claims that various other sums are due him arising out of the cohabitation of the parties. However, at the time of the expenditures, it was not at all clear or unequivocal that the parties had a "meeting of the minds" as to restitution. Indeed, plaintiff kept expending monies despite Kosty's obvious lack of ability or intent to make reimbursement. Moreover, Kosty monetarily contributed to the relationship in other ways which may have served to offset Soderholm's financial advances. To attempt to put judicial sanction on such vague arrangements and financial exchanges is not conceptually valid and cannot expect judicial enforcement. In short, "no specific dollar amounts were ever specified, no time for performance was ever set and no conditions as to the manner of payment were given, nor was anything ever said about what would happen if the relationship between the parties terminated." Without more, these other expenditures, surrounded not by clear or third-party "IOU's," but by cohabitation, love, bliss, "somedays" and borrowed cars, do not a contractual debt make.

Although the court might agree with plaintiff that Kosty may have financially "come out ahead" as a result of this cohabitation experience, it cannot be said that there is any judicially enforceable claim other than the joint tenancy obligation. In a day when even basic family computer legal forms contain "cohabitation agreements" and given the vagaries of love and love lost, this court finds that it continues to be against the public policy of this state to attempt enforcement of plaintiff's other claims. Accordingly, the Court awards the sum of $770.25 and the costs of this action ($15.00) to Soderholm, as and for Kosty's share of the rent. The other claims (including plaintiff's request for "collection costs" not provided for in a contract, as is required in New York), are dismissed.

| DISCUSSION QUESTIONS | FOR *SOLDERHOLM v. KOSTY* |

A. The court states that "basic contract law requires that an agreement spell out a meaningful exchange of promises, clear in their intent and manner of execution. It is not for courts to fashion a contract where the parties have neglected to do so themselves." The court also says that where expenditures are concerned, it must be clear that "the parties had a meeting of the minds as to restitution." It adds that "even an express contract alleged to be verbal in nature presents problems of proof. Particularly in the context of cohabitation, it is subject to a greater risk of emotion-laden afterthought, fraud, ambiguity, and bitterness." Do you agree with these observations? Why shouldn't a court fashion a contract for the parties when their conduct strongly suggests one existed? Isn't the court placing too high a standard when considering enforcement of contracts between cohabiting partners? Would it place the same high standard on commercial contracts?

B. Assume for this hypothetical that a single woman employed by a New York law firm claimed an implied agreement with a married partner with whom she had a personal and sexual relationship for ten years. When the relationship ended, she quit her job. She received further payments for a while from the partner, but when they ceased, she sued. She alleged in her complaint that during their relationship, her former lover promised to provide for her economic security for the rest of her life. The partner denied that any such promise was made. The trial judge ruled that it was impossible to determine if any of the services performed by plaintiff in the course of their relationship were not "rendered gratuitously" and granted summary judgment to the defendant partner. Most likely, how will a New York appellate court rule on the enforceability of the alleged oral agreement? *Kastil v. Carro*, 145 A.D.2d 388 (N.Y.A.D. 1 Dept. 1988).

C. One of the problems with using contract theory as the conceptual underpinning for claims between cohabitating partners is that the parties do not in fact think of their relationship in contract terms. *See* Ira Mark Ellman, *Contract Thinking Was Marvin's Fatal Flaw*, 76 Notre Dame L. Rev. 1365 (2001). Assuming that parties usually are not thinking in contract terms, should the legal system reject the contract analysis and consider an approach that rests primarily upon evidence of status, for example, the amount of time the couple lived together? Whether they had children while living together? However, doesn't the choice not to marry reflect the partners' opposition (or at least of that partner who refuses to marry) to bear the financial burdens imposed on married persons who decide to divorce from their spouses?

14.15 TORT ACTIONS

Background to *Graves v. Estabrook*

Wrongful death claims are entirely statutory, with most statutes strictly limiting the class of persons entitled to recover for negligently causing the death of another. Statutes typically include spouses and immediate family members. Cohabitants who have filed wrongful death claims are seldom successful.

Cohabitants have had only limited success in asserting claims of loss of consortium and negligent infliction of emotional distress. Some courts have held that the relationship between an engaged couple is sufficient for a claim of bystander emotional distress. Other courts have held that only blood or marriage relationships qualify as sufficient relationships and bar a bystander from maintaining a cause of action for emotional distress due to witnessing the death of a fiancée. *See, e.g., Lindsey v. Visitec, Inc.*, 804 F. Supp. 1340 (W.D. Wash. 1992).

GRAVES
v.
ESTABROOK

Supreme Court of New Hampshire
818 A.2d 1255 (N.H. 2003)

DUGGAN, J. . . . Graves was engaged to Brett A. Ennis and had lived with him for approximately seven years. On September 23, 2000, Ennis was riding his motorcycle while Graves followed immediately behind him in a car. At an intersection, Estabrook's vehicle failed to yield at a stop sign and collided with Ennis. As Graves looked on, Ennis flipped over the hood of Estabrook's car and landed on the pavement. Graves immediately stopped her car and ran to the aid of her fiancée. She saw blood coming from his mouth and significant trauma to his head. She followed the ambulance that transported her fiancée to the hospital, stayed by his side while he was being treated, and attempted to comfort his parents and son. Ennis died the next day. Graves alleges that as a result of witnessing the collision and death of her fiancée, she suffered shock, severe mental pain and emotional distress. The issue before us is whether a plaintiff who lived with and was engaged to marry the decedent may recover for negligent infliction of emotional distress. . . .

We conclude that "to foreclose [an unmarried cohabitant] from making a claim based upon emotional harm because her relationship with the injured person does not carry a particular label is to work a potential injustice where the emotional injury is genuine and substantial and is based upon a relationship of significant duration that is deep, lasting and genuinely intimate." *Id.* A number of courts have reached a similar conclusion. *See Thurmon v. Sellers*, 62 S.W.3d 145, 164 (Tenn. App. 2001); *Heldreth v. Marrs*, 425 S.E.2d 157, 162-63 W. Va. (1992); *James v. Lieb*, 375 N.W.2d 109, 115 (Neb. 1985); *Paugh v. Hanks*, 451 N.E.2d 759, 766-67 (Ohio

1983); *Sinn v. Burd*, 404 A.2d 672, 685 (Penn. 1979); *Leong v. Takasaki*, 520 P.2d 758, 766 (Haw. 1974).

DALIANIS, J. dissenting. Because I believe that the class of bystanders who may recover for negligent infliction of emotional distress should be limited to those closely related to the victim by marriage or blood, I respectfully dissent. . . .

The majority's interpretation of the "closely related" factor is "so ambiguous as to limit the class of plaintiffs who could assert a claim for [negligent infliction of emotional distress] only by the imagination of counsel drafting the pleadings." . . . If the emotional connection between the bystander and the victim determines whether they are "closely related," there is no principled distinction, for example, between an unmarried cohabitant who claims to have a sufficiently "intimate" relationship with the victim and close friends who claim the same intimacy. . . . I disagree with the New Jersey Supreme Court's holding in *Dunphy v. Gregor*, 136 N.J. 99, 642 A.2d 372, 378 (1994), that a standard that "take[s] into account the duration of the relationship, the degree of mutual dependence, the extent of common contributions to a life together, [and] the extent and quality of shared experience" properly confines this cause of action within a well-defined boundary. To the contrary, the "application of these factors would not provide a sufficiently definite and predictable test to allow for consistent application from case to case." . . .

If the class of potential plaintiffs who may recover is extended beyond those closely related to the victim by blood or marriage, courts will face difficult problems of proof in determining whether the relationship is sufficiently close to permit recovery. Under the majority's holding, courts will be compelled to define and make findings about the subjective emotional connection between the parties in an attempt to determine whether the plaintiff's emotional trauma was reasonably foreseeable to the defendant. . . .

Thus, I would not expand the class of potential plaintiffs beyond those closely related to the victim by the objective criteria of marriage or blood. While I recognize that "[s]uch limitations are indisputably arbitrary since it is foreseeable that in some cases unrelated persons have a relationship to the victim or are so affected by the traumatic event that they suffer equivalent emotional distress," defining the class of "closely related" bystanders by the depth of their emotional connection to the victim would unreasonably expand the defendant's liability.

 **FOR *GRAVES v. ESTABROOK***

A. Justice Dalianis argues that there is no "principled distinction" between an unmarried cohabitant who claims to have a sufficiently "intimate" relationship with the victim and close friends who claim the same intimacy. Consequently, he maintains that only bystanders related to the victim by marriage or blood should recover. He also maintains that extending redress beyond marriage or blood creates very difficult problems of proof for courts. Do you agree?

B. Would excluding unmarried cohabitants from the realm of potential plaintiffs conform to societal expectations regarding the preferential treatment of married couples? Would it also be less likely to lead to confusion, given that spouses receive preferential treatment in many other contexts, such as intestacy, alimony, and loss of consortium? Furthermore, doesn't the state have strong interest in marriage that draws a bright line in terms of benefits between those married and unmarried? *See Dunphy v. Gregor*, 642 A.2d 372, 382-383 (N.J. 1994) (Garibaldi, J., dissenting).

C. In *Elden v. Sheldon*, 758 P.2d 582, 588 (Cal. 1988), the court stated that "[a]bsent exceptional circumstances, recovery should be limited to relatives residing in the same household, or parents, siblings, children, and grandparents of the victim." Several jurisdictions have followed California's reasoning. *See, e.g., Biercevicz v. Liberty Mut. Ins. Co.*, 865 A.2d 1267, 1272 (Conn. Super. 2004) (fiancé was not "closely-related" to decedent so as to allow bystander emotional distress claim); *Smith v. Toney*, 862 N.E.2d 656, 660-662 (Ind. 2007) (fiancée's relationship to motorist was not analogous to spouse); *Grotts v. Zahner*, 989 P.2d 415, 416 (Nev. 1999) (standing of accident bystander to bring emotional distress claim requires membership in victim's family either by blood or marriage). Are the courts the best equipped body to decide this issue or should the issue be left entirely to state legislatures to decide as a policy matter?

D. In *Onge v. MacDonald*, 917 A.2d 233 (N.H. 2007), the court held that a motorcyclist and a passenger were not "closely related," and failed to satisfy the requirements of *Graves v. Estabrook*, "for bystander recovery in a negligent infliction of emotional distress claim." In making its ruling, the court relied on three factors set out in *Dillon v. Legg*, 441 P.2d 912 (Cal. 1968), to determine whether the harm was foreseeable. That test requires the trial court to determine (1) whether plaintiff was located near the scene of the accident as contrasted with one who was a distance away from it; (2) whether the shock resulted from a direct emotional impact upon plaintiff from the sensory and contemporaneous observance of the accident, as contrasted with learning of the accident from others after its occurrence; and (3) whether plaintiff and the victim were closely related, as contrasted with an absence of any relationship or the presence of only a distant relationship. When determining whether a plaintiff and a victim are "closely related," the trial court is to take into account (1) the duration of the relationship; (2) the degree of mutual dependence; (3) the extent of common contributions to a life together; (4) the extent and quality of shared experience; (5) whether the plaintiff and the injured person were members of the same household; (6) their emotional reliance upon each other; (7) the particulars of their day-to-day relationship; and (8) the manner in which they related to each other in attending to life's mundane requirements. Is this list of factors sufficient to overcome the concern evinced by Justice Dalianis in his dissent?

14.16 DOMESTIC PARTNERSHIPS

Domestic partnership is a legal status recognized by several states, cities, counties, and employers. The phrase "domestic partner" commonly contains the following elements: (1) The partners are at a minimum 18 years old; (2) neither partner is related by blood closer than what is permitted by state law for marriage; (3) the partners share a committed, exclusive relationship; and (4) the partners are financially interdependent. *See* Margaret W. Hickey, *Pitfalls and Promises: Cohabitation, Marriage and Domestic Partnerships, Estate Planning for Cohabitants*, 22 J. Am. Acad. Matrimonial Law. 1, 5 (2009).

It is argued that domestic partnerships are important "to planning for unmarried cohabitants because they may confer certain rights and benefits on those who choose to take advantage of the status." *Id.* at 8. This may include "employment benefits for the domestic partner such as health insurance on a family plan, inclusion in family and medical leave definitions, and other benefits that the employer may offer to an employee's unmarried partner, whether of the same or opposite sex." *Ibid.*

Restatement. The Restatement (Third) of Property §2.2 comment *g* states: "g. Domestic partner. . . . To the extent that a domestic partner is treated as having the status of a spouse, conferring rights on such a partner on the dissolution of the relationship, the domestic partner who remains in that relationship with the decedent until the decedent's death, should be treated as a legal spouse for purposes of intestacy." Statutes in Colorado, Illinois, Maine, Nevada, Wisconsin, and the District of Columbia provide some inheritance rights to unmarried couples who register with the state, without regard to whether the relationship is opposite-sex or same-sex. Illinois provisions appear to provide rights that are equivalent to marriage.

REFLECTIVE QUESTIONS	What social policy is furthered by a state enacting a domestic partnership law?

14.17 PRACTICAL ISSUES: DEAD MAN'S STATUTES

Dead Man's statutes concern whether a witness may testify about conversations or transactions with a decedent. There are a wide variety of Dead Man's statutes. *See* Ed Wallis, *An Outdated Form of Evidentiary Law: A Survey of Dead Man's Statutes and a Proposal for Change*, 53 Clev. St. L. Rev. 75, 75, n.9 (2005-2006). About a dozen states have statutes that prohibit testimony from an interested witness in respect to conversations or transactions with the deceased. Another group of states prohibits the witness from testifying about oral communications with the deceased but allows testimony regarding transactions with the deceased. Some states have provisions declaring that testimony is barred unless there is other corroborative evidence, in which case testimony is allowed.

Tennessee courts take the view that the purpose of a Dead Man's statute is to protect estates from spurious claims. *Morfin v. Estate of Martinez*, 831 N.E.2d 791, 798 (Ind. App. 2005). It is based on the common law principle that an interested party will be powerfully tempted to misrepresent transactions or communications with a deceased person who cannot rebut the party's testimony. *Schimpf v. Gerald, Inc.*, 52 F. Supp. 2d 976, 987 (E.D. Wis. 1999). The Dead Man's statute prevents interested parties from giving self-serving testimony regarding conversations or transactions with the deceased when the testimony involves transactions or statements that would either increase or decrease the deceased's estate. *Cantrell v. Estate of Cantrell*, 19 S.W.3d 842, 846 (Tenn. App. 1999). In *In re Estate of Marks*, 187 S.W.3d 21 (Tenn. App. 2005), the statute was applied to prevent the decedent's fiancée from testifying about her agreement with him.

<table>
<tr><td>

REFLECTIVE
QUESTIONS

</td><td>

Would domestic partners and cohabiting couples be considered interested parties in Wisconsin and Tennessee and their testimony barred in a dispute over the question of who has an interest in an estate left by a partner?

</td></tr>
</table>

14.18 PRACTICAL ISSUES: DRAFTING

Lawyers recommend that cohabiting persons prepare a written contract that specifically sets out each party's rights and responsibilities upon illness, death, or a breakup of the relationship. A written contract may be particularly useful where one party is better educated, possesses greater earning capacity, or owns property at the inception of the relationship.

When cohabitation agreements are prepared, it is suggested that they should be arms' length transactions and demonstrate that each party is receiving some benefit. Should the agreement be challenged in the future, this may shield it from a claim of a lack of legal consideration. Margaret W. Hickey, *supra* at 1, 9. It is also suggested that cohabitant contracts should be treated in the same manner as premarital contracts and that a lawyer normally should refuse to represent both parties. *Id.* at 10. Unfortunately, few cohabitants take the time or make the effort to execute these documents. Consequently, courts are left to do the best they can in weighing competing claims and interests when the relationship breaks up or ends with the death of one of the two.

Where enforced? Cohabitation agreements will generally be enforced in the state where the agreement is executed. Jeanne M. Hannah, *The Law and Living Together*, Family Advocate 28 (Winter 2010).

REFLECTIVE QUESTIONS	Shouldn't states enact statutes that only allow enforcement of cohabitation claims if the parties executed a written agreement as to property and support, with each party represented by a lawyer, before they began their relationship?

14.19 JURISDICTION IN FEDERAL COURT

Cohabitation agreement claims may arrive in federal court based on diversity jurisdiction. Whether federal courts will consider the claims as a pure contract matters and take jurisdiction to hear the dispute, or apply the domestic relations exception to federal jurisdiction and dismiss the action, is not always clear.

The domestic relations exception in federal court reflects the conflict over the relationship between the states and the federal system when family issues are involved. Meredith Johnson Harbach, *Is the Family a Federal Question?*, 66 Wash. & Lee L. Rev. 131 (Winter 2009). The domestic relations exception has been interpreted as meaning that federal courts with jurisdiction will nevertheless refuse to hear cases involving the issuance of a divorce, alimony, or child support order or decree. *Ankenbrandt v. Richards*, 504 U.S. 689, 703 (1992).

The domestic relations exception was raised in *Anastasi v. Anastasi (Anastasi I)*, 532 F. Supp. 720 (D.N.J. 1982). The plaintiff alleged that the parties entered into an oral contract under which, in exchange for life support, the female party agreed to come live with the male party full time and be his helpmate, companion, homemaker, housewife, and cook. The defendant denied the agreement. The federal court considered the dispute and held that a palimony action for breach of an agreement to provide the plaintiff with all her financial support and needs for the rest of her life sounded in contract. Therefore, it was not within the domestic relations exception to diversity jurisdiction. The court noted that it might consider palimony to be within the domestic relations exception if a state exhibited a significant interest in this kind of relationship.

In *Anastasi v. Anastasi (Anastasi II)*, 544 F. Supp. 866 (D.N.J. 1982), the court changed its mind and reversed its earlier ruling on jurisdiction. It based its reversal on a decision by the New Jersey Supreme Court, *Crowe v. DeGioia*, 90 N.J. 126, 447 A.2d 173 (1982). In *Crowe v. DeGioia*, the court declared the State of New Jersey had a significant interest in consensual live-in relationships. The state action persuaded the district court to remand the dispute to state court as within the domestic relations exception to federal jurisdiction notwithstanding that there was diversity of citizenship.

In *Johnson v. Thomas*, 808 F. Supp. 1316, 1320 (W.D. Mich. 1992), the former husband brought an action against his former wife, his wife's current husband, and the wife's attorney arising out of an alleged domestic partnership agreement. In rejecting exercising jurisdiction, the federal court stated: "This function is the same one a court performs when granting a divorce. The fact that the label is different should not defeat the fact that this type of action falls within the exception. Certainly, the court would find that a dissolution case and an annulment case would fall within the exception regardless of the fact that they do not possess the label of divorce. The state courts have an expertise in the delicate situation presented when a domestic relationship is ended." *Ibid.* See *Ankenbrandt v. Richards,* 504 U.S. 689 (1992).

In *Korby v Erickson,* 550 F. Supp. 136 (S.D.N.Y. 1982), the court considered an action for a declaratory judgment where the plaintiff argued he was entitled to the entire proceeds from the sale of shares of a co-operative apartment, which were issued in his name and the name of the woman with whom he lived. The court held the dispute did not come within the domestic relations exception to diversity jurisdiction. The ruling came despite the fact that, as an incident to an alleged agreement to combine their skills, earnings, and investments, the parties also agreed to live together and did live together as husband and wife without being actually married. The court reasoned that, as an incident of the alleged agreement to combine their skills and the like, the parties also agreed to live together, and did live together; this did not create a marital status that came within the exception. The court added that the contract claims were of a common garden variety and did not require the special competence of the state courts, but were routinely determined by federal courts.

REFLECTIVE QUESTIONS	What is the reason for the difference in the jurisdictional outcome in *Anastasi I* and *Anastasi II*?

General Principles

1. Traditionally, courts refused to enforce agreements between unmarried cohabitants because the relationship was viewed as meretricious. Such agreements were invalid as contrary to public policy. They were considered similar to contracts for prostitution, and courts acted to deter immorality.

2. Today, jurisdictions are not in agreement in this area of the law. A minority of jurisdictions adhere to the traditional rule and refuse to recognize support and property division claims brought by cohabitants. Others recognize claims only if based on an express agreement. A third group of jurisdictions recognizes claims if based on express or implied contracts.

3. Implied contracts may be either implied-in-fact or implied-in-law. An implied-in-fact contract is created when the court infers intent from the parties' conduct. An implied-in-law contract is created when a court imposes a remedy to prevent unjust enrichment.

4. In some jurisdictions, such as New York, implied agreements for personal services will not be enforced on the theory that such services are rendered

gratuitously during intimate relationships. Courts fear fraud and find establishing proof of implied promises difficult.

5. Under the *Marvin* doctrine, courts will recognize the rights of nonmarital partners to make express and implied agreements.

6. Under the *Marvin* doctrine, agreements between cohabitants fail only to the extent that they rest on illicit sexual services. Courts will sever any portion of a contract that does not rest on illicit sexual services and enforce it.

7. Under the *Marvin* doctrine, contracts to pool earnings and provide support are not barred by abolition of actions for breach of promise to marry.

8. Some jurisdictions permit cohabitants to recover in tort for injuries caused by a third party such as loss of consortium or negligent infliction of emotional distress; others do not.

9. The ALI *Principles of the Law of Family Dissolution* rejects the contract-based approach of *Marvin*. The ALI recommends recognition of a status relationship.

Chapter Problems

1. Assume that in response to *Marvin*, a state enacts the following Statute of Frauds.

Section A provides:

> If sexual relations between the parties are contemplated, a contract between a man and a woman who are living together in this state out of wedlock, or who are about to commence living together in this state out of wedlock, is enforceable as to terms concerning the property and financial relations of the parties only if:
>
> **1.** the contract is written and signed by the parties, and
> **2.** enforcement is sought after termination of the relationship.

Section B provides:

> Unless the individuals have executed a contract complying with the provisions of section A, the courts of this state are without jurisdiction to hear and shall dismiss as contrary to public policy any claim by an individual to the earnings or property of another individual if the claim is based on the fact that the individuals lived together in contemplation of sexual relations and out of wedlock within or without this state.

Do these provisions eliminate the possibility of implied contract claims in cohabitation disputes in jurisdictions that recognized such causes of action prior to enactment of the statute? Do the provisions eliminate enforcement of expressed oral agreements in those states where such claims were recognized before enactment of the statutes? *See In re Eriksen*, 337 N.W.2d 671 (Minn. 1983).

2. Assume in a hypothetical case a palimony complaint is filed by P that alleges that after the parties first met they "dated, engaged in sexual activities and, in general, acted towards one another as two people do who have discovered a love, one for the other." The complaint also states that the plaintiff orally agreed "to cohabit with the deceased as if they were, in fact, married; that they would hold themselves out to the public at large as cohabiting mates." The complaint states that "plaintiff would render his services to D as a lover, companion, homemaker, traveling companion, housekeeper, and cook in order that plaintiff would be able to devote his time to D's benefit as his lover, companion, homemaker, traveling companion, housekeeper, and cook; that P would abandon his career; that P and D cohabited and lived together and pursuant to and in reliance on the cohabiters' oral agreement, P allowed himself to be known to the general public as the lover and cohabitation mate of D." The complaint is challenged on a summary judgment.

The estate relies on a statement in *Marvin* that "(A) contract between nonmarital partners, even if expressly made in contemplation of a common living arrangement, is invalid only if sexual acts form an inseparable part of the consideration for the agreement. In sum, a court will not enforce a contract for the pooling of property and earnings if it is explicitly and inseparably based upon services as a paramour." Were P's rendition of sexual services to D an inseparable part of the consideration for the "cohabiters' agreement," and the predominant consideration, and should summary judgment be granted? *Compare Bryne v. Laura*, 60 Cal. Rptr. 2d 908 (Cal. App. 1997), *with Jones v. Daly*, 176 Cal. Rptr. 130 (Cal. App. 1981); *see also In re Estate of Quarg*, 938 A.2d 193 (N.J. 2008); *Poe v. Levy's Estate*, 411 So. 2d 253 (Fla. Dist. Ct. App. 1982); *Norton v. McOsker*, 407 F.3d 501 (1st Cir. 2005); *In re Estate of Alexander*, 445 So. 2d 836 (Miss. 1984).

3. Assume that the following facts were presented to a judge in a jurisdiction that follows the *Marvin* doctrine. Frank and Florence were both 70. Their spouses had died and for a variety of reasons, they decide it would be wonderful to live together, but they did not marry. For six years they lived together at Florence's apartment. Florence died at age 76 and left a large estate. Frank seeks his intestate share.

Florence's two daughters challenge Frank's claim. They introduce evidence that Florence's apartment lease, title to her Mercedes automobile, all life insurance policies, and all bank accounts are in her name. Both daughters testify their mother told them that they would get all of the estate "should something happen to me."

Frank testifies that Florence promised that if he lived with her and she predeceased him, that he would receive half of her estate, just as though they were married. Frank also testifies that he was receiving public assistance and if his name was placed on Florence's bank accounts he feared losing this income. Frank introduces a few checks showing that he occasionally paid for groceries and twice paid the rent on the apartment. Finally, he testifies that Florence was receiving a large amount of money in maintenance from her former spouse and under the conditions of the divorce decree, she would lose the funds if she remarried. Frank's son testifies that the couple always "appeared as though they were married" and that on several occasions Frank told him that "Florence will take care of me the rest of my life." How will a court most likely rule on Frank's claim?

4. Assume Nancy and Nick live together without benefit of marriage for 20 years in a jurisdiction that does not recognize common law marriages. Nick is struck and seriously injured by an uninsured motorist while crossing the street. If Nick is Nancy's spouse, he can recover under Nancy's uninsured motorist policy that contains a provision that specifically covers "relatives." Nancy asks a court to declare that Nick is her spouse and covered by the "relative" provision in the insurance policy. What arguments will Nancy make in an effort to persuade the court to rule in her favor? How will a court most likely rule?

5. Jack and Jill lived together out of wedlock at Jill's apartment in a jurisdiction that recognizes the *Marvin* doctrine. After they have lived together for two months, Jack purchased a dry cleaning establishment using $15,000 from his savings. A month later they split up. Jill seeks a 50 percent interest in Jack's dry cleaning establishment based on a promise made by Jack during the relationship that "anything of mine is yours too." How will a court most likely rule on Jill's claim?

6. Assume that Sharon began living with Ted in Ted's apartment. The arrangement lasted eight years. The parties agreed that Ted would pay for the apartment rent, utilities, and groceries for the first two years of their cohabitation. Sharon bought groceries during the other years. For one year while Sharon was unemployed, Ted paid for her health insurance premiums. Sharon testified that she did all the laundry, the ironing, the mending, and the cleaning of the apartment they shared. Ted disagreed and testified that they evenly split the cooking and cleaning duties at the apartment and the cottage and that each was responsible for his or her own laundry and ironing.

During the last year of their relationship, Sharon enrolled in law school and rented a room near the law school, where she spent four days a week, and she spent the remainder at the apartment shared with Ted. The parties kept their finances and property separate throughout their relationship. Sharon made interest-free loans to Ted, which he paid back and for which she never requested interest payment. Sharon testified that throughout most of their relationship, she hoped and believed they would eventually get married, and there was discussion between them regarding marriage. They were never engaged, but at one point Ted talked about purchasing a diamond engagement ring and wedding band. When the relationship broke down, Sharon sued Ted alleging unjust enrichment. She testified that Ted told her she would "share in the appreciation of his wealth, and she therefore provided, without just compensation, services and benefits." At trial, Sharon submitted a calculation of the value of her domestic services to Ted at the apartment at the rate of $6 per hour or $3,000 per year for eight years, for a total amount of about $25,000. The trial court has granted summary judgment in favor of Ted, declaring that on these facts it was unable to conclude there was either an express or implied contract. Has Sharon produced sufficient evidence of the only legal theory left — unjust enrichment?

7. Assume that Rachel and Ronald lived together for three years. Although they never talked about it, Rachel believed that Ronald intended to marry her at some time in the future. Ronald paid for the apartment rent and associated expenses. He also purchased all the food, took Rachel on trips with him, and otherwise provided for her. During the last year of their relationship, Rachel began working as a waitress full time in Ronald's small restaurant. Ronald did not pay Rachel any wages. Rachel believed that she was helping build for the future. However, after an argument over Ronald's relationship with another waitress, Rachel moved out. She now seeks reasonable compensation for the time she worked for Ronald in his restaurant. Most likely, how will a court rule?

8. Assume in this hypothetical that a 67-year-old male, who was earning a modest but respectable living as a travel tour guide, met a wealthy widow with assets in excess of $40,000,000. She began making demands on his time, and allegedly agreed to support him in a luxurious fashion, if he would devote all his time and attention to her. He gave up his business career, in which he was earning no more than $55,000 a year, and became the ever-present companion of the widow. He moved to larger quarters and modified his wardrobe to suit her tastes. He accompanied her to lunch and dinner, escorted her to the theatre and parties, and travelled with her on her trips to Europe. Assume that five years after the relationship began, it broke up. He brings an action in New York alleging an express oral agreement, an implied agreement, and unjust enrichment. He claims he agreed to give up his business and render services to the defendant, in return for which defendant would pay and provide (a) all his costs and expenses incurred in connection with the performance of his services, (b) all his costs and expenses for sumptuous living during the time the services were rendered, and (c) within a reasonable time an amount sufficient to pay for all his costs and expenses for sumptuous living for the rest of his life. He seeks $1.5 million.

The widow maintains that the alleged oral agreement by which defendant would pay an amount sufficient to take care of all of plaintiff's costs and expenses for sumptuous living and maintenance for the remainder of his life was unenforceable due to its vagueness because (a) no specific dollar amount of any future support was ever discussed between them, and (b) no facts were presented in the complaint that would tend to establish a meeting of minds as to the definition of sumptuous living. The widow moves to dismiss the action. How will a New York court most likely rule on the widow's motion? *See Trimmer v. Van Bomel*, 434 N.Y.S.2d 82 (N.Y. Sup. 1980).

Preparation for Practice

1. Assume that your client asks you to draft a cohabitation agreement. Prepare an outline of the document in not more than two pages. Be prepared to discuss the draft.

2. Prepare a PowerPoint presentation explaining your jurisdiction's position on cohabitation contracts. Be prepared to show and discuss your work during class.

3. Assume a legislator has asked you to explain to a legislative committee the difference between the ALI approach to cohabitation contracts and the approach used in your jurisdiction. Prepare an outline not to exceed two pages to explain the differences, if any.

Part V

Protection of Family Members

Chapter 15

Intimate Partner Violence

15.1 INTRODUCTION

This chapter focuses on intimate partner violence occurring between partners and parents. Although the topics are related, this chapter does not explore criminal or tort remedies for abuse. Throughout the chapter, the terms *intimate partner violence* and *domestic violence* are used interchangeably.

Families experiencing intimate partner violence differ significantly from one another, and each case requires special handling and consideration in part because intimate partner violence impacts every aspect of divorce and child custody.

> Domestic violence affects grounds for divorce and strategic questions of whether victims of abuse should seek divorce on no-fault or fault-based grounds. It affects distribution of assets in divorce. It must be taken into consideration when determining custody issues such as joint custody, relocation, and visitation. It affects issues of divorce mediation and parent education. It shapes the panoply of laws that have an impact on women who might need to flee with their children from an abuser. Domestic violence affects the child protective system as well as issues of race and class throughout the family law system generally. Violence is often a part of the lives of poor mothers and can result in neglect and/or abuse petitions, or termination of parental rights resulting in children being sent to foster care. For undocumented women who experience violence, immigration issues pose tremendous barriers.

Elizabeth M. Schneider, *Domestic Violence Law Reform in the Twenty-First Century: Looking Back and Looking Forward*, 42 Fam. L.Q. 353, 359-360 (2011). Professionals working with families should remain cognizant that common expectations about "friendly" parenting, joint physical custody, and substantial contact with both parents may be inapplicable or even dangerous for families with a history of intimate partner violence.

Questions such as the following should come to mind as you study this chapter: How has intimate partner violence been viewed from a historical perspective? How might intimate partner violence affect children and parenting? How will a family attorney discern whether intimate partner violence is an issue? When should a client seek a protective order? What relief can be obtained in a protective order?

REFLECTIVE QUESTIONS	How might intimate partner violence impact the family law topics you have studied so far?

15.2 HISTORICAL VIEW OF INTIMATE PARTNER VIOLENCE

Although the existence of intimate partner violence has been traced as far back as ancient Rome, it was historically viewed as a private family matter and societal intervention was rare. Victims of intimate partner violence had few, if any, legal rights or protections. For example, husbands were historically exempt from prosecution for marital rape. An explanation for this policy posited by Lord Hale states "but a husband cannot be guilty of a rape committed by himself upon his lawful wife, for by their mutual matrimonial consent and contract the wife hath given up herself in this kin unto her husband which she cannot retreat." 1 Hale P.C. 629. This passage is quoted in the case of *Warren v. State*, 336 S.E.2d 221 (1985), where the Georgia Supreme Court ruled that a husband could be criminally liable for raping his wife. Fortunately, during the last half-century, strong advocacy on behalf of victims and heightened societal awareness of intimate partner violence have resulted in significant legal reform.

REFLECTIVE QUESTIONS	What was the historical justification for the common law view that a husband could not be charged with raping his wife?

Background to *State v. Rhodes*

A husband historically possessed the legal right to physically "chastise" his wife, and the extent of this right is explored in the 1868 case of *State v. Rhodes*. Fortunately, intimate partner violence is no longer explicitly approved under the law. Nevertheless, the cases in this chapter should be read with this historical context in mind.

STATE
v.
RHODES

Supreme Court of North Carolina
61 N.C. 453 (1868)

The defendant was indicted for an assault and battery upon his wife, Elizabeth Rhodes. Upon the evidence submitted to them the jury returned the following special verdict:

> We find that the defendant struck Elizabeth Rhodes, his wife, three licks, with a switch about the size of one of his fingers (but not as large as a man's thumb) without any provocation except some words uttered by her and not recollected by the witness.

His Honor was of opinion that the defendant had a right to whip his wife with a switch no larger than his thumb, and that upon the facts found in the special verdict he was not guilty in law. Judgment in favor of the defendant was accordingly entered and the State appealed. . . .

READE, J. The violence complained of would without question have constituted a battery if the subject of it had not been the defendant's wife. The question is how far that fact affects the case.

The courts have been loathe to take cognizance of trivial complaints arising out of the domestic relations — such as master and apprentice, teacher and pupil, parent and child, husband and wife. Not because those relations are not subject to the law, but because the evil of publicity would be greater than the evil involved in the trifles complained of; and because they ought to be left to family government. . . .

In this case no provocation worth the name was proved. The fact found was that it was "without any provocation except some words which were not recollected by the witness." The words must have been of the slightest import to have made no impression on the memory. We must therefore, consider the violence as unprovoked. The question is therefore plainly presented, whether the court will allow a conviction of the husband for moderate correction of the wife without provocation. . . .

Blackstone says "that the husband, by the old law, might give the wife moderate correction, for as he was to answer for her misbehavior, he ought to have the power to control her; but that in the polite reign of Charles the Second, this power of correction began to be doubted." Wharton says, that by the ancient common law the husband possessed the power to chastise his wife; but that the tendency of criminal courts in the present day, is to regard the marital relation as no defence to a battery. Chancellor Walworth says of such correction, that it is not authorized by the law of any civilized country; not indeed meaning that England is not civilized, but referring to the anomalous relics of barbarism which cleave to her jurisprudence. The old law of moderate correction has been questioned even in England, and has been repudiated in Ireland and Scotland. The old rule is approved in Mississippi, but it has met with but little favor elsewhere in the United States. In looking into the discussions of the other States we find but little uniformity.

From what has been said it will be seen how much the subject is at sea. And, probably, it will ever be so: for it will always be influenced by the habits, manners and condition of every community. Yet it is necessary that we should lay down something as precise and practical as the nature of the subject will admit of, for the guidance of our courts. Our conclusion is that family government is recognized by law as being as complete in itself as the State government is in itself, and yet subordinate to it; and that we will not interfere with or attempt to control it, in favor of either husband or wife, unless in cases where permanent or malicious injury is inflicted or threatened, or the condition of the party is intolerable. For, however great are the evils of ill temper, quarrels, and even personal conflicts inflicting only temporary pain, they are not comparable with the evils which would result from raising the curtain, and exposing to public curiosity and criticism, the nursery and the bed chamber. Every household has and must have, a government of its own, modelled to suit the temper, disposition and condition of its inmates. Mere ebullitions of passion, impulsive violence, and temporary pain, affection will soon forget and forgive; and each member will find excuse for the other in his own frailties. But when trifles are taken hold of by the public, and the parties are exposed and disgraced, and each endeavors to justify himself or herself by criminating the other, that which ought to be forgotten in a day, will be remembered for life.

It is urged in this case, that as there was no provocation the violence was of course excessive and malicious; that every one in whatever relation of life should be able to purchase immunity from pain, by obedience to authority and faithfulness in duty. And it is insisted, that in the *State v. Pendegrass*, 2 D. & B., 365, which was the case of a schoolmistress whipping a child, that doctrine is laid down. It is true that it is there said, that the master may be punishable even when he does not transcend the powers granted; i.e., when he does not inflict permanent injury, if he grossly abuse his powers, and use them as a cover for his malice. But observe, the language is, if he grossly abuse his powers. So that every one would say at once, there was no cause for it, and it was purely malicious and cruel. If this be not the rule then every violence which would amount to an assault upon a stranger, would have to be investigated to see whether there was any provocation. And that would contravene what we have said, that we will punish no case of trifling importance. If in every such case we are to hunt for the provocation, how will the proof be supplied? Take the case before us. The witness said, there was no provocation except some slight words. But then who can tell what significance the trifling words may have had to the husband? Who can tell what had happened an hour before, and every hour for a week? To him they may have been sharper than a sword. And so in every case, it might be impossible for the court to appreciate what might be offered as an excuse, or no excuse might appear at all, when a complete justification exists. Or, suppose the provocation could in every case be known, and the court should undertake to weigh the provocation in every trifling family broil, what would be the standard? Suppose a case coming up to us from a hovel, where neither delicacy of sentiment nor refinement of manners is appreciated or known. The parties themselves would be amazed, if they were to be held responsible for rudeness or trifling violence. What do they care for insults and indignities? In such cases what end would be gained by investigation or punishment?

Take a case from the middle class, where modesty and purity have their abode but nevertheless have not immunity from the frailties of nature, and are sometimes moved by the mysteries of passion. What could be more harassing to them, or injurious to society, than to draw a crowd around their seclusion?

Or take a case from the higher ranks, where education and culture have so refined nature, that a look cuts like a knife, and a word strikes like a hammer; where the most delicate attention gives pleasure, and the slightest neglect pain; where an indignity is disgrace and exposure is ruin. Bring all these cases into court side by side, with the same offence charged and the same proof made; and what conceivable charge of the court to the jury would be alike appropriate to all the cases, except, That they all have domestic government, which they have formed for themselves, suited to their own peculiar conditions, and that those governments are supreme, and from them there is no appeal except in cases of great importance requiring the strong arm of the law, and that to those governments they must submit themselves.

It will be observed that the ground upon which we have put this decision, is not, that the husband has the right to whip his wife much or little; but that we will not interfere with family government in trifling cases. We will no more interfere where the husband whips the wife, than where the wife whips the husband; and yet we would hardly be supposed to hold, that a wife has a right to whip her husband. We will not inflict upon society the greater evil of raising the curtain upon domestic privacy, to punish the lesser evil of trifling violence. Two boys under fourteen years of age fight upon the play-ground, and yet the courts will take no notice of it, not for the reason that boys have the right to fight, but because the interests of society require that they should be left to the more appropriate discipline of the school room and of home. It is not true that boys have a right to fight; nor is it true that a husband has a right to whip his wife. And if he had, it is not easily seen how the thumb is the standard of size for the instrument which he may use, as some of the old authorities have said; and in deference to which was his Honor's charge. A light blow, or many light blows, with a stick larger than the thumb, might produce no injury; but a switch half the size might be so used as to produce death. The standard is the effect produced, and not the manner of producing it, or the instrument used. Because our opinion is not in unison with the decisions of some of the sister States, or with the philosophy of some very respectable law writers, and could not be in unison with all, because of their contrariety—a decent respect for the opinions of others has induced us to be very full in stating the reasons for our conclusion. There is no error.

DISCUSSION QUESTIONS FOR *STATE v. RHODES*

A. What is the basis for the court's hesitancy to recognize "trivial complaints" arising out of domestic relations?

B. What was Blackstone's view regarding the right of the husband to correct and control his wife?

C. Although the court criticizes the "rule of thumb," does it go so far as to make violence against a spouse illegal? If not, what reasons does it provide to justify refusal to do so?

D. The court states that the husband's actions would constitute battery *if* the parties were not married. What societal views supported the court in making this distinction? Should violence within the family be treated differently than violence between nonfamily members?

E. The court found that the violence was "unprovoked." What behaviors might constitute provocation? Would the decision have been different if the court believed that the victim provoked the violence? Why were courts at this time concerned with provocation? Should provocation be relevant today? Why or why not?

15.3 REPORTS OF INTIMATE PARTNER VIOLENCE

In some studies of families contesting child custody issues, researchers have found that intimate partner violence was alleged in two-thirds to three-fourths of the cases and that half to three-fourths of the allegations could be in some way substantiated. Janet Johnston et al., *In the Name of the Child: A Developmental Approach to Understanding and Helping Children of Conflicted and Violent Divorce* 308 (2009). This does not mean that the remaining allegations were unfounded — sometimes there are no witnesses to or physical evidence of the abuse.

In some studies of couples entering mediation, over 50 percent report physical violence. Connie J.A. Beck & Chitra Raghavan, *Intimate Partner Abuse Screening in Custody Mediation: The Importance of Assessing Coercive Control*, 48 Fam. Ct. Rev. 555, 560 (2010):

> Although detected rates of IPV vary, it is common to find reported violence rates as high as 50% to 60% in cases presenting for divorce or separation mediation (Pearson, 1997). Newmark, Harrell, and Salem (1995) found that 68% of women and 55% of men reported being the victim of physical violence from the other party. Mathis and Tanner (1998) found that 60% of the cases in their mediation sample had some

violence, and half of the violent couples reported "extreme tactics" such as beating up or using weapons. In a third study, the definition of intimate partner abuse was expanded to include emotional abuse and coercive control (Beck, Walsh, Mechanic, & Taylor, 2010). With this broader definition, 85% of wives and 77% of husbands reported abuse, and only 10% of cases reported no abuse whatsoever by either party.

Robin H. Ballard et al., *Detecting Intimate Partner Violence in Family and Divorce Mediation: A Randomized Trial of Intimate Partner Violence Screening*, 17 Psychol. Pub. Pol'y & L. 241, 243 (2011). Other research in the context of mediation indicates that future male partner violence is associated with past violence, past abuse, emotional dependency, relationship problems, mental health problems, control issues, and substance abuse. Desmond Ellis & Noreen Stuckless, *Domestic Violence, DOVE, and Divorce Mediation*, 44 Fam. Ct. Rev. 658 (2006).

Initial research indicates that intimate partner violence may occur at approximately the same rate in same-gender couples. *See* Joanna Bunker Rohrbaugh, *Domestic Violence in Same-Gender Relationships*, 44 Fam. Ct. Rev. 287 (2006). *See also* Leigh Goodmark, *Transgender People, Intimate Partner Abuse, and the Legal System*, 48 Harv. C.R.-C.L. L. Rev. 51 (2013).

REFLECTIVE QUESTIONS	Are you surprised by the prevalence of intimate partner violence? Why or why not?

15.4 FAMILY-SPECIFIC APPROACH

The terms intimate partner violence and domestic violence refer to a wide range of behaviors. Each situation varies with respect to the perpetrator's intent, the meaning ascribed to the violence, and the effect on the victim or victims. Loretta Frederick, *Questions About Family Court Domestic Violence Screening and Assessment*, 46 Fam. Ct. Rev. 523, 524 (2008).

Intimate partner violence can have a profound effect on families and on the way attorneys and courts handle a case. Because the experiences of families can be so different, experts advise family lawyers to adopt a structured family-specific approach to representation. Such an approach is described below. Gabrielle Davis, *A Systematic Approach to Domestic Abuse-Informed Child Custody Decision-Making in Family Law Cases*, 53 Fam. Ct. Rev. 562 (2015) (explaining and describing the four-part framework for analysis).

Identification of possible domestic abuse. Family law attorneys should screen all clients for intimate partner violence. Some survivors of abuse risk retaliation if they disclose it, and they are understandably hesitant to do so. Such clients are more likely to disclose abuse to an attorney (as opposed to other professionals) because of the confidential nature of the relationship. *See* Margaret Drew, *Lawyer Malpractice* *and Domestic Violence: Are We Revictimizing Our Clients?*, 39 Fam. L.Q. 7 (2005) (exploring malpractice and ethical mistakes likely to occur when representing clients in cases involving domestic violence).

The purpose of the screening inquiry is to ascertain whether intimate partner violence *could* be an issue. If there are indications of possible abuse, additional investigation and assessment will be needed. A screening protocol typically involves confidential face-to-face interviews, use of screening instruments, and ongoing monitoring throughout the case. Nancy Ver Steegh et al., *Look Before You Leap* 972-979 (discussing practices for screening and existing screening instruments).

Understanding who is doing what to whom and with what effect. The impact and implications of intimate partner violence vary depending on its severity, frequency, form, and on the context in which it occurs. For example, consider three situations where partner A pushes partner B. In the first situation, there has been no prior history of violence or intimidation. In the second situation, there has been no previous physical violence, but partner A frequently threatens partner B and insists on knowing B's whereabouts at all times. In the third situation, partner A has a history of violence, including cutting B with a knife and breaking B's jaw. Although the physical act of partner A pushing B is the same in each hypothetical situation, the impact on B and the risk level to B is significantly different. Consequently, it is important to consider the circumstances of the violence in addition to specific physical acts. *See* Nancy Ver Steegh & Clare Dalton, *Report from the Wingspread Conference on Domestic Violence and Family Courts*, 46 Fam. Ct. Rev. 454 (2008).

Special care must be taken to understand the dynamics of coercive controlling abuse, which typically involves a combination of emotional abuse, psychological abuse, isolation of a partner, economic control, and manipulation of children. This abuse is likely to escalate at the time of separation, and it often continues after divorce. A coercive controlling perpetrator may use nonviolent tactics to intimidate the victim, and as a consequence, a larger escalating pattern of coercion might be overlooked. Similarly, coercive controlling perpetrators are likely to appear to be the more cooperative parent, and without investigation, an underlying pattern of threats and manipulation of children might go undetected. *See generally* Evan Stark, *Coercive Control: The Entrapment of Women in Personal Life* (2007); Connie J.A. Beck & Chitra Raghavan, *Intimate Partner Abuse Screening in Custody Mediation: The Importance of Assessing Coercive Control*, 48 Fam. Ct. Rev. 555; Dana Harrington Connor, *Financial Freedom: Women, Money, and Domestic Abuse*, 20 Wm. & Mary J. Women & L. 339 (2014).

Determining the implications of the abuse. Intimate partner violence may have a variety of implications for safety, child custody and access, or participation in dispute resolution processes. The impact and risks are different for each family, and the meaning and significance of the abuse must be evaluated in light of the issues being decided.

Accounting for abuse in actions and decisions. Substantive and procedural decisions should specifically and realistically address the problems created by the abuse. While there are no one-size-fits-all solutions, it may be necessary to limit access to children and/or monitor compliance with protective orders. Participation in dispute resolution processes may be helpful for some parties but could be unproductive or even dangerous for others. As the foregoing illustrates, discernment about the intent, meaning, and effect of intimate partner violence is essential for safe and appropriate decision making with respect to families who have experienced intimate partner violence.

 **REFLECTIVE QUESTIONS** What problems and repercussions are avoided when attorneys use a family-specific structured approach to representation in cases involving intimate partner violence? Why are the areas of inquiry discussed above important?

15.5 LEGAL DEFINITIONS OF INTIMATE PARTNER VIOLENCE

The Model Code on Domestic and Family Violence defines intimate partner violence as follows:

> Domestic or family violence means the occurrence of one or more of the following acts by a family or household member, but does not include acts of self defense:
>
> a) Attempting to cause or causing physical harm to another family or household member;
>
> b) Placing a family or household member in fear of physical harm; or
>
> c) Causing a family or household member to engage involuntarily in sexual activity by force, threat of force, or duress.

Most civil legal definitions of intimate partner violence focus on specific acts of physical violence. Nevertheless, family law professionals are encouraged to remain cognizant of the importance of examining context, particularly in cases involving coercive control:

> Every state requires evidence of physical violence or potential violence. This focus on violence is understandable because oppressive coercion or other non-violent abuse is difficult to quantify and prove. Violence is tangible and is already criminalized, with evidence and elements familiar to courts, lawyers, and police. In order to intercept and prevent abusive coercion, however, these regimes must shed the fixation of physical violence. When civil protection statutes define abuse, in addition to customary definitions of violence or references to criminal codes, the statute should include definitions to encompass non-violent, abusive coercion.
>
> To codify coercive control, drafters must grapple with highly contextualized, subjective, discrete relationships. While seeking to extend civil protection relief to victims who suffer coercive abuse but not violence, drafters must guard against

expanding the definition so far as to interfere with ordinary conflicts in non-abusive relationships. Quantified elements of coercive control might be so broad as to be indistinguishable from common arguments between aggrieved spouses, and they might dilute the promise of civil protection orders for those in legitimate need of relief.

Jeffrey R. Baker, *Enjoining Coercion: Squaring Civil Protection Orders with the Reality of Domestic Abuse*, 11 J.L. & Fam. Stud. 35, 58-59 (2008).

REFLECTIVE QUESTIONS   **What do you think the legal definition of intimate partner violence should be? Should the definition be different depending on whether it is being used in a child custody or criminal statute?**

15.6 CIVIL DOMESTIC ABUSE STATUTES: OVERVIEW

During the 1960s and 1970s, advocates successfully drew attention to the pervasiveness and seriousness of the problem of intimate partner violence. As more victims came forward, volunteers created emergency shelters and began providing other needed services. This movement eventually led to major legal reform, including enforcement of criminal laws and passage of civil intimate partner violence statutes.

In 1976, Pennsylvania became the first state to enact legislation providing for civil domestic violence protective orders. Currently all of the states have civil domestic abuse statutes. National Council of Juvenile and Family Court Judges, A Guide for Effective Issuance and Enforcement of Protection Orders 2 (2005), available at http://www.ncdsv.org/images/ncjfcj_burgundybook.pdf (last visited August 8, 2015).

Typical civil domestic abuse statutes define intimate partner violence and authorize courts to issue emergency and ongoing protective orders that may include prohibition of violence and contact, child custody, use of the residence, child support, and other relief.

States vary in terms of who is covered under the statutes but relief is generally granted to family and household members, spouses and former spouses, and those with a child in common. In some states the statutes apply to people in dating relationships. *See Evans v. Braun*, 12 A.3d 395 (Pa. Super. 2010) ("girlfriend" protected under statute); *J.S. v. J.F.*, 983 A.2d 1151 (N.J. Super. 2009) (dating relationship). *See also* D. Kelly Weisberg, *Lindsay's Legacy: The Tragedy That Triggered Law Reform to Prevent Teen Dating Violence*, 24 Hastings Women's L.J. 27 (2013).

REFLECTIVE QUESTIONS   **From a policy perspective, do you think that protective order relief should be available to people in dating relationships? Why or why not?**

15.7 CIVIL DOMESTIC ABUSE STATUTES: CONSTITUTIONAL CHALLENGES

During the years since their passage, civil domestic violence statutes have been challenged on various constitutional grounds. Recently, for example, in *Crespo v. Crespo*, 972 A.2d 1169 (N.J. Super. 2009), an alleged perpetrator unsuccessfully asserted that (1) his right to due process was violated under the New Jersey Prevention of Domestic Violence Act, which provides for a preponderance standard (rather than a clear and convincing standard); and (2) his Second Amendment right to bear arms was violated by a provision of the act allowing seizure of his firearms.

In emergency situations, civil domestic abuse acts allow victims to file for protective orders without giving prior notice to the respondent. Although the relief granted is typically more limited than when notice is provided, ex parte relief can include an order temporarily removing an alleged perpetrator from a shared home. *See Araya v. Keleta*, 26 A.3d 708 (D.C. Ct. App. 2011) (husband ordered to vacate shared residence titled in his name); *Harris v. Ross*, 2011 WL 825739 (Ohio App. 2011) (protection order could not affect title to real property).

REFLECTIVE QUESTIONS	Why are ex parte protective orders sometimes granted?

Background to *State ex rel. Williams v. Marsh*

In the following case, *State ex rel. Williams v. Marsh*, the Missouri Supreme Court considers the due process rights of an alleged perpetrator who challenges provisions found in a typical domestic abuse act.

STATE EX REL. WILLIAMS
v.
MARSH

Supreme Court of Missouri
626 S.W.2d 223 (1982)

HIGGINS, J. After a hearing on plaintiff's petition for an *ex parte* order of protection, the trial court found:

> plaintiff, Denise Williams, and respondent, Edward M. Williams were married; one child was born of the marriage; the couple had been living separately for approximately five months prior to the hearing, plaintiff having custody of the child; respondent's home

> address was unknown although his place of employment was known and his estimated wages were $1,000 per month; during the separation respondent provided no support or maintenance to plaintiff or the child with the exception of a small amount of clothing for the child; plaintiff leased or rented her residence individually; on November 13, 1980, and on numerous previous occasions, respondent (a 230 lbs., former Golden Gloves boxer) "intentionally, knowingly and wilfully beat petitioner . . . causing . . . serious physical injury . . . requiring petitioner to be hospitalized . . . for 12 days."

The court concluded: "respondent was a former adult household member whose actions constituted abuse; he had purposely placed petitioner in apprehension of immediate physical injury; and thus plaintiff had shown an unqualified right to the temporary relief available under §§455.035 and 455.045."

The court dismissed the petition because it held the Adult Abuse Act, in general and specifically §455.035, 045 and 085, RSMo Supp. 1980 unconstitutional, and thus unenforceable.

The Adult Abuse Act, was adopted by the Missouri Legislature on June 13, 1980, and became effective August 13, 1980. It was adopted by the Missouri Legislature as a result of an increased awareness nationally of the prevalence of domestic violence and of the need to protect the victims of that violence. It is part of a nationwide trend to legislate in this area. Existing remedies such as peace bonds, regular criminal process, and tort law have proved to be less than adequate in aiding the victims of abuse and in preventing further abuse.

An adult who is abused by a present or former adult household member, may petition the circuit court for relief under the Act. Two types of relief are available: *ex parte* orders issued without notice to the respondent or a hearing, and orders issued after notice and an on record hearing. Violation of an *ex parte* order of protection of which the respondent has notice or of a full order of protection is declared to be a class C misdemeanor for which the respondent may be arrested without a warrant. . . .

Studies have shown that the victim of adult abuse is usually a woman. In a large percentage of families, children have been present when the abuse occurred. In one study, fifty-four percent of the battered women interviewed reported that their husbands had committed acts of violence against their children as well as against them. Even if the child is not physically injured, he likely will suffer emotional trauma from witnessing violence between his parents. Abuse appears to be perpetuated through the generations; an individual who grows up in a home where violence occurs is more likely either to abuse others as an adult or to be a victim of abuse. Adult abuse, therefore, is a problem affecting not only the adult members of a household but also the children. The most compelling reason for an abused woman to remain in the home subject to more abuse is her financial dependency; this is particularly true for the women with children. The orders pertaining to child custody, support, and maintenance are all fairly related to and serve the purpose of aiding victims of domestic violence and preventing future incidents of adult abuse.

The court held that §§455.035, 045 of the Act facially violate the due process guarantees of U.S. Const., amend. XIV and Mo. Const. art. I, §10 by permitting a respondent to be deprived of constitutionally protected interests prior to notice or an adversary hearing. The trial court found the *ex parte* orders of protection constitutionally infirm because the Act, on its face, may be applied to exclude a respondent from his home or from contact with his children for a fifteen day period prior to notice or hearing. The trial judge concedes that the goal of the statute is legitimate and important, but nevertheless ruled it unconstitutional because of its impact on important personal rights. He reached this conclusion by finding:

> that the facts upon which an *ex parte* order may be issued are not easily verifiable and thus not appropriate for presentation by affidavit to the court, as required by *Mitchell v. W.T. Grant Co.*, 416 U.S. 600, 617-618 (1974); and that there is no procedure by which the respondent can dissolve the *ex parte* orders.

Sections 455.020-.035, RSMo Supp. 1980 set out the procedure for obtaining an *ex parte* order of protection. The person seeking an order of protection files a verified petition with the clerk of the circuit court or, if the court is unavailable, with "any available circuit or associate circuit judge in the city or county having jurisdiction. . . ." The judge may grant the *ex parte* orders only "for good cause shown" which is defined as "(a)n immediate and present danger of abuse to the petitioner." "Abuse" is defined as "inflicting, other than by accidental means, or attempting to inflict physical injury, on an adult or purposely placing another adult in apprehension of immediate physical injury."

Three orders may be issued *ex parte*: restraining the respondent from further acts of abuse; restraining the respondent from entering the family dwelling unit; and granting temporary custody of any minor children. The statute permits an order restraining the respondent from entering the family dwelling unit to issue in favor of a spouse who otherwise has no property interest in the home. An *ex parte* order of protection remains in effect until the hearing, which is to be held "(n)ot later than fifteen days after the filing of a petition. . . ."

The due process guarantee is intended to protect an individual against arbitrary acts of the government. Furthermore, it protects the right to use and enjoy one's property without governmental interference. Before the guarantee of due process comes into play, however, there must be a deprivation by the government of a constitutionally protected interest. The interests which are subject to temporary deprivation through the issuance of an *ex parte* order constitute significant liberty and property interests falling "within the purview of the Due Process Clause." Thus the procedures available under the Act must meet the constitutional standard.

Notice and an opportunity to be heard must be provided by the state in a meaningful manner prior to deprivation of a protected interest. This rule is not necessarily applied when there is only a temporary taking, as is the case here. Due process is a flexible concept; the same procedures need not be applied in all instances. The extent and nature of procedures depends upon weighing of the private interests affected and the governmental functions involved. The United States Supreme Court in *Mathews v. Eldridge* [424 U.S. 319 (1976)] identified a third factor to be considered in the balancing formula; the risk of erroneous deprivation using the existing procedures.

The first factor is the private interest affected. The respondent has two private interests at stake; a property interest in one's home and a liberty interest in custody of one's children. These interests are significant, the importance of which has been emphasized by the United States Supreme Court.

The second factor in the balancing formula is the governmental interest. The Adult Abuse Act is an exercise of the state's police power. Through the procedures established to aid victims of domestic violence, the legislature promotes the general health, welfare, and safety of its citizens. The magnitude of the problem of domestic violence is evidenced by statistics compiled by the FBI in 1973 which indicate that one-fourth of all homicides in the United States occur within the family. The petitioner's interests which are protected by the state in furthering its interests are the same as those of the respondent. The parties, irrespective of marital status, may own or rent the dwelling jointly, although under the Act this is not required. If it becomes unsafe for both parties to remain in the home, one may need to be excluded. The choice is reduced to the victim of the abuse leaving or the court ordering the abuser to leave. Parents may have an equal interest in maintaining custody of their children. Both interests are important and have been accorded deference by the courts.

The Missouri Legislature has established a mechanism whereby the state can intervene when abuse of one adult by another household member occurs or is threatened and thus prevent further violence. State legislatures have broad power to enact laws to protect the general health, welfare, and safety. States also have been given deference in adopting reasonable summary procedures when acting under their police power.

The third factor in the test in *Mathews v. Eldridge* is "the fairness and reliability of the existing pretermination procedures, and the probable value, if any, of additional procedural safeguards." "The risk of wrongful use of the procedure must also be judged in the context of the issues which are to be determined at that proceeding."

An *ex parte* order of protection is analogous to a temporary restraining order because both are injunctions issued prior to notice or hearing. *Ex parte* orders restraining acts of abuse or entrance into the dwelling are issued upon a showing of "an immediate and present danger of abuse to the petitioner." As in a proceeding to obtain any other restraining order, the petitioner must satisfy the court that grounds exist to justify granting this order. This will, in most instances, require the petitioner to appear personally before the court at which time the credibility of the petitioner can be tested. In addition, the judge may be able to see first hand "the evidence of violence manifested in burns, cuts, bruises, and fractures." If the petitioner is unable to appear because of injuries, this may be alleged and proof thereof will allow the court to determine that there is "(a)n immediate and present danger of abuse."

A protection order, if granted, remains in effect until the hearing which is to be held "(n)ot later than fifteen days after the filing of a petition." This sets a maximum period that the order could be effective without some hearing. Nothing in the statute suggests that the respondent could not obtain an earlier hearing. Concerning other restraining orders, Rule 92.02(b) provides that a party against whom a temporary restraining order has been issued may, upon two days' (or shorter time if the court so prescribes) notice to the opposing party, receive a hearing on the order. This rule is equally applicable to orders issued under the Act. The statute requires that the petition, notice of the hearing date, and any *ex parte* order of protection be served upon the respondent. The court at the same time may include in the notice information regarding the respondent's right to request an earlier hearing and the procedure to be followed. The Supreme Court in *Fuentes v. Shevin*, [407 U.S. 67 (1972)] outlined categories of cases where outright seizures have been allowed. The first is where seizure has been directly necessary to secure an important governmental or general public interest; the second is where there has been a special need for prompt action; the third is where the state has kept strict control over its monopoly of legitimate force: there is a government official responsible for determining that seizure was necessary under standards set out in "narrowly drawn statutes."

The Act meets the foregoing standards. The Act is directly necessary to secure important governmental interests, i.e., protection of victims of abuse and prevention of further abuse. The situation where the challenged Act is to be applied are those where prompt action is necessary, i.e., when there is "(a)n immediate and present danger of abuse" — the only time the *ex parte* order may be issued. The government has kept strict control over its powers. Only a judge in his discretion, may issue the *ex parte* orders. This differs from the procedure where "(p)rivate parties, serving their own private advantage, may unilaterally invoke state power to replevy goods from another" disapproved in *Fuentes v. Shevin*. Under the Adult Abuse Act, the petitioner requests the court to act on his or her behalf. The court, not the clerk, must issue the order and the orders are not to be issued routinely but only after the petitioner has filed a verified petition showing good cause. The burden is on the challenger to show that this exercise of the state's police power is unreasonable, a burden not here carried. The interests and procedures considered, these *ex parte* order provisions comply with due process requirements because they are a reasonable means to achieve the state's legitimate goal of preventing domestic violence, and afford adequate procedural safeguards, prior to and after any deprivation occurs. The presumptive constitutionality of the Adult Abuse Act is not overcome by any of the attacks presented.

DISCUSSION QUESTIONS FOR *STATE EX REL. WILLIAMS v. MARSH*

A. On what basis did the trial court hold that the Missouri statute facially violated the Due Process Clause of the U.S. and state constitutions?

B. How is abuse defined under the Adult Abuse Act in this jurisdiction? What must the victim show in order to obtain a protective order? Who can seek such an order?

C. What procedures did the statute require a person seeking an ex parte order of protection to comply with before the order would issue?

D. What relief may be afforded a person seeking a temporary order? How long does an ex parte order remain in effect?

E. What test did the court use to determine whether the granting of an ex parte order violates due process protections? What are the three factors that the court balances? For each factor, list the arguments made by each side. Do you agree with the reasoning of the court?

F. Most states have adopted statutes similar to Missouri's Adult Abuse Act. Why did this occur? Is relief provided by domestic violence statutes (such as the Missouri statute) that is not otherwise already available to victims through the criminal justice system, the civil tort law, or the family court system?

15.8 ENFORCEMENT OF PROTECTIVE ORDERS

Entry of an order for protection can be an integral part of a victim's safety plan. However, the decision about whether to seek a protective order should be made on a case-by-case basis. Although many victims report that protective orders are effective and empowering, researchers continue to investigate the extent to which protective orders prevent future abuse. In one study, 60 percent of temporary orders were violated within the first year. Victims who were previously more seriously abused suffered more serious violations of the protective order. Also, perpetrators who objected to entry of a protective order were more likely to violate them. Adele Harrel & Barbara E. Smith, *Effects of Restraining Orders on Domestic Violence Victims*, in *Do Arrests and Restraining Orders Work?* (Buzawa & Buzawa eds., 1996). Protective orders may be less effective in cases where the perpetrator has a criminal history, the couple has minor children, or the parties have low incomes. *See* Eve S. Buzawa & Carl G. Buzawa, *Domestic Violence: The Criminal Justice Response* 242-245 (2003).

In some intimate partner violence situations, the police are called to intervene. Historically, they were trained to avoid arresting persons for crimes such as assault, battery, rape, and attempted murder in "domestic" cases, and few perpetrators were criminally prosecuted. This practice changed significantly during the 1980s as a result of heightened awareness of the possible deterrent effect of arrest and a rash of lawsuits filed against police departments. Some police departments reacted by adopting mandatory arrest policies, and some prosecutors instituted "no-drop" prosecution policies. *See* Sara R. Benson, *Failure to Arrest: A Pilot Study of Police Response to Domestic Violence in Rural Illinois*, 17 Am. U. J. Gender Soc. Pol'y & L. 685 (2009). As domestic abuse statutes were passed, they provided that violation of a protective order was in itself a criminal offense.

<table>
<tr><td>REFLECTIVE
QUESTIONS</td><td>What advice should family lawyers give clients
about when police protection should be sought?</td></tr>
</table>

Background to *Town of Castle Rock v. Gonzales*

In the case of *Town of Castle Rock* a restraining order was in effect against Mr. Gonzales at the time he abducted his three children. Throughout the evening of the abduction Mrs. Gonzales repeatedly called the police seeking enforcement of the order, but no action was taken. Despite the tragic outcome in the case, the Supreme Court ruled that a victim of intimate partner violence does not have a personal entitlement to or a property interest in police enforcement of a restraining order.

TOWN OF CASTLE ROCK
v.
GONZALES

Supreme Court of the United States
545 U.S. 748 (2005)

SCALIA, J., delivered the opinion of the Court, in which **REHNQUIST, C.J.,** and **O'CONNOR, KENNEDY, SOUTER, THOMAS,** and **BREYER, JJ.,** joined. **SOUTER, J.,** filed a concurring opinion, in which **BREYER, J.,** joined. **STEVENS, J.,** filed a dissenting opinion, in which **GINSBURG, J.,** joined.

We decide in this case whether an individual who has obtained a state-law restraining order has a constitutionally protected property interest in having the police enforce the restraining order when they have probable cause to believe it has been violated.

The horrible facts of this case are contained in the complaint that respondent Jessica Gonzales filed in Federal District Court. Because the case comes to us on appeal from a dismissal of the complaint, we assume its allegations are true. Respondent alleges that petitioner, the town of Castle Rock, Colorado, violated the Due Process Clause of the Fourteenth Amendment to the United States Constitution when its police officers, acting pursuant to official policy or custom, failed to respond properly to her repeated reports that her estranged husband was violating the terms of a restraining order.

The restraining order had been issued by a state trial court several weeks earlier in conjunction with respondent's divorce proceedings. The original form order, issued on May 21, 1999, and served on respondent's husband on June 4, 1999, commanded him not to "molest or disturb the peace of [respondent] or of any child," and to remain at least 100 yards from the family home at all times. The bottom of the pre-printed form noted that the reverse side contained "IMPORTANT NOTICES FOR RESTRAINED PARTIES AND LAW ENFORCEMENT OFFICIALS." The preprinted text on the back of the form included the following "**WARNING**":

> **A KNOWING VIOLATION OF A RESTRAINING ORDER IS A CRIME**. . . . A VIOLATION WILL ALSO CONSTITUTE CONTEMPT OF COURT. **YOU MAY BE ARRESTED** WITHOUT NOTICE IF A LAW ENFORCEMENT OFFICER HAS PROBABLE CAUSE TO BELIEVE THAT YOU HAVE KNOWINGLY VIOLATED THIS ORDER.

The preprinted text on the back of the form also included a "**NOTICE TO LAW ENFORCEMENT OFFICIALS,**" which read in part:

> YOU SHALL USE EVERY REASONABLE MEANS TO ENFORCE THIS RESTRAINING ORDER. YOU SHALL ARREST, OR, IF AN ARREST WOULD BE IMPRACTICAL UNDER THE CIRCUMSTANCES, SEEK A WARRANT FOR THE ARREST OF THE RESTRAINED PERSON WHEN YOU HAVE INFORMATION AMOUNTING TO PROBABLE CAUSE THAT THE RESTRAINED PERSON HAS VIOLATED OR ATTEMPTED TO VIOLATE ANY PROVISION OF THIS ORDER AND THE RESTRAINED PERSON HAS BEEN PROPERLY SERVED WITH A COPY OF THIS ORDER OR HAS RECEIVED ACTUAL NOTICE OF THE EXISTENCE OF THIS ORDER.

On June 4, 1999, the state trial court modified the terms of the restraining order and made it permanent. The modified order gave respondent's husband the right to spend time with his three daughters (ages 10, 9, and 7) on alternate weekends, for two weeks during the summer, and, "'upon reasonable notice,'" for a mid-week dinner visit "'arranged by the parties'"; the modified order also allowed him to visit the home to collect the children for such "parenting time."

According to the complaint, at about 5 or 5:30 P.M. on Tuesday, June 22, 1999, respondent's husband took the three daughters while they were playing outside the family home. No advance arrangements had been made for him to see the daughters that evening. When respondent noticed the children were missing, she suspected her husband had taken them. At about 7:30 P.M., she called the Castle Rock Police Department, which dispatched two officers. The complaint continues: "When [the officers] arrived . . . , she showed them a copy of the TRO and requested that it be enforced and the three children be returned to her immediately. [The officers] stated that there was nothing they could do about the TRO and suggested that [respondent] call the Police Department again if the three children did not return home by 10:00 P.M."

At approximately 8:30 P.M., respondent talked to her husband on his cellular telephone. He told her "he had the three children [at an] amusement park in Denver." She called the police again and asked them to "have someone check for" her husband or his vehicle at the amusement park and "put out an [all points bulletin]" for her husband, but the officer with whom she spoke "refused to do so," again telling her to "wait until 10:00 P.M. and see if" her husband returned the girls.

At approximately 10:10 P.M., respondent called the police and said her children were still missing, but she was now told to wait until midnight. She called at midnight and told the dispatcher her children were still missing. She went to her husband's apartment and, finding nobody there, called the police at 12:10 A.M.; she was told to wait for an officer to arrive. When none came, she went to the police station at 12:50 A.M. and submitted an incident report. The officer who took the report "made no reasonable effort to enforce the TRO or locate the three children. Instead, he went to dinner." At approximately 3:20 A.M., respondent's husband arrived at the police station and opened fire with a semiautomatic handgun he had purchased earlier that evening. Police shot back, killing him. Inside the cab of his pickup truck, they found the bodies of all three daughters, whom he had already murdered.

On the basis of the foregoing factual allegations, respondent brought an action under Rev. Stat. §1979, 42 U.S.C. §1983, claiming that the town violated the Due Process Clause because its police department had "an official policy or custom of failing to respond properly to complaints of restraining order violations" and "tolerate[d] the non-enforcement of restraining orders by its police officers." The complaint also alleged that the town's actions "were taken either willfully, recklessly or with such gross negligence as to indicate wanton disregard and deliberate indifference to" respondent's civil rights. . . .

The Fourteenth Amendment to the United States Constitution provides that a State shall not "deprive any person of life, liberty, or property, without due process of law." In 42 U.S.C. §1983, Congress has created a federal cause of action for "the deprivation of any rights, privileges, or immunities secured by the Constitution and laws." Respondent claims the benefit of this provision on the ground that she had a property interest in police enforcement of the restraining order against her husband; and that the town deprived her of this property without due process by having a policy that tolerated nonenforcement of restraining orders.

As the Court of Appeals recognized, we left a similar question unanswered in *DeShaney v. Winnebago County Dept. of Social Servs.*, 489 U.S. 189, 109 (1989), another case with "undeniably tragic" facts: Local child-protection officials had failed to protect a young boy from beatings by his father that left him severely brain damaged. We held that the so-called "substantive" component of the Due Process Clause does not "requir[e] the State to protect the life, liberty, and property of its citizens against invasion by private actors." We noted, however, that the petitioner had not properly preserved the argument that—and we thus "decline[d] to consider" whether—state "child protection statutes gave [him] an 'entitlement' to receive protective services in accordance with the terms of the statute, an entitlement which would enjoy due process protection." Our cases recognize that a benefit is not a protected entitlement if government officials may grant or deny it in their discretion. The Court of Appeals in this case determined that Colorado law created an entitlement to enforcement of the restraining order because the "court-issued restraining order . . . specifically dictated that its terms must be enforced" and a "state statute command[ed]" enforcement of the order when certain objective conditions were met (probable cause to believe that the order had been violated and that the object of the order had received notice of its existence). . . .

The critical language in the restraining order came not from any part of the order itself (which was signed by the state-court trial judge and directed to the restrained party, respondent's husband), but from the preprinted notice to law-enforcement personnel that appeared on the back of the order. That notice effectively restated the statutory provision describing "peace officers' duties" related to the crime of violation of a restraining order. At the time of the conduct at issue in this case, that provision read as follows:

> (a) Whenever a restraining order is issued, the protected person shall be provided with a copy of such order. *A peace officer shall use every reasonable means to enforce a restraining order.*
>
> (b) *A peace officer shall arrest, or, if an arrest would be impractical under the circumstances, seek a warrant for the arrest of a restrained person* when the peace officer has information amounting to probable cause that:
>
> (I) The restrained person has violated or attempted to violate any provision of a restraining order; and
>
> (II) The restrained person has been properly served with a copy of the restraining order or the restrained person has received actual notice of the existence and substance of such order.
>
> (c) In making the probable cause determination described in paragraph (b) of this subsection (3), a peace officer shall assume that the information received from the registry is accurate. *A peace officer shall enforce a valid restraining order whether or not there is a record of the restraining order in the registry.* Colo. Rev. Stat. §18-6-803.5(3) (Lexis 1999) (emphases added).

The Court of Appeals concluded that this statutory provision — especially taken in conjunction with a statement from its legislative history, and with another statute restricting criminal and civil liability for officers making arrests — established the Colorado Legislature's clear intent "to alter the fact that the police were not enforcing domestic abuse retraining orders," and thus its intent "that the recipient of a domestic abuse restraining order have an entitlement to its enforcement." Any other result, it said, "would render domestic abuse restraining orders utterly valueless."

This last statement is sheer hyperbole. Whether or not respondent had a right to enforce the restraining order, it rendered certain otherwise lawful conduct by her husband both criminal and in contempt of court. The creation of grounds on which he could be arrested, criminally prosecuted, and held in contempt was hardly "valueless" — even if the prospect of those sanctions ultimately failed to prevent him from committing three murders and a suicide.

We do not believe that these provisions of Colorado law truly made enforcement of restraining orders *mandatory.* A well-established tradition of police discretion has long coexisted with apparently mandatory arrest statutes.

> In each and every state there are long-standing statutes that, by their terms, seem to preclude nonenforcement by the police. . . . However, for a number of reasons, including their legislative history, insufficient resources, and sheer physical impossibility, it has been recognized that such statutes cannot be interpreted literally. . . . [T]hey clearly do not

mean that a police officer may not lawfully decline to make an arrest. As to third parties in these states, the full-enforcement statutes simply have no effect, and their significance is further diminished. 1 ABA Standards for Criminal Justice 1-4.5, commentary, pp. 1-124 to 1-125 (2d ed. 1980).

The deep-rooted nature of law-enforcement discretion, even in the presence of seemingly mandatory legislative commands, is illustrated by *Chicago v. Morales*, 527 U.S. 41 (1999), which involved an ordinance that said a police officer " 'shall order' " persons to disperse in certain circumstances. This Court rejected out of hand the possibility that "the mandatory language of the ordinance . . . afford[ed] the police *no* discretion." It is, the Court proclaimed, simply "common sense that *all* police officers must use some discretion in deciding when and where to enforce city ordinances."

Against that backdrop, a true mandate of police action would require some stronger indication from the Colorado Legislature than "shall use every reasonable means to enforce a restraining order" (or even "shall arrest . . . or . . . seek a warrant"). That language is not perceptibly more mandatory than the Colorado statute which has long told municipal chiefs of police that they "shall pursue and arrest any person fleeing from justice in any part of the state" and that they "shall apprehend any person in the act of committing any offense . . . and, forthwith and without any warrant, bring such person before a . . . competent authority for examination and trial." It is hard to imagine that a Colorado peace officer would not have some discretion to determine that — despite probable cause to believe a restraining order has been violated — the circumstances of the violation or the competing duties of that officer or his agency counsel decisively against enforcement in a particular instance. The practical necessity for discretion is particularly apparent in a case such as this one, where the suspected violator is not actually present and his whereabouts are unknown. *Cf. Donaldson v. Seattle*, 65 Wash. App. 661 (1992) ("There is a vast difference between a mandatory duty to arrest [a violator who is on the scene] and a mandatory duty to conduct a follow up investigation [to locate an absent violator]. . . . A mandatory duty to investigate would be completely open-ended as to priority, duration and intensity").

The dissent correctly points out that, in the specific context of domestic violence, mandatory-arrest statutes have been found in some States to be more mandatory than traditional mandatory-arrest statutes. The Colorado statute mandating arrest for a domestic-violence offense is different from but related to the one at issue here, and it includes similar though not identical phrasing. See Colo. Rev. Stat. §18-6-803.6(1) ("When a peace officer determines that there is probable cause to believe that a crime or offense involving domestic violence . . . has been committed, the officer shall, without undue delay, arrest the person suspected of its commission . . ."). Even in the domestic-violence context, however, it is unclear how the mandatory-arrest paradigm applies to cases in which the offender is not present to be arrested. As the dissent explains, much of the impetus for mandatory-arrest statutes and policies derived from the idea that it is better for police officers to arrest the aggressor in a domestic-violence incident than to attempt to mediate the dispute or merely to ask the offender to leave the scene. Those other options are only available, of course, when the offender is present at the scene. See Hanna, *No Right to Choose: Mandated Victim Participation in Domestic Violence Prosecutions*, 109 Harv. L. Rev. 1849, 1860 (1996) ("[T]he clear trend in police practice is to arrest the batterer *at the scene* . . ." (emphasis added)).

As one of the cases cited by the dissent, recognized, "there will be situations when no arrest is possible, *such as when the alleged abuser is not in the home.*" *Donaldson*, 65 Wash. App., at 674, 831 P.2d, at 1105. That case held that Washington's mandatory-arrest statute required an arrest only in "cases where the offender is on the scene," and that it "d[id] not create an on-going mandatory duty to conduct an investigation" to locate the offender. Colorado's restraining-order statute appears to contemplate a similar distinction, providing that when arrest is "impractical"—which was likely the case when the whereabouts of respondent's husband were unknown—the officers' statutory duty is to "seek a warrant" rather than "arrest." . . .

Even if we were to think otherwise concerning the creation of an entitlement by Colorado, it is by no means clear that an individual entitlement to enforcement of a restraining order could constitute a "property" interest for purposes of the Due Process Clause. Such a right would not, of course, resemble any traditional conception of property. Although that alone does not disqualify it from due process protection, as *Roth* and its progeny show, the right to have a restraining order enforced does not "have some ascertainable monetary value," as even our "*Roth*-type property-as-entitlement" cases have implicitly required. Perhaps most radically, the alleged property interest here arises *incidentally*, not out of some new species of government benefit or service, but out of a function that government actors have always performed—to wit, arresting people who they have probable cause to believe have committed a criminal offense. . . . We conclude, therefore, that respondent did not, for purposes of the Due Process Clause, have a property interest in police enforcement of the restraining order against her husband. . . . The judgment of the Court of Appeals is *Reversed*.

JUSTICE STEVENS, with whom **JUSTICE GINSBURG** joins, dissenting.

Three flaws in the Court's rather superficial analysis of the merits highlight the unwisdom of its decision to answer the state-law question *de novo.* First, the Court places undue weight on the various statutes throughout the country that seemingly mandate police enforcement but are generally understood to preserve police discretion. As a result, the Court gives short shrift to the unique case of "mandatory arrest" statutes in the domestic violence context; States passed a wave of these statutes in the 1980's and 1990's with the unmistakable goal of eliminating police discretion in this area. Second, the Court's formalistic analysis fails to take seriously the fact that the Colorado statute at issue in this case was enacted for the benefit of the narrow class of persons who are beneficiaries of domestic restraining orders, and that the order at issue in this case was specifically intended to provide protection to respondent and her children. Finally, the Court is simply wrong to assert that a citizen's interest in the government's commitment to provide police enforcement in certain defined circumstances does not resemble any "traditional conception of property," in fact, a citizen's property interest in such a commitment is just as concrete and worthy of protection as her interest in any other important service the government or a private firm has undertaken to provide. . . .

DISCUSSION QUESTIONS FOR *TOWN OF CASTLE ROCK v. GONZALES*

A. What was the legal basis for the plaintiff's complaint and what did she allege?

B. The Court discussed *DeShaney v. Winnebago County Dept. of Social Services.* What was the holding in that case?

C. Do you agree with the court of appeals that without an entitlement to enforcement, a domestic abuse restraining order is "utterly valueless"? Is this assertion "sheer hyperbole" as the Supreme Court suggests? What is the value of a domestic abuse restraining order after this decision?

D. According to the Court, what is the tradition regarding police discretion to arrest?

E. In the dissent, Justice Stevens (joined by Justice Ginsburg) writes as follows:

> While Colorado case law does not speak to the question, it is instructive that other state courts interpreting their analogous statutes have not only held that they eliminate the police's traditional discretion to refuse enforcement, but have also recognized that they create rights enforceable against the police under state law. For example, in *Nearing v. Weaver*, 670 P.2d 137 (1983), the court held that although the common law of negligence did not support a suit against the police for failing to enforce a domestic restraining order, the statute's mandatory directive formed the basis for the suit because it was "a specific duty imposed by statute for the benefit of individuals previously identified by judicial order."

Which argument do you find most persuasive?

F. The opinion states: "The modified order gave respondent's husband the right to spend time with his three daughters (ages 10, 9, and 7) on alternate weekends, for two weeks during the summer," and, " 'upon reasonable notice,' for a mid-week dinner visit 'arranged by the parties'; 'the modified order also allowed him to visit the home to collect the children for such parenting time.' " Should visitation have been awarded in this case? How should courts make such decisions? Why was the perpetrator ordered to visit the home to pick up the children?

G. In 2011, the Inter-American Commission on Human Rights (IACHR) held the United States responsible for violating the human rights of Jessica Lenahan

(Gonzalez) and her children. Do you view the failure to enforce the restraining order as a human rights violation? Why or why not? *See Jessica Lenahan (Gonzalez) v. United States*, located at http://www.cidh.org/comunicados/english/2011/92-11eng.htm (last visited August 8, 2015). *See* Caroline Bettinger-Lopez, *Human Rights at Home: Domestic Violence as a Human Rights Violation*, 40 Colum. Hum. Rts. L. Rev. 19 (2008).

15.9 VIOLENCE AGAINST WOMEN ACT

The Violence Against Women Act (VAWA) requires states to enforce protective orders from other states if the issuing court provided due process and had jurisdiction to enter the order. In cases where mutual orders were issued, only the order entered on behalf of the petitioner is enforceable unless the respondent filed a counterpetition and specific findings were made. 18 U.S.C. §2265 (2011). The act also criminalizes possession of a firearm by perpetrators subject to protective orders and provides penalties for crossing state lines to harm an intimate partner or violate a protective order. *See* 18 U.S.C. §§922(g)(8)(9); Lisa D. May, *The Backfiring of the Domestic Violence Firearms Bans*, 14 Colum. J. Gender & L. 1 (2005). Recent amendments focus on the power of tribes to assume jurisdiction over defendants who perpetrate domestic violence or violate protective orders in Indian country. Department of Justice, Violence Against Women Act (VAWA) Reauthorization 2013, available at http://www.justice.gov/tribal/violence-against-women-act-vawa-reauthorization-2013-0 (last visited July 22, 2015).

> **REFLECTIVE QUESTIONS**
>
> Why do you think Congress passed and has reauthorized the Violence Against Women Act? Why do you think that reauthorization has been controversial?

15.10 CHILDREN AND INTIMATE PARTNER VIOLENCE: CONTACT RESTRICTIONS

In about half of the homes where spousal abuse occurs, children are also physically abused. This is referred to as concurrent child abuse. Even if the children are not directly physically abused, they are likely to be exposed to the violence and suffer other consequences from the abuse. *See* Evan Stark & Anne Flitcraft, *Women at Risk* 76 (1996) (discussing relationship between domestic violence and child abuse); Lundy Bancroft & Jay Silverman, *The Batterer as Parent* 42 (2002) (40-70 percent report concurrent child abuse).

The extent of the impact of intimate partner violence on children varies depending on the child's overall situation and the existence of various protective factors. However, infants may exhibit poor health, may have difficulty sleeping, and may be less responsive than other children. Preschoolers sometimes lag developmentally and are likely to cling to their mothers. Older girls may become more passive, while older boys may exhibit more aggressive and hostile behaviors. *See* Jeffrey L. Edleson, *The Overlap Between Child Maltreatment and Woman Abuse* (1999), located at http://www.vawnet.org/applied-research-papers/print-document.php?doc_id=389 (last visited August 8, 2015); Maria Roy, *Children in the Crossfire: Violence in the Home—How Does It Affect Our Children?* (1988). *See also* the Child Exposure to Domestic Violence (CEDV) scale located at http://www.mincava.umn.edu/cedv/index.html (last visited August 8, 2015).

Special care must be taken to fashion parenting plans and court orders regarding child custody when intimate partner violence has occurred. As discussed previously, such situations need to be individually considered in light of the context of the violence. *See* Peter G. Jaffe et al., *Custody Disputes Involving Allegations of Domestic Violence: Toward a Differentiated Approach to Parenting Plans*, 46 Fam. Ct. Rev. 500 (2008).

| REFLECTIVE QUESTIONS | Can you create a hypothetical under which you would favor entry of a "no contact" with parent order? |

Background to *In re Marriage of Stewart*

In some cases involving intimate partner violence, courts limit or suspend the perpetrating parent's contact with the children. In the case of *In re Marriage of Stewart*, the mother sought to bar contact between the father and the children based on psychological harm to the children resulting from the father's violence. The court suspended the father's contact with the children despite the fact that a permanent parenting plan granting him access was in effect.

IN RE MARRIAGE OF STEWART
Court of Appeals of Washington
137 P.3d 25 (2006)

ELLINGTON, J. Nichole and Wilson Stewart have two children, R.S., age 13, and S.S., age 8. The Stewarts dissolved their marriage in 2001. The permanent parenting plan established Nichole as the primary residential parent. Since then, there have been multiple incidents of domestic violence. In February 2002, Nichole picked up R.S. after a school basketball practice. Wilson is the team's coach. He reached into Nichole's car and smeared chewing gum in her hair, berating her in vulgar terms about her romantic life. Both children were present, and R.S. attempted to call 911 on a cell phone. Wilson initially denied the incident occurred, but later pleaded guilty to assault in the fourth degree, and was ordered to participate in domestic violence treatment as part of his sentence. A no-contact order was issued, and Nichole also obtained a permanent restraining order prohibiting Wilson from harassing her, stalking her, or entering her home or workplace without her permission. The order provided that all exchanges of the children occur curbside at each party's residence. Five days later, Wilson violated the order by following Nichole's car in the late evening, leaving messages on her cell phone marking her progress. Nichole contacted police. Wilson denied stalking Nichole or making the calls. After officers listened to the recordings on Nichole's voice mail, they arrested Wilson for violating the protection order.

In July 2003, the parties amended their parenting plan to require co-parent counseling aimed at reaching agreement on minor modifications to the residential schedule, and adding a Starbucks in Bothell as a location for visitation exchanges.

In March 2004, Wilson completed the domestic violence treatment required by the February 2002 protection order. That same month, during a visitation exchange, he is alleged to have shoved his hand down Nichole's pants and then forced his finger into her mouth, in the presence of S.S. In September 2004, Wilson allegedly barged into Nichole's home, accused her of seeing other men, and, with the children present, ripped the comforter off her bed to examine the sheets for evidence of sex. On Christmas Day 2004, the Stewarts were to do a curbside exchange of the children at Wilson's house. When Nichole arrived to drop off the children, Wilson approached and tried to reach her through the car window. He then spat upon her in front of the children. The children apparently confronted Wilson about this incident later in the day. Nichole testified that S.S. telephoned her several times from Wilson's house, crying and then hanging up because she was afraid Wilson would catch her calling Nichole. Wilson was later charged with assault in the fourth degree and violation of the 2002 restraining order. After this incident, Nichole sought the chapter 26.50 RCW domestic violence protection order at issue here. A superior court commissioner granted the order on a temporary basis and suspended the parenting plan pending the statutory 14-day hearing.

At the 14-day hearing on January 26, 2005, Nichole presented her declaration and police reports detailing the incidents of domestic violence. Wilson denied Nichole's allegations, and asserted instead that Nichole had initiated sexual encounters with him. It is apparent from his declaration that Wilson had asked the children about their mother's romantic life. Wilson also acknowledged that the night before the incident, Christmas Eve, he drove past Nichole's house and observed her fiancé's car in the driveway, and that he saw it there again when he drove by at 7:00 A.M. Christmas morning.

The commissioner entered a one-year protection order prohibiting Wilson from contact with Nichole or the children. The order included the following language: "The parenting plan entered in the dissolution action is suspended pending further order through a parenting plan modification action." Wilson moved for revision. Judge Douglass North denied the motion, ruling that: "The court finds the mother's credibility is greater than the father's [and] [t]here is evidence of imminent psychological harm to the children which is a basis for an order of protection as to the children." That afternoon, Nichole filed a formal motion to modify the parenting plan. . . .

Valid Grounds Supported the Protection Order. Wilson first contends that psychological harm to the children is not a proper basis for the issuance of a protection order. RCW 26.50.060 authorizes the court to issue a protection order restraining the respondent from committing acts of domestic violence. The order may restrict contact between a parent and child, in which case the restraint may not exceed a maximum period of one year. RCW 26.50.010(a) defines domestic violence to include: "Physical harm, bodily injury, assault, or the infliction of fear of imminent physical harm, bodily injury or assault, between family or household members."

There is no allegation that Wilson assaulted his children. But the children witnessed Wilson's assaults on Nichole, and were afraid for her. For example, R.S. attempted to call 911 during one assault, and when Wilson invaded Nichole's house "both children were terrified, begging [Wilson] to stop and just leave." In short, there was ample evidence that Wilson caused his children to fear he would assault Nichole. Such fear is indeed psychological harm, as the trial court termed it. It is also domestic violence, and is a statutory basis for an order of protection.

Wilson next contends that complete suspension of contact was not reasonably necessary to prevent the children from witnessing domestic violence between their parents, because third party exchanges would have accomplished the same result. But a protection order proceeding serves to provide a swift response to prevent further domestic abuse. One reason the order must be temporary is that, unlike the family court, the protection order court is necessarily limited in its ability to craft finely tuned solutions. Here, various visitation exchange procedures had been tried. Whether third party exchanges would or could be an effective solution was properly left to the family court. The evidence amply supported the order of protection as to the children. . . .

Wilson next contends a protection order should have only a "fleeting effect" on parental contact. That precisely describes the effect of the order here. In the morning on March 10, 2005, Judge North refused to revise the protection order. The same afternoon, Nichole filed a motion in family court seeking to modify the parenting plan. Wilson could have done the same. If protection order restrictions have more than a very temporary duration, it is because the parties have delayed in seeking resort to family court. Delay is not a result of the protection order.

We agree that a protection order cannot actually suspend a parenting plan. Nor can it impose a long-term restriction on parental contact with a minor child, or otherwise affect the terms of the parenting plan. In purporting to suspend the entire parenting plan, the order here was overbroad. The parties plainly understood, however, that the court intended to suspend only the provisions allowing for contact between Wilson and his children, and they have so litigated the order ever since. That intent and effect were entirely proper under the statute. . . .

| DISCUSSION QUESTIONS | FOR *IN RE MARRIAGE OF STEWART* |

A. The court finds that the father did not physically assault the children. Is a finding that physical harm was inflicted on the children necessary for entry of a protective order on their behalf or for suspension of parenting time?

B. What facts does the court discuss that indicate that the children suffered psychological harm? Do you believe that the children suffered psychological harm in this case? How should psychological harm be defined and proven? Is expert testimony necessary or advisable?

C. The father in this case contended that complete suspension of contact was not reasonably necessary to prevent the children from witnessing domestic violence between their parents, because third-party exchanges would have accomplished the same result. What was the court's response to this argument? Do you agree?

D. The order in this case is valid for one year. Is this too long a period for no contact with the children? Too short?

15.11 CHILDREN AND INTIMATE PARTNER VIOLENCE: PRESUMPTIONS

Courts and legislatures increasingly recognize the impact that intimate partner violence has on children. As states moved away from fault divorce during the 1970s, some courts took the position that the occurrence of intimate partner violence was not relevant to child custody decisions. Other courts viewed it as one factor to be considered among many in determining the best interests of the child. A recent legislative trend involves creation of rebuttable presumptions against awards of child custody to parents who have perpetrated intimate partner violence.

| REFLECTIVE QUESTIONS | Why do you think that intimate partner violence-related presumptions have become more common? |

Background to *Hicks v. Hicks*

In *Hicks v. Hicks*, the trial judge awarded joint custody of the minor children to the parents, with Mr. Hicks designated as the primary custodial parent during the school year and Ms. Hicks acting as the custodial parent during the summer. On appeal Ms. Hicks challenges the ruling granting Mr. Hicks primary custody of the children under a Louisiana statute containing a presumption against awards of sole or joint physical custody to a parent with a history of perpetrating domestic violence. She bases her claim on evidence that Mr. Hicks hit her during pregnancy, causing her to have miscarriages; that he broke several brooms over her; that he picked her up with a two by four under her neck and threw her off the porch; and that he forced her to have sex with him several times against her wishes.

HICKS
v.
HICKS

Court of Appeals of Louisiana
733 So. 2d 1261 (1999)

WOODARD, J. Ms. Teresa Hicks, defendant in this divorce suit, appeals a judgment awarding primary residency of all three of her minor children to her husband, Mr. David Hicks. . . .

The relevant provisions of La. R.S. 9:364 state:

> A. There is created a presumption that no parent who has a history of perpetrating family violence shall be awarded sole or joint custody of children. The court may find a history of perpetrating family violence if the court finds that one incident of family violence has resulted in serious bodily injury or the court finds more than one incident of family violence. The presumption shall be overcome only by a preponderance of the evidence that the perpetrating parent has successfully completed a treatment program as defined in R.S. 9:362, is not abusing alcohol and the illegal use of drugs scheduled in R.S. 40:964, and that the best interest of the child or children requires that parent's participation as a custodial parent because of the other parent's absence, mental illness, or substance abuse, or such other circumstances which affect the best interest of the child or children. The fact that the abused parent suffers from the effects of the abuse shall not be grounds for denying that parent custody. . . .
>
>   C. If the court finds that a parent has a history of perpetrating family violence, the court shall allow only supervised child visitation with that parent, conditioned upon that parent's participation in and completion of a treatment program. Unsupervised visitation shall be allowed only if it is shown by a preponderance of the evidence that the violent parent has completed a treatment program, is not abusing alcohol and psychoactive drugs, and poses no danger to the child, and that such visitation is in the child's best interest.

As this statute is clear and unambiguous, it is to be applied, to the facts in this case and in similar future cases, as written. La. Civ. Code art. 9. Only in this way, can the remedial purposes of the Act, which are to protect battered spouses and their children and insure counseling for those who commit acts of domestic violence, be achieved.

In *Simmons v. Simmons*, 649 So. 2d 799, 802, that court stated its view of some criteria by which to determine the application of the Act:

> In deciding whether a parent has a "history of perpetrating family violence," the trial court should look at the entire chronicle of the family, remaining mindful that the paramount goal of the legislation is the children's best interest. Such factors as the number, frequency, and severity of incidents will be relevant, as well as whether the violence occurred in the presence of the children, and to what extent there existed provocation for any violent act. Stated differently, the determination must be based on a review of the total circumstances of the family, and necessarily involves a weighing of the evidence.

We note that the second circuit reads into the statute that a reviewing court, in the application of the Act, should consider "whether the violence occurred in the presence of the children" and "to what extent there existed provocation for any violent act." We expressly reject that language as being inconsistent with the mandate of the Act and its remedial purposes. It is also inconsistent with the requirements of La. Civ. Code art. 9 that the Act be applied as written.

Once this Act has been triggered, we do not look to the La. Civ. Code art. 134 factors relating to the best interest of the children until the perpetrator has satisfied all requirements delineated in the Act.

Turning to the facts of the case before us, for purposes of analyzing whether the trial judge erred in not applying the Act, we have discounted those acts of violence which Mr. Hicks contradicted, even though Mrs. Hicks provided corroborating evidence for some of them. The only acts we have considered in this review are those which Mr. Hicks did not refute, namely: that he caused the deaths of unborn children; he beat her with brooms; he picked her up with a two by four under her neck and threw her off the porch; he forced her to have sex against her will, on numerous occasions. When such testimony is unrefuted, Ms. Hicks did not have to bring forth corroborating evidence. Nevertheless, she did do so concerning the black eye, the bruises she sustained from time to time, and Mr. Hicks having beaten her with a broom stick on at least one occasion, causing her face to be swollen beyond recognition. For example, her mother testified that one night Ms. Hicks came to her, hysterical and unrecognizable.

> [S]he came through the door and . . . I just looked at her, I didn't even recognize her and I just went on with what I was doing and she said, mother, and, I turned around and looked at her, and I said, oh my goodness, I didn't use quite that word, but she was hysterical. Her eyes were swollen, she was just totally upset. I went up to her and I said, what's wrong and she showed me her back and her arm and I said, what happened and how did you do that? She told me that he had hit her with a broom stick. . . .

Ms. Hicks' mother testified that, also, she had seen bruises on her daughter at other times.

Other corroborating evidence included the testimony of an elderly gentleman, a nonrelative, Mr. Minze, who testified that he saw Ms. Hicks right after Mr. Hicks gave her the black eye and that Mr. Hicks admitted to him that he had done it.

Without considering these corroborated acts of violence, Ms. Hicks has, nevertheless, satisfied her burden of proof under the Act. She has proved, by a preponderance of the evidence, that Mr. Hicks committed, at least, one act of violence against her, resulting in a serious injury—the beatings while she was pregnant which caused miscarriages, resulting in the deaths of unborn children. She also proved more than two acts of violence which were not refuted. The Act only requires one serious act of violence resulting in serious injury, or simply, more than one act of violence to establish a history of violence and to create a presumption that no parent, who has a history of perpetrating family violence, shall be awarded sole or joint custody of children. "The presumption shall be overcome only by a preponderance of the evidence that the perpetrating parent has successfully completed a treatment program. . . ." La. R.S. 9:364(A). Mr. Hicks did not rebut this presumption.

The Post-Separation Family Violence Relief Act, La. R.S. 9:361-369 is clearly applicable in this case. The trial court's failure to apply it requires us to reverse its decision. We award custody of the three children to Ms. Hicks and order that all visitation by Mr. Hicks shall be under supervised conditions until he can prove to the trial court that he has satisfied all requirements of the Act. . . .

The trial court erred in failing to apply the provisions of the Post-Separation Family Violence Relief Act, La. R.S. 9:361-369, to the facts in this case. Accordingly, we reverse its award of joint custody to the parents with Mr. Hicks being designated as the primary custodial parent during the school year and Ms. Hicks custodial parent during the summer. Ms. Hicks is awarded sole custody of the children. All visitation by Mr. Hicks shall be under supervised conditions until such time that he can prove to a court that he has successfully completed a treatment program and satisfied all other requirements of the Act. Mr. Hicks is cast with the costs of this appeal. Reversed And Rendered With Instructions.

DISCUSSION QUESTIONS **FOR *HICKS v. HICKS***

A. The Post-Separation Family Violence Relief Act creates a presumption that "no parent who has a history of perpetrating family violence shall be awarded sole or joint custody of children." What are the arguments in favor of such a presumption? What arguments can be made in opposition?

B. What showing is necessary to trigger the presumption? Is a single violent incident sufficient? Must the children be present and witness the incident? The dissent (not reproduced) argued that the trial judge's ruling should be affirmed because the decision was based "solely on the testimony of witnesses called by each side; no physical evidence was presented." Should corroborating evidence be required in order for the presumption to be applied?

C. Once the presumption is invoked, what showing is required to overcome it?

D. Commentators have raised concerns about unintended consequences associated with the application of presumptions in intimate partner violence–related child custody decision making. As a matter of policy, do you favor or disfavor use of presumptions like that in *Hicks*? *See* Margaret F. Brinig et al., *Perspectives on Joint Custody Presumptions as Applied to Domestic Violence Cases*, 52 Fam. Ct. Rev. 271 (2014).

15.12 THE HAGUE CONVENTION AND INTIMATE PARTNER VIOLENCE

The Hague Convention on the Civil Aspects of International Child Abduction comes into play when there are allegations of parental kidnapping. Some research indicates that some of these cases involve victims of intimate partner violence who cross international borders to keep themselves and their children safe. *See* Jeffrey L. Edleson et al., *Multiple Perspectives on Battered Mothers and Their Children Fleeing to the United States for Safety: A Study of Hague Convention Cases*, available at https://www.ncjrs.gov/pdffiles1/nij/grants/232624.pdf (last visited August 8, 2015).

> **REFLECTIVE QUESTIONS** | What is the purpose of the Hague Convention on the Civil Aspects of International Child Abduction?

Background to *Miltiadous v. Tetervak*

In the following case, a father invokes the Hague Convention to seek the return of his children to Cyprus. The court explains the operation of the Hague Convention and analyzes the mother's grave risk defense.

MILTIADOUS
v.
TETERVAK
United States District Court (E.D. Pa.)
686 F. Supp. 2d 544 (2010)

ROBRENO, J. This is a Petition for Return of Children brought pursuant to the Hague Convention. . . .

II. FINDINGS OF FACT

Petitioner is a citizen of Cyprus and Respondent is a Russian citizen. The two met in Cyprus in 2000 while the Respondent was in Cyprus on a worker's visa. After a brief courtship, Petitioner and Respondent were married on November 29, 2000, in Aradippou, Cyprus, and continued to live together in Cyprus until November 23, 2007. After her marriage to Petitioner, Respondent had temporary resident status in Cyprus that was dependent upon Petitioner signing her visa yearly.

Petitioner and Respondent had two children together, Iliana Miltiadous and Achilleas Miltiadous (jointly referred to as the "children"), born on August 24, 2002, and March 29, 2004, respectively. The children were born in Cyprus and are Cyprus citizens. At the time the instant motion was filed, the children were six and four years old, respectively.

Petitioner and Respondent experienced a violent and tumultuous relationship throughout their marriage. Petitioner was an "avid drinker and habitual drug user," and physically and psychologically abused Respondent "almost throughout the duration of their marriage." Although Petitioner has never physically harmed the children, he has "always harassed the children by yelling at them and threatening them that he would take them away and they would never see their mother again."

On November 23, 2007, the family departed for a temporary vacation to visit extended family in the United States. Return airline tickets were purchased; Petitioner was to return to Cyprus on January 20, 2008, and Respondent and both children were to return on February 24, 2008.

While the family was visiting Respondent's parents in the United States, Petitioner's abusive behavior continued. On December 1, 2007, Petitioner returned to Respondent's parents home drunk and aggressive. Respondent called the police on December 1, 2007, and Petitioner left to stay with his cousins in New Jersey.

Petitioner was served with a "Notice of Hearing and Order" for temporary restraints, issued by the Pennsylvania Court of Common Pleas on December 10, 2007. On December 14, 2007, after a hearing at which both Petitioner and Respondent were represented by counsel, Respondent obtained a Protection from Abuse Order from the Court of Common Pleas in Philadelphia, ordering Petitioner to stay away from Respondent, granting Respondent sole custody of the children, and allowing Petitioner weekly supervised visitation rights with the children. Despite this order, on December 21, 2008, Petitioner called Respondent and left a threatening voicemail, urging her to stop the legal proceedings. Thereafter, Respondent called the police and a warrant was issued for Petitioner's arrest.

Respondent filed for political asylum in the United States on May 9, 2008, seeking permanent asylum for herself and her children due to the fear of imminent physical and mental abuse by her husband in Cyprus. On July 22, 2009, Respondent was granted asylum and her children's immigration status is derived from hers. Respondent and the children currently reside with her parents in Philadelphia, Pennsylvania.

Since returning to Cyprus, Petitioner has spoken with Respondent by telephone and requested that she voluntarily allow the children to return to Cyprus. Respondent has refused this request. On November 14, 2008, Petitioner filed an "Application for

Assistance Under the Hague Convention on Child Abduction from Cyprus to the Central Authority of the United States of America: Request for Return of Child Under Article 12 of the Convention." In addition, Petitioner is pursuing legal action in Cyprus for Respondent's retention of the children in the United States without Petitioner's consent.

III. LEGAL STANDARD UNDER THE HAGUE CONVENTION

1. Background

The Hague Convention on the Civil Aspects of International Child Abduction reflects a universal concern about the harm done to children by parental kidnapping and a strong desire among the Contracting States to implement an effective deterrent to such behavior. Hague Convention, Preamble, 42 U.S.C. §11601(a)(1)-(4). The United States and Cyprus are signatories to this multilateral treaty. The United States Congress implemented the Convention in the International Child Abduction Remedies Act, 42 U.S.C. §11601 et seq.

Pursuant to the preamble of the Hague Convention, there are two main purposes of the Convention: (1) "to ensure the prompt return of children to the state of their habitual residence when they have been wrongfully removed;" and (2) "to ensure that rights of custody and of access under the law of one Contracting State are effectively respected in other Contracting States." The Convention's procedures are not designed to settle international custody disputes, but rather to restore the status quo prior to any wrongful removal or retention, and to deter parents from engaging in international forum shopping in custody cases. *Baxter v. Baxter*, 423 F.3d 363, 367 (3d Cir. 2005).

2. Petitioner's Burden

Any person seeking the return of a child in the United States may commence a civil action under the Convention by filing a petition in a court of the jurisdiction in which the child is located. 42 U.S.C. §11603(b). To obtain an order for the child's return under the Hague Convention, the petitioner bears the burden of proving by a preponderance of the evidence that the removal or retention was "wrongful" under Article 3. 42 U.S.C. §11603(e)(1)(A).

Specifically, a petitioner must show: (1) the child was habitually residing in one State and has been removed to or retained in a different state; (2) the removal or retention was in breach of the petitioner's custody rights under the law of the State of habitual residence; and (3) the petitioner was exercising those rights at the time of the removal or retention. 42 U.S.C. §11603(e)(1)(A).

The Third Circuit highlights these requirements and notes that wrongful removal or retention claims under Article 3 of the Convention typically raise four questions: "(1) When did the removal or retention at issue take place?; (2) Immediately prior to the removal or retention, in which state was the child a habitual resident?; (3) Did the removal or retention breach the rights of custody attributed to the petitioner under the law of the habitual residence?; and (4) Was the petitioner exercising those rights at the time of the removal or retention?" *Karkkainen v. Kovalchuk*, 445 F.3d 280, 287 (3d Cir. 2006) (citing *Baxter*, 423 F.3d at 368).

3. Habitual Residence

A petitioner cannot claim that the removal or retention of a child is "wrongful" unless "the child to whom the petition relates is 'habitually resident' in a State signatory to the Convention and has been removed to or retained in a different State." *Karkkainen*, 445 F.3d at 287 (quoting *Gitter v. Gitter*, 396 F.3d 124, 130 (2d Cir. 2005)). Therefore, determination of a child's habitual residence is a threshold question in deciding a case under the Hague Convention. *Id.* (citing *Feder v. Evans-Feder*, 63 F.3d 217, 222 (3d Cir. 1995)).

In determining a child's habitual residence, the Third Circuit provides, "a child's habitual residence is the place where he or she has been physically present for an amount of time sufficient for acclimatization and which has a degree of 'settled purpose' from the child's perspective. . . . The determination of whether any particular place satisfies this standard must focus on the child and consists of an analysis of the child's circumstances in that place and the parents' present, shared intentions regarding their child's presence there." *Feder*, 63 F.3d at 224.

The inquiry into a child's habitual residence is a fact-intensive determination that cannot be reduced to a predetermined formula and varies with the facts and circumstances of each case. *Whiting v. Krassner*, 391 F.3d 540, 546 (3d Cir. 2004). This standard focuses on the parents' shared intentions, the period of time sufficient for acclimatization and the child's degree of settled purpose. *Harris v. Harris*, No. 03-5952, 2003 WL 23162326, at *6 (E.D. Pa. Dec. 12, 2003).

4. Affirmative Defenses

Once a habitual residence is determined, a court is not required to return a child there, even if it finds that the removal or retention was wrongful. *Karkkainen*, 445 F.3d at 288. After a petitioner demonstrates wrongful removal or retention, the burden shifts to the respondent to prove an affirmative defense against the return of the child to the country of habitual residence. These affirmative defenses are narrowly construed to effectuate the purposes of the Hague Convention and, even where a defense applies, the court has discretion to order the child's return. If a petitioner carries his burden under the Hague Convention and the court finds wrongful removal or retention, the burden shifts to the respondent to provide an affirmative defense, under article 13 of the Convention, against the return of the child to the country of habituation resident.

There are two available affirmative defenses under article 13, each with a different burden of proof: (a) consent or acquiescence to the removal or retention, which must be proven by a preponderance of the evidence; and (b) grave risk of harm that return of child would expose child to physical or psychological harm, which must be proven by clear and convincing evidence. The latter is at issue here.

The grave risk of harm affirmative defense, under Article 13(b) of the Hague Convention, requires proof by clear and convincing evidence. 42 U.S.C.

§11603(e)(2)(A). The Third Circuit Court of Appeals explained that a grave risk of harm exception encompasses "situations in which the child faces a real risk of being hurt, physically or psychologically, as a result of repatriation," but not "situations where repatriation might cause inconvenience or hardship, eliminate certain educational or economic opportunities, or not comport with the child's preferences." *In re Application of Adan*, 437 F.3d 381, 395 (3d Cir. 2006). For the grave risk exception to apply, the respondent must cite specific evidence of potential harm to the child upon his return. *Baxter*, 423 F.3d at 374.

IV. ANALYSIS . . .

2. Grave Risk of Harm Affirmative Defense

As noted above, grave risk requires proof by clear and convincing evidence. 42 U.S.C. §11603(e)(2)(A). This exception has been held to apply in at least two sets of cases: (1) "when return of the child puts the child in imminent danger . . . e.g., returning the child to a zone of war, famine, or disease . . . ;" and (2) "cases of serious abuse or neglect, or extraordinary emotional dependence, when the court in the country of habitual residence, for whatever reason, may be incapable or unwilling to give the child adequate protection." *Baxter*, 423 F.3d at 373 (citing *Friedrich v. Friedrich*, 78 F.3d 1060, 1069 (1996)).

The evidence presented at the evidentiary hearings demonstrates that returning the children to Cyprus poses a grave risk of physical or psychological harm to the children. Petitioner's physical and emotional abuse throughout the duration of the parents' marriage, the inability of the Cyprus authorities to protect Respondent from abuse and Iliana's resulting psychological disorder warrant the grave risk of harm determination.

a. Spousal Abuse

The evidence shows by clear and convincing evidence a grave risk of physical or psychological harm to the children or an otherwise intolerable situation. Respondent testified credibly about extensive physical and emotional abuse she suffered throughout her marriage. She testified that the Petitioner beat her repeatedly and, at one point, broke her nose. She testified that she required surgery on her nose because of this incident.

Respondent also testified that Petitioner would drink heavily and become enraged at Respondent and the children. Respondent testified that Petitioner kept a gun in the house and threatened to kill her. According to Respondent, Petitioner aimed the gun on her several times, but did not shoot.

Petitioner admitted the two argued often and that he hit Respondent, but in self-defense. Petitioner denied abusing Respondent; however, the Court finds his testimony to be not credible.

Respondent's testimony was supported by testimony from her mother, Irene Boritsaya. Ms. Boritsaya testified that, as a result of her visits to Cyprus with Respondent, she suspected there was significant spousal abuse in Cyprus. She added that she witnessed the abuse firsthand while the family was in the United

States on vacation. She testified that at times Petitioner became highly agitated, yelled and cursed at the family. Specifically, Ms. Boritsaya testified that Petitioner also pushed her and threatened to harm her and her family.

Respondent's evidence of spousal abuse compels a finding that the grave risk of harm affirmative defense applies here. *See, e.g., Van De Sande v. Van De Sande*, 431 F.3d 567, 570 (7th Cir. 2005) (reversing order of return where the father had "beat[en] his wife severely and repeatedly in [the children's] presence," and also threatened to kill them); *Walsh*, 221 F.3d at 219-220 (reversing order of return where father was psychologically abusive and had severely beaten the children's mother in their presence); *Elyashiv v. Elyashiv*, 353 F. Supp. 2d 394, 398-400 (E.D.N.Y. 2005) (refusing return where father frequently hit the children, threatened to kill his son, and severely abused their mother in their presence); *Rodriguez v. Rodriguez*, 33 F. Supp. 2d 456, 459-460 (D. Md. 1999) (refusing return where child had been belt-whipped, punched, and kicked, and where the child's mother had been subjected to more serious attacks, including choking her and breaking her nose).

b. Cyprus Authorities

Respondent also testified that while in Cyprus she was afraid to call the authorities because she feared the local police, who were well acquainted with Petitioner, would not help. She testified that she once called the police and filed a police report. However, she testified that the Petitioner threatened to "throw her out of [Cyprus]" and she was forced to recall her complaint. Moreover, Respondent, a Russian citizen, testified that she has no legal citizenship status in Cyprus and was uncertain if she had proper legal standing to fight a custody battle there.

Thus, there is evidence that the Cyprus authorities were unable or would have been unwilling to protect Respondent. *See In re Adan*, 437 F.3d 381, 397 (3d Cir. 2006) (noting that district courts must consider testimony and evidence regarding the willingness and ability of the local authorities in habitual residence to protect the parties from abuse).

c. Iliana's Post Traumatic Stress Disorder

Respondent testified that her daughter, Iliana, began having night terrors and wetting the bed as a result of the stress from the violence she witnessed. The Court heard testimony from Dr. Igor Davidson, a licensed psychologist, who evaluated Iliana. Dr. Davidson submitted a report and testified that Iliana suffers from Chronic Post Traumatic Stress Disorder ("PTSD"). Dr. Davidson's report indicated that "Iliana was referred for a comprehensive psychological evaluation following a period of nervousness, unprovoked crying spells, appearing to be 'in her own world', occasional aggression, fearfulness, nightmares and avoidance."

Dr. Davidson administered two psychological tests, the PTSD Inventory and the Conner's Rating Scale. The PTSD test was designed as a tool for use in diagnosing children with PTSD. Based on the test results, Dr. Davidson testified that "Iliana's signs and symptoms best fit a post traumatic stress disorder of a chronic variety." Dr. Davidson also testified that Iliana's PTSD condition was connected to the family violence she observed.

As part of the PTSD test, Dr. Davidson asked Iliana, "Have you seen a scary thing happen to someone else?" Iliana responded that she had. Dr. Davidson, as per procedure of the PTSD test, asked the follow up question, "tell me about it." Iliana responded, "A long time ago, Mama and Papa were fighting, everybody was screaming. Papa was screaming. He pulled Mama's hair and choked her." Iliana also answered that she was scared and upset when this incident occurred. She admitted that she was having many upsetting thoughts about the incident she described, pictures of the incident keep popping into her head, and she has bad dreams about the incident.

Dr. Davidson confirmed Iliana's responses with reports from Respondent, as well as other information related to the instant case. Dr. Davidson also administered the Conner's Rating Scale to the Respondent and Iliana's schoolteacher. According to the report, "Iliana is functioning in the 'typical score' to 'indicates significant problem' range on all scales of the Connor's Parents Rating Scale. Areas of most concern according to maternal report were Anxious-Shy, Emotional Lability and Hyperactivity."

Dr. Davidson concluded that "Iliana's emotional and psychological problems are founded on the duress she incurred as a witness to her mother's abuse. It appears that in the present day, this condition continues to constitute significant personal distress for Iliana and interfere with adequate social growth with adults and peers." Dr. Davidson recommended a stable, consistent, structured and safe family environment. Finally, Dr. Davidson warned against Iliana's return to Cyprus. "A return to Cyprus will subject Iliana to particularly those persons, places and stimuli which founded her current difficulties and as such is likely to result in severe psychological and emotional duress for Iliana[.]"

Dr. Anthony Pisa, a licensed psychologist, with an expertise in forensic psychology, testified for the Petitioner. Dr. Pisa reviewed Dr. Davidson's report and testified as to some problems in the Davidson report. Dr. Pisa found that Dr. Davidson failed to: (1) evaluate the manner in which Iliana generally perceives her world; (2) explore Iliana's ability to accurately recall recent events as well as other salient events that occurred in her life; (3) explore Iliana's concept of time; (4) fill in an answer for every question on the PTSD test; (5) consider the discrepancies between the teacher's ratings of Iliana's behavior and Mother's rating of Iliana's behavior as the Mother appears to rate Iliana's behavior as more pathological when compared to the teacher's rating; and (6) correctly add points on the Teacher Rating Scale.

Dr. Pisa testified that he never met Iliana or Respondent, nor personally evaluated Iliana. In forming his report, Dr. Pisa relied on Dr. Davidson's report, Petitioner's instant motion, the deposition of the paternal grandmother, the transcript of the Protective Order hearing in the Philadelphia Court of Common pleas and proposed findings of fact and conclusions of law by Petitioner. Dr. Pisa did not read any responses or documents crafted by the Respondent.

Furthermore, Dr. Pisa admitted that he was unable to testify to a degree of medical certainty as to whether or not Iliana is, in fact, suffering from PTSD. Dr. Pisa did not contradict Dr. Davidson's diagnosis of Iliana regarding her Chronic PTSD. Dr. Pisa also admitted that he was unable to testify as to whether or not Iliana needs psychological treatment or make any recommendations for Iliana.

Although Dr. Pisa points out certain irregularities with Dr. Davidson's administration and evaluation of the two tests, the two expert opinions are not irreconcilable.

Dr. Pisa does not conclude that Dr. Davidson's report is fatally flawed, that Iliana does not have PTSD or that Iliana should be returned to Cyprus.

Therefore, the Court relies on Dr. Davidson's expert opinion that Iliana is suffering from Chronic PTSD as a result of the family violence she witnessed in Cyprus. *See Danaipour v. McLarey*, 286 F.3d 1, 17 (1st Cir. 2002) (explaining that a finding that a child suffers from PTSD and would deteriorate if returned to the country of habitual residence could be evidence tending to support a finding of grave risk under Article 13(b)) (citing *Blondin v. Dubois*, 238 F.3d 153 (2d Cir. 2001)); *see also Walsh*, 221 F.3d 204, 211-112, *Elyashiv*, 353 F. Supp. 2d at 398-399 (finding that an expert's opinion that children suffering from PTSD would deteriorate if returned to country of habitual residence warranted the application of grave risk of harm affirmative defense).

Returning Iliana to Petitioner's residence would likely expose her to a grave risk of both physical and psychological harm. This is so, given her witnessing her father's abuse of their mother and the uprooting from her new home in the United States to the country where she observed physical and emotional abuse. This would be coupled with the relapse she would suffer of her PTSD disorder.

Similar to *Blondin*, in light of the sole, unimpeached and uncontroverted testimony of Dr. Davidson that Iliana's return to Cyprus would trigger her PTSD, there is no need for the Court to consider alternative living arrangements or reach out to the Cyprus authorities for their input.

Even though there has been no definitive evidence that Achilleas, the now five-year-old male child of Petitioner and Respondent, suffers from PTSD, returning him to Cyprus would also expose him to a grave risk of physical and psychological harm. In respect to physical harm, Achilleas is not insulated from the likelihood of future abuse, given Petitioner's inability to control his temper, his pattern of domestic abuse and his threats. As for psychological harm, since his sibling, with whom he has lived all of his life, would remain in the United States, and presumably his mother as well, a separation from his mother and sibling is likely to cause him harm.

Under these circumstances, the Court finds that Respondent has satisfied the grave risk of harm affirmative defense by clear and convincing evidence.

DISCUSSION QUESTIONS FOR *MILTIADOUS v. TETERVAK*

A. What is the purpose of the Hague Convention?

B. What is the significance of the child's habitual residence?

C. What must a respondent show to invoke the grave risk of harm affirmative defense? What evidence was presented in this case?

D. Do you agree with the court's decision in this case? Why or why not?

General Principles

1. Intimate partner violence was historically viewed as a private family matter and victims had few, if any, legal rights or protections.
2. Historically, husbands were exempt from prosecution for marital rape.
3. All attorneys should use an intimate partner violence screening protocol, which may include confidential face-to-face interviews, written questionnaires, observation and check-in, and documentary review.
4. Intimate partner violence includes a wide range of behaviors that require family-specific inquiry into the nature and context of the abuse, the meaning and implications of the abuse for the family, and ways to account for the abuse in actions and decisions.
5. Typical civil domestic abuse statutes define intimate partner violence and authorize courts to issue emergency and ongoing protective orders that may include prohibition of violence and contact, child custody, use of the residence, and other relief.
6. States vary in terms of who is covered under civil domestic abuse statutes but relief is generally granted to family and household members, spouses and former spouses, and those with a child in common. In some states the statutes apply to people in dating relationships.
7. Although the relief granted is typically more limited than when notice is provided, temporary protective orders can be issued on an ex parte basis.
8. Protective orders can help protect victims from abuse despite the fact that victims of intimate partner violence do not have personal entitlement to or property interest in police enforcement of a restraining order.
9. In about half of the homes where spousal abuse occurs, children are also physically abused. Even if the children are not directly physically abused, they are likely to be exposed to the violence and suffer other consequences from the abuse. Consequently, courts may limit or suspend a perpetrating parent's contact with children.
10. The Hague Convention on the Civil Aspects of International Child Abduction may be relevant when there are allegations of parental kidnapping. Research shows that some of these cases involve victims of intimate partner violence who cross international borders to keep themselves and their children safe.

Chapter Problems

1. Assume that you represent a victim of intimate partner violence who has been sexually assaulted by her husband, attacked with a weapon, and repeatedly threatened. You petition on her behalf for a protective order, and at the time of the hearing the husband tells the judge that he is willing to agree to entry of a

protective order against him if the court will also enter a protective order against her. How will you counsel your client? What are reasons to accept such a proposal? In what way might such an agreement be problematic? *See Deacon v. Landers*, 587 N.E.2d 395 (Ohio App. 1990); *In re Marriage of Kiferbaum*, 19 N.E.3d 1204 (Ill. App. 2014).

2. Assume that A is repeatedly violent to B and that the young children of the couple have witnessed several severe beatings. If B does not leave the relationship, should child protection authorities intervene? If so, what action should be taken? What reasons might B have for staying in the relationship? *See Nicholson v. Scoppetta*, 820 N.E.2d 840 (N.Y. 2004); Evan Stark, *A Failure to Protect: Unraveling the "Battered Mother's Dilemma,"* 27 W. St. U. L. Rev. 29 (1999-2000).

3. Compare the following cases where the Hague Convention grave risk of harm defense has been invoked in cases involving domestic violence: *Wigley v. Hares*, 2011 WL 3111898 (Fla. App. 2011); *Stewart v. Marrun*, 2009 WL 1530820 (E.D. Tex. 2011); and *Charalambous v. Charalambous*, 627 F.3d 462 (1st Cir. 2010). How do you account for the different results? What factors seem most significant in the deliberations of the various courts?

Preparation for Practice

1. Locate the civil domestic violence statute operative in your state. What relief can be ordered on an ex parte basis? What relief can be ordered after notice? Should the relief that can be ordered be different in the two situations? Why or why not?

2. How is domestic violence defined in your state? What if any changes to the definition would you suggest? Why?

3. Review the practice guides on the Battered Women's Justice Project's National Child Custody website located at http://www.bwjp.org/our-work/projects/national-child-custody-project.html (last visited July 22, 2015).

4. Compare the purposes of various screening tools. How is the focus of each different? *See* Jacqueline C. Campbell, The Danger Assessment, available at http://www.dangerassessment.org/about.aspx (last visited July 21, 2015); Amy Holtzworth-Munroe et al., *The Mediator's Assessment of Safety Issues and Concerns (MASIC): A Screening Interview for Intimate Partner Violence and Abuse Available in the Public Domain*, 48 Fam. Ct. Rev. 646 (2010). *See also* Janet

Johnston et al., *In the Name of the Child: A Developmental Approach to Understanding and Helping Children of Conflicted and Violent Divorce* (2009).

5. Do an Internet search for guides for safety planning with victims of intimate partner violence. How do the guides compare?

6. Explore resources addressing the problem of teen dating violence. *See* D. Kelly Weisberg, *Lindsay's Legacy: The Tragedy That Triggered Law Reform to Prevent Teen Dating Violence*, 24 Hastings Women's L.J. 27 (2013).

Chapter 16

Child Abuse

16.1 INTRODUCTION

This chapter focuses on when and how state actors intervene to protect children who may be abused or neglected by parents. Courts hearing these cases make challenging decisions that significantly impact the lives and well-being of children. Although parents may be criminally prosecuted for child abuse, this chapter concentrates on civil actions brought by state child protection agencies. It is a companion chapter to the one that follows on the subject of termination of parental rights.

Before you read this chapter, consider questions you have about this topic. When can the state intervene in the parent-child relationship? What procedural protections are afforded parents? What legal standards apply? What is the difference between abuse and neglect? What happens to children and parents when state intervention is warranted?

> **REFLECTIVE QUESTIONS**   What are your goals for this chapter?

16.2 SNAPSHOT OF CHILD MALTREATMENT

Child abuse and neglect constitute a serious and widespread problem in the United States. The following are some facts and figures concerning the victims, the perpetrators, and common types of child abuse and neglect as reported in 2013:

- The highest rate of victimization was among children under one year of age;
- Three-quarters of children who died as a result of neglect or abuse were under the age of three;
- Neglect was the most common form of maltreatment (79.5%), followed by physical abuse (18%);
- The racial/ethnic backgrounds of victims were White (44%), Hispanic (22.4%), and African-American (21.2%).

U.S. Dept. of Health and Human Services, Administration for Children and Families, *Child Maltreatment 2013*, ix-x, available at http://www.acf.hhs.gov/sites/default/files/cb/cm2013.pdf (last visited July 27, 2015).

REFLECTIVE QUESTIONS	What surprises you about these statistics?

16.3 HISTORICAL PERSPECTIVE: CAPTA

Historically, children were viewed as the responsibility and exclusive property of their parents, and absent serious injury courts did not interfere with the exercise of parental authority over children. In the late 1800s, private charities and societies began to focus on the plight of abused children, and by 1922 approximately 300 such organizations existed and most of the states had started juvenile courts. John E.B. Myers, *A Short History of Child Protection in America*, 42 Fam. L.Q. 449, 452 (2008). By the late 1960s, private societies had given way to governmental agencies, but services were not comprehensive: "In most states, protective services were not available statewide. Most communities lacked twenty-four hour coverage. Thus, for the first six decades of the twentieth century, protective services in most communities were inadequate and in some places nonexistent." *Id.* at 454.

The passage of The Child Abuse Prevention and Treatment Act (CAPTA) in 1974 heralded a sea change in that the federal government assumed a leadership role in setting expectations and mandates for state and county child protection programs. To receive funding, states were required to align statutory definitions of abuse and neglect with federal ones. CAPTA has been amended over years to include focus on child sexual abuse and preventive programs as well as other activities. Howard Davidson, *Federal Law and State Intervention When Parents Fail: Has National Guidance of Our Child Welfare System Been Successful?*, 42 Fam. L.Q. 481 (2008).

As societal awareness of child abuse increased and child protection laws were strengthened, courts had a clearer basis for intervention in the family when necessary for the protection of children. Nevertheless, intervention remains bounded by strong constitutional protection of a parent's liberty interest in raising and disciplining his or her child. *See Meyer v. Nebraska*, 262 U.S. 390 (1923);

Pierce v. Society of Sisters, 268 U.S. 510 (1925); *Troxel v. Granville*, 530 U.S. 57 (2000).

REFLECTIVE QUESTIONS	Why do you think the federal government became involved in setting child protection policy?

16.4 INDIAN CHILD WELFARE ACT (ICWA)

The Indian Child Welfare Act (ICWA) governs child protection and termination of parental rights proceedings involving American Indian children. It was enacted to prevent disproportionate removal of American Indian children from their homes.

> Prior to 1978, as many as twenty-five to thirty-five percent of Native American children were removed from their parents for alleged neglect or abuse. The majority of these children were placed in non-Indian foster homes, adoptive homes, and institutions. In 1978, Congress enacted the Indian Child Welfare Act (ICWA) to reduce the number of Native American children removed from their homes. Congress recognized, "There is no resource that is more vital to the continued existence and integrity of Indian tribes than their children," and "that an alarmingly high percentage of Indian families are broken up by the removal, often unwarranted, of their children from them by nontribal public and private agencies." To reduce inappropriate removal of Indian children from their homes, ICWA provides that only tribal courts can decide abuse and neglect cases involving children whose permanent residence is a reservation. For Indian children who do not live on a reservation, state juvenile courts can make decisions about removal, but the child's tribe must be notified, and the tribe has the right to intervene in the case.

John E.B. Myers, *A Short History of Child Protection in America*, 42 Fam. L.Q. 449, 457 (2008).

The Indian Child Welfare Act (ICWA) provides special protections for Native American children who may be victims of abuse or neglect. Before such a child is removed from the home, clear and convincing evidence of serious emotional or physical harm must be produced. 25 U.S.C. §1912(e). When children are removed from the home, they are (absent good cause) expected to be placed with extended family, in a tribe-approved foster home, or in an institution operated by an American Indian organization. 25 U.S.C. §1915(b). *See* Howard Davidson, *Federal Law and State Intervention When Parents Fail: Has National Guidance of Our Child Welfare System Been Successful?*, 42 Fam. L.Q. 481 (2008).

REFLECTIVE QUESTIONS	How should a family lawyer identify children who may be partly or fully Native American? Why is it important to do so?

16.5 REPORTING AND INVESTIGATION: DUTY TO PROTECT?

While anyone can report incidents of abuse or neglect to authorities, some specially situated professionals are mandated by statute to report abuse or neglect (and reasonable suspicions of abuse or neglect) that they encounter in the course of their employment. Mandatory reporters typically include social workers, teachers, registered nurses, physicians, therapists, and in some states, clergy and attorneys.

In 2013, people working in professional roles made three-fifths of reports. The Administration for Children and Families breaks down the relative number of reports made by different groups:

> The three largest percentages of report sources were from such professionals as legal and law enforcement personnel (17.5%), education personnel (17.5%) and social services personnel (11.0%). . . . Nonprofessionals—including friends, neighbors, and relatives—submitted one fifth of reports (18.6%).

U.S. Dept. of Health and Human Services, Administration for Children and Families, *Child Maltreatment 2013*, ix-x, available at http://www.acf.hhs.gov/sites/default/files/cb/cm2013.pdf (last visited July 27, 2015).

Once a report is made, the state child protection agency decides what level of investigation, if any, is warranted. After investigation the agency exercises considerable discretion in determining whether and how quickly to intervene in the family.

REFLECTIVE QUESTIONS	Do you think lawyers should be mandatory reporters of child abuse and neglect? Why or why not?

Background to *DeShaney v. Winnebago County Dept. of Social Services*

In the disturbing case of *DeShaney v. Winnebago County Dept. of Social Services*, the Supreme Court considered whether the state has a constitutional duty to protect a child while that child is in the physical care of his or her parent. The case is a particularly difficult one because the child protection agency had ongoing contact with the family over a two-year period but failed to take action that might have protected the child from his father's abuse.

DESHANEY
v.
WINNEBAGO COUNTY DEPT. OF SOCIAL SERVICES
Supreme Court of the United States
489 U.S. 189 (1989)

REHNQUIST, C.J. Petitioner is a boy who was beaten and permanently injured by his father, with whom he lived. Respondents are social workers and other local officials who received complaints that petitioner was being abused by his father and had reason to believe that this was the case, but nonetheless did not act to remove petitioner from his father's custody. Petitioner sued respondents claiming that their failure to act deprived him of his liberty in violation of the Due Process Clause of the Fourteenth Amendment to the United States Constitution. We hold that it did not.

The facts of this case are undeniably tragic. Petitioner Joshua DeShaney was born in 1979. In 1980, a Wyoming court granted his parents a divorce and awarded custody of Joshua to his father, Randy DeShaney. The father shortly thereafter moved to Neenah, a city located in Winnebago County, Wisconsin, taking the infant Joshua with him. There he entered into a second marriage, which also ended in divorce.

The Winnebago County authorities first learned that Joshua DeShaney might be a victim of child abuse in January 1982, when his father's second wife complained to the police, at the time of their divorce, that he had previously "hit the boy causing marks and [was] a prime case for child abuse." The Winnebago County Department of Social Services (DSS) interviewed the father, but he denied the accusations, and DSS did not pursue them further. In January 1983, Joshua was admitted to a local hospital with multiple bruises and abrasions. The examining physician suspected child abuse and notified DSS, which immediately obtained an order from a Wisconsin juvenile court placing Joshua in the temporary custody of the hospital. Three days later, the county convened an ad hoc "Child Protection Team" — consisting of a pediatrician, a psychologist, a police detective, the county's lawyer, several DSS caseworkers, and various hospital personnel — to consider Joshua's situation. At this meeting, the Team decided that there was insufficient evidence of child abuse to retain Joshua in the custody of the court. The Team did, however, decide to recommend several measures to protect Joshua, including enrolling him in a preschool program, providing his father with certain counseling services, and encouraging his father's girlfriend to move out of the home. Randy DeShaney entered into a voluntary agreement with DSS in which he promised to cooperate with them in accomplishing these goals.

Based on the recommendation of the Child Protection Team, the juvenile court dismissed the child protection case and returned Joshua to the custody of his father. A month later, emergency room personnel called the DSS caseworker handling Joshua's case to report that he had once again been treated for suspicious injuries. The caseworker concluded that there was no basis for action. For the next six months, the caseworker made monthly visits to the DeShaney home, during which she observed a number of suspicious injuries on Joshua's head; she also noticed that he had not been enrolled in school, and that the girlfriend had not moved out. The caseworker dutifully recorded these incidents in her files, along with her continuing suspicions that someone in the DeShaney household was physically abusing Joshua, but she did nothing more. In November 1983, the emergency room notified DSS that Joshua had been treated once again for injuries that they believed to be caused by child abuse. On the caseworker's next two visits to the DeShaney home, she was told that Joshua was too ill to see her. Still DSS took no action.

In March 1984, Randy DeShaney beat 4-year-old Joshua so severely that he fell into a life-threatening coma. Emergency brain surgery revealed a series of hemorrhages caused by traumatic injuries to the head inflicted over a long period of time. Joshua did not die, but he suffered brain damage so severe that he is expected to spend the rest of his life confined to an institution for the profoundly retarded. Randy DeShaney was subsequently tried and convicted of child abuse.

Joshua and his mother brought this action under 42 U.S.C. §1983 in the United States District Court for the Eastern District of Wisconsin against respondents Winnebago County, DSS, and various individual employees of DSS. The complaint alleged that respondents had deprived Joshua of his liberty without due process of law, in violation of his rights under the Fourteenth Amendment, by failing to intervene to protect him against a risk of violence at his father's hands of which they knew or should have known. . . .

[N]othing in the language of the Due Process Clause itself requires the State to protect the life, liberty, and property of its citizens against invasion by private actors. The Clause is phrased as a limitation on the State's power to act, not as a guarantee of certain minimal levels of safety and security. It forbids the State itself to deprive individuals of life, liberty, or property without "due process of law," but its language cannot fairly be extended to impose an affirmative obligation on the State to ensure that those interests do not come to harm through other means. Nor does history support such an expansive reading of the constitutional text. Like its counterpart in the Fifth Amendment, the Due Process Clause of the Fourteenth Amendment was intended to prevent government "from abusing [its] power, or employing it as an instrument of oppression." Its purpose was to protect the people from the State, not to ensure that the State protected them from each other. The Framers were content to leave the extent of governmental obligation in the latter area to the democratic political processes.

As we said in *Harris v. McRae*: "Although the liberty protected by the Due Process Clause affords protection against unwarranted government interference, it does not confer an entitlement to such [governmental aid] as may be necessary to realize all the advantages of that freedom." If the Due Process Clause does not require the State to provide its citizens with particular protective services, it follows that the State cannot be held liable under the Clause for injuries that could have been averted had it chosen to provide them. As a general matter, then, we conclude that a State's failure to protect an individual against private violence simply does not constitute a violation of the Due Process Clause.

Petitioners contend, however, that even if the Due Process Clause imposes no affirmative obligation on the State to provide the general public with adequate protective services, such a duty may arise out of certain "special relationships" created or assumed by the State with respect to particular individuals. Petitioners argue that such a "special relationship" existed here because the State knew that Joshua faced a special danger of abuse at his father's hands, and specifically proclaimed, by word and by deed, its intention to protect him against that danger.

Having actually undertaken to protect Joshua from this danger — which petitioners concede the State played no part in creating — the State acquired an affirmative "duty," enforceable through the Due Process Clause, to do so in a reasonably competent fashion. Its failure to discharge that duty, so the argument goes, was an abuse of governmental power that so "shocks the conscience," as to constitute a substantive due process violation.

We reject this argument. It is true that in certain limited circumstances the Constitution imposes upon the State affirmative duties of care and protection with respect to particular individuals. But these cases afford petitioners no help. Taken together, they stand only for the proposition that when the State takes a person into its custody and holds him there against his will, the Constitution imposes upon it a corresponding duty to assume some responsibility for his safety and general well-being. The rationale for this principle is simple enough: when the State by the affirmative exercise of its power so restrains an individual's liberty that it renders him unable to care for himself, and at the same time fails to provide for his basic human needs — e.g., food, clothing, shelter, medical care, and reasonable safety — it transgresses the substantive limits on state action set by the Eighth Amendment and the Due Process Clause.

In the substantive due process analysis, it is the State's affirmative act of restraining the individual's freedom to act on his own behalf — through incarceration, institutionalization, or other similar restraint of personal liberty — which is the "deprivation of liberty" triggering the protections of the Due Process Clause, not its failure to act to protect his liberty interests against harms inflicted by other means.

The *Estelle-Youngberg* analysis simply has no applicability in the present case. Petitioners concede that the harms Joshua suffered occurred not while he was in the State's custody, but while he was in the custody of his natural father, who was in no sense a state actor. While the State may have been aware of the dangers that Joshua faced in the free world, it played no part in their creation, nor did it do anything to render him any more vulnerable to them. That the State once took temporary custody of Joshua does not alter the analysis, for when it returned him to his father's custody, it placed him in no worse position than that in which he would have been had it not acted at all; the State does not become the permanent guarantor of an individual's safety by having once offered him shelter. Under these circumstances, the State had no constitutional duty to protect Joshua.

It may well be that, by voluntarily undertaking to protect Joshua against a danger it concededly played no part in creating, the State acquired a duty under state tort law to provide him with adequate protection against that danger. But the claim here is based on the Due Process Clause of the Fourteenth Amendment, which, as we have said many times, does not transform every tort committed by a state actor into a constitutional violation.

BRENNAN, J. dissenting with **MARSHALL, J.** and **BLACKMUN, J.** "The most that can be said of the state functionaries in this case," the Court today concludes, "is that they stood by and did nothing when suspicious circumstances dictated a more active role for them." . . .

The Court's baseline is the absence of positive rights in the Constitution and a concomitant suspicion of any claim that seems to depend on such rights. From this perspective, the DeShaneys' claim is first and foremost about inaction (the failure, here, of respondents to take steps to protect Joshua), and only tangentially about action (the establishment of a state program specifically designed to help children like Joshua). And from this perspective, holding these Wisconsin officials liable — where the only difference between this case and one involving a general claim to protective services is Wisconsin's establishment and operation of a program to protect children — would seem to punish an effort that we should seek to promote.

I would begin from the opposite direction. I would focus first on the action that Wisconsin has taken with respect to Joshua and children like him, rather than on the actions that the State failed to take. Cases from the lower courts also recognize that a State's actions can be decisive in assessing the constitutional significance of subsequent inaction. For these purposes, moreover, actual physical restraint is not the only state action that has been considered relevant.

Wisconsin has established a child-welfare system specifically designed to help children like Joshua. Wisconsin law places upon the local departments of social services such as respondent (DSS or Department) a duty to investigate reported instances of child abuse. While other governmental bodies and private persons are largely responsible for the reporting of possible cases of child abuse, Wisconsin law channels all such reports to the local departments of social services for evaluation and, if necessary, further action. Even when it is the sheriff's office or police department that receives a report of suspected child abuse, that report is referred to local social services departments for action; the only exception to this occurs when the reporter fears for the child's immediate safety. In this way, Wisconsin law invites — indeed, directs — citizens and other governmental entities to depend on local departments of social services such as respondent to protect children from abuse.

The specific facts before us bear out this view of Wisconsin's system of protecting children. Each time someone voiced a suspicion that Joshua was being abused, that information was relayed to the Department for investigation and possible action. When Randy DeShaney's second wife told the police that he had "hit the boy causing marks and [was] a prime case for child abuse," the police referred her complaint to DSS.

When, on three separate occasions, emergency room personnel noticed suspicious injuries on Joshua's body, they went to DSS with this information. When neighbors informed the police that they had seen or heard Joshua's father or his father's lover beating or otherwise abusing Joshua, the police brought these reports to the attention of DSS. And when respondent Kemmeter, through these reports and through her own observations in the course of nearly 20 visits to the DeShaney home, compiled growing evidence that Joshua was being abused, that information stayed within the Department — chronicled by the social worker in detail that seems almost eerie in light of her failure to act upon it. (As to the extent of the social worker's involvement in, and knowledge of, Joshua's predicament, her reaction to the news of Joshua's last and most devastating injuries is illuminating: "I just knew the phone would ring some day and Joshua would be dead.")

Even more telling than these examples is the Department's control over the decision whether to take steps to protect a particular child from suspected abuse. While many different people contributed information and advice to this decision, it was up to the people at DSS to make the ultimate decision (subject to the approval of the local government's Corporation Counsel) whether to disturb the family's current arrangements. When Joshua first appeared at a local hospital with injuries signaling physical abuse, for example, it was DSS that made the decision to take him into temporary custody for the purpose of studying his situation — and it was DSS, acting in conjunction with the corporation counsel, that returned him to his father. Unfortunately for Joshua DeShaney, the buck effectively stopped with the Department.

In these circumstances, a private citizen, or even a person working in a government agency other than DSS, would doubtless feel that her job was done as soon as she had reported her suspicions of child abuse to DSS. Through its child-welfare program, in other words, the State of Wisconsin has relieved ordinary citizens and governmental bodies other than the Department of any sense of obligation to do anything more than report their suspicions of child abuse to DSS. If DSS ignores or dismisses these suspicions, no one will step in to fill the gap. Wisconsin's child-protection program thus effectively confined Joshua DeShaney within the walls of Randy DeShaney's violent home until such time as DSS took action to remove him. Conceivably, then, children like Joshua are made worse off by the existence of this program when the persons and entities charged with carrying it out fail to do their jobs.

DISCUSSION QUESTIONS **FOR *DESHANEY v. WINNEBAGO COUNTY DEPT. OF SOCIAL SERVICES***

A. The plaintiff argued that the social workers had deprived him of his liberty in violation of the Due Process Clause of the Fourteenth Amendment. According to the Supreme Court, what protections does the Due Process Clause provide and what protections does it not afford?

B. When the state received the complaints about abuse, what "affirmative" steps did it take to protect the minor child? What did the state fail to do to protect Joshua?

C. The plaintiff argued that there were special circumstances that imposed an affirmative obligation on the state to protect him from his father. What were the special circumstances the plaintiff alluded to in his argument?

D. Justice Brennan argues that the Due Process Clause was violated by the state officials. What is Justice Brennan's thesis? How persuasive is it?

E. This case has generated substantial controversy over the years. One commentator challenges the reasoning underlying the majority decision as follows:

> [H]ad the Court found that under applicable law and the facts of the case that Joshua DeShaney had a constitutional right to protection by the DSS from his father, and the only issue was whether the State had violated that right, *Harris* might be applicable. For example, if Joshua DeShaney's mother were claiming that the DSS had to provide him with an armed guard twenty-four hours a day, an analysis under *Harris* would be necessary. *Harris* is not applicable to the preliminary question of the existence of such a right to protection.

Phillip M. Kannan, *But Who Will Protect Poor Joshua DeShaney, A Four-Year-Old Child with No Positive Due Process Rights?*, 39 U. Mem. L. Rev. 543, 572 (2009). Do you agree with this analysis? Why or why not?

16.6 OVERVIEW OF ADJUDICATION, DISPOSITION, AND REVIEW

Civil child protection proceedings generally involve a two-step process of adjudication and disposition. Adjudication is required for the court to establish jurisdiction and determine whether a child meets the relevant statutory definition of abuse or neglect. Nevertheless, the state may take emergency temporary custody of a child prior to adjudication if the child is shown to be in imminent danger. The final adjudication may involve a contested hearing or the parent may agree to the finding.

After adjudication, various dispositions may result, including ongoing supervision in the home or placement with a relative or in foster care. As discussed in the following chapter on termination of parental rights, federal statutes such as the Adoption Assistance and Child Welfare Act (AACWA) and the Adoption and Safe Families Act (AFSA) require that states make "reasonable efforts" to prevent removal of children from the home, and when it occurs, to reunite the family. The state is required to periodically review open cases and undertake "permanency planning" in the event that reunification is not realistic.

| REFLECTIVE QUESTIONS | Why did the federal government believe it necessary to mandate states to make "reasonable efforts" to prevent removal of children and/or reunite them with their families? |

16.7 ALTERNATIVE PROCESSES

Some jurisdictions use mediation and other alternative dispute resolution (ADR) processes in child protection cases to promote communication and involve families in planning. Available research indicates that agreement is reached in 60-80 percent of these cases and that when cases are mediated, extended family members are more likely to be involved and visitation arrangements tend to be more specific. Nancy Thoennes, *What We Know Now: Findings from Dependency Mediation Research*, 47 Fam. Ct. Rev. 21 (2009). *See also* Bernie Mayer, *Reflections on the State of Consensus-Based Decision Making in Child Welfare*, 47 Fam. Ct. Rev. 10 (2009).

In some states if a report involves lower risk to a child, parents are offered services without proceeding to adjudication. Such programs are known as alternative response, family assessment response, or differential response. *See* U.S. Dept. of Health and Human Services, Administration for Children and Families, *Child Maltreatment 2013*, 18-20, available at http://www.acf.hhs.gov/sites/default/files/cb/cm2013.pdf (last visited July 27, 2015). These programs remain controversial.

DR systems are designed to divert some 50-80% of the cases now reported to and investigated by the coercive CPS system to a noncoercive system of supportive services. DR proponents note that a high proportion of CPS cases are closed without provision of services, even though these families often need services, as demonstrated by the fact that roughly one-third of the children in these cases are rereported for maltreatment within about a year. They argue that children and families will be better served by getting the services which could be provided by a nonstigmatizing voluntary system. DR proponents also argue that there is no need for a coercive system to protect these children because a large majority of CPS cases are minor, a claim they say is supported by the fact that a majority of CPS cases are categorized as neglect rather than abuse.

There are many problems with the DR position. First, there is no reason to think that a majority of CPS cases are minor. Most neglect cases involve serious parental substance abuse issues which put children at risk for very real harm, including death at high rates. Many neglect cases are abuse cases categorized as neglect because the latter is easier to prove.

Elizabeth Bartholet, *Creating a Child-Friendly Child Welfare System: Effective Early Intervention to Prevent Maltreatment and Protect Victimized Children*, 60 Buff. L. Rev. 1323, 1335-1336 (2012).

REFLECTIVE QUESTIONS	Do you support the controversial use of alternative responses? Why or why not?

16.8 DEFINING ABUSE, NEGLECT, DEPENDENCY

States define abuse, neglect, and dependency by statute. Generally, abuse involves physical, sexual, and/or serious psychological harm. Neglect arises when parents fail to provide adequate food, housing, medical care, or oversight of education. Dependency similarly involves failure to provide for basic needs, but the failure is not attributed to the fault of the parent. Some states merge the concepts of abuse, neglect, and dependency into a single category, such as "child in need of protection."

REFLECTIVE QUESTIONS	**Why might states separately define abuse and neglect? Why might states adopt a single category such as child in need of protection? Does it matter whether the definitions are merged or viewed as separate?**

16.9 DETERMINATION OF ABUSE: CORPORAL PUNISHMENT

Historians suggest that the practice of using corporal punishment is ancient. For example, the Bible declares in Proverbs 19:18 (King James) the following: "Chasten thy son while there is hope, and let not thy soul spare for his crying." The idea is that such punishment will scare bad behavior out of a child. Matthew A. Menendez, *When to Punish the Punishers: The New Standard of Corporal Punishment*, 10 Loy. J. Pub. Int'l L. 217, n.4 (Spring 2009). In the United States, corporal punishment has been allowed in the home and in the schools. It is estimated that corporal punishment is allowed in schools in almost half of all the states. *Ibid.* Alabama, for example, allows teachers to use appropriate means of discipline up to and including corporal punishment as may be prescribed by the local board of education. Ala. Code §16-28A-1 (2015).

Given the general nature of most definitions of abuse and neglect, courts exercise substantial discretion in determining whether parental abuse or neglect has taken place. Consequently, the level of harm warranting intervention may vary from jurisdiction to jurisdiction.

State and local differences are particularly evident in cases involving corporal punishment. The states authorize parents to use reasonable force to correct a child, and judges are sometimes asked to determine whether the force used by a parent was "reasonable" or whether it constituted child abuse. However, the Supreme Court has never directly addressed the question of whether parents have a fundamental right to use corporal punishment.

| REFLECTIVE QUESTIONS | Do you believe that corporal punishment benefits or harms children? |

Background to *People ex rel. C.F.*

In the next case, a mother used a belt to strike a child six times on the buttocks, and the Supreme Court of South Dakota was asked to review a lower court decision holding that the mother's action was not a reasonable use of force.

PEOPLE EX REL. C.F.
Supreme Court of South Dakota
708 N.W.2d 313 (2005)

GILBERTSON, C.J. . . . C.F. is the eldest of three daughters born to Mother. Mother is married to Stepfather, the biological father of the youngest daughter. At the time of the events in question, C.F. was ten years old.

The family's history with the Department of Social Services (Department) began in November 2003. The Department received a referral from the children's school that there were bruises on C.F.'s younger sister (hereinafter "Sister 1.") Sister 1 and C.F. told a Department social worker that Sister 1 had gotten a "whooping" from Stepfather for bad grades and unfinished homework. The children described a "whooping" as more serious than a spanking or a beating, and that it was administered with a belt. The children described that they were required to put their hands on the bed during a "whooping" so they would remain in one spot, and then they would receive the "whooping" on their buttocks. However, in the November 2003 incident, Sister 1 had moved and was struck on the back of her upper thigh with the belt, which left a six-inch bruise.

That same day the social worker visited with both Mother and Stepfather regarding the incident. The couple stated they believed in and used "whoopings" with a belt as a form of discipline of last resort. They also stated they punished the children by requiring them to stand in a corner on one leg for a specified period of time. After the conference with the social worker, Mother and Stepfather signed a proposed family case plan in which they agreed to attend Common Sense Parenting classes on administering appropriate discipline. The parents also agreed that they would refrain from verbally chastising the children for visiting with the Department social worker, and discontinue the use of the one-legged corner punishment. The family was also referred to Home Base Services for additional information on nonphysical discipline methods. All three children were removed from the home temporarily, and an abuse and neglect petition was filed. The children were returned to the home and the petition was dismissed after the case plan was signed by the parents.

The family's next contact with the Department occurred after a series of events involving C.F. In June 2004, C.F. stole a music CD from a local K-Mart. C.F. lied about stealing the CD. Mother disciplined C.F. by making her return the CD to the store manager, and placing her on two weeks restriction, or grounding. The grounding consisted of the loss of her toys, television viewing, candy and other treats maintained in the home, and outside privileges. The only activity C.F. was allowed to participate in during the summer was swimming lessons. After the two weeks, C.F.'s original grounding was extended when she failed to come home before dark. During the time of the grounding, Mother discovered candy wrappers, and popsicle sticks and wrappers under C.F.'s bed and on the floor of a closet in her room. When confronted by Mother about breaking the rules, C.F. denied it. C.F.'s grounding was extended for several weeks as a result. During the last week of July, Mother discovered green marker scribbles on the carpet and walls of C.F.'s room. Mother and Stepfather asked C.F. to clean the marks and provided C.F. with a cleaning solution in a spray bottle and rag to scrub the carpet.

On August 2, 2004, Stepfather entered C.F.'s bedroom and found the markings had not been cleaned and additional candy and popsicle wrappers under C.F.'s bed. Stepfather again requested that C.F. clean up the markings and C.F. began to cry and deny the accusations against her. Stepfather told C.F. to be quiet and stop crying or he would add to her punishment. C.F. did not quiet down and Stepfather added one day to her restriction, and then a second day when C.F. refused to quiet down. Finally, Stepfather took C.F.'s swimming lessons away after a third warning. Stepfather then left the room and asked C.F. to clean the marks on the carpet and walls, pick up the wrappers and stop crying and screaming. . . .

Blaedorn spoke with Mother over the telephone later that day. Mother admitted to hitting C.F. with a belt approximately six times. Mother also stated she did not think the spanking was abusive as it left no marks on the child. Based on the information given to the Department by C.F. and the confirmation by Stepfather and Mother of the details leading up to the incident and the spanking, C.F. was removed from the home. At the Department's request, C.F. was examined by a physician the following day but no bruising was detected.

On August 2, 2004, the trial court issued a temporary custody directive placing C.F. in the care and custody of the Department. The State filed an abuse and neglect petition on August 4, 2004, alleging Mother abused and neglected C.F. An adjudicatory hearing was held on October 5, 2004.

Mother argued at the adjudicatory hearing that her actions were rendered necessary by C.F.'s misbehavior, and that the amount of force she used was reasonable in manner and moderate in degree within the meaning of SDCL 22-18-5. Mother argued that there was no other alternative available for C.F.'s series of misbehaviors, and that because there was nothing else to take from the child the spanking was necessary. In addition, Mother quantified the amount of force she used as a four on a scale of one to ten. Mother noted she used a belt to administer corporal punishment rather than her hand, as she and Stepfather believe that parents' hands should be used for affection and not punishment. . . .

The trial court found C.F. to be abused and neglected within the meaning of SDCL 26-8A-2 based on Mother striking C.F. six times with a belt to her buttocks as punishment for C.F.'s failure to remove coloring marks from the wall or floor, concealment of candy and ice cream wrappers, and crying and slamming doors after being informed that she would not be allowed to participate in swimming lessons. The trial court held that Mother's act of striking C.F. six times with a belt for the above-mentioned misbehavior was not reasonable in manner and moderate in degree as set forth in SDCL 22-18-5. On November 8, 2004, the trial court signed an order of adjudication and interim disposition and entered adjudicatory findings of fact and conclusions of law. The final dispositional hearing was held on November 30, 2004, at which the trial court returned physical and legal custody of C.F. to Mother. The final dispositional findings of fact and conclusions of law and the final dispositional order were served on December 15, 2004.

Mother appeals one issue: Whether the trial court abused its discretion when it determined C.F. was an abused and neglected child.

Whether a child is abused and neglected is a question of fact that the State must prove by clear and convincing evidence. . . . The trial court's findings of fact are subject to the clearly erroneous standard, and will not be set aside unless "we are left with a definite and firm conviction that a mistake has been made." . . . We will give due regard to the trial court's opportunity to judge the credibility of witnesses. . . .

The State must prove a child is abused or neglected under the criteria set forth in SDCL 26-8A-2. . . .

SDCL 26-8A-2 provides:

In this chapter and chapter 26-7A, the term, abused or neglected child, means a child:

(1) Whose parent, guardian, or custodian has abandoned the child or has subjected the child to mistreatment or abuse;

(2) Who lacks proper parental care through the actions or omissions of the child's parent, guardian, or custodian;

(3) Whose environment is injurious to the child's welfare;

(4) Whose parent, guardian, or custodian fails or refuses to provide proper or necessary subsistence, supervision, education, medical care, or any other care necessary for the child's health, guidance, or well-being;

(5) Who is homeless, without proper care, or not domiciled with the child's parent, guardian, or custodian through no fault of the child's parent, guardian, or custodian;

(6) Who is threatened with substantial harm;

(7) Who has sustained emotional harm or mental injury as indicated by an injury to the child's intellectual or psychological capacity evidenced by an observable and substantial impairment in the child's ability to function within the child's normal range of performance and behavior, with due regard to the child's culture;

(8) Who is subject to sexual abuse, sexual molestation, or sexual exploitation by the child's parent, guardian, custodian, or any other person responsible for the child's care;

(9) Who was subject to prenatal exposure to abusive use of alcohol or any controlled drug or substance not lawfully prescribed by a practitioner as authorized by chapters 22-42 and 34-20B; or

(10) Whose parent, guardian, or custodian knowingly exposes the child to an environment that is being used for the manufacturing of methamphetamines.

"Under SDCL 26-8-6, any one of the eight subparts to that statute standing alone is enough to sustain a dependency and neglect adjudication as long as that ultimate finding is supported by clear and convincing evidence."

This Court has crafted a two-prong inquiry to assess whether a parents' administration of corporal punishment falls under SDCL 22-18-5 and, therefore, is not abuse as defined under SDCL 26-8-6. *In re T.A.*, 2003 SD 56, ¶8, 663 N.W.2d 225, 230. The first prong of the inquiry requires the trial court to determine whether the restraint or corrective measure utilized was "rendered necessary" by the child's actions. *Id.* The second prong requires the trial court to determine whether the force used was "reasonable in manner and moderate in degree." *Id.* . . .

First, Mother argues the spanking was rendered necessary by the misconduct of C.F. over the months of June, July and August of 2004. Mother urges this Court to find the trial court erred when it found that the six strikes were excessive in manner and not moderate in degree for the offense of failing to remove coloring marker from the wall or floor, concealment of candy and ice cream wrappers, and crying and slamming doors after being informed that the child would not be allowed to participate in swimming lessons. Instead, Mother urges this Court to view the series of events as one continuous offense or misbehavior for which progressive discipline was rendered necessary. Under the one continuous offense approach, Mother argues that the disciplinary actions were necessary as C.F.'s misbehavior continuously escalated throughout the summer months and culminated in the episode on August 2, 2004.

Second, Mother argues that the strikes were reasonable in manner and moderate in degree. Mother contends that the force was not excessive, as the strikes were given on the buttocks and over clothing. Furthermore, Mother argues that the strikes were not intended to cause bruising and, in fact, did not cause bruising. Finally, Mother argues that the strength and severity of the strikes were "probably a 4 on a scale of 1 to 10," and therefore not excessive.

The record supports Mother's assertion that C.F.'s behavior on the day in question was disrespectful and defiant, in that C.F. was screaming and crying and slamming doors before the spanking. The trial court noted that C.F.'s behavior had escalated over the summer, and that she had been pushing the issue with her misbehavior. The trial court did not include a finding of fact or conclusion of law concerning the necessity prong of SDCL 22-18-5. However, based on the hearing transcript we conclude that the trial court determined that the punishment was rendered necessary within the meaning of SDCL 22-18-5 by C.F.'s misconduct. It is clear from the evidence presented at the hearing that the trial court did not err in its conclusion that Mother was exercising lawful authority to correct the child.

However, on the day of the spanking, the trial court found that Mother failed to intervene in a manner that permitted her to administer punishment starting from the lower end of the scale, rather than starting at the upper end of the scale that had been established over the course of the summer. While alternative discipline was attempted by Stepfather, Mother did not attempt any other form of discipline before administering the six strikes with a belt. The trial court found that Mother overdid the punishment in that hitting the child six times with a belt was not moderate in degree and reasonable in manner given the facts of the case, such that the amount of force used complied with the second prong of the test for corporal punishment under SDCL 22-18-5. The trial court noted that there were other forms of punishment that Mother could have resorted to rather than starting at the punishment of last resort on the day in question.

The Legislature has determined in this State that corporal punishment will not be absolutely prohibited, nor will it be allowed in all instances with any amount of force a parent decides to use. Instead the Legislature has opted for a middle ground by requiring it be "rendered necessary" and be "reasonable in manner and moderate in degree," in order for such corporal punishment to fall outside the definition of abuse under SDCL 26-8-6.

These requirements are obviously very general in nature, and by their very terms place a large amount of discretion with the trial court to determine whether or not the actions of a parent fall within the definition in SDCL 22-18-5. Such a definition further calls for such a determination by the trial court on a case by case basis. There obviously is no bright line test applicable under a statutory definition such as this. As such, deference for the trial court and its ability to hear the evidence and determine the appropriateness, or lack thereof, of the parents' possessive actions is considerable.

There was no error in the determination by the trial court that the amount of force used by Mother was not "reasonable in manner and moderate in degree." While the spanking left no bruises on C.F., it did leave her with enough pain that she sat down in a guarded manner at the Department's office some thirty to forty-five minutes after the strikes were administered. Despite Mother's assertions that the force of the blow was only a "4 on a scale of 1 to 10," clearly there was enough force behind the blows for the child to experience pain for an extended period of time.

Employing the clearly erroneous standard of review to the trial court's findings of fact, we are not "left with a definite and firm conviction that a mistake has been made." See *In re J.S.B., Jr.*, 691 N.W.2d at 615 (citing *In re T.H.*, 396 N.W.2d at 148.) Therefore, the trial court did not err in finding the amount of force used by Mother was not "reasonable in manner and moderate in degree." We affirm the trial court's holding that C.F. was abused and neglected.

MEIERHENRY, Justice (concurring specially).

In this case, we affirm an abuse and neglect determination based on a parent's use of a belt to spank a child. The case of *In re T.A.* also affirmed a determination of abuse and neglect where a father spanked his child with a belt. In that case, the spanking was unacceptable because the "[p]arents failed to intervene in any manner before resorting to spanking" and because no alternative discipline was attempted prior to the spanking. We also said that the evidence did not support the father's claim that T.A. was "out of control." In addition, the spanking left bruising "on the child's posterior, belt-line and arm." Under the circumstances, the force was not reasonable in manner and moderate in degree under SDCL 22-18-5.

This case, however, presents a different situation. Here, the child's misbehavior leading up to the spanking started when she stole a music CD from a store. Mother required her to return the CD and apologize to the storeowners. Mother also grounded C.F. with loss of toys, television, candy, and treats. The child broke the rules by returning late from swimming and eating candy and popsicles. Additionally, the child scribbled on the carpet and walls of her room with a green marker. As a result, the child was directed to clean the markings and pick up the candy wrappers and other trash she had left on the floor of her closet and behind her bed. Failing to do so, she was admonished by her stepfather. According to Mother, the child's crying and screaming and slamming doors got louder and louder. Mother testified, "C.F. was up there about five minutes or so, she was still screaming and slamming doors and I had had enough. There was nothing else to take from her. I had taken everything she had." Mother saw the child's behavior "as the final straw. There was no talking. Nothing else to take away and her behavior was way beyond unacceptable." Mother said she got a belt, went to the child's room and told the child to turn around and put her hands on the bed. She then spanked the child over her clothing with the belt six times, with a force of four on a scale of one to ten. Mother admitted to administering spankings like this about four times a year. The trial court found that under the circumstances hitting a child six or seven times with a belt was not reasonable in manner and moderate in degree and that Mother had overdone it.

In this case, the parents tried other methods of discipline before the spanking. Evidence indicated the child was out of control—screaming, crying and slamming doors. And despite the spanking administered by Mother, the child showed no bruising. What appears to be unacceptable in this case is that Mother used a belt and hit the child six or seven times with a force that did not leave bruises but made the child uncomfortable. This is certainly a very restricted interpretation of the legal force a parent can use under South Dakota law "in the exercise of a lawful authority to restrain or correct his child . . . if restraint or correction has been rendered necessary by the misconduct of such child . . . or by his refusal to obey the lawful command of such parent." SDCL 22-18-5. Apparently the use of a belt and the number of swats rendered the spanking of C.F. abusive, that is, not "reasonable in manner and moderate in degree." This restricted interpretation could be a very slippery slope for the trial courts. Spanking is out of favor under modern theories of child rearing, yet the Legislature still recognizes the parent's right to enforce physical punishment. Thus, resolution of these conflicting theories is left to the individual judge on a case-by-case basis and indubitably does not give clear direction to parents who might be hauled into court on abuse and neglect claims.

That being said, our standard of review on appeal is whether the trial court's findings are clearly erroneous. Those findings are not to be set aside unless we are definitely and firmly convinced that the trial court made a mistake. Under this standard of review, I agree this matter should be affirmed.

DISCUSSION QUESTIONS	FOR *PEOPLE EX REL C.F.*

A. The court states, "The first prong of the inquiry requires the trial court to determine whether the restraint or corrective measure utilized was 'rendered necessary' by the child's actions." The mother argued that the child's behavior rendered the punishment necessary. What behavior did she base this argument on? Should the child's behavior be the determining factor? In a concurring opinion (not included here) a judge wrote that the mother had "painted herself into a corner" and that there were "other alternatives." Should the mother's parenting skill be considered along with the child's actions?

B. The court states, "The second prong requires the trial court to determine whether the force used was "reasonable in manner and moderate in degree." What did the mother argue with respect to manner and degree? What, if any, specific force would you consider to be reasonable in manner and moderate in degree?

C. The concurring judge suggests that the majority's analysis could be a "very slippery slope" for trial courts. Explain this observation.

D. Countries such as Norway, Denmark, Finland, and Austria prohibit corporal punishment, and the United Nations Convention on the Rights of the Child supports this view. *See* Jaap E. Doek, *What Does the Children's Convention Require?*, 20 Emory Int'l L. Rev. 199 (2006). What are arguments for and against the use of corporal punishment by parents?

E. In *In re Syed I*, 877 N.Y.S.2d 318 (N.Y.A.D. 2009), the father punished the children by hitting them, making them do knee bends, and threatening to withhold food if they did not memorize certain written passages. The father's mental health was deteriorating and the mother feared him. Should the children be removed from both the mother and the father? Or only the father? What is the mother's duty to protect children in this situation? Should the fact that a mother is inexperienced excuse her behavior toward her children? *See In re J.C.*, Slip Copy 2011-Ohio-4933 (Ohio App. 2011).

16.10 DETERMINATION OF NEGLECT: PARENTING, HOUSING, MEDICAL CARE

A typical statute defines child neglect as follows:

> "Child neglect" means harm or threatened harm to a child's health or welfare by a parent . . . that occurs through either of the following: (*i*) Negligent treatment,

including the failure to provide adequate food, clothing, shelter, or medical care. (*ii*) Placing a child at an unreasonable risk to the child's health or welfare by failure of the parent . . . to intervene to eliminate that risk when that person is able to do so and has, or should have, knowledge of the risk.

Mich. Comp. Laws Ann. §722.622(j) (2015). Neglect is often associated with inadequate food, housing, medical care, and supervision and, not surprisingly, low-income families are more likely to fall into this category. *See* Elizabeth Bartholet, *Nobody's Children* 33 (1999).

REFLECTIVE QUESTIONS	Do you believe that the definition quoted above is sufficiently definite to allow for consistent application? How much discretion do you think courts should exercise in this area?

Background to *New Jersey Division of Youth and Family Services v. P.W.R.*

Courts face particular challenges when making decisions about whether physical, medical, educational, or emotional neglect has occurred, and judges are sometimes criticized for applying value-laden standards. In the following case, the Supreme Court of New Jersey considers a case where the family situation of a teenage girl is far from ideal but may not reach the level required for intervention.

NEW JERSEY DIVISION OF YOUTH AND FAMILY SERVICES

v.

P.W.R.

Supreme Court of New Jersey
11 A.3d 844 (2011)

LaVECCHIA, J., . . . [T]he trial court's written order concluding that Alice was abused and neglected listed six findings for its affirmative conclusion: (1) Pam physically abused Alice; (2) Charlie did not intervene when Pam did so; (3) Alice had not been taken to a pediatrician in two years; (4) there was no heat in the home; (5) Pam and Charlie took Alice's paychecks to support themselves; and (6) Pam and Charlie isolated Alice from her extended family. We address each, as to Pam, in turn.

With regard to the trial court's conclusion that Pam physically abused Alice, Title Nine provides that an abused or neglected child is one

whose physical, mental, or emotional condition has been impaired or is in imminent danger of becoming impaired as the result of the failure of his parent or guardian, as herein defined, to exercise a minimum degree of care . . . in providing the child with proper supervision or guardianship, by unreasonably inflicting or allowing to be inflicted harm, or substantial risk thereof, including the infliction of excessive corporal punishment. . . .

[N.J. Stat. Ann. §9:6-8.21(c)(4).]

Pam does not dispute that she occasionally slapped Alice in the face as a form of discipline; what she contests is that her actions constituted "excessive corporal punishment."

Although hardly admirable, we agree that such occasional discipline does not fit a common sense application of the statutory prohibition against "excessive" corporal punishment. There was no evidence developed in this record showing the existence of bruises, scars, lacerations, fractures, or any other medical ailment suffered as a result of Pam's actions. . . . Indeed, DYFS itself found the allegation of physical abuse to be unfounded. That should have put the matter to rest. Before the Family Part, DYFS seemingly agreed; it did not argue that Alice was physically abused. Despite the deferential standard that we apply to the findings of the Family Part courts who hear the oft-difficult and wrenching abuse and neglect actions, we cannot credit the finding of physical abuse made here by the trial court.

A slap of the face of a teenager as a form of discipline — with no resulting bruising or marks — does not constitute "excessive corporal punishment" within the meaning of N.J.S.A. 9:6-8.21(c)(4)(b). That is not to suggest approval of such behavior. But, by qualifying the prohibition with the term, "excessive," the statutory language plainly recognizes the need for some parental autonomy in the child-rearing dynamic that, of necessity, may involve the need for punishment. Limiting state involvement only to interference with excessive corporal punishment requires the exercise of judgment by reviewing courts before a finding of physical abuse is entered against a parent. In this matter, where DYFS labeled the physical abuse "unfounded," the trial court abused its discretion by utilizing the slaps as a basis for a finding of physical abuse. It also caused a fair notice violation because no lay person served with the DYFS complaint in this matter would reasonably read the complaint to indicate that a claim of physical abuse would be advanced at the hearing. But, more importantly, our reversal of this finding goes to its core. The proofs simply were insufficient to support a finding that Pam physically abused Alice.

Second, the fact that there was a problem with the central heat in the home should not, standing alone, constitute neglect. DYFS documents admitted into evidence demonstrated that, per Ms. Rivera's observation, space heaters were in use in the home. The statute provides that a child can be considered abused or neglected if the parents or guardians fail "to exercise a minimum degree of care (a) in supplying the child with adequate food, clothing, shelter, education, medical or surgical care though financially able to do so or though offered financial or other reasonable means to do so. . . ." N.J.S.A. 9:6-8.21(c)(4). There is no evidence in the record that Charlie and Pam were financially able to cure their larger central heating problem but were refusing to do so, nor is there evidence that DYFS made any attempt whatsoever to assist them in fixing the heating problem. The record demonstrated that both Charlie and Pam were temporarily out of work. That DYFS did not make any offer of assistance to remedy the heating problem is troubling, particularly to the extent that the deficient central heating component of the home was used as a basis for removing Alice.

For similar reasons, it is hard to conclude that Alice was abused or neglected simply because Pam and Charlie took some portion of Alice's paychecks to support the family's phone or cable bill, or because she was not taken to a pediatrician in two years. As to the former, impecuniousness cannot be the basis for having one's child taken from him or her. Requiring working-age children to contribute to the support of the family is not an actionable reason to remove the child from the family home. Despite financial difficulties, many parents have raised children appropriately free from state interference. The trial court's citing to the family's demand that Alice contribute to family bills as evidence that she was an abused or neglected child is simply wide of the mark.

Further, with regard to the alleged medical neglect, there was no evidence submitted that Alice's "physical, mental, or emotional condition [was] impaired or [was] in imminent danger of becoming impaired" simply because she had not seen a pediatrician in two years. She had been going with Pam to Planned Parenthood for pregnancy checks and DYFS never demonstrated proof of a physical condition, other than possible pregnancy, for which Alice required pediatric care that was not sought. We also know from this record that Alice had been provided with braces paid for by her parents, but, according to the Law Guardian, she was behind in having them checked for adjustment. Based on their temporary financial setbacks, the parents' judgment to delay completing Alice's teeth-straightening process hardly constituted a form of medical neglect. Again, those complaints neither individually nor collectively reasonably rise to actionable "medical neglect," and the trial court findings to that effect are so wide of the mark as to be unsustainable.

Finally, we cannot agree that Pam and Charlie's decision to limit Alice's contact with her grandfather constituted emotional impairment meant to be actionable by the statutory inclusion of impairment to a child's "emotional condition" in the definition of an abused or neglected child. . . . Parents have a fundamental right to parental autonomy, and with respect to a grandparent's visitation rights, the burden is on the grandparent to establish "by a preponderance of the evidence that visitation is necessary to avoid harm to the child." . . . There was no showing, through expert testimony or otherwise, that Alice actually suffered mental or emotional harm from the restricted contact with her grandfather. Thus, this finding too is unsustainable.

Before closing, we add the following. In child abuse and neglect cases, we recognize the need to evaluate the totality of the proofs because the evidence can be synergistically related. With that in mind, it is impossible to ignore the difficult home environment present in this family's circumstances. Clearly, there were problems within this family. The question, however, is not whether Alice and Pam struggled over the issues between them, but rather, whether Alice's "physical, mental, or emotional condition has been impaired or is in imminent danger of becoming impaired" because of Pam. Despite the long list of Alice's complaints, actionable abuse or neglect was not demonstrated. Most of the allegations were the product of the family's tight financial situation, such as the lack of central heating and the family's apparent need for monetary contribution from Alice's part-time job. The dominant allegation of abuse was that Pam slapped Alice in the face, which conduct, although abhorrent to a sixteen-year-old young woman, and hardly admirable, does not fit within the statutory definition of abuse. The remaining instances of alleged abuse and neglect, while not necessarily paragons of parenting, do not satisfy the standard articulated in N.J.S.A. 9:6-8.21(c)(4).

In sum, although no parenting awards are to be won on this record, neither was actionable abuse or neglect proven. As stated at the outset, DYFS has many serious cases, and even more numerous referrals that necessitate investigations requiring the agency to wade into difficult family problems in order to protect children. Its task is hard and it must be vigilant, but it must be vigilant within the limitations of the law that empowers the agency's actions. The record here simply did not demonstrate proof of actionable abuse or neglect of Alice by Pam. It was an error for the courts below to have sustained the findings of abuse and neglect entered against Pam.

DISCUSSION QUESTIONS FOR *NEW JERSEY DIVISION OF YOUTH AND FAMILY SERVICES v. P.W.R.*

A. What is the definition of abuse and neglect in New Jersey?

B. What constitutes "excessive corporal punishment" in the view of the court?

C. The court was troubled by the fact that DYFS did not offer any assistance with the heating problem prior to bringing an action. What was the court's reasoning? Do you agree? Why or why not?

D. What allegations were made with respect to medical neglect of Alice? What facts might have constituted medical neglect if they had occurred in this case?

E. Do you think that DYFS should have investigated this case? Should they have pursued a finding of neglect? Why or why not?

16.11 DETERMINATION OF NEGLECT: FAILURE TO PROTECT, INTIMATE PARTNER VIOLENCE

Parents have a legal obligation to protect children from reasonably anticipated danger, and a parent who does not do so may be found to have neglected his or her child. For example, a parent who reasonably suspects that a child is being sexually abused is expected to take steps to end the abuse and keep the child safe. If the parent fails to do so, that parent may be legally neglectful.

> | REFLECTIVE QUESTIONS | Can you think of other examples of hypothetical situations where a parent has a duty to protect a child from harm? |

Background to *Nicholson v. Scoppetta*

As discussed in the previous chapter, there is increasing awareness that exposure to intimate partner violence is harmful for children. At the same time, a survivor of intimate partner violence may have difficulty leaving an abusive situation due to threats, intimidation, injury, financial issues, and so forth. In such situations, state child protection agencies may seek removal of children based in part on the victim's failure to protect them from witnessing the violence. This was the situation in the well-known case of *Nicholson v. Scoppetta*. There, victims of intimate partner violence brought a class action lawsuit against the New York City Administration for Children's Services (ACS) challenging the ACS policy of seeking removal of children "solely because the mother is the victim of domestic violence." In its decision, the court of appeals reviews the statutory definition of child neglect and considers the extent to which a child who witnesses intimate partner violence falls within it.

NICHOLSON
v.
SCOPPETTA
Court of Appeals of New York
820 N.E.2d 840 (2004)

KAYE, C.J. . . . In April 2000, Sharwline Nicholson, on behalf of herself and her two children, brought an action pursuant to 42 USC §1983 against the New York City Administration for Children's Services (ACS). . . . Plaintiffs alleged that ACS, as a matter of policy, removed children from mothers who were victims of domestic violence because, as victims, they "engaged in domestic violence" and that defendants removed and detained children without probable cause and without due process of law. That policy, and its implementation — according to plaintiff mothers — constituted, among other wrongs, an unlawful interference with their liberty interest in the care and custody of their children in violation of the United States Constitution. . . .

CERTIFIED QUESTION NO. 1: NEGLECT

"Does the definition of a 'neglected child' under N.Y. Family Ct. Act §1012(f), (h) include instances in which the sole allegation of neglect is that the parent or other person legally responsible for the child's care allows the child to witness domestic abuse against the caretaker?" . . .

We understand this question to ask whether a court reviewing a Family Court Act article 10 petition may find a respondent parent responsible for neglect based on evidence of two facts only: that the parent has been the victim of domestic violence, and that the child has been exposed to that violence. That question must be answered in the negative. Plainly, more is required for a showing of neglect under New York law than the fact that a child was exposed to domestic abuse against the caretaker. Answering the question in the affirmative, moreover, would read an unacceptable presumption into the statute, contrary to its plain language.

Family Court Act §1012(f) is explicit in identifying the elements that must be shown to support a finding of neglect. As relevant here, it defines a "neglected child" to mean:

> a child less than eighteen years of age
> (i) whose physical, mental or emotional condition has been impaired or is in immi-nent danger of becoming impaired as a result of the failure of his parent or other person legally responsible for his care to exercise a minimum degree of care . . .
> (B) in providing the child with proper supervision or guardianship, by unrea-sonably inflicting or allowing to be inflicted harm, or a substantial risk thereof, including the infliction of excessive corporal punishment; or by misusing a drug or drugs; or by misusing alcoholic beverages to the extent that he loses self-control of his actions; or by any other acts of a similarly serious nature requiring the aid of the court.

Thus, a party seeking to establish neglect must show, by a preponderance of the evidence (see Family Ct. Act §1046[b][i]), first, that a child's physical, mental or emo-tional condition has been impaired or is in imminent danger of becoming impaired and second, that the actual or threatened harm to the child is a consequence of the failure of the parent or caretaker to exercise a minimum degree of care in providing the child with proper supervision or guardianship. The drafters of article 10 were "deeply concerned" that an imprecise definition of child neglect might result in "unwarranted state intervention into private family life." . . .

The first statutory element requires proof of actual (or imminent danger of) phys-ical, emotional or mental impairment to the child (see *Matter of Nassau County Dept. of Social Servs. [Dante M.] v. Denise J.*, 661 N.E.2d 138 [1995]). This prerequisite to a finding of neglect ensures that the Family Court, in deciding whether to authorize state intervention, will focus on serious harm or potential harm to the child, not just on what might be deemed undesirable parental behavior. "Imminent danger" reflects the Legislature's judgment that a finding of neglect may be appropriate even when a child has not actually been harmed; "imminent danger of impairment to a child is an independent and separate ground on which a neglect finding may be based." . . . Imminent danger, however, must be near or impending, not merely possible.

In each case, additionally, there must be a link or causal connection between the basis for the neglect petition and the circumstances that allegedly produce the child's impairment or imminent danger of impairment. In *Dante M.*, for example, we held that the Family Court erred in concluding that a newborn's positive toxicology for a controlled substance alone was sufficient to support a finding of neglect because the report, in and of itself, did not prove that the child was impaired or in imminent danger of becoming impaired. . . . We reasoned, "[r]elying solely on a positive toxicology result for a neglect determination fails to make the necessary causative connection to all the surrounding circumstances that may or may not produce impairment or imminent risk of impairment in the newborn child." The positive toxicology report, in conjunction with other evidence — such as the mother's history of inability to care for her children because of her drug use, testimony of relatives that she was high on cocaine during her pregnancy and the mother's failure to testify at the neglect hearing — supported a finding of neglect and established a link between the report and physical impairment.

The cases at bar concern, in particular, alleged threats to the child's emotional, or mental, health. The statute specifically defines "[i]mpairment of emotional health" and "impairment of mental or emotional condition" to include

> "a state of substantially diminished psychological or intellectual functioning in relation to, but not limited to, such factors as failure to thrive, control of aggressive or self-destructive impulses, ability to think and reason, or acting out or misbehavior, including incorrigibility, ungovernability or habitual truancy" (Family Ct. Act §1012 [h]).

Under New York law, "such impairment must be clearly attributable to the unwillingness or inability of the respondent to exercise a minimum degree of care toward the child." Here, the Legislature recognized that the source of emotional or mental impairment — unlike physical injury — may be murky, and that it is unjust to fault a parent too readily. The Legislature therefore specified that such impairment be "clearly attributable" to the parent's failure to exercise the requisite degree of care.

Assuming that actual or imminent danger to the child has been shown, "neglect" also requires proof of the parent's failure to exercise a minimum degree of care. As the Second Circuit observed, "a fundamental interpretive question is what conduct satisfies the broad, tort-like phrase, 'a minimum degree of care.' The Court of Appeals has not yet addressed that question, which would be critical to defining appropriate parental behavior" (344 F.3d at 169).

"[M]inimum degree of care" is a "baseline of proper care for children that all parents, regardless of lifestyle or social or economic position, must meet." . . . Notably, the statutory test is *"minimum degree of care"* — not maximum, not best, not ideal — and the failure must be actual, not threatened (*see, e.g., Matter of Hofbauer*, 393 N.E.2d 1009 [1979] [recognizing, in the context of medical neglect, the court's role is not as surrogate parent and the inquiry is not posed in absolute terms of whether the parent has made the "right" or "wrong" decision]).

Courts must evaluate parental behavior objectively: would a reasonable and prudent parent have so acted, or failed to act, under the circumstances then and there existing. . . . The standard takes into account the special vulnerabilities of the child, even where general physical health is not implicated (*see Matter of Sayeh R.*, 693 N.E.2d 724 [1997] [mother's decision to demand immediate return of her traumatized children without regard to their need for counseling and related services "could well be found to represent precisely the kind of failure 'to exercise a minimum degree of care' that our neglect statute contemplates"]). Thus, when the inquiry is whether a mother — and domestic violence victim — failed to exercise a minimum degree of care, the focus must be on whether she has met the standard of the reasonable and prudent person in similar circumstances.

As the Subclass A members point out, for a battered mother — and ultimately for a court — what course of action constitutes a parent's exercise of a "minimum degree of care" may include such considerations as: risks attendant to leaving, if the batterer has threatened to kill her if she does; risks attendant to staying and suffering continued abuse; risks attendant to seeking assistance through government channels, potentially increasing the danger to herself and her children; risks attendant to criminal prosecution against the abuser; and risks attendant to relocation. Whether a particular mother in these circumstances has actually failed to exercise a minimum degree of care is necessarily dependent on facts such as the severity and frequency of the violence, and the resources and options available to her. . . .

Only when a petitioner demonstrates, by a preponderance of evidence, that both elements of section 1012(f) are satisfied may a child be deemed neglected under the statute. When "the sole allegation" is that the mother has been abused and the child has witnessed the abuse, such a showing has not been made. This does not mean, however, that a child can never be "neglected" when living in a household plagued by domestic violence. Conceivably, neglect might be found where a record establishes that, for example, the mother acknowledged that the children knew of repeated domestic violence by her paramour and had reason to be afraid of him, yet nonetheless allowed him several times to return to her home, and lacked awareness of any impact of the violence on the children, as in *Matter of James M.M.*, 740 N.Y.S.2d 730; or where the children were exposed to regular and continuous extremely violent conduct between their parents, several times requiring official intervention, and where caseworkers testified to the fear and distress the children were experiencing as a result of their long exposure to the violence (*Matter of Theresa C.C.*, 178 A.D.2d 687, 576 N.Y.S.2d 937 [3d Dept. 1991]).

In such circumstances, the battered mother is charged with neglect not because she is a victim of domestic violence or because her children witnessed the abuse, but rather because a preponderance of the evidence establishes that the children were actually or imminently harmed by reason of her failure to exercise even minimal care in providing them with proper oversight. . . .

DISCUSSION QUESTIONS FOR *NICHOLSON V. SCOPPETTA*

A. One of the requirements for finding neglect is proof of actual physical, emotional, or mental impairment. What is the rationale for this element?

B. The court discusses a link or causal connection between the basis for the neglect petition and the circumstances producing the impairment or imminent danger. Provide an explanation and example of the court's view on the link.

C. Assuming that actual or imminent danger to the child has been shown, what other proof is required to show neglect?

D. Under what situations would this court find that failure to prevent a child from witnessing intimate partner violence would constitute neglect?

E. Professor Robin Fretwell Wilson argues that the abusive parent, rather than the child, should be removed from the home. She states:

> . . . ultimatums to parents to exit the home are customary in other countries. In Great Britain the accused parent can be ordered "to leave a dwelling-house in which he is living with the child." This is the "preferred course of action" when a child is at risk from someone living in their home. The United States actually shares more common ground with Great Britain than scholars and caseworkers realize. Nine jurisdictions in the United States explicitly authorize state judges to issue, and CPS agencies to seek, protective orders directing an alleged offender to vacate the home.

Robin Fretwell Wilson, *Removing Violent Parents from the Home: A Test Case for the Public Health Approach*, 12 Va. J. Soc. Pol'y & L. 638 (2005). Do you agree with this approach? Why do you suppose that the more common American practice is to remove the child, rather than the perpetrator, from the home?

16.12 DISPOSITION: SEXUAL ABUSE, CASE PLAN, FOSTER CARE

After a finding of abuse or neglect is made, the case plan may allow the child to remain in the home or the child may be placed outside of the home while the parents attempt to remedy the abusive or neglectful situation. As discussed in Chapter 17, pursuant to a case plan, states are required to make "reasonable efforts" to prevent removal of the children or to reunify the family if children have been placed outside the home.

When children are removed from the home, the state agency attempts to place them with "kin":

A significant percentage of foster children now live with kin. As of September 30, 2006, 24% of children in placement in the United States were living with kin foster parents, and "kin" is regularly defined to include non-genetically related individuals who had established a relationship with the child prior to his or her placement in foster care (e.g., family friend, neighbor). Excluding children who were placed in group homes, institutions, and other non-family home settings, over 32% of children in foster home placements lived with kin foster parents.

David Herring et al., *Evolutionary Theory and Kinship Foster Care: An Initial Test of Two Hypotheses*, 38 Cap. U. L. Rev. 291, 291 (2009).

 **REFLECTIVE QUESTIONS** | **Do you think it is important to place children with "kin"? Are there situations where you think it would be inappropriate to do so?**

Background to *Doe v. South Carolina Department of Social Services*

Under *DeShaney*, the state does not have an affirmative duty to protect children from abuse by their parents. In the following case, the Fourth Circuit considers the extent to which, pursuant to *DeShaney*, the state has an obligation to protect children placed in foster care.

DOE
v.
SOUTH CAROLINA DEPARTMENT OF SOCIAL SERVICES
Court of Appeals of the United States, Fourth Circuit
597 F.3d 163 (2010)

TRAXLER, Chief Judge: On August 9, 1999, SCDSS received a report that four-year-old Jane Doe and her eight-year-old brother, Kameron Cox, were victims of sexual abuse. The report alleged that Kameron had been sexually abused by his mother and that Jane had been sexually abused by her mother's boyfriend and her maternal grandfather. The biological father of the children was incarcerated in another state.

Upon receipt of the report, SCDSS officials took the children into emergency protective custody. During the subsequent investigation, Kameron claimed that his mother had sexually abused him, and denied knowledge of anyone sexually abusing Jane. Jane's mother denied abuse but reported that "Kameron had played with [Jane]'s private but she told him not to do it anymore." Ultimately, the sexual abuse assessments and medical examinations were inconclusive as to whether the children had been sexually abused. However, the South Carolina Family Court found physical neglect and granted SCDSS temporary custody of the children. No findings were made regarding the sexual abuse allegations. Physical custody of the children was initially transferred to a maternal aunt, but she relinquished the children to SCDSS's legal custody in July 2000. They were placed in a group home until September 2000 when they were moved to their first state-approved foster home.

On June 18, 2001, Joy Bennett, the children's therapist, reported that Kameron had become increasingly angry and depressed at his inability to return to his mother's home. She stated that he posed a threat to himself and to Jane, and she recommended psychiatric hospitalization. However, she also recommended that, in order to maintain the bond between Kameron and Jane, the two ultimately should continue to be placed together "if this c[ould] be done safely" for Jane. According to the psychiatric records, Kameron had a history of depression, suicidal and homicidal thoughts, and had become increasingly aggressive and hostile toward Jane. Kameron blamed Jane for their being in foster care "because she made statements that [their] mother, stepfather, and maternal grandfather [had] sexually molested her," but Kameron "d[id] not believe her allegations." The psychiatric records also included a history of sexual experimentation by Kameron and Jane with each other, possible sexual abuse of the children, and possible intergenerational incest.

On May 30, 2001, the defendant Debby Thompson, an employee of SCDSS, was assigned as the Adoption Specialist for the children. On July 5, 2001, Kameron was discharged from the hospital and placed in a foster home separate from Jane. Thompson began visiting the children later that month, but Kameron's threats to Jane necessitated postponement of recruitment efforts for a joint adoption of the siblings "until a determination of the appropriateness of an adoptive placement of [Jane] and Kameron together c[ould] be made." On August 22, 2001, Bennett advised Thompson that Kameron "ha[d] been a danger to [Jane] and she should be protected," but that Bennett had "realistic hope that Kameron c[ould] deal with his emotions and be safely reunited with her." She also noted that Jane "show[ed] some signs of sexual abuse including . . . a history of trying to sneak into Kameron's bed, probably for comfort through sexual contact." Although the exact history of sexual abuse was unclear, Bennett noted that it was "very likely that they ha[d] engaged in inappropriate sexual encounters with adults and with each other." During this period, Jane also began to exhibit acting-out behaviors of a sexual nature, including overly affectionate behavior towards boys and men, as well as anger and aggressiveness when she was frustrated.

On November 26, 2001, Jane was placed in foster care with Bill and Pam Hamerick, where she could be seen by Kameron's therapist, Titsa M. Flesch, and have sibling visits with Kameron, including some overnight visits on weekends and holidays. On September 9, 2002, Kameron was placed in the Hamericks' home as well. By this time, SCDSS had filed an action in family court seeking to legally terminate the parental rights of the biological parents, in order to pursue a joint adoption of the siblings. Following a contested proceeding, the mother voluntarily relinquished her parental rights, and the parental rights of the father were judicially terminated. The family court granted "[c]ustody of the minor children . . . to [SCDSS] with all rights of guardianship, placement, care and supervision, including the authority to approve medical treatment or educational plans, to secure placement for the minor children and the sole authority to consent to any adoption, with the authority to seek such routine and emergency medical care as [SCDSS] deems necessary and in the best interests of said minor children."

Plaintiffs Gregory and Michelle Johnson completed an application for adoption in May 2002. The Johnsons expressed their understanding that the "children [we]re in the system because of abuse, neglect, etc.," and they stated that they "fully underst[oo]d the therapy issues." They were willing to accept a child or children (including a sibling group) with "mild/treatable" sexual abuse, but not a child who was "sexually aggressive" towards other children. In January 2003, Thompson presented a background summary on Kameron and Jane to the Johnsons. Thompson claims that the summary contained all of the information available to her about the children, including the allegations that they had been sexually abused. It stated that the children had been removed from the birth home for allegations of sexual abuse but that Jane had been inconsistent in her reports of abuse, alternatively naming her birth mother, Kameron, her maternal grandfather, and her mother's boyfriend as having been sexually inappropriate or abusive toward her. Kameron had also been inconsistent at times, both denying and admitting inappropriate contact with his mother. He denied knowledge of any inappropriate contact between Jane and the adults. In the end, the Johnsons were advised that SCDSS had been unable to substantiate or rule out sexual abuse of either child. However, the summary represented that "[t]here ha[d] been no reports of any sexually inappropriate behavior from Kameron since entering care" and that "[p]art of his therapy ha[d] been to insure that he understands boundaries, good touch–bad touch rules and appropriate social interactions."

On February 28, 2003, Jane and Kameron were placed with the Johnsons for prospective adoption. Approximately four weeks after the placement, however, the Johnsons chose not to proceed with the adoption of Kameron, and he was removed from the Johnsons' home. Among other things, Kameron was believed to have inappropriately touched the Johnsons' biological son. Jane remained with the Johnsons though, and her adoption was finalized on November 6, 2003.

Approximately one year later, Kameron admitted to his therapist that he had sexually abused Jane prior to SCDSS's removal of them from the birth home. Kameron also claimed to have sexually abused seven foster children while in foster care, both before and after his placement with the Johnsons. Kameron's social worker notified the Johnsons that Kameron had claimed to have had an inappropriate sexual relationship with Jane prior to SCDSS's taking custody of them, but Jane told her therapist "that Kameron was lying and that they were still having 'sex' until they moved in with [the Johnsons]." She also claimed that she told Thompson and Flesch that Kameron had sexually abused her while she was with the Hamericks and at other foster homes that she could not recall, although she was inconsistent as to whom she told first. According to Jane, Thompson "told her not to tell anyone or they would never adopt her." Thompson denies that Jane made any such report to her. She claims that she received no reports of any inappropriate behavior or contact between Jane and Kameron occurring during her relationship with Jane, and represents that she never observed any behavior which would have led her to believe that Jane and Kameron were having sexual or other inappropriate contact at that time.

Since the disclosure, Jane's behavior has significantly deteriorated. According to the Johnsons, she cannot be left alone or trusted, they are unable to obtain any help supervising her, and they cannot leave her alone with other children for fear that she will act out sexually. Among other things, she is physically and sexually aggressive, violent towards the Johnsons and their biological children, and abusive to animals. Her behavior has necessitated therapeutic placements outside the home, and further care and treatment is believed to be indicated.

The Johnsons subsequently filed suit on their own behalf, and as parents and guardians of Jane, against Thompson. They alleged under §1983 that Thompson violated Jane's substantive due process rights under the Fourteenth Amendment by placing her in foster care settings with Kameron knowing that Kameron was sexually abusive toward Jane.

The issue before us today . . . is whether a child who has been involuntarily removed from her home by state officials for abuse or neglect, placed in the legal custody of the SCDSS, and transferred to state-approved foster care by SCDSS officials can state a substantive due process claim against a state social worker for violations of her fundamental right to personal safety and security analogous to that recognized in *Estelle* for prisoners and in *Youngberg* for the involuntarily committed and, if so, what degree of culpability must be demonstrated to subject the social worker to liability under §1983.

As the *DeShaney* Court noted, several circuit courts had already "held, by analogy to *Estelle* and *Youngberg,* that the State may be held liable under the Due Process Clause for failing to protect children in foster homes from mistreatment at the hands of their foster parents." . . .

Since *DeShaney,* additional circuits have also recognized the right of a foster child to bring a substantive due process claim where state officials have taken the affirmative action of involuntarily removing the child from his home and placing him in a known, dangerous foster care environment, in deliberate indifference to the child's right to reasonable safety and security. In *K.H. ex rel. Murphy v. Morgan*, 914 F.2d 846 (7th Cir. 1990), for example, the court distinguished *DeShaney* and applied a custodial exception to recognize a due process claim where a child was involuntarily removed from the custody of his parents and placed by child welfare workers with a foster parent the state knew or suspected to be a child abuser:

> This is not a "positive liberties" case, like *DeShaney,* where the question was whether the Constitution entitles a child to governmental protection against physical abuse by his parents or by other private persons not acting under the direction of the state. The Supreme Court agreed with this court that there is no such entitlement. Here, in contrast, the state *removed* a child from the custody of her parents; and having done so, it could no more place her in a position of danger, deliberately and without justification, without thereby violating her rights under the due process clause of the Fourteenth Amendment than it could deliberately and without justification place a criminal defendant in a jail or

prison in which his health or safety would be endangered, without violating his rights either under the cruel and unusual punishments clause of the Eighth Amendment (held applicable to the states through the Fourteenth Amendment) if he was a convicted prisoner, or the due process clause if he was awaiting trial. In either case the state would be a doer of harm rather than merely an inept rescuer, just as the Roman state was a doer of harm when it threw Christians to lions.

Id. at 848-849; *see Hutchinson ex rel. Baker v. Spink*, 126 F.3d 895, 900 (7th Cir. 1997) ("[O]nce the State removes a child from her natural parents, it assumes at least a rudimentary duty of safekeeping. It cannot place a child in custody with foster parents it knows are incompetent or dangerous"[;] *see also Nicini v. Morra*, 212 F.3d 798, 808 (3d Cir. 2000) (en banc) ("[W]hen [a] state places a child in state-regulated foster care, the state has entered into a special relationship with that child which imposes upon it certain affirmative duties" which, if attended to in a manner deliberately indifferent to the safety of the child, can give rise to liability under §1983); *Norfleet v. Arkansas Dep't of Human Servs.*, 989 F.2d 289, 293 (8th Cir. 1993) ("[A] special custodial relationship . . . was created by the state when it took [a child] from his caregiver and placed him in foster care" where the "child los[t] his freedom and ability to make decisions about his own welfare, and must rely on the state to take care of his needs."); *Yvonne L. v. New Mexico Dep't of Human Servs.*, 959 F.2d 883, 893 (10th Cir. 1992) ("[C]hildren in the custody of a state ha[ve] a constitutional right to be reasonably safe from harm" and "if the persons responsible place children in a foster home or institution that they know or suspect to be dangerous to the children they incur liability if the harm occurs."); *Meador v. Cabinet for Human Res.*, 902 F.2d 474, 476 (6th Cir. 1990) (holding that substantive "due process extends the right to be free from the infliction of unnecessary harm to children in state-regulated foster homes" where the complaint alleged that the state officials "were 'deliberately indifferent' to reports of abuse" in the foster home).

Relying upon a trilogy of cases discussed below, Thompson contends that our circuit, in contrast to our sister circuits, has answered *DeShaney*'s unresolved question in the negative and would not recognize such a claim of deliberate indifference in the foster care placement, and the district court "reject[ed] plaintiffs' attempt to establish a custodial or foster care exception to the *DeShaney* rule," even in the limited context that we face today. While we agree with Thompson's alternative contention that any such right was not clearly established at the time she made her placement decisions in this case, we disagree that they foreclose our recognition of such a right in appropriate cases.

In *Milburn v. Anne Arundel County Department of Social Services*, 871 F.2d 474 (4th Cir. 1989), a minor child who had been voluntarily placed in foster care by his parents sustained significant injuries which were reported by medical providers to social services officials as suspected child abuse. After the fourth such incident, the officials intervened and removed the child from the foster home. Applying *DeShaney*, we held that the child had no substantive due process right to affirmative protection by the state. First, the state "by the affirmative exercise of its power had *not* restrained the [child's] liberty; he was voluntarily placed in the foster home by his natural parents." *Id.* at 476 (emphasis added). In addition, "the injuries to the [child] did not occur while he was in the custody of the State of Maryland, [but] rather while he was in the custody of his foster parents, who were not state actors." *Id.* There being no affirmative exercise of the state's power to restrain the child's liberty in the first instance, there could be no corresponding duty or responsibility on the part of the state officials to protect the child from harm by private parties. *See K.H.*, 914 F.2d at 849 (noting our decision in *Milburn* to be "[c]onsistent with [its custodial] distinction," as *Milburn* "emphasize[d] the state's lack of responsibility for a child's *voluntary* placement by the natural parents in an abusing private foster home"); *cf. Walton v. Alexander*, 44 F.3d 1297, 1303-1304 (5th Cir. 1995) (en banc) ("Since *DeShaney* was decided . . . , we have followed its language strictly and have held consistently that *only* when the state, by its affirmative exercise of power, has custody over an individual *involuntarily or against his will* does a 'special relationship' exist between the individual and the state.").

In *Weller v. Department of Social Services*, 901 F.2d 387 (4th Cir. 1990), we held that a foster child could not maintain a substantive due process claim against state agents who had affirmatively removed the child from the home of his natural father, upon allegations of abuse, where the child was immediately transferred to the custody of his natural grandmother and then to his natural mother. At no point was the child in foster care, nor was there any prior indication that the family members to whom the child was transferred posed any danger to the child. We agreed "that *DeShaney* [was] applicable to the extent that Maryland had no duty to provide [the child] with protective services" in the first instance and held that "the transfer of custody [from one family member to another] did not make the State 'the permanent guarantor' of [the child's] safety." *Id.* at 392 (quoting *DeShaney*, 489 U.S. at 201, 109 S. Ct. 998). Also, as in *Milburn,* any actual physical harm that was inflicted upon the child at the hands of his family members "was not [harm] inflicted by the State." *Id.*

This brings us to the case of *White ex rel. White v. Chambliss*, 112 F.3d 731 (4th Cir. 1997), and the one most analogous to the case before us. In *White*, SCDSS officials involuntarily removed Keena White, a minor child, from the physical custody of her natural mother and placed her in an approved foster home, where she later died from severe blows to the head. The mother brought a §1983 action alleging that the SCDSS officials had a duty to protect Keena from abuse after her placement in foster care and, in the alternative, had been deliberately indifferent in their placement of Keena in the foster home.

We rejected the plaintiff's claim that there was a general duty on the part of the SCDSS workers to protect the child from abuse after she was placed with the foster family because "children placed in foster care ha[ve] no federal constitutional right to state protection" and "the state ha[s] no affirmative constitutional obligation to protect individuals against private violence." *Id.* at 737 (citing *Milburn*, 871 F.2d at 476); *see id.* at 738 ("'[H]arm suffered by [the] child at the hands of h[er] foster parents [wa]s not harm inflicted by state agents,'" (quoting *Weller*, 901 F.2d at 392)). We further noted that, as it pertains to this principle, *Milburn* was not limited in "its application to situations where parents had voluntarily placed their children in foster care." *Id.*

In this case, SCDSS takes the position that no protection means no protection and that Fourth Circuit law allows SCDSS officials to also escape §1983 liability when they affirmatively place a child in a known dangerous environment, including, for example, with a known child predator. However, in *White*, we declined to dispose of the question of whether a §1983 action could be maintained against a social worker who knowingly places a child in a dangerous foster care environment, in deliberate indifference to the child's fundamental right to personal safety and security. Instead, we held that the factual record before us there fell short of demonstrating any such deliberate indifference. *See id.* at 737 ("Whatever the clearly established law on this question, White's claim simply falls short on the facts. The summary judgment record contains no evidence to indicate that any of the DSS defendants knew or suspected that the [foster parents] were abusive foster parents when they placed Keena in their care. Indeed, the [foster parents] were licensed by the DSS, and White points to no evidence indicating that the [foster parents] had previously been accused of, or investigated for, child abuse."). Such "[a] claim of deliberate indifference, unlike one of negligence," we held, "implies at a minimum that defendants were plainly placed on notice of a danger and chose to ignore the danger notwithstanding the notice." *Id.*

We now hold that when a state involuntarily removes a child from her home, thereby taking the child into its custody and care, the state has taken an affirmative act to restrain the child's liberty, triggering the protections of the Due Process Clause and imposing "some responsibility for [the child's] safety and general well-being." *DeShaney*, 489 U.S. at 200, 109 S. Ct. 998. Such responsibility, in turn, includes a duty not to make a foster care placement that is deliberately indifferent to the child's right to personal safety and security. This does not mean that social workers will be duty-bound to protect the child from unknown harm or dangers. Nor "does [it] mean that every child in foster care may prevail in a section 1983 action against state officials based on incidental injuries or infrequent acts of abuse." *Taylor*, 818 F.2d at 797. Negligence, and even carelessness, on the part of such officials that results in harm to the child will not support a claim. But "where it is alleged and the proof shows that the state officials were deliberately indifferent to the welfare of the child," liability may be imposed. *Id.* Such "[a] claim of deliberate indifference, unlike one of negligence, implies at a minimum that defendants were plainly placed on notice of a danger and chose to ignore the danger notwithstanding the notice." *White*, 112 F.3d at 737.

Here, Jane was involuntarily removed from the custody of her natural parents by affirmative state action and ultimately placed in foster care approved by SCDSS. The state filed a complaint in family court alleging abuse, sought emergency and temporary custody and, ultimately, terminated the parental rights of her biological parents by judicial order. *See* S.C. Code Ann. §20-7-1576 ("An order terminating the relationship between parent and child . . . divests the parent and the child of all legal rights, powers, privileges, immunities, duties, and obligations with respect to each other, except the right of the child to inherit from the parent."). Thus, unlike the children in *DeShaney*, *Milburn* and *Weller*, Jane was clearly within the custody and control of the state social services department when foster care placement decisions were made. Accordingly, the state officials responsible for those decisions had a corresponding duty to refrain from placing her in a known, dangerous environment in deliberate indifference to her right to personal safety and security.

WILKINSON, CIRCUIT JUDGE, concurring in the judgment:

. . . The first potential result of today's decision is to dissuade states from assuming legal custody of children altogether. As *DeShaney* made clear, and as the majority admits, if a state avoids taking custody of a child, it cannot be held legally responsible for harm suffered by the child, even if the state knew about the harm and stood by to watch. *DeShaney v. Winnebago County Dep't of Soc. Servs.*, 489 U.S. 189, 201, (1989). A "duty to protect" arises, if at all, "only if the state takes an individual into custody; if there is no custodial relationship, then the state has no duty to protect." *Patten v. Nichols*, 274 F.3d 829, 841 (4th Cir. 2001).

By contrast, if a state takes legal custody of a child, it now potentially faces steep liability. Before this decision, a state taking custody of a child from her biological parents, against the parents' wishes, already risked one form of litigation: a section 1983 suit by the biological parents for a violation of their substantive due process rights to "retain custody over and care for their children, and to rear their children as they deem appropriate." *Jordan ex rel. Jordan v. Jackson*, 15 F.3d 333, 342 (4th Cir. 1994). Now, after this decision, a state taking custody of a child from her biological parents, against the parents' wishes, is subject to a second form of litigation: a section 1983 suit by the child herself, perhaps brought many years after the initiation of custody, for a violation of the child's substantive due process rights to "safety and general well-being." By piling on this additional cause of action, the majority has littered the path to protecting children with section 1983 landmines.

Thus, in deciding whether to assume custody of a child, states are faced with two possible choices: allow the child to continue to suffer, with no accompanying risk of liability, or rescue the child and quite possibly defend against two lawsuits. It doesn't take a Law and Economics scholar to figure out how these prospects will affect rational state actors. The majority's "duty to protect" essentially rewards states for the exact opposite: for not protecting and for doing nothing. . . .

DISCUSSION QUESTIONS   FOR *DOE v. SOUTH CAROLINA DEPARTMENT OF SOCIAL SERVICES*

A. Given the facts as reported in the case, what did the state agency know and when did they have information concerning the dangerousness of the placement?

B. What is the analysis of the majority with respect to the *DeShaney* decision?

C. How does the majority distinguish the cases discussed in this opinion? In what situations would the state not be potentially liable?

D. What are the objections of the concurring judge? Do you agree with them? Why or why not?

General Principles

1. Historically, children were viewed as the responsibility and exclusive property of their parents and absent serious injury courts did not interfere with the exercise of parental authority over children.

2. Parents have a constitutionally protected liberty interest in raising and disciplining their children.

3. The state does not have an affirmative duty to protect children who are in the care of their parents.

4. The Indian Child Welfare Act (ICWA) provides special protections for Native American children who may be victims of abuse or neglect.

5. Some specially situated professionals are required to report abuse or neglect and reasonable suspicions of abuse or neglect encountered in the course of their employment. Mandatory reporters typically include social workers, teachers, registered nurses, physicians, therapists, and in some states, clergy and attorneys.

6. Civil child protection proceedings generally involve a two-step process of adjudication and disposition.

7. States have varying statutory definitions of abuse, neglect, and dependency. Generally, abuse involves physical, sexual, and/or serious psychological harm. Neglect arises when parents fail to provide adequate food, housing, medical care, or oversight of education. Dependency similarly involves failure to provide for basic needs but the failure is not attributed to the fault of the parent.

8. Parents have a legal obligation to protect children from reasonably anticipated danger, and a parent who does not do so may be found to have neglected his or her child.

9. States generally authorize parents to use reasonable force to correct a child but in application, courts may differ concerning whether the force used by a parent was "reasonable" or whether it constituted child abuse.

10. When a state involuntarily removes a child from the care of parents, the state has an obligation to protect the safety of the child.

11. States must make "reasonable efforts" to reunify the family.

Chapter Problems

1. Medical neglect occurs when parents fail to obtain necessary treatment for children. When should courts honor parents' religious views regarding treatment and when should the state intervene on behalf of an ill child?

2. The Child Abuse and Prevention Treatment Act (CAPTA) defines the withholding of medically indicated treatment as follows:

(5) the term "withholding of medically indicated treatment" means the failure to respond to the infant's life-threatening conditions by providing treatment (including appropriate nutrition, hydration, and medication) which, in the treating physician's or physicians' reasonable medical judgment, will be most likely to be effective in ameliorating or correcting all such conditions, except that the term does not include the failure to provide treatment (other than appropriate nutrition, hydration, or medication) to an infant when, in the treating physician's or physicians' reasonable medical judgment—

(A) the infant is chronically and irreversibly comatose;

(B) the provision of such treatment would—

(i) merely prolong dying;

(ii) not be effective in ameliorating or correcting all of the infant's life-threatening conditions; or

(iii) otherwise be futile in terms of the survival of the infant; or

(C) the provision of such treatment would be virtually futile in terms of the survival of the infant and the treatment itself under such circumstances would be inhumane.

42 U.S.C.A. §5106g (2010). What might be the policy reason for the exception?

3. You are contacted by a legislator interested in passing a statute providing that if a pregnant woman uses illegal drugs during pregnancy, the state could remove the child from her care immediately after birth. What policy considerations will you advise the legislator to consider?

Preparation for Practice

1. Locate the statute(s) defining abuse, neglect, and/or dependency in your state. What terms are used?

2. Some states maintain a central registry of abuse reports, involving some credible evidence, for use by prospective employers. What are reasons to keep such a registry? What safeguards should be in place? Might the maintenance of this registry jeopardize the rights of persons whose names appear on them? *See Valmonte v. Bane*, 18 F.3d 992 (2d Cir. 1994) (holding New York registry statute unconstitutional).

3. Review "A Coordinated Response to Child Abuse and Neglect: The Foundation for Practice" (2003) located at http://www.childwelfare.gov/pubs/usermanuals/foundation/index.cfm (last visited August 8, 2015). According to Chapter 16, what factors contribute to child abuse and neglect? How can child abuse and neglect be prevented?

4. Read the executive summary of *Child Welfare Outcomes 2009-2012: Report to Congress* located at http://www.acf.hhs.gov/programs/cb/resource/cwo-09-12 (last visited July 27, 2015). What information, if any, surprises you? Do you think that current efforts to prevent and ameliorate child maltreatment are successful? Why or why not?

Involuntary Termination of Parental Rights

17.1 INTRODUCTION

This chapter deals with unfortunate and often tragic situations where the state intervenes to permanently end a parent-child relationship. As you consider this drastic remedy, you may be curious about the following questions: When can the state seek termination of parental rights? What are the relevant legal standards? What are the consequences of termination? What procedural protections are provided? How does the child protection agency decide whether to continue reunification efforts or seek termination? What special provisions apply to American Indian children?

REFLECTIVE QUESTIONS	What are your goals for this chapter?

17.2 CONSTITUTIONAL PROTECTION: CONSEQUENCES OF TERMINATION

The family unit is a foundational social institution entitled to constitutional protection. Although the Supreme Court has held that natural parents of a child possess a Fourteenth Amendment liberty interest in their care and custody, the liberty interest is not absolute. *See Prince v. Massachusetts*, 321 U.S. 158, 169-170 (1944) (parents have no absolute right to direct activities of their children). A state, by virtue of its *parens patriae* power, may interfere with parental rights in order to preserve and promote the welfare of a child. The most extreme form of state intervention involves the permanent severance of the relationship between a child and his or her parents, that is, a termination of parental rights proceeding.

Termination of parental rights ends the parent-child relationship. Consequently, the parents no longer have the right to care for or visit the child and the child becomes available for adoption. Recognizing the seriousness of termination, one judge wrote:

> As the critical inquiry, a determination of current parental unfitness is not focused upon "whether the parent is a good one, let alone an ideal one; rather, the inquiry is whether the parent is so bad as to place the child at serious risk of peril from abuse, neglect, or other activity harmful to the child." . . . "Parental unfitness . . . means more than ineptitude, handicap, character flaw, conviction of a crime, unusual life style, or inability to do as good a job as the child's foster parent. Rather, the idea of 'parental unfitness' means 'grievous shortcomings or handicaps' that put the child's welfare much at hazard."

In re Adoption of Leland, 842 N.E.2d 962 (Mass. App. 2006).

Background to *In re Desmond F.*

Sometimes parents facing termination actions choose not to contest them. In the case of *In re Desmond F.*, the Supreme Court of Wisconsin considers the rights of parents in such situations and explores the practical and legal consequences of termination of parental rights.

IN RE DESMOND F.
Supreme Court of Wisconsin
795 N.W.2d 730 (2011)

BRADLEY, J. In October 2008, Desmond was adjudged to be a child in need of protection or services. He was placed outside the home, in the care of foster parents. Nine months later, the Brown County Department of Human Services (the County) filed a petition for involuntary termination of Brenda's parental rights. As grounds, the County alleged that Desmond was in continuing need of protection or services and also that Brenda failed to assume parental responsibility for Desmond.

Through her attorney, Brenda opposed the petition, demanded a jury trial for the fact-finding hearing, and waived the statutory time limits. Trial was scheduled for October 6, 2009.

However, at a hearing that took place one day before the scheduled trial, Brenda's attorney advised the court that Brenda intended to plead no contest to the petition's allegation that there were grounds for termination. He explained that Brenda still intended to contest the ultimate disposition:

> My client and I will talk some more but she [has] indicated to me that she understands the procedure 'cuz I explained it to her. . . .
>
> I explained to her the purpose of a jury trial and the rights that go along with it. We've talked. . . .
>
> My client indicates to me that she is going to agree to waive her right to have a jury trial in this case and she [has] made it clear to me that she wishes to contest the ultimate disposition in this case where she would argue to the Court that it's not in the best interests of the child to terminate her parental rights.
>
> She's — she has clearly advised me that she does not want to give up her parental rights and she's made it clear to me after we further discussed this case that she does not wish to have a trial.

The County agreed that if Brenda did not contest that Desmond was in continuing need of protection or services, the County would move to dismiss the remaining alleged ground for termination, failure to assume parental responsibility.

On the following morning, the circuit court placed Brenda under oath and engaged her in a colloquy to determine whether she knowingly, voluntarily, and intelligently intended to plead no contest to grounds for termination. The court's colloquy was lengthy, occupying 20 pages of hearing transcript. Additionally, both Brenda's counsel and counsel for the County addressed Brenda and made extensive inquiries relating to her plea.

The court began by ascertaining Brenda's age, educational level, mental state, satisfaction with her attorney, and ability to read, write, and understand English. Brenda acknowledged that she had reviewed the petition and its attachment with her attorney, and she stated that she did not have any questions.

Brenda informed the court that she wanted to plead no contest to grounds for termination. The court inquired into whether Brenda understood the procedural rights she was waiving by entering the plea, including the right to call witnesses, the right to cross-examine witnesses, and the right to remain silent without having anyone comment upon her silence. It inquired into whether Brenda understood that she was giving up the right to make the County prove the elements of continuing need of protection or services by clear and convincing evidence.

The court explained that the question at the fact-finding hearing would have been whether there were grounds to terminate her parental rights:

> [W]hat this whole hearing would be about is not whether you're terminate — your parental rights should be terminated. That's ultimately my decision in the disposition hearing. I can either grant the petition to terminate your parental rights or dismiss the petition to terminate your parental rights.
>
> What this is — what this trial would be is [to] see if there are facts to terminate your parental rights on. It's called a fact-finding hearing. Do you understand that?

Brenda responded that she understood. The court outlined the jury instructions and the special verdict questions, and Brenda attested that she understood the findings a jury would have to make.

Upon the court's questioning, Brenda indicated she understood that if the court accepted her plea, the court would be required to make a finding of parental unfitness. The court inquired:

> [I]f you make a no contest plea and I accept your plea . . . I have to make a finding of parental unfitness. Do you understand that?

Brenda indicated that she understood.

The court informed Brenda that once grounds for termination were found, the next phase would consist of a dispositional hearing. It explained that at the dispositional hearing, the court could either grant the petition or dismiss the petition, and that decision would be made based on the best interests of the child:

> I can grant the petition at a dispositional hearing or I can dismiss the petition at a dispositional hearing.
>
> Those are the two alternatives and by case law I have to explain to you that those are the alternatives. The standard that I use at the dispositional hearing is different than the standard at a fact-finding hearing. The standard is the best interest of the child.

The court outlined the factors that it would consider at disposition and explained: "I make my decisions based on the best interest of the child." Brenda indicated that she understood the factors that would be considered by the court using the best interests of the child standard.

After the court finished its colloquy with Brenda, counsel for the County questioned Brenda. Among other inquiries, he asked whether she understood that by pleading no contest, she was giving up her right to fight the County's allegation that Desmond was in continuing need of protection or services, and that by giving up her right to fight that allegation, she could lose her parental rights to Desmond at the dispositional hearing:

Q: You understand that by pleading no contest you give up your right to fight the County's allegation that the child is in continuing need of protection or services?

A: Yes.

Q: . . . Do you understand that by giving up your right to fight that allegation you could lose your parental rights to Desmond [] at the dispositional hearing?

A: Yes.

Counsel for the County also inquired about Brenda's understanding of the specific rights she would lose if her parental rights were terminated at the dispositional hearing:

Q: Do you understand that at the dispositional hearing, if the Court terminates your parental rights, you will lose the right to have visitation with your child?
A: Yes.
Q: You will lose the right to know any information about your child including where the child is going to school and information about the child's health?
A: Yes.
Q: Are—that you will lose the right to make any decisions for your child?
A: Yes.
Q: That the child will not have the right to inherit from you?
A: Yes.
Q: That you will not have the right to inherit from your child?
A: Yes.
Q: That you will no longer have the right to custody of the child?
A: Yes.

In response to further questioning by counsel for the County, Brenda acknowledged that she was aware that the County had identified Desmond's current foster mother as a proposed adoptive parent. Likewise, she acknowledged that county employees had discussed various alternatives that might be available for Desmond's custody, including custody with the Department of Human Services, foster home placement, residential care, and institutionalization.

In response to questioning from her own attorney, Brenda professed to understand how termination of parental rights proceedings operate. She acknowledged that she was familiar with the evidence in the case, and she agreed that some of the evidence was positive and some of the evidence was negative.

Before making any findings, the court asked Brenda whether she had any questions, and Brenda responded that she had none. The court then accepted her no contest plea and concluded that it was tendered "freely, voluntarily and intelligently":

> After a discussion with [Brenda] here on the record I asked her a variety of questions, received a variety of responses and [the guardian *ad litem*] made a statement and [Brown County's counsel] made statements and he asked questions as—as well did [Brenda's counsel].
>
> I am finding that she freely, voluntarily and intelligently tendered a plea of no contest to the petition and the supplement too. I do find that there's a factual basis in the petition; in the supplement thereto for a fact-finding under 48.415(2)(a). So I will accept her no contest plea here today.

The court indicated that Brenda was "very composed," that she "articulated well," and that she "appeared to be very confident of her responses" and "asked appropriate questions." It scheduled the dispositional hearing for the following month.

At the scheduled dispositional hearing, the court initially made the finding of unfitness that had been deferred from the grounds phase of the proceedings. Brenda then testified, as did the proposed adoptive mother and the county social worker who had initiated the petition.

In a memorandum decision issued several days later, the circuit court terminated Brenda's parental rights to Desmond. It explained that the "ultimate decision whether to terminate parental rights is discretionary." After discussing the statutory factors, it concluded that terminating Brenda's parental rights was in Desmond's best interests. It transferred parental rights to the State Department of Children and Families pending adoption.

Brenda filed a notice of appeal. On Brenda's request, the court of appeals remanded the matter to the circuit court for further proceedings so that Brenda could file a motion to withdraw her no contest plea. On remand in the circuit court, Brenda argued that the colloquy preceding her no contest plea was deficient in two respects. She contended that the circuit court should have inquired into whether she understood that she was waiving her constitutionally protected right to act as a parent by pleading no contest. Brenda also argued that the circuit court was required to ascertain whether she understood all of the potential dispositions available under Wis. Stat. §48.427. Brenda asserted that she had been unaware of the implications of her no contest plea with respect to these two matters. . . .

III

To provide context to our discussion, we begin by setting forth the nature of parental rights as well as the procedures under Wisconsin statutes by which parental rights may be involuntarily terminated. Then, we turn to address Brenda's arguments about the requirements of a plea colloquy. Finally, we apply the requirements we set forth to the colloquy given in this case.

"A parent's desire for and right to the companionship, care, custody, and management of his or her children is an important interest that undeniably warrants deference and, absent a powerful countervailing interest, protection." . . . The parent-child relationship is recognized as a fundamental liberty interest protected by the Fourteenth Amendment. *Steven V. v. Kelley H.*, 2004 WI 47, ¶22, 271 Wis. 2d 1, 678 N.W.2d 856 (citing *Santosky v. Kramer*, 455 U.S. 745, 753, 102 S. Ct. 1388, 71 L. Ed. 2d 599 (1982)).

Nevertheless, Wisconsin's Children's Code, Wis. Stat. ch. 48, provides that "under certain circumstances" a court "may determine that it is in the best interests of the child for the child to be removed from his or her parents, consistent with any applicable law relating to the rights of parents." Termination of parental rights adjudications are "among the most consequential of judicial acts" because they involve the power of the State to "permanently extinguish[]" any legal recognition of the rights and obligations existing between parent and child. "When the State moves to destroy weakened familial bonds, it must provide the parents with fundamentally fair procedures." . . .

Initially, the parental right is considered paramount "until there has been an appropriate judicial proceeding demonstrating that the state's power may be exercised to terminate that right." . . . A court may not terminate parental rights without first making an individualized determination that the parent is unfit. *Stanley v. Illinois*, 405 U.S. 645, 649, 92 S. Ct. 1208, 31 L. Ed. 2d 551 (1972).

Once an unfitness determination is made, however, it is the best interests of the child rather than the rights of the parent that is considered "paramount." To accommodate the different and sometimes conflicting interests involved, termination of parental rights proceedings are bifurcated into two phases.

The first phase consists of a fact-finding hearing, where the purpose is to determine whether parental unfitness can be proven. During this first phase, the parent receives a full complement of procedural rights. The burden is on the petitioner to demonstrate by clear and convincing evidence that grounds for termination exist. If the petitioner meets that burden, the court must find the parent to be unfit.

An unfitness finding does not predetermine the ultimate outcome of the proceedings. Rather, a finding of unfitness permits the court to move on to the second phase of the proceedings, the dispositional phase. During the dispositional phase, the court determines whether the parent's rights will be terminated and if so, what will happen to the child. It is the best interests of the child that is the "polestar" at the dispositional hearing.

IV

Under the procedures outlined above, it is during the first phase of an involuntary termination of parental rights proceeding that the parent's interest in the parent-child relationship is most jealously protected. A parent who chooses to enter a no contest plea during this phase is giving up valuable protections and must have knowledge of the rights being waived by making the plea.

. . . The circuit court must engage the parent in a colloquy to ensure that the plea is knowing, voluntary, and intelligent. This colloquy is governed by the requirements of Wis. Stat. §48.422(7) and notions of due process.

If the parent can later show that the colloquy was deficient and also alleges that he or she did not know or understand the information that should have been provided, that parent has made a prima facie case that the plea was not knowing, voluntary, and intelligent. At that point, the burden shifts to the petitioner to demonstrate by clear and convincing evidence that the parent knowingly, voluntarily, and intelligently pled no contest.

According to Brenda's argument, the court was obligated to inform her that, upon the finding of unfitness, she would lose her constitutional right to parent Desmond. She asserts that informing a parent that the plea will result in a finding of unfitness is insufficient because it does not fully inform the parent of the more solemn loss of the constitutionally protected right to parent his or her child.

Under our statutory scheme, it is not accurate to say that a parent loses his or her constitutional right to parent if the court accepts a no contest plea during the grounds phase. Rather, the immediate consequence of the plea is that the parent will be found to be unfit. Even after the parent is found to be unfit, however, the circuit court may in its discretion opt to dismiss the petition after the dispositional hearing, leaving all parental rights intact.

Therefore, the court was not obligated to inform Brenda that, upon acceptance of her plea, she would lose her constitutional right to parent Desmond. As the court of appeals persuasively explained in a recent unpublished opinion, "[b]ecause

Wisconsin statutory law does not permit a court to terminate parental rights upon a finding of unfitness without completing the dispositional phase, we see no rationale for requiring a court to inform a parent that a finding of unfitness results in the automatic loss of the constitutional right to parent."

Nevertheless, whenever a parent wishes to plead no contest to grounds for involuntary termination, the parent must be provided with sufficient information to evaluate the stakes involved. Before a no contest plea can be accepted, a parent must understand that the power of the State may be employed to permanently extinguish any legal recognition of the rights and obligations existing between parent and child. The parent must be given sufficient information to understand the rights that could be lost if, during the second phase of the proceedings, the court decides to terminate parental rights.

It is likewise essential for parents to understand that they are agreeing to waive the protections which safeguard parental rights from permanent extinguishment by the State. The parent must be informed that there are a number of procedural trial rights put in place to prevent parental rights from being terminated without cause, and that these rights are waived with the court's acceptance of the plea.

It is important that the parent understand that by pleading no contest to a ground for termination, the parent is waiving the right to make the petitioner prove unfitness by clear and convincing evidence, and that acceptance of the plea will result in a finding that the parent is unfit.

Finally, the parent must be informed that by pleading no contest to grounds for termination, the parent has waived a fact-finding hearing during the phase of the proceedings in which the parent's rights receive the utmost protection under the Constitution. Should a parent wish to contest termination after he or she is found to be unfit, that parent is left with the sole issue of whether termination of parental rights is in the best interests of the child. Once the parent is found to be unfit, it is the court's determination about what is best for the child rather than any concern about protecting the parent's right that drives the outcome.

At oral argument, Brenda's counsel advanced that it was necessary for a court to explain that the right to parent derives from the Constitution. We disagree that the word "constitutional" has the talismanic significance attributed to it by counsel. What is essential is that a parent understands the nature and import of the rights involved — not necessarily the source of those rights.

Accordingly, given that a finding of parental unfitness does not necessarily result in an involuntary termination of parental rights, we determine that the circuit court was not obligated to inform Brenda that by pleading no contest she was waiving her constitutional right to parent. We additionally determine that the court need not explain that the right to parent is a constitutional right. What is important is that the parent understands the import of the rights at stake rather than the sources from which they are derived. . . .

V

In applying the principles discussed above, we do not provide a specific checklist. The questions to be asked depend upon the circumstances of the case. Under the facts presented here, we conclude that the colloquy provided Brenda with sufficient information to understand the import of the rights at stake. Further, we determine that Brenda received sufficient information to understand the potential dispositions.

During the plea, Brenda was informed that at the dispositional hearing, the power of the State could be employed to permanently extinguish legal recognition of the rights and obligations existing between her and Desmond. Counsel for the County asked if Brenda understood that she "could lose [her] parental rights to Desmond at the dispositional hearing," and Brenda stated that she understood.

Through questioning by counsel for the County, Brenda was provided with additional information to understand the consequences that termination of parental rights would have on her relationship with Desmond. Counsel for the County confirmed her understanding that she could lose custody and the right to care for Desmond, the right to make decisions for Desmond, the right to receive information about Desmond, the right to inherit from Desmond, and the right to visit.

Additionally, Brenda was informed that she had a number of procedural rights, and that she was waiving those procedural rights if the court accepted her plea. Specifically, the court informed Brenda that she was waiving the right to call witnesses, the right to cross-examine witnesses, and the right to remain silent without having anyone comment upon her silence.

Brenda also was advised that her parental rights could not be terminated without the County proving unfitness, and that by pleading no contest, she was waiving the right to have the County prove by clear and convincing evidence that Desmond was in continuing need of protection or services. Brenda professed to understand that she was "giv[ing] up [her] right to fight the County's allegation" that Desmond was in continuing need of protection or services, and that acceptance of her plea would result in a finding of unfitness.

Further, the court advised Brenda that the standard at the dispositional hearing differed from the standard at the fact-finding hearing. It explained that at the dispositional hearing, its decision would be made based on Desmond's best interests, and that the court could determine that it would be in Desmond's best interests to terminate her parental rights.

The court informed Brenda that during the dispositional phase of the proceedings, the court could dismiss the petition or terminate Brenda's parental rights. Brenda acknowledged that she was aware of various alternatives that might be available for Desmond's custody, and that Desmond's current foster mother was considered by the County as a proposed adoptive mother.

Under these circumstances, we conclude that Brenda has failed to present a prima facie case that her plea was not entered knowingly, voluntarily, and intelligently. For that reason, the circuit court did not err by denying Brenda's motion to withdraw her no contest plea.

In sum, given that a finding of parental unfitness does not necessarily result in an involuntary termination of parental rights, we determine that the circuit court was not obligated to inform Brenda that by pleading no contest she was waiving her constitutional right to parent. We additionally determine that the court need not explain that the right to parent is a constitutional right. What is important is that the parent understands the import of the rights at stake rather than the sources from which they are derived.

 **FOR *IN RE DESMOND F.***

A. As the court discussed them, what are the consequences of termination of parental rights?

B. What is required for a parent to enter a knowing, voluntary, and intelligent plea in a termination case? Of what must the parent be advised?

C. Do you think that Brenda should have been advised more extensively or differently than she was? What was the role of her lawyer in this process?

D. What was the standard of proof that was required in this case?

E. In a few states, parents whose rights have been terminated have nevertheless been required to continue to pay child support. Do you think this is a sound policy? Why or why not? *See In re Beck*, 793 N.W.2d 562 (Mich. 2010); *In re Ryan B.*, 686 S.E.2d 601 (W. Va. 2009).

17.3 APPOINTMENT OF COUNSEL

In *Lassiter v. Department of Social Services*, 452 U.S. 18 (1981), the Court held that failure to appoint counsel for indigent parents in a termination proceeding did not deprive a parent of due process where the petition contained no allegations upon which criminal charges could be based, no expert witnesses testified, the case presented no specially troublesome points of law, and presence of counsel would not have made a determinative difference for petitioner. Four Justices dissented. *Lassiter* has been interpreted as requiring a case-by-case balancing test. For example, in *In re "A . . ." Children*, 119 Haw. 28 (Haw. App. 2014), the Hawai'i court held that an indigent father was entitled to counsel under *Lassiter*. The action was intended to divest the father of his parental and custodial rights in his two children. He had not graduated from high school or obtained a general-education diploma, and he was described as marginalized and confused during the proceedings.

Despite the *Lassiter* ruling, states generally provide counsel in such cases:

> In child protection cases involving state-initiated actions to terminate parental rights, the right of an indigent parent to appointed counsel continues to be widely recognized. At the time of the decision in *Lassiter*, all but seventeen states had recognized

such rights, either as a matter of constitutional law or statute. Indeed, since 1979, only one state has curtailed rights to counsel available prior to *Lassiter*, and seven states that had previously limited appointments now provide statutorily for the mandatory appointment of counsel in termination cases, either automatically or on request of a financially-eligible parent. As a consequence, despite the limitations of the Fourteenth Amendment described in *Lassiter*, most indigent parents continue to be entitled to free counsel when they are forced to respond to charges of parental unfitness brought by the state.

Bruce Boyer, *Justice, Access to the Courts, and the Right to Free Counsel for Indigent Parents; The Continuing Scourge of Lassiter v. Department of Social Services of Durham*, 36 Loy. U. Chi. L.J. 363, 367 (2005). As the Florida Supreme Court recently held, when counsel is provided in a termination action a parent may challenge the effectiveness of that counsel. *J.B. v. Florida Dept. of Children & Families*, 2015 WL 4112321 (2015) (". . . we hold that the right to counsel in termination of parental right (TPR) proceedings includes the right to effective assistance and requires a means of vindicating that right").

Native Americans. Appointment of counsel is available as a matter of right for an indigent parent or American Indian custodian in any removal, placement, or termination proceeding. Appointment of counsel for an American Indian child is authorized when deemed in the child's best interests. 25 U.S.C.A. §1912(b) (2015); *see In re Welfare of S.L.J.*, 782 N.W.2d 549, 553 (Minn. 2010) (concluding that ICWA required appointment of counsel, and directing counties to pay fees).

REFLECTIVE QUESTIONS   Do you think that all parents should have a constitutionally protected right to counsel in a termination of parental rights case regardless of their financial circumstances? Why or why not?

17.4 STANDARD OF PROOF

The year after *Lassiter* was decided, the Supreme Court considered the standard of proof required as a matter of due process in termination or parental rights cases. At the time, some states terminated parental rights using the "fair preponderance of the evidence" standard. In *Santosky v. Kramer*, 455 U.S. 745 (1982), the Court found that standard to be insufficient in light of parents' liberty interest in the custody of their children. After balancing the private interests at stake, the risk of error, and the countervailing government interest, the Court concluded that involuntary termination cases must be proven by clear and convincing evidence: "For the child, the likely consequence of an erroneous failure to terminate is preservation of an uneasy status quo. For the natural parents, however, the consequence of an erroneous termination is the unnecessary destruction of their natural family.

A standard that allocates the risk of error nearly equally between those two outcomes does not reflect properly their relative severity." *Id.* at 765-766.

REFLECTIVE QUESTIONS	Can you imagine a hypothetical situation where the evidence meets a preponderance of the evidence standard but is not sufficient to constitute clear and convincing evidence?

17.5 GROUNDS FOR TERMINATION OF PARENTAL RIGHTS: TREATMENT PLAN

As discussed in Chapter 16, if a court makes a finding of abuse or neglect a case plan is developed and executed by the parents. In many cases, parents comply with the case plan, the situation is improved, and the children are returned home. In fact, of children exiting foster care in 2010, 51 percent were reunited with a parent or primary caretaker, 8 percent went to live with other relatives, and only 21 percent were adopted. U.S. Department of Health and Human Services, Administration for Children and Families, Administration on Children, Youth and Families, Children's Bureau, The AFCARS Report #21, http://www.acf.hhs.gov/sites/default/files/cb/afcarsreport21.pdf (last visited July 27, 2015).

When children cannot safely be returned to their parent(s) and "reasonable efforts" have been made to reunify the family, an action for involuntary termination of parental rights may be commenced. Typical statutory grounds for termination of parental rights include continued abuse or neglect or abuse or neglect of other children; abandonment; termination of parental rights to a sibling; chronic parental incapacity due to mental illness or alcohol or drug abuse; lack of contact with the child; felony conviction for violence against a family member; or placement in foster care for 15 of the preceding 22 months. Child Welfare Information Gateway, *Grounds for Involuntary Termination of Parental Rights*, available at https://www.childwelfare.gov/pubPDFs/groundtermin.pdf#page=2&view=Grounds%20for%20Termination%20of%20Parental%20Rights (last visited July 27, 2015).

REFLECTIVE QUESTIONS	What kinds of services would you expect to see included in a case or treatment plan for each of the grounds for termination listed above?

Background to *People ex rel. N.A.T.*

In *People ex rel. N.A.T.* the court considers a mother's claim that her parental rights cannot be terminated because she has sufficiently complied with the treatment plan. The court reviews what the state must prove in order to terminate parental rights and discusses the potential availability of a less drastic alternative.

PEOPLE EX REL. N.A.T.
Court of Appeals of Colorado
134 P.3d 535 (2006)

VOGT, J. . . . Mother next contends that the evidence was insufficient to support the criteria for termination of her parent-child legal relationship with N.A.T. and J.M.T., Jr. She asserts that she completed the significant portions of the treatment plan and that she would be available to parent the children within six months. We disagree. To terminate the parent-child legal relationship pursuant to §19-3-604(1)(c), C.R.S. 2005, clear and convincing evidence must establish that the child has been adjudicated dependent or neglected; that an appropriate treatment plan, approved by the trial court, has not been complied with by the parent or has not been successful in rehabilitating the parent; that the parent is unfit; and that the parent's conduct or condition is unlikely to change within a reasonable time.

The parent is responsible for assuring compliance with and success of a treatment plan. . . . Although absolute compliance is not required, partial compliance, or even substantial compliance, may not result in a successful plan that renders the parent fit. . . . In determining whether a parent can become fit within a reasonable time, a trial court may consider whether any change has occurred during the pendency of the dependency or neglect proceeding, the parent's social history, and the chronic or long-term nature of the parent's conduct or condition. A reasonable time is not an indefinite time, and it must be determined by considering the physical, mental, and emotional conditions and needs of the child. See §19-3-604(3), C.R.S. 2005.

The People have the burden to establish the criteria for termination. . . . The credibility of the witnesses and the sufficiency, probative effect, and weight of the evidence, as well as the inferences and conclusions to be drawn from it, are within the discretion of the trial court. Thus, a trial court's findings and conclusions will not be disturbed on review if the record supports them.

Intervention here was necessitated when N.A.T. was hospitalized at the age of two months with bronchitis and appeared malnourished. Two-year-old J.M.T., Jr. was also underweight. In addition, mother had arrived at the hospital smelling of alcohol, appeared to be under the influence of substances, and she admitted that she drank alcohol during her pregnancy with N.A.T.

To address these concerns, the treatment plan required that mother (1) cooperate with the Denver Department of Human Services and all treatment providers; (2) maintain stable housing and employment; (3) complete parenting classes or individual parenting instruction; (4) participate in a mental health evaluation, if deemed necessary, and follow any recommendations; (5) complete a substance abuse evaluation and follow any recommendations; and (6) ensure that the children's physical, developmental, medical, and educational needs were met upon their return to her custody.

Mother partially complied with the treatment plan. However, she did not follow through on a referral for a mental health evaluation, obtain employment, or cooperate with her caseworker or treatment providers. Further, mother repeatedly tested positive for cocaine and was discharged unsuccessfully from outpatient treatment programs. Although she completed a three-week residential substance abuse treatment program, she did not comply with the recommended outpatient treatment after her release and she relapsed within weeks.

The caseworker testified that, despite having completed parenting classes, mother was unable to attend to the children's needs during her visits with them. The children had special developmental and educational needs resulting from pre-natal alcohol exposure and malnourishment. The child protection worker testified that they needed stable permanent homes, with nurturing caregivers, as soon as possible.

Relying on this evidence, the juvenile court found that mother did not successfully comply with the treatment plan; that mother's continuing use of cocaine interfered with her ability to provide reasonable parental care and rendered her unfit; and that, in light of her lack of progress during the pendency of the proceeding, she would not likely change within a reasonable time. These findings have support in the record and therefore will not be disturbed on review.

Mother further contends that the juvenile court erred in failing to consider less drastic alternatives to termination. Again, we disagree.

Implicit in the statutory scheme for termination set forth in §19-3-604(1)(c) is a requirement that the trial court consider and eliminate less drastic alternatives before entering an order of termination. *People in Interest of M.M.*, 726 P.2d 1108 (Colo. 1986). In so doing, the trial court must give primary consideration to the physical, mental, and emotional conditions and needs of the child. *People in Interest of D.B-J.*, 89 P.3d 530 (Colo. App. 2004); *see* §19-3-604(3).

Mother identified her cousin as a possible placement alternative for the children a few days before the termination hearing. The caseworker made an appointment to discuss the matter with the cousin, but the cousin failed to attend. Likewise, the cousin did not appear at the termination hearing or otherwise indicate that she was willing to provide permanent care for the children.

The maternal grandmother was considered as a placement alternative early in the proceeding. However, a home study rejected placement of the children with her because of inadequate housing. When she was contacted later about having another home study, she responded that she still had "several adults living in the home and . . . [wasn't] able to be a placement option for the kids."

A paternal cousin had also been identified as a placement option. However, when contacted, the cousin indicated that she would not be able to care for the children. Thus, the juvenile court's finding that there were no viable alternatives to termination is supported by the evidence. Accordingly, that finding may not be disturbed on review. . . .

 **FOR** *PEOPLE EX REL. N.A.T.*

A. What was the mother required to do under the treatment plan? Do you think that the treatment plan was appropriate? Was it sufficiently clear? Was it realistic?

B. What are the elements that must be proven in order to terminate parental rights in Colorado? Who has the burden of proof?

C. The court states that a parent should have a reasonable amount of time to comply with the treatment plan. How much time do you think would be reasonable in this case?

17.6 GROUNDS FOR TERMINATION: PRIOR RELINQUISHMENT

Some state termination statutes provide that a prior termination of parental rights serves as grounds for termination of parental rights with respect to another child. These statutes have been challenged on constitutional grounds.

In *In re Welfare of Child of R.D.L.*, 853 N.W.2d 127 (Minn. 2014), a Minnesota statute provided that parents who had previously had their parental rights involuntarily terminated were presumed to be palpably unfit to parent other children. A parent challenged the statute on the grounds that it violated the equal protection provisions of the United States and Minnesota Constitutions. Using a strict standard of scrutiny test, the court held that the mother, whose rights were involuntarily terminated, was similarly situated with parents who voluntarily terminated their parental rights. The court held that the rebuttable statutory presumption of unfitness was narrowly tailored to serve a compelling government interest in the best interests of the child.

> **REFLECTIVE QUESTIONS** | How does a prior relinquishment presumption square with the goal of rehabilitating families? What if a parent's circumstances changed?

Background to *In re Interest of Sir Messiah T.*

In the following case, the Supreme Court of Nebraska rules on a constitutional challenge by a mother (Yolanda) to a Nebraska statute making prior neglect of a sibling a ground for termination of parental rights.

IN RE INTEREST OF SIR MESSIAH T.
Supreme Court of Nebraska
782 N.W.2d 320 (2010)

MILLER-LERMAN, J. . . . . Yolanda's overall claim is that §43-292(2) of the parental rights termination statutes is unconstitutional because it allows the State to terminate parental rights based solely upon a finding that a parent has previously neglected and refused to care for a sibling. We logically read "sibling" to include a child of the parent under review, regardless of whether the parental rights to that sibling have been terminated. Yolanda claims that if her reading is correct, §43-292(2) violates her rights under the Due Process Clause of the 14th Amendment to the U.S. Constitution, because it fails to afford her an opportunity to present evidence showing that her current circumstances do not warrant termination. Yolanda misreads §43-292(2), and we reject her argument. . . .

In Nebraska statutes, the bases for termination of parental rights are codified in §43-292. Section 43-292 (Supp. 2009) currently provides 11 separate conditions, any one of which can serve as the basis for the termination of parental rights when coupled with evidence that termination is in the best interests of the child. Section 43-292, which is applicable to each of the 11 bases, states:

> The court may terminate all parental rights between the parents or the mother of a juvenile born out of wedlock and such juvenile when the court finds such action to be in the best interests of the juvenile and it appears by the evidence that one or more of the following conditions exist[.]

Basis number two, §43-292(2), is at issue in this assignment of error and states that termination is authorized where "[t]he parents have substantially and continuously or repeatedly neglected and refused to give the juvenile or a sibling of the juvenile necessary parental care and protection."

By its terms, §43-292 requires a showing of best interests plus 1 of the 11 statutory bases for termination. Section 43-292(2) involves the neglect of the child or a sibling of the child at issue. Unlike the reading urged by Yolanda, §43-292(2) does not dictate that whenever a parent has neglected a sibling in the past, parental rights to any future children will automatically be terminated without giving the parent an opportunity to present evidence of current circumstances. Instead, the statute as a whole states that prior neglect can be a basis for termination only in conjunction with proof by the State which establishes that termination is in the best interests of the minor children involved in the current proceedings. Indeed, as we have emphasized, and we take this opportunity to repeat, a juvenile's best interests are a primary consideration in determining whether parental rights should be terminated as authorized by the Nebraska Juvenile Code. In deciding best interests, the court is obligated to review the evidence presented by all parties relative to the parent's current circumstances and determine if termination is in the best interests of the minor children based on those circumstances.

For completeness, we note that at trial and on appeal, Yolanda has suggested what may be characterized as a substantive due process claim. Yolanda effectively claims that the neglect of a sibling as provided for in §43-292(2) is not a proper fact for consideration in the current proceeding as it bears on her fitness and that such consideration automatically results in termination and prevents her from receiving due process. Yolanda suggests that due to the termination of parental rights as to her three older children, she should be given a "clean slate" with respect to the four juveniles now under consideration, and that prior neglect should be ignored. The intermediate appellate court of this state rejected a similar argument in *In re Interest of Andrew S.*, 14 Neb. App. 739, 714 N.W.2d 762 (2006), and we reject it in the instant case.

In *In re Interest of Andrew S.*, the Nebraska Court of Appeals considered prior relinquishments as they related to the adjudication then at issue. The Court of Appeals stated that the previous relinquishments

> do not bode well for [the parents'] stability and ability as parents, and they serve to convince us that [the current juvenile] is at risk. The fact that a parent has previously relinquished an adjudicated child is relevant evidence in an adjudication proceeding concerning a child born soon thereafter. In short, given the purpose of the juvenile code, one's history as a parent is a permanent record and may serve as a basis for adjudication depending on the circumstances. Relinquishments of parental rights are not any sort of "pardon," which is how [the parents] would have us treat the relinquishments they made. They cite no authority on point for such notion, and while we have found none either, we suggest that one's history as a parent speaks to one's future as a parent.

Id. at 749, 714 N.W.2d at 769-770.

Courts in other jurisdictions have similarly reasoned in related contexts. In *State ex rel. Children, Youth v. Amy B.*, 133 N.M. 136, 141, 61 P.3d 845, 850 (N.M. App. 2002), the court in a juvenile matter reviewed the jurisprudence in this area and stated that "in most of the reported cases, there is a very real relationship between the past conduct and the current abilities." In a juvenile case considering the prospects of future success as a parent, the California Court of Appeals stated, "Experience has shown that with certain parents . . . the risk of recidivism is a very real concern. Therefore, when another child of that same parent is adjudged a dependent child, it is not unreasonable to assume [that future parenting] efforts will be unsuccessful. . . . We agree with this reasoning which recognizes that one's history as a parent speaks to one's future as a parent and reject Yolanda's suggestion that past parenting outcomes should be ignored. Along with other courts, we believe that neglect of a prior sibling is relevant to the current inquiry and that past neglect, along with facts relating to current family circumstances which go to best interests, are all properly considered in a parental termination case under §43-292(2).

Focusing on the procedural due process Yolanda was accorded herein, the record shows that Yolanda was adequately notified in the "Motion for Termination of Parental Rights and Notice of Hearing" that the State sought to terminate her parental rights to the four children in question on the basis, *inter alia*, of §43-292(2) and that the factual basis alleged under §43-292(2) was prior neglect, i.e., the involuntary termination of parental rights for the neglect of three siblings.

Pursuant to the statute, Yolanda was accorded a full evidentiary hearing, at which hearing she was represented by counsel and had the opportunity to present evidence and cross-examine the witnesses, and the State was required to present clear and convincing evidence of neglect of prior siblings and current best interests. The earlier termination of parental rights to the three siblings for neglect was readily established. With respect to best interests, the evidence showed the needs of the four children involved. The evidence also showed that Yolanda was offered numerous reunification plans, and there was ample current evidence that she was not successful in rehabilitation and reunification. This evidence went to present circumstances.

As the Supreme Court of Montana noted in a similar context under a statute with comparable features, "[t]he statutes . . . do not limit the decision to the facts of the prior [neglect]. The district court also considers any available evidence relating to present family circumstances and the specific child at issue." . . . Like the Montana statute, Nebraska's §43-292(2) requires proof of both best interests and neglect of either the child at issue or a sibling. Unlike Yolanda's reading of §43-292(2), termination of parental rights under this section is not based exclusively on neglect of another sibling. Proof of best interests is also required. The State proffered evidence of both, and Yolanda presented evidence on her own behalf. Given the terms of the statute and the scope and safeguards of the evidentiary hearing which were accorded Yolanda, we reject Yolanda's constitutional challenge to §43-292(2).

DISCUSSION QUESTIONS FOR *IN RE INTEREST OF SIR MESSIAH T.*

A. What did the statute being challenged provide as a ground for termination of parental rights?

B. What was the mother's claim and why did the court reject it?

C. What is the policy basis for the statutory provision? What could you argue in support of it and in opposition to it?

D. Could this action have been brought by the state without reference to §43-292(2)?

E. The Nebraska Supreme Court recognized that one's history as a parent speaks to one's future as a parent. A court need not ignore past parenting outcomes. Do you agree that past performance is a good predictor of future conduct? Or is present conduct the best predictor of future conduct? How much weight should a judge give to past conduct? Present conduct?

17.7 REUNIFICATION AND PERMANENCY PLANNING: REASONABLE EFFORTS

Historically, when the state removed a child from the home, the ultimate goal was to return the child safely to the family. Unfortunately, some children were not able to be reunified with their families, and they spent an inordinate amount of time in foster care (commonly referred to as "foster care drift"). Out of concern about the number of children growing up in foster care, Congress passed the Adoption Assistance and Child Welfare Act (AACWA). The act required the states to make "reasonable efforts" to reunify families but it also required states to undertake "permanency planning," usually in the form of adoption, when reunification was not realistic.

In 1997, based on continuing concern about foster care drift, Congress passed the Adoption and Safe Families Act (ASFA). The act requires states to more aggressively seek to free children for adoption. For example, states are to pursue termination of parental rights if a child has been in foster care for 15 of the preceding 22 months, unless the child has been placed with a relative, reunification services have not been provided, or termination would not be in the best interests of the child. Reasonable efforts to reunify the family are required under ASFA, but exceptions are made for cases involving "aggravated circumstances" or when rights to a sibling have previously been terminated.

The median amount of time spent in foster care for children leaving care in 2013 was 13.5 months. Eleven percent of these children were in foster care for less than one month but 5 percent were in foster care for 5 years or more. Child Welfare Information Gateway, Foster Care Statistics 2013 (April 2015), available at https://www.childwelfare.gov/pubPDFs/foster.pdf (last visited July 27, 2015).

REFLECTIVE QUESTIONS	Under what circumstances might termination of parental rights not be in the best interests of a child who has been in foster care for 15 of the preceding 22 months?

Background to *State ex rel. Children, Youth & Families Dept.*

In the next case, a mother whose parental rights have been terminated alleges that the state did not make reasonable efforts to assist her. The court considers the reasonable efforts requirement under both AACWA and ASFA.

STATE EX REL. CHILDREN, YOUTH & FAMILIES DEPT.

Court of Appeals of New Mexico
47 P.3d 859 (2002)

BOSSON, C.J. Patricia H's parental rights in her child, Elizabeth (Child), were terminated by the district court, pursuant to NMSA 1978, Section 32A-4-28(B)(2) (2001). Patricia H. (Mother) contends that the record is not sufficient to support, by clear and convincing evidence, that: (1) the Children, Youth and Families Department (CYFD) made reasonable efforts to assist her in remedying the causes of her neglect of Child, and (2) further efforts would be futile.

CYFD took custody of Child in March of 1998, when she was 41/2 years old. CYFD did so at the request of Mother who stated that she was no longer able to care for Child and expressed extreme frustration with Child's "defiant" behavior. CYFD had previously received referrals related to a lack of adequate supervision in Child's home. At the time she came into CYFD custody, Child was dirty, unkempt, and hungry. Mother pled no contest to Child being without proper parental care or control necessary to her well-being, and a stipulated judgment was entered on May 27, 1998.

At the time Child was taken into CYFD custody, Mother was experiencing serious health problems, including a thyroid disorder, which reportedly caused her to be unusually irritable. Shortly thereafter, Mother was diagnosed with breast cancer, and underwent a mastectomy in April 1998, followed by a course of radiation therapy, which was completed in July 1998. A psychological evaluation of Mother was completed in June 1998, and CYFD developed a treatment plan based on that evaluation. During the first three months that Child was in CYFD custody, CYFD arranged visits between Child and Mother, but Mother did not engage well with Child at that time. Mother had little contact with Child between June and December of 1998. In October 1998, Mother was hospitalized twice for additional surgeries related to her mastectomy, and subsequently received home-based support and case management services until February 1999.

Following a permanency hearing on December 7, 1998, the court found that Mother had made some efforts to comply with treatment, but ordered that Child was to remain in CYFD custody until further order of the court. The permanency plan at that time was for Child eventually to return home with Mother. The CYFD treatment plan included goals related to improving Mother's parenting skills, and called for individual therapy for Mother, as well as work with Child's therapist. The treatment plan was incorporated by reference into the court's order. . . .

Before parental rights may be terminated, New Mexico law requires that CYFD demonstrate, by clear and convincing evidence, that a child has been neglected or abused as defined by Section 32A-4-2. CYFD must also establish that the "causes of the neglect or abuse are unlikely to change in the foreseeable future, despite reasonable efforts by [CYFD] to assist the parent in adjusting the conditions that render the parent unable to properly care for the child." Finally, CYFD must show that the best interests of the child are served by the termination of parental rights. However, the termination of parental rights cannot be based on a best interests determination alone. "The fact that a child might be better off in a different environment is not a basis for termination of parental rights in this state." The statutory prerequisite of reasonable efforts to assist the parent must be satisfied before parental rights may be terminated.

"Once extraordinary circumstances are shown by clear and convincing evidence, the court should then make a determination based on the best interests of the child." What constitutes reasonable efforts may vary with a number of factors, such as the level of cooperation demonstrated by the parent and the recalcitrance of the problems that render the parent unable to provide adequate parenting. For example, in *State ex rel. Children, Youth & Families Dep't v. Tammy S.*, 1999-NMCA-009, 15, 126 N.M. 664, 974 P.2d 158, we held that the "[f]ather's transience, failure to communicate, and lack of cooperation rendered [CYFD's] efforts sufficient." In that case, we affirmed a futility finding where a father was arrested twice for violent crimes, failed to establish a stable residence, and did not participate in the domestic violence counseling, alcohol treatment, or psychological evaluation recommended by CYFD. In *State ex rel. Children, Youth & Families Dep't v. Vanessa C.*, 128 N.M. 701, 997 P.2d 833, we affirmed a finding of futility where, after two years with only limited progress, a mother continued to use drugs, commit crimes, and choose partners who committed acts of domestic violence.

The duration of what constitutes reasonable efforts has changed considerably over the past several years, as CYFD has truncated the length of time it renders assistance to parents. . . .

Changes in federal legislation have unquestionably had an impact on what is regarded as a reasonable effort. In 1980, Congress passed the Adoption Assistance and Child Welfare Act (AACWA), 42 U.S.C. §§670-79 (1994 & Supp. V 1999), which provided that states would receive federal funding for their child welfare programs if they made reasonable efforts to prevent the removal of children from their homes, and to reunify families whenever possible. Following the promulgation of AACWA, the number of children in foster care actually began to increase, as an emphasis on trying to reunify families resulted in children being kept in foster care for longer periods of time.

In 1997, Congress passed the Adoption and Safe Families Act (ASFA), which encourages states to move more quickly to terminate parental rights and gives states a financial incentive to increase the number of adoptions. ASFA also clarifies that states are not required to make reunification efforts for an indefinite period of time. ASFA describes "time-limited reunification services" as those provided within a fifteen-month period following the placement of a child into foster care, and provides federal funding for this time-limited assistance. These services may include individual, group, and family counseling, substance abuse treatment, mental health services, transportation, child care, and other therapeutic services. ASFA has had a significant impact upon the State's responsibility to provide services to children and families, which consequently informs our contemporary understanding of what constitutes a reasonable effort to assist a parent before the State may resort to termination. The fifteen-month period described in ASFA for "time-limited reunification services" provides us some guidance in how we assess the duration of reasonable efforts under state law. In so doing, we must keep in mind that the use of such a guideline needs to remain flexible and must be harmonized with the requirements of state law. We now turn to the efforts provided by CYFD.

The initial services provided Mother were clearly reasonable. During the first few months of Child's CYFD placement, while Mother was grappling with a major medical illness, CYFD appropriately arranged for visitation between Mother and Child, and provided Mother with a psychological evaluation. In late 1998 and early 1999, Mother was provided with transportation assistance and home-based services. CYFD provided Mother the initial five sessions with Ms. Krauss which ended in January 1999 and, shortly thereafter, offered her referrals for a bonding study and parenting training, which she refused. Mother may have had what she considered to be good faith reasons for her refusal, but CYFD is only required to make reasonable efforts, not efforts subject to conditions unilaterally imposed by the parent.

Subsequently, at the second permanency hearing, in mid-1999, the court ordered CYFD to continue to implement the treatment plan by providing referrals as appropriate. Aside from two "courtesy" visits by the social worker, the record does not show that CYFD provided Mother with any assistance after February of 1999 (six months before the second permanency order). Mother makes much of this lack of assistance, arguing in effect that CYFD gave up on her too soon. Mother has a point that CYFD might have done more to help her during the latter period, particularly with the kind of interactive treatment with her Child that she needed. However, our job is not to determine whether CYFD did everything possible; our task is limited by our statutory scope of review to whether CYFD complied with the minimum required under law. We conclude, albeit with some hesitation, that it did.

Following the second permanency order, CYFD was somewhat constrained in what it could do. There were legitimate concerns about the deleterious effect that contact with Mother could have on Child, arising from CYFD's earlier unsuccessful attempts to work jointly with Mother and Child. The court agreed, and the record supports its conclusion, that visitation should be delayed until an expert could be present to determine whether Mother had made sufficient progress through her own therapy, so that such contact would not be harmful to Child. Although the court ordered the 706 expert to move expeditiously and conduct a bonding study to determine whether things had progressed enough so that parent-child contact could be resumed, the report was delayed until so much time had elapsed that the expert felt a bonding study would be pointless. That conclusion was never challenged by Mother below.

Although Mother did not have the opportunity to be seen jointly with Child to address the interactional problems and parenting deficits previously observed by Ms. Krauss, it was not CYFD that stood in her way. The evidence shows quite clearly that Child is unusually fragile and requires highly skilled parenting. Mother has parenting deficits that apparently coincide with those precise areas in which Child's needs are most acute. Mother rebuffed CYFD's earlier efforts at a bonding study. Later, CYFD followed the court's instructions. After the second permanency order, CYFD's responsibility was largely limited to arranging referrals. Mother has not pointed to any referrals that CYFD should have made, given the restrictions the court placed upon it while the 706 report was pending. CYFD was aware during that time that

Mother's need for individual therapy was being met by Dr. Snyder at the Veteran's Administration. . . .

Considering the totality of the circumstances, the trial court could have concluded that CYFD made reasonable efforts to assist Mother, notwithstanding the court's refusal to make a futility finding at the second permanency hearing and the lack of any CYFD assistance to Mother after that time.

LIKELIHOOD OF CHANGE IN THE FORESEEABLE FUTURE

Before parental rights may be terminated, CYFD must demonstrate that the causes of the neglect or abuse are unlikely to change in the foreseeable future, despite the reasonable efforts of CYFD to assist the parent.

The testimony raised significant questions regarding Mother's present ability to meet Child's specialized needs. If a gradual reintroduction were initiated, Dr. Kenney estimated that the process would take about a year, including preparing Mother for visitation, assessing Mother's readiness, and several months of supervised visitation. Furthermore, Dr. Kenney testified that there was no guarantee that it would work.

We have interpreted the term "foreseeable future" to refer to corrective change within "a reasonably definite time or within the near future." We have also noted that "in balancing the interests of the parents and children, the court is not required to place the children indefinitely in a legal holding pattern."

At the time of the termination hearing, Child had already been in CYFD custody for nearly two and a half years. The trial court could have reasonably concluded that another year might well be too long to wait, particularly where there was considerable doubt as to whether the wait would enable Mother to develop the necessary skills. Having determined that CYFD had made reasonable efforts, the trial court could also properly consider the potential hardship to Child, who is less resilient to change than most other children, in attempting a reintroduction process with Mother. Under these circumstances, the trial court did not act unreasonably in concluding that change was unlikely in the foreseeable future.

While affirming, we note for the record our reservations about CYFD's performance in this case. As of the summer of 1999, all parties and the court had decided to rely upon the intervention and guidance of a 706 expert. Lapse of any additional time was a significant concern to all. When the expert became ill, the report was delayed until one of its very purposes—a closely monitored interactional study of both Mother and Child together—was no longer feasible.

Time became an insurmountable obstacle for Mother in this process. Without the necessary joint therapy with her Child, Mother could not prove her fitness to parent; without the 706 report, she could not obtain that therapy. By the time of the final TPR hearing, it was simply too late to change course given the extreme needs of the Child.

Given the time sensitivity of this case, we are troubled by CYFD's lack of initiative from mid-1999 onward. CYFD failed to take charge of the process, to alert the court in a timely manner about unforeseen delays and their prejudicial impact upon Mother. In effect, CYFD appears to have simply let events take their course until termination was inevitable. Although, for the reasons set forth herein, CYFD may have barely satisfied the requirement of reasonable efforts, especially when considered over the entire period of its responsibility, CYFD cannot be proud of its record at the critical juncture when the process bogged down.

The decision of the district court terminating Mother's parental rights in Child is hereby affirmed.

DISCUSSION QUESTIONS FOR *STATE EX REL. CHILDREN, YOUTH & FAMILIES DEPT.*

A. What burden of proof does New Mexico apply at termination proceedings?

B. In order to terminate parental rights involuntarily, what must CYFD demonstrate?

C. List the facts that persuaded the court to terminate the parental rights of the mother in this case. The court indicated that it had reservations about the state's handling of this case. What were those reservations, and should they have caused the court to reverse the trial judge's ruling?

D. What constitutes reasonable efforts by CYFD to assist the parent in correcting the conditions that rendered the parent unable to care for the child properly? How has the duration of these efforts changed?

E. Simultaneously working toward family reunification and termination of parental rights, commonly referred to as concurrent planning, is controversial. Some of the concerns include the following:

> Concurrent planning has not been the panacea that its creators imagined. Instead, it has had the effect of rushing parents through inadequate family reunification with little forethought for appropriate permanent plans for children. In its current state, it is a system that lacks adequate services, de-emphasizes sibling connections, creates legal orphans without a sufficient supply of adoptive parents, and provides few, if any, front-end services to help families avoid court intervention.

William Wesley Patton & Amy Pellman, *The Reality of Concurrent Planning: Juggling Multiple Family Plans Expeditiously Without Sufficient Resources*, 9 U.C. Davis J. Juv. L. & Pol'y 171, 188-189 (2005). Should concurrent planning continue? Based on the comments above, can you suggest safeguards that might be adopted? *See* Barbara Ann Atwood, *Achieving Permanency for American Indian and Alaska Native Children: Lessons from Tribal Traditions*, 37 Cap. U. L. Rev. 239, 256 (2008) (discussing the Fostering Connections to Success and Increasing Adoptions Act of 2008 as supporting kinship options as an alternative to reunification or adoption).

17.8 REUNIFICATION AND PERMANENCY PLANNING: ICWA

As discussed in Chapter 16, the Indian Child Welfare Act (ICWA) applies when proceedings involve an American Indian child. Under ICWA "active efforts" to rehabilitate the family (rather than reasonable efforts pursuant to ASFA) are required prior to termination of parental rights. In addition, a higher burden of proof, the beyond a reasonable doubt standard, is applied to fact situations. Should adoption result, preference is given to extended family, tribal members, and other American Indians. *See* Barbara Ann Atwood, *Achieving Permanency for American Indian and Alaska Native Children: Lessons from Tribal Traditions*, 37 Cap. U. L. Rev. 239 (2008) (comparing provisions of ICWA and AFSA and analyzing how they "interface").

REFLECTIVE QUESTIONS	**Is there a practical difference between "active efforts" and "reasonable efforts" to rehabilitate a family?**

Background to *J.S. v. State*

In *J.S. v. State*, the Alaska Supreme Court considers a situation where compliance with the "active efforts" requirement of ICWA could place the child in danger.

J.S.
v.
STATE

Supreme Court of Alaska
50 P.3d 388 (2002)

CARPENETI, J. Jack's parental rights were terminated as to his sons Avery, Lyle, and Carl after Jack was convicted of five counts of sexual abuse against them. . . .

Jack argues that the proposed case plan offered by the state in response to the superior court's August 24, 1999 order did not comply with ICWA's requirement that active efforts be made to rehabilitate a family prior to the termination of parental rights. The state and the guardian *ad litem* (GAL) argue that the active efforts requirement was complied with. The state and the GAL also argue that ICWA should be interpreted as not requiring active efforts once a family is irrevocably sundered by parental sexual abuse.

The Indian Child Welfare Act requires the state to prove "active efforts . . . to provide remedial services and rehabilitative programs designed to prevent the breakup of the Indian family." We decide whether active efforts have been made on a case-by-case basis. Generally, the state's duty under the active efforts requirement is not affected by a parent's motivation or prognosis before remedial efforts have commenced. We have previously held that "[n]either incarceration nor doubtful prospects for rehabilitation will relieve the State of its duty under ICWA to make active remedial efforts."

However, the enactment of the Adoption and Safe Families Act of 1997 (ASFA) convinces us that it is the policy of Congress to not require remedial measures in situations where a court has determined that a parent has subjected his or her child to sexual abuse. This enactment amended 42 U.S.C. §671 so as not to require reasonable efforts to be made to preserve the family when "a court of competent jurisdiction has determined that . . . the parent has subjected the child to aggravated circumstances," which includes sexual abuse. Although this case is not governed by ASFA, that act is useful in providing guidance to congressional policy on child welfare issues. It suggests that in situations of adjudicated devastating sexual abuse, such as this one, a person's fundamental right to parent is not more important than a child's fundamental right to safety. Therefore, we hold that active efforts to reunify the abusing parent are not required in a situation after there has been a judicial determination that the parent has subjected the child to sexual abuse. . . .

Jack argues that the evidence presented to the superior court by the state was insufficient to meet the beyond a reasonable doubt standard required by ICWA. Specifically, Jack argues that the expert witnesses did not have sufficient knowledge of the specific facts of this case. . . .

The first expert to testify was Pamela A. Robinson, who has a Bachelor of Science degree in sociology with a minor in psychology and a master's degree in counseling psychology. She testified that prior to getting her master's degree she worked for twenty years in early childhood education and child development, and that she has been qualified as an expert in several other cases. At the time of her testimony, she had been counseling Carl for approximately one and one-half years. Upon the initial consultation, she diagnosed Carl with post-traumatic stress disorder, possible major depression, and adjustment disorder. She stated that she believed that Carl could not be transitioned back to Jack without causing Carl emotional harm.

The second expert to testify was Sandra Husted, who has a bachelor's degree in sociology and a master's degree in counseling. She stated that she was a Clinician II at Providence Mental Health Center in Kodiak from January 1998 until January 1999. At the time of the hearing, she had been licensed as a professional counselor in Texas for nine years. She had been qualified as an expert in psychotherapy and crisis emergency in previous court cases. She testified that she treated Avery from February of 1998 until November of 1998 during which time she saw him approximately every three weeks. She testified that Avery could not be transitioned away from his foster family and back to Jack because of the abuse perpetrated by Jack.

Dr. Robert B. Duthie testified next. He holds a Ph.D. in counseling and clinical psychology and has been board certified in forensic psychology since 1987. He stated that he had been qualified as an expert in at least 100 previous cases. He first met Lyle in June of 1998 and had been following the case ever since. He testified that Lyle had post-traumatic stress disorder arising from the sexual abuse by Jack.

He also testified that Lyle could not successfully be placed back into custody with Jack without emotional harm and risk of continued sexual abuse because Jack has not received treatment nor apologized for the previous abuse.

The fourth expert to testify was Dr. Joseph M. Keville, who has a Bachelor of Science degree in social services and a Ph.D. in education; he has been a licensed psychologist in Massachusetts since 1973. He practices in the area of clinical child psychology. He testified that he had treated approximately 1,000 children in the last ten years. He met with Avery on two occasions and testified that he thought that Avery would have a "severe depressive reaction" if he was forced to leave his foster family.

The fifth expert to testify was Dr. Ronald D. Howes, who has a bachelor's degree and master's degree in psychology and a Ph.D. in clinical psychology. He stated that he had completed over 2,000 hours of clinical internship in forensic psychology with the California Department of Corrections and is board certified in trauma psychology with specialties in sex therapy and treatment of sex addictions. He had testified as an expert in court on numerous occasions. He stated that the recidivism rate for a sex offender increased in cases with same gender sexual abuse, lack of a strong family member supervising the family, and where the abuse was not admitted to by the offender. He stated that, given the situation in this case, the rate of recidivism would be over fifty percent.

There was substantial testimony by experts with personal knowledge of the facts of this case and an expert with substantial expertise in sex offender treatment. The superior court's finding beyond a reasonable doubt that placement with Jack would result in serious emotional damage to the boys was therefore not clearly erroneous. We affirm the termination of Jack's parental rights.

DISCUSSION QUESTIONS FOR *J.S. v. STATE*

A. This court seems to accept the proposition that active remedial efforts aimed at reunification of a family are unnecessary once a family is "irrevocably sundered" by parental sexual abuse. Although governed by ICWA, the court looks to AFSA's "aggravated circumstances" analysis. Why did the court do so? Do you think this was appropriate?

B. The state offered five experts who testified at the termination proceeding. How persuasive is their testimony? Should the state have provided Jack, who is indigent, with funds to hire his own experts? Should the case be reversed if the state failed to provide Jack with this assistance?

C. The ICWA requires that evidence presented to the court by the state at a termination proceeding meet the "beyond a reasonable doubt" standard.

In most jurisdictions, termination occurs when the state meets the "clear and convincing" standard. What possible explanation is there for the higher standard under ICWA?

D. Professor Atwood writes that stability and permanency for American Indian children might encompass tribal care-giving practices not necessarily contemplated under AFSA:

> Two federal laws with contrasting approaches to permanency have particular relevance: the Indian Child Welfare Act of 1978 (ICWA) and the Adoption and Safe Families Act of 1997 (ASFA). While permanency, a centerpiece of ASFA, is not mentioned in ICWA, permanency as a goal for Indian children is consistent with the basic themes of ICWA. Examples from tribal law and traditions reveal that tribes themselves value continuity and stability for children in their primary caregiving relationships. At the same time, tribes often embrace more fluid approaches to permanency than are contemplated under ASFA. These alternative conceptions of permanency reflect the tribes' traditions of shared child-rearing and collective responsibility for children. While a few state courts have begun to recognize tribal care-giving traditions in applying ASFA's command to achieve permanency for foster children, child welfare laws across the country still favor the permanency model of parental rights termination followed by adoption.

Barbara Ann Atwood, *Achieving Permanency for American Indian and Alaska Native Children: Lessons from Tribal Traditions*, 37 Cap. U. L. Rev. 239, 240-241 (2008). From a policy perspective should courts be encouraged to take a more expansive view of permanency? Why or why not?

Background to *Adoptive Couple v. Baby Girl*

The United States Supreme Court recently decided a factually dramatic and contentious case involving ICWA. A predominantly Hispanic birth mother and biological father, a member of the Cherokee Nation, were romantically involved and became engaged to marry in 2008. A month after the engagement, Birth Mother told Biological Father that she was pregnant. He asked her to move up their wedding date. He informed her that he wouldn't provide financial support unless they married. The relationship deteriorated, and the engagement was broken off. In June, months before the September birth of a baby girl, Birth Mother sent Biological Father a text message asking if he would rather pay child support or relinquish his parental rights. He responded via text message that he would relinquish his rights.

Birth Mother decided to put the infant up for adoption and contacted an attorney. The attorney, believing Biological Father had Cherokee Indian heritage, contacted the Cherokee Nation to determine whether Biological Father was a formally enrolled member. The inquiry letter from the attorney misspelled Biological Father's first name and incorrectly stated his birthday. The Cherokee Nation responded that, based on the information provided by the attorney, it could not verify Biological Father's membership in the tribal records.

Working with a private adoption agency, Birth Mother selected a husband and wife non–American Indian couple to adopt the infant. The morning following the infant's birth, Birth Mother signed forms relinquishing her parental rights and consenting to the adoption. The couple initiated adoption proceedings in South Carolina a few days later, and returned there with Baby Girl.

During pregnancy and the first four months after Baby Girl's birth, Biological Father provided no financial assistance to Birth Mother or Baby Girl, although he had the ability to do so.

The couple that intended to adopt the infant served Biological Father with notice of the pending adoption. (This was the first notification that they had provided to Biological Father regarding the adoption proceeding.) He signed papers stating that he accepted service and that he was "not contesting the adoption." Biological Father changed his mind after signing the consent documents and contacted a lawyer. The adoption was contested with a trial taking place in Family Court when the child was now two years old.

The Family Court denied the adoption petition and awarded custody to Biological Father. The child was then placed in the custody of Biological Father, whom she had never met. On appeal, the South Carolina Supreme Court, Toal, J., affirmed. The state supreme court held that two separate provisions of the ICWA barred the termination of Biological Father's parental rights. First, the court held that the adoptive couple had failed to show that "active efforts ha[d] been made to provide remedial services and rehabilitative programs designed to prevent the breakup of the Indian family," as required by 25 U.S.C. §1912(d). Second, the court concluded that the adoptive couple had not shown that Biological Father's "custody of Baby Girl would result in serious emotional or physical harm to her beyond a reasonable doubt" (citing 25 U.S.C. §1912(f)). Finally, the court stated that, even if it had decided to terminate Biological Father's parental rights, 25 U.S.C. §1915(a)'s adoption-placement preferences would have applied. The U.S. Supreme Court granted certiorari.

Biological Father argued a more expansive version of the ICWA. That is, the ICWA applies whenever a court is considering whether to terminate parental rights of an American Indian parent. The adoptive parents argued that ICWA's coverage is limited to the kinds of cases that Congress most likely had in mind when it passed ICWA. Those are cases where social workers and other government officials are seeking to remove American Indian children from an existing American Indian family. In a five-to-four opinion, the Court took selected the latter interpretation.

The issues as the Court saw them were: (1) When, if ever, can a Native American biological non-custodial parent invoke ICWA to block an adoption voluntarily and lawfully initiated by a non–American Indian parent under state law? and (2) Does the definition of "parent" under ICWA include an unwed biological father who has not complied with state law rules to attain legal status as a parent?

The Court limited the application of ICWA holding that ICWA protections related to the legal standard for termination, the active efforts requirement, and the adoptive placement preference did not apply to an American Indian biological father who had not previously had legal or physical custody of the child. As a result of the decision, the child was to be returned to the care of the adoptive family.

ADOPTIVE COUPLE
v.
BABY GIRL

Supreme Court of the United States
133 S. Ct. 2552 (2013)

ALITO, J. . . . We need not — and therefore do not — decide whether Biological Father is a "parent." Rather, assuming for the sake of argument that he is a "parent," we hold that neither §1912(f) nor §1912(d) bars the termination of his parental rights.

II

A

Section 1912(f) addresses the involuntary termination of parental rights with respect to an Indian child. Specifically, §1912(f) provides that "[n]o termination of parental rights may be ordered in such proceeding in the absence of a determination, supported by evidence beyond a reasonable doubt, . . . that the *continued custody* of the child by the parent or Indian custodian is likely to result in serious emotional or physical damage to the child." The South Carolina Supreme Court held that Adoptive Couple failed to satisfy §1912(f) because they did not make a heightened showing that Biological Father's "*prospective* legal and physical custody" would likely result in serious damage to the child. That holding was error.

Section 1912(f) conditions the involuntary termination of parental rights on a showing regarding the merits of "*continued* custody of the child by the parent." The adjective "continued" plainly refers to a pre-existing state. . . . The phrase "continued custody" therefore refers to custody that a parent already has (or at least had at some point in the past). As a result, §1912(f) does not apply in cases where the Indian parent *never* had custody of the Indian child.

Biological Father's contrary reading of §1912(f) is nonsensical. Pointing to the provision's requirement that "[n]o termination of parental rights may be ordered . . . in the absence of a determination" relating to "the continued custody of the child by the parent," Biological Father contends that if a determination relating to "continued custody" is inapposite in cases where there is no "custody," the statutory text *prohibits* termination. But it would be absurd to think that Congress enacted a provision that *permits* termination of a custodial parent's rights, while simultaneously *prohibiting* termination of a noncustodial parent's rights. If the statute draws any distinction between custodial and noncustodial parents, that distinction surely does not provide greater protection for noncustodial parents.

Our reading of §1912(f) comports with the statutory text demonstrating that the primary mischief the ICWA was designed to counteract was the unwarranted *removal* of Indian children from Indian families due to the cultural insensitivity and biases of social workers and state courts. The statutory text expressly highlights the primary problem that the statute was intended to solve: "an alarmingly high percentage of Indian families [were being] broken up by the *removal*, often unwarranted, of their children from them by nontribal public and private agencies." . . . In sum, when, as here, the adoption of an Indian child is voluntarily and lawfully initiated by a non-Indian parent with sole custodial rights, the ICWA's primary goal of preventing the unwarranted removal of Indian children and the dissolution of Indian families is not implicated.

The dissent fails to dispute that nonbinding guidelines issued by the Bureau of Indian Affairs (BIA) shortly after the ICWA's enactment demonstrate that the BIA envisioned that §1912(f)'s standard would apply only to termination of a *custodial* parent's rights. Specifically, the BIA stated that, under §1912(f), "[a] child may not be *removed* simply because there is someone else willing to raise the child who is likely to do a better job"; instead, "[i]t must be shown that . . . it is dangerous for the child to *remain* with his or her *present* custodians." Guidelines for State Courts; Indian Child Custody Proceedings, 44 Fed. Reg. 67593 (1979) (hereinafter Guidelines). Indeed, the Guidelines recognized that §1912(f) applies only when there is preexisting custody to evaluate. . . .

Under our reading of §1912(f), Biological Father should not have been able to invoke §1912(f) in this case, because he had never had legal or physical custody of Baby Girl as of the time of the adoption proceedings. As an initial matter, it is undisputed that Biological Father never had *physical* custody of Baby Girl. And as a matter of both South Carolina and Oklahoma law, Biological Father never had *legal* custody either.

In sum, the South Carolina Supreme Court erred in finding that §1912(f) barred termination of Biological Father's parental rights.

B

Section 1912(d) provides that "[a]ny party" seeking to terminate parental rights to an Indian child under state law "shall satisfy the court that active efforts have been made to provide remedial services and rehabilitative programs designed *to prevent the breakup of the Indian family* and that these efforts have proved unsuccessful." The South Carolina Supreme Court found that Biological Father's parental rights could not be terminated because Adoptive Couple had not demonstrated that Biological Father had been provided remedial services in accordance with §1912(d). We disagree.

Consistent with the statutory text, we hold that §1912(d) applies only in cases where an Indian family's "breakup" would be precipitated by the termination of the parent's rights. . . . But when an Indian parent abandons an Indian child prior to birth and that child has never been in the Indian parent's legal or physical custody, there is no "relationship" that would be "discontinu[ed]" — and no "effective entity" that would be "end[ed]" — by the termination of the Indian parent's rights. In such a situation, the "breakup of the Indian family" has long since occurred, and §1912(d) is inapplicable.

Our interpretation of §1912(d) is, like our interpretation of §1912(f), consistent with the explicit congressional purpose of providing certain "standards for the *removal* of Indian children from their families." §1902. In addition, the BIA's Guidelines confirm that remedial services under §1912(d) are intended "to alleviate the need to *remove* the Indian child from his or her parents or Indian custodians," not to facilitate a *transfer* of the child *to* an Indian parent. See 44 Fed. Reg., at 67592.

Our interpretation of §1912(d) is also confirmed by the provision's placement next to §1912(e) and §1912(f), both of which condition the outcome of proceedings on the merits of an Indian child's "continued custody" with his parent. That these three provisions appear adjacent to each other strongly suggests that the phrase "breakup of the Indian family" should be read in harmony with the "continued custody" requirement. . . . None of these three provisions *creates* parental rights for unwed fathers where no such rights would otherwise exist. Instead, Indian parents who are already part of an "Indian family" are provided with access to "remedial services and rehabilitative programs" under §1912(d) so that their "custody" might be "continued" in a way that avoids foster-care placement under §1912(e) or termination of parental rights under §1912(f). In other words, the provision of "remedial services and rehabilitative programs" under §1912(d) supports the "continued custody" that is protected by §1912(e) and §1912(f).

Section 1912(d) is a sensible requirement when applied to state social workers who might otherwise be too quick to remove Indian children from their Indian families. It would, however, be unusual to apply §1912(d) in the context of an Indian parent who abandoned a child prior to birth and who never had custody of the child. The decision below illustrates this point. The South Carolina Supreme Court held that §1912(d) mandated measures such as "attempting to stimulate [Biological] Father's desire to be a parent." But if prospective adoptive parents were required to engage in the bizarre undertaking of "stimulat[ing]" a biological father's "desire to be a parent," it would surely dissuade some of them from seeking to adopt Indian children. And this would, in turn, unnecessarily place vulnerable Indian children at a unique disadvantage in finding a permanent and loving home, even in cases where neither an Indian parent nor the relevant tribe objects to the adoption.

In sum, the South Carolina Supreme Court erred in finding that §1912(d) barred termination of Biological Father's parental rights.

IV

In the decision below, the South Carolina Supreme Court suggested that if it had terminated Biological Father's rights, then §1915(a)'s preferences for the adoptive placement of an Indian child would have been applicable. In so doing, however, the court failed to recognize a critical limitation on the scope of §1915(a).

Section 1915(a) provides that "[i]n any adoptive placement of an Indian child under State law, a preference shall be given, in the absence of good cause to the contrary, to a placement with (1) a member of the child's extended family; (2)

other members of the Indian child's tribe; or (3) other Indian families." Contrary to the South Carolina Supreme Court's suggestion, §1915(a)'s preferences are inapplicable in cases where no alternative party has formally sought to adopt the child. This is because there simply is no "preference" to apply if no alternative party that is eligible to be preferred under §1915(a) has come forward.

In this case, Adoptive Couple was the only party that sought to adopt Baby Girl in the Family Court or the South Carolina Supreme Court. Biological Father is not covered by §1915(a) because he did not seek to *adopt* Baby Girl; instead, he argued that his parental rights should not be terminated in the first place. Moreover, Baby Girl's paternal grandparents never sought custody of Baby Girl. Nor did other members of the Cherokee Nation or "other Indian families" seek to adopt Baby Girl, even though the Cherokee Nation had notice of—and intervened in—the adoption proceedings.

The Indian Child Welfare Act was enacted to help preserve the cultural identity and heritage of Indian tribes, but under the State Supreme Court's reading, the Act would put certain vulnerable children at a great disadvantage solely because an ancestor—even a remote one—was an Indian. As the State Supreme Court read §§1912(d) and (f), a biological Indian father could abandon his child *in utero* and refuse any support for the birth mother—perhaps contributing to the mother's decision to put the child up for adoption—and then could play his ICWA trump card at the eleventh hour to override the mother's decision and the child's best interests. If this were possible, many prospective adoptive parents would surely pause before adopting any child who might possibly qualify as an Indian under the ICWA. Such an interpretation would raise equal protection concerns, but the plain text of §§1912(f) and (d) makes clear that neither provision applies in the present context. Nor do §1915(a)'s rebuttable adoption preferences apply when no alternative party has formally sought to adopt the child. We therefore reverse the judgment of the South Carolina Supreme Court and remand the case for further proceedings not inconsistent with this opinion.

It is so ordered.

SOTOMAYOR, J., with whom **GINSBURG, J.** and **KAGAN, J.** join, and with whom **SCALIA, J.** joins in part, dissenting.

I

Beginning its reading with the last clause of §1912(f), the majority concludes that a single phrase appearing there—"continued custody"—means that the entirety of the subsection is inapplicable to any parent, however committed, who has not previously had physical or legal custody of his child. Working back to front, the majority then concludes that §1912(d), tainted by its association with §1912(f), is also inapplicable; in the majority's view, a family bond that does not take custodial form is not a family bond worth preserving from "breakup." Because there are apparently no limits on the contaminating power of this single phrase, the majority does not stop there. Under its reading, §1903(9), which makes biological fathers "parent[s]" under this federal statute (and where, again, the phrase "continued custody" does not appear), has substantive force only when a birth father has physical or state-recognized legal custody of his daughter.

When it excludes noncustodial biological fathers from the Act's substantive protections, this textually backward reading misapprehends ICWA's structure and scope. Moreover, notwithstanding the majority's focus on the perceived parental shortcomings of Birth Father, its reasoning necessarily extends to *all* Indian parents who have never had custody of their children, no matter how fully those parents have embraced the financial and emotional responsibilities of parenting. The majority thereby transforms a statute that was intended to provide uniform federal standards for child custody proceedings involving Indian children and their biological parents into an illogical piecemeal scheme.

A

. . . ICWA commences with express findings. Congress recognized that "there is no resource that is more vital to the continued existence and integrity of Indian tribes than their children," 25 U.S.C. §1901(3), and it found that this resource was threatened. State authorities insufficiently sensitive to "the essential tribal relations of Indian people and the cultural and social standards prevailing in Indian communities and families" were breaking up Indian families and moving Indian children to non-Indian homes and institutions. See §§1901(4)-(5). As §1901(4) makes clear, and as this Court recognized in *Mississippi Band of Choctaw Indians v. Holyfield*, 490 U.S. 30, 33 (1989), adoptive placements of Indian children with non-Indian families contributed significantly to the overall problem. See §1901(4) (finding that "an alarmingly high percentage of [Indian] children are placed in non-Indian . . . adoptive homes").

Consistent with these findings, Congress declared its purpose "to protect the best interests of Indian children and to promote the stability and security of Indian tribes and families by the establishment of minimum Federal standards" applicable to child custody proceedings involving Indian children. §1902. Section 1903 then goes on to establish the reach of these protections through its definitional provisions. For present purposes, two of these definitions are crucial to understanding the statute's full scope.

First, ICWA defines the term "parent" broadly to mean "any biological parent . . . of an Indian child or any Indian person who has lawfully adopted an Indian child." §1903(9). It is undisputed that Baby Girl is an "Indian child" within the meaning of the statute, see §1903(4); *ante*, at 2557, n.1, and Birth Father consequently qualifies as a "parent" under the Act. The statutory definition of parent "does not include the unwed father where paternity has not been acknowledged or established," §1903(9), but Birth Father's biological paternity has never been questioned by any party and was confirmed by a DNA test during the state court proceedings. . . .

Second, the Act's comprehensive definition of "child custody proceeding" includes not only "'adoptive placement[s],'" "'preadoptive placement[s],'" and "'foster care placement[s],'" but also "'termination of parental rights'" proceedings. §1903(1). This last category encompasses "*any* action resulting in the termination of the *parent-child relationship*," §1903(1)(ii) (emphasis added). So far, then, it is clear that Birth Father has a federally recognized status as Baby Girl's "parent" and that his "parent-child relationship" with her is subject to the protections of the Act.

These protections are numerous. Had Birth Father petitioned to remove this proceeding to tribal court, for example, the state court would have been obligated to transfer it absent an objection from Birth Mother or good cause to the contrary. See §1911(b). Any voluntary consent Birth Father gave to Baby Girl's adoption would have been invalid unless written and executed before a judge and would have been revocable up to the time a final decree of adoption was entered. See §§1913(a), (c). And §1912, the center of the dispute here, sets forth procedural and substantive standards applicable in "involuntary proceeding[s] in a State court," including foster care placements of Indian children and termination of parental rights proceedings. §1912(a). I consider §1912's provisions in order.

Section 1912(a) requires that any party seeking "termination of parental rights t[o] an Indian child" provide notice to both the child's "parent or Indian custodian" and the child's tribe "of the pending proceedings and of their right of intervention." Section 1912(b) mandates that counsel be provided for an indigent "parent or Indian custodian" in any "termination proceeding." Section 1912(c) also gives all "part[ies]" to a termination proceeding — which, thanks to §§1912(a) and (b), will always include a biological father if he desires to be present — the right to inspect all material "reports or other documents filed with the court." By providing notice, counsel, and access to relevant documents, the statute ensures a biological father's meaningful participation in an adoption proceeding where the termination of his parental rights is at issue.

These protections are consonant with the principle, recognized in our cases, that the biological bond between parent and child is meaningful. "[A] natural parent's desire for and right to the companionship, care, custody, and management of his or her children," we have explained, "is an interest far more precious than any property right." *Santosky v. Kramer*, 455 U.S. 745, 758-759 (1982). Although the Constitution does not compel the protection of a biological father's parent-child relationship until he has taken steps to cultivate it, this Court has nevertheless recognized that "the biological connection . . . offers the natural father an opportunity that no other male possesses to develop a relationship with his offspring." *Lehr v. Robertson*, 463 U.S. 248, 262 (1983). Federal recognition of a parent-child relationship between a birth father and his child is consistent with ICWA's purpose of providing greater protection for the familial bonds between Indian parents and their children than state law may afford.

The majority does not and cannot reasonably dispute that ICWA grants biological fathers, as "parent[s]," the right to be present at a termination of parental rights proceeding and to have their views and claims heard there. But the majority gives with one hand and takes away with the other. Having assumed a uniform federal definition of "parent" that confers certain procedural rights, the majority then illogically concludes that ICWA's *substantive* protections are available only to a subset of "parent[s]": those who have previously had physical or state-recognized legal custody of his or her child. The statute does not support this departure.

Section 1012(d) provides that "Any party seeking to effect a foster care placement of, or *termination of parental rights to*, an Indian child under State law shall satisfy the court that active efforts have been made to provide remedial services and rehabilitative programs designed to prevent the breakup of the Indian family and that these efforts have proved unsuccessful."

In other words, subsection (d) requires that an attempt be made to cure familial deficiencies before the drastic measures of foster care placement or termination of parental rights can be taken.

The majority would hold that the use of the phrase "breakup of the Indian family" in this subsection means that it does not apply where a birth father has not previously had custody of his child. But there is nothing about this capacious phrase that licenses such a narrowing construction. . . . So far, all of §1912's provisions expressly apply in actions aimed at terminating the "parent-child relationship" that exists between a birth father and his child, and they extend to it meaningful protections. As a logical matter, that relationship is fully capable of being preserved via remedial services and rehabilitation programs. Nothing in the text of subsection (d) indicates that this blood relationship should be excluded from the category of familial "relationships" that the provision aims to save from "discontinuance."

The majority, reaching the contrary conclusion, asserts baldly that "when an Indian parent abandons an Indian child prior to birth and that child has never been in the Indian parent's legal or physical custody, there is no 'relationship' that would be 'discontinu[ed]' . . . by the termination of the Indian parent's rights." Says who? Certainly not the statute. Section 1903 recognizes Birth Father as Baby Girl's "parent," and, in conjunction with ICWA's other provisions, it further establishes that their "parent-child relationship" is protected under federal law. In the face of these broad definitions, the majority has no warrant to substitute its own policy views for Congress' by saying that "no 'relationship'" exists between Birth Father and Baby Girl simply because, based on the hotly contested facts of this case, it views their family bond as insufficiently substantial to deserve protection. . . .

B

The majority also does not acknowledge the full implications of its assumption that there are some ICWA "parent[s]" to whom §§1912(d) and (f) do not apply. Its discussion focuses on Birth Father's particular actions, but nothing in the majority's reasoning limits its manufactured class of semiprotected ICWA parents to biological fathers who failed to support their child's mother during pregnancy. Its logic would apply equally to noncustodial fathers who have actively participated in their child's upbringing.

Consider an Indian father who, though he has never had custody of his biological child, visits her and pays all of his child support obligations. Suppose that, due to deficiencies in the care the child received from her custodial parent, the State placed the child with a foster family and proposed her ultimate adoption by them. Clearly, the father's parental rights would have to be terminated before the adoption could go forward. On the majority's view, notwithstanding the fact that this father would be a "parent" under ICWA, he would not receive the benefit of either

§1912(d) or §1912(f). Presumably the court considering the adoption petition would have to apply some standard to determine whether termination of his parental rights was appropriate. But from whence would that standard come?

Not from the statute Congress drafted, according to the majority. The majority suggests that it might come from state law. But it is incongruous to suppose that Congress intended a patchwork of federal and state law to apply in termination of parental rights proceedings. Congress enacted a statute aimed at protecting the familial relationships between Indian parents and their children because it concluded that state authorities "often failed to recognize the essential tribal relations of Indian people and the cultural and social standards prevailing in Indian communities and families." 25 U.S.C. §1901(5). It provided a "minimum Federal standar[d]," §1902, for termination of parental rights that is more demanding than the showing of unfitness under a high "clear and convincing evidence" standard that is the norm in the States.

While some States might provide protections comparable to §1912(d)'s required remedial efforts and §1912(f)'s heightened standard for termination of parental rights, many will provide less. There is no reason to believe Congress wished to leave protection of the parental rights of a subset of ICWA "parent[s]" dependent on the happenstance of where a particular "child custody proceeding" takes place. I would apply, as the statute construed in its totality commands, the standards Congress provided in §§1912(d) and (f) to the termination of all ICWA "parent[s']" parent-child relationships. . . .

DISCUSSION QUESTIONS FOR *ADOPTIVE COUPLE v. BABY GIRL*

A. What is the statutory language in §§1912(d) and 1912(f) of ICWA that the Court interprets and applies in this case?

B. What is the dispute between the majority and the dissent concerning the meaning of the term "continued custody"? What meaning does the majority ascribe to this term? In his dissent, Justice Scalia wrote: "I reject the conclusion that the Court draws from the words 'continued custody' in 25 U.S.C. §1912(f) not because 'literalness may strangle meaning,' . . . but because there is no reason that 'continued' must refer to custody in the past rather than custody in the future. I read the provision as requiring the court to satisfy itself (beyond a reasonable doubt) not merely that initial or temporary custody is not 'likely to result in serious emotional or physical damage to the child,' but that continued custody is not likely to do so. . . ." Do you agree that the majority interpretation has been so literal as to "strangle meaning"?

C. After this decision, in what factual circumstances would ICWA apply? In what factual circumstances would ICWA not apply? What is Justice Sotomayor's assertion about who will be excluded from coverage?

D. According to Justice Sotomayor, what specific protections would the biological father have received under ICWA if the majority had ruled that it applied in this case?

E. If ICWA applied in this case, what are examples of the remedial services that the biological father might have received?

F. With respect to the ICWA adoption preferences, the majority relies on the fact that no extended family members or Indian families sought to adopt the child in this case. If ICWA had applied, should the child protection agency have had an affirmative obligation to attempt to locate an Indian adoptive home?

G. In his dissenting opinion, not included here, Justice Scalia wrote: "The Court's opinion, it seems to me, needlessly demeans the rights of parenthood. It has been the constant practice of the common law to respect the entitlement of those who bring a child into the world to raise that child. We do not inquire whether leaving a child with his parents is 'in the best interest of the child.' It sometimes is not; he would be better off raised by someone else. But parents have their rights, no less than children do. This father wants to raise his daughter, and the statute amply protects his right to do so. There is no reason in law or policy to dilute that protection." Do you agree with his conclusion? Why or why not?

H. How does the majority view the natural rights concept of parental possession of a child? When is this natural right forfeited?

General Principles

1. Parents have a Fourteenth Amendment liberty interest in the care and custody of their children but, by virtue of its *parens patriae* power, a state may interfere with parental rights to preserve and promote the welfare of a child.
2. Termination of parental rights ends the parent-child relationship. Subsequently, the parents no longer have the right to care for or visit the child and the child becomes available for adoption.
3. Indigent parents facing termination of their parental rights generally have counsel appointed to represent them, although it is not constitutionally required.
4. Clear and convincing evidence is the standard of proof required for involuntary termination of parental rights.
5. Typical statutory grounds for termination of parental rights include continued abuse or neglect; abandonment; termination of parental rights to a sibling; chronic parental incapacity due to mental illness or alcohol or drug abuse;

lack of contact with the child; felony conviction for violence against a family member; or placement in foster care for 15 of the preceding 22 months.

6. Out of concern about the number of children growing up in foster care, Congress passed the Adoption Assistance and Child Welfare Act (AACWA) requiring states to make "reasonable efforts" to reunify families but also undertake "permanency planning," usually in the form of adoption, when reunification is not realistic.

7. The Adoption and Safe Families Act (ASFA) requires states to more aggressively free children for adoption. States pursue termination of parental rights if a child has been in foster care for 15 of the preceding 22 months, unless the child has been placed with a relative, reunification services have not been provided, or termination would not be in the best interests of the child. Reasonable efforts to reunify the family are required but exceptions are made for cases involving "aggravated circumstances" or when rights to a sibling have previously been terminated.

8. Under the Indian Child Welfare Act (ICWA) "active efforts" to rehabilitate the family (rather than reasonable efforts pursuant to ASFA) are required and a higher burden of proof, the beyond a reasonable doubt standard, is applied in termination cases. Adoptive preference is given to extended family, tribal members, and other American Indians.

9. The Supreme Court recently limited the application of ICWA, holding that ICWA protections related to the legal standard for termination, the active efforts requirement, and the adoptive placement preference did not apply to an American Indian biological father who had not previously had legal or physical custody of the child.

Chapter Problems

1. According to Martin Guggenheim and Christine Gottlieb, the discussion about termination of parental rights has become somewhat polarized.

> An important national debate is raging in the United States over the wisdom of the current direction of child welfare policy. To some, the major problems associated with child welfare remain, as they have for much of the second half of the twentieth century, that states put too many children in foster care unnecessarily and fail to help those children who do go into foster care return to their parents as quickly as possible. To others, the principal problem is that states expend too much effort to keep biological families together and, as a consequence, children suffer by not being adopted as soon as they could be.

Martin Guggenheim & Christine Gottlieb, *Justice Denied: Delays in Resolving Child Protection Cases in New York*, 12 Va. J. Soc. Pol'y & L. 546 (2005). Do you favor an aggressive policy of terminating parental rights and placing children for adoption? What are the policy interests behind this view? Do you believe that states are being required to move too quickly to terminate parental rights? What hypothetical fact situations might concern you?

2. Assume that Paula, age 20, has a record of juvenile and adult prostitution. She is a chronic drug user and has failed on two occasions at rehabilitation. Her first child, Juan, is born, and the local social services agency brings an immediate petition to terminate Paula's rights to the child. She argues that she should be given an opportunity to "turn herself around" and "raise her child." What are some of the arguments that the state and Paula's lawyer will make at the termination proceeding? What is the state's obligation to Paula, if any? Should Paula first have a chance to demonstrate that she can be an acceptable parent?

3. In *River v. Minnich*, 483 U.S. 574 (1987), the Supreme Court held that the Due Process Clause does not require that the "clear and convincing evidence" standard be applied to actions where the paternity of a child is at issue. The Court provided several reasons for this view: (1) The preponderance standard is the one used in most states; (2) an action to terminate parental rights is not analogous to one where there is an effort to create parental rights and obligations; (3) a paternity action is between two parties who have relatively equal interests in the outcome, and it is appropriate that each equally share the risk of an inaccurate factual determination; (4) a paternity action is between two parties who have relatively equal interests in the outcome, while a termination action is between the state with all its resources and a citizen; and (5) paternity actions can be relitigated if there is a finding of nonpaternity, while a termination action is final. Which of these reasons is the most persuasive in support of applying different standards to paternity and termination actions?

4. In some cases, children are not adopted subsequent to the termination of their parents' rights. A commentator suggests that under some circumstances parents should be able to seek reinstatement of their parental rights:

> Though the legal responses to parents' attempts to resuscitate parental rights vary, each attempts to respond to the lack of flexibility inherent in a permanent termination final judgment or order. The courts' lack of explicit statutory authority to modify termination orders when circumstances change has made individual responses necessary. Instead of enacting legislation to require a separate legal proceeding to vacate the order, this article recommends giving courts statutory authority and discretion to enter temporary termination of parental rights orders. These provisional orders would free the child for adoption for a limited time period but would also allow parental rights to be reinstated if the court subsequently determines that the child is no longer adoptable or that adoption is no longer in the child's best interest.

Lashanda Taylor, *Resurrecting Parents of Legal Orphans: Un-Terminating Parental Rights*, 17 Va. J. Soc. Pol'y & L. 318, 320-321 (2010). What are the policy arguments supporting and opposing "un-termination"?

Preparation for Practice

1. Assume that you are appointed by a court to represent a parent whose rights are being terminated because of child sexual abuse. During your interview of your client he discloses that he committed the acts alleged but he is unwilling to voluntarily relinquish his parental rights. You are deeply disturbed by the nature and extent of the abuse. What is your ethical obligation to the client? How will you proceed in this case?

2. Mediation is sometimes used in cases involving abuse and neglect. What might be advantages to using mediation in cases involving termination of parental rights? What problems might result?

3. Does your state appoint guardians *ad litem*, CASAs, or attorneys for children in termination of parental rights cases? Do an Internet search to learn more about these roles and discover what training is required to fulfill them.

Part VI

Legal Recognition of Family Relationships

Chapter 18

Establishing Parentage

18.1 INTRODUCTION

This chapter focuses on the legal issues involving parentage. Usually, but not always, the parentage issue involves a child born out of wedlock, and the question is, who is the child's father?

The chapter examines the historic treatment of children born out of wedlock, the legal changes regarding these children that have occurred in the United States over the last several decades, and the impact of scientific testing on determining parentage.

Some of the questions raised by this chapter include the following: What changes have occurred over the last century in how children born out of wedlock are viewed? What role has the Supreme Court played in removing inheritance barriers for children born out of wedlock? What is Lord Mansfield's presumption, and is it relevant today? When, if ever, should the public pay for genetic testing where an indigent father denies paternity? When does the statute of limitations run that prevents a person from establishing paternity? What is the burden of proof standard used in a parentage action? What is a state parentage registry? Should the government create a national parentage registry? Who is considered a de facto parent? When does a de facto parent have standing in a parentage dispute?

> **REFLECTIVE QUESTIONS** What are your goals for this chapter?

18.2 HISTORICAL DISPARATE TREATMENT OF CHILDREN BORN TO UNMARRIED PARENTS: INHERITANCE

At common law, children born out of wedlock were considered "illegitimate." It was a difficult world for them as they had few of the rights and privileges given to children born to married couples. For example, neither a child born out of wedlock nor the child's mother had a right to seek support from the biological father. Similarly, prior to the mid-1800s a nonmarital child could not inherit from his or her mother. The child was considered *filius nullius* — "the child of no one." The common law view of the rights of nonmarital children influenced the creation of state statutes in the United States until well into the twentieth century.

Supreme Court leads change. The changes in this area of the law were led by the Supreme Court beginning in the 1960s. For example, in *Levy v. Louisiana*, 391 U.S. 68 (1968), five nonmarital children sued for damages as the result of the wrongful death of their mother. Under a Louisiana statute, the children were not recognized as having a legally cognizable interest in the death of the mother because they were born outside marriage. The Court struck down the state statute on equal protection grounds holding that denying nonmarital children the right to recover for wrongful death of their mother on whom they were dependent constituted invidious discrimination. It declared that the statute could not discriminate against the children "when no action, conduct, or demeanor of theirs was relevant to the harm that was done in the matter." *Id.* at 72.

In a somewhat similar case, *Glona v. American Guarantee & Liability Ins. Co.*, 391 U.S. 73 (1968), the mother brought an action for wrongful death of her daughter, who was born out of wedlock. The Court stated that "[w]here the claimant is plainly the mother, the State denies equal protection of the laws to withhold relief merely because the child, wrongfully killed, was born to her out-of-wedlock." In *Gomez v. Perez*, 409 U.S. 535 (1973), the Court established the right of paternal support for a child born outside of marriage. It held that a state may not invidiously discriminate against children born out of wedlock by denying them substantial benefits accorded children generally. Furthermore, the Court stated that once a state posits a judicially enforceable right on behalf of children to needed support from their natural fathers, there is no constitutionally sufficient justification for denying this essential right to a nonmarital child.

Inheritance barrier removed. The question of the constitutionality of state statutes that barred children born out of wedlock from inheriting from their biological father came to the Court in the 1970s. In *Trimble v. Gordon*, 430 U.S. 762 (1977), a deceased biological father had provided support and acknowledged his daughter, who was born out of wedlock. When he died without a will, she was prevented by an Illinois probate statute from inheriting because her parents had not married. The Court held that the provision of the Illinois Probate Act that allowed children born out of wedlock to inherit by intestate succession only from their mothers, while children born in wedlock may inherit by intestate succession from both their mothers and their fathers, denied the children born out of wedlock equal protection. The Court held that any classification based on children born out of wedlock must bear a rational relationship to a legitimate state purpose. It stated that the Illinois probate provision could not be justified on the ground that it promoted a legitimate family relationship. Furthermore, the statute could not be justified because of difficulties in proving paternity in some situations. Finally, the Court rejected the argument that the father could have provided for the child by making a will stating that this possibility did not save the provision from invalidity. The ruling meant that children born out of wedlock could inherit from their mothers and fathers.

In *Reed v. Campbell*, 476 U.S. 852 (1986), the United States Supreme Court again addressed the issue of restrictions placed on a nonmarital child's right to inherit from her father by intestate succession. A Texas statute was challenged that required the parents of a nonmarital child to marry before the child could inherit from the father. After the death of her biological father, the child plaintiff in this case had notified the administratrix and a Texas Probate Court of her claim to the estate. Subsequently, a jury found that the deceased was the father of the nonmarital child but she was denied any interest in the estate because of the Texas statutory disinheritance statute. Texas upheld the statute, and the child brought the matter to the Supreme Court. The Court held that the interest, protected by the Fourteenth Amendment, in avoiding unjustified discrimination against children born out of wedlock required that the child's claim to a share in her father's estate be protected by the full applicability of *Trimble, supra. Id.* at 856.

REFLECTIVE QUESTIONS | Which of the above Supreme Court decisions do you consider the most important?

Background to *Lalli v. Lalli*

A year after the *Trimble* decision the Court, in *Lalli v. Lalli*, 439 U.S. 259 (1978), considered the constitutionality of a state statute that required a judicial order of filiation to be entered during the father's lifetime in order for a nonmarital child to inherit from his or her putative father. In the decision, the Court weighs the considerations underlying the *Trimble* ruling with the goal of providing for a "just and orderly disposition of property at death."

LALLI
v.
LALLI

Supreme Court of the United States
439 U.S. 259 (1978)

POWELL, J. Appellant Robert Lalli claims to be the illegitimate son of Mario Lalli who died intestate on January 7, 1973, in the State of New York. Appellant's mother, who died in 1968, never was married to Mario. After Mario's widow, Rosamond Lalli, was appointed administratrix of her husband's estate, appellant petitioned the Surrogate's Court for Westchester County for a compulsory accounting, claiming that he and his sister Maureen Lalli were entitled to inherit from Mario as his children. Rosamond Lalli opposed the petition. She argued that even if Robert and Maureen were Mario's children, they were not lawful distributees of the state because they had failed to comply with §4-1.2, which provides in part:

> An illegitimate child is the legitimate child of his father so that he and his issue inherit from his father if a court of competent jurisdiction has, during the lifetime of the father, made an order of filiation declaring paternity in a proceeding instituted during the pregnancy of the mother or within two years from the birth of the child.

Appellant conceded that he had not obtained an order of filiation during his putative father's lifetime. He contended, however, that §4-1.2, by imposing this requirement, discriminated against him on the basis of his illegitimate birth in violation of the Equal Protection Clause of the Fourteenth Amendment. Appellant tendered certain evidence of his relationship with Mario Lalli, including a notarized document in which Lalli, in consenting to appellant's marriage, referred to him as "my son," and several affidavits by persons who stated that Lalli had acknowledged openly and often that Robert and Maureen were his children. . . .

We begin our analysis with *Trimble.* At issue in that case was the constitutionality of an Illinois statute providing that a child born out of wedlock could inherit from his intestate father only if the father had "acknowledged" the child and the child had been legitimated by the intermarriage of the parents.

We concluded that the Illinois statute discriminated against illegitimate children in a manner prohibited by the Equal Protection Clause. Although classifications based on illegitimacy are not subject to "strict scrutiny," they nevertheless are invalid under the Fourteenth Amendment if they are not substantially related to permissible state interests. Upon examination, we found that the Illinois law failed that test.

The Illinois statute, however, was constitutionally flawed because, by insisting upon not only an acknowledgment by the father, but also the marriage of the parents, it excluded "at least some significant categories of illegitimate children of intestate men [whose] inheritance rights can be recognized without jeopardizing the orderly settlement of estates or the dependability of titles to property passing under intestacy laws." We concluded that the Equal Protection Clause required that a statute placing exceptional burdens on illegitimate children in the furtherance of proper state objectives must be more "carefully tuned to alternative considerations," than was true of the broad disqualification in the Illinois law.

At the outset we observe that §4-1.2 is different in important respects from the statutory provision overturned in *Trimble.* The Illinois statute required, in addition to the father's acknowledgment of paternity, the legitimation of the child through the intermarriage of the parents as an absolute precondition to inheritance. This combination of requirements eliminated "the possibility of a middle ground between the extremes of complete exclusion and case-by-case determination of paternity." As illustrated by the facts in *Trimble*, even a judicial declaration of paternity was insufficient to permit inheritance.

Under §4-1.2, by contrast, the marital status of the parents is irrelevant. The single requirement at issue here is an evidentiary one — that the paternity of the father be declared in a judicial proceeding sometime before his death. The child need not have been legitimated in order to inherit from his father. Had the appellant in *Trimble* been governed by §4-1.2, she would have been a distributee of her father's estate.

A related difference between the two provisions pertains to the state interests said to be served by them. The Illinois law was defended, in part, as a means of encouraging legitimate family relationships. No such justification has been offered in support of §4-1.2. The Court of Appeals disclaimed that the purpose of the statute, "even in small part, was to discourage illegitimacy, to mold human conduct or to set societal norms." The absence in §4-1.2 of any requirement that the parents intermarry or otherwise legitimate a child born out of wedlock and our review of the legislative history of the statute confirm this view.

Our inquiry, therefore, is focused narrowly. We are asked to decide whether the discrete procedural demands that §4-1.2 places on illegitimate children bear an evident and substantial relation to the particular state interests this statute is designed to serve. The primary state goal underlying the challenged aspects of §4-1.2 is to provide for the just and orderly disposition of property at death.

This interest is directly implicated in paternal inheritance by illegitimate children because of the peculiar problems of proof that are involved. Establishing maternity is seldom difficult. As one New York Surrogate's Court has observed: "[T]he birth of the child is a recorded or registered event usually taking place in the presence of others. In most cases the child remains with the mother and for a time is necessarily reared by her. That the child is the child of a particular woman is rarely difficult to prove." Proof of paternity, by contrast, frequently is difficult when the father is not part of a formal family unit.

Thus, a number of problems arise that counsel against treating illegitimate children identically to all other heirs of an intestate father. These were the subject of a comprehensive study by the Temporary State Commission on the Modernization, Revision and Simplification of the Law of Estates. This group, known as the Bennett Commission, consisted of individuals experienced in the practical problems of estate administration. The Commission issued its report and recommendations to the legislature in 1965. . . .

Although the overarching purpose of the proposed statute was "to alleviate the plight of the illegitimate child," the Bennett Commission considered it necessary to impose the strictures of §4-1.2 in order to mitigate serious difficulties in the administration of the estates of both testate and intestate decedents. The Commission's perception of some of these difficulties was described by Surrogate Sobel, a member of "the busiest [surrogate's] court in the State," a participant in some of the Commission's deliberations:

> An illegitimate, if made an unconditional distributee in intestacy, must be served with process in the estate of his parent or if he is a distributee in the estate of the kindred of a parent. How does one cite and serve an illegitimate of whose existence neither family nor personal representative may be aware? And of greatest concern, how achieve finality of decree in any estate when there always exists the possibility however remote of a secret illegitimate lurking in the buried past of a parent or an ancestor of a class of beneficiaries? Finality in decree is essential in the Surrogates' Courts since title to real property passes under such decree. Our procedural statutes and the Due Process Clause mandate notice and opportunity to be heard to all necessary parties. Given the right to intestate succession, all illegitimates must be served with process. This would be no real problem with respect to those few estates where there are "known" illegitimates. But it presents an almost insuperable burden as regards "unknown" illegitimates. The point made in the [Bennett] commission discussions was that instead of affecting only a few estates, procedural problems would be created for many—some members suggested a majority—of estates.
>
> Even where an individual claiming to be the illegitimate child of a deceased man makes himself known, the difficulties facing an estate are likely to persist. Because of the particular problems of proof, spurious claims may be difficult to expose.

The Bennett Commission therefore sought to protect "innocent adults and those rightfully interested in their estates from fraudulent claims of heirship and harassing litigation instituted by those seeking to establish themselves as illegitimate heirs."

As the State's interests are substantial, we now consider the means adopted by New York to further these interests. In order to avoid the problems described above, the Commission recommended a requirement designed to ensure the accurate resolution of claims of paternity and to minimize the potential for disruption of estate administration. Accuracy is enhanced by placing paternity disputes in a judicial forum during the lifetime of the father. In addition, requiring that the order be issued during the father's lifetime permits a man to defend his reputation against "unjust accusations in paternity claims," which was a secondary purpose of §4-1.2. Commission Report 266.

The administration of an estate will be facilitated, and the possibility of delay and uncertainty minimized, where the entitlement of an illegitimate child to notice and participation is a matter of judicial record before the administration commences. Fraudulent assertions of paternity will be much less likely to succeed, or even to arise, where the proof is put before a court of law at a time when the putative father is available to respond, rather than first brought to light when the distribution of the assets of an estate is in the offing.

Appellant contends that §4-1.2, like the statute at issue in *Trimble*, excludes "significant categories of illegitimate children" who could be allowed to inherit "without jeopardizing the orderly settlement" of their intestate fathers' estates. He urges that those in his position—"known" illegitimate children who, despite the absence of an order of filiation obtained during their fathers' lifetimes, can present convincing proof of paternity—cannot rationally be denied inheritance as they pose none of the risks §4-1.2 was intended to minimize. Our inquiry under the Equal Protection Clause does not focus on the abstract "fairness" of a state law, but on whether the statute's relation to the state interests it is intended to promote is so tenuous that it lacks the rationality contemplated by the Fourteenth Amendment. . . .

As the history of §4-1.2 clearly illustrates, the New York Legislature desired to "grant to illegitimates in so far as practicable rights of inheritance on a par with those enjoyed by legitimate children," while protecting the important state interests we have described. Section 4-1.2 represents a carefully considered legislative judgment as to how this balance best could be achieved.

We conclude that the requirement imposed by §4-1.2 on illegitimate children who would inherit from their fathers is substantially related to the important state interests the statute is intended to promote. We therefore find no violation of the Equal Protection Clause. The judgment of the New York Court of Appeals is affirmed.

DISCUSSION QUESTIONS FOR *LALLI v. LALLI*

A. According to the Court, what is the primary goal of the New York intestacy statute?

B. What is the appellant's constitutional claim? What statutory requirement does the defendant claim the plaintiff/appellant failed to comply with?

C. How did the Court distinguish between the Illinois statute in *Trimble* and the New York statute it was reviewing?

D. What role did the report of the Bennett Commission play in the outcome of this case?

E. Should the advent of reliable genetic testing alter the legal analysis of this case?

18.3 LORD MANSFIELD'S PRESUMPTION

During the eighteenth and nineteenth centuries, a common law rule called Lord Mansfield's presumption was created. The rule was recognized in England and

America. Under Lord Mansfield's presumption, a child born during lawful wedlock was presumed legitimate unless it could be proven that the husband was incapable of procreation or had no access to his wife during the period of conception. The rule prevented a biological mother and her husband at the time the child is conceived from giving testimony that might prove that the child is illegitimate. The presumption was intended to legally protect the family and the children born into it. This marital presumption remains in effect today in many jurisdictions; however, it is rebuttable. For example, the mother or the father of the child may now testify regarding the paternity of the child. *See, e.g.,* Ark. Code Ann. §16-43-901 (2015).

REFLECTIVE QUESTIONS	Does Lord Mansfield's presumption have a place in present family law? Or, is it so outdated that it should be abolished?

Background to *Michael H. v. Gerald D.*

California adopted legislation that allowed determinations of paternity based on scientific testing only during the first two years of the child's life. However, once that time period passed, there was a conclusive statutory presumption that the child is a child of the marriage. Cal. Fam. Code §§7540 and 7541. That conclusive presumption was challenged as unconstitutional in *Michael H. v. Gerald D.* In *Michael H. v. Gerald D.,* the biological father sought an order declaring him the father of a child conceived and born while the mother was married to another man. Her husband objected to the court hearing the claim.

The trial court granted a summary judgment motion filed by the husband. It decided that he was conclusively presumed to be the father under California law because he was married to the mother at the time of the child's birth and he desired to raise the child with the mother as his own. The putative natural father and child appealed. The court of appeal affirmed and the matter was taken to the Supreme Court.

The Court asks the following questions: (1) Does the California statute creating a presumption that a child born to married woman living with her husband is the child of the marriage violate the putative natural father's procedural due process rights? (2) Does the statute violate the putative natural father's substantive due process rights? (3) Does the child have a due process right to maintain a filial relationship with both the putative natural father and the husband? (4) Does the statute violate the child's equal protection rights?

MICHAEL H.
v.
GERALD D.

Supreme Court of the United States
491 U.S. 110 (1989)

SCALIA, J. The facts of this case are, we must hope, extraordinary. On May 9, 1976, in Las Vegas, Nevada, Carole D., an international model, and Gerald D., a top executive in a French oil company, were married. The couple established a home in Playa del Rey, California, in which they resided as husband and wife when one or the other was not out of the country on business. In the summer of 1978, Carole became involved in an adulterous affair with a neighbor, Michael H. In September 1980, she conceived a child, Victoria D., who was born on May 11, 1981. Gerald was listed as father on the birth certificate and has always held Victoria out to the world as his daughter. Soon after delivery of the child, however, Carole informed Michael that she believed he might be the father.

In the first three years of her life, Victoria remained always with Carole, but found herself within a variety of quasi-family units. In October 1981, Gerald moved to New York City to pursue his business interests, but Carole chose to remain in California. At the end of that month, Carole and Michael had blood tests of themselves and Victoria, which showed a 98.07% probability that Michael was Victoria's father. In January 1982, Carole visited Michael in St. Thomas, where his primary business interests were based. There Michael held Victoria out as his child. In March, however, Carole left Michael and returned to California, where she took up residence with yet another man, Scott K. Later that spring, and again in the summer, Carole and Victoria spent time with Gerald in New York City, as well as on vacation in Europe. In the fall, they returned to Scott in California.

In November 1982, rebuffed in his attempts to visit Victoria, Michael filed a filiation action in California Superior Court to establish his paternity and right to visitation. In March 1983, the court appointed an attorney and guardian *ad litem* to represent Victoria's interests. Victoria then filed a cross-complaint asserting that if she had more than one psychological or de facto father, she was entitled to maintain her filial relationship, with all of the attendant rights, duties, and obligations, with both. In May 1983, Carole filed a motion for summary judgment. During this period, from March through July 1983, Carole was again living with Gerald in New York. In August, however, she returned to California, became involved once again with Michael, and instructed her attorneys to remove the summary judgment motion from the calendar.

For the ensuing eight months, when Michael was not in St. Thomas he lived with Carole and Victoria in Carole's apartment in Los Angeles and held Victoria out as his daughter. In April 1984, Carole and Michael signed a stipulation that Michael was Victoria's natural father. Carole left Michael the next month, however, and instructed her attorneys not to file the stipulation. In June 1984, Carole reconciled with Gerald and joined him in New York, where they now live with Victoria and two other children since born into the marriage.

In May 1984, Michael and Victoria, through her guardian *ad litem*, sought visitation rights for Michael *pendente lite.* To assist in determining whether visitation would be in Victoria's best interests, the Superior Court appointed a psychologist to evaluate Victoria, Gerald, Michael, and Carole. The psychologist recommended that Carole retain sole custody, but that Michael be allowed continued contact with Victoria pursuant to a restricted visitation schedule. The court concurred and ordered that Michael be provided with limited visitation privileges *pendente lite.*

On October 19, 1984, Gerald, who had intervened in the action, moved for summary judgment on the ground that under Cal. Evid. Code §621 there were no triable issues of fact as to Victoria's paternity. This law provides that "the issue of a wife cohabiting with her husband, who is not impotent or sterile, is conclusively presumed to be a child of the marriage." Cal. Evid. Code Ann. §621(a) (West Supp. 1989). The presumption may be rebutted by blood tests, but only if a motion for such tests is made, within two years from the date of the child's birth, either by the husband or, if the natural father has filed an affidavit acknowledging paternity, by the wife.

On January 28, 1985, having found that affidavits submitted by Carole and Gerald sufficed to demonstrate that the two were cohabiting at conception and birth and that Gerald was neither sterile nor impotent, the Superior Court granted Gerald's motion for summary judgment, rejecting Michael's and Victoria's challenges to the constitutionality of §621. The court also denied their motions for continued visitation pending the appeal. [The California Court of Appeal affirmed the judgment of the Superior Court and upheld the constitutionality of the statute.]

We address first the claims of Michael.

Michael contends as a matter of substantive due process that, because he has established a parental relationship with Victoria, protection of Gerald's and Carole's marital union is an insufficient state interest to support termination of that relationship. This argument is, of course, predicated on the assertion that Michael has a constitutionally protected liberty interest in his relationship with Victoria.

In an attempt to limit and guide interpretation of the Clause, we have insisted not merely that the interest denominated as a "liberty" be "fundamental" (a concept that, in isolation, is hard to objectify), but also that it be an interest traditionally protected by our society. As we have put it, the Due Process Clause affords only those protections "so rooted in the traditions and conscience of our people as to be ranked as fundamental." Our cases reflect "continual insistence upon respect for the teachings of history [and] solid recognition of the basic values that underlie our society."

This insistence that the asserted liberty interest be rooted in history and tradition is evident, as elsewhere, in our cases according constitutional protection to certain parental rights. Michael reads the landmark case of *Stanley v. Illinois*, and the subsequent cases of *Quilloin v. Walcott, Caban v. Mohammed*, and *Lehr v. Robertson*, as establishing that a liberty interest is created by biological fatherhood plus an established parental relationship — factors that exist in the present case as well. We think that distorts the rationale of those cases. As we view them, they rest not upon such isolated factors but upon the historic respect — indeed, sanctity would not be too strong a term — traditionally accorded to the relationships that develop within the unitary family. In *Stanley*, for example, we forbade the destruction of such a family when, upon the death of the mother, the State had sought to remove children from the custody of a father who had lived with and supported them and their mother for 18 years. As Justice Powell stated for the plurality in *Moore v. East Cleveland*: "Our decisions establish that the Constitution protects the sanctity of the family precisely because the institution of the family is deeply rooted in this Nation's history and tradition."

Thus, the legal issue in the present case reduces to whether the relationship between persons in the situation of Michael and Victoria has been treated as a protected family unit under the historic practices of our society, or whether on any other basis it has been accorded special protection. We think it impossible to find that it has. In fact, quite to the contrary, our traditions have protected the marital family (Gerald, Carole, and the child they acknowledge to be theirs) against the sort of claim Michael asserts.

The presumption of legitimacy was a fundamental principle of the common law. Traditionally, that presumption could be rebutted only by proof that a husband was incapable of procreation or had no access to his wife during the relevant period. As explained by Blackstone, nonaccess could only be proved "if the husband be out of the kingdom of England (or, as the law somewhat loosely phrases it, *extra quatuor maria* [beyond the four seas]) for above nine months." And, under the common law both in England and here, "neither husband nor wife [could] be a witness to prove access or nonaccess." The primary policy rationale underlying the common law's severe restrictions on rebuttal of the presumption appears to have been an aversion to declaring children illegitimate, thereby depriving them of rights of inheritance and succession, and likely making them wards of the state. A secondary policy concern was the interest in promoting the "peace and tranquility of States and families," a goal that is obviously impaired by facilitating suits against husband and wife asserting that their children are illegitimate. Even though, as bastardy laws became less harsh, "[j]udges in both [England and the United States] gradually widened the acceptable range of evidence that could be offered by spouses, and placed restraints on the 'four seas rule,' the law retained a strong bias against ruling the children of married women illegitimate."

We have found nothing in the older sources, nor in the older cases, addressing specifically the power of the natural father to assert parental rights over a child born into a woman's existing marriage with another man. Since it is Michael's burden to establish that such a power (at least where the natural father has established a relationship with the child) is so deeply embedded within our traditions as to be a fundamental right, the lack of evidence alone might defeat his case. But the evidence shows that even in modern times — when, as we have noted, the rigid protection of the marital family has in other respects been relaxed — the ability of a person in Michael's position to claim paternity has not been generally acknowledged. For example, a 1957 annotation on the subject: "Who may dispute presumption of legitimacy of child conceived or born during wedlock," shows three States (including California) with statutes limiting standing to the husband or wife and their descendants, one State (Louisiana) with a statute limiting it to the husband, two States (Florida and Texas) with judicial decisions limiting standing to the husband, and two States (Illinois and New York) with judicial decisions denying standing even to the mother. Not a single decision is set forth specifically according standing to the natural father, and "express indications of the nonexistence of any limitation" upon standing were found only "in a few jurisdictions."

Moreover, even if it were clear that one in Michael's position generally possesses, and has generally always possessed, standing to challenge the marital child's legitimacy, that would still not establish Michael's case. As noted earlier, what is at issue here is not entitlement to a state pronouncement that Victoria was begotten by Michael. It is no conceivable denial of constitutional right for a State to decline to declare facts unless some legal consequence hinges upon the requested declaration. What Michael asserts here is a right to have himself declared the natural father and thereby to obtain parental prerogatives. What he must establish, therefore, is not that our society has traditionally allowed a natural father in his circumstances to establish paternity, but that it has traditionally accorded such a father parental rights, or at least has not traditionally denied them. Even if the law in all States had always been that the entire world could challenge the marital presumption and obtain a declaration as to who was the natural father, that would not advance Michael's claim. Thus, it is ultimately irrelevant, even for purposes of determining current social attitudes towards the alleged substantive right Michael asserts, that the present law in a number of States appears to allow the natural father — including the natural father who has not established a relationship with the child — the theoretical power to rebut the marital presumption. What counts is whether the States in fact award substantive parental rights to the natural father of a child conceived within, and born into, an extant marital union that wishes to embrace the child. We are not aware of a single case, old or new, that has done so. This is not the stuff of which fundamental rights qualifying as liberty interests are made.

We do not accept Justice Brennan's criticism that this result "squashes" the liberty that consists of "the freedom not to conform." It seems to us that reflects the erroneous view that there is only one side to this controversy — that one disposition can expand a "liberty" of sorts without contracting an equivalent "liberty" on the other side. Such a happy choice is rarely available. Here, to provide protection to an adulterous natural father is to deny protection to a marital father, and vice versa. If Michael has a "freedom not to conform" (whatever that means), Gerald must equivalently have a "freedom to conform." One of them will pay a price for asserting that "freedom" — Michael by being unable to act as father of the child he has adulterously begotten, or Gerald by being unable to preserve the integrity of the traditional family unit he and Victoria have established. Our disposition does not choose between these two "freedoms," but leaves that to the people of California. Justice Brennan's approach chooses one of them as the constitutional imperative, on no apparent basis except that the unconventional is to be preferred.

We have never had occasion to decide whether a child has a liberty interest, symmetrical with that of her parent, in maintaining her filial relationship. We need not do so here because, even assuming that such a right exists, Victoria's claim must fail. Victoria's due process challenge is, if anything, weaker than Michael's. Her basic claim is not that California has erred in preventing her from establishing that Michael, not Gerald, should stand as her legal father. Rather, she claims a due process right to maintain filial relationships with both Michael and Gerald. This assertion merits little discussion, for, whatever the merits of the guardian *ad litem*'s belief that such an arrangement can be of great psychological benefit to a child, the claim that a State must recognize multiple fatherhood has no support in the history or traditions of this country. Moreover, even if we were to construe Victoria's argument as forwarding the lesser proposition that, whatever her status vis-a-vis Gerald, she has a liberty interest in maintaining a filial relationship with her natural father, Michael, we find that, at best, her claim is the obverse of Michael's and fails for the same reasons. The judgment of the California Court of Appeal is affirmed.

JUSTICE BRENNAN, with whom **JUSTICE MARSHALL** and **JUSTICE BLACK-MUN** join, dissenting.

In a case that has yielded so many opinions as has this one, it is fruitful to begin by emphasizing the common ground shared by a majority of this Court. Five Members of the Court refuse to foreclose "the possibility that a natural father might ever have a constitutionally protected interest in his relationship with a child whose mother was married to, and cohabiting with, another man at the time of the child's conception and birth." Five Justices agree that the flaw inhering in a conclusive presumption that terminates a constitutionally protected interest without any hearing whatsoever is a procedural one. Four Members of the Court agree that Michael H. has a liberty interest in his relationship with Victoria, and one assumes for purposes of this case that he does.

In contrast, only one other Member of the Court fully endorses Justice Scalia's view of the proper method of analyzing questions arising under the Due Process Clause. Nevertheless, because the plurality opinion's exclusively historical analysis portends a significant and unfortunate departure from our prior cases and from sound constitutional decision making, I devote a substantial portion of my discussion to it. . . .

Once we recognized that the "liberty" protected by the Due Process Clause of the Fourteenth Amendment encompasses more than freedom from bodily restraint, today's plurality opinion emphasizes, the concept was cut loose from one natural limitation on its meaning. This innovation paved the way, so the plurality hints, for judges to substitute their own preferences for those of elected officials. Dissatisfied with this supposedly unbridled and uncertain state of affairs, the plurality casts about for another limitation on the concept of liberty.

It finds this limitation in "tradition." Apparently oblivious to the fact that this concept can be as malleable and as elusive as "liberty" itself, the plurality pretends that tradition places a discernible border around the Constitution. The pretense is seductive; it would be comforting to believe that a search for "tradition" involves nothing more idiosyncratic or complicated than poring through dusty volumes on American history. Yet, as Justice White observed in his dissent in *Moore v. East Cleveland*, "What the deeply rooted traditions of the country are is arguable." Indeed, wherever I would begin to look for an interest "deeply rooted in the country's traditions," one thing is certain: I would not stop (as does the plurality) at Bracton, or Blackstone, or Kent, or even the American Law Reports in conducting my search. Because reasonable people can disagree about the content of particular traditions, and because they can disagree even about which traditions are relevant to the definition of "liberty," the plurality has not found the objective boundary that it seeks.

Even if we could agree, moreover, on the content and significance of particular traditions, we still would be forced to identify the point at which a tradition becomes firm enough to be relevant to our definition of liberty and the moment at which it becomes too obsolete to be relevant any longer. The plurality supplies no objective means by which we might make these determinations. Indeed, as soon as the plurality sees signs that the tradition upon which it bases its decision (the laws denying putative fathers like Michael standing to assert paternity) is crumbling, it shifts ground and says that the case has nothing to do with that tradition, after all. "[W]hat is at issue here," the plurality asserts after canvassing the law on paternity suits, "is not entitlement to a state pronouncement that Victoria was begotten by Michael." But that is precisely what is at issue here, and the plurality's last-minute denial of this fact dramatically illustrates the subjectivity of its own analysis.

It is ironic that an approach so utterly dependent on tradition is so indifferent to our precedents. Citing barely a handful of this Court's numerous decisions defining the scope of the liberty protected by the Due Process Clause to support its reliance on tradition, the plurality acts as though English legal treatises and the American Law Reports always have provided the sole source for our constitutional principles. They have not. Just as common-law notions no longer define the "property" that the Constitution protects, neither do they circumscribe the "liberty" that it guarantees. On the contrary, "'[l]iberty' and 'property' are broad and majestic terms. They are among the '[g]reat [constitutional] concepts . . . purposely left to gather meaning from experience. . . . [T]hey relate to the whole domain of social and economic fact, and the statesmen who founded this Nation knew too well that only a stagnant society remains unchanged.'"

It is not that tradition has been irrelevant to our prior decisions. Throughout our decision making in this important area runs the theme that certain interests and practices — freedom from physical restraint, marriage, childbearing, childrearing, and others — form the core of our definition of "liberty." Our solicitude for these interests is partly the result of the fact that the Due Process Clause would seem an empty promise if it did not protect them, and partly the result of the historical and traditional importance of these interests in our society. In deciding cases arising under the Due Process Clause, therefore, we have considered whether the concrete limitation under consideration impermissibly impinges upon one of these more generalized interests.

Today's plurality, however, does not ask whether parenthood is an interest that historically has received our attention and protection; the answer to that question is too clear for dispute. Instead, the plurality asks whether the specific variety of parenthood under consideration — a natural father's relationship with a child whose mother is married to another man — has enjoyed such protection.

If we had looked to tradition with such specificity in past cases, many a decision would have reached a different result. Surely the use of contraceptives by unmarried couples, *Eisenstadt v. Baird*, 405 U.S. 438, (1972), or even by married couples, *Griswold v. Connecticut*, 381 U.S. 479 (1965); the freedom from corporal punishment in schools, *Ingraham v. Wright*, 430 U.S. 651, (1977); the freedom from an arbitrary transfer from a prison to a psychiatric institution, *Vitek v. Jones*, 445 U.S. 480 (1980); and even the right to raise one's natural but illegitimate children, *Stanley v. Illinois*, 405 U.S. 645 (1972), were not "interest[s] traditionally protected by our society," at the time of their consideration by this Court. If we had asked, therefore, in *Eisenstadt*, *Griswold*, *Ingraham*, *Vitek*, or *Stanley* itself whether the specific interest under consideration had been traditionally protected, the answer would have been a resounding "no." That we did not ask this question in those cases highlights the novelty of the interpretive method that the plurality opinion employs today.

The plurality's interpretive method is more than novel; it is misguided. It ignores the good reasons for limiting the role of "tradition" in interpreting the Constitution's deliberately capacious language. In the plurality's constitutional universe, we may not take notice of the fact that the original reasons for the conclusive presumption of paternity are out of place in a world in which blood tests can prove virtually beyond a shadow of a doubt who sired a particular child and in which the fact of illegitimacy no longer plays the burdensome and stigmatizing role it once did. Nor, in the plurality's world, may we deny "tradition" its full scope by pointing out that the rationale for the conventional rule has changed over the years, as has the rationale for Cal. Evid. Code Ann. §621 (West Supp. 1989); instead, our task is simply to identify a rule denying the asserted interest and not to ask whether the basis for that rule—which is the true reflection of the values undergirding it—has changed too often or too recently to call the rule embodying that rationale a "tradition." Moreover, by describing the decisive question as whether Michael's and Victoria's interest is one that has been "traditionally protected by our society," rather than one that society traditionally has thought important (with or without protecting it), and by suggesting that our sole function is to "discern the society's views," the plurality acts as if the only purpose of the Due Process Clause is to confirm the importance of interests already protected by a majority of the States. Transforming the protection afforded by the Due Process Clause into a redundancy mocks those who, with care and purpose, wrote the Fourteenth Amendment.

In construing the Fourteenth Amendment to offer shelter only to those interests specifically protected by historical practice, moreover, the plurality ignores the kind of society in which our Constitution exists. We are not an assimilative, homogeneous society, but a facilitative, pluralistic one, in which we must be willing to abide someone else's unfamiliar or even repellent practice because the same tolerant impulse protects our own idiosyncrasies. Even if we can agree, therefore, that "family" and "parenthood" are part of the good life, it is absurd to assume that we can agree on the content of those terms and destructive to pretend that we do. In a community such as ours, "liberty" must include the freedom not to conform. The plurality today squashes this freedom by requiring specific approval from history before protecting anything in the name of liberty.

The document that the plurality construes today is unfamiliar to me. It is not the living charter that I have taken to be our Constitution; it is instead a stagnant, archaic, hidebound document steeped in the prejudices and superstitions of a time long past. This Constitution does not recognize that times change, does not see that sometimes a practice or rule outlives its foundations. I cannot accept an interpretive method that does such violence to the charter that I am bound by oath to uphold. . . .

Because the plurality decides that Michael and Victoria have no liberty interest in their relationship with each other, it need consider neither the effect of §621 on their relationship nor the State's interest in bringing about that effect. It is obvious, however, that the effect of §621 is to terminate the relationship between Michael and Victoria before affording any hearing whatsoever on the issue whether Michael is Victoria's father. This refusal to hold a hearing is properly analyzed under our procedural due process cases, which instruct us to consider the State's interest in curtailing the procedures accompanying the termination of a constitutionally protected interest. California's interest, minute in comparison with a father's interest in his relationship with his child, cannot justify its refusal to hear Michael out on his claim that he is Victoria's father. . . .

The atmosphere surrounding today's decision is one of make-believe. Beginning with the suggestion that the situation confronting us here does not repeat itself every day in every corner of the country, moving on to the claim that it is tradition alone that supplies the details of the liberty that the Constitution protects, and passing finally to the notion that the Court always has recognized a cramped vision of "the family," today's decision lets stand California's pronouncement that Michael—whom blood tests show to a 98 percent probability to be Victoria's father—is not Victoria's father. When and if the Court awakes to reality, it will find a world very different from the one it expects.

DISCUSSION QUESTIONS FOR *MICHAEL H. v. GERALD D.*

A. What is Michael's substantive due process argument?

B. The plurality says that the legal issue here is reduced to whether the relationship between Michael and Victoria has been treated as a protected family unit under the historic practices of our society. Isn't seeing the issue through this lens rejecting the changes in society that may have altered those historic practices? Isn't it too narrow? Isn't it relying too much on tradition?

C. What is Victoria's basic claim and why does the plurality reject it?

D. Justice Brennan suggests the plurality found another "limitation on the concept of liberty." What is the limitation Justice Brennan is writing about?

E. What is Justice Brennan illustrating when he cites several cases including *Eisenstadt v. Baird*, 495 U.S. 438 (1972), to rebut Justice Scalia's analysis?

F. In your opinion, should the Court have recognized "multiple fatherhood"? Could the parties have agreed to such an arrangement privately, through mediation or negotiation?

18.4 GENETIC TESTING

In the early twentieth century, scientific proof of paternity was not very reliable. Defendants in criminal paternity proceedings were entitled to jury trials where the evidence might consist of testimony regarding the parents' relationship, the mother's relationships with other potential fathers, and the physical resemblance of the child to the defendant. Without an admission by the alleged father and no blood test, it was difficult to establish paternity.

As science advanced, blood tests became common as a means to exclude men as biological fathers of children. However, the cost of the tests made it difficult, if not impossible, for some parties to obtain them. The issue of whether the state can be required to bear the cost of a blood test where an alleged biological father is indigent was litigated in *Little v. Streater*, 452 U.S. 1 (1981). The question as framed by the Court was whether a statute that provides that in paternity actions the cost of blood grouping tests is to be borne by the party requesting them denies indigent defendants due process of law.

The Court held that to deny blood grouping tests because of a person's lack of financial resources violated the due process guarantee of the Fourteenth Amendment. It stated that because of the unique quality of blood grouping tests, they acted as a source of exculpatory evidence. It also stated that the state's financial interest in avoiding the expenses of blood grouping tests is not significant enough to overcome the substantial private interests involved. This is particularly true, it said, where federal funds are available to help defray such expenses and the state could advance such expenses and then tax them as costs to the parties. The Court also stated that without aid in obtaining blood test evidence in a paternity case, an indigent defendant, who faces the state as an adversary when the child is a recipient of public assistance and who must overcome the evidentiary burden imposed by the state, lacks "a meaningful opportunity to be heard." *Id.* at 6.

REFLECTIVE QUESTIONS	**Given the decision in *Little v. Streater*, should the public pay for DNA testing to establish paternity when requested by an indigent party?**

Background to *Sinicropi v. Mazurek*

Sinicropi v. Mazurek involves a man (Powers) who signed a voluntary acknowledgment of paternity when he believed a child was his issue. However, five years later genetic tests determined that another man (Sinicropi) was the child's biological father. Sinicropi filed a paternity action to establish that he was the father of the child.

SINICROPI
v.
MAZUREK

Court of Appeals of Michigan
729 N.W.2d 256 (2006)

MURPHY, P.J. . . . Pursuant to the plain language of the [Michigan paternity] statute, when Powers and Mazurek executed the acknowledgement of parentage Powers's paternity was established, and the child was in a position identical to one in which the child was born or conceived during a marriage. . . . The Legislature was clearly expressing a public policy position favoring legal protection of a child born out of wedlock, pursuant to which a mother and a man jointly executing an acknowledgment of parentage would be legally recognized as the child's parents without litigation, thereby allowing the parties to seek and the court to enter custody, parenting time, and support orders. . . .

Although Powers may not have had legal rights identical to those of a father whose child is born or conceived within a marriage, the Acknowledgment of Parentage Act bestowed on Powers the designation of "natural father," MCL 722.1003(1), and entitled him to seek custody. Powers was the "legal parent" for purposes of the Child Custody Act. *Killingbeck, supra* at 144, 711 N.W.2d 759 ("Pursuant to the acknowledgment of parentage statute, Killingbeck thus became a 'legal parent' for purposes of the Child Custody Act. . . ."). Moreover, from the child's legal perspective, it was as if he were born in wedlock.

Mazurek made multiple attempts to have Powers's custody action dismissed and the acknowledgment of parentage revoked, which the trial court rejected. With regard to revocation of an acknowledgment of parentage, MCL 722.1011(1) allows certain individuals, including Mazurek as the child's mother but not Sinicropi, to file a claim for revocation. An affidavit signed by the claimant is required and must set forth facts that constitute either a mistake of fact, newly discovered evidence, fraud, misrepresentation, misconduct, or duress relative to the acknowledgment. MCL 722.1011(2). . . .

In *Killingbeck, supra* at 144, 711 N.W.2d 759, this Court emphasized that even where there is clear and convincing evidence that the man who executed the acknowledgment of parentage is not the biological father, revocation of the acknowledgment must also be warranted by the equities in the case. . . .

We conclude that the trial court erred when, after refusing to revoke the acknowledgment of parentage, it nonetheless entertained Sinicropi's paternity action and entered an order of filiation recognizing Sinicropi as the child's legal father as a result of the DNA testing.

We hold that Sinicropi could not obtain an order of filiation because the Paternity Act and the Acknowledgment of Parentage Act, when read and construed together, do not permit the entry of an order of filiation where an unrevoked acknowledgment of parentage is already in place.

As noted above, the Acknowledgment of Parentage Act "*establishes paternity*" and provides a court with the basis and authority to enter orders regarding custody, parenting time, and support. MCL 722.1004. With respect to the Paternity Act, our Supreme Court stated that "[t]he act was created as a procedural vehicle for determining the paternity of children 'born out of wedlock,' and enforcing the resulting support obligation." . . . Thus, the Acknowledgment of Parentage Act and the Paternity Act provide two separate procedures by which to establish paternity and provide support for children born out of wedlock. . . .

It is evident to us that the Paternity Act and the Acknowledgment of Parentage Act constitute legislation envisioning alternative mechanisms to establish paternity where a child is born out of wedlock, i.e., an acknowledgment of parentage is executed or an order of filiation is entered. But the Legislature did not intend the creation of two legal fathers for one child through utilization of both acts, one by acknowledgment and one by order of filiation. A court cannot recognize both. As stated by our Supreme Court in *In re KH*, 469 Mich. 621, 624, 677 N.W.2d 800 (2004), "where a legal father exists, a biological father cannot properly be considered even a putative father."

With the enactment of the revocation provision contained in MCL 722.1011 of the Acknowledgment of Parentage Act, the Legislature astutely envisioned cases in which it is discovered that the biological father is not the same individual who executed the acknowledgment of parentage, yet the Legislature did not provide that the acknowledger is then automatically no longer deemed the natural father and that an order of filiation can be entered in favor of the biological father if known. Rather, the Legislature provided for revocation proceedings that took into consideration biology *and* equity. Construing the Acknowledgment of Parentage Act and the Paternity Act together and harmoniously, there can only be one conclusion with respect to the legislative intent in the context of the facts presented in this case. If an acknowledgment of parentage has been properly executed, subsequent recognition of a person as the father in an order of filiation by way of a paternity action cannot occur unless the acknowledgment has been revoked. Were we to accept Mazurek's and Sinicropi's contention that a biological father is always entitled to commence a paternity action and obtain an order of filiation where a child is born out of wedlock, the revocation provision in the Acknowledgment of Parentage Act, and especially the language regarding the equities of revocation, would be rendered meaningless in a legal battle between a biological father and an acknowledger. Such a position is contrary to the legislative intent as outlined in this opinion. . . .

Here, DNA testing provided clear and convincing evidence that Powers was not the biological father, and the parties present no argument to the contrary. Our discussion regarding the equities of the case first requires us to look at the nature of the trial court's rulings. In the fall of 2004, Mazurek filed a motion to dismiss Powers's custody action and to revoke the acknowledgment of parentage. The trial court denied the motion in a written opinion and order. However, the focus of the court's ruling was not on the "clear and convincing" and equity language contained in MCL 722.1011(3). Instead, the trial court first discussed equitable parenthood and *Van, supra*, which it found distinguishable because here there was an acknowledgment of parentage and a court order providing Powers with joint legal and physical custody. The trial court further determined that Powers was the legal parent and had standing to pursue custody. The trial court then proceeded to rule, on the basis of *Hawkins v.*

Murphy . . . that the doctrines of collateral estoppel and *res judicata* precluded dismissal of Powers's custody action and precluded revocation of the acknowledgment. The trial court essentially ruled that the issue of paternity could not be revisited. Apparently, the trial court was relying on the 2001 consent order of joint custody as support for invoking those doctrines. The trial court did not address the revocation motion as required by MCL 722.1011, specifically subsection 3. . . .

Here, the consent order of joint custody was not the result of litigation over the issue of paternity and therefore did not determine paternity. Paternity was not an issue when Powers filed the motion for custody in 2001 because the acknowledgment of parentage had already established paternity. MCL 722.1004. Of course, the acknowledgment of parentage itself did not constitute prior litigation that could give rise to *res judicata* and collateral estoppels. And the acknowledgment was expressly subject to revocation under MCL 722.1011. Thus, the trial court erred in analyzing the revocation motion in terms of *res judicata* and collateral estoppel instead of taking into consideration the necessary analysis set forth in MCL 722.1011. . . .

We remand this case so that the trial court can revisit the issue of revocation of the acknowledgment of parentage. We do so because the trial court never squarely addressed the issue of revocation within the four corners of the language of MCL 722.1011(3), which requires, in part, that Mazurek prove by clear and convincing evidence that revocation of the acknowledgment is proper "considering the equities of the case." While the trial court's comments in prior proceedings clearly demonstrate the court's position that equity favors Powers, we nevertheless conclude that remand is proper, not only to allow the court to address the issue within the parameters of MCL 722.1011(3) without consideration of *res judicata* and collateral estoppel, but also for the court to render a decision knowing and appreciating full well that if revocation is not permitted this time, Sinicropi shall have absolutely no rights as a father because the order of filiation will be vacated consistently with this opinion.

DISCUSSION QUESTIONS FOR *SINICROPI v. MAZUREK*

A. What are the public policy advantages of providing for voluntary acknowledgment of paternity? Are there disadvantages?

B. Michigan law allows the mother of a child born out of wedlock to file a claim to revoke an acknowledgment of paternity. Why shouldn't Powers and Sinicropi have the same opportunity? Would you change the statute if you were a Michigan legislator?

C. The court says that the Michigan Legislature considered biology and equity when it enacted the revocation provision in Mich. Comp. Laws §722.1011. What is the consequence of this interpretation of the statute where it is clear a person who signed an acknowledgment is not the biological father of the child and a revocation request is filed?

18.5 BURDEN OF PROOF

The burden of proof required in paternity proceedings varies from state to state. When the Court held in *Santosky v. Kramer*, 455 U.S. 745 (1982) that the "clear and convincing" standard must be applied when a civil action is brought to terminate parental rights some believed that this level of proof also applied to paternity actions. That is not the case.

A year after *Santosky* the Court decided *Rivera v. Minnich*, 483 U.S. 574 (1987). It refused to extend *Santosky* to paternity proceedings. This meant that whatever burden of proof a state had already established for determining parentage remained unchanged. The Court distinguished imposition of the legal obligations attending a biological relationship between parent and child from a state's termination of a fully existing parent-child relationship. *Id.* at 579-582. In drawing the distinction, the Court observed that state legislatures had similarly separated the two proceedings in their statutes.

REFLECTIVE QUESTIONS	Do you agree with the Court's reasoning in *Rivera* for distinguishing the burden of proof in a termination of parental rights case from the burden of proof to establish paternity?

18.6 STATUTES OF LIMITATIONS

Historically, a state statute of limitations provision established a narrow window of time, typically two years, to establish paternity. In *Clark v. Jeter*, 486 U.S. 456 (1988), the Supreme Court invalidated state statutes with short windows of opportunity within which to establish paternity holding that they denied nonmarital children equal protection of the law. In *Jeter*, the Court held that Pennsylvania's six-year statute of limitations for paternity actions did not withstand heightened scrutiny under the Equal Protection Clause. The Court suggested that six years does not necessarily provide a reasonable opportunity to assert a claim on behalf of an illegitimate child. A mother, for example, may be unwilling to file a paternity action on behalf of her child. The unwillingness may be based on one of several reasons. It could stem from her relationship with the natural father. Or, it could be caused by the emotional strain of having a child out of wedlock. Or, it could be the result of a desire to avoid community and family disapproval of having a child out of wedlock. A mother might realize belatedly a loss of income attributable to the need to care for the child. Finally, financial difficulties may increase as the child matures and incurs expenses for clothing, school, and medical care. The Court observed that the unwillingness to determine parentage may be exacerbated if the mother is a minor.

In *Mills v. Habluetzel*, 456 U.S. 91 (1992), the Court held that a Texas statute providing that a paternity suit to identify the natural father of a child born out of wedlock for purposes of obtaining child support must be brought before the child is one year old denies equal protection to these children. The Court reasoned that because Texas provided the opportunity for children born during a marriage to obtain parental support for a much greater length of time, it must also grant an identical opportunity to children born out of wedlock.

> **REFLECTIVE QUESTIONS** | Should there be any time limitation that bars a party from establishing paternity?

Background to *In re Parentage of C.S.*

In the following case, the court considers the circumstances of a child born during the marriage who is not the biological child of the husband. The husband sought to rebut the marital presumption that the child was his issue. He filed a motion to disestablish himself as father of the child. The trial court dismissed the action as barred by the statute of limitations. This appeal ensued.

IN RE PARENTAGE OF C.S.
Court of Appeals of Washington
139 P.3d 366 (2006)

ELLINGTON, J. Sherry and Dean married in 1995. The marriage was, by mutual agreement, not sexually monogamous, and the couple belonged to an Internet "swingers" group. At a party sponsored by the group in October 2001, Sherry met Frederick, who was also married but whose wife was unaware of his activities. Sherry and Frederick later met several times at a hotel, as a result of which Sherry became pregnant. Sherry informed Dean of her pregnancy, and also told him he might not be the child's father. C.S. was born on July 17, 2002. Dean was present at the birth, was named as the father on the birth certificate, and the child was given Dean as his middle name.

On August 11, 2002, a DNA test excluded Dean as the biological father. The following month, Sherry and Dean decided to end their marriage. They continued living together for a time in order to make alternative arrangements. Dean states that he has had no involvement in caring for C.S.

In November 2002, Sherry contacted Frederick via e-mail. She claims Frederick lied about his blood type to convince her he could not be C.S.'s father. Frederick then removed his identity from the Internet forum. Sherry did not know Frederick's last name, and was unable to contact him until July 2003, when she recognized him from an Internet personal ad. Frederick once more terminated his Internet identity.

In November 2003, C.S. was scheduled for surgery. After some research, Sherry was able to locate Frederick to seek family medical information. Frederick met with Sherry and C.S., gave Sherry $200, and said he would start a college fund for C.S.

In January 2004, a DNA test confirmed Frederick was C.S.'s father. Frederick started paying Sherry $500 a month. In e-mail correspondence, Frederick generally referred to supporting C.S. for a period of two years, though in one message he agreed to provide $500 monthly for 16 years.

In May 2004, Sherry informed Frederick that she and Dean planned to remove Dean's name from C.S.'s birth certificate, and asked Frederick to replace it with his own. Frederick refused, citing concern that as a public document, the certificate might alert his wife to his infidelity. Frederick, who has a law degree, told Sherry that his legal research indicated Dean could not deny paternity because Dean was the presumed father. Frederick suggested Sherry consult a lawyer.

This situation came to court on August 4, 2004, when Dean filed a petition seeking to disestablish himself as father of C.S., and to adjudicate Frederick as the father. Sherry later joined in the petition, and also asserted a common law action for determination of parentage and a claim of fraud and fraudulent concealment. On Frederick's motion, the trial court dismissed the action as barred by the statute of limitations.

Discovery Rule. Under the Uniform Parentage Act, chapter 26.26 RCW, a man is the presumed father if the child is born during his marriage to the child's mother. A proceeding to adjudicate the parentage of a child who has a presumed father "must be commenced not later than two years after the birth of the child."

Dean and Sherry acknowledge that he is C.S.'s presumed father and that the petition was filed more than two years after C.S. was born. They contend, however, that the discovery rule should apply to toll the statute, and that under the rule, the petition was timely because it was filed less than two years after Dean learned the results of the DNA test excluding him as C.S.'s father. We conclude the legislature intended the limitations period to run from the child's birth, not from acquisition of genetic evidence.

The statute of limitations upon an action generally runs from the time the cause of action accrues. If the discovery rule applies, the limitation period begins to run when the plaintiff discovers, or in the exercise of reasonable diligence should have discovered, the facts giving rise to the cause of action. . . . But the discovery rule is not available where the legislature has clearly delineated the event that starts the running of the limitations period, for there is then no "accrual" to interpret. Such is the case here.

Before Washington revised the Uniform Parentage Act in 2002, a presumed father could seek an adjudication of nonpaternity at any time, so long as the action was filed "within a reasonable time after obtaining knowledge of relevant facts." The former statute thus essentially contained a discovery rule.

In adopting the revised uniform act, however, the legislature established specific rules and processes for adjudicating paternity. The revised statute requires filing such an action within two years of the child's birth (with a single exception not applicable here).

A comment to the Uniform Parentage Act states that after the two-year period, "the presumption [of paternity] is immune from attack by any . . . individuals." The two-year limit was featured prominently in the Washington House and Senate reports. It is evident that the legislature deliberately abandoned the "reasonable time" approach in favor of a strict two-year limitation period. Under these circumstances, there is no room for interpretation and no room for the discovery rule.

Further, even if a discovery rule were available, it could not, consistent with the Uniform Parentage Act, be triggered by acquisition of DNA evidence. The statute permits filing a paternity action even before the child is born, and contemplates that DNA evidence will be presented. Both Dean and Sherry knew during Sherry's pregnancy that C.S. was possibly not his child. They thus knew all the facts necessary to the petition even before the statute began to run. The petition to disestablish Dean as C.S.'s father was time-barred.

Estoppel. The doctrine of estoppel may apply to prevent a fraudulent or inequitable resort to the statute of limitations, such as where a defendant conceals facts or otherwise induces the plaintiff not to bring suit within the limitations period. Dean and Sherry contend there are material questions of fact as to whether Frederick should be estopped from asserting the limitations defense.

For Dean, this argument fails at the threshold. Certainly there was no concealment of the facts. To make out a case for estoppel, therefore, Dean must point to some act of Frederick by which he was induced to refrain from enforcing his rights. But Frederick made no representations to Dean, and Dean states, "[I] did not involve myself with the details of the petitioner's negotiations with [Frederick], as I did not believe that it really concerned me." Dean does not claim that any act of Frederick induced him to refrain from filing this action. Rather, he believed "this was something [Sherry and he] could resolve eventually." Dean can establish no estoppel.

As to Sherry's arguments, it is useful to observe at the outset that the petition in question sought two forms of relief: to *disestablish* Dean and to *establish* Frederick as C.S.'s father. There is no requirement that these issues be combined. The limitations period applies only to the petition to disestablish Dean's presumed paternity, which, once accomplished, would have allowed a petition to establish Frederick's paternity at any time thereafter. Yet most of Sherry's estoppel arguments pertain to establishing Frederick as C.S.'s father, not to disestablishing Dean. . . .

Both Dean and Sherry knew during Sherry's pregnancy that C.S. was possibly not his child. They thus knew all the facts necessary to the petition even before the statute began to run. The petition to disestablish Dean as C.S.'s father was time-barred. . . .

Dean and Sherry urge us to recognize a common law cause of action to adjudicate Frederick as C.S.'s father, arguing that otherwise "the actions and inactions of the adults in this case [will] have . . . deprived C.S. of his own action to adjudicate his biological father as his legal father." As previously discussed, C.S. is not bound by any adjudication to which he was not a party, and may file his own petition at any time. He has thus not been deprived of any legal rights. . . .

This is a troubling set of facts, and leaves the court dismayed at the predicament of a child twice abandoned. The legislative limitations period, however, rests soundly upon the value of stability, and if stability is completely absent here despite the legislature's efforts, that does nothing to diminish the wisdom of the general rule. Dean will thus continue, however unwillingly, to serve as C.S.'s legal father.

DISCUSSION QUESTIONS FOR *IN RE PARENTAGE OF C.S.*

A. Why is the statute of limitations for the purpose of establishing paternity so much longer that the statute of limitations to disestablish paternity? Is this sound public policy?

B. Dean and Sherry argue the discovery rule applies in this case. Explain their argument.

C. Did application of the concept of estoppel prevent Frederick from asserting the statute of limitations?

D. After the decision in this case, does Frederick have any legal obligation to the child? Might he be required to pay child support? Will he be allowed visitation if he makes such a request? Will the child inherit from him?

18.7 ESTABLISHING PATERNITY: PARENTAGE REGISTRY

Under the Uniform Parentage Act (UPA), a man who wishes to be notified of a proceeding for termination of parental rights or adoption regarding a child he may have fathered must enter his name in a paternity registry within 30 days of the birth of the child. In some situations, failure to do so could result in termination of parental rights without notice. UPA §401 et seq.

REFLECTIVE QUESTIONS Consider reviewing the section on the parentage registry in the adoption chapter.

18.8 MATERNITY PRESUMPTION

Historically, a woman who gave birth to a child was presumed to be the child's legal mother. The Uniform Parentage Act (UPA) specifically provides that "[t]he mother-child relationship is established between a woman and a child by: (1) the woman's having given birth to the child. . . ." UPA §201(a)(1).

Several developments have made determinations of maternity more complicated than in the past. First, alternative reproductive technologies have blurred the definition of motherhood. Second, as courts increasingly recognize "social" fathers over biological fathers, women who have established parenting relationships with children have sought recognition as social or intended mothers. Finally, courts have begun to explore the extent to which common law and statutory presumptions of paternity might also apply to questions of maternity.

Background to *Amy G. v. M.W.*

In the following case, *Amy G. v. M.W.*, a stepmother asserts that she, not the biological mother, should be the legal mother of a child.

AMY G.
v.
M.W.

Court of Appeal of California
142 Cal. App. 4th 1 (2006)

KLEIN, P.J. Father is married to Amy. During his marriage to Amy, he had an extramarital relationship with Kim, the real party in interest. That relationship resulted in a child, Nathan. During her relationship with father, Kim was married to Steven, but they were separated at the time of Nathan's conception and birth. Nathan is Kim's only child. Father and Amy have two daughters.

The parties disagree as to their intent and as to the circumstances of Nathan's conception and birth. Father asserts Kim offered to bear a child who would be raised as a child of his marriage to Amy. Kim contends her relationship with father was romantic, the pregnancy was unplanned, and that she expected they would raise Nathan jointly. Kim concealed her pregnancy from business associates, acquaintances, family and friends and left California for Virginia, where she gave birth to Nathan. Kim cared for Nathan during his first month in Virginia.

In June 2003, when Nathan was one month old, father came to Virginia to take him to California. Father met with Kim in a hotel lobby. He presented Kim with an "agreement regarding custody and adoption" (the Agreement), drafted by a Maryland law firm he had retained. The Agreement provided: father would have sole custody over Nathan; Kim would have no visitation; and Kim consented to a stepparent adoption by Amy. The Agreement also contained recitals to the effect that Kim acknowledged and was aware of her right to obtain independent counsel, father's counsel had not provided her with any legal advice in connection with the Agreement, she was executing the Agreement freely and voluntarily, and the Agreement was not the product of any fraud, duress or undue influence. Kim and father signed the Agreement while sitting in father's limousine. Kim did not have a lawyer when she signed the document. She contends she did not understand what she was signing and felt pressured to do so. After signing the Agreement, they returned to the hotel lobby where father picked up Nathan. Kim handed father all of Nathan's clothes, formula, diapers and toys. That evening, father flew with Nathan back to Los Angeles. Since June 29, 2003, Nathan has lived continuously with father and his family and has never been alone with Kim. On September 29, 2003, Kim filed a petition against father to establish parental relationship, seeking child support, custody and visitation. Thereafter, Kim brought an order to show cause. Kim did not serve the papers until November 11, 2003. Father responded, requesting the court to deny Kim the relief she requested and to enter a judgment of parentage recognizing Amy as the mother. . . .

Father and Amy's Arguments Are Unavailing Because Amy Cannot Be Deemed to Be Nathan's Mother. . . . Amy and father advance several arguments as to why Amy can allege status as Nathan's mother. Amy and father allege Amy is Nathan's presumed mother under section 7611, subdivisions (a) and (d). They further allege Amy is conclusively presumed to be Nathan's mother under section 7540. They also take the position Amy is Nathan's natural mother within the meaning of section 7635, subdivision (b). Based on any and all of these claims, Amy and father argue Amy is entitled either to joinder in Kim's action or to standing to bring an independent maternity action. As explained, none of these theories has merit.

Amy Cannot Establish Status as Nathan's Presumed Mother Under Section 7611, Subdivisions (a) and (d). Section 7611 sets forth various circumstances wherein the court will presume a man to be a child's father. "A man is presumed to be the natural father of the child if . . . [¶] (a) He and the child's natural mother are or have been married to each other and the child is born during the marriage. . . ." (§7611, subd. (a).) A man is also presumed to be the natural father of the child if "[h]e receives the child into his home and openly holds out the child as his natural child." (§7611, subd. (d).)

. . . In general, California law only recognizes one mother. (*Johnson v. Calvert* (1993) 851 P.2d 776.) Amy and father do not dispute that Kim gave birth to Nathan, making Kim the natural mother under section 7610, subdivision (a). . . . Amy and father argue Amy is Nathan's presumed mother under section 7611, subdivision (a), by virtue of her marriage to father, and under section 7611, subdivision (d), because she received Nathan into her home and held him out as her own child. Neither the case law nor the statutory framework supports this argument.

In limited circumstances, the presumptions of paternity listed in section 7611 have been interpreted to apply to women. . . .

In *Karen C.*, the birth mother gave her child to another woman when the child was born and subsequently absented herself. . . . The other woman, who took the child into her home and raised the child as her own, was presumed to be the child's mother under section 7611, subdivision (d). . . . Similarly, in *Salvador M.*, where the birth mother was deceased, the child's adult half-sister who raised the child since his mother's death was presumed to be his mother under section 7611, subdivision (d). . . . Thus, in both *Karen C.* and *Salvador M.*, the birth mother was absent and there was no competing claim to maternity.

Elisa B. applied section 7611, subdivision (d), to declare a woman, Elisa, a presumed mother of the twin children born to her same-sex partner, Emily. . . . After the relationship ended, a county district attorney sued Elisa for child support on behalf of the twins. Elisa had actively participated in causing the children to be conceived with the understanding that she would raise the children as her own together with Emily. Once the children were born, Elisa received them into her home and openly held them out as her own. Given these circumstances, the court declared Elisa a presumed mother under section 7611, subdivision (d), perceiving "no reason" why both parents of a child cannot be women. In reaching this conclusion, the court specifically noted there were *"no competing claims to her being the children's second parent."*

Father and Amy rely on *Elisa B.* for the proposition that section 7611 should apply in maternity cases even where the child's birth mother is present and asserts legal parenthood. However, *Elisa B.* is distinguishable. Here, Nathan's natural father is known and present in the action. Nathan only can have one additional parent. Both father and Amy concede that Kim is Nathan's biological mother. By alleging presumed maternity, Amy advances a competing claim to be Nathan's second parent. Because the absence of a competing claim to be the second parent specifically drove the *Elisa B.* court's decision, *Elisa B.* cannot control this case.

The cases cited by Amy and father where the courts applied the presumed father statute, section 7611, to recognize a presumed mother all involved circumstances where there was *no competing claim* to be the child's mother or second parent. . . . Here, unlike those cases, both the child's biological father and biological mother have identified themselves and come forward to assert their legal parentage. Under these circumstances, it is not appropriate to invoke a gender-neutral reading of the paternity presumptions to provide Nathan with another mother. To allow Amy an opportunity to be declared Nathan's mother through a gender-neutral reading of the UPA would arrive at an impracticable result. (§7650, subd. (a).). . . .

Amy Is Not Nathan's Presumed Mother Under Section 7540. Father and Amy alternatively contend Amy is conclusively presumed to be Nathan's mother under section 7540, which provides, *"Except as provided in Section 7541*, the child of a wife cohabiting with her husband, who is not impotent or sterile, is conclusively presumed to be a child of the marriage." (§7540) According to father and Amy, because section 7650, subdivision (a), mandates application of paternity rules to maternity actions, Nathan is conclusively presumed to be a child of father and Amy's marriage under section 7540.

Their argument is without merit. In their interpretation of section 7540, Amy and father overlook the statute's qualifying phrase *"Except as provided in Section 7541. . . ."* (§7540.) Section 7541, subdivision (a), overrides the presumption of paternity under section 7540 if blood tests reveal that the biological mother's husband is not the father of the child. Assuming arguendo, we apply a gender-neutral reading of section 7540, we must also apply a gender-neutral reading of section 7541, which would negate a wife's conclusive presumption of maternity when blood tests reveal she is not the mother of the child.

Here, no blood tests are required. It is undisputed that Kim, not Amy, is Nathan's biological mother. Accordingly, Amy cannot enjoy a conclusive presumption of maternity under section 7540.

Amy Cannot Assert Status as Nathan's Natural Mother. We also reject Amy and father's additional suggestion that Amy is Nathan's natural mother, and therefore can be joined pursuant to section 7635, subdivision (b). While the word "natural" is not always interpreted as synonymous with "biological," . . . the language of section 7635, subdivision (b), expressly refers to the "natural mother" and also differentiates between "each man *presumed* to be the father under Section 7611, and each man alleged to be the *natural* father. . . ." (§7635, subd. (b).) Because the statutory language provides this distinction, we interpret "natural mother" here to refer to the biological mother. Thus, Amy cannot be deemed to be Nathan's natural mother.

Preliminary Conclusion: Trial Court Did Not Err in Refusing to Join Amy or in Granting Kim's Motion to Quash Amy's Separate Action. For the reasons discussed above, we hold, where as here, a birth mother promptly comes forward to assert her legal maternity, and the child's father is undisputed and present in the action, the father's spouse cannot be the child's natural mother or the child's presumed mother through a gender-neutral reading of either section 7611, subdivisions (a) and (d), or section 7540.

Because Amy cannot legally be Nathan's mother under these circumstances, Amy cannot "claim an interest relating to the subject of the action" which would require her joinder under Code of Civil Procedure section 389, subdivision (a). Amy is not Nathan's natural mother or presumed mother and therefore is not a person who may be made a party to the action under section 7635, subdivision (b); for the same reasons, she is not an "interested person" within the meaning of section 7650, subdivision (a); and she cannot claim custody rights under rule 5.158(a) because Nathan is not a child of the marriage between Amy and father.

For these reasons, we find no error in either the trial court's denial of father's motion to join Amy or its grant of Kim's motion to quash Amy's independent action. . . .

FOR *AMY G. v. M.W.*

A. What is the basis of Amy's claims under Cal. Fam. Code §§7611(a) and (d)? What is the basis of her claim under Cal. Fam. Code §7635(b)?

B. The court states as follows: "To allow Amy an opportunity to be declared Nathan's mother through a gender-neutral reading of the UPA would arrive at an impracticable result." Why would such a reading be "impracticable"?

C. What is Amy's argument with respect to the marital presumption? Do you find it persuasive?

D. The court distinguishes cases where there was no competing claim of parentage from this case. Do you agree with the distinction?

18.9 DE FACTO PARENTS

Sometimes an adult with no biological or legal link to a child functions *in loco parentis* to the child. As discussed in the chapter on parenting time and visitation, these caring adults may be awarded de facto legal status and allowed visitation and possibly custody, depending on the applicable state statute.

To gain de facto status, a nonparent must be found by the court to have assumed, on a day-to-day basis, the role of parent. The nonparent should have fulfilled both the child's physical and psychological needs for care and affection, and assumed that role for a substantial period. *See* Cal. Rule of Court 1401(a)(8) (2015). The nonparent should have achieved a close and continuing relationship with the child, which is likely to give the nonparent a unique knowledge about the child and his or her needs.

Once a court recognizes a nonparent as having de facto status, that person gains a protected legal interest in the child. De facto parents become full parties, entitled to be represented by counsel in some states such as California. They also may present evidence in custody, visitation, and dependency actions. *See In re Cynthia C.*, 58 Cal. App. 4th 1479, 1490-1491 (1997).

A nonparent who otherwise meets the description of de facto parent may be denied that status if he or she has betrayed and abandoned, not embraced, the role of parent by inflicting harm on the child or by exposing the child to a risk of serious harm.

> **REFLECTIVE QUESTIONS**   What is the utility of introducing into family law the concept of a "de facto" parent?

Background to *In re Parentage of L.B.*

The combination of the technological advances both of genetic testing and assisted reproduction, along with a change in view from the traditional family concept of prior years, has given rise in the past decade or more to numerous decisions around the country concerned with the issue of whether a person can obtain parental and custodial rights of a child where the child was conceived by assisted reproduction or surrogate relationship during that person's committed intimate domestic relationship with another person of the same sex, and where both of these individuals made a joint decision to cause the birth of the child and thereafter raise the child. Employing legal theories involving psychological parenthood, *in loco parentis* status, de facto parenthood, or parenthood by estoppel, some courts have found that a nonbiologically related or nonadoptive parent involved in such a committed relationship was entitled to rights of custody and visitation.

In *In re Parentage of L.B.*, the Supreme Court of Washington responds to a request from a same-sex partner to recognize her as a common law de facto parent.

IN RE PARENTAGE OF L.B.
Supreme Court of Washington
122 P.3d 161 (2005)

BRIDGE, J. Carvin and Britain became romantically involved in a same-sex relationship in June 1989 and cohabitated from September 1989 until February 2001. In 1994 the couple jointly decided to conceive and raise a child. A close male friend of theirs, John Auseth, agreed to donate sperm to assist in their efforts. The parties conducted the artificial insemination in their home, with Carvin personally inseminating Britain with the donor sperm. Carvin accompanied Britain to her prenatal appointments, and they participated together in prenatal birthing classes. On May 10, 1995, Carvin was present at and assisted in the birth of L.B. When she was born, the parties gave L.B. family names representing both Carvin's and Britain's family. In L.B.'s baby book, Britain listed herself under "mother" and altered "father" to also read "mother," listing Carvin.

For the first six years of L.B.'s life, Carvin, Britain, and L.B. lived together as a family unit and held themselves out to the public as a family. Carvin and Britain shared parenting responsibilities, with Carvin actively involved in L.B.'s parenting, including discipline decisions, day care and schooling decisions, and medical care decisions. Both parties were named as "parents" on L.B.'s kindergarten and first grade records. While the parties now dispute the nature of their relationship and the extent of Carvin's role as a "mother," as the Court of Appeals notes, "the record reflects that Carvin provided much of the child's 'mothering' during the first six years of her life." . . . This conclusion is supported by the fact that L.B., in her interactions with the two women, referred to Carvin as "mama" and Britain as "mommy."

L.B. was nearly six years old when the parties ended their relationship. After initially sharing custody and parenting responsibilities, Britain eventually took measures to limit Carvin's contact with L.B. and in the spring of 2002, unilaterally terminated all of Carvin's contact with L.B. L.B. was then seven years old.

Seeking to continue her relationship with L.B., on November 15, 2002, Carvin filed a petition for the establishment of parentage in King County Superior Court.

[ANALYSIS.] In the face of advancing technologies and evolving notions of what comprises a family unit, this case causes us to confront the manner in which our state, through its statutory scheme and common law principles, defines the terms "parents" and "families." During the first half of Washington's statehood, determinations of the conflicting rights of persons in family relationships were made by courts acting in equity.

But over the past half-century, our legislature has established statutory schemes intended to govern various aspects of parentage, child custody disputes, visitation privileges, and child support obligations . . . yet, inevitably, in the field of familial relations, factual scenarios arise, which even after a strict statutory analysis remain unresolved, leaving deserving parties without any appropriate remedy, often where demonstrated public policy is in favor of redress. . . .

[Common law parentage.] *Common Law:* Carvin asserts that, because she lacks an adequate remedy at law, equity and the common law should accord her standing as a *de facto* parent. Britain objects to the recognition of a common law right, asserting that such considerations are properly the province of our legislature. . . .

Washington courts have consistently invoked their equity powers and common law responsibility to respond to the needs of children and families in the face of changing realities. We have often done so in spite of legislative enactments that may have spoken to the area of law, but did so incompletely. With these common law principles in mind, we turn to whether Washington's common law recognizes *de facto* parents.

Washington's Recognition of Common Law Parentage: Carvin asks this court to affirm the Court of Appeals' holding recognizing a common law *de facto* parent status, asserting that the same is consistent with our jurisprudence and that severing such a parent-child relationship, regardless of its lack of statutory recognition, would be detrimental to the child. Britain counters that because she is the biological mother of L.B. and there has been no finding that she is unfit, the law presumes she acts in the best interests of her child and the state should not interfere in her decisions, regardless of their impact on L.B. (citing *Troxel*, 530 U.S. at 70, 120 S. Ct. 2054). Further she contends that granting parental status to "psychological parents" would have "wide reaching implications" opening the door to claims by "teachers, nannies, parents of best friends, . . . adult siblings, aunts, [] grandparents," and every "third-party . . . caregiver." . . .

Washington courts have long recognized that individuals not biologically or legally related to the children whom they "parent" may nevertheless be considered a child's "psychological parent." . . . Yet Carvin's claim here seeks more than a simple recognition of her status as a psychological parent—she seeks standing as a *de facto* parent.

Two Court of Appeals cases support Carvin's claim that Washington's common law recognizes the status of *de facto* parents. Implicitly recognizing *de facto* parentage status, these courts have awarded custody to nonbiological "parents" over the objection of otherwise fit biological parents. In *In re Marriage of Allen* . . . , noting that "unique circumstances may warrant unique custody decrees," Division Three affirmed a trial court's custody decree in favor of a deaf child's stepmother over the objection of the child's biological father. The stepmother parented the child from age three to age seven, and during that time, due in large part to the stepmother's "dedication, devotion and determination," the child showed "remarkable development." . . . The court recognized that, in custody disputes between parents and nonparents, "[g]reat deference is accorded to parental rights" yet those rights are "balanced by the State's interest as *parens patriae* in the child's welfare." . . . When these interests come into conflict, the parent's rights may be outweighed. . . . The court then found that parental unfitness *or* a determination that "the child's growth and development would be detrimentally affected by placement with an otherwise fit parent" could serve to outweigh parental rights. . . . The Court of Appeals then made two findings: one, that despite the father's fitness as a parent, the child's development would be detrimentally affected if his father was awarded custody, and two, that the child "had become integrated into the family unit" formed by the father and stepmother. . . . With regard to the second finding, it noted:

> Where the reason for deferring to parental rights — the goal of preserving families — would be ill-served by maintaining parental custody, as where a child is integrated into the nonparent's family, the *de facto* family relationship does not exist as to the natural parent and need not be supported. In such a case, custody might lie with a nonparent.

The court concluded that "the psychological relationship [here] is *equivalent* to that of a natural family entity." . . .

Division One reached a similar conclusion in *In re Custody of Stell*. . . . There, the child referred to his aunt as "Mom" and expert testimony established that she had become his "psychological parent." . . . Testimony also showed that because of the child's "special need for stability and consistent parenting," placement with the father "would be detrimental." . . . The Court of Appeals additionally found that the record reflected that the aunt was the "psychological parent" of the child, that the two "represent a family unit," and that "these considerations cannot be ignored." . . . The Court of Appeals thus reversed the trial court's award of permanent custody to the child's father. . . . The cases of *Allen* and *Stell* support the proposition that Washington common law recognizes the significance of parent-child relationships that may otherwise lack statutory recognition. In addition, both cases make clear that individuals may comprise a legally cognizable family through means other than biological or adoptive.

[Legislative pronouncements on parentage.] *Uniform Parentage Act:* In 2000, Washington adopted the then-current version of the UPA to govern statutory determinations of parentage in our state. . . . Several sections of the UPA shed light on our state's public policy concerning disputes which touch on the rights and interests of children. Specifically, the legislature established that questions of parentage are to be considered without differentiation on the basis of the marital status or gender of the child's parent. . . . Additionally, the UPA establishes that at least in the case of artificial insemination, the intent of the parties is the principal inquiry in determining legal parentage. . . . While not directly controlling here, these related policy pronouncements inform our decision making regarding recognition of a common law right to *de facto* parentage.

In defining the scope of the act, the UPA provides that "[t]his chapter governs every determination of parentage in this state." . . . Nevertheless, while attempting to give structure and predictability to such determinations, neither the UPA nor corresponding statutes defining parental rights and responsibilities purport to pre-clude the operation of the common law when addressing situations left unanswered after conducting a strict statutory inquiry. . . . It is important to note that it is the interrelated nature of the UPA and other relevant statutory enactments and common law principles which give the UPA meaning. Thus, a close examination of these related statutes is necessary to determine whether the legislature intended the UPA and the related statutes as the *exclusive* means of obtaining parental rights and enforcing parental responsibilities, and also serves the parallel purpose of dis-cerning the extent of any such rights recognizable by the common law. . . .

[Recognition of common law de facto parentage.] . . . In 1995, the Wis-consin Supreme Court was presented with a situation factually analogous to the one presented here. *See In re Custody of J.S.H.K.* . . . In that case, two women "shared a close, committed relationship for more than ten years" and jointly decided to raise a child. . . . One partner was artificially inseminated with sperm from an anonymous donor, became pregnant, and in December 1988 a child was born. . . . The women gave the child names honoring the families of both partners, held themselves out to the public as a family unit, and actively co-parented the child until their relationship ended in 1993. . . . Three months after the parties separated, the biological mother terminated her former partner's relationship with the child and filed a restraining order seeking to prohibit all contact. . . . In response, the biological mother's former partner filed a petition for visitation and custody.

The Wisconsin Supreme Court determined that under the Wisconsin statutory scheme, the biological mother's former female partner lacked standing to petition for custody or visitation. . . . The relevant custody statute, Wisconsin Statute §767.24 (1991-1992), provided that a nonparent may petition for custody only if a parent is "unfit or unable to care for the child" or other compelling reasons exist. . . . The former partner was unable to meet this standard and thus lacked standing. . . . In addition, the court rejected the former partner's statutory visitation claim because the court determined that the "legislature enacted the ch. 767 visi-tation statute with the dissolution of marriage in mind." . . . Because the parties' dispute did not arise in the context of dissolution of a marriage, a legal impossibility because of their lesbian relationship, statutory visitation was unavailable.

In spite of this determination, the court held that the legislature had not intended to preempt the equitable power of the court in domestic matters so as to preclude a remedy *outside* of the statutory scheme. It then examined the history of that state's visitation law and the relevant legislative enactments to discern whether the statutory scheme was intended as the exclusive means of obtaining visitation rights and con-cluded that "[i]t is reasonable to infer that the legislature did not intend the visitation statutes to bar the courts from exercising their equitable power to order visitation in circumstances not included within the statutes but in conformity with the policy directions set forth in the statutes." . . . The court thus concluded that courts have equitable power to hear a visitation petition if it finds that the nonparent has a "parent-like relationship with the child" and that "a significant triggering event justifies state intervention." *Id.* at 694, 533 N.W.2d 419 (requiring, as a threshold matter, that the legal parent substantially interfere with the petitioner's parent-like relationship and then setting forth the four-part test adopted by our Court of Appeals below).

Again, with facts substantially identical to those present here, in 1999, the Massachusetts Supreme Judicial Court recognized the viability of the common law de facto parent doctrine. See E.N.O. v. L.M.M. . . . There, the former partner of the biological mother sought temporary visitation with the child she had parented from birth until the child was over three years old. . . . The court held that the "equity jurisdiction" of the probate and family court governed resolution of the issue in spite of a lack of statutory authority. . . . It then concluded that the "the best interests of the child require . . . the child's de facto parent[] be allowed . . . visitation with the child." . . . The court found significant the fact that the former lesbian partner "was intimately involved in the decision to bring the child into the world." . . . Additionally, E.N.O. noted that, contrary to cases where a third party nonparent seeks rights vis-à-vis a child, or even where a putative father seeks paternity rights, here the family unit deserving protection was the family unit consisting of the biological mother, the lesbian partner, and the child, . . . and "[t]he child's interest in maintaining his filial ties with the plaintiff counters the [biological mother's] custodial interest." Id. The fact that "[t]he only *family* the child has ever known," id. (emphasis added), could be described as a nontraditional family unit, did not make its disruption any less significant to the child. As such, E.N.O.'s holding principally rested on its conclusion that "recognition of de facto parents is in accord with notions of the modern family," . . . and it is the actual family unit that should ultimately be afforded respect and protected from unreasonable disruption. Numerous other jurisdictions have recognized common law rights on behalf of de facto parents. . . . These cases provide a well reasoned and just template for the recognition of de facto parent status in Washington.

Conclusion: Our state's current statutory scheme reflects the unsurprising fact that statutes often fail to contemplate all potential scenarios which may arise in the ever changing and evolving notion of familial relations. Yet, simply because a statute fails to speak to a specific situation should not, and does not in our common law system, operate to preclude the availability of potential redress. This is especially true when the rights and interests of those least able to speak for themselves are concerned. We cannot read the legislature's pronouncements on this subject to preclude any potential redress to Carvin or L.B. In fact, to do so would be antagonistic to the clear legislative intent that permeates this field of law—to effectuate the best interests of the child in the face of differing notions of family and to provide certain and needed economical and psychological support and nurturing to the children of our state. While the legislature may eventually choose to enact differing standards than those recognized here today, and to do so would be within its province, until that time, it is the duty of this court to "endeavor to administer justice according to the promptings of reason and common sense." . . .

To establish standing as a de facto parent we adopt the following criteria, delineated by the Wisconsin Supreme Court and set forth in the Court of Appeals opinion below: (1) the natural or legal parent consented to and fostered the parent-like relationship, (2) the petitioner and the child lived together in the same household, (3) the petitioner assumed obligations of parenthood without expectation of financial compensation, and (4) the petitioner has been in a parental role for a length of time sufficient to have established with the child a bonded, dependent relationship, parental in nature. . . . In addition, recognition of a de facto parent is "limited to those adults who have fully and completely undertaken a permanent, unequivocal, committed, and responsible parental role in the child's life." . . .

We thus hold that henceforth in Washington, a de facto parent stands in legal parity with an otherwise legal parent, whether biological, adoptive, or otherwise. . . . As such, recognition of a person as a child's de facto parent necessarily "authorizes [a] court to consider an award of parental rights and responsibilities . . . based on its determination of the best interest of the child." . . . A de facto parent is not entitled to any parental privileges, as a matter of right, but only as is determined to be in the best interests of the child at the center of any such dispute.

DISCUSSION QUESTIONS FOR *IN RE PARENTAGE OF L.B.*

A. What is the criteria the court adopts that must be met in order to establish standing as a de facto parent?

B. What is the significance of the distinction between recognizing a psychological parent and a de facto parent?

C. Of what significance to the outcome of this case was the UPA?

D. The court cites *In re Custody of J.S.H.K* for what proposition? How is *E.N.O. v. L.M.M.* used by the court in this opinion?

E. In a part of the majority opinion not included here, the court stated as follows:

> Britain's primary argument is that the State, through judicial action, cannot infringe on or materially interfere with her rights as a biological parent in favor of Carvin's rights as a nonparent third party. However, today we hold that our common law recognizes the status of de facto parents and places them in parity with biological and adoptive parents in our state. Thus, if, on remand, Carvin can establish standing as a de facto parent, Britain and Carvin would both have a "fundamental liberty interest" in the "care, custody, and control" of L.B. . . .
>
> Additionally, contrary to Britain's assertions, *Troxel* does not establish that recognition of a de facto parentage right infringes on the liberty interests of a biological or adoptive parent. First, *Troxel* did not address the issue of state law determinations of "parents" and "families," rather simply disapproved of the grant of visitation in that case, narrowly holding that "[t]he problem . . . is not that the [trial court] intervened" but that, when it did so, "it gave no special weight at all" to the parents' determination

regarding the grandparents' visitation. *Troxel,* 530 U.S. at 69, 120 S. Ct. 2054. Second, addressing the issue of nontraditional families and disputes arising therefrom, Justice Stevens noted that:

Even the Court would seem to agree that in many circumstances, it would be constitutionally permissible for a court to award some visitation of a child to a parent or previous caregiver in cases of parental separation or divorce, cases of disputed custody, cases involving temporary foster care or guardianship, and so forth.

Id. at 85, 120 S. Ct. 2054 (Stevens, J., dissenting).

What is Britain's argument under *Troxel*? Do you find it persuasive?

General Principles

1. At common law, children born outside of marriage were viewed as "illegitimate," and they had few rights and privileges.
2. Because of the harsh treatment "illegitimate" children received at common law, a strong presumption of legitimacy developed in favor of children who were born during marriage. The presumption could be overcome only with proof that the husband was incapable of procreation or had no access to the wife during the period of conception.
3. UPA §505 provides that a man may be "rebuttably identified" as a father based on the results of genetic testing.
4. If properly executed, under the UPA an acknowledgment of paternity is "the equivalent of a judicial adjudication of paternity of the child." UPA §201(b)(2); UPA §305.
5. The applicable standard of proof in parentage cases is preponderance of the evidence.
6. To remain eligible for federal subsidies for child support enforcement, states were required to extend statutes of limitation related to establishment of paternity until age 18 or longer. Different statutes of limitation apply when a presumed or acknowledged father seeks to disestablish, rather than establish, paternity.
7. A woman who gives birth to a child is presumed to be the child's legal mother.

Chapter Problems

1. Assume that Patrick is married to Donna and during the marriage a child, Chris, is born. When Chris is seven years old, Patrick and Donna divorce.

Donna tells Patrick that he is not the father of Chris. Genetic testing confirms that Tom is the biological father. Who is the legal father of Chris? What, if any, additional information do you need to make this determination?

2. A mother alleges that she had intercourse with two men prior to giving birth to a child. The men were identical twins, and genetic testing showed that each had a 99.999 percent genetic probability of being the father. Assume that you are the judge in this case, what kind of evidence will you expect the attorneys to produce? How would you make a decision in this case? *See State of Missouri ex rel. Department of Social Services v. Miller,* 218 S.W.3d 2 (Mo. App. 2007).

3. Historically, jurisdictions allowed jury trials in paternity cases. However, The Personal Responsibility and Work Opportunity Reconciliation Act of 1996 (PRWORA) required states to preclude jury trials in contested paternity cases as a condition of receiving federal funds. Were jury trials more important before the advent of accurate genetic testing? Why might the change have been required?

Preparation for Practice

1. Locate an acknowledgment of paternity form used in your state. What, if any, changes would you recommend making?

2. In cases where paternity is disestablished, the "former father" may attempt, but will not necessarily succeed at, obtaining reimbursement of child support. *See J.S. v. L.S.,* 912 A.2d 180 (N.J. App. 2006); *Wheat v. Commonwealth Cabinet for Health and Family Services,* 217 S.W.3d 266 (Ky. App. 2007); *In re Marriage of Smith,* 7 P.3d 1012 (Colo. App. 1999). What arguments can be made for and against reimbursing child support under these circumstances?

3. Professor Nancy E. Dowd proposes several changes to the Uniform Parentage Act:

> First, I would give stronger recognition to social fathers. I would recognize parentage at birth of a "birthfather," based on a nurture standard. Biological fathers would be presumptive birthfathers. I would not maintain the marital presumption, or alternatively, not give it much weight. Second, I would recognize multiple fathers. Instead of identifying only one legal father, I would recognize genetic and social fathers. Third, I would split parental rights and responsibilities. Economic support of a child would be required of the genetic father. Social rights would be a function of performing social fathering. If a social, non-genetic father voluntarily assumed the economic responsibilities of the genetic father, then the genetic father's legal

fatherhood could be terminated. All of these proposals are centered on the core principle that fatherhood should be defined around nurture.

Nancy E. Dowd, *Parentage at Birth: Birthfathers and Social Fatherhood*, 14 Wm. & Mary Bill Rts. J. 909 (2006). Do you agree that fatherhood should be defined around "nurture"?

4. Professor Harris writes that biology and function are the primary legal bases for determining parentage:

> Child support law has become predominantly welfare-driven; . . . it has taken on characteristics of "public law," regardless of whether it applies to the poor or to the upper classes. The law that governs private disputes over custody, visitation and the like continues to have the characteristics of "private law." The difference in these approaches is especially apparent in the law of parentage. If child support is the ultimate question, parentage will likely be determined according to biology, the principle favored by the "public law approach." If custody or access is the main issue, private law principles, which tend to respect functional parenthood, are more likely to be invoked. And yet, once legal parentage is determined, it applies to determine the rights and duties of the involved adults vis-à-vis the child, regardless of context.

Leslie Joan Harris, *The Basis for Legal Parentage and the Clash Between Custody and Child Support*, 42 Ind. L. Rev. 611, 613-614 (2009). Should parentage be determined differently depending on the purpose of the determination?

5. As parentage determinations have become more complicated, some have argued for recognition of multiple parents. If multiple parents received recognition as legal parents, how should financial responsibility for a child be allocated? *See* Melanie B. Jacobs, *More Parents, More Money: Reflections on the Financial Implications of Multiple Parentage*, 16 Cardozo J.L. & Gender 217 (2010).

Chapter 19

Adoption

19.1 INTRODUCTION

This chapter focuses on situations where, due to the death of a parent or a voluntary or involuntary termination of parental rights, a new legal parent or set of parents is established pursuant to a court order. Although the underlying circumstances giving rise to the adoption may in some cases be tragic, the occasion of adoption can be a joyous one.

The chapter provides basic information about adoption, including its history, the development of constitutional protections for unwed fathers, and the role that race and ethic origin may play in selecting an adoptive parent. Some of the questions the chapter raises include the following: What rights do adoptive children have to inherit from their biological parents? What has been the Supreme Court's role in expanding unwed fathers' rights to their biological children? What role does race and ethnic origin play when deciding who may adopt? Should public policy keep most adoption records secret? What is an open adoption? Is there a need for a national adoption registry? Do Native American children receive special consideration from Congress in adoption cases?

> **REFLECTIVE QUESTIONS**   What are your goals for this chapter?

19.2 ADOPTION DATA

It is difficult to obtain an accurate overall assessment of adoption in the United States. The U.S. Department of Health and Human Services, Administration for Children and Families, Administration on Children, Youth and Families, Children's Bureau, reported that an estimated 50,608 children were adopted with welfare agency involvement in 2013. It also reported that there were 101,840 children waiting to be adopted in that year. Of that number, 58,887 children were available for adoption as the result of legal actions in which the rights of their biological parents had been terminated. *See* http://www.acf.hhs.gov/sites/default/files/cb/afcarsreport21.pdf (last visited August 2015). Of the children waiting for adoption, 42 percent were White, 24 percent were Black or African-American, and 23 percent were Hispanic.

| REFLECTIVE QUESTIONS | Were you surprised by any of the data collected in the above study? |

19.3 HISTORY

Although the practice of adoption dates back to ancient times, there was no legal provision for adoption at common law. It was not until 1851 that the first American adoption statute was passed in Massachusetts. Over the next 25 years, most states passed similar statutes.

The legal attributes of adoption have changed over time. When the early statutes were passed, adopted children were often not provided with the same rights as biological children born to married couples. In addition, some states allowed the return of the child if, unknown to the adoptive parent, the child suffered from conditions such as epilepsy, insanity, or venereal infection.

During the early twentieth century, states began to require investigations of prospective adoptive parents. Adoption records were generally sealed to ensure anonymity, shield the child from potential stigma associated with illegitimacy, and encourage immersion into the adoptive family. By the 1970s, the insistence on secrecy became less rigid as some adopted children sought information concerning their biological parents.

| REFLECTIVE QUESTIONS | Can you think of some reasons why adoptive children would like to have information regarding their biological parents provided to them? What public policy is served by keeping that information secret? |

19.4 LEGAL EFFECT OF AN ADOPTION

Once an adoption occurs, the general rule is that a natural parent is divested of all legal rights and obligations owed to the child and those owed to the parent by the child. After adoption, the child and the parent are legal strangers. Persons who claim rights and obligations derivative of the parent are similarly divested. 2 *Elderlaw Advoc. Aging* §25:32 (2d ed. 2011). Consequently, adoption terminates the legal relationship between the adopted child and the grandparents. These principles apply to issues involving intestate inheritance and interpretation of testamentary documents.

REFLECTIVE QUESTIONS | **What public policy is promoted by divesting the natural parents of all legal rights and obligations toward a child once it is adopted?**

Background to *Hall v. Vallandingham*

Hall v. Vallandingham provides a thumbnail history of adoption in the United States. The court discusses the question of whether under Maryland's statutes, which are similar to those in other states around the country, an adoptive child loses all rights of inheritance from the child's natural parents and their natural collateral and lineal relatives.

HALL
v.
VALLANDINGHAM

Court of Appeals of Maryland
540 A.2d 1162 (1988)

GILBERT, C.J. Adoption did not exist under the common law of England, although it was in use "[a]mong the ancient peoples of Greece, Rome, Egypt and Babylonia." The primary purpose for adoption was, and still is, inheritance rights, particularly in "France, Greece, Spain and most of Latin America." Since adoption was not a part of the common law, it owes its existence in this State, and indeed in this nation, to statutory enactments.

The first two general adoption statutes were passed in Texas and Vermont in 1850. Maryland first enacted an Adoption Statute in Laws 1892, Ch. 244, and that law has continued in existence, in various forms, until the present time. The current statute, Maryland Code, Family Law Article Ann. §5-308 provides, in pertinent part:

(b) [A]fter a decree of adoption is entered:

    (1) the individual adopted:

        (i) is the child of the petitioner for all intents and purposes; and

        (ii) is entitled to all the rights and privileges of and is subject to all the obligations of a child born to the petitioner in wedlock;

    (2) each living natural parent of the individual adopted is:

        (i) relieved of all parental duties and obligations to the individual adopted; and

        (ii) divested of all parental rights as to the individual adopted; and

    (3) all rights of inheritance between the individual adopted and the natural relations shall be governed by the Estates and Trusts Article.

The applicable section of the Md. Estates and Trusts Code Ann., §1-207(a), provides:

> An adopted child shall be treated as a natural child of his adopted parent or parents. On adoption, a child no longer shall be considered a child of either natural parent, except that upon adoption by the spouse of a natural parent, the child shall be considered the child of that natural parent.

With that "thumbnail" history of adoption and the current statutes firmly in mind, we turn our attention to the matter *sub judice*.

Earl J. Vallandingham died in 1956, survived by his widow, Elizabeth, and their four children. Two years later, Elizabeth married Jim Walter Killgore, who adopted the children. In 1983, twenty-five years after the adoption of Earl's children by Killgore, Earl's brother, William Jr., died childless, unmarried, and intestate. His sole heirs were his surviving brothers and sisters and the children of brothers and sisters who predeceased him. Joseph W. Vallandingham, the decedent's twin brother, was appointed Personal Representative of the estate. After the Inventory and First Accounting were filed, the four natural children of Earl J. Vallandingham noted exceptions, alleging that they were entitled to the distributive share of their natural uncle's estate that their natural father would have received had he survived William.

The Orphan's Court transmitted the issue to the Circuit Court for St. Mary's County. That tribunal determined that the four natural children of Earl, because of their adoption by their adoptive father, Jim Walter Killgore, were not entitled to inherit from William M. Vallandingham Jr.

Patently unwilling to accept that judgment which effectively disinherited them, the children have journeyed here where they posit to us:

> Did the trial court err in construing Maryland's current law regarding natural inheritance by adopted persons so as to deny the Appellants the right to inherit through their natural paternal uncle, when said Appellants were adopted as minors by their stepfather after the death of their natural father and the remarriage of their natural mother?

When the four natural children of Earl J. Vallandingham were adopted in 1958 by Jim Killgore, then Md. Ann. Code art. 16, §78(b) clearly provided that adopted children retained the right to inherit from their natural parents and relatives.

That right of inheritance was removed by the Legislature in 1963 when it declared: "Upon entry of a decree of adoption, the adopted child shall lose all rights of inheritance from its parents and from their natural collateral or lineal relatives." Laws 1963, Ch. 174. Subsequently, the Legislature in 1969 enacted what is the current, above-quoted language of Est. & Trusts Art. §1-207(a). Laws 1969, Ch. 3, §4(c).

The appellants contend that since the explicit language of the 1963 Act proscribing dual inheritance by adoptees was not retained in the present law, Est. & Trusts Art. §1-207(a) implicitly permits adoptees to inherit from natural relatives, as well as the adoptive parents.

The right to receive property by devise or descent is not a natural right but a privilege granted by the State. Every State possesses the power to regulate the manner or term by which property within its dominion may be transmitted by will or inheritance and to prescribe who shall or shall not be capable of receiving that property. A State may deny the privilege altogether or may impose whatever restrictions or conditions upon the grant it deems appropriate.

Family Law Art. §5-308(b)(1)(ii) entitles an adopted person to all the rights and privileges of a natural child insofar as the adoptive parents are concerned, but adoption does not confer upon the adopted child more rights and privileges than those possessed by a natural child. To construe Est. & Trusts Art. §1-207(a) so as to allow dual inheritance would bestow upon an adopted child a superior status. That status was removed in Laws 1963, Ch. 174 which, as we have said, expressly disallowed the dual inheritance capability of adopted children by providing that "the adopted child shall lose all rights of inheritance from its parents and from their natural collateral or lineal relatives." We think that the current statute, Est. & Trusts Art. §1-207(a), did not alter the substance of the 1963 act which eliminated dual inheritance. Rather, §1-207(a) merely "streamlined" the wording while retaining the meaning.

Family Law Art. §5-308 plainly mandates that adoption be considered a "rebirth" into a completely different relationship. Once a child is adopted, the rights of both the natural parents and relatives are terminated. *L.F.M. v. Department of Social Services*, 507 A.2d 1151 (1986). Est. & Trusts Art. §1-207(a) and Family Law Art. §5-308 emphasize the clean-cut severance from the natural bloodline. Because an adopted child has no right to inherit from the estate of a natural parent who dies intestate, it follows that the same child may not inherit through the natural parent by way of representation. What may not be done directly most assuredly may not be done indirectly. The elimination of dual inheritance in 1963 clearly established that policy, and the current language of §1-207(a) simply reflects the continuation of that policy.

We hold that because §1-207(a) eliminates the adopted child's right to inherit from the natural parent it concomitantly abrogated the right to inherit through the natural parent by way of representation. "The Legislature giveth, and the Legislature taketh away."

DISCUSSION QUESTIONS FOR *HALL v. VALLANDINGHAM*

A. When did the legislature in this case remove the right of adopted children to inherit from their natural parents and relatives? What arguments do the children make to support their view that the legislation is not retroactive?

B. What rationale does the court use when deciding to apply the statute retroactively?

C. Can you make an argument that the children in this dispute would have been better off if they had not been formally adopted? How did they benefit from being adopted?

D. Assume that this case had been decided so that the adopted children were allowed to inherit from their biological relative. Would this be sound public policy?

19.5 NOTICE AND CONSENT: TERMINATION OF PARENTAL RIGHTS PRIOR TO ADOPTION

Before an adoption occurs, the prospective adoptive child's ties to his or her biological parents must be legally severed. In some cases, the biological parents voluntarily consent to termination of parental rights and to the adoption of the child. States have created procedural requirements aimed at ensuring that consent is deliberative. For example, birth mothers must typically wait one or two days after birth before providing consent to adoption.

In some situations, the parental rights of one or both parents have been involuntarily terminated by the court based on grounds set out by statute. If parental rights are not terminated precisely as prescribed by a state statute, a biological parent may later seek to void the adoption. The result of the challenge can create a frightening and highly emotional state of affairs for the adoptive family.

 **REFLECTIVE QUESTIONS** | Given the brief narrative above, what may concern a lawyer handling an adoption when the natural parental rights to the child involved in the adoption have been terminated by a court?

Background to *In the Interest of B.G.C.*

Problems sometimes arise when a biological father was unknown or unnamed in a termination proceeding. That is the situation in the following case: A man who erroneously believed he was the biological father of a child born out of wedlock consented to termination of his parental rights so the child could be adopted. However, when the biological father discovered he had fathered a child and it was about to be adopted, he challenged the adoption effort. Eventually, both of the child's biological parents sought return of the child, who had already begun living with an adoptive family.

The court considers whether parental rights could be terminated solely on the basis of a child's best interest. The biological father in *B.G.C.* argued that the state's termination statute must be followed "to the letter." The adoptive parents argued that the "best interests" of the child is the test in an adoption proceeding.

IN THE INTEREST OF B.G.C.
Supreme Court of Iowa
496 N.W.2d 239 (1993)

LARSON, J. This case is, we observe thankfully, an unusual one. It involves the future of a baby girl, B.G.C., who was born on February 8, 1991. Her mother, Cara, who was not married, decided to give up the baby for adoption and signed a release of parental rights as provided by Iowa Code section 600A.4 (1991). She named "Scott" as the father of the baby, and Scott signed a release of parental rights. Later, both Cara and Scott signed waivers of notice of the termination hearing. After the hearing, the court ordered the termination of the parental rights of both Cara and Scott. Custody of the child was given to the potential adoptive parents, R.D. and J.D.

Cara moved to set aside the termination, asserting that her release was defective for several reasons. She also asserted, for the first time, that the real father was "Daniel," not Scott. She informed Daniel that he was the father of her child, and Daniel intervened in the adoption proceeding to assert his parental rights. The juvenile court denied Cara's motion to set aside the termination of her parental rights, and she appealed.

In the meantime, the adoption case proceeded. The district court found that Daniel was in fact the real father, that he had not released his parental rights, and that he had not abandoned the baby. The court denied the adoption and ordered the baby to be surrendered to Daniel. R.D. and J.D. appealed and obtained a stay of the district court's order transferring custody. The baby has remained in the custody of R.D. and J.D. virtually from the time of her birth.

The court of appeals reversed the termination of Cara's parental rights and remanded the case to the juvenile court. We granted further review of that decision and consolidated it with R.D. and J.D.'s appeal in the adoption case. . . .

R.D. and J.D., as prospective adoptive parents petitioned to terminate the parental rights of Daniel, the "second" father. The district court heard the petition for termination in conjunction with its hearing on the petition for adoption. The district court therefore acted in a joint role as juvenile court and district court. According to the order of Judge Kilburg, the adoption proceedings by J.D. and R.D. were fatally defective because Daniel established that he was the real father and his rights had not been terminated as required by Iowa Code section 600.3(2) ("An adoption petition shall not be filed until a termination of parental rights has been accomplished except [in adoptions of adults and stepchildren]."). The court concluded that the ground of abandonment had not been established and that the adoption petition must therefore be denied. . . .

The argument that the best interests of the baby are best served by allowing her to stay with R.D. and J.D. is a very alluring argument. Daniel has had a poor performance record as a parent. He fathered two children prior to this child, a son, age fourteen, and a daughter born out of wedlock, now age twelve. The record shows that Daniel has largely failed to support these children financially and has failed to maintain meaningful contact with either of them.

In contrast, as the district court found, R.D. and J.D. "have provided exemplary care for the child [and] view themselves as the parents of this child in every respect."

What R.D. and J.D. ask us to do, however, is to bypass the termination requirements of chapter 600A and order the granting of the adoption without establishment of any of the grounds for termination specified in section 600A.8 because it would be in the baby's best interest.

Their argument is that, although Daniel was not a party to the original termination hearing under chapter 600A (in which Scott was named as father), his rights could, and should, have been terminated by the court in the chapter 600 adoption proceeding. Under chapter 600, they argue, specific grounds for termination need not be established; the best interest of the child determines the issue of termination in an adoption case. We do not believe that our law is capable of this interpretation. Whatever our adoption law was prior to 1976, it is clear that since 1976 termination of parental rights "shall be accomplished only according to the provisions of this division [now chapter 600A]."

The intention of the legislature to link the termination provisions of chapter 600 and 600A is apparent from the fact that the same 1976 Act that made chapter 600A the exclusive vehicle for termination also amended the adoption statute, ch. 600, to require a termination of parental rights prior to the filing of an adoption petition. 1976 Iowa Acts ch. 1229, §12 (now codified in Iowa Code §600.3(2)). The general rule is that:

> [t]he state cannot interfere with the rights of natural parents simply to better the moral and temporal welfare of the child as against an unoffending parent, and, as a general rule, the court may not consider whether the adoption will be for the welfare and best interests of the child where the parents have not consented to an adoption or the conditions which obviate the necessity of their consent do not exist. However, where a parent by his conduct forfeits the right to withhold consent, but nevertheless contests the adoption, the welfare of the child is the paramount issue. 2 C.J.S. Adoption of Persons §67, at 491 (1972).

Our case law is in accord with this view; statutory grounds for termination must be established in addition to establishing the child's best interests in order to terminate. We agree with the district court that under section 600.3(2) parental rights may not be terminated solely on consideration of the child's best interest but that specific grounds for termination under chapter 600A must also be established. Daniel's parental rights had not been terminated, and the adoption proceedings were therefore fatally flawed. Affirmed.

SNELL, J. dissenting. The evidence is sufficient to show abandonment of the baby by Daniel. The record shows he has previously failed to raise or support his other two children. He quit supporting his son, born in 1976, after two years. From 1978 to 1990 he saw him three times. He has another daughter whom he has never seen and has failed to support. He stated he just never took any interest in her. In every meaningful way, he abandoned them.

Daniel knew that Cara was pregnant in December 1990. He saw her in the building where they worked for the same employer. The child was born in February 1991. Having knowledge of the facts that support the likelihood that he was the biological father, nevertheless, he did nothing to protect his rights. The mother, Cara, who knew better than anyone who the father was, named Scott as the father. The legal proceedings logically and reasonably were based on these representations. The termination of parental rights as known to exist at the time were legally completed and an adoption process was commenced.

Daniel's sudden desire to assume parental responsibilities is a late claim to assumed rights that he forfeited by his indifferent conduct to the fate of Cara and her child. The specter of newly named genetic fathers, upsetting adoptions, perhaps years later, is an unconscionable result. Such a consequence is not driven by the language of our statutes, due process concerns or the facts of this case.

I would remand for termination of Daniel's parental rights based on abandonment and denial of Cara's motions. The intervention petition of Daniel in the adoption case should be dismissed on remand and the adoption should proceed.

 **FOR *IN THE INTEREST OF B.G.C.***

A. The dissent argues that Daniel had abandoned the child. Are you persuaded by this argument?

B. Here the adoptive parents have provided the infant exemplary care whereas the biological father fathered two children prior to this child, a son, age 14, and a daughter born out of wedlock, now age 12. He failed to support these children financially and has not maintained meaningful contact with either of them. Should the best interests of the minor child "trump" whatever claim the biological parent may have had to the child?

19.6 NOTICE AND CONSENT: EMERGING CONSTITUTIONAL RIGHTS OF UNMARRIED FATHERS

Historically, unmarried fathers had fewer rights with regard to their children than either unwed mothers or married parents. Over the past several decades, unmarried fathers have sought recognition of their parental rights under the Fourteenth Amendment. Beginning in 1973, in an important line of decisions, the Supreme Court analyzed and radically changed the legal climate with respect to the constitutional rights of unmarried fathers in the context of adoption.

Presumption applied to unwed fathers struck down. In *Stanley v. Illinois*, 405 U.S. 645 (1973), an unwed father, Stanley, lived with his biological children and their mother intermittently for 18 years prior to her death. When their mother died, the children automatically became wards of the state. At the time, Illinois law presumed that Stanley was unfit to care for the children even though there had been no hearing regarding his fitness or any proof of neglect on his part. Stanley sought custody of the children, arguing that he should be afforded a hearing on his fitness. When the Illinois Supreme Court refused to provide him a hearing, the Supreme Court granted review. The Court held that a putative father's interest in the "companionship, care, custody and management" of his children was greater than the state's interest in the children as long as the putative father was a fit parent. It ordered that a hearing be held to determine whether Stanley was in fact fit to have custody of the children. The Court did not, however, articulate the scope of the protection afforded an unwed father. On remand, the trial court found that Stanley was not a fit parent.

Little or no contact waives adoption veto. Five years after *Stanley*, the Supreme Court clarified the principles articulated in that decision in *Quilloin v. Walcott*, 434 U.S. 246 (1977). In *Quilloin* the Court held that a putative father who had little or no contact with his child did not have a constitutional right to veto the child's adoption. A unanimous Court based its decision on the putative father's failure to seek actual or legal custody of the child and the fact he had played no part in the child's daily supervision, education, protection, or care. *Quilloin* established the rule that where there is no significant commitment to the child, the state is not required "to find anything more than that the adoption, and denial of legitimization, were in the 'best interests of the child.'"

Gender-based distinction unconstitutional. In *Caban v. Mohammed*, 441 U.S. 380 (1979), both the mother and the putative father emotionally and financially supported children born to them outside of marriage. When their relationship ended and they separated, the mother married another and then initiated proceedings asking the court to allow her new husband to adopt the children. The putative father filed a cross-petition in which he asked to adopt the children. Under a New York statute, a putative father could not adopt his children without the mother's consent. However, the mother could legally adopt the children without first obtaining the putative father's consent. The trial court permitted the mother and her new husband to adopt the children over their putative father's objection and the Supreme Court granted review. The Court reversed. It held that the New York statute had inappropriately created a gender-based distinction between unwed mothers and unwed fathers, which bore no substantial relation to any legitimate state interest. Because the putative father had demonstrated a substantial interest in his children, the Court said he had certain constitutionally protected rights that the state could not take from him.

No substantial relationship. In *Lehr v. Robertson*, 463 U.S. 248 (1983), the Court considered whether the Due Process and Equal Protection Clauses provided a putative father with the right to notice and an opportunity to be heard before a child is adopted, even if he has not established a substantial relationship with his biological child born outside of marriage. Lehr had never lived with his child or the mother, had never registered with the putative father registry, and had failed to provide any financial support. When the child was eight months old, the mother married and her husband adopted the child. The Court rejected Lehr's constitutional claim that he had a right to notice of the pending adoption proceedings under the Due Process and Equal Protection Clauses of the Constitution. The Court reasoned that his rights had not been violated because he had not developed a substantial relationship with the child. The "mere existence of a biological link," wrote the Court, "does not merit equivalent constitutional protection." *Id.* at 261. The Court also held that Lehr was not denied due process or equal protection since he could have guaranteed that he would receive notice of any adoption proceedings by mailing a postcard to the putative father registry.

Is strength of the relationship is the determining factor? Under *Lehr*, a putative father's legal rights with respect to a biological child may ultimately depend on the strength of the relationship between the putative father, mother, and child. In *Stanley* and *Caban*, the fathers demonstrated the existence of a sufficiently strong relationship that warranted constitutional protection. However, in the absence of such a commitment, there may be no constitutional protection. *See Adoption of Baby Girl P*, 242 P.3d 1168 (Kan. 2010); *Adoption of T.B.*, 232 P.3d 1026 (Utah 2010).

Professor Laura Owen has commented on the problem associated with notice to a putative father of the birth of a child out of wedlock. She writes:

> The line of consent to adoption constitutional decisions left the states without adequate guidance on how to handle unmarried men who have not had time to either meet or fail to meet *Lehr*'s criteria about stepping forward and grasping the unique opportunity of biology. Thus, post-*Lehr* state courts and legislatures are required to make their own decisions about putative fathers who claim that they have been denied their opportunity interest and prevented from developing the kind of relationship that would clearly put them over the constitutional line. The question left open is how does one engage in advanced *Lehr* line drawing that can distinguish the wheat from the chaff among the fathers of newborn and very young children?

Laura Owen, *Unmarried Fathers and Adoption: "Perfecting" or "Abandoning" an Opportunity Interest*, 36 Cap. U. L. Rev. 253, 265-266 (2007).

What is Professor Owen's concern with
constitutional "line drawing"?

19.7 NOTICE AND CONSENT: ADOPTION REGISTRIES

As a result of uncertainty about the constitutional rights of putative fathers, some states have adopted a bright-line approach involving creation of adoption or putative father registries. In order to ensure that he receives notice of a potential adoption, a putative father may be required by the state statute to enter his name on an adoption registry prior to the child's birth or within a prescribed time, typically within 30 days of the birth. *See, e.g.,* Ind. Code §31-19-5-2(a) (2015) (deadline is 30 days after the birth or the date a petition is filed, whichever occurs later). Compliance assures that a putative father will receive notice in the event that a mother does not disclose his name and address in connection with executing her consent to adoption. A father may petition for a parentage hearing after an adoption petition is filed so long as the child is not yet 30 days old. *In re I.J.,* 2015 WL 4111706, _____ N.E.3d _____ (Ind. App. 2015).

Once a father has received notice from the state adoption registry of a prospective adoption, statutes may require that he take action within a certain period of time. For example, Minnesota requires that a father must bring a paternity action within 30 days of receiving the adoption registry notice unless he can show good cause for not doing so. Minn. Stat. §259.52, subd. 10 (2015).

When required by a statute, the failure to register may waive any potential right of the father to notice of an adoption and could constitute irrevocable consent to the adoption. Approximately half of the states have implemented adoption registries. U.S. Dept. of Health and Human Services, Administration for Children and Families, Child Welfare Information Gateway, available at http://www.childwelfare.gov/systemwide/laws_policies/statutes/putative.cfm (last visited June 2015).

In some jurisdictions, upon proof of indigency, a putative father who has registered with the fathers' adoption registry, who has received a notice, and who has timely filed an intent to claim paternal rights will have counsel appointed at public expense. *See, e.g.,* Minn. Stat. §259.52, subd. 12 (2014).

REFLECTIVE QUESTIONS	Why shouldn't every state enact an adoption registry for men who may have fathered a child out of wedlock? Should there be a national registry?

Background to *In re J.D.C.*

States providing that a putative father's failure to register constitutes consent to adoption assert that the requirement is necessary to advance the state's policy interest in prompt and permanent placement of children into stable homes. Nevertheless, in the next case the court considers the petition of a putative father who did not receive notice of adoption and who had failed to enter his name on the adoption registry. As in similar registry disputes, the question is whether failure to register forever bars the putative father from contesting the adoption of the child by the child's stepfather.

IN RE J.D.C.
Court of Appeals of Indiana
751 N.E.2d 747 (2001)

VAIDIK, J. Ronald B. Hunter appeals the trial court's denial of his motion to vacate the Judgment following the adoption of Carrie Colaric's biological child. Hunter claims that, as the putative father, he had a right to receive notice of the adoption proceedings.

The relevant facts reveal that Hunter and Colaric had an intimate relationship in March of 1999. During this relationship, Colaric became pregnant. Hunter knew of Colaric's pregnancy. On November 26, 1999, Colaric gave birth to a child. Two days later, Colaric voluntarily terminated her parental rights and consented to the adoption of the child. She also signed a statement naming Hunter as the putative father, but averring that she did not know of his whereabouts and was unaware of anyone who would be able to locate him. The adoption agency then placed the child with the adoptive couple on the same day.

On December 23, 1999, the adoptive couple petitioned to adopt the child. The putative father's registry was checked while the adoption was pending, but no one, including Hunter, had registered as the child's putative father. The adoption was finalized on March 9, 2000. Hunter never registered with the putative father's registry and was not given notice of the proceedings.

In an effort to balance the competing interests involved in adoption, Indiana established the Indiana Putative Father's Registry in 1994, managed by the Indiana Department of Health. The purpose of the registry is to provide notice to a putative father that a petition for adoption has been filed. A putative father who registers within thirty days after the child's birth or the date the adoption petition is filed, whichever occurs later, is entitled to notice of the child's adoption. A putative father's failure to register not only waives his right to notice of the adoption but also irrevocably implies his consent.

The Indiana Putative Father's Registry was recently upheld in the decision, *In re Paternity of Baby Doe*, 734 N.E.2d 281 (Ind. Ct. App. 2000). We held that a putative father was not entitled to notice of an adoption petition and that his consent was irrevocably implied where the biological mother did not disclose his identity or address and he failed to register with the putative father's registry until six months after the adoption petition was filed.

We reasoned that because "Indiana has a strong interest in providing stable homes for children," early and permanent placement of children with adoptive families is of the utmost importance. If a father fails to register within the specified amount of time allowed under the statute, then "the State's obligation to provide this child with a permanent, capable and loving family becomes paramount." Considering this important State interest, we rejected the putative father's argument that he could not have complied with the statutory requirements because he did not know of the child's existence until after his frame of time to register had passed.

Moreover, other jurisdictions have similarly concluded that a putative father who fails to register with the putative father's registry waives his right to notice of adoption proceedings and impliedly consents to the adoption. For example, our court relied upon *Robert O. v. Russell K.*, 604 N.E.2d 99 (1992) in our holding in *Baby Doe*. In *Robert O.*, the New York Court of Appeals concluded that the putative father's notice or consent was not needed for the adoption where he failed to avail himself of the methods to qualify for notice until some ten months after the adoption became final. The court explained that although the putative father was not immediately aware of the child, not only due to his lack of effort to discover the child but also because of the biological mother's efforts to keep him from knowing about the child,

> [p]romptness is measured in terms of the baby's life not by the onset of the father's awareness. The demand for prompt action by the father at the child's birth is neither arbitrary nor punitive, but instead a logical and necessary outgrowth of the State's legitimate interest in the child's need for early permanence and stability.

Further, our court in *Baby Doe* noted that both the Arkansas Supreme Court and the South Dakota Supreme Court addressed a similar issue and concluded that putative fathers, who failed to avail themselves of statutory procedures for establishing their paternal rights, were not allowed to terminate or intervene in adoption proceedings.

In *S.J.B.*, the Arkansas Supreme Court distinguished the United States Supreme Court decision of *Stanley v. Illinois*, 405 U.S. 645 (1972), which protected an unwed father's rights where he had a substantial relationship with his children. Unlike *Stanley*, where a relationship between the father and his children existed, the court in S.J.B. proclaimed, "the father is merely 'the biological link' which brought the child into existence." Thus, the father was not entitled to notice of the adoption proceedings.

Similarly, in *Baby Boy K.*, the South Dakota Supreme Court was faced with a situation where the biological mother asserted that even if she could identify the father, she could not give his complete name and address. The court held that the putative father, who later discovered that the biological mother had lied about her inability to identify or locate him, could not vacate the termination of his parental rights, reasoning that "[b]ecause children require early and consistent nurturing of their emotional as well as physical needs," an unwed father must quickly grasp his opportunity interest to trigger protection under the law. The court explained that the need for early assurances in a child's life requires that a putative father grasp the fleeting opportunity to take on parenting responsibilities before the opportunity is lost.

Thus, under the Indiana adoption statutes and corresponding case law, Hunter was not entitled to notice of the adoption proceedings because Colaric did not disclose his address to the adoption agency and he failed to preserve his rights by registering in the putative father's registry. An inquiry of his whereabouts was not required due to this failure to register. Affirmed.

DISCUSSION QUESTIONS FOR *IN RE J.D.C.*

A. Weigh the interests of the state in allowing an adoption to go forward and the interests of the biological father who has never been notified of the birth of the child. Which interest do you believe is stronger?

B. Is the use of a putative father's registry realistic, that is, how do potential fathers learn of the registry? Does the existence of a registry suggest that a male should notify a state's registry whenever he has sexual intercourse with a new female partner? Is it realistic to believe that a man who has sex with a woman will sign the registry after every relationship because he is concerned he may have fathered a child who has not yet been born?

19.8 QUALIFICATIONS OF ADOPTIVE PARENTS: AGE AND RACE

In most adoption cases, a home study and background checks are conducted to determine the suitability of potential adoptive parents. After a petition to adopt is filed, children may be placed with the adoptive parent or parents for a probationary period.

Age. States vary with respect to the minimum age requirements for adoptive parents. Some states require prospective parents to be at least 18 years old while others set the minimum age at 21 or 25 years of age. A few states require that the adoptive parent be at least 10 years older than the person to be adopted. Approximately half of the states allow adults to be adopted, regardless of age.

States have not set a statutory maximum age for adoption. However, it is a factor that courts may consider in determining whether the best interests of a child are served by the adoption. For example, in *In re A.C.G.*, 894 A.2d 436 (D.C. 2006), the court allowed a 77-year-old to adopt. It noted that she had established 2 back-up caretakers, aged 67 and 41, who were family members and well known to the child, and who had agreed to rear the child in the event of her death or disability.

Married couple must join. Absent specific statutory exceptions, a decree of adoption by one spouse, when the petitioner's husband or wife does not join in the petition, is considered void.

Race. The extent to which race may be considered in placing children for adoption has been the subject of much debate and resulted in federal legislation in the form of the Multiethnic Placement Act (MEPA). 42 U.S.C. §1996b (2015). MEPA was a reaction by Congress to criticism that there was a widespread preference for placing black children with black parents. This was a practice known as race matching, and Congress was told that it had exacerbated the disproportionate representation of black children among those awaiting adoption from foster care. Critics claimed that social workers would decline to place a child across racial lines even if it meant the child would remain in foster care without a permanent family. Critics also claimed that white foster parents with whom a black child had lived were denied the opportunity to adopt the child. Ralph Richard Banks, *The Multiethnic Placement Act and the Troubling Persistence of Race Matching*, 38 Cap. U. L. Rev. 271 (2009).

The first version of MEPA prohibited officials from delaying or denying the placement of a child "solely on the basis of race." However, after a public outcry, the word "solely" was taken out of the statute.

Today MEPA is viewed as prohibiting states from delaying or denying a child's adoptive placement on the basis of the child's, or the prospective adoptive parent's, race, color, or national origin. It also prohibits states from denying a prospective adoptive parent the opportunity to become a foster or adoptive parent based on the child or adoptive parent's race, color, or national origin. MEPA obligates the states to recruit foster and adoptive parents who reflect the racial and ethnic diversity of the population of children awaiting permanent homes. *See* 42 U.S.C. §622(b)(9).

While a state department of social services cannot routinely consider a child's race, color, or national origin in determining what placement would be in the child's best interests, the law recognizes that there may be exceptional circumstances where the specific needs of an individual child require consideration of these factors. MEPA does not alter the Indian Child Welfare Act (ICWA).

| REFLECTIVE QUESTIONS | What were the concerns about "race matching" that caused Congress to promulgate and then amend the MEPA? |

Background to *Arkansas Department of Human Services v. Cole*

The Arkansas Supreme Court considered the constitutionality of a ballot initiative prohibiting unmarried cohabitants from adopting children. The Arkansas Adoption and Foster Care Act of 2008, also known as Act 1, began as a ballot initiative sent to Arkansas voters in the 2008 election. They approved it and it became law in 2009. Garrett O'Brien, *Recent Developments*, 64 Ark. L. Rev. 541 (2011).

Once the law was in place, the plaintiff, Sheila Cole, and others challenged its constitutionality. *Ibid.* The plaintiffs claimed the provision deprived children of the right of access to suitable homes in violation of the Due Process Clause of the United States Constitution and violated the best interests of children in state custody contrary to their due process rights under articles 8 and 21 of the Arkansas Constitution. They also claimed violations of their fundamental right to parental autonomy under both the United States and Arkansas Constitutions and argued that the provision burdened intimate relationships in violation of due process rights and right of privacy under the United States and Arkansas Constitutions.

The state argued that a fundamental right was not at issue because the statute only proscribed cohabitation. The state also argued that adopting and fostering children are privileges bestowed by the state and are not rights in themselves.

The two issues discussed in the following case excerpt are whether under the Arkansas Constitution sexual cohabitors have the right to engage in private, consensual, noncommercial intimacy in the privacy of their homes and whether the statute at issue precludes them from adopting or serving as foster parents.

ARKANSAS DEPARTMENT OF HUMAN SERVICES
v.
COLE

Supreme Court of Arkansas
380 S.W.3d 429 (2011)

BROWN, J. On November 4, 2008, a ballot initiative entitled "An Act Providing That an Individual Who is Cohabiting Outside of a Valid Marriage May Not Adopt or Be a Foster Parent of a Child Less Than Eighteen Years Old" was approved by fifty-seven percent of Arkansas voters. The ballot initiative is known as the Arkansas Adoption and Foster Care Act of 2008 or "Act 1." Act 1 went into effect on January 1, 2009, and is now codified at Arkansas Code Annotated sections 9-8-301 to -305.

Under Act 1, an individual is prohibited from adopting or serving as a foster parent if that individual is "cohabiting with a sexual partner outside of a marriage that is valid under the Arkansas Constitution and the laws of this state." Ark. Code Ann. §9-8-304(a) (Repl. 2009). This prohibition on adoption and foster parenting "applies equally to cohabiting opposite-sex and same-sex individuals." Ark. Code Ann. §9-8-304(b). Act 1 further provides that the "public policy of the state is to favor marriage as defined by the constitution and laws of this state over unmarried cohabitation with regard to adoption and foster care." Ark. Code Ann. §9-8-302 (Repl. 2009). Act 1 also declares that "it is in the best interest of children in need of adoption or foster care to be reared in homes in which adoptive or foster parents are not cohabiting outside of marriage." Ark. Code Ann. §9-8-301 (Repl. 2009).

II. FUNDAMENTAL RIGHT

The State and FCAC first contend that adoption and fostering are not fundamental rights under the Arkansas Constitution. Cole counters and contends in her complaint that because Act 1 prohibits cohabiting sexual partners from adopting and fostering, this substantially burdens her right to engage in private acts of sexual intimacy with her partner in her home. Specifically, Cole contends that Act 1 forces her to choose between a relationship with a sexual partner on the one hand and adopting or fostering children on the other, thus burdening her right to sexual intimacy. Under Act 1, she claims, she cannot do both. . . .

The State and FCAC do not really contest the fact that cohabiting adults in Arkansas have a fundamental right under *Jegley* to engage in consensual, sexual acts within the privacy of their homes without government intrusion. Their bone of contention is whether this right is indeed burdened by Act 1, and they point to the fact that adopting and fostering children are privileges bestowed by state statutes and not rights in themselves.

The problem with the argument mounted by the State and FCAC is that under Act 1 the exercise of one's fundamental right to engage in private, consensual sexual activity is conditioned on foregoing the privilege of adopting or fostering children. The choice imposed on cohabiting sexual partners, whether heterosexual or homosexual, is dramatic. They must chose either to lead a life of private, sexual intimacy with a partner without the opportunity to adopt or foster children or forego sexual cohabitation and, thereby, attain eligibility to adopt or foster. . . .

Act 1 exerts significant pressure on Cole to choose between exercising her fundamental right to engage in an intimate sexual relationship in the privacy of her home without being eligible to adopt or foster children, on the one hand, or refraining from exercising this fundamental right in order to be eligible to adopt or foster children, on the other. . . . [T]he condition placed on the privilege to foster or adopt thwarts the exercise of a fundamental right to sexual intimacy in the home free from government intrusion under the Arkansas Constitution. . . .

We hold that a fundamental right to privacy is at issue in this case and that, under the Arkansas Constitution, sexual cohabitors have the right to engage in private, consensual, noncommercial intimacy in the privacy of their homes. We further hold that this right is jeopardized by Act 1 which precludes all sexual cohabitors, without exception, from eligibility for parenthood, whether by means of adoption or foster care. We quickly note that in certain instances, such as in custody, visitation, or dependency-neglect matters, the State and the circuit courts of this state have a duty to protect the best interest of the child. We will discuss this issue more fully below.

III. COHABITATION IN FAMILY LAW CASES

The State and FCAC base a considerable part of their argument on their assertion that Arkansas courts disfavor cohabitation by a parent in the presence of children following a divorce and in many cases condition custody of children on non-cohabitation agreements. They then assert that Act 1 is no more an invasion of Cole's privacy rights than non-cohabitation agreements in child-custody cases and corresponding court orders are on divorced biological parents' privacy rights.

On this point, the State and FCAC rely heavily on this court's decision in *Alphin v. Alphin*, 364 Ark. 332, 219 S.W.3d 160 (2005), and quote from it to the effect that extramarital cohabitation in the presence of children "has never been condoned in Arkansas, is contrary to the public policy of promoting a stable environment for children, and may of itself constitute a material change in circumstances warranting a change of custody." *Id.* at 340, 219 S.W.3d at 165. Yet, upon reviewing the change of custody in *Alphin*, this court recognized that the primary consideration in child-custody cases is the best interest of the child and that all other considerations are secondary.

We strongly disagree with the State and FCAC's conclusion that if this court finds that the categorical ban on adoption and fostering for sexual cohabitors put in place by Act 1 violates an individual's fundamental right to sexual privacy in one's home, state courts and DHS will be prohibited henceforth from considering and enforcing non-cohabitation agreements and orders in deciding child-custody and visitation cases as well as dependency-neglect cases. That simply is not the case. The overriding concern in all of these situations is the best interest of the child. *See Alphin v. Alphin, supra.* To arrive at what is in the child's best interest, the circuit courts and state agencies look at all the factors, including a non-cohabitation order if one exists, and make the best-interest determination on a case-by-case basis. Act 1's blanket ban provides for no such individualized consideration or case-by-case analysis in adoption or foster-care cases and makes the bald assumption that in *all* cases where adoption or foster care is the issue it is always against the best interest of the child to be placed in a home where an individual is cohabiting with a sexual partner outside of marriage.

But in addition to case-by-case analysis, there is another difference between cohabitation in the child-custody or dependency-neglect context and cohabiting sexual partners who wish to adopt or become foster parents. Third-party strangers who cohabit with a divorced parent are unknown in many cases to the circuit court and have not undergone the rigorous screening associated with foster care or adoption. By everyone's account, applicants for foster care must comply with a raft of DHS regulations that include criminal background checks, home studies, family histories, support systems, and the like. Adoption, under the auspices of the trial court, requires similar screening. Unsuitable and undesirable adoptive and foster parents are thereby weeded out in the screening process. The same does not pertain to a third-party stranger who cohabits with a divorced or single parent. . . .

V. HEIGHTENED SCRUTINY

. . . We have held in this case that a fundamental right of privacy is at issue and that the burden imposed by the State is direct and substantial. We now hold, as an additional matter, that because of the direct and substantial burden on a fundamental right, the standard to be applied is heightened scrutiny and not a rational-basis standard. Using the heightened-scrutiny standard, because Act 1 exacts a categorical ban against all cohabiting couples engaged in sexual conduct, we hold that it is not narrowly tailored or the least restrictive means available to serve the State's compelling interest of protecting the best interest of the child.

In holding as we do, we first note that Act 1 says "[t]he people of Arkansas find and declare that it is in the best interest of children in need of adoption or foster care to be reared in homes in which adoptive or foster parents are not cohabiting outside of marriage." Ark. Code Ann. §9-8-301 (Repl. 2009). Despite this statement in Act 1, several of the State's and FCAC's own witnesses testified that they did not believe Act 1 promoted the welfare interests of the child by its categorical ban.

Ed Appler, Child Welfare Agency Review Board (CWARB) member and President of Grace Adoptions, said in his deposition taken August 4, 2009, that, as a Review Board Member and as a social worker, he could not identify any child welfare interests that are advanced by Act 1. Sandi Doherty, Division of Children and Family Services (DCFS) Program Administrator and former DCFS Area Director and County Supervisor, in her deposition taken November 17, 2009, stated that in her personal view Act 1 is not consistent with the best practices because it bars placement of children with relatives who are cohabiting with a sexual partner. Marilyn Counts, DCFS Administrator of Adoptions, in her deposition taken December 9, 2009, agreed that she could not identify any child welfare interests that are furthered by categorically excluding unmarried couples from being assessed on an individual basis as to whether they would be a suitable adoptive parent. John Selig, Director of DHS, in his deposition taken December 16, 2009, stated that in his personal opinion, it is not in the best interest of children to have a categorical ban on any cohabiting couple from fostering or adopting children because the case workers should have as much discretion as possible to make the best placement. Moreover, counsel for the State and FCAC admitted at oral argument that some adults cohabiting with their sexual partners would be suitable and appropriate foster or adoptive parents, all of which militates against a blanket ban.

Furthermore, the concerns raised by the State and FCAC and used as justification for Act 1's categorical ban of cohabiting adults, such as (1) unmarried cohabiting relationships are less stable than married relationships, (2) they put children at a higher risk for domestic violence and abuse than married relationships, and (3) they have lower income levels, higher infidelity rates, and less social support than married relationships, can all be addressed by the individualized screening process currently in place in foster and adoption cases. The CWARB has Minimum Licensing

Standards that require it to "select the home that is in the best interest of the child, the least restrictive possible, and is matched to the child's physical and emotional needs. The placement decision shall be based on an individualized assessment of the child's needs." Minimum Licensing Standards for Child Welfare Agencies §200.1.

Prior to placing a child in foster care or in an adoptive home, DCFS conducts an individualized home assessment of each foster or adoptive family. The purpose of this home assessment process "is to educate prospective foster parents on the characteristics of children in out-of-home placement and evaluate their ability to meet those needs, as well as evaluate the applicants' compliance with the Minimum Licensing Standards and DFCS policy requirements for foster homes." Ark. Dept. of Human Services Division of Children and Family Services: Family Services Policy and Procedure Manual (DHS Manual), Policy VII-C: Foster Home Assessment Process, at 144. The home assessment process is a mutual-selection process which involves several components including interviews, background checks, in-home consultation visits, preservice training, home studies, and ongoing consultations with prospective foster parents to ensure that all appropriate criteria related to compliance and quality are met. *Id.* The home study, in particular, is conducted in order to evaluate the prospective foster family's dynamics, including the "motivation for wanting to foster, household composition, housing, safety hazards, income and expenses, health, education, childcare arrangements or plans, child rearing practices, daily schedules, social history, family activities, and support systems." *Id.* at 146, 669 S.W.2d 878.

We have no doubt that this individualized assessment process is a thorough and effective means to screen out unsuitable applicants, depending on the individual case. Jane Huddleston, Assistant Director of DHS, asserted in her deposition that the assessment process is sufficient to screen out unsuitable foster or adoptive parents and that this screening process would not be any less effective to screen out unsuitable cohabiting heterosexual or homosexual couples or individuals. In addition, John Selig testified in his deposition that it cannot be determined whether a particular placement is better or worse for a particular child based solely on the marital status of the couple in the home.

We conclude that the individualized assessments by DHS and our trial courts are effective in addressing issues such as relationship instability, abuse, lack of social support, and other factors that could potentially create a risk to the child or otherwise render the applicant unsuitable to be a foster or adoptive parent. These would be the least restrictive means for addressing the compelling state interest of protecting the welfare, safety, and best interest of Arkansas's children. By imposing a categorical ban on all persons who cohabit with a sexual partner, Act 1 removes the ability of the State and our courts to conduct these individualized assessments on these individuals, many of whom could qualify and be entirely suitable foster or adoptive parents. As a result, Act 1 fails to pass constitutional muster under a heightened-scrutiny analysis.

Because we hold as we do, we need not address the issue of whether Act 1 is rationally related to serving a legitimate government interest. . . .

VII. CONCLUSION

We hold that Cole's fundamental privacy rights, which are implicit in the Arkansas Constitution, are substantially and directly burdened by Act 1's prohibition against the ability of cohabiting sexual partners to foster or adopt children. The State's compelling interest, no doubt, is protection of the welfare of Arkansas's children, but we further hold that under a heightened-scrutiny analysis, which is the standard that applies to this case, the least restrictive means of serving that interest has not been employed; nor has the application of Act 1 been narrowly tailored, as required.

DISCUSSION QUESTIONS **FOR *ARKANSAS DEPARTMENT OF HUMAN SERVICES v. COLE***

A. What public policy did Act 1 purport to further?

B. What fundamental right did Act 1 impinge upon?

C. How did the court arrive at its conclusion that Act 1's "blanket ban" was inconsistent with the best interests standard?

D. The court concludes that the Act 1 ban was not sufficiently tailored to its purpose. What was the purpose?

19.9 UNSEALING OF RECORDS AND OPEN ADOPTION

Although adoption records were historically open, during the 1940s and 1950s states began to close adoption records in order protect the identity of the birth parents and to shield the adopted child from the stigmatization of illegitimacy. The statutory scheme is designed to promote policies and procedures socially necessary and desirable for the protection not only of the adoptive child but also the natural and adopting parents.

In some states, such as Pennsylvania, an adoptee must show that there is good cause for unsealing adoption records, and this must be shown by clear and convincing evidence. *In re Long*, 745 A.2d 673 (Pa. 1999). When considering whether to unseal adoption records, a court will weigh the ramifications to those specifically affected by that unsealing, including the adoptive and biological parents and their families, and the impact on the integrity of the adoption process in general. A court will grant a request to unseal an adoption record only if the adoptee's need for the information clearly outweighs the considerations behind the statute. *Ibid.* For example, in *Scriven v. State*, 769 S.E.2d 569 (Ga. App. 2015), the court held the children had shown good cause to open sealed adoption records. The parents of the children were dead and the children sought information contained in the sealed records, in part for medical reasons to help determine whether they had a marker for a specific form of cancer. In *In re Alice, L.L.T.*, 960 N.Y.S.2d 857 (N.Y. Surr. 2012), the court refused to open sealed adoption records in order to ascertain whether the petitioner's birth mother was of the Jewish faith. However, it did inform the petitioner that her mother was Protestant (Lutheran), which it considered non-identifying information that it could provide while keeping the records sealed.

Open adoption. Some states allow the option of a postadoption contact between the child and the biological parents. Such arrangements are known as "open" adoptions. In open adoptions, it is common for the birth parents and adoptive parents to meet and exchange identifying information, and written agreements setting forth the respective rights of the parties are common. The agreement is signed after the birth and before placement.

New York was one of the first states to recognize "open" adoptions. New York allowed a parent to include a reservation of rights of visitation and communication upon agreement with the adopting party in the document surrendering a child. This changed the traditional rule that an adoption severs all ties with the biological parents.

Mediated open adoptions. In a mediated open adoption, the parties arrange for a method of communication or contact that remains open as the child grows up. Mediators assist the birth parents and the adoptive parents to prepare a mutually acceptable agreement.

REFLECTIVE QUESTIONS

What public policy is furthered by allowing contact between an adopted child and the child's biological parents? When should postadoption contact between the adopted child and the biological parents be allowed? Or, should postadoption contact be barred for life?

Background to *In the Matter of M.B. & S.B. v. Indiana Department of Child Services*

In *In the Matter of M.B. & S.B.*, the Supreme Court of Indiana explores the issue of statutory postadoption privileges and the extent to which they are enforceable. The biological mother signed an addendum to the relinquishment of her child that reserved postadoption visitation privileges. Once her rights to her child were terminated, the visitation provision was also terminated without notice to her. The court considers whether the addendum contravenes Indiana statutory law and public policy and, if so, whether the agreement is rendered void *ab initio* and thus unenforceable as to visitation.

IN THE MATTER OF M.B. & S.B.
v.
INDIANA DEPARTMENT OF CHILD SERVICES
Supreme Court of Indiana
921 N.E.2d 494 (2009)

SULLIVAN, J., . . . We are presented with a situation in which Mother contends that she voluntarily agreed to the termination of her parental rights subject to continued and ongoing visitation with her children, only to have that visitation right terminated at a hearing of which she received no notice and no opportunity to be heard. She asks to restore the *status quo ante* such that all her parental rights would be restored and any termination proceedings would need to begin anew.

Voluntary termination of parental rights severs all legal ties, including visitation rights, between parents and their children. Indiana's "open adoption statutes" (I.C. §§31-19-16-1 & 2), however, provide parents the opportunity to obtain post-adoption visitation privileges under certain circumstances. Indiana Code §31-19-16-1 states in relevant part: "*At the time an adoption decree is entered,* the court entering the adoption decree may grant postadoption contact privileges under section 2 of this chapter to a *birth parent who has*[] . . . *voluntarily terminated the parent-child relationship.*" *Id.* (emphases added). The phrase "section 2 of this chapter" refers to I.C. §31-19-16-2, which delineates the procedures that must be followed before a court may grant postadoption contact privileges to a birth parent who has voluntarily terminated parental rights. Indiana Code §31-19-16-2 states:

> *A court may grant postadoption privileges if:*
>   (1) *the court determines that the best interests of the child would be served by granting postadoption contact privileges;*
>   (2) the child is at least two (2) years of age and the court finds that there is a significant emotional attachment between the child and the birth parent;
>   (3) *each adoptive parent consents to the granting of postadoption contact privileges;*
>   (4) *the adoptive parents and the birth parents:*
>   (A) *execute a postadoption contact agreement; and*
>   (B) *file the agreement with the court;*
>   (5) the licensed child placing agency sponsoring the adoption and the child's court appointed special advocate or guardian *ad litem* appointed under IC 31-32-3 recommends to the court the postadoption contact agreement, or if there is no licensed child placing agency sponsoring the adoption, the county office of family and children or other agency that prepared an adoption report under IC 31-19-8-5 is informed of the contents of the postadoption contact agreement and comments on the agreement in the agency's report to the court;
>   (6) consent to postadoption contact is obtained from the child if the child is at least twelve (12) years of age; and
>   (7) *the postadoption contact agreement is approved by the court.*

Id. (emphases added).

The "Post Adoption Privileges" Addendum in this case explicitly references I.C. §31-19-16-2. It provides that Mother's consent to relinquish her parental rights voluntarily and her consent to adoption were "subject to the Court granting post-adoption privileges and the adoptive parents consenting to post-adoption contact by and between themselves and [M.B.] and [S.B.] pursuant to I.C. 31-19-16-2." Mother contends that there is Court of Appeals precedent "holding that post-adoption contact privileges may be stipulated to and contemplated in the future." She noted that "the Addendum would require the [State] to find adoptive parents willing to allow [Mother] post-adoption contact."

We find that the Addendum's reservation of post-adoption contact privileges is irreconcilably inconsistent with Indiana's open adoption statutes. *See* I.C. §§31-19-16-1 & 2. We agree with the following analysis by the Court of Appeals:

> Indiana Code Section 31-19-16-1 provides that a court entering an adoption decree may grant post-adoption contact privileges under Indiana Code Section 31-19-16-2 to a birth parent who has previously voluntarily relinquished his or her parental rights *"at the time an adoption decree is entered[,]"* and not, as Mother would have us do, prior to, or as a condition precedent to, a parent's voluntary consent to termination. . . . Indiana Code Section 31-19-16-2 requires several pre-conditions to be met before post-adoption visitation may be granted [.] . . . Such conditions can never be satisfied at the time of termination because adoption cannot occur until after the termination of all parental rights of the natural parent.

In re M.B. & S.B., 806 N.E.2d at 7.

The Addendum impermissibly overrides the authority of an adoption court provided by I.C. §31-19-16-2. It requires that "the Court grant[] post-adoption privileges and the adoptive parents consent[] to post-adoption contact[.]"This stipulation removes an adoption court's statutory authority to grant post-adoption contact privileges if it finds that (1) contact would be in the "best interests of the child[,]" I.C. §31-19-16-2(1); and (2) if the child is two years of age or older, "that there is a significant emotional attachment between the child and the birth parent[,]" *id.* §2(2). It also overrides the adoptive parents' statutory right to consent to post-adoption contact privileges, *see id.* §2(3), and the joint responsibility of the consenting adoptive parents and the birth parents to execute a post-adoption contact agreement and file the agreement with the court, *id.* §2(4). Finally, the Addendum does away with an adoption court's statutory authority to give final approval to the parties' agreement. *See id.* §2(7).

We hold that, unless all of the provisions of Indiana's open adoption statutes (I.C. §§31-19-16-1 & 2) are satisfied, the voluntary termination of parental rights may not be conditioned upon post-adoption contact privileges.

The Court of Appeals treated Mother's voluntary termination form and the Addendum as a contract. *In re M.B. & S.B.*, 896 N.E.2d at 6. It held that the Addendum, reserving post-adoption visitation privileges, contravened both Indiana statutory law and public policy and was *"void ab initio* and thus unenforceable as a matter of law." *Id.* at 8. It next considered "whether such a decision renders the entire voluntary consent contract void." *Id.* The court concluded that "severing the addendum does not frustrate the basic purpose of the remainder of the agreement[,]" which it defined as Mother's voluntary consent to the termination of her parental rights. *Id.* at 8-9. It therefore held that "[t]he remaining consent form is . . . enforceable by the trial court." *Id.* at 9.

We agree with the Court of Appeals that the visitation proviso contained in the Addendum was invalid as a matter of Indiana law, *see supra* Part I. We decline to analyze this as a matter of contract law, however, and instead conclude that the Addendum should be honored after taking into account the following three factors.

First, the State accepted the post-adoption visitation proviso at the termination proceeding without objection. Mr. Dechert, Mother's attorney, asked the State whether "at this point in time the department believes it is still in the children's best interest to continue with visitation[.]" Case Manager Scott Simmonds replied, "That's correct." After the proceeding, the State confirmed its acceptance of the Addendum by facilitating Mother's bi-weekly supervised visitation with the Children for three months.

Second, the trial court expressly conditioned the voluntary termination on the post-adoption visitation privileges outlined in the Addendum. During the proceeding, the court asked Mother, "you understand that by giving your consent to the termination of parent/child rights[] . . . it is subject to this reservation of post-adoption privileges . . . ?" Mother replied, "Yes." At the close of the proceedings, the trial court concluded that "the court would show that it would accept the Voluntary Relinquishment of Parental Rights as executed by [Mother], subject to the post-adoption privileges, as filed here today."

Third, while the Addendum impermissibly interferes with the open adoption statutes' grants of authority to adoption courts and of consent rights to adoptive parents, the colloquy between the trial court, Mother, and her counsel clearly indicates that the parties understood that any post-adoption visitation was not unconditional. At the commencement of the termination proceeding, Mother's attorney informed the court that "I . . . told [Mother] that that post-adoption contact would only continue so long as it is in the children's best interest and if at any point in time a court, either this court or another court, determine it is no longer in the children's best interest, she would not be entitled to further visitation[.]" . . . The court then granted Mother visitation rights subject to "a court determining that it's in the child's best interest for such visitation . . . to occur[.]"

Given these three factors—that the State voiced no objection to the visitation proviso and acknowledged and complied with it; the trial court's colloquy with Mother expressly referenced the visitation proviso; and the visitation proviso was not unconditional—it would be inequitable and unjust to hold that Mother's voluntary relinquishment of her parental rights was not subject to ongoing but conditional visitation rights. We hold, on the facts of this case, that Mother's parental rights were terminated as provided in I.C. §§31-35-I-12(2)(A) & (B) except that that she had the right to ongoing periodic visitation with the Children unless and until a court were to determine that such visitation was no longer in the children's best interest. If a court were to make such a determination, she would not be entitled to further visitation.

As described under *Background*, following the termination hearing, the State facilitated Mother's supervised visitations with the Children on a bi-weekly basis for about three months. Then, on September 10, 2007, at a review hearing, the State requested, and the trial court agreed, to terminate Mother's visitation rights. Neither Mother nor her counsel were notified of the hearing and therefore had no opportunity to be heard prior to the termination of her visitation rights. She had a final visit with the Children on September 12, 2007.

Mother contends that "due process would require notice and the opportunity to be heard from the person they seek to void or modify the post-adoption contact with." The State counters that Mother was "not entitled to notice of the periodic case review hearing on September 10, 2007[]" because she was "no longer a party to the CHINS case" as a result of the trial court's order terminating her parental rights.

Indiana Code §31-34-21-4, which governs periodic CHINS review hearings, provides that "at least seven (7) days before the periodic case review [] . . . the department [of child services] *shall* provide notice of the review to . . . (1) The child's parent, guardian, or custodian." I.C. §31-34-21-4(a)(1) (emphasis added). The department "shall present proof of service of the notice . . . at the periodic case review." *Id.* §4(b). Furthermore, I.C. §31-34-21-4(d) provides that in periodic CHINS review hearings, the court "*shall* provide [parents, guardians, and custodians, inter alia] an opportunity to be heard and to make any recommendations to the court[.]" (emphasis added). This includes "the right . . . to submit a written statement to the court" and "the right to present oral testimony to the court and cross examine any of the witnesses at the hearing." *Id.* §(d)(1)-(2).

We acknowledge the State's position that these provisions are not applicable to a parent whose parental rights have been completely and irrevocably terminated. But based on the conclusion that we reached in Part II, that simply is not Mother's situation. She did maintain ongoing visitation rights and we hold that she was entitled to the relevant statutory protections. And given what transpired at the review hearing, we are unable to say that the failure to accord her those protections was harmless.

At the review hearing, the State was represented by counsel, Ms. Rebecca Vent. The State's case manager, Ms. Lee, also made an appearance. After reviewing written reports submitted by Ms. Lee and Ms. Pierson (the CASA), the court raised the issue of "whether or not the visits were in the children's best interest." Ms. Vent replied:

> Well, Judge, based upon the letters presented by both of the therapists for the children, they both are of the opinion that it's no longer in the children's best interest because it's impeding the bonding process with the adoptive family. *There's a difference between their opinions in that one of the therapists believes there should be a phased-out visitation over the course of three separate visitations. The other one is of the opinion that just an immediate termination of the visitations would better suit the child.* So I suppose the department is asking for the termination of the visitation as to both children immediately because one therapist recommends the immediate termination, [and] the other says phase it out, but it would be difficult to separate the two children, one goes for visitation

and one doesn't, so we were hopeful that the court would just grant our recommendation that visitations be terminated.

Given that the State itself indicated that the therapist for one of the Children did not think that visitation rights should be immediately terminated, we cannot say that Mother would not have been able to present evidence that termination would not be in the Children's best interest.

Having found that Mother's voluntary relinquishment of her parental rights was subject to conditional visitation rights, Mother further maintains that because her rights to notice and an opportunity to be heard at the hearing terminating her visitation rights were violated, the earlier termination of her parental rights should also be vacated. We hold that her parental rights remain terminated and that she is entitled to no relief in that regard. She consented to the termination in a proceeding that appears to us to have accorded with all relevant law, save the visitation proviso. While she retains an enforceable right as to the visitation proviso, this does not create any basis for reopening the termination of parental rights proceeding.

BOEHM, J., concurring in result.

I agree with the result reached by the majority in Parts I and II, but I do not agree that a consent with an invalid condition is nonetheless a consent. I would, as the majority puts it, resolve Mother's claim as a matter of contract. Mother consented to termination, but attached an addendum containing a written condition — on its face a perpetual unchallengeable right to visitation — that violated several statutory provisions. A consent with an unacceptable condition is no consent at all. ("If striking the illegal portion defeats the primary purpose of the contract, a court must deem the entire contract unenforceable."). A court may void the invalid condition only "if the parties would have entered the bargain absent the illegal portion of the original agreement." Here, the majority concludes that voiding the addendum does not also void Mother's original consent. I disagree. Mother testified that she would not have voluntarily relinquished her parental rights without the addendum. I do not find her earlier statement that she thought her rights would "be terminated anyway" to be inconsistent with her claim that she would have contested termination without the addendum.

Mother's consent was not required for the court to terminate her parental rights. If the invalid consent were the end of the story, we would be left with trying to figure out what would have happened if Mother had contested termination and what should be done about an invalid consent in light of two years of intervening experience and adoptions on the assumption by all parties that Mother's parental rights had been terminated. But at the termination hearing, Mother explicitly consented to a termination and, contrary to her written submission, unequivocally agreed to subject her visitation rights to future reconsideration. What is said in "open court" controls over pre-hearing documents. *Neal v. DeKalb County Div. of Family and Children*, 796 N.E.2d 280, 285 (Ind. 2003) (holding that a mother's written consent to termination of parental rights was invalid when she later revoked her consent in open court). Having given her consent in open court Mother is estopped from challenging the court's right to revisit and adjust or eliminate her visitation. In short, I do not agree that Mother's written consent is enforceable, but in this case she clearly waived any right to assert a bulletproof right to visitation, and the termination is no longer open to question.

DISCUSSION QUESTIONS	FOR *IN THE MATTER OF M.B. & S.B. v. INDIANA DEPARTMENT OF CHILD SERVICES*

A. What does the Indiana statute provide with respect to adoption privileges?

B. How was the Addendum in this case inconsistent with the Indiana statutory provision?

C. What three factors does the court deem significant when analyzing this case? What determination is made concerning each?

D. Why didn't the court reopen the issue of the termination of parental rights? What is the viewpoint of the concurring judge on this point?

19.10 INDIAN CHILD WELFARE ACT (ICWA)

The Indian Child Welfare Act (ICWA), 25 U.S.C. §1901 et seq., governs the placement of Native American children for adoption. The ICWA provides Native American tribes with the ability to preserve their culture and identity by granting tribal courts either exclusive or concurrent jurisdiction over adoption matters involving an American Indian child. The ICWA recognizes that the tribe possesses an interest in an American Indian child that is distinct from but on a parity with the interest of the parents. The act gives rights not only to parents of American Indian children, but also to their tribes. Congress enacted the law to prevent "wholesale separation of American Indian children from their families" through state court proceedings.

The act presumes that it is in the best interests of a child to retain tribal ties and cultural heritage and that it is in the interest of the tribe to preserve its future generations. It also presumes that protection of the Indian child's relationship to the tribe is in the child's best interests.

An adoption decree entered in violation of the act can be invalidated by the tribe or custodian at any time after the decree is entered. 25 U.S.C. §1913(1). The United States Supreme Court ruled six-to-three in *Mississippi Band of Choctaw Indians v. Holyfield*, 490 U.S. 30 (1989), that the Indian Child Welfare Act gives tribal courts exclusive jurisdiction over custody disputes involving American Indian children.

REFLECTIVE QUESTIONS   What purpose is served by Congress giving tribal courts exclusive jurisdiction over custody (adoption) disputes involving American Indian children?

19.11 INTERNATIONAL ADOPTION

Many couples in the United States have used international adoption as a means of adopting a child or children. The adoption laws of the various countries vary widely. For example, China has relatively well-established rules and procedures for adopters to follow. The United Arab Emirates expressly forbids adoption by foreign citizens. Other countries have long waiting periods that make adoption impracticable.

In 1993, the Hague Convention on Protection of Children and Cooperation in Respect of Intercountry Adoption was promulgated. The Convention is an international treaty between Convention member countries. The treaty provides a process that allows the countries who are members of the Convention to work jointly to ensure certain intercountry adoption procedures are followed. The purpose of the Convention is to prevent abduction, sale, or trafficking in children and to provide adoptees with permanent and loving homes. The Convention facilitates international adoptions by requiring that supervisory authorities determine that adoption is in a child's best interest. The United States ratified the Convention in 2001, making it applicable when the United States and the other country are signatories to the Convention. 42 U.S.C. §§14901-14945 (West 2007).

On November 16, 2007, then-President George W. Bush signed the United States' Instrument of Ratification for the Hague Convention on Intercountry Adoption. This authorized the Department of State to deposit it with designated authorities in the Netherlands. This was the final procedural step for the United States to become a full member of the Hague Convention.

If the Convention is in force between two countries, then any adoption of a child habitually resident in one country by a person habitually resident in another country must comply with the requirements of the Convention.

REFLECTIVE QUESTIONS   What is the purpose of the Hague Convention on Intercountry Adoption?

General Principles

1. Although the practice of adoption dates back to ancient times, there was no legal provision for adoption at common law.

2. When a child is adopted, the adoptive parents are substituted for the biological parents, and they assume the rights and obligations that the biological parents once had.

3. Before a child can be adopted, the child's ties to his or her biological parents must be legally terminated.

4. A putative father's legal rights with respect to a biological child may ultimately depend on the strength of the relationship between the putative father, mother, and child. In *Stanley* and *Caban*, the fathers demonstrated the existence of a sufficiently strong relationship that warranted constitutional protection. However, in the absence of such a commitment, there may be no constitutional protection.

5. In order to ensure that he receives notice of a potential adoption, a putative father may be required to enter his name on an adoption registry prior to the child's birth or within a prescribed time, typically within 30 days of the birth.

6. Today most adoptions are "closed" in that the birth parents are not identified and they have no further contact with the adopted child. Nevertheless, some states allow the option of postadoption contact between the child and the biological parents. Such arrangements are known as "open" adoptions.

7. The Indian Child Welfare Act, 25 U.S.C. §1901 et seq., governs the placement of Native American children for adoption.

Chapter Problems

1. Assume that Pat and Doris have a child named Ann, who is ultimately adopted by Alex and Barbara. Pat and Doris die in a terrible car accident, and Alex and Barbara bring a wrongful death lawsuit on Ann's behalf. Will Ann be allowed to recover?

2. Alice and Bill lived together outside of marriage for four years. During the relationship, two children were born to them. While he and Alice lived together, Bill provided food and clothing for the children. Eleven months ago Bill moved out, leaving Alice with the children, ages one and two. He provided no additional support for the children or Alice. Alice decided it was in their best interests for the children to be adopted. She placed the children for adoption with an adoption agency, which asked her to provide the name and address of their father. Alice lied to the agency, saying she had not seen their father for two years and had no idea of where he lived. The children were placed with Dick and Jane, pending formal adoption. They remained with Dick and Jane for six months. During this period, the agency published the adoption notice in the local legal newspaper and conducted a search for Bill using the telephone and street directories. He could not be located. A court hearing was then held in which Alice testified she understood the consequences of her action and signed a valid document terminating her parental rights. The order was issued, and the children have lived with Dick and Jane for five months. Bill returned to the area from his work on an oil rig in the Gulf of Mexico and contacted Alice, looking for the children. When he learned that she had put them up for adoption, he contacted you asking for legal advice. Was the termination constitutional? What advice will you give Bill?

3. When a child is adopted, should the child have a right to visitation with his or her siblings (assuming they are not adopted into the same family)? In *In re the Matter of D.C. and D.C.*, the New Jersey Supreme Court discussed this issue:

> [S]iblings can petition for visitation with their brothers and sisters who have been adopted by non-relatives, subject to the avoidance of harm standard. We can envision, for example, a case in which pre-teen siblings, raised together in the same household, deeply entwined in each other's lives, are removed due to abuse or neglect. If one is adopted by a non-relative and the other taken in by his grandmother, it seems likely to us that denial of the sibling's application to visit his adopted brother would satisfy the harm threshold. To the contrary, it is less clear that siblings separated at birth and raised in different households with no interaction whatsoever would be able to vault the threshold.

In re the Matter of D.C. and D.C., 4 A.3d 1004, 1007 (N.J. 2010). The court also stated: "All of the attributes of a biological family are applicable in the case of adoption; adoptive parents are free, within the same limits as biological parents, to raise their children as they see fit, including choices regarding religion, education, and association." *Id.* at 1021. If an adoptive parent opposes sibling visitation, whose rights should prevail?

Preparation for Practice

1. Imagine that you are interested in adopting a child. Conduct an Internet search on becoming an adoptive parent in your state. What did you learn?

2. Prepare a checklist of the steps a person in your jurisdiction must take from the time adoption is considered through the final order of adoption. Include an estimate of the approximate time it takes for each step to occur.

3. Does your state have a putative father registry? Go online and search for the registry. What information is provided there?

4. Proposals have been made to establish a national adoption registry:

> The momentum has built towards enactment of a national putative father registry database such that Senator Mary Landrieu introduced one in the United States Senate in 2006 called the PROUD FATHER ACT. While Congress did not

enact it, its legislative intent to protect the parental rights of earnest unwed fathers against interstate adoption, to protect the privacy and safety of birth mothers, and to expedite the prompt stable placement of children justifies its re-introduction and enactment. Only a national registry can accomplish these legislative goals, because relocation across state lines is so common.

Mary Beck, *A National Putative Father Registry*, 36 Cap. L. Rev. 295, 298 (2007). Do you favor or oppose such an approach? Prepare a 250-word essay expressing your position about creating a national registry and share it with the class.

Accuracy of term "surrogate." Some question the accuracy of the term *surrogate* when used to describe a woman who is in fact the actual biological mother of a child. One author expressed the opinion that "[t]he term 'surrogate' mother, coined by advocates of commercial surrogacy, is a misnomer. The woman who bears the child is an actual mother; she is a surrogate 'wife.'" Kathryn D. Katz, *The Public Policy Response to Surrogate Motherhood Agreements: Why They Should Be Illegal and Unenforceable*, N.Y. St. B.J. (May 1988).

Compensation. States do not agree on compensation of surrogate mothers. For example, Illinois expressly permits compensation to surrogate birth mothers. Jennifer L. Watson, *Growing a Baby for Sale or Merely Renting a Womb: Should Surrogate Mothers Be Compensated for Their Services?*, 6 Whittier J. Child & Fam. Advoc. 529, n.29 (Spring 2007).

Several states refuse to enforce any surrogacy agreements, whether compensated or uncompensated. A few have explicitly stated that only unpaid surrogacy agreements are lawful, while some jurisdictions prohibit payment to intermediaries who seek willing surrogates for infertile couples.

Among the obstacles to these contracts is the existence of criminal statutes that ban the payment of compensation in connection with an adoption and others that outlaw child selling. *See* Sarah Mortazavi, *It Takes a Village to Make a Child: Creating Guidelines for International Surrogacy*, 100 Geo. L.J. 2249, 2258-2260 (2012) (categorizing states that either permit, regulate, or ban "commercial" and/or "altruistic" surrogacy contracts). At least three states have exempted commercial surrogacy agreements from statutory provisions criminalizing the sale of babies. *Id.* at n.34.

A majority of states do not have statutes addressing the enforceability of surrogacy agreements in general, whether commercial or noncommercial, which leaves the courts in those states to determine their legality and enforceability.

REFLECTIVE QUESTIONS	**What are some of the differences among the states when considering whether a surrogate may be compensated? What might explain the lack of uniformity about compensation?**

20.7 SURROGACY: HUSBAND'S SPERM, SURROGATE'S EGG

Background to *In the Matter of Baby M*

The New Jersey case, *In the Matter of Baby M*, gained national attention. The husband and wife, Mr. and Mrs. Stern, could not have their own children and sought to have them via a traditional surrogacy arrangement. Pursuant to a written agreement with a surrogate agency, Mr. Stern's sperm fertilized a surrogate's

(Mrs. Whitehead's) eggs. Mrs. Whitehead eventually delivered a baby, but refused to follow the terms of the agreement and claimed that she was legally the mother of the infant.

The trial judge concluded that New Jersey statutes governing baby selling, adoption, and custody disputes between unwed parents did not apply to this type of arrangement. He applied general contract, constitutional, and *parens patriae* doctrines to resolve the case.

IN THE MATTER OF BABY M
Supreme Court of New Jersey
537 A.2d 1227 (1988)

WILENTZ, J. In this matter the Court is asked to determine the validity of a contract that purports to provide a new way of bringing children into a family. For a fee of $10,000, a woman agrees to be artificially inseminated with the semen of another woman's husband; she is to conceive a child, carry it to term, and after its birth surrender it to the natural father and his wife. The intent of the contract is that the child's natural mother will thereafter be forever separated from her child. The wife is to adopt the child, and she and the natural father are to be regarded as its parents for all purposes. The contract providing for this is called a "surrogacy contract," the natural mother inappropriately called the "surrogate mother." . . .

In February 1985, William Stern and Mary Beth Whitehead entered into a surrogacy contract. It recited that Stern's wife, Elizabeth, was infertile, that they wanted a child, and that Mrs. Whitehead was willing to provide that child as the mother with Mr. Stern as the father.

The contract provided that through artificial insemination using Mr. Stern's sperm, Mrs. Whitehead would become pregnant, carry the child to term, bear it, deliver it to the Sterns, and thereafter do whatever was necessary to terminate her maternal rights so that Mrs. Stern could thereafter adopt the child. Whitehead's husband, Richard, was also a party to the contract; Mrs. Stern was not. Mr. Whitehead promised to do all acts necessary to rebut the presumption of paternity under the Parentage Act. Although Mrs. Stern was not a party to the surrogacy agreement, the contract gave her sole custody of the child in the event of Mr. Stern's death. Mrs. Stern's status as a nonparty to the surrogate parenting agreement presumably was to avoid the application of the baby-selling statute to this arrangement.

Mr. Stern, on his part, agreed to attempt the artificial insemination and to pay Mrs. Whitehead $10,000 after the child's birth, on its delivery to him. In a separate contract, Mr. Stern agreed to pay $7,500 to the Infertility Center of New York ("ICNY"). The Center's advertising campaigns solicit surrogate mothers and encourage infertile couples to consider surrogacy. ICNY arranged for the surrogacy contract by bringing the parties together, explaining the process to them, furnishing the contractual form, and providing legal counsel.

The history of the parties' involvement in this arrangement suggests their good faith. William and Elizabeth Stern were married in July 1974, having met at the

University of Michigan, where both were Ph.D. candidates. Due to financial considerations and Mrs. Stern's pursuit of a medical degree and residency, they decided to defer starting a family until 1981. Before then, however, Mrs. Stern learned that she might have multiple sclerosis and that the disease in some cases renders pregnancy a serious health risk. Her anxiety appears to have exceeded the actual risk, which current medical authorities assess as minimal. Nonetheless that anxiety was evidently quite real, Mrs. Stern fearing that pregnancy might precipitate blindness, paraplegia, or other forms of debilitation. Based on the perceived risk, the Sterns decided to forego having their own children. The decision had a special significance for Mr. Stern. Most of his family had been destroyed in the Holocaust. As the family's only survivor, he very much wanted to continue his bloodline.

Initially the Sterns considered adoption, but were discouraged by the substantial delay apparently involved and by the potential problem they saw arising from their age and their differing religious backgrounds. They were most eager for some other means to start a family.

The paths of Mrs. Whitehead and the Sterns to surrogacy were similar. Both responded to advertising by ICNY. The Sterns' response, following their inquiries into adoption, was the result of their long-standing decision to have a child. Mrs. Whitehead's response apparently resulted from her sympathy with family members and others who could have no children (she stated that she wanted to give another couple the "gift of life"); she also wanted the $10,000 to help her family.

Both parties, undoubtedly because of their own self-interest, were less sensitive to the implications of the transaction than they might otherwise have been. Mrs. Whitehead, for instance, appears not to have been concerned about whether the Sterns would make good parents for her child; the Sterns, on their part, while conscious of the obvious possibility that surrendering the child might cause grief to Mrs. Whitehead, overcame their qualms because of their desire for a child. At any rate, both the Sterns and Mrs. Whitehead were committed to the arrangement; both thought it right and constructive.

Mrs. Whitehead had reached her decision concerning surrogacy before the Sterns, and had actually been involved as a potential surrogate mother with another couple. After numerous unsuccessful artificial inseminations, that effort was abandoned. Thereafter, the Sterns learned of the Infertility Center, the possibilities of surrogacy, and of Mary Beth Whitehead. The two couples met to discuss the surrogacy arrangement and decided to go forward. On February 6, 1985, Mr. Stern and Mr. and Mrs. Whitehead executed the surrogate parenting agreement. After several artificial inseminations over a period of months, Mrs. Whitehead became pregnant. The pregnancy was uneventful and on March 27, 1986, Baby M was born.

Not wishing anyone at the hospital to be aware of the surrogacy arrangement, Mr. and Mrs. Whitehead appeared to all as the proud parents of a healthy female child. Her birth certificate indicated her name to be Sara Elizabeth Whitehead and her father to be Richard Whitehead. In accordance with Mrs. Whitehead's request, the Sterns visited the hospital unobtrusively to see the newborn child.

Mrs. Whitehead realized, almost from the moment of birth, that she could not part with this child. She had felt a bond with it even during pregnancy. Some indication of the attachment was conveyed to the Sterns at the hospital when they told

Mrs. Whitehead what they were going to name the baby. She apparently broke into tears and indicated that she did not know if she could give up the child. She talked about how the baby looked like her daughter, and made it clear that she was experiencing great difficulty with the decision. Nonetheless, Mrs. Whitehead was, for the moment, true to her word. Despite powerful inclinations to the contrary, she turned her child over to the Sterns on March 30 at the Whiteheads' home.

The Sterns were thrilled with their new child. They had planned extensively for its arrival, far beyond the practical furnishing of a room for her. It was a time of joyful celebration — not just for them but for their friends as well. The Sterns looked forward to raising their daughter, whom they named Melissa. While aware by then that Mrs. Whitehead was undergoing an emotional crisis, they were as yet not cognizant of the depth of that crisis and its implications for their newly enlarged family.

Later in the evening of March 30, Mrs. Whitehead became deeply disturbed, disconsolate, stricken with unbearable sadness. She had to have her child. She could not eat, sleep, or concentrate on anything other than her need for her baby. The next day she went to the Sterns' home and told them how much she was suffering.

The depth of Mrs. Whitehead's despair surprised and frightened the Sterns. She told them that she could not live without her baby, that she must have her, even if only for one week, that thereafter she would surrender her child. The Sterns, concerned that Mrs. Whitehead might indeed commit suicide, not wanting under any circumstances to risk that, and in any event believing that Mrs. Whitehead would keep her word, turned the child over to her. It was not until four months later, after a series of attempts to regain possession of the child, that Melissa was returned to the Sterns, having been forcibly removed from the home where she was then living with Mr. and Mrs. Whitehead, the home in Florida owned by Mary Beth Whitehead's parents.

The struggle over Baby M began when it became apparent that Mrs. Whitehead could not return the child to Mr. Stern. Due to Mrs. Whitehead's refusal to relinquish the baby, Mr. Stern filed a complaint seeking enforcement of the surrogacy contract. He alleged, accurately, that Mrs. Whitehead had not only refused to comply with the surrogacy contract but had threatened to flee from New Jersey with the child in order to avoid even the possibility of his obtaining custody. The court papers asserted that if Mrs. Whitehead were to be given notice of the application for an order requiring her to relinquish custody, she would, prior to the hearing, leave the state with the baby. And that is precisely what she did. After the order was entered, *ex parte*, the process server, aided by the police, in the presence of the Sterns, entered Mrs. Whitehead's home to execute the order. Mr. Whitehead fled with the child, who had been handed to him through a window while those who came to enforce the order were thrown off balance by a dispute over the child's current name.

The Whiteheads immediately fled to Florida with Baby M. They stayed initially with Mrs. Whitehead's parents, where one of Mrs. Whitehead's children had been living. For the next three months, the Whiteheads and Melissa lived at roughly twenty different hotels, motels, and homes in order to avoid apprehension. From time to time Mrs. Whitehead would call Mr. Stern to discuss the matter; the conversations, recorded by Mr. Stern on advice of counsel, show an escalating dispute about rights, morality, and power, accompanied by threats of Mrs. Whitehead to kill herself, to kill the child, and falsely to accuse Mr. Stern of sexually molesting Mrs. Whitehead's other daughter.

Eventually the Sterns discovered where the Whiteheads were staying, commenced supplementary proceedings in Florida, and obtained an order requiring the Whiteheads to turn over the child. Police in Florida enforced the order, forcibly removing the child from her grandparents' home. She was soon thereafter brought to New Jersey and turned over to the Sterns. The prior order of the court, issued *ex parte*, awarding custody of the child to the Sterns *pendente lite*, was reaffirmed by the trial court after consideration of the certified representations of the parties (both represented by counsel) concerning the unusual sequence of events that had unfolded. Pending final judgment, Mrs. Whitehead was awarded limited visitation with Baby M.

The Sterns' complaint, in addition to seeking possession and ultimately custody of the child, sought enforcement of the surrogacy contract. Pursuant to the contract, it asked that the child be permanently placed in their custody, that Mrs. Whitehead's parental rights be terminated, and that Mrs. Stern be allowed to adopt the child, i.e., that, for all purposes, Melissa become the Sterns' child. . . .

[The trial took 32 days, over a period of more than 2 months, and the trial judge held that the surrogacy contract was valid; he ordered that Mrs. Whitehead's right be terminated and that sole custody of the child be granted to Mr. Stern. Mrs. Whitehead appealed.]

Mrs. Whitehead contends that the surrogacy contract, for a variety of reasons, is invalid. She contends that it conflicts with public policy since it guarantees that the child will not have the nurturing of both natural parents—presumably New Jersey's goal for families. She further argues that it deprives the mother of her constitutional right to the companionship of her child, and that it conflicts with statutes concerning termination of parental rights and adoption. With the contract thus void, Mrs. Whitehead claims primary custody (with visitation rights in Mr. Stern) both on a best interests basis (stressing the "tender years" doctrine) as well as on the policy basis of discouraging surrogacy contracts. She maintains that even if custody would ordinarily go to Mr. Stern, here it should be awarded to Mrs. Whitehead to deter future surrogacy arrangements.

In a brief filed after oral argument, counsel for Mrs. Whitehead suggests that the standard for determining best interests where the infant resulted from a surrogacy contract is that the child should be placed with the mother absent a showing of unfitness. All parties agree that no expert testified that Mary Beth Whitehead was unfit as a mother; the trial court expressly found that she was not "unfit," that, on the contrary, "she is a good mother for and to her older children," and no one now claims anything to the contrary. . . .

The Sterns claim that the surrogacy contract is valid and should be enforced. . . . They claim a constitutional right of privacy, which includes the right of procreation, and the right of consenting adults to deal with matters of reproduction as they see fit. As for the child's best interests, their position is factual: given all of the circumstances, the child is better off in their custody with no residual parental rights reserved for Mrs. Whitehead. . . .

We have concluded that this surrogacy contract is invalid. Our conclusion has two bases: direct conflict with existing statutes and conflict with the public policies of this State, as expressed in its statutory and decisional law.

One of the surrogacy contract's basic purposes, to achieve the adoption of a child through private placement, though permitted in New Jersey "is very much disfavored." Its use of money for this purpose — and we have no doubt whatsoever that the money is being paid to obtain an adoption and not, as the Sterns argue, for the personal services of Mary Beth Whitehead — is illegal and perhaps criminal. In addition to the inducement of money, there is the coercion of contract: the natural mother's irrevocable agreement, prior to birth, even prior to conception, to surrender the child to the adoptive couple. Such an agreement is totally unenforceable in private placement adoption. Even where the adoption is through an approved agency, the formal agreement to surrender occurs only after birth, and then, by regulation, only after the birth mother has been counseled. Integral to these invalid provisions of the surrogacy contract is the related agreement, equally invalid, on the part of the natural mother to cooperate with, and not to contest, proceedings to terminate her parental rights, as well as her contractual concession, in aid of the adoption, that the child's best interests would be served by awarding custody to the natural father and his wife — all of this before she has even conceived, and, in some cases, before she has the slightest idea of what the natural father and adoptive mother are like. . . .

The surrogacy contract's invalidity, resulting from its direct conflict with the above statutory provisions, is further underlined when its goals and means are measured against New Jersey's public policy. The contract's basic premise, that the natural parents can decide in advance of birth which one is to have custody of the child, bears no relationship to the settled law that the child's best interests shall determine custody. ("Whatever the agreement of the parents, the ultimate determination of custody lies with the court in the exercise of its supervisory jurisdiction as *parens patriae*.") The fact that the trial court remedied that aspect of the contract through the "best interests" phase does not make the contractual provision any less offensive to the public policy of this State.

The surrogacy contract guarantees permanent separation of the child from one of its natural parents. Our policy, however, has long been that to the extent possible, children should remain with and be brought up by both of their natural parents. That was the first stated purpose of the previous adoption act: "it is necessary and desirable (a) to protect the child from unnecessary separation from his natural parents." While not so stated in the present adoption law, this purpose remains part of the public policy of this State.

The surrogacy contract violates the policy of this State that the rights of natural parents are equal concerning their child, the father's right no greater than the mother's. "The parent and child relationship extends equally to every child and to every parent, regardless of the marital status of the parents." . . .

As noted before, if termination of Mrs. Whitehead's parental rights is justified, Mrs. Whitehead will have no further claim either to custody or to visitation, and adoption by Mrs. Stern may proceed pursuant to the private placement adoption statute. If termination is not justified, Mrs. Whitehead remains the legal mother, and even if not entitled to custody, she would ordinarily be expected to have some rights of visitation. . . .

Having decided that the surrogacy contract is illegal and unenforceable, we now must decide the custody question without regard to the provisions of the surrogacy contract that would give Mr. Stern sole and permanent custody.

. . . Under the Parentage Act the claims of the natural father and the natural mother are entitled to equal weight, i.e., one is not preferred over the other solely because he or she is the father or the mother. The applicable rule given these circumstances is clear: the child's best interests determine custody. Based on all of this we have concluded, independent of the trial court's identical conclusion, that Melissa's best interests call for custody in the Sterns.

The trial court's decision to terminate Mrs. Whitehead's parental rights precluded it from making any determination on visitation. Our reversal of the trial court's order, however, requires delineation of Mrs. Whitehead's rights to visitation. It is apparent to us that this factually sensitive issue, which was never addressed below, should not be determined de novo by this Court.

[Remanded for visitation hearing.]

DISCUSSION QUESTIONS FOR *IN THE MATTER OF BABY M*

A. When Mrs. Whitehead decided to keep the child, should the court have required her to reimburse the Sterns for the fees they paid her and the surrogate agency?

B. What legal restrictions should apply to surrogacy contracts where all the parties agree to a contract's terms and the contract is carried out? What role should payment to the surrogate play in these cases? The New Jersey court holds that payment to a surrogate is illegal because it constitutes the sale of a child, regardless of the party's wishes. However, isn't such an agreement similar to an adoption agreement, which is not illegal?

C. What is Mr. Stern's legal status with respect to the child? Is this a situation where a woman conceives via AID while married? Isn't Mr. Stern merely a sperm donor with no legal status under AID law?

D. Professor Marjorie Maguire Shultz argues that the *Baby M* "decision ignored and trivialized distinctions between conventional pre-technology procreation and the transactions and relationships in the surrogacy arrangement. To say that the factual issues are 'the same' as if Whitehead and William Stern had simply had a child out of wedlock, ignores the centrally important fact that modern reproductive techniques allow the separation of personal and sexual intimacy from procreation." Professor Shultz says that the court's view "ignores that these reproductive techniques have different meanings and occur in different factual contexts than those contemplated by baby-selling statutes." She also argues that the "court's decision reinforced stereotypes regarding the desirability of segregating women from the market, the unpredictability of women's intentions and decisions, and the givenness of women's biological destiny. Perhaps worst of all, it acted to lock in existing gender-based spheres of influence in our society, refusing to recognize fragile, emergent male efforts to claim a meaningful role in access to and nurture of children." Marjorie Maguire Shultz, *Reproductive Technology and Intent-Based Parenthood: An Opportunity for Gender Neutrality*, 1990 Wis. L. Rev. 297, 376-379. Do you agree with Professor Shultz's perspective?

E. What weight, if any, should a court give to the terms of a surrogate contract when the surrogate is provided independent counsel at the time the contract was executed?

F. The Michigan legislature criminalized "surrogate" parent contracts under which a woman agrees to give birth and then to transfer her child to another for a fee. The statute, known as the Surrogate Parenting Act, declares that "[a] person shall not enter into, induce, arrange, procure, or otherwise assist in the formation of a surrogate parentage contract for compensation." Mich. Comp. Laws Ann. §722.859(1) (2015). The statute makes participation in a surrogacy contract for compensation a misdemeanor, punishable by a fine not greater than $10,000 or imprisonment for not more than a year or both. A person who arranges or procures such a contract is guilty of a felony punishable by a fine of not more than $50,000 or imprisonment for not more than 5 years, or both. Such contracts are "void and unenforceable as contrary to public policy." Mich. Comp. Laws Ann. §722.855 (2015). Isn't Michigan's criminal statute taking the surrogacy prohibition too far?

G. What should public policy be if surrogacy arrangements fail because the intended parties refuse to take the child because it is born with a birth defect?

H. In its analysis, the court in *Baby M* said that in addition to the inducement of money there was "coercion of contract." Explain the court's view regarding "coercion of contract."

I. The court in *Baby M* indicated that the contract involved the adoption of a child through private placement and stated that although private placement is permitted, it is disfavored. What reasons did the court give in support of its view that private placement contracts were disfavored? Are they persuasive?

J. During the court's analysis in *Baby M*, it criticized a provision that allowed the natural parents to decide in advance of birth who is to have custody of the child. What was the court's concern? Is its analysis on this point persuasive?

K. In justifying its decision, the court discussed New Jersey's public policy regarding separating a child from one of its natural parents. What significance did this policy play in the ultimate decision of the case?

L. Proponents of surrogate contracts argue that they are superior to the situation where an adoption follows an unplanned pregnancy because in the surrogacy context consent to adopt is given preconception. Therefore, the financial and emotional stresses present in an unplanned pregnancy/adoption are not present. How much weight should the proponents' view receive in a surrogacy contract dispute?

20.8 SURROGACY: HUSBAND'S SPERM, WIFE'S EGG, THIRD-PARTY GESTATIONAL CARRIER

Background to *Johnson v. Calvert*

As noted earlier, there are two types of surrogacy: gestational and traditional. Gestational surrogacy involves a surrogate who gestates the child but has no genetic relationship with the child. In "traditional" surrogacy, such as we saw in *In the Matter of Baby M*, the surrogate's own egg is used, rendering her both the genetic and the gestational mother.

In *Johnson v. Calvert*, a married couple could not have children naturally because the wife had undergone a hysterectomy. She could, however, produce eggs. The couple entered into a surrogacy agreement with a third-party female, Anna Johnson, who agreed to give birth to a child on their behalf in exchange for $10,000 and other consideration. One of Ms. Calvert's eggs was fertilized with Mr. Calvert's sperm and was successfully implanted in Ms. Johnson's uterus. However, when the relationship between the Calverts and Ms. Johnson deteriorated, litigation over maternity and custody ensued. Under California's version of the Uniform Parentage Act, both genetic consanguinity and giving birth were equally recognized bases for establishing maternity.

The American Civil Liberties Union (ACLU) filed an amicus brief suggesting that the appropriate outcome, where both the gestational mother and the genetic mother desired a continued relationship with the child, was to recognize that the child had two legal mothers. The result of this argument is that a child has three parents: the father, the genetic mother, and the gestational mother.

JOHNSON
v.
CALVERT

Supreme Court of California
851 P.2d 776 (1993)

PANELLI, J. In this case we address several of the legal questions raised by recent advances in reproductive technology. When, pursuant to a surrogacy agreement, a zygote formed of the gametes of a husband and wife is implanted in the uterus of another woman, who carries the resulting fetus to term and gives birth to a child not genetically related to her, who is the child's "natural mother" under California law? Does a determination that the wife is the child's natural mother work a deprivation of the gestating woman's constitutional rights? And is such an agreement barred by any public policy of this state? . . .

Mark and Crispina Calvert are a married couple who desired to have a child. Crispina was forced to undergo a hysterectomy in 1984. Her ovaries remained capable of producing eggs, however, and the couple eventually considered surrogacy. In 1989 Anna Johnson heard about Crispina's plight from a coworker and offered to serve as a surrogate for the Calverts.

On January 15, 1990, Mark, Crispina, and Anna signed a contract providing that an embryo created by the sperm of Mark and the egg of Crispina would be implanted in Anna and the child born would be taken into Mark and Crispina's home "as their child." Anna agreed she would relinquish "all parental rights" to the child in favor of Mark and Crispina. In return, Mark and Crispina would pay Anna $10,000 in a series of installments, the last to be paid six weeks after the child's birth. Mark and Crispina were also to pay for a $200,000 life insurance policy on Anna's life.

The zygote was implanted on January 19, 1990. Less than a month later, an ultrasound test confirmed Anna was pregnant.

Unfortunately, relations deteriorated between the two sides. Mark learned that Anna had not disclosed she had suffered several stillbirths and miscarriages. Anna felt Mark and Crispina did not do enough to obtain the required insurance policy. She also felt abandoned during an onset of premature labor in June.

In July 1990, Anna sent Mark and Crispina a letter demanding the balance of the payments due her or else she would refuse to give up the child. The following month, Mark and Crispina responded with a lawsuit, seeking a declaration they were the legal parents of the unborn child. Anna filed her own action to be declared the mother of the child, and the two cases were eventually consolidated. The parties agreed to an independent guardian ad litem for the purposes of the suit.

The child was born on September 19, 1990, and blood samples were obtained from both Anna and the child for analysis. The blood test results excluded Anna as the genetic mother. The parties agreed to a court order providing that the child would remain with Mark and Crispina on a temporary basis with visits by Anna.

At trial in October 1990, the parties stipulated that Mark and Crispina were the child's genetic parents. After hearing evidence and arguments, the trial court ruled that Mark and Crispina were the child's "genetic, biological and natural" father and mother, that Anna had no "parental" rights to the child, and that the surrogacy contract was legal and enforceable against Anna's claims. The court also terminated the order allowing visitation. Anna appealed from the trial court's judgment. The Court of Appeal for the Fourth District, Division Three, affirmed. We granted review.

Anna, of course, predicates her claim of maternity on the fact that she gave birth to the child. The Calverts contend that Crispina's genetic relationship to the child establishes that she is his mother. Counsel for the minor joins in that contention and argues, in addition, that several of the presumptions created by the Act dictate the same result. As will appear, we conclude that presentation of blood test evidence is one means of establishing maternity, as is proof of having given birth, but that the presumptions cited by minor's counsel do not apply to this case. . . .

Because two women each have presented acceptable proof of maternity, we do not believe this case can be decided without enquiring into the parties' intentions as manifested in the surrogacy agreement. Mark and Crispina are a couple who desired to have a child of their own genetic stock but are physically unable to do so without the help of reproductive technology. They affirmatively intended the birth of the child, and took the steps necessary to effect in vitro fertilization. But for their acted-on intention, the child would not exist. Anna agreed to facilitate the procreation of Mark's and Crispina's child. The parties' aim was to bring Mark's and Crispina's child into the world, not for Mark and Crispina to donate a zygote to Anna. Crispina from the outset intended to be the child's mother. Although the gestative function Anna performed was necessary to bring about the child's birth, it is safe to say that Anna would not have been given the opportunity to gestate or deliver the child had she, prior to implantation of the zygote, manifested her own intent to be the child's mother. No reason appears why Anna's later change of heart should vitiate the determination that Crispina is the child's natural mother.

We conclude that although the [California statutes] recognize both genetic consanguinity and giving birth as means of establishing a mother and child relationship, when the two means do not coincide in one woman, she who intended to procreate the child—that is, she who intended to bring about the birth of a child that she intended to raise as her own—is the natural mother under California law. . . .

In deciding the issue of maternity under the Act we have felt free to take into account the parties' intentions, as expressed in the surrogacy contract, because in our view the agreement is not, on its face, inconsistent with public policy.

Anna urges that surrogacy contracts violate several social policies. Relying on her contention that she is the child's legal, natural mother, she cites the public policy embodied in Penal Code section 273, prohibiting the payment for consent to adoption of a child. She argues further that the policies underlying the adoption laws of this state are violated by the surrogacy contract because it in effect constitutes a prebirth waiver of her parental rights.

We disagree. Gestational surrogacy differs in crucial respects from adoption and so is not subject to the adoption statutes. The parties voluntarily agreed to participate in in vitro fertilization and related medical procedures before the child was conceived; at the time when Anna entered into the contract, therefore, she was not vulnerable to financial inducements to part with her own expected offspring. As discussed above, Anna was not the genetic mother of the child. The payments to Anna under the contract were meant to compensate her for her services in gestating the fetus and undergoing labor, rather than for giving up "parental" rights to the child. Payments were due both during the pregnancy and after the child's birth.

We are, accordingly, unpersuaded that the contract used in this case violates the public policies embodied in Penal Code section 273 and the adoption statutes. For the same reasons, we conclude these contracts do not implicate the policies underlying the statutes governing termination of parental rights.

It has been suggested that gestational surrogacy may run afoul of prohibitions on involuntary servitude. Involuntary servitude has been recognized in cases of criminal punishment for refusal to work. We see no potential for that evil in the contract at issue here, and extrinsic evidence of coercion or duress is utterly lacking. We note that although at one point the contract purports to give Mark and Crispina the sole right to determine whether to abort the pregnancy, at another point it acknowledges: "All parties understand that a pregnant woman has the absolute right to abort or not abort any fetus she is carrying. Any promise to the contrary is unenforceable." We therefore need not determine the validity of a surrogacy contract purporting to deprive the gestator of her freedom to terminate the pregnancy.

Finally, Anna and some commentators have expressed concern that surrogacy contracts tend to exploit or dehumanize women, especially women of lower economic status. Anna's objections center around the psychological harm she asserts may result from the gestator's relinquishing the child to whom she has given birth. Some have also cautioned that the practice of surrogacy may encourage society to view children as commodities, subject to trade at their parents' will.

We are all too aware that the proper forum for resolution of this issue is the Legislature, where empirical data, largely lacking from this record, can be studied and rules of general applicability developed. However, in light of our responsibility to decide this case, we have considered as best we can its possible consequences.

We are unpersuaded that gestational surrogacy arrangements are so likely to cause the untoward results Anna cites as to demand their invalidation on public policy grounds. Although common sense suggests that women of lesser means serve as surrogate mothers more often than do wealthy women, there has been no proof that surrogacy contracts exploit poor women to any greater degree than economic necessity in general exploits them by inducing them to accept lower-paid or otherwise undesirable employment. We are likewise unpersuaded by the claim that surrogacy will foster the attitude that children are mere commodities; no evidence is offered to support it. The limited data available seem to reflect an absence of significant adverse effects of surrogacy on all participants.

The argument that a woman cannot knowingly and intelligently agree to gestate and deliver a baby for intending parents carries overtones of the reasoning that for centuries prevented women from attaining equal economic rights and professional status under the law. To resurrect this view is both to foreclose a personal and economic choice on the part of the surrogate mother, and to deny intending parents what may be their only means of procreating a child of their own genetic stock.

Certainly in the present case it cannot seriously be argued that Anna, a licensed vocational nurse who had done well in school and who had previously borne a child, lacked the intellectual wherewithal or life experience necessary to make an informed decision to enter into the surrogacy contract. . . .

Anna argues at length that her right to the continued companionship of the child is protected under the federal Constitution. . . . First, we note the constitutional rights that are not implicated here.

There is no issue of procedural due process: although Anna broadly contends that the procedures prescribed for adoptions should be followed in the situation of a gestational surrogate's relinquishment to the genetic parents of the child she has carried and delivered, she cites no specific deficiency in the notice or hearing this matter received.

Furthermore, neither Anna nor amicus curiae ACLU articulates a claim under the equal protection clause, and we are unable to discern in these facts the necessary predicate to its operation. This is because a woman who voluntarily agrees to gestate and deliver for a married couple a child who is their genetic offspring is situated differently from the wife who provides the ovum for fertilization, intending to mother the resulting child.

Anna relies mainly on theories of substantive due process, privacy, and procreative freedom, citing a number of decisions recognizing the fundamental liberty interest of natural parents in the custody and care of their children. . . . Most of the cases Anna cites deal with the rights of unwed fathers in the face of attempts to terminate their parental relationship to their children. These cases do not support recognition of parental rights for a gestational surrogate. Although Anna quotes language stressing the primacy of a developed parent-child relationship in assessing unwed fathers' rights (*see Lehr v. Robertson*), certain language in the cases reinforces the importance of genetic parents' rights. . . . ["The significance of the biological connection is that it offers the natural father an opportunity that no other male possesses to develop a relationship with his offspring. If he grasps that opportunity and accepts some measure of responsibility for the child's future, he may enjoy the blessings of the parent-child relationship and make uniquely valuable contributions to the child's development."].

Anna's argument depends on a prior determination that she is indeed the child's mother. Since Crispina is the child's mother under California law because she, not Anna, provided the ovum for the in vitro fertilization procedure, intending to raise the child as her own, it follows that any constitutional interests Anna possesses in this situation are something less than those of a mother. As counsel for the minor points out, the issue in this case is not whether Anna's asserted rights as a natural mother were unconstitutionally violated, but rather whether the determination that she is not the legal natural mother at all is constitutional.

Anna relies principally on the decision of the United States Supreme Court in *Michael H. v. Gerald D.* (1989) 491 U.S. 110, to support her claim to a constitutionally protected liberty interest in the companionship of the child, based on her status as "birth mother." . . . In that case, a plurality of the court held that a state may constitutionally deny a man parental rights with respect to a child he fathered during a liaison with the wife of another man, since it is the marital family that traditionally has been accorded a protected liberty interest, as reflected in the historic presumption of legitimacy of a child born into such a family. The reasoning of the plurality in *Michael H.* does not assist Anna. Society has not traditionally protected the right of a woman who gestates and delivers a baby pursuant to an agreement with a couple who supply the zygote from which the baby develops and who intend to raise the child as their own; such arrangements are of too recent an origin to claim the protection of tradition. To the extent that tradition has a bearing on the present case, we believe it supports the claim of the couple who exercise their right to procreate in order to form a family of their own, albeit through novel medical procedures.

Moreover, if we were to conclude that Anna enjoys some sort of liberty interest in the companionship of the child, then the liberty interests of Mark and Crispina, the child's natural parents, in their procreative choices and their relationship with the child would perforce be infringed. Any parental rights Anna might successfully assert could come only at Crispina's expense. As we have seen, Anna has no parental rights to the child under California law, and she fails to persuade us that sufficiently strong policy reasons exist to accord her a protected liberty interest in the companionship of the child when such an interest would necessarily detract from or impair the parental bond enjoyed by Mark and Crispina.

Amicus curiae ACLU urges that Anna's right of privacy, embodied in the California Constitution (Cal. Const., art. I, §1), requires recognition and protection of her status as "birth mother." We cannot agree. Certainly it is true that our state Constitution has been construed to provide California citizens with privacy protections encompassing procreative decision making — broader, indeed, than those recognized by the federal Constitution. . . . However, amicus curiae fails to articulate persuasively how Anna's claim falls within even the broad parameters of the state right of privacy. Amicus curiae appears to assume that the choice to gestate and deliver a baby for its genetic parents pursuant to a surrogacy agreement is the equivalent, in constitutional weight, of the decision whether to bear a child of one's own. We disagree. A woman who enters into a gestational surrogacy arrangement is not exercising her own right to make procreative choices; she is agreeing to provide a necessary and profoundly important service without (by definition) any expectation that she will raise the resulting child as her own.

Drawing an analogy to artificial insemination, Anna argues that Mark and Crispina were mere genetic donors who are entitled to no constitutional protection. That characterization [is] . . . inaccurate. Mark and Crispina never intended to "donate" genetic material to anyone. Rather, they intended to procreate a child genetically related to them by the only available means. . . .

Finally, Anna argues that the Act's failure to address novel reproductive techniques such as in vitro fertilization indicates legislative disapproval of such practices. Given that the Act was drafted long before such techniques were developed, we cannot agree. Moreover, we may not arrogate to ourselves the power to disapprove them. It is not the role of the judiciary to inhibit the use of reproductive technology when the Legislature has not seen fit to do so; any such effort would raise serious questions in light of the fundamental nature of the rights of procreation and privacy. . . .

The judgment of the Court of Appeal is affirmed.

ARABIAN, J., concurring to opinion by **PANELLI, J.** I concur in the decision to find under the Uniform Parentage Act that Crispina Calvert is the natural mother of the child she at all times intended to parent and raise as her own with her husband Mark, the child's natural father. That determination answers the question on which this court granted review, and in my view sufficiently resolves the controversy between the parties to warrant no further analysis. . . .

KENNARD, J. dissenting. . . .

II. THIS OPINION'S APPROACH

The determination of a question of parental rights to a child born of a surrogacy arrangement was before the New Jersey Supreme Court in *Matter of Baby M.*, a case that received worldwide attention. But in the surrogacy arrangement at issue there the woman who gave birth to the child, Mary Beth Whitehead, had been impregnated by artificial insemination with the sperm of the intending father, William Stern. Whitehead thus provided the genetic material and carried the fetus to term. This case is different, because here those two aspects of the female role in reproduction were divided between two women. This process is known as "gestational" surrogacy, to distinguish it from the surrogacy arrangement involved in *Baby M.*] . . .

. . . In my view, the woman who provided the fertilized ovum and the woman who gave birth to the child both have substantial claims to legal motherhood. Pregnancy entails a unique commitment, both psychological and emotional, to an unborn child. No less substantial, however, is the contribution of the woman from whose egg the child developed and without whose desire the child would not exist. . . .

Surrogacy proponents generally contend that gestational surrogacy, like the other reproductive technologies that extend the ability to procreate to persons who might not otherwise be able to have children, enhances "individual freedom, fulfillment and responsibility." . . . Under this view, women capable of bearing children should be allowed to freely agree to be paid to do so by infertile couples desiring to form a family. . . . The "surrogate mother" is expected "to weigh the prospective investment in her birthing labor" before entering into the arrangement, and, if her "autonomous reproductive decision" is "voluntary," she should be held responsible for it so as "to fulfill the expectations of the other parties." . . .

Surrogacy critics, however, maintain that the payment of money for the gestation and relinquishment of a child threatens the economic exploitation of poor women who may be induced to engage in commercial surrogacy arrangements out of financial need. . . . Some fear the development of a "breeder" class of poor women who will be regularly employed to bear children for the economically advantaged. . . . Others suggest that women who enter into surrogacy arrangements may underestimate the psychological impact of relinquishing a child they have nurtured in their bodies for nine months.

Gestational surrogacy is also said to be "dehumanizing" and to "commodify" women and children by treating the female reproductive capacity and the children born of gestational surrogacy arrangements as products that can be bought and sold. . . . The commodification of women and children, it is feared, will reinforce oppressive gender stereotypes and threaten the well-being of all children. . . . Some critics foresee promotion of an ever-expanding "business of surrogacy brokerage."

Organizations representing diverse viewpoints share many of the concerns highlighted by the legal commentators. For example, the American Medical Association considers the conception of a child for relinquishment after birth to pose grave ethical problems. . . . Likewise, the official position of the Catholic Church is that surrogacy arrangements are "contrary to the unity of marriage and to the dignity of the procreation of the human person." . . .

The policy statement of the New York State Task Force on Life and the Law sums up the broad range of ethical problems that commercial surrogacy arrangements are viewed to present: "The gestation of children as a service for others in exchange for a fee is a radical departure from the way in which society understands and values pregnancy. It substitutes commercial values for the web of social, affective and moral meanings associated with human reproduction. . . . This transformation has profound implications for childbearing, for women, and for the relationship between parents and the children they bring into the world. Surrogate parenting allows the genetic, gestational and social components of parenthood to be fragmented, creating unprecedented relationships among people bound together by contractual obligation rather than by the bonds of kinship and caring. Surrogate parenting alters deep-rooted social and moral assumptions about the relationship between parents and children. [It] is premised on the ability and willingness of women to abdicate [their parental] responsibility without moral compunction or regret [and] makes the obligations that accompany parenthood alienable and negotiable." . . .

Proponents and critics of gestational surrogacy propose widely differing approaches for deciding who should be the legal mother of a child born of a gestational surrogacy arrangement. Surrogacy advocates propose to enforce preconception contracts in which gestational mothers have agreed to relinquish parental rights, and, thus, would make "bargained-for intentions determinative of legal parenthood." . . . Professor Robertson, for instance, contends that "[t]he right to noncoital, collaborative reproduction also includes the right of the parties to agree how they should allocate their obligations and entitlements with respect to the child. Legal presumptions of paternity and maternity would be overridden by this agreement of the parties." . . .

Surrogacy critics, on the other hand, consider the unique female role in human reproduction as the determinative factor of questions of legal parentage. They reason that although males and females both contribute genetic material for the child, the act of gestating the fetus falls only on the female. . . . Accordingly, in their view, a woman who, as the result of gestational surrogacy, is not genetically related to the child she bears is like any other woman who gives birth to a child. In either situation the woman giving birth is the child's mother. . . . Under this approach, the laws governing adoption should govern the parental rights to a child born of gestational surrogacy. Upon the birth of the child, the gestational mother can decide whether or not to relinquish her parental rights in favor of the genetic mother. . . .

Faced with the failure of current statutory law to adequately address the issue of who is a child's natural mother when two women qualify under the UPA, the majority breaks the "tie" by resort to a criterion not found in the UPA—the "intent" of the genetic mother to be the child's mother. This case presents a difficult issue. The majority's resolution of that issue deserves serious consideration. Ultimately, however, I cannot agree that "intent" is the appropriate test for resolving this case.

The majority offers four arguments in support of its conclusion to rely on the intent of the genetic mother as the exclusive determinant for deciding who is the natural mother of a child born of gestational surrogacy. Careful examination, however, demonstrates that none of the arguments mandates the majority's conclusion.

The first argument that the majority uses in support of its conclusion that the intent of the genetic mother to bear a child should be dispositive of the question of motherhood is "but-for" causation. . . . Neither the "but for" nor the "substantial factor" test of causation provides any basis for preferring the genetic mother's intent as the determinative factor in gestational surrogacy cases: Both the genetic and the gestational mothers are indispensable to the birth of a child in a gestational surrogacy arrangement.

Behind the majority's reliance on "but-for" causation as justification for its intent test is a second, closely related argument. The majority draws its second rationale from a student note: "The mental concept of the child is a controlling factor of its creation, and the originators of that concept merit full credit as conceivers." . . .

The problem with this argument, of course, is that children are not property. Unlike songs or inventions, rights in children cannot be sold for consideration, or made freely available to the general public. Our most fundamental notions of personhood tell us it is inappropriate to treat children as property. . . . Accordingly, I cannot endorse the majority's "originators of the concept" or intellectual property rationale for employing intent to break the "tie" between the genetic mother and the gestational mother of the child.

Next, the majority offers as its third rationale the notion that bargained-for expectations support its conclusion regarding the dispositive significance of the genetic mother's intent. . . . The unsuitability of applying the notion that, because contract intentions are "voluntarily chosen, deliberate, express and bargained-for," their performance ought to be compelled by the courts is even more clear when the concept of specific performance is used to determine the course of the life of a child. Just as children are not the intellectual property of their parents, neither are they the personal property of anyone, and their delivery cannot be ordered as a contract remedy on the same terms that a court would, for example, order a breaching party to deliver a truckload of nuts and bolts.

Thus, three of the majority's four arguments in support of its exclusive reliance on the intent of the genetic mother as determinative in gestational surrogacy cases cannot withstand analysis. . . . [B]efore turning to the majority's fourth rationale, I shall discuss two additional considerations, not noted by the majority, that in my view also weigh against utilizing the intent of the genetic mother as the sole determinant of the result in this case and others like it.

First, in making the intent of the genetic mother who wants to have a child the dispositive factor, the majority renders a certain result preordained and inflexible in every such case: as between an intending genetic mother and a gestational mother, the genetic mother will, under the majority's analysis, always prevail. The majority recognizes no meaningful contribution by a woman who agrees to carry a fetus to term for the genetic mother beyond that of mere employment to perform a specified biological function.

The majority's approach entirely devalues the substantial claims of motherhood by a gestational mother such as Anna. True, a woman who enters into a surrogacy arrangement intending to raise the child has by her intent manifested an assumption of parental responsibility in addition to her biological contribution of providing the genetic material. But the gestational mother's biological contribution of carrying a child for nine months and giving birth is likewise an assumption of parental responsibility. . . . A pregnant woman's commitment to the unborn child she carries is not just physical; it is psychological and emotional as well. . . . A pregnant woman intending to bring a child into the world is more than a mere container or breeding animal; she is a conscious agent of creation no less than the genetic mother, and her humanity is implicated on a deep level. Her role should not be devalued. . . .

I find the majority's reliance on "intent" unsatisfactory for yet another reason. By making intent determinative of parental rights to a child born of a gestational surrogacy arrangement, the majority would permit enforcement of a gestational surrogacy agreement without requiring any of the protections that would be afforded by the [Uniform Status of Children of Assisted Conception Act]. . . .

In my view, protective requirements such as those set forth in the USCACA are necessary to minimize any possibility in gestational surrogacy arrangements for over-reaching or abuse by a party with economic advantage. As the New Jersey Supreme Court recognized, it will be a rare instance when a low-income infertile couple can employ an upper-income surrogate. The model act's carefully drafted provisions would assure that the surrogacy arrangement is a matter of medical necessity on the part of the intending parents, and not merely the product of a desire to avoid the inconveniences of pregnancy, together with the financial ability to do so. Also, by requiring both pre-conception psychological counseling for all parties and judicial approval, the model act would assure that parties enter into a surrogacy arrange-ment only if they are legally and psychologically capable of doing so and fully under-stand all the risks involved, and that the surrogacy arrangement would not be substantially detrimental to the interests of any individual. Moreover, by requiring judicial approval, the model act would significantly discourage the rapid expansion of commercial surrogacy brokerage and the resulting commodification of the products of pregnancy. In contrast, here the majority's grant of parental rights to the intending mother contains no provisions for the procedural protections sug-gested by the commissioners who drafted the model act. The majority opinion is a sweeping endorsement of unregulated gestational surrogacy.

The majority's final argument in support of using the intent of the genetic mother as the exclusive determinant of the outcome in gestational surrogacy cases is that preferring the intending mother serves the child's interests, which are "[u]nlikely to run contrary to those of adults who choose to bring [the child] into being."

I agree with the majority that the best interests of the child is an important goal. . . . The problem with the majority's rule of intent is that application of this inflexible rule will not serve the child's best interests in every case. . . .

In the absence of legislation that is designed to address the unique problems of gestational surrogacy, this court should look not to tort, property or contract law, but to family law, as the governing paradigm and source of a rule of decision.

The allocation of parental rights and responsibilities necessarily impacts the wel-fare of a minor child. And in issues of child welfare, the standard that courts fre-quently apply is the best interests of the child. . . . This "best interests" standard serves to assure that in the judicial resolution of disputes affecting a child's well-being, protection of the minor child is the foremost consideration. Consequently, I would apply "the best interests of the child" standard to determine who can best assume the social and legal responsibilities of motherhood for a child born of a gestational surrogacy arrangement. . . .

I would remand the matter to the trial court to undertake that evaluation.

DISCUSSION QUESTIONS FOR *JOHNSON v. CALVERT*

A. The court states that gestational surrogacy differs in crucial respects from adoption and termination of parental rights actions. What are the differences?

B. The majority of the court held that "this issue should be resolved by looking to the intent of the parties" and not merely to genetics. Under such circumstances the intended mother is to be deemed the legal mother. What is the dissent's response to the majority's reliance on the intent of the parties?

C. Why shouldn't a court recognize two legal mothers?

D. Ms. Johnson argued that there were social policies that should be applied to this dispute and favored awarding her the child. What was her argument? Is it persuasive?

E. In arriving at its decision, the majority appears influenced by the fact that the child was the product of an implanted zygote. What is the medical distinction between this case and *In the Matter of Baby M*? Does the medical distinction control the outcome of the case?

F. Opponents of surrogacy arrangements argue that surrogacy contracts tend to "exploit or dehumanize women, especially women of lower economic status." Do you agree with those arguments?

G. Professor R. Alta Charo writes that "California's *Johnson* decision holding that a gestational mother can be no more than a foster parent to her own child is almost without precedent in the world. In fact, policymakers in other countries — including the United Kingdom, the former West Germany, Bulgaria, and New Zealand — have concluded that, in the context of egg donation, the woman who gives birth is the child's mother." R. Alta Charo, *Biological Determinism in Legal Decision Making: The Parent Trap*, 3 Tex. J. Women & L. 265, 294 (Spring 1994). What might explain the apparent international policy differences in the approach to surrogacy?

H. Assume that Alice donated an egg to be fertilized with Bill's sperm. The fetus was to be gestated by Bill's wife Candy. Would Alice or Candy be the child's legal mother under the majority reasoning in *Johnson v. Calvert*?

I. Assume that surrogate Alice was artificially inseminated by Bill. Husband Bill and wife Barbara have executed an agreement with Alice that the child will be turned over to them and Alice will relinquish all rights when it is born. When the child is born, who is the legal mother?

20.9 SURROGACY: KNOWN FEMALE EGG DONOR, ANONYMOUS SPERM DONOR

Background to *K.M. v. E.G.*

In this dispute, a lesbian couple decided to have a child together. One partner provided the eggs, which were fertilized with sperm from an anonymous sperm donor and then implanted in the uterus of the other. Before making the donation, the donor partner signed a contract allegedly waiving any future parental rights to a child or children born from her eggs. Twins were subsequently born, and the couple raised them together for five years. However, the children were never told that the mother who did not give birth to them is actually their genetic mother.

After five years, the couple broke up, and the birth mother argued that she was the twins' only legal parent and sought to prevent any contact between the twins and the genetic mother. The birth mother also argued that California's sperm donor statute, which prevented sperm donors from having standing to assert parental rights, also applied to an egg donor. K.M. contends that she did not intend to donate her ova, but rather provided her ova so that E.G. could give birth to a child to be raised jointly by K.M. and E.G. E.G. contests this, asserting that K.M. donated her ova to E.G., agreeing that E.G. would be the sole parent.

The overarching question in this case appears to be whether a female partner, who donated an egg to her partner, the birth mother, and who signed the consent forms to terminate her parental status, while intending to raise the child in their joint home, was a legal parent. Under California law, a man is not a father of a child if he provides semen to a physician to inseminate a woman who is not his wife. The court is asked whether this law applies to K.M. and E.G.

Note that the dissenting opinion, which is not reproduced here, argued that the decision destabilizes preconception agreements about parental status in the context of ovum donation and surrogacy.

K.M.
v.
E.G.

Supreme Court of California
33 Cal. Rptr. 3d 61 (Cal. 2005)

MORENO, J. . . . Petitioner K.M. filed a petition to establish a parental relationship with twin five-year-old girls born to respondent E.G., her former lesbian partner. K.M. alleged that she "is the biological parent of the minor children" because "[s]he donated her egg to respondent, the gestational mother of the children." E.G. moved to dismiss the petition on the grounds that, although K.M. and E.G. "were lesbian partners who lived together until this action was filed," K.M. "explicitly donated her ovum under a clear written agreement by which she relinquished any claim to offspring born of her donation." . . .

E.G. testified that she first considered raising a child before she met K.M., at a time when she did not have a partner. She met K.M. in October 1992 and they became romantically involved in June 1993. E.G. told K.M. that she planned to adopt a baby as a single mother. E.G. applied for adoption in November, 1993. K.M. and E.G. began living together in March, 1994 and registered as domestic partners in San Francisco.

E.G. visited several fertility clinics in March, 1993 to inquire about artificial insemination and she attempted artificial insemination, without success, on 13 occasions. . . . K.M. accompanied her to most of these appointments. K.M. testified that she and E.G. planned to raise the child together, while E.G. insisted that, although K.M. was very supportive, E.G. made it clear that her intention was to become "a single parent."

In December, 1994, E.G. consulted with Dr. Mary Martin at the fertility practice of the University of California at San Francisco Medical Center (UCSF). E.G.'s first attempts at in vitro fertilization failed because she was unable to produce sufficient ova. In January, 1995, Dr. Martin suggested using K.M.'s ova. E.G. then asked K.M. to donate her ova, explaining that she would accept the ova only if K.M. "would really be a donor" and E.G. would "be the mother of any child," adding that she would not even consider permitting K.M. to adopt the child "for at least five years until [she] felt the relationship was stable and would endure." E.G. told K.M. that she "had seen too many lesbian relationships end quickly, and [she] did not want to be in a custody battle." E.G. and K.M. agreed they would not tell anyone that K.M. was the ova donor.

K.M. acknowledged that she agreed not to disclose to anyone that she was the ova donor, but insisted that she only agreed to provide her ova because she and E.G. had agreed to raise the child together. K.M. and E.G. selected the sperm donor together. K.M. denied that E.G. had said she wanted to be a single parent and insisted that she would not have donated her ova had she known E.G. intended to be the sole parent.

On March 8, 1995, K.M. signed a four-page form on UCSF letterhead entitled "Consent Form for Ovum Donor (Known)." The form states that K.M. agrees "to have eggs taken from my ovaries, in order that they may be donated to another woman." After explaining the medical procedures involved, the form states on the third page:

> It is understood that I waive any right and relinquish any claim to the donated eggs or any pregnancy or offspring that might result from them. I agree that the recipient may regard the donated eggs and any offspring resulting therefrom as her own children.

The following appears on page 4 of the form, above K.M.'s signature and the signature of a witness:

> I specifically disclaim and waive any right in or any child that may be conceived as a result of the use of any ovum or egg of mine, and I agree not to attempt to discover the identity of the recipient thereof.

E.G. signed a form entitled "Consent Form for Ovum Recipient" that stated, in part:

> I acknowledge that the child or children produced by the IVF procedure is and shall be my own legitimate child or children and the heir or heirs of my body with all rights and privileges accompanying such status.

E.G. testified she received these two forms in a letter from UCSF dated February 2, 1995, and discussed the consent forms with K.M. during February and March. E.G. stated she would not have accepted K.M.'s ova if K.M. had not signed the consent form, because E.G. wanted to have a child on her own and believed the consent form "protected" her in this regard.

K.M. testified . . . that she first saw the ovum donation consent form 10 minutes before she signed it on March 8, 1995. K.M. admitted reading the form, but thought parts of the form were "odd" and did not pertain to her, such as the part stating that the donor promised not to discover the identity of the recipient. She did not intend to relinquish her rights and only signed the form so that "we could have children." Despite having signed the form, K.M. "thought [she] was going to be a parent."

Ova were withdrawn from K.M. on April 11, 1995, and embryos were implanted in E.G. on April 13, 1995. K.M. and E.G. told K.M's father about the resulting pregnancy by announcing that he was going to be a grandfather. The twins were born on December 7, 1995. The twins' birth certificates listed E.G. as their mother and did not reflect a father's name. As they had agreed, neither E.G. nor K.M. told anyone K.M. had donated the ova, including their friends, family and the twins' pediatrician. Soon after the twins were born, E.G. asked K.M. to marry her, and on Christmas Day, the couple exchanged rings.

Within a month of their birth, E.G. added the twins to her health insurance policy, named them as her beneficiary for all employment benefits, and increased her life insurance with the twins as the beneficiary. K.M. did not do the same.

E.G. referred to her mother, as well as K.M.'s parents, as the twins' grandparents and referred to K.M.'s sister and brother as the twins' aunt and uncle, and K.M.'s nieces as their cousins. Two school forms listed both K.M. and respondent as the twins' parents. The children's nanny testified that both K.M. and E.G. "were the babies' mother."

The relationship between K.M. and E.G. ended in March, 2001 and K.M. filed the present action. In September, 2001, E.G. and the twins moved to Massachusetts to live with E.G.'s mother. . . .

In *Johnson v. Calvert* it was determined that a wife whose ovum was fertilized in vitro by her husband's sperm and implanted in a surrogate mother was the "natural mother" of the child thus produced. We noted that the UPA states that provisions applicable to determining a father and child relationship shall be used to determine a mother and child relationship "insofar as practicable." We relied, therefore, on the provisions in the UPA regarding presumptions of paternity and concluded that "genetic consanguinity" could be the basis for a finding of maternity just as it is for paternity. Under this authority, K.M.'s genetic relationship to the children in the present case constitutes evidence of a mother and child relationship as contemplated by the Act.

The Court of Appeal in the present case concluded, however, that K.M. was not a parent of the twins, despite her genetic relationship to them, because she had the same status as a sperm donor. Section 7613(b) states:

> The donor of semen provided to a licensed physician and surgeon for use in artificial insemination of a woman other than the donor's wife is treated in law as if he were not the natural father of a child thereby conceived.

In *Johnson*, we considered the predecessor statute to section 7613(b), former Civil Code section 7005. We did not discuss whether this statute applied to a woman who provides ova used to impregnate another woman, but we observed that "in a true 'egg donation' situation, where a woman gestates and gives birth to a child formed from the egg of another woman with the intent to raise the child as her own, the birth mother is the natural mother under California law." We held that the statute did not apply under the circumstances in *Johnson v. Calvert*, because the husband and wife did not intend to "donate" their sperm and ova to the surrogate mother, but rather "intended to procreate a child genetically related to them by the only available means."

The circumstances of the present case are not identical to those in *Johnson v. Calvert*, but they are similar in a crucial respect; both the couple in *Johnson* and the couple in the present case intended to produce a child that would be raised in their own home. In *Johnson*, it was clear that the married couple did not intend to "donate" their semen and ova to the surrogate mother, but rather permitted their semen and ova to be used to impregnate the surrogate mother in order to produce a child to be raised by them. In the present case, K.M. contends that she did not intend to donate her ova, but rather provided her ova so that E.G. could give birth to a child to be raised jointly by K.M. and E.G. E.G. hotly contests this, asserting that K.M. donated her ova to E.G., agreeing that E.G. would be the sole parent. It is undisputed, however, that the couple lived together and that they both intended to bring the child into their joint home. Thus, even accepting as true E.G.'s version of the facts (which the superior court did), the present case, like *Johnson*, does not present a "true 'egg donation' " situation. K.M. did not intend to simply donate her ova to E.G., but rather provided her ova to her lesbian partner with whom she was living so that E.G. could give birth to a child that would be raised in their joint home. Even if we assume that the provisions of section 7613(b) apply to women who donate ova, the statute does not apply under the circumstances of the present case. An examination of the history of 7613(b) supports our conclusion.

The predecessor to section 7613(b), former Civil Code section 7005, was enacted in 1975 as part of the UPA. Section 5, subdivision (b), of the Model UPA states:

> The donor of semen provided to a licensed physician for use in artificial insemination of a married woman other than the donor's wife is treated in law as if he were not the natural father of a child thereby conceived.

The comment to this portion of the model act notes that this provision was not intended to solve all questions posed by the use of artificial insemination:

> This Act does not deal with many complex and serious legal problems raised by the practice of artificial insemination. It was though[t] useful, however, to single out and cover in this Act at least one fact situation that occurs frequently.

Although the predecessor to section 7613 was based upon the Model UPA, the California Legislature made one significant change; it expanded the reach of the provision to apply to both married and unmarried women.

Section 7005 is derived almost verbatim from the UPA as originally drafted, with one crucial exception. The original UPA restricts application of the nonpaternity provision of subdivision (b) to a "married woman other than the donor's wife." The word "married" is excluded from subdivision (b) of section 7005, so that in California, subdivision (b) applies to all women, married or not. Thus, the California Legislature has afforded unmarried as well as married women a statutory vehicle for obtaining semen for artificial insemination without fear that the donor may claim paternity, and has likewise provided men with a statutory vehicle for donating semen to married and unmarried women alike without fear of liability for child support.

Under the Model UPA, a man who donated semen that was used to impregnate a woman who was married to someone other than the donor would not be considered the father of the resulting child. But the provision would not apply, and the semen donor would be considered the father of the child, if the woman impregnated was unmarried. Therefore, this provision of the model act would not apply if a man provided semen that was used to impregnate his unmarried partner in order to produce a child that would be raised in their joint home, and the man would be considered the father of the resulting child.

In adopting the model act, California expanded the reach of this provision by omitting the word "married," so that unmarried women could avail themselves of artificial insemination. This omission was purposeful. . . .

It is clear, therefore, that California intended to expand the protection of the model act to include unmarried women so that unmarried women could avail themselves of artificial insemination. But there is nothing to indicate that California intended to expand the reach of this provision so far that it would apply if a man provided semen to be used to impregnate his unmarried partner in order to produce a child that would be raised in their joint home. It would be surprising, to say the least, to conclude that the Legislature intended such a result. The Colorado Supreme Court considered a related issue and reached a similar conclusion.

In *In Interest of R.C.* the Colorado Supreme Court addressed a Colorado statute identical to section 7613(b), which applied to both married and unmarried women. At issue were the parental rights, if any, of a man who provided semen to a physician that was used to impregnate an unmarried friend of the man. The man claimed that the woman had promised that he would be treated as the child's father. The court recognized that the Model UPA addressed only the artificial insemination of a woman married to someone other than the semen donor, adding that the parental rights of a semen donor are "least clearly understood when the semen donor is known and the recipient is unmarried." The court concluded that the statute did not apply when a man donated semen to an unmarried woman with the understanding that he would be the father of the resulting child:

> [W]e conclude that the General Assembly neither considered nor intended to affect the rights of known donors who gave their semen to unmarried women for use in artificial insemination with the agreement that the donor would be the father of any child so conceived. [The statute] simply does not apply in that circumstance.

The Colorado Supreme Court was thus faced with a situation in which a man provided semen, through a physician, to an unmarried "friend" who allegedly had promised that the man would be the father of the resulting child. The court concluded that the Model UPA, and the Colorado statute based upon it, were not intended to apply to such circumstances. We are faced with an even more compelling situation, because K.M. and E.G. were more than "friends" when K.M. provided her ova, through a physician, to be used to impregnate E.G.; they lived together and were registered domestic partners. Although the parties dispute whether both women were intended to be parents of the resulting child, it is undisputed that they intended that the resulting child would be raised in their joint home. Neither the Model UPA, nor section 7613(b) was intended to apply under such circumstances. . . .

It is true we said in *Johnson* that "for any child California law recognizes only one natural mother." But as we explain in the companion case of *Elisa B. v. Superior Court*, this statement in *Johnson* must be understood in light of the issue presented in that case; "our decision in *Johnson* does not preclude a child from having two parents both of whom are women." . . .

The superior court in the present case found that K.M. signed a waiver form, thereby "relinquishing and waiving all rights to claim legal parentage of any children who might result." But such a waiver does not affect our determination of parentage. Section 7632 provides:

> Regardless of its terms, an agreement between an alleged or presumed father and the mother or child does not bar an action under this chapter.

See In re Marriage of Buzzanca, supra, 61 Cal. App. 4th 1410, 1426 ["It is well established that parents cannot, by agreement, limit or abrogate a child's right to support."]. A woman who supplies ova to be used to impregnate her lesbian partner, with the understanding that the resulting child will be raised in their joint home, cannot waive her responsibility to support that child. Nor can such a purported waiver effectively cause that woman to relinquish her parental rights.

In light of our conclusion that section 7613(b) does not apply and that K.M. is the twins' parent (together with E.G.), based upon K.M.'s genetic relationship to the twins, we need not, and do not, consider whether K.M. is presumed to be a parent of the twins under section 7611, subdivision (d), which provides that a man is presumed to be a child's father if "[h]e receives the child into his home and openly holds out the child as his natural child." The judgment of the Court of Appeal is reversed.

DISCUSSION QUESTIONS FOR *K.M. v. E.G.*

A. How are the circumstances of this case similar to those in *Johnson v. Calvert*? In what crucial respect are they different?

B. Under the Uniform Parentage Act (UPA), which is discussed in *K.M. v. E.G.*, could a man who donated semen that was used to impregnate a woman who was married to someone other than the donor be considered the father of the resulting child? What if the semen was used to impregnate an unmarried woman?

C. What is the main thrust of the discussion of the Colorado decision in this case, *In Interest of R.C.*?

D. The court states that the circumstances of this case are more compelling than those in *R.C.* How does it support this view?

E. The court refused to enforce the waiver form signed by K.M. in which she stated that she was "relinquishing and waiving all rights to claim legal parentage of any children who might result." What is the court's reasoning, and is it persuasive?

F. The dissent's view, which is not included, is that K.M. donated her ova for physician-assisted artificial insemination and implantation in another woman, and knowingly and voluntarily signed a document declaring her intention not to become a parent of any resulting children. Because of the waiver, the dissent argues K.M. cannot be a parent of the twins. How strong is the dissent's argument?

20.10 PROPERTY RIGHTS TO FROZEN EMBRYOS/PREEMBRYOS

"The first pregnancy resulting from the implantation of an embryo that had previously been frozen was reported in Australia in 1983. Since then, the freezing, or cryopreservation, of embryos created through in vitro fertilization (IVF) has become a standard part of the practice of assisted reproductive technologies (ARTs)." Carl H. Coleman, *Procreative Liberty and Contemporaneous Choice: An Inalienable Rights Approach*, 84 Minn. L. Rev. 55 (November 1999).

Cryopreservation has advantages for a woman attempting to achieve pregnancy. It permits her to achieve pregnancy on several successive occasions without surgery to remove ova. It also allows for the possibility of replacing preembryos during a spontaneous ovulatory cycle and avoids the risk of multiple pregnancies that inhere in the simultaneous use of numerous preembryos. Finally, it provides for posthumous reproduction. *See* Anne Reichman Schiff, *Arising from the Dead: Challenges of Posthumous Procreation*, 75 N.C. L. Rev. 901, 903 (1997).

Courts are not in agreement when it comes to classifying embryos and frozen sperm. One court has concluded that frozen sperm of a decedent is property and comes within the state Probate Code. *York v. Jones*, 717 F. Supp. 421 (E.D. Va. 1989). Others have considered frozen embryos as in an interim category between "property" and "persons." In *Davis v. Davis*, 842 S.W.2d 588, 597 (Tenn. 1992), the court said that "[w]e conclude that preembryos are not, strictly speaking, either 'persons' or 'property,' but occupy an interim category that entitles them to special respect because of their potential for human life."

The Tennessee Supreme Court in *Davis* was one of the first state courts to address the question of the custody of cryogenically preserved embryos. The parties in that case had tried for several years to have a child and eventually turned to in vitro fertilization (IVF) to conceive. When they experienced several failed attempts, the clinic offered the couple the opportunity to harvest and fertilize multiple eggs, most of which would be cryogenically frozen and possibly used in later pregnancy attempts should the current efforts fail. During these attempts, the couple did not sign any agreement with the IVF clinic or between themselves specifying the disposition of any frozen embryos.

When the couple divorced, the question became who possessed the embryos. The Tennessee court ultimately decided the dispute on the basis of constitutional privacy rights of procreational autonomy, including the right to procreate and the right to avoid procreation. The court balanced the parties' interests and determined that the husband's wishes to avoid procreation should take precedence.

Other courts have addressed this issue. For example, the Iowa Supreme Court held in *In re Marriage of Witten*, 672 N.W.2d 768 (Iowa 2003), that if the donors cannot reach a mutual decision on disposition, then no transfer, release, disposition, or use of the embryos can occur. The court stated that if a stalemate results, the status quo would be maintained. "The practical effect will be that the embryos are stored indefinitely unless both parties can agree to destroy the fertilized eggs.

Thus, any expense associated with maintaining the status quo should logically be borne by the person opposing destruction." *Id.* at 783.

In *Kass v. Kass*, 696 N.E.2d 174 (N.Y. 1998), the court held that agreements between progenitors, or gamete donors, regarding disposition of their pre-zygotes should generally be presumed valid and binding, and enforced in any dispute between them.

 **REFLECTIVE QUESTIONS** | **When it comes to disposition of frozen embryos involved in a divorce proceeding, what considerations are there that support the right to procreate and the right to avoid procreation?**

Background to *Szafranski v. Dunston*

The ex-boyfriend, Jacob Szafranski, sued his ex-girlfriend, Karla Dunston, seeking to enjoin her from using preembryos created with his sperm and her ova. Dunston counterclaimed, seeking a declaratory judgment granting her sole custody and control over the preembryos. She alleged a breach of contract and requested specific performance. The trial court granted Dunston summary judgment and Szafranski appealed.

SZAFRANSKI
v.
DUNSTON

Appellate Court of Illinois, First District, Second Division
993 N.E.2d 502 (2013)

QUINN, J. . . . [Dunston] was diagnosed with non-Hodgkin's lymphoma and informed that her chemotherapy treatments would likely cause the loss of her fertility. She asked [Szafranski], with whom she was in a relationship, if he would donate his sperm for the purpose of creating pre-embryos with her eggs, and he agreed to do so.

. . . [T]he couple met with physicians and staff at Northwestern regarding the creation of the pre-embryos, and appellant deposited sperm to be frozen and used as a back-up on the date [Dunston's] eggs were retrieved. The couple also signed a document entitled "INFORMED CONSENT FOR ASSISTED REPRODUC-TION" (the informed consent). Besides outlining the risks involved with in vitro fertilization, the informed consent states that "[n]o use can be made of these embryos without the consent of both partners (if applicable). . . . In the event of divorce or dissolution of the marriage or partnership, NMFF [Northwestern Medical Faculty Foundation's Division of Reproductive Endocrinology and Infertility] will abide by the terms of the court decree or settlement agreement regarding the ownership and/or other rights to the embryos." The informed consent contains the following disclaimer as well:

> "The law regarding [in vitro fertilization], embryo cryopreservation, subsequent embryo thaw and use, and parent-child status of any resulting child(ren) is, or may be, unsettled in the state in which either the patient, spouse, partner, or any current or future donor lives, or in Illinois, the state in which the NMFF Program is located. NMFF does not provide legal advice, and you should not rely on NMFF to give you any legal advice. You should consider consulting with a lawyer who is experienced in the areas of reproductive law and embryo cryopreservation as well as the disposition of embryos, including any questions or concerns about the present or future status of your embryos, your individual or joint access to them, your individual or joint parental status as to any resulting child, or about any other aspect of this consent and agreement."

On the day of their meeting at Northwestern, the couple also met with an attorney, Nidhi Desai, to discuss the legal implications of creating pre-embryos, and Desai presented them with two possible arrangements: a co-parent agreement or a sperm donor agreement. . . . [Dunston] sent Desai an e-mail opting for the former, and Desai sent the couple a draft of a co-parent agreement. The stated primary purpose of the co-parent agreement was "to memorialize the Parties' intent and agreement that they shall both be established as the legal co-parents of the Child." The co-parent agreement provided, inter alia, that the couple would attempt to participate in at least one in vitro fertilization and pre-embryo transfer cycle in which appellant would "provide sperm samples to create the pre-embryos," and that [Szafranski] "agrees to undertake all legal, custodial, and other obligations to the Child regardless of any change of circumstance between the Parties." The co-parent agreement also provided that "[a]ny eggs retrieved and cryopreserved as a result of this [in vitro fertilization] retrieval shall be under [Dunston's] sole control" and that "[s]hould the Intended Parents separate, [Dunston] will control the disposition of the pre-embryos." Further, the co-parent agreement provided: "Jacob acknowledges and agrees that Karla is likely to be unable to create new healthy embryos subsequent to the chemotherapy regimen[] she will undergo, and Jacob specifically agrees that Karla should have the opportunity to use such embryos to have a child."

The co-parent agreement was never signed by the couple. Nevertheless, on April 6, 2010, appellant deposited sperm and eight eggs were retrieved from appellee. The couple agreed to fertilize all eight based on the doctor's advice that doing so would be appellee's best chance of having a child, and three of the pre-embryos ultimately survived to viability. The next day, appellee began her chemotherapy treatment.

In May 2010, [Szafranski] sent [Dunston] a text message ending their relationship. On August 22, 2011, he filed a pro se complaint in the circuit court of Cook County seeking to permanently enjoin [Dunston] from using the pre-embryos so as to "preserv[e] [his] right to not forcibly father a child against his will." On September 1, 2011, [Dunston] responded with a three-count verified counterclaim: in count I, she sought a declaratory judgment granting her sole custody and control over the pre-embryos and the right to use them to bear children; in count II, she alleged breach of contract and requested specific performance of the parties' agreement; and in count III, she sought relief under a theory of promissory estoppel.

. . . [Dunston] asserted, inter alia, that [Szafranski] was bound by the terms of the co-parent agreement because, even though he did not sign it, he fully performed his one "critical" obligation under the agreement and provided sperm samples to create the embryos. She also asserted that [Szafranski] induced her to rely on his representation that he would help her have her own children, and that she was harmed by that reliance because now she cannot go back and use a random sperm donor to fertilize her eggs. Additionally, [Dunston] asserted that if the court found that [Szafranski] was not bound by the co-parent agreement or estopped from preventing use of the embryos, the court should follow *Reber v. Reiss*, 42 A.3d 1131 (Pa. Super. Ct. 2012), and balance the interests of the parties, finding that her interest in having her own biological children outweighs [Szafranski's] interest in not fathering a child. [Dunston] attached to her motion a letter from Dr. Eve Feinberg stating that [she] has ovarian failure as a result of her chemotherapy treatment which has "rendered [her] unable to conceive a child with the use of her own oocytes."

. . . [Szafranski] maintained that [Dunston's] motion for summary judgment should be denied because there was a question of fact regarding whether a contract existed.

This case presents an issue of first impression in Illinois; namely, who controls the disposition of cryopreserved pre-embryos created with one party's sperm and another party's ova. Courts in other jurisdictions have addressed this issue under various circumstances and generally conducted three types of analyses in resolving this question: (1) a contractual approach, (2) a contemporaneous mutual consent approach; and/or (3) a balancing approach. *Reber*, 42 A.3d at 1134. Each of these approaches is discussed, in turn, below.

1. THE CONTRACTUAL APPROACH

. . . Under this approach, courts will enforce contracts governing the disposition of pre-embryos which were entered into at the time of in vitro fertilization so long as they do not violate public policy. The benefits of a contractual approach are that it encourages parties to enter into agreements that will avoid future costly litigation, and that it removes state and court involvement in private family decisions. As noted by the Court of Appeals of New York:

> [P]arties should be encouraged in advance, before embarking on [in vitro fertilization] and cryopreservation, to think through possible contingencies and carefully specify their wishes in writing. Explicit agreements avoid costly litigation in business transactions. They are all the more necessary and desirable in personal matters of reproductive choice, where the intangible costs of any litigation are simply incalculable. Advance directives, subject to mutual change of mind that must be jointly expressed, both minimize misunderstandings and maximize procreative liberty by reserving to the progenitors the authority to make what is in the first instance a quintessentially personal, private decision. Written agreements also provide the certainty needed for effective operation of [in vitro fertilization] programs [citations].

> . . .

> . . . To the extent possible, it should be the progenitors—not the State and not the courts—who by their prior directive make this deeply personal life choice. *Kass v. Kass*, 696 N.E.2d 174, 180 (1998).

Criticism of the contractual approach, on the other hand, includes that it "'insufficiently protects the individual and societal interests at stake.'" *Witten*, 672 N.W.2d at 777 (quoting Carl H. Coleman, Procreative Liberty and Contemporaneous Choice: An Inalienable Rights Approach to Frozen Embryo Disputes, 84 Minn. L. Rev. 55, 88-89 (1999)). Among the concerns is that "decisions about the disposition of frozen embryos implicate rights central to individual identity," and that "[o]n matters of such fundamental personal importance, individuals are entitled to make decisions consistent with their contemporaneous wishes, values, and beliefs." . . . Of further concern is that "'requiring couples to make binding decisions about the future use of their frozen embryos ignores the difficulty of predicting one's future response to life-altering events such as parenthood,'" and that "'treating couples' decisions about the future use of their frozen embryos as binding contracts undermines important values about families, reproduction, and the strength of genetic ties.'"

Notwithstanding these criticisms, the contractual approach has been applied/endorsed in five states. . . . (New York); (Oregon); (Tennessee); (Texas); [and] (Washington).

. . .

In *A.Z. v. B.Z.*, 725 N.E.2d 1051 (2000), . . . the Supreme Judicial Court of Massachusetts declined to honor the parties' advance agreement regarding the disposition of pre-embryos on the grounds of public policy. There, a husband and wife underwent in vitro fertilization due to the wife's difficulties conceiving a child. They signed a consent form stating that if they "'[s]hould become separated, [they] both agree[d] to have the embryo(s) . . . return[ed] to [the] wife for implant.'" At the time of their divorce, one vial containing four frozen pre-embryos remained in storage, and the husband filed a motion for a permanent injunction to prohibit the wife from using them. On appeal, the Supreme Judicial Court of Massachusetts initially expressed doubt that the consent form "represent[ed] the intent of the husband and the wife regarding disposition of the preembryos in the case of a dispute between them." The court noted, inter alia:

> [T]he consent form's primary purpose is to explain to the donors the benefits and risks of freezing, and to record the donors' desires for disposition of the frozen preembryos at the time the form is executed in order to provide the clinic with guidance if the donors (as a unit) no longer wish to use the frozen preembryos. The form does not state, and the record does not indicate, that the husband and wife intended the consent form to act as a binding agreement between them should they later disagree as to the disposition. Rather, it appears that it was intended only to define the donors' relationship as a unit with the clinic. *A.Z.*, 725 N.E.2d at 1056.

In any event, the court concluded:

> [E]ven had the husband and the wife entered into an unambiguous agreement between themselves regarding the disposition of the frozen preembryos, we would not enforce an

agreement that would compel one donor to become a parent against his or her will. As a matter of public policy, we conclude that forced procreation is not an area amenable to judicial enforcement.

Thus, while a majority of courts utilize the contractual approach and have sought to give effect to the parties' advance directives regarding the disposition of pre-embryos, there is not a unanimous view that such agreements are within the public interest. The next approach places the emphasis on the contemporaneous desires of the parties.

2. THE CONTEMPORANEOUS MUTUAL CONSENT APPROACH

The second approach applied by courts is known as the contemporaneous mutual consent model. This approach proposes that "'no embryo should be used by either partner, donated to another patient, used in research, or destroyed without the [contemporaneous] mutual consent of the couple that created the embryo.'" Under this approach,

> advance instructions would not be treated as binding contracts. If either partner has a change of mind about disposition decisions made in advance, that person's current objection would take precedence over the prior consent. If one of the partners rescinds an advance disposition decision and the other does not, the mutual consent principle would not be satisfied and the previously agreed-upon disposition decision could not be carried out.
>
> . . .
>
> When the couple is unable to agree to any disposition decision, the most appropriate solution is to keep the embryos where they are — in frozen storage. Unlike the other possible disposition decisions — use by one partner, donation to another patient, donation to research, or destruction — keeping the embryos frozen is not final and irrevocable. By preserving the status quo, it makes it possible for the partners to reach an agreement at a later time.

Like the contractual approach, the contemporaneous mutual consent approach acknowledges that "'decisions about the disposition of frozen embryos belong to the couple that created the embryo, with each partner entitled to an equal say in how the embryos should be disposed.'" However, it addresses many of the concerns with the contractual approach by allowing a party to change his or her mind prior to use of the pre-embryos.

The contemporaneous mutual consent approach is not immune from criticism either, though. While the approach benefits from ease of application and at least the appearance of respecting the rights of the parties involved, the Superior Court of Pennsylvania has aptly noted: "This approach strikes us as being totally unrealistic. If the parties could reach an agreement, they would not be in court."

Iowa is the only state to have expressly adopted the contemporaneous mutual consent approach. In *Witten*, a husband and wife underwent in vitro fertilization because the wife was unable to conceive children naturally. They signed an informed consent document entitled "Embryo Storage Agreement," which stated that " '[t]he

Client Depositors . . . understand and agree that containers of embryos stored pursuant to this agreement will be used for transfer, release or disposition only with the signed approval of both Client Depositors.' " At trial on a dissolution action, the wife sought custody of the pre-embryos to have them implanted in her or a surrogate, but the husband did not want the wife to use them and requested a permanent injunction prohibiting either party from transferring, releasing, or utilizing the pre-embryos without both of their written consents. On appeal, the Supreme Court of Iowa declined to adopt a contractual approach and held that "agreements entered into at the time in vitro fertilization is commenced are enforceable and binding on the parties, 'subject to the right of either party to change his or her mind about disposition up to the point of use or destruction of any stored embryo.' " *Witten*, 672 N.W.2d at 782 (quoting *J.B. v. M.B.*, 170 N.J. 9, 783 A.2d 707, 719 (2001)). The court then noted "grave public policy concerns" with a balancing test, and ultimately adopted the contemporaneous mutual consent approach, holding that there could be no use or disposition of the couple's pre-embryos unless the husband and wife reached an agreement.

One commentator has noted that "the *Witten* opinion puts someone like [the husband] in a particularly powerful position." Mark P. Strasser, You Take the Embryos But I Get the House (and the Business): Recent Trends in Awards Involving Embryos Upon Divorce, 57 Buff. L. Rev. 1159, 1210 (2009). He notes:

> For example, the court said that the party opposing destruction of the embryos would bear the costs of their cryopreservation. Someone who wanted to get back at an ex-spouse might well say that he or she had no interest in cryopreserving the embryos, thereby shifting the costs to his or her ex-spouse. Further, one could imagine such a person imposing continuing psychic damage by hinting that he or she might consent to the ex-spouse's use of the embryos sometime in the future — the ex-spouse might well continue to be on an emotional rollercoaster when considering the possibility of finally becoming a parent. Or the embryos might in effect be held hostage — they would be released for use only if the ex-spouse were willing to give up something valuable in return, for example, in a property settlement or in exchange for more favorable support terms.

In this regard, the contemporaneous mutual consent model "give[s] each progenitor a powerful bargaining chip at a time when individuals might very well be tempted to punish their soon-to-be ex-spouses," "[which] makes no sense and may invite individuals to hold hostage their ex-partner's ability to parent a biologically related child in order to punish or to gain other advantages." The next approach attempts to address these concerns by placing the disposition decision exclusively in the hands of the court.

3. THE BALANCING APPROACH

The third and final approach is for the court to balance the interests of the parties. Under this approach, courts enforce contracts between the parties, at least to a point, then balance their interests in the absence of an agreement. Although this approach allows courts leeway to determine who is entitled to use pre-embryos absent an agreement regarding disposition, the Supreme Court of Iowa has criticized this approach for its internal inconsistency, noting:

> Public policy concerns similar to those that prompt courts to refrain from enforcement of contracts addressing reproductive choice demand even more strongly that we not substitute the courts as decision makers in this highly emotional and personal area. Nonetheless, that is exactly what happens under the decisional framework based on the balancing test because the court must weigh the relative interests of the parties in deciding the disposition of embryos when the parties cannot agree. *Witten*, 672 N.W.2d at 779.

Notwithstanding this concern, the balancing approach has been applied in three states. (New Jersey); (Pennsylvania); (Tennessee).

. . .

Most recently, the Superior Court of Pennsylvania applied a balancing approach in *Reber*. In that case, a husband and wife underwent in vitro fertilization to preserve the wife's ability to conceive a child after she was diagnosed with breast cancer and prescribed cancer treatments. *Reber*, 42 A.3d at 1132-33. The husband subsequently filed for divorce, and the wife sought their pre-embryos for implantation. After balancing the parties' interests, the trial court awarded the wife the pre-embryos based on her inability to achieve biological parenthood without use of the pre-embryos. On appeal, the Superior Court of Pennsylvania noted that it did not need to decide whether to adopt a specific approach because the couple had not signed the portion of the consent form related to the disposition of the pre-embryos in the event of divorce, and "it was quite obvious that Husband and Wife could not come to a contemporaneous mutual agreement regarding the pre-embryos." Under the circumstances, the court found that "the balancing approach [was] the most suitable test" and concluded that the balance of interests weighed in the wife's favor because "Husband and Wife never made an agreement prior to undergoing IVF, and these pre-embryos are likely Wife's only opportunity to achieve biological parenthood and her best chance to achieve parenthood at all."

Courts applying the balancing approach have noted that a party's inability to have a child weighs in his or her favor. See *Davis*, 842 S.W.2d at 604 (noting that "[t]he case would be closer if [wife] were seeking to use the preembryos herself, but only if she could not achieve parenthood by any other reasonable means"); but see *J.B. v. M.B.*, 170 N.J. 9, 783 A.2d 707, 720 (2001) (expressing "no opinion in respect of a case in which a party who has become infertile seeks use of stored preembryos against the wishes of his or her partner, noting only that the possibility of adoption also may be a consideration, among others, in the court's assessment"). However, none of these courts have awarded one party the right to implant pre-embryos in the face of a prior agreement stating that both parties' consents were required to make use of the pre-embryos.

THE PROPER APPROACH

Having considered the arguments of the parties and case law from other jurisdictions, we believe that the best approach for resolving disputes over the disposition of pre-embryos created with one party's sperm and another party's ova is to honor the parties' own mutually expressed intent as set forth in their prior agreements. We therefore join those courts that have held that "[a]greements between progenitors, or gamete donors, regarding disposition of their pre-zygotes should generally be presumed valid and binding, and enforced in any dispute between them." *Kass*, 696 N.E.2d at 180.

We believe that honoring parties' agreements properly allows them, rather than the courts, to make their own reproductive choices while also providing a measure of certainty necessary to proper family planning. We also believe that honoring such agreements will promote serious discussions between the parties prior to participating in in vitro fertilization regarding their desires, intentions, and concerns. The American Medical Association has expressed similar sentiments, stating, "Advance agreements are recommended for deciding the disposition of frozen pre-embryos in the event of divorce or other changes in circumstances. Advance agreements can help ensure that the gamete providers undergo IVF and pre-embryo freezing after a full contemplation of the consequences. . . ." AMA Code of Medical Ethics Op. 2.141 (June 1994). Although we acknowledge the concern that individuals may change their minds regarding parenthood during the process of in vitro fertilization, we note that this concern can be adequately addressed in a contract and should be discussed in advance of the procedure. We do not believe, however, that such a concern should allow one party's indecisiveness to plague a process, fraught with emotions and lifelong repercussions, with uncertainty at another's expense.

In addition to holding that agreements between the parties should be honored, we further hold that where there has been no advance agreement regarding the disposition of pre-embryos, "then the relative interests of the parties in using or not using the preembryos must be weighed." *Davis*, 842 S.W.2d at 604. Although we acknowledge that this is not an ideal way to resolve a dispute implicating reproductive rights, we note that "what is even worse . . . is to give a possibly antagonized ex-spouse the power to either block parentage or to name the price that potential parentage will cost."

. . .

We . . . find no constitutional obstacle to honoring an agreement regarding the disposition of pre-embryos, and where there has been no advance agreement regarding the disposition of pre-embryos, then to balance the parties' interests in the event of a dispute.

. . .

In this case, appellant maintains that the informed consent executed by the parties is a valid contract which prevents use of the pre-embryos without his consent. Specifically, he claims that the informed consent is an expression of both his and appellee's intent that the pre-embryos cannot be used without both of their consents.

Appellee claims that appellant has misinterpreted the informed consent and argues that it is "simply the document by which the hospital sets forth its own policies regarding the control of pre-embryos." She also counters that appellant agreed to the subsequently written co-parent agreement where he promised that he would sign it, then performed his one critical obligation by providing sperm to create the pre-embryos.

Appellant replies that he never promised to sign the co-parent agreement and never agreed to its terms. He also claims that he did not perform under the co-parent agreement because he told appellee that "we needed to discuss it," and he was "simply honoring the prior commitment he had made on March 25."

Being a case of first impression, the circuit court did an admirable job of considering the alternative approaches taken by other states' courts in addressing the issue of how to determine the disposition of cryopreserved pre-embryos created with one party's sperm and another party's ova. Obviously, the parties did not know which approach the circuit court would adopt prior to the circuit court applying the balancing approach and entering summary judgment in favor of the appellee. As we have explained, the proper test to apply is the contractual approach. Consequently, we vacate the entry of summary judgment in favor of the appellee. As the parties were unable to present evidence in support of their respective positions in light of the contractual approach, we remand this matter to the circuit court to apply the contractual approach to any facts previously adduced and to any facts the parties wish to present on remand. This court retains jurisdiction over this matter and we instruct the circuit court and the parties to conclude any additional litigation they deem necessary within 180 days of this court issuing our mandate.

Reversed and remanded with instructions.

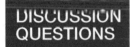 **FOR *SZAFRANSKI v. DUNSTON***

A. Describe each of the three approaches discussed by this court to determine who controls the disposition of cryopreserved preembryos created with one party's sperm and another party's ova.

B. Describe the criticism that has been made of each of the three approaches.

C. What approach did this court adopt to resolve control over disposition of cryopreserved preembryos created with one party's sperm and another party's ova?

D. What facts support the argument that a contract existed between Szafranski and Dunston? What facts support the argument that a contract does not exist between the two? If you were the trial judge on remand, in whose favor would you rule based on the contract arguments?

E. If on remand the trial judge rules there was no contract, does that end the matter? If not, how would you resolve the ultimate interest?

20.11 ABA MODEL ASSISTED REPRODUCTIVE TECHNOLOGIES ACT

A proposed Model Code Governing Assisted Reproduction was drafted by the American Bar Association Family Law Section Committee on Assisted Reproductive Technology and Genetics. The Code was initially approved by the ABA Council in May 2006. A revised draft was approved by the Section Council in February 2007. http://apps.americanbar.org/family/committees/artmodelcode_feb2007.pdf (last visited June 2015). The ABA claims the act "provides a flexible framework that will serve as a mechanism to resolve contemporary controversies, to adapt to the need for resolution of controversies that are envisioned but which may have not yet occurred, and to guide the expansion of ways by which families are formed."

REFLECTIVE QUESTIONS	Consider reviewing the ABA draft by going to the website listed above.

20.12 POSTHUMOUSLY CONCEIVED CHILD AND ELIGIBILITY FOR BENEFITS

There are situations where children are conceived posthumously by the surviving widow using sperm of her deceased husband. When a child is born, one question that has been raised is whether he or she is eligible for survivor benefits under the Social Security Act. Another question is whether the child may participate in the deceased's estate.

Social Security Act. At least five courts have held that a posthumously conceived child is entitled to benefits under the Social Security Act. *See, e.g., Capato ex rel. B.N.C. v. Commr. of Soc. Sec.*, 631 F.3d 626 (3d Cir. 2011). Because the lower federal courts cannot agree on this issue, the final answer to the question of posthumously conceived children and Social Security benefits will eventually be made by the Supreme Court. *See generally* Bruce A. Fowler & Teresa A. Baird, *Frozen in Time: Planning for the Posthumously Conceived Child*, 37-JUN Colo. Law. 45 (June 2008).

Probate matters. State courts have considered posthumously conceived children in the context of probate matters. For example, in Louisiana, a post-conceived child may inherit from his or her father if the father consented in writing to his wife's use of his semen and the child was born within three years of the father's death. The statute also allows a person adversely affected to challenge paternity within one year of such child's birth. La. Civ. Code §9:391.1 (2015).

Various state approaches. Time limitations and a written document requirement have been enacted in some states that focus on posthumously conceived children. For example, in order for a post-conceived child to inherit in the State of California, the parent must have consented in writing to the posthumous use of genetic material and designated a person to control its use. Such designee must be given written notice of the designation, and the child must have been conceived within two years of decedent's death. Cal. Prob. Code §249.5 (2015).

Florida requires a written agreement by the couple and the treating physician for the disposition of their eggs or semen in the event of divorce or death. A post-conceived child may inherit only if the parent explicitly provided for such child under his or her will. Fla. Stat. Ann. §742.17 (2015).

UPA. The Revised UPA allows for the creation of a parent-child relationship between a deceased individual and a posthumously conceived child. Section 707 of the UPA states that when "an individual consents in a record to be a parent by assisted reproduction," but then "dies before placement of eggs, sperm, or embryos," the decedent will not be considered "a parent of the resulting child unless the deceased spouse" agreed, in a record, to be a parent of any child resulting from assisted reproduction that "occur[s] after death."

| REFLECTIVE QUESTIONS | What conditions should a state set before a posthumously conceived child may inherit? |

General Principles

1. Artificial insemination, which some now label "alternative insemination," is primarily used when a husband is sterile, has a low sperm count, or carries a genetically transmissible disease. When a wife is inseminated with the sperm of an anonymous third-party semen donor, this is commonly referred to as AID (artificial insemination by donor). AID raises legal issues of legitimacy and paternity.

2. Artificial insemination is also used to correct some types of female infertility with the wife being inseminated with her husband's semen. This is termed homologous insemination or AIH (artificial insemination by husband). AIH does not raise legal issues of legitimacy and paternity.

3. The original version of the Uniform Parentage Act provided that the husband of a woman who is artificially inseminated by a third party is treated, legally, as if the husband were the natural father if he consents to the procedure and the procedure is carried out under the supervision of a licensed physician.

4. Some jurisdictions have artificial insemination statutes that protect a sperm donor from incurring any obligations such as child support because of a child born as a result of this process. Courts may, however, sometimes distinguish

between a known sperm donor and an anonymous sperm donor when it comes to imposing financial obligations on the donor.

5. Once a husband consents to artificial insemination of his wife, he is liable for supporting the child and his consent is presumed to continue through the time his wife becomes pregnant. To show that he withdrew his consent before she became pregnant, he must present clear and convincing evidence that this occurred.

6. Traditional surrogacy is generally described as a contractual arrangement whereby a woman agrees to be artificially inseminated with the sperm of a man whose wife is unable to conceive or bear a child. As a part of the contract, the surrogate agrees to surrender the ensuing child to the biological father and his wife.

7. Traditionally, surrogacy contracts were considered void as contrary to public policy. They were viewed as violating existing statutes on baby selling and prebirth consent (adoption), while effectively removing from a court its duty to protect the best interests of a child.

8. The revised Uniform Parentage Act authorizes a "gestational agreement" with a surrogate provided a court validates the contract. The act allows for payment to the surrogate mother and the intended parents may be married or unmarried. Judicial validation requires: (1) the court to possess jurisdiction; (2) the intended mother to be unable to bear a child; (3) a home study to demonstrate that the intended parents are fit; (4) the contract to be voluntary and the parties to understand its consequences; (5) there to be no known physical or mental health risks to the gestational mother; (6) adequate provisions for health care expenses to be included; and (7) the payment to the gestational mother who will act as the surrogate to be reasonable. If these requirements are met, a court may issue an order validating the agreement and will declare that the intended parents are the parents of the child.

9. If the surrogate is married, to overcome the presumption of that the surrogate's husband is the natural father of any children who are born during the marriage, the surrogacy contract normally requires that the surrogate's husband be a party to the contract. He must relinquish any parental rights he may have to the child to be carried by his wife as a surrogate mother.

10. In vitro fertilization is a medical procedure involving the surgical removal of ova that subsequently are placed in a laboratory medium, together with sperm, where fertilization takes place. The resulting embryo is implanted in the uterus of either the ovum donor or another woman.

Chapter Problems

1. Assume that Alice and Alfred discussed artificial insemination of Alice with their family physician. The physician artificially inseminated Alice and a child was born. A few weeks after the birth of the child, Alfred filed for divorce. He claimed he did

not have any responsibility for the child. Alfred points out that he never consented to the artificial insemination in writing. If this jurisdiction has adopted the Uniform Parentage Act (2002), is Alfred the child's legal father? If this state has no legislation on artificial insemination, most likely how will a court rule on Alfred's issue?

2. Barbara wanted to conceive a child by artificial insemination and to raise the child jointly with her partner, Betty. Barbara chose Betty's brother, Bill, to act as the semen donor. Barbara became pregnant as a result of artificial insemination by her physician. There was no written agreement.

When the child is born, Bill claims that he and Barbara agreed that he could see the child on a regular basis and would act as a noncustodial father. Barbara says there was no such agreement. Bill produces a birth certificate where his name appears as the child's father. If this state has adopted the Uniform Parentage Act (2002), most likely how will a court rule? If Bill had impregnated Barbara through sexual intercourse, would the result be different? Would the result be different if Bill had signed a document in which he agreed that he waived all of his legal rights to the child?

3. Assume that the husband and wife contracted with an egg donor and an IVF clinic. Before the IVF clinic would work with the couple, it required that they sign a contract declaring that any remaining embryos after the wife's eggs were fertilized would be thawed out and not allowed to undergo further development. Both voluntarily and with full understanding of the language, signed the contract. After the husband's sperm fertilized three of the donor's eggs, the eggs were implanted, resulting in the birth of a child. Before the birth, however, the parties separated, and sued for divorce. At the divorce trial, the wife asked to be awarded the remaining embryos in the IVF clinic's possession to implant in a surrogate. The trial court awarded the embryos to the husband, who wanted to donate them to an out-of-state couple. The appeals court, in reviewing the egg donor contract, noted that it did not provide what would be done with the embryos if the parties could not agree or if they dissolved their marriage. The court concluded that the husband's right not to procreate compelled an award of the embryos to him. Wife appealed. How will the state's highest court most likely resolve the issue?

4. Assume that Harry and Hanna are unable to conceive a child in a jurisdiction that has not taken a position on surrogate contracts. They contact Jane, a college student, and for $50,000 she agrees to become their surrogate. In their contract, Hanna will provide an egg that will be fertilized with Harry's sperm. The embryo will be implanted in Jane, who agrees to carry the child to term and, upon birth, to relinquish it to Harry and Hanna. All goes well until the child is born. Jane refuses to turn the child over to Harry and Hanna, and they bring an action asking the family court to specifically enforce the contract. What arguments will each side make, and most likely, how will a court rule?

5. Assume that Tom and Tina entered into an agreement regarding the disposition of frozen preembryos. The agreement is clear that if there is a divorce, the pre-embryos must be destroyed. Also assume that Tom died while Tom and Tina were married. Six months after his death, Tina decides to implant the frozen preembryos created with the couple's gametes during the marriage. Tom's parents object. How should a court rule?

6. Assume that Alice signed a contract providing that an embryo created by the sperm of Paul and the egg of Pauline would be implanted in Alice and the child born would be taken into Paul and Pauline's home "as their child." Assume that the embryo is implanted and in its sixth month Paul and Pauline divorce. When it is born, both Paul and Pauline argue that the child is Alice's. How should a court rule?

7. Assume that Alice signed a contract providing that an embryo created by the sperm of Paul and the egg of Pauline would be implanted in Alice and the child born would be taken into Paul and Pauline's home "as their child." In the second month of pregnancy, Paul and Pauline change their mind and demand that Alice abort the child. Alice refuses. When the child is born, Paul and Pauline refuse to have anything to do with the child. Alice seeks specific performance of the contract or, in the alternative, child support. How should a court rule?

Preparation for Practice

1. Prepare a paper outlining the legal position taken by your jurisdiction when it comes to AIH, AID, and gestational surrogacy. Does it differ from New York? California? Texas and Ohio?

2. Prepare a short paper explaining whether your jurisdiction follows *Davis v. Davis* or *A.Z. v. B.Z.* If your jurisdiction has not ruled on the issue, your paper should reflect your analysis and conclusion about which view it will take.

3. Prepare a PowerPoint slide outlining the legal principles your jurisdiction applies when considering an alternative reproduction issue.

Part VII

The Changing Role of the Family Lawyer

Chapter 21

Mediation, Collaborative Law, Parenting Coordination, and Arbitration

21.1 INTRODUCTION

Although there are a variety of alternative dispute resolution processes and services available for families today, this chapter focuses on four of them: mediation, collaborative law, parenting coordination, and arbitration.

Couples with children usually continue to interact with each other after divorce, and participation in an alternative dispute resolution process may promote more constructive interactions. However, for some parents, participation in alternative dispute resolution processes may be unsafe and unproductive. Attorneys must consequently facilitate informed client decision making about whether, when, and how to participate in various processes.

As you read this chapter, consider questions such as these: What is mediation, and what is the role of the mediator? What is collaborative law, and what distinguishes it from general practice? What is a parenting coordinator, and when can one be appointed? When can arbitration be used in a family law case? How can the family law attorney assist clients in making informed choices about participation in various processes and services?

REFLECTIVE QUESTIONS	What are your goals for this chapter?

21.2 CHANGED NATURE OF THE FAMILY COURT SYSTEM

Over the past 30 years, court systems have embraced settlement-oriented methods of dispute resolution such that they are now the norm, rather than the "alternative." Some family courts see themselves as providers or coordinators of processes and services aimed at helping families through emotional conflict. This role extends beyond the traditional court focus on resolving legal issues.

> While the delegalization of parenting disputes offers potential benefits for families and children, it also poses significant risks, particularly when coupled with the ambitious agenda of today's family courts. . . . The recharacterization of parenting disputes from legal events to ongoing, multifaceted processes diminishes the importance of legal norms in family dispute resolution. . . . Although judges still service as the ultimate backstop if other dispute resolution mechanisms fail, decision-making functions are increasingly delegated to nonlegal staff who rely on party self-determination or staff evaluation that draws more on psychology and social work than on legal doctrine.

Jane C. Murphy & Jana B. Singer, *Divorced from Reality: Rethinking Family Dispute Resolution* 43 (2015).

With the advent of alternative dispute resolution processes, the role of judges and the court system has undergone change. Various questions have arisen as judges and courts have become case managers in addition to decision makers: (a) Are judges qualified to fulfill the new roles? (b) Will families be given choices about processes or ordered to them? (c) How will services take account of cultural and socioeconomic issues? Nancy Ver Steegh, *Family Court Reform and ADR: Shifting Values and Expectations Transform the Divorce Process*, 42 Fam. L.Q. 659, 669 (2008). *See also* Nancy Ver Steegh et al., *Look Before You Leap: Court System Triage of Family Law Cases Involving Intimate Partner Violence*, 95 Marq. L. Rev. 955 (2012) (endorsing informed decision making by parties concerning participation in dispute resolution processes).

REFLECTIVE QUESTIONS	With the advent of alternative dispute resolution processes, how has the role of a family court judge changed? Or, has it changed?

21.3 FACILITATIVE MEDIATION: PROCESS OVERVIEW

The Model Standards of Practice for Family and Divorce Mediation define mediation as follows:

A process in which a mediator, an impartial third party, facilitates the resolution of family disputes by promoting the participants' voluntary agreement. The family mediator assists communication, encourages understanding and focuses the participants on their individual and common interests. The family mediator works with the participants to explore options, make decisions and reach their own agreements.

Andrew Schepard, *An Introduction to the Model Standards of Practice for Family and Divorce Mediation*, 35 Fam. L.Q. 1, 3 (2001).

Mediation is a structured problem-solving process in which couples identify issues, gather facts and information about the issues, establish standards of fairness, brainstorm about possible solutions, analyze the repercussions of various choices, and make decisions for the future. For example, a couple dividing property might list and provide verification for all of their assets, discuss whether they want to divide the total estate in half or make some other arrangement, imagine a variety of ways to divide the property, explore the consequences to each concerning various divisions, and decide on which option best meets the needs of both.

Mediation is an interest-based process and the parties are discouraged from adopting a win-lose framework focused on protecting their own "rights." Instead, they are encouraged to identify and express their underlying needs and interests. For example, parents have a strong mutual desire to ensure that their children are secure and nurtured. As a result, they can be encouraged to work together to meet the children's needs rather than arguing about who is a better parent.

Most mediated agreements involving children include detailed parenting plans that directly address points of potential conflict. In addition, where permitted by state law, parents can avoid the use of sometimes contentious custody labels and instead focus on parenting time schedules and specific agreements about decision making. Throughout the process, the mediator focuses the parties on the needs of their children and encourages them to view decisions through the children's eyes. Parents are given information about the impact of divorce on children, the developmental needs of children at various ages, and the effect of continuing parental conflict on children. If necessary, a neutral child psychologist or related professional can be brought into the mediation session to advise the parents on the children's needs.

Agreements reached in mediation are not final and enforceable until the court formally approves them. Courts vary concerning the level of scrutiny with which they review proposed mediated settlements. *See In re Lee*, 411 S.W.3d 445 (Tex. 2013) (review of mediated agreement).

| REFLECTIVE QUESTIONS | How does mediation differ from negotiation by the parties? |

21.4 FACILITATIVE MEDIATION: THE ROLE OF THE MEDIATOR

A *mediator* is a neutral facilitator of the mediation process. Unlike a judge or arbitrator, the mediator does not make a decision or express an opinion about the substantive issues being discussed. The mediator does, however, guide and structure the process so that the parties can more easily reach agreement. The mediator does this, in part, by establishing and enforcing ground rules, focusing discussion, balancing the participation of each party, and reframing points of contention as problems to be solved. The mediator models conflict resolution skills that the couple can later use on their own.

The mediator may draft a memorandum of agreement setting forth the decisions made by the parties, but the mediator will not file pleadings or finalize the divorce in court. Even if the mediator is a licensed attorney, he or she functions as a neutral facilitator in mediation and does not represent either party. Couples are encouraged to seek legal advice from an attorney throughout the mediation process as well as after a final agreement has been reached. Attorneys representing the parties may attend mediation sessions in some cases. As the number of unrepresented parties increases, mediators must remain attuned to professional boundaries and ethical obligations. *See* Amy G. Applegate & Connie J.A. Beck, *Self-Represented Parties in Mediation: Fifty Years Later It Remains the Elephant in the Room*, 51 Fam. Ct. Rev. 87 (2013).

Family mediation is a multidisciplinary practice in that, by background, mediators may be psychologists, social workers, lawyers, or other professionals. Because mediators come from different professions and the practice is relatively new, the field struggles to promote quality practice while encouraging professional diversity and continued innovation. The Model Standards of Practice for Family and Divorce Mediation suggest as minimum qualifications that mediators should:

1. have knowledge of family law;
2. have knowledge of and training in the impact of family conflict on parents, children, and other participants, including knowledge of child development, domestic abuse, and child abuse and neglect;
3. have education and training specific to the process of mediation; and
4. be able to recognize the impact of culture and diversity.

Model Standards of Practice for Family and Divorce Mediation, Standard X (2001).

| REFLECTIVE QUESTIONS | Do you think that the outcomes of family law cases differ depending on whether decisions are made in mediation or pursuant to a court hearing? |

Background to *Vitakis-Valchine v. Valchine*

Available research shows that many mediators are impartial, sensitive, and skilled. *See* Joan B. Kelly, *A Decade of Divorce Mediation Research: Some Answers and Questions*, 34 Fam. & Conciliation Cts. Rev. 373, 378 (1996). However, the following case illustrates inappropriate mediator conduct rising to such a level that the court was asked to intervene.

VITAKIS-VALCHINE
v.
VALCHINE
Court of Appeals of Florida
793 So. 2d 1094 (2001)

STEVENSON, J. This is an appeal from a final judgment of dissolution which was entered pursuant to a mediated settlement agreement. The wife argues that the trial court erred in affirming the recommendations of the general master and in denying her request to set aside the settlement agreement on the grounds that it was entered into under duress and coercion. The wife also alleges that the mediator committed misconduct during the mediation session, including but not limited to coercion and improper influence, and that she entered into the settlement agreement as a direct result of this misconduct.

By August of 1999, Kalliope and David Valchine's divorce proceedings to end their near twelve-year marriage had been going on for one and a half to two years. On August 17, 1999, the couple attended court-ordered mediation to attempt to resolve their dispute. At the mediation, both parties were represented by counsel. The mediation lasted seven to eight hours and resulted in a twenty-three page marital settlement agreement. The agreement was comprehensive and dealt with alimony, bank accounts, both parties' IRAs, and the husband's federal customs, postal, and military pensions. The agreement also addressed the disposition of embryos that the couple had frozen during in vitro fertilization attempts prior to the divorce. The agreement provided in this regard that "the Wife has expressed her desire to have the frozen embryos, but has reluctantly agreed to provide them to the husband to dispose of."

THIRD PARTY COERCION

As a general rule under Florida law, a contract or settlement may not be set aside on the basis of duress or coercion unless the improper influence emanated from one of the contracting parties—the actions of a third party will not suffice. In this case, the record adequately supports the finding that neither the husband nor the husband's attorney was involved in any duress or coercion [or] had [any] knowledge of any improper conduct on the part of the mediator.

THE FORMER WIFE'S CLAIMS

The wife testified that the eight-hour mediation, with Mark London as the mediator, began at approximately 10:45 A.M., that both her attorney and her brother attended, and that her husband was there with his counsel. Everyone initially gathered together, the mediator explained the process, and then the wife, her attorney and her brother were left in one room while the husband and his attorney went to another. The mediator then went back and forth between the two rooms during the course of the negotiations in what the mediator described as "Kissinger-style shuttle diplomacy."

With respect to the frozen embryos, which were in the custody of the Fertility Institute of Boca Raton, the wife explained that there were lengthy discussions concerning what was to become of them. The wife was concerned about destroying the embryos and wanted to retain them herself. The wife testified that the mediator told her that the embryos were not "lives in being" and that the court would not require the husband to pay child support if she were impregnated with the embryos after the divorce. According to the wife, the mediator told her that the judge would never give her custody of the embryos, but would order them destroyed. The wife said that at one point during the discussion of the frozen embryo issue, the mediator came in, threw the papers on the table, and declared "that's it, I give up." Then, according to the wife, the mediator told her that if no agreement was reached, he (the mediator) would report to the trial judge that the settlement failed because of her. Additionally, the wife testified that the mediator told her that if she signed the agreement at the mediation, she could still protest any provisions she didn't agree with at the final hearing — including her objection to the husband "disposing" of the frozen embryos.

With respect to the distribution of assets, the wife alleges that the mediator told her that she was not entitled to any of the husband's federal pensions. She further testified that the mediator told her that the husband's pensions were only worth about $200 per month and that she would spend at least $70,000 in court litigating entitlement to this relatively modest sum. The wife states that the mediation was conducted with neither her nor the mediator knowing the present value of the husband's pensions or the marital estate itself. The wife testified that she and her new attorney had since constructed a list of assets and liabilities, and that she was short-changed by approximately $34,000 — not including the husband's pensions. When asked what she would have done if Mr. London had told her that the attorney's fees could have amounted to as little as $15,000, the wife stated, "I would have took [sic] it to trial."

Finally, the wife testified that she signed the agreement in part due to "time pressure" being placed on her by the mediator. She testified that while the final draft was being typed up, the mediator got a call and she heard him say "have a bottle of wine and a glass of drink, and a strong drink ready for me." The wife explained that the mediator had repeatedly stated that his daughter was leaving for law school, and finally said that "you guys have five minutes to hurry up and get out of here because that family is more important to me." The wife testified that she ultimately signed the agreement because

[I] felt pressured. I felt that I had no other alternative but to accept the Agreement from the things that I was told by Mr. London. I believed everything that he said.

COURT-ORDERED MEDIATION

Mediation is a process whereby a neutral third party, the mediator, assists the principals of a dispute in reaching a complete or partial voluntary resolution of their issues of conflict. Mandatory, court-ordered mediation was officially sanctioned by the Florida legislature in 1987, and since then, mediation has become institutionalized within Florida's court system. All twenty judicial circuits in Florida utilize some form of court-connected mediation to assist with their caseloads. The process is meant to be non-adversarial and informal, with the mediator essentially serving as a facilitator for communications between the parties and providing assistance in the identification of issues and the exploration of options to resolve the dispute. Ultimate authority to settle remains with the parties. Mediation, as a method of alternative dispute resolution, potentially saves both the parties and the judicial system time and money while leaving the power to structure the terms of any resolution of the dispute in the hands of the parties themselves.

Mediation, pursuant to chapter 44, is mandatory when ordered by the court. Any court in which a civil action, including a family matter, is pending may refer the case to mediation, with or without the parties' consent. Communications during the mediation sessions are privileged and confidential. During court-ordered mediation conducted pursuant to the statute, the mediator enjoys "judicial immunity in the same manner and to the same extent as a judge." The mediation must be conducted in accordance with rules of practice and procedure adopted by the Florida Supreme Court.

Comprehensive procedures for conducting the mediation session and minimum standards for qualification, training, certification, professional conduct, and discipline of mediators have been set forth by the Florida Supreme Court in the Florida Rules for Certified and Court-Appointed Mediators, Rule 10. Predecessors to these rules initially took effect in 1987 and were amended in February 2000. One of the hallmarks of the process of mediation is the empowerment of the parties to resolve their dispute on their own, agreed-upon terms. While parties are required to attend mediation, no party is required to settle at mediation.

Decision-making. Decisions made during a mediation are to be made by the parties. A mediator shall not make substantive decisions for any party. A mediator is responsible for assisting the parties in reaching informed and voluntary decisions while protecting their right of self-determination.

Fla. R. Med. 10.310(a). The committee notes to the rule provide in part that

While mediation techniques and practice styles may vary from mediator to mediator and mediation to mediation, a line is crossed and ethical standards are violated when any conduct of the mediator serves to compromise the parties' basic right to agree or not to agree. Special care should be taken to preserve the party's right to self-determination if the mediator provides input to the mediation process.

In keeping with the notion of self-determination and voluntary resolution of the dispute at court-ordered mediation, any improper influence such as coercion or duress on the part of the mediator is expressly prohibited:

> Coercion Prohibited. A mediator shall not coerce or improperly influence any party to make a decision or unwillingly participate in a mediation.

Fla. R. Med. 10.310(b). Likewise, a mediator may not intentionally misrepresent any material fact in an effort to promote or encourage an agreement:

> Misrepresentation Prohibited. A mediator shall not intentionally or knowingly misrepresent any material fact or circumstance in the course of conducting a mediation.

Fla. R. Med. 10.310(c).

Other sections of Rule 10 address the rendering of personal or professional opinions by the mediator, and one section specifically provides that a mediator shall not offer a personal or professional opinion as to how the court in which the case has been filed will resolve the dispute. Fla. R. Med. 10.370(c).

Under this section, the committee notes caution that

> While mediators may call upon their own qualifications and experience to supply information and options, the parties must be given the opportunity to freely decide upon any agreement. Mediators shall not utilize their opinions to decide any aspect of the dispute or to coerce the parties or their representatives to accept any resolution option.

The question we are confronted with in this case is whether a referring court may set aside an agreement reached in court-ordered mediation if the court finds that the agreement was reached as a direct result of the mediator's substantial violation of the rules of conduct for mediators. We believe that it would be unconscionable for a court to enforce a settlement agreement reached through coercion or any other improper tactics utilized by a court-appointed mediator. When a court refers a case to mediation, the mediation must be conducted according to the practices and procedures outlined in the applicable statutes and rules. If the required practices and procedures are not substantially complied with, no party to the mediation can rightfully claim the benefits of an agreement reached in such a way. During a court-ordered mediation, the mediator is no ordinary third party, but is, for all intent and purposes, an agent of the court carrying out an official court-ordered function. We hold that the court may invoke its inherent power to maintain the integrity of the judicial system and its processes by invalidating a court-ordered mediation settlement agreement obtained through violation and abuse of the judicially-prescribed mediation procedures.

We hasten to add that no findings were made as to whether the mediator actually committed the alleged misconduct. Nevertheless, at least some of the wife's claims clearly are sufficient to allege a violation of the applicable rules. On remand, the trial court must determine whether the mediator substantially violated the Rules for Mediators, and whether that misconduct led to the settlement agreement in this case. Affirmed in part, reversed in part, and remanded.

DISCUSSION QUESTIONS FOR *VITAKIS-VALCHINE v. VALCHINE*

A. What is the wife's claim, and what relief is she seeking?

B. How long did the mediation last?

C. List the behaviors of the mediator that were considered to be inappropriate by the court. Do you agree with the court's analysis? What should be the proper role of the mediator in a dispute like this?

D. Not all states regulate the practice of mediation as Florida does in this case. What qualifications and education do you think a mediator should have? Should all mediators be required to be lawyers? Should all mediators be required to be mental health professionals? Should states license mediators?

E. Many mediators are mental health professionals but not attorneys. Did the mediator in this case give legal advice? If he was not an attorney, was this practicing law without a license? If he was an attorney, whom did he represent?

F. Was the wife represented by an attorney at the mediation? What role should an attorney play in the mediation process?

G. Mediation was mandatory in this case. Why do some states mandate mediation? What are the pros and cons of this policy?

21.5 MEDIATION: TESTIMONY BY THE MEDIATOR

In order for mediation to be successful, parties are encouraged to pool information, brainstorm, and speak with candor about their situation. This free flow of information and ideas will not occur if the parties fear that their statements could later be used against them. Consequently, if an impasse is reached, mediators resist being called as witnesses in a later court proceeding. *See Powell v. Fackler*, 891 N.E.2d 1091, 1097 (Ind. App. 2009) (ADR rules provide that parties may not waive confidentiality); *Horner v. Carter*, 981 N.E.2d 1210 (Ind. 2013) (party statements made during mediation were not admissible in court).

> REFLECTIVE
> QUESTIONS
>
> Can you make an argument that statements made during mediation sessions should be admissible at trial if the case is not settled?

Background to *Marchal v. Craig*

The following case discusses a situation in which a mediator was allowed to testify at trial and the trial court relied extensively on the opinion of the mediator as to the ultimate issues in the case. The appellate court discusses the need to protect the integrity of the mediation process.

MARCHAL
v.
CRAIG

Court of Appeals of Indiana
681 N.E.2d 1160 (1997)

ROBERTSON, J. . . . Keith A. Marchal (Father) appeals the denial of his petition for the modification of the child custody arrangement with respect to the child born of his marriage to Paula Craig (Mother).

The dispositive facts are largely undisputed. Father and Mother are the parents of one child, a boy born in 1988. The parents divorced in 1991. The divorce decree, entered pursuant to a settlement agreement, provided that the parents would have joint legal custody of the child but that Father had the right to make all major decisions regarding the child, including those related to his educational training and religious upbringing. The agreement provided that the parties would share physical custody of the child on approximately a 50-50 basis.

After various conflicts and additional litigation, Father petitioned the trial court to order mediation. As a result, the parties entered into a written agreement on January 12, 1993, signed by both parties and their attorneys and entered on the court's docket, which reads in pertinent part as follows:

> With the assistance of [Dr. John Ehrmann, a clinical psychologist], the [parties] shall attempt to jointly resolve all child related issues; but that if agreement cannot be reached, Dr. Ehrmann has authority to resolve the dispute considering [the child's] best interests, and his resolution shall be determinative.

On April 12, 1993, Dr. Ehrmann submitted a letter to Mother's attorney which read, in pertinent part, as follows:

> I met with [Father and Mother] on March 3rd of 1993 to begin mediation per the agreed entry. . . . I see no other course at this point other than to move forward in a legal arena.

Mediation had failed, and the litigation resumed. Ultimately, both parties, through counsel, stipulated that Dr. Ehrmann would be an acceptable witness for both parties. Father, through counsel, had filed a proposed witness list which included Dr. Ehrmann. Later, Father, through counsel, filed a supplemental list of exhibits which included:

1. All tape recordings made by [Father] of Dr. John Ehrmann's sessions pertaining to the evaluation, mediation, and counseling of the parties herein and the minor child.
2. All correspondence, by either the mail services or by facsimile transmission from the [Father] to Dr. John Ehrmann.

Father's attorney withdrew from the case and Father proceeded to trial pro se. At trial, Father objected to the testimony of Dr. Ehrmann based upon the then effective version of Ind. Alternative Dispute Resolution Rule 2.8 which read as follows:

A person who has served as a mediator in a proceeding may act as a mediator in subsequent disputes between the parties, and the parties may provide for a review of the agreement with the mediator on a periodic basis. However, the mediator shall decline to act in any capacity, except as mediator, unless the subsequent association is clearly distinct from the mediation issues. The mediator is required to utilize an effective system to identify potential conflict of interest at the time of appointment. The mediator may not subsequently act as an investigator for any court-ordered report or make any recommendations to the court regarding the mediated litigation.

Subsection 12 (A.D.R. 2.12) provided for the confidentiality of mediation communications and provided that:

Mediators shall not be subject to process requiring the disclosure of any matter discussed during the mediation, but rather, such matter shall be considered confidential and privileged in nature. The confidentiality requirement may not be waived by the parties, and an objection to the obtaining of testimony or physical evidence from mediation may be made by any party or by the mediators.

The trial court overruled Father's objection to Dr. Ehrmann's testimony on the basis that the parties had stipulated that Dr. Ehrmann would be an acceptable witness for both parties.

At trial, Dr. Ehrmann gave extensive evidence highly prejudicial to Father which supported Mother's request for the sole legal custody of the child. The trial court's findings and judgment, awarding sole legal custody of the child to Mother, relied extensively on the evidence provided by Dr. Ehrmann.

This appeal ensued. . . . The Alternative Dispute Resolution rules governing the confidentiality and privileged nature of mediation communications are unequivocal. The preamble defining the purpose of mediation states that mediation "involves the confidential process by which a neutral mediator assists the litigants in reaching a mutually acceptable agreement." (A.D.R. 2.1). The parties to mediation seek to resolve their dispute unhindered by the threat of subsequent litigation. Accordingly, the mediator should be perceived as impartial and willing to protect the confidentiality of the process. It is therefore essential that the confidentiality of the process be protected on two levels — first, that which is disclosed during the private caucus sessions will not be revealed to the opponent during the mediation, and second, that which transpires during the mediation is not used in any subsequent trial or other proceeding. In the landmark decision of *N.L.R.B. v. Joseph Macaluso, Inc.*, 618 F.2d 51 (9th Cir. 1980), the court held that the public interest in maintaining the perceived and actual impartiality of mediators outweighed any benefit to be derived from the testimony which could be obtained from mediators.

As set out above, the rules governing alternative dispute resolution strictly prohibit mediators from providing evidence in the cases they have attempted to mediate. All matters discussed in mediation are strictly confidential and privileged. Moreover, and dispositive in the present case, the A.D.R. rules expressly provide that the confidentiality requirement may not be waived by the parties and that an objection to the obtaining of testimony or physical evidence from mediation may be made by any party. We must conclude that these provisions are designed to protect the integrity of the mediation process itself and that they are operational despite any attempt by the parties to override them.

Mother argues 1) that Dr. Ehrmann was not a mediator subject to the A.D.R. rules because he was not an attorney, and 2) that Father invited any error due to his attorney's stipulation and the fact that he had included Dr. Ehrmann on his witness list and evidence derived from mediation in his lists of exhibits to be presented at trial. First, Dr. Ehrmann, Ph.D., as a person who has a bachelor's degree from an accredited institution of higher learning, is qualified to serve as a mediator in a domestic relations case. Second, as discussed above, the A.D.R. rules provide that confidentiality may not be waived. Moreover, Father raised an objection to the evidence at trial. Therefore, we cannot conclude that error was either waived or invited.

The A.D.R. rules involved here are designed to protect the mediation process itself. Therefore, we hold the trial court erred by permitting the introduction of Dr. Ehrmann's evidence despite the parties' former stipulation. [W]e reverse and remand for retrial.

 **FOR *MARCHAL v. CRAIG***

A. What was the basis on which the trial judge allowed Dr. Ehrmann to testify at the trial regarding the mediation?

B. The mother claimed that Dr. Ehrmann was not a mediator subject to the ADR rules because he was not an attorney. What was the response of the appellate court to this argument?

C. Mediators believe that confidentiality is vital to the mediation process because it allows the participants to speak freely and with candor during mediation sessions. Why is that important?

D. What if during a mediation session, one party admits past child abuse or physically threatens the other spouse? Should the mediator report this information? Should mediators ever be allowed to testify in court?

E. Mediators remain neutral in that they do not express opinions or take sides with either party during mediation sessions. Why is this important? Should mediators be allowed to give status reports to the court? What if the judge wants to hear the mediator's opinion on an issue?

21.6 MEDIATION: POTENTIAL BENEFITS

Proponents of mediation believe that it is beneficial for many families. For example, in a long-term study comparing couples assigned randomly to mediation and litigation, mediating nonresidential parents maintained more contact with their children than those who litigated. Robert E. Emery et al., *Child Custody Mediation and Litigation: Custody, Contact, and Coparenting 12 Years After Initial Dispute Resolution*, J. Consulting & Clinical Psychol. 69, 323-332 (2001).

In some cases, mediation has proven to be less expensive and less time-consuming than traditional litigation. More time and money is saved if the couple enters mediation early in the divorce process. When a couple participates in mediation there may be less involvement by attorneys and consequently fewer attorney hours are billed. In addition, couples save money by using neutral experts instead of each party hiring his or her own expert witnesses. When necessary, a single neutral expert, such as a child psychologist or accountant, will advise the couple during a mediation session. *See* Joan B. Kelly, *A Decade of Divorce Mediation Research: Some Answers and Questions*, 34 Fam. & Conciliation Cts. Rev. (1996).

Although mediation programs differ significantly from each other, on average couples reach agreement through mediation between 40 and 80 percent of the time. More than two-thirds of couples participating in mediation express satisfaction with the process. Some research shows that couples who mediate are more likely to comply with the resulting agreements than those who do not mediate. Similarly, mediating couples may be less likely to return to court during the first few years after divorce. *See* Desmond Ellis & Noreen Stuckless, *Mediating and Negotiating Marital Conflicts* (1996); Jessica Pearson & Nancy Thoennes, *Divorce Mediation: Reflections on a Decade of Research*, in *Mediation Research* (Kenneth Kressel et al. eds., 1989).

| REFLECTIVE QUESTIONS | What are possible benefits of participating in family mediation? |

21.7 MEDIATION: READINESS FOR PARTICIPATION

For mediation to be beneficial, participation must be safe as well as knowing and voluntary. Parties must act in good faith and deal fairly with each other. Each party must be able to make autonomous decisions. Whenever these conditions do not exist, participation in mediation may not be appropriate. Gabrielle Davis et al., *Practice Guides for Family Court Decision-Making in Domestic Abuse-Related Child Custody Matters* 48 (2015), available at http://www.bwjp.org/our-work/projects/national-child-custody-project.html (last visited August 1, 2015) (Readiness for Mediation Assessment Guide). *See also* Connie J.A. Beck & Lynda E. Frost, *Defining a Threshold for Client Competence to Participate in Divorce Mediation*, 12 Psychol. Pub. Pol'y & L. 1 (2006).

REFLECTIVE QUESTIONS	Create a hypothetical situation where the benchmarks for mediation described above are not met. Describe a situation where mediation is clearly inappropriate.

21.8 MEDIATION: INTIMATE PARTNER VIOLENCE

Mediation is particularly controversial in cases involving intimate partner violence. Commentators express concerns about safety, coercion, and retribution linked to the dynamics of some violent relationships. A large number of divorcing couples, including couples who mediate, have experienced intimate partner violence. *See* Amy Holtzworth-Munroe et al., *The Mediator's Assessment of Safety Issues and Concerns (MASIC): A Screening Interview for Intimate Partner Violence and Abuse Available in the Public Domain*, 48 Fam. Ct. Rev. 646, 647 (2010) (studies show rates of 40-50% for couples entering mediation).

Screening for possible abuse. It is critical that mediators and lawyers conduct ongoing screening for intimate partner violence, and for this purpose various protocols and tools have been developed. *See* Amy Holtzworth-Munroe et al., *The Mediator's Assessment of Safety Issues and Concerns (MASIC): A Screening Interview for Intimate Partner Violence and Abuse Available in the Public Domain*, 48 Fam. Ct. Rev. 646 (2010). Unfortunately, for various reasons, mediators sometimes fail to detect intimate partner violence. Robin H. Ballard et al., *Detecting Intimate Partner Violence in Family and Divorce Mediation: A Randomized Trial of Intimate Partner Violence Screening*, 17 Psychol. Pub. Pol'y & L. 241, 256 ("despite premediation preparation and talking to the parties about their concerns during intake and mediation, mediators did not report the presence of IPV in more than half the cases in which the parties themselves reported physical violence on a short, behaviorally specific screening questionnaire").

Informed decision making about participation in mediation. Lawyers and mediators should counsel clients regarding potential participation in mediation and other alternative dispute resolution processes. In addition to safety concerns, both parties must be willing and able to negotiate in good faith and make autonomous decisions. Factors such as the following will have an impact on whether mediation might be safe and appropriate when intimate partner violence is an issue: frequency and severity of abuse; history of coercive controlling abuse; health status of the victim; likely abuser response; quality of the mediation process available; availability of legal representation; presence of children; state law; financial resources; and preferred decision-making approach. *See* Nancy Ver Steegh, *Yes, No, and Maybe: Informed Decision Making About Divorce Mediation in the Presence of Domestic Violence*, 9 Wm. & Mary J. Women & L. 145 (2003).

Will safeguards effectively address concerns? If mediation occurs in a case involving intimate partner violence, special precautions, ground rules, and procedures should be tailored to meet specific concerns. For example, requiring separate arrival and departure from mediation sessions will not address concerns about retaliation occurring between sessions. *See* Desmond Ellis & Noreen Stuckless, *Domestic Violence, DOVE, and Divorce Mediation*, 44 Fam. Ct. Rev. 658, 659 (2006) (empirically validated intimate partner violence screening instrument which "links violence prevention interventions with: (a) level of risk; (b) the presence of specific types of predictors; and (c) types and levels of violence and abuse" in the mediation setting).

Is participation voluntary? Jurisdictions that mandate participation in mediation may make exceptions for cases involving intimate partner violence. Typical "opt-out" provisions are only partially effective because they require survivors to make disclosures that may put them and their children in danger. Other jurisdictions have adopted a "victim choice" system similar to that provided in the Model Code on Domestic and Family Violence (1994). *See* Model Standards of Practice for Family and Divorce Mediation III.C. Supporting parties in making informed decisions about "opting in" to mediation is safer and more consistent with the underlying values of mediation.

REFLECTIVE QUESTIONS	What steps should an attorney take to assure that a client with a history of intimate partner violence is making an informed choice about participation in mediation? What, if anything, should an attorney do if the attorney disagrees with a client's decision about participation?

21.9 COLLABORATIVE LAW

Collaborative law is a model of practice in which each party is represented by a designated collaborative lawyer. These attorneys use interest-based cooperative problem-solving techniques to assist the parties in settling the case. From the outset, the parties and lawyers agree that they will not seek court assistance in resolving the case. Consequently, if court intervention is sought by either party, the collaborative lawyers withdraw from the case and litigation counsel is substituted. *See* Pauline H. Tessler, *Collaborative Family Law*, 4 Pepp. Disp. Resol. L.J. 317 (2004). Professional responsibility issues connected with collaborative law practice are discussed in Chapter 22.

Research indicates that there are various models of collaborative practice and that collaborative lawyers differ, for example, concerning the extent to which they involve coaches and experts, meet with clients outside of negotiation sessions, and disclose information. *See* Julie Macfarlane, *The Emerging Phenomenon of Collaborative Family Law (CFL): A Qualitative Study of CFL Cases* 13-14 (2005), available at http://www.justice.gc.ca/eng/rp-pr/fl-lf/famil/2005_1/pdf/2005_1.pdf (last visited August 8, 2015).

UCLR and UCLA. The Uniform Law Commission recently approved the Uniform Collaborative Law Rules (UCLR) and Uniform Collaborative Law Act (UCLA), text available at http://www.uniformlaws.org/Act.aspx?title=Collaborative%20Law%20Act (last visited August 1, 2015). The UCLR and the UCLA clarify and attempt to standardize significant features of collaborative law practice. The UCLR and the UCLA provide best practices for collaborative lawyers in a number of areas, including decision making about use of collaborative law in situations where there is a history of coercion or violence between the parties. *See* Nancy Ver Steegh, *The Uniform Collaborative Law Act and Intimate Partner Violence: A Roadmap for Collaborative (and Non-Collaborative) Lawyers*, 38 Hofstra L. Rev. 699 (2009).

> **REFLECTIVE QUESTIONS** | What is the difference between collaborative law practice and "ordinary" family law practice?

Background to *In re Mabray*

While some lawyers engage in the practice of collaborative law, others prefer a "cooperative law" model. Cooperative lawyers function much like collaborative lawyers except that they are not required to withdraw from representation if court intervention is sought by either party. In the following case an appellate court compares the two processes and the differing obligations of the attorneys.

IN RE MABRAY
Court of Appeals of Texas
2010 WL 3448198 (2010)

HIGLEY, J., On February 12, 2009, the parties and their counsel signed a four page document titled "Cooperative Law Dispute Resolution Agreement" ("the Agreement"). The Agreement states that the parties agreed to "effectively and honestly communicate with each other with the goal of efficiently and economically settling the terms of the dissolution of the marriage."

The Agreement forbids formal discovery unless agreed upon, relying instead on "good faith" informal discovery. Specifically, the Agreement provides:

> No formal discovery procedure will be used unless specifically agreed to in advance. The parties will be required to sign a sworn inventory and appraisement if requested by the other party.
>
> We acknowledge that, by using informal discovery, we are giving up certain investigative procedures and methods that would be available to us in the litigation process. We give up these measures with the specific understanding that the parties will make to each other a complete and accurate disclosure of all assets, income, debts, and other information necessary for us to reach a fair settlement. Participation in this process is based on the assumptions that we have acted in good faith and that the parties have provided complete and accurate information to the best of their ability.

Neither party requested a sworn inventory and appraisement.

COLLABORATIVE AND COOPERATIVE LAW

The case before us concerns the legitimacy of cooperative law. Because cooperative law is untreated in Texas case law, and its more established cousin, collaborative law, only receives minor treatment, a brief exposition of each is warranted.

Collaborative law is codified in the Texas Family Code, which provides, in part:

> (a) On a written agreement of the parties and their attorneys, a dissolution of marriage proceeding may be conducted under collaborative law procedures.
>
> (b) Collaborative law is a procedure in which the parties and their counsel agree in writing to use their best efforts and make a good faith attempt to resolve their dissolution of marriage dispute on an agreed basis without resorting to judicial intervention except to have the court approve the settlement agreement, make the legal pronouncements, and sign the orders required by law to effectuate the agreement of the parties as the court determines appropriate. The parties' counsel may not serve as litigation counsel except to ask the court to approve the settlement agreement.
>
> (c) A collaborative law agreement must include provisions for:
>
> (1) full and candid exchange of information between parties and their attorneys as necessary to make a proper evaluation of the case;
>
> (2) suspending court intervention in the dispute while the parties are using collaborative law procedures;
>
> (3) hiring experts, as jointly agreed, to be used in the procedure

(4) *withdrawal of all counsel involved in the collaborative law procedure if the collaborative law procedure does not result in settlement of the dispute;* and

(5) other provisions as agreed to by the parties consistent with a good faith effort to collaboratively settle the matter. . . .

Tex. Fam. Code Ann. §6.603 (Vernon 2006) (emphasis added).

Collaborative law is a variety of alternative dispute resolution, used most commonly in the context of divorce, that "provides for an advance agreement entered into by the parties and the lawyers in their individual capacities, under which the lawyers commit to terminate their representations in the event the settlement process is unsuccessful and the matter proceeds to litigation." Stephanie Smith and Janet Martinez, *An Analytic Framework for Dispute System Design,* 14 Harv. Negot. L. Rev. 123, 166 (2009). Developed in Minnesota in 1990, collaborative law attempts to foster an amiable rather than an adversarial atmosphere by creating a "four-way" agreement between each party and their attorneys "in which all are expected to participate actively." John Lande and Gregg Herman, *Fitting the Forum to the Family Fuss,* 42 Fam. Ct. Rev. 280, 283 (2004).

The presence of a disqualification agreement is widely held to be the minimum qualification for calling a practice collaborative law. *Id.; see also* Pauline Tesler, *Collaborative Law: Achieving Effective Resolution in Divorce Without Litigation* 5-6 (American Bar Association 2008) ("There is really only one irreducible minimum condition for calling what you do 'collaborative law': you and the counsel for the other party must sign papers disqualifying you from ever appearing in court on behalf of either of these clients against the other."). Specifically, collaborative law attorneys cannot represent their collaborative clients in litigation if the collaborative process fails, but collaborative law clients retain their right to pursue litigation with new counsel. John Lande, *Possibilities for Collaborative Law: Ethics and Practice of Lawyer Disqualification and Process Control in a New Model of Lawyering,* 64 Ohio St. L.J. 1315, 1322 n.20 (2003). . . .

Akin to collaborative law, cooperative law "is a process which incorporates many of the hallmarks of Collaborative Law but does not require the lawyer to enter into a contract with the opposing party providing for the lawyer's disqualification." Smith and Martinez, 14 Harv. Negot. L. Rev. at 166. "Cooperative law includes a written agreement to make full, voluntary disclosure of all financial information, avoid formal discovery procedures, utilize joint rather than unilateral appraisals, and use interest-based negotiation." Lande and Herman, 42 Fam. Ct. Rev. at 284. Put simply, cooperative law agreements mirror collaborative law agreements in spirit and objective, but lack the disqualification clause unique to collaborative law agreements. . . .

Here, we do not weigh the legitimacy of collaborative law; it already has been adopted in Texas. Instead, we examine whether the collaborative law statute excludes the use of cooperative agreements and whether Texas public policy permits cooperative law, a matter of first impression in this court. According to experts, cooperative law is a small but legitimate movement akin to collaborative law. *See, e.g.,* Hon. Tommy Bryan, *Saying "No" to Court?,* 70 Ala. Law. 434, 436 (2009);

Lande and Herman, 42 Fam. Ct. Rev. at 284. Like collaborative law, it possesses both benefits and detriments. For example, the absence of a disqualification agreement offers advantages but also poses disadvantages. Lande and Herman, 42 Fam. Ct. Rev. at 284. Specifically, "parties and lawyers may act reasonably only if they face a credible threat of litigation." *Id.* Additionally, cooperative law clients are less likely to feel mired in the cooperative process because they need not hire and educate new lawyers should litigation ensue. *See* Bryan, 70 Ala. Law. at 436. Conversely, collaborative law clients may feel unduly pressured to complete the collaborative process rather than pursue litigation because of the cost and inconvenience of hiring and educating a new attorney. *Id.* Of course, cooperative law threatens to "taint the negotiation by undermining a problem-solving atmosphere." Lande, 42 Fam. Ct. Rev. at 284.

While we have not encountered cooperative law's codification in any state's code, neither have we encountered its prohibition. In fact, as we have observed, it has been found to be a better system in at least one jurisdiction. *See* Colo. Bar Ass'n Ethics Comm., Formal Op. 115.

Against this general backdrop, we must determine whether the collaborative law statute controls this agreement and, if not, whether a cooperative law agreement is void as a matter of public policy within the State of Texas. We will first consider whether the collaborative law statute controls before determining whether cooperative law agreements violate public policy.

APPLICABILITY OF THE COLLABORATIVE LAW STATUTE

In her first point of error, Mary asserts that Keen must be disqualified because Keen's continued representation of Gary violates the Texas collaborative law statute. Specifically, Mary contends that "[u]sing a slightly different title for the ADR agreement does not avoid the protections of the statute." Gary responds that the collaborative law statute is inapplicable to a cooperative law agreement.

The trial court determined that the Agreement is a cooperative law agreement, not a collaborative law agreement, and therefore need not conform to Texas's collaborative law statute. The Agreement does not suffer from a crisis of identity; it does not reference collaborative law or the collaborative law statute.

Mary contends that "leaving out a required element does not avoid a statute; it violates it." In order for this to be true, however, the statute would either have to mandate its application or forbid the use of cooperative law agreements. We hold that it does neither.

It is clear by its plain language that the collaborative law statute is elective, not mandatory. Subsection (a) of the statute explicitly provides that "a dissolution of marriage proceeding *may* be conducted under collaborative law procedures." Tex. Fam. Code Ann. §6.603(a) (emphasis added). Nothing in the statute mandates its usage. Instead, parties that elect to follow its procedures obtain certain benefits from the trial court. The parties can obtain a judgment on their collaborative law agreement by signing the settlement agreement and including a boldfaced, capitalized, or underlined statement that the agreement is not subject to revocation. *Id.*

§6.603(d). If the parties provide proper notice to the trial court, the court is precluded from setting a hearing or trial in the case, imposing discovery deadlines, requiring compliance with scheduling orders, or dismissing the case while the parties are using the process. *Id.* §6.603(e). Additionally, the statute incorporates the provisions for confidentiality of alternative dispute resolution procedures as provided in Chapter 154 of the Civil Practices and Remedies Code for collaborative law procedures. *Id.* §6.603(h).

In order to obtain these benefits, the parties must enter into an agreement providing for (1) a full and candid exchange of information; (2) suspending court intervention in the dispute while the parties are using collaborative law procedures; (3) hiring any experts jointly; (4) withdrawal of all counsel in the collaborative law procedure if the collaborative law procedure does not result in settlement of the dispute; and (5) other provisions agreed to by the parties that are consistent with a good faith effort to collaboratively settle the suit. *Id.* §6.603(c). The Agreement signed by Mary and Gary does not require the withdrawal of counsel if settlement is not obtained, the fourth requirement for application of the collaborative law statute. Accordingly, by the plain language of the statute, the collaborative law procedures and resulting benefits do not apply to the Agreement.

Additionally, nothing in the statute or in its legislative history leads us to the conclusion that the collaborative law statute forbids parties in Texas from entering into cooperative law agreements. It has been the stated policy of Texas from at least 1987 "to encourage the peaceable resolution of disputes . . . and the early settlement of pending litigation through voluntary settlement procedures." Tex. Civ. Prac. & Rem. Code Ann. §154.002 (Vernon 2005). There is no statute or case law in Texas that explicitly prohibits any specific form of alternative dispute resolution.

The collaborative law statute is one of four alternative dispute resolution processes that the Texas legislature specifically encourages parties in divorce proceedings to utilize. The four processes are arbitration, mediation, collaborative law, and informal settlement conferences. Tex. Fam. Code Ann. §6.601-.604 (Vernon 2006). Nothing in these statutes states that they are the exclusive forms of alternative dispute resolution available to parties to a divorce.

Even if these were the exclusive forms of alternative dispute resolution available to parties to a divorce, the Agreement specifically cites to sections 6.601 and 6.604 of the Family Code. Those are the arbitration and informal settlement conference provisions, respectively. Tex. Fam. Code Ann. §§6.601, .604.

In an informal settlement conference, "[t]he parties to a suit for dissolution of a marriage may agree to one or more informal settlement conferences and may agree that the settlement conferences may be conducted with or without the presence of the parties' attorneys, if any." Tex. Fam. Code Ann. §6.604(a). The legislature did not in any other way limit or constrict the parties' abilities to determine how informal settlement conferences would be conducted. Because this statute is deliberately silent as to the procedures that can be used in informal settlement conferences, we must conclude that the legislature meant to cast a wide net and give the parties wide latitude in deciding how to structure them, including structuring them through a cooperative law agreement.

The dissent argues that the legislature's enacting of the collaborative law statute is proof that they meant to exclude cooperative law agreements. We cannot agree. The legislature knows how to conscribe permissible actions when other related actions would be in violation of public policy. *See, e.g.,* Tex. Bus. & Com. Code Ann. §15.05 (Vernon 2002) (mandating every contract in restraint of trade is unlawful), §15.50 (Vernon Supp. 2009) (providing strict requirements for covenants not to compete to avoid violation of public policy). The legislature has taken no such action here. Instead, it has determined that alternative dispute resolution is beneficial and encourages it. Tex. Civ. Prac. & Rem. Code Ann. §154.002. Given the legislature's broad approval of alternative dispute resolution, we find no reason to determine that it meant to prohibit parties from entering into cooperative law agreements.

DISCUSSION QUESTIONS FOR *IN RE MABRAY*

A. How is acting as a collaborative lawyer different than functioning as a cooperative lawyer in a case?

B. Does the Texas collaborative law statute govern the practice of cooperative law? Why or why not?

C. What are the four alternative dispute resolution processes that the legislature encourages?

D. Are there cases where use of cooperative law is not appropriate? Describe such a case.

E. How do mediation, collaborative law, and cooperative law compare? As a lawyer, how would you counsel clients concerning the processes?

21.10 PARENTING COORDINATION

Sometimes parents who experience a high degree of ongoing conflict seek additional parenting assistance during or after divorce. In such situations, a parenting coordinator may be appointed to function much like a special master. Parenting coordination is defined as

> a child-focused alternative dispute resolution process in which a mental health or legal professional with mediation training and experience assists high conflict parents to implement their parenting plan by facilitating the resolution of their disputes in a timely manner, educating parents about children's needs, and with prior approval

of the parties and/or the court, making decisions within the scope of the court order or appointment contract.

Association of Family and Conciliation Courts Task Force on Parenting Coordination, *Parenting Coordination: Implementation Issues*, 41 Fam. Ct. Rev. 533 (2003).

The role of parenting coordinator is relatively new, and only a handful of states (such as Colorado, Florida, Idaho, Louisiana, North Carolina, Oklahoma, Oregon, and Texas) have statutes defining and regulating the practice. Leta Parks et al., *Defining Parenting Coordination with State Laws*, 49 Fam. Ct. Rev. 629, 630 (2011) (comparing statutory provisions).

In a recent national survey of parenting coordinators researchers found that parenting coordinators are a multidisciplinary group of professionals including psychologists (44 percent), M.S.W. social workers (19 percent), LPC counselors (15 percent), B.A.-level practitioners (11 percent), and attorneys (11 percent). All the parenting coordinators surveyed work only by court order or under mutually signed consent decrees. Most use written parenting coordinator agreements that include the basis and scope of authority, advise that communications are not confidential, and clarify that the parenting coordinator will not provide therapy or give legal advice. Karl Kirkland & Matthew Sullivan, *Parenting Coordination (PC) Practice: A Survey of Experienced Professionals*, 46 Fam. Ct. Rev. 622 (2008).

REFLECTIVE QUESTIONS	What is the primary role of a parenting coordinator? Why do you think so few states have adopted parenting coordination statutes?

Background to *Barnes v. Barnes*

Oklahoma was one of the first states to adopt a parenting coordination statute and in the following case, the Oklahoma Supreme Court considers a constitutional challenge to it.

BARNES
v.
BARNES

Supreme Court of Oklahoma
107 P.3d 560 (2005)

HARGRAVE, J. Mother was given custody of the two-year-old child in April of 1999 in an agreed decree of divorce, and Father was given standard visitation with extended summer visitation. In June of 2000, Father asked the court to further expand his visitation to one-half of the summer and for right of first refusal to care for the child when the mother could not. Father also requested a modification of child support. Testimony at the hearing demonstrated that there had been a deterioration in communication between the parties since they had both been remarried and Father's visitation with the child had become more difficult for the Father to procure. The mental health expert who evaluated the family agreed and recommended the appointment of a parenting coordinator to assist the parents with communication, with their visitation problems, to help them negotiate agreements, and to advise them what was in the best interest of the child. Father stated that he would not object to the appointment of a parenting coordinator. Mother testified that she was willing to follow the recommendations in the psychologist's report, and that she had discussed with her counsel the functions of a parenting coordinator. She testified that she was willing to use a parenting coordinator.

An order modifying the divorce decree was entered and filed on July 9, 2002. The trial court found a substantial, material and permanent change of circumstances and made modifications in visitation and the amount of child support paid. The order modifying appointed a parenting coordinator which is the main basis of the present appeal. An Order Appointing Parenting Coordinator was also entered. In that order, the parenting coordinator was given specific issues which outlined his decision-making power. These issues are as follows:

> Issues Subject to Parent Coordination:
>   A. The following specific issues are hereby submitted to the Parenting Coordinator:
>   (1) To assist the parties in communications,
>   (2) To resolve minor issues,
>   (3) To monitor problems, if any, and transitions, and,
>   (4) To make recommendations regarding shared parenting time.
>   B. The Parenting Coordinator may not make any decisions outside of the scope of the issues submitted above, unless both parties agree.

The trial court, after hearing the testimony of the parties and the psychologist, waived the parties' signature on the Order Appointing Parenting Coordinator. Mother now appeals the appointment of the parenting coordinator as she argues such appointment is unconstitutional. . . .

DUE PROCESS

To determine that there was a violation of due process on substantive grounds we must ascertain that in the instant matter, absent some jeopardy to the health and safety of children, the government intruded into the familial relationship by requiring the Mother to participate with a parental coordinator to assist in communications and aid the court in the furtherance of post-divorce visitation. However, in determining whether the order or statute constituted a substantive due process violation, a balance must be struck between the right protected and the demands of society. . . .

The mother in the instant matter seems to argue that there are no limitations on the parenting coordinator. She argues that the coordinator somehow micromanages the family thus taking away her rights as custodial parent to make decisions. However, the order appointing the coordinator in the instant matter is limited to matters that aid in the communication of the parties and the enforcement of the court's order of custody, visitation or guardianship.

The Statute that grants the power to Oklahoma Courts to appoint Parenting Coordinators puts strict guidelines on their use. 43 O.S. Supp. 2003 §120.3 provides:

A. In any action for dissolution of marriage, legal separation, paternity, or guardianship where minor children are involved, the court may, upon its own motion, or by motion or agreement of the parties, appoint a parenting coordinator to assist the parties in resolving issues and decide disputed issues pursuant to the provisions of the Parenting Coordinator Act related to parenting or other family issues in the case except as provided in subsection B of this section, and subsection A of Section 120.5 of this title.

B. The court shall not appoint a parenting coordinator if any party objects, unless:

1. The court makes specific findings that the case is a high-conflict case; and

2. The court makes specific findings that the appointment of a parenting coordinator is in the best interest of any minor child in the case.

C.

1. The authority of a parenting coordinator shall be specified in the order appointing the parenting coordinator and limited to matters that will aid the parties in:

a. identifying disputed issues,

b. reducing misunderstandings,

c. clarifying priorities,

d. exploring possibilities for compromise,

e. developing methods of collaboration in parenting, and

f. complying with the court's order of custody, visitation, or guardianship.

2. The appointment of a parenting coordinator shall not divest the court of its exclusive jurisdiction to determine fundamental issues of custody, visitation, and support, and the authority to exercise management and control of the case.

3. The parenting coordinator shall not make any modification to any order, judgment or decree; however, the parenting coordinator may allow the parties to make minor temporary departures from a parenting plan if authorized by the court to do so. The appointment order should specify those matters which the parenting coordinator is authorized to determine. The order shall specify which determinations will be immediately effective and which will require an opportunity for court review prior to taking effect.

D. The parties may limit the decision-making authority of the parenting coordinator to specific issues or areas if the parenting coordinator is being appointed pursuant to agreement of the parties.

E. Meetings between the parenting coordinator and the parties need not follow any specific procedures and the meetings may be informal. All communication between the parties and the parenting coordinator shall not be confidential.

F. Nothing in the Parenting Coordinator Act shall abrogate the custodial or noncustodial parent's rights or any court-ordered visitation given to grandparents or other persons except as specifically addressed in the order appointing the parenting coordinator.

G.

1. Except as otherwise provided by this subsection, the court shall reserve the right to remove the parenting coordinator in its own discretion.

2. The court may remove the parenting coordinator upon the request and agreement of both parties. Upon the motion of either party and good cause shown, the court may remove the parenting coordinator.

Mother does not outline how the custodial parent's rights have been abrogated by the issues to be decided. She has not shown that the order in the instant case or the statute itself gives the parenting coordinator authority to hear and decide more than issues limited to matters that aid in the communication of the parties and the enforcement of the court's order. The extent to which a parent may be inconvenienced by cooperating with a parenting coordinator is subordinate to the need to protect the child's welfare. We find that the parenting coordinator act is not unconstitutional on procedural or substantive due process grounds. We also find that the actions of the trial court did not wrongfully assign the rights of the custodial parent to third parties.

 **DISCUSSION QUESTIONS** FOR *BARNES v. BARNES*

A. What is the role of the parenting coordinator? What decisions can the parenting coordinator make or not make?

B. What was the mother's objection to the appointment of a parenting coordinator?

C. Can a parenting coordinator be appointed even though one or both of the parties oppose the appointment? *But see Bower v. Bournay-Bower*, 15 N.E.3d 745 (Mass. 2014) (addressing consent requirement in Massachusetts).

D. Early research shows that use of parenting coordination may reduce post-divorce relitigation:

> Results of this study seem to indicate that litigating divorced/separated couples do, in fact, file fewer motions in the domestic relations court when utilizing the services of a PC. Over 60% of couples filed fewer total motions in the first year parenting coordination was court ordered, including 75% fewer child-related motions and 40% non-child-related motions. These findings are substantial in terms of the time saved

by all involved in the court system, including the judges, lawyers, support staff, and the parents themselves.

Wilma Henry et al., *Parenting Coordination and Court Relitigation: A Case Study*, 47 Fam. Ct. Rev. 682, 690 (2011). Why do you think return visits to court may be decreased?

E. Do you think more states should adopt the role of parenting coordinator? Why or why not?

F. Commentators suggest that states drafting parenting coordination (PC) statutes consider the following issues:

1. Whether parents must agree to the order or the judge can impose the service on parents;
2. Whether the goals of the intervention are treatment, educational, legal problem solving, or forensic in nature;
3. Whether or under what circumstances the PC's records and testimony of private sessions with parents/children can be used in the litigation process;
4. Whether the PC can be given judicial authority to impose decisions on parents; and
5. What training requirements are necessary for competent and ethical practice of PC.

Leta Parks et al., *Defining Parenting Coordination with State Laws*, 42 Fam. Ct. Rev. 629, 635 (2011). Imagine that you are in the role of advising legislators on adopting a parenting coordinator statute. What would you recommend on each of these questions and why?

G. To whom should parenting coordinators be accountable? *See Vangelder v. Johnson*, 827 N.W.2d 430 (Minn. App. 2013) (parenting coordinator had quasi-judicial immunity).

21.11 ARBITRATION

In contrast to the role of the mediator, who does not make decisions for the parties, an arbitrator is a sort of "private judge" who may be empowered to make binding decisions on some or all, of the issues.

> **REFLECTIVE QUESTIONS**   Can you think of a situation where you would favor resolving a family law issue through arbitration, as opposed to participation in mediation or going to trial?

Background to *Johnson v. Johnson*

States differ with respect to whether child custody and parenting time decisions may be submitted to arbitration. For example, in *Kelm v. Kelm*, 749 N.E.2d 299 (2001), the Supreme Court of Ohio disapproved arbitration of custody and parenting time issues, as opposed to property and support decisions, stating: "[W]e hold that in a domestic relations case, matters of child custody and parental visitation are not subject to arbitration. The authority to resolve disputes over custody and visitation rests exclusively with the courts. Any agreement to the contrary is void and unenforceable." Similarly in *Toiberman v. Tisera*, 998 So. 2d 4 (Fla. App. 2008), the appellate court enforced a statutory prohibition of arbitration of child custody, parenting time, and child support.

In contrast to the foregoing cases, in the following case, the Supreme Court of New Jersey reaches a different conclusion.

JOHNSON
v.
JOHNSON

Supreme Court of New Jersey
9 A.3d 1003 (2010)

LONG, J. The case arose as follows: David Johnson and Molly V.G.B. Johnson were married on October 26, 1994, and divorced on August 16, 2005. Two children were born during the marriage: Amelia, on February 9, 2001, and Elsie, on January 30, 2003. In May 2005, the couple separated; Ms. Johnson elected to move out of the marital home and ceded residential custody of the children to Mr. Johnson. From May 2005 until November 2005, Ms. Johnson spent parenting time at the marital residence while she lived in an apartment with roommates. When she purchased her current home, the children began to spend time with her there.

The final judgment of divorce incorporated a May 24, 2005, property settlement agreement, which provided that the parties would share joint legal custody of the children and that Mr. Johnson would continue as the residential custodial parent. According to the informal parenting schedule the parties agreed on, Mr. Johnson had the children from Sunday evening to Tuesday evening (5:30 P.M.); Wednesday evening to after school Thursday; and alternate weekends from Friday evening until Sunday evening. Ms. Johnson had the children from Tuesday evening until Wednesday evening (5:30 P.M.); Thursday after school until Friday evening (5:30 P.M.); and alternate weekends from Friday evening until Sunday evening. Holidays were alternated and each party had one week of vacation with the children per year.

Following the divorce, the parties encountered difficulties with the parenting schedule and thereafter consented to resolving those issues in arbitration. Pursuant to a consent order, the parties chose to be governed by the APDRA. Their agreement was extremely thorough and explained what the parties viewed as the issue and how they intended the APDRA to operate. The agreement began by identifying the issue:

> 1A] The parties are the parents of AMELIA JOHNSON, age six, and ELSIE JOHNSON age four. For several years [they] have experienced on-going difficulties in resolving differing parenting approaches and Parenting Time Schedules that will advance their children's best interests.

The agreement went on to detail the parties' expectations regarding how the case was to be conducted:

> 1B] To resolve parenting differences and Parenting Time scheduling issue[s] *in futuro*, the parties have agreed to utilize the Arbitration services of MARK WHITE, Ph.D. It is *not* the intent of the parties and recognized and acknowledged that Dr. WHITE shall not provide any therapeutic or other psychological services in this case; as serving in this dual role would place Dr. WHITE in a conflict situation. Rather it is envisaged that Dr. WHITE shall initially meet with the parties and counsel; and thereafter meet with both parties on one or more occasions as he shall deem necessary in his sole discretion. Dr. WHITE shall receive position papers of the parties which may be prepared with the assistance of and prepared by their attorneys. The position papers may include examples of the difficulties the parties have faced, citing examples, findings of facts that are requested to be made by Dr. WHITE, as well as [the] law of the State of New Jersey applicable to such facts. Dr. WHITE will observe the children in the presence of the parents. With this input and without the necessity of taking formal testimony of the parties in the presence of their attorneys, it is anticipated that Dr. WHITE will have sufficient information to craft a decision intend[ed] to resolve the parenting issues and scheduling issues that currently [exist]. It is not envisaged that Dr. WHITE will require formal Arbitration in the presence of both parties and counsel to make findings of fact in this case; although he shall have the power and authority to do so, in his sound discretion. It is required that Dr. WHITE create a scheduling calendar, with the intent of limiting future parenting schedule controversy to a minimum. The fact that testimony of the parties in each other's presence and counsel's presence was not adduced by the Arbitrator/Umpire shall not constitute a good cause grounds for reversing the Arbitration Award.

In addition, the agreement vested the arbitrator with the duty to make findings of relevant material facts and legal determinations; provided that the arbitrator would make an award on all submitted issues in accordance with applicable principles of New Jersey substantive law, as required by N.J.S.A. 2A:23A-12(e); afforded a right to file a motion for reconsideration of the award and for modification, pursuant to N.J.S.A. 2A:23A-12(d); limited the parties' right to appeal to the issue of whether the arbitrator properly applied the law to the factual findings and issues presented for resolution; and specified that there would be no transcript of proceedings and that the detailed findings of the arbitrator would constitute the record, as supplemented by the written certified statements submitted by the parties prior to arbitration. The agreement was explicit that testimony outside a party's or counsel's presence would not constitute good cause grounds for reversing any award. Finally, the parties waived their rights to a trial on the merits and preserved the right to appeal the award within the constraints of the APDRA.

As anticipated by the agreement, over the course of several months the arbitrator conducted various interviews, including those with Mr. Johnson (multiple), his new wife, Sara Johnson, Ms. Johnson (multiple), Amelia and Elsie, a psychologist (Dr. Sandra Sessa), and a clinical social worker (Ms. Cheryl Daniel) who had previously counseled the parties. In addition, he observed the children in both home settings and reviewed their school records.

In April 2008, the arbitrator issued his award. At the outset, he detailed the parties' proposals, which were not vastly different from what was in effect at the time:

Proposal of Mr. Johnson
The children would be at the home of Mr. Johnson Sunday night through Friday afternoon, and every other weekend. Alternation of parenting time during the two extended winter and spring breaks from school. Alternation of holidays. One week vacation with each parent. Sunday evening overnights with Ms. Johnson before all Monday holidays when the children are off from school. Children to be returned by noon Monday. Dinner with Ms. Johnson one night during the week, to be scheduled "based upon the best arrangement factoring everyone's schedule."

Proposal of Ms. Johnson
The weekend the children are with Ms. Johnson should be extended to include Sunday overnights, and then drop off at schools Monday mornings. Scheduling of activities for the children only upon mutual consent of both parents. Pick up of the children from schools on Thursdays.

The arbitrator then recounted the substance of every interview and observation he undertook, including a particularized recitation of the parties' claims about their different approaches to parenting and the problems with scheduling transitions. Mr. Johnson, who remains angry at his former wife over the divorce, contended that she is unreliable and frequently late picking up the children; that she tends to drop the children off without remembering to bring their things; that the children are not dressed and ready when he picks them up or when their mother drops them off; that they are not ready for school on mornings after they stay with their mother; that they eat snacks at her house before dinner at his house; that Ms. Johnson creates emotionally dramatic transfers; that she is routinely five to ten minutes late; that she is more than ten minutes late almost twenty percent of the time; and that she has issues with boundaries (for example, she allows the girls to sleep with her) that cause problems in his home. The interview with Mr. Johnson's new wife, Sara Johnson, supported Mr. Johnson's claims regarding Ms. Johnson's unreliability.

Ms. Johnson countered that her former husband is rigid; has excessive control over the children's schedules; arranges activities during her parenting time; and that he has otherwise decreased the amount of time the children spend with her. She further claimed that he over schedules the children (e.g., dance, violin, swimming, T-ball, soccer), and that there is poor communication between the parties in that

Mr. Johnson fails to convey essential information to her and verbally attacks her when the subject of increased parenting time comes up.

Ms. Johnson also contended that she had made the children late only a few times in two years; that the children benefit from the less structured, more creative environment at her home; that Mr. Johnson does not give her open phone access to the children; and that he does not consult her on scheduled activities. Following that interview, Ms. Johnson sent the arbitrator a long letter reiterating all of her concerns, in particular, that her former husband's actions have the effect of "marginalizing" her. The arbitrator recounted the contents of the letter in his decision.

The home visits, according to the arbitrator, were uneventful — with both homes, though very different, fully appropriate for the girls. The arbitrator perceived the girls as well-adjusted, but affected by the parenting conflicts and the amount of moving around required.

The arbitrator reported Dr. Sessa's conclusion that the parties are opposite in nature, Ms. Johnson — "artsy, come-a-day, go-a-day" — and Mr. Johnson — "structured, highly organized, logical and linear." Yet, the psychologist expressed that she had no concern about either party's parenting abilities, though Ms. Johnson's organization could be improved upon. The psychologist did note significant animosity between the parties.

The arbitrator also detailed the results of his consultation with Ms. Daniel who had seen the parties several times in 2006. Like the psychologist, she noted the obvious stylistic differences between the parties and Mr. Johnson's continuing emotional response to the divorce. Despite Mr. Johnson's efforts to the contrary, she likewise found no basis to question Ms. Johnson's parental capacity. The arbitrator recapitulated the children's scholastic records from the 2007-2008 school year, which revealed that Amelia was tardy on six days, all of which followed overnights with her mother.

The arbitrator concluded that both parties are decent, well-intentioned, non-pathological parents and that the children are positively developing in their care. He proceeded to evaluate the case in terms of how the parties' behavior imposed on their daughters' experiences. He noted that it was his "fervent hope" that his involvement would "result in the prevention of escalation of the family system factors that could elevate the probability of [the girls] developing psychological symptoms later in their childhoods."

To accomplish that goal, the arbitrator stated that Ms. Johnson needed to accept responsibility for leaving the marriage and for her lackadaisical approach, evidenced by her tardiness and inefficiency which prevented a "more robust co-parenting alliance," and that Mr. Johnson needed to confront and resolve his anger towards Ms. Johnson over the divorce. In addition, the arbitrator reasoned that the children were too young to experience so many transitions, particularly in light of the "intrinsic tension" between their parents and the "dissimilarity of the home cultures." Accordingly, he set forth a decision "[i]n the hope that both parties will accept [the provisions] in the child-protective spirit in which they are offered."

With a view toward carrying out what the parties had commissioned him to do — "create a scheduling calendar, with the intent of limiting future parenting schedule controversy to a minimum," the arbitrator increased the amount of uninterrupted weekly time the children spent with Mr. Johnson, but extended the weekend and holiday time spent with Ms. Johnson. Specifically, the arbitrator expanded Ms. Johnson's weekends with the children to Sunday overnights and limited her weekday overnights to Wednesdays only. He compensated for the time that the girls lost with their mother by providing her with a majority of three-day, four-overnight weekends and additional time during school vacations.

In addition, he referred Ms. Johnson to a neuropsychologist for an evaluation for Attention Deficit Hyperactivity Disorder based upon her "time management and attentional difficulties." He also referred Mr. Johnson to counseling for his unresolved emotions related to the divorce. Specifically addressing Ms. Johnson's concern that the children were overly programmed, the arbitrator limited them to one scheduled activity in a given season.

The award left open Ms. Johnson's request for expanded time with the children to be reconsidered after she had undergone her evaluation and demonstrated that Amelia could attend school for three consecutive months without receiving a tardy notice. The decision also permitted future meetings between the arbitrator and the parties starting around October 1, 2008, to consider further modifications.

Ms. Johnson filed a motion for reconsideration of the entire decision or clarification of the extent of her vacation time custody. The gravamen of the motion was that she did not "feel as though [her] viewpoints and concerns were considered. . . ." In response, the arbitrator prepared an eleven-point decision in which he reaffirmed his conclusion that both parents are well-intentioned and deeply invested in their children's welfare. He noted that he considered the extent and severity of both parties' accusations in a neutral fashion, and recounted Ms. Johnson's basic allegation that Mr. Johnson is overly controlling and Mr. Johnson's counter-allegation that Ms. Johnson is unreliable. He pointed to his recommendation that Mr. Johnson seek psychotherapy and that Ms. Johnson submit to a neuropsychological evaluation because of the empirical data that Amelia's six tardies in first grade occurred after nights she spent with her mother.

The arbitrator explained that changes in the schedule were based on the children's needs rather than any conclusion about Ms. Johnson's ability to parent. It was his explicit intention "to prevent the post-divorce version of the Johnsons' inability to collaboratively solve problems from metastasizing to a level that will represent a pathogenic risk to their beautiful daughters." The arbitrator stated that divorce and remarriage "necessitates the need to more clearly establish boundaries between Mom's house and Dad's house."

As an addendum to the decision, the arbitrator delayed implementation of the new schedule from the original decision because "stresses attendant to changing Amelia's schedule so late in the school year" outweighed the benefits of implementation. The arbitrator remained open to meeting with the parents prior to the start of the next school year to rebalance the children's time at each home and determine the advisability of a parent coordinator. He observed that the "ultimate goal . . . was to foster good faith in their post-divorce parenting alliance. Otherwise, a more adversarial and conflict-enhancing option would have been selected for resolution of their custody/visitation issues." He noted that such a climate of cooperation would be of immeasurable value to the girls' psychological development.

In July 2008, Ms. Johnson sought the arbitrator's removal based on the Appellate Division's decision in *Fawzy v. Fawzy*, 400 N.J. Super. 567, 948 A.2d 709 (App. Div. 2008), which had held that parties cannot agree to binding arbitration in a custody matter. In response, Mr. Johnson filed a motion to confirm the arbitrator's decision. Ms. Johnson filed a cross-motion requesting modification of the parenting time schedule or a plenary hearing to determine custody and parenting time.

Judge Robert A. Coogan presided over the proceedings in the Family Division. After a hearing, he confirmed the arbitrator's award. In ruling, the judge examined the award in terms of the children's interests and characterized both parties as "good parents." Because he determined that the girls "have a difficult time transitioning from one house to another," the judge faulted the prior custody schedule with its frequent shuttling back and forth several times during the week and concluded that it was reasonable for the arbitrator to extend Ms. Johnson's weekends and expand Mr. Johnson's weekday overnights. Further, he noted that the arbitrator was even-handed in recommending that Ms. Johnson see a neuropsychologist specializing in Attention Deficit Hyperactivity Disorder and that Mr. Johnson attend counseling to address his unresolved anger. Finally, the judge concluded that there was a sufficient record made by the arbitrator to permit judicial review. Therefore, he denied Ms. Johnson's parenting schedule proposal and both parties' counsel fee requests and confirmed the arbitrator's award.

Ms. Johnson appealed. Meanwhile, we issued our opinion in *Fawzy*. Based on *Fawzy*, the appellate panel reversed the trial court decision and remanded the case for a plenary hearing because the procedural requirements set forth in *Fawzy* were not satisfied. In particular, because there was no verbatim record of testimony, the panel concluded that the trial court had no basis on which to evaluate the threat of harm to the children or confirm the award. The panel determined that this case was not distinguishable from *Fawzy*, which involved the Arbitration Act, and not the APDRA, because the acts "are similar" and "neither is immune to public policy concerns." We granted Mr. Johnson's petition for certification.

II

The parties differ essentially over the applicability of *Fawzy* to this APDRA arbitration; over whether, if applicable, *Fawzy* requires reversal on the basis of the absence of a verbatim transcript; and over whether Ms. Johnson's claims of harm were sufficient to trigger substantive judicial review.

We begin with a recap of *Fawzy*. On the day that their divorce trial was to occur, the Fawzys agreed to binding arbitration and selected the recently appointed guardian *ad litem* to serve as the arbitrator on all issues. In the parties' interim arbitration order, they agreed to be governed by the Arbitration Act.

Between the time that the arbitration proceedings began and the taking of testimony, Mr. Fawzy filed an order to show cause seeking to restrain the arbitrator from deciding any parenting-time or custody issues on the grounds that our prior decision in *Faherty v. Faherty*, [477] A.2d 1257 (1984), precluded arbitration of such issues. He further claimed that he had been rushed into agreeing to arbitrate, and had done so because he believed he would be viewed as uncooperative otherwise. The judge denied the application. Thereafter, the arbitrator awarded the parties joint legal custody and designated Mrs. Fawzy as the primary residential parent. Mr. Fawzy filed a second order to show cause, arguing that he did not understand the rights he was waiving when he agreed to arbitrate. The trial judge denied that application and confirmed the award.

Mr. Fawzy appealed, arguing that permitting parties to submit custody issues to binding arbitration deprives the court of exercising its *parens patriae* jurisdiction to protect children's best interests. The Appellate Division agreed, reversed the trial court's ruling, and remanded the case for a plenary hearing on the custody and parenting-time issues. On certification, we affirmed that judgment, although on different grounds.

In *Fawzy* we recognized the benefits of arbitration in the family law setting and, in particular, the potential to "minimize the harmful effects of divorce litigation on both children and parents." We further noted the wide-ranging scholarly support for such arbitration that had developed since the issue was left open in *Faherty. Id.* at 471-472, 973 A.2d 347.

In ruling, we reaffirmed the constitutional right to parental autonomy in child-rearing:

> Deference to parental autonomy means that the State does not second-guess parental decision making or interfere with the shared opinion of parents regarding how a child should be raised. Nor does it impose its own notion of a child's best interests on a family. Rather, the State permits to stand unchallenged parental judgments that it might not have made or that could be characterized as unwise. That is because parental autonomy includes the "freedom to decide wrongly."

[*Id.* at 473-474, 973 A.2d 347.]

At the same time, we recognized that "[t]he right of parents to the care and custody of their children is not absolute," *id.* at 474, 973 A.2d 347 (quoting *V.C. v. M.J.B.*, [748] A.2d 539 (2000)), and that "the state has an obligation, under the *parens patriae* doctrine, to intervene where it is necessary to prevent harm to a child." As we said in *Moriarty v. Bradt*, [827] A.2d 203 (2003), "interference with parental autonomy will be tolerated only to avoid harm to the health or welfare of a child." *Id.* at 115, 827 A.2d 203. Indeed, that harm standard "is a constitutional necessity because a parent's right to family privacy and autonomy are at issue." In short, potential harm to a child is the constitutional imperative that allows the State to intervene into the otherwise private and protected realm of parent-child relations. With that as a backdrop, we concluded that

> the bundle of rights that the notion of parental autonomy sweeps in includes the right to decide how issues of custody and parenting time will be resolved. Indeed, we have no hesitation in concluding that, just as parents "choose" to decide issues of custody and parenting time among themselves without court intervention, they may opt to sidestep the judicial process and submit their dispute to an arbitrator whom they have chosen.

[*Fawzy, supra*, 199 N.J. at 477, 973 A.2d 347.]

We then turned to the standard of review of a child custody arbitration award and concluded that

> where no harm to the child is threatened, there is no justification for the infringement on the parents' choice to be bound by the arbitrator's decision. In the absence of a claim of harm, the parties are limited to the remedies provided in the Arbitration Act. On the contrary, where harm is claimed and a prima facie case advanced, the court must determine the harm issue. If no finding of harm ensues, the award will only be subject to review under the Arbitration Act standard. If there is a finding of harm, the presumption in favor of the parents' choice of arbitration will be overcome and it will fall to the court to decide what is in the child's best interests.

[*Id.* at 478-479, 973 A.2d 347 (citation omitted).]

However, we expressed concern in *Fawzy* over the court's ability to intervene, where necessary, to prevent harm to the child,

> in light of the fact that the Arbitration Act does not require a full record to be kept of arbitration proceedings. Nor does it compel the recordation of testimony or a statement by the arbitrator of his findings and conclusions beyond the issuance of an award, N.J.S.A. 2A:23B-19(a), although parties are free to agree upon other procedures, *see* N.J.S.A. 2A:23B-4.

[*Id.* at 480, 973 A.2d 347.]

Because of that, and because we determined that an empty record, like the one before us in *Fawzy*, could provide no basis for a harm review, we said:

> We therefore direct that when parties in a dissolution proceeding agree to arbitrate their dispute, the general rules governing the conduct of arbitration shall apply, N.J.S.A. 2A:23B-1 to -32. However, in respect of child-custody and parenting-time issues only, a record of all documentary evidence shall be kept; all testimony shall be recorded verbatim; and the arbitrator shall state in writing or otherwise record his or her findings of fact and conclusions of law with a focus on the best-interests standard. It is only upon such a record that an evaluation of the threat of harm can take place without an entirely new trial. Any arbitration award regarding child-custody and parenting-time issues that results from procedures other than those that we have mandated will be subject to vacation upon motion.

[*Id.* at 480-481, 973 A.2d 347.]

We then set forth the minimum elements of an agreement to arbitrate a child custody dispute, including that it

> must be in writing or recorded in accordance with the requirements of N.J.S.A. 2A:23B-1. In addition, it must state in clear and unmistakable language: (1) that the parties understand their entitlement to a judicial adjudication of their dispute and are willing to waive that right; (2) that the parties are aware of the limited circumstances under which a challenge to the arbitration award may be advanced and agree to those limitations; (3) that the parties have had sufficient time to consider the implications of their decision to

arbitrate; and (4) that the parties have entered into the arbitration agreement freely and voluntarily, after due consideration of the consequences of doing so.

[*Id.* at 482, 973 A.2d 347.]

Because the record in *Fawzy* was inadequate to assure that the parties fully understood the consequences of removing their custody dispute from the judicial arena into binding arbitration, we affirmed the decision of the appellate panel that had reversed the arbitration award and remanded for a new trial.

As a matter of practice, *Fawzy* plays out this way: When a child custody or parenting time arbitration award issues, one party will ordinarily move for confirmation. If there is no challenge, the award will be confirmed. If there is a challenge that does not implicate harm to the child, the award is subject to review under the limited standards in the relevant arbitration statute or as agreed by the parties. If a party advances the claim that the arbitration award will harm the child, the trial judge must determine whether a prima facie case has been established. In other words, is there evidence which if not controverted, would prove harm? If that question is answered in the negative, for example, where a claim of harm is insubstantial or frivolous (e.g., not enough summer vacation), the only review available will be that provided in the relevant arbitration act or as otherwise agreed. If, on the other hand, the claim is one that, if proved, would implicate harm to the child, the judge must determine if the arbitration record is an adequate basis for review. If it is, the judge will evaluate the harm claim and, if there is a finding of harm, the parents' choice of arbitration will be overcome and it will fall to the judge to decide what is in the children's best interests. If the arbitration record is insufficient, the judge will be required to conduct a plenary hearing. That is the backdrop for our inquiry. . . .

IV

We turn, finally, to Mr. Johnson's contention that Ms. Johnson's claim of harm was insufficient to tee up the issue of entitlement to judicial review. We agree. For that conclusion, we hearken back to our directive in *Fawzy*:

> Mere disagreement with the arbitrator's decision obviously will not satisfy the harm standard. The threat of harm is a significantly higher burden than a best-interests analysis. Although each case is unique and fact intensive, by way of example, in a case of two fit parents, a party's challenge to an arbitrator's custody award because she would be "better" is not a claim of harm. Nor will the contention that a particular parenting-time schedule did not include enough summer vacation time be sufficient to pass muster. To the contrary, a party's claim that the arbitrator granted custody to a parent with serious substance abuse issues or a debilitating mental illness could raise the specter of harm. Obviously, evidential support establishing a prima facie case of harm will be required in order to trigger a hearing. Where the hearing yields a finding of harm, the court must set aside the arbitration award and decide the case anew, using the best-interests test.

[*Fawzy, supra*, 199 N.J. at 479, 973 A.2d 347.]

Here, neither party raised any real claim of unfitness. They agreed that there was "a lot of love in both homes and consistency between the homes in parenting, relative to a sense of respect, the importance of getting work done and manners." The issue was always parenting style, not capacity, and the arbitrator's commission was to create a schedule that would minimize conflicts and problems in the face of such different parenting styles. His new schedule was nothing more than a tweaking of an agreed-upon parenting time schedule to minimize disruption for the children. Simply put, that does not begin to approach a showing of harm sufficient to warrant judicial inquiry beyond what is provided in the APDRA.

V

One final note. Our holding that Ms. Johnson's contentions fell short of triggering a substantive judicial review of the arbitration award is without prejudice to her pursuing an application for expanded parenting time as anticipated in the arbitrator's award. Much has transpired since the award issued in April 2008. The girls are growing up and how the parties have fared with the parenting time schedule during the interim period should be factored into any revised award. Either party may request such reconsideration.

VI

For the foregoing reasons, the judgment of the Appellate Division is reversed and the order of the trial judge confirming the arbitration award is reinstated.

 **FOR** *JOHNSON v. JOHNSON*

A. Arbitration and mediation are both alternative dispute resolution methods. How are they different from each other? How might couples decide which might be more helpful to them?

B. Why do you think some courts allow arbitration of property and support issues but not child custody and parenting time questions?

C. What is the role of parental autonomy and best interests of the child in the *Johnson* decision?

D. Should disputes be submitted to arbitration if mediation fails? Why or why not? If this occurs, should the mediator be permitted to act as the arbitrator? Why or why not?

General Principles

1. Mediation is a structured problem-solving process in which couples identify issues, gather facts and information about the issues, establish standards of fairness, brainstorm about possible solutions, analyze the repercussions of various choices, and make decisions for the future.

2. A mediator guides and structures the mediation process by setting the agenda, establishing and enforcing ground rules, focusing discussion on the future, balancing the relative power of participants, and turning points of contention into problems to be solved. The mediator models conflict resolution skills that the couple can later use on their own.

3. Mediation has been particularly controversial in cases involving intimate partner violence because of concerns about safety, coercion, and retribution linked to the dynamics of some violent relationships. Lawyers and mediators should screen for intimate partner violence and counsel clients regarding potential participation in mediation and other alternative dispute resolution processes. If mediation or other ADR processes are used in a case involving intimate partner violence, special precautions, ground rules, and procedures should be implemented.

4. Collaborative lawyers use interest-based problem-solving techniques to assist the parties in settling a case. If court intervention is sought by either party, the collaborative lawyers withdraw from the case and litigation counsel is substituted.

5. Parenting coordination is "a child-focused alternative dispute resolution process in which a mental health or legal professional with mediation training and experience assists high conflict parents to implement their parenting plan by facilitating the resolution of their disputes in a timely manner, educating parents about children's needs, and with prior approval of the parties and/or the court, making decisions within the scope of the court order or appointment contract." Association of Family and Conciliation Courts Task Force on Parenting Coordination, *Parenting Coordination: Implementation Issues*, 41 Fam. Ct. Rev. 533 (2003).

6. An arbitrator makes decisions in a manner similar to that of a judge but states vary concerning whether child custody and parenting time disputes may be submitted to arbitration.

Chapter Problems

1. Does mediation differ significantly from collaborative law? How are the two processes similar and how are they different?

2. How does parenting coordination compare to mediation and arbitration?

3. An increasing number of people seeking divorces are not represented by attorneys, usually because of the expense involved in hiring an attorney. Sometimes one spouse will be represented and the other will not be represented. Is mediation a more or less desirable alternative for pro se litigants?

4. Assume that you practice family law and also work as a family mediator. After mediation has been completed, can you represent either or both parties to have the divorce decree finalized in court? Could you represent one of the parties in an unrelated matter? *See* 2002 Model Rules of Professional Conduct, Rules 1.12 and 2.4.

Preparation for Practice

1. What is required in your state to become a mediator?

2. There is little uniformity among the states about the licensing and regulation of mediators. Should mediators be required to attain a certain educational level? Should they be required to be attorneys? Should a period of supervised practice be required?

3. If a client of yours wants to mediate, how would you go about finding a skilled mediator?

4. What factors should a lawyer and client discuss when deciding whether an alternative dispute resolution process is appropriate?

5. Assume that you are a lawyer representing a divorce client whose case will be mediated. What is your role in the mediation? How will you prepare your client for the mediation sessions?

6. Review the provisions of the state parenting coordination statutes compared in Leta Parks et al., *Defining Parenting Coordination with State Laws*, 42 Fam. Ct. Rev. 629 (2011). Which state scheme do you prefer? Why?

7. Assume that you have been asked to draft a parenting coordination agreement. What topics should be covered? What terms would you include? *See* Karl Kirkland & Matthew Sullivan, *Parenting Coordination (PC) Practice: A Survey of Experienced Professionals*, 46 Fam. Ct. Rev. 622 (2008).

8. Review the Model Family Law Arbitration Act published by the American Academy of Matrimonial Lawyers located at http://www.aaml.org/library/publications/21215/model-family-law-arbitration-act. What does it provide?

Should states adopt acts such as this? Why or why not? *See* Lynn P. Burleson, *Family Law Arbitration: Third Party Alternative Dispute Resolution*, 30 Campbell L. Rev. 297 (2008) (discussing state matrimonial arbitration statutes).

9. The Uniform Law Commission has drafted a Family Arbitration Act. Check on the content and status of the Act at http://www.uniformlaws.org/Committee.aspx?title=Family%20Law%20Arbitration (last visited August 1, 2015).

Chapter 22

Professional Responsibility

This chapter explores issues of professional responsibility that particularly pertain to family lawyers. Family lawyers recognize that they confront special challenges because of the emotional nature of domestic relations work. *See* Sandra Day O'Connor, *Remarks: The Supreme Court and the Family*, 3 U. Pa. J. Const. L. 573, 573, 576 (2001). In fact, parties ending a relationship may view separation or divorce as one of the most difficult experiences of their lives. They may never have consulted with a lawyer or appeared in a courtroom before. They may feel bitterness, anger, disillusionment, fear, and distrust as they deal with potentially overwhelming situations and financial costs. The consequences of a family breakup may extend beyond the couple involved to other family members, friends, and business associates. As a result, the actions of a family lawyer take on special significance and may have a lasting impact on the futures of the parties involved.

Some lawyers believe that attorneys engaged in family practice are at a higher risk for disciplinary and malpractice actions than lawyers practicing in other areas of the law. *See* Barbara Glesner Fines & Cathy Madsen, Symposium: Ethics of Family Representation, *Caring Too Little, Caring Too Much: Competence and the Family Law Attorney*, 75 UMKC L. Rev. 965, 971 (Summer 2007). Practitioners attribute the number of complaints to clients' unrealistic expectations and to the emotional turmoil that clients often experience at the time of divorce. Nevertheless, all too often, family law clients report that their attorneys do not communicate effectively with them, fail to include them in decision making, and do not pay sufficient attention to their cases. *See* Andrew Schepard, *The Evolving Judicial Role in Child Custody Disputes: From Fault Finder to Conflict Manager to Differential Case Management*, 22 U. Ark. Little Rock L. Rev. 395, 410 (2000); Susan Daicoff,

Lawyer Know Thyself: A Review of Empirical Research on Attorney Attributes Bearing on Professionalism, 46 Am. U. L. Rev. 1337 (1997); Marsha Kline Pruett & Tamara D. Jackson, *The Lawyer's Role During the Divorce Process: Perceptions of Parents, Their Young Children, and Their Attorneys*, 33 Fam. L.Q. 283, 297 (1999).

While studying this topic you may want to consider questions such as the following: How often should family lawyers communicate with clients? Can contingent fee arrangements be used in divorce actions? How do conflicts of interest typically arise? Can a family attorney represent both spouses in a divorce? Can a family law attorney represent a person with whom he or she is having a sexual relationship? Can an attorney ethically serve as a mediator or collaborative lawyer? How should a family lawyer deal with unrepresented parties?

> **REFLECTIVE QUESTIONS**
>
> What concrete steps might a family lawyer take to stay in communication with clients, involve clients in decision making, and assure that he or she is paying sufficient attention to cases?

22.2 SELF-REPRESENTED LITIGANTS (SLRs)

An increasing number of family litigants are not represented by counsel. A 1990 American Bar Association study conducted in Arizona found that at least one party was unrepresented in 88 percent of divorce cases. Steven K. Berenson, *A Family Law Residency Program: A Modest Proposal in Response to the Burdens Created by Self-Represented Litigants in Family Court*, 33 Rutgers L.J. 105, 109 (2001).

> As study after study found, "the percentage of cases in which one or both of the parties appears without a lawyer is significantly higher in family law cases than in any other area of the law," and the number is increasing. In San Diego, for example, the number of divorce filings involving at least one pro se litigant rose from forty-six percent in 1992 to seventy-seven percent in 2000. In the eight-year period from 1996 to 2004, the percentage of SRLs in family court for one Wisconsin district increased from forty-three percent to sixty-three percent. While statistics vary by state, depending on the type of proceeding, studies show that in between fifty-five and eighty percent of family law matters, at least one party appears pro se. In part as a result of the growing number of SRLs in family court, family law cases overall now comprise more than one-third of all civil filings nationally and continue to grow. It is not just that SRLs are a growing phenomena, it is that they now represent a significant majority of litigants in family court.

Jim Hilbert, *Educational Workshops on Settlement and Dispute Resolution: Another Tool for Self-Represented Litigants in Family Court*, 43 Fam. L.Q. 545, 548-549 (2009).

Research on self-representation. A recent Canadian study confirmed that cost is the primary reason that parties are not represented. Parties who had been represented for some period of time also expressed concerns about lawyer inactivity, failure to pursue settlement, and not being listened to or consulted. According to the study:

> Finally, many SRL's sought some type of "unbundled" legal services from legal counsel; for example, assistance with document review, writing a letter, or appearing in court. Relatively few were successful in accessing legal services on this basis despite a sustained effort. This was perplexing to many respondents, who could not afford to pay a traditional retainer and envisaged that they could undertake some parts of the necessary work themselves, with assistance.

Julie Macfarlane, The National Self-Represented Litigants Project: Final Report (Executive Summary) available at https://representingyourselfcanada.files.wordpress.com/2014/06/executive-summary.pdf (last visited August 2, 2015).

Attorney obligations when dealing with self-represented parties. Attorneys have special obligations when dealing with an unrepresented party. Model Rule 4.3 provides as follows:

> In dealing on behalf of a client with a person who is not represented by counsel, a lawyer shall not state or imply that the lawyer is disinterested. When the lawyer knows or reasonably should know that the unrepresented person misunderstands the lawyer's role in the matter, the lawyer shall make reasonable efforts to correct the misunderstanding. The lawyer shall not give legal advice to an unrepresented person, other than the advice to secure counsel, if the lawyer knows or reasonably should know that the interests of such a person are or have a reasonable possibility of being in conflict with the interests of the client.

Need for pro bono representation. Family lawyers have a responsibility to provide some pro bono representation to potential clients who are unable to afford an attorney. The Model Rules of Professional Conduct, Rule 6.1 (2010), suggests that lawyers provide at least 50 hours of uncompensated service per year.

 **REFLECTIVE QUESTIONS** | What challenges do unrepresented parties face as they navigate the court system? What court system reforms might be helpful to assist unrepresented parties involved in a family law case?

22.3 DUAL REPRESENTATION BY AN ATTORNEY

Attorneys are sometimes asked to represent both parties in a divorce action, particularly if the parties are involved in a no-fault divorce, have limited funds, and appear to be cooperative. There are, however, obvious pitfalls that confront a lawyer agreeing to such an arrangement. They include the fact that the attorney-client privilege will not attach between commonly represented clients. *See* Comment [30] to Model Rule of Professional Conduct 1.7. Furthermore, if during representation the parties cannot agree on an issue, the lawyer must withdraw from representing either party. Dual representation also makes it more likely that an agreement by the parties could be overturned after the divorce or separation based on overreaching. *See Logiudice v. Logiudice*, 67 A.D.3d 544, 545 (N.Y.A.D. 2009).

Model Rule. Model Rule of Professional Conduct 1.7(b)(3) (2010), available at http://www.americanbar.org/groups/professional_responsibility/publications/model_rules_of_professional_conduct/rule_1_7_conflict_of_interest_current_clients.html (last visited August 2, 2015), disapproves of representation that involves "the assertion of a claim by one client against another client represented by the lawyer in the same litigation or other proceeding before a tribunal."

State views. State courts are not in complete agreement over dual representation in divorce proceedings. West Virginia has taken the position that dual representation is improper at any stage of a divorce proceeding. *Walden v. Hoke*, 429 S.E.2d 504 (W. Va. 1993). "It is improper for a lawyer to represent both the husband and the wife at any stage of the separation and divorce proceeding, even with full disclosure and informed consent. The likelihood of prejudice is so great with dual representation so as to make adequate representation of both spouses impossible, even where the separation is friendly and the divorce uncontested." *Id.* at 509; *Ware v. Ware*, 687 S.E.2d 382 (W. Va. 2009) (one attorney may not represent, nor purport to counsel, both parties to a prenuptial agreement as in a divorce, the likelihood of prejudice is so great with dual representation so as to make adequate representation of both parties impossible). California Rules of Professional Conduct, Rule 3-310, provides: "(C) A member shall not, without the informed written consent of each client: (1) Accept representation of more than one client in a matter in which the interest of the clients potentially conflict; or (2) Accept or continue representation of more than one client in a matter in which the interests of the clients actually conflict." *See In re Marriage of Friedman*, 122 Cal. Rptr. 2d 412 (Cal. App. 2002).

REFLECTIVE QUESTIONS	**What are the potential costs and benefits of dual representation? What should an attorney consider when asked to undertake representation of both parties?**

Background to *Disciplinary Proceedings Against Gamino*

In the following case, the Supreme Court of Wisconsin considers the issue of dual representation and the competency of an attorney. At the time of the proceeding the Wisconsin rule on conflict of interest provided that "(a) A lawyer shall not represent a client if the representation of that client will be directly adverse to another client, unless: (1) the lawyer reasonably believes the representation will not adversely affect the relationship with the other client; and (2) each client consents in writing after consultation."

DISCIPLINARY PROCEEDINGS AGAINST GAMINO
Supreme Court of Wisconsin
753 N.W.2d 521 (2008)

PER CURIAM. We review the recommendation of the referee, Dennis J. Flynn, that the license of Attorney Carlos A. Gamiño to practice law in this state be suspended for a period of 18 months due to his professional misconduct and that he should also be required to complete 24 continuing legal education (CLE) credits approved for ethics and pay the costs of this disciplinary proceeding. . . .

Attorney Gamiño was licensed to practice law in Wisconsin in 1997. His law license was suspended for six months effective January 24, 2006, because he was found to have engaged in a sexual relationship with a client in one matter and a sexual relationship with a juvenile client's mother in another matter. He also made false representations about his conduct to a court and to the Office of Lawyer Regulation (OLR) investigators in that matter. Attorney Gamiño was publicly reprimanded on April 28, 2006, for failure to act with reasonable diligence, failure to immediately refund unearned fees, contacting a client after receiving notice that successor counsel had been retained in one matter, and for a trust account violation. Attorney Gamiño's petition for reinstatement was granted by this court on September 5, 2007.

The misconduct at issue in this proceeding occurred in 2004, about the same time as the incidents giving rise to his prior discipline for professional misconduct.

On or about April 20, 2004, Attorney Gamiño met with N.B. and E.B. to discuss helping them finalize their divorce action that had then been pending for about seven months. The couple had been married since February 1979.

When they met with Attorney Gamiño, both N.B. and E.B. had separate attorneys. The husband, E.B., suggested they find one attorney to represent them both in order to save money. Attorney Gamiño agreed to represent both N.B. and E.B. He sent separate stipulations and orders for substitution of counsel to the attorneys of record for both N.B. and E.B. However, he did not obtain either party's written consent to the dual representation and he failed to file the stipulations with the court.

At the time Attorney Gamiño undertook the representation, a court trial in the divorce proceeding was scheduled for June 22, 2004. On June 21, 2004, Attorney Gamiño's office contacted the court requesting an adjournment of the court trial. The court denied the request because Attorney Gamiño was not counsel of record because he had failed to file the substitution of counsel documents with the court. On June 22, 2004, the case was placed on the dismissal calendar because neither party appeared. A notice of dismissal was sent to the parties advising them that the action was set for the July 6, 2004, dismissal calendar. Attorney Gamiño claims that he did not receive a copy of the notice of hearing of the dismissal matter. No one appeared in court on July 6, 2004, and the case was dismissed for failure to prosecute. Attorney Gamiño did not inform N.B. that the divorce action had been dismissed.

On September 28, 2004, Attorney Gamiño filed a motion to reopen the divorce case. A hearing on the motion was scheduled for January 3, 2005. Attorney Gamiño appeared at the hearing on behalf of E.B. N.B. did not appear at this hearing; she alleged that Attorney Gamiño failed to tell her about it. The court granted the motion to reopen the matter and the divorce hearing was scheduled for February 3, 2005.

At the February 3, 2005, final divorce hearing, Attorney Gamiño told the court that N.B. was appearing pro se and that he was representing E.B. N.B. later testified that until that date, she believed that Attorney Gamiño was representing her as well as E.B. Attorney Gamiño disputes this claim, stating that he informed N.B. he would not represent her during a December 2004 telephone conversation. However, he could produce no written documentation to support this assertion.

Attorney Gamiño prepared the joint financial disclosure statement using information he received from the parties. His office also prepared the marital settlement agreement. Subsequently, a number of problems were identified with these documents that were disadvantageous to N.B. For example, the value of E.B.'s retirement accounts was never listed and certain monies the parties had agreed would go to N.B. were not mentioned in the marital settlement agreement.

The joint financial disclosure statement was signed on April 24, 2004. The court commissioner granted the divorce judgment and directed the marital settlement agreement be part of that judgment.

After the divorce, Attorney Gamiño received a letter from N.B.'s post-divorce attorney requesting a copy of her file. He did not comply with that request. He later explained that he opted not to comply because E.B. had not authorized him to release the file documents.

The OLR complaint in this matter was filed on October 6, 2006, and alleged seven counts of professional misconduct committed in connection with the divorce proceeding. The referee ultimately concluded that Attorney Gamiño committed five of the seven counts and exonerated him on the remaining two counts.

At the evidentiary hearing, the referee heard extensive expert testimony regarding Attorney Gamiño's handling of the divorce matter. Attorney Cheryl Gemignani provided expert testimony and opined that:

1. The marital settlement agreement was signed on April 22, 2004. It could not have been signed before the preparation of the joint financial disclosure statement dated April 24, 2004. The documents, she believes, were falsified.
2. Attorney Gamiño had a duty to ascertain a fair market value of all of E.B.'s retirement accounts and other assets in order to comply with the law in Wisconsin regarding a presumptive equal division of the marital estate. This was not done.
3. It is misconduct for an attorney to present for the first time the complete joint financial disclosure statement to the clients at the time of the final divorce hearing as stated by N.B.
4. Attorney Gamiño stated he did not know the difference between a defined benefit and a defined contribution plan. He had a duty to consult with other professionals to get this information. He did not do so.

Attorney Margaret Wrenn Hickey also provided expert testimony and opined that Attorney Gamiño's legal representation was deficient in the following respects:

1. Attorney Gamiño represented both parties when their interests were adverse. This conflict situation was not waivable. Even if the condition was waivable, Attorney Gamiño did not obtain a written waiver.
2. The parties were not on an equal footing. N.B. was the victim of domestic violence, in poor health, and her education and experience in financial and business matters was not equal to E.B.'s.
3. Attorney Gamiño did not reasonably communicate with his clients regarding the divorce dismissal, the motion to reopen, the marital settlement agreement, the joint financial disclosure agreement, and the notice regarding the final divorce hearing.
4. Securing only three years of maintenance for this long-term marriage is not reasonable. It does not reasonably consider the medical disabilities of N.B., and the final maintenance award was indefinite.
5. A patently unfair settlement (maintenance and property division) can only occur through a knowing waiver. That waiver did not occur in this case. Attorney Gamiño has a duty of loyalty to his client and it was not honored.
6. Attorney Gamiño did not inform himself on the actual situation of his client (asset verification, health condition of N.B., discussion of law relative to 50-50 division of marital estate and maintenance) and as a result, the clients were not able to make informed decisions regarding their rights. One meeting with clients is not enough. Separate meetings are needed with each client. Meetings to review marital settlement agreement are needed with each client.
7. The marital settlement agreement did not include all of the assets listed in the joint financial disclosure and the list of assets prepared by E.B. This focuses on the $98,000 N.B. was to get regarding the pension.
8. Attorney Gamiño failed to reasonably notify his clients that at trial he would only represent E.B. and not N.B. There was no written consent or waiver by clients. No waiver was possible in this case as Attorney Gamiño had critical knowledge as to N.B. and thus the conflict he had could never be ameliorated.
9. The matter regarding the embryos was never resolved between the parties in the marital settlement agreement. Attorney Gamiño has a duty to resolve all matters in conflict to the extent possible.
10. Attorney Gamiño failed to obtain the files of the two prior attorneys who represented the parties in this divorce. Critical information regarding the marital estate would perhaps be disclosed.

The referee considered the testimony of other witnesses as well, including Attorney Gamiño's family members. Ultimately, the referee found that Attorney Gamiño failed to obtain information essential to ensuring an equitable division of property in this divorce proceeding. More specifically, Attorney Gamiño failed to:

(1) Obtain financial documents and information needed to establish N.B.'s interests in an equitable division of marital property and maintenance;
(2) Inquire about N.B.'s domestic situation, which included medical complications and a history of domestic abuse by E.B.;
(3) Inform N.B. and E.B. of the presumption in Wisconsin that their property, including retirement assets, would be divided equally between them;
(4) Inquire about the dissipation of assets;

(5) Address the division of E.B.'s pension, savings plan and other retirement savings in the marital settlement agreement;

(6) Address the subject of retirement plans and/or qualified domestic orders;

(7) Remove N.B. from a mortgage note for property awarded to E.B.;

(8) Advise N.B. regarding her rights to maintenance, particularly in light of her disability and receipt of public aid;

(9) Obtain N.B.'s written consent for continued representation of E.B. only in the divorce action;

(10) Return N.B.'s case file after she requested it through her new attorney;

(11) Notify N.B. of his withdrawal as her counsel and give her ample time to secure a new attorney; and

(12) Give proper information to the court and district committee regarding the marital settlement agreement, when it was signed, and knowledge of E.B.'s retirement accounts.

The referee was not persuaded by Attorney Gamiño's assertion that it was not his responsibility to ensure an equitable division of property in this divorce proceeding. Attorney Gamiño argued that N.B. and E.B. had separate attorneys and he thought that they had resolved all divorce matters before coming to see him. He explained that N.B. and E.B. simply wanted him to secure their divorce by stipulation under agreements that had been reached by their prior attorneys. Attorney Gamiño said he informed the parties that if a dispute arose he would only represent one party and the parties agreed that would be E.B.

Attorney Gamiño testified further that he did try to explain the law regarding maintenance and property division to the parties but they were not interested in that information. He admitted that he did not have the parties sign any consent to allow him to represent both the wife and husband in this divorce matter. He acknowledged that he did not recognize the disparities between N.B.'s and E.B.'s income, education, and work background. Attorney Gamiño testified that he trusted his clients regarding the retirement information and did not check into it himself.

Turning to the allegations in the OLR complaint, the referee concluded that Attorney Gamiño violated former SCR 20:1.7(a), by representing both N.B. and E.B. in their divorce proceeding when Attorney Gamiño could not have reasonably believed that N.B.'s interests would not be adversely affected by failing to obtain written consent to the dual representation. In reaching this conclusion, the referee observed that the record is clear that Attorney Gamiño knowingly represented both parties in an adverse divorce proceeding and never sought to obtain any consent or waiver from the clients regarding this situation.

The referee also concluded that Attorney Gamiño failed to keep N.B. reasonably informed about the status of her divorce case in violation of SCR 20:1.4. The referee explained:

N.B. first learned of the fact that Attorney Gamiño was only going to represent E.B. just before going into court for the default divorce on February 3, 2005. E.B.'s testimony corroborates this. Attorney Gamiño's contentions to the effect that he advised E.B. and N.B. orally about the dismissal of the divorce due to non-prosecution, that he advised N.B. orally about the motion to reopen and the date for that hearing, and that he orally told N.B. in December 2004 that he was going to represent E.B. only in the divorce and that she should get her own attorney are rejected. . . . N.B.'s testimony on these issues is more credible than that of Attorney Gamiño.

The referee also concluded that Attorney Gamiño violated SCR 20:1.1 which provides that a lawyer shall provide competent representation to a client because Attorney Gamiño did not make an adequate inquiry into E.B.'s retirement assets, N.B.'s health condition, her disability status, or the domestic violence that she had experienced in the past from E.B. The referee noted that, "The fact that N.B. was receiving Social Security disability income should have alerted him to make some further inquiry into her medical and work history insofar as maintenance was concerned." He found that "the credible evidence establishes that Attorney Gamiño did nothing to advise N.B. of her rights in this area. . . . [H]e did not discuss with N.B. her rights to fair maintenance in this long-term marriage."

As such, the referee concluded that "OLR has established by clear, satisfactory and convincing evidence that Attorney Gamiño failed to provide competent legal representation to his clients in this divorce matter" in violation of SCR 20:1.1.

Similarly, the referee found that the "credible evidence establishes that Attorney Gamiño did not advise N.B. before the final hearing that he would not be representing her in the divorce action." Attorney Gamiño thus violated SCR 20:1.9(a), which provides that a lawyer who has formerly represented a client in a matter shall not represent another person in the same or a substantially similar matter in which the person's interests are materially adverse to the interests of the former client unless the former client consents in writing after consultation. The referee observed:

> N.B. had no real information regarding her husband's pension accounts. She was disabled under Social Security and likely could not work. She had been a past victim of domestic abuse by E.B. The marital settlement agreement did not give her the $98,000 that she was to get from her husband's known pension accounts. Under the guise of maintenance, she was to get $500 per month toward her share (the $98,000) of the property division. However, those payments were not guaranteed in the event of E.B.'s death. This approach meant that the alleged maintenance was a tax deductible expense for E.B. and N.B. would be obligated to pay taxes on what in fact were payments to her over time of her share of the marital estate. Attorney Gamiño knew or should have known all of this information. It was as expert witness Hickey said. The conflict was not waivable by Attorney Gamiño regarding the adverse position of these parties. Under Attorney Gamiño's duty of loyalty to N.B., he was obligated to disabuse N.B. as to the patently unfair divorce agreement that was being offered to the court. N.B. could potentially waive the conflict had she been informed of her rights, but there was no such advice given to N.B. by Attorney Gamiño and no written waiver ever was prepared or signed. Attorney Gamiño had critical knowledge as to N.B. that created an insurmountable conflict and made it impossible for him to continue to represent E.B., an adverse party to N.B., his former client, in the divorce.

Thus, the referee concluded that the OLR established by clear, satisfactory and convincing evidence that Attorney Gamiño violated SCR 20:1.9(a).

The referee also concluded that Attorney Gamiño violated SCR 20:1.16(d) by failing to provide N.B.'s file to her new attorney when a request was made on June 6, 2005, after his representation of N.B. had terminated. Indeed, Attorney Gamiño never even responded to the file request. Thus, the referee found that the OLR established by clear, satisfactory and convincing evidence that Attorney Gamiño violated 20:1.16(d).

The referee also concluded that the OLR failed to meet its burden of proof with respect to the claim that Attorney Gamiño failed to timely file documents and make necessary court appearances. The referee stated, "The credible evidence does not establish, to the level of clear, satisfactory and convincing, that Attorney Gamiño failed to act with reasonable diligence and promptness in representing N.B. and/ or E.B. regarding their divorce." Finally, the referee found that OLR had not established that Attorney Gamiño knowingly gave false information during the course of the investigation into this matter. Rather, the referee was of the opinion that Attorney Gamiño's oversights were based on ignorance. The referee found further that there was inadequate information in the record to ascertain exactly when the agreements in question were signed.

We accept the referee's findings of fact, and we agree with his conclusions of law. Accordingly, we turn to the question of the appropriate discipline for Attorney Gamiño's misconduct.

The OLR requested a two-year suspension of Attorney Gamiño's license to practice law. Attorney Gamiño requested a public reprimand. The referee ultimately recommended an 18-month suspension and recommended further that Attorney Gamiño complete 24 credits of CLE courses approved for ethics education, and pay the costs of this proceeding. The referee concluded restitution was not appropriate in this matter.

Attorney Gamiño's prior disciplinary history is troubling, but we note that the conduct at issue here occurred around the same time as the incidents giving rise to his prior discipline. On balance, we agree that the recommended sanction is not inconsistent with other cases involving similar misconduct. We therefore accept the recommended discipline. Attorney Gamiño's license to practice law will be suspended for 18 months. We direct Attorney Gamiño to complete 24 credits of approved coursework in the area of legal ethics and professional responsibility and to pay the costs of this proceeding.

DISCUSSION QUESTIONS FOR *DISCIPLINARY PROCEEDINGS AGAINST GAMINO*

A. What are the 12 obligations outlined by the referee that the attorney failed to fulfill? What possible harm could come to a client as a result of them? What should the attorney have done to provide competent representation?

B. Under the Wisconsin rule in effect at the time of the case, could the attorney have represented both parties? Would the answer to this question be the same or different under Model Rule of Professional Conduct 1.7(b)(3)? Why or why not?

C. Do you agree with the penalty imposed in this case? Why or why not?

22.4 CONTINGENT FEES

Under a contingent fee arrangement, a lawyer and client agree that the lawyer will receive a fixed percentage of the client's recovery in a settlement or judgment. If there is no recovery, the lawyer takes nothing. Occasionally, a lawyer will charge an hourly fee, but will receive a bonus for a specified favorable results.

Model Rule. Under Model Rule of Professional Conduct 1.5(d)(1) (2010) lawyers are prohibited from charging a fee "contingent upon the securing of a divorce or upon the amount of alimony or support, or property settlement in lieu thereof. . . ." However, this provision does not preclude contingent fees for recovery of post-judgment amounts due under court orders for support, alimony, and some other financial issues.

Rationale. Concerns about use of contingent fee arrangements for clients seeking a divorce stem in part from fears that attorneys who have a financial stake in the outcome of the divorce might discourage reconciliation of parties. *See Maxwell Schuman & Co. v. Edwards*, 663 S.E.2d 329 (N.C. App. 2008).

AAML view. The American Academy of Matrimonial Lawyers, Bounds of Advocacy are less restrictive than the Model Rules. AAML goal 4.5 states that a lawyer should not charge a fee that is contingent on (a) obtaining a divorce; (b) particular custody or visitation provisions; or (c) the amount of alimony or child support awarded. An attorney may charge a contingent fee for all other matters (such as property distribution issues), provided that the client is informed of the right to have the fee based on an hourly rate, and that the client has an opportunity to seek independent legal advice concerning the desirability of the contingent fee arrangement.

REFLECTIVE QUESTIONS	Do you think that family attorneys should be able to charge a contingent fee? Why should they or why shouldn't they?

22.5 SEXUAL RELATIONSHIPS WITH CLIENTS

Rule 1.8(j) of the Model Rules of Professional Conduct (2010) provides that "[a] lawyer shall not have sexual relations with a client unless a consensual sexual relationship existed between them when the client-lawyer relationship commenced." Comment [17] explains that a lawyer engaged in a sexual relationship with a client may find that his or her independent professional judgment is impaired and that the attorney-client evidentiary privilege has been compromised.

REFLECTIVE QUESTIONS	How might the attorney-client privilege be impaired because an attorney has a sexual relationship with a client?

Background to *In re Tsoutsouris*

As explained in the next case, *In re Tsoutsouris*, a sexual relationship with a client can be especially problematic in family law cases. If, for example, child custody is at issue, the lawyer's relationship with the client may become evidence in the case and could ultimately adversely affect the outcome.

IN RE TSOUTSOURIS
Supreme Court of Indiana
748 N.E.2d 856 (2001)

PER CURIAM. . . . [A] client hired the respondent in 1994 to represent her in a child support modification action filed by her first husband. The client paid the respondent a total fee of $350. While that child support matter was pending, the client also hired the respondent to represent her in a dissolution action against her second husband.

While the respondent was representing the client in the fall of 1994, the respondent and the client began dating and engaged in consensual sexual relations several times. The respondent did not inform the client how a sexual relationship between them might impact his professional duties to her or otherwise affect their attorney/client relationship.

The respondent ended the sexual relationship a few weeks after it began in 1994. The client hired the respondent for a third legal matter in 1996. In 1997, the client sought psychological treatment. One of the subjects discussed during that treatment was her personal relationship with the respondent three years earlier.

In his Petition for Review, the respondent contends his consensual sexual relationship with his client during his representation of her does not violate the Rules of Professional Conduct. He bases that argument on the lack of evidence establishing that his sexual relationship with the client impaired his ability to represent the client effectively. The respondent contends that a sexual relationship between attorney and client in Indiana is professional misconduct only when it affects the quality of the attorney's representation of the client.

Rule 1.7(b) prohibits representation of a client if the representation "may be materially limited by the lawyer's own interests." Although the rule contains general exceptions in instances where the lawyer reasonably believes that the representation will not be adversely affected and the client consents after consultation, these exceptions will not generally avail when the "lawyer's own interests" at issue are those related to a lawyer/client sexual relationship.

Twenty-five years ago this Court suspended a lawyer for sexual misconduct with clients and warned of the professional conflicts such intimate associations create. In a subsequent case involving the same attorney accused of similar misconduct, this Court ruled that the intermission of a lawyer's professional duties with the lawyer's personal sexual interests creates a situation where "the exercise of professional judgment on behalf of a client would be affected by personal interests" in violation of Rule 5101(A).

Six years after our second *Wood* decision, the American Bar Association issued an ethics opinion on the subject of sexual relationships between attorneys and clients. ABA Formal Ethics Opinion No. 92364, Sexual Relations with Client. The ABA made it clear that attorneys should avoid sexual contact with their clients. While the ABA Model Rules of Professional Conduct do not explicitly prohibit a sexual relationship between an attorney and client, we note that such relationships have been unequivocally discouraged, as noted in ABA Ethics Opinion 92364:

> First, because of the dependence that so often characterizes the attorney client relationship, there is a significant possibility that the sexual relationship will have resulted from the exploitation of the lawyer's dominant position and influence and, thus, breached the lawyer's fiduciary obligations to the client. Second, a sexual relationship with a client may affect the independence of the lawyer's judgment. Third, the lawyer's engaging in a sexual relationship with a client may create a prohibited conflict between the interests of the lawyer and those of the client. Fourth, a nonprofessional, yet emotionally charged, relationship between attorney and client may result in confidences being imparted in circumstances where the attorney client privilege is not available, yet would have been, absent the personal relationship.
>
> We believe the better practice is to avoid all sexual contact with clients during the representation.

This position is further bolstered by the recent proposed revisions of the ABA Model Rules of Professional Conduct resulting from a three year comprehensive study and evaluation by the ABA Commission on Evaluation of the Rules of Professional Conduct (commonly referred to as the "Ethics 2000" Commission). These revisions include a proposed new rule explicitly declaring that "A lawyer shall not have sexual relations with a client unless a consensual sexual relationship existed between them when the client lawyer relationship commenced." Proposed Model Rule 1.8(j). The proposed rule is further supported by commentary reflecting important policy considerations. Proposed Comment 17 to Rule 1.8 states:

> The relationship between lawyer and client is a fiduciary one in which the lawyer occupies the highest position of trust and confidence. The relationship is almost always unequal; thus, a sexual relationship between lawyer and client can involve unfair exploitation of the lawyer's fiduciary role, in violation of the lawyer's basic ethical obligation not to use the trust of the client to the client's disadvantage. In addition, such a relationship presents a

significant danger that, because of the lawyer's emotional involvement, the lawyer will be unable to represent the client without impairment of the exercise of independent professional judgment. Moreover, a blurred line between the professional and personal relationships may make it difficult to predict to what extent client confidences will be protected by the attorney client evidentiary privilege, since client confidences are protected by privilege only when they are imparted in the context of the client lawyer relationship. Because of the significant danger of harm to client interests and because the client's own emotional involvement renders it unlikely that the client could give adequate informed consent, this Rule prohibits the lawyer from having sexual relations with a client regardless of whether the relationship is consensual and regardless of the absence of prejudice to the client.

In *Matter of Grimm*, 674 N.E.2d 551 (Ind. 1996), this Court found an attorney's "sexual relationship with his client during the pendency of dissolution and post-dissolution matters materially limited his representation of her," thereby violating Prof. Cond. R. 1.7(b). *Grimm*, 674 N.E.2d at 554. We explained:

In their professional capacity, lawyers are expected to provide emotionally detached, objective analysis of legal problems and issues for clients who may be embroiled in sensitive or difficult matters. Clients, especially those who are troubled or emotionally fragile, often place a great deal of trust in the lawyer and rely heavily on his or her agreement to provide professional assistance. Unfortunately, the lawyer's position of trust may provide opportunity to manipulate the client for the lawyer's sexual benefit. Where a lawyer permits or encourages a sexual relationship to form with a client, that trust is betrayed and the stage is set for continued unfair exploitation of the lawyer's fiduciary position. Additionally, the lawyer's ability to represent effectively the client may be impaired. Objective detachment, essential for clear and reasoned analysis of issues and independent professional judgment, may be lost.

Grimm is one of several cases decided under the Rules of Professional Conduct in which this Court has held that consensual sexual relationships with clients constitute professional misconduct. In *Matter of Hawkins*, 695 N.E.2d 109 (Ind. 1998), we found a violation of Rule 1.7(b) and held that, by "having sexual relations with his client, the respondent promoted and served his own interests and thereby threatened material limitation of his representation of her." See also *Matter of Bamberth*, 737 N.E.2d 1157 (Ind. 2000) ("By having a consensual sexual relationship with a client during the pendency of the representation, the respondent engaged in an impermissible conflict of interest in violation of Ind. Professional Conduct Rule 1.7(b)").

We hold that the respondent violated Prof. Cond. R. 1.7(b) and prejudiced the administration of justice in violation of Prof. Cond. R. 8.4(d). It is, therefore, ordered that the respondent is hereby suspended from the practice of law in Indiana for 30 days, effective July 23, 2001, at the conclusion of which he shall be reinstated automatically.

 **FOR** *IN RE TSOUTSOURIS*

A. The American Bar Association (ABA) has expressed a number of concerns about attorneys engaging in a sexual relationship with a client. What are they? What is the ABA's view of the power relationship between an attorney and a client?

B. The present version of Rule 1.8(j) does not forbid consensual sexual relationships that existed prior to the formation of the attorney-client relationship. Comment [18] explains that "[i]ssues relating to the exploitation of the fiduciary relationship and client dependency are diminished." What argument can you make that all sexual relationships with clients should be prohibited, including previously existing relationships?

C. The respondent was suspended from practice for 30 days. Do you believe the sanction was appropriate?

22.6 COMMUNICATION WITH CLIENTS

Model Rule of Professional Conduct 1.4 (2010) requires attorneys to keep clients "reasonably informed" about their cases and to "comply with reasonable requests for information."

Unfortunately, family law clients sometimes recount that their lawyers fail to return phone calls promptly and otherwise sufficiently communicate with them. Because lawyers routinely deal with family law issues, they sometimes underestimate the personal turmoil and emotional intensity that clients experience. In addition, some family lawyers are uncomfortable with client emotions and avoid client contact by not responding to requests. *See* Barbara Glesner Fines & Cathy Madsen, *Caring Too Little, Caring Too Much: Competence and the Family Law Attorney*, 75 KMKC L. Rev. 965 (2007) (discussing attorney skill at dealing with emotions).

An effective practitioner educates clients from the outset concerning the nature and frequency of lawyer contact they might expect. A skilled family lawyer is also prepared to refer troubled clients to mental health professionals who specialize in coaching clients through the divorce process.

| REFLECTIVE QUESTIONS | What steps might a family lawyer take to assure effective communication with clients? |

Background to *Bach v. State Bar of California*

The following case illustrates an extreme situation involving "lack of communication" with a client.

BACH
v.
STATE BAR OF CALIFORNIA
Supreme Court of California, *en banc*
805 P.2d 325 (1991)

We review the recommendation of the State Bar Court that petitioner John Nicholas Bach, admitted to practice in 1964, be suspended from the practice of law for 12 months, that execution of the suspension be stayed, that petitioner be placed on probation for that period and that he be actually suspended for the first 30 days and until proof is made of restitution of certain unearned fees.

Following three days of hearings, a State Bar referee concluded that petitioner had repeatedly and with reckless disregard failed to perform legal services competently for one of his clients in an uncontested marital dissolution proceeding by failing over a period of two and a half years to pursue the case to a conclusion; that he had failed to communicate with his client over much of that time; had withdrawn his representation without the client's consent or court approval; and had failed to refund unearned fees paid to him in advance. The referee further found that petitioner violated provisions of the Business and Professions Code in failing to respond to two written inquiries from a State Bar investigator requesting information relating to his representation of the complaining client.

After weighing evidence in mitigation of these conclusions and circumstances in aggravation, the referee made the disciplinary recommendations summarized above; by a vote of 8 to 2, the Review Department of the State Bar (review department) adopted the findings and conclusions of the referee as well as his recommendation as to discipline.

The notice to show cause issued against petitioner alleged, and the evidence before the referee showed, that on August 9, 1984, Barbara Hester retained petitioner to obtain a dissolution of her marriage, paying him $3,000 in advance; that petitioner thereafter failed to communicate with Ms. Hester for months at a time despite repeated telephone calls and office visits; never obtained the dissolution; and purported to withdraw from the dissolution proceeding in March of 1987 without the consent of either Ms. Hester or the superior court and without returning the unearned portion of the fees advanced.

Petitioner contends that the evidence before the referee was insufficient to sustain the findings with respect to his conduct in the Hester dissolution, claiming that Ms. Hester lacked credibility. We disagree. As is our practice in disciplinary matters, we have weighed the evidence before the referee and independently conclude that it was more than sufficient to sustain each of the referee's findings with respect to the Hester matter. Petitioner's case is not aided by his insistence on rearguing his version of events or by asking us to overturn credibility determinations. His briefing fails to carry his burden of demonstrating that the referee's findings are not supported by substantial evidence.

The charge of noncooperation . . . arose from petitioner's failure to respond to two successive letters of inquiry mailed well after the alleged telephone call. The letters advised petitioner that a complaint had been filed by Ms. Hester, summarized its nature, requested a response within three weeks, and invited petitioner's attention to section 6068, subdivision (i). Neither letter having been returned and no reply from petitioner having been received, in the absence of a credible alternative account of the matter, the referee was entitled to conclude from the evidence that petitioner had ignored the two requests and thus breached his duty to cooperate in the disciplinary investigation. Under these circumstances, petitioner's efforts to portray the State Bar as itself uncooperative in failing to follow up on petitioner's telephonic "leads," are unconvincing.

Finally, petitioner contends that the recommended discipline is excessive in light of his record of no prior discipline, other factors in mitigation, and published disciplinary guidelines. He relies on the definition of "mitigating circumstance" in standard 1.2(e) of the Standards for Attorney Sanctions for Professional Misconduct of division V of the Rules of Procedure of the State Bar (hereafter the standards) and suggests that a private admonition is the appropriate sanction, assuming any culpability at all.

Although arising out of a single case of client neglect, petitioner's difficulties have multiplied apparently as a result of a persistent lack of insight into the deficiencies of his professional behavior. He has denied any responsibility for the inordinate delay and substantial cost, anxiety, and inconvenience imposed on Ms. Hester by his nonperformance, refused to participate in mandatory fee arbitration proceedings on essentially specious grounds, and declined to respond to successive requests from the State Bar for information concerning the matter although reminded of his duty to do so.

Despite this record, petitioner invokes our discretion over discipline by suggesting that the following factors in mitigation itemized under standard 1.2(e) of the standards are present in his case: that his conduct was "not deemed serious"; that he acted in "good faith"; that the record shows a "lack of harm to the client"; that he displayed "spontaneous candor and cooperation" during the investigation and disciplinary proceedings; and that these proceedings were excessively delayed without his fault and to his prejudice. We find none of these factors presented by this record.

Moreover, the attitude toward discipline betrayed by petitioner's feckless suggestion that these factors are present strengthens the case for a period of actual suspension, however brief, followed by supervised probation. Our independent review of the record and exercise of our own judgment confirms the appropriateness of the recommendation of the review department. We adopt it as our own.

It is ordered that petitioner be suspended from the practice of law for 12 months from the date this order is final but that execution of the suspension order be stayed and that he be placed on probation for 12 months on all the conditions of probation adopted by the review department at its meeting of August 31, 1989, including actual suspension for the first 30 days of the probationary period and until petitioner makes restitution to Barbara Hester in the sum of $2,000 together with interest at 7 percent per annum from February 5, 1987.

It is further ordered that John Nicholas Bach shall take and pass the Professional Responsibility Examination administered by the National Conference of Bar Examiners within one year of the effective date of this order. This order is effective upon the finality of this decision in this court.

DISCUSSION QUESTIONS FOR *BACH v. STATE BAR OF CALIFORNIA*

A. Do you believe that the sanctions in this case were appropriate? Do the sanctions adequately protect future clients? Can you think of other disciplinary measures that should be considered in a case like this?

B. Some family law clients desire frequent contact with their attorneys, and some family law lawyers have high-volume practices. What law office procedures might family law practitioners institute in order to avoid the kind of misconduct alleged in this case?

22.7 COLLABORATIVE LAWYERING

Collaborative law is discussed more fully in Chapter 21. As explained there, collaborative lawyers employ interest-based cooperative problem-solving techniques to settle cases. Before entering into the process the parties and lawyers agree that they will not seek court assistance. Consequently, if court intervention is sought by either party, a disqualification agreement comes into play and the collaborative lawyers must withdraw from the case.

Background for Formal Opinion 07-447

The following is an ethical opinion regarding collaborative law issued by the American Bar Association Standing Committee on Ethics and Professional Responsibility. It explores some of the ethical questions raised about collaborative law practice.

FORMAL OPINION 07-447
Ethical Considerations in Collaborative Law Practice
August 9, 2007

Before representing a client in a collaborative law process, a lawyer must advise the client of the benefits and risks of participation in the process. If the client has given his or her informed consent, the lawyer may represent the client in the collaborative law process. A lawyer who engages in collaborative resolution processes still is bound by the rules of professional conduct, including the duties of competence and diligence.

In this opinion, we analyze the implications of the Model Rules on collaborative law practice. Collaborative law is a type of alternative dispute resolution in which the parties and their lawyers commit to work cooperatively to reach a settlement. It had its roots in, and shares many attributes of, the mediation process. Participants focus on the interests of both clients, gather sufficient information to insure that decisions are made with full knowledge, develop a full range of options, and then choose options that best meet the needs of the parties. The parties structure a mutually acceptable written resolution of all issues without court involvement. The product of the process is then submitted to the court as a final decree. The structure creates a problem-solving atmosphere with a focus on interest-based negotiation and client empowerment.

Since its creation in Minnesota in 1990, collaborative practice has spread rapidly throughout the United States and into Canada, Australia, and Western Europe. Numerous established collaborative law organizations develop local practice protocols, train practitioners, reach out to the public, and build referral networks. On its website, the International Academy of Collaborative Professionals describes its mission as fostering professional excellence in conflict resolution by protecting the essentials of collaborative practice, expanding collaborative practice worldwide, and providing a central resource for education, networking, and standards of practice.

Although there are several models of collaborative practice, all of them share the same core elements that are set out in a contract between the clients and their lawyers (often referred to as a "four-way" agreement). In that agreement, the parties commit to negotiating a mutually acceptable settlement without court intervention, to engaging in open communication and information sharing, and to creating shared solutions that meet the needs of both clients. To ensure the commitment of the lawyers to the collaborative process, the four-way agreement also includes a requirement that, if the process breaks down, the lawyers will withdraw from representing their respective clients and will not handle any subsequent court proceedings.

Several state bar opinions have analyzed collaborative practice and, with one exception, have concluded that it is not inherently inconsistent with the Model Rules. Most authorities treat collaborative law practice as a species of limited scope representation and discuss the duties of lawyers in those situations, including communication, competence, diligence, and confidentiality. However, even those opinions are guarded, and caution that collaborative practice carries with it a potential for significant ethical difficulties.

As explained herein, we agree that collaborative law practice and the provisions of the four-way agreement represent a permissible limited scope representation under Model Rule 1.2, with the concomitant duties of competence, diligence, and communication. We reject the suggestion that collaborative law practice sets up a non-waivable conflict under Rule 1.7(a)(2).

Rule 1.2(c) permits a lawyer to limit the scope of a representation so long as the limitation is reasonable under the circumstances and the client gives informed consent. Nothing in the Rule or its Comment suggest that limiting a representation to a collaborative effort to reach a settlement is per se unreasonable. On the contrary, Comment [6] provides that "[a] limited representation may be appropriate because the client has limited objectives for the representation. In addition, the terms upon which representation is undertaken may exclude specific means that might otherwise be used to accomplish the client's objectives."

Obtaining the client's informed consent requires that the lawyer communicate adequate information and explanation about the material risks of and reasonably available alternatives to the limited representation. The lawyer must provide adequate information about the rules or contractual terms governing the collaborative process, its advantages and disadvantages, and the alternatives. The lawyer also must assure that the client understands that, if the collaborative law procedure does not result in settlement of the dispute and litigation is the only recourse, the collaborative lawyer must withdraw and the parties must retain new lawyers to prepare the matter for trial.

The one opinion that expressed the view that collaborative practice is impermissible did so on the theory that the "four-way agreement" creates a non-waivable conflict of interest under Rule 1.7(a)(2). We disagree with that result because we conclude that it turns on a faulty premise. As we stated earlier, the four-way agreement that is at the heart of collaborative practice includes the promise that both lawyers will withdraw from representing their respective clients if the collaboration fails and that they will not assist their clients in ensuing litigation. We do not disagree with the proposition that this contractual obligation to withdraw creates on the part of each lawyer a "responsibility to a third party" within the meaning of Rule 1.7(a)(2). We do disagree with the view that such a responsibility creates a conflict of interest under that Rule. A conflict exists between a lawyer and her own client under Rule 1.7(a)(2) "if there is a significant risk that the representation [of the client] will be materially limited by the lawyer's responsibilities to . . . a third person or by a personal interest of the lawyer." A self-interest conflict can be resolved if the client gives informed consent, confirmed in writing, but a lawyer may not seek the client's informed consent unless the lawyer "reasonably believes that [she] will be able to provide competent and diligent representation" to the client. According to Comment [1] to Rule 1.7, "[l]oyalty and independent judgment are essential elements in the lawyer's relationship to a client." As explained more fully in Comment [8] to that Rule, "a conflict exists if there is a significant risk that a lawyer's ability to consider, recommend or carry out an appropriate course of action for the client will be materially limited by the lawyer's other responsibilities or interests. . . . The conflict in effect forecloses alternatives that would otherwise be available to the client."

On the issue of consentability, Rule 1.7 Comment [15] is instructive. It provides that "[c]onsentability is typically determined by considering whether the interests of the clients will be adequately protected if the clients are permitted to give their informed consent to representation burdened by a conflict of interest. Thus, under paragraph (b)(1), representation is prohibited in the circumstances the lawyer cannot reasonably conclude that the lawyer will be able to provide competent and diligent representation."

Responsibilities to third parties constitute conflicts with one's own client only if there is a significant risk that those responsibilities will materially limit the lawyer's representation of the client. It has been suggested that a lawyer's agreement to withdraw is essentially an agreement by the lawyer to impair her ability to represent the client. We disagree, because we view participation in the collaborative process as a limited scope representation.

When a client has given informed consent to a representation limited to collaborative negotiation toward settlement, the lawyer's agreement to withdraw if the collaboration fails is not an agreement that impairs her ability to represent the client, but rather is consistent with the client's limited goals for the representation. A client's agreement to a limited scope representation does not exempt the lawyer from the duties of competence and diligence, notwithstanding that the contours of the requisite competence and diligence are limited in accordance with the overall scope of the representation. Thus, there is no basis to conclude that the lawyer's representation of the client will be materially limited by the lawyer's obligation to withdraw if settlement cannot be accomplished. In the absence of a significant risk of such a material limitation, no conflict arises between the lawyer and her client under Rule 1.7(a)(2). Stated differently, there is no foreclosing of alternatives, i.e., consideration and pursuit of litigation, otherwise available to the client because the client has specifically limited the scope of the lawyer's representation to the collaborative negotiation of a settlement.

DISCUSSION QUESTIONS FOR FORMAL OPINION 07-447

A. What are the core elements of collaborative law? How does it differ from traditional family law practice?

B. What is a limited-scope representation?

C. What advice must a lawyer give to a client considering the collaborative law process? What informed consent is required?

D. The opinion notes that one state (Colorado) expressed the contrary view that the "four-way agreement" creates a nonwaivable conflict of interest. What was the reasoning behind this view?

E. The opinion states that even with the disqualification agreement, there is no foreclosing of alternatives in collaborative practice. Explain.

F. What arguments are made that the practice of collaborative law is inconsistent with the Rules of Professional Conduct? Do you find these arguments persuasive?

G. Colorado issued an ethical opinion favoring the use of "cooperative law" as opposed to collaborative law. Cooperative law uses a similar approach to collaborative law but does not require a disqualification agreement in the event that the parties seek judicial intervention. Why do collaborative lawyers use a disqualification agreement? *See* Colorado Bar Assn. Ethics Comm., Op 115 (2-24-07); John Lande, *Practical Insights from an Empirical Study of Cooperative Lawyers in Wisconsin*, 2008 J. Dispute Resol. 203 (2008); David A. Hoffman, *Cooperative Agreements: Using Contracts to Make a Safe Place for a Difficult Conversation*, in *Innovations in Family Law Practice* 63 (Kelly Browe Olson & Nancy Ver Steegh eds., 2008).

22.8 LAWYER AS MEDIATOR

Today's family lawyers choose from an array of professional opportunities including traditional practice, cooperative law, collaborative law, mediation, provision of "unbundled" legal services, parenting coordination, and parenting education. Many of these roles and processes are explored in Chapter 21. New lawyers should consider which roles are most consistent with their interests, skills, and personal values.

Model Rule. All practitioners need to remain alert to professional responsibility obligations related to various roles and focus continuously on which function they serve in a given case. Model Rule of Professional Conduct 2.4 discusses issues for lawyers who serve as neutrals in cases:

> Rule 2.4 Lawyer Serving As Third-Party Neutral
> (a) A lawyer serves as a third-party neutral when the lawyer assists two or more persons who are not clients of the lawyer to reach a resolution of a dispute or other matter that has arisen between them. Service as a third-party neutral may include service as an arbitrator, a mediator or in such other capacity as will enable the lawyer to assist the parties to resolve the matter.
> (b) A lawyer serving as a third-party neutral shall inform unrepresented parties that the lawyer is not representing them. When the lawyer knows or reasonably should know that a party does not understand the lawyer's role in the matter, the lawyer shall explain the difference between the lawyer's role as a third-party neutral and a lawyer's role as one who represents a client.

Do lawyers require special training to be effective third-party neutrals? What type of training would be helpful?

Background to SODR-2010-1

Below is an excerpt of an advisory response to questions posed to the ABA Section of Dispute Resolution Committee on Mediator Ethical Guidance concerning appropriate activities for a lawyer functioning as a mediator. The full response and other advisory responses can be found at http://apps.americanbar.org/dch/committee.cfm?com=DR018600 (last visited August 2, 2015).

ABA SECTION OF DISPUTE RESOLUTION COMMITTEE ON MEDIATOR ETHICAL GUIDANCE

SODR-2010-1

Questions: A married couple with one minor child has decided that they would like to get an uncontested no-fault divorce and want joint custody over their minor child. The parties have decided to jointly retain you as a Mediator to mediate the terms of a property settlement, custody, and support agreement. The mediation is successful, and the parties reach an agreement concerning the division of all of their property and the custody, visitation arrangements, and child support for their minor child. The parties then want the Mediator to prepare the agreement for them. Neither party wants to retain his or her own attorney to prepare the agreement or to have their attorneys review the agreement if prepared by the Mediator.

Question 1A: If the Mediator is a lawyer, should he or she prepare the agreement under these circumstances and if so, what are the ethical responsibilities and constraints, if any, that should be considered in connection with the preparation of the agreement?

Question 1B: What are the Mediator's ethical duties and responsibilities with respect to the parties under these circumstances?

Question 1C: Would the ethical considerations be different if the mediation only involved the division of property and not custody, visitation, and support for the minor child also? . . .

Authority Referenced: Model Standards of Conduct for Mediators 2005, Preamble, Standards I(A), I(A)(2); II(B); II(C); III(A); III(D); IV(A)(1); IV(B); VI(A)(5); VI(A)(8); VI(C).

Summary: The Committee answers the posed questions mindful of the specific context of the inquiry. It posits that the unrepresented parties in a divorce mediation specifically seek out a lawyer-mediator with the expectation that he or she will provide substantive drafting services and that the parties will not retain an attorney to review the mediator's work product or otherwise advise the parties about their legal rights. In answering the questions, the Committee does not endorse any particular style or orientation of the mediator, and it does not analyze the questions by defining the proposed services as facilitative or evaluative in nature.

The Committee also notes that the aspirational Model Standards of Practice for Family and Divorce Mediation (Family Standards) would apply to family law practitioners. It advises those practitioners to be guided first by the Family Standards, relevant provisions of which specifically permit certain drafting activities by family mediators. While it is not within the purview of this Committee to interpret the Family Standards, the Committee has provided citations in the footnotes to provisions found in those standards that are parallel to the applicable provisions of the Model Standards.

Question 1A: A lawyer-mediator may act as a "scrivener" to memorialize the parties' agreement without adding terms or operative language. A lawyer-mediator with the experience and training to competently provide additional drafting services could do so, if done consistent with the Model Standards governing party self-determination and mediator impartiality. Arguably, before taking on any new role in the process, the mediator must explain the implications of assuming that role and get the consent of the parties to provide those services. The mediator should also advise parties of their right to consult other professionals, including lawyers, to help them make informed choices.

Question 1B: The Model Standards arguably also permit a lawyer-mediator to provide legal information to the parties. If, however, the mediator provides legal advice or performs other tasks typically done by legal counsel, the mediator runs a serious risk of inappropriately mixing the roles of legal counsel and mediator, thereby raising ethical issues under the Model Standards. At a minimum, the lawyer-mediator must disclose the implications of shifting roles and receive consent from the parties. The lawyer-mediator should also consider legal ethics provisions governing, among other things, joint representation of legal clients and the unauthorized practice of law (UPL) in a state in which the lawyer is not licensed.

Question 1C: The ethical considerations do not differ under the Model Standards even if the mediation only involves the division of property. . . .

DISCUSSION QUESTIONS FOR SODR-2010-1

A. What is the distinction made between a lawyer-mediator acting as a "scrivener" and "drafting"? Why does it matter? What are examples of each?

B. What is the difference between providing "legal information" and "legal advice"? Why does the distinction matter?

C. Under this response, what must lawyer-mediators explain and disclose to parties?

22.9 LAWYER AS CHILDREN'S REPRESENTATIVE

In child protection proceedings, a court may appoint a lawyer or other adult to speak on behalf of the child or in the child's interest. States use different terminology to describe these roles and consequently there may be confusion about expectations.

ABA standards. The American Bar Association (ABA) has attempted to clarify the situation in the context of child protection by defining two distinct roles that lawyers might play. The first role is that of the child's attorney: "The term 'child's attorney' means a lawyer who provides legal services for a child and who owes the same duties of undivided loyalty, confidentiality, and competent representation to the child as is due an adult client." Thus, the child's attorney is charged with carrying out the child's wishes. The second role is that of guardian *ad litem*: "A lawyer appointed as 'guardian *ad litem*' for a child is an officer of the court appointed to protect the child's interests without being bound by the child's expressed preferences." American Bar Association, Standards of Practice for Lawyers Who Represent Children in Abuse and Neglect Cases (1996), http://www.a-banet.org/family/reports/standards_abuseneglect.pdf (last visited October 6, 2011).

Contrasting values. The different roles stem from competing values with respect to children's rights. On one hand, a child is given voice when an attorney carries out his or her wishes. On the other hand, some children may not be willing or able to appropriately direct counsel. Professor Atwood summarizes the conflict in the field in the context of family court:

> Despite the position of the AAML and numerous children's rights advocates, the laws of most states in the United States continue to permit children's lawyers to engage in best interests representation. Judicial opinions have recognized with evident approval that the central role of a child's representative is not to zealously advocate what the child wants, but to advocate "what the lawyer believes to be in the client's best interests, even when the lawyer and the client disagree." States vary in their approach to child representation in family court, with the majority authorizing the discretionary appointment of a legal representative — whether denominated an attorney or a guardian ad litem — to represent the child's best interests. Importantly, some states authorize the appointment of either a traditional attorney or a best interests representative, or both, at the court's discretion.

Barbara A. Atwood, *Representing Children Who Can't or Won't Direct Counsel: Best Interests Lawyering or No Lawyer at All?*, 53 Ariz. L. Rev. 381, 391-392 (2011). *See also American Academy of Matrimonial Lawyers Representing Children: Standards for Attorneys for Children in Custody or Visitation Proceedings with Commentary*, 22 J. Am. Acad. Matrimonial Law. 227 (2009).

REFLECTIVE QUESTIONS | Can a lawyer simultaneously function as the child's attorney and the best interests attorney?

Background to *Aksamit v. Krahn*

In the following case, an appellate court defines three roles that may be played by lawyers in a divorce case: best interests attorney, child's attorney, and court-appointed advisor.

AKSAMIT
v.
KRAHN

Court of Appeals of Arizona
227 P.3d 475 (2010)

BARKER, J. The issue before us in this opinion is the proper role of a best interests attorney ("BIA") in family court proceedings. For the following reasons, and those set forth in a simultaneously filed memorandum decision, we affirm in part, vacate in part and remand for a new trial on custody.

FACTS AND PROCEDURAL BACKGROUND

Patricia K. Aksamit ("Mother") filed a petition for dissolution of her marriage to Greg Krahn ("Father") in August 2007. Father and Mother are the parents of two minor children, ages eight and five when the petition was filed. In her petition, Mother sought joint legal custody and primary physical custody of the children. Father sought sole legal custody with parenting time for Mother. In a separate pretrial statement, Mother amended her request and sought sole legal custody for herself with parenting time for Father.

At a hearing on temporary orders, the court appointed a BIA to represent the minor children's best interests. In pertinent part the order provided:

> According to Rule 10(E), Arizona Rules of Family Law Procedure effective January 1, 2006, . . . a *Best Interests Attorney shall participate in the conduct of the litigation to the same extent as an attorney for any party.* The Best Interests Attorney shall attend all hearings and participate in trials or evidentiary hearings by offering evidence, examining witnesses, etc. The *Best Interests Attorney shall not submit a report or testify in court.* . . .
>
> *The Best Interests Attorney* shall attend all court hearings concerning the children unless excused by the Court upon written motion, and *shall participate in the conduct of litigation to the extent authorized by Rule 10, Arizona Rules of Family Law Procedure.*

(Emphasis added.)

At the trial to the court, Mother and Father were the only two sworn witnesses. At the outset of the trial, the court asked the BIA to "give me a report." The BIA then orally responded.

After the trial, the court issued its decree, granting Mother sole custody of the children with Father receiving parenting time. The court's findings make multiple, specific references to the information conveyed by the BIA in her report, including the following:

Custody and Parenting Time

In determining custody and parenting time, the Court is guided by the factors set forth in A.R.S. Section 403(A). Those factors, and the Court's findings thereon, are as follows:

The wishes of the child's parent or parents as to custody

Mother requests sole custody as the parents are unable to communicate with each other regarding major issues involving the minor children. *This view is supported by the opinion and experience of the Best Interests Attorney ["BIA"], who told the Court that although Father has come a long way* from the beginning of the case in his residential stability and in his volatility regarding his ability to discuss issues regarding his children, *he remains bitter and angry at Mother to the extent that he is unable or unwilling to focus on the children's best interest much of the time.* Father is also requesting sole custody of the children. . . .

The interaction and interrelationship of the child with the child's parent or parents, the child's siblings and any other person who may significantly affect the child's best interest

Mother has two older sons from another relationship, Scott (18) and Steven (almost 17) who live with her and have good relationships with their younger brothers, providing some caretaking support to the minor children. *The BIA indicates that she could find no deficiencies in the caretaking abilities of the older boys nor any problems in the relationships between the siblings.*

(Emphasis added in italics.)

Discussion

Father argues the court erred by considering the BIA's report when determining child custody. We agree. Because the error was prejudicial, we vacate the custody order. . . .

1. The Framework Provided in the Rules

To resolve this matter we first turn to the rule permitting the appointment of a BIA. Rule 10(A)(1) provides as follows:

> 1. The court may appoint one or more of the following:
>   a. a best interests attorney;
>   b. a child's attorney; or
>   c. a court-appointed advisor.

Thus, there are three specific positions to which the court may appoint qualified individuals under circumstances specified in the rule. *See* Ariz. R. Fam. L.P. 10(A)(2) (setting forth bases for appointment by the court of an attorney to represent a child or a court-appointed advisor); Ariz. R. Fam. L.P. 10(B), (C) (qualifications of an appointed child's attorney, best interests attorney, or a court-appointed advisor).

As one would suspect, the three positions have different duties and responsibilities. Before setting forth the rule's delineation of duties, it is helpful to consider the descriptive nature of the titles for each of the three different positions. Two of the positions are specifically designated as "attorney" positions: "A best interests *attorney*" and "a child's *attorney.*" As the title suggests, the duties of each of these two positions are those consistent with that of an attorney, one who acts in a representative capacity, as contrasted with a witness, who testifies based on his or her knowledge and experience. On the other hand, the third position is designated "a court-appointed *advisor.*" Similarly, the duties of an advisor are generally viewed as one who provides counsel or input, a witness rather than one who acts in a representative capacity as does an attorney.

With that background, we turn to Rule 10(E) for the specific delineation of the duties and responsibilities that pertain to each position:

E. Participation in Proceeding by Child's Attorney, Best Interests Attorney, And Court-Appointed Advisor

1. A child's attorney or best interests attorney shall participate in the conduct of the litigation to the same extent as an attorney for any party.

2. A child's attorney, best interests attorney, and court-appointed advisor may not engage in *ex parte* contact with the court except as authorized by law other than this rule.

3. A court-appointed advisor may not take any action that may be taken only by a licensed attorney, including making opening and closing statements, examining witnesses, and engaging in discovery other than as a witness.

4. The court shall ensure that any court-appointed advisor for a child has an opportunity to testify or submit a report setting forth:

    a. the court-appointed advisor's recommendations regarding the best interests of the child; and

    b. the basis for the court-appointed advisor's recommendations.

5. In a proceeding, a party, including a child's attorney or best interests attorney, may call any court-appointed advisor for the child as a witness for the purpose of cross-examination regarding the advisor's report without the advisor's being listed as a witness by a party.

6. An attorney appointed as child's attorney or best interests attorney may not:

    a. be compelled to produce the attorney's work product developed during the appointment;

    b. be required to disclose the source of information obtained as a result of the appointment;

    c. submit a report into evidence; or

    d. testify in court.

7. Subdivision 6 does not alter the duty of an attorney to report child abuse or neglect under applicable law.

As can be seen from the rule, there are two key differences between a child's attorney and a BIA, as contrasted with a court-appointed advisor. First, the court "*shall ensure*" that a court-appointed advisor "has an opportunity to testify or submit a report," Rule 10(E)(4) (emphasis added), whereas one who serves as a child's attorney or BIA "*may not* . . . submit a report into evidence" or "testify in court." Ariz. R. Fam. L.P. 10(E)(6) (emphasis added). Second, while a child's attorney or BIA "*shall participate* . . . to the same extent as an *attorney* for any party," Rule 10(E)(1) (emphasis added), a court-appointed advisor "*may not* take any action" that is only permitted by a licensed attorney. Ariz. R. Fam. L.P. 10(E)(3) (emphasis added). Thus, there are bright line delineations provided in the rule: a child's attorney or BIA may act in a representative capacity and urge the court to reach a particular result based upon the evidence presented. However, like any other attorney functioning in a representative capacity, the argument and positions taken by the attorney do not themselves constitute evidence.

Though the rule provides bright line delineations between a child's attorney and a BIA as contrasted with a court-appointed advisor, the rule does not delineate the differences between a child's attorney and a BIA. The committee comment, however, is helpful. In pertinent part it provides:

> The American Bar Association Standards of Practice for Lawyers Representing Children in Custody Cases ["ABA Standards"], adopted August 2003, provides guidance to the court, counsel, and litigants about the appointment of attorneys for children. The Standards include suggestions about when and how an attorney should be appointed, and in which capacity, and detail what the attorney's responsibilities are to the court and the client.

Ariz. R. Fam. L.P. 10, cmt. Thus, we turn to the ABA Standards.

As to the distinction between a child's attorney and a BIA, the ABA Standards provide as follows:

> B. Definitions
>   1. "Child's Attorney": A lawyer who provides independent legal counsel for a child and who owes the same duties of undivided loyalty, confidentiality, and competent representation as are due an adult client.
>   2. "Best Interests Attorney": A lawyer who provides independent legal services for the purpose of protecting a child's best interests, without being bound by the child's directives or objectives.

ABA Standards §II(B)(1), (2). As the commentary to the ABA Standards states:

> The essential distinction between the two lawyer roles is that the Best Interests Attorney investigates and advocates the best interests of the child as a lawyer in the litigation, while the Child's Attorney is a lawyer who represents the child as a client.

ABA Standards §II(B), cmt. Thus, a trial court will consider appointment of a child's attorney, for an older child who has judgment and maturity, to represent that child's views. On the other hand, a BIA will be appointed when the court determines, due to the child's lack of maturity or judgment or other circumstances, that it is more appropriate for a lawyer to be appointed to discern—and then advocate—the child's best interests. As the Commentary provides "[n]either kind of lawyer is a witness." ABA Standards §II(B), cmt. Indeed, the ABA Standards are in express conformity with our rules in precluding either type of attorney from acting as a witness:

> B. Lawyer's Roles
>   A lawyer appointed as a Child's Attorney or Best Interests Attorney should not play any other role in the case, and should not testify, file a report, or make recommendations.

ABA Standards §III(B). The commentary to this standard provides:

> Neither kind of lawyer should be a witness, which means that the lawyer should not be cross-examined, and more importantly should neither testify nor make a written or oral report or recommendation to the court, but instead should offer traditional evidence-based legal arguments such as other lawyers make. However, explaining what result a client wants, or proffering what one hopes to prove, is not testifying; those are things all lawyers do.

ABA Standards §III(B), cmt. We do not, as Rule 10 did not, *adopt* the ABA Standards as a whole as binding upon us. The committee comment indicates that the ABA Standards "provide [] guidance" and "include suggestions." *Id.* We employ them in that fashion here and find them persuasive as to the points referenced.

Thus, the express language of our rules, as well as the guidance we receive from the ABA Standards, make it plain that a child's attorney, a BIA, and a court-appointed advisor have distinct and separate roles with definite parameters that apply to their involvement in family court proceedings.

2. Application of Rule 10 to the Proceedings Here

In this case there was a clear departure from the permissible role of the BIA. As a practical matter, the BIA functioned as a court-appointed advisor, giving a substantive report that was treated as evidence, even though the minute entry appointing her and the terms of Rule 10 expressly precluded her from acting in that role.

Specifically, the trial court asked for, and the BIA gave, "a report." The exchange began with "I'm gonna ask [the BIA] to give me a report." It concluded with the BIA saying, "So that's my report and my recommendations to the Court." In between, the BIA spoke for what now comprises six transcript pages of substantive information based upon the BIA's own investigation in meetings with the parents, caretakers, and other relevant individuals. For instance, the BIA told the court:

> I'm supporting the mother's request for sole custody. . . . There have been allegations that mother's home is unfit. CPS has been involved. My social worker at the time was [sic] to the home. I have met the boys very often. . . .

I've met with the older boys which were an issue for Mr. Krahn in terms of the older boys helping their single mom watch the boys while she's at work. . . . I do not feel that the boys are at risk in the mother's home at all. I don't think her home poses a risk. . . .

In my interaction with [Father] he was extremely volatile and angry.

While Father, I believe, from what he has told me, is back on his meds . . . he's very bitter. He's very angry. He does not focus. . . . Their [Mother's and Father's] communication is not good at all. And so for them to try to make some decisions that may come up about the boys, I don't see them co-parenting.

These statements by the BIA clearly violated the requirement of Rule 10(E)(6)(c) and (d) specifying that a BIA "may not . . . submit a report into evidence" or "testify in court."

Mother argues, however, that the BIA's oral report was not formally offered "into evidence" and that the BIA did not "testify" because she was not sworn before offering her report. Regardless, as we discuss below, it is clear that the trial court relied on the report as though it was evidence and as though the BIA had been sworn. The use of the report violates the rule.

There was nothing inappropriate about the BIA's statement to the court that "I'm supporting the mother's request for sole custody." This advocacy statement was within the clear parameters of the rule. As the BIA, she was charged with presenting her *position* to the court with regard to what is in the children's best interests. Taking sides and supporting a particular position is what a BIA is called upon to do. If, in her so-called "report" she had referred to evidence that would properly come before the court from a source other than herself, her "report" would have been the equivalent of an opening statement or closing argument and would have been quite proper. The error here is that both the BIA and the trial court treated the information or report from the BIA (however it is denominated) as *evidence* upon which, at least in part, the child custody decision was based. This is completely contrary to both the BIA's order of appointment and Rule 10.

That the trial court relied upon the BIA's report as evidence is plain. As noted earlier, in its written findings, the trial court indicated that Mother's request for sole custody "is supported by the opinion and experience of the [BIA], who told the Court that [Father] . . . remains bitter and angry at Mother to the extent that he is unable or unwilling to focus on the children's best interest much of the time." In short, the court relied upon the BIA's custody opinion to decide the custody question. Father had cited to the caretaking done by Mother's older sons as a reason he should have sole custody. As to this contested issue, the trial court expressly found that "[t]he BIA indicates that she could find no deficiencies in the caretaking abilities of the older boys nor any problems in the relationships between the siblings." Although Mother attempts to depict the record as showing that the BIA merely functioned as an attorney pointing to other evidence, the record simply does not permit that conclusion. The trial court expressly based its finding as to custody on "the opinion and experience of the [BIA]." . . .

On core issues in the case, whether Father or Mother should have sole custody and the extent to which the older siblings were permissible caretakers, the

BIA offered information based upon a series of interactions and interviews that took place over a period of weeks and gave her own opinion regarding custody. The court expressly relied upon the BIA's information and opinion in coming to its conclusions. The error was prejudicial and we must vacate the order as to custody and parenting time.

DISCUSSION QUESTIONS FOR *AKSAMIT v. KRAHN*

A. What is the role of the best interests attorney?

B. What is the role of the child's attorney?

C. What is the role of the court-appointed advisor?

D. What was the problem with the participation of the best interests attorney in this case? Do you agree that the error was prejudicial? How?

E. Which of these roles would you prefer to play in a case? Why?

General Principles

1. Model Rule of Professional Conduct 1.7(b)(3) (2010) disapproves of dual representation that involves "the assertion of a claim by one client against another client represented by the lawyer in the same litigation or other proceeding before a tribunal."

2. Under Model Rule of Professional Conduct 1.5(d)(1) (2010), lawyers are prohibited from charging a fee "contingent upon the securing of a divorce or upon the amount of alimony or support, or property settlement in lieu thereof. . . ."

3. Rule 1.8(j) of the Model Rules of Professional Conduct (2010) provides that "[a] lawyer shall not have sexual relations with a client unless a consensual sexual relationship existed between them when the client-lawyer relationship commenced."

4. Model Rule of Professional Conduct Rule 1.4 (2010) requires attorneys to keep clients "reasonably informed" about their cases and to "comply with reasonable requests for information."

5. The American Bar Association Standing Committee on Ethics and Professional Responsibility approves of the practice of collaborative law in circumstances where clients give informed consent to participation.
6. Lawyers may serve as third-party neutrals in matters where they do not represent either party as a client.
7. The American Bar Association Standards of Practice for Lawyers Representing Children in Custody Cases provides for the role of child's attorney and best interests attorney.
8. Model Rule of Professional Conduct 6.1 (2010) suggests that lawyers provide at least 50 hours of uncompensated service per year.

Chapter Problems

1. Model Rule of Professional Conduct 2.1 discusses the role of an attorney as an advisor:

> In representing a client, a lawyer shall exercise independent professional judgment and render candid advice. In rendering advice, a lawyer may refer not only to law but to other considerations such as moral, economic, social and political factors, that may be relevant to the client's situation.

In a divorce case, should you counsel your client about (a) whether the parties should reconcile; (b) how your client can be a better parent; (c) the impact of divorce on children; (d) the likely outcome of the case; (e) how to adjust his or her budget in order to pay your fee; (f) whether he or she should sell the house; or (g) what he or she should tell people about the divorce?

2. Assume that you are a practicing family law attorney. A prospective client comes to see you because she has been sued for divorce. The client recently learned that her husband was engaged in an affair of long duration and that he has a child with his mistress. The husband is seeking a divorce in order to marry this other woman. Your client and her husband have three children under the age of ten. The client feels humiliated and ashamed and wants you to do the following: (a) stop the divorce from occurring; (b) substantially slow the progress of the divorce; (c) file extensive discovery requests in order to make the divorce painful and expensive for the husband; (d) seek a very large amount of alimony; and (e) make sure the judge knows of the husband's unfaithful conduct. How will you respond to the client?

3. Assume that you and your partner, Steven, specialize in family law and you have been practicing together for five years. Steven informs you that he is falling in love with a client whose divorce he is handling. Fortunately, there is little more to do in the case than a final meeting to sign a property settlement agreement. What will you advise your partner?

4. Assume the following findings are made concerning an applicant for admission to the bar:

> [X] exhibited abusive behavior toward four women with whom he had previous relationships. In each case, the version of events provided by the woman describes [X]'s actions toward her as intimidating, violent, assaultive, unlawful, perverted, and demonstrating an abuse of his authority. In each instance, [X] provides an explanation differing from that given by the woman.

In re Application of Anthony Ybarra for Admission to the Nebraska State Bar on Examination, 781 N.W.2d 446, 767-768 (Neb. 2010). Will X pass the character and fitness requirement?

Preparation for Practice

1. Does your community have a self-help center aimed at providing information for self-represented litigants? If so, what assistance does it provide? How do self-represented litigants find out about it?

2. The practice of family law is increasingly interdisciplinary. Family lawyers frequently work with professionals from disciplines such as psychology, psychiatry, medicine, social work, accounting, and financial planning. Consequently, family lawyers need to have a working knowledge of these fields and the capacity to communicate effectively with other professionals. If you practice in the area of family law, how will you go about selecting other professionals to involve in cases or recommend to clients?

3. As family law professional roles have expanded, law schools have expanded their curriculum to include skills education related to conflict resolution, interest-based negotiation, and creative problem solving. *See* Mary E. O'Connell & J. Herbie DiFonzo, *The Family Law Education Reform Project Final Report*, 44 Fam. Ct. Rev. 524 (2006). As discussed in this chapter and in the previous chapter, practicing family law attorneys increasingly characterize their role as client counselor rather than zealous advocate:

> The traditional view of the matrimonial lawyer (a view still held by many practitioners) is of the "zealous advocate" whose only job is to win. However, the emphasis on zealous representation of individual clients in criminal and some civil cases is not always appropriate in family law matters. Public opinion . . . has increasingly supported other models of lawyering and goals of conflict resolution in appropriate cases. A counseling, problem-solving approach for people in need of help in

resolving difficult issues and conflicts within the family is one model; this is sometimes referred to as "constructive advocacy." Mediation and arbitration offer alternative models.

American Academy of Matrimonial Lawyers, *The Bounds of Advocacy.* Are there times when a family law attorney should advise against participation in alternative dispute resolution processes? What factors would influence your judgment about whether to proceed to trial and/or negotiate in a given case?

Table of Cases